THROUGH THE EYES OF A CHILD

The Hello, Goodbye Window

Norton Juster Chris Raschka

Through the Eyes of a Child

An Introduction to Children's Literature

Seventh Edition

Donna E. Norton
Texas A & M University

Saundra E. Norton

PEARSON
Merrill
Prentice Hall

Upper Saddle River, New Jersey
Columbus, Ohio

Library of Congress Cataloging-in-Publication Data

Norton, Donna E.
  Through the eyes of a child: an introduction to children's literature/Donna E. Norton.—
7th ed.
    p. cm.
  Includes bibliographical references and index.
  ISBN 0-13-220296-4
    1. Children—Books and reading—United States. 2. Children's literature—History and
criticism. I. Title.
Z1037.A1N68 2007
028.1'62—dc22

2005054994

Vice President and Executive Publisher: Jeffery W. Johnston
Senior Editor: Linda Ashe Bishop
Senior Development Editor: Hope Madden
Senior Production Editor: Mary M. Irvin
Design Coordinator: Diane C. Lorenzo
Senior Editorial Assistant: Laura Weaver
Production Coordination: Carlisle Publishing Services
Cover Designer: Kristina Holmes
Cover Image: Robert Sabuda
Production Manager: Pamela D. Bennett
Director of Marketing: David Gesell
Marketing Manager: Darcy Betts Prybella
Marketing Coordinator: Brian Mounts

This book was set in Goudy Old Style BT by Carlisle Publishing Services. It was printed and bound by R. R. Donnelley & Sons Company. The cover was printed by Phoenix Color Corp.

Cover Image Credit: Reprinted by permission of Atheneum Books for Young Readers, an imprint of Simon & Schuster Children's Publishing Division from ARTHUR AND THE SWORD retold and illustrated by Robert Subuda. Copyright © 1995 by Robert Sabuda.

Photo Credits: p. 24, Courtesy of Robert Sabuda; p. 84, Courtesy of HarperCollins Publishers; p. 136, © Suki Coughlin, Courtesy of G. P. Putnam's; p. 187, Courtesy of Simon & Schuster; p. 252, Courtesy of Tom Tingle; p. 295, by Ralph DeFelice; p. 322, Courtesy of Random House Children's Books; p. 399, Courtesy of Macmillan; p. 420, Courtesy of Houghton Mifflin Company; p. 478, Courtesy of David Adler; p. 520, Courtesy of Laurence Pringle.

Pearson Education Ltd.
Pearson Education Singapore Pte. Ltd.
Pearson Education Canada, Ltd.
Pearson Education—Japan

Pearson Education Australia Pty. Limited
Pearson Education North Asia Ltd.
Pearson Educación de Mexico, S. A. de C. V.
Pearson Education Malaysia Pte. Ltd.

10 9 8 7 6 5 4 3 2
ISBN: 0-13-220296-4

Preface

What do you need to share a love of literature with children? The short answer: just a love of literature. But what if you want to pass on something meaningful, to help children find the best literature, the kind of books that will be favorite friends for a lifetime? What if you are looking for a way to engender a passion for reading, and even hope to use these books as a starting point for even greater learning? You would need to know how to choose the best books—books children could love and be moved by. You would need an understanding of children's interests and the criteria that make great books great. A tool to help you find the best books would be invaluable. Ideas for extending books into the school curriculum to deepen children's understanding of both the book and their content areas would be important. In short, information and resources to help you understand, find, evaluate, and extend children's literature as well as match that literature to potential readers would be invaluable to your purpose.

The seventh edition of *Through the Eyes of a Child: An Introduction to Children's Literature* was crafted with the single purpose of helping you make the absolute most of sharing literature with children. You will get to know the literature and what is required of a book to be considered great. You'll get background information and insight from the best children's authors, and you'll learn the criteria to use to determine the best of the best. It will also become clear how and where to find the titles you'll want to share. Successful strategies for implementing literature study in the classroom will round out the picture.

Through the Eyes of a Child: An Introduction to Children's Literature continues to be the visually stunning, theoretically sound, comprehensive overview of children's literature you have come to expect. The new edition has been updated and honed to prepare you to better appreciate, evaluate, and share children's literature. You'll develop these skills by examining the most important elements of the literature and by addressing the interests and needs of its young readers.

Evaluating, Choosing, and Sharing

No text better prepares you for evaluating, choosing, and sharing quality children's literature than *Through the Eyes of a Child*.

- Chapter 3, Evaluating and Selecting Literature for Children, lays the groundwork upon which each subsequent chapter builds. This chapter, devoted entirely to the discussion of evaluating and choosing literature

for children, will provide you with a foundation of moving beyond an appreciation of what is "cute" and on to a deep appreciation of the quality and value to be found in excellent literature for children.

- *Evaluation Criteria* boxes in every genre chapter build on the foundation laid in Chapter 3, outlining exactly what you need to look for to find quality literature in every genre.

UNIQUE! • *In-Depth Analysis* features take you deep into an exemplary title, using a single book to explore the topics being covered in the chapter. This exercise will help you discover the elements that compose quality literature.

Books and Audience

The seventh edition of the text broadens its look at the literature that appeals to and nourishes children and adolescents.

NEW! • Every chapter looks at *Young Adult Literature*, examining the ways to intrigue and nurture young adult readers, to evaluate titles for this audience, and to integrate these quality titles into your teaching. Studies show that students' interest in reading wanes in the adolescent years, so it is particularly important for you to be familiar with the titles that will keep this audience interested. You will also need to know how to find truly quality literature for adolescents.

NEW! • The text's long-known, respected coverage of multicultural literature has been embedded in the genre chapters. Rest assured that this important topic is discussed with the same detail and thoughtfulness found in previous editions. But to encourage appreciation and integration of multicultural titles in the classroom, it was important to embed these titles and discussions. Look for the *Multicultural Literature* logo to find specific coverage.

MULTICULTURAL LITERATURE

NEW! • Because of the increased popularity, quality, and proliferation of nonfiction titles, nonfiction coverage has been expanded to two chapters. Biographies (Chapter 11) and Informational Books (Chapter 12) will guide you to a better understanding of what is available in these areas and help you to match these books with readers as you learn to utilize these titles to enrich your content area teaching.

- *Through the Eyes of an Author* features invite you into the world of some of children's literature's greatest storytellers and artists. Five new authors share a personal statement about their writing in the new edition. Look for each feature's Video Profile section to learn which authors are included in segments on the video available to adopting professors.
- *Through the Eyes of a Child* features expand on the chapter's *Through the Eyes of an Author* feature by exhibiting a piece of student writing that discusses a title from the chapter's highlighted author. You'll see how excited children can get with the right books in their hands.
- As in past editions, new titles have been carefully selected and included in the new edition, while out-of-print books have been culled. The books discussed in this edition were chosen for their quality and to create a balance between the most contemporary titles and classics that have passed the test of time.

Extending the Literature

UNIQUE! • A unique feature of this text, beginning in Chapter 3 and extending through Chapter 12, places the characteristics, history, and titles of each genre next to the appropriate strategies for involving children in that genre. *Teaching With* sections at the end of every genre chapter cover strategies that have been field tested at the university, secondary, and elementary school levels, and during in-service training for teachers and librarians.

- *Issues* features in certain chapters help you look closely at the controversies that can arise from the choices you make with books, and provide topics for in-depth class discussions that will broaden your understanding of literature.
- *Suggested Activities* at the end of chapters are designed to foster your understanding of children's literature and help you develop children's appreciation for the genres.

Integrating Media

By incorporating media, the seventh edition gives you the tools to stay up to date, do research, and utilize technology to enrich your learning and teaching.

UNIQUE! • A completely redesigned *A Database of Children's Literature* on CD-ROM accompanies the text. This tool provides you easily accessible information on thousands of excellent titles worth sharing with children and adolescents in an intuitive, user-friendly format. Along with the database you'll find *Through the Eyes of a Teacher* features that model the use of literature in classroom teaching, as well as links to all major literature award sites and the text's Companion Website.

UNIQUE! • *Technology Resource* features throughout chapters help you make the most of the media available with the text, providing specific ideas for integrating the technology into teaching.

- A robust *Companion Website* containing online activities, CD activities, self-assessment opportunities, and valuable links to literature-related sites gives you the tools to enrich your study of children's literature.

This comprehensive new edition of *Through the Eyes of a Child: An Introduction to Children's Literature* focuses squarely on selecting and evaluating quality literature to share with children, and guiding children to appreciate and respond to that literature. With a solid, infused consideration of multicultural literature and a new, thorough look at books appropriate for young adult readers, the text will help you learn how to find all the best literature available as it models the skills you'll need to share that literature in meaningful ways with children and adolescents.

Supplements for the Student

CD-ROM

A *Database of Children's Literature* accompanies every copy of the text. This resource, filled with excellent ideas for classroom lessons as well as the database itself, contains thousands of titles at a glance. The newly revised, easily navigated database helps you find titles for a lesson, a unit, a text set, or for one specific reader. Search by topic, author, genre, title, and even determine what awards each title has received.

Companion Website

This robust electronic ancillary, available at *www.prenhall.com/norton*, has been completely revised to meet changes in the literature and literacy communities.

You'll find

- Objectives to help you organize chapter information
- Multiple choice quizzes to gauge your understanding of chapter concepts
- Essay questions to allow you reflective consideration of chapter topics
- Web links to connect you to important literature-related sites
- CD activities to help you make use of this valuable resource
- Internet activities to use yourself and in your own classroom
- Lessons appropriate for each chapter's concepts, ready for you to take into your classroom

Supplements for the Professor

Video

Conversations with Children's Authors and Illustrators, free to adopting professors, gives you intimate access to the creative processes used by exemplary storytellers, poets, illustrators, and children's literature writers, including many features in the text's *Through the Eyes of an Author* features. Hear from Joseph Bruchac, Brian Pinkney, Eve Bunting, Gary Soto, and more.

Instructor Resource Center

The Instructor Resource Center at *www.prenhall.com* has a variety of print and media resources available in downloadable, digital format—all in one location. As a registered faculty member, you can access and download pass-code protected resource files, course management content, and other premium online content directly to your computer.

Digital resources available for *Through the Eyes of a Child: An Introduction to Children's Literature* include:

- Text-specific PowerPoint Lectures
- An online Instructor's Manual
- An online Test Bank

To access these items online, go to *www.prenhall. com* and click on the Instructor Support button and then go to the Download Supplements section. Here you will be able to log in or complete a one-time registration for a user name and password. If you have any questions regarding this process or the materials available online, please contact your local Prentice Hall sales representative.

Acknowledgments

I thank the reviewers of the seventh edition for their thoughtful responses and meaningful suggestions regarding this revision: Daniel Holm, Indiana University South Bend; Olivia Saracho, University of Maryland; and Sharron Mcelmeel, University of Wisconsin–Stout–Grant Wood AEA, Nancy Thornberry of Texas A&M University.

Thank you to the librarians who were so gracious with their time and thoughts as I revised this text. In particular, I would like to thank Texas A&M Librarians: Jane Smith, Director, Education Reference Library, and Halbert Hall, Senior Scholar and Bibliographer; University of Wisconsin, Madison, Cooperative Children's Book Center: Kathleen T. Horning, Merri V. Lindgren, Hollis Rudiger, and Megan Schliesman; Madison, Wisconsin Public Library–Children's Librarians: Linda Olson–Director of Children's Division, Kelly Verheyden, Amy Brandt, Carolyn Forde, Alice Oakey, Jill Olig, and Bridget Zinn; Children's Book Sellers, Borders Books, Madison, Wisconsin: Laurie Rosengren and Jayne Rowsan.

I wish to thank Robert Sabuda for sharing his wonderful image from *Arthur and the Sword*, which graces the cover of this text and suggests the awe you can find in literature if you look through the eyes of a child.

Thanks again to Mr. Sabuda, as well as David A. Adler, Cynthia DeFelice, Laurence Pringle, and Tim Tingle for taking the time to speak with me about their work. The experience was as enlightening as it was enjoyable, and I hope the readers of this text get as much from the words of these magnificent artists as I did.

Finally, I wish to dedicate this book to my husband, Verland, and my children, Saundra and Bradley, for their constant support, immense understanding, and insightful viewpoints.

TEACHER PREP

**MERRILL
PRENTICE HALL**

See a demo at
www.prenhall.com/teacherprep/demo

Your Class. Their Careers. Our Future. Will your students be prepared?

We invite you to explore our new, innovative and engaging website and all that it has to offer you, your course, and tomorrow's educators! Organized around the major courses pre-service teachers take, the Teacher Preparation site provides media, student/teacher artifacts, strategies, research articles, and other resources to equip your students with the quality tools needed to excel in their courses and prepare them for their first classroom.

This ultimate on-line education resource is available at no cost, when packaged with a Merrill text, and will provide you and your students access to:

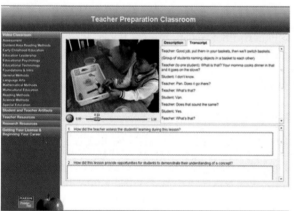

Online Video Library. More than 150 video clips—each tied to a course topic and framed by learning goals and Praxis-type questions—capture real teachers and students working in real classrooms, as well as in-depth interviews with both students and educators.

Student and Teacher Artifacts. More than 200 student and teacher classroom artifacts—each tied to a course topic and framed by learning goals and application questions—provide a wealth of materials and experiences to help make your study to become a professional teacher more concrete and hands-on.

Research Articles. Over 500 articles from ASCD's renowned journal *Educational Leadership*. The site also includes Research Navigator, a searchable database of additional educational journals.

Teaching Strategies. Over 500 strategies and lesson plans for you to use when you become a practicing professional.

Licensure and Career Tools. Resources devoted to helping you pass your licensure exam; learn standards, law, and public policies; plan a teaching portfolio; and succeed in your first year of teaching.

How to ORDER Teacher Prep for you and your students:
For students to receive a *Teacher Prep* Access Code with this text, instructors **must** provide a special value pack ISBN number on their textbook order form. To receive this special ISBN, please email **Merrill.marketing@pearsoned.com** and provide the following information:
- Name and Affiliation
- Author/Title/Edition of Merrill text

Upon ordering *Teacher Prep* for their students, instructors will be given a lifetime *Teacher Prep* Access Code.

Brief Contents

Chapter 1
The Child Responds to Literature 1

Chapter 2
The History of Children's Literature 43

Chapter 3
Evaluating and Selecting Literature
for Children 73

Chapter 4
Artists and Their Illustrations 117

Chapter 5
Picture Books 163

Chapter 6
Traditional Literature 207

Chapter 7
Modern Fantasy 271

Chapter 8
Poetry 315

Chapter 9
Contemporary Realistic Fiction 361

Chapter 10
Historical Fiction 415

Chapter 11
Biographies 461

Chapter 12
Informational Books 499

Contents

Chapter 1

The Child Responds to Literature 1

Values of Literature for Children   3
Promoting Child Development Through Literature   4
  Language Development, 4 ▪ Cognitive Development, 11 ▪
  Personality Development, 20 ▪ Social Development, 29
Children's Responses to Literature   36
  Factors Within Readers, 37 ▪ Factors Within Texts, 37 ▪
  Factors Within Contexts, 37 ▪ Responses, 38 ▪ Analyzing
  Responses, 39 ▪ The Role of Motivation, 39
Suggested Activities   41

Chapter 2

The History of Children's Literature 43

Milestones in the History of Children's Literature   45
  The Oral Tradition, 45 ▪ Early Printed Books, 46 ▪ The
  Puritan Influence, 48 ▪ John Locke's Influence on Views of
  Childhood, 49 ▪ Charles Perrault's Tales of Mother Goose,
  49 ▪ The Adventure Stories of Defoe and Swift, 49 ▪
  Newbery's Books for Children, 50 ▪ Rousseau's Philosophy
  of Natural Development, 51 ▪ William Blake's Poetry
  About Children, 52 ▪ The Fairy Tales of Andersen and the
  Brothers Grimm, 52 ▪ Early Illustrators of Children's Books,
  53 ▪ The Victorian Influence, 56 ▪ Fantasy, Adventure, and
  Real People, 58
Standards for Evaluating Young Adult Literature   64
The History of Censorship   65
Children and the Family in Children's Literature   67
  The Child and the Family, 1856–1903, 67 ▪ The Child and
  the Family, 1938–1960, 68 ▪ The Child and the Family,
  1969–Present, 69
Suggested Activities   71

Chapter 3

Evaluating and Selecting Literature for Children 73

Standards, Literary Elements,
and Book Selection   74
Evaluation Criteria—Literary Criticism: Questions to
  Ask Myself When I Judge a Book   75
Standards for Evaluating Books and Literary
  Criticism   75
Standards for Evaluating Multicultural Literature   77
  Values of Multicultural Literature, 77 ▪ Literary Criticism:
  Evaluating Multicultural Literature, 78

Evaluation Criteria—Literary Criticism: Multicultural
    Literature   79
Literary Elements   79
    Plot, 79 ▪ Characterization, 84 ▪ Setting, 87 ▪ Theme, 91 ▪
    Style, 93 ▪ Point of View, 96
The Right Book for Each Child   99
    Accessibility, 99 ▪ Readability, 99 ▪ Interest and Reader
    Response, 100
The Child as Critic   100

   Teaching With Literary Elements   103
Involving Children in Plot   103
Involving Children in Characterization   104
    Characterization Techniques, 105 ▪ Modeling
    Inferencing, 105
Involving Children in Setting   106
    Settings That Create Moods, 106 ▪ Settings That Develop
    Antagonists, 107 ▪ Settings That Develop Historical and
    Geographical Backgrounds, 108 ▪ Settings That Are
    Symbolic, 108
Involving Children in Theme   108
Involving Children in Style   109
    Personification, 109 ▪ Pleasing Style, 110
Webbing the Literary Elements   110
Suggested Activities   110
Children's Literature   111

Chapter 4

Artists and Their Illustrations 117

   Understanding Artists and Their Illustrations   118
Evaluating the Illustrations in Children's
    Books   118
Evaluation Criteria—Illustrations   119
Visual Elements: The Grammar of Artists   119
    Line, 119 ▪ Color, 121 ▪ Shape, 122 ▪ Texture, 124
Design: Organizing the Visual Elements   125
Artistic Media   127
    Lines and Washes, 128 ▪ Watercolors, Acrylics, Pastels, and
    Oils, 128 ▪ Woodcuts, 130 ▪ Collage, 131
Artistic Style   133
    Representational Art, 133 ▪ Abstract Art, 134
Outstanding Illustrators of Children's Books   134
    Barbara Cooney, 135 ▪ Tomie dePaola, 135 ▪ Leo and
    Diane Dillon, 136 ▪ Ezra Jack Keats, 137 ▪ Robert
    McCloskey, 138 ▪ Alice and Martin Provensen, 138 ▪
    Maurice Sendak, 138 ▪ Chris Van Allsburg, 139 ▪
    David Wiesner, 139

   Teaching With Artists and Their Illustrations   140
Using Art Education Books   140
Aesthetic Scanning   141
Studying Inspirations for Art   143
Investigating the Works of Great Artists   145
Suggested Activities   153
Children's Literature   154

Chapter 5

Picture Books 161

   A Book Is More Than Words   162
What a Picture Book Is   162
Literary Criticism: Evaluating Picture
    Books   163
Evaluation Criteria—Selecting High-Quality Picture
    Books   163
Mother Goose   163
    Appealing Characteristics, 164 ▪ Collections, 164 ▪ Books
    That Illustrate One Rhyme or Tale, 166 ▪ Nursery Rhymes
    in Other Lands, 166
Toy Books   166
Alphabet Books   168
    Animal Themes, 169 ▪ Other Alphabet Books, 169
Counting Books   171
Concept Books   173
Wordless Books   174
Evaluation Criteria—Selecting High-Quality Wordless
    Books   176
Easy-to-Read Books   177
Picture Storybooks   178
    Elements in Picture Storybooks, 178 ▪ Typical Characters
    and Situations, 184

   Teaching With Picture Books   191
Sharing Mother Goose   192
Sharing Wordless Books   192
    Stimulating Cognitive and Language Development, 192 ▪
    Motivating Writing and Reading, 193
Reading to Children   193
    Choosing the Books, 194 ▪ Preparing to Read Aloud, 195 ▪
    The Reading Itself, 195
Developing Aesthetic Sensitivity   195
Motivating Writing With Picture Storybooks   196
Suggested Activities   197
Children's Literature   197

Chapter 6

Traditional Literature 207

   Of Castle and Cottage   208
Our Traditional Literary Heritage   208
Types of Traditional Literature   209
    Folktales, 209 ▪ Fables, 211 ▪ Myths, 211 ▪
    Legends, 212
Values of Traditional Literature for Children   212
    Understanding the World, 212
Evaluation Criteria—Literary Criticism: Increasing
    World Understanding Through Traditional
    Tales   212
    Identifying With Universal Human Struggles, 213 ▪
    Pleasure, 213
Authenticating the Folklore   214

Folktales   214
Characteristics, 214 ■ Motifs, 218
Fables   240
Characteristics, 240 ■ Contemporary Editions, 240
Myths   242
Greek and Roman Mythology, 242 ■ Norse
Mythology, 244
Legends   247
Additional Traditional Literature With Religious
Themes   250

Teaching With Traditional Literature   252

Telling Stories   252
Choosing a Story, 253 ■ Preparing the Story for Telling, 254
■ Sharing the Story With an Audience, 254 ■ Observing
Children's Responses to Storytelling, 255 ■ Encouraging
Children to Be Storytellers, 255 ■ Using Feltboards to Share
Folktales, 255
Motivating Writing Through Traditional Tales   261
Developing Critical Evaluators for Fables   261
Suggested Activities   261
Children's Literature   262

Chapter 7
Modern Fantasy 271

Time, Space, and Place   272

Evaluating Modern Fantasy   273
Suspending Disbelief: Plot, 273
Evaluation Criteria—Selecting Modern Fantasy   273
Suspending Disbelief: Characterization, 273 ■ Creating a
World: Setting, 274 ■ Universality: Themes, 275 ■
Suspending Disbelief: Point of View, 275
Bridges Between Traditional and Modern
Fantasy   275
Literary Folktales, 276 ■ Religious and Ethical
Allegory, 278 ■ Mythical Quests and Conflicts, 280
Categories of Modern Fantasy   284
Articulate Animals, 285 ■ Toys, 290 ■ Preposterous
Characters and Situations, 291 ■ Strange and Curious
Worlds, 292 ■ Little People, 293 ■ Spirits Friendly and
Frightening, 294 ■ Time Warps, 296 ■ Science
Fiction, 297

Teaching With Modern Fantasy   301

Helping Children Recognize, Understand, and Enjoy
Elements in Fantasy   301
Interpreting Modern Fantasy by Identifying Plot
Structures   303
Involving Children With Science Fiction   304
Interdisciplinary Studies: Interaction Between Social
Studies and Science Fiction, 304
Unit Plan: Using One Book of Modern Fantasy   305
Oral Discussion, 305 ■ Artwork, 307 ■ Creative
Dramatization, 307
Suggested Activities   309
Children's Literature   309

Chapter 8
Poetry 315

Rhythmic Patterns of Language   316

The Values of Poetry for Children   316
What Poetry Is   317
Characteristics of Poems That Children Prefer   318
Criteria for Selecting Poetry for Children   319
Elements of Poetry   319
Evaluation Criteria—Literary Criticism: Selecting Poetry
for Children   319
Rhythm, 319 ■ Rhyme and Other Sound Patterns, 320 ■
Repetition, 321 ■ Imagery, 323 ■ Shape, 324
Forms of Poetry   325
Lyric Poetry, 325 ■ Narrative Poetry, 326 ■ Ballads, 327 ■
Limericks, 328 ■ Concrete Poems, 329 ■ Haiku, 329
Poems and Poets   330
Nonsense and Humor: Poems for Starting Out Right, 330 ■
Nature Poems, 333 ■ Animals, 336 ■ Science, 338 ■
Characters, Situations, and Locations, 339 ■ Moods and
Feelings, 341

Teaching With Poetry   346

Listening to Poetry   347
Moving to Poetry   347
Dramatizing Poetry   347
Developing Choral Speaking   348
Refrain Arrangement, 349 ■ Line Arrangement, 349 ■
Antiphonal, or Dialogue, Arrangement, 349 ■ Cumulative
Arrangement, 349 ■ Unison Arrangement, 350
Choosing Poetry to Accompany Content   350
Writing Poetry   351
Motivations, 351 ■ Oral Exchanges of Ideas, 352 ■
Transcriptions, 352 ■ Sharing, 352 ■ Various Forms of
Poetry, 352 ■ Poetry Writing Exercises, 354
Suggested Activities   354
Children's Literature   355

Chapter 9
Contemporary Realistic Fiction 361

Window on the World   362

What Contemporary Realistic Fiction Is   362
Values of Realistic Fiction   363
Literary Elements—Evaluating Realistic Fiction   364
Plot, 364 ■ Characterization, 364
Evaluation Criteria—Literary Criticism:
Realistic Fiction   365
Theme, 365 ■ Style, 366
How Realistic Fiction Has Changed   368
Literary Criticism: New Realism and the
Problem Novel   368
Controversial Issues   369
Sexism, 369 ■ Sexuality, 370 ■ Violence, 371 ■ Profanity,
372 ■ Family Problems and Other Controversial Issues, 372

Literary Criticism: Guidelines for Selecting Controversial
    Fiction   372
Evaluation Criteria—Literary Criticism: Controversial
    Books   373
Subjects in Realistic Fiction   373
    Family Life, 373 ■ Growing Up, 376 ■ Survival, 379 ■
    Death, 383 ■ People as Individuals, Not Stereotypes, 384
Animal Stories, Mysteries, Sports Stories,
    and Humor   395
    Animals, 395 ■ Mysteries, 396 ■ Sports, 397 ■
    Humor, 398

Teaching With Realistic Fiction   401
Using Role Playing   402
Using Survival Stories to Motivate Reading and
    Interaction With Literature   403
    Interdisciplinary Unit: Island Survival, 403
Developing Questioning Strategies   407
    Literal Recognition, 407 ■ Inference, 407 ■
    Evaluation, 408 ■ Appreciation, 408
Suggested Activities   409
Children's Literature   409

Chapter 10
HISTORICAL FICTION 415

The People and the Past Come Alive   416
Values of Historical Fiction for Children   416
Literary Criticism: Using Literary Elements to Evaluate
    Historical Fiction   417
    Plot, 417
Evaluation Criteria—Literary Criticism: Historical
    Fiction   417
    Characterization, 418 ■ Setting, 419 ■ Theme, 420 ■
    Style, 422
Historical Authenticity   422
A Chronology of Historical Fiction   424
    Ancient Times Through the Middle Ages, 424 ■ The Salem
    Witch-Hunts, 430 ■ The American Revolution, 431 ■ Early
    Expansion of the United States and Canada, 432 ■ The
    Western Frontier, 437 ■ The Early 20th Century, 443 ■
    World War II, 444

Teaching With Historical Fiction   452
Providing Background Through Illustrations   452
Interdisciplinary Unit: Looking at Pioneer
    America   452
    Values From the Past, 453 ■ The Pioneer
    Environment, 454 ■ Trails in Westward Expansion, 455 ■
    Research Skills, 455 ■ Additional Activities, 455 ■
    A Culminating Activity, 456
Creating a Historical Fiction "Books on the Move"
    Source   456
Suggested Activities   457
Children's Literature   457

Chapter 11
BIOGRAPHIES 461

People Who Change Lives   462
Changing Ideas About Biographies for Children   462
Literary Criticism: Evaluating Biographies   464
Evaluation Criteria—Literary Criticism:
    Biography   464
    Characterization, 464 ■ Factual Accuracy, 465 ■
    Worthiness of Subject, 466 ■ Balance Between Fact and
    Story Line, 466 ■ Biographies in Picture-Book Format, 466
Biographical Subjects   469
    Explorers of Earth and Space, 469 ■ Political Leaders and
    Social Activists, 471 ■ Artists and Authors, 478 ■ People
    Who Have Persevered, 483

Teaching With Biographies   488
Unit Plan: Using Biographies in Creative
    Dramatizations   488
Reader Response: Developing Hypothetical Interviews
    With Authors   489
    Imaginary Conversations Between People of Two Time
    Periods, 490
Common Themes in Lives of Scientists
    and Inventors   490
Developing Comprehension Through Time Lines of
    Biographical Characters   491
Analyzing Values and Beliefs   491
Motivating Additional Reading and Discussion   492
Developing Appreciation for the Lives and the Music of
    Biographical Characters   493
Suggested Activities   494
Children's Literature   494

Chapter 12
INFORMATIONAL BOOKS 499

From History to How Things Work   500
Values of Informational Books   500
Evaluating Informational Books   502
    Accuracy, 502
Evaluation Criteria—Literary Criticism: Informational
    Books   502
    Stereotypes, 504 ■ Illustrations, 504 ■ Analytical
    Thinking, 504 ■ Organization, 505 ■ Style, 506
History and Culture   507
    The Ancient World, 507 ■ The Modern World, 510
Nature   517
    The Human Body, 517 ■ Animals, 518 ■ Plants, 524 ■
    Geology and Geography, 524
Discoveries and How Things Work   526
    Discoveries, 526 ■ How Things Work, 527

Hobbies, Crafts, and How-To Books   527
    Creative Arts, 528

Teaching With Informational Books   531

Incorporating Literature Into the Science
    Curriculum   531
    Using the Parts of a Book, 532 ■ Locating Sources of
    Information, 532 ■ Using Science Vocabulary, 532 ■
    Reading for Meaning, 533 ■ Evaluating Science
    Materials, 534
Suggested Activities   535
Children's Literature   535

References 543

Author, Illustrator, and Title Index I-1

Subject Index I-43

Credits C-1

About the Authors

Special Features

Through the Eyes of . . .

. . . an Artist: Robert Sabuda 24
. . . an Author/Illustrator: Steven Kellogg 61
. . . an Author: David Wisniewski 84
. . . an Illustrator: Tomie dePaola 136
. . . an Illustrator: E. B. Lewis 187
. . . a Storyteller: Tim Tingle 252
. . . an Author: Cynthia DeFelice 295
. . . a Poet: Jack Prelutsky 322
. . . an Author: Eve Bunting 399
. . . an Author: Mary E. Lyons 420
. . . a Biographer: David A. Adler 478
. . . an Author: Laurence Pringle 520

Through the Eyes of a Child

Jacob on Robert Sabuda 25
Sam on Steven Kellogg 62
Andersen on David Wisniewski 86
Lauryn on Tomie dePaola 137
Kelly on E. B. Lewis 189
Donovan on Tim Tingle 253
Sarah on Cynthia DeFelice 296
Katie on Jack Prelutsky 323
Riley on Eve Bunting 400
Lindsay on Mary E. Lyons 421
Julia on David A. Adler 479
Caleb on Laurence Pringle 521

Multicultural Literature

Standards for Evaluating
Multicultural Literature 77
History of a Culture as Reflected
in Art: A Multicultural Approach . . . 146
Folktales From Around the World . . . 220
Native American Myths 245
Myths From Other Cultures 246
Comparing Folktales From Different
Countries 256
Investigating Themes or Motifs Found in
Tales From Many Cultures 259
Investigating Folktales From a Single
Country 259
Many Voices: Poetry for Young Adults 344
Multicultural Topics in Realistic Fiction 386

Developing Understanding of Point of View

Developing Understanding of Point of View
and Motivating Writing With a Native
American Story 409
Changes in the Old World and Encounters
With the New World 428
Slavery, the Civil War, and Overcoming
Segregation 434
Pioneers and Native Americans 441
Internment of Japanese Americans and the
Pacific Conflict 449
Recognizing Similarities 456
Civil Rights Leaders 477
History of Civil Rights for African
Americans 516

Young Adult Literature

Young Adults and Language Development 11
Reading Interests of Young Adults 100
Studying Art With Older Students 150
Picture Storybooks for Young Adults 190
Folklore for Young Adults 250
Modern Fantasy and Science Fiction for Young
Adults 300
Analytical Reading of Nancy Farmer's
The House of the Scorpion 307
Poetry for Young Adults 345
Contemporary Realistic Fiction for Young
Adults 398
Historical Fiction for Young Adults 450
Biographies Written for Young Adults 486
Motivating Discussions With Young Adult
Readers 493
Informational Books for Young Adults 530

Issues

The Content of Children's Books: Pleasure
Versus the Message 101
Picture Books and Controversy 175
Whose Cultural Values and Belief Systems
Should Be Reflected in Folklore? 213
Harry Potter and Censorship 286
Unbalanced Viewpoints in Historical
Fiction 435

Is There a Shortage of History Books for
Children? Should Authors of History Books
for Children Include Controversial
Subjects? 508
Who Should Write Science Information
Books for Children? 528

In-Depth Analysis Features

What Is the Future of Children's Book
Publishing and Literacy? 70
The Plot and Conflict in One Book 81
Characterization in One Book 85
Setting in One Book 87

Theme in One Book 92
Author's Use of Style in One Book 95
Point of View in One Book 97
Aesthetic Scanning in One Book 142
A Folklore Collection 236
Fantasy in the Writings of One Author 284
A Contemporary Realistic Fiction Novel 367
A Contemporary Realistic Fiction Novel
for Young Adults 401
One Example of Multicultural Literature—
Native American 442
One Book of Historical Fiction. 445
A Biography 474
An Informational Book. 506

1 THE CHILD RESPONDS TO LITERATURE

From So You Want to Be President? by Judith St. George, illustrated by David Small. Copyright © 2000 by David Small, illustrations. Used by permission of Philomel Books, an imprint of Penguin Putnam Books for Young Readers, a division of Penguin Putnam Inc.

CHAPTER OUTLINE

- ## Values of Literature for Children

- ## Promoting Child Development Through Literature

- ## Children's Responses to Literature

iterature entices, motivates, and instructs. It opens doors to discovery and provides endless hours of adventure and enjoyment. Children need not be tied to the whims of television programming nor wait in line at the theater to follow a rabbit down a hole into Wonderland, save a wild herd of mustangs from slaughter, fight in the Revolutionary War, learn about a new hobby that will provide many enjoyable hours, or model themselves after real-life people of accomplishment. These experiences are available at any time on the nearest bookshelf.

Adults have a responsibility to help children become aware of the enchantment in books. However, the extent to which books play a significant role in the life of young children depends upon adults. Adults provide the books and, through sharing literature, they transmit the literary heritage contained in nursery rhymes, picture storybooks, and traditional tales. The important role of adults in developing a love of literature is found in the response of the Madison, Wisconsin, library director when asked why the city was ranked fourth in the nation for having an outstanding reading culture. She stated: "People here understand the importance of establishing a love of books early in life, so they read to their children and bring them to story time at the public library" (Ingersoll, 2004, p. A1).

Teachers also have a major role in developing a love of books. Patricia Cunningham and Richard Allington (2003) identify characteristics of classrooms in which children are successful: "Children who are successful at becoming literate view reading and writing as authentic activities from which they get information and pleasure, and by which they communicate with others. . . . The teachers know that it is important to take the time to read to children each day. They know it is important to have a time each day in which children read materials that they have selected for themselves" (p. 2). Alleen Pace Nilsen (2005) adds to the role of literature when she says, "The younger and more deprived the children are, the more reward—the more pleasure—they need to see coming from the printed word. . . . I am saddened by the way current instructional practices are nibbling away on the few short years during which people can read and appreciate children's literature through the eyes of a child" (p. 39).

As you read this book, you will gain knowledge about literature so that you can share stimulating books and book-related experiences with children. This chapter introduces various values of literature for children to help you search for books that can play significant roles in children's lives. It also looks at the importance of considering children's stages of language, cognitive, personality, and social development when selecting literature for children and suggests books that reflect children's needs during different stages of the maturing process. All of these developmental areas influence children's understanding and appreciation of literature and their responses to literature.

Values of Literature for Children

Following a rabbit down a rabbit hole or walking through a wardrobe into a mythical kingdom sounds like fun. There is nothing wrong with admitting that one of the primary values of literature is pleasure, and there is nothing wrong with turning to a book to escape or to enjoy an adventure with new or old book friends. Time is enriched, not wasted, when children look at beautiful pictures and imagine themselves in new places. When children discover enjoyment in books, they develop favorable attitudes toward them that usually extend into a lifetime of appreciation.

Books are the major means of transmitting our literary heritage from one generation to the next. Each new generation can enjoy the words of Lewis Carroll, Louisa May Alcott, Robert Louis Stevenson, and Mark Twain. Through the work of storytellers such as the Brothers Grimm, each generation can also experience the folktales originally transmitted through the oral tradition. Anita Silvey (2004) emphasizes the importance of this literary heritage, especially for young children: "Because children are young for such a short time, we need to give them their literary heritage during these brief years. Just as every literate adult knows certain books, every child should know specific children's books. If we fail to present these books to children, they reach adulthood without a basic literary heritage" (p. xi).

Literature plays a strong role in helping us understand and value our cultural heritage as well. Developing positive attitudes toward our own culture and the cultures of others is necessary for both social and personal development. Carefully selected literature can illustrate the contributions and values of the many cultures. It is especially critical to foster an appreciation of the heritage of the ethnic minorities in American society. A positive self-concept is not possible unless we respect others as well as ourselves; literature can contribute considerably toward our understanding and thus our respect.

The vicarious experiences of literature result in personal development as well as pleasure. Without literature, most children could not relive the European colonists' experiences of crossing the ocean and shaping a new country in North America; they could not experience the loneliness and fear of a fight for survival on an isolated island; they could not travel to distant places in the galaxy. Historical fiction provides children with opportunities to live in the past. Science fiction allows them to speculate about the future. Contemporary realistic fiction encourages them to experience relationships with the people and the environment of today. Because children can learn from literature how other people handle their problems, characters in books can help children deal with similar problems, as well as understand other people's feelings.

Another value of literature is that of developing emotional intelligence. Daniel Golman (1995) identifies five basic elements of emotional intelligence that children need: self-awareness, managing emotions, handling anxiety in appropriate ways, motivating oneself, and sensitivity toward others. Marjorie N. Allen (1999) states that children's literature is an excellent source for helping adolescents deal with emotions because "books are a way to face grief, deal with perceived differences, and gain self-confidence. When written well, they create empathy and understanding at a time when young people are trying to adjust to the unexpected complexities of growing up" (p. 87).

Informational books relay new knowledge about virtually every topic imaginable, and they are available at all levels of difficulty. Biographies and autobiographies tell about the people who gained knowledge or made discoveries. Photographs and illustrations show the wonders of nature or depict the processes required to master new hobbies. Realistic stories from a specific time bring history to life. The use of concept books that illustrate colors, numbers, shapes, and sizes may stimulate the cognitive development of even very young children. On the flyleaf of his *A History of Reading*, Alberto Manguel (1996) summarizes the values gained through literature. He states:

> At one magical instant in your early childhood, the page of a book—that string of confused, alien ciphers—shivered into meaning. Words spoke to you, gave up their secrets; at that moment, whole universes opened. You became, irrevocably, a reader.

Any discussion about the values of literature must stress the role that literature plays in nurturing and expanding the imagination. Books take children into worlds that stimulate additional imaginative experiences when they tell or write their own stories and interact with each other during creative drama inspired by what they have read. Both well-written literature and illustrations, such as those found in picture books and picture storybooks, can stimulate aesthetic development. Children enjoy and evaluate illustrations and can explore artistic media by creating illustrations of their own. Shirley Brice Heath (2004) found that young artists were reading for pleasure nearly twice as much as students in comparative classes. She concludes that students benefit when they have opportunities for "drawing in collaboration with writing, creative writing for production or complement to visual arts, and dramatic renderings of children's literature and young adult publications" (p. 341).

The values gained from literature in childhood often have profound influences on adults. David L. Russell (1999) chronicles the importance of reading to historical fiction author Scott O'Dell. Russell states:

> O'Dell's early formal education had little impact on him, but he always enjoyed reading. When he was 10, his parents gave him the works of his ancestor Sir Walter Scott, and he fell in love with them. Perhaps from that time forward he was destined to be a historical novelist himself. (p. 3)

Poet Eloise Greenfield may provide one of the greatest benefits for reading through her poem "Story," found in *In the Land of Words: New and Selected Poems*. The poem is printed in the form of steps:

Story
I step into the story,
I leave my world behind,
I let the walls of story
Be the walls around my mind.

    New faces and new voices,
    I listen and I see,
    and people I have never met
    mean everything to me.

        I worry when they worry,
        I quake when danger's near,
        I hold my breath and hope
        that all their troubles disappear.

            I don't know what will happen,
            I never know what I'll find,
            when I step into a story
            and leave my world behind.

Promoting Child Development Through Literature

Research in child development has identified stages in the language, cognitive, personality, and social development of children. Not all children progress through these stages at the same rate, but all children do pass through each stage as they mature. The general characteristics of children at each developmental stage provide clues for appropriate literature. Certain books can benefit children during a particular stage of development, helping them progress to the next stage. Understanding the types and stages of child development is useful for anyone who works with children.

Language Development

Literature has profound influences on children's language development. Chart 1.1 lists characteristics, teaching recommendations, and books that are appropriate for language development.

Preschool Children. During their first few years, children show dramatic changes in language ability. Most children learn language very rapidly. They speak their first words at about 1 year of age; at about 18 months, they begin to put words together in two-word combinations. Speech during this stage of language development consists of nouns, verbs, and adjectives; it usually contains no prepositions, articles, auxiliary verbs, or pronouns. When children say "pretty flower" or "milk gone," they are using telegraphic speech. The number of different two-word combinations increases slowly, then it shows a sudden upsurge around age 2.

Speech usually becomes more complex by age 3, when most children have added adverbs, pronouns, prepositions, and more adjectives to their vocabularies. Children also enjoy playing with the sounds of words at this stage of language development. By age 4, they produce grammatically correct sentences. This stage is a questioning one, during which language is used to ask why and how.

Literature and literature-related experiences can encourage language development in preschool children. Steve Herb (1997) reviews research findings and concludes, "Children's early experiences with books directly relate to their success in learning to read in school," and "storybook reading is a more effective influence on literacy development when children have opportunities to engage in conversation about the story" (p. 23).

Book experiences in the home, at the library, and at preschool can help children use language to discover the world, identify and name actions and objects, gain more complex speech, and enjoy the wonder of language. Many children first experience literature through picture books, which help them give meaning to their expanding vocabularies. For example, children who are just learning to identify their hands and other parts of their bodies may find these parts in drawings of children. Parents of very young children can share Helen Oxenbury's excellent baby board books. (Board books are toy books made of cardboard for young children.) *Dressing,* for example, includes a picture of a baby's clothing, followed by a picture of the child dressed in those items. The illustrations are sequentially developed to encourage talking about the steps in dressing.

Young children can identify actions in pictures such as those found in Carolyn Curtis's *I Took the Moon for a Walk.* The book includes both the language in rhyming text and the journey that takes the child past locations such as a steeple that snags the moon, "rust-bellied robins," and clouds as "fragile as lace."

Kevin Henkes's *Kitten's First Full Moon* is another highly illustrated book that focuses on interactions with the moon. This humorous story introduces each action with repetitive phrases as the kitten tries to catch the elusive moon. The author uses language such as "So she chased it—down the sidewalk, through the garden, past the field, and by the pond" (unnumbered). Stars provide the repetition in Lauren Thompson's *Polar Bear Night* as they are compared to snowflakes, falling, falling, falling.

Many excellent books allow children to listen to the sounds of language and experiment with these sounds. For example, Woody Guthrie's *Woody's 20 Grow Big Songs* includes songs that contain both repetition and actions that younger children enjoy.

Books with repetitive language are excellent for enticing listeners to join in during oral reading. In *Off We Go!,*

CHART 1.1   Language development (pp. 5–7)

Characteristics	Teaching Recommendations	Literature Suggestions
Preschool: Ages 2–3		
1 Very rapid language growth occurs. By the end of this period, children have vocabularies of about 900 words.	1 Provide many activities to stimulate language growth, including picture books and Mother Goose rhymes.	Ho, Minfong. *Hush!: A Thai Lullaby*. Lewis, Kim. *Good Night, Harry*. Lobel, Arnold. *The Random House Book of Mother Goose*. O'Connell, Rebecca. *The Baby Goes Beep*. Simmons, Jane. *Daisy Says "Coo!"*.
2 Children learn to identify and name actions in pictures.	2 Read books that contain clear, familiar action pictures; encourage children to identify actions.	Baicker, Karen. *Tumble Me Tumbily*. Fleming, Denise. *In the Tall, Tall Grass*. Opie, Iona. *Here Comes Mother Goose*.
3 Children learn to identify large and small body parts.	3 Allow children to identify familiar body parts in picture books.	Oxenbury, Helen. *Dressing*.
Preschool: Ages 3–4		
1 Vocabularies have increased to about 1,500 words. Children enjoy playing with sound and rhythm in language.	1 Include opportunities to listen to and say rhymes, poetry, and riddles.	Gerber, Carole. *Leaf Jumpers*. Griego, Margot C., et al. *Tortillitas Para Mama*. Krauss, Ruth. *Bears*. Rosen, Michael. *We're Going on a Bear Hunt*. Whybrow, Ian. *The Noisy Way to Bed*. Wilson, Karma. *Bear Snores On*. Yolen, Jane. *The Three Bears Rhyme Book*.
2 Children develop the ability to use past tense but may overgeneralize the *ed* and *s* markers. 3 Children use language to help find out about the world.	2 Allow children to talk about what they did yesterday; discuss actions in books. 3 Read picture storybooks to allow children to find out about and discuss pets, families, people, and the environment.	Cooper, Helen. *Pumpkin Soup*. Hill, Eric. *Spot Goes to School*. Keats, Ezra Jack. *The Snowy Day*. Fleming, Denise. *In the Small, Small Pond*. Markes, Julie. *Shhhh! Everybody's Sleeping*. Potter, Beatrix. *The Tale of Peter Rabbit*. Shannon, David. *Alice the Fairy*. Tafuri, Nancy. *Early Morning in the Barn*. Thompson, Lauren. *Polar Bear Night*. Waddell, Martin. *Let's Go Home, Little Bear*.
4 Speech becomes more complex, with more adjectives, adverbs, pronouns, and prepositions.	4 Expand the use of descriptive words through detailed picture books and picture storybooks. Allow children to tell stories and describe characters and their actions.	Barton, Byron. *Machines at Work*. Narahashi, Keiko. *I Have a Friend*. Rohman, Eric. *My Friend Rabbit*.
Preschool: Ages 4–5		
1 Language is more abstract; children produce grammatically correct sentences. Their vocabularies contain approximately 2,500 words.	1 Children enjoy books with slightly more complex plots. Ask them to tell longer and more detailed stories. They enjoy retelling folktales and can tell stories using wordless books.	Brett, Jan. *Goldilocks and the Three Bears*. Fleischman, Paul. *Sidewalk Circus*. Haas, Irene. *A Summertime Song*. McCully, Emily Arnold. *School*. Wiesner, David. *Free Fall*. ———. *Tuesday*.

(continues)

CHART 1.1   Continued

Characteristics	Teaching Recommendations	Literature Suggestions
2 Children understand the prepositions *over, under, in, out, in front of,* and *behind.* 3 Children enjoy asking many questions, especially those related to *why* and *how.*	2 Use concept books or other picture books in which prepositions can be reinforced. 3 Take advantage of natural curiosity and find books to help answer children's questions. Allow them to answer each other's questions.	Henkes, Kevin. *Kitten's First Full Moon.* hooks, bell. *Skin Again.* Hutchins, Pat. *What Game Shall We Play?* Juan, Ana. *The Night Eater.* Noll, Sally. *Watch Where You Go.*
Preschool–Kindergarten: Ages 5–6 I Most children use complex sentences frequently and begin to use correct pronouns and verbs in present and past tense. They understand approximately 6,000 words. 2 Children enjoy taking part in dramatic play and producing dialogue about everyday activities such as those at home and at the grocery store. 3 Children are curious about the written appearance of their own language.	I Give children many opportunities for oral language activities connected with literature. 2 Read stories about the home and community. Allow children to act out their own stories. 3 Write chart stories using the children's own words. Have children dictate descriptions of pictures.	Aardema, Verna. *Bringing the Rain to Kapiti Plain.* Appelt, Kathi. *Where, Where Is Swamp Bear?* Cronin, Doreen. *Click, Clack, Moo: Cows That Type.* Gág, Wanda. *Millions of Cats.* Katz, Bobbi. *Pocket Poems.* Moss, Lloyd. *Zin! Zin! Zin! A Violin.* Opie, Iona. *My Very First Mother Goose.* Taback, Simms. *There Was an Old Lady Who Swallowed a Fly.* Demarest, Chris. L. *Firefighters A to Z.* Hurd, Edith Thacher. *I Dance in My Red Pajamas.* Martin, Rafe. *Will's Mammoth.* Seeber, Dorothea. *A Pup Just for Me: A Boy Just for Me.* Seuss, Dr. *And to Think That I Saw It on Mulberry Street.* Sturges, Philemon. *She'll Be Comin' 'Round the Mountain.* Baker, Jeannie. *Window.* Edwards, Pamela Duncan. *The Neat Line.* McCully, Emily Arnold. *Picnic.* Newman, Lesléa. *Cats, Cats, Cats!* Willard, Nancy. *Night Story.*
Early Elementary: Ages 6–8 I Language development continues. Children add many new words to their vocabularies. 2 Most children use complex sentences with adjectival clauses and conditional clauses beginning with *if.* The average oral sentence length is seven and one half words.	I Provide daily time for reading to children and allow for oral interaction. 2 Read stories that provide models for children's expanding language structure.	DeFelice, Cynthia. *Willy's Silly Grandma.* George, Kristine O'Connell. *Toasting Marshmallows: Camping Poems.* Hoberman, Mary Ann. *You Read to Me, I'll Read to You.* Joosse, Barbara. *Hot City.* Lewin, Hugh. *Jafta.* Myers, Tim. *Basho and the River Stones.* Silverstein, Shel. *A Light in the Attic.* Washington, Donna L. *A Pride of African Tales.* Burton, Virginia Lee. *The Little House.* Curtis, Carolyn. *I Took the Moon for a Walk.* McCloskey, Robert. *Make Way for Ducklings.*

CHART 1.1   Continued

Characteristics	Teaching Recommendations	Literature Suggestions
Middle Elementary: Ages 8–10 1 Children begin to relate concepts to general ideas. They use connectors such as *meanwhile* and *unless*. 2 The subordinating connector *although* is used correctly by 50% of children. Present participle active and perfect participle appear. The average sentence length is nine words.	1 Supply books as models. Let children use these terms during oral language activities. 2 Use written models and oral models to help children master their language skills. Literature discussions allow many opportunities for oral sentence expansion.	Schotter, Roni. *Nothing Ever Happens on 90th Street.* Steptoe, John. *Mufaro's Beautiful Daughters: An African Tale.* Young, Ed. *Lon Po Po: A Red Riding Hood Story From China.* DiCamillo, Kate. *The Tale of Despereaux.* Kennedy, Caroline. *The Best-Loved Poems of Jacqueline Kennedy Onassis.* Levine, Arthur A. *The Boy Who Drew Cats: A Japanese Folktale.* Paolilli, Paul, and Dan Brewer. *Silver Seeds: A Book of Nature Poems.* Sandburg, Carl. *More Rootabagas.* Sierra, Judy. *Tasty Baby Belly Buttons.* Walter, Mildred Pitts. *Brother to the Wind.*
Upper Elementary: Ages 10–12 1 Children use complex sentences with subordinate clauses of concession introduced by *nevertheless* and *in spite of.* Auxiliary verbs *might, could,* and *should* appear frequently.	1 Encourage oral language and written activities that permit children to use more complex sentence structures.	Dunleavy, Deborah. *The Jumbo Book of Drama.* Lehman, Barbara. *The Red Book.* L'Engle, Madeleine. *A Swiftly Tilting Planet.* McKinley, Robin. *The Hero and the Crown.* Paulsen, Gary. *Hatchet.* _____. *The Winter Room.* Pullman, Philip. *The Golden Compass.* Rogers, Gregory. *The Boy, The Bear, The Baron, The Bard.* Whelan, Gloria, *Homeless Bird.*
Adolescence: Ages 12–18 1 Students have a better understanding of figurative language such as metaphors and hyperbole. 2 Students acquire vocabulary related to academic disciplines.	1 Read and discuss poetry that uses figurative language. Use in creative writing. 2 Identify and use the specific vocabulary associated with each discipline. Read a wide variety of nonfictional materials.	Grimes, Nikki. *Bronx Masquerade.* Janeczko, Paul, (Ed.). *Blushing: Expressions of Love in Poems & Letters.* _____. *Worlds Afire.* Nelson, Marilyn. *Carver: A Life in Poems.* Thomas, Dylan. *A Child's Christmas in Wales.* Burleigh, Robert. *The Sea: Exploring Life on an Ocean Planet.* Kermode, Frank. *The Age of Shakespeare.* *Oxford Spanish Dictionary.*

Sources: Bartel (1995); Brown (1973); Gage and Berliner (1992); Hendrick (1996); and Loban (1976).

From A CHILD'S CHRISTMAS IN WALES. Text Copyright © 1954 by New Directions. Illustrations Copyright © 2004 by Chris Raschka. Published under an agreement with New Directions Publishing Corporation and the Trustees for the copyrights of Dylan Thomas. Reproduced by permission of the publisher Candlewick Press. Inc.

Jane Yolen creates a rhythmic, rhyming text as various animals move off to find grandmother's house. For example, notice the appealing language as "Slither-slee, slithery slee. Down the branch and round the tree" (unnumbered) goes the little snake in search of grandmother. There are numerous rhyming sentences: Frogs slop, stop; moles sleep, creep; ducks scratch, hatch; and spiders crawl, fall. Another good source of a rhythmic text to read to young children is Lesléa Newman's *Cats, Cats, Cats!*, in which cats are tucked in tight every night and *fiddle dee dee* is rhymed with *me*. Rhythmic language that invites children to join in is an enjoyable feature in Philemon Sturges's *She'll Be Comin' 'Round the Mountain*; the text is based on the folk song. The poems in Lee Bennett Hopkins's *Hanukkah Lights: Holiday Poetry* include rhyming texts and lines that lend themselves to acting out. For example, "Dizzy," by Maria Fleming, contains rhyming words such as *giggly* and *wiggly* and lines that encourage children to feel twirly, whirly, and squiggly inside, just like a dizzy top. Children can respond in both Spanish and English when they interact with the rhymes in *Tortillitas Para Mama*, by Margot C. Griego et al.

Books that encourage children to play with and appreciate language are also excellent for language development. The vivid language in Lloyd Moss's *Zin! Zin! Zin! A*

Violin is especially appealing. Children can join in as the trombone plays mournful tones by "gliding, sliding" or the oboe plays "gleeful, bleating, sobbing, pleading." This book provides an excellent source for acting out the sounds and movements related to the instruments of the orchestra.

Unusual words and stories in rhyme encourage children to play with language. In *Good Zap, Little Grog*, Sarah Wilson uses unusual language to create a story in rhyme; as the fantasy story progresses, ooglets are tuzzling, parobbies are churling, and glipneeps are jumping. Rob and Amy Spence's *Clickety Clack* includes both a story in rhyme and rhythm associated with a railroad. Children can easily join in with all the words that rhyme with *clack*, such as *track, back, yak, quack, crack*, and *attack*. Considerable onomatopoeia provides humor in Libba Moore Gray's language for *When Uncle Took the Fiddle*, as the strings on the violin go "zee zee, saw saw, and ziggle, ziggle, zang" and gourds shake "click and clatter, shu, sha, shu, and rick-a-rack-a MEW!" (unnumbered).

Some stories in rhyme encourage children to fill in the missing rhyming word. In Ian Whybrow's *The Noisy Way to Bed*, for example, the author uses a series of rhyming verses that all rhyme with *bed*.

The poems in Jane Dyer's collection *Animal Crackers: A Delectable Collection of Pictures, Poems, and Lullabies*

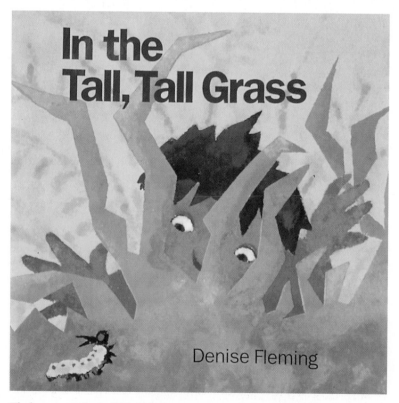

The language in In the Tall, Tall Grass *encourages both observation and play with words. From* In the Tall, Tall Grass, *by Denise Fleming. Copyright © 1991 by Denise Fleming. Reprinted by permission of Henry Holt and Company, Inc.*

for the Very Young include rhythm, rhyme, and sound patterns that appeal to young children.

Elementary-Age Children. Of course, language development continues as children enter school and progress through the grades. Walter Loban (1976) conducted the most extensive longitudinal study of language development in school-age children. This study is so important that Marilyn Hanf Buckley (1992) states that Loban's work established the firm relationship between oral language development and success at reading and writing and "provided the base upon which our present-day thinking about the integrated language arts curriculum rests" (p. 622). Loban examined the language development of the same group of more than 200 children from age 5 to age 18. He found that children's power over language increases through successive control over different forms of language, including pronouns, verb tenses, and connectors, such as *meanwhile* and *unless.*

Loban (1976) identified dramatic differences between children who ranked high in language proficiency and those who ranked low: The high group reached a level of oral proficiency in 1st grade that

Folklore elements and important themes are developed in this southern tale. (From The Talking Eggs: A Folktale from the American South, *retold by Robert D. San Souci, pictures by Jerry Pinkney. Pictures copyright © 1989 by Jerry Pinkney. Reprinted by permission of Dial Books for Young Readers.)*

the low group did not attain until 6th grade and a level of written proficiency in 4th grade that the low group did not attain until 10th grade. Those who demonstrated high language proficiency excelled in the control of ideas expressed, showing unity and planning in both their speech and their writing. These students spoke freely, fluently, and easily, using a rich vocabulary and adjusting the pace of their words to their listeners. They were attentive and creative listeners themselves, far outranking the low group in listening ability. The oral communication of those with low language proficiency was characterized by rambling and unpurposeful dialogue that demonstrated a meager vocabulary.

Children who were superior in oral language in kindergarten and first grade also excelled in reading and writing in sixth grade. They were more fluent in written language than were the low-ranked children, used more words per sentence, showed a richer written vocabulary, and were superior in using connectors and subordination to combine thoughts into complex forms of expression. Given the demonstrated connection between oral and written language skills, Loban (1976) concluded that teachers, librarians, and parents should give greater attention to developing children's oral language. Discussion should be a vital part of elementary school and library pro-

grams because it helps children organize ideas and make complex generalizations. Unfortunately, however, Marie Clay (1991) concludes, "While teachers see oral language as central to writing and reading acquisition, they often do not recognize the need to foster its further development" (p. 41).

Stories in rhyme written for elementary-age children may combine both history and rhyming language, as found in Jill Esbaum's *Ste-e-e-e-eam Boat A-Comin'!* The text and story follow the activities surrounding a Mississippi River steamboat in 1867. The rhyming text includes words appropriate for the time such as "shouts and roustabouts." The illustrations show the *S. L. Clemens* and an Illinois town as the people meet the steamboat and trade for the goods it brought.

Wordless picture books are excellent stimuli for oral and written language. Some excellent examples of wordless picture books include Emily Arnold McCully's *School*, which follows the exploits of the littlest mouse child, who discovers what happens during a real school day. Peter Collington's *The Angel and the Soldier Boy* provides an exciting adventure, in which an angel and a soldier rescue a coin from pirates and return it to a sleeping child. Older students can go back to the time of Shakespeare and the Globe Theatre to tell the story that accompanies the illustrations in the wordless book *The Boy, The Bear, The Baron, The Bard,* illustrated by Gregory Rogers.

Books that are written in two languages allow children to see and hear another language as well as read or hear their own language. For example, James Rumford's *Sequoyah: The Cherokee Man Who Gave His People Writing* has parallel text written in Cherokee.

David Wiesner is renowned for his mastery with wordless picture books. His *Free Fall* shows the adventures that are possible within dreams. Wiesner's *Tuesday* is a story filled with surprising and unexpected elements as frogs fly around the neighborhood. Readers enjoy extending the book into the next Tuesday. Wiesner's final illustration shows that now the pigs have their opportunity to fly, to explore the neighborhood, and to baffle the people. The book provides an interesting stimulus for oral stories, creative writing, and drawing illustrations and for children to create their own stories about "The Night the Pigs Could Fly."

Books with vivid language, similes, and metaphors stimulate language development and appreciation for literary style. The text for Jane Yolen's *Owl Moon* is filled with figurative language that personifies trees, dogs, and shadows. For example, footprints in the snow "follow us," shadows "bumped after me," and cold places an "icy hand . . . palm-down on my back." Similes and metaphors produce vivid comparisons; voices in the night fade away "as quiet as a dream," snow is "whiter than milk in a cereal bowl," and an owl moves "like a shadow without a sound." The vivid language in Nancy Willard's *Pish, Posh, Said Hieronymus Bosch* presents a fantasy world in which the housekeeper wrestles with dragons "while the cats chase the cucumbers, slickity-slink."

Poetry collections are another good source for language development. *Silver Seeds: A Book of Nature Poems,* by Paul Paolilli, encourages readers to view nature in new ways as the poems use vivid metaphors to describe such common natural occurrences as the stars, the moon, and the clouds. When reading or listening to poetry, students may need guidance to understand the poetic forms. In *A Child's Introduction to Poetry,* Michael Driscoll presents definitions for and examples of different types of poetry, such as villanelle, limerick, haiku, narrative verse, and lyric verse. In addition, he provides a CD of the poems read by professional actors. The cover includes words that suggest the motivational power of the poems: "Listen while you learn about the magic words that have moved mountains, won battles and made us laugh and cry."

Literature is a crucial resource, providing both a model for language and a stimulus for oral and written activities. This text suggests a wealth of literature: literature to be read aloud to children; literature to provide models for expanding language proficiency; and literature to stimulate oral discussion, creative dramatics, creative writing, and listening enjoyment.

Literature provides stimulus for the dramatic play and creative dramatics that inspire children in the primary grades to express themselves verbally with much enjoyment. For example, in Maurice Sendak's *Where the Wild Things Are,* Max gets into so much mischief when he is wearing his wolf suit that his mother sends him to his room without any supper. His vivid imagination turns the room into a forest inhabited by wild things. Max stays in the forest and becomes its king, but finally, he gets lonely and wants to return to the land where someone loves him. Children can relate to Max's experience and use it to stimulate their own wild experiences. Children enjoy using their imaginations and turning common occurrences into creative experiences.

Books that encourage children to make up their own stories are also excellent for language development. Authors may develop their books on the premise of what would happen if a character from a book came to life. In Susan Cooper's *Matthew's Dragon,* the dragon from a boy's favorite book comes to life, and the boy and the dragon share an adventure. By reading and viewing *The Flying Dragon Room,* text by Audrey Wood and illustrations by Mark Teague, children can use their imaginations to create their own fantasy worlds inhabited by strange animals and unusual experiences, or they can pretend that they are riding the flying dragon or sailing on the Jolly Mermaid. In *Edward and the Pirates,* David McPhail uses a young boy's love for reading and his powerful imagination to create adventures. Any of these books can encourage children to create their own stories. For example, children can choose a figure from a fictional book and pretend that it comes to life. What would happen? What might the figure do for good or for bad? How would they control the figure?

"What if" stories may encourage children to explore new worlds vicariously and to tell about experiences if they could accompany the literary characters. Paul Fleischman's *Time Train* provides a marvelous opportunity for children to enter the Rocky Mountain Unlimited and to go back in time chronologically until they finally enter a tropical world inhabited by dinosaurs. Jon Scieszka's *Your Mother Was a Neanderthal* allows children to accompany a time-warp trio back to the time of woolly mammoths and saber-toothed tigers. Alison Lester's *The Journey Home* encourages readers to accompany two children who dig a hole that takes them to the other side of the world; they have numerous adventures as they explore the earth in their endeavor to reach home. These books encourage children to create imaginative fantasies.

Young Adults and Language Development

Not only does language development continue, but language requirements increase as students progress into junior high and high school. Chart 1.1 (see pp. 5–7) shows some of the characteristics of the adolescent or young adult reader, teaching recommendations, and literature examples. The books they read and the activities associated with literature will encourage literary appreciation as well as understanding.

Some of the books available for young adults are written by outstanding authors whose craft is a model for language. For example, Marilyn Nelson's *Carver: A Life in Poems* and *Fortune's Bones: The Manumission Requiem* highlight the work of the Poet Laureate of the State of Connecticut and a three-time National Book Award finalist. Likewise, Diane McWhorter, the author of *A Dream of Freedom: The Civil Rights Movement From 1954 to 1968*, won the Pulitzer Prize for her adult book on the civil rights movement.

In addition, some of the authors of young adult literature use writing styles that may help students understand the writing process. For example, in *Project Mulberry*, Linda Sue Park allows her teenage protagonist to interact with the author: Following each chapter, she creates dialogue between herself, as author, and the teenage Korean American protagonist. This style allows the author to illuminate her writing process as well as highlight the difficulties of a teenage girl trying to overcome prejudice.

Cognitive Development

Factors related to helping children remember, anticipate, integrate perceptions, and develop concepts fill numerous textbooks and have been the subject of both research and conjecture. Jean Piaget and B. Inhelder (1969) maintained that the order in which children's thinking matures is the same for all children, although the pace varies from child to child. Stimulation also is necessary for cognitive development. Children who grow up without a variety of experiences may be 3 to 5 years behind other children in developing the mental strategies that aid recall. Chart 1.2 lists books that can promote cognitive development in children.

According to child development authority David Shaffer (1989), cognitive development "refers to the changes that occur in children's mental skills and abilities over time" (p. 306). Shaffer states, "We are constantly attending to objects and events, interpreting them, comparing them with past experiences, placing them into categories, and encoding them into memory" (p. 306). Mussen, Conger, and Kagan (1989) define cognition as the process involved in

(1) perception—the detection, organization, and interpretation of information from both the outside world and the inter-

nal environment, (2) memory—the storage and retrieval of the perceived information, (3) reasoning—the use of knowledge to make inferences and draw conclusions, (4) reflection—the evaluation of the quality of ideas and solutions, and (5) insight—the recognition of new relationships between two or more segments of knowledge.

George Maxim (1993) emphasizes cognitive development that includes two major areas: physical knowledge and logicomathematical ability. Physical knowledge is gained through observing properties of objects within the child's experience: The child learns about the physical environment through observation and experimentation. Logicomathematical ability includes the ability to classify or group objects on some common criterion; to arrange objects according to size, quality, or quantity and then compare similarities and differences among objects in the same category and order them according to relative differences; to understand spatial relations in terms of direction, distance, and perspective; to understand temporal relations that allow perception of time sequences; and to conceptualize properties of objects.

Scientist and author Chet Raymo (1992) highlights the role of children's books in developing a scientific imagination. He states, "Creative science depends crucially upon habits of mind that are most readily acquired by children: curiosity; voracious observation; sensitivity to rules and variations within the rules; and fantasy. Children's books that instill these habits of mind sustain science" (p. 561).

All of the preceding processes are essential for success in both school and adult life. Each is also closely related to understanding and enjoying literature. Without visual and auditory perception, literature could not be read or heard; without memory, there would be no way to see the relationships among literary works and to recognize new relationships as experiences are extended. Literature also is important in stimulating cognitive development by encouraging the oral exchange of ideas and the development of thought processes. Children's literature is especially effective for developing the basic operations associated with thinking: (1) observing, (2) comparing, (3) classifying, (4) hypothesizing, (5) organizing, (6) summarizing, (7) applying, and (8) criticizing.

Observing. Colorful picture books are excellent vehicles for developing observational skills in both younger and older children. Suse MacDonald's *Alphabatics* encourages young children to observe how a letter changes within three or four drawings to a picture of an object that begins with that letter. Keith Baker's *Hide and Snake* encourages viewers to search through the illustrations to find the snake that is mixed in with colored yarns, curled around hats, wrapped among presents, and napping with cats. The colors of the snake blend with the colors in the illustrations; consequently, this book becomes a game of hide-and-seek. Using Stephen T. Johnson's *Alphabet City*,

CHART 1.2   Cognitive development (pp. 12–15)

Characteristics	Teaching Recommendations	Literature Suggestions
Preschool: Ages 2–3		
1 Children learn new ways to organize and classify their worlds by putting together things that they perceive to be alike. 2 Children begin to remember two or three items.	1 Provide opportunities for children to discuss and group things according to color, shape, size, or use. Use picture concept books with large, colorful pictures. 2 Exercise children's short-term memories by providing opportunities to recall information.	Crews, Donald. *Freight Train.* Hoban, Tana. *Look! Look! Look!* _____. *Of Colors and Things.* _____. *1, 2, 3.* Gunson, Christopher. *Over on the Farm: A Counting Picture Book Rhyme.*
Preschool: Ages 3–4		
1 Children develop an understanding of how things relate to each other: how parts go together to make a whole, and how they are arranged in space in relation to each other. 2 Children begin to understand relationships and classify things according to certain perceptual attributes that they share, such as color, size, shape, and what they are used for. 3 Children begin to understand how objects relate to each other in terms of number and amount. 4 Children begin to compare two things and tell which is bigger and which is smaller.	1 Give children opportunities to find the correct part of a picture to match another picture. Use simple picture puzzles. 2 Share concept books on color, size, shape, and use. Provide opportunities for children to group and classify objects and pictures. 3 Give picture counting books to children. Allow them to count. 4 Share and discuss books that allow comparisons in size, such as a giant and a boy, a big item and a small item, or a series of animals.	Hutchins, Pat. *Changes, Changes.* Oxenbury, Helen. *I See.* Carle, Eric. *My Very First Book of Colors.* Hoban, Tana. *Shapes, Shapes, Shapes.* _____. *So Many Circles, So Many Squares.* Seeger, Laura Vaccaro. *Lemons Are Not Red.* Bang, Molly. *Ten, Nine, Eight.* Carle, Eric. *My Very First Book of Numbers.* Christelow, Eileen. *Five Little Monkeys Jumping on the Bed.* Fleming, Denise. *Count!* Reiser, Lynn. *Ten Puppies.* Campbell, Rod. *Dear Zoo.* Voake, Charlotte. *Mrs. Goose's Baby.*
Preschool: Ages 4–5		
1 Children remember to do three things told to them or retell a short story if the material is presented in a meaningful sequence. 2 Children increase their ability to group objects according to important characteristics but still base their rules on how things look to them. 3 Children pretend to tell time but do not understand the concept. Things happen "now" or "before now."	1 Tell short, meaningful stories and allow children to retell them. Use flannelboard and picture stories to help children organize the story. Give practice in following three-step directions. 2 Provide many opportunities to share concept books and activities designed to develop ideas of shape, color, size, feel, and use. 3 Share books to help children understand sequence of time and when things happen, such as the seasons of the year and different times of the day or different days of the week.	Asbjørnsen, Peter Christen. *Three Billy Goats Gruff.* Gág, Wanda. *Millions of Cats.* Cullen, Catherine Ann. *Thirsty Baby.* Galdone, Paul. *The Gingerbread Boy.* Carle, Eric. *My Very First Book of Shapes.* Hoban, Tana. *Circles, Triangles, and Squares.* Nye, Naomi Shihab. *Baby Radar.* Sís, Peter. *Trucks Trucks Trucks.* Peters, Lisa Westberg. *October Smiled Back.* Rockwell, Anne. *First Comes Spring.*

CHART 1.2 Continued

Characteristics	Teaching Recommendations	Literature Suggestions
Preschool–Kindergarten: Ages 5–6		
1 Children learn to follow one type of classification (such as color or shape) through to completion without changing the main characteristic partway through the task.	1 Continue to share concept books and encourage activities that allow children to group and classify.	Leuck, Laura. *One Witch.* Lobel, Arnold. *On Market Street.*
2 Children count to 10 and discriminate 10 objects.	2 Reinforce counting skills with counting books and other counting activities.	Carle, Eric. *10 Little Rubber Ducks.* Parker, Vic. *Bearobics: A Hip-Hop Counting Story.* Sierra, Judy. *Counting Crocodiles.*
3 Children identify primary colors.	3 Reinforce identification through the use of color concept books and colors found in other picture books.	Hutchins, Pat. *Changes, Changes.*
4 Children learn to distinguish between "a lot of" something and "a little of" something.	4 Provide opportunities for children to identify and discuss the differences between concepts.	Rumford, James. *Calabash Cat and His Amazing Journey.* Zemach, Margot. *It Could Always Be Worse.*
5 Children require trial and error before they can arrange things in order from smallest to biggest.	5 Share books that progress from smallest to largest. Have children retell stories using flannelboard characters drawn in appropriate sizes.	Galdone, Paul. *The Three Billy Goats Gruff.* Jenkins, Steve. *Big & Little.*
6 Children still have vague concepts of time.	6 Share books to help children understand time sequence.	Moser, Barry. *The Three Little Pigs.* Young, Ed. *I, Doko: The Tale of a Basket.*
Early Elementary: Ages 6–8		
1 Children are learning to read; they enjoy reading easy books and demonstrating their new abilities.	1 Provide easy-to-read books geared to children's developing reading skills.	Byars, Betsy. *My Brother, Ant.* Lobel, Arnold. *Frog and Toad All Year.* Rylant, Cynthia. *Henry and Mudge and the Long Weekend.* _____. *Mr. Putter and Tabby Pour the Tea.* Seuss, Dr. *The Cat in the Hat.*
2 Children are learning to write and enjoy creating their own stories.	2 Allow children to write, illustrate, and share their own picture books. Use wordless books to suggest plot.	Van Leeuwen, Jean. *Oliver Pig at School.* Fleischman, Paul. *Sidewalk Circus.* Van Allsburg, Chris. *The Mysteries of Harris Burdick.* Wiesner, David. *Free Fall.* _____. *Sector 7.* _____. *Tuesday.*
3 Children enjoy longer stories than they did when they were 5 because their attention spans are increasing.	3 Read longer storybooks to children, such as books in which the chapters can be completed in a short time.	Alexander, Lloyd. *The Fortune-Tellers.* Lester, Julius. *The Last Tales of Uncle Remus.* Milne, A. A. *The House at Pooh Corner.* San Souci, Robert. *The Talking Eggs: A Folktale From the American South.* Van Allsburg, Chris. *The Polar Express.*

(continues)

CHART 1.2   Continued

Characteristics	Teaching Recommendations	Literature Suggestions
Early Elementary: Ages 6–8		
4 Children under 7 still base their rules on immediate perception and learn through real situations.	4 Provide experiences that allow children to see, discuss, and verify information and relationships.	Andrews-Goebel, Nancy. *The Pot That Juan Built.* Emberley. Ed. *The Wing on a Flea: A Book About Shapes.* hooks, bell. *Skin Again.* Micklethwait, Lucy. *A Child's Book of Play in Art: Great Pictures Great Fun.* Peters, Lisa Westberg. *The Sun, the Wind and the Rain.* Priceman, Marjorie, *How to Make an Apple Pie and See the World.*
5 Sometime during this age, children pass into the stage that Piaget refers to as concrete operational. Children have developed a new set of rules, called groupings, so they don't have to see all objects to group; they can understand relationships among categories.	5 Provide opportunities for children to read and discuss concept books.	Anno, Mitsumasa. *Anno's Counting Book.* _____. *Anno's Math Games II.* Feelings, Muriel. *Moja Means One: Swahili Counting Book.* Grossman, Bill. *My Little Sister Ate One Hare.* Haskins, Jim. *Count Your Way Through Italy.* Hoban, Tana. *26 Letters and 99 Cents.* Inkpen, Mick. *Kipper's A to Z: An Alphabet Adventure.* Kalman, Maira. *What Pete Ate From A–Z (Really!).* McMillan, Bruce. *Eating Fractions.* Wells, Rosemary. *Emily's First 100 Days of School.*
Middle Elementary: Ages 8–10		
1 Children's reading skills improve rapidly, although there are wide variations in reading ability among children within the same age group.	1 For independent reading, provide books at appropriate reading levels. Allow children opportunities to share their book experiences with peers, parents, teachers, and other adults.	Blume, Judy. *Tales of a Fourth Grade Nothing.* Cleary, Beverly. *Ramona and Her Father.* Lowry, Lois. *Attaboy, Sam!* Nichol, Barbara. *Beethoven Lives Upstairs.* Wilder, Laura Ingalls. *Little House in the Big Woods.*
2 Children's level of interest in literature may still be above their reading levels.	2 Provide a daily time during which children can listen to a variety of books being read aloud.	Burnett, Frances Hodgson. *The Secret Garden.* Christelow, Eileen. *Vote.* Cooper, Michael L. *Dust to Eat: Drought and Depression in the 1930s.* Gantos, Jack. *Joey Pigza Loses Control.* Grahame, Kenneth. *The Wind in the Willows.* Konigsburg, E. L. *The View From Saturday.* Lewis, C. S. *The Lion, the Witch and the Wardrobe.* White, E. B. *Charlotte's Web.*
3 Memory improves as children learn to attend to certain stimuli and ignore others.	3 Help children set purposes for listening or reading before the actual literature experience.	Ammon, Richard. *Valley Forge.* Freedman, Russell. *The Wright Brothers: How They Invented the Airplane.* Koscielniak, Bruce. *The Story of the Incredible Orchestra.* Martin, Laura. *Nature's Art Box.*

CHART 1.2   Continued

Characteristics	Teaching Recommendations	Literature Suggestions
Upper Elementary: Ages 10–12		
1 Children develop an understanding of the chronological ordering of past events.	1 Encourage children to read historical fiction and books showing historical changes to help them understand differing viewpoints and historical perspectives.	Forbes, Esther. *Johnny Tremain.* McCurdy, Michael. *Escape From Slavery: The Boyhood of Frederick Douglass in His Own Words.* Meyer, Carolyn, and Charles Gallenkamp: *The Mystery of the Ancient Maya.* Schanzer, Rosalyn. *George vs. George: The American Revolution as Seen From Both Sides.* Speare, Elizabeth George. *The Sign of the Beaver.* Stolley, Richard B. *Life: Our Century in Pictures for Young People.* Orlev, Uri. *The Man From the Other Side.*
2 Children apply logical rules, reasoning, and formal operations to abstract problems.	2 Use questioning and discussion strategies to develop higher-level thought processes. Children enjoy more complex books.	Avi. *Nothing But the Truth: A Documentary Novel.* *Beowulf.* Blumberg, Rhoda. *The Incredible Journey of Lewis & Clark.* Freedman, Russell. *Lincoln: A Photobiography.* Grimes, Nikki. *Tai Chi Morning: Snapshots of China.* Jackson, Donna M. *In Your Face: The Facts About Your Features.*
Adolescence: Ages 12–18		
1 Most students have the ability to attend to a task for longer periods.	1 Give assignments that require focusing on a task for longer periods.	Clee, Paul. *Photography and the Making of the American West.* Hill, Laban Carrick. *Harlem Stomp! A Cultural History of the Harlem Renaissance.* Holzhey, Magdelena. *Frida Kahlo: The Artist in the Blue House.*
2 Many students can integrate knowledge and understand relationships.	2 Encourage students to conduct research and to use inquiry approaches.	Oppel, Kenneth. *Airborne.* Lauber, Patricia. *Who Came First? New Clues to Prehistoric Americans.* Venezia, Mike. *Diego Velázquez.*

Sources: Maxim (1997); Mussen, Conger, and Kagan (1989); and Piaget and Inhelder (1969).

students can search for the various letters of the alphabet captured through paintings of various scenes. For example, the letter A is a construction sawhorse, the letter M is a bridge structure, and the letter Z is formed with fire escapes. The illustrations in Lucy Micklethwait's *A Child's Book of Play in Art: Great Pictures, Great Fun* encourage children to find details, imitate sounds, adapt patterns, and interpret costumes.

Paul Fleischman's wordless book *Sidewalk Circus* provides many opportunities for observation and compar-

isons. The story begins as a girl watches activities across the street from her bus stop. A marquee reads: "World-Renowned Garibaldi Circus!!!! Coming Soon." Kevin Hawkes's illustrations show that workers in the town are already performing as tightrope walkers, strong men, sword swallowers, and clowns. Children can describe how the illustrations show each of these circus acts in real life. They can also observe their own towns and relate to Kevin Hawkes when he describes how he prepared for the illustrations: "As I worked on *Sidewalk Circus,* I spent a lot of

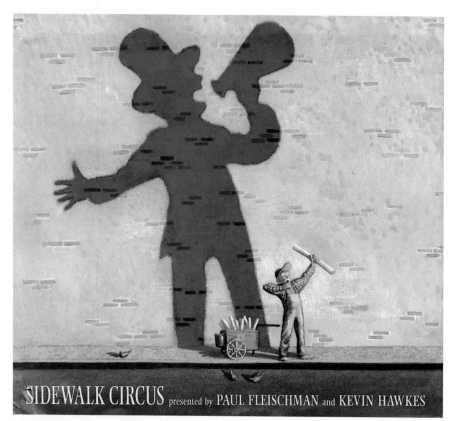

From SIDEWALK CIRCUS. Story and text copyright © 2004 Paul Fleischman. Illustrations copyright © 2004 Kevin Hawkes. Reproduced by permission of the publisher Candlewick Press, Inc.

in about 1485 by Sandro Botticelli. Browne uses a similar approach in *The Shape Game:* Now he transplants elements of the family who are visiting a museum into the paintings. The shape game continues as the family travels home. Now one person draws an abstract shape and another member changes the shape into something they recognize. Anthony Browne uses experiences he gained as a writer-and-illustrator-in-residence at the Tate gallery in London. In *I Spy Shapes in Art,* Lucy Micklethwait places reproductions of art on the right side of the page and asks an "I spy" question on the left side. For example, "I spy ten circles. What do you spy?" (unnumbered).

Comparing. Picture books and other literature selections provide opportunities for comparing. For example, comparisons between two points of view can be made using Dorothea P. Seeber's *A Pup Just for Me; A Boy Just for Me.* Two stories are told

time in Portland, Maine. I was amazed by all the things going on in the city, and all the people and things I had never really noticed before. I am grateful to Paul Fleischman for opening my eyes" (unnumbered book cover).

Amy Schwartz's *What James Likes Best* encourages young listeners to choose what they believe the young boy will like the best.

Older children enjoy searching for art objects, literary and historical characters, and present-day personalities in Mitsumasa Anno's detailed wordless books, such as *Anno's U.S.A. Lentil,* by Robert McCloskey, contains excellent drawings of a Midwestern town in the early 1900s: the town square, the houses on the streets, the interior of the schoolhouse, the train depot, and a parade. Single lines of text accompany each picture, but the pictures show the lifestyles and the emotions of the characters in the story. Kathy Jakobsen's *My New York* encourages children to locate the narrator within each picture and to describe the detailed New York settings.

Anthony Browne's *Willy's Pictures* provides an observational task in which readers are asked to identify the artistic works that inspired Browne's illustrations. The book concludes with copies of the original paintings. For example, one of Browne's illustrations includes a shell that is similar to the shell in "The Birth of Venus," painted

in the book, one from the point of view of a boy who wants a puppy and the other from that of a puppy who wants a kind, loving master.

Comparisons between work activities and nature activities can be made as the characters in D. B. Johnson's *Henry Hikes to Fitchburg* wager who will travel the 30 miles first: the one who walks and enjoys nature along the way or the one who works for money for the train ticket. The illustrator has contrasted the activities of the two characters. For example, one paints a fence while the other walks on stone walls and looks at nature through a magnifying glass; one sits on a train in a crowd of people while the other picks and eats blackberries in a berry patch. Readers can also decide if Henry David Thoreau was correct when he decided that walking was the best way to enjoy nature.

Different artists' renditions of the same story provide opportunities for artistic comparisons. For example, there are several illustrated versions of Margery Williams's *The Velveteen Rabbit,* originally published in 1922, including those by Allen Atkinson, Michael Hague, and Ilse Plume. Students can consider the impact of color, line, design, and media on the interpretation of the text, as well as evaluate the accuracy of the illustrations. In addition to comparing artists' renditions, children can compare traditional versions of the tales and those adapted by authors such as William J. Brooke in *Untold Tales*, Jon Scieszka in *The Stinky Cheese Man and Other Fairly Stupid Tales*, and Eugene Trivizas in *The Three Little Wolves and the Big Bad Pig*.

Tales From Shakespeare, retold by Tina Packer, is a collection of 10 Shakespearean tales retold for ages 9–12; each of the tales is illustrated by a different artist. Comparisons can be made between these illustrations and how the illustrators have matched the moods of the plays. For example, Gail de Marcken creates a light fairy tale atmosphere for "A Midsummer Night's Dream," and P. J. Lynch's illustrations for "Hamlet" and Barry Moser's illustrations for "Macbeth" develop much darker moods that correspond to the contents of the plays. This edition for younger readers, published in 2004, can be compared with other retellings of Shakespearean plays such as the 1807 version, *Tales From Shakespeare*, retold by Charles and Mary Lamb, E. Nesbit's *Beautiful Stories From Shakespeare for Children*, published in the early 1900s, and Leon Garfield's *Shakespeare Stories*, published in 1985.

A poetry collection, *Jump Back, Honey: The Poems of Paul Laurence Dunbar*, provides an interesting comparative activity. The poems are illustrated by different artists, including Ashley Bryan, Carol Byard, Jan Spivey Gilchrist, Brian Pinkney, Jerry Pinkney, and Faith Ringgold. Viewers can compare the various artistic styles. Three editions of "Aesop's Fables," all published in 2000, provide interesting comparisons. Jerry Pinkney's *Aesop's Fables* is a large collection of 60 fables illustrated in watercolors. Each fable concludes with a moral. Doris Orgel's *The Lion & the Mouse and Other Aesop Fables* presents 12 fables, each of which includes sidebars with information about ancient Greece rather than the more typical moral. The fables in Tom Lynch's *Fables From Aesop* are illustrated with fabric collages. Each fable ends with a short moral. Children can compare the styles of the retellings and the impact of the illustrations.

Upper-elementary children can compare the main characters, their struggles for survival, and their growing up in books such as Maia Wojciechowska's *Shadow of a Bull* and Elizabeth George Speare's *The Bronze Bow*. They can compare one author's depiction of characters and survival in Gary Paulsen's *Hatchet* and *The Voyage of the Frog*. They can compare themes, characterizations, and person-against-self conflicts in Marion Dane Bauer's *On My Honor* and Paula Fox's *One-Eyed Cat*. Comparisons of the Dust Bowl also can be made between Michael L. Cooper's *Dust to Eat: Drought and Depression in the 1930s* and Karen Hesse's *Out of the Dust*.

Two other interesting comparisons can be accomplished using Lois Duncan's *The Magic of Spider Woman* and Shonto Begay's *Navajo: Visions and Voices Across the Mesa*. Students can compare the similarities in values, beliefs, and themes in Duncan's folklore with the values, beliefs, and themes expressed in three poems in Begay's text: "Echoes," "Creation," and "Mother's Lace."

Classifying. Concept books provide excellent stimuli for classifying. Children must be able to classify objects or ideas before seeing or understanding the relationships among them. Various concept books use different levels of abstractness to introduce children to such concepts as color, shape, size, and usefulness. Eric Carle allows children to match blocks of color with the color shown in an illustration in his *My Very First Book of Colors* and illustrates the colorful story of a chameleon who wants to change his appearance in *The Mixed-Up Chameleon*.

Shape concept books vary in level of difficulty. Carle's *My Very First Book of Shapes* encourages children to match black shapes with similar shapes in color. John Reiss's *Shapes* presents shapes, their names, and their three-dimensional forms. Photographs in Tana Hoban's *Shapes, Shapes, Shapes* encourage children to search for circles, rectangles, and ovals.

Many other types of books can be used to develop children's classification skills and responses to literature. For example, after listening to the folktale "The Three Bears," children can classify the bears, porridge bowls, chairs, and beds according to their size and then identify which bear could best use a particular bowl, bed, or chair. (Flannelgraph characters and objects make classification more concrete for young children.) Stories can be classified using a category for wild animals or pets; a boy or girl

A boy turns a day in the snow into a very imaginative experience. Illustration by Stephen Gammell, reproduced with permission of G. P. Putnam's Sons from Will's Mammoth, *by Rafe Martin, illustrations copyright © 1989 by Stephen Gammell.*

category for the main character; or a category for settings such as country or city. Characteristics of a story can also be used for classification: realistic or unrealistic; likable or unlikable; happy or sad; and funny or serious. For example, children can compare the realistic and unrealistic qualities found in Patricia Lauber's *The News About Dinosaurs,* Henry Schwartz's *How I Captured a Dinosaur,* and Rafe Martin's *Will's Mammoth.*

Hypothesizing. Several illustrated books encourage younger children to hypothesize about what they will find when they turn the page. In *Look! Look! Look!,* Tana Hoban uses cutout squares to reveal portions of pictures; the total picture appears on the page following the portions. At a more complex level, students must turn the page to determine the possible dialogue in Chris Van Allsburg's *The Z Was Zapped.*

Hypothesizing is stimulated as children search for clues in pictures and text to answer various questions. In *Joseph Had a Little Overcoat,* Simms Taback uses cutouts in illustrations to provide clues about the next, always smaller, item that he makes out of the material that was once his old and worn jacket. In Mary Serfozo's *What's What?: A Guessing Game,* readers hypothesize about the answer to a question such as "What's light?" After they guess, they can turn the page to discover the artist's answer. Finding objects may encourage both hypothesizing about the potential for the object and expanding the imagination. When a young girl finds a red ribbon on the ground in Carole Lexa Schaefer's *The Squiggle,* she twists and twirls the ribbon as she imagines it to be objects such as a thunder cloud and a dragon. In Edith Baer's *This Is the Way We Go to School: A Book About Children Around the World,* readers must locate clues in the illustrations and then identify where in the world the children attend school. A map with the correct answers appears in the back of the book.

Books that encourage hypothesizing include texts or illustrations in which children are asked to speculate about what may happen next. For example, young children can hypothesize about what will happen next when *The Red Book* is picked up by the boy on the bicycle in Barbara Lehman's text. Adults who read Janet Stevens's *Tops & Bottoms* could stop after the second time in which Hare tricks Bear by getting the best part of the vegetable crop. Adults can ask students to speculate about how Hare will trick Bear during the third year, when Bear states that he wants both the tops and bottoms. In a humorous ending, Hare plants corn so that Bear gets the roots (bottoms) and the tassels (tops), and Hare gets the ears of corn (middles). Before reading Betty Levin's *Shadow Catcher,* children can speculate about the content of this book set in the 1890s. The book is a mystery in which considerable insights and knowledge are gained as the protagonist sees life through the camera's lens.

Hypothesizing about the subject, plot, or characters in a story helps children develop their cognitive skills and interests. It also motivates them to read or listen to literature. For example, before reading Ian Strachan's *The Flawed Glass,* older children can speculate about the author's purposes for using a plot that parallels the struggles of a girl with a physical handicap that makes it difficult to walk and speak and the struggles of a weak eagle that tries to survive on the island.

Descriptive chapter titles and titles to subsections of books are excellent stimuli for verbal or written speculations by older children. For example, before reading or listening to Kathryn Lasky's *Think Like an Eagle: At Work With a Wildlife Photographer,* children can discuss what information they believe will be in each of the following sections: "A Walk Through the Night," "A Key to the Forest," "Dreams of Birds," "Corkscrew Swamp," "Thinking Like a Beaver," "Another Wilderness," and "The Last Golden Days." After reading each section, they can review the accuracy of their predictions.

Organizing. Books that allow children to follow changes in seasons increase their understanding about sequences of time. In *Sky Tree: Seeing Science Through Art,* Thomas Locker follows the seasonal cycle of a tree beginning in summer and progressing through the seasons until the tree again experiences summer. Lisa Westberg Peters's *October Smiled Back* portrays each of the months in both text and illustrations. Longer sequences of time are also presented in many books. For example, the organizational structure in Donald Hall's *Old Home Day* follows the evolution of a pond in New Hampshire from the Ice Age to the late 1990s. Patricia Lauber's *What You Never Knew About, Tubs, Toilets, and Showers* begins with the Stone Age and then traces the development of these "fictures" through time and different civilizations. For older children, Kathryn Lasky's *Sugaring Time* follows the sequential order in which maple syrup is collected and processed, and Russell Freedman's *The Wright Brothers: How They Invented the Airplane* traces the major events in the lives of these two inventors.

Anne Millard's *A Street Through Time: A 12,000-Year Walk Through History* includes detailed illustrations that depict the same street from the Stone Age to modern times. Considerable opportunities exist for observation as readers are asked to locate Henry Hyde, who is hidden in the pictures from each historical period.

Younger students can reinforce concepts of time by reading Kes Gray's *Cluck O'Clock;* the text and illustrations follow a group of hens and a rooster as they go through their day from 4 o'clock in the morning until 12 o'clock midnight. Along the way, the rooster outmaneuvers Olga, the fox, who would like to get into the hen house. In *I, Doko: The Tale of a Basket,* Ed Young tells a Nepalese story through the viewpoint of a basket that is used by three generations of a family.

Some nonfiction books provide visual guides that help students understand a sequence of events. For example, in *Valley Forge,* Richard Ammon presents details associated with the Revolutionary War through timelines; the text uses sidebars that focus on personalities of the time period. Henry Sayre's *Cave Paintings to Picasso: The Inside Scoop on 50 Art Masterpieces* includes a time line for the art examples that range from 22,000 B.C. to 1964 A.D.; an asterisk marks the date of a specific piece. The book provides a vivid introduction to art history, and the time lines help students follow the organizations. Photographs also may provide visual guides. A sequence of photographs show the construction process in Elizabeth Mann's *Empire State Building: When New York Reached for the Skies*. Diagrams and close-up photographs help readers understand the role of blood in Paul Shower's *A Drop of Blood*.

Summarizing. Summarizing skills can be developed with literature of any genre or level of difficulty. Children can summarize stories orally or in writing. Oral summaries may motivate other children to read the same books or stories. After a recreational reading period in the classroom, library, or home, members of the group can retell a story, retell the part of the story they liked best, discuss the most important information that they learned, describe the funniest part of the story, discuss the most exciting part, and describe the actions of the character they admired the most or the least.

Summaries can be related to specific content. For example, children can summarize the most important historical information in Rhoda Blumberg's *The Incredible Journey of Lewis & Clark* and *Commodore Perry in the Land of the Shogun,* or the most important scientific information in Patricia Lauber's *Volcano: The Eruption and Healing of Mount St. Helens.* They can summarize the major contributions of Theodore Roosevelt after reading Jean Fritz's *Bully for You, Teddy Roosevelt!* or of Eleanor Roosevelt after reading Russell Freedman's *Eleanor Roosevelt: A Life of Discovery.*

Applying and Responding. Young children need many opportunities to apply the skills, concepts, information, or ideas in books. When children read concept books, for example, they should see and manipulate concrete examples, not merely look at pictures. Children who read

Tana Hoban's *26 Letters and 99 Cents* can count and group objects. Using Anita Lobel's *One Lighthouse, One Moon,* readers can respond to colors, days of the week, months, and numbers from 1 to 10.

Humorous situations provide opportunities to discover unusual ways to apply knowledge. Paul Fleischman uses such a technique in *Weslandia* when his main character, Wesley, discovers that "He could actually use what he'd learned that week for a summer project that would top all others. He would grow his own staple food crop— and found his own civilization!" (unnumbered). This text could also stimulate interesting discussions in science and social studies.

How-to books provide numerous opportunities for applying directions. *Ed Emberley's Picture Pie 2: A Drawing Book and Stencil* includes a group of stencils and directions for turning the stencil drawings into various animal forms such as birds, lions, and mice. The step-by-step instructions show which shape to use, its color, its size, and where to place it. Denis Roche's *Loo-Loo, Boo, and Art You Can Do* includes step-by-step instructions for making 11 art projects such as face masks, potato prints, and papier-mâché.

Books that not only enhance children's appreciation of nature but also provide directions for science projects are excellent sources. For example, in *Butterfly House*, Eve Bunting presents directions for "How to Raise a Butterfly." Vivian French's *Growing Frogs* provides directions for collecting frogs' eggs, watching tadpoles develop, and

The wheels on a train, the hole in a key.

The Wing on a Flea introduces the concept that geometric forms are all around us. From The Wing on a Flea, *by Ed Emberley. Text and illustrations copyright © 2001 by Ed Emberley. Reprinted by permission of Little, Brown & Company.*

releasing frogs back into the environment. Kathryn Lasky's *Science Fair Bunnies* shows that even two first-grade bunny friends can solve a problem when it appears that their science fair project has failed. Lasky shows that if students apply their knowledge and imagination to problems, they can succeed. Using Ed Emberley's *The Wing on a Flea: A Book About Shapes,* students can search for examples of rectangles, triangles, and circles found in the world around them.

Criticizing.   Neither adults nor children should be required or encouraged to accept everything that they hear or read without criticism. Children should be given many opportunities to evaluate critically what they read or hear. They develop critical evaluation skills when they sense the appropriateness, reliability, value, and authenticity of literature selections. For older readers, evaluation might include assessing the authenticity of biographies, such as Gary Schwartz's *Rembrandt,* or informational books, such as Francine Jacobs's *The Tainos: The People Who Welcomed Columbus.* Research indicates that the levels and types of questioning strategies used with children affect their levels of thinking and their development of critical evaluative skills.

Books provide many opportunities for students to critically evaluate the effectiveness of the literature. For example, older students can summarize the development of themes in Sharon Creech's *Walk Two Moons* and critically evaluate the effectiveness of the messages in developing themes, conflict, and characterization. Using Lloyd Alexander's *The Arkadians,* students can search for and critically evaluate the effectiveness of Alexander's use of Greek mythology in this modern fantasy. Using Carol Fenner's *Yolonda's Genius,* students can critically evaluate the effectiveness of Fenner's use of music to develop themes and characterizations.

Historical fiction texts provide many opportunities to critically evaluate the accuracy of the historical content. For example, students can evaluate the accuracy of Japanese American internment camps during World War II by reading David Patneaude's *Thin Wood Walls.* The book also includes numerous references to the time period, such as President Roosevelt's speech after Pearl Harbor, cultural icons such as Captain Midnight comics, and World War II actions such as the Bataan Death March and D-Day landings on the beaches of Normandy. Sylvie Weil's *My Guardian Angel,* set in 1096, provides an opportunity to authenticate the Jewish experience in Troyes, France, during the Crusades. Gennifer Choldenko's *Al Capone Does My Shirts* could be authenticated for either the 1935 setting on Alcazar Island or the autistic characteristics of one of the characters.

Personality Development

According to George Maxim (1993), personality characteristics are "the traits that give each person a unique style

of reacting to other people, places, things, and events" (p. 81). To acquire these traits, children go through many stages of personality development. They gradually learn to express emotions acceptably, experience empathy toward others, and develop feelings of self-esteem.

Child development authority Joanne Hendrick (1992) states that children "pass through a series of stages of emotional development wherein basic attitudes are formed. Early childhood encompasses three of these: the stages of trust versus mistrust, autonomy versus shame and doubt, and initiative versus guilt" (p. 112). Hendrick maintains that people who work with children must foster mental health in young children by providing many opportunities to develop healthy emotional attitudes. Slowly, with guidance, children learn to handle their emotions productively rather than disruptively. Expanded experiences, adult and sibling models, and personal success show positive ways of dealing with emotions.

Overcoming fears, developing trust, relinquishing the desire to have only one's own way, and learning acceptable forms of interaction with both peers and adults inevitably involve traumatic experiences. Progressing through the stages of personality development is part of the maturing process, and books can play a very important role in that process. Chart 1.3 lists the stages of personality development and suggests books to present during each stage.

Bibliotherapy is interaction between readers and literature. In bibliotherapy, the ideas inherent in the reading materials have a therapeutic effect. Experts in child development frequently suggest bibliotherapy to help children through various times of stress, such as hospitalization, loss of a friend, and parents' divorce. Although the emotional problems that young children experience are not all as severe as coping with loss and separation, all children must face numerous smaller crises that require personal adjustment. Literature can help children understand their feelings, identify with characters who experience similar feelings, and gain new insights into how others have coped with the same problems. According to Masha Rudman and Anna Pearce (1988), "books can serve as mirrors for children, reflecting their appearance, their relationships, their feelings and thoughts in their immediate environment" (p. 159). In addition, books can act as windows on the world, inviting children to look beyond themselves and to form bonds with characters and circumstances.

Technology Resources   **CW**

Link to the Enriching Materials module in Chapter 1 on the Companion Website at www.prenhall.com/norton for more resources on promoting children's personality development with literature.

CHART 1.3   Personality development

Characteristics	Teaching Recommendations	Literature Suggestions
Preschool: Ages 2–3 1 Some children show anxiety when encountering strangers. 2 Children begin to understand that they can influence caregivers. 3 Most children develop secure attachments and realize that parents will return when they leave their children with caregivers.	1 Realize that young children may be cautious or fearful in new situations. 2 Respond to genuine needs by showing warmth. 3 Establish a routine when leaving and when returning.	Fox, Mem. *Night Noises.* Waddell, Martin. *Tiny's Big Adventure.* Gág, Wanda. *Millions of Cats.* Whybrow, Ian. *The Noisy Way to Bed.* Brown, Marc. *Kiss Hello, Kiss Good-bye.* Harris, Robie H. *Don't Forget to Come Back.*
Preschool: Ages 3–4 1 Children talk about emotions and realize that emotions are connected to people's desires. 2 Children tend to go to adults for reassurance, and they seek support from parents. 3 Children develop egocentric feelings and consider themselves the center of the universe.	1 Help children by modeling ways to express feelings. 2 Share books that show warm relationships. 3 Develop warm, loving environments that show families value children.	Kasza, Keiko. *A Mother for Choco.* Wormell, Mary. *Why Not?* Bang, Molly. *Goose.* Greenspun, Adele. *Grandparents Are the Greatest Because . . .* Curtis, Jamie Lee. *Tell Me Again About the Night I was Born.* Yolen, Jane. *Owl Moon.*
Preschool–Kindergarten: Ages 5–6 1 Beginning in preschool years, boys show more anger than girls. 2 Children are shy about interacting with new groups. 3 Many children need reassurances before they are comfortable with new experiences.	1 Help children develop appropriate ways to handle their emotions. 2 Help them enter into groups on the playground and in school. 3 Share books in which characters face similar problems.	Newman, Lesléa. *The Best Cat in the World.* Rotner, Shelley. *Lots of Feelings.* Dyer, Jane. *Little Brown Bear Won't.* Wells, Rosemary. *My Kindergarten.* Recorvits, Helen. *My Name Is Yoon.* Stadler, Alexander. *Beverly Billingsly Can't Catch.*
Early Elementary: Ages 6–8 1 For emotional stability, children want to do activities that emphasize their strengths. 2 Boys begin to put on a self-confident front when they feel vulnerable. 3 Girls respond more negatively to failure. 4 Children tend to base self-evaluations on their own improvements over time.	1 Help children identify their strengths, but also work on less developed areas. 2 Share books in which boys overcome difficulties and show success. 3 Share books in which girls overcome failure and show success. 4 Easy-to-read books help students evaluate their own improvements.	Leedy, Loreen. *Look at My Book: How Kids Can Write and Illustrate Terrific Books.* Schwartz, Amy. *Things I Learned in Second Grade.* Krull, Kathleen. *The Boy on Fairfield Street.* Barasch, Lynn. *Knockin' on Wood.* Geeslin, Campbell. *Elena's Serenade.* O'Neill, Alexis. *Loud Emily.* McMullan, Kate. *Pearl and Wagner: Three Secrets.* Van Leeuwen, Jean. *Oliver the Mighty Pig.*

(continues)

CHART 1.3   Continued

Characteristics	Teaching Recommendations	Literature Suggestions
Middle Elementary: Ages 8–10		
1 Experiences help children develop a positive or negative sense of their worth. 2 Children may minimize the mistakes they make in ways that enhance their sense of self. 3 Major family disruptions such as divorce or death may undermine children's security.	1 Children who are treated warmly by others tend to develop positive feelings about self-worth. 2 Praise children for their accomplishments in numerous areas. 3 Discuss feelings of characters in literature to help children understand how other children face emotional experiences.	Bernier-Grand, Carmen. *Yes, We Can.* Napoli, Donna Jo. *North.* Jacobson, Jennifer. *Truly Winnie.* Kimmel, Eric A. *Don Quixote and the Windmills.* Bredsdorff, Bodil. *The Crow-Girl: The Children of Crow Cove.* Dennison, Amy, et al. *Our Dad Died.*
Early Adolescence: Ages 10–14		
1 Adolescents tend to be more emotionally volatile and experience more anxieties. 2 Boys especially may hide their emotions in order to appear "cool." 3 Adolescents may feel self-conscious and awkward.	1 Be supportive when they want to share their anxieties. 2 Help students discover that some moodiness is normal and it is all right to express emotions. 3 Share books that show that many people have these feelings.	Creech, Sharon. *Granny Torrelli Makes Soup.* Tolan, Stephanie S. *Surviving the Applewhites.* Yep, Laurence. *Skunk Scout.* Choldenko, Gennifer. *Al Capone Does My Shirts.* Lowry, Lois. *See You Around, Sam!* Patneaude, David. *Thin Wood Walls.* Henkes, Kevin. *Olive's Ocean.* Little, Jean. *Willow and Twig.* Ryan, Pam Muñoz. *Becoming Naomi León.*
Late Adolescence: Ages 14–18		
1 Adolescents may find their needs and desires conflict with authority figures. 2 Conflicts with peers may cause inner turmoil. 3 Many adolescents perceive their lives as stressful and believe they are unable to cope with problems. 4 Puberty results in gender differences: Girls may experience moodiness and depression; boys, aggressiveness and rebelliousness.	1 Share books and discuss ways to deal with conflicts. 2 Discuss instances of conflict and how the conflicts can be eliminated. 3 Share books that show students coping with problems and encourage outlets from stress such sports and hobbies. 4 Help students consider controlling emotions as skills that improve over time.	Donnelly, Jennifer. *A Northern Light.* Konigsburg, E. L. *The Outcasts of 19 Schuyler Place.* Myers, Walter Dean. *Shooter.* Rosoff, Meg. *How I Live Now.* Shea, Pegi Deitz. *Tangled Threads: A Hmong Girl's Story.* Stolz, Joëlle. *The Shadows of Ghadames.* Almond, David. *The Fire-Eaters.* Myers, Walter Dean. *Bad Boy, a Memoir.* Orr, Tamara. *Violence in Our Schools.* Hutchin, Megan, et al. *Choose the Right College & Get Accepted!* Ojeda, Auriana. *Teens at Risk: Opposing Viewpoints.* Smith, Charles. *Hoop Kings.* Armstrong, Thomas. *You're Smarter Than You Think.* Creech, Sharon. *Heartbeat.* Myracle, Lauren. *ttyl.* Paulsen, Gary. *How Angel Peterson Got His Name: And Other Outrageous Tales About Extreme Sports.* Vecchione, Patrice (Ed.). *Revenge and Forgiveness.*

Joan Glazer (1991) identifies four ways in which literature contributes to the emotional growth of children. First, literature shows children that many of their feelings are common to other children and that those feelings are normal and natural. Second, literature explores a feeling from several viewpoints, giving a fuller picture and providing a basis for naming the feeling. Third, actions of various characters show options for ways of dealing with particular emotions. Fourth, literature makes clear that one person experiences many emotions and that these emotions sometimes conflict.

One of the best-known theories related to personality development is Erik Erikson's (1972) psychological theory based on the premise that individuals progress through the following eight stages of development:

1. *Infancy (Birth–1½ years)—Trust Versus Mistrust:* Children learn to have confidence in others. During this time, they develop feelings of security or become fearful and unsure of their environment and the people around them.

2. *Toddler Years (1½–3 years)—Autonomy Versus Shame and Doubt:* Children learn to make decisions and accept independence or become inhibited and lack self-esteem.

3. *Preschool Years (3–6 years)—Initiative Versus Guilt:* Children learn to plan and carry out their own activities and attempt to master new challenges. In contrast, they may learn to fear failure if it leads to punishment and feelings of guilt.

4. *Elementary School Years—Industry Versus Inferiority:* Children seek recognition by learning the skills of a culture that lead to success and a positive self-concept. Or they may find that lack of recognition and failure lead to feelings of inadequacy and inferiority.

5. *Adolescence—Identity Versus Role Confusion:* Children try to identify who they are and how they fit into the adult world by exploring and using many different types of activities that help them achieve a sense of who they are and who they hope to become. In contrast, there may be role confusion that leads to feelings of bewilderment.

6. *Young Adult—Intimacy Versus Isolation:* Young people have established their identities and are capable of intimacy as they form reciprocal relationships with other people. Adults who cannot form relationships may feel a sense of isolation.

7. *Middle Age—Generativity Versus Stagnation:* The primary developmental tasks are contributing to society and family and developing a sense of productivity and accomplishment. In contrast, people who are unwilling to help society may develop feelings of stagnation and dissatisfaction because of lack of production.

8. *Retirement Years—Integrity Versus Despair:* Individuals look back at their lives and develop feelings of contentment or a sense of distress because they believe their lives are filled with disappointments and inability to achieve goals.

Contemporary realistic fiction is filled with primary and secondary characters whose actions represent these various stages of development. As with all development, there are those who believe that Erikson's stages are representative of beliefs about attachment, self-concepts, and identity, and also those who argue that Erikson's theory does not describe emotional development in some cultures. As you read literature for children and young adults, try to identify when Erikson's stages of development seem to apply and when they do not. Are there differences depending on the cultural group identified in the literature?

Animal characters in books for young children frequently act very much like people. The problems the characters face, especially their fears, can assist the personality development of young children. Books with animal characters are very satisfying for readers because the authors allow the animal characters to face and overcome common fears and emotions. For example, Martin Waddell's *Can't You Sleep, Little Bear?* focuses on a young bear's fear of the dark. In *Let's Go Home, Little Bear,* Waddell's characters focus on overcoming fears of sounds. In both books, Big Bear's compassion and understanding help the young

In *Can't You Sleep, Little Bear?, a young bear experiences fears that are similar to those expressed by children. Illustration from* Can't You Sleep, Little Bear?, *by Martin Waddell. Illustration © 1988 Barbara Firth. Used by permission of Candlewick Press, Cambridge, MA.*

Through the Eyes of an ARTIST

Robert Sabuda

Visit the CD-ROM that accompanies this text to generate a complete list of titles written and/or illustrated by Robert Sabuda.

Selected Titles by Robert Sabuda:

- Arthur and the Sword
- America the Beautiful: A Pop-Up Book
- The Wonderful Wizard of Oz: A Commemorative Pop-Up
- Alice's Adventures in Wonderland: A Pop-Up Adaptation
- Encyclopedia Prehistoria Dinosaurs: The Definitive Pop-Up
- Winter's Tale

I've always thought of books as more than words and pictures. The hope of a good book is that it really transports you to another place or another state of mind. And for me, it didn't just have to be a cerebral place. I wondered why it couldn't be an actual place. That's what has led me to keep making my own world in books. A lot of the work I do, I have to tell you, I do because I like it and I want to do it. Many people ask me who the audience or the market is, but I don't really worry about that. If the book lover boy in me wants to see it happen, I make it happen.

The paper engineer in me always works in white at first. I don't add the color to the pop-up books until after; I use white card stock and look at shadows and look through holes and doors and windows and see depth. The book is very intriguing to me, so with *America the Beautiful,* I left it white. People have really embraced that simplicity to the point that many people see it as paper sculpture.

I used to really be a chameleon with the illustrating. I would get bored. A lot of people get comfortable with a style; it flows out of them like water from a pitcher. But the projects I worked on were so different from each other that a different approach seemed more natural. With *Arthur and the Sword,* stained glass felt right. It felt comfortable. I'd rather do something that feels right and fail than do the same thing over and over again.

And I've made pop-up books since I was a boy, so I was really waiting for the opportunity. I've always loved books that excite one step beyond the normal. I remember distinctly the first time I got a scratch-and-sniff book as a boy. I know that sounds silly, but it was the involvement of two more senses that excited me. It was totally cool, you go these extra steps and get this great surprise, and as a boy I just thought that was so great. And I was interested right away in creating these books that could just go one step beyond.

One of the things about being a paper engineer is that it's a very small community. On the planet there are probably three dozen paper engineers—that's sort of scary. The pop-up books I've done might provide young artists with the idea that this is a wide-open, thriving field of children's book illustration, and you should take advantage of it! It's important to us in the studio to have more young people working with their hands with books. And that's become another large part of my work. I love to teach, and so many people have shared with me that I really felt a need to give that back.

Video Profile: The accompanying video contains conversations with illustrators Molly Bang, Floyd Cooper, Keith Baker, and more.

---

bear overcome his fears. The kitten in Mary Wormell's *Why Not?* learns a lesson about not bothering other animals and about listening to her mother.

Searching for identity is a common theme in books with young animal characters. In Molly Bang's *Goose,* a goose egg falls out of the nest, and the baby is raised by a loving family of woodchucks. The baby goose feels like an outsider, however, until she discovers that she has her own special abilities: She can fly. Now she is able to be herself and return to her adoptive family. The main character in Bob Graham's *Benny: An Adventure Story* discovers pride in his abilities and a family who loves a dancing dog.

As stated, many of these books satisfy readers because the animal characters face and overcome identifiable emotions. For example, *In the Rain With Baby Duck,* by Amy Hest, allows Baby Duck to discover that when his mother was little, she also disliked rain, puddles, mud, and getting her feet wet; Grampa Duck solves the problem by giving Baby Duck the umbrella and boots that his mother wore when she was young. This text shows that two generations had the same feelings about going out in the rain. In Helen Lester's *Hooway for Wodney Wat,* a rodent with a speech impediment discovers that he can be a hero when his speech difficulty helps him overcome the class bully.

Jealousy is an emotion that is familiar to most children when they feel threatened by a new baby. Books about new babies can help children express their fears and realize that their parents still love them but that it is not unusual to feel fearful about a new relationship. Ezra Jack Keats's *Peter's Chair* shows how one child handles fear and jealousy when he not only gets an unwanted baby sister but also sees his own furniture painted pink for the new arrival. The older sister in Lenore Look's *Henry's First-Moon Birthday* discovers that her baby brother is not as bad as she thought when she becomes involved in the preparations for his 1-month birthday.

Many children fear going to school for the first time or moving into a new school or neighborhood. In *Miss Bindergarten Gets Ready for Kindergarten,* Joseph Slate creates two parallel stories as both the teacher, who is a black-and-white dog, and a group of animals prepare for the first day of school. All the animals except a reluctant iguana discover a very satisfying experience. In Kathryn Lasky's *Lunch Bunnies,* Clyde worries about all the terrible things that might happen during lunch on his first day of school. Fortunately, the experience is more pleasant than he imagined. Eric Carle's *Do You Want to Be My Friend?,* Miriam Cohen's *Will I Have a Friend?,* and Rosemary Wells's *Timothy Goes to School* present heroes who successfully cope with this problem. The conflict between in-

Through the Eyes of a Child

Jacob
Grade 1

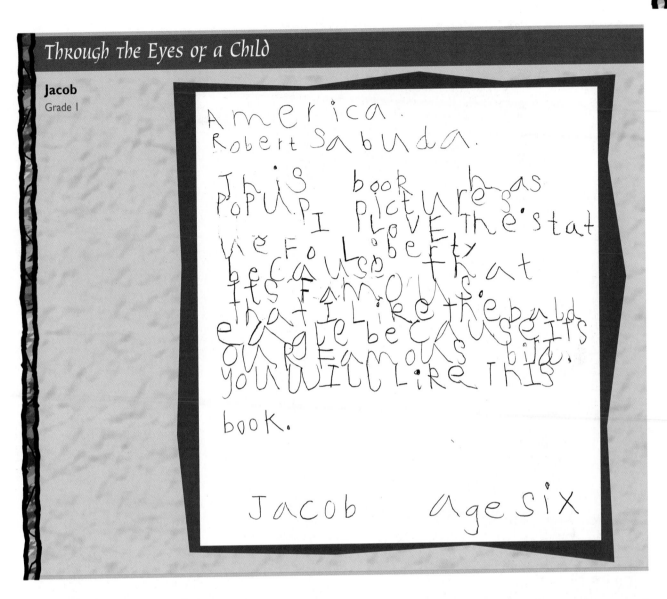

America.
Robert Sabuda.

This book has
POPUP. I PLOVE the stat
we Fo Libetty
because that
its FamoUs
that I Like the bald
eagle because Its
our Famous bird.
YOU WILL LIKE THIS
book.

Jacob   Age SIX

dividuality and conformity provides the plot in Peggy Rathmann's *Ruby the Copycat*. Many children who are unsure of their capabilities relate to this story of a girl who feels so unsure of herself that she copies a classmate's actions. By the end of the story, the girl discovers that she has her own creative resources. In fact, she is so good at hopping that the class now copies her. In Kevin Henkes's *Chrysanthemum*, a mouse child experiences problems adjusting to other children in school who make fun of her name. An understanding adult helps her learn to appreciate her name.

Literature can play an important role in helping children develop positive and realistic self-concepts. Infants do not think of themselves as individuals. Between the ages of 2 and 3, children slowly begin to realize that they have identities separate from those of other members of the family. By age 3, with the assistance of warm, loving environments, most children have developed a set of feelings about themselves; they consider themselves "I."

Egocentric feelings continue for several years, and children consider themselves the center of the universe. If the development of self-esteem is to progress positively, children need to know that their families, friends, and the larger society value them. Jane Yolen's *Owl Moon* and Karen Ackerman's *Song and Dance Man* are books in which children are valued by family members.

Books also show children that it is all right to be different from their families. Jan Mark's *Fun* shows that a boy who prefers quiet, contemplative activities can be happy living with an active, boisterous mother and father.

Picture storybooks written for younger children may help children cope with loss. Books written for younger children frequently stress overcoming loss associated with the loss of a pet. For example, the plot in Lesléa Newman's *The Best Cat in the World* deals with grief after the loss of a beloved cat, Charlie. The young boy goes through several stages of grief as he cries for 2 days and tries to talk to his cat who is buried near a rosebush. He eventually accepts a new kitten from the vet. At first, he does not like the

A young girl discovers the first Ichthyosaur remains and surprises the scientific world of the early 19th century. From The Fossil Girl: Mary Anning's Dinosaur Discovery. *Text and illustrations © 1999 by Catherine Brighton. Published by the Millbrook Press. Reprinted by permission.*

From The Best Cat in the World. *Written by Lesléa Newman. Illustrated by Ronald Himler. Copyright 2004. Published by Eerdmans Publishing Co. (800)253-7521. www.eerdmans.com/youngreaders. Used by permission, all rights reserved.*

From Lots of Feelings *by Shelly Rotner. Copyright © 2003 by Shelly Rotner. Reprinted with the permission of The Millbrook Press, a division of Lerner Publishing Group. All rights reserved. No part of this text excerpt may be used or reproduced in any manner whatsoever without prior written permission of The Millbrook Press.*

kitten because it does not act like Charlie. Eventually, the boy accepts the new kitten and realizes that the two pets are not alike. But each of the cats has its own personality and brings joy to the boy.

In a book for slightly older readers, *When Dinosaurs Die: A Guide to Understanding Death,* Laurie Krasny Brown and Marc Brown provide a more detailed exploration of death by asking and answering questions such as "Why does someone die?" and "What does dead mean?" Various emotions and feelings about death are explored through the text. The book concludes with a positive section, "Ways to Remember Someone."

Divorce is another emotional and stressful experience faced by many children. Fred Rogers's *Let's Talk About It: Divorce* provides examples of ways that children can deal with their emotions. Through such statements as "Their divorce is not your fault," Rogers approaches one of the greatest concerns of young children and provides them with reassurance. Rogers recommends that adults use this book to discuss the topic with children. Photographs show three families whose members are experiencing divorce.

Adoption is another emotional experience. In *Tell Me Again About the Night I Was Born,* Jamie Lee Curtis tells a story that depicts a loving relationship between the child and the adoptive parents. This book encourages children to overcome fear by celebrating adoption and suggesting that it is a very important decision for both parents and children.

Several excellent books for older children are based on the themes of overcoming problems. In Scott O'Dell's *Island of the Blue Dolphins,* a girl survives alone on an island off the coast of California. She is not rescued for 18 years and must overcome loneliness, develop weapons that violate a taboo of her society, and create a life for herself. Gary Paulsen's *Hatchet* follows a boy as he learns about personal and physical survival in the Canadian wilderness. *Call It Courage,* by Armstrong Sperry, is another survival book. In this book, a boy must overcome his fear of the sea before he can return home. Survival during the Holocaust is developed in Livia Bitton-Jackson's *I Have Lived a Thousand Years: Growing Up in the Holocaust* as the heroine survives the ghetto, labor camps, and Auschwitz. Her bravery and determination help her realize that she is happy to be Jewish.

All children must feel pride in their accomplishments and their cultural heritage and must develop positive sex-role identifications. Those who develop positive feelings of self-worth will be able to assume responsibility for their own successes and failures. Literature can help young children discover the capabilities they have and realize that acquiring some skills takes considerable time. For example, in Ezra Jack Keats's *Whistle for Willie,* Peter tries and tries to whistle; after considerable practice, he finally learns this skill. The importance of feeling pride in one's accomplishments is developed in Florence Parry Heide and Judith Heide Gilliland's *The Day of Ahmed's Secret.* This story, set in Cairo, follows a boy through his day of work and encourages readers to empathize with his excitement as he shares his secret with his family: He can write his own name.

The importance of being independent and developing your own interests is developed in Laurence Anholt's biography *Stone Girl, Bone Girl: The Story of Mary Anning.* The author focuses on the characteristics of a young girl who continues her hunt for fossils even though she is teased by children of the village. Her persistence pays off when she finds a large ichthyosaur skeleton. Her various finds increase her interest in paleontology and eventually enable her to make a living in that field. You can compare Anholt's biography with Catherine Brighton's *The Fossil Girl: Mary Anning's Dinosaur Discovery.*

Using talent and wisely pursuing one's dreams are important themes in Oliver Dunrea's *The Painter Who Loved Chickens.* In this story, the painter discovers that it is possible to both live where he wants to live—on a farm—and paint the subjects he wants to paint—chickens. Dunrea develops this important message when "The painter became famous. And he never again painted anything that he did not love to paint" (unnumbered). Helen Lester's *Author: A True Story* focuses on how the author overcame both learning disabilities as a child and rejection slips as an adult to become an author of children's books. Kathleen Krull's *Wilma Unlimited: How Wilma Rudolph Became the World's Fastest Woman* provides an excellent model for achievement through overcoming obstacles that would discourage many people. Wilma overcame polio, competed in a male-dominated sport, and as an African American grew up in the segregated South of the 1940s. Another book that emphasizes the accomplishments of female sports stars is Sue Macy's *Winning Ways: A Photohistory of American Women in Sports.*

Personality development in children is extremely important: If children do not understand themselves and believe that they are important, how can they value anyone else? Many literary selections and literature-related experiences reinforce positive personality development. Such experiences include reading orally in a warm and secure environment, discussing and acting out various roles from literature, and simply enjoying a wide variety of literature.

Social Development

According to David Shaffer (1989), socialization "is the process by which children acquire the beliefs, values, and behaviors deemed significant and appropriate by the older members of their society" (p. 560). Shaffer identifies three ways in which socialization serves society: (1) as a means of regulating children's behavior and controlling their undesirable or antisocial impulses, (2) as a way to promote the personal growth of the individual, and (3) as a means to perpetuate the social order. George Maxim (1993) emphasizes the role of literature in influencing positive racial and cultural attitudes. He believes that we must start to enhance self-concepts and cultural identity, develop social skills and responsibility, broaden the cultural base of the curriculum, and study particular groups by integrating multicultural education into the curriculum of the very young. To meet this multicultural component, Maxim recommends reading or telling stories that describe the lives of people in other cultures, inviting guest speakers from other cultures, visiting museums, and playing with games and toys from various cultures. Chart 1.4 lists books that can promote the social development of children.

Socialization.   Socialization is said to occur when children learn the ways of their groups so that they can function acceptably within those groups. Children must learn to exert control over aggressive and hostile behavior if they are to have acceptable relationships with family members, friends, and the larger community. Acceptable relationships require an understanding of the feelings and viewpoints of others. Quite obviously, socialization is a very important part of child development. Understanding the processes that influence social development is essential for anyone who works with children. Researchers have identified three processes influential in the socialization of children.

First, reward or punishment by parents and other adults reinforces socially acceptable attitudes and behaviors and discourages socially unacceptable ones. For example, a child who refuses to share a toy with another child may be deprived of the toy, whereas appropriate sharing may be rewarded with a hug and a favorable comment.

Second, observation of others teaches children the responses, behaviors, and beliefs considered appropriate within their culture. Children learn how to act and what to believe by imitating adults and peers. For example, a girl may learn about gender distinctions in our culture by observing and trying to copy her mother's role in the family. Children also observe what other members of the family fear and how members of their group react to people who belong to different racial or cultural groups.

The third process, identification, may be the most important for socialization: It requires emotional ties with models. Children's thoughts, feelings, and actions become similar to those of people they believe are like them.

Children's first relationships usually occur within the immediate family, then extend to a few friends in the neighborhood, to school, and finally to the broader world. Literature and literature-related activities can aid in the development of these relationships by encouraging children to become sensitive to the feelings of others.

Books for younger children frequently deal with such problems as developing satisfactory relationships with family, friends, and neighbors. In Martin Waddell's *You and Me, Little Bear,* the author develops the importance of

CHART 1.4   Social development (pp. 30–33)

Characteristics	Teaching Recommendations	Literature Suggestions
Preschool: Ages 2–3		
1 Children learn to organize and represent their world; they imitate actions and behaviors they have observed. 2 Children transform things into make-believe: a yardstick may be a horse.	1 Encourage children to role-play so they can begin to take others' points of view and learn about other behavior. 2 Provide objects and books that suggest creative interpretations.	Burningham, John. *Mr. Gumpy's Outing.* Carle, Eric. *The Mixed-Up Chameleon.* Oxenbury, Helen. *Family.* Hutchins, Pat. *Changes, Changes.*
Preschool: Ages 3–4		
1 Children begin to realize that other people have feelings, just as they do. 2 Children enjoy playing together and develop strong attachments to other children. 3 Children begin to enjoy participating in group activities and group games. 4 Children begin to identify others' feelings by observing facial expressions.	1 Encourage children to talk about how they felt when something similar happened to them; provide books that show feelings. 2 Encourage the growing social skills of sharing, taking turns, and playing cooperatively. 3 Let children be both leaders and followers during group activities after reading a book. 4 Encourage children to become sensitive to their own and others' feelings by talking about the feelings that accompany different facial expressions in books.	Keats, Ezra Jack. *Peter's Chair.* Winthrop, Elizabeth. *Bear and Mrs. Duck.* Hoban, Russell. *Best Friends for Frances.* Lindgren, Barbro. *Sam's Ball.* Bemelmans, Ludwig. *Madeline.* Henkes, Kevin. *Jessica.* Hutchins, Pat. *Where's the Baby?* Schaefer, Carol Lexa. *Snow Pumpkin.* Wells, Rosemary. *Bunny Cakes.*
Preschool: Ages 4–5		
1 Children start to avoid aggression when angry and instead look for compromises. They are, however, frequently bossy, assertive, and prone to using alibis. 2 Children begin to understand consequences of good and bad behavior and may engage in unacceptable behavior to elicit reactions. 3 Children seldom play alone, but they begin to work by themselves. 4 Children increase their awareness of the different roles people play—nurse, police officer, grocery clerk, man, woman, etc. 5 Children exhibit unreasonable fears, such as fear of the dark, thunder, and animals.	1 Praise children for talking out anger, help them to calm down and talk about the situation, direct them toward finding solutions. Choose books in which aggression is avoided. 2 Explain actions in terms that children understand. Let children discuss alternative actions. 3 Encourage persistence; let children work at something until it is completed to their satisfaction. This is crucial for problem solving and self-directed learning. 4 Provide opportunities to meet different kinds of people through real life and books; encourage dramatic play around different roles. 5 Help children overcome fears by sharing experiences of others who had fears but overcame them.	Bloom, Suzanne. *A Splendid Friend, Indeed.* Reiser, Lynn. *Best Friends Think Alike.* Galdone, Paul. *The Little Red Hen.* Howe, James. *Horace and Morris But Mostly Dolores.* Burton, Virginia Lee. *Mike Mulligan and His Steam Shovel.* Horse, Harry. *Little Rabbit Goes to School.* Banks, Kate. *Mama's Coming Home.* Bunting, Eve. *Ghost's Hour, Spook's Hour.* Ernst, Lisa Campbell. *Ginger Jumps.*
Preschool–Kindergarten: Ages 5–6		
1 Children like to help parents around the house; they are developing dependable behavior.	1 Allow children to be responsible for jobs that they can realistically complete. Read stories about children helping.	Rylant, Cynthia. *When I Was Young in the Mountains.* Spinelli, Eileen. *Night Shift Daddy.* Williams, Vera B. *A Chair for My Mother.*

CHART 1.4   Continued

Characteristics	Teaching Recommendations	Literature Suggestions
2 Children protect younger brothers and sisters and other children.	2 Let children help and read to younger children; encourage them to become aware that they are growing into independent people. Share reasons why all people need security.	Chen, Chih-Yuan. *Guji Guji.* Krauss, Ruth. *Bears.*
3 Children are proud of their accomplishments; they take pride in going to school and in their possessions.	3 Encourage a feeling of self-worth: Praise accomplishments, encourage children to share school and home experiences, and allow them to talk about their possessions.	Forward, Toby. *What Did You Do Today?* Kraus, Robert. *Leo the Late Bloomer.* Schwartz, Amy. *Annabelle Swift, Kindergartner.*
4 Children continue to show anxiety and unreasonable fear.	4 Help children overcome their fears and anxieties; stress that these are normal.	Leaf, Munro. *The Story of Ferdinand.* Wells, Rosemary. *Timothy Goes to School.*
5 Children enjoy playing outside on their favorite toys, such as tricycles and sleds.	5 Provide opportunities for play, discussions about play, reading and drawing about outside play, and dictating stories about outside play.	Keats, Ezra Jack. *The Snowy Day.* Martin, Rafe. *Will's Mammoth.* Smalls-Hector, Irene. *Jonathan and His Mommy.*
6 Children enjoy excursions to new places and familiar ones.	6 Plan trips to zoos, fire stations, historic sites, and such. Read about these places, and encourage children to tell about family trips.	Asch, Frank. *Moonbear's Pet.* Griffith, Helen V. *Grandaddy's Place.* McCloskey, Robert. *Make Way for Ducklings,*
7 Children enjoy dressing up, role playing, and creative play.	7 Provide opportunities for children to dress up and play different roles. Read stories that can be used for creative play.	Aardema, Verna. *Who's in Rabbit's House?*
Early Elementary: Ages 6–8		
1 Children may defy parents when they are under pressure; they have difficulty getting along with younger siblings.	1 Encourage children to become more sensitive to family needs and to talk and read stories about similar situations. Direct children toward finding solutions.	Blume, Judy. *The One in the Middle Is the Green Kangaroo.* Hartmann, Wendy, and Niki Daly. *The Dinosaurs Are Back and It's All Your Fault Edward!* Hoberman, Mary Ann. *Mr. and Mrs. Muddle.* Ness, Evaline. *Sam, Bangs, and Moonshine.* Nomura, Takaaki. *Grandpa's Town.* Sendak, Maurice. *Where the Wild Things Are.* Zalben, Jane. *Baby Babka, the Gorgeous Genius.*
2 Children want to play with other children but frequently insist on being first.	2 Encourage children to both lead and follow; read books in which children overcome similar problems.	Hughes, Shirley. *Ella's Big Chance.* Rodman, Mary, Ann. *My Best Friend.*
3 Children respond to teachers' help or praise. They try to conform and please teachers.	3 Allow children to share work and receive praise. Show-and-tell is especially enjoyable for 6- and 7-year-olds. Praise their reading and sharing of books.	Henkes, Kevin. *Lilly's Purple Plastic Purse.* Lobel, Arnold. *Frog and Toad All Year.* Van Leeuwen, Jean. *More Tales of Oliver Pig.*
4 Children enjoy sitting still and listening to stories read at school, at home, or in the library.	4 Provide frequent storytelling and story-reading times.	Fleischman, Sid. *The Scarebird.* Orgel, Doris. *The Bremen Town Musicians.* Young, Ed. *Seven Blind Mice.* Polacco, Patricia. *The Butterfly.* Say, Allen. *Grandfather's Journey.*

(continues)

CHART 1.4   Continued

Characteristics	Teaching Recommendations	Literature Suggestions
5 Children have definite, inflexible ideas of right and wrong.	5 Discuss attitudes and standards of conduct in books.	Demi. *The Hungry Coat.* Friedman, Ina R. *How My Parents Learned to Eat.* Hanson, Regina. *The Face at the Window.* Schotter, Roni. *Captain Snap and the Children of Vinegar Lane.* Wild, Margaret. *Mr. Nick's Knitting.*
Middle Elementary: Ages 8–10 1 Concepts of right and wrong become more flexible; the situation in which the wrong action occurred is taken into consideration. 2 Children begin to be influenced by their peer groups. 3 Children's thinking is becoming socialized; they can understand other people's points of view. They feel that their reasoning and solutions to problems should agree with others.	 1 Provide experiences and books to help children relate to different points of view; they begin to realize there are attitudes, values, and standards different from those their parents stress. 2 Read and discuss books in which peer groups become more important; these groups can influence attitudes, values, and interests. 3 Provide many opportunities for children to investigate differing points of view. Literature is an excellent source.	Adler, David A. *America's Champion Swimmer: Gertrude Ederle.* Coerr, Eleanor. *Sadako and the Thousand Paper Cranes.* Goble, Paul. *The Girl Who Loved Wild Horses.* Say, Allen. *Kamishibai Man.* Ahlberg, Allan. *The Children Who Smelled a Rat.* Edwards, Michelle. *Stinky Stern Forever.* Soto, Gary. *Taking Sides.* Byars, Betsy. *The Animal, the Vegetable, and John D. Jones.* Kerley, Barbara. *Walt Whitman: Words for America.* Monjo, F. N. *The Drinking Gourd.* Peet, Bill. *Bill Peet: An Autobiography.* Prelutsky, Jack. *The New Kid on the Block.*
Upper Elementary: Ages 10–12 1 Children have developed racial attitudes; low-prejudiced children increase in perception of nonracial characteristics; high-prejudiced children increase in perception of racial characteristics. 2 Children want to do jobs well instead of starting and exploring them; feelings of inferiority and inadequacy may result if children feel that they cannot measure up to their own personal standards. 3 Children have a sense of justice and resist imperfections in the world.	 1 Provide literature and instructional activities to develop multiethnic values and stress contributions of ethnic minorities. 2 Encourage expansion of knowledge in high-interest areas; provide books in these areas; provide assistance and encouragement to allow children to finish jobs to meet their expectations. 3 Read and discuss stories where people overcome injustice, improve some aspect of life, or raise questions about life.	Bat-Ami, Miriam. *Two Suns in the Sky.* Curtis, Christopher Paul. *Bud, Not Buddy.* Freedman, Russell. *An Indian Winter.* Highwater, Jamake. *Anpao—An American Indian Odyssey.* McKissack, Patricia, and Fredrick McKissack. *The Civil Rights Movement in America From 1865 to the Present.* Paulsen, Gary, *Dogsong.* Soto, Gary. *Neighborhood Odes.* Giblin, Jame Cross. *The Century That Was: Reflections on the Last One Hundred Years.* Macaulay, David. *The New Way Things Work.* Micklethwait, Lucy. *A Child's Book of Art.* Arnold, Caroline. *Saving the Peregrine Falcon.* DiCamillo, Kate. *Because of Winn-Dixie.* Lasky, Kathryn. *The Night Journey.* Lowry, Lois. *Number the Stars.* Sachar, Louis. *Holes.* Severance, John B. *Gandhi, Great Soul.* Yates, Elizabeth. *Amos Fortune, Free Man.*

CHART 1.4 Continued

Characteristics	Teaching Recommendations	Literature Suggestions
4 Peer groups exert strong influences on children; conformity to parents decreases and conformity to peers increases in social situations. Children may challenge their parents.	4 If differences between peer and family values are too great, children may experience conflicts. Provide literature selections and discussions to help.	Brooks, Bruce. *The Moves Make the Man.* Byars, Betsy. *The Cybil War.* Greenberg, Jan. *The Iceberg and Its Shadow.* Hahn, Mary Downing. *Stepping on the Cracks.* Lisle, Janet Taylor. *Afternoon of the Elves.*
5 Children have developed strong associations with gender-typed expectations: Girls may fail in "masculine" tasks, boys in "feminine" tasks.	5 Provide books and discussions that avoid sex-stereotyped roles; emphasize that both sexes can succeed in many roles.	Cleary, Beverly. *A Girl From Yamhill: A Memoir.* Cummings, Pat. *Talking With Artists.* Freedman, Russell. *Eleanor Roosevelt: A Life of Discovery.* Johnson, Rebecca L. *Braving the Frozen Frontier: Women Working in Antarctica.* Macy, Sue. *Winning Ways: A Photohistory of American Women in Sports.* Weil, Sylvie. *My Guardian Angel.*
6 Boys and girls accept the identity of the opposite sex. Girls more than boys begin to feel that marriage would be desirable.	6 Provide books that develop relationships with the opposite sex; such books interest girls especially.	Cole, Brock. *The Goats.* Cooper, Susan. *Seaward.* Lunn, Janet. *The Root Cellar.* MacLachian. Patricia. *The Facts and Fictions of Minna Pratt.*
Adolescence: Ages 12–18		
1 Students recognize that people may have conflicting emotions and purposes.	1 Discuss controversial points of view in historical materials and science fiction.	Aleshire, Peter. *Reaping the Whirlwind: The Apache Wars.* Almond, David. *The Fire-Eaters.* Bat-Ami, Miriam. *Two Suns in the Sky.* Farmer, Nancy. *Scorpion House.* Haskins, James. *Freedom Riders.* Napoli, Donna Jo. *Bound.* Shea, Pegi Deitz. *Tangled Threads: A Hmong Girl's Story.* Sheth, Kashmira. *Blue Jasmine.*
2 Students recognize that rules help society and themselves and the legislative process.	2 Discuss books in which rules help society make important decisions.	Giblin, James Cross. *The Century That Was: Reflecting on the Last One Hundred Years.* Stolley, Richard B. *Our Century in Pictures for Young People.*

Sources: Mussen et al. (1989). Piaget and Inhelder (1969); and Shaffer (1989).

loving parent-and-child relationships as Little Bear wants to play, but Big Bear has work to do. Both the text and Barbara Firth's illustrations reflect the warm relationships between the two animals and the possibilities of resolving these types of family conflicts. In *Guess How Much I Love You,* Sam McBratney creates a loving bond between two rabbits as the father and son try to explain the measure of their love for each other.

In Leah Komaiko's *Just My Dad & Me,* a young girl wishes she could spend the day alone with her father only to find many extended family members joining them on

the water. After a fanciful dive alone in the ocean, she discovers that she needs her family, especially her father. Aliki's *Those Summers* details the carefree times at the beach and the interactions with children and adults. This book could be used to motivate discussions about special times during the summer.

Close relationships with a grandmother are important in Lenore Look's *Love as Strong as Ginger.* This Chinese American story was inspired by the author's grandmother, who worked in a cannery in Seattle in the 1960s and 1970s. The girl learns a very important lesson

From Jim Thorpe's Bright Path. *Text copyright © 2004 by Joseph Bruchac. Illustrations copyright © 2004 by S. D. Nelson. Permission arranged with Lee & Low Books, Inc., New York, NY 10016.*

family, but he discovers that he actually misses Stevie when Stevie leaves.

Many books for preschool and early-primary children deal with various emotions related to friendship. Best friends may have strong attachments with each other, as shown in Russell Hoban's *Best Friends for Frances.*

What happens to people when they want to be different from those around them is the subject of Toni Morrison's *The Big Box.* The story, told as a poem, provides interesting discussions as children are placed in a box because they cannot handle their freedom and act differently than their teachers and parents desire.

Social development includes becoming aware of and understanding the different social roles that people play. One of the greatest contributions literature and literature-related discussions make is the realization that both boys and girls can succeed in a wide range of roles. Books that emphasize nonstereotyped sex roles and achievement are excellent models that can stimulate discussion. Biographies about female leaders and authors show that women have made many important contributions, even during historical time periods when women did not usually have leadership roles. For example, Diane Stanley and Peter Vennema's *Good Queen Bess: The Story of Elizabeth I of England* presents a strong female who overcame many obstacles to rule her people. Biographies such as Norma Johnston's *Louisa May: The World and Works of Louisa May Alcott* and Angelica Shirley Carpenter and Jean Shirley's *Frances Hodgson Burnett: Beyond the Secret Garden* show that there were important female authors even during a time when writing was dominated by male authors.

Becoming aware of different views of the world is important in socialization, and literature can help accomplish this. Children can sympathize with the Native American girl who loves her family but longs for a free life among the wild horses in *The Girl Who Loved Wild Horses,* by Paul Goble. They can view a cross-cultural Christmas as they read Allen Say's *Tree of Cranes* and become involved in a Christmas celebration that includes elements

from her grandmother when she discovers that it is important to become whatever you dream. Relationships with a neighbor who becomes a mentor are very important in Nikki Grimes's *My Man Blue.* Through a series of poems, Grimes develops this strengthening relationship until the boy concludes that someday he wants to be just like his friend Blue: gentle, trustworthy, and wise.

In *Skin Again,* bell hooks develops a book that celebrates what makes us unique and different. Chris Raschka's illustrations show individuals with different skin colors, and the text states that "the skin I'm in will always be just a covering. It cannot tell my story. If you want to know who I am you have to come inside" (unnumbered).

Overcoming problems related to sibling rivalry is a frequent theme in children's books and is one that children can understand. In *Stevie,* by John Steptoe, Robert is upset when his mother takes care of a child from another

Grandpa's Town

By Takaaki Nomura

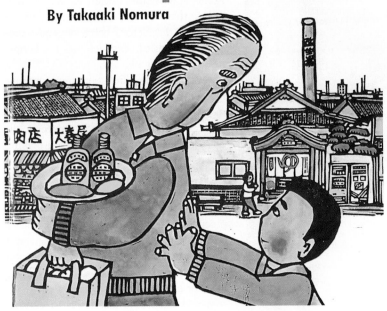

In Grandpa's Town, *a close and understanding relationship is shown between a boy and his grandfather. Illustration from* Grandpa's Town © 1989 Takaaki Normura, *translated by Amanda Mayer Stinchecum.*© 1991 Kane/Miller Book Publishers. *Used by permission of Kane/Miller Book Publishers.*

from both the Japanese and American cultures. They can understand the slave's viewpoint and the consequences of prejudice when they read F. N. Monjo's *The Drinking Gourd.* Older children discover the consequences of prejudice when they read Mildred Taylor's *Let the Circle Be Unbroken,* Belinda Hurmence's *A Girl Called Boy,* or Virginia Hamilton's *Many Thousand Gone: African Americans From Slavery to Freedom.* When children read Ellen Levine's *Freedom's Children: Young Civil Rights Activists Tell Their Own Stories,* they can empathize with young people who worked for civil rights in the 1950s and 1960s.

Patricia Polacco's *The Butterfly,* helps readers visualize the conflict and fear surrounding people during the German occupation of France during World War II. This story of friendship between a Jewish and a French family highlights the significance of strong social values during times of inhumanity. Louise Borden's *The Greatest Skating Race* also develops strong social values.

Moral Development. Acquiring moral standards is an important part of each child's social development. Preschool children start to develop concepts of right and wrong when they identify with their parents and with parental values, attitudes, and standards of conduct. A 2-year-old, for example, knows that certain acts are wrong. According to Piaget and Inhelder (1969), children younger than 7 or 8 have rigid and inflexible ideas of right and wrong, which they have learned from their parents. Piaget and Inhelder suggest that between the ages of 8 and 11, many changes occur in the moral development of children. At this time, children start to develop a sense of equality and to take into account the situation in which a wrong action occurs. Children become more flexible and realize that there are exceptions to their original strict rules of behavior; at this time, peer groups begin to influence conduct.

Lawrence Kohlberg (1981) defines the stages of moral judgment of adults and children according to the choices made when two or more values conflict. Kohlberg considers the moral decisions made, as well as the reasons for the decisions, when he identifies the stages in moral development. At Stages 1 and 2, Kohlberg's "preconventional" level, a child responds to external, concrete consequences. During Stage 1, a child chooses to be good, or to obey rules, in order to escape physical punishment. During Stage 2, a child obeys or conforms in order to obtain rewards. Kohlberg's stages and children's ages cannot be equated because some people progress more rapidly through the sequence. However, Stages 1 and 2 apparently dominate the behavior of most children during the primary grades.

At Stages 3 and 4, Kohlberg's "conventional" level, a child is concerned with meeting the external social expectations of family, group, or nation. During Stage 3, a child desires social approval and consequently makes decisions according to the expectations of the people who are important to him or her. Stage 4 has a law-and-order orientation; a child conforms because of a high regard for social order and for patriotic duty. Although one stage builds on another, the transition between stages is gradual: Stage 3 behaviors usually begin in the upper-elementary grades, and Stage 4 behaviors usually emerge in adolescence.

Stages 5 and 6 (which may be incorporated into a single stage) are at the "postconventional," autonomous, or principled level. At this level, a person establishes his or her own moral values. At Stage 5, a person responds to equal rights and consequently avoids violating the rights of others. At Stage 6, an individual conforms to his or her inner beliefs in order to avoid self-condemnation. Kohlberg estimates that only 25% of the population moves on in late adolescence or adulthood to a morality of equal rights, justice, and internal commitment to the principles of conscience.

Kohlberg suggested that a Stage 7 in moral development is the highest level of ethical and religious thinking. He

The characters' actions in this book set during World War II demonstrate Kohlberg's stages of development. From The Butterfly, by Patricia Polacco. Copyright © 2000 by Patricia Polacco. Used by permission of Philomel Books, an imprint of Penguin Putnam Books for Young Readers, a division of Penguin Putnam, Inc.

refers to this stage as one of qualitatively new insight and perspective, in which a person experiences wholeness—a union with nature, a deity, and the cosmos. Although Kohlberg recognizes Stage 7 as an aspiration rather than as a complete possibility, he maintains that Stage 7 behaviors support individuals through experiences of suffering, injustice, and death.

Children's literature contains numerous moments of crisis, when characters make moral decisions and contemplate the reasons for their decisions. If adults expect children to understand the decision-making process of characters in a story, they should be aware of the level of the decisions that the characters are making and consider whether the children are at a stage when they can appreciate those decisions. Teachers or other adults may need to help children understand decision making if the decisions are beyond their moral development.

For example, let us consider the decision making by the characters in Patricia Polacco's *The Butterfly*. At Stage 1, punishment and obedience, Monique obeys her mother and does not argue when she is told to go to school. At Stage 3, the maintaining of good relations, the children pretend they do not see the Nazi soldiers: "Don't look for too long. . . . If we do they'll come for us." At Stage 5, the morality of contract, Monique is upset when a Jewish shopkeeper is arrested. She worries that the Nazis will treat him the way they treated the butterfly they killed. At Stage 6, the morality of individual principles of conscience, Monique understands the sadness in her mother's eyes and realizes that she must protect the Jewish family hiding in her basement. She understands the importance of being free as a butterfly, and she gives away her cat as a symbol of friendship. Now consider which of these decisions might require adults to help children understand the moral development.

Children's Responses to Literature

Encouraging children to respond to the literature they read is one of the most important tasks for adults who interact with children and literature. Thomas W. Bean and Nicole Rigoni (2001) state that "intergenerational studies of reader responses to literature show the tremendous potential these exchanges have for increasing reader interest, engagement, and critical thinking" (p. 235). Lee Galda (1988) states, however:

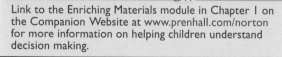

Technology Resources   CW

Link to the Enriching Materials module in Chapter 1 on the Companion Website at www.prenhall.com/norton for more information on helping children understand decision making.

Responding to literature is a complex process involving readers, texts, and contexts. Responding to literature has to do with what we make of a text as we read, how it becomes alive and personal for us, the pleasure and satisfaction we feel, and the way in which we display these feelings. Our responses to the books we read are influenced by many factors and come in many forms. (p. 92)

Cedric Cullingford (1998) emphasizes the complexities associated with children's responses when he states: "The more that the responses of readers are studied the more complicated they become. Readers bring all their idiosyncrasies to bear. They do not become the text, but connect the text to their own ways and to their own interpretations" (p. 1).

This section discusses each of the factors involved in literature responses and relates the factors to specific literature.

Factors Within Readers

Readers bring past experiences, present interests, and expectations of stories with them when they read a selection. Consequently, different readers often read, interpret, and respond to the same piece of literature in different ways. The stories children hear lead them to expectations about what a story should be and about what new stories will be like. Thus, early and continual reading to children is extremely important.

In addition, children's responses to literature are influenced by the developmental factors discussed in this chapter. Children's language, cognitive, personality, social, and moral development affect the ways in which they interpret and respond to a story. In a review of response research, Miriam Martinez and Nancy Roser (2003) state that numerous reader characteristics influence response, including reader beliefs and expectations, reading ability, socioeconomic status, cultural background, cognitive development, sex, and personal style. Robert Probst (1991) adds that insights gained from Piaget's work on cognitive development and Kohlberg's research on the development of moral reasoning are important for understanding and examining children's responses to literature.

As children bring their developmental, emotional, cultural, and scholastic backgrounds to their reading of literature, they approach the reading with their previous knowledge of the subject, their purposes for reading that literature, and their various strategies for gaining meaning from text. Rewarding interpretations of literature require personal responses that allow readers to connect experiences, emotions, and text; to understand and appreciate the unique requirements of different literary elements and genres; and to use various types of responses to expand their reactions to the literature. Consequently, the descriptions of various types of development and knowledge gained from the age and stage charts in this chapter will add to your knowledge of factors that influence readers and the examples of literature that you can use at different stages of development to enhance children's responses to literature.

Factors Within Texts

Literature texts vary from fairly simple narrative structures in folktales to elaborate novel-length plots with interwoven themes, detailed characterizations, and vivid, complex styles and language. In addition, each of the genres of literature has unique requirements: Poetry has a form different from that of biography; expository texts have reading requirements and purposes different from those of realistic fiction; and mythology has a fundamental belief system different from that of fantasy. Even within expository writing, texts vary from simple, literal descriptions to structures that develop complex ideas such as cause and effect.

Galda (1988) states that factors in texts are important because "the text guides the response of the reader in that it presents content in a specific style and form which generate and modify expectations as a reader reads" (p. 98). Galda then identifies specific characteristics that influence response. The characteristics that influence readers' emotional involvement include aspects of style and characterization, the point of view of the story, the level of abstraction, and the complexity of the syntax. The age and maturation level of the main character frequently influence interest in the story and the type of response generated. The genre of the literature also influences types of responses. For example, fantasy frequently elicits a type of response different from that of realistic fiction. Likewise, readers may respond to poetry in different ways than they respond to biography.

Factors Within Contexts

The literature environment influences children's responses to literature. When adults support and encourage growth in children's responses and provide numerous experiences with many types of literature, they create an environment that stimulates children's responses. Martinez and Roser (2003) summarized some of the context factors that influence children's responses within home and school settings. They found that adults who positively influence children's responses make books accessible to children, select titles that emphasize quality and that allow children to make connections among literature selections, read to children daily, discuss books using critical terminology, suggest literature-related activities and share the results of those activities with peers, plan numerous experiences with literature, provide repeated opportunities for children to interact with the same books, and model personal responses to literature for the children. Martinez and Roser report research that shows students use discussions to make "connections to the literary elements in the story, connections to the illustrations, connections to the lives of authors and illustrators, and connections with the children's own life experiences and other texts" (p. 809).

To enrich your study of children's literature in today's global and media-savvy environment, I have included a CD-ROM database as well as a robust Companion Website to accompany this text.

Use the CD-ROM to
1.   search the database of thousands of children's literature titles for appropriate books to share with students;
2.   generate lists of books by specific authors or illustrators, or to fit a particular theme or topic;
3.   explore classrooms that have used children's literature to great success in the Through the Eyes of a Teacher feature;
4.   find Enriching Materials—resources to give depth to many topics you'll discover in this text;
5.   link to children's literature awards sites.

Visit the Companion Website at www.prenhall.com/norton to link to some of the wonderful children's literature–related opportunities available on-line.
•   Internet activities connect you with valuable tools and ideas for integrating this exciting technology in your classroom.
•   Self-assessments help you gauge your understanding of chapter concepts.
•   Chapter objectives serve as useful concept organizers for your study.
•   CD activities help you integrate the two media components with your teaching.

Look for Technology Resources in every chapter to lead you through the many possibilities these media offer.

FIGURE 1.1   Technology resources

A report published in *Reading Today* (2001) highlights the importance of this literary environment for reading achievement. Factors attributed to achievement include reading for fun; discussing studies at home; and having books, magazines, newspapers, and encyclopedias in the home.

Responses

When literary critics and authorities discuss responses related to literature, they frequently emphasize two major types of responses: efferent and aesthetic. Rosenblatt (1985) distinguishes between the two when she states that efferent reading focuses attention on "actions to be performed, information to be retained, conclusions to be drawn, solutions to be arrived at, analytic concepts to be applied, propositions to be tested" (p. 70). Aesthetic reading, according to Rosenblatt, focuses on "what we are seeing and feeling and thinking, on what is aroused within us by the sound of the words, and by what they point to in the human and natural world" (p. 70).

A worthy literature program should include both efferent and aesthetic responses to literature. Robert Ruddell (1992) explains:

A critical issue in this process is for the teacher to recognize the instructional stance taken toward literature in the classroom. One stance focuses attention on aesthetic-type reading, leading to identification with story characters, personal interpretation, and transaction with the text as the child steps through the "magic curtain" into the book with the character. A different stance, however, may focus attention on efferent-type reading, emphasizing content and informa-

tion to be "taken away" from the book. Both aesthetic and efferent stances are needed in the instructional setting but serve very different purposes. Our overall literacy program must have balance across these two stances. (p. 615)

Alan C. Purves and Dianne L. Monson (1984) also emphasize the importance of encouraging both efferent and aesthetic responses within a literature program. They emphasize the relationships between texts and readers as the readers draw meaning. They describe two important functions in any literature program that prepares readers through a transactional approach. First, the program provides a broad background of literary genres and allows the students to talk about books using words such as *plot, metaphor, characterization, theme, style,* and *tone.* This function encourages students to understand the reasons for deciding that one book is better than another book (efferent responses). The program also exposes students to a variety of approaches and critical questions that allow the students to consider "How does the literature or character affect me? What does it mean? How good is it?" Such responses allow aesthetic involvement and individual transactions. Notice how Purves and Monson (1984) stress both the efferent and the aesthetic responses to literature:

It would seem therefore that students should be exposed to a variety of critical questions, including those which are personal and affective, those which are analytical, those which are interpretive, and those which are evaluative. Each of these questions can be answered intelligently and answering each can help a student learn to read and think and feel. And you can teach your students how to answer them. (p. 189)

Cedric Cullingford (1998) states that teachers should consider the "development of a reader who is aware and discriminating, who can analyze as well as react to what is read. Our first concern is to bring out the critical abilities of the reader, without which no demanding text can be enjoyed" (p. 193).

Analyzing Responses

Using realistic fiction and other types of books for role playing and bibliotherapy is more effective when there is a general understanding of children's responses to literature. Louise Rosenblatt (1978) states that literature selection "should not be thought of as an object, an entity, but rather as an active process lived through during the relationship between a reader and a text" (p. 12). Readers bring past experiences, present interests, and expectations that influence their responses to texts.

Studies of children's oral and written responses to literature analyze the types of comments that children make when they retell a selection or talk about a story. In a review of children's responses to literature, Purves and Monson (1984) identify characteristic responses of children in different grades. For example, children up to the third grade tend to respond to and retell literal aspects of a story. In addition to literal responses, fourth- and fifth-grade students tend to elaborate by placing themselves in the roles of the characters, comparing themselves to the characters, and talking about their personal reactions. By sixth grade, students begin to emphasize and interpret characters. In seventh and eighth grades, students increase their interpretations and frequently emphasize meaning and understanding in their evaluations. Eighth-grade students begin to look for deeper or hidden meanings in stories.

Working with children and literature, you can learn a great deal about children's responses to literature by analyzing what they choose to say or write about when they discuss literature. Purves and Monson (1984) recommend a classification system to use when analyzing children's comments about literature (see Chart 1.5).

Robert B. Ruddell (2003) emphasizes the importance of both efferent and aesthetic responses when he states, "These stances have different purposes and influence the way readers respond to text. An efferent stance shifts the reader's thinking to content and the analytical search for information to be retained. An aesthetic stance draws the reader into the text" (p. 225).

The Role of Motivation

Motivation is especially important in the aesthetic response to literature. Ruddell (2003) emphasizes that in the aesthetic approach, adults help students identify with the story characters and text topics. He states, "Your ability to do this will depend not only on your knowledge of children and their motivations and inter-

CHART 1.5 Classifying children's responses to books

Type of Response	Examples
Descriptive	Retelling the story, naming the characters, listing the media used in illustration.
Analytic	Pointing to the uses of language, structure, point-of-view in the work.
Classificatory	Placing the work in its literary historical context.
Personal	Describing the reader's reactions to the work and the emotions and memories that have been evoked.
Interpretive	Making inferences about the work and its parts, relating the work to some way of viewing phenomena (e.g., psychology).
Evaluative	Judging the work's merit on personal, formal, or moral criteria.

Source: From Alan C. Purves and Dianne L. Monson. *Experiencing Children's Literature.* Glenview, Ill.: Scott, Foresman, 1984, p. 143.

ests but also on your knowledge of children's literature. Your goal should be to connect students with literary work through discussions that link students' background knowledge, personal interests, and responses to the story characters, plot, language, format, and illustrations" (p. 226).

Problem-resolution books encourage readers to see themselves as successful problem solvers. In this response, readers relate to characters who are able to solve or resolve problems and vicariously associate with successful characters. Young children, for example, can become successful problem solvers as they respond to the boy who uses his wits to encourage the king to leave the bathtub in Audrey Wood's *King Bidgood's in the Bathtub.*

Older children can see themselves as successful problem solvers by responding to E. L. Konigsburg's protagonist in *The Outcasts of 19 Schuyler Place* as she rescues a work of art. With Molly Cone's *Come Back Salmon,* children can associate with the members of a fifth-grade class who cleaned up a salmon stream in Washington. With Susan Cooper's *The Boggart,* children can accompany three Canadian children as they figure out how to send a mischievous spirit back to his castle. With E. B. White's *Charlotte's Web,* children can respond to Charlotte, certainly one of the most successful problem solvers in children's fantasy.

The internal motivation of prestige enables a child to vicariously become a person of significance, who receives attention and exerts influence and control. Through picture *storybooks*, children can visualize themselves as heroines or heroes.

Highly illustrated biographies allow children to respond to characters who have had prestige in history, such as those in Diane Stanley and Peter Vennema's *Good Queen Bess: The Story of Elizabeth I of England*, *Bard of Avon: The Story of William Shakespeare*, and *Shaka: King of the Zulus*. The prestige of an artist may appeal to readers who can associate themselves with the successful career of an animator for Disney Studios and an illustrator of children's books in Bill Peet's *Bill Peet: An Autobiography*. Pat Cummings's *Talking With Artists* presents interviews with 14 illustrators of children's books and shows examples of their works. Jeanette Winter's *My Name Is Georgia* follows the life of Georgia O'Keeffe and shows how she drew her inspiration from nature.

Aesthetic motivation involves the elevation of an aesthetic sense and ranges from appreciation of beauty in nature to the enjoyment of family harmony and interaction. Children are motivated to respond to both the aesthetic beauty in nature and the beauty of language when they read Jane Yolen's *Owl Moon*. In Munro Leaf's *The Story of Ferdinand*, children can respond to a bull who prefers the aesthetic response to nature to the glory of the bullring. Aesthetic responses to beautiful language are heightened through poetry books such as Nancy Willard's *Pish, Posh, Said Hieronymus Bosch* and Stephen Dunning, Edward Lueders, and Hugh Smith's *Reflections on a Gift of Watermelon Pickle . . . and Other Modern Verse*. Enjoyment of family harmony and interactions are found in Pat Mora's *A Birthday Basket for Tía*. This book depicts loving relationships between a Latina girl and her aunt. Laura Ingalls Wilder's *Little House in the Big Woods* describes strong family relationships in pioneer times.

Escape literature enables readers to vicariously accompany literary characters to unfamiliar or even fantasy places. Readers can escape to Africa with a carpenter who discovers how to tell fortunes in Lloyd Alexander's *The Fortune-Tellers*. Africa is also the escape location for an African American girl who imagines what it would be like to live in East Africa in Virginia Kroll's *Masai and I*. The illustrations in David Wiesner's *Free Fall* allow readers to escape through a character's dreams. Gregory Rogers's *The Boy, The Bear, The Baron, The Bard* takes readers back to Tudor London. Books such as A. A. Milne's *Winnie-the-Pooh* allow readers to escape to the Hundred Acre Wood of personified toys. J. R. R. Tolkien's *The Hobbit* takes children into Middle Earth and allows them to become heroes as they accomplish their quest and regain the realm of the dwarfs.

Fiction and nonfiction set in other time periods encourage children to vicariously escape into those times. Avi's *Who Was That Masked Man, Anyway?* takes children back to World War II and allows them to interact with a boy who is infatuated with the radio shows of that time. Tracy Barrett's *Anna of Byzantium* takes readers back to the intrigue of the 11th-century Byzantine Empire to discover a princess who wanted to write history. Classics such as Robert Louis Stevenson's *Treasure Island* have encouraged generations to escape into the adventures that are possible with treasure maps, mysterious islands, and questionable characters.

The motivator of intellectual curiosity encourages inquisitive minds to explore and learn about new words and new ideas. Some picture books, such as Arthur Geisert's *Pigs From 1 to 10*, challenge readers to find animals that are hiding within the illustrations. Numerous nonfiction books also encourage intellectual curiosity. Lois Ehlert's *Red Leaf, Yellow Leaf* follows a child's curiosity as she plants a sugar maple tree and discovers how the seedling arrived at the nursery. Joanna Cole's *The Magic School Bus on the Ocean Floor* presents science facts through an amusing excursion through the ocean. Anne Baird's *Space Camp: The Great Adventure for NASA Hopefuls* includes numerous photographs and descriptions that will motivate and excite future astronauts. Kathryn Lasky's *Think Like an Eagle: At Work With a Wildlife Photographer* challenges readers to think like animals in order to acquire the best photographs.

Understanding of self is a powerful motivator. Books allow children to understand and respond to personal motivations and the motivations that influence others. Many books can be used to elicit and increase personal responses to literature because they depict emotions that children experience. In Cynthia Rylant's *Missing May*, a girl faces her aunt's death and makes discoveries about herself and those whom she loves. Avi's *Nothing But the Truth: A Documentary Novel* elicits very personal responses and insights into the motives of older students. Memos, letters, diary pages, phone and personal conversations, speeches, and telegrams encourage readers to develop and defend their own point of view about which character is telling the truth.

Throughout this book are many literature recommendations and literature-related activities that entice and enhance children's responses to literature. These recommendations encourage both efferent and aesthetic responses to literature. For example, through oral responses such as drama, discussions, role playing, and storytelling, children can respond to and critically evaluate development of the literary elements such as plot, conflict, characterization, and theme (efferent responses) and can provide personal reactions to those literary elements (aesthetic responses). Likewise, readers can evaluate the effectiveness of the setting and mood as created by the author or illustrator (efferent responses) and provide personal responses that emphasize emotional reactions through their own drawings (aesthetic responses).

Suggested Activities

For more suggested activities, visit the Companion Website at www.prenhall.com/norton

CW

- Select several books, such as Eve Rice's *Oh, Lewis!*, to encourage young children to identify familiar actions in books. Share these books with a few preschool children and let them interact orally with the text.

- With a group of your peers, compile a list of picture books that would be useful when developing one of the following cognitive skills: observing, comparing, hypothesizing, organizing, summarizing, applying, or criticizing. Share your findings with your class.

- Read several books in which young children must overcome such problems as jealousy, fear, or anger. Compare the ways in which the authors have allowed the children to handle their problems. Do the feelings seem normal and natural? Is more than one aspect of a feeling developed? Are options shown for handling each emotion?

- The cover of *School Library Journal* for September 2000 carries the headline "You Are What You Read." Conduct your own research on your reading habits. What literature influenced you at different times in your life? By looking at your list, how would you answer the question: What do my reading habits reveal about me?

All literature discussed in Chapter 1 can be found in the appropriate genre chapters as well as in the appropriate Children's Literature lists at the end of Chapters 3 through 12.

For an extensive list of children's literature, visit the CD-ROM that accompanies this book.

2 THE HISTORY OF CHILDREN'S LITERATURE

From The Pied Piper of Hamelin, by Robert Browning. Illustrated by Kate Greenaway. Copyright © 1986 by F. Warne, London. Used by permission.

CHAPTER OUTLINE

- Milestones in the History of Children's Literature
- Standards for Evaluating Young Adult Literature
- The History of Censorship
- Children and the Family in Children's Literature

When students of children's literature look at the beautiful books published to meet children's needs, interests, and reading levels, many are amazed to learn that not long ago, books were not written specifically for children. Changes in printing technology provided affordable books, but more important were changes in social attitudes toward children. When society looked upon children as little adults who must rapidly step into the roles of their parents, children had little time or need to read books. But when childhood began to be viewed as a special part of the human life cycle, literature written specifically for children became very important.

Within the context of human history as a whole, the history of children's literature is very short. Neither early tales told through the oral tradition nor early books were created specifically for children. When children's books were eventually written, they usually mirrored the dominant cultural values of their place and time. Thus, a study of children's literature from the 15th century through contemporary times reflects both changes in society as a whole and changes in social expectations of children and the family.

Literature researchers view children's literature as a vehicle for studying social values and changing attitudes. Robert Gordon Kelly's (1970) "Mother Was a Lady: Self and Society in Selected American Children's Periodicals, 1865–1890," Mary Lystad's (1980) *From Dr. Mather to Dr. Seuss: Two Hundred Years of American Books for Children*, Cedric Cullingford's (1998) *Children's Literature and Its Effects*, and Gwen Athene Tarbox's (2000) *The Clubwomen's Daughters: Collective Impulses in Progressive-Era Girl's Fiction, 1890–1940* are examples of research of children's literature as an index to the social attitudes of a particular time.

Numerous edited texts are available that collect writings of various researchers and critics. For example, *Aspects and Issues in the History of Children's Literature*, edited by Maria Nikolajeva (1995), includes articles on theories and methods of conducting studies on the history of children's literature and aspects of national histories. *Literature and the Child: Romantic Continuations, Postmodern Contestations*, edited by James Holt McGavran (1999), provides articles on topics such as "Romanticism Continuing and Contested" and "Romantic Ironies, Postmodern Texts." *Children's Book Publishing in Britain Since 1945*, edited by Kimberley Reynolds and Nicholas Tucker (1998), includes critical articles on topics such as picture books and movable books. Holly Koelling's (2004) *Classic Connections: Turning Teens on to Great Literature* presents a discussion of and a guide to using classic literature with young adults.

Milestones in the History of Children's Literature

This chapter first considers some milestones in the development of children's literature, then it looks at changing views of children and the family as reflected in early books for children and in more contemporary stories. Chart 2.1 provides an overview of the historical milestones.

The Oral Tradition

Long before recorded history, family units and tribes shared their group traditions and values through stories told around the campfire. On every continent around the globe, ancient peoples developed folktales and mythologies that speculated about human beginnings, attempted to explain the origins of the universe and other natural phenomena, emphasized ethical truths, and transmitted history from one generation to the next. When hunters

returned from their adventures, they probably told about the perils of the hunt and hostile encounters with other tribes. Heroic deeds were certainly told and retold until they became a part of a group's heritage. This tradition has existed since the first oral communication among human beings and goes back to the very roots of every civilization on earth. These tales were not told specifically to children, but children were surely present—listening, watching, learning, and remembering.

The various native peoples of North America developed mythologies expressing their reverence for the rolling prairies, lush forests, ice floes, deserts, and blue lakes of their continent. In Central and South America, storytellers of the Yucatán Peninsula and the Andes chronicled the rise of Mayan, Aztec, and Incan empires, wars of expansion, and, eventually, the Spanish conquest of their homelands. Across Africa, highly respected storytellers developed a style that encouraged audiences to interact with storytellers in relating tales of dramatic heroes, personified animals, and witty tricksters. In the

CHART 2.1   Early historical milestones in children's literature

———	The Oral Tradition
	    "Beowulf"
	    "Jack the Giant Killer"
		1800s	The Romantic Movement in Europe
			    The Brothers Grimm
			    Hans Christian Andersen

1400s	Early Books
	    Hornbooks
	    Caxton's Printing Press—1476
			The Impact of Illustrators on Children's
			        Books
			    Walter Crane

1500s	The Introduction of Chapbooks
	    "Jack the Giant Killer"
			Randolph Caldecott
			    Kate Greenaway

1600s	The Puritan Influence
	    Spiritual Milk for Boston Babes in Either
	        England, Drawn From the Breasts of Both
	        Testaments for Their Souls' Nourishment
	    Pilgrim's Progress
		1860s	The Victorian Influence
			    Charlotte Yonge's *The Daisy Chain* and *The*
			        Clever Woman of the Family

1693	A View of Childhood Changes
	    John Locke's *Some Thoughts Concerning Ed-*
	        ucation
		1840–1900	Childhood Seen as an Adventure, Not a
			        Training Ground for Adulthood
			    Fantasy

1697	First Fairy Tales Written for Children
	    Charles Perrault's *Tales of Mother Goose*
			Lewis Carroll's *Alice's Adventures in Won-*
			        derland.
			    Edward Lear's *A Book of Nonsense*

1719	Great Adventure Stories
	    Daniel Defoe's *Robinson Crusoe*
	    Jonathan Swift's *Gulliver's Travels*
			Adventure
			    Robert Louis Stevenson's *Treasure Island*
			    Howard Pyle's *The Merry Adventures of*

1744	Children's Literature: A True Beginning
	    John Newbery's *A Little Pretty Pocket Book*
	        and *History of Little Goody Two-Shoes*
	        (1745)
			Robin Hood
			    Jules Verne's *Twenty Thousand Leagues Un-*
			        der the Sea
			    Real People

1762	Guidance of Children in Their Search for
	        Knowledge
	    Jean-Jacques Rousseau's *Emile*
			Margaret Sidney's *The Five Little Peppers*
			        and How They Grew
			    Louisa May Alcott's *Little Women*

1789	Poetry About Children William Blake's *Songs of Innocence*		Johanna Spyri's *Heidi*

ancient cultures of Asia, from Mesopotamia to Japan, early myths and folktales were eventually incorporated into the complex mythologies and philosophical tenets of Taoism, Confucianism, Hinduism, and Buddhism. In Europe, the earliest oral traditions of the Celts, Franks, Saxons, Goths, Danes, and many other groups eventually influenced one another as a result of migration, trade, and warfare; and the mythologies of ancient Greece and Rome became widely influential as the Roman Empire expanded over much of the continent.

The European oral tradition, according to Robert Leeson (1977), reached its climax in the feudal era of the Middle Ages. What are often called *castle tales* and *cottage tales* provided people with literature long before those tales were widely accessible in writing or print. The ruling classes favored poetic epics about the reputed deeds of the lord of the manor or his ancestors. In the great halls of castles, minstrels or bards accompanied themselves on lyers or harps while singing tales about noble warriors, such as Beowulf and King Arthur, or ballads of chivalrous love in regal surroundings, such as those found in the French version of *Cinderella*.

Around cottage fires or at country fairs, humbler people had different heroes: Storytellers shared folktales about people much like the peasants themselves, people who daily confronted servitude, inscrutable natural phenomena, and unknown spiritual forces. In these tales, even the youngest or poorest person had the potential to use resourcefulness or kindness to go from rags to riches and to live "happily even after." Often, such achievement required outwitting or slaying wolves, dragons, malevolent supernatural beings, or great lords.

By whatever name they were known—bards, minstrels, or devisers of tales—the storytellers of medieval Europe were entertainers: If they did not entertain, they lost their audiences or even their meals and lodging. Consequently, they learned to tell stories that had rapid plot development and easily identifiable characters. These storytellers also possessed considerable power. Sir Philip Sidney (1595), a 16th-century English poet, described storytellers as able to keep children away from their play and old people away from their chimney corners. Whether woven from imagination or retold from legends and stories of old, the tales of storytellers could influence the people who heard them. Thus, if a minstrel's story offended or discredited a lord, the minstrel could be punished. By the end of the 14th century, feudal authority sought to control the tales being told and often jailed storytellers who angered either a ruler or the church.

German scholar August Nitschke (1988) describes the role of fairy tales in earlier times. He states:

> In the fifteenth and sixteenth centuries fairy tales were told to children, but grown men took fairy tales so seriously that they would interpret them symbolically. Geiler of Kaiserberg, for instance, and Martin Luther were able to interpret the Cinderella story in such a way. They foretold a good future for those persons working in the kitchen as humbly and shyly as Cinderella did. Others such as Cardinal Giovanni Dominici opposed fairy tales because he thought they could foster vanity such as toys might—like the wooden horses or the pretty trumpets or the artificial birds or the golden drums—or because they might frighten children. (p. 164)

Today, many early European folktales, myths, and legends are considered ideal for sharing with children, but this was not the attitude of feudal Europe. Storytellers addressed audiences of all ages. A child was considered a small adult who should enter into adult life as quickly as possible, and stories primarily for young people were considered unnecessary. Consequently, the stories about giants, heroes, and simpletons that relieved the strain of adult life also entertained children. These favorite tales, which had been told and retold for hundreds of years, were eventually chosen for some of the first printed books in Europe.

Early Printed Books

Prior to the mid-1400s, the literary heritage of Europe consisted of the oral tradition and parchment manuscripts laboriously handwritten by monks and scribes. Manuscript books were rare and costly, prized possessions of the nobles and priests, who were among the few Europeans able to read and write. To the extent that these books were meant for the young, they were usually designed to provide instruction in rhetoric, grammar, and music for the children privileged enough to attend monastery schools. Children were rarely trusted with the books themselves and usually wrote on slates as monks dictated their lessons.

A significant event occurred in the 1450s, when the German Johannes Gutenberg discovered a practical method for using movable metal type, which made possible the mass production of books. After learning the printing process in Germany, William Caxton established England's first printing press in 1476. The use of printing presses led to the creation of hornbooks, which were printed sheets of text mounted on wood and covered with translucent animal horn. The books were in the shape of a paddle. Hornbooks were used to teach reading and numbers. Gillian Avery (1995) states that "this convenient and relatively indestructible form of presenting the alphabet (followed by a syllabary, invocation to the Trinity, and the Lord's Prayer) was in common use from the sixteenth century until well on in the eighteenth" (p. 3).

Hornbooks remained popular into the 1700s, when the battledore, a lesson book made of folded paper or cardboard, became more prevalent. Like hornbooks, battledores usually contained an alphabet, numerals, and proverbs or prayers.

When William Caxton opened his printing business in 1476, most of the books used with children were not written for their interest. Instead, books for children adhered to the sentiment that young readers should read

The hornbook, which was used for instruction, usually contained the alphabet, numerals, and the Lord's Prayer. (Photo courtesy of The Horn Book, Inc.)

This lesson book, or battledore, was made from folded paper or cardboard. (Courtesy of The Horn Book, Inc.)

only what would improve their manners or instruct their minds. *Caxton's Book of Curtesye,* first printed in 1477 (Furnivall, 1868), contained directions for drawing readers away from vice and turning them toward virtue. Verses guided readers toward personal cleanliness (comb your hair, clean your ears, clean your nose but don't pick it), polite social interactions (look people straight in the face when speaking, don't quarrel with dogs), suitable reverence in church (kneel before the cross, don't chatter), and correct table manners (don't blow on your food or undo your girdle at the table).

The majority of books that Caxton published were not meant to be read by children, but three of his publications are now considered classics in children's literature. In 1481, Caxton published the beast fable *Reynart the Foxe* (*The History of Reynard the Fox*), a satire of oppression and tyranny. This tale of a clever fox who could outwit all his adversaries became popular with both adults and children.

Caxton's most important publication may be *The Book of the Subtyle Historyes and Fables of Esope* (*The Fables of Aesop*), which Caxton translated from a manuscript by the French monk Machault in 1484. These fables about the weaknesses of people and animals were popular with readers of various ages and are still enjoyed by children. Caxton's publication in 1485 of Sir Thomas Malory's *Le Morte d'Arthur* (*The Death of Arthur*) preserved the legendary story of King Arthur and his

knights, which has been published since in many versions suitable for young readers.

Caxton's translations, standardization of English, and literary style had a major impact on English literature, according to Jane Bingham and Grayce Scholt (1980). Cornelia Meigs et al. (1969) also stress Caxton's importance in creating the first printed books in the English language. In outward form, these books were of a standard not easily equaled. The ample pages, the broad margins, and the black-letter type that suggested manuscript contributed to their beauty, dignity, and worthiness to be England's first widespread realization of her own literature.

Caxton's books were beautiful, but they were too expensive for the common people. Soon, however, peddlers (or chapmen) were selling crudely printed chapbooks for pennies at markets and fairs, along with ribbons, patent medicines, and other wares. Customers could also go directly to a printer and select from large uncut sheets of as many as 16 pages of text, which then were bound into a hardcover book.

Some of the first chapbooks were based on ballads, such as "The Two Children in the Wood," and traditional tales, such as "Jack the Giant Killer." According to Lou J. McCulloch (1979), the content of chapbooks fell into the following categories: religious instruction, interpretations of the supernatural, romantic legends, ballad tales, and historical narratives. John Ashton's (1882) *Chap-Books of the Eighteenth Century* includes religious titles, such as "The History of Joseph and His Brethren" and "The Unhappy Birth, Wicked Life, and Miserable Death of the Vile Traytor and Apostle Judas Iscariot"; traditional tales, such as "Tom Thumb" and "A True Tale of Robin Hood"; and supernatural tales, such as "The Portsmouth Ghost."

From the 16th to the 19th centuries, peddlers sold inexpensive chapbooks in Europe and North America. (From Chap-Books of the Eighteenth Century, by John Ashton. Published by Chatto and Windus, 1882. From the John G. White Collection, Cleveland Public Library.)

Chapbooks were extremely popular in both England and the United States during the 1700s, but their popularity rapidly declined during the early 1800s. Zohar Shavit (1995) states that "during the eighteenth century, chapbooks became the most important reading material for children. However, neither the religious nor the educational establishment were delighted about the reading of chapbooks by children. On the contrary, the more important the child's education (and consequently his reading matter) became, the less the educational establishment was ready to accept children's reading of chapbooks. When the religious establishment began to scrutinize the education of children as well as their reading material, chapbooks had to retreat underground" (p. 31).

The Puritan Influence

According to Bingham and Scholt (1980), political upheaval, religious dissent, and censorship affected English literature in the 1600s. As printing increased and literacy spread, the British monarchy realized the power of the press. In 1637, it decreed that only London, Oxford, Cambridge, and York could have printing establishments.

According to Anne Scott MacLeod (1995), "the story of children's reading in America begins with the Puritans. . . . From the beginning, Puritans thought about the children and provided for their schooling, at home and in the tiny communities they called towns. By the 1640s, Massachusetts laws required heads of families to teach their children and apprentices to read" (p. 102).

The beliefs of the Puritans, dissenters from the established Church of England who were growing in strength and numbers in England and North America, also influenced literature of the period. Puritans considered the traditional tales about giants, fairies, and witches found in chapbooks to be impious and corrupting. They urged that children not be allowed to read such materials and instead be provided with literature to instruct them and reinforce their moral development. Puritans expected their offspring to be children of God first and foremost. Bernard J. Lonsdale and Helen K. Macintosh (1973) explain:

> Family worship, admonitions from elders, home instruction, strict attendance at school, and close attention to lessons all were aimed at perpetuating those ideals and values for which the parents themselves had sacrificed so much. To the elders, the important part of education was learning to read, write, and figure. Only literature that would instruct and warn was tolerated. (p. 161)

Awesome titles for books that stressed the importance of instructing children in moral concerns were common in Puritan times. In 1649, the grandfather of Cotton Mather (a Puritan who was influential during the Salem witch-hunts in New England) wrote a book called *Spiritual Milk for Boston Babes in Either England, Drawn From the Breasts of Both Testaments for Their Souls' Nourishment.* In 1671, the leading Puritan writer, James Janeway, published a series of stories about children who had led saintly lives until their deaths at an early age. His *A Token for Children, Being an Exact Account of the Conversion, Holy and Exemplary Lives, and Joyful Deaths of Several Young Children* was meant not for enjoyment, but to instruct Puritan children in moral development.

The most influential piece of literature written during this period was John Bunyan's *The Pilgrim's Progress from this world, to that which is to come. Delivered under the similitude of a Dream. Wherein is discovered, the manner of his setting out, his dangerous journey and safe arrival at the Desired Country,* or *Pilgrim's Progress,* published in England in 1678. Although moral improvement was the primary purpose of this book, *Pilgrim's Progress* also contained bold action that appealed to both children and older readers, some of whom adopted it for its entertainment, as well as religious, value. Bunyan's hero, Christian, experiences many perilous adventures as he journeys alone through the Slough of Despond and the Valley of Humiliation in his search for salvation. Characters such as Mr. Valiant-for-Truth and Ignorance appear in such settings as the Valley of the Shadow of Death, the Delectable Mountains, and the Celestial City. Christian acquires a companion, Faithful, who is executed in the town of Vanity Fair. Then another companion, Hopeful, helps him fight the giant Despair and finally reach his goal.

A	In *Adam's* Fall We Sinned all.
B	Thy Life to Mend This *Book* Attend.
C	The *Cat* doth play And after flay.
D	A *Dog* will bite A Thief at night.
E	An *Eagles* flight Is out of fight.
F	The Idle *Fool* Is whipt at School.

The New England Primer *taught both Puritan ideals and the alphabet. (From* The New England Primer, Enlarged, Boston, *1727 edition. From the Rare Books and Manuscript Division, The New York Public Library, Astor, Lenox, and Tilden Foundations.)*

Pilgrim's Progress and the *Spiritual Milk for Boston Babes in Either England* were required reading for colonial children in North America. Another important book in colonial homes was *The New England Primer*, a combination alphabet and catechism designed to teach Puritan ideals. The primer was written in such a way that spiritual instruction was the main theme. The primer appeared around 1690 and was printed in hundreds of editions until 1830. According to Cornelia Meigs et al. (1969), the influence of the primer lasted so long because in that era, "the chance of life for young children was cruelly small" (p. 114), and spiritual preparation for an early death was thus imperative.

John Locke's Influence on Views of Childhood

In a social environment that viewed children as small adults and expected them to behave accordingly, few considered that children might have interests and educational needs of their own. The Puritans and other Calvinist Christians believed that everyone was born predestined to achieve either salvation or damnation: thus, all must spend their lives attempting to prove predestined worthiness to be saved.

The English philosopher John Locke, however, envisioned the child's mind at birth as a *tabula rasa*, a blank page on which ideas were to be imprinted. In *Some Thoughts Concerning Education* (1910), published in

1693, Locke stressed the interrelatedness of healthy physical development and healthy mental development, and he advocated milder ways of teaching and bringing up children than had been recommended previously. According to John Rowe Townsend (1975), Locke believed that children who could read should be provided with easy, pleasant books suited to their capacities—books that encouraged them to read and rewarded them for their reading efforts but that did not fill their heads with useless "trumpery" or encourage vice.

Locke found a grave shortage of books that could provide children with pleasure or reward, but he did recommend *Aesop's Fables* and *Reynard the Fox* for the delight they offered children and the useful reflections they offered the adults in children's lives. Locke's attitude was quite enlightened for his time: It provided a glimmer of hope that children might be permitted to go through a period of childhood rather than immediately assume the same roles as their parents. Although 17th-century European and North American culture contained few books appropriate for children, a realization dawned that children might benefit from books written to encourage their reading.

Charles Perrault's Tales of Mother Goose

An exciting development in children's literature occurred in 17th-century France: Charles Perrault, a gifted member of the Académie Française, published a book called *Contes de ma Mère l'Oye (Tales of Mother Goose)*. The stories in this collection were not those normally referred to as Mother Goose rhymes today: Instead, they were well-known fairy tales, such as "Cinderella," "Sleeping Beauty," "Puss in Boots," "Little Red Riding Hood," and "Blue Beard." Perrault did not create these tales; he retold stories from the French oral tradition that had entranced children and provided entertainment in the elegant salons of the Parisian aristocracy for generations.

Perrault was one of the first writers to recognize that fairy tales have a special place in the world of children. Readers can thank Perrault or, as many scholars (Muir, 1954) now believe, his son Pierre Perrault d'Armancour, for collecting these tales, which have been translated and retold by many contemporary writers and illustrators of children's books. At last, entertainment was written for children rather than adopted by them because nothing else was available.

The Adventure Stories of Defoe and Swift

Two adventure books that appeared in the early 18th century were, like virtually all literature of the time, written for adults, but these two were quickly embraced by children. A political climate that punished dissenters by placing them into prison molded the author of the first great adventure story, *Robinson Crusoe*, which was published in 1719. Daniel Defoe was condemned to Newgate Prison after he wrote a fiery pamphlet responding to the political

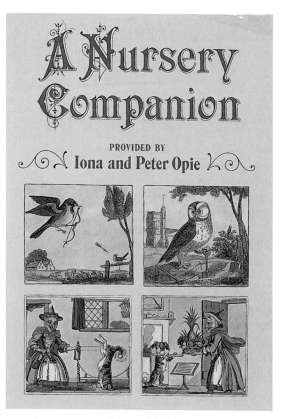

A Nursery Companion *is a collection of Mother Goose rhymes that were originally published in the early 1800s. (From A* Nursery Companion, *by Iona and Peter Opie, Oxford University Press, 1980.)*

and religious controversies of his time. However, Defoe wrote constantly, even while in jail.

Defoe was motivated to write *Robinson Crusoe* when he read the personal accounts of a Scottish sailor, Alexander Selkirk, who had been marooned on one of the Juan Fernandez Islands, located off the coast of Chile. This Scottish sailor had deserted ship after a disagreement with the captain and had lived alone on the island for 4 years before he was discovered by another ship and taken back to England. Defoe was so captivated by Selkirk's experience that he wrote an adventure story to answer his questions about how a person might acquire food, clothing, and shelter if shipwrecked on an island. The resulting tale appeared first in serial publication and then in a book. Children and adults enjoyed the exciting and suspenseful story.

According to Brian W. Alderson (1959), *Robinson Crusoe* reflects an era in Western history when people had begun to believe in the natural goodness of human beings uninfluenced by corruption in the world around them. *Robinson Crusoe* became and remained so popular that it stimulated a whole group of books written about similar subjects, which came to be known as Robinsonades. The most popular Robinsonade was Johann Wyss's *The Swiss Family Robinson.* Susan Naramore Maher (1988) states:

Robinsonades commanded an eager juvenile readership ready to devour the latest fiction about castaways, no matter how didactic or improbable the tale. In the nineteenth century, *Robinson Crusoe* itself became a prized nursery book, favored by children for its detail and adventure, by parents for its religious sentiment and work ethic. (p. 169)

The second major adventure story written during the early 18th century also dealt with the subject of shipwreck. Jonathan Swift's *Gulliver's Travels*, published in 1726, described Gulliver's realistic adventures with strange beings encountered in mysterious lands: tiny Lilliputians, giant Brobdingnagians, talking horses, and flying islands. Swift wrote *Gulliver's Travels* as a satire for adults. Children, however, thought of the story as an enjoyable adventure and adopted Gulliver as a hero.

These adventure stories must have seemed truly remarkable to children otherwise surrounded by literature written only to instruct or to moralize. The impact of these 18th-century writers is still felt today, as 21st-century children enjoy versions of the first adventure stories.

Newbery's Books for Children

The 1740s are commonly regarded as the time when the idea of children's books began in Europe and North America. New ways of thought emerged as the middle class became larger and strengthened it social position. Because more people had the time, money, and education necessary for reading, books became more important. Middle-class life also began to center on the home and family rather than on the marketplace or the great houses of nobility. With the growing emphasis on family life, a realization began that children should be children rather than small adults.

Into this social climate came John Newbery, an admirer of John Locke and an advocate of a milder way of educating children. Newbery was also a writer and publisher, who began publishing a line of books for children in 1744 with *A Little Pretty Pocket Book.* "Although his work reflected the didactic tone of the time," say Jane Bingham and Grayce Scholt (1980), "his books were not intended to be textbooks. Their gilt-paper covers, attractive pages, engaging stories and verses—and sometimes toys which were offered with the books—provided 'diversion' for children of the English-speaking world" (p. 86). *A Little Pretty Pocket Book* included a letter from Jack the Giant Killer written to both instruct and entertain children. Modern readers would not consider this early book for children very entertaining compared with books written to amuse today's children, but it must have been revolutionary for

Technology Resources

Use the CD-ROM that accompanies this text to generate a list of Newbery award and Newbery Honor winners. Just search under Awards and type "New" in the field.

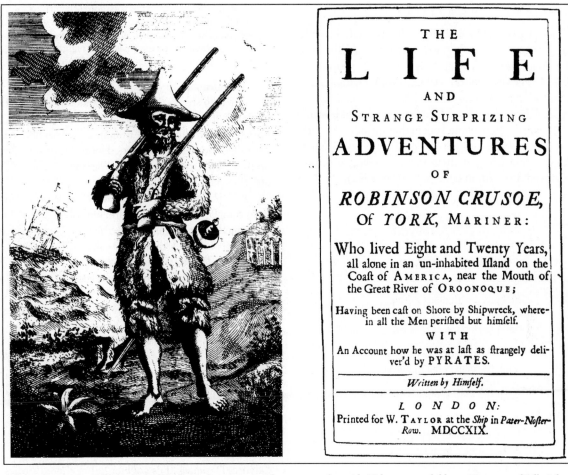

THE

LIFE

AND

STRANGE SURPRIZING

ADVENTURES

OF

ROBINSON CRUSOE,

Of *YORK*, MARINER:

Who lived Eight and Twenty Years,
all alone in an un-inhabited Ifland on the
Coaft of AMERICA, near the Mouth of
the Great River of OROONOQUE;

Having been caft on Shore by Shipwreck, wherein all the Men perifhed but himfelf.

WITH

An Account how he was at laft as ftrangely deliver'd by PYRATES.

Written by Himfelf.

LONDON:

Printed for W. TAYLOR at the *Ship* in *Pater-Nofter-
Row.* MDCCXIX.

Although not written for children, Daniel Defoe's adventure story became popular with 18th-century children. (Courtesy of Lilly Library, Indiana University, Bloomington, Indiana.)

its time. In 1765, Newbery published a more famous book, *History of Little Goody Two-Shoes,* a fictitious story by Oliver Goldsmith.

Newbery's company, set up in London, became a success. His accomplishments are often attributed to his bustling energy, his interest in literature and writers, his love for children, and his taking note of children's tastes as measured by the popularity of their favorite chapbooks. Newbery's publications included *Nurse Truelove's New Year's Gift, Mother Goose, Tom Thumb's Folio,* and old favorites, such as *Aesop's Fables, Robinson Crusoe,* and *Gulliver's Travels.* Because of Newbery's success, publishers realized that there was indeed a market for books written specifically for children. It is fitting that the coveted award given annually to the outstanding author of a children's literature selection bears Newbery's name.

Rousseau's Philosophy of Natural Development

Whereas John Locke had advocated a milder and more rational approach to educating children, Jean-Jacques Rousseau recommended a totally new approach: Locke believed that children should be led in their search for knowledge, but Rousseau believed that they should merely be accompanied. He maintained that children could and should develop naturally, with gentle guidance from wise adults who could supply necessary information.

In his *Emile,* published in 1762, Rousseau described stages of children's growth, stressing the importance of experiences in harmony with children's natural development physically and mentally. Rousseau's stages progressed from early sensory motor development, through a concrete learning period, into a period where intellecual conceptualization was possible. Rousseau believed that Daniel Defoe's *Robinson Crusoe* was the most important piece of literature because it emphasized the necessity of using one's own ideas to cope with one's environment. His impact on parents' attitudes toward children was "forceful and unmistakable," says Margaret C. Gillespie (1970). "Now children were looked upon as 'little angels' who could do no wrong. They were permitted to be children rather than 'little adults.' They became the center of the educational scene rather than satellites around the curriculum" (p. 23).

William Blake's Poetry About Children

The English poet William Blake, who is credited with writing verses as if a child had written them, published his *Songs of Innocence* in 1789 and his *Songs of Experience* in 1794. F. J. Harvey Darton (1932, 1966) characterizes Blake in the spiritual sense as "a child happy on a cloud, singing and desiring such songs as few but he could write" (p. 179). Blake's often-quoted poem that introduces *Songs of Innocence* provides readers an opportunity to visualize this happy child (the punctuation and spelling are from the engraved first edition cited in Darton, 1932):

Introduction

Piping down the valleys wild
Piping songs of pleasant glee
On a cloud I saw a child.
And he laughing said to me.

Pipe a song about a Lamb:
So I piped with merry chear,
Piper pipe that song again—
So I piped, he wept to hear.

Drop thy pipe thy happy pipe
Sing thy songs of happy chear.
So I sung the same again
While he wept with joy to hear.

Piper sit thee down and write
In a book that all may read—
So he vanish'd from my sight.
And I pluck'd a hollow reed

And I made a rural pen,
And I stain'd the water clear,
And I wrote my happy songs,
Every child may joy to hear.

The Fairy Tales of Andersen and the Brothers Grimm

Sir Walter Scott's novels about the Middle Ages, enthusiasm for Gothic architecture and lyrical ballads, and Rousseau's philosophy of a return to nature typified the Romantic Movement in late-18th-century Europe. This atmosphere encouraged an interest in folk literature.

In the early 1800s, two German scholars, Jacob and Wilhelm Grimm, became interested in collecting folktales that reflected the ancient German language and tradition. In researching their subject, the brothers listened to tales told by Dortchen and Gretchen Wild; the Wilds' maid, Marie; a farmer's wife called Frau Viehmännin; and other storytellers from throughout Germany. Although scholars disagree about how exactly the Brothers Grimm transcribed the tales they heard, Bettina Hürlimann (1980) maintains that the brothers

> did not just write down what they heard. Even for the first edition they did a lot of revising, comparing with other sources, and trying to find a simple language which was at the same time full of character. With time and with later editions

it became clear that Jacob, the more scholarly, tried to keep the tales in the most simple, original form, more or less as they had heard them, and that Wilhelm, more of a poet, was for retelling them in a new form with regard to the children. (p. 71)

The Grimms' first edition of tales, published in 1812, contained 85 stories, including "Cinderella," "Hansel and Gretel," "Little Red Riding Hood," and "The Frog Prince." According to Hürlimann, the second edition, published in 1815, was designed more specifically for children, with illustrations and a minimum of scholarly comment on the tales it contained.

In 1823, the tales collected by the Brothers Grimm were translated into English and published under the title *German Popular Stories.* Since that time, artists in many countries have illustrated such tales as "Snow White and the Seven Dwarfs," "Rumpelstiltskin," and "The Elves and the Shoemaker," which have become part of our literary heritage.

Most of the published folktales and fairy tales discussed thus far were written down by either Charles Perrault or the Brothers Grimm. The stories had been told in castles and cottages for many generations. Hans Christian Andersen, however, is generally credited with being the first to create and publish an original fairy tale. Andersen used his own experiences to stimulate his writing. "The Ugly Duckling," "The Little Mermaid," and "The Red Shoes" are among Andersen's famous stories.

Andersen was born to a poor but happy family in Odense, Denmark. His cobbler father shared stories with him and even built a puppet theater for Andersen. Even when his father died and it seemed that he would have to learn a trade, Andersen retained his dream of becoming an actor. During these poverty-stricken years, he tried to forget his troubles by putting on puppet shows and telling stories to children.

Because Andersen wanted to write stories and plays, he returned to school to improve his writing skills. While there, he suffered from cruel jokes about his looks; he was thin and had large feet and a large nose. (Doesn't this sound like a theme for one of his fairy tales?)

In 1828, when Andersen was 23, he began to write stories and poems. Five years later, he was recognized as a promising writer by the Danish government, whose financial support allowed him to travel and write about his experiences. When his *Life in Italy,* a rather scholarly work, was published, Andersen at last started to make money. His next book was far different: It was the first of his famous fairy tale books, and it was written in the same colloquial language used to tell stories.

When *Fairy Tales Told for Children* was published, a friend told Andersen that his *Life in Italy* would make him famous but his fairy tales would make people remember him forever. Although Andersen did not believe his fairy tales were as good as his other books, he enjoyed writing them and produced a new fairy tale book each Christmas

German Popular Stories, *such as this 1826 edition, introduced the Grimms' folktalés to English-speaking children. (Courtesy of Lilly Library, Indiana University, Bloomington, Indiana.)*

as a gift to children of all ages. When Andersen was 62, he was invited back to Odense, the town in which he had known happiness, poverty, and sadness. This time, however, he was the honored guest at a celebration that lasted for an entire week.

Andersen's fairy stories are still popular; newly illustrated versions are published every year, and his influence can be seen in modern children's literature as well. Naomi Lewis (2004) states that "every children's book whose characters are non-human but whose story reflects the range of human behavior is descended from Andersen" (p. 9).

Early Illustrators of Children's Books

The identity of the first picture book for children is debated. Eric Quayle (1971) identifies *Kunst und Lehrbüchlein* (*Book of Art and Instruction for Young People*), published in 1580 by the German publisher Sigmund Feyerabend, as the "first book aimed at the unexplored juvenile market" (p. 11). The detailed, full-page woodcuts showing European life were the work of Jost Amman. Of particular interest are the pictures of a young scholar reading a hornbook and of a child holding a doll.

Johann Amos Comenius, a Moravian teacher and former bishop of the Bohemian Brethren, is usually cred-

ited with writing the first nonalphabet picture book that strove to educate children. Bettina Hürlimann (1980) describes Comenius as a great humanist, who wanted children to observe God's creations—plants, stars, clouds, rain, sun, and geography—rather than to memorize abstract knowledge.

To achieve this goal. Comenius took children out of the conventional classrooms and into the natural world. He then wrote down their experiences in simple sentences, using both Latin and the children's own language. He published these simple sentences and accompanying woodcuts in 1658 as *Orbis Pictus* (*Painted World*). Educational historian Ayers Bagley (1985) identifies allegorical meanings in the illustrations and text: Accoring to Bagley, Comenius saw true understanding, right action, and correct speech as important contributors to the attainment of wisdom.

Scholars disagree about whether Comenius drew the illustrations for *Orbis Pictus* himself or whether he instructed artists in their exection; Jane Bingham and Grayce Scholt (1980) credit the woodcuts in the 1658 edition to Paul Kreutzberger and the wood engravings in the 1810 American edition to Alexander Anderson. Whoever the artist was, Hürlimann emphasizes that "the pictures are in wonderful harmony with the text, and the

A typical woodcut from Orbis Pictus, *the first picture book for children. (A reprint of the* Orbis Pictus *has been published by Singing Tree Press, Gale Research Company, Detroit, Michigan.)*

book was to become for more than a century the most popular book with children of all classes" (p. 67).

Most book illustrations before the 1800s, especially those in the inexpensive chapbooks, were crude woodcuts. If color was used, it was usually hand applied by amateurs who filled in the colors according to a guide. Thomas Bewick is credited with being one of the earliest artists to illustrate books for children. His skillfully executed woodcuts graced *The New Lottery Book of Birds and Beasts*, published in 1771, and *A Pretty Book of Pictures for Little Masters and Misses; or Tommy Trip's History of Beasts and Birds*, published in 1779.

Three 19th-century English artists had enormous impact on illustrations for children's books. According to Ruth Hill Viguers in the introduction to Edward Ernest's (1967) *The Kate Greenaway Treasury*, the work of these artists "represents the best to be found in picture books for children in any era: the strength of design and richness of color and detail of Walter Crane's pictures; the eloquence, humor, vitality, and movement of Randolph Caldecott's art; and the tenderness, dignity, and grace of the very personal interpretation of Kate Greenaway's enchanted land of childhood" (p. 13).

Walter Crane's *The House That Jack Built*, published in 1865, was the first of his series of toy books, the name used for picture books published for young children. These books, engraved by Edmund Evans, are credited with marking the beginning of the modern era in color illustrations. From 1865 through 1898, Crane illustrated more than 40 books, including folktales, such as *The Three Bears* and *Cinderella*, and alphabet books, such as *The Farmyard Alphabet* and *The Absurd ABC*.

Many of Crane's illustrations reflect his appreciation of Japanese color prints. Crane (1984) specified this appreciation in lectures that he gave before the Society of Arts in 1889, when he stated that Japanese art was "a living art, an art of the people, in which traditions and craftsmanship were unbroken, and the results full of attractive variety, quickness, and naturalistic force" (p. 133).

Randolph Caldecott's talent was discovered by Edmund Evans, the printer. Caldecott's illustrations for *The Diverting History of John Gilpin*, printed by Evans in 1878, demonstrated his ability to depict robust characters, action, and humor. (The Caldecott Medal for children's book illustration, named for the artist, is embossed with the picture of Gilpin galloping through an English village.) Caldecott's lively and humorous figures jump fences, dance to the fiddler, and flirt with milkmaids in such picture books as *The Fox Jumps Over the Parson's Gate, Come Lasses and Lads,* and *The Milkmaid.*

Caldecott's picture books are now reissued by Frederick Warne. Brian Alderson's (1986) *Sing a Song of Sixpence* provides a pictorial history of English picture books and Randolph Caldecott's art.

Printer and engraver Edmund Evans also encouraged and supported the work of Kate Greenaway. Delighted by Greenaway's drawings and verses, Evans printed

Walter Crane's illustrated texts, characterized by subdued colors, strong design, and rich detail, are credited with marking the beginning of the modern era in color illustrations. (From The Baby's Own Aesop. *Repreduced by permission of the Department of Special Collections, Research Library, University of California, Los Angeles.)*

Randolph Caldecott's illustrations suggest action and vitality. (From The Hey Diddle Diddle Picture Book, *by Randolph Caldecott. Reprodced by permission of Frederick Warne & Co., Inc., Publishers.)*

able to get so much joy out of things that are always there to give it, and do not change? What a great pity my hands are not clever enough to do what my mind and eyes see, but there it is! (Ernest, 1967, p. 19)

Other picture books illustrated by Greenaway include *Kate Greenaway's Birthday Book* (1880), *Mother Goose* (1881), *The Language of Flowers* (1884), and Robert Browning's *Pied Piper of Hamelin* (1880). Greenaway's name, like Caldecott's, has been given to an award honoring distinguished artistic accomplishment in the field of children's books: The Kate Greenaway Medal is given annually to the most distinguished British illustrator of children's books.

By the late 1800s, when Crane, Caldecott, and Greenaway began drawing for children, European and North American attitudes toward children were also changing. According to Frederick Laws (1980), these three artists

her first book, *Under the Window*, in 1878. It was so successful that 70,000 English editions and more than 30,000 French and German editions were sold.

Greenaway continued illustrating books that reflected happy days of childhood and the blossoming apple trees and primroses that dotted the English countryside of her youth. In a letter to her friend John Ruskin, Greenaway described her view of the world:

I go on liking things more and more, seeing them more and more beautiful. Don't you think it is a great possession to be

were under no public compulsion to be morally edifying or factually informative. Children were no longer supposed to be "young persons" whose taste would be much the same whether they were five or fifteen. So long as they pleased children, artists were free; indeed, Crane wrote that "in a sober and matter-of-fact age Toybooks afford perhaps the only outlet for unrestricted flights of fancy open to the modern illustrator who likes to revolt against the despotism of facts." (p. 318)

This brief discussion of illustrators does not mention all of the artists who made contributions in the 19th century, but it does outline the early history of children's book illustration. Chart 2.2 summarizes some milestones in the illustration of children's books from the 15th century into the early 20th century.

CHART 2.2 Milestones in the history of children's illustration

1484	William Caxton, *Aesop's Fables*, contained woodcuts.	1878	Randolph Caldecott, *The Diverting History of John Gilpin*, the first of sixteen picture books.
1658	Johann Amos Comenius, *Orbis Pictus* (Painted World), considered by many to be the first picture book for children.	1878	Kate Greenaway, *Under the Window*.
		1883	Howard Pyle, *The Merry Adventures of Robin Hood*.
1771	Thomas Bewick, *The New Lottery Book of Birds and Beasts*.	1900	Arthur Rackham, illustrations for Grimms' *Fairy Tales*.
1784	Thomas and John Bewick, *The Select Fables of Aesop and Others*.	1901	Beatrix Potter, *The Tale of Peter Rabbit*.
1789	William Blake, *Songs of Innocence*.	1924	E. H. Shepard, illustrations for A. A Milne's *When We Were Very Young*.
1823	George Cruikshank, translation of Grimms' *Fairy Tales*.	1933	Kurt Wiese, illustrations for Marjorie Flack's *The Story of Ping*.
1853	George Cruikshank, *Fairy Library*.	1933	E. H. Shepard, illustrations for Kenneth Grahame's *The Wind in the Willows*.
1865	John Tenniel, illustrations for Lewis Carroll's *Alice's Adventures in Wonderland*.	1937	Dr. Seuss, *And to Think That I Saw It on Mulberry Street*.
1865	Walter Crane, *The House That Jack Built*, the first of the toy books engraved by Evans.		

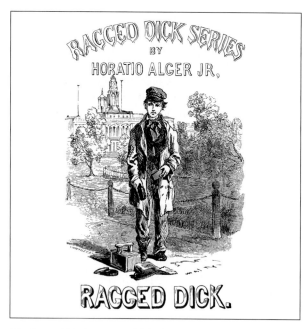

The Ragged Dick series, published in 1868, told of the sad plight of children who tried to survive in a city without family or friends.

without family or friends. They often worked long hours in factories or on farms; many died. Horatio Alger, Jr., wrote the series in the hope that readers would be sympathetic to the cause of poor children and the Children's Aid Society. Since 1854, the society has been finding homes for abandoned children.

Horatio Alger, Jr.'s *Frank's Campaign* (1864) was the first of a series of books in which poor American youths went from rags to riches. Other books by Alger that have a similar theme include *Fame and Fortune* (1868), *Sink or Swim* (1870), *Strong and Steady* (1871), *Brave and Bold* (1874), *Risen From the Ranks* (1874), and *From Farm Boy to Senator: Being the History of the Boyhood and Manhood of Daniel Webster* (1882).

Reissues of lesser known books and stories published during the Victorian period provide opportunities for further study. For example, *What I Cannot Tell My Mother Is Not Fit for Me to Know* is a collection of stories, poems, and songs selected by Gwladys and Brian Rees-Williams (1981) from texts published in the 19th century. Andrew Tuer's *Stories From Forgotten Children's Books* (1986) is a facsimile edition of a book published in 1898.

Fantasy, Adventure, and Real People

As the world was changing, so were views of childhood. Emphases in children's literature mirrored the new attitudes and world developments. Childhood was becoming, at least for middle- and upper-class children, a more carefree and enjoyable period of life, and this change was reflected in the increase in fantasy stories for children. As adventurers explored unknown areas of the world, their experiences inspired new adventure stories. Also, the characters of specific families and localities were captured in the growing popularity of literature about ordinary people, places, and events in sometimes extraordinary circumstances.

Fantasy. By the mid-1800s, the puritanical resistance to fantasy in children's literature was on its way toward extinction in most segments of European and North American society. Children had been reading and enjoying the folktales of Perrault and the Brothers Grimm, and Andersen's stories had been translated into English. More and more educators and parents believed that literature should entertain children rather than merely instruct them.

According to Raymond Chapman (1968), fantasy created a world where fears could be projected onto impossible creatures of the imagination while a child remained safe. Brian W. Alderson (1959) describes the creation of one of the landmarks in fantasy and nonsense:

> One summer's day on the river at Oxford [England] a thirty-year-old lecturer in mathematics at Christ Church was taking the three daughters of his Dean, Edith, Lorina, and Alice, out for a row. His name was Charles Lutwidge Dodgson. The day was hot and the children wanted to have a story told them, a thing they had come to expect from Mr. Dodgson. So the young lecturer complied, his mind relaxing in the drowsy heat and his thoughts, which did not tire so easily, following paths of their own making. (p. 64)

The paths led directly down the rabbit hole and into adventures in Wonderland with the Cheshire Cat, the Queen of Hearts, and the Mad Hatter. The story told that afternoon in 1862 made such an impression on Alice that she pestered Dodgson to write it down. He wrote it for her, gave it to her as a gift, and, after it had been thoroughly enjoyed by many people, published it for others under the pseudonym Lewis Carroll.

According to Cornelia Meigs et al. (1969), the revolutionary nature of Lewis Carroll's *Alice's Adventures in Wonderland* and *Through the Looking Glass*, when compared with earlier books written for children, is due to "the fact that they were written purely to give pleasure to children. . . . Here . . . for the first time we find a story designed for children without a trace of a lesson or moral" (p. 194).

Edward Lear, the other great writer of fantasy for children in the 19th century, created absurd and delightful characters in nonsense verses. Lear's *A Book of Nonsense* appeared in 1846, his *More Nonsense* in 1872. *Nonsense Songs, Botany and Alphabets*, published in 1871, contained Lear's "Nonsense Stories," "Nonsense Geography," "Natural History," and "Nonsense Alphabets." *Laughable Lyrics* (1877) included the nonsense verses "The Quangle-Wangle's Hat," "The Dong with the Luminous Nose," and "The Youghy-Bonghy-Bo."

Lear's work, like Carroll's, was popular with both young and adult readers. Today, both writers are often

The illustrations and text for Alice's Adventures in Wonderland *were designed to give pleasure, not to teach a lesson. (Illustrated by John Tenniel. From* Alice's Adventures in Wonderland, *by Lewis Carroll. Published by Macmillan and Co., 1865. Courtesy of Lilly Library, Indiana University, Bloomington, Indiana.)*

There was an Old Person of Pinner,
As thin as a lath, if not thinner;
They dressed him in white,
And roll'd him up tight,
That elastic Old Person of Pinner.

Edward Lear's illustrations heightened the humor of his limericks. (From A Book of Nonsense, *by Edward Lear. Published by Heinrich Hoffman, 1846. Courtesy of Lilly Library, Indiana University, Bloomington, Indiana.)*

quoted and are enjoyed as much as they were when their works were created.

Adventure.   The 19th century saw many real-life adventures: Explorers were seeking the North Pole, Florence Nightingale was poineering for female independence as a director of nursing in the Crimean War, and a railroad was being constructed across the United States. If a person could not go to a remote region and overcome the perils lurking there, the next best adventure was the vicarious one offered through books.

Robert Louis Stevenson was the master of the adventure stories written during this time. When *Treasure Island* was published, it was considered the greatest adventure story for children since *Robinson Crusoe.*

Stevenson was born in Edinburgh, Scotland, the son of a lighthouse engineer. When he was a young boy, his father told him bedtime tales filled with "blood and thunder," and his nurse told him stories of body snatchers, ghosts, and martyrs. As an adult, Stevenson traveled to many lands, but he still loved the lochs, islands, and misty forests of his home. His early experiences are evident in his two most famous adventure stories, *Treasure Island* and *Kidnapped.*

Treasure Island had an interesting beginning: While trying to entertain his stepson, Stevenson drew a watercolor map of an island, then followed his drawing with the now famous story of pirates, buried treasure, and a young boy's adventures. Both *Treasure Island* and *Kidnapped* have the ingredients of outstanding adventure literature: action, mystery, and pursuit and evasion in authentic historical settings. Stevenson believed that an adventure story should have a specific effect on its readers: It should absorb and delight them, fill their minds with a kaleidoscope of images, and satisfy their nameless longings. According to Bernard J. Lonsdale and Helen K. Macintosh (1973), Stevenson believed that Robinson Crusoe discovering a footprint on his lonely beach, Achilles shouting against the Trojans, and Ulysses bending over his great bow were culminating moments that have been printed in the mind's eye forever. In addition, according to Brian W. Alderson (1959), Stevenson believed that children and adults should demand such moments in their literature; Stevenson achieved that quality in tales of "treasure and treachery . . . the comings and goings of . . . pirates, the ominous hints of the fearful events which are to come" (p. 257).

While Robert Louis Stevenson wrote of pirates and buried treasure in the not-so-distant past, Howard Pyle took readers back to the Middle Ages to fight evil, overcome Prince John's injustice, and have a rollicking good time in the green depths of Sherwood Forest. Pyle's *The Merry Adventures of Robin Hood,* published in 1883, retold the old English ballad about Robin Hood, Little John, Friar Tuck, and the other merry men who robbed the rich

The historical novel became popular in the 1800s with the publication of stories by Sir Walter Scott and Charlotte Yonge.

to give to the poor and constantly thwarted the evil plans of the Sheriff of Nottingham. Here was swashbuckling entertainment that also provided children with a glimpse of an early period in European history.

The historical novel became popular in the 1800s with the publication of stories by Sir Walter Scott. Scott's story of medieval English life, *Ivanhoe: A Romance* (1820), was often used as a school assignment for older children. Other popular books by Scott included *The Lady of the Lake* (1810), *Waverly: Or, 'Tis Sixty Years Since* (1814), *Rob Roy* (1818), and *Tales of the Crusaders* (1825).

The Industrial Revolution, the invention of the steam engine, and the prevalent feeling of new possibilities always just around the corner laid the groundwork for a new kind of adventure story in the last half of the 19th century. Jules Verne's science fiction adventure stories can certainly be classified as another benchmark in children's literature. Verne envisioned submarines, guided missiles, and dirigibles long before such things were possible. His first science fiction book, *Five Weeks in a Balloon,* was published in France in 1863. His two most famous books, *Twenty Thousand Leagues Under the Sea,* published in 1869, and *Around the World in Eighty Days,* published in 1872, have also been immortalized on film. Consequently, the heroes of these books, Captain Nemo and Phileas Fogg, are well known to both readers and movie fans.

Verne admired the work of an earlier author, Daniel Defoe, and Verne's *The Mysterious Island,* published in 1875, was written because of Verne's interest in *Robinson Crusoe.* Verne's genius can be seen in the popularity of his works even today, after his glorious inventions have be-

come reality. Verne's detailed descriptions are so believable they seem as modern now as they did when they were published in the 1800s. The popularity of Verne's literature also caused other authors to write science fiction and to expand the new genre.

Real People.   During the late 19th and early 20th centuries, the local-color story came into its own. Realistic situations and people are the settings and subjects of such stories, in which place, plot, and characters are tightly integrated. According to James H. Fraser (1978), "This integration, which reveals the complex involvement of human, cultural, and geographical influences, produces a rich literature—peculiarly rich for the student of American culture, and extraordinarily rich for the young persons fortunate enough to read it" (p. 55). The diversity of American geography and people are found in books such as Edward Eggleston's *The Hoosier School Boy* (rural Indiana), Thomas Bailey Aldrich's *The Story of a Bad Boy* (a New England seafaring town), Kate Douglas Wiggins's *Rebecca of Sunnybrook Farm* (rural Maine), Mark Twain's *The Adventures of Huckleberry Finn* (Mississippi River towns), and Frances Courtenay Baylor's *Juan and Juanita* (the American Southwest). Fraser maintains that these local-color stories also transmit a conservative, traditional view of American life to the next generation. Their characters are "carryovers from an earlier age, an agrarian, preindustrial age, which the stories sentimentalize for their modern readers" (p. 59).

The greatest American writer of realistic adventure in this period was Mark Twain (Samuel Clemens). While Robert Louis Stevenson was writing about adventures on far-off islands, Twain was immortalizing life on the Mississippi River before the Civil War. Twain captured the human, cultural, and geographical influences that affected a boy's life in this era of American history. Twain grew up in the river town of Hannibal, Missouri, where he lived many of the adventures he later wrote about: He explored the river, raided melon patches, and used a cave as a rendezvous to plan further adventures and mischief with his friends. These adventures made Tom Sawyer and Huckleberry Finn come alive for many adventure-loving children. Twain's heroes did not leave the continent, but they did have exciting adventures on a nearby island, return in time to hear plans for their own funerals, and then attend those momentous occasions. Characters such as Injun Joe, Aunt Polly, Tom Sawyer, Becky Thatcher, and Huckleberry Finn still provide reading pleasure for children and adults. Donald A. Barclay (1992) concludes that Mark Twain's *The Adventures of Huckleberry Finn* is also one of the most frequently illustrated novels in history. Barclay estimates that there are approximately 800 editions of the novel, most of which are illustrated.

Many American books in the Victorian era took the family as their subject, and series stories dealing with the

Through the Eyes of an AUTHOR/ILLUSTRATOR

Steven Kellogg

Visit the CD-ROM that accompanies this text to generate a complete list of Steven Kellogg titles.

Selected Titles by Steven Kellogg:
Yankee Doodle
Jack and the Beanstalk
Paul Bunyan
The Mystery of the Missing Red Mitten
Ralph's Secret Weapon

I think one of the functions of literature is to keep legends, tales, myths, and old ballads alive and re-create them in new forms for succeeding generations. I think one of the roles of the author, the storyteller, or the artist is to keep our heritage alive and pass it on, and encourage the people to whom you pass it on to do the same thing for the generation that comes after them. Our American tall tale literature really is our mythology, our folklore. Actually it was an editor who mentioned to me quite a number of years ago that it had been somewhat overlooked in the picture-book form, and he was anxious that I undertake a picture book retelling the adventures of Paul Bunyan. That was the beginning of the tall tale series that I've been working on, on and off ever since, for more than twenty-five years now.

These tales were oral to begin with. Then they were printed in some anthologies earlier on, but they tended to be underillustrated, illustrated with small black-and-white line drawings. One of the exciting things that has been happening to picture books in the last 30 years is that there have been great advances in full-color printing, so there have been a lot of opportunities open to artists that were not there before. Full-color printing is a lot less expensive now, and it became possible to obtain really high-quality results without the enormous financial investment that had been commanded earlier. So there was a real renaissance in picture books in terms of the quality of their illustrations, and a lot more artists were drawn to express themselves in that format.

Also, there's been a growing awareness of the importance of literature to children and that they are shaped by the stories they're exposed to. So there was a real desire to make available to them the highest quality writing and artwork so their aesthetic judgment would respond to that and they would enjoy literature and the arts on that level, we hope, for the rest of their lives.

When I write, I think a lot about the audience, which is, of course, primarily the kids, and I really want them to have as many positive experiences as possible during these years of crucial development. This is really important, especially because they are still learning the nuts and bolts of reading and mastering all the nuances of language and the complexities of verbal communication. We want to present that in as appealing a way as possible. So I think I lean in the direction of making the books really welcoming, positive, enjoyable, and fun so that the kids will find them compelling and really be drawn to them.

The *Jack and the Beanstalk* that I did, though, like a lot of fairy tales, has a lot of very dark overtones to it. I tried to really honor that and not shy away from it—to capture the moments of Jack's distress when he is trapped in the ogre's house and feeling very vulnerable and very frightened. I tried to really capture that feeling because I know that's important. You want to deal with real feelings, not just the lighthearted, positive ones, by giving readers a chance to explore the darker corridors as well.

Yankee Doodle has so much vitality and so much energy that I tried to infuse the illustrations with the same kind of really exuberant activity, the explosive energy and frenetic cadence of the song and the whole upbeat quality of it. I tried to capture that in the illustrations and have that harmonize with the text.

My own illustrations come from a lot of background work, and thought, and sketching, and trial and error, by trying out different pictorial compositions and then altering them in a way that seems to make them more effective and harmonize more completely with the text, and also to give nuances and meaning to the text that are only hinted at or not even there. A picture book is really a duet between the two voices, the verbal and the visual. They both make a very important contribution, but don't necessarily rehash the same material. The pictures bring different meaning to the story. Sometimes it's the way the two combine that is really the essence of the picture book as a storytelling form.

Video Profiles: The accompanying video contains conversations from such authors and illustrators as Jack Gantos, Roland Smith, Molly Bang, and Floyd Cooper.

---

everyday lives of large families became popular. Margaret Sidney, for example, wrote a series of books about the five little Peppers. The first book, *The Five Little Peppers and How They Grew*, published in 1881, was followed by *The Five Little Peppers Midway* and *The Five Little Peppers Grown Up*.

Louisa May Alcott's account of family life in *Little Women*, published in 1868, is so real that readers feel they know each member of the March family intimately. In many ways, Alcott's life was quite different from the usual Victorian model, which accounts for the ways in which *Little Women* was ahead of its time. Alcott's father believed in educating his daughters. Consequently, Alcott was first educated at home by her father and then sent to the district school.

In 1867, a publisher asked Alcott to write a book for girls, and she decided to write about her own family. The resulting book, *Little Women*, was an overwhelming success. Readers enjoyed the intimate details of a warm, loving, and very human family. The most popular character, Jo, shares many characteristics with Alcott herself. Jo is courageous, tender, and honest, but she has a quick temper that often gets her into difficulty. She also leaves home to earn a living as a writer and to help support her family. *Little Women* was so popular that in 1869, Alcott wrote a sequel, *Little Women, Part II*. She also wrote other favorites, such as *An Old-Fashioned Girl*, *Little Men*, and *Eight Cousins*.

One very popular realistic story published in the 19th century had a setting foreign to most readers of its English

Through the Eyes of a CHILD

Sam
Grade 3

TITLE: Paul Bunyam
AUTHOR: Steven Kellogg

I like this book because I like the monsters. They were cool looking. The monsters captured Paul Bunyan's gang. I would recken-and this book to my friends.
Sam

Mark Twain wrote adventures about life in the Mississippi River environment in which he himself had grown up. (From The Adventures of Huckleberry Finn, by Mark Twain. Published by Charles L. Webster and Co., 1885. Courtesy of Lilly Library, Indiana University, Bloomington, Indiana.)

translation: Mountains that climb into the sky, sheepherders, tinkling bells, rushing streams, flower-strewn meadows, a hut with a bed of fresh hay, and the freedom to wander in delightful Swiss surroundings were found in Johanna Spyri's *Heidi*, published in Switzerland in 1880 and translated into English in 1884. Spyri based her book on her own childhood experiences in the Swiss Alps, which may help explain its realistic appeal.

Actual experience in a foreign land was not the only basis that an author had for providing a believable setting. Mary Mapes Dodge, for example, used research and imagination to provide credible background and characters in *Hans Brinker, or the Silver Skates, a Story of Life in Holland*. Readers in the Netherlands accepted this story as authentic in 1865, even though Dodge had never visited their country.

Space does not allow a complete discussion of all the books written for children or written for adults and read by children in earlier eras of our history. Chart 2.3 lists some previously discussed literature that brings the world of children's books into the 21st century. As you read this chart, however, remember that book publishing for children is a fairly recent activity. As Betsy Hearne (1988) points out, the first children's book department to be established in a publishing house in the United States was Macmillan's children's book department, established in 1918. Although children's books were published prior to this date, this is certainly a milestone in the publication of children's literature.

CHART 2.3 Notable authors of children's literature

1477	William Caxton, *Caxton's Book of Curtesye*
1484	William Caxton, *The Fables of Aesop*
1485	William Caxton, *Le Morte d'Arthur*
1678	John Bunyan, *Pilgrim's Progress*
1698	Charles Perrault or Pierre Perrault d'Arman-cour, *Tales of Mother Goose*
1719	Daniel Defoe, *Robinson Crusoe*
1726	Jonathan Swift, *Gulliver's Travels*
1744	John Newbery, *A Little Pretty Pocket Book*
1789	William Blake, *Songs of Innocence*
1812	First volume of Grimm Brothers' fairy tales, *Kinder-und Hausmärchen*
	Johann Wyss, *Swiss Family Robinson*
1820	Sir Walter Scott, *Ivanhoe: A Romance*
1823	Clement G. Moore, *A Visit From St. Nicholas*
1826	James Fenimore Cooper, *The Last of the Mohicans*
1843	Charles Dickens, *A Christmas Carol*
1846	Edward Lear, *A Book of Nonsense*
	Hans Christian Andersen's fairy tales in English translations
1851	John Ruskin, *King of the Golden River*
1856	Charlotte Yonge, *The Daisy Chain*
1862	Christina Georgina Rossetti, *Goblin Market*
1863	Charles Kingsley, *The Water Babies*
1865	Lewis Carroll, *Alice's Adventures in Wonderland*
	Mary Elizabeth Mapes Dodge, *Hans Brinker, or the Silver Skates, a Story of Life in Holland*
1868	Louisa May Alcott, *Little Women*
1870	Thomas Bailey Aldrich, *The Story of a Bad Boy*
1871	George MacDonald, *At the Back of the North Wind*
1872	Jules Verne, *Around the World in Eighty Days*
1873	*St. Nicholas: Scribner's Illustrated Magazine for Girls and Boys*, edited by Mary Mapes Dodge
1876	Mark Twain, *The Adventures of Tom Sawyer*
1877	Anna Sewell, *Black Beauty*
1881	Margaret Sidney, *The Five Little Peppers and How They Grew*
	Joel Chandler Harris, *Uncle Remus; His Songs and Sayings: The Folklore of the Old Plantation*
1883	Howard Pyle, *Merry Adventures of Robin Hood of Great Renown, in Nottinghamshire*
	Robert Louis Stevenson, *Treasure Island*
1884	Johanna Spyri, *Heidi: Her Years of Wandering and Learning*
1885	Robert Louis Stevenson, *A Child's Garden of Verses*
1886	Frances Hodgson Burnett, *Little Lord Fauntleroy*
1889	Andrew Lang. *The Blue Fairy Book*
1892	Carlo Collodi, *The Adventures of Pinocchio*
	Arthur Conan Doyle, *The Adventures of Sherlock Holmes*
1894	Rudyard Kipling, *The Jungle Book*
1901	Beatrix Potter, *The Tale of Peter Rabbit*

1903	L. Leslie Brooke, *Johnny Crow's Garden*
	Kate Douglas Wiggins, *Rebecca of Sunnybrook Farm*
	J. M. Barrie, *Peter Pan; or The Boy Who Would Not Grow Up*
1904	Howard Garis, *The Bobbsey Twins; or Merry Days Indoors and Out* (There are over seventy books in the series.)
1908	Kenneth Grahame, *The Wind in the Willows*
1911	Frances Hodgson Burnett, *The Secret Garden*
1913	Eleanor H. Porter, *Pollyanna*
1918	O. Henry, *The Ransom of Red Chief*
1921	Hendrik Willem Van Loon, *The Story of Mankind* (One of the first informational books attempting to make learning exciting; first Newbery Medal, 1922)
1922	Margery Williams Bianco, *The Velveteen Rabbit*
1924	A. A Milne, *When We Were Very Young*
1926	A. A. Milne, *Winnie-the-Pooh*
1928	Wanda Gág, *Millions of Cats*
	Carl Sandburg, *Abe Lincoln Grows Up*
1929	Rachel Field, *Hitty, Her First Hundred Years*
1932	Laura Ingalls Wilder, *Little House in the Big Woods*
	Laura E. Richards, *Tirra Lirra: Rhymes Old and New*
1933	Jean de Brunhoff, *The Story of Babar*
1937	Dr. Seuss, *And to Think That I Saw It on Mulberry Street*
	John Ronald Reuel Tolkien, *The Hobbit*
1939	James Daugherty, *Daniel Boone*
1940	Armstrong Sperry, *Call It Courage*
	Doris Gates, *Blue Willow*
1941	Lois Lenski, *Indian Captive, The Story of Mary Jemison*
	Robert McCloskey, *Make Way for Ducklings*
1942	Virginia Lee Burton, *The Little House*
1944	Robert Lawson, *Robbit Hill*
1946	Esther Forbes, *Johnny Tremain*
1947	Marcia Brown, *Stone Soup*
1950	Beverly Cleary, *Henry Huggins*
1951	Olivia Coolidge, *Legends of the North*
1952	Lynd Ward, *The Biggest Bear*
	E. B. White, *Charlotte's Web*
	David McCord, *Far and Few*
1953	Mary Norton, *The Borrowers*
1954	Rosemary Sutcliff, *The Eagle of the Ninth*
1955	L. M. Boston, *The Children of Green Knowe*
1957	Else Holmelund Minarik, *Little Bear*
1958	Jean Fritz, *The Cabin Faced West*
	Elizabeth George Speare, *The Witch of Blackbird Pond*
1959	Leo Lionni, *Little Blue and Little Yellow*
	Jean George, *My Side of the Mountain*

(continues)

CHART 2.3 Continued

1960	Michael Bond, *A Bear Called Paddington*
	Scott O'Dell, *Island of the Blue Dolphins*
1961	C. S. Lewis, *The Lion, the Witch and the Wardrobe*
1962	Ronald Syme, *African Traveler, The Story of Mary Kingsley*
	Madeleine L'Engle, *A Wrinkle in Time*
	Ezra Jack Keats, *The Snowy Day*
1964	Louise Fitzhugh, *Harriet the Spy*
	Irene Hunt, *Across Five Aprils*
	Lloyd Alexander, *The Book of Three*
1967	John Christopher, *The White Mountains*
	E. L. Konigsburg, *Jennifer, Hecate, MacBeth, William McKinley and Me, Elizabeth*
	Virginia Hamilton, *Zeely*
1969	John Steptoe, *Stevie*
	William H. Armstrong, *Sounder*
	Theodore Taylor, *The Cay*
	Vera and Bill Cleaver, *Where the Lilies Bloom*
	William Steig, *Sylvester and the Magic Pebble*
1970	Betsy Byars, *Summer of the Swans*
	Judy Blume, *Are You There God? It's Me, Margaret*
1971	Arnold Lobel, *Frog and Toad Are Friends*
	Muriel Feelings, *Moja Means One: Swahili Counting Book*
	Robert Kraus, *Leo, the Late Bloomer*
1972	Judith Viorst, *Alexander and the Terrible, Horrible, No Good, Very Bad Day*
1973	Doris Smith, *A Taste of Blackberries*
1974	Janet Hickman, *The Valley of the Shadow*
1975	Laurence Yep, *Dragonwings*
1976	Mildred Taylor, *Roll of Thunder, Hear My Cry*
1977	Jamake Highwater, *Anpao: An Indian Odyssey*
	Patricia Clapp, *I'm Deborah Sampson; A Soldier in the War of the Revolution*
	Katherine Paterson, *Bridge to Terabithia*
	Margaret Musgrove, *Ashanti to Zulu: African Traditions*
1978	Tornie dePaola, *The Clown of God*
1979	José Aruego and Ariane Dewey, *We Hide, You Seek*
1981	Nancy Willard, *A Visit to William Blake's Inn*
1982	Nina Bawden, *Kept in the Dark*
	Laurence Pringle, *Water: The Next Great Resource Battle*
	Cynthia Rylant, *When I Was Young in the Mountains*
1984	Paula Fox, *One-Eyed Cat*
1985	Rhoda Blumberg, *Commodore Perry in the Land of the Shogun*
1986	Jean Fritz, *Make Way for Sam Houston*
1987	Russell Freedman, *Lincoln: A Photobiography*
1988	Paul Fleischman, *Joyful Noise: Poems for Two Voices*
1989	Janet Taylor Lisle, *Afternoon of the Elves*
1990	Dr. Seuss, *Oh, the Places You'll Go!*
1991	Avi, *Nothing But the Truth: A Documentary Novel*
1993	Lois Lowry, *The Giver*
1997	E. L. Konigsburg receives her Second Newbery Medal for *The View From Saturday*
1999	Louis Sachar's *Holes* receives both the Newbery Medal and the National Book Award
2001	Richard Peck, *A Year Down Yonder*
2003	Kate DiCamillo, *The Tale of Despereaux*
2004	Jim Murphy, *An American Plague*
2005	J. K. Rowling, *Harry Potter and the Half-Blood Prince*

Standards for Evaluating Young Adult Literature

When evaluating literature written for young adults, the books should adhere to the same high-quality literary standards as presented in this chapter. Literature written for young adults, however, usually has more mature themes and characters who face complex issues that may be faced by contemporary young adults. Consequently, fictional literature selected for young adults needs to have believable plots and conflicts and characters who overcome problems in ways that are believable to the readers. Books should have the power to allow readers to place themselves in the role of the characters, to emphasize with the protagonists and antagonists, and to understand points of view that may be different from their own.

When evaluating nonfiction literature such as biographies and nonfiction literature, the books should, as recommended by Ann W. Moore (2005), motivate, inspire, and instruct. Biographies should bring characters to life so that young adults understand that individuals have survived even when they faced and overcame enormous challenges. Informational books should be both accurate and up-to-date. The books should allow readers to become engrossed in a topic and add to their growing knowledge associated with an academic discipline.

The charts in Chapter 1 identified characteristics of young adults, implications for literature selections, and recommendations for literature. These charts also suggest evaluative standards for young adult literature. For example, books selected for social development should encourage students to read about and discuss controversial points of view in historical materials and discuss books in which rules help society make important decisions. Implications for personality development also suggest evaluative criteria as young adults read and discuss books that deal with how characters overcome different types of conflict and show how characters cope with problems. Selecting and discussing literature that helps young adults understand that controlling their emotions is important. But, like characters in many books, it is a skill that improves over time. This is a valuable lesson to be learned.

The questions in the Evaluation Criteria feature on this page are helpful when selecting literature for young adults.

Evaluation Criteria

Literary Criticism: Young Adult Literature

1. Do the characters face issues and problems that are believable for and interesting to young adult readers?

2. Do the characters overcome these problems in ways that allow them to gain insights into different ways of handling problems?

3. Are the major characters many sided individuals who experience emotions and conflicts that are meaningful to the young adult readers? Do the characters have both strengths and weaknesses?

4. Does the setting and the issues in literature set in historical times allow readers to gain understandings about the changes in society and to realize that people during those times may reflect different historical points of view?

5. Does the author develop multi-leveled themes that allow young adults to think about and discuss the complexities of life reflected in those themes?

6. Does the literature encourage readers to use higher thought process such as making inferences, evaluating what they read, and authenticating the content?

7. Is the literature free from negative stereotypes? Does the literature show that both males and females have unique personalities and capabilities?

8. Does the literature motivate and inspire students?

9. If the literature is nonfiction, does it provide accurate and motivating information that expands the young adult readers' knowledge of the academic field?

The History of Censorship

According to *Webster's Dictionary: The New Lexicon of the English Language*, 1988 edition, a censor is "a person empowered to suppress publications or excise any matter in them thought to be immoral, seditious, or otherwise undesirable" (p. 158). What is considered immoral, seditious, or undesirable changes, however, with various time periods and with political and social attitudes.

According to Kirk Polking (1990), although "censorship has always existed to some degree, the criteria for proposing that books be banned seem to shift with social trends. In the late 1960s and early 1970s, racism, sexism, and other forms of discrimination were considered objectionable; in the 1980s, it was material alleged to be anti-American, anti-family, or obscene that was challenged. While educators traditionally have chosen books for use by school children for their literary value and for their handling of controversial topics in what they consider to be a tasteful manner, some conservative lobbying groups emerged in the early 1980s as opponents of certain works of literature" (p. 67). Peter Hunt (1997) identifies two limitations on the freedom to read that he considers to be serious invisible censorship that influences the availability of books in both Great Britain and the United States: "What is available for British children to read is severely circumscribed by a combination of two silent forces: government policies, which have in recent years severely cut school library budgets and school library services, and (as in the U.S.) the selection procedures of those powerful bookselling companies that dominate the market" (p. 96).

In his book *A History of Reading*, Alberto Manguel (1996) identifies some of the milestones in the history of censorship beginning in 411 B.C. and relates censorship with power. He states, "Censorship, therefore, in some form or another, is the corollary of all power, and the history of reading is lit by a seemingly endless line of censors' bonfires, from the earliest papyrus scrolls to the books of our time" (p. 283). Another source for milestones in the history of censorship is Gail Blasser Riley's (1998) *Censorship*. Riley includes legal issues in a chapter, "The Law of Censorship," and a section on "How to Research Censorship."

In Chart 2.4, the milestones in the history of censorship include some of the landmarks identified by Manguel in his chapter, "Forbidden Reading" and listings in Anne Lyon Haight's *Banned Books: 387 B.C. to 1978 A.D.* (1978) and in William Noble's *Bookbanning in America: Who Bans Books?—and Why* (1990). Additional milestones in censorship that specifically influenced children's literature have also been added to the list. As you read the list of books in the chart, try to identify the social, religious, or political attitudes that might have been behind these actions.

CHART 2.4   Milestones in the history of censorship

411 B.C.	Works of Protagoras were burned in Athens.
387 B.C.	Plato suggested expurgating Homer's *The Odyssey* for immature readers.
213 B.C.	Chinese Emperor Shih Huang-ti tried to burn all the books in his realm because he disapproved of the traditional Chinese culture.
168 B.C.	Jewish library in Jerusalem was destroyed during the Maccabean uprising.
1st century	Augustus exiled poets and banned their works. Emperor Caligula ordered books by Homer and Virgil burned.
A.D. 303	Diocletian condemned and burned all Christian books.
1497	Works of Ovid and Dante were burned in Florence.
1559	The Sacred Congregation of the Roman Inquisition published the first *Index of Forbidden Books*—books considered dangerous to the faith and morals of Roman Catholics (abandoned in 1996).
1624	The Bible, translated by Martin Luther in 1534, was burned in Germany.
1660	Charles II of England decreed that the Council for Foreign Plantations instruct natives, servants, and slaves of the British colonies in the precepts of Christianity by teaching them to read. But British slave owners feared literate blacks might find dangerous revolutionary ideas in books.
1713	Daniel Defoe was prosecuted and imprisoned by the Whigs for writing treasonable anti-Jacobite pamphlets. In 1720, his *Robinson Crusoe* was placed on the *Index of Forbidden Books*.
1726	*Gulliver's Travels,* by Jonathan Swift, was denounced as wicked and obscene because of its satire on courts, political parties, and statesmen.
1760	South Carolina passed strict laws forbidding all blacks from being taught to read.
1762	Jean-Jacques Rousseau's *Emile* was condemned and burned by Parliament of Paris.
1872	Anthony Comstock founded in New York the Society for the Suppression of Vice. This was the first effective censorship board in the United States.
1884	Mark Twain's *Huckleberry Finn* was banned in Massachusetts. The sales of the book increased.
1925	John Scopes was found guilty of teaching evolution based on *The Origin of Species*.
1933	In Berlin, propaganda minister Paul Goebbels spoke during the burning of more than 20,000 books while a crowd of more than 100,000 cheered.
	Rudolf Frank was arrested in Germany for writing *No Hero for the Kaiser,* a juvenile literature book with an anti-war theme.
1942	In Athens, performances of classic Greek plays were banned by Nazi occupation authorities.
1955	In Connecticut, African Americans protested against a dramatized version of Harriet Beecher Stowe's *Uncle Tom's Cabin, or Life Among the Lowly.*
1957	New York City dropped works of Mark Twain from lists of approved books for junior and senior high schools because of racial language.
1980	Parents took Hawkins County Tennessee Public Schools to court because an elementary school series was believed to violate their fundamentalist religious beliefs.
1984	*The Adventures of Huckleberry Finn* was removed from the high school reading list in Waukegan, Illinois.
1989	A survey of schools showed that Mark Twain's *The Adventures of Huckleberry Finn* was one of the most read books in high schools.
1994–95	List compiled by People for the American Way of the 10 leading books that various groups tried to ban during the year and the reasons for the banning:
	Alvin Schwartz. *More Scary Stories to Tell in the Dark* (supernatural tales).
	Alvin Schwartz. *Scary Stories to Tell in the Dark* (supernatural tales).
	Maya Angelou. *I Know Why the Caged Bird Sings* (sexual content).
	Lois Lowry. *The Giver* (profanity, violence, depressing story).
	Eve Merriam. *Halloween ABC* (supernatural theme).
	Alvin Schwarts. *Scary Stories 3: More Tales to Chill Your Bones* (supernatural tales).
	Katherine Paterson. *Bridge to Terabithia* (sexual content, profanity, "satanic" material).
	Robert Cormier. *The Chocolate War* (profanity, violence, sexual content).
	John Steinbeck. *Of Mice and Men* (profanity, sexual content).
	Christopher and James Lincoln Collier. *My Brother Sam Is Dead* (profanity, violence, challenge to patriotism, challenge to parental authority).
2005	Although frequently censored, *The Adventures of Huckleberry Finn* ranks 7th on a list of the top 1,000 titles owned by libraries.

Children and the Family in Children's Literature

As has already been discussed, attitudes toward children's place in the family have changed considerably over time. Before the Middle Ages, children were not greatly valued, and infanticide was a regular practice. During the Middle Ages, poor children shared the poverty and hard work of their parents, and children from the upper class and nobility spent most of their childhood separated from their families, receiving instruction and training in the roles that they would assume as adults. Not until relatively recently has childhood become the time for the close family interaction that we are familiar with today.

Books written for children or adopted by children during the last few centuries have usually reflected views of childhood and the family typical of their time. Researchers are increasingly viewing children's literature as an important source of information about these changing attitudes.

Unsurprisingly, a prominent theme in children's literature has been the relationships of children within the family. Changing views about children and the family over time necessarily reflect other social attitudes as well. The following time periods reflect the publication dates of a few popular American children's books in eras otherwise not easily demarcated by precise years. All of these books are available today; the older books have been published in reproductions by Garland Publishing Company of New York and London.

The Child and the Family, 1856–1903

An emphatic sense of duty to God and parents, the rise of the public school and Sunday School movements, and the beginning of a belief that children are individuals in their own right are among the characteristics of the Victorian era identifiable in children's literature of the time. According to Karen I. Adams (1989), "In the latter half of the nineteenth century and early decades of the twentieth century, religion was most often represented by the moralizing of Louisa May Alcott in *Little Women*" (p. 5). Much Victorian children's literature stresses the development of conscience, the merit of striving for perfection, and the male and female roles exemplified by family members. Illuminating examples of the social attitudes of this period can be drawn from Charlotte Yonge's *The Daisy Chain* (1856), Louisa May Alcott's *Little Women* (1868), Thomas Bailey Aldrich's *The Story of a Bad Boy* (1870), Margaret Sidney's *The Five Little Peppers and How They Grew* (1880), and Kate Douglas Wiggins's *Rebecca of Sunnybrook Farm* (1903).

Although these books have their differences, all of them stress the importance of accepting responsibility, whether for one's family, the poor and unfortunate, or self-improvement. For example, the older children in *The Daisy Chain* assume the task of raising the younger children when their mother dies; their greatest concerns are instilling Christian goodness in their siblings and living up to their father's wishes. Likewise, the children in *Little Women* and *The Five Little Peppers and How They Grew* feel responsible for their siblings and their mothers. Rebecca, in *Rebecca of Sunnybrook Farm*, feels this responsibility to such an extent that she completes 4 years of work at the academy in 3 years so that she can earn a living and help educate her siblings.

The characters in these books respect adult authority. Children strive to live up to their parents' ideals or want the acceptance and respect of their parents. The protagonist in *The Story of a Bad Boy* may not always ask or follow his grandfather's advice, but he admits that he deserves the terrible things that usually happen to him when he disobeys.

Respect for authority is underscored by the characteristic religious emphasis in these books. In *The Daisy Chain*, family members read the Bible together, discuss the meaning of the minister's sermons, debate the relative importance of the temptations in their lives, and organize a church and school for the poor. In *Little Women*, the family members receive strength from prayer and Bible reading. In *The Story of a Bad Boy*, Sundays are solemn days in which the family attends church, reads the scriptures, and eats food prepared the day before. The five little Peppers voice admiration for the clergy and want to become "good." Rebecca of Sunnybrook Farm's aunt, like her father before her, is an influential member of her church.

Family life in these books reiterates the definite social roles assigned to males and females in the Victorian era: Females usually run the household and make decisions related to everyday life, but the husband and father is usually the undisputed head of the family. The author may even state this fact point-blank, so there is no misunderstanding on the part of readers—as Louisa May Alcott does in *Little Women*:

> To outsiders, the five energetic women seemed to rule the house, and so they did in many things; but the quiet scholar, sitting among his books, was still the head of the family, the household conscience, anchor, and comforter: to him the busy, anxious women always turned in troublous times, finding him, in the truest sense of those sacred words, husband and father. (p. 294)

Males and females attend separate schools in *The Story of a Bad Boy*, and only male characters attend the university in *The Daisy Chain* and *Little Women*. Education may also stress different objectives for males and females. Yonge's heroine in *The Daisy Chain* completes her brother's school assignments but is not expected to understand mathematical concepts. Aldrich's hero wants training in manly arts, such as boxing, riding, and rowing. In contrast, drawing, writing, and music are desired accomplishments for the females in *Little Women*, piano

May Alcott's illustrations for her sister Louisa May Alcott's Little Women *reinforce the vision of a warm, loving Victorian family. (Illustration by May Alcott. From* Little Women or, Meg, Jo, Beth and Amy, *by Louisa M. Alcott. Published by Roberts Brothers, 1868. Courtesy of Lilly Library, Indiana University, Bloomington, Indiana.)*

lessons are sought by the oldest female Pepper, and writing is Rebecca's desire.

Insights about the children and families in these books are gained by viewing the problems that the heroes and heroines experience. Many of these problems involve attempts to abide by the period's standards of moral rectitude. Yonge's heroine, for example, strives to raise her family and help the poor. She works to keep the youngest baby an "unstained jewel" until the baby returns to her mother. She and her brother also face the problems associated with providing spiritual guidance to the poor. Many of Jo's problems in *Little Women* are related to controlling her "unfeminine" high energy and self-assertiveness. Jo looks to her pious mother for guidance in how to be "good":

> Jo's only answer was to hold her mother close, and, in the silence which followed, the sincerest prayer she had ever prayed left her heart without words; for in that sad, yet happy hour, she had learned not only the bitterness of remorse and despair, but the sweetness of self-denial and self-control; and, led by her mother's hand, she had drawn nearer to the Friend who welcomes every child with a love stronger than that of any father, tenderer than that of any mother. (p. 103)

Rebecca of Sunnybrook Farm also confronts problems caused by the conflicts between her own high-spirited nature and adults' strict expectations about a young girl's behavior: She, too, experiences personal misgivings when her actions do not live up to her desire to be good. The advantages of these conflicts, however, are stated by Rebecca's English teacher at the academy: "Luckily she attends to her own development. . . . In a sense she is independent of everything and everybody; she follows her saint without being conscious of it."

The problems that Thomas Bailey Aldrich creates for his protagonist allow the "bad" boy to consider and strengthen his own moral code. Although he has several unhappy and even disastrous experiences, the boy does not dwell on them, believing that they have caused him to become more manly and self-reliant.

Overcoming problems related to poverty and growing up without a father are major concerns of the Pepper children, but Margaret Sidney has their mother encourage them in this way: "You keep on a-tryin', and the Lord'll send some way; don't you go to botherin' your head about it now . . . it'll come when it's time." The family's financial problems are finally solved when a wealthy old gentleman invites them to share his home.

The Child and the Family, 1938–1960

The 1900s brought much change to the lives of American children: Many states passed child labor laws, John Dewey's influential theories encouraged a more child-centered educational philosophy, the quality and extent of public education improved, and religious training placed less emphasis on sinfulness and more emphasis on moral development and responsibility toward others. Children's literature reflected these changes, and children's book publishing expanded to meet the needs of an increasingly literate youthful population. Optimism was a keynote in the 20th-century "Age of Progress," and, especially after World War II, "children's book editors saw a bright future for the children of this country and the world" (McElderry, 1974, p. 89).

This optimism is reflected in the views of the children and families depicted in American children's books of the late 1930s through the beginning of the 1960s. John Rowe Townsend's (1975) conclusions about depictions of family life in children's literature of the 1950s apply to earlier literature as well: Children live in stable communities, where most children are happy and secure, the older generations are wise and respected, and the generations follow one another into traditional social roles in an orderly way.

The following books, written by award-winning authors, characterize the social values, the stability of family life, and the types of personal relationships depicted in children's literature of this period: Elizabeth Enright's *Thimble Summer* (1938), Eleanor Estes's *The Moffats* (1941), Sydney Taylor's *All-of-a-Kind Family* (1951), and

Madeleine L'Engle's *Meet the Austins* (1960). The families in these books live in different locations around the United States and range from lower-middle class to upper-middle class, but the values that they support are similar. The characters admire and emulate the traditional family model of breadwinning father, housewife mother, and their children, living together in one place for a number of years.

Family members have happy and secure relationships with one another, complemented by mutual respect, warmth, and humor. The actions of the Moffats express confidence and trust in the family unit. The children in *All-of-a-Kind Family* cannot imagine what it would be like not to have a family. In *Meet the Austins,* Vicky is pleased because her mother looks just the way that she believes a mother should look.

Religious values are suggested in these stories by Sunday School attendance, preparation for the sabbath, or prayers before meals. Dignity is stressed. The family in *Thimble Summer* brings an orphaned boy into its home on trust without checking his background. The parents in *All-of-a-Kind Family* tell their children to accept people and not to ask them about their personal lives. The Austin family feels empathy for others' problems, and the parents include their children in serious discussions.

Patriotism is strong in all of the books, and the law is respected. Education is considered important; children enjoy reading, go to school with the expectation that it will increase their understanding, and finish their homework before playing. Families prize even small collections of books. The work ethic is a powerful force in the lives of these families: Children talk about saving their money to buy a farm, a mother takes in sewing to keep the family together, and a father works long hours, saving for the day when he can make life better for his family. Children respect adult wisdom and authority; they obey rules, minding their teachers and complying with parental desires. Children also enjoy listening to their elders tell about their own experiences.

Unsurprisingly, given their secure lives and confident adherence to established social standards, the children in these books have few emotional problems. They usually feel good about themselves and other family members. Their actions suggest dependence on the family for emotional stability, but independence in their daily experiences, as they move without fear around the neighborhood, city, or countryside.

The Child and the Family, 1969–Present

Researchers who have analyzed children's literature over time have identified the 1960s, 1970s, and 1980s as decades in which traditional social, family, and personal values appeared to be changing. Alma Cross Homze (1963) found that in the late 1950s, adult characters in children's books were becoming less authoritarian and critical in their relationships with children, and children were becoming more outspoken, independent, and critical of adults. John Rowe Townsend (1975) later concluded that children's literature of the 1960s suggested an erosion of adult authority and a widening of the generation gap. When Beverly Young (1985) compared female protagonists of the 1930s, the 1950s, and the 1970s, she concluded that the characters had become increasingly protest oriented. Craig Werner and Frank Riga (1989) used religious questions developed by authors in the late 1900s to analyze changes in questions pertaining to religious matters in literature written in the 1800s. They found that 19th-century authors such as George MacDonald addressed questions such as "What must I do to enter the kingdom of God?" or "How should I pray?" In contrast, contemporary authors such as Cynthia Rylant and M. E. Kerr address questions such as "Is there a Kingdom of God?" or "Does it do any good to pray?" Werner and Riga conclude that the questions have shifted radically from the searchable to the searching because modern authors present partial answers, "not the full-blown declarations of faith that characterized earlier religious writings for children" (p. 2).

Binnie Tate Wilkin (1978) connects these trends in the children's literature of the 1960s and 1970s with changing "educational, social and political, and economic concerns" (p. 21), citing as examples the civil rights movements, protest marches, and assassinations of the period. Wilkin says:

> Almost all levels of society were challenged to respond to the activism. Book publishers responded with new materials reflecting dominant concerns. Distress about children's reading problems, federal responses to urban unrest, the youth movements, new openness about sexuality, religious protest, etc. were reflected in children's books. (p. 21)

In 1981, polls quoted by John F. Stacks (1981) showed that about 20% of Americans still expressed belief in most of the traditional values of hard work, family loyalty, and sacrifice, although the majority of respondents embraced only some of those values, doubted that self-denial and moral rectitude were their own rewards, and held tolerant views about abortion, premarital sex, remaining single, and not having children. Still, Stacks concluded that people who believed in traditional values were becoming an increasingly vocal group that "could set to a significant degree the moral tone for the 1980s" (p. 18).

Statistics cited by Nancy Lee Cecil and Patricia L. Roberts (1998) to support their view of the changing American family show the rapid decline of the former typical family of two parents—a father who works outside the home and a mother who is a homemaker. They cite Census Bureau reports that indicate that 26% of the U.S. population consists of married couples with at least one child living at home. Single-parent households now make up 29% of the households. Of these households, 90% have women as the head of the family.

ISSUE What Is the Future of Children's Book Publishing and Literacy?

In an article edited by Diane Roback and Shannon Maughan,[1] several publishers and editors speculate about the future of children's book publishing. Many of these speculations provide issues that can be analyzed, researched, and discussed in children's literature courses. For example, the following quotes and concerns provide interesting discussion topics:

Stephen Roxburgh, president and publisher, Front Street Books, provides two issues that are of interest. First, he maintains that we are currently dealing with an industry that has changed from privately held to publicly held businesses whose investors demand return on their money. He states, "The potential for profit and growth is enormous, hence, the headlong rush and ruthless tactics" (p. 152). Second, he believes that the old publishing model based on serving libraries has been replaced by the media industry model that sells entertainment to the masses. He states, "Those who publish books supported primarily by the institutions (hardcover fiction, nonfiction, poetry, 'high-end' picture books) will find themselves under siege to justify their existence" (p. 152).

Tracy Tang, vice president and publisher, Puffin Books, discusses the results of the market-driven type of publishing that may cause publishers to lose sight of more traditional, book-based publishing. She states, "I'm speaking optimistically when I say I hope that there will be a return to publishing books for the strength of their story and their illustrations" (p. 153). Tang's second issue focuses on the quality of the huge numbers of paperbacks for middle-grade and young adult series. She states, "A lot of people are trying to clone Goosebumps and the Baby-sitters Club. I think it's safe to say that most of these series aren't working as well as publishers hoped. I'm not sure that there will ever be fewer new series being published, but hopefully we'll see more high-quality, author-based series" (p. 153).

Jasan Higgins, vice president and director of marketing of children's books, William Morrow, discusses the impact on purchasing power for both public and school libraries. She emphasizes the controversy between book and technology purchases as the libraries try to stretch dollars to meet both demands.

David Ahlender, vice president and editorial director, Children's Book-of-the-Month Club, argues for the future of books and literacy. He believes that "it really does come down to a book and a child. Parents today cannot take literacy for granted the way they used to; they need to provide books in the home if they want their children to be literate. Our industry has a tremendous cultural relevance and a bright future. I hope that publishers will take that as a cause and a mission, because that's what really matters" (p. 153).

There are differences of opinion in these comments by publishers. Their comments, however, provide interesting topics for discussion and debate. You may consider questions such as the following: What is the impact on children's literature of each of these positions? How does the newer impact of a market-driven economy influence the types of books that will be published? How can the public ensure that there will be high-quality books for children? What will happen to children's literacy if there is a reduction in higher quality books? What do you believe will be the outcome of the debate between book purchases and technology?

The authors of *Media and Literacy*[2] speculate about the future of technology and literacy: "As new interlocking technologies shape our future, it is important to explore the possibilities and the problems. The power of today's information, communications, and networking media requires special attention. But it would be foolish to provide too warm a welcome without more serious thought. Will developing multimedia technology provide a transforming vision and a new awareness? Possibly. But developments have been moving so fast that few have taken the time to consider where we are going or where we might end up" (pp. 3–4).

[1]Roback, Diane, & Maughan, Shannon (Eds.). (1996, July 22). Fall 1996 children's books: The road ahead. *Publishers Weekly, 243*, 151–153.
[2]Adams, Dennis, & Hamm, Mary, (2000). *Media and literacy* (2nd ed.). Springfield, IL: Charles C. Thomas.

A William A. Galston article published in *The Family* (Mary E. Williams, 1998) discusses the changing influences of divorce on families. He states, "Since the 1960s, the number of children directly touched by divorce has jumped from 485,000 to one million a year. The percentage of children living in mother-only households has more than doubled, and about 40 percent of children have not seen their fathers during the past year" (p. 81).

Comparison of children's literature written between the 1930s and the early 1960s with children's literature written in the 1970s through the 1990s reveals both similarities and differences between the American families in the two periods. Many books still portray strong family ties and stress the importance of personal responsibility and human dignity, but the happy, stable unit of the earlier literature is often replaced by a family in turmoil as it adjusts to a new culture, faces the prospects of surviving without one or both parents, handles the disruption resulting from divorce, or deals with an extended family, exemplified by grandparents or a foster home. Later literature also suggests that many acceptable family units do not conform to the traditional American model.

Although many children's books could be selected for this discussion, the following books contain some of the diverse attitudes toward family and children in the period from 1969 to today: Vera and Bill Cleaver's *Where the Lilies Bloom* (1969), Norma Klein's *Mom, the Wolf Man, and Me* (1972), Paula Fox's *The Moonlight Man* (1986), Ruth White's *Belle Prater's Boy* (1996), Jack Gantos's *Joey Pigza Loses Control* (2000), and Meg Rosoff's *How I Live Now* (2004). Whereas children in the literature of the 1940s and 1950s had few personal and emotional problems, children between 1969 and today may have much responsibility and may experience emotional problems as they try to survive. The strongest character in *Where the Lilies Bloom* attempts to hold the family together, but she discovers that she needs people outside her immediate family. The heroine of *Mom, the Wolf Man, and Me* fears that her life will change if her mother marries. The main character in *The Moonlight Man* must accept her father and his behavior as well as her parents' divorce. The main characters in *Belle Prater's Boy* learn how to overcome the inner hurt caused by the suicide of a parent and the disappearance of another parent. The main characer in *Joey Pigza Loses Control* has a hyperactive disorder, divorced parents, and an alcoholic father.

Characters in the literature of this period may express concern about equal opportunities and question respect for the law, education, and adult authority. In *Mom, the Wolf Man, and Me,* the mother is a sucessful photographer who allows her daughter to accompany her on women's rights and peace marches.

The strongest story related to the dignity of human beings and acceptance of responsibility is Vera and Bill Cleaver's *Where the Lilies Bloom,* which is about the proud, independent mountain people who earn their livings through wildcrafting (the gathering of wild plants for human use). Before the father dies, he asks his daughter to keep the family together without accepting charity and to instill in the children pride in having the name Luther. Also *Belle Prater's Boy* is a strong story about the dignity of human beings as the children discover the truth in Grandpa's belief that what is in the heart is what counts.

An opposite condition is found in *The Moonlight Man.* The father is an alcoholic, and when his daughter says, "See you," as she leaves him, he whispers, "Not if I see you first" (p. 179). The father in *Joey Pigza Loses Control* is an alcoholic who needs help but refuses to accept assistance. They happy ending occurs when Joey returns home with his mother and realizes that he is not like his father. *How I Live Now* includes family traumas associated with living through a terrorist attack. Clearly, children's literature now presents a greater range and more realistic representations of family diversity.

Suggested Activities

For more suggested activities for understanding the history of children's literature, visit the Companion Website at www.prenhall.com/norton

- Investigate the life and contributions of William Caxton. What circumstances led to his opening a printing business in 1476? Why were *Reynart the Foxe, The Book of the Subtyle Historyes and Fables of Esope,* and *Le Morte d'Arthur* considered such important contributions to children's literature?

- Choose a tale published by Charles Perrault in his *Tales of Mother Goose,* such as "Cinderella," "Sleeping Beauty," "Puss in Boots," "Little Red Riding Hood," "Blue Beard," or "Little Thumb." Compare the language and style of Perrault's early edition with the language and style in a 21st-century version of the same tale. What differences did you find? Why do you believe the changes were made?

- Choose one of the following great 19th-century English artists who had an impact on children's illustrations: Kate Greenaway, Walter Crane, or Randolph Caldecott. Read biographical information and look at examples of their illustrations. Share your information and reactions with your literature class.

- Read Mark Twain's *The Adventures of Tom Sawyer* or *The Adventures of Huckleberry Finn.* Consider the controversy about racism in Twain's work. Compare Mark Twain's writing for the 19th century with writing for the 21st century.

3 Evaluating and Selecting Literature for Children

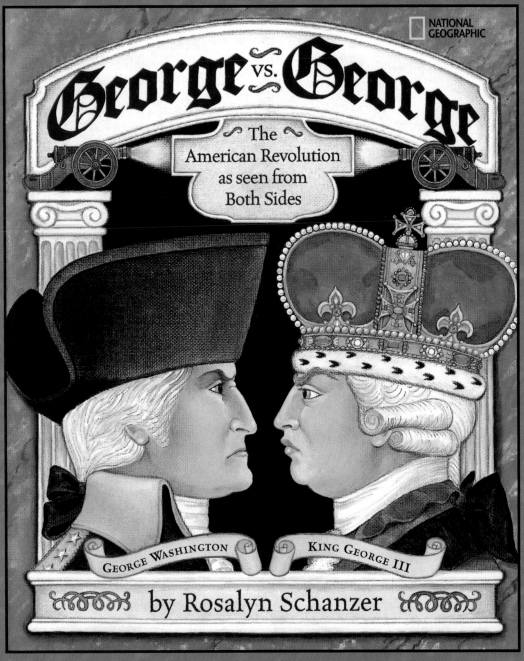

Cover from George vs. George: The American Revolution as Seen from Both Sides by Rosalyn Schanzer. Jacket illustration copyright © 2004 Rosalyn Schanzer, jacket copyright © 2004 National Geographic Society. Reprinted by permission.

CHAPTER OUTLINE

Standards, Literary Elements, and Book Selection

- Standards for Evaluating Books and Literary Criticism
- Standards for Evaluating Multicultural Literature
- Literary Elements
- The Right Book for Each Child
- The Child as Critic

Teaching With Literary Elements

- Involving Children in Plot
- Involving Children in Characterization
- Involving Children in Setting
- Involving Children in Theme
- Involving Children in Style
- Webbing the Literary Elements

Standards, Literary Elements, and Book Selection

Because thousands of books have been published for children, selecting books appropriate to the needs of children can be difficult. Teachers and librarians, who share books with groups of children as well as with individual children, should select books that provide balance in a school or public library. The objectives of literature programs also affect educators' selections of children's books.

A literature program should have five objectives. First, a literature program should help students realize that literature is for entertainment and can be enjoyed throughout their lives. Literature should cater to children's interests as well as create interest in new topics. Consequently, educators must know these interests and understand ways to stimulate new ones.

Second, a literature program should acquaint children with their literary heritage. To accomplish this, literature should foster the preservation of knowledge and allow its transmission to future generations. Therefore, educators must be familiar with fine literature from the past and must share it with children.

Third, a literature program should help students understand the formal elements of literature and lead them to prefer the best that our literature has to offer. Children need to hear and read fine literature and to appreciate authors who not only have something to say but also say it extremely well. Educators must be able to identify the best books in literature and share these books with children.

Fourth, a literature program should help children grow up understanding themselves and the rest of humanity. Children who identify with literary characters confronting and overcoming problems like their own learn ways to cope with their own problems. Educators should provide literature that introduces children to people from other times and nations and that encourages children to see both themselves and their world in a new perspective.

Fifth, a literature program should help children evaluate what they read. Literature programs should extend children's appreciation of literature and their imaginations. Therefore, educators should help students learn how to compare, question, and evaluate the books they read.

Rosenblatt (1991) adds an important sixth objective, encouraging "readers to pay attention to their own literary experiences as the basis for self-understanding or for comparison with others' evocations. This implies a new, collaborative relationship between teacher and student. Emphasis on the reader need not exclude application of various approaches, literary and social, to the process of critical interpretation and evaluation" (p. 61). Children need many opportunities to respond to literature.

Susan Wise Bauer (2003) presents a powerful objective for a literature study that encourages readers to understand, evaluate, and express opinions about what is read. This final objective of a literature program, as recommended by Bauer, is to train readers' minds by teaching them how to learn. To accomplish this objective, she recommends a study of literature that progresses from first reading a book to get a general sense of the story and the characters; to rereading the book to analyze the story, discover the author's techniques, and analyze any arguments the author developed; and, finally, to deciding such questions as Did I sympathize with the characters? Why or why not? Did I agree or disagree with the ideas in the book?

If children are to gain enjoyment, knowledge of their heritage, recognition and appreciation of good literature, and understanding of themselves and others, they must explore balanced selections of literature. A literature program thus should include classics and contemporary stories, fanciful stories as well as realistic ones, prose as well as poetry, biographies, and books containing factual information. To provide this balance, educators must know about many kinds of literature. Alan Purves (1991) identifies basic groups of items usually found in literature programs: literary works, background information, literary terminology and theory, and cultural information. He states that some curricula also include the responses of the readers themselves.

This chapter provides information about numerous types of books written for children, and looks at standards for evaluating books written for children. It presents and discusses the literary elements of plot, characterization, setting, theme, style, and point of view. It also discusses children's literature interests, characteristics of literature found in books chosen by children, and procedures to help children evaluate literature.

Standards for Evaluating Books and Literary Criticism

According to Jean Karl (1987), in true literature, "there are ideas that go beyond the plot of a novel or picture book story or the basic theme of a nonfiction book, but they are presented subtly and gently; good books do not preach; their ideas are wound into the substance of the book and are clearly a part of the life of the book itself" (p. 507). Karl maintains that in contrast, mediocre books overemphasize their messages or they oversimplify or distort life; mediocre books contain visions that are too obvious and can be put aside too easily. If literature is to help develop children's potential, merit rather than mediocrity must be part of children's experiences with literature. Both children and adults need opportunities to evaluate literature. They also need supporting context to help them make accurate judgments about quality.

Evaluation Criteria

Literary Criticism: Questions to Ask Myself When I Judge a Book

1. Is this a good story?
2. Is the story about something I think could really happen? Is the plot believable?
3. Did the main character overcome the problem, but not too easily?
4. Did the climax seem natural?
5. Did the characters seem real? Did I understand the characters' personalities and the reasons for their actions?
6. Did the characters in the story grow?
7. Did I find out about more than one side of the characters? Did the characters have both strengths and weaknesses?
8. Did the setting present what is actually known about that time or place?
9. Did the characters fit into the setting?
10. Did I feel that I was really in that time or place?
11. What did the author want to tell me in the story?
12. Was the theme worthwhile?
13. When I read the book aloud, did the characters sound like real people actually talking?
14. Did the rest of the language sound natural? (Norton, 1993)

Literary critic Anita Silvey (1993) provides both a useful list for the qualities of a reviewer and questions for the reviewer to consider. She first identifies the characteristics of fine reviewers and fine reviews; these include a sense of children and how they will respond to the book as well as an evaluation that, if the book is good, will make readers want to read the book. The review should evaluate the literary capabilities of the author and also be written in an enjoyable style. The reviewer needs a sense of the history of the genre and must be able to make comparisons with past books of the author or illustrator. This sense of genre also requires knowledge of contemporary adult literature, art, and film so that the reviewer is able to place the book in the wider context of adult literature and art. The review should also include a balance between a discussion of plot and critical commentary. A sense of audience requires that the reviewer understand what the audience knows about books. Finally, Silvey recommends that a reviewer have a sense of humor; especially when evaluating books that are themselves humorous.

Silvey's list of questions that the reviewer should consider is divided according to literary questions (How effective is the development of the various literary elements?), artistic questions (How effective are the illustrations and the illustrator's techniques?), pragmatic questions (How accurate and logical is the material?), philosophical questions (Will the book enrich a reader's life?), and personal questions (Does the book appeal to me?).

Northrop Frye, Sheridan Baker, and George Perkins (1985) identify five focuses of all literary criticism, two or more of which are usually emphasized in an evaluation of a literary text:

(1) The work in isolation, with primary focus on its form, as opposed to its content; (2) its relationship to its own time and place, including the writer; the social, economic, and intellectual milieu surrounding it; the method of its printing or other dissemination; and the assumptions of the audience that first received it; (3) its relationship to literary and social history before its time, as it repeats, extends, or departs from the traditions that preceded it; (4) its relationship to the future, as represented by those works and events that come after it, as it forms a part of the large body of literature, influencing the reading, writing, and thinking of later generations; (5) its relationship to some eternal concept of being, absolute standards of art, or immutable truths of existence. (p. 130)

The relative importance of each of the preceding areas to a particular critic depends on the critic's degree of concern with the work itself, the author, the subject matter, and the audience.

Book reviews and longer critical analyses of books in the major literature journals are valuable sources for librarians, teachers, parents, and other students of children's literature. As might be expected from the five focuses of Frye, Baker, and Perkins, reviews emphasize different aspects of evaluation and criticism. Phyllis K. Kennemer (1984) identified three categories of book reviews and longer book analyses: (1) descriptive, (2) analytical, and (3) sociological. Descriptive reviews report factual information about the story and illustrations of a book. Analytical reviews discuss, compare, and evaluate literary elements (plot, characterization, setting, theme, style, and point of view), the illustrations, and relationships with other books. Sociological reviews emphasize the social context of a book, concerning themselves with characterizations of particular social groups, distinguishable ethnic characteristics, moral values, possible controversy, and potential popularity.

Although a review may contain all three types of information, Kennemer concludes that the major sources of information on children's literature emphasize one type of evaluation. For example, reviews in the *Bulletin of the Center for Children's Books* tend to be descriptive, but they also mention literary elements. Reviews in *Booklist, The Horn Book, Kirkus Reviews,* and *The School Library Journal* chiefly analyze literary elements. *The School Library Journal* also places great emphasis on sociological analysis.

The "Annual Policy Statement" for *The School Library Journal* (Jones, 2005) states the selection and evaluation criteria for the journal: "SLJ's reviews are written by librarians working directly with children and young adults in schools or public libraries, library-school educators, teachers of children's literature, and subject specialists. They evaluate books in terms of literary quality, artistic merit, clarity of presentation, and appeal to the intended audience. They also make comparisons between new titles and materials already available in most collections and mention curriculum connections" (p. 84).

For example, the following analysis for Uri Schulevitz's *The Travels of Benjamin of Tudela: Through Three Continents in the Twelfth Century* was written by Margaret A. Chang (April 2005). As you read this analysis of a book that merited a starred review, notice the type of information the reviewer provides:

Grade 4–8—Benjamin, a Spanish Jew, left his native town of Tudela in 1159 to embark on a 14-year journey across the Middle East. His *Book of Travels,* written in Hebrew, recounts his grueling, often-dangerous journey through what is modern-day France, Italy, Greece, Cyprus, Israel, Syria, Iraq, Iran, and Egypt. Encounters with warring Crusaders and Muslims, rapacious pirates, and bandits added to his hardships. Shulevitz recreates this epic journey in a picture book of epic proportions, adapting Benjamin's account into a detailed, first-person narrative, accompanied by large, ambitious illustrations that evoke the landscapes, people, architecture, and history of the places that Benjamin saw. Darker, freer, and more impressionistic than Shulevitz's familiar work, the art is often indebted to medieval manuscript painting and Persian miniatures. Meticulously researched, with a long bibliography, lengthy author's note, and brief insets containing information that complements Benjamin's descriptions, this oversize picture book is obviously a labor of love. Wherever he went, Benjamin visited Jewish communities. Shulevitz's retelling stands as a testimony to the history, wisdom, and fortitude of those medieval Jews living precariously under Christian or Muslim rule. Both art and text will help readers imagine life during that time, and perhaps provide a context for the contemporary turmoil in the lands Benjamin visited so long ago (p. 142).

Selection criteria and reviews in specific journals also emphasize the particular content and viewpoints of the group that publishes the journal. For example, each year, the National Council for the Social Studies selects books for grades 4–8 that emphasize human relations and are sensitive to cultural experiences, present an original theme, are of high literary quality, and have a pleasing format and illustrations that enrich the text.

Reading and discussing excellent books as well as analyzing book reviews and literary criticism can increase one's ability to recognize and recommend excellent literature for children. Those of us who work with students of children's literature are rewarded when for the first time people see literature with a new awareness, discover the techniques that an author uses to create a believable plot or memorable characters, and discover that they can provide rationales for why a book is excellent, mediocre, or poor. Ideally, reading and discussing excellent literature can help each student of children's literature become a worthy critic. The Evaluation Criteria presented on

Technology Resources

You can use the CD-ROM that accompanies this text to print a list of Carnegie award winners: Simply search under Awards, type in "Crn" (award name abbreviations are listed under Field Information on the Help menu).

page 75 suggest the type of criteria that are useful for both teachers and librarians when selecting books and for students when they are criticizing the books they read.

In addition to books that are chosen for various literary awards such as the Newbery, the Carnegie, and the Hans Christian Andersen Award, students of children's literature can consider and discuss the merits of books identified by Karen Breen, Ellen Fader, Kathleen Odean, and Zena Sutherland (2000) on their list of the 100 books that they believe were the most significant for children and young adults in terms of shaping the 20th century. When citing their criteria for these books, they state: "We decided that our list should include books with literary and artistic merit, as well as books that are perennially popular with young readers, books that have blazed new trails, and books that have exerted a lasting influence on the world of children's book publishing" (p. 50).

CHART 3.1 Twenty-three significant children's books that shaped the 20th century

Author	Book Title
Natalle Babbitt	Tuck Everlasting
Ludwig Bemelmans	Madeline
Judy Blume	Are You There God? It's Me, Margaret
Margaret Wise Brown	Goodnight Moon
Robert Cormier	The Chocolate War
Louise Fitzhugh	Harriet the Spy
Anne Frank	Anne Frank: The Diary of a Young Girl
Russell Freedman	Lincoln: A Photobiography
Jean Craighead George	Julie of the Wolves
Ezra Jack Keats	The Snowy Day
E. L. Konigsburg	From the Mixed-Up Files of Mrs. Basil E. Frankweiler
Madeleine L'Engle	A Wrinkle in Time
C. S. Lewis	The Lion, the Witch and the Wardrobe
Arnold Lobel	Frog and Toad Are Friends
Patricia MacLachlan	Sarah, Plain and Tall
A. A. Milne	Winnie-the-Pooh
Scott O'Dell	Island of the Blue Dolphins
Katherine Paterson	Bridge to Terabithia
Beatrix Potter	The Tale of Peter Rabbit
Maurice Sendak	Where the Wild Things Are
Dr. Seuss	The Cat in the Hat
E. B. White	Charlotte's Web
Laura Ingalls Wilder	Little House in the Big Woods

Of the 100 books on the list, 23 were selected unanimously by all four of the experts on the first round of balloting: these 23 are listed in Chart 3.1. As you may notice when you read this list, the books range from picture storybooks for young children to novels for older readers. They also include all of the various genres of literature that are discussed in this textbook. The list provides an interesting discussion for literary elements: Why are these particular books included on such a distinguished list?

Alleen Pace Nilsen and Kenneth L. Donelson (2001) warn that adults add another element when evaluating literature: "We should caution, however, that books are selected as 'the best' on the basis of many different criteria, and one person's best is not necessarily yours or that of the young people with whom you work. We hope that you will read many books, so that you can recommend them not because you saw them on a list, but because you enjoyed them and believe they will appeal to a particular student" (p. 11).

Standards for Evaluating Multicultural Literature

Multicultural literature is literature about racial or ethnic minority groups that are culturally and socially different from the white Anglo-Saxon majority in the United States, whose largely middle-class values and customs are most represented in American literature. Violet Harris (1992) defines multicultural literature as "literature that focuses on people of color, on religious minorities, on regional cultures, on the disabled, and on the aged" (p. 9).

Values of Multicultural Literature

Many of the goals for multicultural education can be developed through multicultural literature. For example, Rena Lewis and Donald Doorlag (1987) state that multicultural education can restore cultural rights by emphasizing cultural equality and respect, enhancing the self-concepts of students, and teaching respect for various cultures while teaching basic skills. These goals for multicultural education are similar to the following goals of the UN Convention of the Rights of the Child and cited by Doni Kwolek Kobus (1992):

1. understanding and respect for each child's cultural group identities;

2. respect for and tolerance of cultural differences, including differences of gender, language, race, ethnicity, religion, region, and disabilities;

3. understanding of and respect for universal human rights and fundamental freedoms;

4. preparation of children for responsible life in a free society; and

5. knowledge of cross-cultural communication strategies, perspective taking, and conflict

management skills to ensure understanding, peace, tolerance, and friendship among all peoples and groups. (p. 224)

Through multicultural literature, children who are members of racial or ethnic minority groups realize that they have a cultural heritage of which they can be proud, and that their culture has made important contributions to the United States and to the world. Pride in their heritage helps children who are members of minority groups improve their self-concepts and develop cultural identity. Learning about other cultures allows children to understand that people who belong to racial or ethnic groups other than theirs are individuals with feelings, emotions, and needs similar to their own—individual human beings, not stereotypes. Through multicultural literature, children discover that although not all people share their personal beliefs and values, individuals can and must learn to live in harmony.

Multicultural literature teaches children of the majority culture to respect the values and contributions of minority groups in the United States and those of people in other parts of the world. In addition, children broaden their understanding of history, geography, and natural history when they read about cultural groups living in various regions of their country and the world. The wide range of multicultural themes also helps children develop an understanding of social change. Finally, reading about members of minority groups who have successfully solved their own problems and made notable achievements helps raise the aspirations of children who belong to a minority group.

Literary Criticism: Evaluating Multicultural Literature

To develop positive attitudes about and respect for individuals in all cultures, children need many opportunities to read and listen to literature that presents accurate and respectful images of everyone. Because fewer children's books in the United States are written from the perspective of racial or cultural minorities and because many stories perpetuate negative stereotypes, you should carefully evaluate books containing nonwhite characters. Outstanding multicultural literature meets the literary criteria applied to any fine book, but other criteria apply to the treatment of cultural and racial minorities. The following criteria related to literature that represents African Americans, Native Americans,* Latino Americans, and Asian Americans reflect the recommendations of the research studies and evaluations compiled by Donna Norton (2005):

Are African, Native, Latino, and Asian Americans portrayed as unique individuals, with their own thoughts,

emotions, and philosophies, instead of as representatives of particular racial or cultural groups?

Does a book transcend stereotypes in the appearance, behavior, and character traits of its nonwhite characters? Does the depiction of nonwhite characters and lifestyles imply any stigma? Does a book suggest that all members of an ethnic or racial group live in poverty? Are the characters from a variety of socioeconomic backgrounds, educational levels, and occupations? Does the author avoid depicting Asian Americans as workers in restaurants and laundries, Latinos as illegal alien unskilled laborers, Native Americans as bloodthirsty warriors, African Americans as menial service employees, and so forth? Does the author avoid the "model minority" and "bad minority" syndrome? Are nonwhite characters respected for themselves, or must they display outstanding abilities to gain approval from white characters?

Is the physical diversity within a particular racial or cultural minority group accurately portrayed in the text and the illustrations? Do nonwhite characters have stereotypically exaggerated facial features or physiques that make them all look alike?

Will children be able to recognize the characters in the text and the illustrations as African Americans, Latinos, Asian Americans, or Native Americans and not mistake them for white? Are people of color shown as gray—that is, as simply darker versions of Caucasian-featured people?

Is the culture of a racial or ethnic minority group accurately portrayed? Is it treated with respect, or is it depicted as inferior to the majority white culture? Does the author believe the culture worthy of preservation? Is the cultural diversity within African American, Asian American, Latino, and Native American life clearly demonstrated? Are the customs and values of those diverse groups accurately portrayed? Must nonwhite characters fit into a cultural image acceptable to white characters? Is a nonwhite culture shown in an overexotic or romanticized way instead of being placed within the context of everyday activities familiar to all people?

Are social issues and problems related to minority group status depicted frankly and accurately, without oversimplification? Must characters who are members of racial and cultural minority groups exercise all of the understanding and forgiveness?

Do nonwhite characters handle their problems individually, through their own efforts, or with the assistance of close family and friends, or are problems solved through the intervention of whites? Are nonwhite characters shown as the equals of white characters? Are some characters placed in submissive or inferior positions? Are white people always the benefactors?

Are nonwhite characters glamorized or glorified, especially in biography? (Both excessive praise and excessive deprecation of nonwhite characters result in unreal and unbalanced characterizations.) If the book is a biography, are

---

*This book primarily uses the term *Native Americans* to denote the people historically referred to as *American Indians*. The term *Indian* is sometimes used interchangeably with *Native American* and in some contexts is used to name certain tribes of Native Americans.

Evaluation Criteria

Literary Criticism: Multicultural Literature

1. Are the characters portrayed as individuals instead of as representatives of a group?

2. Does the book transcend stereotypes?

3. Does the book portray physical diversity?

4. Will children be able to recognize the characters in the text and illustrations?

5. Is the culture accurately portrayed?

6. Are social issues and problems depicted frankly, accurately, and without oversimplification?

7. Do nonwhite characters solve their problems without intervention by whites?

8. Are nonwhite characters shown as equals of white characters?

9. Does the author avoid glamorizing or glorifying nonwhite characters?

10. Is the setting authentic?

11. Are the factual and historical details accurate?

12. Does the author accurately describe contemporary settings?

13. Does the book rectify historical distortions or omissions?

14. Does dialect have a legitimate purpose, and does it ring true?

15. Does the author avoid offensive or degrading vocabulary?

16. Are the illustrations authentic and nonstereotypical?

17. Does the book reflect an awareness of the changed status of females?

both the personality and the accomplishments of the main character shown in accurate detail and not oversimplified?

Is the setting of a story authentic, whether past, present, or future? Will children be able to recognize the setting as urban, rural, or fantasy? If a story deals with factual information or historical events, are the details accurate? If the setting is contemporary, does the author accurately describe the situations of nonwhite people in the United States and elsewhere today? Does a book rectify historical distortions and omissions?

If dialect is used, does it have a legitimate purpose? Does it ring true and blend in naturally with the story in a nonstereotypical way, or is it simply used as an example of substandard English? If non-English words are used, are they spelled and used correctly? Is offensive or degrading

vocabulary used to describe the characters, their actions, their customs, or their lifestyles?

Are the illustrations authentic and nonstereotypical in every detail?

Does a book reflect an awareness of the changing status of females in all racial and cultural groups today? Does the author provide role models for girls other than subservient females?

Notice in the Evaluation Criteria for multicultural literature that in addition to specific concerns about evaluating cultural content, there is also an evaluation of the literary elements of plot, conflict, characterization, setting, theme, style, and point of view. Also notice that several of the In-Depth Analysis features in this text are about multicultural titles.

Literary Elements

To effectively evaluate literature, readers must look at the ways in which authors of children's books use plot, characterization, setting, theme, style, and point of view to create memorable stories.

Plot

Plot is important in stories, whether the stories reflect the oral storytelling style of Chaucer's *The Canterbury Tales* or the complex interactions in a mystery. When asked to tell about a favorite story, children usually recount the plot, or plan of action. Children want a book to have a good plot: enough action, excitement, suspense, and conflict to develop interest. A good plot also allows children to become involved in the action, feel the conflict developing, recognize the climax when it occurs, and respond to a satisfactory ending. Children's expectations and enjoyment of conflict vary according to their ages: Young children are satisfied with simple plots that deal with everyday happenings, but as children mature, they expect and enjoy more complex plots.

Following the plot of a story is like following a path winding through it; the action develops naturally. If the plot is well developed, a book will be difficult to put down unfinished; if the plot is not well developed, the book will not sustain interest or will be so prematurely predictable that the story ends long before it should. The author's development of action should help children enjoy the story.

Developing the Order of Events. Readers expect a story to have a good beginning, one that introduces the action and characters in an enticing way; a good middle section, one that develops the conflict; a recognizable climax; and an appropriate ending. If any element is missing, children consider a book unsatisfactory and a waste of time. Authors can choose from any of several approaches for presenting the events in a credible plot. In children's literature, events usually happen in chronological order. The author reveals the plot by presenting the first happening, followed by the second happening, and so forth, until the story is completed. Illustrations reinforce the chronological order in picture storybooks for younger children.

Very strong and obvious chronological order is found in cumulative folktales. Actions and characters are related to each other in sequential order, and each is mentioned again when new action or a new character is introduced. Children who enjoy the cumulative style of the nursery rhyme "The House That Jack Built" also enjoy a similar cumulative rhythm in Verna Aardema's *Bringing the Rain to Kapiti Plain: A Nandi Tale*. Cumulative, sequential action may also be developed in reverse, from last event to first, as in Verna Aardema's *Why Mosquitoes Buzz in People's Ears*.

Authors of biographies frequently use chronological life events to develop plot. Jean Fritz, for example, traces the life of a famous president and constitutional leader in *The Great Little Madison*. In *Lincoln: A Photobiography*, Russell Freedman begins with Lincoln's childhood and continues through his life as president. In *The Wright Brothers: How They Invented the Airplane*, Freedman follows the lives of the Wright brothers and emphasizes major changes in aeronautics, and in *Eleanor Roosevelt: A Life of Discovery*, Freedman follows the life of one of the great women in American history. Dates in these texts help readers follow the chronological order.

The events in a story also may follow the maturing process of the main character. In *The Borning Room*, Paul Fleischman begins with the birth of the heroine in a borning room on a farm in Ohio in 1851. The plot then develops according to major events that occurred in the borning room as the family uses the special room at times of births and deaths. The book concludes as the heroine, after years of a rewarding life, is herself waiting in the borning room for her probable death.

Books written for older readers sometimes use flashbacks in addition to chronological order. At the point when readers have many questions about a character's background or wonder why a character is acting in a certain way, the author may interrupt the order of the story to reveal information about a previous time or experience. For example, memories of a beloved aunt allow readers to understand the character and the conflict in Cynthia Rylant's *Missing May*. The memories of 12-year-old Summer allow readers to understand the grief following the aunt's death and to follow Summer and her uncle as they try to overcome the grief and begin a new life for themselves. Without the memories, readers would not understand May's character.

Developing Conflict. Excitement in a story occurs when the main characters experience a struggle or overcome conflict. Conflict is the usual source of plots in literature. According to Rebecca J. Lukens (1999), children's literature contains four kinds of conflict: (1) person against person, (2) person against society, (3) person against nature, and (4) person against self. Plots written for younger children usually develop only one kind of conflict, but many of the stories for older children use several conflicting situations.

Person Against Person. One person-against-person conflict that young children enjoy is the tale of that famous bunny, Peter Rabbit, by Beatrix Potter. In this story. Peter's disobedience and greed quickly bring him into conflict with the owner of the garden, Mr. McGregor, who has sworn to put Peter into a pie. Excitement and suspense develop as Peter and Mr. McGregor proceed through a series of life-and-death encounters: Mr. McGregor chases Peter with a rake, Peter becomes tangled in a gooseberry net, and Mr. McGregor tries to trap Peter inside a sieve. Knowledge of Peter's possible fate increases the suspense of these adventures. The excitement intensifies each time Peter narrowly misses being caught, and young readers' relief is great when Peter escapes for good. Children also sympathize with Peter when his disobedience results in a stomachache and a dose of chamomile tea.

Conflicts between animals and humans, or animals and animals, or humans and humans are common in children's literature, including many popular folktales. Both Little Red Riding Hood and the three little pigs confront a wicked wolf, Cinderella and Sleeping Beauty are among the fairytale heroines mistreated by stepmothers, and Hansel and Gretel are imprisoned by a witch.

A humorous person-against-person conflict provides the story line in Beverly Cleary's *Ramona and Her Father*. Seven-year-old Ramona's life changes drastically when her father loses his job and her mother must work full-time. Ramona's new time with her father is not as enjoyable as she had hoped it would be, however: Her father becomes tense and irritable as his period of unemployment lengthens. Ramona and her father survive their experience, and by the end of the story, they have returned to their normal, warm relationship.

Katherine Paterson develops a more complex person-against-person conflict for older children in *Jacob Have I Loved*. In this story, one twin believes that she is like the despised Esau in the Old Testament, whereas her sister is the adored favorite of the family. The unhappy heroine's descriptions of her early experiences with her sister, her growing independence as she works with her father, and her final discovery that she, not her sister, is the strong twin create an engrossing plot and memorable characters.

Person Against Society. Conflicts also develop when the main character's actions, desires, or values differ from those of the surrounding society. This society may consist of groups of children who cannot tolerate children who are different from themselves. In Brock Cole's *The Goats*, a boy and a girl who are considered social outcasts by their peers at camp are stripped of their clothing and marooned

An In-Depth Analysis of the Plot and Conflict in One Book

Christopher Paul Curtis's *The Watsons Go to Birmingham—1963*, a 1996 Newbery Honor book, provides an excellent source for both literary analysis and historical authenticity. It is a book that changes mood at about the halfway point in the story. At the beginning of the book, the author depicts a typical African American family who lives and works in Flint, Michigan. The problems of the various characters are typical for many families. The main character, 10-year-old Kenny, is a bright boy who reads very well. Kenny's scholastic achievements frequently place him in conflict with his older brother, Bryon, whose escapades vary from the humorous to the more serious. At the point in which the parents decide that Bryon is heading for a life of delinquency, they decide that he should spend time with his strict grandmother in Birmingham.

When they decide to travel to Alabama, the tone of the book changes. In this time of racial tension, person-against-society conflict is the most prominent. The racial conflict is developed early in the story when the mother wants to go from Flint to Birmingham because life is slower in Alabama and the people are friendlier. Dad responds, "'Oh yeah, they're a laugh a minute down there. Let's see, where was that 'Coloreds Only' bathroom downtown?'" (p. 5). The culmination of this person-against-society conflict results toward the end of the book when a church is bombed and several African American children are killed.

Curtis develops parallels between the person-against-society and person-against-self conflicts. As Kenny tries to understand the hatred that could cause such deaths he also, with the help of his older brother, reaches a point where he releases his personal feelings and begins to cry. The author shows the impact of this release in the following quote: "He knew that was some real embarrassing stuff so he closed the bathroom door and sat on the tub and waited for me to stop, but I couldn't. I felt like someone had pulled a plug on me and every tear inside was rushing out" (p. 199).

At the moment of complete self-understanding, Kenny admits to his brother that he was no longer afraid of the bombing incident; instead, he was ashamed of himself because he ran from the church rather than try to find his sister, who he believed was inside the church. His older brother helps him clarify the situation and makes him realize that he has no reason for embarrassment.

The themes and language in the book also relate to the person-against-society and person-against-self conflicts. Through the actions of various characters, we learn that prejudice and hatred are harmful and destructive forces. To increase understanding of these conflicts, Curtis effectively uses comparative language and symbolism. For example, he compares the steering of a big car to being grown up when the father tells Kenny that both are scary at first, but that with a lot of practice, the car and life are under control. The symbolism of the Wool Pooh (Winnie-the-Pooh's evil twin brother) is of particular interest: When Kenny swims in dangerous waters, he almost drowns. He believes it is the Wool Pooh who is trying to kill him. Later, in the bombed church, he believes he sees this same faceless monster. Students of literature may find interesting comparisons for discussion as they analyze the possible significance of this evil symbolism as it relates to both the conflicts and themes developed in the book.

When using this book with older students, adults can ask them to trace the parallels between person-against-society and person-against-self conflicts, conduct historical studies to analyze the 1963 setting and conflicts for authenticity and to relate them to the church bombings in 1996, and trace the emergence of the themes. Curtis's text provides an interesting discussion to show the relationships among conflict, theme, and author's style. Students then can read Janice N. Harrington's *Going North* to compare the experiences of an African American family who decides to leave Alabama in the 1960s and move north to Nebraska.

on a deserted island. The author reveals the social attitudes of this camp when girls are classified as queens, princesses, dogs, and real dogs; the girl on the island is considered a real dog. Cole reveals the feelings of the children through their ordeal when he uses terms such as *they* and *them* to identify the society. When the girl wants the boy to leave her, his actions, thoughts, and dialogue reveal the strength of his dislike for the society that placed him in this isolation: " 'I'm afraid. Maybe you'd better go without me.' 'No,' he said. He didn't try to explain. He knew he was afraid to leave her alone, but even more important, it wouldn't be good enough. He wanted them both to disappear. To disappear completely" (p. 16).

Children's books often portray person-against-society conflicts that result from being different from the majority in terms of race, religion, or physical characteristics. Gary Paulsen's *Nightjohn* develops the brutality of a society that mistreats slaves. Life for 12-year-old Sarney becomes even more miserable when Nightjohn secretly teaches her how to read and both of them are punished for this action. Judy Blume's *Blubber* shows the cruelty to which a fat child is subjected by her peers. For the conflict between person and society in such books to be believable, the social setting and its values must be presented in accurate detail.

Numerous survival stories set in wartime develop person-against-society conflicts. In Uri Orlev's *The Island on Bird Street,* the conflict is between a Jewish boy and the society that forces him to live in loneliness and starvation rather than surrender. Throughout the story, Orlev describes the boy's fear and the society that causes him to

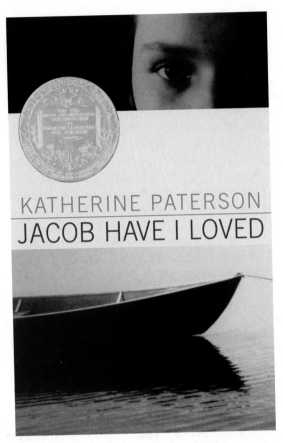

KATHERINE PATERSON
JACOB HAVE I LOVED

Complex person-against-person conflict develops between twin sisters in Jacob Have I Loved *by Katherine Paterson. (Jacket by Kinoko Craft, Thomas Y. Crowell Co. Copyright © 2001 by Hilary Zarycky. Used by permission of HarperCollins Publishers.)*

feel and respond in this way. For example, in the following quote, notice how Orlev describes the actions of the society and the boy's responses to that society when a group of Jewish people are found living in a hidden bunker:

> Its inhabitants began to come out. It took a long while for the last of them to emerge. The Germans and the policemen kept shouting and footsteps kept crossing the ruins from the cellar to the front gate. Now and then someone stumbled. . . . Somebody fell once or maybe twice. A shot rang out. Nobody screamed, though. Even the children had stopped crying. The last footsteps left the building. I heard voices in the street and an order to line up in threes. The same as had been given us. Then they were marched away. A few more shots. Finally, the car started up and drove away. . . . It was strange to think that all those people had been hiding with me in one house without us even knowing about each other. . . . They'd never take me away like that. (p. 81)

Holocaust stories, with their strong anti-Semitism, create some of the strongest person-against-society conflicts. In *Daniel Half Human and the Good Nazi*, David Chotjewitz creates a believable antagonist through reactions of the family toward knowledge that Daniel is half Jewish. The mother declares: "She was terrified. . . . She could feel how her son, at this very moment, would be distancing himself from her" (p. 60). The author uses news-

paper headlines that call upon the nation to boycott Jewish businesses, class essays from students in which they express their hatred of the Jews, attitudes of Nazi officers toward the Jews, and descriptions of such experiences as the Night of the Broken Glass to encourage readers to visualize the society.

The author uses statements of Daniel's mother to describe the changes in the society: "A pestilence had broken out, a terrible disease, and no one had noticed. It has infected everyone, and now it's an epidemic. . . . It was as though the Germany she'd known had vanished. No, worse—as though it had decided to obliterate itself. The strength and the spirit that had once created art, poetry, and science were now spent creating the worst of all possible worlds" (pp. 159–160).

Person Against Nature.   Nature—not society or another person—is the antagonist in many memorable books for older children. When the author thoroughly describes the natural environment, readers vicariously travel into a world ruled by nature's harsh laws of survival. This is the case in Jean Craighead George's *Julie of the Wolves*. Miyax, a 13-year-old Eskimo girl also called by the English name Julie, is lost and without food on the North Slope of Alaska. She is introduced lying on her stomach, peering at a pack of wolves. The wolves are not her enemy, however. Her adversary is the vast, cold tundra that stretches for hundreds of miles without human presence, a land so harsh that no berry bushes point to the south, no birds fly overhead so that she can follow, and continuous summer daylight blots out the North Star that might guide her home:

> No roads cross it; ponds and lakes freckle its immensity. Winds scream across it, and the view in every direction is exactly the same. Somewhere in this cosmos was Miyax; and the very life in her body, its spark and warmth, depended upon these wolves for survival. And she was not so sure they would help. (p. 6)

The constant wind; the empty sky; and the cold, deserted earth are ever present as Miyax crosses the Arctic searching for food, protecting herself from the elements, and making friends with the wolves, who bring her food. The author encourages readers to visualize the power and beauty of this harsh landscape and to share the girl's sorrow over human destruction of this land, its animals, and the Eskimo way of life.

Another book that pits a young person against the elements of nature is Armstrong Sperry's *Call It Courage*. The hero's conflict with nature begins when the crashing, stormy sea—"a monster livid and hungry"—capsizes Mafatu's canoe during a hurricane:

> Higher and higher it rose, until it seemed that it must scrape at the low-hanging clouds. Its crest heaved over with a vast sigh. The boy saw it coming. He tried to cry out. No sound issued from his throat. Suddenly the wave was upon him. Down it crashed. Chaos! Mafatu felt the paddle torn from his hands. Thunder in his ears. Water strangled him. Terror in his soul. (p. 24)

The preceding quote makes clear that there are two adversaries in the story: The hero is in conflict with nature and also in conflict with himself. The two adversaries are interwoven in the plot as Mafatu sails away from his island in order to prove that he is not a coward. Each time the boy wins a victory over nature, he also comes closer to his main goal, victory over his own fear. Without victory over fear, the boy cannot be called by his rightful name, Mafatu, "Stout Heart," nor can he have the respect of his father, his Polynesian people, and himself.

In *A Girl Named Disaster*, Nancy Farmer develops a survival story set in Mozambique and Zimbabwe. As the heroine struggles to escape starvation on her lonely journey, she discovers that the spirits of her ancestors help both her physical and her emotional survival.

You can compare Farmer's story of survival with Anton Quintana's *The Baboon King*, set in the African land of the Kikuyu and the Masai. Quintana also depicts the need for both physical and emotional survival after a young man is banished by his people. The author describes not only the physical geography of the landscape but also the predators that might attack a lone hunter. The need for emotional survival is developed as the young man joins a baboon troop in order to regain the companionship that he lost.

Authors who write strong person-against-nature conflicts use many of the techniques shown in the quotes by George and Sperry. Personification gives human actions to nature, vivid descriptions show that characters are in a life-and-death struggle, sentences become shorter to show increasing danger, and actions reveal that characters know they are in serious conflict with nature.

Person Against Self. In *Hatchet*, Gary Paulsen develops person-against-self and person-against-nature conflicts for his major character, 13-year-old Brian; these two major conflicts are intertwined throughout the book. For example, Paulsen creates an excellent transition between unconsciousness at the end of Chapter 3 and consciousness at the beginning of Chapter 4. In the following quote, notice how Paulsen ties together the two most destructive experiences in Brian's life: the plane crash that could have killed him and the secret about his mother that caused his parents' divorce.

> Without knowing anything. Pulling until his hands caught at weeds and muck, pulling and screaming until his hands caught at last in grass and brush and he felt his chest on land, felt his face in the coarse blades of grass and he stopped; everything stopped. A color came that he had never seen before, a color that exploded in his mind with the pain and he was gone, gone from it all, spiraling out into the world, spiraling out into nothing. Nothing. (p. 30, end of chapter 3)
>
> The Memory was like a knife cutting into him. Slicing deep into him with hate. The Secret. (p. 31, beginning of chapter 4)

Symbolically, the secret is the first thing Brian remembers after waking from unconsciousness. Paulsen reveals the destructive nature of the secret through flashbacks, as Brian's memory returns, and through comparisons between the hate that cut him like a knife and the sharp pain caused by the crash. As Brian gains confidence and ability to survive in the Canadian wilderness, he gains understanding about his parents' conflict and his ability to face his own person-against-self conflict.

The main character in Michael Morpurgo's young adult novel *Private Peaceful* faces an even more dramatic person-against-self secret. Notice in the following quote how the author uses the symbolism of the burial and the drifting away from the cemetery to reveal a terrible secret: "The earth thuds and thumps down on the coffin behind us as we drift away, leaving him. We walk home together along the deep lanes, Big Joe plucking at the foxgloves and the honeysuckle, filling Mother's hands with flowers, and none of us has any tears to cry or words to say. Me least of all. For I have inside me a secret so horrible, a secret I can never tell anyone, not even Charlie. Father needn't have died that morning in Ford's Cleave Wood. He was trying to save me. If only I had tried to save myself, if I had run, he would not now be lying dead in his coffin. As Mother smoothes my hair and Big Joe offers her yet another foxglove, all I can think is that I have caused this. I have killed my own father" (p. 12).

Although few children face the extreme personal challenges described in *Hatchet, Call it Courage*, and *Julie of the Wolves*, all children must overcome fears and personal problems while growing up. Person-against-self conflict is a popular plot device in children's literature. Authors of contemporary realistic fiction often develop plots around children who face and overcome problems related to family disturbances. For example, the cause of the person-against-self conflict in Jerry Spinelli's *Wringer* is a boy's realization that if he does not accept the violence associated with killing pigeons, he must find the courage to oppose the actions and attitudes expressed by both his friends and the town. In Ruth White's *Belle Prater's Boy*, the characters struggle to understand the suicide of the girl's father and desertion by the boy's mother.

Good plots do not rely on contrivance or coincidence; they are credible to young readers because many of the same conflicts occur in the children's own lives. Credibility is an important consideration in evaluating plot in children's books. Although authors of adult books often rely on sensational conflict to create interest, writers of children's books like to focus on the characters and the ways in which they overcome problems.

Pete Hautman's character in his young adult novel *Godless* faces person-against-self and person-against-society issues related to faith. In this National Book Award winner, the main character, Jason Bock, overcomes his lack of belief in organized religion by inventing a new god—the town's water tower. He and a few recruits develop their own religious doctrine complete with rules for worship. Jason faces his worst person-against-self dilemma when things

Through the Eyes of an AUTHOR

David Wisniewski

Visit the CD-ROM that accompanies this text to generate a complete list of David Wisniewski titles.

Selected Titles by David Wisniewski:
- Golem
- Sundiata, Lion King of Mali
- Rain Player
- The Warrior and the Wise Man
- The Secret Knowledge of Grown-Ups: The Second File

The world of children's literature lost an inspired writer and remarkable illustrator in 2002 when Caldecott winner David Wisniewski died in his Maryland home. Creator of stunningly crafted folktales, such as the award-winning Golem and Sundiata, Lion King of Mali, as well as clever comic pieces, exemplified by his two-part series, The Secret Knowledge of Grown-Ups, Wisniewski made an indelible mark on publishing. His painstaking and inspired illustrative style of layered cut paper became his unmistakable calling card, drawing attention to a wonderful body of work to be shared with children for generations.

Being in contact with kids and performing for them give you a sense of what they want in a story. *The Warrior and the Wise Man,* which was my first book, came out of my background in puppetry doing folktales. It seemed only natural to use a folktale or a folkloric tale to capitalize on that familiarity. And I also did not want to do anything trivial. I wanted to do something that had a point, but I also knew enough from puppetry that if you are going to make a point, it has to be demonstrated by the story plot and character. It cannot be laid on top.

I learned from the puppetry that if you are going to have a point, it has to be organically built into the tale and demonstrated by the tale, not preached at you. So with *The Warrior and the Wise Man,* I started off with the point that it's better to think your way through a problem than fight your way through a problem. Knowing that, I knew I could set the story in Japan, because they had two classes: They had the Samurai and they had the Shinto monks coming into Japanese history at the same time. So I could have a dichotomy already set up there. By making my characters twins, I start them off evenly. By making them sons of the emperor vying for the throne, then I've got what Alfred Hitchcock called "the maguffin." I had the point of the story set up.

Because it is a nature-oriented religion, the Shinto religion provided my wind/water/fire—all those elements required by the twins in order to gain the throne. And then the final inspiration was the kids game of "Scissors/Paper/Rock," which was one element canceling out another element. And then the twist at the end was really not something I had planned. That was a bright idea that came to me. What I like about this story is that the warrior is not evil. He simply has what has proved to be an inferior way of doing things. And that's brought up at the very end—being strong is nice, but unless that strength is directed intelligently, its worthless.

So that is what got me started on the culturally entrenched tales with a sensible way of working. I came up with the idea that I needed to know what point I wanted the story to make. Where is the culture that supports the point of my story? What culture could this story have happened in? And then I do research from there to make sure that I'm not breaking any cultural norms that would preclude the use of my original tale in it.

Video Profiles: The accompanying video contains conversations from such authors and illustrators as Roland Smith, the late Paula Danziger, and E. B. Lewis.

---

begin to get out of hand and very dangerous: The new congregation climbs to the top of the water tower, everyone jumps into the water in the tank, and one member is seriously hurt. Now Jason faces both society's outrage in the form of his father, the church, and the police department and his own inner conflicts as he debates what has happened to his friends because of his actions. He battles within himself as he debates what he will do in his need to have faith in something.

Characterization

A believable, enjoyable story needs main characters who seem lifelike and who develop throughout the story. Characterization is one of the most powerful of the literary elements, whether the story is a contemporary tale in which characters face realistic problems or an adaptation of classic literature.

The characters whom we remember fondly from our childhood reading usually have several sides; like real people, they are not all good or all bad, and they change as they confront and overcome their problems. Laura, from the various "Little House" books by Laura Ingalls Wilder, typifies a rounded character in literature: She is honest,

trustworthy, and courageous, but she can also be jealous, frightened, or angry. Her character not only is fully developed in the story but also changes during its course.

One child who enjoyed Wilder's books described Laura this way: "I would like Laura for my best friend. She would be fun to play with but she would also understand when I was hurt or angry. I could tell Laura my secrets without being afraid she would laugh at me or tell them to someone else." Any writer who can create such a friend for children is very skilled at characterization.

Rosemary Chance (1999) reported on a study analyzing the characteristics of novels that were on the list of young adult choices, and she found that characterization was the most important criterion. Protagonists in these books are dynamic and well developed. The majority of the novels included conflicts that center on people, including person-against-self and person-against-person conflicts. It would appear from such studies and comments from readers that memorable characterization is one of the most important literary elements.

How does an author develop a memorable character? How can an author show the many sides of a character as well as demonstrate believable change as this character

An In-Depth Analysis of Characterization in One Book

Carol Fenner, the author of one of the 1996 Newbery Honor books, *Yolonda's Genius,* uses several techniques to develop the characteristics of two African American children, bright, fifth-grade Yolonda and her slower younger brother, Andrew. For example, the author reveals both Yolonda's intelligence and her strategy for retaliation after she is teased about her size by being called a whale: Yolonda tells her fellow bus rider that he knows nothing about whales because "whales are the most remarkable mammals in the ocean—all five oceans" (p. 16). She then provides information about whales, such as "The whales sank, lifting their tails high above the water like a signal. Deep in the ocean, their voices sent out a high swelling cry, sharing their message of victory for a hundred miles" (p. 17). We learn later that Yolonda goes to the library each week to learn new facts.

Yolonda's positive attitudes and Andrew's possible musical genius are developed as Yolonda shares Andrew's abilities. She reviews what Andrew can do and not what he cannot do when she thinks, "If there was music on the TV or the blaster, he could keep it company by beating out a rhythm on anything—his knees, a table, a wall. Or he could play a sweet line of sound on his harmonica just underneath the music, like water under a bridge. He played people's voices—an argument, cries of surprise, hushed conversation. The harmonica lived in his pocket. He fell asleep with it in his hand" (p. 38).

Later, Yolonda's actions show both her respect for Andrew's talents and her dislike for those who torment her younger brother because he is a slower learner in school and gains his enjoyment from playing his harmonica. Yolonda takes vengeance on the three boys who destroy Andrew's harmonica. She does this while Andrew is watching because she wants it to be Andrew's vengeance as well as her own.

The author continues to show characterization through the symbolism of music. Andrew makes discoveries about people through sounds, he learns the alphabet after a teacher relates the alphabet to the instruments, and he eventually plays his harmonica to reveal the character of Yolonda. As you read the following quote, analyze how the author describes Yolonda through Andrew's music: "Yolonda walking, a steady, strong beat—great big moves, slow, making waves of air pass by. Yolonda eating a chocolate eclair—full mouth—soft and happy. Yolonda reading to him, voice purring around the big words, Yolonda dancing. This is the sound of Yolonda's body—large, gobbling, space, powerful and protecting—great like a queen, frightening everyone with a scowl and a swelling of her shoulders" (p. 203).

Notice in this example how the author uses several different techniques to develop the characterizations of Yolonda and her brother. After reading the book, readers understand that both characters have well-rounded personalities.

---

matures? The credibility of a character depends on the writer's ability to reveal that character's full nature, including strengths and weaknesses. An author can achieve such a three-dimensional character by describing the character's physical appearance, recording the conversations of the character, revealing the character's thoughts, revealing the perceptions of other characters, and showing the character in action.

In *Call It Courage*, Armstrong Sperry uses all of these methods to reveal Mafatu's character and the changes that occur in him as he overcomes his fears. Sperry first tells readers that Mafatu fears the sea. Then, through narration, Sperry shows the young child clinging to his mother's back as a stormy sea and sharks almost end their lives. Mafatu's memories of this experience, revealed in his thoughts and actions, make him useless in the eyes of his Polynesian tribe, as Sperry reveals through the dialogue of other characters: "That is woman's work. Mafatu is afraid of the sea. He will never be a warrior" (p. 12).

The laughter of the tribe follows, and Sperry then describes Mafatu's inner feelings:

Suddenly a fierce resentment stormed through him. He knew in that instant what he must do: he must prove his courage to himself, and to the others, or he could no longer live in their midst. He must face Moana, the Sea God—face him and conquer him. (p. 13)

Sperry portrays Mafatu's battle for courage through a combination of actions and thoughts: Terror and elation follow each other repeatedly as Mafatu lands on a forbidden island used for human sacrifice, dares to take a ceremonial spear even though doing so may mean death, confronts a hammerhead shark that circles his raft, and then overcomes his fear and attacks the shark to save his dog. Mafatu celebrates a final victory when he kills a wild boar, whose teeth symbolize courage. Mafatu's tremendous victory over fear is signified by his father's statement of pride: "Here is my son come home from the sea. Mafatu, Stout Heart. A brave name for a brave boy" (p. 115).

In *The Moves Make the Man*, Bruce Brooks develops character through basketball terminology. Brooks uses the words of Jerome Foxworthy, a talented black student, to express these thoughts about his own character:

Moves were all I cared about last summer. I got them down, and I liked not just the fun of doing them, but having them too, like a little definition of Jerome. Reverse spin, triple jump, reverse dribble. . . . These are me. The moves make the man, the moves make me, I thought, until Mama noticed they were making me something else. (p. 44)

Brooks uses contrasting attitudes toward fake moves in basketball to reveal important differences between Jerome and Bix Rivers, a talented but disturbed white athlete.

Through The Eyes of a CHILD

Andersen

Grade 2

Author: David wishiewski
Title: the worrior and the wise man
I like this book because it
is a interesting book. My favorite
part is when they go to
the wind demend because I
like wind. My favorite character
is Toe mon because he's nice. The
demends are not scary at all! They
are nice if your nice to them!
There is a big twist at the
end but I'm not gunna tell you!
You should read it some time!

ANDERSEN

In *The Wanderer,* Sharon Creech introduces the main character by emphasizing the girl's father's description of her as a person who has many sides. Notice in the following quote how Creech describes both the father's and the girl's interpretation of her character:

> I am not always such a dreamy girl, listening to the sea calling me. My father calls me Three-Sided Sophie: One side is dreamy and romantic; one is logical and down-to-earth; and the third side is hardheaded and impulsive. He says I am either in dreamland or earthland or mule-land, and if I ever get the three together, I'll be set, though I wonder where I will be then. If I'm not in dreamland or earthland or mule-land, where will I be? (p. 3).

By the end of the book, the author shows the main character's progression through these same three characteristics. She now answers her own question when she realizes: "I'm not in dreamland or earthland or muteland. I'm just right here, right now. When I close my eyes, I can still smell the sea, but I feel as if I've been dunked in the clear cool water and I've come out all clean and new." (p. 305).

This textbook discusses many memorable characters in children's literature. Some of these characters—such as the faithful spider Charlotte and a terrific pig named Wilbur, in E. B. White's *Charlotte's Web,* Max, in Maurice Sendak's *Where the Wild Things Are,* and Karana, in Scott O'Dell's *Island of the Blue Dolphins*—are old favorites who have been capturing children's imaginations for decades. Others—such as Harry Potter, in J. K. Rowling's fantasy series, Ida B, from Katherine Hannigan's *Ida B . . . and Her Plans to Maximize Fun, Avoid Disaster, and (Possibly) Save the World,* and Margaret Rose Kane, in E. L. Konigsburg's *The Outcasts of 19 Schuyler Place*—are more recent arrivals in the world of children's books. Authors of picture storybooks, historical fiction, science fiction, fantasy, and contemporary realistic fiction have created characters who are likely to be remembered long after the details of their stories have been forgotten.

SETTING

The setting of a story—its location in time and place—helps readers share what the characters see, smell, hear, and touch, and also makes the characters' values, actions, and conflicts more understandable. For example, notice in the following description of setting how Gary D. Schmidt, in the 2005 Newbery Honor book *Lizzie Bright and the Buckminster Boy*, allows readers to experience the setting: "Turner Buckminster had lived in Phippsburg, Maine, for fifteen minutes shy of six hours. He had dipped his hand in its waves and licked the salt from his fingers. He had smelled the sharp resin of the pines. He had heard the low rhythm of the bells on the buoys that balanced on the ridges of the sea. He had seen the fine clapboard parsonage beside the church where he was to live. . . . He didn't know how much longer he could stand it" (p. 1). Whether a story takes place in the past, present, or future, its overall credibility may depend on how well the plot, characterizations, and setting support one another. Different types of literature—picture storybooks, fantasy, historical fiction, and contemporary realistic fiction—have their own requirements as far as setting is concerned. When a story is set in an identifiable historical period or geographical location, details should be accurate.

Jean Craighead George (1991), author of numerous survival stories, emphasizes the setting for a book. To do this, George walks through the setting, smells the environment, looks at the world to see careful details, and searches for protagonists. During her final writing, she closes her eyes and recreates in her imagination the land, the people, and the animals. George states:

> I strive to put the reader on the scene. I want to make each child feel that he is under a hemlock tree with Sam Gribley in *My Side of the Mountain* or on his hands and knees talking to the tundra wolves in *Julie of the Wolves*. I want my reader to hear and see the ice on the Arctic Ocean in *Water Sky*. (p. 70)

In some books, setting is such an important part of the story that the characters and plot cannot be developed without understanding the time and place. In other stories, however, the setting provides only a background.

An In-Depth Analysis of Setting in One Book

The settings in Philip Pullman's award-winning fantasy from England, *The Golden Compass*, reveal several purposes for setting that can be found in the same book. For example, in the beginning of the book, notice how the author creates a suspenseful setting through the following quote showing the characters' actions: "'Behind the chair—quick!' whispered Pantalaimon, and in a flash Lyra was out of the armchair and crouching behind it. It wasn't the best one for hiding behind: she'd chose one in the very center of the room, and unless she kept very quiet . . . " (p. 4).

On the pages that follow, readers discover how dangerous this setting might be for Lyra: "What she saw next, however, changed things completely. The Master took from his pocket a folded paper and laid it on the table beside the wine. He took the stopper out of the mouth of a decanter containing a rich golden wine, unfolded the paper, and poured a thin stream of white powder into the decanter before crumpling the paper and throwing it into the fire. Then he took a pencil from his pocket, stirred the wine until the powder had dissolved, and replaced the stopper" (p. 6).

As the story moves from England to the far north, the setting frequently becomes an antagonist as Lyra faces both the cold and the fear found in the wilderness. Pullman creates both of these moods in quotes such as the following: "The other girls went on talking, but Lyra and Pantalaimon nestled down deep in the bed and tried to get warm, knowing that for hundreds of miles all around her little bed there was nothing but fear" (p. 246).

Pullman's settings both create a realistic background and suggest the fantasy settings of other worlds. For example, the fol-lowing quote provides realistic background for a small town in the far north; it also allows readers to visualize, hear, and even smell the setting: "Directly ahead of the ship a mountain rose, green flanked and snowcapped, and a little town and harbor lay below it: wooden houses with steep roofs, an oratory spire, cranes in the harbor, and clouds of gulls wheeling and crying. The smell was of fish, but mixed with it came land smells too: pine resin and earth and something animal and musky, and something else that was cold and blank and wild: it might have been snow. It was the smell of the North" (p. 168).

Many of Pullman's settings also reflect a universe inhabited by witches and supernatural beings, and incorporate parallel worlds. Pullman describes this parallel world in this way: "The city hanging there so empty and silent looked new-made, waiting to be occupied; or asleep, waiting to be woken. The sun of that world was shining into this, making Lyra's hands golden, melting the ice on Roger's wolfskin hood, making his pale cheeks transparent, glistening in his open sightless eyes" (p. 397).

Pullman concludes his fantasy in a way that prepares readers for the next book in the series by summarizing some of the moods found in the previous settings and foreshadowing the fantasy to come: "She turned away. Behind them lay pain and death and fear; ahead of them lay doubt, and danger, and fathomless mysteries. But they weren't alone. So Lyra and her deamon turned away from the world they were born in, and looked toward the sun, and walked into the sky" (p. 399). To continue analyzing Pullman's fantasy setting, read *The Subtle Knife* and *The Amber Spyglass*, sequels to *The Golden Compass*.

In fact, some settings are so well known that just a few words place readers immediately into the expected location. "Once upon a time," for example, is a mythical time in days of yore when it was possible for magical spells to transform princes into beasts or to change pumpkins into glittering carriages. Thirty of the 37 traditional fairy tales in Andrew Lang's *The Red Fairy Book* begin with "Once upon a time." Magical spells cannot happen everywhere; they usually occur in "a certain kingdom," "deep in the forest," in "the humble hut of a wise and good peasant," or "far, far away, in a warm and pleasant land." Children become so familiar with such phrases—and the visualizations of setting that they trigger—that additional details and descriptions are not necessary.

Even a setting that is described briefly can serve several purposes: It can create a mood, provide an antagonist, establish historical background, or supply symbolic meanings.

Setting as Mood.   Authors of children's literature and adult literature alike use settings to create moods that add credibility to characters and plot. Readers would probably be a bit skeptical, for example, if a vampire appeared in a sunny American kitchen on a weekday morning while a family was preparing to leave for school and work; the same vampire would seem more believable in a moldy castle in Transylvania at midnight. The illustrations and text can create the mood of a location. Readers can infer the author's and illustrator's feelings about the setting. For example, Cynthia Rylant's text and Barry Moser's illustrations for *Appalachia: The Voices of Sleeping Birds* provide a setting that radiates warm feelings about the varied people, their strengths, and their way of life.

The illustrations create a nostalgic look at childhood in In Coal Country. *(From* In Coal Country *by Judith Hendershot, illustrated by Thomas B. Allen. Illustration copyright © 1987 by Thomas B. Allen. Reprinted by permission of Alfred A. Knopf.)*

The mood in David Almond's *The Fire-Eaters*, 2003 winner of the Whitbread Children's Book Award, matches the strong antiwar theme in this story set in 1962 at the time of the Cuban missile crisis. Notice how Almond develops a frightening mood and sets the stage for a person-against-society conflict in the following quote:

> The air grew cold. Dad threw more sea coal and lumps of driftwood onto the fire. I sat with him and watched TV. There'd been more nuclear bomb tests in Russia and the US. President Kennedy stood at a lectern, whispered to a general, shuffled some papers and spoke of his resolution, our growing strength. He said there were no limits to the steps we'd take if we were pushed. Khrushchev made a fist, thumped a table and glared. Then came the pictures that accompanied such reports: the missiles that would be launched, the planes that would take off, the mushroom clouds, the howling winds, the devastated cities. (p. 19)

What mood did Almond develop with the reference to the nuclear bomb tests, the mushroom clouds, and the devastated cities? What is the significance of the air growing colder and the thumping of fists?

In the following quote found in the first paragraph of *From the Lighthouse*, Liz Chipman shows the mood of her character by describing the unhappy impact of a beautiful autumn season:

> Autumn used to be my favorite time of year. I don't like it so much anymore. It's lost some of its luster. Autumn leaves on the Hudson weren't enough to make Ma stay. And what am I, compared to the bright yellow-orange-red of an October riverbank, the sun lighting up the sky, shining warm love on the whole entire earth? Not much: A knobby-kneed thirteen-year-old girl with black hair and the two biggest front teeth in the entire town of Hudson, New York. Foolish to think I could be enough to make Ma want to stay if the leaves couldn't. (p. 5)

A setting that would normally reflect a happy mood becomes one of loss. The mood of the character also introduces a major person-against-self conflict as the girl tries to understand what caused her mother to leave her, her three brothers, her father, and the lighthouse that is home to the family.

Setting as Antagonist.   Setting can be an antagonist in plots based on person-against-society or person-against-nature conflict. The descriptions of the Arctic in Jean Craighead George's *Julie of the Wolves* are essential; without them, readers would have difficulty understanding the life-and-death peril facing Miyax. These descriptions make it possible to comprehend Miyax's love for the Arctic, her admiration of and dependence on the wolves, and her preference for the old Eskimo ways.

Sharon Creech's descriptions of the ocean during a storm in *The Wanderer* provide a vivid antagonist. For example, notice how Creech uses descriptive language and frightening similes in the following quotes: "Now the waves are more fierce, cresting and toppling over, like leering drooling monsters spewing heavy streaks of foam

The paintings depict the terrible destruction associated with a tornado in Irene Trivas's illustrations for George Ella Lyon's One Lucky Girl. *(From* One Lucky Girl *by George Ella Lyon. Copyright © 2000 by Dorling Kindersley Limited, London. Reprinted by permission of Dorling Kindersley.)*

through the air" (p. 185) and "But this wave was unlike any other. It had a curl, a distinct high curl. I watched it growing up behind us, higher and higher, and then curled over *The Wanderer*, thousands of gallons of water, white and lashing" (p. 208).

The setting in Ida Vos's *Hide and Seek* provides the antagonist, the Netherlands during German occupation. In the foreword to the text. Vos introduces the setting for the story and helps readers understand that the setting is the antagonist:

> Come with me to a small country in Western Europe. To the Netherlands, a land also known as Holland. Come with me, back to the year 1940. I am eight years old. German soldiers are parading through the Dutch streets. They have helmets on their heads and they are wearing black boots. They are marching and singing songs that have words I don't understand. "They're going to kill all the Jews!" shouts my mother. I am afraid, I have a stomachache. I am Jewish. (p. vii)

The reactions of the characters and the descriptions of the occupation in the remainder of the book leave no doubt that this setting is an antagonist. Vos based *Hide and Seek* on her family's life during World War II.

Authors of nonfiction who write about horrific periods in history may also introduce their subjects with the setting as the antagonist. For example, notice how Jim Murphy prepares readers for the turmoil to come in *An American Plague: The True and Terrifying Story of the Yellow Fever Epidemic of 1793*: "Saturday, August 3, 1793. The sun came up, as it had every day since the end of May, bright, hot, and unrelenting. The swamps and marshes south of Philadelphia had already lost a great deal of wa-

ter to the intense heat, while the Delaware and Schuylkill Rivers had receded to reveal long stretches of their muddy, root-choked banks. Dead fish and gooey vegetable matter were exposed and rotted, while swarms of insects droned in the heavy, humid air. . . . Mosquitoes were everywhere, though their high-pitched whirring was particularly loud near rain barrels, gutters, and open sewers" (p. 1).

Illustrated picture books also may develop the setting as antagonist. For example, Irene Travas's illustrations for George Ella Lyon's *One Lucky Girl* depict the destruction associated with a tornado.

Setting as Historical Background. Accuracy in setting is extremely important in historical fiction and in biography. Conflict in the story and the actions of the characters may be influenced by the time period and the geographical location. However, unless authors describe settings carefully, children cannot comprehend unfamiliar historical periods or the stories that unfold in them. *A Gathering of Days*, by Joan W. Blos, is an example of historical fiction that carefully depicts setting—in this case, a small New Hampshire farm in the 1830s. Blos brings rural 19th-century America to life through descriptions of little things, such as home remedies, country pleasures, and country hardships.

Blos describes in detail the preparation of a cold remedy: The character goes to the pump for water, blows up the fire, heats a kettle of water over the flames, wrings out a flannel in hot water, sprinkles the flannel with turpentine, and places it on the patient's chest. Blos also describes discipline and school life in the 1830s. Disobedience can result in a thrashing. Because of their sex, girls are excused from all but the simplest arithmetic. Readers vicariously join the characters in breaking out of the snow with a team of oxen, tapping the maple sugar trees, and collecting nuts. Of this last experience, the narrator says, "O, I do think, as has been said, that if getting in the corn and potatoes are the prose of a farm child's life, then nutting's the poetry" (p. 131).

The setting in Joëlle Stolz's *The Shadows of Ghadames* is 19th-century Libya. The author develops a historical background for this Muslim country by focusing on the very traditional and often hidden lives of women in Ghadames, where "the men are often away on the desert tracks while the women wait for them on the rooftops" (p. 3). The author makes this a believable setting by describing cultural details such as the rooftop world of the women where they cook and weave, the belief in spirits, the treatment for illnesses, the authority of men in the family and in the culture, the women's baths, and the conflict caused by two wives living in the same family. The author concludes with a theme that suggests that changes are coming to this Islamic world. An interesting cultural comparison to this book is Suzanne Fisher Staples's *Shabanu: Daughter of the Wind*, a story of a Muslim family

NUMBER THE STARS
a novel by Lois Lowry

Lois Lowry develops a setting that is historically accurate for World War II Denmark. (From Number the Stars by Lois Lowry, copyright © 1989. Reproduced with permission of Houghton Mifflin Co.)

who lives in the Cholistan Desert in Pakistan. Staples's novel is discussed in Chapter 9, "Contemporary Realistic Fiction."

In *Number the Stars*, set in Copenhagen during the 1940s, Lois Lowry develops a fictional story around the actions of the Danish Resistance. Actions of King Christian add to the historical accuracy of the time period. In addition to depicting historically accurate backgrounds, Lowry develops the attitudes of the Danish people. Consequently, readers understand why many Danes risked their lives to relocate the Jewish residents of Denmark.

Detailed illustrations by Steve Noon for Anne Millard's *A Street Through Time: A 12,000-Year Walk Through History* allow viewers to identify many aspects of life as it would appear in the same setting beginning in 10,000 B.C. and progressing into a modern town. Text covering early periods such as "Roman Times," "Viking Raiders," and "Medieval Village" provide numerous details that could clarify nonillustrated books of historical fiction.

The authors of historical fiction and biography must not only depict the time and location but also be aware of values, vocabulary, and other speech patterns consistent with the time and location. To do this, the authors must be immersed in the past and do extensive research. For ex-

ample, Joan Blos researched her subject at the New York Public Library, libraries on the University of Michigan campus, and the town library of Holderness, New Hampshire. She also consulted town and county records in New Hampshire and discussed the story with professional historians. Lois Lowry visited Copenhagen and researched documents about the leaders of the Danish Resistance.

Setting as Symbolism. Settings often have symbolic meanings that underscore what is happening in the story. Symbolism is common in traditional folktales, where frightening adventures and magical transformations occur in the deep, dark woods, and splendid castles are the sites of "happily ever after." Modern authors of fantasy and science fiction for children often borrow symbolic settings from old folktales to establish moods of strangeness and enchantment, such as the parallel universes created in the high fantasies by authors such as J. K. Rowling in *Harry Potter and the Goblet of Fire* and Philip Pullman in *The Golden Compass*, but authors of realistic fiction also use subtly symbolic settings to accentuate plot or help develop characters.

In one children's classic, *The Secret Garden*, by Frances Hodgson Burnett, a garden that has been locked behind a wall for 10 years symbolizes a father's grief after the death of his wife, his son's illness, and the emotional estrangement of the father and son from each other. The first positive change in the life of a lonely, unhappy girl occurs when she discovers the buried key to the garden and opens the vine-covered door: "It was the sweetest, most mysterious-looking place anyone could imagine. The high walls which shut it in were covered with the leafless stems of climbing roses which were so thick that they were matted together" (p. 76). Finding the garden, working in it, and watching its beauty return bring happiness to the girl, restore health to the sick boy, and reunite the father and son. The good magic that causes emotional and physical healing in this secret kingdom is symbolized by tiny new shoots emerging from the soil and the rosy color that the garden's fresh air brings to the cheeks of two pale children.

In a later book, Katherine Paterson's *Bridge to Terabithia*, a secret kingdom in the woods is the "other world" shared by two young people who do not conform to the values of rural Virginia. The boy, Jess, would rather be an artist than follow the more masculine aspirations of his father, who accuses him of being a sissy. Schoolmates taunt the girl, Leslie, because she loves books and has no television. Jess and Leslie find that they have much in common, so they create a domain of their own, in which a beautiful setting symbolizes their growing sense of comradeship, belongingness, and self-love.

Even the entrance to their secret country is symbolic: "It could be a magic country like Narnia, and the only way you can get in is by swinging across on this enchanted rope" (p. 39). They grab the old rope, swing across the creek, and enter their stronghold, where streams of light

A boy and girl create a secret kingdom in which they can escape the problems of the real world. (Illustration by Donna Diamond from Bridge to Terabithia *by Katherine Paterson. Copyright © 1977 by Katherine Paterson. A Newbery Medal winner. By permission of Thomas Y. Crowell, Publishers.)*

Theme

The theme of a story is the underlying idea that ties the plot, characters, and setting together into a meaningful whole. When evaluating themes in children's books, consider what the author wanted to convey about life or society and whether that theme is worthwhile for children. A memorable book has a theme—or several themes—that children can understand because of their own needs. Laurence Perrine (1983) states:

> There is no prescribed method for discovering theme. Sometimes we can best get at it by asking in what way the main character has changed in the course of a story and what, if anything, the character has learned before its end. Sometimes the best approach is to explore the nature of the central conflict and its outcome. Sometimes the title will provide an important clue. (p. 110)

Authors of children's books often directly state the theme of a book, rather than imply it as authors commonly do in books for adults. For example, Wendy Anderson Halperin's *Love Is . . .* develops various definitions of love, such as "Love is kind." On one side of the double page, the artist depicts the consequences when that type of love is not present; the facing page depicts the consequences when that love is added. Theme may be stated by characters or through the author's narrative. The characters' actions and the outcome of the story usually develop and support the theme in children's literature. Picture storybooks, with their shorter texts and fewer themes, allow readers to analyze, trace, and discuss evidence of theme in a briefer, whole story. For example, many readers identify the theme in Patricia Polacco's *Appelemando's Dreams* as "It is important to dream." The following evidence from the book supports this theme:

1. The boy who does not have anything to do in a drab village makes his life interesting by dreaming about magic chariots pulled by galloping hues of color.
2. Appelemando shares his beautiful colored dreams with his friends and makes them happy.
3. The friends try to capture Appelemando's dreams on paper so that they can keep them forever.
4. The children fear that they will lose Appelemando's dreams after the villagers angrily make them wash the dreams off the village walls.
5. The dreams allow the children to be found after they lose their way in the forest.
6. The villagers weep for joy after they follow Appelemando's vision and find the children.
7. The villagers conclude, "Never again would they question the importance of dreams" (p. 28, unnumbered).
8. The village becomes a colorful and dreamy place that people enjoy visiting.

dance through the leaves of dogwood, oak, and evergreen, fears and enemies do not exist, and anything they want is possible. Paterson develops credible settings as Jess and Leslie go from the world of school and home to the world they make for themselves in Terabithia.

A dilapidated house, with its uncared-for backyard, becomes a symbolic setting in Janet Taylor Lisle's *Afternoon of the Elves.* In this setting, two girls, Hillary and Sara-Kate, make discoveries about each other and the importance of accepting people who are different. The girls work together in a miniature village that Sara-Kate maintains was built by elves. Like Paterson, Lisle creates two credible settings: (1) Hillary's normal world of school and home and (2) the almost otherworldly existence of a yard that is entered through a thick hedge. Like many other authors of books that have symbolic settings, Lisle relates the settings to the theme.

An In-Depth Analysis of Theme in One Book

Sharon Creech's 1995 Newbery Medal winner, *Walk Two Moons,* allows readers to analyze the effectiveness of the author's use of theme and to consider how it relates to 13-year-old Sal, her grandparents, her friend, her father, and her mother, who has left home. The themes in Creech's book tie the plot, characters, and setting together into a meaningful whole. For example, Creech uses mysterious messages left by a stranger to tie together the plot, characters' actions, and motivation. The messages are also written in the form of themes.

The first message is "Don't judge a man until you have walked two moons in his moccasins" (p. 51). Father then interprets the meaning of the message on page 61. The second message is "Everyone has his own agenda" (p. 60). This message is tied to Gramps's interpretation of the message (p. 60), Prudence's and Sal's actions (p. 104), and Phoebe's thoughts about her agenda (p. 140). The third message is "In the course of a lifetime what does it matter?" (p. 105). This message is related to Sal's thoughts about the meaning of the message (p. 106). The fourth message is "You can't keep the birds of sadness from flying over your head, but you can keep them from nesting in your hair" (p. 154). This message is related to Phoebe's story (p. 155), Phoebe's father's response (p. 162), Phoebe's crying and Sal's response (p. 169), hope related to the story of Pandora's box (pp. 174–175), the birds of sadness around Phoebe's family (p. 189), and the birds of sadness around Mrs. Cadaver (p. 220). The fifth message is "We never know the worth of water until the well runs dry" (p. 198). This message is related to the discussion about Mrs. Cadaver's and Sal's realization that the messages have changed the way they look at life.

The final and sixth message is the same as the first: "Don't judge a man until you have walked two moons in his moccasins" (p. 252). The importance of this message is developed when Gramps and Sal play the moccasin game in which they take turns pretending they are walking in someone else's moccasins (p. 275) and when Gramps's gift to Sal is to let her walk in her mother's moccasins. This book provides an interesting source for tracing the emergence of themes and the relation of those themes to various characters and conflicts developed in the text.

Themes in books written for younger children frequently develop around experiences and emotions that are important to the younger readers. For example, James Howe's *Horace and Morris But Mostly Dolores* develops the very understandable theme that friendship is important. The theme in Douglas Wood's *What Dads Can't Do* develops the importance of a father's love by showing numerous father-and-child relationships.

In contrast, themes developed in books written for older readers frequently focus on human development and the consequences that may result from choices. For example, Suzanne Fisher Staples's heroine in *Shiva's Fire* discovers "'That is a basic human frailty—we always want to know what will happen if we do one thing rather than another. Not knowing is the mystery of destiny. If you are still for a moment, no doubt you will hear your heart tell you what you must do'" (p. 264). Human frailty is also revealed in the concluding volume to Philip Pullman's trilogy, *The Amber Spyglass.*

Theme Revealed by Changes in Characters. In *The Whipping Boy,* Sid Fleischman develops the theme that friendship is important. He shows how the main characters change in their attitudes toward each other. For example, the names that the main characters call each other progress from hostility to comradeship. At the beginning of the story, Jemmy thinks of the prince as "Your Royal Awfulness." Likewise, the prince refers to Jemmy as "Jemmy-from-the-Street" and "contrary rascal." As the story progresses and the two characters learn to respect and admire each other, Jemmy refers to the prince as "friend" and the prince calls himself "Friend-o-Jemmy's."

Theme and the Nature of Conflict. Stories set in other time periods frequently develop themes by revealing how the main characters respond to conflicts caused by society. For example, Rudolf Frank's *No Hero for the Kaiser,* set in World War I, develops several antiwar themes. Frank depicts the harsh nature of war by exploring the actions and responses of a boy who is unwittingly drawn into battle. Through the viewpoint of the boy. Frank reveals that it takes more courage not to fight than to fight, that it is important to respect oneself, and that "guns never go off by themselves" (p. 13). Frank reinforces these themes through symbolism, similes, and contrasts. The contrasts are especially effective as Frank compares the same soldiers at home and on the battlefield and contrasts peacetime and wartime meanings for terms such as *bull's-eye, shot,* and *field.*

Prejudice is a harmful force in historical fiction, such as Elizabeth George Speare's *The Witch of Blackbird Pond,* Paula Fox's *The Slave Dancer,* Mary Stolz's *Cezanne Pinto: A Memoir,* Uri Orlev's *The Island on Bird Street,* and Mildred D. Taylor's *Roll of Thunder, Hear My Cry.* The theme of prejudice as a harmful force is also found in biographies such as Russell Freedman's *The Voice That Challenged a Nation: Marian Anderson and the Struggle for Equal Rights* and in informational books such as Diane McWhorter's *A Dream of Freedom: The Civil Rights Movement From 1954 to 1968.*

The Theme of Personal Development. Literature offers children opportunities to identify with other people's experiences and thus better understand their own growing up. Consequently, the themes of many children's books deal with developing self-understanding. In an early study, Gretchen Purtell Hayden (1969) concluded that the following themes related to personal development are predominant in children's books that had received the Newbery Medal up to that time: difficulties in establishing good relationships between adults and children, the need for morality to guide one's actions, the importance of support from other people, an acceptance of oneself and others, a respect for authority, the ability to handle problems, and the necessity of cooperation. As you read more current books, search to see if these themes are still found in the literature.

In Robert O'Brien's *Mrs. Frisby and the Rats of NIMH*, intellectually superior rats search for a moral code to guide their actions. They have studied the human race and do not wish to make the same mistakes, but they soon realize how easy it is to slip into dishonest behavior. Some equipment that they find allows them to steal electricity, food, and water from human society, which then makes their lives seem too easy and pointless. Eventually, the rats choose a more difficult course of action, moving into an isolated valley and working to develop their own civilization.

One book that develops the importance of support from another human being is Theodore Taylor's *The Cay*. When Phillip and his mother leave Curaçao to find safety in the United States, their boat is torpedoed by a German submarine. Phillip, a white boy, and Timothy, a black West Indian, become isolated first on a life raft and then on a tiny Caribbean island. Their need for each other is increased when Phillip becomes blind after a blow to the head and, in spite of his racial prejudice, must rely on Timothy to survive. Phillip's superior attitudes gradually vanish, as he becomes totally dependent on another person. When Phillip is finally rescued. He treasures the way in which a wonderful friend has helped change his life for the better.

The Cay also stresses the theme of accepting oneself and others, as does Joan W. Blos's *A Gathering of Days*, in which Catherine experiences injustice for the first time when she and her friends secretly help a runaway slave. Catherine learns to respect authority as well when after years of responsibility for her widowed father and little sister, she must trust and obey her new stepmother.

Many children's books deal in some way with the necessity of overcoming problems. Characters may confront problems within themselves or in their relationships with others, or problems caused by society or nature. Memorable characters face their adversaries, and through a maturing process, they learn to handle their difficulties. Handling problems may be as dramatic and planned as Mafatu's search for courage in Armstrong Sperry's *Call It Courage* or may result from accident, as in Theodore Taylor's *The Cay*.

Cooperation, the importance of personal growth, and the need for kindness and sharing are all themes in E. L. Konigsburg's *The View From Saturday*. These themes are developed as a group of sixth graders form a winning team for the Academic Bowl.

Technology Resources

CW

The *Bulletin of the Centre for Children's Books* is a review journal, providing starred reviews, editorials, and author/illustrator profiles. You can link to this valuable site from the Companion Website at www.prenhall.com/norton

Style

Authors have a wide choice of words to select from and numerous ways to arrange words to create plots, characters, and settings and to express themes. Many authors use words and sentences in creative ways. To evaluate style, read a piece of literature aloud; the sound of a story should appeal to your senses and be appropriate to the content of the story. The language should help develop the plot, bring the characters to life, and create a mood. For example, Ruth Krauss's *Bears* uses an appealing rhyming text, as bears are in such locations as on the stairs and under the chairs.

The Girl Who Loved Wild Horses, by Paul Goble, was a Children's Choice selection. The most frequent reason that children give for choosing this book is the author's use of language. Goble uses precise similes to evoke a landscape of cliffs and canyons, beautiful wild horses, and the high-spirited Indian girl who loves them. One stallion's eyes are "cold stars," and his floating mane and tail are "wispy clouds." During a storm, the horses gallop "faster and faster, pursued by thunder and lightning . . .

Superior rats consider the morality of their actions in a complex plot. (Illustration by Zena Bernstein from Mrs. Frisby and the Rats of NIMH *by Robert C. O'Brien. Copyright © 1971 by Robert C. O'Brien. [New York: Charles Scribner's Sons, 1971]. Reprinted with the permission of Atheneum Publishers.)*

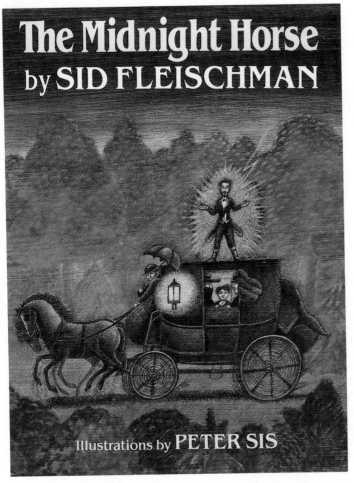

The Midnight Horse
by SID FLEISCHMAN

Illustrations by PETER SIS

Cover from The Midnight Horse *by Sid Fleischman. Text Copyright ©
1990 by Sid Fleischman, Inc. Illustrations copyright © 1990 by Peter Sis.
Reprinted by permission of Greenwillow Books, New York.*

Figurative language also helps develop characters, plot, and setting in Jan Hudson's *Sweetgrass*, a historical novel about the Blackfoot, set on the Canadian prairies. Early in the story, for example, sweet berries symbolize a young girl's happiness and hopes: "Promises hung shimmering in the future like glowing berries above sandy soil as we gathered our bags for the walk home" (p. 12). Later, the same girl's acceptance of a disillusioning reality is symbolized again by berries, which are then bitter.

Authors also may select words and sentence structures with rhythms evoking different moods. Armstrong Sperry creates two distinct moods for Mafatu in *Call It Courage*. As Mafatu goes through the jungle, he is preoccupied and moves leisurely. Sperry uses long sentences to set this mood: "His mind was not in this business at all: he was thinking about the rigging of his canoe, planning how he could strengthen it here, tighten it there" (p. 77). This dreamy preoccupation changes rapidly as Mafatu senses danger. Sperry's verbs become harsh and his sentences short and choppy as Mafatu's tension builds: "The boar charged. Over the ground it tore. Foam flew back from its tusks. The boy braced himself" (p. 78).

Kate DiCamillo, winner of the 2004 Newbery Medal for *The Tale of Despereaux*, uses an unusual style in which the narrator interjects comments by talking to the reader; this usually happens at the end of a chapter. For example, after the father declares that the mouse, Despereaux, cannot live, the narrator states, "But reader, he did live. This is his story" (p. 15). Or the narrator may intervene when readers should think about a word meaning, such as, "At least Lester had the decency to weep at his act of perfidy. Reader, do you know what 'perfidy' means? I have a feeling you do, based on the little scene that has just unfolded here. But you should look up the word in your dictionary, just to be sure" (p. 45).

DiCamillo reveals her purpose for writing in this style in an interview when she states that she uses it so the narrator can help readers navigate the complexity of the plot with its multiple story lines (Horning, 2004): "When Despereaux goes down to the dungeon both times, you as the reader don't feel abandoned because the narrator is there with you. It's kind of like somebody who's taking the journey with you but who knows a little bit more than you do, and implicitly says, 'It's going to be all right.' Kids seem to enjoy it" (p. 46).

Linda Sue Park also interjects the voice of the author in her *Project Mulberry*. At the end of each chapter, she inserts a dialogue between the main character, Julia Song, and herself as author, Ms. Park. Julia states: "If you're interested in learning about how this book was written—background information, mistakes, maybe even a secret or

like a brown flood across hills and through valleys" (p. 12, unnumbered).

Sid Fleischman uses many metaphors and similes to create the setting in *The Midnight Horse*, such as "It was raining bullfrogs. The coach lurched and swayed along the river road like a ship in rough seas. Inside clung three passengers like unlashed cargo. One was a blacksmith, another was a thief, and the third was an orphan boy named Touch" (p. 1).

Fleischman also uses similes to develop characters. For example, Touch, the orphan, is described as "skinny and bareheaded, with hair as curly as wood shavings" (p. 1), and "he chose to bring himself up, free as a sail to catch any chance wind that came along" (p. 29). Compare these similes with those for Otis Cratt, the thief, who is described as a long-armed man who looked "like a loosely wrapped mummy" (p. 3), was drawn to the blacksmith's billfold "like a compass needle to true north" (p. 4), and ran "like a wolf returning to its den" (p. 29). Fleischman uses similes that relate to the actions of each character within the story.

An In-Depth Analysis of Author's Use of Style in One Book

Gloria Whelan, the author of a National Book Award winner, *Homeless Bird,* develops a strong heroine who must overcome the traditional life dictated for her by India's tradition of arranged marriages and lower esteem for women. One of the strengths of Whelan's book is her use of figurative language through similes, metaphors, and symbolism; this is especially important in the references to birds and the title of the book. Notice in the following quote how Koly uses positive comparisons to describe her father's writing: "I watched as the spoken words were written down to become like caged birds, caught forever by my clever baap" (p. 2). In another place, the author uses a comparison with caged animals to reveal Koly's feelings of being trapped: "As I lay there in the strange house, I felt like a newly caged animal that rushes about looking for the open door that isn't there" (p. 24). The theme of the lonely and trapped feelings associated with a homeless bird is developed throughout the book to describe Koly's emotions until at the end of the book, she finds happiness at last and the homeless bird is allowed to fly to its home.

The author also uses very descriptive similes and metaphors to portray Koly's feelings as the time of her arranged marriage approaches. When she realizes that the family of her prospective bridegroom is more interested in her dowry than in her, the author uses a simile that foreshadows Koly's future. Now she thinks, "Was my marriage to be like the buying of a sack of yams in the marketplace?" (p. 13). After her marriage, the author again uses a reference to the marketplace as her mother-in-law holds her arm "as I have seen women in the marketplace holding a chicken's neck before they killed it" (p. 22).

When Koly realizes fully the disastrous consequences of her marriage, the author compares her feelings to those of a small fly caught in the web of a cunning spider. After Koly discovers that her husband has tuberculosis and will probably die, the author again describes her feelings through a vivid simile: "My hope slipped away like a frightened mouse into a dark hole" (p. 42). After Koly's husband dies, the author uses numerous comparisons to develop characterizations: Koly's mother-in-law is suspicious of books, and she treats them like scorpions that might sting. Later, her mother-in-law is compared to little red ants that swarm all over you and continually bite. When her mother-in-law deserts her in a town filled with begging widows, Koly feels like a kitten who has been dropped down a well.

The mood, developed through figurative language, changes after Koly discovers hope in a home for widows that is founded to help people like her gain respect and an ability to earn a living. Notice how the mood of the comparisons changes as Koly also discovers hope: When with relief she takes off her widow's sari, she feels like the snake that rids itself of its confining skin. Later, the author uses Koly's considerable ability with embroidery to show that if we use our talents, life can be like a beautiful tapestry.

The idea for a tapestry also becomes symbolic for the changes in Koly's life. In the following quote, the author uses the symbolism of quilting to show the changes in Koly's life as she progresses from sadness to happiness: "Once again I began to quilt for my dowry. My first quilt was stitched as I worried about my marriage to Hari, the second in sorrow at Hari's death. Chandra's quilt was stitched to celebrate her happiness. This time as I embroidered, I thought only of my own joy. 'When it's finished,' I wrote Raji, 'we'll be married.' In the middle of the quilt, spreading its branches in all directions, I put a tamarind tree to remind me of the tree in my maa and baap's courtyard and the tree in the home I was going to. . . . I stitched a rickshaw and Raji in the fields and me embroidering in the room Raji had made for me. Around the quilt for a border I put the Yamuna River, the reeds and herons beside it" (pp. 207–208).

In addition to the symbolism found in embroidery, the author uses references to Indian poetry and mythology to develop the story's style. As students of children's literature, you might consider the importance of the author's references to this poetry. In the author's note, the poet is identified as Rabindranath Tagor, who lived between 1861 and 1941 and was considered one of India's greatest poets. He also wrote plays and stories, composed music, and was an advocate for India's independence from Great Britain. In 1913, he received the Nobel Prize for literature.

---

two—you've come to the right place. Some people like that sort of thing. It's mostly conversations between me and the author, Ms. Park. We had a lot of discussions while she was writing. Here we go" (p. 12).

Both Nikki Grimes and Marilyn Nelson adopt a style that effectively uses poetry to develop characterization. In *Bronx Masquerade,* Grimes develops the power of poetry as African American students expand a poetry assignment and use poetry for self-evaluation. In this fictional story, the author gives a short introduction to a character who attends a Bronx high school, presents a poem that this student might have written as part of a poetry assignment, and then includes peer responses to the poetry. For example, following a section about Janelle Battle and a poem, "Inside," that she might have written, Grimes includes this reaction by Tyrone after he hears the poem: "You never think other folks got feelings. Like Janelle. I must've cracked wise a hundred times about her weight. Never even thought about it. It was just something I did for a laugh. Listen to her now, it doesn't seem all that funny" (p. 50). In *Carver: A Life in Poems,* Marilyn Nelson uses poetry to tell segments of George Washington Carver's life as an African American poet, painter, musician, botanist, and naturalist.

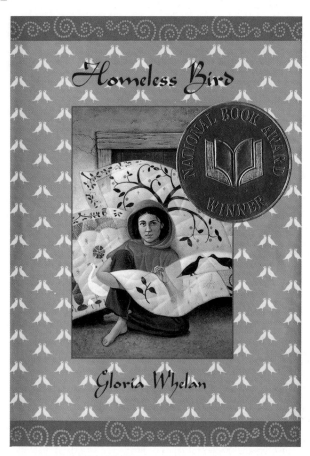

The author's style develops a strong heroine and reflects a vivid setting. (From Homeless Bird by Gloria Whelan. Copyright © 2000 by Gloria Whelan. Published by HarperCollins. Reprinted by permission of the publisher.

Cover from THE TALE OF DESPEREAUX. Text copyright © 2003 by Kate DiCamillo. Illustrations copyright © 2003 by Timothy Basil Ering. Reproduced by permission of the publisher Candlewick Press, Inc.

Chris Raschka's newly illustrated version of Dylan Thomas's *A Child's Christmas in Wales* provides readers and listeners with a way to enjoy Thomas's vivid language that captures his childhood memories. For example, notice how he uses all the senses in the introduction to his book:

> All the Christmases roll down toward the two-tongued sea, like a cold and headlong moon bundling down the sky that was our street; and they stop at the rim of the ice-edged, fish-freezing waves, and I plunge my hands in the snow and bring out whatever I can find. In goes my hand into that wool-white bell-tongued ball of holidays resting at the rim of the carol-singing sea, and out come Mrs. Prothero and the fireman. (unnumbered)

Karen Cushman's style in *Rodzina*, historical fiction set on an orphan train heading west in the 19th century, includes storytelling. The author uses this technique to relate prior experiences and to entertain the worried orphans. Notice in the following quote how the author portrays the historical period and relates a humorous story meant to entertain the orphans:

> I'll tell you about the time my papa won a pig in a raffle. He thought he'd lead it home on a string like a dog, but the pig,

being no dog, just grunted and sat down. Papa tried to carry it. The pig squealed and squirmed so much, Papa dropped it and had to chase after it through the muddy streets until he caught it again. Papa decided he and the pig would take a streetcar. . . . [To take the pig on the streetcar] he went into a bakery and got a flour sack. He put the pig in the sack, tied it up tight with a string, and waited for a trolley. He paid his nickel, sat down, and shoved the pig underneath his seat. The pig began to squeal, and to cover the noise, Papa began to sing. (p. 77)

The story continues as the children laugh and start to tell their own stories. Many of these stories are exaggerated, such as one about a mother who knitted socks in her sleep or a father who was so lazy that he hired someone to do his snoring. The stories, told in the language of the pioneers, help depict the historical period.

POINT OF VIEW

Different people may describe an incident in different terms: The feelings they experience, the details they mention, and their judgments about what occurred may vary because of their backgrounds, values, and perspectives.

An In-Depth Analysis of Point of View in One Book

The point of view developed in Richard Peck's 2001 Newbery Medal winner, *A Year Down Yonder,* enables readers to analyze the effectiveness of several of the purposes for establishing a point of view. Readers may also develop an understanding of the techniques the author used to make them care about the characters and what will happen in the story.

First, the author builds on his previous book, *A Long Way From Chicago,* which was a 1999 Newbery Honor book and a National Book Award finalist. In the first book, the author develops the characters of two children who during each summer of the Depression travel from Chicago to a small town in southern Illinois to visit their grandmother. Peck involves readers by making them care about the boy and the girl. Through the details he chooses to describe, we have a strong feeling about the backgrounds, values, and perspectives of the main characters, especially the feisty grandmother.

In *A Year Down Yonder,* Peck focuses on 15-year-old Mary Alice and her grandmother, who spend a year together during the recession of 1937. The book begins as Mary Alice is asked to live with her grandmother after her father loses his job. Let us begin our discussion of point of view with Lauber's (1991) concern that a major purpose of point of view is to make readers care about the characters and how the story will develop. A considerable portion of Peck's novel is told through Mary Alice's point of view. Most readers will immediately sympathize with her and understand her feelings when she thinks: "Oh, didn't I feel sorry for myself when the Wabash Railroad's Blue Bird train steamed into Grandma's town. . . . My trunk thumped out onto the platform from the baggage car ahead. There I stood at the end of the world with all I had left. Bootsie [her cat] and my radio" (p. 4). In the first chapter, Peck develops Mary Alice's point of view about the town as a place where everyone knows everything about you, about going to a school where she knows nobody and where the students do not want to make friends with a new girl they consider a rich city girl, about missing her brother who always stuck up for her, and about her view of her grandmother who has definite opinions of her own and is considered not only feisty but also difficult to get along with.

Tracing how Peck uses Mary Alice's changing point of view about her grandmother is an interesting way to show the importance of point of view. Through Mary Alice's point of view, we understand how she goes from someone who fears her grandmother and does not want to be with her to someone who understands and respects her grandmother's actions, beliefs, and values. Early in the novel, Peck describes Grandma's actions toward Halloween tricksters, her interpretation of being able to gather all the nuts on the ground in a neighbor's yard, and her attitude toward borrowing pumpkins from a neighbor's garden and then baking them into pies to donate to a school function. We discover through Mary Alice's point of view that "to Grandma, Halloween wasn't so much trick-or-treat as it was vittles and vengeance. Though she'd have called it justice" (p. 38).

Peck continues to develop a plot that focuses on Mary Alice's growing understanding of and respect for her feisty grandmother's actions, beliefs, and values. By the end of the book, we as readers care about both Mary Alice and her grandmother and what will happen to them. The closeness of the two characters is revealed when Mary Alice leaves school during a tornado alert because she wants to "come home" and make sure that her grandmother is all right. This closeness is again reinforced when Mary Alice realizes: "Sometimes I thought I was turning into her. I had to watch out not to talk like her. And I was to cook like her for all the years to come" (p. 123). This closeness is again highlighted through Mary Alice's first-person point of view when she declares, "'Grandma, I don't want to go back to Chicago. I want to stay here with you'" (p. 126).

By developing this relationship through Mary Alice's point of view, Peck helps us understand the changes that allow Mary Alice to progress from someone who thought she was at the end of the world with no one to care about her to a character who shows considerable love, respect, and admiration for her grandmother. Peck's last two pages are situated in the future when, years later, Mary Alice returns to her grandmother's house to be married.

As students of children's literature, you may wish to consider how Peck uses point of view to develop characterizations and plot in *A Long Way From Chicago.* Could you predict any of the happenings in *A Year Down Yonder?* Does Peck use any of the same techniques to develop point of view in *A Long Way From Chicago?*

Consequently, the same story may change drastically when told from another point of view. How would Peter Rabbit's story be different if Beatrix Potter had told it from the viewpoint of the mother rabbit? How would Armstrong Sperry's *Call It Courage* differ if told from the viewpoint of a Polynesian tribesman who loves the sea rather than from that of a boy who fears it? Author Patricia Lauber (1991) emphasizes the importance of point of view when she states, "The best stories have a point of view. They involve readers by making them care—care about the characters, whether people or animals, care about a town, care about an idea, and most of all, care about how it all comes out" (p. 46).

Avi's *Nothing But the Truth: A Documentary Novel* stimulates interesting discussions about point of view and fosters responses to literature. The book, a fictional novel written in documentary format, allows readers to interpret each incident, draw their own conclusions about the

the sequel to the Newbery Honor–winning A LONG WAY FROM CHICAGO

A Year Down Yonder
—RICHARD PECK

In this book, set in the depression in 1937, the author develops several strong points of view. (Cover Art by Steve Cieslawski, copyright © 2000 by Steve Cieslawski, cover art, from A Year Down Yonder, by Richard Peck. Used by permission of Dial Books for Young Readers, a division of Penguin Putnam, Inc.

truthfulness of the documents, and decide which characters are changed the most. As a consequence, readers gain insights into how emotions can define and distort the truth.

As children read this novel, they can analyze how Avi documents various reactions to and points of view on the same incident through the use of memos, letters, diary pages, discussions, phone and personal conversations, speeches, and telegrams. Avi also develops characters, conflicts, and various emotional responses through these same documents. Consequently, the book can be used to stimulate personal responses among readers.

Paul Fleischman's *Bull Run* is a story of the first battle of the Civil War. It is unique because Fleischman develops the story around the points of view of 16 people involved in the battle: Eight characters tell their story from the perspective of the Union, and eight others reflect the perspective of the Confederacy. Fleischman's characters range from generals to foot soldiers. Some of the characters tell their stories while waiting for men to return from

battle, and others are artists, photographers, and doctors who observe or play important parts in the battle. By the end of the book, all of the characters reflect the disillusionment and horror associated with this first battle.

Rosalyn Schanzer's *George vs. George: The American Revolution as Seen From Both Sides* is also unique because the author contrasts the point of view of George Washington and King George III. The author shows the different views about topics that led to the Revolutionary War, such as differing beliefs about taxation and forms of government. The text format that alternates between the two sides provides an excellent way for readers to contrast the views and the consequences of the differing viewpoints. The author's use of historical sources shows readers the importance of research when writing about controversy. Readers also discover that there are two sides to most issues.

The resolution of the conflict in Bruce Edward Hall's *Henry and the Kite Dragon* illustrates the importance of understanding another's perspective if conflict is to be eliminated. The story is set in Chinatown in the 1920s. Conflict arises when the boys from Little Italy throw rocks at Grandfather Chin's dragon kite. It is not until Henry and Grandfather discover that the boys from Little Italy raise homing pigeons and the dragon kite frightens the pigeons that the two sides reach a compromise: The kites will fly in the morning and the homing pigeons will fly in the afternoon. After reading this book, students hopefully understand the importance of identifying point of view when solving problems.

An author has several options when selecting point of view. A *first-person* point of view speaks through the "I" of one of the characters. An author who wishes to use a first-person narrative must decide which character's actions and feelings should influence the story. An *objective* point of view lets actions speak for themselves; the author describes only the characters' actions, and readers must infer the characters' thoughts and feelings.

An *omniscient* point of view tells the story in the third person ("they," "he," or "she"). The author is not restricted to the knowledge, experiences, and feelings of one person; the feelings and thoughts of all characters can be revealed. A *limited omniscient* point of view, however, concentrates on the experiences of one character but has the option to be all-knowing about other characters. A limited omniscient point of view may clarify conflicts and actions that would be less understandable in a first-person narrative.

Although no point of view is preferred for all children's literature, an author's choice can affect how much children of certain ages believe and enjoy a story. Contemporary realistic fiction for children age 8 and older often uses a first-person or a limited omniscient point of view that focuses on one child's experiences. Older children often empathize with one character if they have had similar experiences.

Consistency of point of view encourages readers to believe in a story. Such belief is especially crucial in modern fantasy, where readers are introduced to imaginary worlds, unusual characters, and magical incidents. A writer may describe a setting as if it were being viewed by a character only a few inches tall. To be believable, however, the story cannot stray from the viewpoint of the tiny character: The character's actions, the responses of others toward the character, and the setting must be consistent.

The Right Book for Each Child

Because of developmental stages, children have different personal and literary needs at different ages. Children in the same age group or at the same stage of development also have diverse interests and reading abilities that you must consider. Understanding why and what children read is necessary in order to help them select materials that stimulate their interests and enjoyment. Studies show that the most powerful determinants of adult reading are accessibility, readability, and interest; these factors also influence children's reading. If developing enjoyment through literature is a major objective of your reading program for children, you must make available many excellent books, consider children's reading levels, and know how to gain and use information about children's reading interests.

Accessibility

Literature must be readily accessible if children are to read at all. To determine which books interest them, learn about their heritage, recognize and appreciate good literature, and understand themselves and others through literature, children must have opportunities to read and listen to many books. As suggested, a literature program for children should include a wide variety of high-quality literature, both old and new. Unfortunately, as a result of various legislative mandates that vie for classroom time, children may not have enough opportunities to read literature in school.

Accessibility in the home is also important for developing interest in books. In a review of studies of children who read early and who do voluntary reading, Lesley Mandel Morrow (1991) discusses environments that foster children's early interest in books. She concludes that the environments must have a large supply of accessible books, plus parents who read to children regularly and who are responsive to their children's questions about books. In addition, these parents must serve as models by reading a great deal themselves. In a panel discussion on the importance of reading during the summer, educators interviewed by Eden Ross Lipson (2001) stressed the value of reading for pleasure during this time because children gain a love for reading and also return to school as better readers.

A survey by Susan Swanton (1984) showed that gifted students owned more books and used public libraries more than did other students. Fifty-five percent of the gifted students whom Swanton surveyed identified the public library as their major source of reading materials, as opposed to only 33% of the other students, most of whom identified the school library as their major source for books. Thirty-five percent of the gifted children owned more than 100 books. Only 19% of other students owned an equal number of books. Swanton made the following recommendations for cooperation between public libraries and schools:

1. Promote students' participation in summer reading programs that are sponsored by public libraries.
2. Inform parents about the value of reading aloud to children, of giving children their own books, and of parents as role models for developing readers.
3. Encourage school librarians to do book talks designed to entice children into reading.
4. Provide field trips to public libraries.
5. Advertise public library programs and services.
6. Make obtaining the first library card a special event.

These recommendations have not changed. Nilsen and Donelson (2001) stress many of the same activities to promote reading by young adults, especially the need to match books with readers, provide book talks, make displays to promote books, and develop programs to interest readers.

Readability

Readability is another major consideration in choosing literature for children: A book must conform to a child's reading level in order for the child to read independently. Children become frustrated when books contain too many words that they don't know. A child is able to read independently when he or she can pronounce about 98–100% of the words in a book and answer 90–100% of the comprehension questions asked about it. Reading abilities in any one age group or grade level range widely, so adults working with children must provide and be familiar with an equally wide range of literature. Many children have reading levels lower than their interest levels. Thus, they need many opportunities to listen to, and otherwise interact with, fine literature.

Books listed in the bibliographies at the end of the chapters in this book are identified by grade level and readability, although a book will not be applicable to every child in the grade indicated.

Interest and Reader Response

Interests also are extremely important when developing literature programs. Margaret Early (1992/1993) states, "Decades of experience have shown that children are more likely to develop as thoughtful readers when they are pursuing content that interests them" (p. 307). You can learn about children's interests from studies of children's interests and from interest inventories. You should consider information gained from each source.

Dianne Monson and Sam Sebesta (1991) reviewed the research on children's interests and reading preferences. They conclude, "The results of a good number of studies reveal agreement of types of subject matter that appeal to students of a particular age level and support the notion that interests change with age" (p. 667). However, although research on reader interest can provide some general ideas about what subjects and authors that children of certain ages, sexes, and reading abilities prefer, it is important not to develop stereotyped views about children's preferences. Without asking questions about interests, there is no way to learn, for example, that a fourth-grade boy is a Shakespeare buff, because research into children's interests does not indicate that a fourth grader should like Shakespeare's plays. Or consider a first-grade girl whose favorite subject is dinosaurs, which she can identify by name: Discovering this would be impossible without an interview, because research does not indicate that first-grade girls are interested in factual, scientific subjects. These two cases point to the need to discover children's interests before helping them select books. Informal conversation is one of the simplest ways to uncover children's interests: Ask a child to describe what he or she likes to do and read about. Usually, you should record the information when working with a number of children.

Reading Interests of Young Adults

Young adult literature refers to the books that have the widest appeal to older adolescents. These books are usually of interest to students from junior high through high school; the ages are usually from 12 to 18. Alleen Pace Nilsen and Kenneth Donelson (2001) provide the following characteristics of young adult literature that also match young adults' reading interests: (1) The literature is written from the viewpoint of young people; (2) the main characters frequently overcome problems without the help of their parents; (3) the story lines are fast paced; (4) the literature includes a variety of genres and subjects; (5) many different ethnic and cultural groups are represented in the literature; (6) the books are usually optimistic, and the characters make worthy accomplishments; and (7) the books deal with emotions and problems that are important to young adults.

A study of Canadian adolescent boys and literacy (O'Donnell, 2005) identified several common themes that are of interest to boys and keep them reading: personal interest, action, and success. Notice how these themes are related to many of the characteristics just listed. The authors of the study recommend that teachers use these themes to interest boys in their reading.

Other studies of favorite books identified by young people suggest the range of genres and subject matter that older readers select. For example, an interesting reading promotion and survey of best-loved books was conducted in the United Kingdom by the BBC. This large survey received almost a million votes and resulted in the identification of 200 top books selected by voters. The following books are the top 10 titles listed in order of their popularity (*Reading Today*, February/March 2004):

1. J. R. R. Tolkien's *The Lord of the Rings*
2. Jane Austen's *Pride and Prejudice*
3. Philip Pullman's *His Dark Materials*
4. Douglas Adams's *The Hitchhiker's Guide to the Galaxy*
5. J. K. Rowling's *Harry Potter and the Goblet of Fire*
6. Harper Lee's *To Kill a Mockingbird*
7. A. A. Milne's *Winnie-the-Pooh*
8. George Orwell's *Nineteen Eighty-Four*
9. C. S. Lewis's *The Lion, The Witch and the Wardrobe*
10. Charlotte Bronte's *Jane Eyre*

A number of these books are discussed in the various genre chapters of this textbook. The books also indicate that the selection criteria associated with conflict, plot, characterization, setting, theme, point of view, and author's style are just as important when selecting and evaluating books for young adults as they are when selecting literature for younger readers. The range of books also suggests that it is important to select books that match the interests of the readers.

The Child as Critic

Children are the ultimate critics of what they read, and you should consider their preferences when evaluating and selecting books to share with them. For the last few years, a joint project of the International Reading Association and the Children's Book Council has allowed approximately 10,000 children from around the United States to evaluate children's books published during a given year. Each year, their reactions are recorded, and a research team uses this information to compile a list called "Children's Choices" in the following categories: beginning independent reading, younger children, middle grades, older readers, informational books,

ISSUE The Content of Children's Books: Pleasure Versus the Message

"Read This, It's Good for You" is the title of a critical evaluation of books. Children's author Natalie Babbitt[1] discusses books that have messages about instructing children in the values of reading. She asks, "What's the use of writing a story for children about the value of reading when it will be read only by those children who are already readers?" (p. 23). She argues that in many books, there is no story. Instead, there is a message about the way life is supposed to be. In place of books whose main purpose is delivering a message, Babbitt wants children to learn to love reading by reading books such as *Millions of Cats, Make Way for Ducklings,* and *Where the Wild Things Are.*

Babbitt concludes, "Good stories are always a pleasure to read, and we like pleasure, regardless of our ages. The risk with message books, and message attitudes, is that children's books will get classed with broccoli and end up shoved under the mashed potatoes of television" (p. 24).

Author John Neufeld[2] provides a contrasting view for evaluating books in an article titled "Preaching to the Unconverted." He states, "I have often been criticized for being didactic. Sometimes that criticism has been warranted. At other times, I have felt that reviewers were unable to distinguish between information offered—valuable information for young people—and what they perceive as a Message. . . . I may direct a reader's attention to, or help focus it on, an idea or problem, but I can only induce readers to decide whether that story applies to their lives" (p. 36).

Neufeld believes that the stories that last are the ones that encourage readers to think about what they would do in similar circumstances. Neufeld concludes. "Stories about young people, for young people, are feasts authors serve their youthful readers. I like to think that some of what we offer sticks to their bones" (p. 36).

As you read and evaluate children's literature, consider the impact of the content to bring pleasure and increase joy in reading versus the importance of the message. Which is more important, pleasure or message? Which type of book do you remember from your own childhood? What was the impact of the book on you?

[1]Babbitt, Natalie. (1997, May 18). Read this, it's good for you. *The New York Times Book Review,* 23–24.
[2]Neufeld, John. (1996, July). Preaching to the unconverted. *School Library Journal, 42,* 36.

---

and poetry. This very useful annotated bibliography is published each year in the October issue of *The Reading Teacher,* and it can be obtained from the Children's Book Council, 67 Irving Place, New York, NY 10003.

A summary of children's reading choices by Christine Hall and Martin Coles (1999) provides an interesting list for discussion. They conclude:

1. Children read fewer books as they grow older.

2. In the Children's Reading Choices Survey, the average number of books read in the month prior to the survey was 2.52.

3. Children at ages 10, 12, and 14 are eclectic in their reading habits.

4. Strongly plotted adventure stories are popular at all ages.

5. Ten-year-olds choose to read poetry, but interest in poetry declines with age.

6. Most children respond positively when asked their views about reading.

7. Younger children spend more of their leisure time reading than do older children.

Children choose books from a wide variety of genres. Some are on lists of highly recommended children's books; others are not. Many educators and authorities on children's literature are concerned about the quality of books that children read. To improve their ability to make valid judgments about literature, children must experience good books and investigate and discuss the elements that make books memorable. Young children usually just enjoy and talk about books, but older ones can start to evaluate what they do and do not like about literature.

Ted Hipple and Amy B. Maupin (2001) discuss the importance of encouraging students to find the artistry in the details of a novel. They state, "It is a good teaching tactic to ask students to find selections—passages, individual sentences, even single words—they like. When enough students have responded positively to something, that something, even a required novel, may suddenly take on a new significance: peers like it, too" (p. 41). In addition, they recommend that students read Lois Lowry's *The Giver,* Karen Hesse's *Out of the Dust,* and Louis Sachar's *Holes* and compare and contrast the measures of quality in the books using plots, characters, themes, artistry in details, and emotional impact. These books are excellent choices because they have been identified as popular with readers as well as winners of the Newbery award.

One sixth-grade teacher encouraged her students to make literary judgments and to develop a list of criteria for selecting good literature (Norton, 1993); the motivation for this literature study began when the students wondered what favorite books their parents might have read when they were in the same grade. To answer this question, the children interviewed their parents and other adults, asking them which books and characters were their favorites. The children listed the books, characters, and number of people who recommended each book on a large chart.

Each student then read a book that a parent or another respected adult had enjoyed. (Many adults also reread these books.) Following their reading, the children discussed the book with the adult, considering what made or did not make the book memorable for them. At this time, the teacher introduced the concepts of plot, characterization, setting, theme, and style. The children searched the books they had read for examples of each

The 1998 Newbery winner, Karen Hesse's Out of the Dust, is the story of 14-year-old Billie Jo's pain, forgiveness, and growth after the accidental death of her mother in Depression-era Oklahoma. (Out of the Dust, by Karen Hesse. Copyright © 1997. New York, Scholastic Press. Reprinted by permission of Scholastic, Inc.)

CHART 3.2   Best books recommended by authors

Recommending Author	Recommended Book
David Almond	Kevin Henkes's *Lily's Purple Plastic Purse*
Eve Bunting	Katherine Paterson's *Bridge to Terabithia*
Susan Cooper	David Almond's *Skellig*
Nancy Farmer	Peggy Rathmann's *The Day the Babies Crawled Away*
Paul Fleischman	William Steig's *Abel's Island*
Karen Hesse	Richard Mosher's *Zazoo*
Patrice Kindi	Nancy Farmer's *The Ear, the Eye and the Arm*
E. L. Konigsburg	Judith Viorst's *The Tenth Good Thing About Barney*
Leonard Marcus	Don Brown's *Uncommon Traveler*
Marilyn Singer	Patrice Kindle's *Owl in Love*
Peter Sís	William Steig's *Doctor De Soto*
Ruth White	Lois Lowry's *The Giver*
Virginia Euwer Wolff	Brian Pinkney's *Max Found Two Sticks*

CHART 3.3   Examples from the Cuffie Awards

Award	Title
Picture Book	Sarah Stewart's *The Friend*
Novel	Gennifer Choldenko's *Al Capone Does My Shirts*
	Melina Marchetta's *Saving Francesca*
Vote to Win Newbery	Nancy Farmer's *The Sea of Trolls*
Vote to Win Caldecott	Sarah Stewart's *The Friend*
Most Memorable Character	Katherine Hannigan's *Ida B . . . and Her Plans to Maximize Fun, Avoid Disaster, and (Possibly) Save the World*
Funniest Book	Jon Scieszka's *Science Verse*
Best Nonfiction	Phillip Hoose's *The Race to Save the Lord God Bird*
Best Anthology	Helen Ward's *Unwitting Wisdom: An Anthology of Aesop's Fables*

element. Finally, they listed questions to ask themselves when evaluating a book; see the Evaluation Criteria at the beginning of the chapter.

A review of 14 questions shows how closely they correspond to the criteria that should be used in evaluating plot, characterization, setting, theme, and style.

There are numerous lists of "Best Books" that can be used to motivate students to read, critically evaluate, and select their own lists of best books. For example, Rick Margolis (2004) asked well-known authors of children's literature to select current books that they believe will be classics in future years; Chart 3.2 lists his findings. Ask students to read some of those books and discuss how they would rate them. Students also can develop their own lists of books and discuss why they chose them.

Another listing of books that makes interesting sources for students to discuss and evaluate is the "Off the Cuff" awards, in which children's booksellers vote for their picks of books in various categories. This listing is usually printed in *Publishers Weekly*. For example, Chart 3.3 pre-

sents a few of those listed for "The 2004 Cuffies," from the January 10, 2005, issue. (These books are all discussed in the various genre chapters in this text.)

When children are encouraged to share, discuss, and evaluate books and are given opportunities to do so, they are able to expand their reading enjoyment and to select worthwhile stories and characters. Sharing and discussion can take place in the library, in the classroom, or at home.

Teaching With Literary Elements

Whether developing a literature program, developing literature-based reading instruction, or sharing literature on a one-to-one basis, remember the dual roles of literature: providing enjoyment and developing understanding. If you want children to respond to, love, and appreciate literature, provide them with a varied selection of fine literature and give them many opportunities to read, listen to, share, discuss, and respond to literature.

Involving Children in Plot

Creative drama interpretations based on story texts help children expand their imaginations, stimulate their feelings, enhance their language, and clarify their concepts. Through the playmaking process, children discover that plot provides a framework, that there is a beginning in which the conflict is introduced, a middle that moves the action toward a climax, and an end with a resolution to the conflict.

Nursery rhymes are excellent for introducing both younger and older children to the concept that a story has several parts—a beginning, a middle, and an end. The simple plots in many nursery rhymes make them ideal for this purpose. For example, "Humpty Dumpty" contains three definite actions that cannot be interchanged and still retain a logical sequence: (1) a beginning—"Humpty Dumpty sat on a wall," (2) a middle—"Humpty Dumpty had a great fall," and (3) an end—"All the king's horses and all the king's men couldn't put Humpty Dumpty together again." Children can listen to the rhyme, identify the actions, discuss the reasons for the order, and finally act out each part. Encourage them to extend their part by adding dialogue or characters to the beginning, middle, or ending incident. Other nursery rhymes illustrating sequential plots include "Jack and Jill," "Pat-a-Cake, Pat-a-Cake, Baker's Man," and "Rock-a-Bye Baby."

After children understand the importance of plot structure in nursery rhymes, proceed to folktales, such as "Three Billy Goats Gruff," in which there also is a definite and logical sequence of events. Divide the children according to the beginning incidents, middle incidents, and ending incidents. After each group practices its part, put the groups together into a logical whole. To help children learn the importance of order, have them rearrange the incidents: They will discover that if the ending incidents are acted out first, the story is over and there is no rising action or increasing conflict.

Diagramming plot structures is another activity that helps children appreciate and understand that many stories follow a structure in which the characters and the problems are introduced at the beginning of the story, the conflict increases until a climax or turning point is reached, and then the conflict ends. Have children listen to or read stories and then discuss and identify the

The rhyme "Humpty Dumpty" contains three definite actions that cannot be interchanged and still retain a logical sequence. (From Humpty Dumpty.)

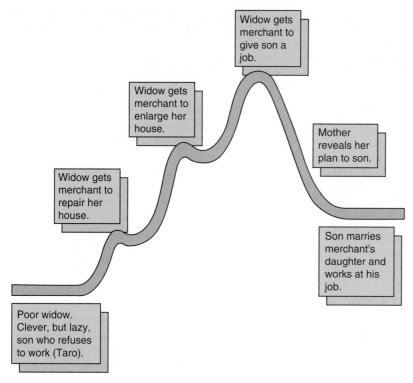

Widow gets merchant to give son a job.

Widow gets merchant to enlarge her house.

Mother reveals her plan to son.

Widow gets merchant to repair her house.

Son marries merchant's daughter and works at his job.

Poor widow. Clever, but lazy, son who refuses to work (Taro).

FIGURE 3.1   Plot diagram for Dianne Snyder's *The Boy of the Three-Year Nap*

important incidents. For example, the important incidents in Dianne Snyder's *The Boy of the Three-Year Nap* are placed on the plot diagram in Figure 3.1.

Stories in which the conflict results because characters must overcome problems within themselves can also be placed on plot diagrams. Caron Lee Cohen (1985) identifies four major components in the development of person-against-self conflicts: (1) problem, (2) struggle, (3) self-realization, and (4) achievement of peace or truth. Literature selections such as Marion Dane Bauer's *On My Honor,* in which the author develops struggles within the main characters, are good for this type of discussion and plot diagramming. In this plot structure, identify (1) the problem and the characters, (2) the incidents that reflect increasing struggle with self, (3) the point of self-realization, and (4) the point at which the main character attains peace or truth. Because person-against-self conflicts are frequently complex, lead students in identifying significant incidents and ask them to provide support for these major struggles.

For example, in *On My Honor,* the problem results for Bauer's character Joel because he betrays his parents' trust and swims with his friend in a treacherous river. The struggle continues as Joel feels increasing guilt, tries not to accept his friend's disappearance and probable death, and blames his father for allowing the two boys to go on a bike ride in the first place. Self-realization begins when Joel admits that Tony drowned and realizes that his father is not the cause of his problem: "But even as he slammed

through the door and ran up the stairs to his room, he knew. It wasn't his father he hated. It wasn't his father at all. He was the one. . . . Tony died because of him" (p. 81).

Peace and truth begin, although the seriousness of the problem does not allow complete resolution. After Joel sobbingly tells his father the whole truth, he feels "tired, exhausted, but tinglingly aware" (p. 89). Even though there cannot be a total resolution of the conflict, because Joel's father cannot give him the reassurance he desires or take away his pain, Joel forgives his father and asks him to stay in the room until he (Joel) falls asleep.

Students can compare Bauer's person-against-self conflict with that in Paula Fox's *One-Eyed Cat* (see Chapter 9). Additional person-against-self conflicts for older students include Cynthia Rylant's *A Fine White Dust,* a traumatic story in which a 13-year-old boy becomes involved with an unscrupulous traveling evangelist and struggles to understand his own beliefs; Karen Hesse's *Out of the Dust,* a story in which the protagonist blames herself and her father for her mother's accidental death; and Audrey Couloumbis's *Getting Near to Baby,* in which the protagonist must overcome her grief and gain insights into the healing process following the death of the baby in the family.

Although many of the books with person-against-self conflicts are written for older students, several books can be used with younger students. For example, Arthur Yorinks's *Hey, Al* is a picture storybook in which Al and his dog, Eddie, overcome dissatisfaction and decide that "Paradise lost is sometimes Heaven found" (p. 27, unnumbered). Evaline Ness's *Sam, Bangs & Moonshine* is a picture storybook in which the main character faces the consequences of her lies.

Involving Children in Characterization

Authors of books with notable characters develop three-dimensional personalities that allow readers to gain insights into those characters' strengths, weaknesses, pasts, hopes, and fears. You can help students understand how authors develop characters by discussing books in which the authors use several characterization techniques. You can also help students understand the often complex nature of inferencing about characters by modeling activities in which you analyze evidence from the text and speculate about the characters.

Characterization Techniques

Have students search for examples in which an author reveals a character through such techniques as narration, thoughts, actions, and dialogue. Have them list examples in which each of these techniques is used and identify what each example reveals. Have the students summarize what they know about a specific character and discuss whether the characterization is flat or rounded.

A group of students led by Diana Vrooman (1989) used this approach to identify and discuss the characterization of Sarah in Patricia MacLachlan's *Sarah, Plain and Tall*. First, Vrooman introduced the story and reviewed the techniques that authors may use to develop characters. Second, she listed on the board the techniques that MacLachlan uses to reveal Sarah's character in *Sarah, Plain and Tall*. Third, she read the first chapter aloud and asked students to identify the examples in the chapter and to stipulate what they learned about Sarah from those examples. Fourth, she asked the students to complete the search for other examples of Sarah's characterization in the remaining chapters. Finally, she asked the students to summarize Sarah's characterization and to defend whether they believed that Sarah was a rounded character. Chart 3.4 shows a few of the characterizations and proofs for Sarah.

The students concluded that Sarah was a fully developed, three-dimensional character. In addition, they discovered the techniques that authors use to develop such well-rounded characters. The same book can be used to analyze the characterization of the young boy, Caleb, or the young girl, Anna.

Modeling Inferencing

Some of MacLachlan's characterizations in *Sarah, Plain and Tall* are stated, but others are implied. Students frequently need much assistance in analyzing implied characterizations. Researchers such as Laura Roehler and Gerald Duffy (1984) and Christine Gordon (1985) have developed modeling approaches that place an adult in an active role with students and that show the adult's thought processing to the students. Modeling is one of the most effective ways to improve comprehension (Dole, Duffy, Roehler, & Pearson, 1991) and to help students understand characterization (Norton, 1992). The following activity demonstrates the modeling process with Patricia MacLachlan's *Sarah, Plain and Tall*.

Requirements for Effective Reasoning. Effective inferencing requires readers to go beyond the information that an author provides in a text. Readers must use clues from the text to hypothesize about a character's emotions, beliefs, actions, hopes, and fears. They must also be aware that authors develop characters through narration, a character's thoughts or the thoughts of others about the character, the character's actions, and the dialogue between the characters.

An Introduction to Inferencing. Review characterization by asking students to identify how authors develop three-dimensional, believable characters; share examples of each technique of characterization as part of this review. Also explain that students will listen as you ask a question, answer the question, provide evidence from the story that supports the answer, and share the reasoning process you used to reach the answer. Explain that after students have listened to you proceed through the sequence, they will use the same process to answer questions, identify evidence, and explore their own reasoning processes. As part of this introduction, discuss the meanings of *evidence* and *reasoning*. Encourage the students to identify evidence about a character in the literature and to share how to use this evidence.

The Importance of Inferencing. Ask students to explain why it is important to be able to make inferences

---

CHART 3.4 Revealing characterization in Patricia MacLachlan's *Sarah, Plain and Tall*

Author's Technique	Characterization	Evidence
Narration	Plain and tall	"She was plain and tall." (p. 19)
	Loved by animals	"The dogs loved Sarah first." (p. 22)
	Loved animals	"The sheep made Sarah smile. . . . She talked to them." (p. 28)
	Intelligent	"Sarah was quick to learn." (p. 52)
Thoughts about the character	Loved the sea	Anna thought: "Sarah loved the sea, I could tell." (p. 12)
	Homesick	Anna thought: "Sarah was not smiling. Sarah was already lonely." (p. 20)
The character's actions	Adventurous	Sarah answers an advertisement asking for a wife. (p. 9)
	Sense of humor	When Sarah finished describing seals, she barked like one. (p. 27)
	Hardworking	Sarah learned how to plow the fields. (p. 33)
Dialogue	Strong	"I am strong and I work hard." (p. 9)
	Independent	Papa tells Sarah that the cat will be good in the barn. Sarah tells Papa that the cat will be good in the house. (p. 19)
	Confident	"I am fast and I am good." (p. 46)

about characters. Encourage them to discuss how inferencing characterizations makes a story more exciting, enjoyable, and believable.

An Introduction to the Story.   There are two important settings in *Sarah, Plain and Tall*: (1) the pioneer setting in one of the prairie states and (2) the pioneer setting in Maine. To identify students' understandings of these locations and time periods, ask them to pretend that they are sitting on the front porch of a cabin in one of the prairie states in the 1800s, to look away from the cabin, and to describe what they see; make sure that they describe prairie grass, wheat fields, few trees, a dirt road, and flat or gently rolling land. Ask them to tell which colors they see. Then ask them to turn around and describe what they see through the open door of the cabin; make sure that they describe a small space, a fireplace, and characteristic furnishings, such as wooden chairs and a wooden table.

The Maine setting is also important to this story because Sarah's conflict results from love of a very different setting. Ask the students to pretend that they are sitting on the coast of Maine, to look out at the ocean, and to describe what they see. Next, have them turn toward the land and describe the setting. Discuss with students the differences between the prairie and the Maine coast and consider whether the differences in these settings could cause conflicts for a character.

The First Modeling Example.   Read orally from the beginning of the book through the line, "That was the worst thing about Caleb," on page 5. Ask, "What was Anna's attitude toward her brother, Caleb, when he was a baby?" Answer, "Anna disliked her brother a great deal. We might even say she hated him." Provide the evidence. Say, "Anna thinks that Caleb is homely, plain, and horrid smelling. She associates Caleb with her mother's death." Provide the reasoning you used to reach the answer. For example, "The words Anna uses, especially *horrid*, are often associated with things that we do not like. I know from the reference to the happy home that Anna loved her mother. When she says that her mother's death was the worst thing about Caleb, I believe that she blamed him for the death."

The Second Modeling Example.   At this point, verify that the students understand the procedure. If they do not, continue by completely modeling another example. If the students understand the process, let them join the discussion by providing an answer, the evidence, and the reasoning. It is advisable to have the students jot down brief answers to the questions, evidence, and reasoning; these notes will increase the quality of the discussion that follows each question.

The next logical discussion point occurs at the bottom of page 5. Read through the line, "And Papa didn't sing." Ask students the question, "What is Anna really telling us about her inner feelings?" They should provide answers similar to this one: "She believes that nothing can replace her lost mother and that the home will not be happy again." Ask the students to provide evidence, such as, "The author tells us that the relatives could not fill the house. The days are compared to long, dark, winter days. The author states that Papa did not sing." Next, ask them to provide reasoning, such as, "The author created a very sad mood. We see a house filled with relatives that do not matter to Anna. I know what long, dark, winter days are like. I can visualize a house without singing. I think Anna is very unhappy, and it may take her a long time to get over her loss."

Continue this process, having the students discuss the many instances of implied characterization in the book. The letters Sarah writes to Mr. Wheaton (p. 9), to Anna (pp. 9–10), and to Caleb (p. 11) are especially good for inferencing about the characters because students need to infer what was in the letters written by Anna and Caleb. To help the students infer the contents of those letters, ask them to write the letters themselves.

Longer stories, such as *Sarah, Plain and Tall*, lend themselves to discussions according to chapters. Students can read and discuss several chapters each day. After each session, however, ask the students to summarize what they know about Sarah, Anna, Caleb, and Papa. Ask them, "What do you want to know about these characters?"

Involving Children in Setting

Believable settings place readers in geographic locations and time periods that they can see, hear, and even feel. In literature, authors use settings for four purposes: (1) creating appropriate moods, (2) developing antagonists, (3) developing historical and geographical backgrounds, and (4) suggesting symbolic interpretations.

Settings That Create Moods

Authors use settings to create moods. Through word choices and the visual pictures the words produce, authors create moods that range from humorous and happy to frightening and foreboding. Asking students to tell their reactions to words and illustrations and comparing words and illustrations in a text help them understand and evaluate the appropriateness of a mood. For example, students can respond to the frightening, eerie mood created by Marcia Brown's illustrations for Blaise Cendrars's poem *Shadow* and examine the influence in it of words, such as *prowler*, and descriptions, such as "teeming like snakes." When a house sits precariously under a wave, as in Shelley Jackson's *The Old Woman and the Wave*, readers can respond to the frightening mood or the more symbolic fear of the unknown.

Teachers can use illustrated texts, such as Karen Ackerman's *Song and Dance Man*, to show students very different moods. Stephen Gammell's illustrations create a warm, happy mood as children watch their beloved grandfather re-create the joyful days of his youth. The transition from a common, dreary, crowded attic to an uncommon experience is enhanced by the artist's drawing of a brightly colored, shadowy shape.

Additional literature selections that develop warm, happy moods through both illustrations and text are Cynthia Rylant's *When I Was Young in the Mountains*, Kate Banks's *And If the Moon Could Talk*, Margaret Wild's *Our Granny*, and Alexandra Day's *Frank and Ernest Play Ball*. Funny, even absurd, moods are created in both the text and illustrations of Doreen Cronin's *Click, Clack, Moo: Cows That Type*, Simms Taback's *There Was an Old Lady Who Swallowed a Fly*, Patricia Polacco's *Meteor!*, Susan Meddaugh's *Martha Speaks*, Kevin Henkes's *Owen*, and Angela Johnson's *Julius*.

Authors of fantasy frequently prepare their readers for the fantastical experiences to come by creating settings and moods in which fantasy seems possible. Sharing and discussing introductions to fantasies allow students to appreciate and understand the techniques that authors use to prepare them for both fantasy and conflict. For example, read and discuss the following introduction to Natalie Babbitt's *Tuck Everlasting*:

> The road that led to Treegap had been trod out long before by a herd of cows who were, to say the least, relaxed. It wandered along in curves and easy angles, swayed off and up in a pleasant tangent to the top of a small hill, ambled down again between fringes of bee-hung clover, and then cut sidewise across a meadow. Here its edges blurred. It widened and seemed to pause, suggesting tranquil bovine picnics: slow chewing and thoughtful contemplation of the infinite. And then it went on again and came at last to the wood. But on reaching the shadows of the first trees, it veered sharply, swung out in a wide arc as if, for the first time, it had reason to think where it was going, and passed around.
>
> On the other side of the wood, the sense of easiness dissolved. The road no longer belonged to the cows. It became, instead, and rather abruptly, the property of people. And all at once the sun was uncomfortably hot, the dust oppressive, and the meager grass along its edges somewhat ragged and forlorn. On the left stood the first house, a square and solid cottage with a touch-me-not appearance, surrounded by grass cut painfully to the quick and enclosed by a capable iron fence some four feet high which clearly said, "Move on—we don't want you here." So the road went humbly by and made its way, past cottages more and more frequent but less and less forbidding, into the village. But the village doesn't matter, except for the jailhouse and the gallows. The first house only is important; the first house, the road, and the wood. (pp. 5–6)

After you read this introduction, to enhance personal response, have the students consider the effect of the contrasts Babbitt used, the influence of personification, and the impact of wording such as "tranquil bovine picnics," "veered sharply," "touch-me-not," and "grass cut painfully to the quick." Have the students speculate about the changing mood in the introduction and the type of story that might follow. Of course, have them read the story to verify their predictions.

Settings That Develop Antagonists

Authors of both historical fiction and contemporary adventure stories frequently develop plots in which nature or society is the antagonist. Vivid descriptions of either nature or society are essential if readers are to understand why and how the setting has created conflicts or even life-and-death perils.

Sharing and discussing quotations will help students identify, respond to, and appreciate vivid descriptions. Kevin Crossley-Holland's *Storm* is written for young readers. The author, however, vividly describes a frightening storm and a girl who fears the storm and faces her fears of a ghostly creature who supposedly roams the English marshlands. Crossley-Holland uses personification and metaphor to develop believable settings. For example, he says that the storm "whistled between its salty lips and gnashed its sharp teeth" (p. 14) and "gave a shriek" (p. 27). Other elements in nature respond: The moon "seemed to be speeding behind grey lumpy clouds, running away from something that was chasing it" (p. 23). The young girl responds in ways that suggest fear: "Annie felt a cold finger slowly moving from the base of her spine up to her neck and then spread out across her shoulders" (p. 12), and she swayed in the saddle as she "thought she could bear it no longer—the furious gallop, the gallop of the storm, the storm of her own fears" (p. 35). By the end of the story, Annie has faced her fears of both the storm and the ghost.

It is more difficult for students to understand the setting if society, and not nature, causes the conflict because they must understand both the larger societal attitudes and the reasons that the characters are in conflict with those attitudes. Thematic studies that allow students to read from several genres are usually best for developing understanding about complex subjects, such as anti-Semitism or slavery. In thematic studies, students can use nonfictional sources to authenticate the settings in historical fiction. For example, a series of books about the Holocaust might include nonfiction, biography, historical fiction, and even time-warp fantasy. Beginning with Barbara Rogasky's nonfictional *Smoke and Ashes: The Story of the Holocaust*, students can discover the historical background of the time period, the roots of anti-Semitism, the development of ghettos and concentration camps, and the tragic consequences. Have the students read Milton Meltzer's nonfictional *Rescue: The Story of How Gentiles Saved Jews in the Holocaust* to provide historical background about heroic people who risked their own lives to save other people, and Michael Leapman's *Witnesses to War: Eight True-Life Stories of Nazi Persecution*. Next, have the students read Albert Marrin's biographical text, *Hitler*. Pages 17–20 are especially revealing: In them, Marrin discusses the roots of Hitler's anti-Semitism and his developing hatred. For example:

> Once Adolph began to hate, it became harder and harder to stop hating. From the age of nineteen, his hatred deepened, grew stronger, until it passed the bounds of sanity. He had only to hear Jews mentioned, to see them or think he saw them, to lose self-control. . . . One day, he vowed, he'd get even with them. They'd pay, every last one of them, for the humiliation they'd caused him. (p. 20)

Have the students read Uri Orlev's historical fiction, *The Island on Bird Street* and *The Man From the Other Side*; Lois Lowry's historical fiction about the Danish resistance, *Number the Stars*; and Jane Yolen's time-warp story, *The Devil's Arithmetic*. Then have the students use the background information from the first three books to evaluate the authenticity of the settings that cause so much conflict in the fictional books.

Settings That Develop Historical and Geographical Backgrounds

Settings in historical fiction and biography should be so integral to the story and so carefully developed that readers can imagine the sights, sounds, and even smells of the environment. For example, have groups of students choose one of the settings developed in Elizabeth George Speare's *The Sign of the Beaver*, such as the log cabin, the wilderness, or the Penobscot village. Lead them to discover as much information as possible about the sights, sounds, and even tastes associated with that environment, and have them identify and analyze quotations that describe the setting.

Students enjoy creating maps and illustrations depicting well-defined settings. Have students use details from historical fiction or fantasy to draw maps, homes, or other settings. Carefully crafted fantasy worlds provide evidence for map locations and show the importance of settings in creating believable worlds. For example, after students read J. R. R. Tolkien's *The Hobbit*, ask them to draw maps of Middle Earth. C. S. Lewis's *The Lion, the Witch and the Wardrobe* includes detailed information about Narnia. Likewise, Lewis Carroll's *Alice's Adventures in Wonderland* provides descriptions of Wonderland.

After students have read literature with well-developed settings, divide the class into groups and ask each group to draw a map so that visitors to the land would be able to travel through it. Ask the students to defend their map locations by providing evidence from the literature. After the maps are completed, ask each group to share its map with the larger group and to defend why it placed landmarks in specific places.

Two sources provide interesting stimulation for these drawing tasks. Alberto Manguel and Gianni Guadalupi's *The Dictionary of Imaginary Places* (2000) includes maps and descriptions of numerous fantasy worlds. Rosalind Ashe and Lisa Tuttle's *Children's Literary Houses: Famous Dwellings in Children's Fiction* (1984) includes interpreta-

tions of the homes found in Frances Hodgson Burnett's *The Secret Garden*, T. H. White's *The Sword in the Stone*, Esther Forbes's *Johnny Tremain*, and Louisa May Alcott's *Little Women*.

Settings That Are Symbolic

The easiest symbolic setting for students to understand is probably the once-upon-a-time setting found in folktales; readers know that "once upon a time" means much more than long ago. When they close their eyes, they often visualize deep woods or majestic castles, where enchantment, magic, and heroic adventures are expected. Folktale settings are excellent introductions to symbolic settings.

Authors of other types of literature also use symbolic settings to develop understanding of plots, characters, and themes. Frances Hodgson Burnett's *The Secret Garden* is one of the best literature selections for showing symbolic settings. Students can trace parallel changes that take place in the garden and in the people living in Misselthwaite Manor. For example, the story begins in a cold, dreary mansion surrounded by gardens that are dormant from winter. The characters are equally unresponsive. Mary is "the most disagreeable-looking child ever seen. . . . She had a little thin face and a little thin body, thin light hair and a sour expression" (p. 1). Colin is an unpleasant invalid, Mr. Craven is still in mourning for his dead wife, and Colin and his father are estranged. However, the setting and the people begin to change after Mary finds the door to the secret garden. Finding the key to the garden is the symbolic turning point, after which the characters and the garden are slowly nurtured back to both physical and emotional health.

As students trace the parallel changes in the garden and in the people, they can ask themselves the following questions: Why does the author focus attention on a garden that has been locked and mostly uncared for for 10 years? What is the significance of a key that opens a door? How do the people change, and what happens to the garden? Why does the author draw parallels between nurturing a garden and healing people both physically and emotionally? Does the garden meet Perrine's requirements for symbolism in literature? Is the garden a good symbolic setting for both characterization and plot development? Why or why not?

Students also can explore the symbolism of gardens in Philippa Pearce's *Tom's Midnight Garden* and other books.

Involving Children in Theme

Students need many opportunities to read and discuss literature in order to identify controlling ideas or central concepts in stories. Themes are difficult because they frequently are implied rather than directly stated. Students learn about themes, however, by studying the actions of characters, analyzing the central conflict, and considering the outcome of a story.

When looking for theme, it is important to consider how the main character changes in the story, what conflicts are found in the story, what actions are rewarded or punished, and what the main character has learned as a result. Even the title may provide clues to the theme.

The following sequence of events develops an understanding of theme in Ann Grifalconi's *Darkness and the Butterfly*. First, explain to the students that theme is the controlling idea or central concept in a story. Themes often reveal important beliefs about life, and a story may contain more than one theme. When searching for theme, ask, "What is the author trying to tell us that would make a difference in our lives?" Review some of the ways in which authors reveal themes, such as through conflict, the characters' actions, the characters' thoughts, the outcome of the story, the actions that are rewarded or punished, and narrative. In addition, the title and illustrations may provide clues.

Next, read *Darkness and the Butterfly* aloud. Ask the students, "What is the author trying to tell us that would make a difference in our lives?" They will probably identify two important themes: (1) It is all right to have fears—we all may have fears that cause us problems—and (2) we can and must overcome our fears.

After the students have identified the themes, read them the story a second time. This time, have them search for proof that the author is developing these themes. Their discussion and evidence probably will include some of the following examples:

1. It is all right to have fears; we all may have fears that cause us problems.

    a. The illustrations show contrasts between the beauty of the world in the day, which is without fear, and the monsters that surface in Osa's mind at night.

    b. The actions of the mother show that she is understanding. She even gives beads to help Osa feel less fearful.

    c. The actions of Osa show that she is a normal child during the day but a fearful child at night.

    d. The wise woman tells Osa that she was once afraid, "'specially at night!"

2. We can and must overcome our fears.

    a. The author tells the story of the yellow butterfly, the smallest of the small, as it flies into the darkness.

    b. The butterfly story is based on an important African proverb, "Darkness pursues the butterfly."

    c. The wise woman tells Osa. "You will find your own way."

    d. The wise woman compares finding your way to the wings of the butterfly.

    e. The dream sequence reveals the beauties of the night.

    f. The actions of the butterfly show that it is not afraid.

    g. Osa reveals her self-realization: "I can go by myself. I'm not afraid anymore."

    h. The author states that Osa, the smallest of the small, "found the way to carry her own light through the darkness."

    i. The butterfly symbolizes that the smallest, most fragile being in nature can light up the darkness, trust the night, and not be afraid.

    j. The title of the book is *Darkness and the Butterfly*.

Folktales, with their easily identifiable conflicts and characterizations, are excellent for developing understanding of theme. For example, when searching for themes in John Steptoe's *Mufaro's Beautiful Daughters*, students discover that greed and selfishness are harmful and that kindness and generosity are beneficial.

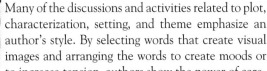

Involving Children in Style

Many of the discussions and activities related to plot, characterization, setting, and theme emphasize an author's style. By selecting words that create visual images and arranging the words to create moods or to increase tension, authors show the power of carefully chosen words and sentence structures. When reading carefully crafted stories, you may not even notice the techniques that authors use. When you read aloud a carefully crafted story and one that is not so well developed, however, the differences become obvious. This section looks at developing students' appreciation for personification through narrative stories and for pleasing style.

Personification

Many of the most enjoyable books read to and by younger children develop characterizations through personification. This is probably so believable because children tend to give human characteristics to their pets and toys. Personification is an excellent introduction to style for younger children because the texts that include personification of objects and animals often are reinforced through illustrations that also personify the subjects.

Virginia Lee Burton's *The Little House* provides an enjoyable introduction to personification. As you read aloud appropriate pages, ask students: What pronoun is used when the author talks about the house? What actions can the house do that are similar to your actions? What feelings does the house express that are similar to your feelings? What causes the house to have each of these feelings? When have you had similar feelings? How do the illustrations help you understand the house's feelings and character? After the students have discussed the answers to these questions, share with them that the author is giving the house human feelings and behaviors through both the text and the illustrations.

Extend this understanding of personification in *The Little House* by asking the students to use pantomime or creative drama to act out the feelings expressed in the book. For example, have them listen to the text being read and pantomime the feelings expressed by the house. Have them create conversations that might occur between the house and her country or city neighbors. Have them tell the story from the point of view of one of the other objects found in the story.

Use similar discussions with books in which toys are personified, such as Anthony Browne's *Gorilla* and Margery Williams's *The Velveteen Rabbit*. Books in which animals are personified include Alexandra Day's *Frank and Ernest on the Road*, Diana Engel's *Josephina Hates Her Name*, and Lillian Hoban's *Arthur's Great Big Valentine*.

Pleasing Style

Jette Morache (1987) recommends having older students collect and share quotations from literature that they find pleasing or that support other literary elements, such as characterization, setting, and theme. Morache recommends having students work in groups to find quotes that illustrate a certain technique, to compare and discuss the quotes chosen by their group and other groups, to compile a page of quotes that they find particularly appealing, and to develop a list of qualities that make a "quotable quote." This type of activity is appropriate for developing appreciation for any of the literary elements discussed in this chapter. Have students find quotes to support characterization, setting, and theme.

Quotes also can emphasize specific literary techniques, such as personification, symbolism, simile, or metaphor. Older students might read Henry Wadsworth Longfellow's "Hiawatha" and Jamake Highwater's *Anpao: An American Indian Odyssey* to find examples of personification in nature. Jan Hudson's *Sweetgrass* is filled with symbolism, similes, and metaphors. Cynthia Voigt's *Dicey's Song* has many references to music, a sailboat, and a tree as symbols.

Students can also search books to find introductory paragraphs in which the author's style heightens their interest and makes them want to know more about the character and the story. For example, Tomie dePaola provides a vivid setting through words and references to known literature in *26 Fairmount Avenue*.

Webbing the Literary Elements

Webbing is an excellent way to help children understand important characteristics of a story (Norton, 1992). Webbing also helps students increase their appreciation of literature and improve their reading and writing competencies. In addition, webbing helps students understand the interrelationships among the literary elements. Prior to the webbing experience, introduce the literary elements of setting, characterization, conflicts (plot), and themes by including many of the activities previously discussed in this chapter. To introduce the idea of webbing literary elements, first read and discuss folktales with the children. Then, draw simple webs with the title of the book in the center and the elements of setting, characterization, conflicts, and themes on spokes that extend from the center. Lead discussions that help students identify the important characteristics being placed on the web.

Figure 3.2 is a complex web for Karen Cushman's *Catherine, Called Birdy*, a historical fiction novel set in medieval England. Notice on the web that the story takes place in an English manor. It also has strong characterizations, conflicts, and themes. An interesting comparison can be made by also webbing Cushman's *The Midwife's Apprentice*, a tale set in the same time period but with a heroine from the lowest level of society.

Suggested Activities

For more suggested activities for evaluating and selecting children's literature, visit the Companion Website at www.prenhall.com/norton

- Find examples of person-against-person, person-against-society, person-against-nature, and person-against-self conflicts in children's literature. Do some books develop more than one type of conflict? What makes the conflict believable? Share these examples with your class.
- Read one of Laura Ingalls Wilder's "Little House" books. Do you agree with the child who said that she would like the character Laura for her best friend? How has the author developed Laura into a believable character? Give examples of techniques that Wilder uses to reveal Laura's nature.
- The following five authors or illustrators from the United States have won the Hans Christian Andersen Award: Virginia Hamilton, Paula Fox, Meindert Dejong, Maurice Sendak, and Scott O'Dell. Pretend that you are a member of the worldwide committee. What qualities encourage you to select books of these authors and illustrators?
- Compare the top teachers' choices and the top children's choices ("Going Places," *Reading Today*, 2001). The top adult choices: E. B. White's *Charlotte's Web*, Chris Van Allsburg's *The Polar Express*, Dr. Seuss's *Green Eggs and Ham*, Maurice Sendak's *Where the Wild Things Are*, Robert N. Munsch's *Love You Forever*, Shel Silverstein's *The Giving Tree*, Eric Carle's *The Very Hungry Caterpillar*, Wilson Rawls's *Where the Red Fern Grows*, and Jan Brett's *The Mitten*. The top children's choices include J. K. Rowling's "Harry Potter" series, R. L. Stine's "Goosebumps" series, Dr. Seuss's *Green Eggs and Ham*, Dr. Seuss's *The Cat in the Hat*, Marc Brown's "Arthur" series, E. B. White's *Charlotte's Web*, Phyllis Reynold Naylor's "Shiloh" trilogy, Gary Paulsen's *Hatchet*, Louis Sachar's *Holes*, and Lois Lowry's *The Giver*.

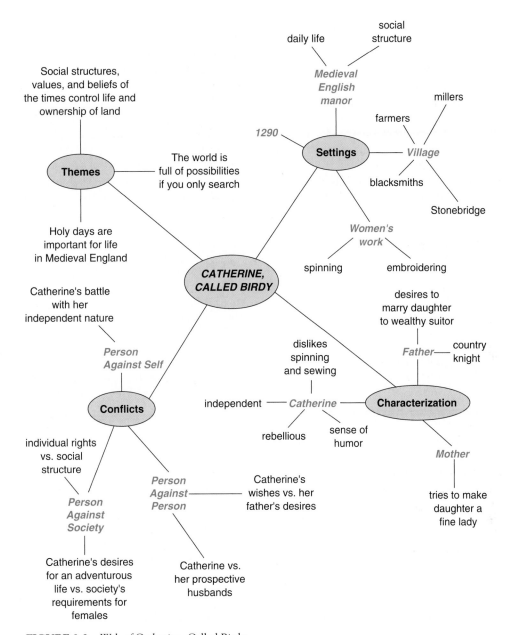

FIGURE 3.2 Web of Catherine, Called Birdy.
Source: Donna E. Norton's *The Effective Teaching of Language Arts,* 6th edition. Merrill, 2004.

Children's Literature

For full descriptions, including plot summaries and award winner notations, of these and other titles for enhancing children's understanding of literary elements, please visit the CD-ROM that accompanies this book.

Aardema, Verna. *Bringing the Rain to Kapiti Plain: A Nandi Tale.* Illustrated by Beatriz Vidal. Dial, 1981 (I:5–8 R:6).

_____. *Why Mosquitoes Buzz in People's Ears.* Illustrated by Leo & Diane Dillon. Dial, 1975 (I:5–9 R:6).

Ackerman, Karen. *Song and Dance Man.* Illustrated by Stephen Gammell. Knopf, 1988 (I:3–8 R:4).

Alcott. Louisa May. *Little Women.* Little, Brown, 1868 (I:10+ R:7).

Alexander, Lloyd. *The Arkadians.* Dutton, 1995 (I:10+ R:6).

Almond, David. *The Fire-Eaters.* Delacorte, 2003 (I:12–YA R:7).

Avi. *Nothing but the Truth: A Documentary Novel.* Orchard, 1991 (I:12+).

_____. *The True Confessions of Charlotte Doyle.* Orchard, 1990 (I:10+ R:6).

Babbitt, Natalie. *Tuck Everlasting.* Farrar, Straus & Giroux, 1975 (I:8–12 R:6).

Banks, Kate. *And If the Moon Could Talk.* Illustrated by Georg Hallensleben. Farrar, Straus & Giroux, 1998 (I:3–6 R:4).

Barrett, Tracy. *Anna of Byzantium.* Delacorte, 1999 (I:10+ R:5).

Barton, Byron. *I Want to Be an Astronaut.* Crowell, 1988 (I:2–6).

Chapter3 header icon

Bat-Ami, Miriam. *Two Suns in the Sky.* Front Street, 1999 (I:12+ R:6).

Bauer, Joan. *Hope Was Here.* Putnam, 2000 (I:10+ R:5).

Bauer, Marion Dane. *On My Honor.* Clarion, 1986 (I:10+ R:4).

Bemelmans, Ludwig. *Madeline.* Viking, 1939, 1977 (I:4–9 R:5).

Ben-Ezer, Ehud. *Hosni the Dreamer.* Illustrated by Uri Shulevitz. Farrar, Straus & Giroux, 1997 (I:5–9 R:5).

Benjamin, Carol Lea. *The Wicked Stepdog.* Crowell, 1982 (I:9–12 R:4).

Berenzy, Alix. *A Frog Prince.* H. Holt, 1989 (I:6–10 R:6).

Blos, Joan W. *A Gathering of Days.* Scribner, 1979 (I:8–14 R:6).

Blume, Judy. *Are You There God? It's Me, Margaret.* Bradbury, 1970 (I:10+ R:6).

_____. *Blubber.* Bradbury, 1974 (I:10+ R:4).

Bober, Natalie. *Countdown to Independence: A Revolution of Ideas in England and Her American Colonies: 1760–1776.* Simon & Schuster, 2001 (I:12+ R:6).

Brooks, Bruce. *The Moves Make the Man.* Harper & Row, 1984 (I:10+ R:7).

_____. *What Hearts.* HarperCollins, 1992 (I:10+ R:6).

Brown, Margaret Wise. *Goodnight Moon.* Illustrated by Clement Hurd. Harper, 1947 (I:2–7).

Browne, Anthony. *Gorilla.* Watts, 1983 (I:3–8 R:4).

Bunting, Eve. *The Wednesday Surprise.* Illustrated by Donald Carrick. Clarion, 1989 (I:3–9 R:5).

Burnett, Frances Hodgson. *The Secret Garden.* Illustrated by Tasha Tudor. Lippincott, 1911, 1938, 1962 (I:8–12 R:7).

Burton, Virginia Lee. *The Little House.* Houghton Mifflin, 1942 (I:3–7 R:3).

Cadnum, Michael. *In a Dark Wood.* Orchard, 1998 (I:10+ R:6).

Carrick, Carol. *Stay Away From Simon!* Illustrated by Donald Carrick. Clarion, 1985 (I:7–10 R:3).

Carroll, Lewis. *Alice's Adventures in Wonderland.* Illustrated by John Tenniel. Macmillan, 1866; Knopf, 1984 (I:8+ R:6).

Cendrars, Blaise. *Shadow.* Illustrated by Marcia Brown. Scribner, 1982 (I:all).

Chaucer, Geoffrey. *The Canterbury Tales.* Retold by Barbara Cohen. Illustrated by Trina Schart Hyman. Lothrop, Lee & Shepard, 1988 (I:8+ R:5).

Chipman, Liz. *From the Lighthouse.* Dutton, 2004 (I:12–YA R:6).

Chotjewitz, David. *Daniel Half Human and the Good Nazi.* Translated by Doris Orgel. Atheneum, 2005 (I:12–YA R:7).

Cleary, Beverly. *The Mouse and the Motorcycle.* Illustrated by Louis Darling. Morrow, 1965 (I:7–11 R:3).

_____. *Ramona and Her Father.* Illustrated by Alan Tiegreen. Morrow, 1977 (I:7–12 R:6).

_____. *Ramona Quimby, Age 8.* Illustrated by Alan Tiegreen. Morrow, 1981 (I:7–12 R:6).

Cole, Brock. *The Goats.* Farrar, Straus & Giroux, 1987 (I:8+ R:5).

Cooper, Helen. *Pumpkin Soup.* Doubleday, 1999 (I:3–8).

Cormier, Robert. *The Chocolate War.* Laureleaf, 1999.

Couloumbis, Audrey. *Getting Near to Baby.* Putnam, 1999 (I:10+ R:4).

Creech, Sharon. *Heartbeat.* HarperCollins, 2004 (I:10–YA).

_____. *Walk Two Moons.* HarperCollins, 1994 (I:12+ R:6).

_____. *The Wanderer.* HarperCollins, 2000 (I:10+ R:6).

Cronin, Doreen. *Click, Clack, Moo: Cows That Type.* Illustrated by Betsy Lewin. Simon & Schuster, 2000 (I:4–7).

Crossley-Holland, Kevin. *Storm.* Illustrated by Alan Marks. Heinemann, 1985 (I:6–12 R:5).

Curtis, Christopher Paul. *The Watsons Go to Birmingham—1963.* Delacorte, 1995 (I:10+ R:6).

Cushman, Karen. *Catherine, Called Birdy.* Clarion, 1994 (I:12+ R:9).

_____. *The Midwife's Apprentice.* Clarion, 1995. (I:12+ R:7)

_____. *Rodzina.* Houghton Mifflin, 2003 (I:8–12 R:5).

Dabcovich, Lydia. *Sleepy Bear.* Dutton, 1982 (I:3–6 R:1).

Day, Alexandra. *Frank and Ernest Play Ball.* Scholastic, 1990 (I:5–8 R:5).

_____. *Frank and Ernest on the Road.* Scholastic, 1994 (I:5–8 R:5).

dePaola, Tomie. *26 Fairmount Avenue.* Putnam, 1999 (I:6+).

DiCamillo, Kate. *The Tale of Despereaux.* Illustrated by Timothy Basil Ering. Candlewick, 2003 (I:8+ R:4).

Dorris, Michael. *Morning Girl.* Hyperion, 1992 (I:8+ R:4).

Edmonds, Walter D. *The Matchlock Gun.* Dodd, Mead, 1941 (I:8+ R:5).

Engel, Diana. *Josephina Hates Her Name.* Morrow, 1989 (I:5–8 R:4).

Farmer, Nancy. *A Girl Named Disaster.* Orchard, 1996 (I:10+ R:6).

Fenner, Carol. *Yolonda's Genius.* McElderry, 1995 (I:10+ R:3).

Fitzhugh, Louise. *Harriet the Spy.* Harper & Row, 1964 (I:8–12 R:3).

Fleischman, Paul. *The Borning Room.* HarperCollins, 1991 (I:10+ R:5).

_____. *Bull Run.* Illustrated by David Frampton. HarperCollins, 1993 (I:10+ R:5).

_____. *Dateline: Troy.* Illustrated by Gwen Frankfeldt & Glenn Morrow. Candlewick, 1996 (I:12+ R:7).

Fleischman, Sid. *The Midnight Horse.* Illustrated by Peter Sís. Greenwillow, 1990 (I:8–12 R:5).

_____. *The Whipping Boy.* Illustrated by Peter Sís. Greenwillow, 1986 (I:8+ R:5).

Forbes, Esther. *Johnny Tremain.* Illustrated by Lynd Ward. Houghton Mifflin, 1943 (I:10+ R:6).

Foreman, Michael. *War Boy: A Country Childhood.* Little, Brown, 1990 (I:all R:6).

Fox, Paula. *Monkey Island.* Orchard, 1991 (I:10+ R:6).

_____. *One-Eyed Cat.* Bradbury, 1984 (I:10+ R:5).

_____. *The Slave Dancer.* Illustrated by Eros Keith. Bradbury, 1973 (I:12+ R:7).

Frank, Anne. *Anne Frank: The Diary of a Young Girl.* Edited by Otto H. Frank & Mirjam Pressler. Translated by Susan Massotty. Doubleday, 1995 (I:12+ R:5).

Frank, Rudolf. *No Hero for the Kaiser.* Translated by Patricia Crampton. Illustrated by Klaus Steffens. Lothrop, Lee & Shepard, 1986 (I:10+ R:7).

Freedman, Russell. *Eleanor Roosevelt: A Life of Discovery.* Clarion, 1993 (I:10+ R:6).

_____. *Lincoln: A Photobiography.* Clarion, 1987 (I:8+ R:6).

_____. *The Voice That Challenged a Nation: Marian Anderson and the Struggle for Equal Rights.* Clarion, 2004 (I:10+ R:6).

_____. *The Wright Brothers: How They Invented the Airplane.* Holiday House. 1991 (I:8+ R:5).

Fritz, Jean. *Bully for You, Teddy Roosevelt!* Illustrated by Mike Wimmer. Putnam, 1991 (I:8+ R:5).

_____. *The Cabin Faced West.* Illustrated by Feodor Rojankousky. Coward, McCann, 1958 (I:7–10 R:5).

_____. *The Great Little Madison.* Putnam, 1989 (I:10+ R:6).

_____. *Make Way for Sam Houston.* Illustrated by Elise Primavera. Putnam, 1986 (I:9+ R:6).

_____. *Traitor: The Case of Benedict Arnold.* Putnam, 1981 (I:8+ R:5).

George, Jean Craighead. *Julie of the Wolves.* Illustrated by John Schoenherr. Harper & Row, 1972 (I:10–13 R:7).

_____. *My Side of the Mountain.* Dutton, 1959 (I:10+ R:6).

_____. *Water Sky.* Harper & Row, 1987 (I:10+ R:6).

Gipson, Fred. *Old Yeller.* Illustrated by Carl Burger. Harper & Row, 1956 (I:10+ R:6).

Goble, Paul. *The Girl Who Loved Wild Horses.* Bradbury, 1978 (I:6–10 R:5).

Grahame, Kenneth. *Wind in the Willows.* Illustrated by E. H. Shepard. Scribner, 1908 (I:7–12 R:7).

Grifalconi, Ann. *Darkness and the Butterfly.* Little, Brown, 1987 (I:4–8 R:4).

Grimes, Nikki. *Bronx Masquerade.* Dial, 2002 (I:10–YA R:5).

Grimm, Brothers. *Rumpelstiltskin.* Retold and illustrated by Paul O. Zelinsky. Dutton, 1986 (I:all R:5).

Hall, Bruce Edward. *Henry and the Kite Dragon.* Illustrated by William Low. Philomel, 2004 (I:5–9 R:4).

Halperin, Wendy Anderson. *Love Is . . .* Simon & Schuster, 2001 (I:all).

Hamilton, Virginia. *Anthony Burns: The Defeat and Triumph of a Fugitive Slave.* Knopf, 1988 (I:9+ R:6).

_____. *Many Thousand Gone: African Americans From Slavery to Freedom.* Illustrated by Leo & Diane Dillon. Knopf, 1993 (I:8+ R:5).

Hannigan, Katherine. *Ida B . . . and Her Plans to Maximize Fun, Avoid Disaster, and (Possibly) Save the World.* Greenwillow, 2004 (I:8+ R:5).

Hansen, Joyce. *I Thought My Soul Would Rise and Fly: The Diary of Patsy, A Freed Girl.* Scholastic, 1997 (I:10+ R:4).

Harrington, Janice N. *Going North.* Illustrated by Jerone Lagarrigue. Farrar, Straus & Giroux, 2004 (I:8–10 R:4).

Hastings, Selina, retold by. *Sir Gawain and the Loathly Lady.* Illustrated by Juan Wijngaard. Lothrop, Lee & Shepard, 1985 (I:9–12 R:6).

Hautman, Pete. *Godless.* Simon & Schuster, 2004 (I:14–YA R:6).

Henkes, Kevin. *Owen.* Greenwillow, 1993 (I:3–7 R:4).

Hesse, Karen. *Out of the Dust.* Scholastic, 1997 (I:10+ R:6).

_____. *Stowaway.* Simon & Schuster, 2000 (I:10+ R:6).

Highwater, Jamake. *Anpao: An American Indian Odyssey.* Illustrated by Fritz Scholder. Lippincott, 1977 (I:12+ R:5).

Hoban, Lillian. *Arthur's Great Big Valentine.* Harper & Row, 1989 (I:5–7 R:2).

Howe, James. *Horace and Morris But Mostly Delores.* Illustrated by Amy Waldo. Atheneum, 1999 (I:4–8).

Hudson, Jan. *Sweetgrass.* Tree Frog, Philomel, 1984, 1989 (I:10+ R:4).

Hurmence, Belinda. *A Girl Called Boy.* Houghton Mifflin, 1982 (I:10+ R:6).

Ibbotson, Eve. *Journey to the River Sea.* Dutton, 2002 (I:10+ R:5).

Jackson, Shelley. *The Old Woman and the Wave.* DK, 1998 (I:4–7 R:4).

Johnson, Angela. *Julius.* Illustrated by Dav Pilkey. Orchard, 1993 (I:3–7 R:4).

_____. *Tell Me a Story, Mama.* Illustrated by David Soman. Watts, 1989 (I:3–7 R:4).

Keats, Ezra Jack. *The Snowy Day.* Viking, 1962 (I:2–6 R:2).

Konigsburg, E.L. *From the Mixed-Up Files of Mrs. Basil E. Frankweiler.* Atheneum, 1967 (I:9–12 R:7).

_____. *Journey to an 800 Number.* Atheneum, 1982 (I:10+ R:6).

_____. *The Outcasts of 19 Schuyler Place.* Atheneum, 2004 (I:8+ R:5).

_____. *The View From Saturday.* Atheneum, 1996 (I:10+ R:6).

Lamb, Charles, & Mary Lamb, retold by. *Tales From Shakespeare.* Illustrated by Elizabeth Shippen Green Elliott. Crown, 1988 (I:8+).

Lang, Andrew. *The Red Fairy Book.* Illustrated by H. J. Ford & Lancelot Speed. McGraw-Hill, 1967 (I:all R:6).

Leapman, Michael. *Witnesses to War: Eight True-Life Stories of Nazi Persecution.* Puffin, 2000.

L'Engle, Madeleine. *A Wrinkle in Time.* Farrar, Straus & Giroux, 1962 (I:10+ R:5).

Levine, Ellen. *Freedom's Children: Young Civil Rights Activists Tell Their Own Stories.* Putnam, 1993 (I:all).

Levine, Gail Carson. *Ella Enchanted.* HarperCollins, 1997 (I:10+ R:6).

Lewis, C.S. *The Lion, the Witch and the Wardrobe.* Illustrated by Pauline Baynes. Macmillan, 1950 (I:9+ R:7).

Lisle, Janet Taylor. *Afternoon of the Elves.* Watts, 1989 (I:10+ R:5).

Lobel, Arnold. *Frog and Toad Are Friends.* Harper & Row, 1970 (I:5–8 R:1).

Lowry, Lois. *The Giver.* Houghton Mifflin, 1993 (I:10+ R:5).

_____. *Number the Stars.* Houghton Mifflin, 1989 (I:8–12 R:5).

Lyon, George Ella. *One Lucky Girl.* Illustrated by Irene Trivas. Dorling Kindersley, 2000 (I:6+ R:4).

MacLachlan, Patricia. *The Facts and Fictions of Minna Pratt.* Harper & Row, 1988 (I:7–12 R:4).

_____. *Mama One, Mama Two.* Illustrated by Ruth Lercher Bornstein. Harper & Row, 1982 (I:5–7 R:2).

_____. *Sarah, Plain and Tall.* Harper & Row, 1985 (I:7–10 R:3).

Marrin, Albert, *Hitler.* Viking Kestrel, 1987 (I:10+ R:7).

Maruki, Toshi. *Hiroshima No Pika.* Lothrop, Lee & Shepard, 1982 (I:8–12 R:4).

McCully, Emily Arnold. *The Ballot Box Battle.* Knopf, 1996 (I:7–9 R:4).

McKinley, Robin. *The Hero and the Crown.* Greenwillow, 1984 (I:10+ R:7).

McKissack, Patricia C. *The Dark-Thirty: Southern Tales of the Supernatural.* Illustrated by Brain Pinkney. Knopf, 1992 (I:all R:5).

McWhorter, Diane. *A Dream of Freedom: The Civil Rights Movement From 1954 to 1968.* Scholastic, 2004 (I:12–YA R:6).

Meddaugh, Susan. *Martha Speaks.* Houghton Mifflin, 1992 (I:4–8 R:4).

Meltzer, Milton. *Rescue: The Story of How Gentiles Saved Jews in the Holocaust.* Harper & Row, 1988 (I:10+ R:6).

_____. *Thomas Jefferson: The Revolutionary Aristocrat.* Watts, 1991 (I:10+ R:6).

_____, ed. *The Black Americans: A History in Their Own Words 1619–1983.* Crowell, 1984 (I:10+).

Merriam, Eve. *Halloween ABC.* Illustrated by Lane Smith. Macmillan, 1987 (I:all).

Millard, Anne. *A Street Through Time: A 12,000-Year Walk Through History.* Illustrated by Steve Noon. DK, 1998 (I:all).

Milne, A. A. *Winnie-the-Pooh.* Illustrated by Ernest H. Shepard. Dutton, 1926, 1954 (I:6–10 R:5).

Morpurgo, Michael. *Kensuke's Kingdom.* Illustrated by Michael Foreman. Mammoth, 2000 (I:8+ R:5).

_____. *Private Peaceful.* Scholastic, 2003 (I:12–YA R:6).

Mowat, Farley. *Lost in the Barrens.* Illustrated by Charles Geer. McClelland & Stewart, 1956, 1984 (I:9+ R:6).

Murphy, Jim. *An American Plague: The True and Terrifying Story of the Yellow Fever Epidemic of 1793.* Clarion, 2004 (I:12+ R:6).

Myers, Walter Dean. *Now Is Your Time The African-American Struggle for Freedom.* HarperCollins, 1991 (I:10+ R:6).

Naylor, Phyllis Reynolds. *Shiloh.* Atheneum, 1991 (I:8+ R:5).

Nelson, Marilyn. *Carver: A Life in Poems.* Front Street, 2001 (I:12–YA R:8).

Ness, Evaline. *Sam, Bangs & Moonshine.* Holt, Rinehart & Winston, 1966 (I:5–9 R:3).

North, Sterling. *Rascal.* Dutton, 1963 (I:10+ R:6).

Noyes, Alfred. *The Highwayman.* Illustrated by Charles Keeping. Oxford, 1981 (I:10+).

O'Brien, Robert C. *Mrs. Frisby and the Rats of NIMH.* Illustrated by Zena Bernstein. Atheneum, 1971 (I:8–12 R:4).

O'Dell, Scott. *Island of the Blue Dolphins.* Houghton Mifflin, 1960 (I:10+ R:6).

Orlev, Uri. *The Island on Bird Street.* Translated by Hillel Halkin. Houghton Mifflin, 1984 (I:10+ R:6).

_____. *The Man From the Other Side.* Translated by Hillel Halkin. Houghton Mifflin, 1991 (I:10+ R:6).

Park, Linda Sue. *Project Mulberry.* Clarion, 2005 (I:9–YA R:5).

Paterson, Katherine. *Bridge to Terabithia.* Illustrated by Donna Diamond. Crowell, 1977 (I:10–14 R:6).

_____. *Jacob Have I Loved.* Crowell, 1980 (I:10 R:6).

Paulsen, Gary. *Hatchet.* Bradbury, 1987 (I:10+ R:6).

_____. *Nightjohn.* Delacorte, 1993 (I:12+ R:6).

Pearce, Philippa. *Tom's Midnight Garden.* Illustrated by Susan Einzig. Lippincott, 1958 (I:8+ R:6).

Peck, Richard. *A Long Way From Chicago.* Dial, 1998 (I:10+ R:5).

_____. *A Year Down Yonder.* Dial, 2000 (I:10+ R:5).

Pienkowski, Jan. *Haunted House.* Dutton, 1979 (I:all).

Polacco, Patricia. *Appelemando's Dreams.* Philomel, 1991 (I:6–9 R:5).

_____. *Meteor!* Dodd, Mead, 1987 (I:6–10 R:7).

Potter, Beatrix. *The Tale of Peter Rabbit.* Warne, 1902 (I:2–7 R:5).

Pullman, Philip. *The Amber Spyglass.* Knopf, 2000 (I:10+ R:7).

_____. *The Golden Compass.* Knopf, 1996 (I:10+ R:7).

_____. *The Subtle Knife.* Knopf, 1997 (I:10+ R:7).

Quintana, Anton. *The Baboon King.* Translated by John Nieuwenhuizen. Walker, 1999 (I:10+ R:5).

Raskin, Ellen. *The Westing Game.* Dutton, 1978 (I:10–14 R:5).

Rathmann, Peggy. *Ruby the Copycat.* Scholastic, 1991 (I:5–8 R:3).

Rodowsky, Colby. *Sydney Herself.* Farrar, Straus & Giroux, 1989 (I:11+ R:6).

Rogasky, Barbara. *Smoke and Ashes: The Story of the Holocaust.* Holiday House, 1988 (I:10+ R:6).

Rowling, J. K. *Harry Potter and the Goblet of Fire.* Scholastic, 2000 (I:9+ R:5).

Rylant, Cynthia. *Appalachia: The Voices of Sleeping Birds.* Illustrated by Barry Moser. Harcourt Brace, 1991 (I:all R:5).

_____. *A Fine White Dust.* Bradbury, 1986 (I:10+ R:6).

_____. *The Islander.* DK, 1998 (I:10+ R:6).

_____. *Missing May.* Orchard, 1992 (I:10+ R:6).

_____. *When I Was Young in the Mountains.* Illustrated by Diane Goode. Dutton, 1982 (I:4–7 R:3).

Sachar, Louis. *Holes.* Farrar, Straus & Giroux, 1998 (I:10+ R:5).

Salisbury, Graham. *Under the Blood-Red Sun.* Doubleday, 1995 (I:10+ R:5).

San Souci, Robert D. *Cendrillon . . . A Caribbean Cinderella.* Illustrated by Brian Pinkney. Simon & Schuster, 1998 (I:all).

Schanzer, Rosalyn. *George vs. George: The American Revolution as Seen From Both Sides.* National Geographic, 2004 (I:8+ R:5).

Schmidt, Gary D. *Lizzie Bright and the Buckminster Boy.* Clarion, 2004 (I:10–YA R:6).

Scieszka, Jon. *The Stinky Cheese Man and Other Fairly Stupid Tales.* Illustrated by Lane Smith. Viking, 1992 (I:all R:4).

Seeber, Dorothea P. *A Pup Just for Me: A Boy Just for Me.* Illustrated by Ed Young. Philomel, 2000 (I:6+).

Sendak, Maurice. *Where the Wild Things Are.* Harper & Row, 1963 (I:4–8 R:6).

Seredy, Kate. *The White Stag.* Viking, 1937; Puffin, 1979 (I:10–14 R:7).

Seuss, Dr. *The Cat in the Hat.* Random House, 1957 (I:4–7 R:1).

Shulevitz, Uri. *The Travels of Benjamin of Tudela: Through Three Continents in the Twelfth Century.* Farrar, Straus and Giroux, 2005 (I:10–YA R:6).

Snyder, Dianne. *The Boy of the Three-Year Nap.* Illustrated by Allen Say. Houghton Mifflin, 1988 (I:4–9 R:4).

Speare, Elizabeth George. *The Sign of the Beaver.* Houghton Mifflin, 1983 (I:8–12 R:5).

_____. *The Witch of Blackbird Pond.* Houghton Mifflin, 1958 (I:9–14 R:4).

Sperry, Armstrong. *Call It Courage.* Macmillan, 1940 (I:9–13 R:6).

Spinelli, Jerry. *Wringer.* HarperCollins, 1997 (I:9+ R:4).

Staples, Suzanne Fisher. *Shabanu: Daughter of the Wind.* Farrar, Straus & Giroux, 1996 (I:12+ R:6).

_____. *Shiva's Fire.* Farrar, Straus & Giroux, 2000 (I:10+).

Steptoe, John. *Mufaro's Beautiful Daughters: An African Tale.* Lothrop, Lee & Shepard, 1987 (I:all R:4).

Stolz, Joëlle. *The Shadows of Ghadames.* Delacorte, 2004 (I:10–YA R:6).

Stolz, Mary. *Cezanne Pinto: A Memoir.* Knopf, 1994 (I:10+ R:6).

Strachan, Ian. *Flawed Glass.* Little, Brown, 1990 (I:10+ R:6).

Taback, Simms. *There Was an Old Lady Who Swallowed a Fly.* Viking, 1997 (I:all).

Taylor, Mildred D. *Roll of Thunder, Hear My Cry.* Dial, 1976 (I:10+ R:6).

Taylor, Theodore. *The Cay.* Doubleday, 1969 (I:8–12 R:6).

Thomas, Dylan. *A Child's Christmas in Wales.* Illustrated by Chris Raschka. Candlewick, 2004 (I:all).

Tolkien, J. R. R. *The Hobbit.* Houghton Mifflin, 1938 (I:9–12 R:6).

Trivizas, Eugene. *The Three Little Wolves and the Big Bad Pig.* Illustrated by Helen Oxenbury. Macmillan, 1993 (I:4–8 R:5).

Turner, Megan Whalen. *The Thief.* Greenwillow, 1996 (I:11+ R:6).

Voigt, Cynthia. *Bad Girls.* Scholastic, 1996 (I:9+ R:7).

_____. *Dicey's Song.* Atheneum, 1982 (I:10+ R:5).

Vos, Ida. *Hide and Seek.* Translated by Terese Edelstein & Inez Smidt. Houghton Mifflin, 1991 (I:8–12 R:5).

Wells, Rosemary. *Max's Chocolate Chicken.* Dial, 1989 (I:2–6).

Whelan, Gloria. *Homeless Bird.* HarperCollins, 2000 (I:10+ R:5).

White, E. B. *Charlotte's Web.* Illustrated by Garth Williams. Harper & Row, 1952 (I:7–11 R:3).

_____. *Trumpet of the Swan.* Puffin, 1970 (I:7–11 R:5).

White, Ruth. *Belle Prater's Boy.* Farrar, Straus & Giroux, 1996 (I:10+ R:6).

White, T. H. *The Sword in the Stone.* Collins, 1938 (I:10+ R:7).

Wild, Margaret. *Our Granny.* Illustrated by Julie Vivas. Ticknor & Fields, 1994 (I:3–6 R:5).

Wilder, Laura Ingalls. *Little House in the Big Woods.* Harper & Row, 1932 (I:8–12 R:6).

Williams, Margery. *The Velveteen Rabbit.* Illustrated by William Nicholson. Doubleday, 1958 (I:6–9 R:5).

Williams, Vera B. *Stringbean's Trip to the Shining Sea.* Illustrated by Vera B. Williams & Jennifer Williams. Greenwillow, 1988 (I:5–10).

Wood, Douglas. *What Dads Can't Do.* Illustrated by Doug Cushman. Simon & Schuster, 2000 (I:3–8).

Yolen, Jane. *The Devil's Arithmetic.* Viking Kestrel, 1988 (I:8+ R:5).

Yorinks, Arthur. *Hey, Al.* Illustrated by Richard Egielski. Farrar, Straus & Giroux, 1986 (I:all).

Chapter Outline

Understanding Artists and Their Illustrations

- Evaluating the Illustrations in Children's Books
- Visual Elements: The Grammar of Artists
- Design: Organizing the Visual Elements
- Artistic Media
- Artistic Style
- Outstanding Illustrators of Children's Books

Teaching With Artists and Their Illustrations

- Using Art Education Books
- Aesthetic Scanning
- Studying Inspirations for Art
- Investigating the Works of Great Artists

Understanding Artists and Their Illustrations

Many young children mention the illustrations when asked what attracted them to a book. The bright colors of an East African setting may entice children into searching for camouflaged animals. Jagged lines and dark colors may excite children with the prospect of dangerous adventures, and delicate lines and pastel colors may set children to dreaming about fairyland. The textures in illustrations may invite children to "feel" a bear's fur or an eagle's feathers. In these and many other ways, illustrations are integral to picture books for young children. Outstanding artists illustrate books for older chilren—such as Laura Ingalls Wilder's "Little House" series—but in such books, the text can stand on its own. In picture books, however, the illustrations join the text in telling the stories.

This chapter discusses the visual elements, media, and styles used by illustrators of all books for children, but it focuses on the special requirements of picture books. It suggests criteria for evaluating illustrations in picture books, provides examples of high-quality books, and looks at some outstanding illustrators to see how they create memorable picture books.

Evaluating the Illustrations in Children's Books

The collaborative process of creating picture books for children makes special demands on artists. Even when illustrator and author are the same person, the artist is a partner to the writer and must place his or her talents in the service of a certain story. David Saylor (2000), the creative director for Scholastic, provides the following evaluation for picture books: "The best picture-book art tells a story of its own; it creates a visual world that enlarges, expands, sharpens, and reinforces an author's words. With this in mind, does the composition help us focus on the important moment in a scene? Does the color enhance the mood? Do the light and shadow help stir up drama? Does the line give us the telling details that conjure up a vivid character or a believable world?" (p. 37).

Another viewpoint that you can consider when evaluating illustrations in children's books is the one presented by Maurice Sendak in an interview with Hazel Rochman (1992b). When Sendak was asked "What makes a good illustrated book?", he responded:

> The illustrations don't simply, prosaically echo the verse. . . . The only thing you can do is to use the verse as a springboard

Evaluation Criteria

Illustrations

1. The illustrator's use of visual elements—line, color, shape, texture—and of certain artistic media should complement or even extend the development of plot, characterization, setting, and theme in the text.

2. The design of the illustrations—individually and throughout an entire book—should reinforce the text and convey a sense of unity that stimulates aesthetic appreciation.

3. The artistic style the illustrator chooses should enhance the author's literary style.

4. The illustrations should help the readers anticipate the unfolding of a story's action and its climax.

5. The illustrations should convincingly delineate and develop the characters.

6. The illustrations should be accurate in historical, cultural, and geographical detail, and they should be consistent with the text.

for personal interpretation, so that what you offer is a surprise, at best as surprising and amusing or serious as the verse, but at the very least a counterpoint, an interpretation, a variation of the verse. (p. 1848)

Consider the accompanying Evaluation Criteria when evaluating the illustrations in picture books for children.

Visual Elements: The Grammar of Artists

Writers create compelling stories by arranging words; artists arrange visual elements to create pictures that complement stories. A visual grammar consists of the elements of line, color, shape, and texture. Artists who organize these elements into unified wholes create visual designs that convey meaning.

Line

Artists use line to suggest direction, motion, energy, and mood. Artist William A. Herring (1997) defines the importance of line when he states: "I regard line as essential to beauty in any work of art" (p. 40). Lines can be thin or wide, light or heavy, feathery or jagged, straight or curved. H. W. Janson and Anthony F. Janson (1999) maintain that line is the most basic visual element: "A majority of art is initially conceived in terms of contour line. Its presence is often implied even when it is not actually used to describe form" (p. 17). According to these authorities in art and art

history, drawings represent line in its purest form and artists commonly treat drawing as a form of note taking. Artists such as Michelangelo based their finished art on carefully developed drawings, but line is also extremely important in children's book illustration. According to Edmund Burke Feldman (1992), line is the most crucial visual element for several reasons:

1. Line is familiar to virtually everyone because of experience with drawing and writing.

2. Line is definite, assertive, intelligible (although its windings and patternings may be infinitely complex); it is precise and unambiguous; it commits artists to specific statements.

3. Line conveys meaning through its identification with natural phenomena.

4. Line leads the eye and involves viewers in the line's "destiny."

5. Line permits the eyes to do as children do when getting to know the world: handle objects and feel their contours. The outlines of things eventually become more important than their color, size, or texture as means of identifying them.

Feldman's discussion of the relationship between line and natural phenomena is especially interesting to people involved with children and the illustrations found in literature for them. Experiences with common natural phenomena may help children relate meaningfully to works of art. Vertical lines, for example, look like trees in a windless landscape or like people who stand rather than move. Consequently, they suggest lack of movement.

Horizontal lines, such as the surface of a placid lake or a flat horizon, suggest calm, sleep, stability, and an absence of strife. Most young children use a horizontal baseline in their drawings to convey the idea of the firm ground they walk on.

Vertical lines and horizontal lines joined at right angles depict artificial elements that differ considerably from the natural world of irregular and approximate shapes. Two vertical lines connected by a horizontal line at the top give the feeling of a solid, safe place: a doorway, house, or building.

In contrast, diagonal lines suggest loss of balance and uncontrolled motion—unless they form a triangle that rests on a horizontal base, which suggests safety. In both human design and nature, jagged lines have connotations of breakdown and destruction. Consequently, jagged lines suggest danger.

People see curved lines as fluid because of their resemblance to the eddies, whirlpools, and concentric ripples in water: Because of this, circles and curved lines seem less definite and predictable than do straight lines.

In *The Girl Who Loved Wild Horses*, Paul Goble uses line effectively to depict the natural setting of a Native

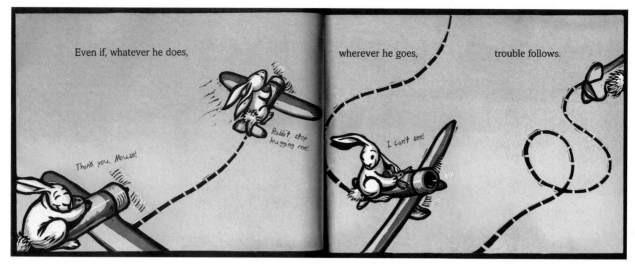

Illustration from MY FRIEND RABBIT *by Eric Rohmann. Copyright 2002 by Eric Rohmann, reprinted by permission of Henry Holt and Company.*

American folktale. Goble introduces readers to the main character as she goes down to the river at sunrise to watch the wild horses. The illustration shows a calm, nonthreatening scene. The lines of the horses' legs are vertical, since the horses are quietly drinking from the river. The calm mood is supplemented by the reflections in the water; not even a ripple breaks the tranquillity.

On the next page, the girl rests in a meadow close to home. Goble illustrates the triangular shapes of teepees sitting securely on the ground. The text relates, however, a rumble while the girl sleeps. The outlines of the clouds suggest this break in a peaceful afternoon: They are still rounded, but they also are heavy, with protrusions jutting into the sky.

Movement in the story and in the illustrations becomes more pronounced as lightning flashes and as the horses rear and snort in terror. Sharp lines of lightning extend from black, rolling clouds to the ground. Even the lines of the plants are diagonal, suggesting dangerous wind as the horses gallop away in front of the storm. When night falls and the storm is over, the tired girl and horses stop to rest. Goble illustrates the hills with vertical lines connected by horizontal lines, suggesting the new feeling of safety and shelter under the moon and the stars.

In contrast to Paul Goble's depiction of familiar natural phenomena, the soft, delicate lines of Marcia Brown's illustrations for Charles Perrault's *Cinderella* create a mythical kingdom that could exist only "once upon a time." The drawing of Cinderella's fairy godmother transforming her into a beautiful princess has an ethereal quality, as if the scene were floating on air. Because these illustrations seem to be almost as diaphanous and changeable as clouds, viewers are not surprised when a pumpkin turns into a coach and a rat becomes its driver. Even the architecture has a magical quality: Delicately curved windows, softly flowing draperies, and graceful pillars provide fitting backgrounds for a favorite fairy tale.

Marjorie Priceman's illustrations for Lloyd Moss's *Zin! Zin! Zin! A Violin* create a flowing movement and a feeling that matches the text. For example, on the page in which the text reads, "And soaring high and moving in, With Zin! Zin! Zin! A Violin" (unnumbered), the violinist seems to float across the pages. Even the cats illustrated in the top of the illustration create a similar flowing movement as they chase a mouse across the page.

In *Kitten's First Full Moon*, the 2005 Caldecott Award winner, Kevin Henkes uses gouache and pencil to depict the strong, heavy lines that outline the kitten and the moon; these uses of heavy line highlight the main objects in this book for younger readers. A strong use of circles in the moon, the lightning bugs, the kitten's eyes, the reflection of the moon in the pond, and the round bowl of milk provide a sense of unity. In an interview (Wiineke, 2005), Henkes explains his use of simple, bold lines and black-and-white illustrations in this book: "I love to use color—even bright color—in most of my picture books, but for this book color seems unnecessary. I thought that by keeping everything as simple and spare as possible, a better, tighter, more complete book would result. I liked the idea of having a white moon, a white cat and a white bowl of milk surrounded by the black night" (p. C1). When looking at the illustrations, notice how the use of white space suggests the distance between the kitten and the moon, how lines suggest movement as the kitten springs toward the moon in the sky and the reflection of the moon in the pond, how the vertical lines of the tree bring the viewer's eyes down to the larger reflection of the moon in the pond, and how the two circular shapes of the moon and the bowl of milk in the final two illustrations bring the story to a warm conclusion.

In *Michael Foreman's Mother Goose,* Michael Foreman uses line to suggest movement and to take viewers into the next picture. Soldiers or animals move from one page to the next, lines continue on the next illustration, and hills or houses introduced on one page become the source for the action on the next page.

Even invisible lines, or suggestions of lines, have impact in illustrations. Lyn Ellen Lacy (1986) emphasizes the role of invisible vertical and horizontal lines as directional influences. For example, when analyzing pages 43 and 44 in Robert McCloskey's *Make Way for Ducklings,* Lacy states:

> Tethered to a top coat button, the whistle manages to fly behind Michael like a free pixie spirit. It points in the direction opposite Michael's intended hasty path. Literally, it points toward the townscape; figuratively, it points our way back into the picture in case we missed something. We do not then turn the page too soon, but instead we follow the whistle's path of gesture along an invisible line, back into the maze of buildings whose vertical lines have a downward thrust to the sidewalk. This underlying structure in the picture is a gentle reminder that there are minute spots on the sidewalk. McCloskey did not want us to miss them. (p. 47)

The minute spots prove to be mother duck and her ducklings.

Color

Color plays an extremely important role in illustration. Janson and Janson (1999) contrast the role of line and color when they state, "The role of color in art rests primarily on its sensuous and emotive appeal, in contrast to the more cerebral quality generally associated with line" (p. 19).

Combining line and color is perhaps the most common way in which artists convey mood and emotion in picture books. Describing picture books of the 1990s, Dilys Evans (1992) emphasizes the roles of line and color in the illustrations of David Wiesner, Lane Smith, and David Wisniewski. Evans states, "Now the world of children's book illustration is witnessing bold new visual voices as they surface upon the page with bright vibrating color, strong black containing lines, and a new reverence for black as color" (p. 760).

Many colors are associated with natural phenomena. Reds, yellows, and oranges are most associated with fire, sun, and blood, and they usually have warm or hot connotations: friendliness, high energy, or anger. Blues, greens, and some violets are most associated with air, water, and plant life, and their coolness or coldness can suggest moods and emotions ranging from tranquility to melancholy.

To evaluate an illustrator's use of color, consider how well the color language of the artist conveys or complements the mood, characters, setting, and theme that the writer develops in words. Marcia Brown complements the delicate lines in her illustrations for Charles Perrault's *Cinderella* by using soft pastels, bringing a

Cover from Leaf Jumpers, *by Carole Gerber. Text copyright © 2004 by Carole Gerber. Illustrations copyright © 2004 by Leslie Evans. Used with permission of Charlesbridge Publishing, Inc. All rights reserved.*

shimmering radiance to the pictures. In contrast, Paul Goble uses bright colors and black, in addition to strong line, to illustrate a desert setting and the tension and movement of animals and forces of nature in *The Girl Who Loved Wild Horses.*

Color can reflect the mood of a story. In *Ox-Cart Man,* Barbara Cooney uses pastels and muted hues of darker colors to translate Donald Hall's gentle story about a quieter time in American history. Cooney portrays the hills of rural New England in the early 1800s as gentle curves of green, gray, and blue. The deep rusts, blues, and greens of the clothing look authentic for the time period.

Cooney's color choices also show the passing of time. When the farmer begins his journey over hills and past villages, the countryside is aflame with the rusts and oranges of fall. When he reaches Portsmouth, the trees have only a few brown leaves. As he returns home, a soft, brown land awaits the first snowfall. The scene turns white in winter. Then, soft greens cover the hills before the trees explode with white and pink apple blossoms. One child said that the pictures made her feel homesick because she had lived in an area that had hills, valleys, quiet farms, and distinct seasons.

Geefwee Boedoe's use of line and color in *Arrowville* supports both the plot of the story and the characters. The citizens of Arrowville, who are always disagreeing and arguing, are drawn in shades of blue with pointed heads. Even the directions of the buildings seem to clash with each other and support the disagreements. In contrast, the Targets, friendly tourists who arrive for a vacation, are drawn in red-and-white circles with bullseyes that make them targets for the Arrowvilles. The illustrator uses color and circular lines to help the Targets show that they are actually friendly by giving away round lollypops that resemble the Targets. The illustrations correspond with the conclusion as "Arrowville was much the same and always on the go, with hustle, bustle, arguing, and racing to and fro. But, all of Arrowville agreed—east, west, and up and down, that smack-dab in the middle was the sweetest spot in town" (unnumbered). The concluding illustration shows a red-and-white Target house with a Target character selling red-and-white lollypops to a line of blue residents of Arrowville.

Rich, vivid colors attract attention and reinforce the happy mood of exploration in Denise Fleming's *In the Small, Small Pond.* Printed in deep black, the text stands out against the colorful illustrations.

Artists may use changes in color to contrast moods within a book. For example, Donald Carrick's illustrations for Eve Bunting's *Ghost's Hour, Spook's Hour* use color to create moods. The dark shades in the early illustrations develop and reinforce the scary environment and the young boy's fear of the dark. When the father rescues his frightened son, the father is shown in an open doorway that has a warm yellow background. The warm yellows are retained as the boy is comforted by his parents and joins them in the big couch bed.

Artists may also use contrasts in illustrations to create drama and complement plot. Helen Oxenbury's illustrations for Michael Rosen's *We're Going on a Bear Hunt* alternate between black and white and color. On the pages with black-and-white illustrations, the characters chant the portion of the bear hunt that they are about to experience. The color illustrations show the family swishing through long grass, splashing across a river, squishing in mud, and stumbling through a dark forest.

Black-and-white photographs may also reflect differences in mood. Interesting comparisons can be made between the effects of painterly photographs and photographs that are in sharp focus by viewing the photographs in Susan Goldman Rubin's photobiography *Margaret Bourke-White: Her Pictures Were Her Life.* For example, Rubin contrasts two photographs of the Terminal Tower, Cleveland, 1929. The photograph reproduced on page 28 shows a "painterly photograph" in soft focus. The photograph on page 29 is labeled "This image of the Terminal Tower, as viewed through the arches of a railroad viaduct, is in sharp focus."

Shape

Lines join and intersect to suggest shapes, and areas of color meet to produce shapes. Organic shapes, irregular and curving, are common in nature and in handmade objects. Geometric shapes—exact, rigid, and often rectangular—usually have mechanical origins. As discussed in relation to line, different shapes have different connotations. Illustrators may use organic, free-form shapes to convey anything from receptivity and imagination to frightening unpredictability. They may use geometric shapes to connote complexity, stability, assertion, or severity.

Gerald McDermott, illustrator and author of *Arrow to the Sun,* uses traditional Native American patterns of line and color to create shapes that draw readers into a desert world where humans, nature, and spiritual forces intertwine. Rich yellow, orange, and brown rectangles depict the pueblo home of the people. This building constructed by humans from natural materials is separated by a black void from the circular orange-and-yellow sun, which is the people's god. The people worship this god in the kiva, a circular ceremonial

Jacket art copyright © 2004 by Geefwee Boedoe. Used by permission of HarperCollins Publishers.

Geometric shapes and sunny colors give a powerful feeling to a Native American tale from the southwestern United States. (From Arrow to the Sun by Gerald McDermott. Copyright © 1974 by Gerald McDermott. Used by permission of Viking Penguin, an imprint of Penguin Putnam Books for Young Readers, a division of Penguin Putnam Inc.)

chamber. A rectangular ray from the sun to the pueblo represents the spark of life that becomes the sun god's earthly son. He is illustrated as a black-and-yellow rectangle, but his mother's form is more circular. Black-and-yellow rectangles predominate in the illustrations until the son decides to search for his father and takes on the sun's power as well as the rainbow of colors available to the sun. He returns to earth as an arrow, and his people, now illustrated in all of the colors that he has brought with him, celebrate with the dance of life.

A person's shape says much about self-image. In *Crow Boy,* Taro Yashima uses line and color to create shapes that emphasize a small boy's growth from fright and alienation to self-confidence. Yashima first draws the boy as a small, huddled shape isolated from his classmates in white space. As an understanding teacher helps Crow Boy become more self-assured, his shape on the page becomes larger,

more outreaching, and closer to the shapes of other characters. Yashima also stresses Crow Boy's transformation by outlining his new form with shades of white that suggest shimmering light.

Shape provides the most important element in alphabet books such as David Pelletier's *The Graphic Alphabet* and Stephen T. Johnson's *Alphabet City.* In *The Graphic Alphabet,* Pelletier relates the shape of the letters to meaning. For example, the letter *f* reflects the meaning of *fire* by showing red flames emerging from the top of the letter. There is no text in *Alphabet City.* Consequently, all of the paintings reflect the shapes of various letters of the alphabet.

Shape is another way to emphasize the mood of a picture and story. According to illustrator Uri Shulevitz (1985), two areas are related to shape and mood: (1) the overall form of an illustration if viewed as a silhouette (with no interior details) and (2) the edges of the picture, which can be hard, soft, jagged, or straight. Shulevitz states that symmetrical picture shapes, such as rectangles, squares, circles, and ovals, are calm and solid, and asymmeterical picture shapes are unbalanced, irregular, and dynamic.

Stephen Savage's use of lines, colors, and simple shapes in his illustrations for Lauren Thompson's *Polar Bear Night* creates contrasts between the warm cave that shelters a bear cub and her mother and the clear, cold night that beckons the curious cub to explore. In the beginning illustration, notice how the lines from the moon focus attention on the simple shape of the cave. On the next two-page spread, the light from the moon focuses attention on the cub, who is the center of the story. Circular shapes radiate from the sleeping mother bear. The colors go from warm to cool blue as the bear cub leaves the shelter of the cave. There is strong emphasis on shape as the cub sees the animals of the night, including a sleeping walrus, the seals, and whales. Rectangular shapes depict the feeling of an ice-logged setting as the little bear climbs higher and higher on a mountain of snow. The jagged lines of the mountain of snow suggest possible danger if the little bear follows her path. The movement of the star showers brings the reader's interest back to the earth where the action is happening, and takes readers back to the snug den where the mother is safely sleeping. The illustrator changes the color of the little bear from cold white to a warmer pink; this color change suggests that the little bear is ready to return to the warm cave and sleep with mother. On the way back, the curved lines suggest a return to peace and tranquility. Circular shapes suggest safety as little bear reaches home and mother.

To evaluate the impact of shape on mood in illustrated books, analyze several award-winning books and books on the Children's Literature Association's touchstone list. Consider David Wisniewski's illustrations for *Golem,* David Diaz's illustrations for Eve Bunting's *Smoky Night,* Stephen Gammell's illustrations for Karen

Ackerman's *Song and Dance Man*, John Schoenherr's illustrations for Jane Yolen's *Owl Moon*, Richard Egielski's illustrations for Arthur Yorinks's *Hey, Al*, Emily Arnold McCully's illustrations for *Mirette on the High Wire*, Paul O. Zelinsky's illustrations for Grimms' *Rapunzel*, David Small's illustrations for Sarah Stewart's *The Gardener*, and Simms Taback's illustrations for *There Was an Old Lady Who Swallowed a Fly.* Earlier illustrated books on the touchstone list include Robert McCloskey's *Make Way for Ducklings*, Dr. Seuss's *The 500 Hats of Bartholomew Cubbins*, L. Leslie Brooke's *Johnny Crow's Garden*, Kate Greenaway's *A: Apple Pie*, Walter Crane's *The Baby's Opera*, and Wanda Gág's *Millions of Cats.* Do the shapes reinforce the moods of these texts?

TEXTURE

Looking at an object for the first time, a child usually wants to touch it to know how it feels. Experience in touching rough bark, smooth skin, sharp thorns, and soft fur enables children later to imagine how something feels without actually touching it. Illustrators use such visual elements as line, color, and shape to create textural imagery.

Frequently, illustrators who depict the wonders of nature use line to show texture in their illustrations. In Jane Yolen's *Owl Moon*, John Schoenherr (1988) re-creates the texture of the woods outside his studio windows. Viewers can almost feel the tree trunks, the snow-covered landscapes, the small animals peeking from behind trees, and the ultimate owl. Similarly, the thick textures of animals are almost felt in Jon Van Zyle's illustrations for Debbie S. Miller's *A Woolly Mammoth Journey.* The many textures of nature are felt through the watercolors used by Jerry Pinkney in his illustrations for Hans Christian Andersen's *The Ugly Duckling.* The textures range from the feathers of the mother duck to the almost transparent wings of a dragonfly.

The textures associated with the geography and the animals found in the Australian bush are found in Christian Birmingham's illustrations for Michael Morpurgo's *Wombat Goes Walkabout.* The textures range from the wombat's soft fur and whiskers to the spiky undergrowth, allowing readers to vicariously experience the wilderness environment of the Healesville Sanctuary in Australia.

In *The Story of Jumping Mouse*, John Steptoe uses line and shades of black and white to create textures ranging from sharp spikes on cacti to delicate petals on flowers. John Sanford's oil paintings emphasize the textures found in nature in Judit Z. Bodnár's *Tale of a Tail.* The fur of bear and fox, the hatched roof of fox's cottage, and the rough-

For one minute,
three minutes,
maybe even a hundred minutes,
we stared at one another.

Lines and color re-create the texture of an owl. (From Owl Moon *by Jane Yolen. Illustrated by John Schoenherr, text copyright 1987, by Jane Yolen, illustrations © 1987 by John Schoenherr. Reprinted by permission of Philomel books.)*

ness of tree bark all seem very appropriate for this Hungarian folktale.

A child's response to Kenneth Lilly's illustrations in Joyce Pope's *Kenneth Lilly's Animals: A Portfolio of Paintings* shows how effective texture can be in an informational book: The child did not want to put the book away because "I was there with the animals, I kept touching the koala bears to see if they were real."

Design: Organizing the Visual Elements

Design, or composition, is the way in which artists combine the visual elements of line, color, shape, and texture into a unified whole. When an illustration has an overall unity, balance, and sense of rhythm, viewers experience aesthetic pleasure, but when the design is weak, viewers often feel that they are looking at an incomplete, incoherent, or boring picture.

Just as authors develop stories around characterization and plot, illustrators of children's books emphasize certain characters, develop main ideas, and provide background information. They also organize their illustrations so that viewers can identify the most important element in a picture and follow a visual sequence within the picture. Artists show dominance in their work by emphasizing size (the largest form is seen first), contrasting intense colors (an intense area of warm color dominates an intense area of cool color of the same size), placing the most important item in the center, using strong lines to provide visual pathways, and emphasizing nonconformity (viewers' eyes travel to an item that is different). When evaluating illustrations in children's books, consider whether the dominant images are consistent with those of the story.

Tomie dePaola achieves balance through symmetry in his illustrations for Clement Moore's *The Night Before Christmas*. The strong vertical lines of the central fireplace are reinforced by stockings hanging beneath the mantle, candles on the mantle, rows of trees in a picture over the mantle, and the legs of a chair and a table in the room. To the left and the right of the fireplace, portraits face the center of the illustration, where Santa stands on the hearth. For further emphasis, Santa's beard and the fur on his jacket are strikingly white against the rich reds and greens of the room.

Both authors and illustrators of children's books use repetition for emphasis. In illustrations, repetition can create rhythms and provide visual pathways. Virginia Lee Burton's illustrations are excellent examples of this technique. Burton's background in ballet and interest in the spatial concepts of dance may help account for her success in capturing rhythm and move-

DePaola achieves balance through symmetry. Notice the lines of the trees in the painting over the fireplace, the pictures on each side of the fireplace, and the fireplace decorations. (Copyright © 1980 by Tomie dePaola. Reprinted from The Night Before Christmas *by permission of Holiday House, Inc.)*

ment on paper. In *The Little House,* for example, she shows the house sitting on a hill and trees on either side. A row of trees follows the curve of several hills behind the house. On each hill are progressively smaller trees, houses, people, and animals. Beyond the last curving line of trees, the text tells us, lies the city that will soon spread out and surround the little house with traffic and skyscrapers.

Page design, illustrations, and poetic text provide a humorous, unifying whole in Lisa Wheeler's *Seadogs: An Epic Ocean Operetta.* The story of Old Seadog and his friends, Brave Beagle and Dear Dachshund, is written in poetic form as the characters face stormy seas and pirates. The poetry is surrounded by Mark Siegel's cartoonlike illustrations that bring a comic-book feeling to this operatic farce.

Page design can provide a unifying quality. Jeanne McLain Harms and Lucille J. Lettow (1998) emphasize the importance of borders in book and page design when they conclude: "These designs decorate, depict folk designs of a culture, focus on story elements, predict emerging plots, extend the messages of a text, bind the text and illustrations, and break the frame. Cameos in borders and margins of illustrations can play a supporting role by portraying minor elements of the story" (p. 23).

Several artists develop visual continuity by framing text pages or illustrations. For example, Trina Schart

Repetition and line provide a visual pathway and suggest movement. (Illustration by Virginia Lee Burton from The Little House. *Copyright 1942 by Virginia Lee Demetrios. Copyright renewed 1969 by George Demetrios. Reprinted by permission of Houghton Mifflin Co.)*

Hyman frames each text page in Margaret Hodges's *Saint George and the Dragon* with drawings of plants that are indigenous to the British Isles. In the illustrations for *Sindbad: From the Tales of the Thousand and One Nights,* Ludmila Zeman uses rich borders that reflect the Persian influence of the setting. Laszlo Gal borders each illustration in Eva Martin's *Canadian Fairy Tales* with lightly penciled sketches of objects chosen from the appropriate story. In *Hiawatha's Childhood,* derived from Henry Wadsworth Longfellow's famous poems, artist Errol LeCain borders each page with the tall birch trees shown in the cover illustration. Helen Davie uses Native American designs to add authenticity to the borders in Barbara Esbensen's *The Star Maiden.*

Page and book design are especially effective when the design matches and adds to the content of the book. For example, the page design in Janet Stevens's *Tops & Bottoms* provides an interesting topic for discussion as readers consider the impact of the book's design, which is illustrated and printed from top to bottom, with the book bound at the top instead of the normal side-to-side page turning. Notice how Helen Cooper, in *Pumpkin Soup* and in *A Pipkin of Pepper for the Pumpkin Soup,* places the text in different formats and changes the size and density of the text to match the story's actions. J. Alison James's text for *The Drums of Noto Hanto* uses a similar approach, in which the words representing the

sounds of the drums become larger and darker as the drums boom.

In addition to providing unifying qualities, page design should reflect the level of formality of the text. Lyn Ellen Lacy (1986) emphasizes choosing levels of formality that are in harmony with the text. She identifies five levels of formality in book and page design. As you look at total book design, analyze the impact and the appropriateness of each of the levels of formality. First, text placed opposite illustrations on adjacent pages is considered the most formal arrangement. *Saint George and the Dragon,* by Margaret Hodges, has such an arrangement; each text page is blocked in black type and surrounded by a formal border. To add to this formal feeling, each illustrated page is also bounded by a consistent border. The resulting text provides the formal feeling of a traditional legend. Likewise, in *Fables,* Arnold Lobel carefully balances the text and illustrations on facing pages and places them within a border.

Second, text positioned above or beneath illustrations is considered formal. The text for Sid Fleischman's *The Scarebird* is consistently placed under Peter Sís's illustrations. Notice how texts such as *The Scarebird* and Donald Hall's *Ox-Cart Man* still appear formal but not as formal as *Saint George and the Dragon* and *Fables.* Similarly, the text for Virginia Hamilton's *The People Could Fly: The Picture Book* may be either below or above the illustrations. Both the text and Leo and Diane Dillon's illustrations are framed in a colored border that unifies the book. The endpapers are embossed with shiny, black feathers; the feathers reinforce the flight that is found in the title.

Third, text shaped with irregular boundaries to fit inside, between, around, or beside illustrations is considered informal. For example, notice how the text is shaped in Virginia Lee Burton's *The Little House* or in Wanda Gág's *Millions of Cats.*

Fourth, text combined with two or more arrangements is very informal. Julian Scheer's *Rain Makes Applesauce* is a good example of a very informal arrangement: The text is printed in different forms, colors, and sizes, and it appears to be part of Marvin Bileck's illustrations. This level of informality seems appropriate for a nonsense poem.

Finally, absence of text, such as in wordless books and almost-wordless books, is considered the most informal. *Will's Mammoth,* with Rafe Martin's text and Stephen Gammell's illustrations, has such a level of informality. The words that introduce an imaginary experience are printed in different sizes and colors. The illustrations then continue the story wordlessly. Words again written in different sizes and colors conclude the story. This combination is appropriate for a text that encourages imaginative play. As you look at page design, consider the different responses that are possible.

ARTISTIC MEDIA

The elements of line, color, shape, and texture are expressed through the materials and techniques that artists use in illustrating. Ink, wood, paper, paint, and other media can create a wide variety of visual effects. Artist Harry Borgman (1979) indicates a few of the possibilities in stating his own preferences:

> If I want a bright, translucent wash tone, I would either use watercolor or dyes. For an opaque paint that is water resistant, I would use acrylics. If I want to draw a line that will dissolve a bit when water is washed over it, I would use a Pentel Sign pen. (113)

Borgman's remarks suggest the importance of choosing the media and artistic techniques most appropriate for conveying characterization, setting, and mood in a particular story.

Different types of artistic media can be viewed over time using Henry Sayre's *Cave Paintings to Picasso: The Inside Scoop on 50 Art Masterpieces*. The text uses an art history approach to discuss the paintings, and the author presents reproductions of the paintings to explain such artistic techniques as sculpture, woodblock, paint-

ing, and carving. Sayre provides the motivation for writing the book in the following introduction: "This book is inspired by the love, as children, that my brothers and sister and I felt for those pictures. It is, first of all, a picture book. But it is also a book of stories—stories about art that parents can read to their curious children or older kids can read for themselves, and perhaps even come away with a sense of the history of art as a whole. This book is, I hope, above all, a book of discovery, a guide to the magical wonders of the world of art" (p. 9) The author, a Distinguished Professor of Art History, develops the book in chronological order from 22,000 B.C. to a 1964 painting. Each of the mainly two-page spreads includes a time line, a copy of the artwork, and a discussion of the work. The author also provides a glossary of terms and an index.

The Art of Reading: Forty Illustrators Celebrate RIF's 40th Anniversary, edited by Reading Is Fundamental, is an excellent source for studying the range of artistic media and how books provide inspiration for art. Forty illustrators of children's books were asked to reimagine a classic book from their childhood, write a short essay about how the book inspired them, and create an illustration that could accompany the book. Interesting comparisons can be made between the original texts and the artists' current interpretation, for example, Eric Rohmann's illustration accompanying his essay about Wanda Gág's *Millions of Cats*, Steven Kellogg's illustration for Anna Sewell's *Black Beauty*, and Richard Egielski's illustration for *Moby*

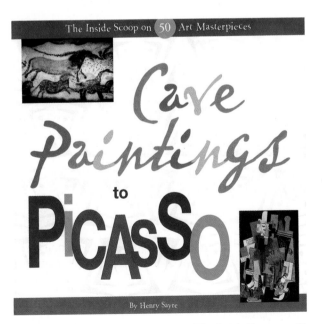

Cover from Cave Paintings to Picasso: The Inside Scoop on 50 Art Masterpieces by Henry Sayre. Text © 2004 by Henry Sayre. Reprinted by permission of Chronicle Books LLC, San Francisco. Visit ChronicleBooks.com

Dick. Comparisons can also be made between the media and style of illustrations that are found in the artists' other works and the example shown in this book. The text concludes with "About the Illustrators"; these brief summaries, which include listings of their illustrated books and any awards and honors presented to them, are very helpful when readers wish to locate additional texts illustrated by the artists.

Lines and Washes

Many illustrations discussed in this chapter rely on lines drawn in ink to convey meaning and develop the mood. For example, the crisp lines and repetition in Wanda Gág's pen-and-ink drawings help readers visualize and believe in a world inhabited by *Millions of Cats*, each of which has special qualities appealing to an old man.

Ink is a versatile medium; it can be applied with brush, sponge, cloth, or even fingers, as well as with pen. In the artist's note about the illustrations for Doreen Cronin's *Click, Clack, Moo: Cows That Type,* Betsy Lewin states that she applied watercolor washes to the black drawings.

Artists also use varying qualities of pen-and-ink line to convey emotions corresponding to characterizations in books. Ray Cruz's drawings for Judith Viorst's *Alexander and the Terrible, Horrible, No Good, Very Bad Day* communicate the essence of a boy who experiences unhappy and frustrating emotions. The scowling expressions and hair on end convey the spirit of a boy who has lost his best friend and doesn't have any dessert in his lunch box.

Shades of water-thinned ink, sparely drawn figures, and textured paper suggest a traditional Japanese setting in Sumiko Yagawa's *The Crane Wife.* Illustrator Suekichi Akaba's traditional Japanese painting techniques complement the story of a transformed crane who rewards a poor farmer for his care but returns to animal form when the young man becomes greedy and breaks his promise.

Watercolors, Acrylics, Pastels, and Oils

Watercolor is one of the most common artistic media chosen by illustrators of children's books. According to art director Lucy Bitzer (1992), "the opportunities offered by the luminous and transparent hues of the watercolor medium make this form a pliant choice to evoke mood, mystery, and timelessness. Specifically, it allows the structure of descriptive drawing to hold its own against a color style" (p. 227). Bitzer identifies Arthur Rackham, who illustrated books in the late 1800s and early 1900s, as one of the first illustrators to recognize the transparent qualities obtainable with watercolors. Edmund Dulac was an-

Strong line and repetition in pencil-and-ink drawings complement a story. (Illustration by Wanda Gág from Millions of Cats. *Copyright 1928; renewed 1956, by Wanda Gág. Reprinted by permission of Coward McCann & Geoghegan, Inc.)*

The illustrations for Jennifer Armstrong's Pierre's Dream *provide a good source for viewing the effectiveness of acrylics. (From* Pierre's Dream *by Jennifer Armstrong, pictures by Susan Gaber. Copyright © 1999 by Susan Gaber, pictures. Used by permission of Dial Books for Young Readers, an imprint of Penguin Putnam Books for Young Readers, a division of Penguin Putnam Inc.)*

other early artist who used watercolors, especially when illustrating folktales.

Laurel Molk's watercolors for Jane Yolen's *Off We Go!* suggest a close relationship with nature. The transparent qualities are especially noticeable in an illustration depicting a fragile spider's web with blues and greens in the background.

David Wiesner's *Tuesday* is an excellent example of watercolors in illustration: The paintings go from the transparency of a curtain to the heavy leaves and trees of the outdoor setting. Likewise, the lighting changes from dark shadows to brilliant moonlight. In Frances Ward Weller's *I Wonder If I'll See a Whale*, Ted Lewin's illustrations contrast the colors of life above the sea and the blues and greens of life below the sea. Several pictures create a feeling of looking through the water with its levels of color and changes in current.

Greg Couch's watercolors used to illustrate Jane Cutler's *The Cello of Mr. O.* exemplify the range of moods that can be created by this medium. There is the desolation of a war-torn city, but also the glowing feelings associated with music. When Mr. O begins playing, the paintings take on an almost transparent appearance as birds and flowers rise out of the instrument. The illustrations match the moods that go from fear to happiness.

Humor can also be created through the use of watercolors, as shown in James Marshall's illustrations for Edward Lear's *The Owl and the Pussycat*. Read the comments written by Maurice Sendak in the Afterword of the book and see if you agree with his conclusion: "There never was such an Owl and Pussycat, certainly not since Edward Lear, and for my money James surpasses Lear's original pictures in sheer giddy humor and heartfeltness" (unnumbered).

The effects of three color media—watercolors, pastels, and acrylics—are seen in Leo and Diane Dillon's illustrations for Margaret Musgrove's *Ashanti to Zulu: African Traditions*. Vibrantly colored jewelry and designs on artifacts contrast with the soft shades of the flowing garments. The river in the illustration that depicts the Lozi people is so transparent that the bottom of the boat shimmers through the water. In other pictures, the sky vibrates with heat from the sun, and jewel-like tones express the breathtaking beauty of exotic birds and plants.

James Rumford's illustrations for *Sequoyah: The Cherokee Man Who Gave His People Writing* are a combi-

The transparent quality of watercolors suggests a close relationship with nature in this spider's web in Laurel Molk's illustrations for Jane Yolen's Off We Go! *(From* Off We Go!, *by Jane Yolen. Text copyright © 2000 by Jane Yolen. Illustrations © 2000 by Laurel Molk. Published by Little, Brown & Company. Reprinted by permission of the publisher.)*

nation of watercolor, pastel, pencil, and ink. A textured feeling is developed by creating the illustrations on a rough piece of wood. Alison Jay used oils painted on paper with a crackling varnish to illustrate Carolyn Curtis's *I Took the Moon for a Walk*.

Brightly colored illustrations result from the use of acrylics and crayons in Ana Juan's illustrations for Campbell Geeslin's *Elena's Serenade*. The resulting stylized folk art develops the mood of this story set in Mexico. The technique seems very appropriate to illustrate a story about a young girl's desire to create her own artistic works.

According to an interview with Marisa Bulzone (1993), illustrator Gary Kelley is inspired by oil paintings, but he creates his works in pastels. Kelley used pastels in the illustrations for Washington Irving's *The Legend of Sleepy Hollow* because he was influenced by the paintings

Hand holding hand through the starry night sky   when I took the Moon for a walk.

Illustration from I Took the Moon for a Walk, *written by Carolyn Curtis, text copyright © 2004 Carolyn Curtis. Illustrated by Alison Jay. Illustrations copyright © 2004 Alison Jay. Reprinted by permission of Barefoot Books.*

of John Singleton Copley, Charles Wilson Peale, and the Hudson River and Naive schools of painting. He states, "I wanted my illustrations to reflect their color palettes and the way these painters handled similar subject matter" (p. 96). As you look at illustrations by Gary Kelley, try to analyze how he was influenced by oil paintings.

Paul O. Zelinsky's full-page oil paintings create a somber mood for *Hansel and Gretel*, as told by the Brothers Grimm. Zelinsky's woods are menacing, where evil is likely to exist. The rich highlights that are possible with oil are shown in Zelinsky's illustrations for the Brothers Grimm's *Rumpelstiltskin* and *Rapunzel*. Likewise, Thomas Locker's full-page oil paintings for Jean Craighead George's *The First Thanksgiving* show the shadings, highlights, colors, and textures possible with oils. Lane Smith (1993), the illustrator of Jon Scieszka's *The True Story of the 3 Little Pigs!* and *The Stinky Cheese Man and Other Fairly Stupid Tales*, describes how he uses oil paint on illustration board to acquire the desired effects:

> Everything I do is oil paint on board. I get texture from a variety of means. Usually it involves some sort of acrylic paints or sprays to cause a reaction. . . . Sometimes, if the painting gets really thick, I'll sand down areas to another layer. I've always been attracted to texture. (p. 70)

Woodcuts

Woodcuts are among the oldest and most influential artistic media in both Western and Eastern cultures. In the 15th century, the black-and-white woodcuts of the German artist Albrecht Dürer brought this medium to a new level of sophistication in Europe. These early woodcuts, which were often drawings of animals, influenced the ways in which people saw and thought about nature (Quammen, 1993). The first printed books, including the earliest books for children, were illustrated with black-and-white woodcuts. Later, Japanese artists pioneered in the creation of full-color woodcuts, inspiring other artists in Europe and North America, such as the famous French artist Paul Gauguin.

To create a woodcut, an artist draws an image on a block of wood and cuts away the areas around the design. After rolling ink onto this raised surface, the artist presses the woodblock against paper, transferring the image to the paper. Color prints require a different woodblock for each color in the picture. Woodcuts can be printed in colors with varying degrees of transparency, and the grain and texture of the wood can add to the effect of the composition. Carol Finley's *Art of Japan* focuses on the woodblock prints made in Japan between 1600 and 1868. The paint-

Dark, somber tones in full-page oil paintings create an appropriately menacing setting for a dramatic folktale. (From Hansel and Gretel. *Illustrated by Paul O. Zelinsky and retold by Rika Lesser. Illustrations copyright © 1984 by Paul O. Zelinsky, Dodd Mead. Reprinted by permission.*

ings reproduced in the book show landscapes that celebrate the beauty and meditative quality of nature, birds, and flowers, and the dramatic style of Kabuki acting. The author also describes the creation of the woodblock prints as well as how this period in Japanese art influenced European artists.

The strong lines and bold colors of woodcuts create a simplicity often desired by illustrators of folktales. Gail Haley used woodcuts to illustrate her version of an African folktale, *A Story, a Story.* The grain of the wood replicates the texture of native huts and communicates the earthy nature of a traditional setting.

The effects of Betsy Bowen's woodcuts can be analyzed in her illustrations for Lise Lunge-Larsen's *The Troll With No Heart in His Body and Other Tales of Trolls From Norway.* The rough texture seems very appropriate for illustrating hags, shaggy goats, and all types of trolls.

Kevin Crossley-Holland illustrates his story set in the Middle Ages, *Arthur: The Seeing Stone,* with woodcuts from the publication "Medieval Life Illustrations." The use of these reproductions of early woodcuts adds a sense of authenticity to a book set in England and Wales in

1199. Christopher Wormell's linoleum block prints for his *Teeth, Tails, & Tentacles: An Animal Counting Book* suggest a three-dimensional quality that invites readers to touch the body and teeth of the crocodile or the suckers on an octopus's tentacles.

Collage

Collage—a word derived from the French word *coller,* meaning "to paste" or "to stick"—is a recent addition to the world of book illustration. Pasting and sticking are exactly what artists do when using this technique. Any object or substance that can be attached to a surface can be used to develop a design; artists may use cardboard, paper, cloth, glass, leather, metal, wood, leaves, flowers, or even butterflies. They may cut up and rearrange their own paintings or use paint and other media to add background. When photographically reproduced, collages still communicate texture.

Eric Carle, a popular artist of picture books for children, is known for his striking colorful storybooks; *The Very Hungry Caterpillar* won the American Institute of Graphic Art's award for 1970. Carle develops his collages through a three-step process. He begins by applying acrylic paints to tissue paper. Then, he uses rubber cement to paste the paper into the desired designs. Finally, he applies colored crayon to provide accents. In *Eric Carle's Animals Animals,* tissue-paper collage creates a dazzling array of animals. In Laura Whipple's *Eric Carle's Dragons Dragons & Other Creatures That Never Were,* Carle painted on thin tissue papers and then cut or tore the papers into shapes and glued them onto the illustration boards; the painted tissue papers create smooth and silky illustrations. Carle's collages for *From Head to Toe* compare movements among animals and children. Carle adds a sensory feature to his large, colorful collages in *The Very Clumsy Click Beetle:* Readers can hear a loud click as the beetle overcomes his clumsiness and learns how to accomplish somersaults. In *Mister Seahorse,* Carle uses painted tissue paper to create his very colorful collages. Cut-paper collages also provide color, light, and texture in Carle's *10 Little Rubber Ducks.*

Cut-paper collages using different types and thicknesses of paper form Javaka Steptoe's illustrations for Karen English's *Hot Day on Abbott Avenue.* To suggest perspiration on the clothes, the artist uses sheer crepe paper, and to suggest the texture of jump ropes, she uses twists of raffia and twine.

Melissa Sweet's illustrations for Jacqueline Davies's *The Boy Who Drew Birds: A Story of John James Audubon* show the various textures that are possible with collage. As is appropriate for a book about a young man who observed nature and drew birds, the collages develop a strong feeling of nature in illustrations that include bird nests, feathers, and bits of bark.

Another artist who illustrates with collage is Ezra Jack Keats. In *Peter's Chair,* lace looks realistic as it cascades

The collage illustrations reflect the changing moods of the Mississippi River. (From Steamboat! The Story of Captain Blanche Leathers, by Judith Heide Gilliland, illustrated by Holly Meade. Copyright © 2000 by DK Publishing. Reprinted by permission of the publisher.)

From Bridges Are to Cross by Philemon Sturges. Text copyright © 1998 by Philemon Sturges. Illustrations © 1998 by Giles Laroche. Used by permission of Putnam's Sons, a division of Penguin. Putnam, Inc.

from the inside of a bassinet. On the same page, pink wallpaper with large flowers provides the background for the baby sister's room. Keats also combines paints and collage in his illustrations, which he used effectively in *The Trip*, where the illustrations have a three-dimensional quality appropriate for a story about a boy who builds his old neighborhood within a box and then visits it in his imagination. A humorous mood is created by Simms Taback in *Joseph Had a Little Overcoat*. The artist uses a combination of collage, watercolor, gouache, pencil, and ink; cut shapes in the pages provide an additional sense of mystery as Joseph recycles his overcoat into smaller and smaller objects.

Marcia Brown uses collage and paint to match the mood of the text in Blaise Cendrars's *Shadow*. Brown's strong, dark images of the nighttime forest and her wispy ghosts strongly reinforce the spell cast by the storyteller.

Illustrators use numerous materials to produce three-dimensional pictures. In the illustrations for Eve Bunting's *Smoky Night*, David Diaz uses cut fragments of glass, scattered cereals, burned matches, and jagged paper to create a feeling of confusion and terror associated with the Los Angeles riots.

Richard Keep's collage illustrations for *Clatter Bash! A Day of the Dead Celebration* complement the text that depicts the rhythmic and joyous Mexican holiday. The illustrations show playful skeletons who rise from their graves and party by singing, dancing, and telling stories. Keep states that he chose a "traditional Mexican approach to create the cut-paper montage illustrations in this book, using simple materials at hand such as painted papers, papel picado (perforated paper), a mate bark paper (hand made by Otomi artisans), acrylic and watercolor paints, pens, and markers" (About the Author and Illustrator, unnumbered).

David Wisniewski uses cut-paper illustrations very effectively in *Rain Player*, a Mayan tale. In the author's note, Wisniewski describes his technique:

The pictures were first drawn on layout paper in pencil, then drawn more tightly with a technical pen on tracing paper. . . . Each portion was transferred to the back of colored papers with carbon paper, then cut out with a #11 X-Acto blade.

The pieces were assembled with double-stick photo mountings and foam tape. The finished artwork was then photographed, with each piece lit to provide the most dramatic shadows. (author's note)

You can compare the moods of David Wisniewski's collages in *Golem*, a Jewish tale, with those of the collages he created for Aaron Shepard's *Master Man: A Tale of Nigeria*.

Artistic Style

Every artist has a style that distinguishes his or her artistic vision, serving as that person's signature. Numerous artists, however, gravitate toward similar ways of making visual statements through the use of line, color, shape, and texture. The many different styles of visual art identified by art critics and historians are too complex for this text to discuss in detail. This section, however, considers two very general categories of artistic style, the *representational* and the *abstract*.

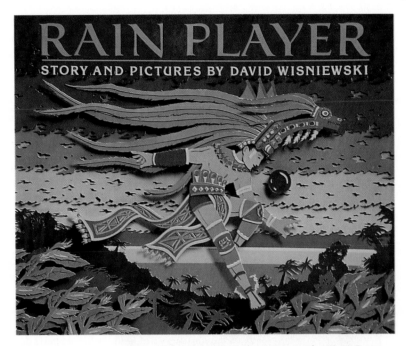

Cut-paper illustrations provide color and dimension for a Mayan tale. (From Rain Player *by David Wisniewski. Copyright © 1991 by David Wisniewski. Used by permission of Clarion Books/Houghton Mifflin Co. All rights reserved.*)

Representational Art

Representational art, sometimes also called realistic art, depicts subjects as they are seen in everyday life. Representational artists do not necessarily attempt to create photographically exact images of their subjects. Instead, they create compositions that refer clearly to people, objects, or natural phenomena in realistic ways. Many of the paintings and sculptures most familiar to us, such as Leonardo da Vinci's *Mona Lisa* and Auguste Rodin's *The Thinker*, are representational in style.

Since the first books for children were illustrated, the pictures in most children's books have been representational, as examples throughout this text show. Realistic imagery helps children identify with and learn more about things in their environments, giving them familiar bases from which to expand their understanding of the world. Lynd Ward's illustrations for *The Biggest Bear* are excellent examples of the use of representational art to create the details of a realistic story. Readers can almost feel the rough shingles and unpainted siding on the buildings, and the wheat looks ripe enough to harvest. When the bear cub runs in to claim the mash prepared for the chickens, several frightened chickens look as if they will fly off the page.

Author-illustrator Holling Clancy Holling combines imaginative fiction with factual information in beautifully illustrated books that take their themes from North American history and geography. Holling's detailed, realistic illustrations draw older children into both new adventure and new learning. In *Paddle-to-the-Sea*, a Native American boy in the Canadian wilderness carves a wooden canoe and "paddle person," which he launches on a journey from Lake Superior to the Atlantic Ocean. *Seabird* is an ivory gull carved by a young sailor on a whaling vessel. The gull accompanies several generations of one American family on their ocean voyages around the world. In each book, full-page realistic paintings in color encourage readers to enter the different settings of the story, and detailed black-and-white drawings on the text pages show, for example, how a sawmill turns logs into boards and how volcanoes in an ocean create islands.

Modern book illustrators, like most contemporary artists, have been profoundly influenced by stylistic innovations that have occurred over the last 100 years. Nineteenth-century French artist Claude Monet was among those who initiated a new approach to representational art, known as *impressionism* (originally a derogatory term applied by a disapproving critic). Impressionists departed from the tradition of representing the world in complex detail; instead, they focused on the play of light over objects in the natural environment. Usually working from outdoor subjects, they experimented with breaking up colors and shapes to create an *impression* of the scintillating, changeable quality of light. "Monet's goal was to capture a visual 'impression' of what the eye sees, regardless of subject. Traditional critics were as upset by this attitude to subject matter as they were by Monet's loose brushstrokes" (Wilkins, Schultz, & Linduff, 2005). Whatever the original criticism, impressionism has had considerable influence on contemporary illustrators of children's books.

An oil painting reflecting impressionist style depicts a sunset landscape and a tranquil mood. (From Sailing With the Wind *by Thomas Locker, copyright © 1986 by Thomas Locker. Reprinted by permission of Dial Books for Young Readers.)*

Thomas Locker's oil paintings for *Where the River Begins* reveal impressionist influences on this modern artist. Locker's magnificent landscapes shimmer with sunlight emerging through mist, the moon illuminating rushing water, and the reflection of sunset on billowing clouds.

Expressionism, a later stylistic development in representational art, uses visual elements to express artists' deepest inner feelings. Expressionist paintings by such artists as Vincent van Gogh and Edvard Munch reverberate with the rhythm of intense emotion expressed through emphatic color, texture, and movement of line. Such art begins to move away from the representational into the more abstractly symbolic. (Later, 20th-century artists such as Jackson Pollock developed a style known as *abstract expressionism*.)

Expressionistic influences are vividly evident in Toshi Maruki's illustrations for her book *Hiroshima No Pika (The Flash of Hiroshima)*. Maruki's uses of color and shape reinforce the emotional impact of horrific devastation, as a mother and child experience the aftereffects of the atomic bomb. Swirling red flames pass over the forms of fleeing people and animals. Black clouds cover the forms of huddling masses and destroyed buildings. A more realistic rendering of this holocaust would probably be far less powerful.

Leonard Fisher's expressionistic paintings complement the mood of Myra Cohn Livingston's poems in *A Circle of Seasons*. Whites and pinks suggest apple blossoms

and dogtooth violets. Greens and yellows symbolize the warming sun, the rain, and awakening earth in spring. Hot sun reds, watery blues, and corn-ripened yellows seem appropriate for paintings accompanying summer poems, and the oranges, reds, and shimmering frost against a dark blue sky suggest changing moods of autumn. In winter paintings, white squares against shades of blue and purple suggest ice crystals and snowflakes converging on a bleak winter world. The wintery mood is supplemented by hoarfrost, icicles, and frosted windowpanes that gleam in silvery needle shapes against a dark blue background.

ABSTRACT ART

Some abstract art takes ordinary things as subjects but emphasizes certain characteristics by changing or distorting the usual images. Pablo Picasso's abstract paintings, for example, reduce people and familiar objects to angular forms and shifting planes. The work of other modern artists has become so abstract—focusing on pure form and representing no actual person, place, or thing—that art experts describe it as *nonrepresentational*. For example, Piet Mondrian's famous geometrical compositions in oil show the artists's attempts at visual statements that have "little or no reference to the appearance of natural objects" (Janson & Janson, 2006, p. 651).

The elimination of representational images characteristic of abstract art is evident in Beverly Brodsky McDermott's illustrations for *The Golem*, a Jewish legend about a rabbi who uses a magic spell to create a man out of clay. McDermott (1976) says:

> As I explored the mysteries of the Golem, an evolution took place. At first, he resembled something human. Then he was transformed. His textured body became a powerful presence lurking in dark corners, spilling out of my paintings. In the end he shatters into pieces of clay-color and returns to the earth. All that remains is the symbol of silence. (foreword)

Both expressionist and abstract influences are apparent in Leo Lionni's illustrations. Lionni uses watercolors, textured collages, and thickly painted surfaces to recreate the feeling of a watery world in *Swimmy*. This is not a realistic world of easily discernible water plants and animals: Seaweed has the texture of painted doilies, and fish are only suggestive outlines.

Janice Hartwick Dressel (1984) presents arguments for and against using abstract art in children's books. She concludes that exposing children to such sophisticated, symbolical art may encourage higher levels of thinking and may enhance aesthetic response to all art.

Outstanding Illustrators of Children's Books

A close look at several artists reveals the wide range of excellence in children's book illustration and the ways in which individuals fluent in artistic grammar create visual narratives that appeal to young children.

The artists discussed in this chapter use the elements of line, color, shape, and texture to create memorable illustrations that highlight the moods of the texts. These illustrations provide numerous opportunities for both children and adults to interact with visual elements and to improve their appreciation of art.

Barbara Cooney

Barbara Cooney's illustrations for Donald Hall's *Ox-Cart Man* use gentle colors and rounded shapes to evoke the peaceful countryside. Cooney creates the same mood in *Island Boy:* Soft colors and curved landscapes add to the feeling of an unhurried way of life in which a young boy can explore the joys of his New England home. In Cooney's illustrations for *Chanticleer and the Fox,* however, bold, black lines create a strutting, vain rooster in the earlier portion of the book and a frightened, humble one as the story reaches its climax in the life-and-death struggle between Chanticleer and his enemy, the fox.

Cooney is skilled in using artistic techniques that best complement a particular text. Her illustrations for Margot Griego et al.'s *Tortillitas Para Mama and Other Spanish Nursery Rhymes* re-create the varied settings associated with Latin American nursery rhymes. Warm browns depict the interior of a Mexican home, cool blues warmed by the shining moon suggest a village by the water, and warm fuchsia pinks reflect the warmth of a mother and father sharing a quiet time with their baby.

Cooney's illustrations for Jane Yolen's *Letting Swift River Go* take viewers back to the rural life in western Massachusetts and to the memories of a town that was submerged when the Quabbin Reservoir was formed. Before illustrating Michael Bedard's *Emily,* Cooney conducted research at Emily Dickinson's home in Amherst, Massachusetts. Cooney painted the illustrations for *Emily* on China silk mounted on illustration board, using liquitex acrylic paints, prismacolor, and Derwent colored pencils and pastels. Cooney also illustrates the earlier rural setting of Columbia County, New York, for Mary Lyn Ray's *Basket Moon.*

Tomie dePaola

Tomie dePaola has illustrated, or written and illustrated, more than 100 books, including traditional folktales from Italy, Scandinavia, and Mexico; informational books; realistic fiction; and Bible stories.

DePaola's illustations for *The Clown of God* reveal the influence of two pre-Renaissance artists, Giotto and Fra Angelico, whose simplicity and strength of line dePaola admires: "I almost reduce features to a symbol. And yet I think of my faces as good and warm. I try to show expression in very few lines" (Hepler, 1979, p. 299). For *The Clown of God,* dePaola first penciled in the lines and then went over the sketches with raw sienna waterproof ink, a

Barbara Cooney uses gentle colors and rounded shapes to re-create the feeling of an earlier rural setting in Mary Lyn Ray's Basket Moon. *(From* Basket Moon *by Mary Lyn Ray. Text copyright © 1999 by Mary Lyn Ray, illustrations copyright © 1999 by Barbara Cooney. Published by Little, Brown & Company. Reprinted by permission of the publisher.)*

Through the Eyes of an ILLUSTRATOR

Tomie dePaola

Visit the CD-ROM that accompanies this text to generate a complete list of Tomie dePaola titles.

Selected Titles by Tomie dePaola
- Strega Nona
- Clown of God: An Old Story
- The Mysterious Giant of Barletta
- The Art Lessons
- Nana Upstairs & Nana Downstairs

Illustrating and Books

I am a doodler. In fact, I *love* to doodle. I always have. I keep pads of scratch paper and black and red fine-line markers by the telephones, at my drawing table, on my desk, in my carry-on bag when I fly; and when I was teaching, I never went to a meeting (faculty, committee, etc.) without my handy pad and markers.

Growing up, coloring books were absent from our house . . . at least, in my room. My tools were plain paper, pencils, and my trusty Crayolas. After all, I was going to be an artist when I grew up. And besides, my own drawings and doodles seemed to be far more interesting to me, and those around me, than the simple coloring book images. (My mother also admitted that plain paper was lots cheaper.)

I learned at an early age that there was a definite difference between out-and-out drawing and serious doodling. A drawing had more structure, more directiion. A definite idea was usually the beginning of a drawing. For example, I might say, "I think I will do a drawing of a girl ice skating, wearing a fancy Ice Follies–type costume." (Yes, the Ice Follies were around way back then.) Then the problem would be to try to do a drawing that coincided with my original idea or vision.

Doodles were (and are) totally different. I would just put pencil to paper and see what happened. All sorts of interesting images would result. I might start out not really concentrating on my doodle but on what else I was doing at the time. Talking on the phone was a very good activity for doodling. Late at night under the covers with a flashlight and listening to the radio was another activity that produced more terrific doodles—some actually on sheets rather than on paper. The "state of the art" doodles of this period, though, appeared as if by early magic on my arithmetic papers. There would be columns of figures copied from the blackboard and before I knew it, the paper would be covered with pictures with no room for the answers. My teachers—well, at least, a few of them—were *not* amused. They warned me. I'd never learn to add, subtract, multiply, etc. They were right, but for me as an artist, the doodling proved to be a far more important activity. I was able to buy a cal-

culator with a royalty check, and now, I have an accountant.

"Meeting doodles," especially faculty meeting doodles, proved to be among the most valuable for me. It was during a college faculty meeting that was about the same issues the previous dozen meetings had been about that "Strega Nona" appeared on my pad. I didn't know who she was at that moment, but a few months on my studio wall, and she soon let me know all about herself.

I've just opened a drawer and found some doodles that were done several years ago. (I stash doodles in different drawers so they can show up later and surprise me. My assistant saves all the phone-call doodles for me. My mother and an old friend both have doodles of mine in special drawers, waiting for the day they can cash in on them.)

The newfound doodles are on the wall of my studio. There is a rather fetching sheep and two classy cats, dressed to kill. Who knows . . . someday. . . . But remember! You read about them here first!

Video Profiles: The accompanying video contains conversations from such children's book artists as E. B. Lewis, Molly Bang, Floyd Cooper, and Lynne Cherry.

---

second brown pencil line, and brown ink. He completed the artwork with watercolors.

DePaola emphasizes that his great love of folk art is a strong element in his work. Consequently, according to Masha Rudman (1993b), he was inspired by the early works of Alice and Martin Provensen. Strong feelings for Americana are found in dePaola's *An Early American Christmas*. Many of dePaola's illustrations and texts such as *Christopher: The Holy Giant* reflect his belief that children and adults should be exposed to the rich heritage of ethnic folklore. In his illustrations for *The Legend of the Bluebonnet, The Legend of the Indian Paintbrush*, and numerous folktales from various European countries, dePaola combines folk art and folktale.

DePaola also values his theater experience and makes use of it in his illustrations: "There are so many ways picture books are like theater-scenes, settings, characterization. A double page spread can be like a stage" (Hepler, 1979, p. 300). DePaola's illustrations often have the symmetry of stage settings, with actions that appear to take place in front of a backdrop. *Giorgio's Village*, for example,

a pop-up book that re-creates an Italian Renaissance village, is itself a stagelike setting in which windows open and tabs allow movement. Some of the illustrations in *Tomie dePaola's Mother Goose* also have the appearance of stage settings.

Other books show the influence of films. In *Watch Out for the Chicken Feet in Your Soup*, the action in the story and illustrations starts before the title page, which becomes part of both the narrative and the action. In these and other ways, dePaola's large body of work demonstrates his belief that children should be exposed to many types of visual imagery.

Leo and Diane Dillon

Leo and Diane Dillon's strong interest in the folklore of traditional peoples is evident in their award-winning books. Their work reflects careful research into the decorative motifs of many cultures and helps re-create and preserve traditional ways of life.

The text for Mildred Pitts Walter's *Brother to the Wind* is rich in folklore, symbols, and dreams. The Dillons

Through the Eyes of a CHILD

Lauryn
Grade I

TITLE: Stagestruck
AUTHOR: Tomie DePaola

I licked this book beckebkus I l liked the piekchres. I liked the colres and bunnies. It made me feel happy. It was a store about a boy that liked to be on stage.

Laulyn

use light and dark, pastels and deep colors, to contrast a boy's mythical quest to fly and the earthbound unbelievers who are sure that he will fail. In one illustration, the wind, which makes it possible for the boy to fly, is a transparent woman whose color and shape blend into the pale, cloudy sky. Viewers are given the impression that only they and the boy, not the doubting villagers, can see the wind.

Leo and Diane Dillon have illustrated the title tale from Hamilton's book *The People Could Fly: American Black Folktales* in *The People Could Fly: The Picture Book.* The illustrations and the text develop a formal presentation of the story, with both text and illustrations bordered on three sides. The expressions on the faces show the human torture of people bound in chains and the joy that comes with flying away from bondage into freedom. Their illustrations for Verna Aardema's *Why Mosquitoes Buzz in People's Ears* re-create the setting of a traditional African folktale. In Virginia Hamilton's *Her Stories: African American Folktales, Fairy Tales, and True Tales*, the artists painted with acrylics on illustration board. Acrylics are also used to illustrate Howard Norman's *The Girl Who Dreamed Only Geese and Other Tales of the Far North.* In every case, careful research preceded the Dillons' illustrations.

Ezra Jack Keats

Ezra Jack Keats combines collage, paint, and empathy for children's needs and emotions in compositions that portray inner-city life. Sometimes, the environment is peaceful, as in *The Snowy Day,* where Keats uses brilliantly white torn paper to convey the snow covering chimneys and rooftops as Peter looks out on a fresh, white world. Later, shadowy blue footprints bring the text and the illustrations together, asking readers to look at Peter's footprints in the snow. Snowbanks are rounded shapes, and buildings are rectangles of color in the background. Peter's simple, red-clad figure stands out against the snowy background.

Keats evokes quite a different mood with collage and paint in *Goggles!* Here, two children confront harsher realities, as they try to escape from bigger boys who want their possessions. The colors are dark, and the collages include thrown-away items that one might find in back alleys. Keats shows the frightening big boys as almost featureless. In one picture, a hole in a piece of wood frames the scene as the two small boys look through it and plan how to get home. In other books—such as *Louie, The Trip,* and *Peter's Chair*—illustrations by Keats complement the loneliness, daydreams, or jealousy described in the text.

Joseph Schwarcz (1982) believes that children respond to books by Keats, such as *Apt. 3,* because

the illustrations dramatize the lyrical mood, probably also making it more easily accessible for the younger reader. The gestures and postures of the people in the story are down to earth, outspoken. The important visual motifs are the ones we know well. The apartment building is muddy and ugly.

The large shapes of the boys, painted from a close angle, evoke intimacy. From the beginning there is visual metaphor. (p. 188)

Robert McCloskey

Robert McCloskey's illustrations present the real world of boys, girls, families, and animals. Detailed black-and-white drawings depict the settings in most of his books, although McCloskey also uses color to evoke the essence of an island susceptible to forces of nature in *Time of Wonder*. In that book, McCloskey's watercolors first depict a serene world. When gentle rain approaches, the painting is so transparent that the first thing seen is a thin mist descending. Later, diagonal lines of raindrops break the surface of the peaceful water, and light fog surrounds two children, who experience the whispering sound of growing ferns. The island is not always serene, however: A hurricane bends the lines of the trees, as the illustrations themselves almost move on the page. McCloskey's use of line is so compelling that Lyn Ellen Lacy (1986) uses page-by-page discussion of *Make Way for Ducklings* and *Time of Wonder* to analyze line in McCloskey's Caldecott Award–winning books.

Black-and-white drawings illustrate McCloskey's delightful *Blueberries for Sal*. The child, whether stealing berries from a pail or mistakenly following a mother bear instead of her own mother, looks as if she could walk right off the page.

Alice and Martin Provensen

Color, symmetry, and effective use of space are noteworthy elements in the work of Alice and Martin Provensen. Many illustrations by the Provensens, whose collaborative effects include more than 50 books, reflect the world in earlier times or worlds of fantasy. The Provensens create a feeling of flying through space in their book about the first flight across the English Channel, *The Glorious Flight Across the Channel With Louis Bleriot, July 25, 1909*. Consecutive illustrations proceed from a close-up of the plane before it soars to a wide-angle view of the small plane surrounded by clouds and sky. The corresponding text reveals that Louis Bleriot is alone, lost in a world of swirling fog. The illustrators' use of space and color reinforces this mood of danger and exhilaration.

The impact of symmetry in design is felt in several of the Provensens' illustrations for Nancy Willard's *A Visit to William Blake's Inn: Poems for Innocent and Experienced Travelers*. In one illustration, for example, the Wonderful

Car hovers over buildings that provide a visual center for the car; the steps of the flying vehicle lead viewers toward the passengers; and the two smaller sets of propeller blades balance the larger center blade.

Maurice Sendak

Time magazine has called Maurice Sendak "the Picasso of children's books." Sendak's artistic versatility in using color, line, and balance is evident in the many books that Sendak has illustrated or written and illustrated, including Janice Udry's *The Moon Jumpers*. One of Sendak's primary aims in illustrating a text is to make "the pictures so organically akin to the text, so reflective of its atmosphere, that they look as if they could have been done in no other way. They should help create the special world of the story . . . creating the air for a writer" (Moritz, 1968, p. 352).

Sendak's special relationship between text and illustrations may be most apparent in *Outside Over There* and *Where the Wild Things Are*. Sendak (Davis, 1981) described the steps he took in creating the illustrations for *Outside Over There*, which he considers his best and most significant children's book. One of his first concerns was drawing 10-year-old Ida holding a baby. To reproduce realistic body postures, Sendak made photographs of a child holding a baby. The baby kept slipping out of the child's arms, so that the clothes on both children drooped and became disheveled. Sendak referred to watercolors by the British poet and artist William Blake for inspiration in choosing colors that communicate the setting, characterization, and mood:

> The colors belong to Ida. She is rural, of the time in the country when winter sunsets have that certain yellow you never see in other seasons. There's a description of women's clothing, watered silk, and that's what those skies are like—moist, sensuous, silken, almost transparent—the color I copied in the cape Ida wears and in other things showing up against soft mauve, blue, green, tan—all part of the story's feeling. (p. 46)

The illustrations for *Where the Wild Things Are* are totally integrated with the text and play a crucial role in the plot and characterization, as well as the setting. When Max is banished to his room for bad behavior, the room gradually becomes the kingdom of the wild things, with trees growing naturally out of the bedposts and the shag rug turning into grass. As the story progresses, the illustrations cover more and more of the page; when Max becomes king of the wild things, six pages of illustrations are uninterrupted by text. Sendak creates a believably mischievous boy and humorous but forceful wild things with terrible rolling eyes and horrible gnashing teeth.

Brian Alderson (1993b) maintains that with the illustration of *Where the Wild Things Are*, Sendak shifted the load-bearing responsibility in his books from words to pictures. As you look at books illustrated by Maurice Sendak, notice how much of the story is extended, or even totally told, through the illustrations. The illustrations are espe-

---

Technology Resources

Use the CD-ROM that accompanies this text to generate a list of works by your favorite illustrator. You can add your own comments concerning individual titles in the comment field at the bottom of the record.

cially important in Sendak's *We Are All in the Dumps With Jack and Guy*, where Sendak uses two nursery rhymes to provide minimal text. The illustrations, however, develop a contemporary story about the harsh reality of homelessness and poverty. Even the newspapers used as protection emphasize the contemporary social conflict between wealth and poverty.

Selma Lanes's *The Art of Maurice Sendak* (1980) provides biographical information as well as examples from Sendak's numerous books. Sendak's *Posters by Maurice Sendak* (1986) provides examples from many occasions. The posters also show how important wild things are in Sendak's art.

Chris Van Allsburg

Chris Van Allsburg's *The Garden of Abdul Gasazi, Jumanji, The Mysteries of Harris Burdick*, and *The Widow's Broom* demonstrate the effectiveness of black-and-white illustrations. Both line and subtle shading focus attention along a visual pathway in the illustrations for *The Garden of Abdul Gasazi*. In one picture, the main character is framed by a central doorway. On either side of the doorway, bright statues against dark leaves point down a black tunnel toward a circle of white. This circle represents the garden in which the story line develops. (Symmetry is one way that artists create balance in their designs.)

In *The Wreck of the Zephyr*, Van Allsburg uses line to create movement and color to convey mood. As the story begins, rolling waves and billowing dark clouds suggest movement and the ominous forces of angry sea and sky.

Symmetry of design directs viewers toward the distant garden. (Illustration by Chris Van Allsburg from The Garden of Abdul Gasazi. *Copyright 1979 by Chris Van Allsburg. Reprinted by permission of Houghton Mifflin Company.)*

Later, the mood changes to fantasy, and Van Allsburg uses color to create a calm sea sparkling with light, a fantasy harbor town seen through shadows, soft clouds tinged with sunset, and a star-studded sky.

Compare Van Allsburg's use of line and shading in his black-and-white illustrations with his use of line and color in *The Wreck of the Zephyr, The Polar Express, The Wretched Stone*, and *The Sweetest Fig*. In *The Polar Express*, Van Allsburg uses line to create the furry textures of lean wolves roaming the dark forests and the feathery texture of newly fallen snow; even Santa Claus's beard and mittens seem to have texture. Van Allsburg also uses contrasting light and dark colors and shadings effectively. Moonlight focuses attention on the boy in his darkened bedroom, train windows glow with warmth as the train winds through cold forests and up snow-covered mountains, and city lights stream from windows to pierce the darkness.

David Wiesner

David Wiesner is best known for his wordless books, Caldecott Medal winner *Tuesday* and Caldecott Honor book *Free Fall*. In an interview conducted by Susan Caroff and Elizabeth Moje (1992/1993), Wiesner states:

Wordless books have been my passion for a long time. It's something that goes way back. I've always liked telling stories with pictures, more than just painting a single painting. If I came up with an image that I liked—I would always be interested in seeing what had happened before or after the particular image I had painted. (p. 284)

Wiesner is pleased when his wordless books are used to stimulate creativity. He maintains that his books need readers because the author's voice is not there in the form of text. Words do not anchor the stories to reality; instead, readers must interpret the illustrations themselves and create their own interpretations.

In *Free Fall*, Wiesner's illustrations seem to move into the next page. As you look at these illustrations, notice how the squares in the boy's blanket become the fields in a countryside divided into geometric shapes and then become a lifelike chess board. When the boy returns from his fantasy experience, the squares return to the bed covering. Flying shapes are important in creating the fantasy in both Wiesner's *Tuesday* and *June 29, 1999*.

Wiesner uses color to create moods appropriate for the settings. In *Tuesday*, blues and greens create the coolness of the night and provide an appropriate background for a story in which frogs explore their environment at night.

The glowing colors and contrasts between light and dark are appropriate for a children's fantasy. (Illustrations from The Polar Express *by Chris Van Allsburg, copyright © 1985 by Chris Van Allsburg. Reproduced with permission from Houghton Mifflin Co.)*

Teaching With Artists and Their Illustrations

 growing trend is helping children appreciate, respond to, and understand art. Children's librarian and author Sylvia S. Marantz (1992) argues that to awaken their visual perceptions, children need experiences designed to help them learn. She states:

> Unfortunately most of their experience comes to them through a barrage of photographed images from a television screen. The children have no opportunity to examine what they see, to question its form or validity, to compare or contrast it critically with other pictures their eyes are receiving or with those their imaginations might provide if given the chance. (p. v)

Marantz uses her experience with children and books to recommend a program in which children, with the aid of adults, examine, discuss, question, and compare the illustrations in books and accomplish art activities that relate to the specific illustrations. Marantz progresses through a series of activities that focus on the book jacket, the front endpapers, the title page, and each illustration, leading children to understand and appreciate such elements as color, movement, page design, and format. She recommends viewing and discussing additional books by the same illustrator and books to use for comparisons.

Susan Boulanger (1996) emphasizes using art education books that provide "opportunities for sharing the experience of looking at, thinking about, and discussing art" (p. 298). Such books allow children living in all locations to develop an appreciation for and an understanding of art, even if museum collections are not available.

In her author's note to *Art of the Far North: Inuit Sculpture, Drawing, and Printmaking,* Carol Finley provides another reason for studying art: "One way to learn about the traditions of another people is to study their art. It could be said that art is a universal language and a window into cultures different from our own" (unnumbered).

This section of the chapter presents a few of the ways that you can help children experience "breathtaking, ingenious aspects of pictures" (Nodelman, 1984a, p. 40): using art education books, using aesthetic scanning, studying inspirations for art, investigating the works of great artists, exploring the history of a culture through art, and using a viewer's response approach.

Using Art Education Books

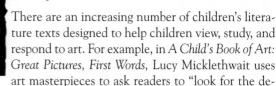 There are an increasing number of children's literature texts designed to help children view, study, and respond to art. For example, in *A Child's Book of Art: Great Pictures, First Words,* Lucy Micklethwait uses art masterpieces to ask readers to "look for the details, talk about the colors, discuss the clothes or the weather, or talk about how the picture makes you feel. Babies may respond to highly detailed pictures with precise lines, colors, and patterns. Young children may have fun making the noises of the animals depicted or talking about the shapes and colors in an abstract painting. Older children may appreciate the use of space in a Japanese print or the feeling of springtime in an Impressionist painting" (p. 4). In addition, the book expands vocabulary and gen-

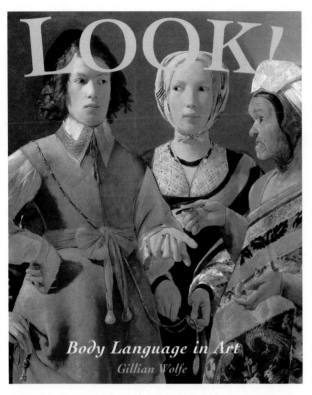

Cover from Look! Body Language in Art, by Gillian Wolfe. Copyright © Frances Lincoln Limited 2004. Text copyright © Gillian Wolfe 2004. Distributed in the USA by Publisher's Group West. Used by permission.

eral knowledge because each painting is labeled with a term that suggests what the viewers should search for in the painting. The book also uses art to introduce action words such as *dancing* and *swimming* and concepts such as shapes and opposites.

Gillian Wolfe's *Look: Body Language in Art* introduces 17 paintings and asks readers to search each painting for emotions and meanings depicted in faces, hands, and body poses. In a section titled "Look for the Message," there is a full-page reproduction of "The Fortune Teller," by Georges de La Tour, on one page; the facing page is titled "Look for the Message: Crafty Crooks." Portions of the painting are highlighted to help readers interpret their meaning. The author also suggests the following creative writing activity and a viewer's response activity to accompany the painting: "How would you finish this story? Write your own ending or draw a picture of what you think happened next," and "Does this scene make you feel worried about the fate of the young man? Will he realize in time that he is being tricked?" (p. 29).

In *Art Up Close: From Ancient to Modern*, Claire d'Harcourt presents 23 art masterpieces and enlarges some of the details. She tells readers, "It's your job to locate all of the details in each picture" (p. 3). This becomes a flap book when at the end of the text, readers can look under flaps to see if they have located all of the details in the pictures. In addition to having readers search for de-

tails, the author presents information about the lives of the artists.

The in-depth activities recommended in these books provide an excellent introduction to aesthetic scanning, discussed in the next section.

Aesthetic Scanning

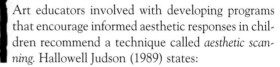

Art educators involved with developing programs that encourage informed aesthetic responses in children recommend a technique called *aesthetic scanning*. Hallowell Judson (1989) states:

> Aesthetic scanning consists of locating and identifying the aesthetic properties of an artwork while looking at it. It is a pedagogical version of what artists do when they are making art and what connoisseurs do when contemplating it. The aesthetic properties involved in aesthetic scanning include the sensory, the formal, the expressive, and the technical. (p. 62)

The sensory properties include the visual elements of art, such as line, color, shape, and texture. The formal properties include the principles of art used to organize or compose art, such as balance, repetition, variety, and contrast. Expressive qualities are visual characteristics used to express feelings or ideas, such as mood, conflict, energy, and meaning. The technical properties are the media, such as watercolor and chalk, and techniques used by artists.

Judson recommends using the aesthetic scanning approach developed by H. S. Broudy (1981) and described by Gloria J. Hewett and Jean C. Rush (1987) when encouraging students to respond to the illustrations in children's literature. Hewett and Rush also identify two rules for this type of treasure hunt: (1) the aesthetic property must be in the artwork and observable by others, and (2) the viewer must be able to identify and describe the property. Chart 4.1 presents examples of questions that adults can ask to encourage children to examine a work of art carefully and to volunteer information based on their own perceptions. Hewett and Rush recommend that adults build confidence by beginning with easier questions. Notice that the questions are presented in order of difficulty; the questions toward the end of the chart require higher levels of artistic knowledge and lead to better informed aesthetic responses. As children become experienced at looking at art and talking about aesthetic properties, expect longer, more detailed descriptions of the properties and ask more open-ended questions.

Hewett and Rush (1987) also recommend encouraging students to expand their responses by asking them questions that clarify and elaborate the responses. They warn, however, that the questions in the chart are merely examples to be modified, amended, changed, or rearranged to meet the goals of instruction. They state that if the questions are followed mechanically or methodically and are used with every lesson, discussions may be limited rather than enhanced. Remember that questions should expand children's responses to art.

An In-Depth Analysis of Aesthetic Scanning in One Book

Many books provide opportunities for developing aesthetic scanning and cultural understanding. Paul Goble's *The Girl Who Loved Wild Horses* includes excellent examples of visual elements and illustrations that develop understanding of the Native American culture, specifically that of the Plains Indians. (Although the pages in the book are unnumbered, page numbers here refer to pages as if the title page were page 1.)

Endpapers, both front and back. The color red develops a feeling of warmth and provides a harmonious introduction to the title page, on which red also dominates. Consider the possible mood for a book that is introduced by red.

Page 1, the title page. The title here is written in the same form as it is on the cover of the book. The color red develops a feeling of warmth and high energy. The sun in this illustration shines on a Native American girl riding her Appaloosa stallion. According to Goble (1978), the geometric sun design comes from the Plains Indians; women painted this geometric sun design on buffalo robes that men wore. The circle surrounded by white space creates a sense of balance. The plants in the foreground increase this sense of balance.

Pages 2 and 3. The horizontal lines suggest calm, sleep, and stability. The vertical lines in the plants and the horses' necks suggest absence of movement and reinforce the feeling of calm. The sleeping girl adds to this total, nonthreatening scene.

Pages 6 and 7. The running buffalo herd creates the sense of movement and direction. According to Goble, the buffalo hunters approach the sacred buffalo on the right side so that they can use the bow and arrow to the best effect. Several hunters are trying to help the hunter who has had a mishap.

Pages 8 and 9. This two-page spread uses horizontal and vertical lines to create a peaceful, nonthreatening scene. Notice that the horizontal lines of the horses are reflected in the surface of the lake. Not a ripple mars the tranquility. Also notice that the vertical lines of the cattails and the horses' manes mirror the peaceful setting described in the text. Because the horses are not frightened by the girl, we can infer a close relationship. The gold colors in the aspens show that it is autumn. According to Goble, reflection, as seen through the water, is a theme found in Indian painting. The quill and beadwork designs frequently have reflections (or up-and-down motifs), which symbolize sky and earth.

Pages 10 and 11. The teepees sitting securely on the ground suggest a safe place. Changes in color and movement, however, are found in the far left. The black, circular clouds suggest changes. The jagged lines protruding from the clouds even indicate the direction that the storm is moving. These changes of color and line foreshadow danger.

Pages 12 and 13. Diagonal lines suggest loss of balance and uncontrolled motion. Notice the jagged diagonal line of the lightning. Feelings of fear explode in this picture because lightning is one of nature's most fearsome elements. The danger is imminent because the black clouds cover almost half of the two-page spread. Notice that the lines of the birds, the horses' legs, and the horses' manes suggest movement and danger.

Pages 14 and 15. Notice that Goble depicts movement and direction through the horses, other animals, and even the plants leaning away from the wind. The jagged yellow lines and the black clouds approach and cover portions of the sun that earlier provided warmth.

Pages 16 and 17. Horizontal lines on the mountain tops and on the horses' backs show that the danger is over and that peace and tranquillity exist once again. The high canyon walls have a special awe and quietness at night. The stars and the sky are important in this illustration. According to Goble, much Native American mythology concerns the Sky World. When a person dies, his spirit walks along the Milky Way to the world above. A sense of peace in the dark is provided by knowing that one has relatives in the sky and by remembering that the moon is the sun's wife.

Pages 20 and 21. According to Globe, pairs of scouts were sent out to find the buffalo herds so that when returning to camp, each scout could vouch for the truth of the other's report. The stallion takes a position of defense at the rear of his mares, whom he drives in front of him.

Pages 24, 25, 26, and 27. According to Goble, this is a Blackfoot camp. Looking at all four pages at the same time, one sees half of the camp circle. Each teepee design is divinely revealed. The top portion represents the sky, the cross at the very top symbolizes the morning star and a wish for wisdom and good dreams, and the discs represent stars. The middle portion of the teepee contains the animals, who have their feet on earth and their heads in heaven. These designs display vital tracts, kidneys, and leg joints because they are sources of the animals' power. The bottom border of the teepee represents the earth, and the projecting triangles or rounded shapes represent mountains or hills. Such lodges are still held sacred by the Blackfoot Indians.

Pages 30 and 31. According to Globe, these pages parallel page 1. The girl, however, may have become a horse. The figures share the warmth of each other and the sun. The crocuses and the bluebirds show that winter is over and springtime is here.

After discussing the illustrations in his book, ask students to respond to and compare the illustrations in other books by Paul Goble.

CHART 4.1 Aesthetic scanning: Initiating questions

Kind of Question*	Properties	Sample Questions
Leading (Agreement, disagreement)	Sensory	This painting has a lot of red, doesn't it?
	Formal	The balance in this fabric pattern is symmetrical, isn't it?
	Expressive	Don't you agree that the smooth shapes in this sculpture convey a feeling of peace?
	Technical	You can feel how rough the surface texture of this pot is, can't you?
Selective (Choice)	Sensory	Do you see more red or blue in this painting?
	Formal	Is this balance symmetrical or asymmetrical?
	Expressive	Do the shapes make you feel peaceful or upset?
	Technical	Is the surface texture rough or smooth?
Parallel (Additional information)	Sensory	What other colors are there in this painting besides red?
	Formal	Is there any kind of balance here other than symmetrical?
	Expressive	What else might these smooth shapes suggest?
	Technical	Are there more smooth surfaces on this clay piece than rough ones?
Constructive (Specific new information)	Sensory	What colors can you find in this painting?
	Formal	What kinds of balance do you see here?
	Expressive	What kinds of shapes can you find in this sculpture, and what mood do they evoke?
	Technical	How has the artist treated the surface of this clay pot?
Productive (General new information)	Sensory	How would you describe one of the painting's sensory properties?
	Formal	Can you describe one of the formal properties in this fabric pattern?
	Expressive	What does this sculpture express?
	Technical	What medium and techniques did the artist use in constructing this pot?

*Initiating questions are presented in order of how difficult they are to answer.
Reprinted from Gloria J. Hewett and Jean C. Rush, "Finding Buried Treasures: Aesthetic Scanning With Children," *Art Education, 40* (January 1987).

Use the information presented earlier in this chapter on various artistic elements, design, artistic media, artistic styles, and outstanding illustrators of children's books to help you select interesting artwork from children's illustrators and to develop your own treasure hunt. In addition, Lyn Ellen Lacy's *Art and Design in Children's Picture Books* (1986) provides in-depth suggestions for analyzing the visual elements in several Caldecott Medal–winning illustrations. Use Chart 4.1 to help you include questions related to sensory, formal, expressive, and technical aspects of the artistic work. Many children enjoy developing their own observations and formulating questions that allow them to interact with art.

Studying Inspirations for Art

After children have had many opportunities to look at and to discuss the art in picture books, make connections between artists' illustrations and the artists' inspirations. Lynn Hoffman (2000) emphasizes that "picture book illustration is not separate from other art forms; rather, it copies and imitates and pays homage to the body of work that has come before it, just as in other art forms" (p. 16). Hoffman describes the effectiveness of displays that pair illustrations from children's books with examples from traditional fine art. It is interesting to discover what artists, artistic time periods, artistic styles, or works have inspired contemporary artists and to compare the picture-book illustrations.

For example, for *Outside Over There*, Maurice Sendak was inspired, as we have discussed, by the watercolors of British poet and artist William Blake in his choice of colors. H. W. Janson and Anthony F. Janson (1995) describe Blake, who lived from 1757 to 1827, as a painter of the Romantic movement who was inspired by literature to develop new ranges of subjects, emotions, and attitudes. Encourage children to discuss Sendak's illustrations in *Outside Over There* and to compare them with illustrations by William Blake in art texts.

Help children make connections between the art of Maurice Sendak and the art of Randolph Caldecott, who lived from 1846 to 1886. In a review of Sendak's *We Are*

All in the Dumps With Jack and Guy, Brian Alderson (1993a), the children's book editor of *The Times of London*, states: "Put it all down to Randolph Caldecott. As you may know, Maurice Sendak is a devotee of that Victorian picture-book artist, and indeed he designated an early book, *Hector Protector*, 'an intentionally contrived homage to this beloved teacher'" (p. 17). Like Caldecott, Sendak transforms rhymes into epics by introducing a pictorial narrative inspired by the slender texts of the rhymes. Alderson compares Sendak and Caldecott because "Caldecott loved to play with such visual counterpointing (the tragic demise of the dish eloping with the spoon; the decrepit beggar man fiddling while bonny lasses and lads dance around the maypole). The exercise probably helped to keep up his interest in his rudimentary copy" (p. 17). As discussed earlier, many reissues of Caldecott's books are available.

There are interesting connections between Clement Hurd's illustrations for Margaret Wise Brown's *Goodnight Moon* and a painting by Goya. Leonard S. Marcus (1991) describes how Hurd created the illustrations:

> All March and for the rest of the spring, the artist worked on the illustrations for *Goodnight Moon*. Margaret had not given him many suggestions for the art, as she sometimes did. She simply scribbled a few brief notes and, along with them, offered inspiration in the form of a small color reproduction of Goya's dashing *Boy in Red*, which she pasted onto the notebook's front cover. (p. 20)

Ask students to look carefully at Hurd's illustrations for *Goodnight Moon* and respond to the mood created by colors, lines, shapes, and light, then have them aesthetically scan Goya's painting and discuss the sensory and expressive qualities found in that art (see Ann Waldron's *Francisco Goya*). Are there any similarities between Goya's and Hurd's works? Was Hurd motivated by the *Boy in Red*? Why do you believe that Margaret Wise Brown sent Hurd the photo?

In an interview with David Wiesner, Susan Caroff and Elizabeth Moje (1992/1993) report that the greatest impact on Wiesner's work and the ways in which he tells stories is a book illustrated by Lynd Ward, *Mad Man's Drum*. Ward developed this novel for adults completely in woodcuts, without words. Wiesner states that he was very impressed with Ward's ability to develop a complex story dealing with complicated themes and imagery in a 250-page book with no words. Encourage students to either compare Ward's and Wiesner's illustrations or analyze Wiesner's ability to convey themes and imagery through wordless books.

Jennifer M. Brown's interview with Ian Falconer (2000) identifies the children's books that most influenced the author/illustrator of *Olivia*. Encourage students to analyze the following books and discuss how they might have influenced Falconer: Ludwig Bemelman's *Madeline*, Robert McCloskey's *One Morning in Maine* and *Blueberries for Sal*, Dr. Seuss's *The 500 Hats of Bartholomew Cubbins*, Jean de Brunhoff's *The Story of Babar*, and John Tenniel's drawings for *Alice in Wonderland*.

Quite different artworks influenced artist Lane Smith (1993). Smith states that he was influenced by Monty Python, *Mad* magazine, and comic books. He adds:

> I think my palette, my sensibilities, and my composition were greatly influenced by films I saw as a child, especially the old Disney films like *Snow White* and *The Jungle Book*. Some of my work in *The Stinky Cheese Man*—the ugly duckling sequence in particular—is directly influenced by Tex Avery. He was an animation director from the forties—the one who always had his cartoon characters' eyeballs popping right out of their heads. All his work was very exaggerated. (p. 68)

Encourage students to compare Lane Smith's illustrations with those that inspired his art.

Christopher Wormell, a British wood engraver and linoleum block illustrator, credits the British wood engraver Thomas Bewick (1753–1828) for his inspiration. His *An Alphabet of Animals* is a winner of the Graphics Prize at the Bologna International Children's Book Fair, and *The New York Times* named his *Teeth, Tales, & Tentacles: An Animal Counting Book* one of the 2004 Best Illustrated Books.

In *Celebrate America: In Poetry and Art*, Nora Panzer pairs poetry and art to show readers how the two art forms build on each other and are related. In *Heart to Heart: New Poems Inspired by Twentieth-Century American Art*, an anthology by Jan Greenberg, poets respond to a varied collection of art ranging from folk art to contemporary works. Creating a peaceful world for children is the ultimate dream of Jella Lepman, the founder of the International Board on Books for Young People (IBBY). To promote this goal, the organization published *Under the Spell of the Moon: Art for Children From the World's Great Illustrators*, edited by Patricia Aldana. In this text, artists from around the world were asked to choose a text such as a poem, nursery rhyme, or song and to use it as inspiration to create art that promotes a peaceful world for children.

You can use many additional illustrators for similar activities. For example, Peter Sís (1992) states that he has always admired medieval artists such as Bosch and Breughel and artists from the German Gothic school. Henrik Drescher's illustrations have been compared to those of Paul Klee and the German expressionists. John Steptoe, who illustrated *Stevie*, has been compared to the French painter Georges Rouault. According to Herbert R. Lottman (1993), illustrator Satomi Ichikawa was motivated to illustrate books after she discovered the art of Maurice Boutet de Monvel. In an interview with Masha Kabakow Rudman (1993b), Ashley Bryan says that he was inspired by early religious books printed by hand using woodcuts when he illustrated texts based on African American spirituals, such as *I'm Going to Sing: Black American Spirituals*. Lois Ehlert states that her inspiration for *Leaf Man* is nature and the beautiful autumn leaves she collected.

Investigating the Works of Great Artists

Many books currently published for children encourage the children to make discoveries about the history of art, to learn about elements and style in art, and to explore the art of renowned artists. Art history is introduced in Henry Sayre's *Cave Paintings to Picasso: The Inside Scoop on 50 Art Masterpieces.* Students can investigate the chronologcial order of artworks and artists from "Woman From Brassempowy," 22,000 B.C., to René Magritte's "The Son of Man," 1964. This book provides a fascinating beginning for historical research because each painting is placed into a time line of history. One of these times is represented by the wall paintings found in the tomb of Nebamum, a member of the Egyptian nobility who died about 1360 B.C. Students who are interested in searching for the art of ancient Egypt can read Emily Sands's *Egyptology: Search for the Tomb of Osiris.* The following note from the publisher provides an intriguing motivation for students to conduct research and determine what parts of the text are accurate: "This book is the facsimile of a journal supposedly written in 1926. As there is scant evidence to back up this claim, it must be enjoyed solely on its own merits" (inside cover).

The illustrations in Anthony Browne's *Willy's Pictures,* winner of the Hans Christian Andersen Medal for excellence in illustrations, feature items from original paintings

LOTS AND LOTS AND LOTS OF DOTS
We gradually started to notice some
very strange things in the park.

Viewers can search for aspects of origional paintings found in the illustrations such as this one based on Sunday Afternoon on the Island of LaGrande Jatte *by George Seurat. (From* Willy's Pictures *by Anthony Browne. Copyright © 2000 by Anthony Browne. Reproduced by permission of the publisher, Candlewick Press, Inc., Cambridge, MA.*

by artists such as Henri Rousseau, Vincent van Gogh, and Edouard Manet. Readers are asked to look carefully at each of Browne's illustrations and then search the copies of the original paintings reprinted at the end of the book.

You can use Jill Bossert's (1998) *Children's Book Illustration: Step By Step Techniques* to explore the artistic styles and techniques developed by nine artists, including Charles Santore, Emily Arnold McCully, and Jerry Pinkney. Younger children can follow the techniques described by Debra Cooper-Solomon (1999) as she uses the illustrations of Eric Carle to introduce collage. Cooper-Solomon presents detailed guidelines for developing an art project following the reading of Carle's *The Mixed-Up Chameleon*.

Have students investigate specific artistic styles using Jude Welton's *Impressionism*, in which he interweaves biographical information about the artists with color reproductions of their paintings. Use this book for introductory research on artistic style or to stimulate students to conduct further research into the lives and works of specific artists.

For example, in *The Pot That Juan Built*, Nancy Andrews-Goebel explores how Mexican artist Juan Quezada discovered pottery shards from an ancient culture, experimented to re-create the lost art, and taught villagers and family members to create pottery using the lost art. This book could be paired with Linda Sue Park's *A Single Shard*, a historical fiction novel set in medieval Korea in which an orphan boy works with one of the most famous potters in Korea. The story is based on the celadon potters of the Korya era (918–1392 A.D.). From these two books, readers gain an understanding of the importance of pottery in two ancient cultures.

Mexico's most renowned female painter is the topic of Magdalena Holzhey's *Frida Kahlo: The Artist in the Blue House*. Spain's 16th-century artist *Diego Velázquez* is highlighted in the text by Mike Venezia. The author includes reproductions of Velázquez's paintings as well as biographical sketches. In *Degas and the Dance: The Painter and the Petits Rats, Perfecting Their Art*, Susan Goldman Rubin presents a look at the artist's obsession with the ballet and the demands placed on the dancers. Rubin includes numerous reproductions of Degas's impressionistic paintings. In *Runaway Girl: The Artist Louise Bourgeois*, Jan Greenberg and Sandra Jordan incorporate both Bourgeois's art and the background experiences that shaped it.

You can use numerous highly illustrated books for research projects in which students investigate the works of one artist. One of the most interesting books for all children is Christina Björk's *Linnea in Monet's Garden*. Along with Linnea, readers can learn about Monet and discover the excitement of visualizing nature and paintings in new ways. After children read *Linnea in Monet's Garden*, have them conduct their own research into the work and life of Monet. Jude Welton's *Monet* is a source for numerous re-productions of paintings, discussions about the paintings, and biographical information about Monet.

Use *Linnea in Monet's Garden* as a model to stimulate students to create stories in which they make discoveries about great artists. Leonardo da Vinci is an excellent subject for such a visual journey. For this task, have students use Richard McLanathan's *Leonardo da Vinci*, Diane Stanley's *Leonardo da Vinci*, Rosabianca Skira-Venturi's *A Weekend With Leonardo da Vinci*, or Robert Byrd's *Leonardo: Beautiful Dreamer*.

Christina Björk's *Vendela in Venice* can be used to motivate children to research and write stories in which they explore architecture, painting, statues, and sculptures associated with a location. The four golden horses and the numerous statues of lions are of special interest. There is also enough mystery associated with the creation of the horses (Greece, 300 B.C., or Rome, 300 A.D.) to stimulate speculation and creative writing. The dates at the end of the book could motivate additional creative stories as told through the possible viewpoints of the horses.

The Treasury of Saints and Martyrs provides a source for a study of early artwork associated with the history of art. Margaret Mulvihill's text, written for older readers, includes numerous labeled reproductions of artworks proceeding from the early centuries through modern times. The picture acknowledgements include the locations of the original art.

For a focus on illustrators of children's books, have students begin their study with Pat Cummings's *Talking With Artists*. This book provides information on 14 artists, including Leo and Diane Dillon, Steven Kellogg, Jerry Pinkney, Lane Smith, Chris Van Allsburg, and David Wiesner. Throughout this text are suggestions for motivating children to respond to literature through artistic interpretations of books or to create their own illustrations using specific art media.

History of a Culture as Reflected in Art: A Multicultural Approach

This chapter presents activities and sources for books that develop children's appreciation for and understanding of art, artists, and texts. We also can use art to foster understanding of specific cultures and the artists whose works represent them. Authors of many art texts designed for adults emphasize that an understanding of the culture and history of a people is best developed through their art. For example, Richard J. Powell highlights this viewpoint in the title of his book *Black Art: A Cultural History* (2002). In *History of Japanese Art* (2005), Penelope Mason points out that it is through art that we discover characteristics of a people whose history and culture, for long periods of time, were not open to Westerners. Janson and Janson (1992) state: "Art history is more than a stream of art objects cre-

CHART 4.2   African American culture and history through art

Author/Artist	Texts	Author/Artist	Texts
Ancient Africa: The Foundations		Tonya Bolden	*Wake Up Our Souls: A Celebration of Black American Artists*
Tom Phillips (adult)	*Africa: The Art of a Continent*	Jonny Hannah	*Hot Jazz Special*
		Laban Carrick Hill	*Harlem Stomp! A Cultural History of the Harlem Renaissance*
Years of Slavery			
Romare Bearden	*Li'l Dan the Drummer Boy*	**Civil Rights Movement**	
Tom Feelings	*The Middle Passage*		
Susan Goldman Rubin	*Art Against the Odds: From Slave Quilts to Prison Paintings*	Rosemary Bray	*Martin Luther King*
		Wade and Cheryl Hudson	*In Praise of Our Fathers and Our Mothers: A Black Family Treasury by Outstanding Authors and Artists*
Renaissance: The Awakening			
Amalia K. Amaki (adult)	*A Century of African American Art*	Toni Morrison	*Remember: The Journey to School Integration* (photographs)
Charles Miers (adult)	*Harlem Renaissance: Art of Black America*	Winfred Rembert	*Don't Hold Me Back: My Life and Art*
Richard Powell (adult)	*Black Art: A Cultural History*	Faith Ringgold	*My Dream of Martin Luther King*

ated over time. It is intimately related to history itself, that is, the recorded evidence of human events" (p. 29). Consequently, by studying the art created by people during different time periods, we gain an understanding of their culture and their history and how that culture and history have changed over time.

For this study, we focus on art from African American, Asian, Jewish, Latino, Middle Eastern, and Native American cultures and history; we identify both adult art books that include illustrations that are open to any age group and illustrated books written for children and young adults. Teachers can focus on one culture at a time, or older students can divide into groups, investigate books related to the cultures, and report their findings to the class. Charts 4.2–4.7 provide suggested sources of books. A variety of levels of books are listed, from adult art books to highly illustrated books for younger children. The books include photographs as well as other forms of art.

To introduce this study of a culture through art, students can either brainstorm ideas about what they could learn from viewing the art of a culture, or teachers can provide suggestions about what students might consider. These suggestions could include the following:

- What was the function of art within the culture during this time period? For example, what might be the importance in prehistoric cultures of art depicting the animal world such as that found in animals painted on walls of caves or carved in stone or wood? Could there be a spiritual connection between the art and the beliefs of the people?

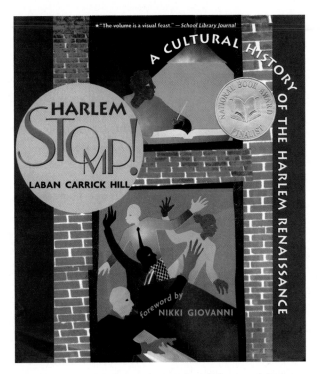

Cover art from Harlem Stomp! A Cultural History of the Harlem Renaissance, *by Laban Carrick Hill. Little Brown, 2003. Text copyright © 2003 by Laban Carrick Hill. Cover illustration copyright © 2003 by Christopher Myers. Used by permission of Little, Brown and Company.*

CHART 4.3 Asian culture and history through art

Author/Artist	Texts
Early Cultures and History	
Sherman E. Lee (adult)	*A History of Far Eastern Art*
Penelope Mason (adult)	*History of Japanese Art*
David G. Wilkins et al. (adult)	*Art Past Art Present* (ancient China, Vietnam)
Rhoda Blumberg	*Commodore Perry in the Land of the Shogun* (reproductions of original drawings)
John S. Major	*The Silk Route: 7,000 Miles of History*
Ed Young	*I, Dako: The Tale of a Basket*
World War II	
Tatsuharu Kodama	*Shin's Tricycle*
Toshi Maruki	*Hiroshima No Pika*
Modern Asia	
National Geographic (adult)	*Through the Lens: National Geographic Greatest Photographs* (Asia)
Emigration to North America	
Diane Hoyt-Goldsmith	*Hoang Anh: A Vietnamese-American Boy* (photographs)
Patricia McMahon	*Chi-Hoon: A Korean Girl* (photographs)
Allen Say	*Grandfather's Journey*
Ian Wallace	*Chin Chiang and the Dragon's Dance*
Kate Waters & Madeline Slovenz-Law	*Lion Dancer: Ernie Wan's Chinese New Year*

CHART 4.4 Jewish culture and history through art

Author/Artist	Texts
Ancient Culture	
Ellen Frankel (adult)	*The Jewish Spirit: A Celebration in Stories and Art*
Sharon Keller (adult)	*The Jews: A Treasury of Art and Literature*
Eric A. Kimmel	*Wonders and Miracles: A Passover Companion* (art spans 3,000 years)
Karla Kuskin	*Jerusalem, Shining Still*
Neil Waldman	*The Golden City: Jerusalem's 3,000 Years*
Emigration	
Dorothy and Thomas Hoobler	*The Jewish American Family Album* (photographs)
Patricia Polacco	*The Keeping Quilt*
The Holocaust	
Guggenheim Museum (adult)	*Marc Chagall and the Jewish Theater*
Chana Byers Abells	*The Children We Remember* (photographs)
Susan D. Bachrach	*Tell Them We Remember: The Story of the Holocaust* (photographs)
Tony Kushner/Maurice Sendak	*Brundibar*
Barbara Rogasky	*Smoke and Ashes: The Story of the Holocaust* (photographs)
Marisabina Russo	*Always Remember Me: How One Family Survived World War II*
Hana Volavkova	*. . . I Never Saw Another Butterfly . . . Children's Drawings and Poems From Terezin Concentration Camp, 1942–1944*

- What were the forms of the art and the media used? What does this tell us about the culture?

- What might have been the occupations of the men and women who created the art? What occupations are depicted through various media?

- What techniques or methods were used to create the art? What does this tell us about the technology of the culture at a given time?

- What is the evidence that the society is becoming more complex over time?

- What types of intellectual or physical activities are shown in the art?

- What social levels of the people are reflected in the art? Does this change? What does this tell us about the people who may have hired the artist to create the art?

- How is religion reflected in the art? How does the depiction of religion change over time?

- How is the politics of the culture reflected in the art? How does this change over time?

- How does known history, especially conflicts within the culture, influence the artist and the art? For example, how does slavery, the Holocaust, or World War II influence the art of the culture?

- How do details in the art relate to the social and educational levels of the people in the culture? For example, how are the people dressed, and what activities are they doing?

Jacket cover, "The Butterfly" by Pavel Friedman, from I NEVER SAW ANOTHER BUTTERFLY by U.S. Holocaust Memorial Museum, edited by Hana Volavkova, copyright © 1978, 1993 by Artia Prague. Compilation © 1993 by Schocken Books. Used by permission of Schocken Books, a division of Random House, Inc.

CHART 4.5 Latino culture and history through art

Authors/Artists	Texts
Ancient World	
Art Museum, Princeton Univ. (adult)	The Olmec World: Ritual and Rulership
Jay Levenson (adult)	Circa 1492: Art in the Age of Exploration
Jean Fritz et al.	The World in 1492
Cultural Celebrations	
June Behren	Fiesta! (Cinco de Mayo)
Marie Hall Ets and Aurora Labastida	Nine Days to Christmas: A Story of Mexico
Richard Keep	Clatter Bash! A Day of the Dead Celebration
Nancy Luenn	A Gift for Abuelita: Celebrating the Day of the Dead
Contemporary Lives and Artists	
Luis-Martin (adult)	Frida Kahlo
Keto von Waberer (adult)	Frida Kahlo Masterpieces
Martha Zamora (adult)	Frida Kahlo: The Brush of Anguish
S. Beth Atkin	Voices From the Fields: Children of Migrant Farmworkers Tell Their Stories (photographs)
Eve Bunting	Going Home
James Cockcroft	Diego Rivera
Rachel Crandell	Hands of the Maya: Villagers at Work and Play (photographs)
Camen Lomas Garza	Family Pictures
Robyn Montana Turner	Frida Kahlo: Portraits of Women Artists for Children

- How, if at all, does the art reflect influences from other cultures?
- What social and cultural conflicts are reflected in the art?
- What is the purpose for the art during the time period? For example, is it to honor the animal or spiritual world, create a symbol for religious worship, honor a person through portraits, tell about a historical event, or provide a source for meditation and enjoyment?
- What are the levels of engineering depicted in the art? For example, what engineering ability is required to build the pyramids or construct a mosque? What does this reveal about the culture?

As these suggested topics for investigating art indicate, this study of a culture through its art is closely related to the social studies and history curriculums in upper

Readers are asked to respond to Diego Rivera's painting, Piñata. (From Come Look With Me: World of Play by Gladys S. Blizzard. Published by Thomasson-Grant, 1993. Diego Rivera Piñata 1953. Tempera on canvas 97" × 171 1/2" Hospital Infantil de Mexico "Federico Gomez," Mexico City. Reproduced by permission of the hospital.)

CHART 4.6   Middle Eastern culture and history through art

Author/Artist	Texts	Author/Artist	Texts
Early History		Nicholas Reeves	*Into the Mummy's Tomb: The Real-Life Discovery of Tutankhamun's Treasures*
David G. Wilkins et al. (adult)	*Art Past Art Present* (Sumerian, Egyptian, Persian, Islamic)	David Macaulay	*Mosque*
Sheila Blair and Jonathan Bloom (adult)	*The Art and Architecture of Islam 1250–1800*	Fiona Macdonald	*A 16th Century Mosque*
H. W. and Anthony F. Janson	*History of Art for Young People* (Egypt, Near East)	Emily Sand	*Egyptology*
Sir Richard F. Burton	*The Arabian Nights: Tales From a Thousand and One Nights*	**Contemporary Life**	
		National Geographic (adult)	*Through the Lens: National Geographic Greatest Photographs* (Middle East)
Edmund Dulac	*Sinbad the Sailor and Other Stories From the Arabian Nights* (art inspired by Persian miniatures)	Naomi Shihab Nye	*The Space Between Our Footsteps: Poems and Paintings From the Middle East*

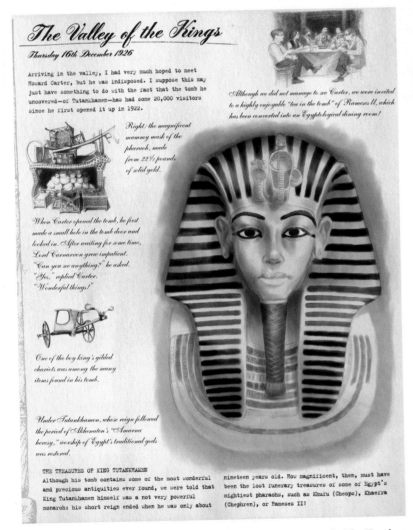

Illustration from EGYPTOLOGY. Text and design copyright © 2004 by The Templar Company. Illustration copyright © 2004 by Ian Andrew, Nick Harris and Helen Ward. Reproduced by permission of the publisher Candlewick Press, Inc.

elementary and middle school. It can also be related to the history curriculum studied by young adults.

Studying Art With Older Students

The heavily illustrated books discussed in this chapter can also be used with older students and young adults as they learn to analyze, criticize, and evaluate the art. Two approaches are especially useful when guiding students in their analysis of art: a viewer's response approach, and focusing on economic and social conditions when evaluating art. Both approaches are recommended by art historians who focus on thinking and writing about art. The approaches also can relate to using art in the study of social studies, history, and political science.

Using a Viewer's Response Approach

Adults can use the recommendations of art historian Donna K. Reid (2004) to guide the study of art and to help viewers appreciate, respond to, and understand art. These recommendations can be used with a single piece of art or with a heavily illustrated book. They are useful with reproductions of classical art or with contemporary works, and they can be adapted to meet the needs and back-

CHART 4.7 Native American culture and history through art

Authors/Artists	Texts
Early History	
Jay Levenson (adult)	*Circa 1492: Art in the Age of Exploration*
Edward Field	*Magic Words*
Jean Fritz et al.	*The World in 1492*
Jennifer Owings Dewey	*Stories on Stone: Rock Art: Images From the Ancient Ones*
Paul Goble	*Mystic Horse*
Time of European Expansion	
Russell Freedman	*An American Winter*
Russell Freedman	*Buffalo Hunt*
Laurie Lawlor	*Shadow Catcher: The Life and Work of Edward S. Curtis (photographs)*
Nancy Wood	*The Serpent's Tongue: Prose, Poetry, and Art of the New Mexico Pueblos*
Contemporary Art and Life	
Shonto Begay	*Navajo: Visions and Voices Across the Mesa*
Tricia Brown	*Children of the Midnight Sun: Young Native Voices of Alaska (photographs)*
Carol Finley	*Art of the Far North: Inuit Sculpture, Drawing, and Printmaking*
George Littlechild	*This Land Is My Land*
Chief Jake Swamp	*Giving Thanks: A Native American Morning Message*

the shade and warmth you give us.
Thank you, all the birds in the world, for singing your beautiful songs for all to enjoy.

From GIVING THANKS: A NATIVE AMERICAN GOOD MORNING MESSAGE. *Text copyright © 1995 by Chief Jake Swamp. Illustrations copyright © 1995 by Erwin Printup, Jr. Permission arranged with Lee & Low Books, Inc., New York, NY 10016.*

grounds of various ages. Reid recommends the following four steps when approaching a work of art: respond, reflect, research, and revisit the work of art.

1. *Respond:* What is your initial reaction to the work of art? This response correlates reader response theory and art response theory. According to Anne D'Alleva (2005), "a number of art historians have adapted reader-response theory to the study of visual art—and, indeed, we regard a 'text' as an image, sound, gesture, or any other cultural phenomenon to be interpreted" (p. 115). Just as in reader response theory with an implied reader, in art response theory, there is an implied beholder who is involved in a particular viewing experience; the viewer brings his or her past experiences and knowledge to the interpretation. D'Alleva states that works of art are often used "to emphasize schemata and are meant to trigger particular responses in the viewer" (p. 116).

D'Alleva suggests questions that viewers can ask to increase an understanding of art response, such as: Is there an implied viewer for the work? If so, how is that viewer established—is there an implied gender, class, or historical background? What is the effect of the artwork on the viewer? How might this particular art help the viewer understand or deal with human relationships or self-discovery? If there is conflict in the work, how does it influence the viewer? How does the art challenge the viewer's assumptions? How does your own understanding of culture, gender, and society shape your responses to the work?

2. *Reflection:* To encourage reflection, the viewer considers how the artist's artistic choices influenced the viewer's responses. What caused the specific reaction to the art? What knowledge do you have that will help you understand the work? What questions need to be answered about the work? What are the basic facts about the work such as its title, the significance of the title, identity of the artist, when and why the art was completed, the subject for the art, the artist's message, the artist's

¡Gracias!

Illustration from Clatter Bash! A Day of the Dead Celebration, *by Richard Keep. Peachtree Publishers 2004. Text and illustrations copyright © 2004 by Richard Keep. Permission to reprint granted by Peachtree Publishers.*

ing a record of "Mood Indigo," recorded by Duke Ellington. Another illustration shows Paul Robeson as a much larger figure than the little girl. What might the difference in size say about the importance of Robeson in the African American community? What is the viewer response to an illustration of DuBois in which another figure shows him considerable respect? In another illustration, what is the response to the young girl's view that she is living in the company of men who changed the world? What might be the reaction to the men playing cards? Are they gambling for power? What is the response to the picure on the wall of African American athletes? Might the artist use this as a symbol to suggest that African American athletes were more apt to succeed during this time period than were other African Americans? Another illustration shows two men having a political discussion while they are eating. What is the viewer's response to the subject that might be discussed? What is the viewer's response to illustrations that focus on inclusion, not exclusion? What is the message that the artist may be delivering? Why did the artist believe the message was important? What is the response to the author's inclusion of the words to "Mood Indigo" at the end of the book? This book could be used to motivate a study of different African American personages. The author includes pictures and short biographical sketches of the people who are illustrated in the text.

The art selections for an activity that emphasizes responding to illustrations could be located in two sources of award-winning illustrated books: the Caldecott Award and Honor Books and the Best Illustrated Books selected from the *New York Times Book Review.* Choose books from these two sources for the same year, respond to the books, and compare the results. Award-winning books for 2005 include:

Caldecott Award and Honor Books

Kevin Henkes's *Kitten's First Full Moon* (Caldecott Award)
Barbara Lehman's *The Red Book*
Jacqueline Woodson's *Coming On Home Soon,* illustrated by E. B. Lewis
Mo Willems's *Knuffle Bunny: A Cautionary Tale*

Ten Best Illustrated Books

Doreen Cronin's *Duck for President,* illustrated by Betsy Lewin
Geefwee Boedoe's *Arrowville*
Dylan Thomas's *A Child's Christmas in Wales,* illustrated by Chris Raschka
Christopher Wormell's *Teeth, Tales, & Tentacles: An Animal Counting Book*
Virginia Hamilton's *The People Could Fly: The Picture Book,* illustrated by Leo and Diane Dillon
Barbara Kerley's *Walt Whitman: Words for America,* illustrated by Brian Selznick
Kevin Henkes's *Kitten's First Full Moon*

technique, how the work fits into the artist's career, how the work relates to the artist's life, critical reactions to the work, formal evaluation of the artistic elements (line, shape, color, texture, etc.)?

3. *Research:*   Seek answers to the reflection questions and read art criticism associated with the work that might include a critic's evaluation of areas such as the impact on viewers, original and creative significance of the work, effective use of the medium, technical skill of the artist, successful use of design and form, significant message, memorable image, and value for repeated viewing.

4. *Revisit:*   Return to the work of art after the reflection and research. Does the response to the work change? If so, what caused the change? Will the work of art stand the test of time?

Illustrated books that have won awards are ideal for this study of art because there are usually published critical evaluations of the books that can be used during the research stage of the response to art. For example, Kadir Nelson, illustrator of *Ellington Was Not a Street,* by Ntozake Shange, won the Coretta Scott King Award for African-American illustrators. Response theory could relate the illustrations to the historical background and the time of such personages as Duke Ellington, W. E. B. DuBois, and Dizzy Gillespie. When responding to this book, viewers could consider their reactions to the title and to the cover illustration that shows a young girl hold-

Gregory Rogers's *The Boy, The Bear, The Baron, The Bard*

Vladimir Radunsky's *The Mighty Asparagus*

Lauren Thompson's *Polar Bear Night*, illustrated by Stephen Savage

This type of activity could address the award-winning books for any year. Good sources for reviews include *School Library Journal*, *The Horn Book*, and *Publishers Weekly*; these journals provide reviews that focus on literary elements and appropriateness for a specific age level. The reviews of many older books are found in Anita Silvey's *100 Best Books for Children* (2004). Her chapter on "Picture Books" includes numerous award-winning books.

Focusing on Economic and Social Conditions in Art Criticism

Another approach to the study of art is recommended by Stephen F. Eisenman and Thomas Crow (2002), who use art criticism that focuses on the relationship between the art and ideology, the economic and social conditions expressed in the art (a Marxist approach to criticism). Anne D'Alleva (2005) suggests using the following types of questions, which focus on how the art is shaped by ideology and social and economic power, to analyze the economic and social conditions expressed in the art:

Use the time period developed in the art to answer: What would be the social status of the artist during this time period?

What role does class play in the work of both the artist and the viewer?

In what way might the artwork serve as propaganda?

What does the work say about social conflicts?

What ideologies—on the part of the painter, the patron, and the intended audience—shaped the creation of the art?

Why did the artist choose to depict this particular time in the life of a subject?

What qualities does this particular moment emphasize?

What is the dominant ideology that the artist challenged?

What do paintings reveal about the society they are depicting?

Books that have a historical setting or that develop a political conflict provide excellent sources for this activity. It would be interesting to compare analyses of these books using a viewer's response approach and a Marxist criticism approach. For example, Ntozake Shange's *Ellington Was Not a Street*, illustrated by Kadir Nelson, with its Civil Rights background, could be analyzed. Mordicai Gerstein's *The Man Who Walked Between the Towers* was illustrated following the 9/11 attacks; the book ends with an illustration of the two towers drawn from memory. Eve Bunting's *Smoky Night*, illustrated by David Diaz, depicts the Los Angeles riots. David Wisniewski's *Golem* is a Jewish legend that takes place in 16th-century Prague. Peter Sís's *Starry Messenger* is the story of the Italian astronomer Galileo Galilei. Barbara Kerley's *The Dinosaurs of Waterhouse Hawkins*, illustrated by Brian Selznick, is the story of a Victorian artist who created the first life-sized models of dinosaurs. Virginia Hamilton's *The People Could Fly: The Picture Book*, illustrated by Leo and Diane Dillon, is an African American folktale set in the time of slavery.

Both the viewer's response approach and the Marxist criticism approach allow much more sophisticated evaluations of art that are suitable for older students. These approaches encourage them to look with new viewpoints at the heavily illustrated books that are frequently shared with younger students. Hopefully, you will get the same response that I received when I shared illustrated books with middle school and high school students. After using these approaches, several students said, "I had no idea that there was so much information found in the illustrations for books that I thought were only written for young children."

Suggested Activities

For more suggested activities for understanding artists and their illustrations, visit the Companion Website at www.prenhall.com/norton.

- With some of your peers, select one of the following criteria for evaluating the illustrations and narrative portions of a picture book, find books that clearly exemplify the criteria, and share them with the class:
  a. The illustrations help readers anticipate both the action of the story and the climax (for example, Richard Egielski's illustrations for Arthur Yorinks's *Hey, Al* or Maurice Sendak's illustrations for *Where the Wild Things Are*).
  b. The pictures help create the basic mood of the story (for example, Paul Goble's *The Girl Who Loved Wild Horses*; Marcia Brown's illustrations for *Cinderella*, by Charles Perrault; or Mo Willems's *Knuffle Bunny*).
  c. The illustrations portray convincing characters (for example, Taro Yashima's *Crow Boy*).
  d. All pictures are accurate and consistent with the text (for example, Barbara Cooney's illustrations for Donald Hall's *Ox-Cart Man*).
- Consider the ways in which lines are related to natural phenomena. Look carefully at the illustrations in several books. Are there examples in which vertical lines suggest lack of movement, horizontal lines suggest calmness or an absence of strife, vertical and horizontal lines connected at the top suggest stability and safety, diagonal lines suggest motion, and jagged lines symbolize danger?

- Ian Falconer (Brown, 2000) discusses the power of red in his illustrations for *Olivia*. He cites the influence of traditional Russian political posters, which use black and white and red. Research the traditional political posters and compare them with Falconer's illustrations.
- Choose an outstanding illustrator of children's books, and find as many of the illustrator's works as you can. Analyze the artist's use of the elements of art—line, color, shape, and texture—and the various media and styles. Compare the books: Does the artist use a similar style in all works, or does the style change with the subject of the text? Compare earlier works with later ones: Are there any changes in the use of artistic elements, style, or media?

Children's Literature

For full descriptions, including plot summaries and award winner notations, of these and other titles for teaching children about artists and their illustrations, visit the CD-ROM that accompanies this book.

Aardema, Verna. *Why Mosquitoes Buzz in People's Ears.* Illustrated by Leo & Diane Dillon. Dial, 1975 (I:5–9 R:6).

Abells, Chana Byers. *The Children We Remember: Photographs From the Archives of Yad Vashem, the Holocaust Martyrs' and Heroes' Remembrance Authority, Jerusalem, Israel.* Greenwillow, 1986 (I:all).

Ackerman, Karen. *Song and Dance Man.* Illustrated by Stephen Gammell. Knopf, 1988 (I:3–8 R:4).

Aldana, Patricia, ed. *Under the Spell of the Moon: Art for Children From the World's Great Illustrators.* House of Anansi, 2005 (I:all).

Andersen, Hans Christian. *The Nightingale.* Retold by Eva LeGalliene. Illustrated by Nancy Ekholm Burkert, Harper & Row, 1968 (I:6–12 R:8).

_____. *The Ugly Duckling.* Adapted and illustrated by Jerry Pinkney. Morrow, 1999 (I:6–9 R:7).

Andrews-Goebel, Nancy. *The Pot That Juan Built.* Illustrated by David Diaz. Lee & Low, 2002 (I:all).

Arkhurst, Joyce Cooper, retold by. *The Adventures of Spider: West African Folktales.* Illustrated by Jerry Pinkney, Little, Brown, 1992 (I:8–11 R:4+).

Armstrong, Jennifer. *Pierre's Dream.* Illustrated by Susan Gaber, Dial, 1999 (I:6+ R:5).

Aylesworth, Jim. *Country Crossing.* Illustrated by Ted Rand. Atheneum, 1991 (I:3–7).

_____. *The Full Belly Bowl.* Illustrated by Wendy Anderson Halperin. Atheneum, 1999 (I:5–8 R:4).

Bachrach, Susan D. *Tell Them We Remember: The Story of the Holocaust.* Little, Brown, 1994 (I:all).

Baker, Jeannie. *Where the Forest Meets the Sea.* Greenwillow, 1988 (I:4–10).

_____. *Window.* Greenwillow, 1991 (I:all).

Baker, Olaf. *Where the Buffaloes Begin.* Illustrated by Stephen Gammell, Warne, 1981 (I:8+ R:7).

Banks, Kate. *And If the Moon Could Talk.* Illustrated by Georg Hallensleben, Farrar, Straus & Giroux. 1998 (I:3–6 R:4).

Bearden, Romare. *Li'l Dan the Drummer Boy: A Civil War Story.* Simon & Schuster, 2003 (I:8+).

Beckett, Sister Wendy. *A Child's Book of Prayer in Art.* Dorling Kindersley, 1995 (I:all).

Bedard, Michael. *Emily.* Illustrated by Barbara Cooney, Doubleday, 1992 (I:all).

Begay, Shonto. *Navajo: Visions and Voices Across the Mesa.* Scholastic, 1995 (I:all, YA).

Behren, June. *Fiesta!* Photographs by Scott Taylor. Children's Book Press, 1978 (I:5–8).

Bemelmans, Ludwig. *Madeline.* Viking, 1939, 1977 (I:4–9 R:5).

_____. *Madeline in London.* Viking, 1961, 1977 (I:4–9 R:3).

Björk, Christina. *Linnea in Monet's Garden.* Illustrated by Lena Anderson, Farrar, Straus & Giroux, 1987 (I:all R:6).

_____. *Vendela in Venice.* Translated by Patricia Crampton, Illustrated by Inga-Karin Eriksson, R&S, 1999 (I:8+ R:5).

Blizzard, Gladys S. *Come Look With Me: World of Play.* Thomasson-Grant, 1993 (I:all).

Blumberg, Rhoda. *Commodore Perry in the Land of the Shogun.* Lothrop, Lee & Shepard, 1985 (I:8+).

Bodnár, Judit Z. *Tale of a Tail.* Illustrated by John Sandford. Lothrop, Lee & Shepard, 1998 (I:4–8 R:4).

Boedoe, Geefwee. *Arrowville.* HarperCollins, 2004 (I:3–7).

Bolden, Tonya. *Wake Up Our Souls: A Celebration of Black American Artists.* Abrams, 2004 (I:all, YA).

Bowen, Betsy. *Antler, Bear, Canoe: A Northwoods Alphabet Year.* Little, Brown, 1991 (I:all).

Bray, Rosemary L. *Martin Luther King.* Illustrated by Malcah Zeldis. Greenwillow, 1995 (I:7–10).

Brett, Jan. *Berlioz the Bear.* Putnam, 1991 (I:5–8 R:6).

Brooke, L. Leslie. *Johnny Crow's Garden.* Warne, 1903, 1986 (I:all).

Brown, Laurene Krasny, & Marc Brown. *Visiting the Art Museum.* Dutton, 1986 (I:6+).

Brown, Marcia. *Once a Mouse.* Scribner, 1961 (I:3–7 R:6).

Brown, Margaret Wise. *Goodnight Moon.* Illustrated by Clement Hurd. Harper, 1947 (I:2–7).

Brown, Tricia. *Children of the Midnight Sun: Young Native Voices of Alaska.* Photographs by Roy Corral. Alaska Northwest, 1998 (I:8+ R:6).

Browne, Anthony. *Willy's Pictures.* Candlewick, 2000 (I:all).

Bryan, Ashley. *I'm Going to Sing: Black American Spirituals,* Vol. 2. Atheneum, 1982 (I:all).

Bunting, Eve. *Ghost's Hour, Spook's Hour.* Illustrated by Donald Carrick, Clarion, 1987 (I:2–7 R:2).

_____. *Going Home.* Illustrated by David Diaz. HarperCollins, 1996 (I:3–6 R:4).

_____. *Smoky Night.* Illustrated by David Diaz. Harcourt Brace, 1994 (I:all).

Burton, Sir Richard F., translated by. *The Arabian Nights: Tales From a Thousand and One Nights.* Excalibur, 1985 (I:YA).

Burton, Virginia Lee. *The Little House.* Houghton Mifflin, 1942 (I:3–7 R:3).

_____. *Mike Mulligan and His Steam Shovel.* Houghton Mifflin, 1939 (I:3–7 R:3).

Byrd, Robert. *Leonardo: Beautiful Dreamer.* Dutton, 2003 (I:10–14).

Caldecott, Randolph. *Come Lasses and Lads.* New Orchard, 1988.

_____. *The Fox Jumps Over the Parson's Gate.* New Orchard, 1988.

_____. *A Frog He Would A-Wooing Go.* New Orchard, 1988.

_____. *Hey Diddle Diddle and Baby Bunting.* New Orchard, 1988.

_____. *Ride a Cock Horse to Banbury X & a Farmer Went Trotting Upon His Grey Mare.* New Orchard, 1988.

Carle, Eric. *Catch the Ball.* Philomel, 1982 (I:3–6).

_____. *Eric Carle's Animals Animals.* Philomel, 1989 (I:3–9).

_____. *From Head to Toe.* HarperCollins, 1997 (I:3–7).

_____. *Mister Seahorse.* Philomel, 2004 (I:3–6).

_____. *The Honeybee and the Robber: A Moving/Picture Book.* Philomel, 1981 (I:3–6):

_____. *Let's Paint a Rainbow.* Philomel, 1982 (I:3–6).

_____. *The Mixed-Up Chameleon.* Crowell, 1975, 1984 (I:3–6).

_____. *10 Little Rubber Ducks.* HarperCollins, 2005 (I:4–6).

_____. *The Very Clumsy Click Beetle.* Philomel, 1999 (I:1–5).

_____. *The Very Hungry Caterpillar.* Crowell, 1971 (I:2–7).

Carroll, Colleen. *How Artists See Animals: Mammal Fish Bird Reptile.* Abbeville, 1996 (I:8–12).

_____. *How Artists See the Elements: Earth Air Fire Water.* Abbeville, 1996 (I:8–12).

_____. *How Artists See People: Boy Girl Man Woman.* Abbeville, 1996 (I:8–12).

_____. *How Artists See the Weather: Sun Rain Wind Snow.* Abbeville, 1996 (I:8–12).

Carroll, Lewis. *Alice in Wonderland.* Illustrated by John Tenniel, Grossett & Dunlap, 1946 (I:5–8 R:8+).

Carter, David A., & James Diaz. *The Elements of Pop-Up.* Simon & Schuster, 1999 (I:10+).

Catalanotto, Peter. *Emily's Art.* Simon & Schuster, 2001 (I:4–8).

Cendrars, Blaise. *Shadow.* Illustrated by Marcia Brown. Scribner, 1982 (I:all).

Chaucer, Geoffrey. *Canterbury Tales.* Adapted by Barbara Cohen, Illustrated by Trina Schart Hyman. Lothrop, Lee & Shepard, 1988 (I:8+).

Cockcroft, James. *Diego Rivera.* Chelsea House, 1991 (I:10–YA).

Cooney, Barbara. *Chanticleer and the Fox.* Adapted from Geoffrey Chaucer. Crowell, 1958 (I:5–10 R:4).

_____. *Eleanor.* Viking, 1996 (I:6–8 R:4).

_____. *Island Boy.* Viking Kestrel, 1988 (I:3–8 R:3).

Cooper, Helen. *A Pipkin of Pepper for the Pumpkin Soup.* Farrar, Straus & Giroux, 2005 (I:3–7).

_____. *Pumpkin Soup.* Doubleday, 1999 (I:3–7).

Crandell, Rachel. *Hands of the Maya: Villagers at Work and Play.* Holt, 2002 (I:all).

Crane, Walter. *The Baby's Opera.* Simon & Schuster, 1981 (I:all).

Cronin, Doreen. *Click, Clack, Moo: Cows That Type.* Illustrated by Betsy Lewin. Simon & Schuster, 2000 (I:4–7).

_____. *Duck for President.* Illustrated by Betsy Lewin. Simon & Schuster, 2004 (I:4–7 R:4).

Crossley-Holland, Kevin. *Arthur: The Seeing Stone.* Orion, 2000 (I:8+ R:6).

_____. *Beowulf,* Illustrated by Charles Keeping. Oxford, 1982 (I:10+ R:6).

_____. *How Many Miles to Bethlehem?* Illustrated by Peter Malone. Scholastic, 2004 (I:5–8).

Cummings, Pat, ed. *Talking With Artists.* Bradbury, 1992 (I:8+).

Curtis, Carolyn. *I Took the Moon for a Walk.* Illustrated by Alison Jay. Barefoot, 2004 (I:4–8).

Cutler, Jane. *The Cello of Mr. O.* Illustrated by Greg Couch. Dutton, 1999 (I:7+ R:5).

Davies, Jacqueline. *The Boy Who Drew Birds: A Story of John James Audubon.* Illustrated by Melissa Sweet. Houghton Mifflin, 2004 (I:7–10 R:5).

Day, Nancy Raine. *The Lion's Whiskers: An Ethiopian Folktale.* Illustrated by Ann Grifalconi. Scholastic, 1995 (I:5–8 R:5).

de Brunhoff, Jean. *The Story of Babar, the Little Elephant.* Translated by Merle S. Haas. Random House, 2002 (I:3–9 R:4).

dePaola, Tomie. *Big Anthony and the Magic Ring.* Harcourt Brace, 1979 (I:5–9 R:3).

_____. *Charlie Needs a Cloak* Prentice Hall, 1973 (I:3–6 R:4).

_____. *Christopher: The Holy Giant.* Holiday House, 1994 (I:4–8 R:4).

_____. *The Clown of God.* Harcourt Brace, 1978 (I:all R:4).

_____. *An Early American Christmas.* Holiday House, 1987 (I:4–7 R:6).

_____. *Giorgio's Village.* Putnam, 1982 (I:all).

_____. *Helga's Dowry: A Troll Love Story.* Harcourt Brace, 1977 (I:5–9 R:4).

_____. *The Legend of the Bluebonnet.* Putnam, 1983 (I:all R:6).

_____. *The Legend of the Indian Paintbursh,* Putnam, 1987 (I:all R:6).

_____. *Tomie dePaola's Mother Goose.* Putnam, 1985 (I:2–6).

_____. *Watch Out for the Chicken Feet in Your Soup.* Prentice Hall, 1974 (I:3–7 R:2).

Dewey, Jennifer Owings. *Stories on Stone: Rock Art: Images From the Ancient Ones.* Little, Brown, 1996 (I:all).

d' Harcourt, Claire. *Art Up Close: From Ancient to Modern.* Chronicle, 2003 (I:8–12).

Dickens, Charles. *Christmas Carol.* Illustrated by Roberto Innocenti. Stewart, Tabori & Chang, 1990 (I:10+ R:6).

Duggleby, John, *Artist In Overalls: The Life of Grant Wood.* Chronicle, 1995 (I:8+ R:8).

Dulac, Edmund. *Sinbad the Sailor and Other Stories From the Arabian Nights.* Omega, 1986.

Dunbar, Paul Laurence. *Jump Back, Honey: The Poems of Paul Laurence Dunbar.* Hyperion, 1999 (I:all).

Dunrea, Olivier. *The Trow-Wife's Treasure.* Farrar, Straus & Giroux. 1998 (I:4–8).

Ehlert, Lois. *Cuckoo/Cucu.* Harcourt Brace, 1997 (I:4–7).

_____. *Leaf Man.* Harcourt, 2005 (I:all).

_____. *Red Leaf, Yellow Leaf.* Harcourt Brace, 1991 (I:3–7).

Emberley, Barbara. *Drummer Hoff.* Illustrated by Ed Emberley. Prentice Hall, 1967 (I:3–7 R:6).

Emberley, Ed. *Ed Emberley's Picture Pie 2: A Drawing Book and Stencil.* Little, Brown, 1996 (I:all).

English, Karen. *Hot Day on Abbott Avenue.* Illustrated by Javaka Steptoe. Clarion, 2004 (I:4–8).

Esbensen, Barbara. *The Star Maiden.* Illustrated by Helen Davie. Little, Brown, 1988 (I:all).

Ets, Marie Hall, & Aurora Labastida. *Nine Days to Christmas: A Story of Mexico.* Illustrated by Marie Hall Ets. Viking, 1959 (I:5–8).

Everett, Gwen, *Li'l Sis and Uncle Willie: A Story Based on the Life and Paintings of William H. Johnson.* Illustrated by William H. Johnson, Rizzoli, 1992 (I:5–8 R:5).

Fain, Moira. *Snow Day.* Walker, 1996 (I:6–10 R:4).

Falconer, Ian. *Olivia.* Simon & Schuster, 2000 (I:3–8 R:4).

Feelings, Tom. *The Middle Passage: White Ships/Black Cargo.* Dial 1995 (I:10–YA).

Field, Edward. *Magic Words: Poems.* Illustrated by Stefano Vitale. Harcourt Brace, 1998 (I:all).

Field, Eugene. *Wynken, Blynken and Nod.* Illustrated by Susan Jeffers. Dutton, 1982.

Finley, Carol. *Art of Japan.* Lerner, 1998 (I:10 + R:6).

_____. *Art of the Far North: Inuit Sculpture, Drawing, and Printmaking.* Lerner, 1998 (I:8+ R:6).

Fleischman, Sid. *The Scarebird.* Illustrated by Peter Sís. Greenwillow, 1988 (I:7+ R:4).

Fleming, Denise. *In the Small, Small Pond.* Holt. 1993 (I:3–6).

Flournoy, Valerie. *The Patchwork Quilt.* Illustrated by Jerry Pinkney. Dial, 1985 (I:7–10 R:5).

_____. *Tanya's Reunion.* Illustrated by Jerry Pinkney. Dial, 1995 (I:7–10 R:4).

Foreman, Michael. *Michael Foreman's Mother Goose.* Harcourt Brace, 1991 (I:6+).

Frampton, David, *The Whole Night Through.* HarperCollins, 2001 (I:3–7).

Freedman, Russell. *Buffalo Hunt.* Holiday, 1988 (I:8+).

Freedman, Russell. *An Indian Winter.* Illustrated by Karl Bodmer. Holiday, 1992 (I:8+).

Fritz, Jean, et al. *The World in 1492.* Illustrated by Stefano Vitale. Holt, 1992 (I:8–YA).

Gág, Wanda. *Millions of Cats.* Coward, McCann, 1928 (I:3–7 R:3).

Garza, Carmen Lomas. *Family Pictures / Cuadros de familia.* Children's Book Press, 2005 (I:all).

Gauch, Patricia Lee. *Presenting Tanya the Ugly Duckling.* Illustrated by Satomi Ichikawa. Philomel, 1999 (I:6+).

Geeslin, Campbell. *Elena's Serenade.* Illustrated by Ana Juan. Simon & Schuster, 2004 (I:5–9).

Gelman, Rita Golden. *Doodler Doodling.* Illustrated by Paul O. Zelinsky. Greenwillow, 2004 (I:all).

George, Jean, Craighead. *The First Thanksgiving.* Illustrated by Thomas Locker. Philomel, 1993 (I:all).

Gerstein, Mordicai. *The Man Who Walked Between the Towers.* Roaring Brook, 2003 (I:all, YA).

Gilliland, Judith Heide. *Steamboat! The Story of Captain Blanche Leathers.* Illustrated by Holly Meade. DK, 2000 (I:7+).

Goble, Paul, *Beyond the Ridge.* Bradbury, 1989 (I:all R:5).

_____. *Buffalo Woman.* Bradbury, 1984 (I:all R:6).

_____. *Death of the Iron Horse.* Bradbury, 1987 (I:8+ R:5).

_____. *The Gift of the Sacred Dog.* Bradbury, 1980 (I:all R:6).

_____. *The Girl Who Loved Wild Horses.* Bradbury, 1978 (I:6–10 R:5).

_____. *Iktomi and the Berries.* Watts, 1989 (I:4–10 R:4).

_____. *Iktomi and the Boulder: A Plains Indian Story.* Orchard; 1988 (I:4–10 R:4).

_____. *Mystic Horse.* HarperCollins, 2003 (I:all).

_____. *Star Boy.* Bradbury, 1983 (I:6–10 R:5).

Goldin, Barbara Diamond. *Journeys With Elijah: Eight Tales of the Prophet.* Illustrated by Jerry Pinkney. Harcourt Brace, 1998 (I:all).

Greenaway, Kate. *A: Apple Pie.* Castle, 1979 (I:all).

_____. *Kate Greenaway.* Rizzoli, 1977 (I:all).

Greenburg, Jan, ed. *Heart to Heart: New Poems Inspired by Twentieth-Century American Art.* Abrams, 2001 (I:10+).

_____, & Sandra Jordan. *Runaway Girl: The Artist Louise Bourgeois.* Abrams, 2003 (I:13+ R:7).

Griego, Margot C., Betsy L. Bucks, Sharon S. Gilbert, & Laurel H. Kimball. *Tortillitas Para Mama and Other Spanish Nursery Rhymes.* Illustrated by Barbara Cooney. Holt, Rinehart & Winston, 1981 (I:3–7).

Grimes, Nikki. *My Man Blue.* Illustrated by Jerome Lagarrigue. Dial, 1999 (I:all).

_____. *A Pocketful of Poems.* Illustrated by Javaka Steptoe. Clarion, 2001 (I:6–10).

Grimm, Brothers. *The Golden Bird,* retold by Neil Philip. Illustrated by Isabelle Brent. Little, Brown, 1995 (I:all).

_____. *Hansel and Gretel.* Illustrated by Susan Jeffers. Dial, 1980 (I:5–9 R:6).

_____. *Hansel and Gretel.* Retold by Rika Lesser. Illustrated by Paul O. Zelinsky. Dodd, Mead, 1984 (I:all R:6).

_____. *Little Red Riding Hood.* Illustrated by Trina Schart Hyman. Holiday House, 1983 (I:6–9 R:7).

_____. *Rapunzel.* Retold and illustrated by Paul O. Zelinsky. Dutton, 1997 (I:all).

_____. *Rumpelstiltskin.* Retold and illustrated by Paul O. Zelinksky. Dutton, 1986 (I:all).

_____. *Snow White and the Seven Dwarfs.* Illustrated by Nancy Ekholm Burkert. Farrar, Straus & Giroux, 1972 (I:7–12 R:6).

Grimm, Wilhelm. *Dear Mili.* Translated by Ralph Manheim, Illustrated by Maurice Sendak. Farrar, Straus & Giroux, 1988 (I:all R:6).

Guarnieri, Paolo. *A Boy Named Giotto.* Illustrated by Bimba Landman. Farrar, Straus & Giroux, 1999 (I:5–8 R:4).

Haley, Gail E. *A Story, a Story.* Atheneum, 1970 (I:6–10 R:6).

Hall, Donald. *Ox-Cart Man.* Illustrations by Barbara Cooney. Viking, 1979 (I:3–8 R:5).

Halperin, Wendy Anderson. *Love Is . . .* Simon & Schuster, 2001 (I:all).

Hamilton, Virginia. *Her Stories: African American Folktales, Fairy Tales, and True Tales.* Scholastic, 1995 (I:all).

_____. *The People Could Fly: American Black Folktales.* Illustrated by Leo & Diane Dillon. Knopf, 1985 (I:9+ R:6).

_____. *The People Could Fly: The Picture Book.* Illustrated by Leo & Diane Dillon. Knopf, 2004 (I:all, YA).

Hannah, Jonny, *Hot Jazz Special.* Candlewick, 2005 (I:8–YA).

Henkes, Kevin. *Kitten's First Full Moon.* Greenwillow, 2004 (I:3–5).

Hill, Laban Carrick. *Harlem Stomp! A Cultural History of The Harlem Renaissance.* Little, Brown, 2003 (I:9–YA).

Ho, Minfong. *Hush! A Thai Lullaby.* Illustrated by Holly Meade. Orchard, 1996 (I:3–8).

Hoban, Tana. *Shadows and Reflections.* Greenwillow, 1990 (I:all).

Hodges, Margaret. *Saint George and the Dragon.* Illustrated by Trina Schart Hyman. Little, Brown, 1984 (I:9+ R:7).

Holling, Holling Clancy. *Paddle-to-the-Sea.* Houghton Mifflin, 1941 (I:7–12 R:4).

_____. *Seabird.* Houghton Mifflin, 1948 (I:7–12 R:4).

Holzhey, Magdelena. *Frida Kahlo: The Artist in the Blue House.* Prestel, 2003 (I:10–YA).

Hoobler, Dorothy, & Thomas Hoobler. *The Jewish American Family Album.* Oxford University Press, 1995 (I:all).

Howitt, Mary. *The Spider and the Fly.* Illustrated by Tony Diterlizzi, Simon & Schuster, 2002 (I:all, YA).

Hoyt-Goldsmith, Diane. *Hoang Anh: A Vietnamese-American Boy.* Photographs by Lawrence Migdale. Holiday House, 1992 (I:5–9 R:4).

Hudson, Wade, & Cheryl Willis Hudson, compiled by. *In Praise of Our Fathers and Our Mothers: A Black Family Treasury by Outstanding Authors and Artists.* Just Us Books, 1997 (I:10–YA).

Hughes, Langston. *The Sweet and Sour Animal Book.* Illustrated by students from the Harlem School of Arts. Oxford University Press, 1994 (I:all).

Innocenti, Roberto. *Rose Blanche.* Stewart, Tabori & Chang, 1990 (I:8+ R:4).

Irving, Washington. *The Legend of Sleepy Hollow.* Illustrated by Gary Kelley, Creative Education, 1990 (I:9+).

_____. *The Legend of Sleepy Hollow.* Illustrated by Will Moses. Philomel, 1995 (I:all).

Isaacs, Anne. *Swamp Angel,* Illustrated by Paul O. Zelinsky. Dutton, 1994 (I:all).

James, J. Alison. *The Drums of Noto Hanto.* Illustrated by Tsukushi. DK, 1999 (I: all).

Janson, H. W., & Anthony F. Janson. *History of Art for Young People,* 5th Ed. Abrams, 1997 (I:10+).

Jeffers, Susan. *Brother Eagle, Sister Sky.* Dial, 1991 (I:all).

_____. *Three Jovial Huntsmen.* Bradbury, 1973 (I:4–8).

Jenkins, Steve. *The Top of the World: Climbing Mount Everest.* Houghton Mifflin, 1999 (I:7+).

Johnson, James Weldon. *The Creation.* Illustrated by Carla Golembe, Little, Brown, 1993 (I:all).

Johnson, Stephen T. *Alphabet City.* Viking, 1995 (I:all).

Johnston, Tony. *Desert Song.* Illustrated by Ed Young. Sierra Club, 2000 (I:all).

Keats, Ezra Jack. *Apt. 3.* Macmillan, 1974 (I:3–8 R:3).

_____. *Goggles!* Macmillan, 1969 (I:5–9 R:3).

_____. *Louie.* Greenwillow, 1975 (I:3–8 R:2).

_____. *Peter's Chair.* Harper & Row, 1967 (I:3–8 R:2).

_____. *Regards to the Man in the Moon.* Four Winds, 1981 (I:4–8 R:3).

_____. *The Snowy Day.* Viking, 1962 (I:2–6 R:2).

_____. *The Trip.* Greenwillow, 1978 (I:3–8 R:2).

Keep, Richard. *Clatter Bash! A Day of the Dead Celebration.* Peachtree, 2004 (I:4–9).

Kerley, Barbara. *The Dinosaurs of Waterhouse Hawkins.* Illustrated by Brian Selznick, Scholastic, 2001 (I:all, YA).

_____. *Walt Whitman: Words for America.* Illustrated by Brian Selznick. Scholastic, 2004 (I:9–YA).

Kimmel, Eric A. *Wonders and Miracles: A Passover Companion.* Scholastic, 2004 (I:all, YA).

Kleven, Elisa. *Hooray, A Pinata!* Dutton, 1996 (I:4–7).

Knox, Bob. *The Great Art Adventure.* Rizzoli, 1992 (I:all).

Kodama, Tatsuharu. *Shin's Tricycle.* Illustrated by Noriyuki Ando. Translated by Kazuko Hokumen-Jones. Walker, 1995 (I:all).

Kolar, Bob. *Do You Want to Play? A Book About Being Friends.* Dutton, 1999 (I:all).

Krauss, Ruth. *A Hole Is to Dig.* Illustrated by Maurice Sendak. Harper & Row, 1952 (I:2–6 R:2).

Krensky, Stephen. *Breaking Into Print: Before and After the Invention of the Printing Press.* Illustrated by Bonnie Christensen. Little, Brown, 1996 (I:7–10 R:4).

Kushner, Tony. *Brundibar.* Illustrated by Maurice Sendak. Hyperion, 2003 (I:all, YA).

Kuskin, Karla. *Jerusalem Shining Still.* Illustrated by David Frampton. Harper & Row, 1987 (I:8+).

Lawlor, Laurie. *Shadow Catcher: The Life and Work of Edward S. Curtis.* University of Nebraska Press, 2005 (I:10+ R:7).

Lawson, Robert. *Ben and Me.* Little, Brown, 1939 (I:7–11 R:6).

_____. *Rabbit Hill.* Viking, 1944 (I:7–11 R:7).

Leaf, Munro. *The Story of Ferdinand.* Illustrated by Robert Lawson. Viking, 1936. (I:4–10 R:6).

Lear, Edward. *The Owl and The Pussycat.* Illustrated by James Marshall. HarperCollins, 1998 (I:all).

Leedy, Loreen. *Look at My Book: How Kids Can Write & Illustrate Terrific Books.* Holiday House, (I:7–10).

Lehman, Barbara. *The Red Book.* Houghton Mifflin, 2004 (I:all).

Lenski, Lois. *Sing a Song of People.* Illustrated by Giles Laroche. Little, Brown, 1987 (I:all).

Lent, Blair. *Bayberry Bluff.* Houghton Mifflin, 1987 (I:3–8 R:6).

Lester, Julius. *The Tales of Uncle Remus: The Adventures of Brer Rabbit as Told by Julius Lester.* Illustrated by Jerry Pinkney. Dial, 1987 (I:6–9 R:4).

_____. *Further Tales of Uncle Remus: The Misadventures of Brer Rabbit, Brer Fox, the Doodang and All the Other Creatures.* Illustrated by Jerry Pinkney. Dial, 1990 (I:6–11 R:5).

_____. *Sam and the Tigers: A New Telling of Little Black Sambo.* Illustrated by Jerry Pinkney. Dial, 1996 (I:6–9 R:4).

Lewis, Paul Owen. *Storm Boy.* Beyond Words. 1995 (I:7+ R:6).

Lindbergh, Reeve. *Johnny Appleseed.* Illustrated by Kathy Jakobsen, Little Brown, 1990 (I:all).

Lionni, Leo. *Alexander and the Wind-up Mouse.* Pantheon, 1969 (I:3–6 R:3).

_____. *A Color of His Own.* Random House, 1975 (I:2–7 R:5).

_____. *Swimmy.* Pantheon, 1963 (I:2–6 R:3).

Littlechild, George. *This Land Is My Land.* Children's Book Press,1993 (I:8+).

Livingston, Myra Cohn. *A Circle of Seasons.* Illustrated by Leonard Everett Fisher. Holiday House, 1982 (I:all).

Lobel, Arnold. *Fables.* Jonathon Cape, 1980 (I:all).

Locker, Thomas. *Sailing with the Wind.* Dial, 1986. (I:all).

_____. *Where the River Begins.* Dial, 1984 (I:all).

London, Jonathan. *Baby Whale's Journey.* Illustrated by Jon Van Zyle, Chronicle. 1999 (I:all).

Longfellow, Henry Wadsworth. *Hiawatha.* Illustrated by Susan Jeffers. Dial, 1983 (I:all).

_____. *Hiawatha's Childhood.* Illustrated by Errol LeCain. Farrar, Straus & Giroux, 1984 (I:all).

Luenn, Nancy. *A Gift for Abuelita: Celebrating the Day of the Dead.* Illustrated by Robert Chapman. Rising Moon, 1998 (I:7+ R:4).

Lunge-Larsen, Lise, retold by. *The Troll With No Heart in His Body and Other Tales of Trolls From Norway.* Illustrated by Betsy Bowen. Houghton Mifflin, 1999 (I:7+).

Macaulay, David. *Mosque.* Houghton Mifflin, 2003 (I:all, YA).

Macdonald, Fiona. *A 16th Century Mosque.* Illustrated by Mark Bergin. Peter Bedrick, 1994 (I: all).

MacDonald, Suse. *Look Whooo's Counting.* Scholastic, 2000 (I:3–6).

MacGill-Callahan, Sheila. *The Children of Lir,* Illustrated by Gennady Spirin. Dial, 1993 (I:6+ R:5).

MacLachlan, Patricia. *What You Know First.* Illustrated by Barry Moser. HarperCollins, 1995 (I:all).

Major, John S. *The Silk Route: 7,000 Miles of History.* Illustrated by Stephen Fleser. HarperCollins, 1995 (I:8–12).

Mallat, Kathy, and Bruce McMillan. *The Picture That Mom Drew.* Walker, 1997 (I:8+).

Marcus, Leonard S. *A Caldecott Celebration: Six Artists and Their Paths to the Caldecott Medal.* Walker, 1998 (I:8+ R:5).

Martin, Eva. *Canadian Fairy Tales,* Illustrated by Laszlo Gal. Douglas & McIntyre, 1984 (I:7–16 R:4).

Martin, Rafe. *Will's Mammoth.* Illustrated by Stephen Gammell. Putnam, 1989 (I:2–7).

Maruki, Toshi. *Hiroshima No Pika.* Lothrop, Lee & Shepard, 1982 (I:8–12 R:4).

McCloskey, Robert. *Blueberries for Sal.* Viking, 1948 (I:4–8 R:6).

———. *Lentil.* Viking, 1940 (I:4–9 R:7).

———. *Make Way for Ducklings.* Viking, 1941 (I:4–8 R:4).

———. *One Morning in Maine.* Viking, 1952 (I:4–8 R:3).

———. *Time of Wonder.* Viking, 1957 (I:5–8 R:4).

McCully, Emily Arnold. *The Ballot Box Battle.* Knopf, 1996 (I:4–8 R:5).

———. *The Bobbin Girl.* Dial, 1996 (I:6–9 R:5).

———. *Mirette on the High Wire.* Putnam, 1992 (I:all).

McDermott, Beverly Brodsky. *The Golem,* Lippincott, 1976 (I:9–14 R:5).

McDermott, Gerald. *Arrow to the Sun.* Viking, 1974 (!:3–9 R:2).

McLanathan. Richard, *Leonardo da Vinci,* Abrams, 1990 (I:10+).

McMahon, Patricia. *Chi-Hoon: A Korean Girl.* Photographs by Michael O'Brien. Caroline House, 1993 (I:8+).

Meryman, Richard. *Andrew Wyeth.* Abrams, 1991 (I:10+).

Micklethwait, Lucy. *A Child's Book of Art: Great Pictures, First Words.* Dorling Kindersley, 1993 (I:all).

Miller, Debbie S. *A Polar Bear Journey.* Illustrated by Jon Van Zyle. Little, Brown, 1997 (I:6–9 R:5).

———. *A Woolly Mammoth Journey.* Illustrated by Jon Van Zyle. Little, Brown, 2001 (I:6–9 R:5).

Moore, Clement. *The Night Before Christmas.* Illustrated by Tomie dePaola. Holiday House, 1980 (I:all).

Morpurgo, Michael. *Wombat Goes Walkabout.* Illustrated by Christian Birmingham. Candlewick, 2000 (I:4–8).

Morrison, Toni. *Remember: The Journey to School Integration.* Houghton Mifflin, 2004 (I:all).

Mosel, Arlene. *Tikki Tikki Tembo.* Illustrated by Blair Lent. Holt, Rinehart & Winston, 1968 (I:5–9 R:7).

Moser, Barry, retold by. *The Three Little Pigs.* Little, Brown, 2001 (I:4–8).

Moss, Lloyd. *Zin! Zin! Zin! A Violin.* Illustrated by Marjorie Priceman. Simon & Schuster, 1995 (I:all).

Mulvihill, Margaret. *The Treasury of Saints and Martyrs.* Consultant David Hugh Farmer. Viking, 1999 (I:10+ R:7).

Musgrove, Margaret. *Ashanti to Zulu: African Traditions.* Illustrated by Leo & Diane Dillon. Dial, 1976 (I:7–12).

Myers, Christopher. *Wings.* Scholastic, 2000 (I:all).

Newberry, Clare Turlay. *Marshmallow.* Harper & Row, 1942 (I:2–7 R:7).

Nister, Ernest. *Animal Tales.* London: Benn, 1981.

Norman, Howard, retold by. *The Girl Who Dreamed Only Geese and Other Tales of the Far North.* Illustrated by Leo & Diane Dillon. Harcourt Brace, 1997 (I:9+ R:6).

Noyes, Alfred. *The Highwayman.* Illustrated by Charles Keeping. Oxford, 1981 (I:10+).

Nye, Naomi Shihab. *The Space Between Our Footsteps: Poems and Paintings From the Middle East.* Simon & Schuster, 1998 (I:all, YA).

Oppenheim, Joanne. *Have You Seen Trees?* Illustrated by Jean & Mou-sien Tseng. Scholastic, 1995 (I:all).

Panzer, Nora, ed. *Celebrate America: In Poetry and Art.* Hyperion, 1994 (I:all).

Park, Linda Sue. *A Single Shard.* Clarion, 2001 (I:10+ R:5).

Peet, Bill. *Bill Peet's Autobiography.* Houghton Mifflin, 1989 (I:all R:5).

Pelletier, David. *The Graphic Alphabet.* Orchard, 1996 (I:all).

Perrault Charles. *Cinderella.* Adapted by Amy Ehrlich. Illustrated by Susan Jeffers. Dial, 1985 (I:5–8 R:4).

———. *Cinderella.* Illustrated by Marcia Brown. Harper & Row, 1954 (I:5–8 R:5).

Pope, Joyce. *Kenneth Lilly's Animals: A Portfolio of Paintings.* Illustrated by Kenneth Lilly. Lothrop, Lee & Shepard, 1988 (I:all).

Potter, Beatrix. *The Tale of Peter Rabbit.* Warne, 1902, 1986 (I:all).

Priceman, Marjorie. *Froggie Went A-Courting.* Little, Brown, 2000 (I:3–5).

Provensen, Alice, & Martin Provensen. *The Glorious Flight Across the Channel With Louis Bleriot, July 25, 1909.* Viking, 1983 (I:all R:4).

Pyle, Howard, *Bearskin.* Illustrated by Trina Schart Hyman. Morrow, 1997 (I:6–9 R:5).

Quiller-Couch, Sir Arthur, retold by. *The Sleeping Beauty and Other Fairy Tales.* Illustrated by Edmund Dulac. London: Hodder and Stoughton, 1981.

Ransome, Arthur. *The Fool of the World and the Flying Ship.* Illustrated by Uri Shulevitz. Farrar, Straus & Giroux, 1968 (I:6–10 R:6).

Radunsky, Vladimir. *The Mighty Asparagus.* Harcourt, 2004 (I:all).

Ray, Mary Lyn. *Basket Moon.* Illustrated by Barbara Cooney. Little, Brown, 1999 (I:all).

Reading Is Fundamental. *The Art of Reading.* Dutton, 2005 (I:all).

Reeves, Nicholas. *Into the Mummy's Tomb: The Real-Life Discovery of Tutankhamun's Treasures.* Scholastic, 1992 (I:8+).

Rembert, Winfred. *Don't Hold Me Back: My Life and Art.* Cricket, 2003 (I:all, YA).

Ringgold, Faith. *My Dream of Martin Luther King.* Crown, 1995 (I:5–9).

Rogasky, Barbara. *The Golem.* Illustrated by Trina Schart Hyman. Holiday, 1996 (I:9+ R:5).

———. *Smoke and Ashes: The Story of the Holocaust.* Holiday House, 1988 (I:10–YA).

Rogers, Gregory. *The Boy, The Bear, The Baron, The Bard.* Roaring Brook, 2004 (I:all, YA).

Rohmann, Eric. *My Friend Rabbit.* Roaring Brook, 2002 (I:3–6).

Rosen, Michael. *We're Going on a Bear Hunt.* Illustrated by Helen Oxenbury. Macmillan, 1989 (I:2–6).

Rubin, Susan Goldman. *Art Against the Odds: From Slave Quilts to Prison Paintings.* Crown, 2004 (I:9–14).

_____. *Degas and the Dance: The Painter and the Petits Rats Perfecting Their Art.* Abrams, 2002 (I:10–YA).

_____. *Margaret Bourke-White: Her Pictures Were Her Life: Photographs by Margaret Bourke-White.* Abrams, 1999 (I:10+).

Rumford, James. *Sequoyah: The Cherokee Man Who Gave His People Writing.* Translated into Cherokee by Anna Sixkiller Huckaby. Houghton Mifflin, 2004 (1:6–9).

Russo, Marisabina. *Always Remember Me: How One Family Survived World War II.* Atheneum, 2005 (I:8+).

Rylant, Cynthia. *In November.* Illustrated by Jill Kastner. Harcourt Brace, 2000 (I:4–7).

Sabuda, Robert, *The Blizzard's Robe.* Atheneum, 1999 (I:all).

Sands, Emily. *Egyptology.* Candlewick, 2004 (I:all).

Say, Allen. *Allison.* Houghton Mifflin, 1997 (I:4–8 R:4).

_____. *Grandfather's Journey.* Houghton Mifflin, 1993 (I:all).

Sayre, Henry. *Cave Paintings to Picasso: The Inside Scoop on 50 Art Masterpieces.* Chronicle, 2004 (I:10+, YA).

Scheer, Julian. *Rain Makes Applesauce.* Illustrated by Marvin Bileck. Holiday House, 1964 (I:3–8).

Schroeder, Alan. *Minty: A Story of Young Harriet Tubman.* Illustrated by Jerry Pinkney. Puffin, 1996 (I:8–11 R4+).

Schwartz, Gary. *Rembrandt.* Abrams, 1992 (I:10+ R:7).

Scieszka, Jon. *The Stinky Cheese Man and Other Fairly Stupid Tales.* Illustrated by Lane Smith. Viking, 1992 (I:all).

_____. *The True Story of the 3 Little Pigs!* Illustrated by Lane Smith. Viking, 1989 (I:all).

_____, & Lane Smith. *Seen Art?* Museum of Modern Art/Viking, 2005 (I:all).

Sendak, Maurice. *In The Night Kitchen.* Harper & Row, 1970 (I:5–7).

_____. *Outside Over There.* Harper & Row, 1981 (I:5–8 R:5).

_____. *We Are All in the Dumps With Jack and Guy.* HarperCollins, 1993 (I:all).

_____. *Where the Wild Things Are.* Harper & Row, 1963 (I:4–8 R:6).

Seuss, Dr. *The 500 Hats of Bartholomew Cubbins.* Vanguard, 1938 (I:4–9 R:4).

Shange, Ntozake. *Ellington Was Not a Street.* Illustrated by Kadir Nelson. Simon & Schuster, 2004 (I:all, YA).

Shannon, George. *Dance Away.* Illustrated by Jose Aruego and Ariane Dewey. Greenwillow, 1982 (I:2–6).

Shepard, Aaron, retold by. *Master Man: A Tall Tale of Nigeria.* Illustrated by David Wisniewski. HarperCollins, 2001 (I:all).

_____. retold by. *The Sea King's Daughter: A Russian Legend.* Illustrated by Gennady Spirin. Atheneum, 1997 (I:7+ R:5).

Simon, Seymour. *Jupiter.* Morrow, 1985 (I:all R:7).

Simont, Marc. *The Goose That Almost Got Cooked.* Scholastic, 1997 (I:3–7 R:4).

Singer, Isaac Bashevis. *The Golem.* Illustrated by Uri Shulevitz. Farrar, Straus & Giroux, 1982 (I:81 R:5).

_____. *Zlateh the Goat.* Illustrated by Maurice Sendak. Harper & Row, 1966 (I:6–10 R:6).

Sís, Peter. *Starry Messenger: Galileo Galilei.* Farrar, Straus & Giroux, 1996 (I:all).

Skira-Venturi, Rosabianca. *A Weekend With Leonardo da Vinci.* Translated by Ann Keay Beneduce. Rizzoli, 1992 (I:10+).

Spier, Peter. *The Fox Went Out on a Chilly Night.* Doubleday, 1961 (I:all).

_____. *Noah's Ark.* Doubleday, 1977 (I:3–9).

_____. *The Star-Spangled Banner.* Doubleday, 1973 (I:8+).

Stanley, Diane. *Leonardo da Vinci.* Morrow, 1996 (I:8+ R:6).

_____. *Saving Sweetness.* Illustrated by G. Brian Karas. Putnam, 1996 (I:5–8 R:5).

Steig, William. *The Amazing Bone.* Farrar, Straus & Giroux, 1976 (I:6–9 R:5).

Steptoe, Javaka. *In Daddy's Arms I Am Tall: African Americans Celebrating Fathers.* Lee & Low, 1997 (I:all).

Steptoe, John. *Stevie.* Harper & Row, 1969 (I:3–7 R:3).

_____. *The Story of Jumping Mouse.* Lothrop, Lee & Shepard, 1984 (I:all R:4).

Stevens, Janet. *Tops & Bottoms.* Harcourt Brace, 1995 (I:4–7).

Stevenson, Robert Louis. *My Shadow.* Illustrated by Ted Rand. Putnam, 1990 (I:all).

Stewart, Sarah. *The Gardener.* Illustrated by David Small. Farrar, Straus & Giroux, 1997 (I:5–8 R:4).

Strickland, Carol. *The Annotated Mona Lisa: A Crash Course in Art History From Prehistoric to Post-Modern.* Andrews and McMeel, 1992 (I:10+).

Swamp, Chief Jake. *Giving Thanks: A Native American Morning Message.* Illustrated by Erwin Printup Jr. Lee & Sow, 1995 (I:5–8).

Sykes, Julie. *This and That.* Illustrated by Tanya Linch. Farrar, Straus & Giroux, 1996 (I:4–7).

Taback, Simms. *Joseph Had a Little Overcoat.* Viking, 1999 (I:all).

_____. *There Was an Old Lady Who Swallowed a Fly.* Viking, 1997 (I:all).

Thomas, Dylan. *A Child's Christmas in Wales.* Illustrated by Chris Raschka. Candlewick, 2004 (I:all, YA).

Thompson, Lauren. *Polar Bear Night.* Illustrated by Stephen Savage. Scholastic, 2004 (I:3–6).

Tseng, Grace, retold by. *White Tiger, Blue Serpent.* Illustrated by Jean & Mou-sien Tseng. Lothrop, Lee & Shepard, 1999 (I:all).

Turner, Robyn Montana. *Frida Kahlo: Portraits of Women Artists for Children.* Little, Brown, 1993 (I:all).

_____. *Georgia O'Keeffe.* Little, Brown, 1991 (I:9+ R:5).

Udry, Janice May. *The Moon Jumpers.* Illustrated by Maurice Sendak. Harper & Row, 1959 (I:3–9 R:2).

Van Allsburg, Chris. *The Garden of Abdul Gasazi.* Houghton Mifflin, 1979 (I:5–8 R:5).

_____. *Jumanji.* Houghton Mifflin, 1981 (I:5–8 R:6).

_____. *The Mysteries of Harris Burdick.* Houghton Mifflin, 1984 (I:all).

_____. *The Polar Express.* Houghton Mifflin, 1985 (I:5–8 R:6).

_____. *The Sweetest Fig.* Houghton Mifflin, 1993 (I:all R:6).

_____. *The Widow's Broom.* Houghton Mifflin, 1992 (I:5–8 R:6).

_____. *The Wreck of the Zephyr.* Houghton Mifflin, 1983 (I:5–8 R:6).

_____. *The Wretched Stone.* Houghton Mifflin, 1991 (I:5–8 R:6).

Venezia, Mike. *Diego Velázquez.* Children's Press 2004 (I:8+).

Viorst, Judith. *Alexander and the Terrible, Horrible, No Good, Very Bad Day.* Illustrated by Ray Cruz. Atheneum, 1972 (I:3–8 R:6).

Volavkova, Hana, ed. *. . . I Never Saw Another Butterfly . . . Children's Drawings and Poems From Terezin Concentration Camp, 1942–1944.* Schocken, 1993 (I:all, YA).

Waber, Bernard. *The Lion Named Shirley Williamson.* Houghton Mifflin, 1996 (I:5–8 R:5).

Waddell, Martin. *Farmer Duck.* Illustrated by Helen Oxenbury. Candlewick, 1992 (I:4–7).

Waldman, Neil. *The Golden City: Jerusalem's 3,000 Years.* Atheneum, 1995 (I:8–12).

Waldron, Ann. *Francisco Goya.* Abrams, 1992 (I:10+).

Wallace, Ian. *Chin Chiang and the Dragon Dance.* Atheneum, 1984 (I:6–9).

Walter, Mildred Pitts. *Brother to the Wind.* Illustrated by Diane & Leo Dillon. Lothrop, Lee & Shepard, 1985 (I:all R:3).

Ward, Lynd. *The Biggest Bear.* Houghton Mifflin, 1952 (I:5–8 R:4).

Waring, Richard. *Hungry Hen.* Illustrated by Caroline Jayne Church. HarperCollins, 2002 (I:4–8).

Waters, Kate, & Madeline Slovenz-Low. *Lion Dancer: Ernie Wan's Chinese New Year.* Photographs by Martha Cooper. Scholastic, 1990 (I:5–8).

Weller, Frances Ward. *I Wonder If I'll See a Whale.* Illustrated by Ted Lewin. Philomel, 1991 (I:6–10 R:4).

Welton, Jude. *Impressionism.* Kindersley/The Art Institute of Chicago, 1993 (I:10+).

_____. *Monet.* Kindersley/The Musee Marmottan, Paris, 1992 (I:10+).

Wheeler, Lisa. *Seadogs: An Epic Ocean Operetta.* Illustrated by Mark Siegel. Atheneum, 2004 (I:7–10).

Whipple, Laura, complied by. *Eric Carle's Dragons Dragons & Other Creatures That Never Were.* Illustrated by Eric Carle. Philomel, 1991 (I:all).

Wiesner, David. *Free Fall.* Lothrop, Lee & Shepard, 1988 (I:all).

_____. *June 29, 1999.* Clarion, 1992 (I:all).

_____. *Tuesday.* Clarion, 1991 (I:all).

Wild, Margaret. *Let the Celebrations BEGIN!* Illustrated by Julie Vivas. Orchard, 1991 (I:all).

Wildsmith, Brian. *Exodus.* Eerdmans, 1998 (I:all).

Willard, Nancy. *Pish, Posh, Said Hieronymus Bosch.* Illustrated by Leo & Diane Dillon. Harcourt Brace, 1991 (I:all).

_____. *A Visit to William Blake's Inn: Poems for Innocent and Experienced Travelers.* Illustrated by Alice & Martin Provensen. Harcourt Brace, 1981 (I:all).

Willems, Mo. *Knuffle Bunny: A Cautionary Tale.* Hyperion, 2004 (I:2–4).

Winter, Jonah. *Diego.* Translated by Amy Prince. Illustrated by Jeanette Winter. Knopf, 1991 (I:6–10 R:5).

Wisniewski, David. *Golem.* Clarion, 1996 (I:all).

_____. *Rain Player.* Clarion, 1991 (I:5–8 R:5).

Wolfe, Gillian. *Look: Body Language in Art.* Frances Lincoln, 2004 (I:all).

Wood, Audrey. *King Bidgood's in the Bathtub.* Illustrated by Don Wood. Harcourt Brace, 1985 (I:6–9 R:1).

Wood, Douglas. *Old Turtle.* Illustrated by Cheng-Khee Chee. Pfeifer-Hamilton, 1992 (I:all).

Wood, Nancy, ed. *The Serpent's Tongue: Prose, Poetry, and Art of the New Mexico Pueblos.* Dutton, 1997 (I:8+).

Woodson, Jacqueline. *Coming on Home Soon.* Illustrated by E. B. Lewis. Putnam, 2004 (1:5–8).

Wormell, Christopher. *An Alphabet of Animals.* Dial, 1990 (I:all).

_____. *Teeth, Tails, & Tentacles: An Animal Counting Book.* Running Press, 2004 (I:3–8).

Wright, Patricia. *Manet.* Kindersley/National Gallery, London, 1993 (I:10+).

Yagawa, Sumiko. *The Crane Wife.* Translated by Katherine Paterson. Illustrated by Suekichi Akaba. Morrow, 1981 (I:all R:6).

Yashima, Taro. *Crow Boy.* Viking, 1955 (I:4–8 R:4).

_____. *Umbrella.* Viking, 1958 (I:3–7 R:7).

Yolen, Jane. *Letting Swift River Go.* Illustrated by Barbara Cooney. Little, Brown, 1992 (I:all).

_____. *Off We Go!* Illustrated by Laurel Molk. Little, Brown, 2000 (I:3–5).

_____. *Owl Moon.* Illustrated by John Schoenherr. Philomel, 1987 (I:all).

Yorinks, Arthur. *Hey, Al.* Illustrated by Richard Egielski. Farrar, Straus & Giroux, 1986 (I:all).

_____. *The Miami Giant.* Illustrated by Maurice Sendak. HarperCollins, 1995 (I:all).

Young, Ed. *I, Doko: The Tale of a Basket.* Philomel, 2004 (I:all).

_____, translated by. *Lon Po Po: A Red-Riding Hood Story From China.* Philomel, 1989 (I:all R:5).

_____. *Seven Blind Mice.* Philomel, 1992 (I:all).

Zeman, Ludmila, retold and illustrated by. *Sinbad: From the Tales of the Thousand and One Nights.* Tundra, 1999 (I:all).

Zheng, Zhensun, & Alice Low. *Young Painter: The Life and Paintings of Wang Yani—China's Extraordinary Young Artist.* Scholastic, 1991 (I:all R:5).

Zolotow, Charlotte. *Mr. Rabbit and the Lovely Present.* Illustrated by Maurice Sendak. Harper & Row, 1962 (I:3–8 R:2).

_____. *When the Wind Stops.* Illustrated by Stefano Vitale. HarperCollins, 1995 (I:4–8).

Illustration from Storm Boy, written and illustrated by Paul Owen Lewis, copyright © 1995 by Paul Owen Lewis. Beyond Words Publishing, Inc., 1-800-284-9673.

CHAPTER OUTLINE

A Book Is More Than Words

- What a Picture Book Is
- Literary Criticism: Evaluating Picture Books
- Mother Goose
- Toy Books
- Alphabet Books
- Counting Books
- Concept Books
- Wordless Books
- Easy-to-Read Books
- Picture Storybooks

Teaching With Picture Books

- Sharing Mother Goose
- Sharing Wordless Books
- Reading to Children
- Developing Aesthetic Sensitivity
- Motivating Writing With Picture Storybooks

A Book Is More Than Words

The thought of a child, a lap, and a picture book arouses warm feelings and recollections in many adults. When a loving adult provides opportunities for a child to experience the enchantment found in picture books, both the child and the adult benefit.

The books included in the genre of picture books have many values in addition to pleasure. The rhythm, rhyme, and repetition in nursery rhymes stimulate language development as well as auditory discrimination and attentive listening skills in young children. Alphabet books reinforce ability to identify letter/sound relationships and help expand vocabularies. Concept books enhance intellectual development by fostering understanding of abstract ideas. Wordless books encourage children to develop their observational skills, descriptive vocabularies, and abilities to create stories characterized by logical sequence. Illustrations found in picture books stimulate sensitivity to art and beauty. Well-written picture storybooks encourage children to appreciate literary style. Thus, picture books have important roles in children's development.

What a Picture Book Is

Most children's books are illustrated, but not all illustrated children's books are picture books. As Perry Nodelman (1990) points out, picture books "communicate information or tell stories through a series of many pictures combined with relatively slight texts or no texts at all" (p. VII, preface).

In picture books, the illustrations are as important as or even more important than the text. Because children respond to stories told visually as well as verbally, some picture books are quite effective with no words at all. Many picture books, however, maintain a balance between the illustrations and the text, so that neither is completely effective without the other.

Thus the term *picture books* covers a wide variety of children's books, ranging from Mother Goose books and toy books for very young children to picture storybooks with plots that satisfy more experienced, older children. Many of the picture books discussed in this chapter rely heavily on illustrations to present content. In some, each scene or rhyme is illustrated; other books, with more complex verbal story lines, are not so dependent on pictures to develop their plots.

Many picture books have a characteristic not often shared by other children's books: The writer and the illustrator may be the same person. Well-known artists often create picture books. This chapter emphasizes authors, author-illustrators, and their literature.

LITERARY CRITICISM: Evaluating Picture Books

Because the text and the illustrations in picture books should complement each other, consider the relationships between the words and pictures when evaluating a picture book. Zena Sutherland (1997) makes recommendations for evaluating picture books written for young children. She states:

> A story should be brief and straightforward if it is for young children; it should contain few concepts and none that are beyond comprehension if they are not familiar concepts; it should be written in a direct and simple style; and it should have illustrations that complement the text and are not in conflict with it. (p. 64)

The questions in the Evaluation Criteria box on this page can help you select high-quality picture books for children.

Educators, researchers, and authorities in children's literature are increasingly interested in children's responses to picture books and in the characteristics of picture books that appeal to children. You should consider children's own evaluations when selecting picture books to share with children.

The first interactions of a very young child with a picture book are largely physical, as the child investigates the size, shape, texture, and moving parts of the unfamiliar object. The child may stick the book into his or her mouth to become acquainted with it or turn the pages even if the book is upside down. With adult guidance, the child soon learns the specific purposes and pleasures associated with books and responds to the symbolic nature of books, focusing on the content of the pictures and connecting illustrated objects and concepts with the sounds and names given to them. The child quickly begins to assume that books will contain stories.

As a sense of time develops, a child begins to see connections among past, present, and future in pictures and text and to expect that a story will have a beginning, a middle, and an end. Finally, after time and experience with both books and everyday living, a child evaluates book text and illustrations in terms of his or her own view of reality and his or her own feelings and desires. Thus, different types of books and book-related experiences are appropriate for children at different ages and stages of development.

Patricia Cianciolo (1997) identified four major factors that influence how a child perceives and evaluates the illustrations in picture books: (1) the child's age and stage of cognitive and social development, (2) the way in which an adult has (or has not) prepared the child for the experience with a picture book, (3) the child's emotional state of readiness, and (4) the number of times the child looks at the illustrations. Cianciolo's (1983) analysis of picture

Evaluation Criteria

Selecting High-Quality Picture Books

1. Are the illustrations accurate, and do they correspond to the content of the story?
2. Do the illustrations complement the setting, plot, and mood of the story?
3. Do the illustrations enhance the characterizations?
4. Do both the text and illustrations avoid stereotypes of race and sex?
5. Will the plot appeal to children?
6. Is the theme worthwhile?
7. What is the purpose for sharing this book with children or recommending that they read it?
8. Are the author's style and language appropriate for the children's interests and age levels?
9. Are the text, the illustrations, the format, and the typography in harmony?

books listed in the Children's Choices also reveals that children prefer illustrations that depict here-and-now situations, fantasies of all kinds, and humorous exaggerations and slapstick; illustrations that are colorful and add more detail to the descriptions of characters, action, and setting in the text; and illustrations that are drawn in either a realistic or a cartoonlike style. Such preferences may help adults select picture books for children, but Cianciolo stresses that adults can and should also use books and book-related activities to teach children "how to be more evaluative and discriminating in their selections" (p. 28).

Additional insights into evaluating picture books are gained by analyzing picture books that are highly rated in journals that review books written for children. Journals such as *The Horn Book, School Library Journal, Publishers Weekly,* and *Booklist* provide extensive reviews; each of these journals includes starred reviews of books that the reviewers consider to have exceptional merit.

Most of the reviews for outstanding picture books emphasize a close integration between the illustrations and text as well as author style that excites readers. As you read picture books, decide whether you agree with reviewers.

MOTHER Goose

Mother Goose rhymes are the earliest literature enjoyed by many young children; the rhymes, rhythms, and pleasing sounds of these jingles appeal to young children, who are experimenting with their own language patterns, and they aid children's language development. Betsy Hearne (1992)

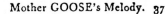

Mother GOOSE's Melody. 37

*J*ACK and *Gill*
Went up the Hill,
To fetch a Pail of Water;
Jack fell down
And broke his Crown,
And *Gill* came tumbling after.

Maxim.

The more you think of dying, the better
you will live.

ARISTOTLE'S

38 Mother GOOSE's Melody.

ARISTOTLE'S STORY.
THERE were two Birds fat on
a Stone,
Fa, la, la, la, lal, de;   [one,
One flew away, and then there was
Fa, la, la, la, lal, de;
The other flew after,
And then there was none,
Fa, la, la, la, lal, de;
And fo the poor Stone
Was left all alone,
Fa, la, la, la, lal, de.

This may ferve as a Chapter of Confequence
in the next new Book of Logick.

*Mother Goose rhymes, which contained maxims or morals, were popular in both Great Britain and North America. (*The Original Mother Goose's Melody *printed in London by John Newbery, 1760.)*

emphasizes the appeal of Mother Goose when she states, "Nursery rhymes are only a step away from song in their changing cadence and compressed story elements" (p. 22). A brief review of the basic characteristics of nursery rhymes indicates why children enjoy them, as well as why nursery rhymes encourage language development in children.

Appealing Characteristics

The rhythm in many nursery rhymes almost forces children to react. For example, children may clap their hands or jump up and down to the rhythm of this jingle:

Handy dandy, Jack-a-Dandy
Loves plum cake and sugar candy;
He bought some at a grocer's shop
And out he came, hop, hop, hop.

Rhyme is another aspect of many nursery verses that children enjoy. Rhyming words, such as *dandy* and *candy,* and *shop* and *hop,* invite children to join in and add the rhyming word or to make up their own rhymes. Rhymes enhance the adventures of many favorite characters: "Little Miss Muffet sat on a tuffet"; "Jack and Jill went up the hill"; "Bobby Shafto's gone to sea, Silver buckles on his knee." Many verses rhyme at the end of each line, but some verses also use internal rhyming elements: "Hickory, dickory, dock, the mouse ran up the clock" and "Rub, a dub, dub, three men in a tub." To test the influence of these rhyming verses, ask older children to share one of their favorite Mother Goose rhymes: They can probably say several, although they may not have heard or recited them for years.

Children also respond to the repetition of sounds in a phrase or line of a nursery rhyme. Alliteration, the repetition of an initial consonant in consecutive words, creates phrases that children enjoy repeating just to experience the marvelous feelings that result from the repetition of beginning sounds: "One misty, moisty, morning"; "Sing a song of sixpence"; and "Diddle, diddle, dumpling." Sentences that contain a great deal of alliteration become tongue twisters. Children love the challenge of this jingle:

Peter Piper picked a peck of pickled
   peppers.
A peck of pickled peppers Peter Piper
   picked,
If Peter Piper picked a peck of pickled
   peppers,
Where's the peck of pickled peppers
   Peter Piper picked?

Humor is another great appeal of Mother Goose verses for children:

Hey, diddle, diddle!
The cat and the fiddle.
The cow jumped over the moon;
The little dog laughed
To see such sport,
And the dish ran away with the spoon.

This verse is also an example of hyperbole, the use of exaggeration for effect, which is common in Mother Goose rhymes. Children appreciate exaggerated, ridiculous situations, such as an old woman's living in a shoe with so many children she doesn't know what to do, a barber's trying to shave a pig, or Simple Simon's going for water with a sieve:

He went for water with a sieve,
But soon it ran all through:
And now poor Simple Simon
Bids you all adieu.

Rhyme, repetition of sounds, humor, and exaggeration combine to create appealing subjects for young children.

Collections

The many different collections of Mother Goose rhymes contain more or less the same verses, but their formats, sizes, and illustrations are quite different. Some editions contain several hundred verses in large-book format, but others have fewer verses and are small enough for a young child to hold. Some editions have illustrations reminiscent of 18th-century England, and others have modern illustrations.

TOMMY was a silly boy.
"I can fly," he said ;
He started off, but very soon
He tumbled on his head.

His little sister Prue was there,
To see how he would do it ;
She knew that, after all his boast,
Full dearly Tom would rue it !

Kate Greenaway was an influential illustrator of children's books in the 19th century. (From Kate Greenaway's Mother Goose, copyright © 1988. Reprinted by permission of Dial Books for Young Readers.)

Two popular early editions, John Newbery's *The Original Mother Goose's Melody* and *Kate Greenaway's Mother Goose: Or, the Old Nursery Rhymes*, continue to be reissued. Newbery's edition may be of greater interest to adults than to children (the text contains a history of Mother Goose), although many older children enjoy looking at the early orthography in Newbery's edition and comparing the verses and illustrations with contemporary editions, which do not share Newbery's tendency to add a moral to the close of each nursery rhyme. In Newbery's edition, for example, "Ding, dong, bell, the cat is in the well," is followed by this maxim: "He that injures one threatens a Hundred" (p. 25).

The edition illustrated by the well-known author-illustrator Kate Greenaway was first published in 1881. Greenaway's book is a small text suitable for sharing with one child. She illustrates the nursery rhymes with pictures of delicate children that appeal to the sentiments of most readers.

Collections assembled by Iona and Peter Opie provide older children and adults with an opportunity to examine early illustrated versions of Mother Goose. *A Nursery Companion* is a large, highly illustrated collection of nursery rhymes originally published in the early 1800s. *The Oxford Nursery Rhyme Book* contains 800 rhymes cat-

egorized according to contents; black-and-white woodcuts, from both earlier editions and newly created works, illustrate this large volume. An informative preface and a list of sources for the illustrations increase its usefulness for those who wish to study early editions of nursery rhymes. *Tail Feathers From Mother Goose: The Opie Rhyme Book* is a collection of lesser-known rhymes, many of which are previously unpublished. The rhymes are illustrated by contemporary artists.

In *I Saw Esau: The Schoolchild's Pocket Book*, the Opies assemble a collection of rhymes, chants, and riddles that are appropriate for various ages. The illustrations by Maurice Sendak and the rhymes appeal to younger children. Older children and adults benefit from the notes section, which explains the origins of the rhymes.

A contemporary city setting forms the background for Nina Crews's *The Neighborhood Mother Goose*. This collection of 41 Mother Goose rhymes has a rhyme on each page that is accompanied by a photograph. The book is large enough to use with a group of students, who can describe the settings as well as listen to and join in with the reading.

Pamela Duncan Edwards adds a problem-solving twist to the nursery rhymes in *The Neat Line: Scribbling Through Mother Goose*. In an unusual approach to Mother Goose, after considerable practice, a baby's scribbling turns into a neat line. Now the line is able to turn into something that solves a problem, such as a horn for Little Boy Blue or a path leading up a hill for Jack and Jill. In a satisfying ending, the line draws itself into the Man in the Moon and switches off the light.

Arnold Lobel's *Gregory Griggs and Other Nursery Rhyme People* contains rhymes about lesser-known characters, such as Theophilus Thistle, the successful thistle sifter; Gregory Griggs, who had 27 wigs; Charley, Charley, who stole the barley; Michael Finnegan, who grew a long beard right on his chinnigan; and Terence McDiddler, the three-stringed fiddler. The language and strong rhyming patterns in these verses make the book appropriate for reading aloud. The humorous, nonsensical rhymes are enriched by Lobel's pastel illustrations: Each rhyme is illustrated with a large picture, making it especially good for sharing with a group of children.

The placement of illustrations next to the matching nursery rhyme, the large-page format, and the humorous folk-art illustrations make *Tomie dePaola's Mother Goose* especially appealing to younger children. The pictures that accompany multiple verses illustrate the sequential development in longer rhymes, such as "Simple Simon." The plots of some of the rhymes are extended through the illustrations; for example, the illustrations accompanying "Jack and Jill" show the actions on a marionette stage.

Michael Foreman's Mother Goose, selected and illustrated by Michael Foreman, is another large collection of

Hey diddle, diddle,
The cat and the fiddle,
The cow jumped over the moon;
The little dog laughed
To see such sport,
And the dish ran away with the spoon.

Humorous illustrations and a large-book format provide an appealing volume for young children. (Illustration by Tomie dePaola reprinted by permission of G. P. Putnam's Sons from Tomie dePaola's Mother Goose. Copyright © 1985 by Tomie dePaola.)

nursery rhymes. Because of the visual links, the illustrations provide interesting opportunities to increase observational abilities and interactions. For example, the illustration on page 23 shows someone falling off the wall in front of the Pretty Maid, who is gathering roses in her garden. When readers turn the page, they find that the legs belong to Humpty Dumpty, who now cannot be put back together again.

In *We Are All in the Dumps With Jack and Guy*, a potentially controversial Mother Goose, Maurice Sendak provides social commentary in illustrations showing newspaper headlines on papers worn by homeless children. Sendak's images, which reflect poverty, crime, AIDS, and unemployment, should encourage much discussion. Figure 5.1 presents the responses and reactions of some fifth graders to this book.

Books That Illustrate One Rhyme or Tale

Children often want to know more about their favorite nursery rhyme characters. The humor and simple plots found in nursery rhymes lend themselves to expansion into picture storybook format. Each verse of Sarah Josepha Hale's *Mary Had a Little Lamb* has several full-page color illustrations of 19th-century farm and school settings by Tomie dePaola.

Picture storybook versions of Mother Goose rhymes may stimulate creative interpretations if children think about what might happen, expanding and illustrating the plots in other nursery rhymes. Texts that extend the story line beyond that found in the Mother Goose rhyme provide motivation for children to create their own expanded story lines of other favorite Mother Goose rhymes.

"Old MacDonald Had a Farm" provides the foundations for Jan Ormerod's *Ms. MacDonald Has a Class*. In this variant of the rhyme, Ms. MacDonald's class takes a field trip to a farm and then prepares a show that depicts their adventures. Young children enjoy joining in with a "Here a hop, there a waddle, everywhere a quack quack" (unnumbered). This variant can also be compared with the original rhyme.

Nursery Rhymes in Other Lands

Traditional nursery rhymes and jingles for children are found in many lands. The language and style may differ from the English Mother Goose, but the content is amazingly alike: Nursery rhymes everywhere tell about good and bad children, wise and foolish people, animals, and nature.

Robert Wyndham has translated Chinese nursery rhymes into English versions that are designed to appeal to English-speaking readers and listeners. *Chinese Mother Goose Rhymes* are about dragons, Buddhas, carriage chairs, the Milky Way, and ladybugs, which seem to fascinate children of many nationalities. Each of the sprightly rhymes is shown in both English and Chinese, with a simple, colorful drawing to illustrate it. Turning games and nonsense words are well represented, as they are in English nursery rhymes.

Gee lee, gu lu, turn the cake,
Add some oil, the better to bake.
Gee lee, gu lu, now it's done;
Give a piece to everyone. (p. 40, unnumbered)

Margot C. Griego et al. have collected nursery rhymes and lullabies from Mexico and Spanish-speaking communities in the United States. *Tortillitas Para Mama and Other Spanish Nursery Rhymes* contains finger plays, counting rhymes, and clapping rhymes written in both Spanish and English.

Nursery rhymes from many nations are important contributions to our cultural heritage. They foster the self-esteem and language skills of the children who are members of ethnic minorities in the United States, and they help all American children appreciate the values and contributions of cultures other than their own.

Toy Books

An increasing number of toy books, including board books, pop-up books, flap books, cloth books, and plastic books, entice children into interacting with stories, developing their vocabularies, counting,

Responses to Maurice Sendak's We Are All in the Dumps With Jack and Guy

Maurice Sendak's book *We Are All in the Dumps With Jack and Guy* has received considerable attention. It has been featured in *The New York Times Book Review* and *The New Yorker* magazine, as well as in journals that review children's literature. Reviewers usually comment on the relevancy of the subject, but some question whether older elementary children will appreciate and understand the message, which is a plea for social responsibility. This plea is developed through the details in the illustrations, which include newspaper headlines, pictures of homeless children, and references to landmarks, art, and even the Holocaust. The images provide numerous topics to study and discuss.

In an effort to discover how children respond to this book, we shared the book with a group of gifted fifth-grade children in a suburb of Dallas, Texas. To obtain responses that were not influenced by the other children, we first asked each child to respond individually to the book. Then the children shared their responses orally with the group. Each child responded to the pictures and told why he or she liked or did not like the book. It is interesting to note that all of these fifth-grade children liked the book.

First, consider their impression of the total book and then identify what images influenced them as they looked at the illustrations and read the text. As you read the following reasons, notice why the children liked the story and what made it popular:

"I liked the book because I like books that need a sharp reader and have hidden messages in the pictures."
"I liked it because you had to piece the story together."
"I loved the significance and the pictures. But, the story about being poor is very sad."
"I liked the way he put the story together and how things in the book fit together."

Next, consider some of the characteristics of the book that encouraged responses: The first characteristic of the book several students noted was the quality of the endpapers. One girl commented that they were like recycled paper bags. She thought the endpapers were appropriate because the story also used a recycling rhyme. She said, "Recycled paper, recycled rhymes, give a modern story that tells about hunger and homelessness. I think it is important."

On the dedication page, the children discussed the possible significance of the stars in the sky and the rope that several thought looked like the Star of Bethlehem. They speculated about why the star was either broken or being used to hang clothes for the homeless.

All of the children responded to the child calling for help and the other children in the dump. They thought it was important that the child calling for help was black because "there is a great deal of hunger in Africa." They noticed the boy identifying his own private property while living in the crowded conditions of the dump. The children said it is important for everyone to identify what is "mine," even if it is only a box or a sack.

The children all commented on the moon's changing expressions: It seemed to show sadness, anger, and tears. They thought the moon was sad because "he sees these kids, their hunger, and their homelessness and no one seems to be doing anything to help them." They also noted that as life became more difficult for the children, the moon became angrier, until he finally changed into a cat and came to earth to rescue the children.

The rats caused much speculation. Several children thought the rats were probably in disguise because they had hands. They worried about what the rats would do to the kittens and to the boy. The fact that they seemed to be gambling over the fate of their captives caused concern.

These fifth graders were interested in every detail in the book. They found "Trumped Tower" and discussed the significance of placing the homeless children below this setting. They were particularly interested in reading the newspaper headlines that formed both the clothes of and shelter for many of the children. They discussed the importance of the changing headlines that went from the availability of expensive housing to chaos in shelters, job layoffs, and AIDS. Several of the children concluded that one cannot create a strong shelter with newspapers. They discussed the possible connections between a bakery and an orphanage and noticed how the black smoke from the building partially covered the face of the moon. They were pleased that at the end of the story, the boy and the kittens were saved (one child referred to the moon, the kittens, and the boy as "the moon's family"), but they were not pleased that the final setting in the book was again the dump.

When asked if there is a message in this book, the children provided several important ones. One child stated, "We must remember to give money to the poor and to try to change their lives." Another child said, "The moon is watching over all of us." Still another felt that rats should not be able to take kids away. When asked what age children they thought should read the book, most of them responded with age 10. They thought that children much younger than 10 would not understand the message in the book or recognize the symbolism. As you read *We Are All in the Dumps With Jack and Guy,* compare your responses with those of these fifth-grade children.

FIGURE 5.1   Children respond to Maurice Sendak's We Are All in the Dumps With Jack and Guy

Cover art from Teeth, Tails, & Tentacles: An Animal Counting Book, *by Christopher Wormell. Running Press 2004. Copyright © 2004 by Christopher Wormell. Reprinted by permission of Running Press Kids, an imprint of Running Press Book Publishers.*

Count and See and *26 Letters and 99 Cents*, by Tana Hoban, are simple counting books with easy-to-identify number concepts that also extend to sets and higher numbers. In *Count and See*, each number, its corresponding written word, and a circle or circles illustrating the number appear in white on a black background. On the opposite page, a photograph illustrates the number with things found in the environments of many children: 1 fire hydrant, 2 children, . . . 20 watermelon seeds, . . . 40 peanuts shown in groups of 10, . . . and 100 peas shown in pods of 10 each. The book also can be used for counting and grouping concrete items. (Counting and grouping aid cognitive development.) This book can be used as either a counting book or an alphabet book. In one direction, the illustrations and text emphasize counting, and in the other direction, it is an alphabet book.

Emily's First 100 Days of School, by Rosemary Wells, introduces the numbers from 1 to 100 through various activities associated with a young bunny as she experiences her days at school. The numbers are introduced as the teacher tells the class that each morning they will learn a new number and create their own number notebook. Some of the activities are associated with school ("There are nine planets in our solar system"), and others relate to home ("I collect twenty-five Japanese beetles from the garden") (unnumbered).

Handtalk Birthday: A Number & Story Book in Sign Language, by Remy Charlip, Mary Beth Miller, and George Ancona, presents an unusual story: It is about a surprise party for a deaf woman. Photographs show the characters using sign language as the woman guesses the contents of her presents and the guests question her about her age.

Muriel Feeling's *Moja Means One: Swahili Counting Book* is the counting-book partner to her Swahili alphabet book. Each two-page spread provides a numeral from 1 to 10, the Swahili word for the number, a detailed illustration (by Tom Feelings) that depicts animal or village life in Africa, and a sentence describing the contents of the illustration. This book may be more appropriate for stimulating interest in an African culture or

Cover art from 10 Little Rubber Ducks, by Eric Carle.
Copyright © 2005 by Eric Carle. Used by permission of
HarperCollins Publishers.

providing information for older children than for presenting number concepts to younger children.

Counting concepts in English and Spanish are reinforced in Ginger Foglesong Guy's *¡Fiesta!* The text develops counting and vocabulary concepts as children go through a village gathering items for a fiesta. The items eventually become the objects in a piñata, which is broken during the party.

Jim Haskins's *Count Your Way Through Italy* is part of the "Count Your Way Through" series of counting books. Haskins develops counting concepts from 1 through 10 in Italian. He then provides background information about Italian culture and geography. Beth Wright's illustrations depict the numbers and the text for such things as Mount Etna (1), the products for which Italy is known (9), and the horses that are chosen to race in the Corsa del Palio (10). Additional books in this series provide counting opportunities through Africa, the Arab world, Canada, China, Germany, Japan, Korea, Mexico, and Russia.

Counting books may also be written for older students. *The History of Counting,* by Denise Schmandt-Besserat, is a fascinating book that describes the evolution of counting, including examples of body counting, concrete counting, and abstract counting.

Concept Books

Many of the books recommended for use in stimulating the cognitive development of children are concept books. These books rely on well-chosen illustrations to help children grasp both relatively easy concepts, such as *red* and *circle,* and more abstract concepts (which may be difficult for children to comprehend), such as prepositions (*through,* for example) and antonyms (*fast* and *slow,* for example). Like counting books, concept books come in various degrees of difficulty, so teachers should consider a child's level of understanding when selecting concept books.

Numerous books have been designed to help young children learn basic concepts, such as colors and shapes. Eric Carle's *My Very First Book of Colors* is a simple, wordless book that asks a child to match a block of color with the picture of an object illustrated in that color. In *Of Colors and Things,* Tana Hoban uses both colors and photographs of objects to invite children to search for matching colors. In *Shapes, Shapes, Shapes,* she uses photographs to depict such shapes as circles, rectangles, and ovals. Photographs also depict shapes in Hoban's *So Many Circles, So Many Squares.* These books also encourage readers to look for similar shapes in their own environments. In *Over, Under and Through and Other Spatial Concepts,* Tana Hoban uses photographs that show children jumping *over* fire hydrants, walking *under* outstretched arms, and crawling *through* large pipes. Shelley Rotner also uses photographs of children in *Lots of Feelings* to reflect opposite expressions such as *happy–sad, angry–loving,* and *serious–silly.*

Basic colors are introduced for very young children in Laura Vaccaro Seeger's *Lemons Are Not Red.* For example, a yellow lemon is on one side of a page and a red apple is on the opposite side; the text reads, "Lemons are yellow, apples are red" (unnumbered).

Food for Thought: The Complete Book of Concepts for Growing Minds, by Saxton Freymann, presents easily recognized labeled illustrations; the large, clever illustrations are created by foods that emphasize shapes, colors, numbers, letters, and opposites. For example, four ants are created from cherries and stems; the label reads "4 four ants." Luch Micklethwait's *I Spy Shapes in Art* is an interactive book that asks readers to locate different geometric shapes in paintings. This is also an art appreciation book because each painting is labeled with the painter's name and title of the work. An author's note provides additional information about the artist and the location of the original painting.

Like Hoban, Donald Crews familiarizes children with various concepts in *Freight Train.* The cars of the train are different colors, and the movement of the train *across* trestles, *through* cities, and *into* tunnels encourages understanding of spatial concepts and of opposites, such as *darkness* and *daylight.* Trains fascinate many young chil-

Angela stays overnight. She is now my best friend. We count eighty-seven stars in the sky. My mama says Australian stars are all different, but the moon is the same.

Readers find many opportunities to apply their counting skills as found in this illustration from Emily's First 100 Days of School. *(From* Emily's First 100 Days of School *by Rosemary Wells. Copyright © 2000 by Rosemary Wells. Reprinted by permission of Hyperion Books for Children.)*

dren, and children eagerly learn concepts while enjoying the colors, movements, and sounds developed in this book. Similarly, Brian Floca uses trucks at an airport in *Five Trucks* to introduce concepts associated with trucks such as *large* and *heavy*, *small* and *quick*, and *long* and *straight*. The activities of trucks are shown as airplanes are prepared for takeoff.

Wordless Books

In another type of picture book, the illustrations tell the whole story, without words. Children enjoy the opportunity to provide the missing text for wordless books—an excellent way of developing their oral

and written language skills. Wordless books stimulate creative thinking and enhance visual literacy abilities, because children must watch the pages for clues to the action. Wordless books are especially valuable because they allow children of different backgrounds and reading levels to enjoy the same book.

Wordless books have various degrees of detail and plot complexity. Some contain much detail, but others do not. Some develop easily identifiable plots, but others can be interpreted in many different ways. Some are large, making them appropriate for sharing with a group, and others are small, easily held by one child or one adult with a child in the lap. You should consider all of these characteristics when choosing wordless books for children of different ages, reading levels, and interests.

Pat Hutchins's *Changes, Changes* is a simple wordless book that appeals to preschoolers and kindergartners who enjoy building with blocks. The illustrations show two wooden dolls building a house of blocks, coping with a fire by turning the house into a fire truck, solving the problem of too much water by building a boat, reaching land by constructing a truck, and eventually rebuilding their home. The large and colorful pictures make actions easily identifiable. The book stimulates oral language, as well as problem solving manipulation of children's own blocks.

Realistic humor is a popular theme of wordless books for young children. A series of wordless books by Mercer Mayer shows the humorous adventures of a boy, a dog, and a frog. *Frog Goes to Dinner*—the most detailed book in the series and, to many children, the funniest—illustrates the humorous disruptions that can occur if a frog hides in a boy's pocket and accompanies a family to a fancy restaurant. Each of Mayer's books is small, just the right size for individual enjoyment or for sharing with an adult. The illustrations are expressive and contain sufficient detail to stimulate language development and enjoyment.

Several wordless books develop plots involving the antics of animals from the world of fantasy. Emily Arnold McCully's *Picnic* follows a family of mice as they jubilantly go on a picnic, unhappily discover that a small mouse is missing, and joyfully reunite the whole family. McCully's *School* follows the same family as they experience common occurrences. The illustrations depict enough plot to stimulate the creation of narrative even by older children.

ISSUE Picture Books and Controversy

Several books discussed in this chapter have stirred controversy and subsequently have been removed from library shelves. Other books have had illustrations altered to meet specific standards.

In the 1960s, Garth Williams's *The Rabbit's Wedding* was criticized because the illustrations showed the marriage of a black rabbit and a white rabbit. In 1969, William Steig's *Sylvester and the Magic Pebble* was criticized because some parents objected to his portrayal of police officers as pigs, and others objected to his having the mother do housework while Sylvester and his father relaxed.

When Maurice Sendak's *In the Night Kitchen* was published in 1970, some parents, teachers, and librarians decried the child's nudity. In several incidents, the nudity was covered with a drawn-on washcloth or the book was removed from the shelf. Also in the 1970s, some people criticized *Changes, Changes,* by Pat Hutchins, because the man has a more active role than does the woman: He drives and decides what to make from the blocks, and the woman pulls the train whistle and hands him the blocks.

One book not discussed in this chapter illustrates the changing sensitivities of Americans toward certain social issues. Helen Bannerman's *Little Black Sambo* (1899) was popular for many years. Eventually, however, many people considered the crudely drawn features of the characters and the story line to be offensive, and the book was taken off many library shelves.

As you evaluate picture books, consider which books might be controversial and the reasons for the controversy. Does controversy change with the times? What subjects might have caused controversy in picture books published in the 1950s, 1960s, 1970s, 1980s, 1990s, or 2000s? Are those subjects still controversial? Are any new areas of controversy developing today?

The sequential organization and detail of the illustrations provide a story line that stimulates language development. (Illustration on unnumbered page 11 from Picnic, *by Emily Arnold McCully. Copyright © 1984 by Emily Arnold McCully. Reprinted by permission of Harper & Row Publishers, Inc.)*

Barbara Lehman's *The Red Book* develops the power of stories in books as a girl gets lost in a book; this book then transports her to another location where she finds a book with a map, an island, a beach, and a boy. When the boy finds the book on the beach, he discovers city scenes and the girl. The theme of the book emphasizes what is possible when a book takes readers out of the real world.

In his author's note, Paul Fleischman states where he got the idea for his *Sidewalk Circus:* "It came out of the blue. A vision of a ringmaster standing on a city street, describing the sun rising and the clouds changing color as if they were circus acts. Eventually, I decided to leave him out of the story. And then I decided to leave the words out as well" (fly of book cover). Kevin Hawkes's illustrations tell the story by showing details such as a delivery man who could be a strongman in the circus and a construction worker who is like a tightrope walker in a circus. The book is excellent for enhancing observation skills because it is only a young girl waiting for a bus who makes the connections and not the adults, who are completely oblivious to the real-life circus that is going on around them.

A dream sequence forms the plot in David Wiesner's *Free Fall.* This beautifully illustrated, wordless book takes the dreamer on a fantasy in which he explores uncharted lands. Interestingly, many of the objects that seem so real in his dream are by his bed when he awakes.

Plots in wordless books frequently take characters on magical excursions. Wiesner's *Sector 7* encourages viewers to accompany a boy in a fantasy during which he discovers how clouds are shaped and sent throughout the country. In Lisa Maizlish's *The Ring,* a boy finds a magical object in a New York City park, puts it on, and flies through the air; photographs follow the boy and reveal his adventures. Ask students to compare the influence of the illustrator's use of black-and-white and color photographs. In *Tuesday,* Wiesner uses the wordless format and glowing watercolors to create a book filled with surprising and unexpected elements. Readers enjoy not only creating their own story to accompany the illustrations but also extending the book into the next Tuesday. Wiesner's final illustration shows the following Tuesday, when

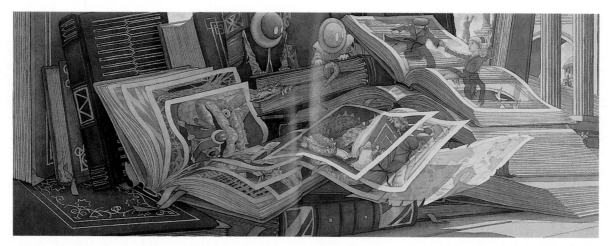

The illustrations show the dream world of the boy in Free Fall, *by David Wiesner. (Illustration by David Wiesner from* Free Fall, *by David Wiesner. Copyright © 1988 by David Wiesner. Reprinted by permission of Lothrop, Lee and Shepard Books, a division of William Morrow & Co., Inc.)*

the pigs have their opportunity to fly, to explore the neighborhood, and to baffle the people. The book provides interesting stimuli for creative writing and illustrating, allowing students to create their own stories about "The Night the Pigs Could Fly."

Peter Spier's *Noah's Ark* is another excellent picture book. The only words occur at the beginning of the book. The pictures show the building of the ark, the boarding of the animals, the long wait, and the starting of life again on the land, which is plowed and cultivated. The pictures contain so much detail that children can discover something new each time they read the book.

Jeannie Baker's *Window* is an exceptional example of collage illustrations that explore textures found in various settings. The illustrations use a window to show the changes that occur in an Australian neighborhood. These changes, which are shown through the growth of a child and the changing view from the window, also develop a strong environmental theme: People affect the environment. By tracing the changes, the artist shows how rapidly a community can change from rural to urban and investigates the possible consequences of moving to a rural area again. The artist reinforces the theme through her endnotes when she states, "By understanding and changing the way we personally affect the environment, we can make a difference."

Several beautifully illustrated wordless books by Mitsumasa Anno also encourage oral discussion and storytelling by older children. The detailed drawings in *Anno's Journey,* for example, are the result of the artist's travels through the countryside, villages, and larger towns of Europe. Anno adds to the enjoyment by suggesting that readers look for certain details in the pictures, such as paintings and characters from children's literature. The pictures are detailed enough to keep even adults occupied. The illustrations in Peter Sís's *Dinosaur!* provide opportunities for children to identify specific types of di-

nosaurs as a young boy takes his toy dinosaur into the tub, only to be joined by many other dinosaurs. The dinosaurs are identified inside the front and back covers.

Many wordless books are ideal for promoting oral language development. Others, however, are so obscure in story line that children may be frustrated when asked to tell the story. When choosing wordless books, consider the questions posed in the Evaluation Criteria box on this page.

The varied levels of complexity found in wordless books indicate that wordless books are appropriate for young children as well as older ones. This same complexity, however, means that adults must select the materials carefully. As an example of the differences in wordless

---

Evaluation Criteria

Selecting High-Quality Wordless Books

1. Is there a sequentially organized plot that provides a framework for children who are just developing their own organizational skills?

2. Is the depth of detail appropriate for the age level of the children? (Too much detail will overwhelm younger children, but not enough detail may bore older ones.)

3. Do the children have enough experiential background to understand and interpret the illustrations? Can they interpret the book during individual reading, or is adult interaction necessary?

4. Is the size of the book appropriate for the purpose? (Larger books are necessary for group sharing.)

5. Will the subject appeal to the children?

books and relationships with age, compare wordless books for young readers, such as those by Mercer Mayer, with Tom Feelings's *The Middle Passage: White Ships/Black Cargo*, a wordless book about the slave trade.

Easy-to-Read Books

Easy-to-read books are designed to be read by children with beginning reading skills. Like picture storybooks, these books contain many pictures designed to suggest the story line. Unlike picture storybooks, however, the vocabulary is controlled so that young readers can manage independently. However, controlling the vocabulary to fit the needs of beginning readers may result in contrived language, because it is difficult to write stories that sound natural if all of the words must be selected from the easiest level of readability.

Authors, teachers, and librarians use several readability formulas to determine the approximate level of reading skill required to read a book. The Fry Readability Formula (Fry, 1977), for example, measures the reading level by finding the average number of sentences and syllables per 100 words; these averages are plotted on a graph that identifies the corresponding grade level for the book. Readability experts assume that easier books have shorter sentences and more monosyllabic words. As the reading level increases, the sentences become longer and multisyllabic words become more numerous.

Compare the readability of an easy-to-read book and another picture storybook. A 100-word selection from one popular easy-to-read book, Dr. Seuss's *The Cat in the Hat*, shows 16 sentences and 100 syllables for those 100 words. The sentences are very short and all words are of one syllable. Plotting these two findings on the Fry graph indicates a first-grade reading level. In contrast, a picture storybook also written for first-grade interests by Dr. Seuss, *And to Think That I Saw It on Mulberry Street*, has seven and one half sentences and 126 syllables in a 100-word selection. The reading level for this book is fifth grade. Although both books appeal to children of about the same age, children themselves usually read the first book, and adults usually read the second to children.

Even though easy-to-read books may not meet all standards for literary quality, they may meet the needs of beginning readers. Because children need experiences with books that allow them to reinforce their reading skills independently and to develop pride in their accomplishments, you should include easy-to-read books in every book collection for primary-age children. Easy-to-read books are also helpful to students in remedial reading classes who need successful experiences. Because of controlled use of language and sentence structure, easy-to-read books are less appropriate for adults to read aloud to children, although children may enjoy reading them aloud to appreciative adults.

Animal antics appeal to young children, and many favorite easy-to-read books have animals as the main characters. In Dr. Seuss's *The Cat in the Hat*, a cat amazes and entertains two children when he balances a fish bowl, a bottle of milk, and a cake simultaneously. Dr. Seuss's humorous illustrations and rhyming dialogue appeal to children. The cat emphasizes this enjoyment:

> Look at me!
> Look at me!
> Look at me Now!
> It is fun to have fun
> But you have to know how. (p. 8)

Arnold Lobel has written and illustrated several enchanting easy-to-read books. The soft brown-and-green illustrations in Lobel's stories about Frog and Toad recreate the atmosphere of a woodland setting and show the friendship felt by these two characters. In *Frog and Toad Are Friends*, Frog tries to entice Toad out of his home in order to experience the new spring season. Children enjoy Toad's reactions when Frog knocks on the door:

> "Toad, Toad," shouted Frog,
> "wake up. It is spring!"
> "Blah," said a voice
> from inside the house.

In Lobel's *Grasshopper on the Road*, a curious insect decides to follow a winding country lane just to discover where it leads. Lobel's characterization is fuller than that found in many other easy-to-read books. He has the grasshopper encounter the rural inhabitants and then try to change their behaviors.

Easy-to-read books may be series books, such as those written by Cynthia Rylant. Rylant includes several books in her Henry and Mudge series. *Henry and Mudge and the Happy Cat* develops the new relationship between the dog, Mudge, and a stray cat. *Henry and Mudge and the Bedtime Thumps* is set in Grandmother's house in the country. A strange noise shows Henry and Mudge that it is better to be together during scary times. In *Henry and Mudge and the Long Weekend*, Rylant tells a warm story in which boredom and "February cranks" are overcome by creating a castle out of large boxes. An elderly man and an old, yellow-and-white cat form a strong companionship in *Mr. Putter and Tabby Pour the Tea* and *Mr. Putter and Tabby Walk the Dog*. *Poppleton* presents stories about a pig. Rylant's easy-to-read books are unique because of their interesting stories and their descriptive language.

Charlotte Pomerantz's "I Can Read Book" *Outside Dog* takes place in a Puerto Rican neighborhood. Pomerantz has incorporated Spanish words and phrases into the text.

Ready . . . Set . . . Read! is an anthology of easy-to-read stories, poems, and games compiled by Joanna Cole and Stephanie Calmenson; the stories are written by such well-known authors as Dr. Seuss, Else Minarik, Arnold Lobel, Joanna Cole, and Bernard Wiseman. This anthology lets students of children's literature analyze and compare several sources of this type of literature.

Picture Storybooks

A characteristic common to many picture books discussed thus far is the use of illustrations to present all or most of the content of a book. Reliance on pictures is especially crucial in concept books, counting books, a majority of the alphabet books, and all wordless picture books. Many of these books do not have continuous story lines; instead, the illustrations are grouped according to common themes or are presented in numerical or alphabetical sequence.

Although picture storybooks contain many illustrations, they also develop strong story lines in text. In a well-written picture storybook, the text and narrative complement each other, so children cannot deduce the whole story merely by viewing the pictures. The illustrations are integral to the story line, enhancing the actions, settings, and characterizations.

Elements in Picture Storybooks

When adults think about enjoyable book experiences shared by adults and children during story hour or at bedtime, they usually remember picture storybooks. Childhood would be less exciting without friends such as Knuffle Bunny, Max, and Duck who decides to run for president. What makes some books so memorable for both children and adults? Originality and imagination are crucial in outstanding picture books, but so are strong plot, characterization, setting, theme, style, and humor.

Originality and Imagination. A man and his dog discover that "Paradise lost is sometimes Heaven found"; a child's bedroom becomes the kingdom of wild things; and a trickster fox cannot outwit a poet. Some adults never lose touch with the dreams, fears, and fantasies of childhood and, as authors of picture storybooks for children, they create imaginative new worlds in which the impossible becomes both real and believable.

In *Hey, Al*, Arthur Yorinks's plot helps a janitor and his dog find a more satisfying way of life. Through experience in a beautiful location, where they do not need to work, they discover that beautiful places can have dangerous secrets.

The format of a trickster tale provides the structure for Tim Myers's *Basho and the River Stones*. This tale set in Japan tells the story of a trickster fox who tries to outwit one of Japan's greatest poets. The trick does not work because the poet appreciates the beauty of the stones that replace the promised gold coins. After the tricks fail, the two characters learn to live in harmony.

David Shannon uses wishes of many young children to develop the plot in *Alice the Fairy*. Alice uses her wand and her imagination to accomplish tasks such as changing Dad into a horse (she rides on his back) and making herself disappear (turning off the light switch with her wand). The text and illustrations show her trying to make clothes get up off the floor and line up in the closet. She concludes that she will probably be a temporary fairy forever because she cannot perform enough magic to become a permanent one.

A child's imagination structures the delightful story in Maurice Sendak's *Where the Wild Things Are*. Only in such fantasy can young children who have been disciplined turn their rooms into kingdoms inhabited by other wild things like themselves and then return home in safety before their suppers get cold.

The moral in *Joseph Had a Little Overcoat*, by Simms Taback, states: "You can always make something out of nothing . . . over and over again!" (unnumbered). In this humorous and imaginative story, the main character keeps recycling his old overcoat into smaller and smaller objects until he loses the final object. But all is not lost because he makes a book about it, which proves "You can always make something out of nothing."

Picture storybooks and their accompanying illustrations are filled with many imaginative episodes. They provide hours of enjoyment and are excellent for stimulating children's imaginations during creative play, storytelling, and creative writing.

Plot. The short attention spans of children who read or hear picture storybooks place special demands on plot development. The plots of picture storybooks are usually simple, clearly developed, and brief; they involve few subplots or secondary characters. Such plots usually allow young children to become involved with the action, identify the problem, and solve it rapidly.

For example, in the first three pages of Maurice Sendak's *Where the Wild Things Are*, children know that Max is in so much trouble that he has been sent to bed without supper. Even though the 37 words used thus far do not reveal what Max has done, the pictures explain his problems: Children see him standing on books, hammering nails into the wall, and chasing the dog with a fork. The plot is swiftly paced, and children rapidly join Max in his imaginary world, as the room becomes wilder and wilder.

Sendak introduces additional conflict and excitement when Max encounters the wild things and overcomes them with a magic trick. Children empathize with Max when he has played long enough, sends his new subjects off to bed, and returns home to his mother's love and his supper. With only 38 words to tell what happens between the time Max leaves the wild things and returns home, this book is an excellent example of the important relationship between illustrations and plot development: The illustrations become larger and larger as the drama increases and then become smaller again as Max returns to his everyday life.

The original plot suggests that beautiful places may be dangerous. (Illustrations from Hey, Al, *by Arthur Yorinks. Illustrated by Richard Egielski. Illustrations copyright © 1986 by Richard Egielski. Reprinted by permission of Farrar, Straus & Giroux, Inc.)*

It is interesting to compare Sendak's illustrations with Richard Egielski's for *Hey, Al.* Both illustrators increase the sizes of their illustrations as conflict develops, use two-page spreads at the height of interest, and include much information about characters and settings within the illustrations.

Some picture books have plots that are very similar to those found in folktales. For example, in Brock Cole's humorous *Buttons,* three daughters are asked to go on a quest in search of buttons to replace those destroyed when their father pops the buttons on his britches. The eldest seeks a husband who will give her buttons in exchange for her hand in marriage. The second decides to join the army to find buttons on a soldier's uniform. The youngest runs through a meadow with her apron held before her, expecting buttons to drop from the sky. As in many humorous folktales, it is the least likely plan that brings buttons to the father and happiness to the family.

Other picture books deal with children's problems in more realistic plots. In *Like Jake and Me,* Mavis Jukes portrays the strained relationship between Alex and his big, powerful stepfather, Jake, who refuses to allow Alex to help with various chores. When a large, hairy spider crawls into Jake's clothes, Alex discovers that even a powerful, ex-rodeo cowboy can be afraid, and Jake discovers that even a small boy can provide assistance. In Ana Zamorano's *Let's Eat!* a boy experiences grown-up responsibilities when Mama is expecting a baby.

Whether a plot is based on fantasy or realism, it usually involves a rapid introduction to the action, a fast pace, and a strong, emotionally satisfying climax. In Patricia Polacco's *Thunder Cake,* a grandmother and her granddaughter assemble a special cake as a thunderstorm grows nearer. These actions help the girl realize that she is brave enough to face the storm. In *Yo! Yes?,* Chris Raschka uses

only 34 words to show the beginning of friendship when an African American boy and a white boy meet on the street. Their brief exchanges, accompanied by cartoonlike illustrations, show many universal feelings and emotions as the two boys become acquainted.

Characterization. The characters in picture storybooks must have specific traits that make them appealing to young children and that meet the demands of the short format. Because a short story does not allow for the fully developed characters that older children and adults prefer, the characters in picture storybooks must experience situations and emotions immediately familiar and credible to the children.

Maurice Sendak, for example, did not need to describe Max, the wild things, or the rumpus that takes place between them; his illustrations show these effectively. Likewise, Stephen Gammell's illustrations for Karen Ackerman's *Song and Dance Man* re-create the magic of vaudeville and express the love between grandchildren and their grandfather.

Any child can understand the feelings of Judith Viorst's hero in *Alexander and the Terrible, Horrible, No Good, Very Bad Day.* Alexander wakes up with gum in his hair, does not get a prize in his cereal when everyone else does, receives reprimands from his teacher, loses his best friend, has a cavity filled by the dentist, gets into trouble for making a mess in his dad's office, has to eat lima beans for dinner, and is ignored by the cat, who goes to sleep with his brother. In this book, as in most picture storybooks, the illustrations supplement the characterizations in the text by showing the characters' actions and reactions.

Children can understand stories about loneliness and friendship. In *The Scarebird,* Sid Fleischman develops a

Children and an old man develop a warm relationship. (From Captain Snap and the Children of Vinegar Lane, *by Roni Schotter, illustrated by Marcia Sewall. Copyright © 1989 by Roni Schotter, illustrations copyright © 1989 by Marcia Sewall. Published by Orchard Books/Scholastic Inc. Used by permission.)*

story of friendship between a lonely older farmer and his creation, a lifelike scarecrow, and then between the farmer and an equally lonely and homeless young farm worker. As the human friendship increases, the farmer takes needed objects from the scarecrow and gives them to the boy. Robie H. Harris's character in *Don't Forget to Come Back!* suffers the type of separation anxiety many young children experience when parents leave them with a babysitter. The story has a happy ending, however, as the girl learns that someone will always be there for her.

Children frequently have close attachments with older people and want to hear more about their lives. Such a character is presented in Gloria Houston's *My Great-Aunt Arizona*. The tone of Houston's text and Susan Condie Lamb's illustrations develop the loving character of a woman who gave her life to teaching. Houston tells readers that although she never traveled from the Blue Ridge Mountains, she educated generations of children and touched their lives wherever they traveled.

Many storybooks contain animal characters that act and speak like humans. Margaret Wise Brown's *The Runaway Bunny* uses a credible little bunny to demonstrate a child's need for independence and love. The dialogue between the mother rabbit and the bunny stresses the bunny's desire to experience freedom by running away. Each time he suggests ways to run away, however, the mother rabbit counters with actions that she would take to get him back. The love between the two animals is vis-

ible in the dialogue and pictures, and the bunny decides to stay with the mother who loves him.

Doreen Cronin's character in *Duck for President* is a very sophisticated barnyard animal who decides that the chores the animals do for Farmer Brown are too demanding. Consequently, Duck runs for election on the platform of having a kinder, gentler farm. The text and illustrations proceed as the animals work together in Duck's campaign and they register voters and conduct an election. Unfortunately, Duck discovers that running a farm is very hard work, so he and his animal staff develop Duck's campaign for governor. Cronin's text and Betsy Lewin's illustrations take readers through the election process as Duck marches in parades, goes to town meetings, and gives speeches. Then Duck discovers that running a state government is very hard work, so he decides to run for president. In a dramatic ending, Duck finds that this job also is hard work; he leaves the government in charge of the vice president and returns to the farm, where he is working on his autobiography.

Setting.   In picture storybooks, as in all literature, setting is used to establish the location of a story in time and place; create a mood; clarify historical background, if necessary; provide an antagonist; and emphasize symbolic meaning. Picture storybooks, however, rely strongly on illustrations to serve these functions. Many books, such as Judith Viorst's *Alexander and the Terrible, Horrible, No Good, Very Bad Day* and Vera Williams's *Something Special for Me*, take place in the familiar contemporary world of television sets, blue jeans, and shopping centers. Other books take place in locations or times unfamiliar to the readers. For example, Carole Byard's illustrations for Sherley Anne Williams's *Working Cotton* create the world of an African American child as she labors in the migrant farming fields of central California. Holly Meade's illustrations for Minfong Ho's *Hush! A Thai Lullaby* create the environment of rural Thailand.

Ntozake Shange's text and Kadir Nelson's illustrations for *Ellington Was Not a Street* is a tribute to the African American community and culture surrounding civil rights workers, composers, and writers such as Paul Robeson and Duke Ellington. The text, written from the viewpoint of a young girl, describes listening to the political discussions and being in the company of individuals who changed the world.

In *Sky Dancers*, Connie Ann Kirk uses a 1930s–1940s city setting and Native American values to develop a story that focuses on the history of Mohawk Indians who were expert steelworkers. The author introduces the Native American values as the protagonist, John Cloud, feels the strength and wisdom of a tree as he climbs higher and higher and realizes that "the tree and Mother Earth and Father Sky would let him know when it was time to go higher" (unnumbered). The author depicts the importance of these workers who were able to walk high across the sky. Again, the author reinforces the Native Americans' connection to the earth when the father tells why he is able to balance on high beams: "I listen to Mother Earth and Father Sky. If you trust them, they will hold you in their embrace just as they did our ancestors who built the bridge over the Great River years ago" (unnumbered). The author's note adds to the importance of this setting when she states that it is based on the Mohawk (Iroquois) steelworkers who built many of the skyscrapers in New York City.

Ronald Himler's illustrations for Byrd Baylor's *The Best Town in the World* show how important illustrations are for illuminating time in picture storybooks. The brief poetic text alone cannot describe the details of a turn-of-the-century general store, the warmth created by a kerosene lamp, and the many activities associated with a picnic celebration in the days when a picnic was a major social event.

In *The Wreck of the Zephyr*, Chris Van Allsburg's illustrations create a light mood, subtly mixing reality and make-believe: A boy who dreams of becoming the best sailor in the world experiences a calm sea sparkling with light and a star-studded night disturbed only by a magical ship flying through the sky. The illustrations in all such worthy picture storybooks enhance the times, places, conflicts, and moods of the stories.

Theme. The themes in picture storybooks for young children are closely related to children's needs and what they understand. Adjusting to new siblings and the need for security are popular themes in books. In *Darcy and Gran Don't Like Babies*, Jane Cutler uses a unique approach to help Darcy accept the new baby: When Gran arrives for a visit, Gran agrees with Darcy as they discuss what they do not like about babies. After they have a fun-filled day together, however, Gran gently helps Darcy understand that she will eventually like the baby.

Numerous picture storybooks develop themes related to security in stories about human and animal characters. For example, Martin Waddell develops this theme in *Tiny's Big Adventure* by creating a plot in which Tiny's big sister, Katy, takes him to a field that might be dangerous to a small mouse. But it is not dangerous as long as Katy is along to reassure him. In *Polar Bear Night*, Lauren Thompson also develops a theme related to the need for secure environments and the need to satisfy curiosity. When the little bear wakes in the warm den, something beckons from outside. She satisfies her curiosity by creeping across the snow and sees seals, whales, and star showers. When the stars stop falling, she realizes that she is ready to sleep. In a satisfying ending, she makes her way back to the den and her mother's soft, warm fur.

In *Owen*, Kevin Henkes also explores the need for security. The mouse child outmaneuvers his parents in their efforts to take away his security blanket, but in a very sat-isfying ending, the mother mouse cuts the blanket into handkerchiefs so that Owen can take his security with him wherever he goes.

Having someone who cares about you is a frequent theme in books for young children. In *Good Night Harry*, Kim Lewis develops this theme as two toy friends, a lamb and a bear, try to help Harry, an elephant, go to sleep. In a gentle plot that is just right for a bedtime story, the elephant's friends curl around him in bed and they all fall asleep.

The importance of happy and secure moments between father and child provides the theme in Eileen Spinelli's *Night Shift Daddy*. Warm, loving relationships are shown as the father tucks the little girl in at night and then she tucks her father in bed when he comes home from work.

An important theme in some picture storybooks is the joy and pleasure that can be obtained from reading. Barbara Joosse develops this theme in *Hot City* by showing two African American children who go to the library to escape the heat only to discover the delightful imaginary world of princesses and dinosaurs. Another book that develops the theme that reading is enjoyable is Pat Mora's *Thomas and the Library Lady*, in which a Latino boy discovers the pleasures found in reading.

Themes related to friendship also figure prominently in picture storybooks. *Hot Day on Abbott Avenue*, by Karen English, supplies the perfect setting for a story about the importance of friendship. The story begins as two African American friends quarrel and refuse to do activities they love to do together because it is a "never-speak-to-her-again-even-if-she-was-the-last-person-on-earth day." The author's style is filled with double-dutch rhymes such as "She asked her mother, mother, mother for fifty cents, cents, cents to see the elephant, elephant, elephant jump over the fence, fence, fence" (unnumbered). The conflict between the two friends eases as they join other neighborhood children in jumping rope to the rhymes. The final return to friendship results when the two girls divide the last purple Popsicle, which is so juicy that the day becomes "a forgetting-all-about-what-you-were-mad-about day."

The need to try new experiences and to expand friendships are themes that are important to the socialization of young children. *Wallace's Lists*, by Barbara Bottner and Gerald Kruglik, explores what happens when Wallace, a young mouse, will not try new experiences unless they are on his carefully prepared list. When he meets a new friend, he discovers that he will need to add to the list or risk missing out on new, exciting experiences.

A theme that expresses the value of friendship and the adverse consequences of misunderstandings is developed in Geefwee Boedoe's *Arrowville*. When peaceful strangers, the Targets, come to town, they are misunderstood. The townspeople believe the Targets are kidnappers until the

Targets show them that they really are friendly. As a consequence of this experience, the mood of the townspeople changes from one of constant arguing to one of laughter and agreement.

The role of friendships during times of great stress is a theme found in storybooks set during World War II. In *The Butterfly*, Patricia Polacco develops a close friendship between a Jewish girl and the daughter of a French family who protects and hides the Jewish family. The author's note stresses the importance of the French underground and resistance in helping Jewish families during the Nazi occupation.

In addition to friendship, the need to respect others and the necessity for conducting wise negotiations are important themes found in picture books. Peggy Rathmann's *Officer Buckle and Gloria* develops a theme about the importance of friendship as the story concludes with the safety tip, "Always Stick With Your Buddy!" (unnumbered). Lynn Reiser's *Best Friends Think Alike*, A. M. Monson's *Wanted: Best Friend*, and Mary Ann Rodman's *My Best Friend* stress friendship, the obligations of friendship, and the often difficult task of sharing.

The need to overcome racial stereotypes is addressed in several books for young children. For example, *Skin Again*, by bell hooks, develops the theme that to understand someone, you must go inside the person, past the skin that is just covering the inside, and open your heart to what is the real person. This book, which has very large print and only about six words per page, would be an excellent introduction to racial understanding.

Style.   Because a picture storybook contains so few words, its author must select those words very carefully. In an interview with Carolyn Phelan (1993), author Mem Fox emphasizes the need for rhythm when writing for children: "I think rhythm is important in all writing, but I think it's of particular importance in a picture book because of the deep-seated, collective unconscious need for rhythm" (p. 29). The presence of rhythm in many of the Mother Goose rhymes, discussed earlier, indicates just how important this rhythm is in books for young children. A storybook also must be designed to catch children's attention and to stimulate their interest when adults read the story aloud. Adults can evaluate the effectiveness of style by reading a storybook orally to themselves or to a child.

Karen Beaumont follows the rhythm of the folk song "It Ain't Gonna Rain No More" in her picture storybook *I Ain't Gonna Paint No More!* This humorous rhythm and David Catrow's illustrations appeal to preschool children who may get into trouble for painting in the wrong place. Jill Esbaum develops a story in rhyme in her historical setting for *Ste-e-e-eam Boat A-Comin'!*. The language matches the style of a riverboat arriving in an Illinois village on the banks of the Mississippi River in 1867. The author depicts the steamboat as a "floating palace, white and red, chimneys belching overhead" (unnumbered). The rhyming text continues as the townspeople go to the wharf where they buy the merchandise.

Authors of picture storybooks frequently repeat single words or phrases to create stronger impressions when the books are read aloud. African folktales, for example, sometimes repeat words several times. In Gail E. Haley's *A Story, a Story*, the Sky God describes Ananse, the tiny spider man, as "so small, so small, so small." Similar use of repetition conveys the impression of a dancing fairy and rain on a hornet's nest. Verna Aardema uses this form of repetition to make a strong statement stronger in *Why Mosquitoes Buzz in People's Ears:* When a mother owl finds her dead baby, she is "so sad, so sad, so sad." The night that doesn't end is described as "long, long, long."

Young children enjoy listening to words that create vivid images. In the preface to *A Story, a Story*, Gail Haley says that many African words are found in the book and asks readers to listen carefully to the sounds so they can tell what the words mean. Haley uses many unknown words to describe the movements of animals. For example, a python slithers "wasawusu, wasawusu, wasawusu" down a rabbit hole; a rabbit bounds "krik, krik, krik" across an open space; and sticks go "purup, purup" as they are pulled out of the iguana's ears. Minfong Ho uses a similar style in *Hush! A Thai Lullaby* as the various animals are introduced with the sounds they might create. For example, a monkey goes "Jiak-jiak! Jiak-jiak!" and a water buffalo goes "MAAAU, MAAAU."

Authors of picture storybooks frequently use words that create vivid images. Carolyn Curtis's text and Alison Jay's illustrations for *I Took the Moon for a Walk* provide a style that invites readers or listeners to go on a fantasy walk where the moon follows along like a summer kite through a country landscape. The pictures add to the story by providing details that are not in the text.

Humor.   Selecting and sharing books that contribute to merriment are major goals of any literature program. Research shows that humorous literature is particularly effective in attracting children to the pleasures of reading and writing. In a study of children's reading preferences, Dianne Monson and Sam Sebesta (1991) identified humor as a very important element in books that children prefer. They state:

> Some forms of humor seem to have greatest appeal and perhaps are better understood by children in elementary and junior high school than others. The totally ridiculous situation and humorous characters are well liked, as is the humor associated with exaggeration, a surprising event, and play on words. (p. 668)

Many elements in picture storybooks can cause children to laugh out loud. An investigation by Sue Anne Martin (1969) concluded that humor in books awarded the Caldecott Medal had five general sources: (1) word play and nonsense, (2) surprise and the unexpected,

(3) exaggeration, (4) the ridiculous and caricatures, and (5) superiority.

Word Play and Nonsense.   Theodor Geisel, better known as Dr. Seuss, is one of the most popular authors of books for children and was an undisputed authority on word play and nonsense. Dr. Seuss often made up totally new words and names to describe the animals found in his imagination. In *Good Zap, Little Grog,* Sarah Wilson uses a style similar to that of Dr. Seuss, creating new words for her story in rhyme. Here little Grog must "zoodle opp," the "ooglets are tuzzling," and "smibblets are giggling." A "Grog Guide" at the end of the book reveals the identity of the various animals in this fantasy world.

In Seuss's *If I Ran the Zoo,* Gerald McGrew's imaginary zoological garden contains an elephant-cat, a bird known as a Bustard, a beast called Flustard, and bugs identified as thwerlls and chugs. Of course, no one could find such animals in the usual jungles, so Gerald must search for them in Motta-fa-Potta-fa-Pell, in the wilds of Nantasket, and on the Desert of Zind. Children enjoy not only the nonsense found in the rhyming text but also the nonsensical illustrations of these strange animals.

Bill Peet's nonsense rhymes and nonsensical illustrations in *No Such Things* also appeal to children. Peet uses both internal and end-of-line rhyming to create text such as the following:

> The blue-snouted Twumps feed entirely on weeds,
> And along with the weeds they swallow the seeds.
> Eating seeds causes weeds to sprout on their backs,
> Till they look very much like walking haystacks. (p. 5)

Surprise and the Unexpected.   Both Audrey Wood's text and Mark Teague's illustrations in *The Flying Dragon Room* create surprise and the unexpected. In this fantasy world of a bored child are rooms in which people slide down a snake, fly through the air in the jumping room, sail into a world inhabited by friendly alligators, and give carrots to Tyrannosaurus Rex. The illustrations in Peggy Rathmann's *Officer Buckle and Gloria* add considerable humor and unexpected situations when the police dog performs behind Officer Buckle's back as he gives safety tips to school children. The dog's actions, unknown by Officer Buckle, change a presentation from dull to exciting.

What difficulties might arise if cows could type and hens decided to go on strike unless the farmer meets their demands? This is the unexpected plot developed by Doreen Cronin in *Click, Clack, Moo: Cows That Type.* The story ends with a what-could-happen-next experience: After the cows and hens receive their demands, the ducks now go "Click, clack, quack./Click, clack, quack./Clickety, clack, quack" (unnumbered) and demand a diving board because the pond is too boring.

Irony creates surprise and the unexpected in Amy Hest's *In the Rain With Baby Duck.* Hest tells the story of a duck who dislikes to get wet feet, hop in puddles, or waddle through the water. The idea of a duck who dislikes water adds light and unexpected humor. Instead of loving rainy weather, he dawdles, dallies, pouts, and drags behind his parents who are thoroughly enjoying the setting. In a satisfying conclusion, Grampa gives Baby Duck a red umbrella and matching boots that once belonged to Baby Duck's mother, who also did not like the rain. Now Grampa and Baby Duck enjoy the weather together.

Problems associated with bringing a new baby into a house that includes pets is a common plot in stories. But what happens when the story is told from the perspective of Nigel, a cat, and Julia, a dog? This is the approach used by Patricia and Emily MacLachlan in *Bittle.* The story follows the pets as they slowly make adjustments to the baby and eventually develop love for the child.

Ducks, led by a uniformed Duck master, strutting through a hotel lobby on a red carpet to the music of a John Philip Sousa march sound like fantasy. Patricia Polacco develops her story, *John Philip Duck,* on the foundations of an activity that started at the Peabody Hotel in Memphis, Tennessee, during the Depression and continues today. The story tells how Edward Pembroke trained an orphan duck, took him to work, and began the tradition where ducks walk across the carpet, swim in the fountain, and return at night to their home on the rooftop of the hotel.

Exaggeration.   Children's imaginations are often filled with exaggerated tales about what they can do or would like to do. In James Stevenson's *Could Be Worse!,* however, the grandfather is the one who exaggerates. Grandpa does and says the same things day after day. Whenever anyone complains, Grandpa responds, "Could be worse." When he overhears his grandchildren commenting on his dull existence, he tells them what happened to him the previous evening: He was captured by a large bird and dropped in the mountains, where he encountered an abominable snowman. Then, he crossed a burning desert, escaped from a giant animal, landed in the ocean, and finally returned home on a paper airplane. After the grandchildren hear his story, they respond with his favorite expression, "Could be worse!"

Patricia Polacco uses exaggeration to develop her humorous *Meteor!* After a meteor lands on a farm, the whole town exaggerates its power: People claim that it gives the ability to play a trumpet, create a marvelous recipe, and even see extraordinary distances. The book is humorous because readers know that such an incident might really happen.

Exaggeration is the source of humor in both Anne Isaacs's text and Paul O. Zelinsky's illustrations in *Swamp Angel.* This tall-tale story set in the American frontier portrays a female character with unusual powers, such as the ability to wrestle a bear. The exaggeration begins on the day of her birth, when "the newborn was scarcely taller than her mother and couldn't climb a tree without help" (unnumbered). The story concludes when Swamp Angel turns Thundering Tarnations (the bear) into a rug. Unfortunately, the bear skin is too big for Tennessee, so she moves to Montana where she can spread the rug on the ground in front of her cabin. "Nowadays, folks call it the Shortgrass Prairie" (unnumbered).

A humorous exaggerated experience accompanies a young boy when he has a sleepover at his grandmother's in Kate Lum's *What! Cried Granny: An Almost Bedtime Story.* The story takes on tall-tale characteristics when Grandmother answers each of the child's protests about going to bed by completing an almost impossible task. For example, because he has no bed, she cuts down a tree and makes him one. She also shears sheep and knits a blanket. The final humor results when she tells him to go to bed but he cannot because it is now morning.

The Ridiculous and Caricatures. The consequences of having antlers suddenly appear on a young girl's head provide the humor in *Imogene's Antlers,* in which author David Small caricatures the ridiculousness of some people's fears. To extend the humor, the story concludes with another what-if: The antlers disappear, but an even more beautiful appendage replaces the antlers.

Foolishness and ridiculous situations may change to wisdom, as shown in Eric Kimmel's *The Chanukkah Tree.* In this Jewish tale, the people of Chelm believe a peddler when he sells them a Christmas tree as "a Chanukkah tree. From America. Over there Chanukkah trees are the latest thing" (unnumbered). The townspeople decorate the tree with potato latkes and candles. The only star that they can find for the top is on a door, so they place the whole door on top of the tree. When they discover that the peddler has duped them, they are unhappy at first. Later, birds take sanctuary on the tree during a snowstorm, and the people discover that their tree is not so ridiculous: The potato latkes feed the birds, the candles warm them, and the door protects them.

The humor in Janet Stevens's *Tops & Bottoms* results from the ridiculous situation and foolish actions of rich, lazy Bear when he is tricked out of the garden produce by Hare, who uses his wits to secure the best portions of the crop. The illustrations of Bear are particularly interesting as they epitomize this humorous and ridiculous situation.

Superiority. Some humorous picture storybooks gratify the desire of young children to be superior to everyone else for a change or to easily overcome their problems. When a town simpleton surpasses not only his clever brothers but also the czar of the land, the result is an unusual tale of humorous superiority. Arthur Ransome's *The Fool of the World and the Flying Ship* is a Russian tale. In it, the good deeds performed by a simple lad allow him to obtain a flying ship, discover companions who have marvelous powers, overcome obstacles the czar has placed in his path, win the hand of the czar's daughter, and live happily ever after.

A singing cow solves her problems through superiority against a greedy human in Lisa Campbell Ernst's *When Bluebell Sang.* When the cow and the farmer become tired of being taken advantage of by a talent agent, the cow hides herself among a herd of cows, where the agent cannot identify her without her dress, hat, and shoes.

Typical Characters and Situations

Children's picture storybooks include stories about people disguised as animals, talking animals with human emotions, personified objects, humans in realistic situations, and humorous and inventive fantasies. This section discusses stories by some outstanding writers of books on these subjects.

People Disguised as Animals. Many children's stories with animal characters are so closely associated with human lifestyles, behavior patterns, and emotions that it is difficult to separate them from stories with human characters. If these stories were read without reference to the illustrations or to specific type of animal, children might assume that the stories are about children and adults like themselves. These stories may be popular with children because they can easily identify with the characters' emotions and the actions.

Russell Hoban's Frances the badger, for example, lives in a nice house with her two parents, loves bread and jam, and feels jealous when she gets a new baby sister. Children identify with Frances when, in *Bread and Jam for Frances,* she refuses to eat anything but her two favorite foods. Hoban has her parents, like good human parents, carefully guide Frances into her decision that eating only bread and jam is boring and that trying different foods is pleasant.

In *A Baby Sister for Frances,* the young badger decides to run away from home when her mother becomes busy with the new baby. She packs a lunch to take with her on her journey, but she goes only as far as the next room, from which she looks longingly at her parents and her sister. In this warm story, Hoban shows how Frances's need for her family helps her overcome her jealousy and decide to accept the new arrival. The warmth is expressed in Hoban's choice of language:

> Big sisters really have to stay
> At home, not travel far away.
> Because everybody misses them
> And wants to hug-and-kisses them. (p. 26, unnumbered)

In *Leo the Late Bloomer,* Robert Kraus develops a credible character through experiences shared by many children: Leo, a young tiger, cannot read, write, draw, talk, or even eat neatly. One of Leo's parents worries, but the other suggests that Leo is merely a late bloomer. Kraus uses repetition to emphasize Leo's problem as the seasons go by: "But Leo still wasn't blooming." A satisfactory ending results in both the text and the illustrations when Leo finally discovers that he can do everything that he couldn't do before, and a happy father and mother hear their happy child declare, "I made it!" Ian Falconer's heroine, *Olivia*, is a precocious pig who believes she can do anything that she desires to accomplish: The feisty heroine sees herself as a prima ballerina, a builder of great buildings, and even an artist. Of course, when she paints a wall at home, she earns very childlike punishment: a time-out.

Fears and experiences that result in temporary unhappiness are popular causes of conflict in stories about animals disguised as people. In *Owen*, Kevin Henkes uses a mouse child's fear of losing his security blanket to create a story that could be about any young child. In *Off to School, Baby Duck!* Amy Hest develops a story that could easily be about a human child as Baby Duck has jitters in her stomach and shows reluctance to go to school on the first day. It is Grampa who introduces Miss Posy, the teacher, to Baby Duck and talks with her about all the fun she will have in school.

Many authors of books for young children develop plots that focus on fears associated with going to school for

Grampa Duck helps Baby Duck overcome his fear of going to school in Off to School, Baby Duck! *(From* Off to School, Baby Duck!, *by Amy Hest. Text copyright © 1999 by Amy Hest, illustrations copyright © 1999 by Jill Barton. Reproduced by permission of the publisher Candlewick Press, Inc., Cambridge, MA.)*

the first time. The protagonist in Harry Horse's *Little Rabbit Goes to School* shows the same fears many young children express. He tries to overcome his fears by taking his toy horse to school even though his mother objects. Unfortunately, the toy misbehaves. However, when Little Rabbit is safely home, he decides that although the toy is not ready for school, he is ready to return without his toy. In Jane Dyer's *Little Brown Bear Won't Go to School!*, Little Bear explores different jobs rather than go to school. After a day of exploring these jobs, Little Bear goes to school and realizes that school is the job for him.

The setting for Rosemary Wells's *My Kindergarten* shows various animals in kindergarten as they do activities that accompany their first year of school, such as singing number songs and creating a "Museum of Things." This is another book that can prepare students for an enjoyable school experience. An older brother helps his little sister by providing positive reasons that she should go to school in Lauren Child's *I Am Too Absolutely Small for School*. The protective big brother produces the winning reason for his sister to go to school: Her invisible friend is starting school and she will be lonely without her.

Family relationships and typical vacation activities form the plots of the stories in Bob Graham's *Tales From the Waterhole*. The short stories feature animals doing activities that will be familiar to many children. The book is suitable for beginning readers.

D. B. Johnson uses the human nature of and the characteristics associated with Henry David Thoreau to create the story *Henry Hikes to Fitchburg*. Two animal friends complete a wager in which they determine who will be the first to arrive in Fitchburg, 30 miles away: Henry decides to walk so he can see and enjoy the country, and his friend decides to work to buy a train ticket. The illustrations show the contrasting activities. For example, while the friend fills a woodbox, Henry is hopping from rock to rock across a river, and while the friend is pulling weeds in a garden, Henry is picking flowers and pressing them into a book to keep. At the conclusion, his friend states that the train was faster but Henry concludes, "I know. I stopped for blackberries" (unnumbered). The author provides information "About Henry" that includes an excerpt from *Walden* in which Henry David Thoreau discusses the pleasures of walking and enjoying nature.

In Marc Brown's *Arthur's Family Vacation*, the aardvark family plans and goes on a vacation to the seashore. Like many human vacations, their vacation at first looks like a disaster because it rains every day, the motel room is too small, the pool is not as large as a bathtub, and the children complain that their friends are not with them. The disaster is averted when Arthur decides to plan field trips for the family. Trips to a cow festival, Gatorville, Flo's Fudge Factory, and Jimmy's Jungle Cruise provide entertainment until the last day, when the sun shines and the family spends a glorious day at the beach. Children respond to the experiences and the problem solving by the oldest aardvark child. If the book were read without pictures, however, the story could be about any family.

Talking Animals With Human Emotions. In other animal stories, the animals live in traditional animal settings, such as meadows, barnyards, jungles, and zoos. The animals in these stories display some animal traits, but they still talk like humans and have many human feelings and problems.

Although the main characters in Martin Waddell's *Can't You Sleep, Little Bear?* live in a cave in the woods, the cave has furnishings, the bears talk, and they express emotions that are very human. The universal fear of darkness and the need to be comforted by a caring adult provide the story line in this warm, loving story. The father, who continually leaves his book to soothe the child and provide security, fosters a good response among children. In a totally satisfying ending, "Big Bear carried Little Bear back into the Bear Cave, fast asleep, and he settled down with Little Bear on one arm and the Bear Book on the other, cozy in the Bear Chair by the fire" (p. 25, unnumbered).

The main character in Munro Leaf's *The Story of Ferdinand* lives in a meadow with his mother and other cattle. Leaf develops contrasts between Ferdinand, who sits under his favorite cork tree smelling the flowers, and the bulls who run, jump, and butt their heads together practicing for the bullring. The theme of the story is relevant to any human child: All individuals should be themselves, and being different is not wrong. Leaf allows Ferdinand to remain true to his individual nature: When Ferdinand is taken to the bullring, he merely sits and smells the flowers.

Jean de Brunhoff uses a variety of emotional experiences in the various Babar books. Emotionally, Babar grows up; grieves when his mother dies; runs away to the city; returns to the jungle, where he is crowned king; and raises a family.

In Roger Duvoisin's *Petunia,* a goose becomes conceited when she finds a book and believes that merely carrying it around gives her wisdom. Petunia's advice creates an uproar in the barnyard when she maintains that firecrackers discovered in the meadow are candy and thus good to eat. Her true wisdom begins when she discovers that books have words and that she will need to learn to read if she really wants to be wise.

Many young children like a combination of fast, slapstick adventure and an animal with easily identifiable human characteristics, such as Hans Rey's *Curious George.* Readers are introduced to this comedic monkey as he observes a large yellow hat lying on the jungle floor. His curiosity gets the better of him, he is captured by the man with the yellow hat, and his adventures begin. The text and illustrations depict one mishap after another: George tries to fly but falls into the ocean, grabs a bunch of balloons and is whisked away by the wind, and is finally rescued again by the man with the yellow hat. The rapid verbal and visual adventures bring delight to young children, who are curious about the world around them and would like to try some of the same activities.

Other picture storybooks with animal characters satisfy children's desires for absurd situations, flights of fancy, and magical transformations. In William Steig's *Sylvester and the Magic Pebble,* for example, a young donkey accidentally changes himself into a rock and must figure out how to communicate with his grieving parents and return to his donkey form.

The absurd situation in Chih-Yuan Chen's *Guji Guji* results when one of the creatures mother duck raises from an egg is actually a crocodile. Everything is fine with the arrangement until three crocodiles try to convince Guji Guji that he must deliver the duck family to them to provide a duck dinner. In a happy ending, Guji Guji tricks the waiting crocodiles and saves his duck family.

Personified Objects. The technique of giving human characteristics to inanimate objects is called *personification.* Children usually see nothing wrong with a house that thinks, a doll that feels, or a steam shovel that responds to emotions. Virginia Lee Burton, a favorite writer for small children, is the highly skilled creator of things that have appealing personalities and believable emotions. In Burton's *Katy and the Big Snow,* an extraordinary red tractor named Katy responds to calls for help from the chief of police, the postmaster, the telephone company, the water department, the hospital, the fire chief,

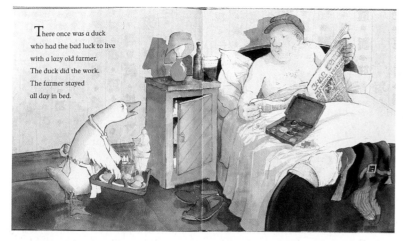

The animals in Farmer Duck *display human emotions and traits. (Reproduced from* Farmer Duck, *by Martin Waddell, with permission from Candlewick Press, Cambridge, MA. Illustration copyright © by Helen Oxenbury.)*

Through the Eyes of an ILLUSTRATOR

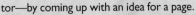

E. B. Lewis

Visit the CD-ROM that accompanies this text to generate a complete list of titles illustrated by E. B. Lewis.

Selected Titles by E. B. Lewis:
• Fire on the Mountain
• Big Boy
• Little Cliff and the Porch People
• The Other Side
• My Best Friend
• Virgie Goes to School with Us Boys

Since I am the illustrator, I'm going to basically tell you how an illustrator works. Basically we start from an idea; sometimes we start with a manuscript. A manuscript is something that's sent to an illustrator and has only words; no pictures. I have to create pictures to go with these words. This is how I start as an illustra-

tor—by coming up with an idea for a page.

I get the manuscript and read the story, for example, *Fire on the Mountain*. This is a story about a little boy who loses his parents in Ethiopia and goes out to find his sister to tell her the news. He encounters his sister, who works for a rich man, and together they end up working for this rich man. The rich man tries to outwit the little boy, to take advantage of him. Together, the boy and his sister conspire to get him back. It's a great little Ethiopian folktale—it tells the reader than if you're truthful and honest, your hopes and dreams will come true.

I go to the library in Philadelphia—I'm from Philadelphia—where there is a department called the Print and Picture Department, and in that department I do my research. Since this is an Ethiopian folktale, that means I have to do all kinds of research on Ethiopia, the country—what the terrain is like, what the people are like, and what have you. The people who work in the department bring me a pho-

tograph or samples of artwork from which I can choose.

The next part of the process is to find a model. Since this is an Ethiopian folktale and I wanted my book to be authentic to Ethiopia, I had to go find a model. I went to a community here in Philadelphia, an Ethiopian community, and I found a little boy.

And since I did the research, I knew what the terrain was like in Ethiopia and found that a forest in back of the Philadelphia Museum of Art closely resembled the terrain in Ethiopia. So I took my model and placed him in that terrain and took photographs. I work from photographs as an artist.

Video Profile: The occompanying video contains more of this conversation with E. B. Lewis, as well as conversations with Molly Bang, Leonard Everett Fisher, Keith Baker, and Brian Pinkney on illustrating children's books.

Technology Resources CW

Visit a great site dedicated to the work of Eric Carle by linking to the Companion Website at www.prenhall.com/norton

---

and the airport. "Sure," she says, and digs the town of Geoppolis out from a big snow that is two stories deep. When city departments believe in Katy, it is easy for the readers to believe in her also.

In *Mike Mulligan and His Steam Shovel*, also by Burton, Mike's best friend is a large piece of machinery named Mary Anne. A suspenseful story unfolds as the two friends try to dig the basement of Popperville's town hall in only one day. *The Little House* is a heroine who is strong and also needs love. In this story, a growing city encroaches upon the house, and she becomes dilapidated and lonely. Like a real person, the house proceeds through a series of emotions until she is moved away from the city and settles down happily on a new foundation, where "once again she was lived in and taken care of" (p. 39).

Humans in Realistic Situations. Young children enjoy stories about other children who share their concerns, problems, and pleasures. The numerous books written and illustrated by Ezra Jack Keats, for example, easily draw young children into the private worlds of other children. Louie, one of Keats's realistic heroes, is very lonely when his family moves to a new neighborhood. He solves his problems in *The Trip* by building a model of his old

neighborhood and going on an imaginative adventure with his old friends. In *Regards to the Man in the Moon*, other children tease Louie because his father is a junk dealer. His father's advice—that Louie build a spacecraft from junk—and his own imagination allow Louie and a friend to experience flight into outer space. When the other children hear of these adventures, they want to take part in them also.

Whereas Keats's books usually have inner-city settings, the settings created by another well-known children's author are usually the country or the coast of Maine. Robert McCloskey stresses warm family relationships in books such as *Blueberries for Sal*. This delightful story allows readers to share the berry-picking expeditions of a human mother and daughter and a mother bear and her cub. McCloskey develops drama when the youngsters get mixed up and start following the wrong parent. He provides a satisfying ending as both children are reunited with their mothers.

Young children understand the emotional trauma that results from losing a treasured possession. The toddler in Mo Willems's *Knuffle Bunny: A Cautionary Tale* accidentally leaves the toy at the laundromat when she helps her father wash clothes. Her father does not understand the problem, and the child is extremely unhappy until Mom realizes that the toy is missing. The author shows the importance of the toy when the child says her first words, "Knuffle Bunny," after she is reunited with the stuffed toy.

Cover from KNUFFLE BUNNY by Mo Willems. Text and illustration copyright © 2004. Reprinted by permission of Hyperion Books for Children.

Stories about relationships between grandparents and grandchildren are also popular in current picture storybooks. In *The Day Gogo Went to Vote: South Africa, April 1994*, Elinor Batezat Sisulu tells the story of how Thembi's great-grandmother, who has not left the house in years, casts her vote for the first time. This story, told through Thembi's viewpoint, shows the importance of this milestone in South African history.

Vera Williams's *A Chair for My Mother* shows that even a young child can help her mother fulfill a dream. After a fire destroys the family's furniture, Williams's heroine earns money to help fill the large coin jar that represents her mother's and grandmother's desire: a new, soft, comfortable chair. This goal is not easily reached, however; mother and daughter must work together.

Emily Arnold McCully's heroine in *Mirette on the High Wire* is an independent female protagonist. When Mirette meets a retired high-wire walker, the Great Bellini, she wants to learn the art. Despite his refusal, Mirette practices and teaches herself. Later, Mirette rescues her friend from the high wire by helping him overcome his fear. In the sequel, *Starring Mirette & Bellini*, McCully develops the theme about the importance of freedom.

In Sharon Bell Mathis's *The Hundred Penny Box*, a young boy develops an important relationship with his Great-great-aunt Dew, who moves into his home with an old box containing a penny for every year of her long life. This is one of many picture storybooks, such as those of Ezra Jack Keats, that share with children of all backgrounds the warm relationships in nonwhite families. Close relationships between a young Chinese girl and her grandfather are depicted in Margaret Holloway Tsubakiyama's *Mei-Mei Loves the Morning*. The text and illustrations show activities such as preparing breakfast, riding to the park on a bicycle, and doing tai-chi with friends.

Of course, young children also confront problems in their families, including sex-role biases. In Charlotte Zolotow's *William's Doll*, a young boy wants a doll to hug, cradle, and play with. His brother calls him a creep, and his neighbor calls him a sissy. His father tries to interest him in "masculine" toys and brings him a basketball and an electric train. William enjoys both toys but still wants a doll. When his grandmother visits, he explains his wish to her, shows her that he can shoot baskets, and tells her that his father does not want him to play with a doll. Grandmother understands William's need, buys him a baby doll, and then explains to William's upset father that William wants and needs a doll so that he can practice being a father just like his own father. Tomie dePaola deals with a similar situation in *Oliver Button Is a Sissy*. Such books can reassure children that there is nothing wrong with non-stereotypical behavior.

Some picture storybooks that deal with more or less realistic situations show protagonists trying to solve their own problems. In Sonia Manzano's *No Dogs Allowed!*, a Puerto Rican family living in New York City decide to go on a picnic at a state park; they take everything they think would make an enjoyable day, including the dog. When they arrive at the park, they see a sign that reads "No Dogs Allowed." In a humorous set of circumstances, they decide to stay in the parking lot with the dog, El Exigente, until they figure out what to do. Family members take turns entertaining the dog, each person sharing with the dog what he or she enjoys doing: hair styling by Carmen, reading by Martha, feeding by Don Joe, dancing with Aunt Tuta, playing dominoes with the Wise Old People, paw reading by the sister, and hugging and kissing by the dog's owner, Iris. The book has a happy ending as the family realizes that they have solved their problem and actually had a very nice picnic, even though it was in the parking lot outside the park.

Two picture storybooks about the Holocaust show that the realistic situations in picture books may sometimes be about very serious subjects. These books also make interesting comparisons for both content and illustrations. In *Rose Blanche*, Roberto Innocenti develops a strong protagonist who discovers the concentration camp near her home in Germany during World War II. As a consequence, she hides food and takes it to the Jewish prisoners. Unfortunately, Rose Blanche is killed by stray bullets as she stands in the woods. The somber colors in the illustrations reflect the sadness of both the concentration camps and Rose Blanche's death. In *Let the Celebrations Begin!*, Margaret Wild focuses on the same time in history. In Wild's book, however, the Jewish prisoners are preparing for soldiers to liberate the camp. Compared with Innocenti's somber shades, Julie Vivas's illustrations for *Let the Celebrations Begin!* are colorful pastels. As you read these two books, compare the illustrations and the contents. Both books have received some criticisms. Is *Rose Blanche* too depressing for children? Do the pastel illustrations and the party preparations found in *Let the Cele-*

Through the Eyes of a CHILD

Kelly
Grade 4

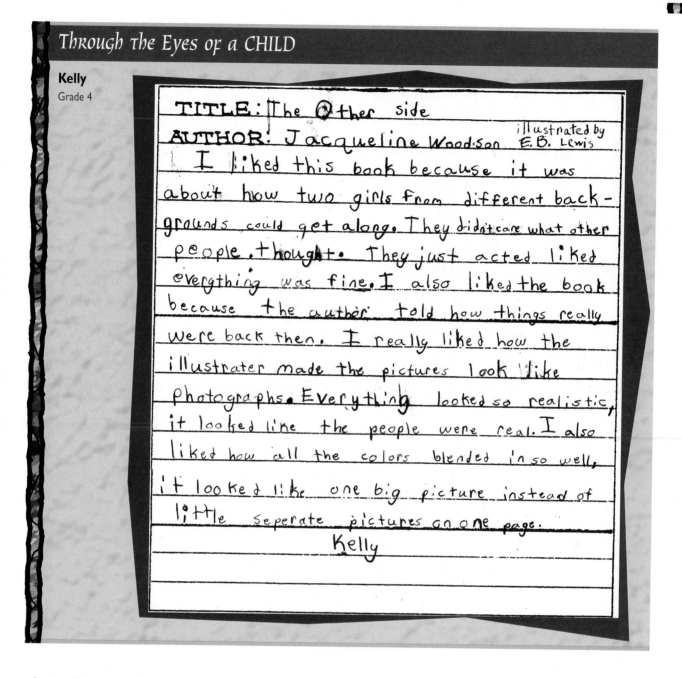

TITLE: The Other side
AUTHOR: Jacqueline Woodson   illustrated by E.B. Lewis

I liked this book because it was about how two girls from different backgrounds could get along. They didn't care what other people thought. They just acted liked everything was fine. I also liked the book because the author told how things really were back then. I really liked how the illustrater made the pictures look like photographs. Everything looked so realistic, it looked like the people were real. I also liked how all the colors blended in so well, it looked like one big picture instead of little seperate pictures on one page.

Kelly

brations Begin! trivialize a very serious subject? You decide as you read the two books.

The 50th anniversary of the end of World War II saw numerous books produced about the time period. Topics in current picture storybooks include war exeperiences in both Europe and Japan. For example, Jo Hoestlandt's *Star of Fear, Star of Hope* is set in Nazi-occupied France on the eve of Helen's 9th birthday. Her best friend, Lydia, is Jewish and leaves Helen's celebration to go home to warn her family that the Nazis are forcibly collecting the Jewish residents of the city. Helen feels abandoned by her friend and lets her know that she is no longer her friend. Unfortunately, Helen never sees Lydia again. Now, years later, Helen hopes that her best friend will see the message in the book and call her. The story ends with an important message that is also one of the themes of the book: "I'll always

have hope . . . " (unnumbered). In Tatsuharu Kodama's *Shin's Tricycle,* a young atomic bomb victim in Hiroshima is remembered through his tricycle, which is now on display at the Peace Museum. Both of these books about different World War II experiences are reminders of the tragedy of war.

Jacqueline Woodson sets her World War II picture book, *Coming On Home Soon,* at a time when a mother leaves home to look for a job because she learns, "They're hiring colored women in Chicago since all the men are off fighting the war" (unnumbered). The text shows what happens as the daughter and her grandmother wait longingly at home until a letter finally arrives with money and the message that mother is coming home soon. This is a tender story that shows how one African American family coped with the war.

From COMING ON HOME SOON by Jacqueline Woodson, illustrated by E. B. Lewis, copyright © 2004 by E. B. Lewis, illustrations. Used by permission of G. P. Putnam's Sons, A Division of Penguin Young Readers Group. A Member of Penguin Group (USA) Inc., 345 Hudson Street, New York, NY 10014. All rights reserved.

Humorous and Inventive Fantasies. Many picture storybooks use fantastical situations to engage readers. In Dr. Seuss's *The 500 Hats of Bartholomew Cubbins*, both conflict and humor result when the king orders a peasant to remove his magical hat. Every time Bartholomew tries to remove one hat, another hat appears. When the number reaches 157 hats, the magicians cast a spell:

> Dig a hole five furlongs deep,
> Down to where the night snakes creep,
> Mix and mold the mystic mud,
> Malber, Balber, Tidder, Tudd. (p. 31, unnumbered)

As the hats begin to number in the hundreds, the king threatens Bartholomew with execution. Then, hat number 500 is so beautiful that the king offers to buy it for 500 gold pieces. With that offer, the spell is broken and a rich Bartholomew returns home.

Several of Dr. Seuss's characters face moral issues. In *Horton Hatches the Egg*, Horton the elephant remains 100 percent faithful to his promise to hatch a lazy bird's egg in spite of jeering bystanders and other unpleasant experiences. He gains his reward when the egg hatches and is an elephant-bird.

Chris Van Allsburg's *Jumanji* begins with a realistic scene involving two children who are asked to keep the house neat until their parents return with guests. Bored, the children make a mess with their toys and then go to the park, where they find instructions for a jungle adventure game that cannot be ended until one player reaches the golden city. When the children take the game home, they realize the consequences of the rules: A lion appears on the piano and chases one of them around the house, and other jungle animals and jungle-related actions enter the scene each time the children frantically throw the dice. Van Allsburg ends the story on a note of suspense and speculation: The children return the game, but two other children, who are notorious for never reading directions, pick up the game and run through the park.

The plot in Van Allsburg's fantasy *The Widow's Broom* develops after a witch leaves her broom with a widow, Minna Shaw. As in all fantasies with witches, the broom has special powers and does Minna's work for her. Complications arise when suspicious neighbors express fear of the broom and then burn it. In a happy ending, the broom arises, rejoins the widow, and plays music for their pleasure.

Picture Storybooks for Young Adults

Picture storybooks frequently relate to the subjects read by or studied in the curriculum of young adults. For example, *A Child's Christmas in Wales*, by Welsh poet Dylan Thomas, is found in a highly illustrated text with paintings by Chris Raschka. Thomas's text for this illustrated version was first published in *Harper's Bazaar* magazine in 1950; an earlier edition was a BBC radio broadcast in 1945. The text can be used to motivate a dramatic reading of the book as if it were a radio broadcast. Or students can read and discuss Thomas's poems.

Gregory Rogers's wordless book *The Boy, The Bear, The Baron, The Bard* is set in the Globe Theater during the time of Shakespeare. This book has been used by middle school and high school students to develop the words for a play that could accompany the illustrations. A high school drama teacher found the book to be an excellent and humorous introduction to Shakespeare's plays and Tudor London. Students could also respond to Rogers's introduction when he states why he has been fascinated by everything Elizabethan and grasp the considerable research that was required to illustrate the book.

The content of some picture books, especially if the topic is about harsh times in history, is frequently more appropriate for young adults. For example, even though it is a wordless book, Tom Feelings's *The Middle Passage: White Ships/Black Cargo* is such a text. The content of the illustrations is clarified in Feelings's introduction when he visualizes the images that motivated the text about slave ships and their human cargo: "Muted images

Illustration from THE BOY, THE BEAR, THE BARON, THE BARD by Gregory Rogers. Copyright © 2004 by Gregory Rogers. Reprinted by permission of Henry Holt and Company, LLC.

flashed across my mind. Pale white sailing ships like huge white birds of prey, plunging forward into mountainous rising white foaming waves of cold water, surrounding and engulfing everything. Our ancestors, hundreds of them locked in the belly of each of these ships, chained together like animals throughout the long voyage from Africa toward unknown destinations, millions dying from the awful conditions in the bowels of the filthy slave galleys" (unnumbered).

Brundibar, retold by Tony Kushner with illustrations by Maurice Sendak, is another picture book about a harsh time in history. The opera on which the book is based was performed by the children of Terezin, the Nazi concentration camp during World War II. The Jewish creator of the original opera, Hans Krasa, was killed in Auschwitz in 1944. The illustrations are filled with references to the Czech Republic, such as a drawing of the Prague Town Square, the Jewish cemetery, and documents showing the destruction of the Jewish people. Both Feelings's book and *Brundibar* require reader background knowledge about the time periods. These picture storybooks provide a source for discussion and additional research.

Teaching With Picture Books

o truly share picture books, you must care enough to select books and prepare book-related activities that children find stimulating and enjoyable. Picture-book experiences involve sharing nursery rhymes to stimulate oral language development and dramatization; wordless books that encourage children to find objects in pictures, tell their own stories, or write creatively; picture storybooks ideal for reading aloud; illustrations that encourage aesthetic sensitivity; and picture books of all sorts that encourage children to join in with songs and movement.

Picture books are important for developing experiences with song and story because, according to Betsy Hearne (1992), "meaning emerges from experience patterned by artistry, an artistry in association with the senses. Song and story are sensuous. . . . Children's books are the continuation of speech, song, and story" (p. 31).

Patricia Cianciolo (1990) argues strongly for using picture books with students at all grade levels, from 3-year-olds who cannot yet read to sophisticated young adults who can analyze the illustrations and grasp new meaning and significance. Cianciolo states:

> In these picture books the illustrations are superbly accomplished works of visual and graphic art, and the texts are written in beautifully expressive language. . . . In addition to bringing out and emphasizing the text, they convey other meanings and impressions that readers would not have envisioned from the verbal information on its own. They encourage higher-level thinking and imaginative thinking. Readers can and do grasp their meaning and significance and can go well beyond what the illustrator and author suggested. (p. 2)

Whatever the book, if it is worth sharing, the sharing experience is worth thoughtful preparation. This section discusses a few of the many ways in which you can use picture books to enhance personal development in children and to increase children's responses to literature.

Sharing Mother Goose

Mother Goose rhymes are natural means of stimulating language development and listening appreciation in very young children because the rhymes include a simple story line that encourages finger play, a story or song with a repeated chorus, a verse with nonsense words, a description of daily actions, and a choral reading in which children join in with the rhyming words. Even 2- and 3-year-olds thoroughly enjoy and respond to the rhyme, rhythm, and nonsense found in nursery rhymes. Because passive listening may not encourage language development, adults must create experiences that motivate children to interact with the verses in enjoyable ways. Once children have heard the simpler Mother Goose rhymes several times, they usually can help you finish the verses by filling in missing words or rhyming elements: "Jack and Jill, went up the _____ to fetch a pail of water. Jack fell down, and broke his _____, and Jill came tumbling after." In addition to providing enjoyment during shared experience, this activity encourages auditory discrimination and attentive listening, skills necessary for later successes in reading and language arts.

You can also insert an incorrect word into a familiar rhyme and have the children correct the error. Children especially enjoy this exercise when the nursery rhyme book has large, colorful illustrations in which they can point out what is wrong with your version. For example, say, "Jack be nimble, Jack be quick, Jack jump over a pumpkin," or "Little Boy Blue come blow your horn. The pig's in the meadow, the chick's in the corn." Many children also enjoy making up their own incorrect versions.

Young children enjoy creative play and can spontaneously dramatize many of their favorite rhymes. Dramatization allows children to explore body movements, develop their senses, expand their imaginations and language, and experiment with characterization. Read or tell various nursery rhymes while children pretend to be each character in the rhyme and perform the actions expressed in the verses. Following each line, allow enough time for the children to act out each part. Children especially enjoy acting out such action rhymes as "Little Miss Muffet," "Jack Be Nimble," and "Hey Diddle Diddle."

You can encourage children to expand upon one of their favorite nursery rhymes, as do some delightful picture books devoted to one rhyme. Mother Goose rhymes that lend themselves to extended oral, written, or artistic versions are "Old Mother Hubbard," "Old King Cole," and "Simple Simon." After sharing one of these books or rhymes with children, ask them if they would like to know more about any other Mother Goose characters.

A discussion with first graders, for example, revealed that several children wanted to know what it would be like to live in a pumpkin. They talked about how they might decorate its interior, what they could do inside a pumpkin, and how neighbors might react to a pumpkin in the neighborhood. They dictated their story to the teacher and divided it into separate sentences, each written and illustrated on tagboard by one child and then placed in the classroom library. This book was read by many children and became one of the most popular picture storybooks in the classroom. When more children created their own books, the children's librarian developed a library display of both commercially published Mother Goose books and books printed and illustrated by the children. In a similar activity, after children read Pamela Duncan Edwards's *The Neat Line: Scribbling Through Mother Goose*, they can choose a rhyme and solve a problem by drawing a line object.

Sharing Wordless Books

Wordless books are ideal for encouraging language growth, stimulating intellectual development, motivating creative writing, developing text for reading, and evaluating language skills. Consider children's ages and the complexity of plot or details when choosing wordless books. Some wordless books have much detail, which stimulates observational skills and descriptive vocabularies. Other wordless books are more appropriate for encouraging understanding and interpretation of sequential plot.

Stimulating Cognitive and Language Development

Literature is valuable in promoting cognitive development in children. Several skills associated with the thinking process—observing, comparing, and organizing—can be developed through the use of wordless books. Children can describe what is happening in each picture and the details that they observe, compare pictures or changes that occur, and express their thoughts in sequentially well-organized stories. Describing, comparing, and storytelling also help children expand their vocabularies.

Children can describe the action in each detailed picture in Peter Spier's *Noah's Ark,* for example, as they follow the building of the ark; the loading of food, utensils, and animals; the problems that develop inside the ark; and the final landing and starting of life anew. One group of 7-year-olds did the following:

1. Identified the animals they recognized in a two-page spread showing animals boarding the ark.

2. Described the color, size, mode of travel, and natural habitat of the animals.

3. Identified humorous details in the illustrations.

4. Identified Noah's problems and suggested possible causes and solutions.

5. Speculated about Noah's feelings as he tried to rid the roof of too many birds, dealt with a reluctant donkey, and finally closed the doors of the ark.

6. Thought of descriptive words for the animals, such as *slithering* for snakes, *leaping* for frogs, and *lazy, brown* for monkeys.

7. Compared the positions of the snails in the illustrations at the beginning and at the end of the book.

8. Chose one picture each and told or wrote a detailed description of the picture.

Spier's wordless book can be compared with Lisbeth Zwerger's illustrations in Heinz Janisch's *Noah's Ark.* Mercer Mayer's funny wordless book *Frog Goes to Dinner* encourages before-and-after comparisons. People enjoy a leisurely meal in one picture, for example, and in the next experience the disruptions caused by Frog. A first grader made this comparison when he discussed two pictures of the band:

> The band was playing beautifully. They had their eyes closed and were enjoying the music. All of a sudden the frog jumped in the saxophone. Now the saxophone player tried to play but couldn't. His face puffed out and he looked funny. The other players jumped. The frog made the drum player fall into his drum. The horn player thought it was funny.

The detailed illustrations in Jeannie Baker's *Window* are excellent for encouraging comparisons of the same setting across time. Children can observe, describe, and compare the illustrations that show changes in the Australian environment and ecology over a period of 24 years.

Motivating Writing and Reading

Educators in reading and language arts frequently recommend the use of language experiences that stimulate children's oral language and writing by exploring ideas and expressing feelings. These experiences in turn provide the content for group and individual stories composed by children and recorded by adults, who then use these stories for reading instruction.

Many teachers introduce students to the language experience approach to literature through group chart stories. These activities are appropriate for all age groups, but they are used most as reading-readiness or early reading activities in kindergarten or first grade. Usually, an entire group (guided by the teacher) writes a chart story after a shared motivational experience, such as a field trip, an art project, a film, music, or a story. Many of the wordless books discussed in this text are excellent sources for motivational activities.

If you use a wordless book to motivate the writing of a chart story, first share the book with the group. Following oral discussion, have the children dictate the story as you record it on posterboard, the chalkboard, or large sheets of newsprint, repeating each word aloud. (Some teachers identify each child's contribution to the chart story by placing the child's name after the contribution.) It is essential that children be able to see each word as it is written. As you write the chart story, children will see that sentences flow from the top to the bottom on a page, follow a left-to-right sequence, begin with capital letters, and end with periods. After completing the chart story, read the whole story, then ask the children to reread it with you. Following this experience, some individual children may choose to read the whole story aloud, and others may choose to read only their own contributions.

Place wordless books and their accompanying chart stories in areas easily accessible to children, so that they can enjoy reading the stories by themselves. Some teachers tape-record the children's reading of the chart stories and then place the recordings, the chart stories, and the wordless books in a listening center. The stories can also be read to children in other classes or added to the library.

Picnic and *School,* by Emily Arnold McCully, provide opportunities for children to write dialogue, describe settings, develop conflicts and characterizations, and discuss themes. David Wiesner's *Free Fall* encourages children to write interpretations of a fanciful dream. University students report that Chris Van Allsburg's *The Mysteries of Harris Burdick* is one of the most enticing nearly wordless books for older elementary students. Children can speculate about each fantasy in Van Allsburg's book, write their own stories, and share the stories with other children who have different interpretations. Because there is no correct answer, children may choose to write more than one story about a picture.

Reading to Children

An adult who reads to children accepts an opportunity and a responsibility for sharing a marvelous experience. Author and illustrator Leo Lionni (quoted by Smith, 1991) states this very well when he describes the role of children's books in children's lives:

> When a child is four or five, he has lived four or five years in a totally chaotic verbal environment. The picture book is the first thing that gets into his head where he is confronted with a verbal structure. If it's a good book, it has a beginning, a middle and an end. It's the first time that he will say "more, again" after the reading is over. Now he knows what the end and the beginning is—just think of what a complicated notion that is. Which means that he also has a notion of what's in between, so that he has a sense of whole. He's not conscious of it, but for the first time, he's faced with structure. That I think is an enormously convincing consideration on the importance of the picture book. (p. 119)

There is probably no better way to interest children in the world of books than to read to them. Listening to books read aloud is a way for children to learn that literature is a form of pleasure. June Brown (1999) emphasizes that because younger children's listening level is greater than their reading level, "reading aloud can build background knowledge, teach new words, and provide a positive role model. It also hooks children on quality literature, demonstrates the pleasure involved in the process, and motivates them to read alone" (p. 520). Without parents, librarians, or other adults, a very young child would not experience nursery rhymes or such stories as Beatrix Potter's *Peter Rabbit,* and younger elementary children would not experience the marvelous verses and stories of A. A. Milne or enter the joyous world of Dr. Seuss. For children just struggling to learn to read, a book may not be a source of happiness. In fact, books actually arouse negative feelings in many children. Being read to helps beginning readers develop an appreciation for literature that they could not manage with their own reading abilities.

The pleasure of the listening experience usually motivates children to ask for a book again or to read it themselves. Very young children may ask for a book to be reread so many times that they memorize it and then feel proud of being able to "read" it. When a teacher reads a particularly enjoyable selection to children in an elementary classroom, the children tend to check out all copies of that book in the class or school library.

Choosing the Books

An appropriate book for reading aloud depends, of course, on the ages of the children, their interests, the need to balance the types of literature presented, the number of children who will share the listening experience, and the quality of the literature. A book selected for reading aloud should be worthy of the time spent by the readers and listeners. It should not be something picked up hurriedly to fill in time.

The style and the illustrations are both considerations when choosing books to read aloud. Mary Ann Hoberman's *You Read to Me, I'll Read to You: Very Short Stories to Read Together* is designed especially for pairing beginning readers with older children or adults. Humorous selections encourage children to share the experience, and Michael Emberley's humorous cartoon illustrations add to the fun. The language in A. A. Milne's *Winnie-the-Pooh* and Dr. Seuss's *The 500 Hats of Bartholomew Cubbins* appeals to young listeners. The rhyming text in Linnea Riley's *Mouse Mess* is fun to listen to and read aloud. Likewise, young children enjoy illustrations that are integral to the story. For example, illustrations in Robert McCloskey's *Lentil* help children visualize a midwestern town in the early 1900s.

Children's ages, attention spans, and reading ability are also important when selecting stories to be read aloud. The books chosen should challenge children to improve their reading skills and to increase their appreciation of outstanding literature. The numerous easy-to-read books should usually be left for children to read independently. Young children respond to short stories; in fact, 4- or 5-year-olds may benefit from several short story times a day rather than one 20- or 30-minute period. Books such as Michael Rosen's *We're Going on a Bear Hunt,* Lloyd Moss's *Zin! Zin! Zin! A Violin,* Robert Kraus's *Leo the Late Bloomer,* and Doreen Cronin's *Click, Clack, Moo: Cows That Type* are short and have colorful pictures. *We're Going on a Bear Hunt* uses repetitive language to encourage children to join in during reading. *Zin! Zin! Zin! A Violin* uses rhyming words and sounds of instruments.

As children enter kindergarten and advance into first grade, they begin to enjoy longer picture storybooks with more elaborate plots. Robert McCloskey's *Make Way for Ducklings* and the various Dr. Seuss books are favorites with beginning elementary school children. Books such as William Steig's *Caleb & Kate,* Eugene Trivizas's *The Three Little Wolves and the Big Bad Pig,* Peggy Rathmann's *Officer Buckle and Gloria,* and Tim Myers's *Basho and the River Stones* have enough plot to appeal to second-grade children. Steven Kellogg's humorous exploits of a Great Dane in *A Penguin Pup for Pinkerton* encourages listeners to enjoy Pinkerton's antics as he decides that a football is really a penguin egg and that it is his responsibility to care for the egg.

By the time children reach the third grade, they are ready for stories read a chapter at a time. (A reading period should not end in the middle of a chapter.) Third graders usually enjoy E. B. White's *The Trumpet of the Swan, Charlotte's Web,* and *Stuart Little.* Fourth and fifth graders often respond to books such as Madeleine L'Engle's *A Wrinkle in Time* and C. S. Lewis's *The Lion, the Witch and the Wardrobe.* Armstrong Sperry's *Call It Courage,* Esther Forbes's *Johnny Tremain,* the various "Harry Potter" books by J. K. Rowling, Louis Sachar's *Holes,* and Gloria Whelan's *Homeless Bird,* discussed in other chapters in this text, often appeal to sixth- and seventh-grade students.

Reading to students should not end in the elementary grades. Unfortunately, June Brown (1999) reports that many upper-grade teachers have abandoned the practice of reading aloud. Without enjoyable oral listening experiences, many older children are not exposed to good literature because they cannot read it independently. Alleen Pace Nilsen and Kenneth L. Donelson (2001) make a strong case for reading aloud to older students:

> English teachers ought to know enough about dramatic techniques and oral interpretation to be comfortable reading aloud to students. We need teachers eager and able to read material to students that just might interest, intrigue, amuse, or excite them, material that might make young people aware of new or old books or writers or techniques or ideas. . . . Poetry must be read aloud. So must drama. Reading fiction aloud is half the fun of teaching short stories. If students are to learn how to read poetry or drama, it will come from English teachers comfortable with their own oral reading. (p. 358)

Preparing to Read Aloud

Many adults mistakenly believe that children's stories are so simple that there is no need for an adult to read a selection before reading it to children. However, many embarrassing situations, such as being unable to pronounce a word or selecting an inappropriate book, can be avoided if you first read the story silently—in order to understand it, identify the sequence of events, recognize the mood, and identify any problems with vocabulary or concepts—and then read it aloud to practice pronunciation, pacing, and voice characterization. Adults with little or no experience in reading to children can listen to themselves on tape recorders. You also should decide how to introduce the story and what type of discussion or other activity, if any, to use following the reading.

The Reading Itself

What makes the story hour a time of magic or an insignificant part of the day? An effective reading experience begins with adult knowledge of the story and is enhanced through child involvement, eye contact, expressive reading, pointing to meaningful words or pictures, and highlighting words and pictures. You should consider all of these factors when preparing for an oral presentation and when actually reading a story to an audience of children. Properly prepared, you can take children on a much-appreciated literary journey.

Let us consider an example of a reading aloud experience that accompanies a book for early elementary students.

While reading Michael Rosen's *We're Going on a Bear Hunt* to kindergarten or first-grade students, emphasize the repetitive language and the descriptive words. Show the students that the illustrator, Helen Oxenbury, places the repetitive verses on black-and-white backgrounds and the descriptive action words on colored backgrounds. Ask the students: "Why would an illustrator choose both black-and-white and colored backgrounds in the same book? How should we read this story to show the differences between black-and-white and colored

backgrounds?" After orally reading the first series of repetitive text, encourage the students to join in the reading. On the colored action pages, ask them to predict the sounds that the family will make as they go through each obstacle. Have them notice that each action is expressed three times and that each line increases in size. Ask the students: "Why would an author increase the size of the letters? How could we use our voices and actions to show this increasing size?" Then have the students read and act out the lines such as:

> *Splash splosh!*
> *Splash splosh!*
> *Splash splosh!*

Students enjoy acting out this whole rhyme as they start the bear hunt, swishy swashy through the grass, splash splosh through the river, squelch squerch through the mud, stumble trip through the forest, hoooo woooo through the snowstorm, tiptoe through the cave, discover the bear, and then go back through each obstacle until they reach the safety of home and bed. This book encourages students to become involved in the text and their own vocabulary development as they join in the repetitive language, act out the action words, and discover how an author and an illustrator might show how words should be spoken by changing the size of the text or by alternating the backgrounds.

Renea Arnold (2005) describes the advantages of using "dialogic reading" during a reading-aloud experience. In this approach, an adult interrupts the oral reading at strategic points to ask "what" questions that have specific answers, to pose "open-ended" questions that do not have right or wrong answers and cannot be answered with single-word responses, and to "expand" on what children answer by asking them to add to their answers.

Developing Aesthetic Sensitivity

If the word *aesthetic* denotes sensitivity to art and beauty, then looking at the beautiful illustrations in children's books must be aesthetic. Children learn to appreciate the artistic media used in book illustrations when they are given the stimulation and the time to become actively involved in making their own illustrations. Some artistic media are too complex for very young children, of course, but Debra Cooper-Solomon (1999) believes that collage is an ideal medium for stimulating creative interpretations of literature and for developing fine-motor skills. In the process of making their own collages and reacting to the collages in book illustrations, children can also improve their vocabularies and oral discussion skills. Ezra Jack Keats, Leo Lionni, Jeannie Baker, and David Wisniewski are among the well-known illustrators of children's books who use collage. Adults can use works of such artists first to enlighten themselves and then as sources of material for children to discuss and compare. (Jeannie Baker's collage illustrations for *Where the Forest Meets the Sea* and *Window* are fine sources of inspiration for both adults and children because Baker uses many different textures to create large, colorful pictures.)

You might use the following sequence when introducing children to collage:

1. Encourage children to experiment with the collage technique by having them tear and cut shapes and pictures from plain paper or magazines and then paste the shapes onto another piece of paper.

2. Provide opportunities for children to experience different textures in the world around them and then use those textures in collages. Have the children take a texture exploration walk, for example, during which they feel and describe the textures of tree bark, leaves, grass, flowers, sidewalks, building materials, fabrics, paper, foods, and so forth. After they have experienced and discussed various textures, have them collect items with different textural qualities to use in charts and texture collages. Encourage the children to touch their collage experiments, look at the textures carefully, and discuss their reactions to different texture combinations.

3. Have the children create their own collages or series of collages using as many different textures as they wish. Then ask the children to share these illustrations with one another, along with accompanying stories or descriptions.

4. Share with the children a picture book illustrated with collage. While reading the story and showing the pictures, ask the children to recognize the collage technique, discuss the feelings each collage object produces, tell why they think the illustrator chose a certain material to represent it, and describe the texture they would feel if they could touch the original collage. Let them decide whether the collage illustrations make the story better.

Some illustrations combine other artistic media with collage. Ezra Jack Keats's illustrations for *Maggie and the Pirate* are brightly colored combinations of collage and painting. Keats's *The Trip* even illustrates a young boy working with various colors and shapes of paper as he creates his own neighborhood within a box; this book can stimulate experimentation with both collage and painting. In his illustrations for Eve Bunting's *Smoky Night*, David Diaz uses photographs, broken glass, and materials such as pieces of plastic bags to re-create a feeling of the Los Angeles riots. Christopher Myers's collage illustrations for Walter Dean Myers's *Harlem* developed feelings for an inner-city setting.

Experimenting with simple cartoon techniques is another way that children can begin to develop their artistic skills and aesthetic sensitivities because cartoons are very popular with children. After experimenting with their cartoons, children can look with new understanding and appreciation at picture storybooks illustrated by well-known cartoonists, such as James Stevenson's *Could Be Worse!*, Helen V. Griffith's *Grandaddy's Place*, and William Steig's *Caleb & Kate* and *Spinky Sulks*. Have the children discuss how well the cartoons complement the text and compare the effectiveness of cartoons and that of other types of book illustration. Also, have the children write stories and illustrate them with cartoons. Children enjoy creating their own cartoon books or creating a newspaper format that combines cartoons drawn by all of the children in a group.

MOTIVATING WRITING WITH PICTURE STORYBOOKS

Picture storybooks provide many sources for expressive and imaginative writing. For example, writing letters to friends, relatives, teachers, librarians, authors, or even imaginary people is an excellent way to encourage expressive writing in children (Norton, 2004). Use stories that include situations in which characters write letters to motivate children to write letters of their own. Introduce younger children to letters through Janet and Allan Ahlberg's *The Jolly Postman*. In this book, the postman delivers letters to fairy-tale characters, such as Cinderella and the three bears.

Several books use trips or moving as reasons for letter writing. For example, in Vera Williams's *Stringbean's Trip to the Shining Sea*, a boy writes a series of postcards during a camping trip across the western United States.

Use picture storybooks that have mysterious endings or that develop speculations to encourage children's imaginative writing. David Wiesner's *June 29, 1999* is an excellent book for stimulating children's speculations about the mysterious vegetables and to motivate children to write and illustrate their own science fiction stories. Wiesner's *Sector 7* can be used to encourage children to speculate about the formation of clouds. Pictures in Quint Buchholz's *The Collector of Moments* provide many opportunities for speculation and creative writing. For example, how do you know that the boy's music is in each of the pictures? Why did the artist show a horse on the lighthouse? What will happen to the huge musical instrument that is flying toward the coast?

Use Barbara Lehman's wordless book, *The Red Book*, to motivate readers to write about their own "what if" adventure. In the book, a city girl finds a red book tucked into a snow drift. When she opens the book, she discovers pictures of a boy walking on a desert island. As he walks along the beach, he finds a red book partially buried in the sand. His book shows pictures of the girl, the city, and snow falling. By attaching herself to balloons, the girl floats to the boy's location, and they meet in a happy reunion. But the story does not end there: Before leaving the city, the girl drops the book and a boy in the city picks it up and bicycles away with it under his arm. Students can extend the adventure by writing and illustrating the next installment. What will appear in the boy's red book? In what part of the world will the story take place? What will happen when the boy interacts with the new setting and people? This ending is similar to the conclusion in Chris Van Allsburg's *Jumanji:* They both have "what-might-happen-next" endings.

Stimulate imaginative writing by asking children to write a story in a point of view that is different from the one developed by the author. For example, read aloud Reeve Lindbergh's humorous *The Day the Goose Got Loose,* and allow children to respond to the humorous situations and illustrations. After they have discussed their responses to the book, ask them, "Who is telling the story about the goose—a human or the goose? How can you tell?" Reread the page on which grandmother asks, "I wonder what thoughts went through her head?" (p. 21, unnumbered). Ask the children why the grandmother is asking this question about the goose. Ask them, "How could we write this story if we were to tell it through the goose's point of view? Why did she do these actions? What was she thinking about as she _____? How did she see each of the people and animals who chased her? How did she feel when she _____?" Finally, encourage the children to write their own stories about *The Day the Goose Got Loose* but to tell the incidents through the goose's point of view. (Notice that this writing also emphasizes personification because the children must retell the story through the point of view of the goose.)

For a similar activity, use Eric Kimmel's *The Chanukkah Guest.* After sharing and discussing the book, ask the children to imagine what the bear must have been thinking as the old woman, Bubba Brayna, mistakes him for the rabbi, feeds him potato latkes, and gives him a warm woolen scarf. Have the children rewrite or retell the story from the time that the bear approaches the house, or have them tell the story through the dreams the bear has after he returns to his den in the deep forest and falls asleep with his stomach full of potato latkes and his neck wrapped in the warm scarf.

Suggested Activities

For more suggested activities for understanding picture books, visit the Companion Website at www.prenhall.com/norton

- Read a journal that evaluates children's literature, such as *The Horn Book Guide to Children's and Young Adult Books.* Select two picture books that are highly rated and two books that are not, and compare the literary elements and the illustrations in the books. Do you agree with the evaluation of the journal? Why or why not?

- Choose several editions of Mother Goose that contain the same nursery rhymes. Compare the artists' interpretations of these characters.

- Select a common animal or object that often appears in books for children. Find several picture books that develop a story about that animal or object, and compare the ways in which the different artists depict the animal or object through the illustrations and the ways in which the writers describe the animal or object and develop the plots.

- This text includes various responses to Maurice Sendak's *We Are All in the Dumps With Jack and Guy.* Respond to the illustrations and text in *The Miami Giant,* written by Arthur Yorinks and illustrated by Maurice Sendak. This book has also received mixed reviews. As you read the book, analyze the effectiveness of the satire.

Children's Literature

For full descriptions, including plot summaries and award winner notations, of these and other titles for teaching children with picture books, visit the CD-ROM that accompanies this book.

MOTHER GOOSE

Beaton, Clare, compiled by *Mother Goose Remembers.* Barefoot, 2000 (I:2–6).

Cole, Joanna, and Stephanie Calmenson, compiled by. *Miss Mary Mac: And Other Children's Street Rhymes.* Illustrated by Alan Tiegreen. Morrow, 1990 (I:4–8).

Crews, Nina. *The Neighborhood Mother Goose.* Greenwillow, 2004 (I:4–8).

dePaola, Tomie. *Tomie dePaola's Mother Goose.* Putnam, 1985 (I:2–6).

Edens, Cooper, ed. *The Glorious Mother Goose.* Atheneum, 1988 (I:all).

Edwards, Pamela Duncan. *The Neat Line: Scribbling Through Mother Goose.* Illustrated by Diana Caine Bluthenthal. HarperCollins, 2005 (I:4–7).

Foreman, Michael. *Michael Foreman's Mother Goose.* Harcourt Brace, 1991 (I:6+).

Greenaway, Kate. *Mother Goose: Or, the Old Nursery Rhymes.* Warne, 1881 (I:3–7).

Griego, Margot C., Betsy L. Bucks, Sharon S. Gilbert, & Laurel H. Kimball, *Tortillitas Para Mama and Other Spanish Nursery Rhymes.* Illustrated by Barbara Cooney. Holt, Rinehart & Winston, 1981 (I:3–7).

Hale, Sarah Josepha. *Mary Had a Little Lamb.* Illustrated by Tomie dePaola. Holiday House, 1984 (I:3–7).

_____. *Mary Had a Little Lamb.* Photographs by Bruce McMillan. Scholastic, 1990 (I:3–8).

Lobel, Arnold, *Gregory Griggs and Other Nursery Rhyme People,* Greenwillow, 1978 (I:4–7).

_____. *The Random House Book of Mother Goose.* Random House, 1986 (I:2–6).

I = Interest by age range.
R = Readability by grade level.

Newbery, John. *The Original Mother Goose's Melody.* Reissue. Gale, 1969 (I:all).

Opie, Iona, ed. *Here Comes Mother Goose.* Illustrated by Rosemary Wells. Candlewick, 1999 (I:2–8).

Opie, Iona, & Peter Opie. *I Saw Esau: The Shoolchild's Pocket Book.* Illustrated by Maurice Sendak. Candlewick, 1992 (I:all).

_____. *My First Mother Goose.* Illustrated by Rosemary Wells. Candlewick, 1996 (I:2–8).

_____. *A Nursery Companion.* Oxford University Press, 1980 (I:all).

_____. *The Oxford Nursery Rhyme Book.* Illustrated by Joan Hassall. Oxford University Press, 1955, 1984 (I:all).

_____. *Tail Feathers From Mother Goose: The Opie Rhyme Book.* Little, Brown, 1988 (I:all).

Ormerod, Jan. *Ms. MacDonald Has a Class.* Clarion, 1996 (I:5–8).

Sendak, Maurice. *We Are All in the Dumps With Jack and Guy.* HarperCollins, 1993 (I:all).

Wyndham, Robert. *Chinese Mother Goose Rhymes.* Illustrated by Ed Young. World, 1968; Philomel, 1982 (paperback) (I:4–7).

TOY BOOKS

Allen, Kit. *Galoshes.* Houghton Mifflin, 2003 (I:1–3).

_____. *Longiohns.* Houghton Mifflin, 2003 (I:1–3).

_____. *Sweater.* Houghton Mifflin, 2003 (I:1–3).

_____. *Swimsuit.* Houghton Mifflin, 2003 (I:1–3).

Brown, Marc. *Kiss Hello, Kiss Good-bye.* Random, 1997 (I:2–5).

_____. *Say the Magic Word.* Random, 1997 (I:2–5).

Brown, Margaret Wise. *The Goodnight Moon Room: A Pop-Up Book.* Illustrated by Clement Hurd. Harper & Row, 1984 (I:2–4).

Campbell, Rod. *Dear Zoo.* Four Winds, 1982 (I:2–4).

Carle, Eric. *The Very Clumsy Click Beetle.* Philomel, 1999 (I:1–5).

_____. *The Very Quiet Cricket.* Philomel, 1997 (I:1–5).

Cousins, Lucy. *Count With Maisy.* Candlewick, 1997 (I:2–4).

_____. *Maisy Goes to the Playground.* Candlewick, 1992 (I:2–4).

_____. *Maisy Goes to School.* Candlewick, 1992 (I:2–4).

_____. *Maisy's Colors.* Candlewick, 1997 (I:2–4).

Crowley, Joy. *Mrs. Wishy-Washy's Scrubbing Machine.* Illustrated by Elizabeth Fuller. Philomel, 2005 (I:1–3).

_____. *Mrs. Wishy-Washy's Splishy-Sploshy.* Illustrated by Elizabeth Fuller. Philomel, 2005 (I:1–3).

Emberley, Barbara. *Drummer Hoff.* Illustrated by Edward Emberley. Simon & Schuster, 1997 (I:3–7).

Fatus, Sophie. *Holes.* Abbeville, 1997 (I:2–6).

_____. *Spots.* Abbeville, 1997 (I:2–6).

_____. *Squares.* Abbeville, 1997 (I:2–6).

_____. *Stripes.* Abbeville, 1997 (I:2–6).

Fox, Mem. *Time for Bed.* Harcourt, 2005 (I:6 mo.–3).

Graham, Bob. *Benny: An Adventure Story.* Candlewick, 1999 (I:3–7).

Henkes, Kevin. *Julius's Candy Com.* Greenwillow, 2003 (I:2–5).

_____. *Wemberly's Ice-Cream Star.* Greenwillow, 2003 (I:2–5).

Hill, Eric. *Spot Goes to School.* Putnam, 1984 (I:2–4).

_____. *Spot's Birthday Party.* Putnam, 1982 (I:2–4).

_____. *Where's Spot?* Putnam, 1980 (I:2–4).

Hoban, Tana. *Look! Look! Look!* Greenwillow, 1988 (I:3–6).

Jeffrey, Sean. *Franklin's Big Search-and-Solve Flap Book.* Kids Can, 2005 (I:4–8).

Julian, Russell. *Busy Dog.* Egmont, 2005 (I:2–3).

_____. *Happy Cockerel.* Egmont, 2005 (I:2–3).

_____. *Hungry Pig.* Egmont, 2005 (I:2–3).

_____. *Lost Calf.* Egmont, 2005 (I:2–3).

Lindgren, Barbro. *Sam's Ball.* Illustrated by Eva Eriksson. Morrow, 1983 (I:2–4).

_____. *Sam's Bath.* Illustrated by Eva Eriksson. Morrow, 1983 (I:2–4).

Lionel. *Peekaboo Babies: A Counting Book.* Orchard, 1997 (I:2–6).

Oxenbury, Helen. *Dressing.* Wanderer Books, 1981 (I:1–3).

_____. *Family.* Wanderer Books, 1981 (I:1–3).

_____. *I Hear.* Random House, 1986 (I:1–3).

_____. *I See.* Random House, 1986 (I:1–3).

_____. *Playing.* Wanderer Books, 1981 (I:1–3).

_____. *Working.* Wanderer Books, 1981 (I:1–3).

Parr, Todd. *Big & Little.* Little, Brown, 2001 (I:2–4).

_____. *Black & White.* Little, Brown, 2001 (I:2–4).

Reed, Nathan. *My Little Toolbox.* Little Simon, 2005 (I:2–5).

Seeber, Dorothea P. *A Pup Just for Me: A Boy Just for Me.* Illustrated by Ed Young. Philomel, 2000 (I:3–7).

Shannon. David. *Oh, David!* Scholastic, 2005 (I:3–5).

_____. *Oops!* Scholastic, 2005 (I:3–5).

Simmons, Jane. *Daisy's Day Out.* Little, Brown, 2000 (I:2–4).

_____. *Daisy's Hide-and-Seek.* Little, Brown, 2001 (I:2–4).

_____. *Daisy Says Goo!* Little, Brown, 2000 (I:2–4).

Sís, Peter. *Trucks Trucks Trucks.* Greenwillow, 1999 (I:2–6).

Stadler, John. *Take Me Out to the Ball Game.* Little Simon, 2005 (I:4–8).

Wells, Rosemary. *Max's Both.* Dial, 1985 (I:1–3).

_____. *Max's Bedtime.* Dial, 1998 (I:1–3).

_____. *Max's Breakfast.* Dial, 1998 (I:1–3).

Ziefert, Harriet, *Baby Buggy.* Illustrated by Richard Brown. Houghton Mifflin, 1997 (I:2–6).

_____. *Night Knight.* Illustrated by Richard Brown. Houghton Mifflin, 1997 (I:2–6).

ALPHABET BOOKS

Aylesworth, Jim, *The Folks in the Valley: A Pennsylvania Dutch ABC.* Illustrated by Stefano Vitale. HarperCollins, 1992 (I:3–7).

Baldwin, Ruth M. *One Hundred Nineteenth-Century Rhyming Alphabets in English.* Southern Illinois University, 1972 (I:all).

Bowen, Betsy. *Antler, Bear, Canoe: A Northwoods Alphabet Year.* Little, Brown, 1991 (I:all).

Bryan, Ashley. *Ashley Bryan's ABC of African American Poetry.* Simon & Schuster, 1997 (I:all).

Chin-Lee, Cynthia. *A Is for Asia.* Illustrated by Yumi Heo. Orchard, 1997 (I:5–10).

Cook, Lyn. *A Canadian ABC.* Penumbra, 1990 (I:all).

Demarest, Chris L. *Firefighters A to Z.* Simon & Schuster, 2000 (I:5–8).

Ehlert, Lois. *Eating the Alphabet: Fruits and Vegetables From A to Z.* Harcourt Brace, 1989 (I:3–6).

Feelings, Muriel. *Jambo Means Hello: Swahili Alphabet Book.* Dial, 1974 (I:all).

Geisert, Arthur. *Pigs From A to Z.* Houghton Mifflin, 1986 (I:all).

Greenaway, Kate. *A—Apple Pie.* Warne, 1886 (I:3–8).

Hague, Kathleen. *Alphabears: An ABC Book.* Illustrated by Michael Hague. Holt, Rinehart & Winston, 1984 (I:3–7).

Heller, Nicholas. *Ogres! Ogres! Ogres!: A Feasting Frenzy from A to Z.* Illustrated by Jos. A. Smith. Greenwillow, 1999 (I:all).

Hepworth, Cathi. *Antics!* Putnam, 1992 (I:all).

Hoban, Tana. *A, B, See!* Greenwillow, 1982 (I:4–6).

Horenstein, Henry. *A Is for . . . ?: A Photographer's Alphabet of Animals.* Harcourt Brace, 1999 (I:all).

Hunt, Jonathan. *Bestiary: An Illuminated Alphabet of Medieval Beasts.* Simon & Schuster, 1998 (I:6–12).

Inkpen, Mick. *Kipper's A to Z: An Alphabet Adventure.* Harcourt, 2001 (I:3–7).

Johnson, Jean. *Postal Workers A to Z.* Walker, 1987 (I:all).

Johnson, Stephen T. *Alphabet City.* Viking, 1995 (I:all).

Jonas, Ann. *Aardvarks, Disembark!* Greenwillow, 1990 (I:all).

Kitchen, Bert. *Animal Alphabet.* Dial, 1984 (I:all).

Lear, Edward. *An Edward Lear Alphabet.* Illustrated by Carol Newsom. Lothrop, Lee & Shepard, 1983 (I:3–7).

Lobel, Anita. *Alison's Zinnia.* Greenwillow, 1990 (I:5–8).

Lobel, Arnold. *On Market Street.* Illustrated by Anita Lobel. Greenwillow, 1981 (I:4–7).

Lowe, Warren, and Sylvia Lowe. *Leroy's Zoo.* Illustrations by Leroy Ramon Archuleta. Black Belt, 1997 (I:all).

MacDonald, Suse. *Alphabatics.* Bradbury, 1986 (I:all).

Magee, Doug, and Robert Newman. *Let's Fly from A to Z.* Cobblehill, 1992 (I:all).

Martin, Bill, Jr., & John Archambault. *Chicka Chicka Boom Boom.* Simon & Schuster: 1989 (I:4–8).

Martin, Cyd. *A Yellowstone ABC.* Rinehart, 1992 (I:all).

Merriam, Eve. *Halloween ABC.* Illustrated by Lane Smith, Macmillan, 1987 (I:6–12).

Micklethwait, Lucy. *I Spy: An Alphabet of Art.* Greenwillow, 1992 (I:all).

Musgrove. Margaret. *Ashanti to Zulu: African Traditions.* Illustrated by Leo & Diane Dillon. Dial, 1976 (I:7–12).

Owens, Mary Beth. *A Caribou Alphabet.* Dog Ear, 1988 (I:all).

Pelletier, David. *The Graphic Alphabet.* Orchard, 1996 (I:all).

Pomeroy, Diana. *Wildflower ABC: An Alphabet of Potato Prints.* Harcourt Brace, 1997 (I:all).

Pratt, Kristin Joy. *A Walk in the Rainforest.* Dawn, 1992 (I:all).

Rosen, Michael. *Michael Rosen's ABC.* Illustrated by Bee Willey. Millbrook. 1997 (I:3–6).

Seeger, Laura Vaccaro. *The Hidden Alphabet.* Roaring Brook, 2003 (I:4–7).

Thornhill, Jan. *The Wildlife ABC: A Nature Alphabet Book.* Simon & Schuster, 1990 (I:all).

Van Allsburg. Chris. *The Z Was Zapped.* Houghton Mifflin, 1987 (I:all).

Viorst, Judith. *The Alphabet From Z to A (With Much Confusion on the Way).* Illustrated by Richard Hull. Atheneum, 1994 (I:7–10).

Whatley, Bruce, and Rosie Smith. *Whatley's Quest.* Illustrated by Bruce Whatley. HarperCollins, 1995 (I:all).

Wilbur, Richard. *The Disappearing Alphabet.* Illustrated by David Diaz. Harcourt Brace 1998 (I:7+).

Winter, Jeanette. *Calavera Abecedario: A Day of the Dead Alphabet Book.* Harcourt Brace, 2004 (I:all)

COUNTING BOOKS

Anno, Mitsumasa. *Anno's Counting Book.* Crowell, 1977 (I:3–7).

Bang, Molly. *Ten, Nine, Eight.* Greenwillow, 1983 (I:3–6).

Carle, Eric. *My Very First Book of Numbers.* Crowell, 1974 (I:3–6).

_____. *10 Little Rubber Ducks.* HarperCollins, 2005 (I:4–6).

_____. *The Very Hungry Caterpillar.* Crowell, 1971 (I:2–7).

Charlip, Remy, Mary Beth Miller, & George Ancona. *Handtalk Birthday: A Number & Story Book in Sign Language.* Four Winds, 1987 (I:all).

Christelow, Eileen. *Five Little Monkeys Jumping on the Bed.* Clarion, 1989 (I:2–6).

Cohen, Caron Lee. *How Many Fish?* Illustrated by S. D. Schindler, HarperCollins, 1998 (I:3–6).

Feelings, Muriel. *Moja Means One: Swahili Counting Book.* Illustrations by Tom Feelings. Dial, 1971 (I:all).

Fleming, Denise. *Count!* Holt. Rinehart & Winston, 1992 (I:2–7).

Geisert, Arthur. *Pigs From I to 10.* Houghton, 1992 (I:2–7).

Giganti, Paul. Jr. *Each Orange Had Eight Slices: A Counting Book.* Illustrated by Donald Crews. Greenwillow, 1992 (I:5–9).

_____. *How Many Snails? A Counting Book.* Illustrated by Donald Crews. Greenwillow, 1988 (I:3–6).

Grossman, Bill. *My Little Sister Ate One Hare.* Illustrated by Kevin Hawkes. Crown, 1996 (I:5–8).

Guettier, Bénédicte. *The Father Who Had 10 Children.* Dial, 1999 (I:3–5).

Guy, Ginger Foglesong. *¡Fiesta!* Illustrated by Rene King Moreno. Greenwillow, 1996 (I:5–8).

Haskins, Jim. *Count Your Way Through Italy.* Illustrated by Beth Wright. Carolrhoda, 1990 (I:all).

Hoban, Tana. *Count and See.* Macmillan, 1972 (I:4–7).

_____. *26 Letters and 99 Cents.* Greenwillow, 1987 (I:4–7).

Knight. Hilary. *Hilary Knight's The Twelve Days of Christmas.* Macmillan, 1981 (I:all).

Lavis, Steve. *Cock-A-Doodle-DOO.* Lodestar, 1997 (I:2–6).

Leuck, Laura. *One Witch.* Illustrated by S. D. Schindler. Walker, 2003 (I:5–8).

Lobel, Anita. *One Lighthouse, One Moon.* Greenwillow, 2000 (I:4–7).

MacDonald, Suse. *Look Whooo's Counting.* Scholastic, 2000 (I:3–6).

McMillan, Bruce. *Eating Fractions.* Scholastic, 1991 (I:5–8).

Morales, Yuyi. *Just a Minute: A Trickster Tale and Counting Book.* Chronicle, 2003 (I:4–7).

Reiser, Lynn. *Ten Puppies.* Greenwillow, 2003 (I:3–6).

Sayre, April Pulley, and Jeff Sayre. *One Is a Snail, Ten Is a Crab: A Counting by Feet Book.* Illustrated by Randy Cecil. Candlewick, 2003 (I:4–8).

Schmandt-Besserat, Denise. *The History of Counting.* Illustrated by Michael Hays. Morrow, 1999 (I:8+)

Sierra, Lucy. *Counting Crocodiles.* Illustrated by Will Hillenbrand. Harcourt Brace, 1997 (I:3–7).

Sturges, Philemon. *Ten Flashing Fireflies.* Illustrated by Anna Vojtech. North-South, 1995 (I:3–7).

Tafuri, Nancy. *Who's Counting?* Greenwillow, 1986 (I:3–6).

Walsh, Ellen Stoll. *Mouse Count.* Harcourt Brace, 1991 (I:3–6).

Wells, Rosemary. *Emily's First 100 Days of School.* Hyperion, 2000 (I:4–8).

Wormell, Christopher. *Teeth, Tails, & Tentacles: An Animal Counting Book.* Running Press, 2004 (I:3–8).

CONCEPT BOOKS

Barton, Byron. *Machines at Work.* Crowell, 1987 (I:2–6).

Carle, Eric. *The Grouchy Ladybug.* Crowell, 1971 (I:4–7).

_____. *The Mixed-Up Chameleon.* Crowell, 1975 (I:2–6).

_____. *My Very First Book of Colors.* Crowell, 1974 (I:3–6).

_____. *My Very First Book of Shapes.* Crowell, 1974 (I:4–7).

Crews, Donald. *Carousel.* Greenwillow, 1982 (I:4–8).

_____. *Freight Train.* Greenwillow, 1978 (I:3–7).

_____. *Harbor.* Greenwillow, 1982 (I:3–7).

Falwell, Cathryn. *Shape Space.* Clarion, 1992 (I:4–7).

Floca, Brian. *Five Trucks.* DK, 1999 (I:2–5).

Freymann, Saxton, *Food for Thought: The Complete Book of Concepts for Growing Minds.* Scholastic, 2005 (I:3–7).

Gibbons, Gail. *Trains.* Holiday House, 1987 (I:4–7).

Hoban, Tana. *Circles, Triangles, and Squares.* Macmillan, 1974 (I:4–8).

_____. *Look! Look! Look!.* Greenwillow, 1988 (I:3–6).

_____. *Of Colors and Things.* Greenwillow, 1989 (I:3–6).

_____. *Over, Under and Through and Other Spatial Concepts.* Macmillan, 1973 (I:3–7).

_____. *Shapes, Shapes, Shapes.* Greenwillow, 1986 (I:3–8).

_____. *So Many Circles, So Many Squares.* Greenwillow, 1998 (I:4–8).

Hutchins, Pat. *What Game Shall We Play?* Greenwillow, 1990 (I:3–7).

Jenkins, Steve. *Big & Little.* Houghton Mifflin, 1996 (I:3–6).

Kalan, Robert. *Blue Sea.* Illustrated by Donald Crews. Greenwillow, 1979 (I:3–7).

Micklethwait, Lucy. *I Spy Shapes in Art.* Greenwillow, 2004 (I:4–10).

Rockwell, Anne. *First Comes Spring.* Crowell, 1985 (I:3–6).

Rotner, Shelley. *Lots of Feelings.* Millbrook, 2003 (I:3–8).

Seeger, Laura Vaccaro. *Lemons Are Not Red.* Roaring Brook, 2004 (I:2–6).

Serfozo, Mary. *What's What? A Guessing Game.* Illustrated by Keiko Narahashi. Simon & Schuster, 1996 (I:2–5).

WORDLESS BOOKS

Anno, Mitsumasa. *Anno's Journey.* Philomel, 1978 (I:6–12).

Baker, Jeannie. *Window.* Greenwillow, 1991 (I:all).

Carle, Eric. *Do You Want to Be My Friend?* Crowell, 1971 (I:3–7).

dePaola, Tomie. *The Hunter and the Animals: A Wordless Picture Book.* Holiday House, 1981 (I:5–9).

_____. *Pancakes for Breakfast.* Harcourt Brace, 1978 (I:3–7).

Feelings, Tom. *The Middle Passage: White Ships/Black Cargo.* Dial, 1995 (I:10+).

Fleischman, Paul. *Sidewalk Circus.* Illustrated by Kevin Hawkes. Candlewick, 2004 (I:all).

Hutchins, Pat. *Changes, Changes.* Macmillan, 1971 (I:2–6).

Lehman, Barbara. *The Red Book.* Houghton Mifflin, 2004 (I:all).

Maizlish, Lisa. *The Ring.* Greenwillow, 1996 (I:all).

Mayer, Mercer. *A Boy, a Dog, a Frog, and a Friend,* Dial, 1971 (I:5–9).

_____. *A Boy, a Dog and a Frog.* Dial, 1967 (I:5–9).

_____. *Frog Goes to Dinner.* Dial, 1974 (I:6–9).

_____. and Marianna Mayer. *One Frog Too Many.* Dial, 1975 (I:5–9).

McCully, Emily Arnold. *Four Hungry Kittens.* Dial, 2001 (I:3–7).

_____. *Picnic.* Harper & Row, 1984 (I:3–7).

_____. *School.* Harper & Row, 1987 (I:3–8).

Rogers, Gregory. *The Boy, The Bear, The Baron, The Bard.* Roaring Brook, 2004 (I:all).

Sís, Peter, *Dinosaur!* Greenwillow, 2000 (I:3–8).

Spier, Peter. *Noah's Ark.* Doubleday, 1977 (I:3–9).

Van Allsburg, Chris. *The Mysteries of Harris Burdick.* Houghton Mifflin, 1984 (I:all).

Wiesner, David. *Free Fall.* Lothrop, Lee & Shepard, 1988 (I:all).

_____. *Sector 7.* Clarion, 1999 (I:all).

_____. *Tuesday.* Clarion, 1991 (I:all).

EASY-TO-READ BOOKS

Allen, Laura Jean. *Rollo and Tweedy and the Ghost at Dougal Castle.* HarperCollins, 1992 (I;5–9).

Benchley, Nathaniel. *Oscar Otter.* Illustrated by Arnold Lobel. Harper & Row, 1966 (I;5–9 R:2).

_____. *Small Wolf.* Illustrated by Joan Sandin. Harper & Row, 1972 (I;6–10 R:3).

Bonsall, Crosby. *The Case of the Hungry Stranger.* HarperCollins, 1992 (new edition of 1963 publication) (I:5–9).

Brenner, Barbara. *Wagon Wheels.* Illustrated by Don Bolognese. Harper & Row, 1978 (I:6–9 R:1).

Bulla, Clyde Robert. *Daniel's Duck.* Illustrated by Joan Sandin. Harper & Row, 1979 (I:6–9 R:2).

Byars, Betsy. *My Brother, Ant.* Illustrated by Marc Simont. Viking. 1996 (I:6–8 R:2).

Cole, Joanna, & Stephanie Calmenson. *Ready . . . Set . . . Read!* Doubleday, 1990 (I:5–8).

Cushman, Doug. *Inspector Hopper's Mystery Year (An I Can Read Book).* HarperCollins, 2003 (I:5–8).

Griffith, Helen V. *Alex and the Cat.* Illustrated by Joseph Low. Greenwillow, 1982 (I:5–8 R:1).

Hoff, Syd. *Chester.* Harper & Row, 1961 (I:5–8 R:1).

_____. *Sammy the Seal.* Harper & Row, 1959 (I:5–8 R:1).

Hopkins, Lee Bennett, ed. *Surprises.* Illustrated by Megan Lloyd. Harper & Row, 1984 (I:5–9).

Kessler, Leonard. *Kick, Pass, and Run.* Harper & Row, 1966 (I:5–8 R:1).

Levinson, Nancy Smiler. *Snowshoe Thompson.* Illustrated by Joan Sandin. HarperCollins. 1992 (I:5–8).

Little, Jean. *Emma's Strange Pet (An I Can Read Book).* Illustrated by Jennifer Plecas. HarperCollins, 2003 (I:5–8).

Lobel, Arnold, *Frog and Toad All Year.* Harper & Row, 1976 (I:5–8 R:1).

_____. *Frog and Toad Are Friends.* Harper & Row, 1970 (I:5–8 R:1).

_____. *Frog and Toad Together.* Harper & Row, 1972 (I:5–8 R:1).

_____. *Grasshopper on the Road.* Harper & Row, 1978 (I:5–8 R:2).

_____. *Owl at Home.* Harper & Row, 1975 (I:5–8 R:2).

_____. *Uncle Elephant.* Harper & Row, 1981 (I:5–8 R:2).

Marshall, Edward. *Four on the Shore.* Illustrated by James Marshall. Dial, 1985 (I:5–9 R:1).

Milgrim, David. *See Pip Point (Ready-to-Read).* Atheneum, 2003 (I:4–6).

Pomerantz, Charlotte. *Outside Dog.* Illustrated by Jennifer Plecas. HarperCollins, 1993 (I:5–8 R:2).

Rylant, Cynthia. *Henry and Mudge and the Bedtime Thumps.* Illustrated by Sucie Stevenson. Bradbury, 1991 (I:5–8).

_____. *Henry and Mudge and the Great Grandpas.* Illustrated by Sucie Stevenson. Simon & Schuster, 2005 (I:5–8).

_____. *Henry and Mudge and the Long Weekend.* Illustrated by Sucie Stevenson. Bradbury, 1992 (I:5–8).

_____. *Mr. Putter and Tabby Pour the Tea.* Illustrated by Arthur Howard. Harcourt Brace, 1994 (I:6–9).

_____. *Mr. Putter and Tabby Walk the Dog.* Illustrated by Arthur Howard. Harcourt Brace, 1994 (I:6–9).

_____. *Poppleton.* Illustrated by Mark Teague. Scholastic, 1997 (I:4–7).

Schwartz, Alvin. *In a Dark, Dark Room.* Illustrated by Dirk Zimmer. Harper & Row, 1984 (I:6–9 R:2).

Seuss, Dr. *The Cat in the Hat.* Random House, 1957 (I:4–7 R:1).

_____. *The Cat in the Hat Comes Back.* Random House, 1958 (I:4–7 R:1).

Van Laan, Nancy. *Busy Busy Moose.* Illustrated by Amy Rusch. Houghton Mifflin, 2003 (I:4–6).

Van Leeuwen, Jean. *More Tales of Oliver Pig.* Dial, 1981 (I:5–7 R:2).

_____. *Oliver and Amanda's Halloween.* Illustrated by Ann Schweninger. Dial, 1992 (I:5–8).

_____. *Oliver Pig at School.* Illustrated by Ann Schweninger. Dail, 1990 (I:5–8).

_____. *Tales of Oliver Pig.* Illustrated by Arnold Lobel. Dial, 1979 (I:5–7 R:2).

Wiseman, Bernard. *Morris Goes to School.* Harper & Row, 1970 (I:5–8 R:1).

PICTURE STORYBOOKS

Aardema, Verna. *Why Mosquitoes Buzz in People's Ears.* Illustrated by Leo & Diane Dillon, Dial, 1975 (I:5–9 R:6).

Ackerman, Karen. *Song and Dance Man.* Illustrated by Stephen Gammell. Knopf, 1988 (I:3–8 R:4).

Adoff, Arnold. *Black Is Brown Is Tan.* Illustrated by Emily Arnold McCully. Harper & Row, 1973 (I:3–7).

Ahlberg, Janet, and Allan Ahlberg. *Each Peach Pear Plum: An I-Spy Story.* Viking, 1978 (I:3–7).

_____. *The Jolly Postman.* Little, Brown, 1986 (I:3–8).

Appelt, Kathi. *Where, Where Is Swamp Bear?* Illustrated by Megan Halsey. HarperCollins, 2002 (I:4–7).

Asch, Frank. *Moonbear's Pet.* Simon & Schuster, 1997 (I:4–6).

Auch, Mary Jane. *The Easter Egg Farm.* Hoilday House, 1992 (I:3–7 R:4).

_____. *Peeping Beauty.* Hoilday House, 1993 (I:4–8 R:4).

Babbitt. Natalie. *BUB: Or the Very Best Thing.* HarperCollins, 1994 (I:all).

Baker, Jeannie. *Where the Forest Meets the Sea.* Greenwillow, 1988 (I:4–10 R:5).

Baker, Keith. *Little Green.* Harcourt, 2001 (I:2–5).

Bang, Molly. *Goose.* Scholastic, 1996 (I:4–7).

Bannerman, Helen. *The Story of Little Babaji.* Illustrated by Fred Marcellino. HarperCollins, 1996 (I:all).

Baylor, Byrd. *The Best Town in the World.* Illustrated by Ronald Himler. Scribner. 1983 (I:all).

Beaumont, Karen. *I Ain't Gonna Paint No More!* Illustrated by David Catrow. Harcourt, 2005 (I:6–9).

Bedard, Michael. *Emily.* Illustrated by Barbara Cooney. Doubleday, 1992 (I:all).

Best, Cari. *Shrinking Violet.* Illustrated by Giselle Potter. Farrar, Straus & Giroux, 2001.

Bloom, Suzanne. *A Splendid Friend, Indeed.* Boyds Mills, 2005 (I:4–6).

Boedoe, Geefwee. *Arrowville.* HarperCollins, 2004 (I:all, YA).

Bogacki, Tomek. *Cat and Mouse.* Farrar, Straus & Giroux, 1996 (I:3–5).

Bottner, Barbara, and Gerald Kruglik. *Wallace's Lists.* Illustrated by Olof Landstrom. HarperCollins, 2004 (I:5–8).

Brown, Marc. *Arthur's Baby.* Little, Brown, 1987 (I:3–6 R:3).

_____. *Arthur Goes to Camp.* Little, Brown, 1982 (I:3–6 R:3).

_____. *Arthur's Family Vacation.* Little, Brown, 1993 (I:3–6 R:3).

Brown, Margaret Wise. *On Christmas Eve.* Illustrated by Nancy Edwards. Calder, 1996 (I:5–8).

_____. *The Runaway Bunny.* Rev. ed. Illustrated by Clement Hurd. Harper & Row, 1972 (I:2–7 R:6).

_____. *The Important Book.* Illustrated by Leonard Weisgard. Harper, 1949 (I:3–8 R:4).

Buchholz, Quint. *The Collector of Moments.* Translated by Peter F. Neumeyer. Farrar, Straus & Giroux, 1999 (I:all).

Bunting, Eve, *Flower Garden.* Illustrated by Kathryn Hewitt. Harcourt Brace, 1994 (I:3–6).

_____. *Ghost's Hour, Spook's Hour.* Illustrated by Donald Carrick. Clarion, 1987 (I:2–7 R:2).

_____. *The Mother's Day Mice.* Illustrated by Jan Brett. Clarion, 1986 (I:3–6).

_____. *My Backpack.* Illustrated by Maryann Cocca-Leffler. Boyds Mills, 1997 (I:4–8).

_____. *Smoky Night.* Illustrated by David Diaz. Harcourt Brace, 1994 (I:all).

_____. *The Wednesday Surprise.* Illustrated by Donald Carrick. Clarion, 1989 (I:3–9 R:5).

Burton, Virginia Lee. *Katy and the Big Snow.* Houghton Mifflin, 1943, 1971 (I:2–6 R:4).

_____. *The Little House.* Houghton Mifflin, 1942 (I:3–7 R:3).

_____. *Mike Mulligan and His Steam Shovel.* Houghton Mifflin, 1939 (I:2–6 R:4).

Calmenson, Stephanie, and Joanna Cole. *Rockin' Reptiles.* Illustrated by Lynn Munsinger. Morrow, 1997 (I:7–9 R:4).

Cannon, Janell, *Verdi.* Harcourt Brace, 1997 (I:4–10 R:5).

Carlstrom, Nancy White, *Jesse Bear, What Will You Wear?* Illustrated by Bruce Degen. Macmillan, 1986 (I:3–6).

Cazet, Denys, *A Fish in His Pocket.* Watts, 1987 (I:3–6 R:4).

Cendrars, Blaise, *Shadow.* Illustrated by Marcia Brown. Scribner, 1982 (I:all).

Chen, Chih-Yuan. *Guji Guji.* Kane/Miller, 2004 (I:4–8).

Child, Lauren. *I Am Too Absolutely Small for School*. Candlewick, 2004 (I:4–7).

Cole, Brock *Buttons*. Farrar, Straus & Giroux, 2000 (I:6+ R:4).

Condra, Estelle, *See the Ocean*. Illustrated by Linda Crockett-Blassingame. Ideals, 1994. (I:6–10 R:4).

Conrad, Pam. *Call Me Ahnighito*. llustrated by Richard Egielski. HarperCollins, 1995 (I:7+ R:5).

Cook, Sally. *Good Night Pillow Fight*. Illustrated by Laura Cornell. HarperCollins, 2004 (I:4–8).

Cooney, Barbara. *Miss Rumphius*. Viking, 1982 (I:5–8).

Cooper, Helen. *The Boy Who Would Not Go to Bed*. Dial, 1997 (I:3–6).

Crews, Donald. *Night At the Fair*. Greenwillow, 1998. (I:4–7).

_____. *Shortcut*. Greenwillow, 1992 (I:4–8 R:4).

Cronin, Doreen, *Click, Clack Moo: Cows That Type*. Illustrated by Betsy Lewin. Simon & Schuster, 2000 (I:4–7).

_____. *Duck for President*. Illustrated by Betsy Lewin. Simon & Schuster, 2004 (I:4–8).

Crunk, Tony. *Big Mama*. Illustrated by Margot Apple. Farrar, Straus & Giroux, 2000 (I:5–8 R:4).

Curtis, Carolyn. *I Took the Moon for a Walk*. Illustrated by Alison Jay. Barefoot, 2004 (I:5–8).

Curtis, Jamie Lee. *Tell Me Again About the Night I Was Born*. Illustrated by Laura Cornell. HarperCollins, 1996 (I:4–7 R:4).

Cutler, Jane, *The Cello of Mr. O*. Illustrated by Greg Couch. Dutton, 1999 (I:7+ R:5).

_____. *Darcy and Gran Don't Like Babies*. Illustrated by Susannah Ryan. Scholastic, 1993 (I:3–7 R:3).

Dadey, Debbie. *Shooting Star: Annie Oakely, the Legend*. Illustrated by Scott Goto. Walker, 1997 (I:5–9 R:5).

de Brunhoff, Jean. *The Story of Babar*. Random House, 1933, 1961 (I:3–9 R:4).

_____., and Laurent de Brunhoff. *Babar's Anniversary Album: 6 Favorite Stories*. Random House, 1981 (I:3–9 R:4)

DeFelice, Cynthia. *Willy's Silly Grandma:* Illustrated by Shelley Jackson, Orchard, 1997 (I:5–8 R:4).

dePaola, Tomie. *The Clown of God*. Harcourt Brace, 1978 (I:all R:4).

_____. *An Early American Christmas*. Holiday House, 1987 (I:4–7 R:6).

_____. *Nana Upstairs & Nana Downstairs*. Putnam, 1973 (I:3–7 R:6).

_____. *Oliver Button Is a Sissy*. Harcourt Brace, 1979 (I:5–8 R:2).

Duvoisin, Roger. *Petunia*. Knopf, 1950 (I:3–6 R:6).

Dyer, Jane. *Little Brown Bear Won't Go to School!* Little, Brown, 2003 (I:3–6).

Ehlert, Lois. *Mole's Hill*. Harcourt Brace, 1994 (I:3–8).

Emberley, Barbara. *Drummer Hoff*. Illustrated by Ed Ernberley. Prentice Hall, 1967 (I:3–7 R:6).

Engel, Diana. *Josephina Hates Her Name*. Morrow, 1989 (I:5–8 R:4).

English, Karen. *Hot Day on Abbott Avenue*. Illustrated by Javaka Steptoe. Clarion, 2004 (I:5–8).

Ericsson, Jennifer A. *No Milk!* Illustrated by Ora Eitan. Tambourine, 1993 (I:3–8).

Ernst. Lisa Campbell. *Walter's Tail*. Bradbury, 1992 (I:4–8 R:4).

_____. *When Bluebell Sang*. Bradbury, 1989 (I:4–8 R:5).

Esbaum, Jill. *Ste-e-e-eam Boat A-Comin'!* Illustrated by Adam Rex. Farrar, Stratus & Giroux, 2005 (I:7–9).

Falconer, Ian, *Olivia*. Simon & Schuster. 2000 (I:3–8 R:4).

_____. *Olivia Saves the Circus*. Simon & Schuster, 2001 (I:3–8 R:4)

Fleischman, Paul. *Time Train*. Illustrated by Claire Ewart. HarperCollins, 1991 (I:4–8 R:4).

_____. *Weslandia*. Illustrated by Kevin Hawkes. Candlewick, 1999 (I:8+ R:5).

Fleischman, Sid. *The Scarebird*. Illustrated by Peter Sís. Greenwillow, 1988 (I:5–9 R:5).

Fleming, Candace. *The Hatmaker's Sign: A Story by Benjamin Franklin*. Illustrated by Robert Andrew Parker. Orchard, 1998 (I:5–9 R:5).

_____. *When Agnes Caws*. Illustrated by Giselle Potter. Atheneum, 1999 (I:4–9 R:4).

_____. *Muncha! Muncha! Muncha!* Illustrated by G. Brian Karas. Atheneum, 2002 (I:5–8).

Fleming, Denise. *Lunch*. Holt, 1992 (I:2–7).

Fletcher, Ralph. *Twilight Comes Twice*. Illustrated by Kate Kiesler. Clarion, 1997 (I:6–10 R:3).

Fox, Mem, *Hattie and the Fox*. Illustrated by Patricia Mullins. Bradbury, 1987 (I:3–7).

_____. *Night Noises*. Illustrated by Terry Denton. Harcourt Brace, 1989 (I:3–8 R:5).

_____. *Wombat Divine*. Illustrated by Kerry Argent. Harcourt Brace, 1996 (I:4–7).

Frank, John. *The Toughest Cowboy: Or How the West Was Won*. Illustrated by Zachary Pullen. Simon & Schuster, 2004 (I:5–8).

Gág, Wanda. *Millions of Cats*. Coward, McCann, 1929 (I:3–7 R:3).

Galbraith, Kathryn O. *Laura Charlotte*. Illustrated by Floyd Cooper. Putnam, 1990 (I:4–6 R:4).

Gammell, Stephen. *Wake Up Bear . . . It's Christmas!* Lothrop, Lee & Shepard, 1981 (I:5–8 R:4).

Gantos, Jack, *Rotten Ralph's Rotten Romance*. Houghton Mifflin, 1997 (I:4–8 R:4).

Gauch, Patricia Lee. *Christina Katerina and the Time She Quit the Family*. Illustrated by Elise Primavera. Putnam, 1987 (I:4–8 R:6).

Geeslin, Campbell. *Elena's Serenade*. Illustrated by Ana Juan. Simon & Schuster, 2004 (I:5–9).

Giovanni, Nikki. *Rosa*. Illustrated by Brian Collier, Henry Holt, 2005.

Graham, Bob. *Benny: An Adventure Story*. Candlewick, 1999 (I:3–7 R:4).

_____. *Tales From the Waterhole*. Candlewick, 2004 (I:5–8).

Gray, Libba Moore. *My Mama Had a Dancing Heart*. Illustrated by Raúl Colón. Orchard, 1995 (I:7–11 R:5).

Griffith, Helen V. *Grandaddy and Janetta*. Illustrated by James Stevenson. Greenwillow, 1993 (I:6–10 R:5).

_____. *Grandaddy's Place*. Illustrated by James Stevenson. Greenwillow, 1987 (I:4–8 R:4).

Haas, Irene. *A Summer Song*. Simon & Schuster, 1997 (I:4–8 R:4).

Haley, Gail E. *A Story, a Story*. Atheneum, 1970 (I:6–10 R:6).

Hall, Bruce Edward. *Henry and the Kite Dragon*. Illustrated by William Low. Philomel, 2004 (I:5–8).

Hanson, Regina. *The Face at the Window*. Illustrated by Linda Saport. Clarion, 1997 (I:5–8 R:4).

Harris, Robie H. *Don't Forget to Come Back!* Illustrated by Harry Bliss. Candlewick, 2004 (I:4–8).

Hartmann, Wendy, & Niki Daly. *The Dinosaurs Are Back and It's All Your Fault Edward!* McElderry, 1997 (I:5–8 R:4).

Henkes, Kevin, *Jessica*. Greenwillow, 1989 (I:3–6 R:5).

_____. *Kitten's First Full Moon*. Greenwillow, 2004 (I:3–5).

_____. *Lily's Purple Plastic Purse*. Greenwillow, 1996 (I:4–8 R:4).

_____. *Owen*. Greenwillow, 1993 (I:2–5 R:4).

Herriot, James. *Moses the Kitten*. Illustrated by Peter Barrett. St. Martin's, 1984 (I:all R:5).

Hest, Amy. *Baby Duck and the Bad Eyeglasses*. Illustrated by Jill Barton. Candlewick. 1996 (I:3–8 R:5).

_____. *In the Rain With Baby Duck*. Illustrated by Jill Barton. Candlewick, 1995 (I:3–8 R:5).

_____. *Off to School, Baby Duck!* Illustrated by Jill Barton. Candlewick. 1999 (I:3–6 R:4).

Hicks, Barbara Jean, and Alexis Deacon. *Jitter-Bug Jam: A Monster Tale*. Illustrated by Alexis Deacon. Farrar, Straus & Giroux, 2005 (I:4–8).

Ho, Minfong. *Hush! A Thai Lullaby*. Illustrated by Holly Meade. Orchard, 1996 (I:3–8).

Hoban, Russell. *A Baby Sister for Frances*. Illustrated by Lillian Hoban. Harper & Row, 1964 (I:5–8 R:4).

_____. *A Bargain for Frances*. Illustrated by Lillian Hoban. Harper & Row, 1970 (I:4–8 R:2).

_____. *Best Friends for Frances*. Illustrated by Lillian Hoban. Harper & Row, 1969 (I:4–8 R:4).

_____. *Bread and Jam for Frances*. Illustrated by Lillian Hoban. Harper & Row, 1964 (I:4–8 R:4).

Hoberman, Mary Ann. *You Read to Me, I'll Read to You: Very Short Stories to Read Together*. Illustrated by Michael Emberley. Little, Brown, 2001 (I:4–8).

Hoestlandt. Jo. *Star of Fear, Star of Hope*. Illustrated by Johanna Kang. Walker. 1995 (I:all).

hooks, bell. *Skin Again*. Illustrated by Chris Raschka. Hyperion, 2004 (I:3–5).

Horse, Harry. *Little Rabbit Goes to School*. Peachtree, 2004 (I:4–6).

Houston, Gloria. *My Great-Aunt Arizona*. Illustrated by Susan Condie Lamb. HarperCollins, 1992 (I:5–9 R:5).

Hughes, Shirley, *Alfie Gives a Hand*. Lothrop, Lee & Shepard, 1983 (I:3–6 R:4).

Hunter, Anne. *Possum's Harvest Moon*. Houghton Mifflin, 1996 (I:3–6).

Hurd, Edith Thacher. *I Dance in My Red Pajamas*. Illustrated by Emily Arnold McCully. Harper & Row, 1982 (I:3–7 R:3).

Hutchins, Pat. *Happy Birthday, Sam*. Greenwillow, 1978 (I:3–6 R:4).

_____. *Where's the Baby?* Greenwillow, 1988 (I:3–6 R:4).

_____. *The Wind Blew*. Macmillan, 1974 (I:3–6 R:4).

Innocenti, Roberto. *Rose Blanche*. Stewart, Tabori & Chang, 1985 (I:all).

Isaacs. Anne. *Swamp Angel*. Illustrated by Paul O. Zelinsky. Dutton, 1994 (I:all).

Isadora, Rachel. *Young Mozart*. Viking, 1997 (I:4–8 R:5).

James, Simon. *Dear Mr. Blueberry*. Macmillan, 1991 (I:4–7 R:4).

Janisch, Heinz, *Noah's Ark*. Illustrated by Lisbeth Zwerger. Translated by Rosemary Lanning. North-South, 1997 (I:6–9).

Johnson, Angela, *Julius*. Illustrated by Dav Pilkey. Orchard, 1993 (I:3–8 R:4).

_____. *The Rolling Store*. Illustrated by Peter Catalanotto. Orchard, 1997 (I:4–8 R:4).

Johnson, D. B. *Henry Hikes to Fitchburg*. Houghton Mifflin, 2000 (I:4–8 R:5).

Johnson, Paul Brett. *The Cow Who Wouldn't Come Down*. Orchard, 1993 (I:5–8 R:5).

Joosse, Barbara. *Hot City*. Illsutrated by R. Gregory Christie. Philomel, 2004 (I:5–9).

Jorgensen, Gail. *Gotcha!* Illustrated by Kerry Argent. Scholastic, 1997 (I:3–7).

Joyce, William. *Dinosaur Bob and His Adventures With the Family Lazardo*. Harper & Row, 1988 (I:5–9 R:5).

_____. *Santa Calls*. HarperCollins, 1993 (I:4–9 R:6).

Jukes, Mavis. *Like Jake and Me*. Illustrated by Lloyd Bloom. Knopf, 1984 (I:6–9 R:4).

Juster, Norton. *The Hello, Goodbye Window*. Illustrated by Chris Raschka. Hyperion, 2005 (I:4–8).

Keats, Ezra Jack. *Dreams*. Macmillan, 1974 (I:3–8 R:3).

_____. *Goggles!* Macmillan, 1969 (I:5–9 R:3).

_____. *A Letter to Amy*. Harper & Row, 1968 (I:3–8 R:3).

_____. *Maggie and the Pirate*. Four Winds, 1979 (I:4–8 R:3).

_____. *Peter's Chair*. Harper & Row, 1967 (I:3–8 R:2).

_____. *Regards to the Man in the Moon*. Four Winds, 1981 (I:4–8 R:3).

_____. *The Trip*. Greenwillow, 1978 (I:3–8 R:2).

Kellogg, Steven. *I Was Born About 10,000 Years Ago*. Morrow, 1996 (I:all).

_____. *A Penguin Pup for Pinkerton*. Dial, 2001 (I:4–8 R:3).

_____. *A Rose for Pinkerton*. Dial, 1981 (I:4–8 R:3).

Kessler, Christina, *Jubela*. Illustrated by JoEllen McAllister Stammen. Simon & Schuster, 2001 (I:4–8).

Khalsa, Dayal Kaur. *I Want a Dog*. Clarkson, 1987 (I:4–7 R:5).

Kimmel, Eric A. *The Chanukkah Guest*. Illustrated by Giora Carmi. Holiday House, 1990 (I:5–9 R:5).

_____. *The Chanukkah Tree*. Illustrated by Giora Carmi. Holiday House, 1988 (I:5–9 R:5).

Kirk, Connie Ann. *Sky Dancers*. Illustrated by Christy Hale. Lee & Low, 2004 (I:7–9).

Kleven, Elisa. *The Puddle Pail*. Dutton, 1997 (I:4–8).

Kodama, Tatsuharu. *Shin's Tricycle*. Illustrated by Noriyuki Ando. Walker, 1995 (I:all).

Kraus, Robert. *Leo the Late Bloomer*. Illustrated by Jose & Ariane Aruego. Windmill, 1971 (I:2–6 R:4).

Kurtz, Jane. *Faraway Home*. Illustrated by E. B. Lewis. Harcourt, 2000 (I:5–8 R:5).

Kushner, Tony. *Brundibar*. Illustrated by Maurice Sendak. Hyperion, 2003 (I:9+).

Leaf, Munro. *The Story of Ferdinand*. Illustrated by Robert Lawson. Viking, 1936 (I:4–10 R:6).

L'Engle, Madeleine. *The Other Dog*. Illustrated by Christine Davenier. North-South, 2001 (I:5–8).

Lester, Helen, *Hooway for Wodney Wat*. Illustrated by Lynn Munsinger. Houghton Mifflin, 1999 (I:6+).

Lester, Julius. *Sam and the Tigers: A New Tale of Little Black Sambo*. Illustrated by Jerry Pinkney. Dial, 1996 (I:all).

Lewis, Kim. *Good Night Harry*. Candlewick, 2004 (I:2–5).

Lewis, Paul Owen. *Storm Boy*. Beyond Words, 1995 (I:7+ R:5).

Lindbergh, Reeve. *The Day the Goose Got Loose.* Illustrated by Steven Kellogg. Dial, 1990 (I:5–8 R:4).

Lionni, Leo. *Alexander and the Wind-up Mouse.* Pantheon, 1969 (I:3–6 R:3).

Littlesugar, Amy. *Marie in Fourth Position: The Story of Degos' "The Little Dancer."* Illustrated by Ian Schoenherr. Philomel, 1996 (I:6–8).

Loomis, Christine. *Astro Bunnies.* Illustrated by Ora Eitan. Putnam, 2001 (I:4–7).

Lum, Kate. *What! Cried Granny: An Almost Bedtime Story.* Illustrated by Adrian Johnson. Dial, 1999 (I:2–6 R:4).

Lyon, George Ella. *Come a Tide.* Illustrated by Stephen Gammell. Orchard, 1990 (I:5–8 R:5).

_____. *Dreamplace.* Illustrated by Peter Catalanotto. Orchard, 1993 (I:all).

Macaulay, David. *Why the Chicken Crossed the Road.* Houghton Mifflin, 1987 (I:5–9 R:6).

MacLachlan, Patricia, and Emily MacLachlan. *Bittle.* Illustrated by Dan Yaccarino. HarperCollins, 2004 (I:3–7).

Manzano, Sonia. *No Dogs Allowed!* Illustrated by Jon J. Muth. Atheneum, 2004 (I:5–8).

Marshall, James. *George and Martha One Fine Day.* Houghton Mifflin, 1978 (I:3–8).

Martin, Bill, and John Archambault. *Up and Down on the Merry-Go-Round.* Illustrated by Ted Rand. Holt, Rinehart & Winston, 1988 (I:3–8).

Martin, Jacqueline Briggs. *Buzzy Bones and the Lost Quilt.* Illustrated by Stella Ormai. Lothrop, Lee & Shepard, 1988 (I:4–8 R:6).

_____. *Good Times on Grandfather Mountain.* Illustrated by Susan Gaber. Orchard, 1992 (I:4–8 R:4).

Martin, Rafe. *Will's Mammoth.* Illustrated by Stephen Gammell. Putnam, 1989 (I:2–8).

Maruki, Toshi. *Hiroshima No Pika.* Lothrop, Lee & Shepard, 1982 (I:10+ R:4).

Mathis, Sharon Bell. *The Hundred Penny Box.* Illustrated by Leo & Diane Dillon. Viking, 1975 (I:6–9 R:3).

Mayer, Mercer. *There's a Nightmare in My Closet.,* Dial, 1969 (I:3–7 R:3).

McCloskey, Robert. *Blueberries for Sal.* Viking, 1948 (I:4–8 R:6).

_____. *Lentil.* Viking, 1940 (I:4–9 R:7).

_____. *Make Way for Ducklings.* Viking, 1941 (I:4–8 R:4).

_____. *One Morning in Maine.* Viking, 1952 (I:4–8 R:3).

_____. *Time of Wonder.* Viking, 1957 (I:5–8 R:4).

McCully, Emily Arnold. *Mirette on the High Wire.* Putnam, 1992 (I:5–9 R:5).

_____. *Starring Mirette & Bellini.* Putnam, 1997 (I:all).

McDonald, Megan. *The Great Pumpkin Switch.* Illustrated by Ted, Lewin. Orchard, 1992 (I:5–8 R:4).

McKissack, Patricia. *The Honest-to-Goodness Truth.* Illustrated by Giselle Potter. Atheneum, 2000 (I:5–9 R:4).

_____. *Nettie Jo's Friends.* Illustrated by Scott Cook. Knopf, 1989 (I:5–9 R:5).

McPhail, David. *Edward and the Pirates.* Little, Brown, 1997 (I:5–8 R:4).

_____. *Fix-it.* Dutton, 1984 (I:3 R:2).

Meddaugh, Susan. *The Best Place.* Houghton Mifflin, 1999 (I:4–8 R:4).

_____. *Martha Speaks.* Houghton Mifflin, 1992 (I:4–8 R:4).

Melmed, Laura Krauss. *The First Song Ever Sung.* Illustrated by Ed Young. Lothrop, Lee & Shepard, 1993 (I:3–6).

Milne, A. A. *Winnie-the-Pooh.* Illustrated by Ernest H. Shepard. Dutton, 1926, 1954 (I:6–10 R:5).

Monson, A. M. *Wanted: Best Friend.* Illustrated by Lynn Munsinger. Dial, 1997 (I:4–8 R:4).

Moss, Lloyd. *Zin! Zin! Zin! A Violin.* Illustrated by Marjorie Priceman. Simon & Schuster, 1995 (I:all).

Murphy, Mary. *I Like It When . . .* Harcourt Brace, 1997 (I:3–5).

Muth, Jon J. *Zen Shorts.* Scholastic, 2005 (I:all).

Myers, Tim. *Basho and the River Stones.* Illustrated by Oki S. Han. Marshall Cavendish, 2004 (I:6–10).

Myers, Walter Dean. *Harlem.* Illustrated by Christopher Myers. Scholastic, 1997 (I:all).

Naylor, Phyllis Reynolds. *Keeping a Christmas Secret.* Illustrated by Lena Shiffman. Atheneum, 1989 (I:3–7 R:3).

Ness, Evaline. *Sam, Bangs & Moonshine.* Holt, Rinehart & Winston, 1966 (I:5–9 R:3).

Newman, Lesléa. *Cats, Cats, Cats!* Illustrated by Erika Oller. Simon & Schuster, 2001 (I:4–8).

Nivola, Claire. *Elisabeth.* Farrar, Straus & Giroux, 1997 (I:4–8 R:4).

Numeroff, Laura. *The Chicken Sisters.* Illustrated by Sharleen Collicott. HarperCollins, 1997 (I:4–7).

Pak, Soyung. *Sumi's First Day of School Ever.* Illustrated by Joung Un Kim. Viking, 2003 (I:5–8).

Paz, Octavio. Translated by Catherine Cowan. *My Life with the Wave.* Illustrated by Mark Buehner. Lothrop, Lee & Shepard, 1997 (I:4–8).

Peet, Bill. *Cyrus the Unsinkable Sea Serpent.* Houghton Mifflin, 1975 (I:5–9 R:7).

_____. *The Gnats of Knotty Pine.* Houghton Mifflin, 1975 (I:5–9 R:6).

_____. *No Such Things.* Houghton Mifflin, 1983 (I:4–8 R:6).

Plourde, Lynn. *Pigs in the Mud in the Middle of the Rud.* Illustrated by John Schoenherr. Scholastic, 1997 (I:3–7).

Polacco, Patricia. *Appelemando's Dreams.* Philomel, 1991 (I:6–9 R:5).

_____. *Babushka Baba Yaga.* Philomel, 1993 (I:5–8 R:5).

_____. *The Bee Tree.* Philomel, 1993 (I:5–8 R:5).

_____. *The Butterfly.* Philomel, 2000 (I:6–9 R:5).

_____. *John Philip Duck.* Philomel, 2004 (I:5–8).

_____. *Meteor!* Dodd, Mead, 1987 (I:6–10 R:7).

_____. *Thunder Cake.* Philomel, 1990 (I:5–8 R:5).

Porte, Barbara Ann. *Harry in Trouble.* Illustrated by Yossi Abolafia. Greenwillow, 1989 (I:3–7 R:2).

Purdy, Carol. *Least of All.* Illustrated by Tim Arnold. Macmillan, 1987 (I:5–8 R:5).

Ransome, Arthur. *The Fool of the World and the Flying Ship.* Illustrated by Uri Shulevitz. Farrar, Straus & Giroux, 1968 (I:6–10 R:6).

Raschka, Chris. *Yo! Yes?* Orchard, 1993 (I:3–7).

Rathmann, Peggy. *Officer Buckle and Gloria.* Putnam, 1995 (I:all).

Reiser, Lynn. *Best Friends Think Alike.* Greenwillow, 1997 (I:3–6).

Rey, Hans. *Curious George.* Houghton Mifflin, 1941, 1969 (I:2–7 R:2).

Riley, Linnea. *Mouse Mess.* Scholastic, 1997 (I:4–7).

Rodman, Mary Ann. *My Best Friend.* Illustrated by E. B. Lewis. Viking, 2005 (I:5–7).

Rosen, Michael. *We're Going on a Bear Hunt.* Illustrated by Helen Oxenbury. Macmillan, 1989 (I:2–7).

Rylant, Cynthia. *Mr. Griggs' Work.* Illustrated by Julie Downing. Watts, 1989 (I:4–8 R:5).

———. *The Old Woman Who Named Things.* Illustrated by Kathryn Brown. Harcourt Brace, 1996 (I:4–8).

———. *When I Was Young in the Mountains.* Dutton, 1985 (I:4–7 R:3).

Schotter, Roni. *Captain Snap and the Children of Vinegar Lane.* Illustrated by Marcia Sewall. Orchard, 1989 (I:5–9 R:5).

———. *Nothing Ever Happens on 90th Street.* Illustrated by Kyrsten Brooker. Orchard, 1997 (I:6–9 R:4).

Schwartz, Amy. *Annabella Swift, Kindergartner.* Orchard, 1988 (I:4–7 R:4).

Sendak, Maurice. *In the Night Kitchen.* Harper & Row, 1970 (I:5–7).

———. *Seven Little Monsters.* Harper & Row, 1977 (I:5–8).

———. *The Sign on Rosie's Door.* Harper & Row, 1960 (I:5–9 R:2).

———. *Where the Wild Things Are.* Harper & Row, 1963 (I:4–8 R:6).

Seuss, Dr. *And to Think That I Saw It on Mulberry Street.* Vanguard, 1937 (I:3–9 R:5).

———. *The 500 Hats of Bartholomew Cubbins.* Vanguard, 1938 (I:4–9 R:4).

———. *Horton Hatches the Egg.* Random House, 1940, 1968 (I:3–9 R:4).

———. *Hunches in Bunches.* Random House, 1982 (I:6–10 R:4).

———. *If I Ran the Zoo.* Random House, 1950 (I:4–10 R:3).

Shange, Ntozake. *Ellington Was Not a Street.* Illustrated by Kadir Nelson. Simon & Schuster, 2004 (I:all).

Shannon, David. *Alice the Fairy.* Scholastic, 2004 (I:4–8).

Sharmat, Marjorie Weinman. *The Best Valentine in the World.* Illustrated by Lilian Obligado. Holiday House, 1982 (I:3–7 R:4).

Simont, Marc, retold by. *The Stray Dog: From a True Story by Reiko Sassa.* HarperCollins, 2001 (I:4–8 R:4).

Sis, Peter. *Starry Messenger.* Farrar, Straus & Giroux, 1996 (I:all).

Sisulu, Elinor Batezat. *The Day Gogo Went to Vote: South Africa, April 1994.* Illustrated by Sharon Wilson. Little, Brown, 1996 (I:4–8 R:5).

Small, David *Imogene's Antlers.* Crown, 1985 (I:5–8 R:6).

So, Meilo. *Gobble, Gobble, Slip, Slop: A Tale of a Very Greedy Cat.* Knopf, 2004 (I:5–8).

Spier, Peter. *The Star-Spangled Banner.* Doubleday, 1973 (I:8+).

Spinelli, Eileen. *Night Shift Daddy.* Illustrated by Melissa Iwa. Hyperion, 2000 (I:3–6).

Steig, William. *The Amazing Bone.* Farrar, Straus & Giroux, 1976 (I:6–9 R:3).

———. *Caleb & Kate.* Farrar, Straus & Giroux, 1977 (I:6–9 R:3).

———. *Spinky Sulks.* Farrar, Straus & Giroux, 1988 (I:3–7 R:5).

———. *Sylvester and the Magic Pebble.* Simon & Schuster, 1969 (I:6–9 R:5).

———. *Toby Where Are You?* Illustrated by Teryl Euvremer. Harcourt Brace, 1997 (I:3–6).

Stevens, Janet. *Tops & Bottoms.* Harcourt Brace, 1995 (I:4–7).

Stevenson, James. *Could Be Worse!* Greenwillow, 1977 (I:5–9 R:3).

———. *Don't You Know There's a War On?* Greenwillow, 1992 (I:all).

———. *July.* Greenwillow, 1990 (I:5–8 R:4).

Stewart, Sarah. *The Gardener.* Illustrated by David Small. Farrar, Straus & Giroux, 1997 (I:5–8 R:4).

Sykes, Julie. *Dora's Eggs.* Illustrated by Jane Chapman. Little Tiger, 1997 (I:3–7 R:4).

Taback, Simms, *Joseph Had a Little Overcoat.* Viking, 1999 (I:all).

Thomas, Dylan. *A Child's Christmas in Wales.* Illustrated by Chris Raschka. Candlewick, 2004 (I:8–YA).

Thompson, Lauren. *Polar Bear Night.* Illustrated by Stephen Savage. Scholastic, 2004 (I:3–6).

Trivizas, Eugene. *The Three Little Wolves and the Big Bad Pig.* Illustrated by Helen Oxenbury. Macmillan, 1993 (I:4–9 R:4).

Tsubakiyama, Margaret Holloway. *Mei-Mei Loves the Morning.* Illustrated by Cornelius Van Wright & Ying-Hwa Hu. Albert Whitman, 1999.

Turner, Ann. *Shaker Hearts.* Illustrated by Wendell Minor. HarperCollins, 1997 (I:all).

Ungerer, Tomi. *The Beast of Monsieur Racine.* Farrar, Straus & Giroux, 1971 (I:5–9 R:5).

Van Allsburg, Chris. *Jumanji.* Houghton Mifflin, 1981 (I:5–8 R:6).

———. *The Polar Express.* Houghton Mifflin, 1985 (I:5–8 R:6).

———. *The Sweetest Fig.* Houghton Mifflin, 1993 (I:all R:6).

———. *The Widow's Broom.* Houghton Mifflin, 1992 (I:5–8 R:5).

———. *The Wreck of the Zephyr.* Houghton Mifflin, 1983 (I:5–8 R:6).

———. *The Wretched Stone.* Houghton Mifflin, 1991 (I:5–8 R:5).

Viorst, Judith. *Alexander and the Terrible, Horrible, No Good, Very Bad Day.* Illustrated by Ray Cruz. Atheneum, 1972 (I:3–8 R:6).

Voake, Charlotte. *Mrs. Goose's Baby.* Little, Brown, 1989 (I:2–6).

Waber, Bernard. *A Lion Named Shirley Williamson.* Houghton Mifflin, 1996 (I:4–7 R:4).

Waddell, Martin. *Can't You Sleep, Little Bear?* Illustrated by Barbara Firth. Candlewick, 1992 (I:2–4 R:4).

———. *Farmer Duck.* Illustrated by Helen Oxenbury. Candlewick, 1992 (I:4–7 R:3).

———. *Let's Go Home, Little Bear.* Illustrated by Barbara Firth. Candlewick, 1993 (I:2–4 R:4).

———. *Tiny's Big Adventure.* Illustrated by John Lawrence. Candlewick, 2004 (I:3–7).

———. *What Use Is a Moose?* Illustrated by Arthur Robins. Candlewick, 1996 (I:5–8 R:4).

———. *You and Me, Little Bear.* Illustrated by Barbara Firth. Candlewick, 1996 (I:3–6 R:4).

Ward, Lynd. *The Biggest Bear.* Houghton Mifflin, 1952 (I:5–8 R:4).

Waring, Richard. *Hungry Hen.* Illustrated by Caroline Jayne Church. HarperCollins, 2002 (I:5–7).

Wayland, April Halprin. *To Rabbittown.* Illustrated by Robin Spowart. Scholastic, 1989 (I:3–8 R:5).

Wegman, William. *William Wegman's Farm.* Hyperion, 1997 (I:all).

Wells, Rosemary. *Bunny Cakes.* Dial, 1997 (I:2–6).

_____. *McDuff Moves In.* Illustrated by Susan Jeffers. Hyperion, 1997 (I:2–5).

_____. *My Kindergarten.* Hyperion, 2004 (I:3–6).

_____. *Timothy Goes to School.* Dial, 1981 (I:4–7 R:4).

Wiesner, David. *June 29, 1999.* Clarion, 1992 (I:all).

Wild, Margaret. *Let the Celebrations Begin!* Illustrated by Julie Vivas. Orchard, 1991 (I:all).

_____. *Mr. Nick's Knitting.* Illustrated by Dee Huxley. Harcourt Brace, 1989 (I:4–8 R:4).

Willems, Mo. *Knuffle Bunny: A Cautionary Tale.* Hyperion, 2004 (I:1–6).

Williams, Garth. *The Rabbit's Wedding.* Harper, 1958 (I:3–7).

Williams, Sherley Anne. *Working Cotton.* Illustrated by Carole Byard. Harcourt Brace, 1992 (I:all).

Williams, Vera. *A Chair for My Mother.* Greenwillow, 1982 (I:3–7 R:6).

_____. *Something Special for Me.* Greenwillow, 1983 (I:3–7 R:6).

_____. *Stringbean's Trip to the Shining Sea.* Greenwillow, 1988 (I:all).

Wilson, Sarah, *Good Zap, Little Grog.* Illustrated by Susan Meddaugh. Candlewick, 1995 (I:3–8).

Wood, Audrey. *The Flying Dragon Room.* Illustrated by Mark Teague. Scholastic, 1996 (I:4–8 R:6).

_____. *The Red Racer.* Simon & Schuster, 1996 (I:4–8 R:5).

Wood, Don. *Piggies.* Harcourt Brace, 1991 (I:2–7).

Woodson, Jacqueline. *Coming On Home Soon.* Illustrated by E. B. Lewis. Putnam, 2004 (I:5–8).

_____. *The Other Side.* Illustrated by E. B. Lewis. Putnam, 2001 (I:6–8 R:4).

Yolen, Jane. *Letting Swift River Go.* Illustrated by Barbara Cooney. Little, Brown, 1992 (I:5–8 R:5).

_____. *Owl Moon.* Illustrated by John Schoenherr. Philomel, 1987 (I:all).

_____. *Welcome to the Sea of Sand.* Illustrated by Laura Regan. Putnam, 1996 (I:5–8 R:4).

Yorinks, Arthur. *Hey, Al.* Illustrated by Richard Egielski. Farrar, Straus & Giroux, 1986 (I:all R:5).

_____. *The Miami Giant.* Illustrated by Maurice Sendak. HarperCollins, 1995 (I:all).

Zalben, Jane Breskin. *Baby Babka, The Gorgeous Genius.* Illustrated by Victoria Chess. Clarion, 2004 (I:5–8).

Zamorano, Ana. *Let's Eat!* Illustrated by Julie Vivas. Scholastic, 1997 (I:4–7 R:4).

Zemach, Margot. *It Could Always Be Worse: A Yiddish Folktale.* Farrar, Straus & Giroux, 1976 (I;5–9 R:2).

Zimmerman, Andrea, & David Clemesha. *My Dog Toby.* Illustrated by True Kelley, Harcourt, 2000 (I:4–8).

Zolotow, Charlotte. *William's Doll.* Illustrated by William Péne du Bois. Harper & Row, 1972 (I:4–8 R:4).

Illustration from Papa Gatto, An Italian Fairy Tale, *retold by Ruth Sanderson, copyright © 1995 by Ruth Sanderson. Used by permission of Little, Brown and Company.*

Chapter Outline

Of Castle and Cottage

- Our Traditional Literary Heritage
- Types of Traditional Literature
- Values of Traditional Literature for Children
- Authenticating the Folklore
- Folktales
- Fables
- Myths
- Legends
- Additional Traditional Literature With Religious Themes

Teaching With Traditional Literature

- Telling Stories
- Motivating Writing Through Traditional Tales
- Developing Critical Evaluators for Fables

Of Castle and Cottage

Enchanted swans who regain human form because of a sister's devotion, a brave boy who climbs into the unknown world at the top of a beanstalk, witches, warriors, supernatural animals, royal personages, and humans are brought to life in traditional literature. Such literature contains something that appeals to all interests: humorous stories, magical stories, and adventure stories. The settings of the stories are as varied as the enchanted places in the human imagination and as the geography of our world, from scorching deserts to polar icecaps. Regardless of location or subject, such tales include some of the most beloved and memorable stories of everyone's childhood. This chapter discusses the nature of our traditional literary heritage—its basic forms and themes and what it has to offer children.

Our Traditional Literary Heritage

The quest for traditional literary heritage takes students of children's literature to times before recorded history and to all parts of the world. Tales of religious significance allowed ancient people to speculate about their beginnings. Mythical heroes and heroines from all cultures overcame supernatural adversaries to gain their rewards. Stories of real people who performed brave deeds probably gratified the rulers of ancient tribes. According to folklorist Stith Thompson (1977), similarities in the types of tales and in the narrative motifs and content of traditional stories from peoples throughout the world constitute tangible evidence that traditional tales are both universal and ancient.

Traditionally, young and old alike heard the same tales, but each social class cultivated the art of storytelling, reflecting the culture, natural environment, and social contacts of the storyteller and the audience. For example, storytellers who earned their livings in medieval European castles related great deeds of nobility. The English court heard about King Arthur, Queen Guinevere, and the Knights of the Round Table, and the French court heard stories of princely valor, such as "The Song of Roland." In ancient China, stories for the ruling classes often portrayed benevolent dragons, symbols of imperial authority.

Commoners in medieval Europe lived lives quite different from those of the nobility, and their traditional stories differed accordingly. The stories that peasants told one another reflected the harsh, unjust, and often cruel circumstances of their existence as virtual slaves to the nobles. A common theme in their folktales is overcoming social inequality to attain a better way of life. In many tales, a poor lad outwits a nobleman, wins his daughter in marriage, and gains lifelong wealth. This theme is found in "The Flying Ship," a Russian tale; "The Golden Goose," a German tale; and "The Princess and the Glass Hill," a Norwegian tale.

Other traditional stories, such as the English "Jack the Giant Killer," tell of overcoming horrible adversaries with cunning and bravery. The peasants in these stories are not always clever. The consequences of stupidity are emphasized, for example, in the Norwegian tale "The Husband Who Has to Mind the House" and in the Russian tale "The Falcon Under the Hat." In place of the benevolent imperial dragon, the tales of early China's common people often involved cruel and evil dragons, whose power the heroines or heros overcame.

In the 17th century, the Puritans of England and its colonies considered folktales about giants, witches, and enchantment to be immoral for everyone. They maintained that children in particular should hear and read only what instructed them and reinforced their moral development. Other social groups in Europe and North America felt differently, however. In 1697, the Frenchman Charles Perrault published a collection of folktales called *Tales of Mother Goose*, which included "Cinderella" and "Sleeping Beauty."

More than 100 years later, the Romantic movement in Europe generated enthusiasm for exploring folklore to discover more about the roots of European languages and traditional cultures. In Germany, the Brothers Grimm carefully collected and transcribed oral tales from the storytellers themselves; these tales have been retold or adapted by many contemporary writers. Perrault and the Brothers Grimm thus brought new respect to traditional tales and ensured their availability for all time. Their work influenced collectors in other countries, as well as writers of literature.

By the end of the 19th century, European and North American societies generally considered childhood a distinct, necessary, and valuable stage in the human life cycle. Improved technology created more leisure hours for the middle and upper classes and a need for literature to entertain children. Traditional literature became a valuable part of the childhood experience.

According to Betsy Hearne (1988), a significant happening in children's book publishing in the early 1900s also influenced the availability of traditional literature: Numerous children's book departments were established. The editors were drawn from librarians who had knowledge of storytelling and the tales from the oral tradition. At the same time, illustrators with close cultural ties to their folklore and art immigrated from Europe. Consequently, newly illustrated folktales became an important part of the children's literature market.

Today, folk literature is considered an important part of every child's cultural heritage. It is difficult to imagine the early childhood and elementary school years of Amer-

ican children without "The Little Red Hen," "The Three Bears," and "Snow White and the Seven Dwarfs." The literary experiences of older children would not be complete without tales of Greek and Norse mythology.

Types of Traditional Literature

Traditional tales have been handed down from generation to generation by word of mouth. In contrast to a modern story, a traditional tale has no identifiable author. Instead, storytellers tell what they have received from previous tellers of tales. Folklorists and others interested in collecting and analyzing traditional literature do not always agree about how to categorize and define different types of traditional tales. This text discusses four types of traditional tales—folktales, fables, myths, and legends—drawing on definitions recommended by folklorist William Bascom (1965). Chart 6.1 summarizes and clarifies the differences among folktales, fables, myths, and legends, providing examples of each type of traditional literature.

Folktales

According to Bascom, folktales are "prose narratives which are regarded as fiction. They are not considered as dogma or history, they may or may not have happened, and they are not taken seriously" (p. 4). Because the tales are set in any time or place, they seem almost timeless and placeless. Folktales usually tell the adventures of animal or human characters. They contain common narrative motifs—such as supernatural adversaries (ogres, witches, and giants), supernatural helpers, magic and marvels, tasks and quests—and common themes—such as reward of good and punishment of evil. (Not all themes and motifs are found within one tale.) Subcategories of folktales include cumulative tales, humorous tales, beast tales, magic and wonder tales, *pourquoi* tales, and realistic tales.

Cumulative Tales. Tales that sequentially repeat actions, characters, or speeches until a climax is reached are found among all cultures. Most cumulative tales give their main characters—whether animal, vegetable, human, or inanimate object—intelligence and reasoning ability. Adults often share these stories with very young children because the structure of cumulative tales allows children to join in as each new happening occurs. A runaway baked food is a popular, culturally diverse subject for cumulative tales. It is found in not only the German "Gingerbread Boy" but also a Norwegian version, "The Pancake"; an English version, "Johnny Cake"; and a Russian version, "The Bun." In each of these tales, the repetition builds until the climax. Other familiar cumulative tales include the English "Henny Penny"; "The Fat Cat," a Danish tale; and "Why Mosquitoes Buzz in People's Ears," an African tale.

Cumulative tales are excellent for storytelling because they encourage listeners to interact with the storyteller by joining in with the repetitive lines and by saying

CHART 6.1 Characteristics of folktales, fables, myths, and legends

Form and Examples	Belief	Time	Place	Attitude	Principal Characters
Folktale	**Fiction**	**Anytime**	**Anyplace**	**Secular**	**Human or Nonhuman**
1. "Snow White and Seven Dwarfs" (European)	Fiction	"Once upon a time"	"In the great forest"	Secular	Human girl and dwarfs
2. "The Crane Wife" (Asian)	Fiction	Long ago	"In a faraway mountain village"	Secular	Human man, supernatural wife
3. "Why Mosquitoes Buzz in People's Ears" (African)	Fiction	"One morning"	In a forest	Secular	Animals
Fable	**Fiction**	**Anytime**	**Anyplace**	**Secular/Allegorical**	**Animal or Human**
1. "The Hare and the Frog" (Aesop)	Fiction	"Once upon a time"	On the shore of a lake	Allegorical	Animals
2. "The Tyrant Who Became a Just Ruler" (Panchatantra—India)	Fiction	"In olden times"	In a kingdom	Allegorical	Human king
Myth	**Considered Fact**	**Remote Past**	**Other World or Earlier World**	**Sacred**	**Nonhuman**
1. "The Warrior Goddess: Athena" (European)	Considered fact	Remote past	Olympus	Deities	Greek goddess
2. "Zuñi Creation Myth" (Native American)	Considered fact	Before and during creation	Sky, earth, and lower world	Deities	Creator Awonawilona, Sun Father, Earth Mother
Legend	**Considered Fact**	**Recent Past**	**World of Today**	**Secular or Sacred**	**Human**
1. "King Arthur Tales" (European)	Considered fact	Recent past	Britain	Secular	King
2. "The White Archer" (Native American)	Considered fact	Recent past	Land of Eskimos	Secular	Indian who wanted to avenge parents' death

the cumulative verses. For example, in *Gobble, Gobble, Slip, Slop: A Tale of a Very Greedy Cat* Meilo So retells a tale from India that uses both repetition and a cumulative style; the lines "gobble, gobble, slip, slop" are repeated frequently. The cumulative text begins, "I've eaten five hundred cakes, I've eaten my friend the parrot, and I can eat you too, I can, I can" (unnumbered). The cumulative text continues as the cat eats the old woman, the farmer and his donkey, the sultan and his wedding procession, and two crabs.

Humorous Tales. Folktales allow people to laugh at themselves as well as at others, an apparently universal pleasure. In tales such as the Russian "The Peasant's Pea Patch," the humor results from absurd situations or the stupidity of the characters. Human foolishness resulting from unwise decisions provides the humor and a moral in the English folktale "Mr. and Mrs. Vinegar" and in the Norwegian tale "The Husband Who Has to Mind the House."

Beast Tales. Beast tales are among the most universal folktales, being found in all cultures. For example, the coyote is a popular animal in Native American tales, and the fox and wolf are found in many European tales. The rabbit and the bear are popular characters in the folktales of African American culture. Beasts in folktales often talk and act quite like people. In some stories, such as "The Bremen Town Musicians," animal characters use their wits to frighten away robbers and claim wealth. In other tales, such as "The Three Billy Goats Gruff," animals use first their wits and then their strength to overcome an enemy. Still other animals win through industrious actions, such as those in "The Little Red Hen." Tales about talking animals may show the cleverness of one animal and the stupidity of another.

Magic and Wonder Tales. The majority of magic and wonder tales contain some element of magic: The fairy godmother transforms the kind, lovely, mistreated girl into a beautiful princess ("Cinderella"), the good peasant boy earns a cloth that provides food ("The Lad Who Went to the North Wind"), a kindhearted simpleton attains a magical ship ("The Fool of the World and the Flying Ship"), or the evil witch transforms the handsome prince into a beast ("Beauty and the Beast"). Transformations from humans to animals and animals to humans are also common in folktales. Mingshui Cai (1993) describes the relationships between humans and animals in both Eastern and Western folktales. He describes several tales in which magical animals become brides for humans. Cai categorizes these bride stories as brides from the sky, as in the Japanese story "The Crane Wife"; brides from the earth, as in the Native American folktale "The Serpent of the Sea"; and brides from the water, as in the Japanese story "Urashima Taro." Magic in wonder tales can be good or bad. When it is good, the person who benefits has usu-

ally had misfortune or is considered inferior by a parent or by society. When it is bad, love and diligence usually overcome the magic—as in the German tale "The Six Swans" and the Norwegian tale "East of the Sun and West of the Moon."

Pourquoi Tales. *Pourquoi* tales—or "why" tales, in an English translation of the French word—answer a question or explain how animals, plants, or humans were created and why they have certain characteristics. For example, why does an animal or a human act in a certain way? Children enjoy *pourquoi* tales and like to make up their own stories about why animals or humans have certain characteristics.

Realistic Tales. The majority of folktales include supernatural characters, magic, or other exaggerated incidents. A few tales, however, have realistic plots and involve people who could have existed. One such tale, "Dick Whittington," tells about a boy who comes to London looking for streets paved with gold. He doesn't find golden streets, but he does find work with an honest merchant, and eventually, he wins his fortune. Some versions of this story suggest that at least parts of it are true—a Dick Whittington was lord mayor of London.

Fables

Fables are brief tales in which animal characters that talk and act like humans indicate a moral lesson or satirize human conduct. For example, in the familiar "The Hare and the Tortoise," the hare taunts the tortoise about her slow movements and boasts about his own speed. The tortoise then challenges the hare to a race. The hare starts rapidly and is soon far ahead, but he becomes tired and, in his confidence, decides to nap. Meanwhile, the tortoise, keeping at her slow and steady pace, plods across the finish line. When the hare awakens, he discovers that the tortoise has reached the goal. The moral of this fable is that perseverance and determination may compensate for lack of other attributes.

Myths

According to Bascom (1965), myths are

> prose narratives which, in the society in which they are told, are considered to be truthful accounts of what happened in the remote past. They are accepted on faith; they are taught to be believed; and they can be cited as authority in answer to ignorance, doubt, or disbelief. Myths are the embodiment of dogma; they are usually sacred; and they are often associated with theology and ritual. (p. 4)

Myths account for the origin of the world and humans; for everyday natural phenomena, such as thunder and lightning; and for human emotions and experiences, such as love and death. The main characters in myths may be animals, deities, or humans. The actions take place in an earlier world or another world, such as the underworld or the sky. Many ancient Greek myths, for example, explain the creation of the world, the creation of the gods and goddesses who ruled from Mount Olympus, and the reasons for natural phenomena. The myth about Demeter and Persephone, for example, explains seasonal changes.

Legends

Legends, Bascom says, are

> prose narratives which, like myths, are regarded as true by the narrator and his audience, but they are set in a period considered less remote, when the world was much as it is today. Legends are more often secular than sacred, and their principal characters are human. (p. 4)

Many legends embroider the historical facts of human wars and migrations, brave deeds, and royalty. Legends from the British Isles tell about Robin Hood, the protector of the poor in the Middle Ages, who may have been an actual person. Legends from France tell about the miraculous visions of Joan of Arc, who led French armies into battle against the English. Legends from Africa describe how the prophet Amakosa saved the Juba people from extinction.

Values of Traditional Literature for Children

Traditional literature helps children understand the world and identify with universal human struggles. It also provides pleasure.

Understanding the World

Traditional tales help children improve their understanding of the world. Storyteller Diane Wolkstein (1992) declares, "Every story is rooted in a culture, and the world of culture is limitless" (p. 704). (See the Evaluation Criteria on this page.) In her introduction to *The Troll With No Heart in His Body and Other Tales of Trolls From Norway*, Lise Lunge-Larsen emphasizes that "telling or reading folktales is one way to cultivate a child's soul and humanity. With their ancient symbolic images, such stories reach deep inside children to connect them with their essential nature" (p. 9).

Children's world understanding is increased as they learn about early cultural traditions, read about cultural diffusion in variants of tales, develop appreciation of culture and art from different countries, and become familiarized with many languages and dialects of cultures around the world.

Betsy Hearne (1993a) considers the identification of cultural sources in folktales so important that she makes the following proposals: "that the producers of picture-book folktales provide source notes that set these stories in their cultural context; that those of us who select these materials for children judge them, at least in part, on how well their authors and publishers meet this responsibility"

Evaluation Criteria

Literary Criticism: Increasing World Understanding Through Traditional Tales

1. Does the literature help children better understand the nonscientific cultural traditions of early humanity?
2. Does the literature show the interrelatedness of various types of stories and narrative motifs?
3. Does the literature help explain how different versions of a tale are dispersed?
4. Does the literature help children learn to appreciate the culture and art of a different country?
5. Does the literature provide factual information about a different country?
6. Does the literature familiarize children with another language or dialect of the world?
7. Can the literature be used to stimulate creative drama, writing, and other forms of artistic expression?
8. Does the literature encourage children to realize that people from another part of the world have inherent goodness, mercy, courage, and industry?

(p. 22). Without cultural knowledge, readers cannot speculate about cultural diffusion. The similarities among tales indicate movement of people through migration and conquests. They also emphasize that humans throughout the world have had similar needs and problems. Some folktales from different countries are almost identical; for example, the German tale "The Table, the Donkey, and the Stick" is very similar to both the Norwegian tale "The Lad Who Went to the North Wind" and the English folktale "The Donkey, the Table, and the Stick." Also, almost every country has its traditional trickster, such as the fox in Palestine and the mousedeer in Malaysia; its stupid, easily fooled creature, such as the bear in Lapland and the giraffe in West Africa; and its benevolent, good-natured animal, such as the kangaroo in Australia. The tales are very similar, although the animals and the settings are characteristic of the countries in which they are told.

Traditional tales encourage children to realize that people from all over the world have inherent goodness, mercy, courage, and industry. In a Chinese tale, a loving brother rescues his sister from a dragon; in a German tale, a sister suffers 6 years of ordeals in order to bring her brothers back to human form. A Jewish folk character works hard to cultivate fig trees that may benefit his descendants but not himself, and the Norse Beowulf's strength of character defeats evil monsters.

ISSUE Whose Cultural Values and Belief Systems Should Be Reflected in Folklore?

One of the issues we face as we read and evaluate folklore from around the world is whose cultural values and belief systems the tales should reflect. Should the stories be rewritten to reflect current American beliefs, or should the tales reflect their original cultures in both text and illustrations? Comments in articles by Nina Jaffe[1] and David Sacks[2] provide interesting points for discussion.

Jaffe evaluates the work of Harold Courlander as he collected and retold tales that preserved the values of the cultures. Jaffe highlights Courlander's difficulties in his desire to retain authenticity. She quotes his difficulties with editors who frequently wanted him to change style or content. Courlander states, "In one collection, there was a Hottentot tale. It was about how people die and don't live again. That was the theme of it—how that came about. It was a kind of how it began story. An editor I was dealing with said. 'A lot of people

don't believe that, they believe you do live again.' And I have to be adamant about it and say, 'This is the story!' They didn't think it was suitable for children. Well too bad, they have to learn other people don't think the same way as we do—that's what it's all about" (p. 133). Jaffe believes that retellers can have creative integrity "as long as values of respect, sensitivity, and self-knowledge are present in the interpretation, research, and retelling" (p. 133).

Sacks provides an equally strong argument for using myths and other literature reflecting ancient Greece and Rome. He believes in retaining the authenticity even in highly illustrated books. He states, "In a collection of myths for elementary-aged audiences, it could mean using illustrations that convey immortal grandeur, not a trivializing goofiness" (p. 38). He then presents an annotated list of myths, history, and historical fiction that he recommends.

As you consider Jaffe and Courlander's concerns for cultural authenticity in the tales and Sacks's concern for cultural authenticity in the illustrations, ask yourself: What do you believe is the value in reading tales from another culture? Should the tales reflect the values and beliefs of the original culture, or should they be rewritten to reflect the values and beliefs of contemporary American audiences? What happens to our understandings of earlier and frequently different cultures if the stories are changed? How does authenticity in illustrations add to or detract from folktales?

[1] Jaffe, Nina. (1996, September). Reflections on the work of Harold Courlander. *School Library Journal, 42,* 132–133.
[2] Sacks, David. (1996, November). Breathing new life into ancient Greece and Rome. *School Library Journal, 42,* 38–39.

Identifying With Universal Human Struggles

In *The Uses of Enchantment: The Meaning and Importance of Fairy Tales*, Bruno Bettelheim (1976) provides strong rationales for using traditional tales with children. In his psychoanalytic approach to traditional tales, Bettelheim claims that nothing is so enriching as traditional literature. To reinforce this claim, he argues that traditional tales allow children to learn about human progress and possible solutions to problems. Because tales state problems briefly, children can understand them. In addition, traditional tales subtly convey the advantages of moral behavior. Children learn that struggling against difficulties is unavoidable, but they can emerge victorious if they directly confront hardships.

Traditional tales present characters who are both good and bad. According to Bettelheim, children gain the conviction that crime does not pay. The simple, straightforward characters in traditional tales allow children to identify with the good and to reject the bad. Children empathize with honorable characters and their struggles, learning that although they may experience difficulty or rejection, they, too, will be given help and guidance when needed. Author and folklorist Gail E. Haley (1986) emphasizes the importance of reading about heroes in folklore because

> heroes of the past teach us solutions for coping with today and tomorrow. They were synthesized out of the dreams and wishes of the people who created and consumed them. Those that survive are those whose faces, forms, and stature have fulfilled the nature and needs of succeeding generations. We still need heroes. (p. 118)

Pleasure

Traditional literature is extremely popular with children. In particular, folktales—with their fast-paced, dramatic plots and easily identifiable good and bad characters—are among the types of literature most appealing to young audiences. Although folktales may appeal primarily to young children, children of various ages and interests find them enjoyable. Animal tales, such as "The Three Little Pigs," "The Little Red Hen," and "The Three Bears," have been illustrated in picture-book format for young children, and fairy tales, such as "Beauty and the Beast," are of interest to upper-elementary school children.

F. André Favat (1977) reviewed the relevant research and reached the following conclusions about interest in folktales among children of different ages:

1. Children between the ages of 5 and 10—or roughly from kindergarten through the fifth grade—are highly interested in folktales, whether they select books or are presented with books and asked for their opinions.

2. This interest follows a curve of reading preference—that is, children's interest in folktales emerges at a prereading age and gradually rises to a peak between the approximate ages of 6 and 8. It then gradually declines.

3. Interest in realistic stories emerges as interest in folktales declines.

Favat maintains that the characteristics of folktales correspond with the characteristics that Jean Piaget ascribed to children. First, children believe that objects, actions, thoughts, and words can exercise magical influence over events in their own lives. Folktales are filled with such occurrences, as spells turn humans into animals, or vice versa, and humble pumpkins become gilded coaches.

Second, children believe that inanimate objects and animals have consciousness much like that of humans. In folktales, the objects and animals that speak or act like people are consistent with children's beliefs.

Third, young children believe in punishment for wrongdoing and reward for good behavior. Folktales satisfy children's sense of justice. The good Goose Girl, for example, is rewarded by marrying the prince, and her deceitful maid is punished harshly.

Fourth, the relationship between heroes and heroines and their environments is much the same as the relationship between children and their own environments. Children are the center of their universes, and heroes and heroines are the centers of their folktale worlds. For example, when Sleeping Beauty sleeps for 100 years, so does the whole castle.

Authenticating the Folklore

If students are to gain the values associated with folklore, especially those concerned with understanding a culture that is different from their own, they require literature that depicts the values, beliefs, and cultural backgrounds of various groups. The need for accuracy and authenticity is emphasized in numerous articles. For example, two articles by Betsy Hearne emphasize the importance of authenticity in picture books. In "Cite the Source: Reducing Cultural Chaos in Picture Books, Part One" (1993a), Hearne states: "How do you tell if a folktale in picture-book format is authentic, or true to its cultural background? What picture books have met the challenge of presenting authentic folklore for children? These two questions . . . are especially pressing in light of our growing national concern about multicultural awareness. And they generate even broader questions: How can an oral tradition survive in print? How do children's books pass on—and play on—folklore?" (p. 22).

In her second article, "Respect the Source: Reducing Cultural Chaos in Picture Books, Part Two" (1993b), Hearne discusses the importance of establishing cultural authority, citing the sources for folklore, and training adults who select and interact with the literature. She concludes her article with the following statements: "We can ask for source citations and more critical reviews; we can compare adaptations of their printed sources (interlibrary loan works for librarians as well as their patrons) and see what's been changed in tone and content; we can consider what context graphic art provides for a story; we can make more informed selections, not by hard and fast rules, but by judging the balance of each book. . . . We can, in

short, educate ourselves on the use and abuse of folklore at an intersection of traditions" (p. 37).

Retellers of folklore are incorporating more information that readers and critics can use to evaluate the authenticity of the folktales. For example, Paul Robert Walker provides considerable information in his retelling of *Little Folk: Stories From Around the World:* an author's note, a discussion about the tale following each story, and a bibliography of sources for each of the tales. Consider in the excerpts from the following discussion of the retelling of "Rumpelstiltskin" how you might use this information when checking the authenticity of the tale:

> "Rumpelstiltskin" was included in the first volume of the first edition of folktales by Jacob and Wilhelm Grimm, published in 1812 as *Kinderund Hausmarchen* (The Children's and Household Tales). . . . In this telling, I have generally followed the Grimms' tales, but I've added ideas from a version of "Tom Tit Tot" collected in Suffolk County, England, and first published in 1878. . . . The most significant addition is that the king—rather than a messenger—happens upon the strange little man singing his song, to my mind at least, makes for a better story. (p. 13)

The sources cited in the bibliography identify enough original editions that evaluators can make their own decisions about the cultural authenticity of this retelling.

For an in-depth look at how you might conduct an authenticity project, consult Norton's *Multicultural Literature: Through the Eyes of Many Children* (2005), which includes examples of authenticating an African folktale (pp. 31–32), a Mayan folktale (pp. 151–152), and a Jewish folktale (pp. 257–258).

Folktales

Many folktales have similar characteristics and motifs. The folktales discussed in this section have many similar characteristics. They also reflect cultural differences. Chart 6.2 summarizes some of these similarities and differences by comparing tales from several cultures. This section looks at British, French, German, Norwegian, Russian, Jewish, Asian, Middle Eastern, African, Latino, African American, and Native American tales. You can analyze other tales from each culture to identify common characteristics.

Characteristics

Because folktales differ from other types of literature, they have characteristics related to plot, characterization, setting, theme, and style that may differ from other types of children's stories.

Plot.   Conflict and action abound in folktales. The nature of the oral tradition made it imperative that listeners be brought quickly into the action. Consequently, even in written versions, folktales immerse readers into the major conflict within the first few sentences. For example, the conflict in Paul Galdone's *The Little Red Hen* is between

CHART 6.2 Comparisons of folktales from different cultures

Culture and Examples	Portrayal of Hero or Heroine	Portrayal of Other Characters	Setting	Ending
British "Jack the Giant Killer"	The simple peasant lad rids the kingdom of giants. **Qualities portrayed:** intelligence and bravery	The giants are evil. The king is weak.	Mountain cave	Happy: The hero is rewarded with knighthood when the villains are slain.
French "Sleeping Beauty"	A threatened girl is rescued by a noble prince. **Qualities portrayed:** beauty, wit, grace, singing, and dancing	The fairy is wicked. The father cannot protect his daughter.	Castle with a series of rooms similar to Versailles	Happy: The prince and princess are married.
German "Hansel and Gretel"	The woodcutter's abandoned children outwit the wicked witch. **Qualities portrayed:** caring and cleverness	The stepmother is uncaring. The father is weak. The witch is wicked.	Forest	Happy: The children are rewarded with jewels after the witch is burned to death.
Norwegian "The Lad Who Went to the North Wind"	The simple but honest peasant boy sets out to retrieve a lost object. **Qualities portrayed:** honesty and kindness	The north wind is powerful. The mother is scolding. The innkeeper is dishonest and greedy.	Rural Far North	Happy: The boy beats the innkeeper and is rewarded with magical objects.
Russian "The Fool of the World and the Flying Ship"	A foolish but kindhearted boy sets out on a quest. He is aided by a magical ship and companions. **Qualities portrayed:** kindness and honesty	The czar is dishonorable. The four companions have great powers.	Rural countryside and the czar's palace	Happy: The peasant marries royalty.
Jewish "Mazel and Shlimazel"	A simple boy is accompanied by good luck and then bad luck on a series of quests. **Qualities portrayed:** diligence, honesty, sincerity, and helpfulness	The spirit of good luck is happy and attractive. The spirit of bad luck is slumped and angry.	King's court and the countryside	Happy: The hero marries the princess and eventually becomes the wisest of prince consorts.
Chinese "The Golden Sheng"	A young boy goes on a quest to save his sister from a dragon. **Qualities portrayed:** helpfulness, diligence, and loyalty	The girl is helpless. The dragon is evil and cruel.	Rural	Happy: After the dragon whirls itself to death, the brother and sister return to their mother.
African "How Spider Got a Thin Waist"	The greedy spider does not work; instead, he plays in the sun. **Qualities portrayed:** industriousness	The villagers are hardworking.	Forest and village	Unhappy: The greedy spider gets a thin waist.
Native American "The Fire Bringer"	A Paiute Indian boy, concerned about his people, sets out with a coyote to get fire. **Qualities portrayed:** intelligence, swiftness and bravery.	The coyote is intelligent. The runners are swift.	Mesa and mountain	Happy: The boy and the coyote are honored.

laziness and industriousness. The first sentence introduces the animals who live together in a little house; the second sentence introduces the lazy cat, dog, and mouse, and the third sentence introduces the industrious hen and the conflict. The remainder of the story develops the conflict between the lazy animals and the industrious fowl. The conflict is resolved when the hen eats her own baking and doesn't share it with her lazy friends.

Conflict between characters representing good and characters representing evil is typical of folktales. Even though the odds are uneven, the hero overcomes the giant in "Jack the Giant Killer," the girl and boy outsmart the witch in "Hansel and Gretel," the intelligent animal outwits the ogre in "Puss in Boots," and a brother saves his sister from a dragon in "The Golden Sheng."

Actions that recur in folktales have been the focus of several researchers. Vladimir Propp (1968) analyzed 100 Russian folktales and identified 31 recurring actions that account for the uniformity and repetitiveness of folktales. Although not all tales included all actions, actions occurred in the same sequence in most tales. More important, Propp discovered that similar patterns were apparent in non-Russian tales. He concluded that consistency of action in folktales does not result from the country of origin; instead, consistency results because the tales remain true to the folk tradition.

F. André Favat (1977) summarized Propp's findings and analyzed French and German tales according to their actions. The following list of recurring sequential actions that may be found in various combinations is adapted from Favat. In some tales, females are the primary actors, but most folktales, reflecting the values and social realities of their times and places of origin, assign actions primarily to male characters.

1. One family member leaves home.

2. The hero or heroine is forbidden to do some action.

3. The hero or heroine violates an order by doing something forbidden.

4. The villain surveys the situation.

5. The villain receives information about the victim.

6. The villain attempts to trick or deceive the victim in order to possess the victim or the victim's belongings.

7. The victim submits to deception and unwittingly helps the enemy.

8. The villain causes harm or injury to a member of a family.

9. One family member either lacks something or desires to have something.

10. A misfortune or lack is made known; the hero or heroine is approached with a request or command; and he or she is allowed to go or is sent on a mission.

11. The seeker agrees to, or decides upon, a counteraction.

12. The hero or heroine leaves home.

13. The hero or heroine is tested, interrogated, or attacked, which prepares the way for him or her to receive a magical agent or a helper.

14. The hero or heroine reacts to the actions of the future donor.

15. The hero or heroine acquires a magical agent.

16. The hero or heroine is transferred, delivered, or led to the whereabouts of an object.

17. The hero or heroine and the villain join in direct combat.

18. The hero or heroine is marked.

19. The villain is defeated.

20. The initial misfortune or lack is eliminated.

21. The hero or heroine returns.

22. The hero or heroine is pursued.

23. The hero or heroine is rescued from pursuit.

24. The hero or heroine, unrecognized, arrives home or in another country.

25. A false hero or heroine presents unfounded claims.

26. A difficult task is proposed to the hero or heroine.

27. The task is resolved.

28. The hero or heroine is recognized.

29. The false hero/heroine or the villain is exposed.

30. The hero or heroine is given a new appearance.

31. The villain is punished.

32. The hero or heroine is married and ascends to the throne.

Many of the folktales discussed in this chapter contain various combinations of these actions. All folktales have similar endings, just as they have similar beginnings and plot development, and most tales end with some version of "and they lived happily ever after."

Characterization. Folktale characters are less developed than characters in other types of stories. Because oral storytellers lacked the time to develop fully rounded characters, characters in folktales are essentially symbolic and flat—that is, they have a limited range of personal characteristics and do not change in the course of the story. A witch is always wicked, whether she is the builder of gingerbread houses in the German tale "Hansel and Gretel" or the fearsome Baba Yaga in the Russian "Maria Morevna." Other unchangeably evil characters include giants, ogres, trolls, and stepmothers.

Characters easily typed as bad are accompanied by those who are always good: The young heroine is fair, kind, and loving; the youngest son is honorable, kind, and unselfish even if he is considered foolish. Isaac Bashevis Singer's *Mazel and Shlimazel, or the Milk of the Lioness* demonstrates characteristic differences between good and bad characters: Mazel, the spirit of good luck, is young, tall, and slim, with pink cheeks and a jaunty stride; Shlimazel, the spirit of bad luck, is old, pale-faced, and angry-eyed, with a crooked red nose, a beard as gray as a spider's web, and a slumping stride.

Folktales usually establish the main characters' natures early on, as Charles Perrault does in the first paragraph of "Cinderella: or The Little Glass Slipper":

> There was once upon a time, a gentleman who married for his second wife the proudest and most haughty woman that ever was known. She had been a widow, and had by her former husband two daughters of her own humor, who were exactly like her in all things. He had also by a former wife a young daughter, but of an unparalleled goodness and sweetness of temper, which she took from her mother, who was the best creature in the world. (*Histories or Tales of Past Times*, p. 73)

The characteristics of two female characters in an Italian folktale reveal honored and disrespected human characteristics in folktales: The actions of Sophia, who is beautiful, greedy, and lazy, and Beatrice, who is plainer but generous, loving, and hardworking, provide the plot and develop the theme in Ruth Sanderson's *Papa Gatto: An Italian Fairy Tale*. The two girls either prove their worthlessness or their worth when they each take care of Papa Gatto's family of kittens. Even though Sophia tries to trick both her stepsister and a handsome prince, it is Beatrice's kind and generous nature that wins the prince, because "he knew he would do all in his power to win the one whose beauty shone from within" (unnumbered).

Children easily identify the good and bad characters in folktales. This easy identification of heroes and heroines, as well as lively action, may account for the popularity of folktales with young children.

Setting. Setting in literature involves both time and place. The time in folktales is always the far-distant past, usually introduced by some version of "once upon a time." The first line of a folktale usually places listeners into a time when anything might happen. A Russian tale, "The Firebird," begins "Long ago, in a distant kingdom, in a distant land, lived Tsar Vyslar Andronovich." Native American folktales may begin with some version of "When all was new, and the gods dwelt in the ancient places, long, long before the time of our ancients." A French tale is set "on a day of days in the time of our fathers," and a German tale begins "In the olden days when wishing still helped one." These introductions inform listeners that enchantment and overcoming obstacles are possible in the tales about to unfold.

The symbolic settings found in many folktales are not carefully described because there is no need for description. One knows immediately that magic can happen in the great forest of the Grimms' "Snow White and the Seven Dwarfs" or in the great castle of Madame de Beaumont's version of "Beauty and the Beast." The title of a Romanian tale, "The Land Where Time Stood Still," establishes a setting where the imagination will accept and expect unusual occurrences.

The introduction that places the folktale in the far-distant past may also briefly sketch the location. For example, a Chinese tale, "The Cinnamon Tree in the Moon," suggests a nature setting, "where not even a soft breeze stirs the heavens and one can see the shadows in the moon." After introducing such settings, folktales immediately identify the characters and develop the conflict.

Theme. Folktales contain universal truths and reflect the values of the times and societies where they originated, many of which are still honored today. The characters, their actions, and their rewards develop themes related to moral and material achievement: Good overcomes evil; justice triumphs; unselfish love conquers; intelligence wins out over physical strength; kindness, diligence, and hard work bring rewards. The tales also show what happens to those who do not meet the traditional standards: The jealous queen is punished, the wicked stepsisters are blinded by birds, the foolish king loses part of his fortune or his daughter, and the greedy man loses the source of his success or his well-being.

The universality of these themes suggests that people everywhere have responded to certain ideals and beliefs. Consider, for example, the universality of the theme that intelligence is superior to physical strength. The hero in the English "Jack the Giant Killer" outwits the much larger and less intelligent giant. In the African tale "A Story, a Story," Spider outwits a series of animals and wins his wager with the being who controls stories. The hero in the Jewish "The Fable of the Fig Tree" is rewarded because he considers the long-range consequences of his actions. The heroine in the Chinese "The Clever Wife" uses her wits to bring the family power.

A theme found in many folktales is that love and honor can overcome the fiercest of obstacles. For example, in the Brothers Grimm tale *The Lady & the Lion*, retold by Laurel Long and Jacqueline K. Ogburn, the heroine travels the world trying to save her beloved husband from the evil enchantress who first turns him into a lion and then into a dove. This tale that combines elements of "Beauty and the Beast" and "East of the Sun, West of the Moon" includes helpers such as the Sun, the Moon, and the North Wind who recognize the heroine's honorable character and help her overcome the enchantress and change the prince back into his human form.

Style. Charles Perrault, the famed collector of French fairy tales in the 17th century, believed "that the best stories are those that imitate best the style and the simplicity of children's verses" (Hearn, 1977, p. viii). Such style permits few distracting details or unnecessary descriptions.

Simplicity is especially apparent in the thoughts and dialogues of characters in folktales: They think and talk like people. For example, the dialogue in the Grimms' "The Golden Goose" sounds as if the listener were overhearing a conversation: The little old gray man welcomes the first son with "Good morning. Do give me a piece of that cake you have got in your pocket, and let me have a draught of your wine—I am so hungry and thirsty." The clever, selfish son immediately answers, "If I give you my cake and wine I shall have none left for myself; you just go your own way." Disaster rapidly follows this exchange.

When Dullhead, the youngest, simplest son, begs to go into the woods, his father's response reflects his opinion of his son's ability: "Both your brothers have injured themselves. You had better leave it alone; you know nothing about it." Dullhead begs hard, and his father replies, "Very well, then—go. Perhaps when you have hurt yourself, you may learn to know better." This German folktale is filled with rapid exchanges as Dullhead is rewarded with the golden goose and moves humorously on toward his destiny with the king and the beautiful princess.

The language of folktales is often enriched with simple rhymes and verses. In "Jack and the Beanstalk," the giant chants:

> Fee, fi-fo-fum,
> I smell the blood of an Englishman,
> Be he alive, or be he dead,
> I'll have his bones to grind my bread.

The enchanted frog from the Grimms' "The Frog King" approaches the door of the princess with these words:

> Princess! Youngest princess!
> Open the door for me!
> Dost thou not know what thou saidst to me
> Yesterday by the cool waters of the fountain?
> Princess, youngest princess!
> Open the door for me!

Likewise, the witch asks Hansel and Gretel:

> Nibble, nibble, gnaw,
> Who is nibbling at my little house?

As the story nears its end, another rhyme asks the duck for help:

> Little duck, little duck, dost thou see
> Hansel and Gretel are waiting for thee?
> There's never a plank or bridge in sight,
> Take us across on thy back so white.

The simple style, easily identifiable characters, and rapid plot development make folktales appropriate for sharing orally with children.

MOTIFS

Kind or cruel supernatural beings, magical transformations of reality, and enchanted young people who must wait for true love to break spells that confine them are elements that take folktales out of the ordinary and encourage people to remember and repeat them. Folklorists have identified hundreds of such elements, or motifs, found in folktales.

Although a folktale may be remembered for one dramatic story element, most tales have multiple elements. Consider the following motifs in "Jack and the Beanstalk": (1) The hero makes a foolish bargain, (2) the hero acquires a magical object, (3) a plant has extraordinary powers, (4) the ogre repeats "fee-fi-fo-fum," (5) the ogre's wife hides the hero, (6) the hero steals a magical object from the ogre, (7) the magical object possesses the power of speech, and (8) the hero summons the ogre.

Researchers use motifs to analyze and identify the similarities in tales from various cultures. Some motifs are practically universal, suggesting similar thought processes in people living in different parts of the world. Other motifs help trace diffusion from one culture to another or identify a common source. Chart 6.3 summarizes the discussion of motifs and demonstrates that folktales from many parts of the world contain the same motifs. The search for common motifs is enlightening and rewarding for children as well as adults. Some of the most common motifs in folktales are supernatural beings; extraordinary animals; and magical objects, powers, and transformations.

Supernatural Adversaries and Helpers. Supernatural beings in folktales are usually either adversaries or helpers. The wicked supernatural beings, such as ogres and witches, may find heroines or heroes, entice them into their cottages or castles, and make preparations to feast upon them. The main character may deliberately seek out the adversary, as in the Chinese tale "Li Chi Slays the Serpent," found in Moss Roberts's *Chinese Fairy Tales & Fantasies,* or the encounter with the evil being may be the result of an unlucky chance meeting, as in "Hansel and Gretel." Fortunately, the intended victims usually outwit the adversaries. In addition to being evil, supernatural adversaries are usually stupid; consequently, they are overcome by characters who use wit and trickery.

Supernatural helpers support many folklore heroes and heroines in their quests. For example, seven dwarfs help Snow White in her battle against her evil stepmother. A supernatural old man causes hardships to the selfish older brothers and rewards the generous younger brother in the Russian tale "The Fool of the World and the Flying Ship." The same motif is found in tales from western Asia, eastern Europe, and India.

Extraordinary Animals. Whether cunning or stupid, deceitful or upstanding, extraordinary animals are popular characters in the folktales of all cultures. In the English and German versions of "Little Red Riding Hood," the wolf plays the role of ogre, deceives a child, and is eliminated. In Japanese folklore, the fox has a malicious nature:

CHART 6.3   Common motifs in folktales from different cultures

Common Motif	Culture	Folktale
Supernatural Adversaries		
Ogre	England	"Jack the Giant Killer"
Ogress	Italy	"Petrosinella"
Troll	Norway	"Three Billy Goats Gruff"
Giant	Germany	"The Valiant Little Tailor"
Dragon	China	"The Golden Sheng"
Witch	Africa	"Marandenboni"
Supernatural Helpers		
Fairies	France and Germany	"The Sleeping Beauty"
Jinni	Arabia	"The Woman of the Well"
Cat (fairy in disguise)	Italy	"The Cunning Cat"
Deceitful or Ferocious Beasts		
Wolf	Germany	"The Wolf and the Seven Little Kids"
Wolf	France	"Little Red Riding Hood"
Wolf	England	"The Three Little Pigs"
Wild hog, unicorn, and lion	United States	"Jack and the Varmints"
Magical Objects		
Cloak of invisibility	Germany	"The Twelve Dancing Princesses"
Magical cloth	Norway	"The Lad Who Went to the North Wind"
Magical lamp	Arabia	"Aladdin and the Magic Lamp"
Magical mill	Norway	"Why the Sea Is Salt"
Magical Powers		
Granted wishes	Germany	"The Fisherman and His Wife"
Wish for a child	Russia	"The Snow Maiden"
Humans with extraordinary powers	Mexico	"The Riddle of the Drum"
Humans with extraordinary powers	Russia	"The Fool of the World and the Flying Ship"
Magical Transformations		
Prince to bear	Norway	"East of the Sun and West of the Moon"
Prince to beast	France	"Beauty and the Beast"
Bird to human	Japan	"The Crane Wife"
Human to animal	United States (Native American)	"The Ring in the Prairie"

It can assume human shape, and it has the power to bewitch humans. Tricky foxes and coyotes are important characters in African American and Native American folktales as well.

Some extraordinary animals are loyal companions and helpers to deserving human characters. The cat in the French "Puss in Boots" outwits an ogre and provides riches for his human master. The German version of "Cinderella" collected by the Brothers Grimm contains no fairy godmother; instead, white doves and other birds help Cinderella complete the impossible tasks that her wicked stepmother requires. The variety of extraordinary animals is apparent in texts such as Margaret Mayo's *Mythical Birds & Beasts From Many Lands*. Mayo presents folktales and mythology as well as notes on the stories.

Magical Objects, Powers, and Transformations. The possession of a magical object or power is crucial in many folktales. When all seems lost, the hero may don the cloak of invisibility and follow "The Twelve Dancing Princesses" to solve a mystery and win his fortune, or the heroine's loving tears may fall into her true love's eyes and save him from blindness, as in "Rapunzel."

Folktale characters often obtain magical objects in extraordinary manners, lose them or have them stolen, and eventually recover them. This sequence occurs in the Norwegian "The Lad Who Went to the North Wind," in which a boy goes to the North Wind demanding the return of his meal, is given a magical object, loses it to a dishonest innkeeper, and must retrieve it. The dishonest innkeeper is eventually punished. In folktales, stealing a magical object often results in problems for the thief.

Magical spells and transformations are also common in folktales around the world. The spell of a fairy godmother turns a pumpkin into a golden coach, and the spell of a witch puts a princess to sleep for 100 years. One of the most common transformation motifs is the transformation of a prince into an animal ("The Frog Prince") or a beast-like monster ("Beauty and the Beast"). A gentle, unselfish youngest daughter usually breaks the enchantment when she falls in love with the animal or beast. In a Basque tale, the beast is a huge serpent; a Magyar Hungarian tale has the prince transformed into a pig; and a Lithuanian tale tells of a prince who becomes a white wolf. "The Crane Wife," a Japanese folktale, contains another example of the transformation from animal to human, as a poor farmer gains a wife when a wounded crane he cares for transforms herself into a lovely woman.

Many Native American tales include humans who are transformed into animals. "The Ring in the Prairie," a Shawnee Indian tale, includes transformations of humans and sky dwellers: A human hunter transforms himself into a mouse to capture a girl who descends from the sky, and the sky dwellers secure part of an animal and are transformed into that specific animal. Many of the Native American transformation stories suggest close relationships between humans and animals.

Folktales From Around the World

Folktales From the British Isles

MULTICULTURAL
LITERATURE

British folktales about ogres, giants, and clever humans were among the first stories published as inexpensive chapbooks in the 1500s. Joseph Jacobs collected the tales, and in 1890, he published more than 80 of them as *English Fairy Tales*. In 1892, Jacobs published a collection of Celtic fairy tales. These books, in reissue or modern editions, are still available today. The fast plots and unpromising heroes of British tales are popular with children. For example, the various "Jack" tales—including "Jack the Giant Killer" and "Jack and the Beanstalk"—develop plots around villainous ogres or giants who terrorize a kingdom and the heroes who overcome their adversaries with trickery and cleverness rather than magical powers.

Steven Kellogg retells "Jack and the Beanstalk," which was first collected by Jacobs. Kellogg's illustrations reinforce the gentle mood of the cow, Milky-White, and the contrasting villainous mood of the ogre, whose food preferences include young boys. The story defines good and bad characters clearly and shows that a person with physical strength does not always succeed.

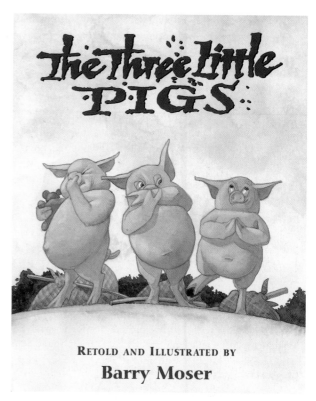

Moser's version of The Three Little Pigs *includes all of the characters found in the classic folktale. (From* The Three Little Pigs. *Copyright © 2001 by Barry Moser. Published by Little, Brown and Company. Reprinted by permission of Little, Brown and Company.)*

Other villains in British folktales play adversarial roles similar to those of giants and ogres. For example, "Three Little Pigs" must outwit a wolf, and a young girl is frightened by "The Three Bears." Glen Rounds's *Three Little Pigs and the Big Bad Wolf* includes a huffing, puffing wolf who fails to lure the wittier third pig out of his home. Steven Kellogg's *The Three Little Pigs* includes a strong and industrious mother and a wolf that is not as bad as that portrayed in usual versions.

A wicked queen who casts a spell on her beautiful and virtuous stepdaughter is the villain in David Wiesner's retelling of Joseph Jacobs's *The Loathsome Dragon*. This evil spell changes the lovely princess into a slithering, fearsome dragon that terrifies the kingdom. According to the spell, she will remain a dragon forever unless her brother, Prince Richard, saves her by kissing the dragon three times. Wiesner uses a rhythmic style that matches the mood of the tale. When Prince Richard sees the fearsome dragon, he questions that it could be his sister and draws his sword until her voice says:

> "Oh, quit your sword, forget your fear,
> And give me kisses three,
> For though I am a loathsome beast,
> No harm I'll do to thee." (unnumbered)

In addition to clearly defined good and bad characters, repetitive language in many British folktales appeals to storytellers and listeners. In "The Three Little Pigs," the wolf threatens, "I'll huff and I'll puff and I'll blow your house in," and the pig replies, "Not by the hair on my chinny chin chin." "Goldilocks and the Three Bears" repeats chairs, bowls of porridge, and beds, and the three bears' questions: Who has been sitting in my chair? Who has been eating my porridge? Who has been sleeping in my bed? Several versions of this folktale appeal to young children. Paul Galdone's *The Three Bears*, which can be used to develop size concepts, has pictures that differentiate the sizes of bears, bowls, beds, and chairs. The characters in James Marshall's *Goldilocks and the Three Bears* frolic in humorous illustrations. Jan Brett's *Goldilocks and the Three Bears* includes large, detailed illustrations on pages bordered with objects and characters from the story.

The consequences of greed, a universal motif in folktales from many countries, are found in Susan Cooper's *The Silver Cow: A Welsh Tale*. In this tale, the magic people, the Tylwyth Teg, send a marvelous cow out of Bearded Lake as a reward for a young boy's music. The greed of the boy's father causes the cow and her offspring to return to the lake, where they are turned into water lilies.

An impossible task created by foolish boasting is a motif in Harve Zemach's *Duffy and the Devil*, a Cornish tale resembling "Rumpelstiltskin." An inefficient maid named Duffy misleads her employer about her spinning ability and makes an agreement with the devil, who promises to do the knitting for 3 years. At the end of that time, she must produce his name or go with him. When the time arrives, the squire goes hunting and overhears the festivities of the witches and the devil as the little man with the long tail sings this song:

Tomorrow! Tomorrow! Tomorrow's the day!
I'll take her! I'll take her! I'll take her away!
Let her weep, let her cry, let her beg, let her pray—
She'll never guess my name is . . . Tarraway!
(unnumbered)

Thus, Duffy learns the magic name and cheats the devil from claiming her soul. The importance of a secret name is reflected in folktales from many cultures. In the English version of "Rumpelstiltskin," the name is Tim Tit Tot; a Scottish secret name is Whuppity Stoorie; a tale from Nigeria is "The Hippopotamus Called Isantim."

A Cinderella-type story is found in several British folktales. In "Tattercoats," recorded by Joseph Jacobs in *More English Fairy Tales*, the heroine is mistreated by her grandfather, who mourns his daughter's death in childbirth and rejects the child who survived, and by the grandfather's cruel servants. In this British version, the prince invites her to attend the ball even though she is dressed in her rags. Only after she is at the ball does the gooseherd transform her into a beautifully dressed lady. Kevin Crossley-Holland's "Mossycoat," found in his *British Folk Tales*, is also mistreated by servants before she marries the young master.

A Cinderella variant, "Fair, Brown, and Trembling," is included in *Celtic Fairy Tales*, retold by Neil Philip. In this variant from Ireland, a hen wife provides beautiful clothes for Trembling so that she can go to church, with the admonition that she must not go inside the church and must rush home when people rise at the end of the service. During the third visit to the church, the son of a king takes her shoe and then searches for the owner. Trembling's two sisters hide her until she is finally discovered by the nobleman. In this variant, after the wedding, Trembling is pushed into the sea by her wicked sister, swallowed by a whale, and must be rescued by her husband.

Folktales from Ireland are filled with fairies, leprechauns, and other little people. Jacobs's "Guleesh," found in *Celtic Fairy Tales*, shows that the fairies do not always outwit people. A young man races with the "shee-hogues," tricks those fairy hosts out of a captured princess, and breaks a spell so that the princess can speak. This tale has an ending characteristic of Irish folk literature: "But I heard it from a birdeen that there was neither cark nor care, sickness nor sorrow, mishap nor misfortune on them till the hour of their death, and may the same be with me, and with us all!" (p. 25).

Colorful language is a style of many Irish folktales. For example, Brendan Behan introduces *The King of Ireland's Son* in this way: "Once upon a time houses were whitewashed with buttermilk and the pigs ran around with knives and forks in their snouts shouting, 'Eat me, eat me!'" (unnumbered).

Peasants rather than royalty are usually the heroes and heroines in folktales of the British Isles. Consequently, readers or listeners can learn much about the problems, beliefs, values, and humor of common people in early British history. Themes in British folktales suggest that intelligence wins over physical strength, that hard work and diligence are rewarded, and that love and loyalty are basic values for everyone.

French Folktales

The majority of French folktales portray splendid royal castles rather than humble peasant cottages. Charles Perrault, a member of the Académie Française, collected and transcribed many of these tales. In 1697, he published a collection of folktales called *Tales of Mother Goose*, which included "Cinderilla" (original spelling), "Sleeping Beauty," "Puss in Boots," "Little Red Riding Hood," "Blue Beard," "Little Thumb," and "Diamond and the Toads." These stories had entertained children and adults of the Parisian aristocracy and, consequently, are quite different from tales that stress wicked, dishonest kings being outwitted by simple peasants. These folktales collected by Perrault provide the foundation for most of the French folktales published today.

Many illustrators and translators of French fairy tales depict royal settings. For example, Marcia Brown's

Cinderella (based on Charles Perrault's version) is quite different from the German version. Cinderella has a fairy godmother who grants her wishes. A pumpkin is transformed into a gilded carriage, six mice become beautiful horses, a rat becomes a coachman with an elegant mustache, and lizards turn into footmen who are complete with fancy livery and lace. Cinderella is dressed in a beautiful gown, which is embroidered with rubies, pearls, and diamonds. This version also has the magical hour of midnight, when everything returns to normal. Perrault's *Cinderella* contains stepsisters who are rude and haughty, but they are not as cruel as they are in the German version. Cinderella even finds it possible to forgive them:

> Now her stepsisters recognized her. Cinderella was the beautiful personage they had seen at the ball! They threw themselves at her feet and begged forgiveness for all their bad treatment of her. Cinderella asked them to rise, embraced them and told them she forgave them with all her heart. She begged them to love her always. (p. 27)

The French version of "Sleeping Beauty" suggests traditional French values. Seven good fairies bestow the virtues of intelligence, beauty, kindness, generosity, gaiety, and grace on the infant princess. David Walker's version, *The Sleeping Beauty*, shows his background in theatrical set and costume design: His illustrations create the feeling of a stage setting, especially as his fairies dance lightly across the great hall of the castle. The collaboration between Lincoln Kirstein's retelling and Alain Vaïs's illustrations for *Puss in Boots* also shows the influence of backgrounds

The illustrations in this version of Puss in Boots *feature 17th-century architecture. (From* Puss in Boots, *by Lincoln Kirstein. Text copyright © 1992 by Lincoln Kirstein. Illustrations copyright © 1992 by Alain Vaïs. Reprinted by permission of Little, Brown and Company.)*

that come from the New York City Ballet. The text includes fast-paced storytelling, and the illustrations develop a world of baroque splendor that could provide stage settings for ballet. In addition, the common French motifs of enchantment and animals that help their masters attain high goals are developed through both the text and the illustrations. Readers will also enjoy searching the illustrations to find examples of 17th-century architecture and figures from art history.

Diane Goode has translated and illustrated an edition of Madame de Beaumont's *Beauty and the Beast*. Meant for the wealthy classes in French society, de Beaumont's tale begins with the traditional "Once upon a time," but it provides descriptions tailored for an aristocratic audience. For example, Beauty enjoys reading, playing the harpsichord, and singing while she spins. When she enters the beast's castle, he provides her with a library, a harpsichord, and music books. Goode's illustrations create the magical settings in which Beauty eventually loves the beast for his virtue, although he lacks good looks and wit. Beauty's moral discrimination permits the beast's transformation back into a handsome prince.

French folktales contain more enchantment than do tales from other countries. The motifs in these tales include fairy godmothers, other fairies, remarkable beasts who help their young masters, unselfish girls who break enchantments, and deceitful beasts.

German Folktales

The following words bring to mind one of the most popular childhood tales:

> Mirror, mirror on the wall.
> Who is the fairest of them all?

German folktales—whether they are about enchanted princesses and friendly dwarfs, clever animals, or poor but honest peasants—are among the most enjoyed folktales in the world. German scholar August Nitschke (1988) emphasizes the role of the German folktales historically. He states that by telling folktales, German "mothers allowed their children to come to an understanding of the world in which familiar and discomforting aspects were clearly separated, thus reaffirming that these two states of community existed" (p. 173). According to Nitschke, the storytelling and the stories allowed both mother and child to gain courage.

The accessibility of German folktales to modern audiences comes from the work of Wilhelm and Jacob Grimm, German professors who researched the roots of the German language through the traditional tales, which had been told orally for generations. The Grimms asked village storytellers throughout Germany to tell them tales, then they wrote down the stories and published them as *Kinder-und Hausmärchen*. The stories ultimately were translated into many languages and became popular in Europe, North America, and elsewhere.

A wolf is the villain in several German folktales that young children enjoy. Wolves in these tales are cunning and dangerous, and they receive just punishments. Trina Schart Hyman's version of *Little Red Riding Hood* is involved and more appropriate for older children. In addition to the story, Hyman stresses the importance of a moral in the Grimms' folktales. The incident with the dangerous wolf teaches Red Riding Hood a lesson: "I will never wander off the forest path again, as long as I live. I should have kept my promise to my mother."

Quite a different mood is created by James Marshall's humorous text and cartoon-type illustrations in his *Red Riding Hood*; the last page even includes a crocodile. Little Red Riding Hood has learned her lesson, however, and refuses to speak to him. For another mood, see William Wegman's *Little Red Riding Hood*, which contains photographs of dogs in the various roles.

Not all animals in German folklore are as fearsome as the wolf. For example, in "The Bremen Town Musicians," old animals about to be destroyed by their owners have humorously appealing human qualities. *The Bremen Town Musicians and Other Animal Tales From Grimm*, retold by Doris Orgel, presents six tales. Some of them, such as the "Bremen Town Musicians" and "The Wolf and the Seven Young Kids," are found in numerous editions. Other tales, such as "The Hare and the Hedgehog," "King of the Birds," "When the Birds and the Beasts Went to War," and "The Fox and the Geese," are less well known. Orgel includes useful information about morals in the tales as well as any changes she made in the retellings. For example, she includes the following morals for "The Hare and the Hedgehog": "The story has two morals: First, no one, regardless how highly he rates himself, should make fun of someone he thinks less of, even if that someone is a hedgehog. And second: If you're looking to get married, and might someday race with a hare, you'd better choose a mate who looks a lot like you" (p. 24). Orgel also describes how she changed the story: In the original tale, the husband masterminds the race and the wife does what she is told, but in her retelling, the wife masterminds the plot.

Poor peasants and penniless soldiers are common heroes in German folklore. The peasant may not be cunning, but he is usually good. In "The Golden Goose," for example, the youngest son is even called Simpleton. When his selfish brothers leave home, their parents give each one a fine, rich cake and a bottle of wine, which they refuse to share with anyone. The despised Simpleton, however, is generous with the cinder cake and sour beer that his parents give him. His kind heart is rewarded when he acquires a golden goose with magical powers that allow him to marry a princess.

"Hansel and Gretel" is the classic tale of an evil witch, a discontented and selfish mother, an ineffectual father, and two resourceful children. Rika Lesser's *Hansel and Gretel*, with Paul O. Zelinsky's illustrations, provides a rich retelling of this favorite tale. James Marshall adds humorous text and cartoon-type illustrations to his *Hansel and Gretel*. In comparing these two books, consider the impact of illustrations on the mood of the tales.

Many of the best-loved German folktales are stories of princesses who sleep for 100 years, have wicked stepmothers, and are enchanted by witches. One lovely version of the Grimms' "Snow White" is translated by Randall Jarrell and illustrated by Nancy Ekholm Burkert. Burkert undertook research in German museums and visited the Black Forest before creating her drawings for *Snow White and the Seven Dwarfs*, which portrays every aspect of the mystical forest, the dwarfs' cottage, and the wicked stepmother's secret tower room. Samuel Denis Fohr (1991) argues that "Snow White" is filled with spiritual symbolism. He states: "The changed mother in 'Snow White' not only represents the world but also worldliness. Similarly, Snow White not only symbolizes human beings but also the innocence or non-worldliness of youth" (p. 85). He argues that the story is consequently of value for adults as well as for children. The text and illustrations in the Jarrell and Burkert editions can be compared with *Snow White* translated by Paul Heins and illustrated by Trina Schart Hyman. Another folktale featuring a sleeping female is Trina Schart Hyman's retelling of Grimms' *The Sleeping Beauty*.

The German version of "Cinderella" in *The Complete Brothers Grimm Fairy Tales* differs from the French rendering of this tale in both detail and mood. A bird in the hazel tree growing by her mother's grave, not a fairy godmother, gives Cinderella a dress made of gold and silver and satin slippers for the ball. When Cinderella is united with the prince, no softness of heart leads her to forgive her cruel stepsisters: On her wedding day, the sisters join the bridal procession, but doves perched on Cinderella's shoulders peck out their eyes.

Breaking enchantments through unselfish love is another common theme in German folklore. In the Grimms' "The Six Swans," also from *The Complete Brothers Grimm Fairy Tales*, the heroine can restore her brothers to human form only by sewing six shirts out of starwort. She cannot speak during the 6 years required for her task, and she suffers many ordeals before she is successful.

The author's note in *The Lady & The Lion*, retold by Laurel Long and Jacqueline K. Ogburn, contains valuable information for those who wish to authenticate the tale: The tale also is known as "The Singing, Springing Lark." According to the retellers, the story combines "Beauty and the Beast" and "East of the Sun, West of the Moon." The oil paintings depict the grandeur of a once-upon-a-time castle. The ending is a typical happily-ever-after ending: "Into the light of the new day, the lady and her prince flew the griffin across the wide world to their home where the flowers bloomed all year long. And they lived happily forever after" (unnumbered).

German folktales are ideal candidates for storytelling: Their speedy openings, fast-paced plots, and drama keep

Four illustrations of a familiar tale show the impact of the pictures on the moods of the story. A, The formal border and illustration style create a traditional mood in the illustrations from Little Red Riding Hood. (Illustrations from Little Red Riding Hood, by Trina Schart Hyman, copyright © 1983 by Trina Schart Hyman. Reprinted by permission of Holiday House.) B, The way the wolf is illustrated by Nicoletta Ceccoli for Josephine Evetts-Seeker's Little Red Riding Hood suggests a beast that is almost encircling the girl. (From Little Red Riding Hood, retold by Josephine Bretts-Seeker, illustrated by Nicoletta Ceccoli, Barefoot Books, 2004). C, James Marshall's cartoon illustrations add a humorous context to Little Red Riding Hood. (From Little Red Riding Hood, by James Marshall. Illustrated by James Marshall, Dial Books for Young Readers. Copyright © 1987.) D (p. 225), Dark colors and frightened girls suggest the dangerous nature of the tale. (From Lon Po Po: A Red-Riding Hood Story From China, translated and illustrated by Ed Young, copyright © 1989 by Ed Young. Reprinted by permission of Philomel Books.)

A

B

C

Shang listened through the door. "Po Po," she said, "why is your voice so low?"

"Your grandmother has caught a cold, good children, and it is dark and windy out here. Quickly open up, and let your Po Po come in," the cunning wolf said.

Tao and Paotze could not wait. One unlatched the door and the other opened it. They shouted, "Po Po, Po Po, come in!"

At the moment he entered the door, the wolf blew out the candle.

"Po Po," Shang asked, "why did you blow out the candle? The room is now dark."

The wolf did not answer.

D

The tale of enchanted princesses emphasizes a regal setting. (From Twelve Dancing Princesses, *retold by Marianna Mayer. Illustrated by K.Y. Craft. Text © 1989 by Marianna Mayer. Illustrations © 1989 by K.Y. Craft Reprinted by permission of Morrow Junior Books, a division of William Morrow & Co.)*

listeners entertained for story after story. In these tales, adversaries include devils, witches, and wolves. The good-hearted youngest child is often rewarded, but selfishness, greed, and discontent are punished. The noble character frequently wins as a result of intervention by supernatural helpers, and magical objects and spells are recurring motifs.

Norwegian Folktales

Norwegian scholars Peter Christen Asbjørnsen and Jørgen Moe's interest in collecting the traditional tales of the Norwegian people was stimulated by reading the Grimms' *Kinder-und Hausmärchen.* They were also inspired by the renaissance that was then sweeping Europe. Asbjørnsen and Moe's collection of traditional tales was published in 1845 under the title *Norwegian Folk Tales.*

The first translation of the tales into English was by Sir George Webbe Dasent in 1859. According to Naomi Lewis (1991),

It was not surprising that Dasent was so captivated by Scandinavia. The plots of fairy tales everywhere have many likenesses; what changes them is the place where they are told—the country and the people. Wherever the landscape is wild, the winters long and bitter, and the villages small and isolated, magic and mystery thrive. Why should the folk there doubt that trolls live in the forest, as well as wolves and bears; or that animals, who share the same scene and hardships, can speak if they will, and even change into humans and back again? (Introduction)

It is interesting to compare Norwegian story elements with those of other European cultures. Consider, for example, Mercer Mayer's *East of the Sun and West of the Moon*. The story in this tale is similar to those in the French "Beauty and the Beast" and other tales of human enchantment and lost loves: An enchanted human demands a promise in return for a favor; the promise is at first honored; the maiden disenchants the human; he must leave because she does not honor her promise; she searches for him; and she saves him finally. The adversaries and helpers in this tale reflect a northern climate and culture. The human is enchanted by a troll princess who lives in a distant, icy kingdom. The loving maiden receives help from, among others, Father Forest, who understands the body of earth and stone; Great Fish, who knows the blood of salt and water; and North Wind, who understands the mind of the earth, the moon, and the sun. The gifts that each helper gives to the maiden allow her to overcome the trolls and free the prince. A tinderbox makes it possible to melt the ice encasing the youth, a shot from the bow and arrow causes the troll princess to turn to wood, and reflections in the fish scale cause the remaining trolls to turn to stone. Mayer's illustrations of snowy winters, creatures frozen in ice, icy mountains, and tree-covered landscapes also evoke northern settings.

In *East O' the Sun and West O' the Moon*, translated by George Webbe Dasent and illustrated by P. J. Lynch, a white bear offers a family riches if its youngest daughter is allowed to live in his castle. In *East of the Sun & West of the Moon: A Play*, Nancy Willard develops a style that is appropriate for oral presentations, as shown in the song that the woodcutter's daughter sings as she goes to the bear's palace:

> When you go through the forest at midnight,
> and your friends and relations are few,
> just remember the crow and the cricket
> are twice as nervous as you. (p. 17)

Lise Lunge-Larsen's collection of Norwegian folktales found in *The Troll With No Heart in His Body and Other Tales of Trolls From Norway* focuses on nine tales that feature hags, trolls, and enchantments in rugged, mountainous settings. There are well-known stories in the collection, such as "The Three Billy Goats Gruff" and "The Boy and the North Wind." There are also less-known tales, such as "The Boy Who Became a Lion, a Falcon, and an Ant." All of the stories, however, have certain characteristics in common: It is possible to overcome even the worst evil by using intelligence, courage, persistence, and kindness.

The northern climate is found throughout the illustrations for this Norwegian tale. (Illustration from East O' the Sun and West O' the Moon, *with an introduction by Naomi Lewis. Illustration © 1991 P. J. Lynch. Used by permission of Candlewick Press, Cambridge, MA.)*

In *The Hidden Folk: Stories of Fairies, Dwarves and Other Secret Beings* Lise Lunge-Larsen reveals in her source note that these are the stories she was told as a child "so that I would know what the world is really like and what I could find if I paid close attention." One of the most charming tales, "The Ivory Cups," reveals how flower fairies saved the life of a young knight who was wounded while fighting a dragon. According to the tale, the fairies filled their little ivory cups with the water of life found in a spring deep in the forest and used the liquid to revive the knight. They each hung their cups on a blade of grass as they waited for the knight to recover. Because the fairies were frightened away by approaching villagers, they left their little cups on the blades of grass. This story becomes a *pourquoi* tale: When the sun rises and shines on the cups, they become the flowers we know as lilies of the valley.

Another favorite for storytelling and creative drama is "Taper Tom," found in Asbjørnsen and Moe's *Norwegian Folk Tales*, whose hero is the characteristic youngest son. Tom sits in a chimney corner amusing himself by grubbing in the ashes and splitting tapers for lights. His family laughs at his belief that he can win the hand of the princess in marriage and half of the kingdom by making the princess laugh. With the assistance of a magical golden goose who does not relinquish anyone who touches her, Tom forms a parade of unwilling followers: an old woman, an angry man who kicks at the woman, a smithy who waves a pair of tongs, and a cook who runs after them waving a ladle of porridge. At the sight of this ridiculous situation, the sad princess bursts into laughter. Tom wins the princess and half of the kingdom. Compare this tale with the Grimms' "The Golden Goose."

Norwegian folktales help children appreciate Norwegian traditions as well as provide them with pleasure and excitement. Themes suggest the rewarding of unselfish love and the punishment of greed. The sharp humor, the trolls, and the poor boys who overcome adversity are excellent elements for storytelling.

Russian Folktales

Heroes and heroines who may be royalty or peasants, settings that reflect deep snows in winter, dark forests, the wooden huts of peasants, the gilded towers of palaces, and villains such as the witch Baba Yaga and dishonest nobility or commoners are found in Russian folktales. Talent, beauty, and kindness are usually appreciated and rewarded. In contrast, foolish actions, greed, broken promises, and jealousy are usually condemned. Peasants sometimes outwit tsars (or *czars*), and females are often strong and resourceful. Lenny Hort's retelling of Alexander Nikolayevich Afanasyév's *The Fool and the Fish: A Tale From Russia* shows that even a peasant can be accepted by the tsar and marry his daughter. The humor of the fool's actions expresses the universal need to laugh at oneself and others. The illustrations by Russian artist Gennady Spirin depict a prerevolutionary Russia. Compare Spirin's illustrations in this book with his illustrations in Aaron Shepard's retelling of *The Sea King's Daughter*.

Many Russian folktales are complex stories of quests, longing, and greed. Ruth Sanderson's *The Golden Mare, the Firebird, and the Magic Ring* includes a greedy tsar, a young horseman, and a magical horse whose talents allow the young man to succeed. The mare comes to the rescue even when the tsar demands such impossible tasks as capturing the firebird.

J. Patrick Lewis's adaptation of *At the Wish of the Fish: A Russian Folktale* shows that even a simpleton can be rewarded for his kindness. At the conclusion of the tale, after he has won the tsar's daughter, he asks the pike to make him less a fool. The tale ends. "The once-upon-a-time simpleton never forgot the great good fortune bestowed upon him by the pike. And often he was heard to say, as he strolled through the gardens in his princely caftan, 'By the will of a fish, I have done all I wish'" (unnumbered).

Universal folktale themes found in Russian folktales include a desire for children, developed in a story about a childless couple who create "The Snow Maiden," and hatred of a beautiful child by her stepmother and stepsisters, developed in "Vassilissa the Fair," a Russian version of the Cinderella story. The latter tale and six others are collected in Alexander Nikolayevich Afanasyév's *Russian Folk Tales*, with illustrations by Ivan Bilibin, the late-19th-century Russian illustrator, who depicts traditional costumes and early Russian settings.

Alexander Pushkin was one of the first Russian writers to transcribe the orally transmitted folktales of his country. Four of Pushkin's tales are found in *The Golden Cockerel and Other Fairy Tales*, originally published in French in 1925. This translation includes "The Dead Princess and the Seven Heroes," a tale similar to the German "Snow White."

The familiar theme of kindness rewarded and the motifs of magical powers and foolish but kindhearted peasants are found in Arthur Ransome's *The Fool of the World and the Flying Ship*. The tsar has offered his daughter's hand in marriage to anyone who can build a flying ship. Kindness to an old man provides a magical ship to a man who aspires to be more than a peasant. Companions with

This Russian folktale depicts magic and brave deeds. (From The Golden Mare, the Firebird, and the Magic Ring, *by Ruth Sanderson. Copyright © 2001 by Ruth Sanderson. Reprinted by permission of Little, Brown and Company.)*

extraordinary powers also aid the peasant in his quest. This tale implies that the tsar does not want a peasant to marry his daughter.

Russian protagonists may be strong and resourceful females. Josepha Sherman's *Vassilisa the Wise: A Tale of Medieval Russia* shows that a clever and courageous female is able to outwit the prince and save her unwise husband from the prince's dark dungeon.

These and many other Russian folktales reflect a vast country containing numerous cultures. Talent, beauty, and kindness are appreciated and rewarded. People must pay the consequences for foolish actions, greed, broken promises, and jealousy. Humor suggests the universal need to laugh at oneself and others.

Jewish Folktales

Folktales, according to Rahel Musleah (1992), can be identified as Jewish if they contain any one of the following elements:

> The components are a Jewish place (under a wedding canopy; in a synagogue); a Jewish character (King Solomon instead of a nameless judge); Jewish time (a holiday or life-cycle event); and most importantly, a Jewish message (faith, learning, remembrance, hospitality, family). (p. 42)

Jewish folktales are filled with stories in which sincerity, unselfishness, and true wisdom are rewarded. The stories also contain bunglers, ironic humor, and human foibles. According to Charlotte Huck, Susan Hepler, and Janet Hickman (1997), Jewish folktales "have a poignancy, wit, and ironic humor that is not matched by any other folklore" (p. 289). Wit and humor are found in Margot Zemach's *It Could Always Be Worse*. This Yiddish folktale relates the story of nine unhappy people who share a small, one-room hut. The father desperately seeks the advice of the rabbi, who suggests that he bring a barnyard animal inside. A pattern of complaint and advice continues until most of the family's livestock is in the house. When the rabbi tells the father to clear the animals out of the hut, the whole family appreciates its large, peaceful home.

Advice from a rabbi is a frequent story plot technique that develops both the ridiculous situation and the moral of the story in Jewish folktales. Joan Rothenberg's *Yettele's Feathers* is a cautionary tale against spreading rumors and gossip. When the situation becomes extreme and no one will speak to Yettele Babbelonski, she asks the rabbi for advice. When Yettele declares that words are like feathers and not like rocks because words and feathers cannot hurt anyone, the rabbi tells her to cut off the top of her largest goose feather pillow and bring it to him. When the wind snatches the pillow from her arms, she is lost in a blizzard of feathers. Now the rabbi tells her he will help her after she retrieves all of the feathers. After Yettele becomes extremely fatigued trying to gather the feathers, she concludes that in a lifetime she could never put all the feathers back into the pillow. Now the rabbi uses her own

words to teach the moral of the story: "And so it is with those stories of yours, my dear Yettele. Once the words leave your lips, they are as impossible to put back as those feathers" (p. 31).

Isaac Bashevis Singer's *Mazel and Shlimazel, or the Milk of the Lioness* is longer and more complex. It pits Mazel, the spirit of good luck, against Shlimazel, the spirit of bad luck. To test the strength of good luck versus bad, the two spirits decide that each of them will spend a year manipulating the life of Tam, a bungler who lives in the poorest hut in the village.

Singer's *When Shlemiel Went to Warsaw & Other Stories* contains several folktales that reflect both human foibles and folklore themes. For example, "Shrewd Todie & Lyzer the Miser" pits foolish, greedy actions against cunning and trickery. To his discomfort, the miser learns, "If you accept nonsense when it brings you profit, you must also accept nonsense when it brings you loss" (p. 12).

My Grandmother's Stories: A Collection of Jewish Folk Tales, retold by Adele Geras, contains 10 tales about wise rabbis as well as the fools of Chelm. One tale reveals the reasoning a dove uses to select the best plant in the garden. Her reasons for selecting the olive tree reveal the themes about the olive tree found in Jewish folklore: The tree nourishes, it is kind, and it is a symbol of peace.

As you read Jewish folktales, notice how this spirit of Chelm emerges from the tales. Additional stories of

These Jewish tales collected from many countries reflect many of the values of the Jewish people. (From The Diamond Tree: Jewish Tales From Around the World, *selected and retold by Howard Schwartz and Barbara Rush. Copyright © 1991 by Uri Shulevitz. Used by permission of HarperCollins Publishers.)*

Chelm are found in Francine Prose's *The Angel's Mistake: Stories of Chelm.*

The fools of Chelm as well as stories about witches, goblins, and King Solomon are found in Howard Schwartz and Barbara Rush's collection of stories, *The Diamond Tree: Jewish Tales From Around the World.* These 15 tales originated in many countries, including Palestine, Iraq, Turkey, Babylon, and Poland. The text concludes with sources and commentary that are extremely useful to scholars and others who are interested in evaluating the sources of the stories. In addition, each tale is classified according to the Aarne-Thompson (AT) system. (Aarne-Thompson is a folklorist who identified tales according to specific characteristics.) For example, notice the useful information found in the notations for "The Bear and the Children" (Eastern Europe):

> From *Yiddisher Folklor* (Yiddish), edited by Yehuda L. Cahan (Vilna: 1931). AT 123.
>
> This is probably the best-known Jewish nursery tale of Eastern Europe—with the exception of the song "Had Gadya" ("One Kid"), sung at the end of the Passover seder. The story offers young children the assurance that if there is danger, their parents will do everything possible to save them. It is a variant of "The Wolf and the Seven Kids" from *Grimms' Fairy Tales.* (p. 119)

Asian Folktales

Asian folktales, like other folktales, portray the feelings, struggles, and aspirations of common people; depict the lives of the well-to-do; and reflect the moral values, superstitions, social customs, and humor of the times and societies in which they originated. Like medieval Europe, ancient Asia contained societies in which royalty and nobles led lives quite different from those of peasants. Females had less freedom and social influence than did males. Asian tales tell about the rich and the poor, the wise and the foolish, mythical quests, lovers, animals, and supernatural beings and powers, motifs common to all folklore, but they also reflect the customs and beliefs of specific cultures.

Chinese Folktales. Traditional Chinese sayings (Wyndham, 1971) suggest Chinese values and philosophical viewpoints expressed in Chinese folktales over the centuries, for example: "A teacher can open the door, but the pupil must go through it alone," and "The home that includes an old grandparent contains a precious jewel."

According to Louise and Yuan-hsi Kuo (1976), Chinese tales often develop universal themes and contain roguish humor. Respect for ancestors, ethical standards, and conflict between nobility and commoners are popular topics in Chinese tales.

A dislike for imperial authority is evident in several Chinese equivalents to the cottage tales of medieval European peasants. The defeat of an evil ruler is the main conflict in Rosalind C. Wang's *The Treasure Chest: A Chinese Tale.* The hero in this tale is a poor widow's son who rescues a fish and earns the gratitude of the Ocean King. The gift from the King of three bamboo sticks helps the young man save the woman he loves from Funtong, the evil ruler who desires the young woman.

The hero in Grace Tseng's *White Tiger, Blue Serpent* is a Chinese boy who faces perils when he tries to rescue a beautiful brocade woven by his mother from the greedy goddess; the boy's efforts free the animals and beautiful vegetation captured within the brocade. In addition to defeating the goddess, the boy's bravery makes it possible for "Kai and his mother to live happily in the beauty of the magnificent brocade" (unnumbered).

Marilee Heyer's *The Weaving of a Dream: A Chinese Folktale* reveals rewarded behavior: bravery, unselfish love, understanding, respect for one's mother, faithfulness, and kindness. In contrast, disrespect for one's mother and selfishness are punished. This tale also shows the power of a dream and the perseverance that may be required to gain the dream. Ed Young's *Lon Po Po: A Red-Riding Hood Story From China* shows that the cleverness of the eldest daughter and the cooperation of the three sisters are powerful enough to outwit the intentions of the evil wolf.

In *Tiger Woman,* Laurence Yep uses a rhyming format to retell a Shantung folktale in which selfishness is punished and sharing is rewarded. When a beggar approaches a selfish woman and asks for some of her bean curd, she replies that she will not give up any of her food because she is a tiger when she is famished. The beggar then casts a spell so that whatever the selfish woman says she becomes. Consequently, she becomes an ox, a bird, an elephant, and a sow. At that point when she almost becomes a pork roast, she repents and turns back into a human. Now she realizes the importance of sharing her food.

In *Two of Everything,* Lily Toy Hong depicts the importance of both humor and wisdom. A poor farmer and his wife discover the unusual characteristics of a brass pot that the farmer unearths in his garden: If one item is placed in the pot, two identical items appear. This happy situation continues until the wife falls head first into the pot, but the woman uses her wits and solves the problem.

Laurence Yep's *The Rainbow People* is a collection of 20 Chinese folktales from Chinese Americans in the United States. The text is divided according to tales about tricksters, fools, virtues and vices, Chinese America, and love. Yep has included introductory comments for each of the sections.

Japanese Folktales. In her introduction to Grace James's *Green Willow and Other Japanese Fairy Tales* (1987), Ellen S. Shapiro summarizes some of the characteristics of Japanese folktales. According to Shapiro, the stories include appreciation for the beauty and mystery of life, belief in the power of the spirit to accomplish its will, and ridicule for pretensions. Shapiro states that within Japanese folktales, "anything is possible; magic abounds, as long as it is faithful to the truths of the heart. Some

"Ah!" came a voice from within. At the same time Yohei cried out in horror and fell back from the doorway.

What Yohei saw was not human. It was a crane, smeared with blood, for with its beak it had plucked out its own feathers to place them in the loom.

At the sight Yohei collapsed into a deep faint.

From The Crane Wife, *retold by Sumiko Yagawa, illustrated by Suekichi Akaba, © 1979. English translation copyright © 1981 by Katherine Peterson. Published by William Morrow and Company, Inc. Reprinted by permission.*

stories are light-hearted, others disturbing, but all reveal the deep human values underlying the apparent transience of the physical world" (p. viii). In her discussion of style associated with Japanese folktales, Shapiro emphasizes that short phrases and repetitive sentences have great emotional impact, as in this quote from "The Wind in the Pine Tree": "the heavenly deity descended. Lightly, lightly he came by way of the Floating Bridge, bearing the tree in his right hand. Lightly, lightly his feet touched the earth" (p. x).

Chinese culture influenced Japanese culture, and thus many Japanese tales are similar to Chinese tales. Dragons, for example, are common in tales from both countries. The tiger, usually considered a symbol of power, is a creature often found in Japanese tales. The cat is important in *The Boy Who Drew Cats: A Japanese Folktale*, retold by Arthur Levine. When a boy paints cats on screens after he is trapped in an abandoned temple, the cats come to life to save him from a giant rat.

Japanese folktales reflecting respected values and disliked human qualities include Katherine Paterson's *The Tale of the Mandarin Ducks*. Paterson develops strong messages, such as that kindness will be rewarded, creatures cannot survive when held captive, honor is important, and sharing helps people through trouble. These respected values are depicted when two servants help a coveted mandarin duck, which has been captured by a greedy lord. When the kitchen maid releases the duck against the lord's command, she and another servant are sentenced to death. The grateful drake and his mate, however, outwit the lord and reward the kindness of the servants.

Cranes, like sparrows, are frequently important in Japanese folktales. Molly Bang's *The Paper Crane* suggests the desirability of friendship between humans and supernatural creatures. A hungry man rewards a restaurant owner with a paper crane that can be brought to life by clapping hands, and this attraction creates many customers for the business.

Dianne Snyder's *The Boy of the Three-Year Nap* has a strong female protagonist who outwits her lazy son. The tale is a humorous match of wits. The lazy son tries to trick a wealthy merchant into letting him marry the merchant's daughter. The mother, however, shows that she is the equal of the son. She not only convinces the merchant to repair and enlarge her house but also tricks her son into getting a job. Another strong female protagonist is found in Judy Sierra's *Tasty Baby Belly Buttons*, in which a girl battles the terrible oni, whose favorite food is human navels. The author uses words such as *boro, boro* and *zushin, zushin*, which are part of the oral vocabulary of traditional Japanese storytellers.

According to Eric A. Kimmel, his retelling of the folktale *Three Samurai Cats: A Story From Japan* is based on the teaching of Zen Buddhism, which emphasizes stillness, meditation, and harmony with nature. These values are revealed when a monk clarifies why the old samurai is able to defeat a ferocious rat when the two younger samurai are defeated: "The first two cats tried to overcome the rat with force. Neko Roshi, on the other hand, allowed his opponent to defeat himself. It is the lesson we teach here all the time, though few ever truly understand it. Draw strength from stillness. Learn to act without acting. And never underestimate a samurai cat" (unnumbered).

Seeking inspiration in nature and capturing the spirit of the subject is the focus of Elizabeth Partridge's artist character in *Kogi's Mysterious Journey*. This is a tale of transformation, as an artist endeavors to capture the essence and spirit of his subjects. As he tries to perfect his images of fish, he undergoes a transformation and swims freely with the fish. As a concluding spirit of nature, the artist releases his fish paintings into the freedom of real water and then joins them in fish form in order to understand the joyful spirit of nature.

Strong associations with nature and ecology are developed in Sheila Hamanaka's *Screen of Frogs*. A landowner responds favorably when a large frog appears in a dream and begs the man not to sell his home. Through the dream, the frog stresses the disasters that will occur if the frogs do not retain their land. As a reward for not selling the land, a tattered white screen belonging to the man is transformed into a beautifully painted screen of frogs.

Other Asian Folktales. The Asian Cultural Centre for UNESCO has published a series of five books called *Folk Tales From Asia for Children Everywhere*. The series contains stories from many Asian countries. For example, a story from Burma, "The Four Puppets," stresses the harm that wealth and power can bring if they are not tempered with wisdom and love. "The Carpenter's Son," a tale from Afghanistan, is similar to the Arabian story of Aladdin and his magic lamp.

Many folktales from India are included in a series of animal stories traditionally known as the *Panchatantra*. The original tales were moralistic and included reincarnations of the Buddha. English translations, however, usually delete the morals and the references to Buddha; consequently, the stories have characteristics of folktales. In Judith Ernst's retelling of *The Golden Goose King: A Tale Told by the Buddha*, the storyteller uses a tale told by the Buddha to reveal how a golden goose instructs the king and queen how to rule wisely.

Nami Rhee's *Magic Spring: A Korean Folktale* develops both humorous irony and the consequences of greed. When a poor, older couple discover a magic spring in the forest, they learn that a drink returns them to their youth. When their rich, greedy neighbor learns about their secret, he goes in search of the spring. Unfortunately, his greed causes him to drink too much water, and he becomes an infant. The renewed couple find him in the forest and raise him as their own child.

Laurence Yep's *The Khan's Daughter: A Mongolian Folktale* develops both a quest motif and a change in character as Mongke, a shepherd boy, accomplishes three trials in order to win the Khan's daughter. Two of the trials are imposed by the girl's mother: He must demonstrate proof of strength and proof of bravery. The third trial is formulated by the Khan's daughter. It is this third trial that shows both the character of the girl in determining her own destiny and the changes in Mongke as he goes from a rather foolish and boastful character to one who is both contrite and filled with considerable wisdom.

Ed Young's *I, Doko: The Tale of a Basket* is a story from Nepal. Told from the viewpoint of a basket that has been in the family for three generations carrying grain from the field, transporting a child, and bringing wood for the fire, the tale develops a powerful moral about the need to care for and respect the elderly when the son decides to use the basket to carry and leave his elderly father on the temple steps where the priests will care for him. The grandson expresses the moral of the tale when he tells his father to bring the basket back so that "I won't need to buy another Doko when you are old and it is time to leave you on the temple steps" (unnumbered). The father realizes his mistake and takes his elderly father back to his home.

Eastern folktales contain such universal motifs as reward for unselfishness, assistance from magical objects, cruel adversaries, and punishment for dishonesty. The tales also emphasize the traditional values of the specific people: Homage is paid to ancestors, knowledge and cleverness are rewarded, and greed and miserly behavior are punished.

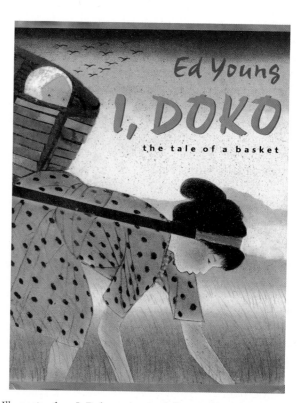

Illustration from I, Doko, *written and illustrated by Ed Young. Copyright © 2004 by Ed Young. Used by permission of Philomel Books, a division of Penguin Putnam, Inc.*

Middle Eastern Folktales

According to Inea Bushnaq, in *Arab Folktales*, the collection of Arab tales began as early as the eighth century by scholars centered in Baghdad. In 1704, *The Arabian Nights or The Thousand and One Nights* was translated from Arabic into French. This translation introduced Persian tales into Europe. Between 1885 and 1888, Sir Richard Francis Burton, the British consul in Trieste, translated the text from Arabic to English. Burton's translation is a primary source for many retellings in English.

In *Arab Folktales*, Bushnaq identifies the following categories for Arabic tales: Bedouin tales told by desert nomads; tales of magic and supernatural or household tales that include djinn, ghouls, and afreets; animal tales, which include fables and anecdotes; famous fools and rascals; religious tales and moral instruction; and tales of wit and wisdom that tell about clever men and wily women. We use Bushnaq's categories because much of the folklore published for children falls into these categories.

The Bedouin tales collected from the nomadic peoples of the desert include characteristics such as generosity in which a person's worth is counted not by what he owns but by what he gives to others; hospitality to those who enter the home and encampment (traditionally, the period of Bedouin hospitality is 3⅓ days); the importance of ancestry and birth in a culture in which the family is the most important social unit; and pride, independence, and self-sufficiency of the nomadic characters. Many Bedouin tales reflect these values when the storyteller concludes with a sentence such as "So it is when men are noble."

Generosity and hospitality are the major values depicted in Bushnaq's "The Last Camel of Emir Hamid." In this tale from Saudi Arabia, a reward is given for generosity. Hospitality is important in "The Boy in Girl's Dress," a story from Syria that shows the value of hospitality in a treeless, waterless region in which to deny food and shelter could mean denying life.

Many of the highly illustrated single-volume stories are tales of magic and supernatural. Eric A. Kimmel's *The Three Princes: A Tale From the Middle East* has a characteristically vague, contradictory opening: "Once there was and once there was not a princess who was as wise as she was beautiful" (p. 1). The princess challenges her three suitors to bring back the rarest things they find in their yearlong travels and promises to marry the prince who returns with the greatest wonder. In a dramatic ending, the prince who returns with the orange that cures any illness uses the fruit to heal the princess and thus wins her for his wife. The importance of generosity, sacrifice, and wisdom is revealed as the princess chooses the prince who sacrificed the most.

Neil Philip's *The Arabian Nights* presents several magical tales, including a variant of the Cinderella story. This variant incorporates both motifs related to Cinderella and motifs that are characteristic of Arabic folklore. Notice how the following motifs suggest that this is an Arabic story: A plot with a jinni provides the heroine with whatever she fancies, including anklets studded with diamonds. The heroine enters the King's harem where the women's part of the entertainment is held. In her haste to leave the feast, she drops the diamond anklets. The queen organizes a search party for the person who can wear the anklets. After the girl is found, she is taken back to the palace where the celebration lasts for 40 days and 40 nights while the wedding is prepared. The evil sisters learn the secret of the jinni and turn their younger sister into a white dove by jabbing her with diamond pins. The prince sends out search parties. Without the heroine, he begins to sicken and waste away. Every day, the white dove comes to the prince's window, and the prince grows to love the bird. The prince finds the diamond pins, pulls them out, and the bride reappears. You can compare this "Cinderella" variant with another tale from the Middle East: Rebecca Hickox's *The Golden Sandal: A Middle Eastern Cinderella Story.*

The stories told by Shahrazad to King Shahriyar are popular for retelling and illustrating. *Sindbad: From the Tales of the Thousand and One Nights*, retold and illustrated by Ludmila Zeman, includes a tale of adventure, magic, and wonder. The author's note relates the Sindbad tales to actual historical routes and stresses that they may contain a mixture of fact and fiction. Zeman states: "Their route resembled that of Sindbad. They sailed on the Arabian Sea around India and Sri Lanka. In Sindbad's adventures, we visit the Valley of Diamonds, possibly the island of Sri Lanka, known for precious stones, such as rubies, blue sapphires, and topazes. Later, Sindbad is captured by manlike creatures—could they be the orangutans that Arabian sailors first encountered in Sumatra?" (author's note). The illustrations in the text reflect the Persian influence.

Aladdin and the Enchanted Lamp, retold by Philip Pullman, is another story told as part of the "Arabian Nights." When reviewing the book, Daniel Handler (2005) states: "The acknowledgment of patronage is one of Pullman's few additions to the age-old tale; otherwise his version is basically streamlined from those found in 'Arabian Nights' and other earlier texts" (p. 39). This is the story in which a poor tailor's son who, with the help of a jinnee from a magic lamp, wins a both a princess and some wisdom along the way. Notice how Aladdin's changing character from a lazy, shiftless boy is revealed in the ending of the story: "So he and Badr-al-Budur were reunited, and they loved each other more than ever. And when at last the Sultan died, Aladdin inherited the kingdom. He ruled justly and well all his life long . . . he had many children and grandchildren, some of them almost as naughty as he had once been, but all of them brave, and beautiful, and greatly loved" (p. 71).

According to Bushnaq, the favorite type of animal story in Arabic is a trickster tale in which two animals, or a human and an animal, try to outwit each other. These tales usually end with a punch line that is wise and witty. For example, "The Cat Who Went to Mecca," an animal tale from Syria, concludes: "The king of the mice jumped back into his hole and rejoined his subjects. 'How is the king of the cats after his pilgrimage?' they asked. 'Let's hope he has changed for the better.' 'Never mind the pilgrimage,' said the king of the mice.' 'He may pray like a Hajji but he still pounces like a cat' " (p. 216).

Demi's *The Hungry Coat: A Tale From Turkey* reveals the wisdom of Nasrettin Hoca, a 13th-century Turkish philosopher, teacher, and humorist. When the wise man in the story is unable to change his old clothes before going to a banquet in a rich man's house, he is avoided and treated with disgust. He goes home, changes into fine clothing, and returns to the dinner where he is welcomed with respect. He then feeds his coat because he believes it is his splendid coat that was invited and not himself.

Demi's afterword includes information about the original teller, Nasrettin Hoca (1208–1284 A.D.). As you read the following information, notice how Demi provides details about this man who was known for his common sense and droll sense of humor. The afterword also reveals values associated with Hoca's life and tales: "Stories about his adventures and wisdom became true folktales, told and embellished by adults and children alike for over seven hundred years. . . . With their universal themes of societal roles, survival, the joys and sorrows of daily life, and the relationships between people, people and objects, and people and animals, the stories center around Nasrettin Hoca himself as a symbol of common sense, clear wisdom, and good-natured humor. . . . Many of the stories end with a moral or clever epigram meant to teach the listener or reader a valuable lesson" (unnumbered).

As you notice from these stories, tales from the Middle East include the importance of generosity and hospitality, using wit and wisdom, and they may include moral instruction.

African Folktales

Africa has a long and rich history of oral literature. In 1828, the first known collection of African tales was published for European audiences. This collection, *Fables Sénégalaises, Recueillies de l'Ouolof,* was translated into French by the Baron Jacques-François Roger, the French Commandant of Senegal. More collections appeared as administrators, traders, and missionaries collected traditional African stories for various purposes. Like other traditional lore, African folklore reveals ancient beliefs in the origins of natural and tribal worlds, as well as certain physical and spiritual traits.

As you read the stories, try to identify the characters, symbols, truths, values, and beliefs that are important to the African people and to those from around the world. Nelson Mandela (2002) identifies the following characters and symbols found in African folktales: "There is the cunning creature that manages to outsmart, including much bigger opponents: the hare, sly little rascal that he is; the cunning jackal, most often in the role of a trickster; the hyena (sometimes associated with the wolf) in the role of the underdog; the lion as ruler and distributor of gifts to the animals; the snake, which inspires fear, but is also a symbol of healing power, often in conjunction with the power of water; magic spells that bring either doom or freedom; people and animals undergoing metamorphoses; gruesome cannibals who terrorize both great and small" (pp. 7–8). Some of the tales explore societal problems and provide possible solutions. For example, Verna Aardema's *Bringing the Rain to Kapiti Plain: A Nandi Tale* shows that individuals have obligations for the betterment of the people, the environment, and the animals that provide their welfare. Ashley Bryan's "The Husband Who Counted the Spoonfuls," found in *Beat the Story-Drum, Pum-Pum,* develops a need for stability in marital relationships. The importance of solving family relationships is the theme found in Nancy Raines Day's *The Lion's Whiskers: An Ethiopian Folktale.* In this tale, a caring stepmother discovers how to make her elusive stepson respond to her.

Ann Grifalconi's *The Village of Round and Square Houses* reveals how a social custom began. In this case, a volcanic eruption in the distant past leaves only two houses within the village: one round and one square. To meet the needs of the village, the women and children move into the round house and the men stay in the square house. According to the tale, the custom continues today because people "live together peacefully here— Because each one has a place to be apart, and a time to be together. . . . And that is how our way came about and will continue—Til Naka speaks again!" (unnumbered). The illustrations in *The Village of Round and Square Houses* add to the feeling of place.

As you read collections of African folktales, notice the values and beliefs presented, such as the importance of maintaining friendship, a need for family loyalty, the desirability of genuine hospitality, the use of wit and trickery in unequal relationships, a strict code for ownership and borrowing, gratitude for help rendered, high risk in excessive pride, care for the feelings of those in authority, respect for individuality, and appropriate awe of the supernatural.

Values such as the use of wit and trickery as appropriate actions when dealing with larger and unequal beings are found in Verna Aardema's *Anansi Does the Impossible: An Ashanti Tale.* Now the little spider must outwit a python, a fairy, and 47 hornets in order to bring them to the Sky God in exchange for the Sky God's stories. With the help of his wife, Aso, Anansi succeeds in accomplishing the three impossible tasks and consequently brings the stories to the people.

John Steptoe's *Mufaro's Beautiful Daughters: An African Tale* shows the importance of kindness and generosity toward others and the harmful results of greed and selfishness. The folktales in Brent Ashabranner and Russell Davis's *The Lion's Whiskers and Other Ethiopian Tales* reveal important values, such as courage and wisdom. *East African Folktales*, retold by Vincent Muli Wa Kituku, is a collection of 18 tales retold in both English and the Kamba language from Kenya. Each of the tales concludes with a moral that helps readers interpret the tales and understand the values and messages developed in them.

Verna Aardema's *Why Mosquitoes Buzz in People's Ears* explains why mosquitoes are noisy. Written as a cumulative tale, it is excellent for sharing orally with children; it suggests a rich language heritage and a respect for storytelling. Ashley Bryan's retelling of Nigerian tales in *The Story of Lightning & Thunder* also reflects this rich language tradition, as is revealed in the introduction to the tale "Ma Sheep Thunder and Son Ram Lightning": "A long time ago, I mean a long, long, time ago, if you wanted to pat Lighting or chat with Thunder; you could do it. Uh-huh, you could."

Aaron Shepard's retelling of *Master Man: A Tall Tale of Nigeria* reveals both why there is thunder in the sky and the foolish consequences resulting from bragging: "Two fools fighting forever to see which one is Master Man." David Wisniewski's collage illustrations add power to this tale. In addition, a useful Author's Note provides information about the Hausa people and identifies the sources used for retelling.

Symbolism is important in both the text and illustrations in many African folktales. Baba Wague Diakite provides interpretations for the symbolism found in the illustrations in *The Magic Gourd*, a tale from the Bamana people of Mali, West Africa. Diakite lists page-by-page interpretations, such as that "The Sickle Blade" and "Calabash Flower" signify hard work and happy family and the "Crooked Road Walker" signifies dishonest actions.

The six tales in Donna L. Washington's *A Pride of African Tales* each have an introduction that identifies the type of folktale, such as a trickster tale, and the country of the original source. Valuable source notes are included. For example, to accompany the first tale, "Anansi's Fishing Expedition," the author states: "The Asante, or Ashanti, nation, where people first told stories about Anansi, is located in southwest Ghana. Stories about Anansi can be found all over Africa as well as in the Caribbean. Anansi is most often depicted as a spider and is sometimes called Grandfather Spider. But in spider or human form, Anansi is always the same—wily, conniving, and full of schemes" (p. 69). The author includes lists of additional sources for each of the tales in her collection.

Nelson Mandela's Favorite African Folktales presents 32 tales from identified countries throughout Africa. He begins his collection with a map of Africa that shows the location of each folktale. Each story includes an introduc-

The consequences of bragging are presented through Master Man: A Tall Tale of Nigeria, *told by Aaron Shepard. (Cover art from* Master Man: A Tall Tale of Nigeria, *told by Aaron Shepard. Jacket illustrations © 2001 by David Wisniewski. Jacket © 2001 by HarperCollins Publishers. Used by permission of HarperCollins Publishers.)*

tion, such as this one for "The Message": "A Nama variation on the theme of how death came into the world, retold here by poet, novelist, and short-story writer George Weideman who heard it from Grandma Rachel Eises. In the countless versions of this ancient tale the message is sometimes brought by the chameleon and the lizard, while sometimes the hare bungles the message all by himself. In this variation Tick and Hare are the messengers. Illustrator: Robert Hichens" (p. 23).

Latino Folklore

The wide cultural areas for Latino folklore include Mexico, South and Central America, Cuba, and the American Southwest. The folklore incorporates pre-Spanish tales of the Aztecs, Maya, and Incas. The Spaniards colonized the earlier populations, and different groups, such as the Apache and Pueblo Indians, interacted. As in other cultures, there are myths that explain (*ejemplos*), as well as folktales and fairy tales (collectively called *cuentos*).

Many of the early Aztec and Mayan tales were recorded for European audiences by Spaniards in the 16th century. Others were written down by Aztecs who learned to read and write in the Texcoco Seminary. These tales were illustrated in pictographic forms on codices and provide many of the sources used by current folklorists and retellers of the tales.

Tales in John Bierhorst's *The Monkey's Haircut and Other Stories Told by the Maya*, collected from the Maya in Guatemala and southeastern Mexico, indicate many of the traditional Mayan values and cultural characteristics. For example, the extensive use of riddles in the folklore shows that the people value cleverness. In "Rabbit and Coyote," double meanings allow Rabbit to dupe Coyote and to escape from his cage. The plot of "Tup and the Ants" hinges on a pun. Cultural characteristics are shown in other tales, such as "The Mole Catcher," in which a husband must pay a price for his wife through a bride service. In *Song of Chirimia—A Guatemalan Folktale*, Jane Anne Volkmer retells the story of a young man who goes on a quest to win a Mayan princess. The illustrations based on ancient stone carvings provide a feeling for the Mayan civilization. The text is printed in both English and Spanish.

The author's note in Gerald McDermott's *Musicians of the Sun* states that the tale is a fragment from the mythological tradition of the Aztecs. The tale reveals how Tezcatlipoca, Lord of the Night, commands Wind to fly to the house of the Sun and free the four musicians who are held prisoner: Red, Yellow, Blue, and Green. This becomes a creation myth as Wind overcomes Sun's power, frees the musicians, and brings color and music to earth. The importance of the four directions is emphasized because each color faces a different direction.

Two highly illustrated books written by Nancy Van Laan and Pleasant DeSpain present Brazilian folktales for younger readers. Van Laan's *So Say the Little Monkeys* uses a rhyming text that incorporates the sounds of the mischievous and active monkeys with the sounds of the jungle. DeSpain's *The Dancing Turtle: A Folktale From Brazil* develops the theme that survival requires courage and wit.

Lois Ehlert's *Moon Rope* is adapted from a Peruvian tale called "The Fox and the Mole," in which Fox convinces Mole that they should try to climb to the moon on a rope woven of grass. The story ends as a *pourquoi* tale because after falling off the rope, Mole prefers to stay in the earth and come out only at night, avoiding other animals and never having to listen to Fox. The text, written in both English and Spanish, is illustrated with pictures inspired by ancient Peruvian textiles, jewelry, ceramics, sculpture, and architectural detail. Ehlert's *Cuckoo: A Mexican Folktale* is another *pourquoi* tale written in both English and Spanish.

Barbara Knutson's *Love and Roast Chicken: A Trickster Tale From the Andes Mountains* pits Cuy, a small guinea pig who uses his brains instead of force, against Tio Antonio, a fox who is trying to eat the guinea pig.

Many of the folktales from Mexico, South and Central America, and Latino cultures in the United States reflect a blending of cultures. For example, John Bierhorst's *Spirit Child: A Story of the Nativity* shows the fusion of

Illustration from Love and Roast Chicken: A Trickster Tale From the Andes Mountains. *Text and illustrations copyright © 2004 by Barbara Knutson. Reprinted by permission of Carolrhoda Books, Inc.*

Christian and Aztec beliefs. The text describes, and Barbara Cooney's illustrations depict, an Aztec setting for the birth of the Christ child. Extensive Aztec beliefs are infused in the tale. Likewise, various versions of "The Virgin of Guadalupe" represent the merger of Spanish-Catholic and Aztec Indian heritages.

Tomie dePaola's *The Lady of Guadalupe*, a retelling of a Mexican tale, develops the connection between the people and their religious faith. According to the tale, the Lady of Guadalupe, now the patron saint of Mexico, appeared to a poor Mexican Indian on a December morning in 1531. Juan Diego, "He-who-speaks-like-an-eagle," was walking toward the Church of Santiago when he saw a hill covered with a brilliant white cloud. Out of the cloud came a gentle voice calling Juan's name and telling him that a church should be built on that site so that the Virgin Mary could show her love for Juan's people, the Indians of Mexico. DePaola says that he has had a lifelong interest in the tale of the Lady of Guadalupe. His drawings, based on careful research, depict the dress and architecture of 16th-century Mexico.

Two traditional tales adapted by Harriet Rohmer originate with the Miskito Indians of Nicaragua. *The Invisible Hunters* reflects the impact of European cultures on the Miskito people. The three hunters are punished when they break their promise and forsake their people. European traders influence the hunters' actions and create and expand their greed. *Mother Scorpion Country* is a tale of love. In this tale, a husband tries to accompany his wife into the land of the dead. According to the author's notes, "the compassionate figure of Mother Scorpion reflects a pre-Christian matriarchal past" (p. 32).

Both of Rohmer's texts provide information about the author's research. For example, Rohmer began her research for *The Invisible Hunters* in anthropological archives, visited the Miskito communities in the company of an Afro-Indian Catholic priest, learned more details of the story from an elder Miskito Catholic deacon, and finally met a Miskito bishop of the Moravian Church, who provided many additional details. During this final contact, Rohmer was told, "According to the stories I heard as a child the Dar has a voice. I can take you to people who say they have heard that voice" (p. 31). In *Mother Scorpion Country*, Rohmer traces the story to the endeavors of a young Moravian minister who recorded the stories and customs of the Miskito Indians in the early 1900s.

Two retellers of Latino folklore have chosen to retell various versions of the story of "La Llorona," the woman who killed her children and now wanders crying through the night; it is believed that because of loneliness, she kidnaps children. *Prietita and the Ghost Woman*, by Gloria Anzaldua, is a story about a girl who goes in search of herbs to cure her mother and becomes lost in the woods. She has always heard about the ghost woman who steals children; now she may be meeting the ghost woman. Rudolfo Anaya's *Maya's Children: The Story of La Llorona* tells about a Mayan woman who is immortal. When the god is angered by her immortality, he threatens to destroy her children. When she tries to trick the god, her children perish. Readers can compare the retellings and the illustrations in these two books.

North American Folktales

Many North American folktales have roots in the cultures of other parts of the world or have been influenced by written literature and characters created by professional writers. Consequently, identifying tales that began in a specifically North American oral tradition is often difficult or impossible.

Folklorists identify four types of folktales found in North America: (1) Native American (and Native Canadian) tales that were handed down over centuries of tribal storytelling; (2) folktales of African Americans that reflect African and European themes but that were changed as slaves faced difficulties in a new land; (3) variants of European folktales containing traditional themes, motifs, and characters that were changed to meet the needs of a robust, rural North America; and (4) boisterous, boastful tall tales that originated on this continent. Some collections of folktales, such as Amy L. Cohn's *From Sea to Shining Sea: A Treasury of American Folklore and Folk Songs*, include all of these types of tales. Other sources contain only one type of tale.

An In-Depth Analysis of a Folklore Collection

Tales From the Rain Forest is a collection of stories from the Amazonian Indians of Brazil as retold by Mercedes Dorson and Jeanne Wilmot. The collection begins with a detailed introduction of the cultural source of the stories: "The Brazilian Indians of Amazonia are the descendants of the Amerindian population that created and passed along the tales told in this book" (p. xv). The authors then provide historical background about the Brazilian Indians.

The introduction also focuses on the importance of the theme that emphasizes the need to respect the jungle:

> The message common in so many of the tales retold in these pages is the importance of respecting the needs of the formidable jungle. . . . The tales of the Brazilian Indians are dominated by animals, humans of animal ancestry, and even humans transformed into plants. Time is not linear. It is marked by the cycles of nature such as the ripening of fruit or the season of flood waters. Anything can be transformed or metamorphosized into anything else. A star can turn into a woman, a boy into a plant, a serpent can have a human daughter and a jaguar can be more civilized than a man. The animate and inanimate are interchangeable in a way that resists logical comprehension. (p. xix)

The authors also tell readers to be prepared to read stories that tell how various animals were created, how night was born, how fire was acquired, and how various aspects of the natural world originated. To further prepare readers or listeners, they explain that in the original stories, the storytellers used pantomime, repetition, and mimicry.

The collection presents 10 stories about motifs associated with creation. Each of the tales concludes with a comment that discusses the source of the tale and provides clarifying background information. Some of the comments, such as the one associated with the tale "The Creation of Night," encourage understanding by defining the Water Serpent as the father of the sorceress and a symbol for the mobility between human and animal form and the feelings of equality with animals. Other comments, such as those accompanying "The Young Man and the Star Maiden," clarify beliefs associated with cultivation, plant and animal management, and conservation.

The authors include a glossary, sources for each of the tales, a list of sources for illustrations, and a bibliography. The author information states that one of the authors was born in Brazil, has traveled in the Amazon region, and spent time among the Brazilian Indians. All of this information adds authenticity to the tales and could be used to further evaluate the stories and the illustrations.

Native American Folktales. Native American tales show that the North American continent had traditional tales centuries old before the European settlers arrived. Critics and reviewers of the literature emphasize the complexity of the tales, the various tribes whose values and beliefs are developed through the tales, and the need for authenticity in texts and in illustrations. In an evaluation of children's literature about Native Americans, Clifford E. Trafzer (1992) emphasizes the need for citing tribal sources and creating works that are culturally authentic for the tribe.

Native American traditional literature is an excellent source for identifying and understanding tribal traditional values and beliefs. In the introduction to *Echoes of the Elders: The Stories and Paintings of Chief Lelooska* (1997), Stephen Dow Beckham states: "The stories were the primary means of passing on the tribal memory. They recounted how the world had come to be, why things were named as they were, and how humans should act. They speak through time to listeners and readers today" (p. 5).

Many of the Native American traditional values, such as living in harmony with nature, viewing religion as a natural phenomenon closely related to nature, showing respect for wisdom gained through age and experience, acquiring patience, and emphasizing group and extended family needs rather than individual needs, are also dominant themes in traditional tales from various tribal regions. As you read Native American tales, see if you can identify these values.

For example, living in harmony with nature is a dominant theme in Tomie dePaola's retelling of the Comanche tale *The Legend of the Bluebonnet*. The theme is developed when selfishly taking from the land is punished by drought, and unselfishly giving a prized possession is rewarded with bluebonnets and rain. The name change in the main character as she goes from She-Who-Is-Alone to One-Who-Dearly-Loved-Her-People supports the emphasis on extended family rather than on the individual.

The interactions between buffalo and Great Plains Indians are depicted in Olaf Baker's *Where the Buffaloes Begin* and Paul Goble's *Buffalo Woman*. In *Where the Buffaloes Begin*, Stephen Gammell's marvelous black-and-white drawings capture the buffaloes surging out of a mythical lake after their birth, rampaging across the prairie, and eventually saving Little Wolf's people from their enemies; in traditional tales from the Great Plains, the buffalo people frequently save those who understand and respect them. Goble's tale ends with why the relationship between the Great Plains Indians and the buffaloes is so important: "The relationship was made between the People and the Buffalo Nation; it will last until the end of time. It will be remembered that a brave young man became a buffalo because he loved his wife and little child. In return, the Buffalo People have given their flesh so that little children,

and babies still unborn, will always have meat to eat. It is the Creator's wish" (unnumbered).

Showing respect for animals, keeping one's word, and listening to elders are interrelated themes in Frank Cushing's "The Poor Turkey Girl," found in *Zuni Folk Tales*. In this Cinderella-type tale, a Zuni maiden who cares for the turkeys is helped to go to a festival by old Gobble and the other turkeys. When the girl does not heed old Gobble's admonition to return on time to feed the turkeys, she loses everything because "after all, the gods dispose of men according as men are fitted; and if the poor be poor in heart and spirit as well as in appearance, how will they be aught but poor to the end of their days? Thus shortens my story" (p. 64).

Native American trickster tales reveal both good and bad conduct. John Bierhorst (1976) states; "The trickster tale affords the narrator an opportunity to flirt with immoral or antisocial temptations" (p. 6) in humorous ways. Trickster characters are found throughout North America. On the northwestern coast of the Pacific Ocean, the trickster is called Raven. When evaluating the role of Raven, Bierhorst (1993) states: "Raven is tough. Whatever is ascribed to him, he can survive it. And when we look back on what has been said of him, we may find that there is more wisdom to these tales than we had realized. As for Raven himself, he is always off on a new adventure. One of the old Tsimshian narrators used to say that after each scrape Raven doggedly 'journeys on.' Or as another old text once phrased it, the trickster simply 'put on his raven garment and flew away.'"

Raven the trickster is the central character in Gerald McDermott's *Raven: A Trickster Tale From the Pacific Northwest*. In this tale, to bring light from Sky Chief, Raven changes himself into a pine needle that is in a drinking cup of Sky Chief's daughter. After swallowing the needle, she eventually gives birth to a child who is really Raven in human form. Thus, Raven is able to acquire the sun that is in a set of nested boxes found in the sky lodge and bring light to the earth.

Iktomi is the Sioux name for "trickster." In *Iktomi and the Boulder: A Plains Indian Story*, Paul Goble describes the fair and foul side of Iktomi, who is "beyond the realm of moral values. He lacks all sincerity. Tales about Iktomi remind us that unsociable and chaotic behavior is never far below the surface. We can see ourselves in him. Iktomi is also credited much greater things: in many of the older stories, the Creator entrusts him with much of Creation. People say that what seem to be the 'mistakes' and 'irrational' aspects of Creation, such as earthquakes, floods, disease, flies, and mosquitoes, were surely made by Iktomi" (introduction).

In Goble's version of the Sioux tale, conceited Iktomi first gives his blanket to a boulder and then deceitfully takes the blanket back when he needs it for protection. He uses trickery to save himself from the angry boulder. Even though he eventually wins the confrontation, he is frightened and momentarily humbled by his experience. Goble's *Iktomi and the Berries* provides another humbling experience for the trickster character.

Numerous Native American tales depict crossing various thresholds; transformations that allow characters to go into and out of the animal world are especially popular in stories retold for children. For example, Paul Goble's *Buffalo Woman* uses transformations to show the bond between Native Americans and animals. Goble's retelling of a tale from the Great Plains reflects a bond between the humans and the buffalo herds, essential if both the people and the buffaloes were to prosper.

In *Beyond the Ridge*, Goble's main character goes from the land of the living to the spirit world. An elderly Plains Indian experiences the afterlife as believed by her people; on her way, she discovers Owl Maker. The spirits of individuals who have led good lives pass Owl Maker to the right, toward Wanagiyata, Land of Many Tipis. However, Owl Maker pushes the spirits of those who have led bad lives to the left, along a short path where they fall off, landing back on earth to wander for a time as ghosts.

Lois Duncan's *The Magic of Spider Woman* is an explanatory tale and a cautionary tale. It is a tale about how Wondering Girl came to be known as Weaving Woman and also of the consequences when she disobeys Spider Woman.

African American Folktales. New folktales developed when Africans became slaves in North America, as Virginia Hamilton (1985) points out in her introduction to *The People Could Fly: American Black Folktales*: "Out of the contacts the plantation slaves made in their new world, combined with memories and habits from the old world of Africa, came a body of folk expression about the slaves and their experiences. The slaves created tales in which various animals . . . took on characteristics of the people found in the new environment of the plantation" (p. x). For example, the favorite Brer Rabbit, who was small and apparently helpless when compared with the more powerful bear and fox, was smart, tricky and clever, and usually won out over larger and stronger animals. The slaves, who identified with the rabbit, told many tales about his exploits.

Virginia Hamilton's collection of tales *The People Could Fly: American Black Folktales*, is divided into four parts: (1) animal tales, (2) extravagant and fanciful experiences, (3) supernatural tales, and (4) slave tales. The collection provides sources for listening, discussing, and comparing. For example, readers can compare the folklore elements, plot, and themes in Hamilton's "The Beautiful Girl of the Moon Tower," a folktale from the Cape Verde Islands, and elements and motifs found in European folktales.

One of the folktales from Hamilton's collection is found in a single-story edition, *The People Could Fly: The Picture Book*. Hamilton's author's note reveals that the story "is a detailed fantasy tale of suffering, of magic power exerted against the so-called Master and his underlings. Finally, it is a powerful testament to the millions of slaves who never had the opportunity to 'fly' away. They remained slaves, as did their children. 'The People Could Fly' was first told and retold by those who had only their imaginations to set them free" (unnumbered).

Hamilton's *When Birds Could Talk & Bats Could Sing: The Adventures of Bruh Sparrow, Sis Wren, and Their Friends* is a collection of retellings of eight folktales from the southern United States. The tales are written in the form of fables, with each fable ending with a moral. Like the African folktales, these tales are filled with rhyming and singing. Barry Moser's watercolors provide visual characterizations of the animals.

The most famous African American folktales originating in the southern United States are the stories originally collected and retold by Joel Chandler Harris's "Uncle Remus" in the late 19th century. Again, that "monstrous clever beast," Brer Rabbit, always survives by using his cunning against stronger enemies. Two authors, Van Dyke Parks and Julius Lester, have adapted highly acclaimed versions of the Uncle Remus stories originally written down by Harris. The combination of Parks's text and Barry Moser's illustrations for *Jump! The Adventures of Brer Rabbit* and *Jump Again! More Adventures of Brer Rabbit* makes for highly readable and visually satisfying experiences. It is interesting to analyze the animal characters, consider the social impact of slavery as depicted in the stories, identify values that are similar to those found in African tales, compare similar tales from other cultures or in other versions of the Uncle Remus stories, and consider the impact of the authors' styles.

For example, Brer Rabbit is considered a character who can use his head, outdo and outwit all other creatures, and rely on trickery if necessary. In this role, Brer Rabbit uses trickery if he is in conflict with bigger and more powerful characters, but he also represents what happens when folks are full of conceit and pride. They "are going to get it taken out of them. Brer Rabbit did get caught up with once, and it cooled him right off" (*Jump!*, p. 19). Notice that rejecting conceit and pride is also found in African folklore. In addition, the tales reflect changes caused by the new environment, where the storytellers are influenced by slavery and European colonization and the need to protect their families and develop friendships that are tempered with distrust.

Symbolism, onomatopoeia, and personification add to Parks's storytelling style. For example, Parks uses symbolic meaning to contrast the length of night and day in *Jump!*: "When the nights were long and the days were short, with plenty of wood on the fire and sweet potatoes in the embers, Brer Rabbit could outdo all the other creatures" (p. 3). Onomatopoeia is used to imitate actions. Brer Rabbit relies on his "lippity-clip and his blickety-blick" (p. 3). Personification is found in descriptions of nature: "Way back yonder when the moon was bigger than he is now . . ." (p. 3).

Make comparisons within and across cultures. For example, compare the stories retold in Parks's version, stories retold in Lester's *The Tales of Uncle Remus: The Adventures of Brer Rabbit*, and stories in earlier versions retold by Joel Chandler Harris. Make cross-cultural comparisons by analyzing "Brer Rabbit Finds His Match" (*Jump!*) and the Aesop fable "The Tortoise and the Hare."

African American folktales are filled with symbolism and alternate meanings. Rex M. Ellis interprets symbolic meanings in many of the African American folktales in his introductions to tales in *Beneath the Blazing Sun* (1997). For example, he states in "The Wolf and the Dog": "The following story addresses this phenomenon [symbolism and alternate meanings] using the character of a wolf, who, like many blacks of the period, chose to live a life of freedom, a life of running away and hiding out—with little comfort—and the dog who embraced a life of comfort—albeit accompanied by humiliation, degradation, and contempt" (p. 51).

American Variants of European Tales. The traditional literatures of the United States and Canada contain many variants of traditional European folktales. European settlers from England, France, and elsewhere brought their oral traditions with them, then they adapted the stories to reflect a new environment. Consequently, many North American folktales involve familiar European themes, motifs, and characters in settings that portray the unknown wilderness and harsh winters confronted by the early colonizers of North America. The only indigenous Canadian traditional literature comes from the Native Canadian and Inuit peoples.

Eva Martin's *Canadian Fairy Tales* contains 12 French-Canadian and English-Canadian variations of traditional European tales. The tales contain several familiar story elements. The lazy fellow kills 1,000 flies with one blow, uses his wits to capture a unicorn and steal a giant's seven-league boots, and eventually marries the princess. In the Canadian variant of "Beauty and the Beast," the enchanted beast is female and the prince stays in her castle. William H. Hooks's *Moss Gown* is an adaptation of the English Cinderella tale that also contains elements of King Lear and the plantation South.

The best-known North American variants of European tales belong to the Jack cycle. In these tales, a seemingly nonheroic person overcomes severe obstacles and outwits adversaries. The American "Jack and the Varmits," for example, is similar to the English "The Brave Little Tailor." In keeping with the European tradition, the American Jack is rewarded by a king. Instead of a giant, Jack must overcome a wild hog, a unicorn, and a lion. The influences of rural America are found in both the setting and language: The lion, who was killing cattle, horses, and humans, came over the mountains from Tennessee, and both the king and Jack speak in frontier dialect. Gail E. Haley's *Jack and the Bean Tree* is an Appalachian variant of "Jack and the Beanstalk." Haley's *Mountain Jack Tales*, a collection of stories from the Jack cycle, has foundations in the mountain regions of America. A resourceful female becomes the heroine in Mary Pope Osborne's variant of "Jack and the Beanstalk," *Kate and the Beanstalk*. There is also considerable humor in this story.

Tall Tales. Boastful frontier humor is found in North American tall tales. These tales reflect the hardships of settlers, who faced severe climatic changes, unknown territory, and people whose lives reflected strange cultures. Exaggerated claims in tall tales—such as those found in Walter Blair's *Tall Tale America: A Legendary History of Our Humorous Heroes*—declare that the American soil is so rich that fast-growing vines damage pumpkins by dragging them on the ground; that frontier people are so powerful that they can lasso and subdue cyclones; and that the leader of the riverboaters can outshoot, outfight, outrun, and outbrag everyone in the world.

The North American heroes and heroines who faced extremes in weather, conquered humans and beasts, and subdued the wilderness are not the godlike heroes and heroines of European mythology. Instead, their lives reflect the primitive virtues of brute force, animal cunning, and courage. The characters and situations in tall tales reflect frontier idealism: People are free to travel; they live self-sufficient lives and are extremely resourceful.

American tall tales contain both fictional heroes and heroes based on real people. Hardworking, persevering characters—such as Johnny Appleseed, who considered it his mission to plant apple trees across the country—demonstrate duty and endurance. Boisterous, bragging roughnecks—such as Davy Crockett, Calamity Jane, and Paul Bunyan—perform otherwise impossible feats, outshooting a thousand enemies or conquering mighty rivers and immense forests. Other characters—such as the steel-driving man, John Henry—reflect a country that was changing from a rural and agricultural way of life to an urban and mechanized one. *John Tabor's Ride*, by Edward C. Day, reflects the whaling industry and the yarns told by whalers in New England. *Mike Fink: A Tall Tale*, retold by Stephen Kellogg, is another story that emphasizes numerous fantastic feats.

Robert D. San Souci's *Cut From the Same Cloth: American Women of Myth, Legend, and Tall Tale* is an excellent tall-tale collection about women in heroic conflicts. San Souci presents tales from different regions and ethnic groups. He also includes source notes and a bibliography. Nancy Van Laan's *With a Whoop and a Holler: A Bushel of Lore From Way Down South* is an anthology of tales from the Bayou region, the deep South, and Appalachia. Scott Cook's illustrations add humor to many of the tall tales. The author includes a list of source notes. These stories would be especially good for oral storytelling.

Fables

Legend credits the origin of the fable in Western culture to a Greek slave named Aesop, who lived in the sixth century B.C. Aesop's nimble wit supposedly got Aesop's master out of numerous difficulties. Verónica Uribe (2004) states that Aesop was the most popular teller of fables because "his fables, transmitted orally, were used in ancient Greece as exercises in rhetoric and grammar. Philosophers had their students memorize and recite the fables, and urged them to come up with their own versions" (p. 122). Aesop may not have been one person, however; several experts attribute the early European fables to various sources. Fables are found worldwide; the traditional literatures of China and India, for example, contain fables similar to Aesop's. Whatever their origins, fables are excellent examples of stories handed down over centuries of oral and written literary tradition.

Characteristics

According to R. T. Lenaghan (1967), in his introduction to *Caxton's Aesop*, fables have the following characteristics: (1) They are fiction in the sense that they did not really happen; (2) they are meant to entertain; (3) they are poetic, with double or allegorical significance; and (4) they are moral tales, usually with animal characters. In fables, animals usually talk and behave like humans and possess other human traits. Fables are short, and they usually have no more than two or three characters. These characters perform simple, straightforward actions that result in a single climax. Fables also contain human lessons expressed through the foibles of personified animals.

The characteristics of fables apparently appealed to traditional storytellers around the world. In 15th-century England, fables were among the first texts that William Caxton printed on his newly created printing press. Lenaghan (1967) credits the popularity of fables to their generic ambiguity: They could be used as entertaining stories, teaching devices, or sermons. They could also reach people of various degrees of intelligence, be bluntly assertive or cleverly ironic, and be didactic or skeptical. Storytellers could emphasize whatever functions they chose.

The continuing popularity of fables led Randolph Caldecott to create his own edition of Aesop in the 19th century. *The Caldecott Aesop,* first published in 1883 and reissued in 1978, allows modern readers to enjoy fables accompanied by hand-colored drawings of a great illustrator of children's books. Caldecott's illustrations show first the animals in a fable, then the people replacing the animals. Sir Roger L'Estrange's 17th-century translation of *Aesop's Fables* is also available in a reissued text.

Contemporary Editions

Helen Ward's introduction to *Unwitting Wisdom: An Anthology of Aesop's Fables* provides an excellent introduction to the purposes and values of fables. She states: "All use animals as the central characters in place of people, thereby avoiding the distractions of race or class, age or gender. As such, the experiences described apply to us all and the lessons learned are both timeless and universal. Each creature comes to symbolize in its own way some particular aspect of the human condition—the sly, sidling fox; the silly crow; the majestic lion; all acting out their parts, uncomprehending the great game of life. . . . In Aesop's fables . . . the animals' reactions are always predictable. They have no choice; they cannot be anything but themselves. They are never more or less, and that is the great lesson and the essence of the fable" (unnumbered, introduction).

Young children like the talking animals and the often humorous climaxes. Authors and illustrators of fables for young children sometimes expand fables into longer, more detailed narrative stories. For example, in *The Tortoise and the Hare,* Janet Stevens expands the story line of the fable by including the exercises Tortoise undertakes to prepare for the race and the actions of Tortoise's friends as they try to deter Hare.

Numerous collections of Aesop's fables have been compiled and illustrated for slightly older children, too. It is interesting to compare the various editions to see how the fables have been interpreted

¶ **Here begynneth the book**
of the subtyl historyes and Fables
of Esope whiche were translated
out of Frensshe in to Englysshe
by william Caxton

At Westmynstre In the yere of oure Lorde
.m. cccc.lxxxiij

The Book of the subtyl historyes and Fables of Esope, *published in the 15th century, is considered one of William Caxton's most important contributions to European literature. (The Book of the Subtyl Historyes and Fables of Esope, by William Caxton, published in the 15th century.)*

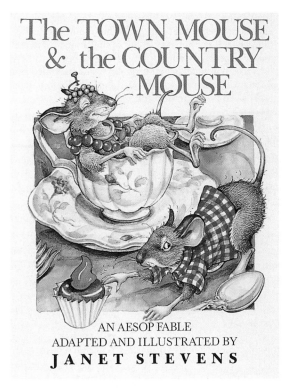

The TOWN MOUSE & the COUNTRY MOUSE

AN AESOP FABLE
ADAPTED AND ILLUSTRATED BY
J A N E T   S T E V E N S

The author has expanded on a fable to create a picture storybook in The Town Mouse & the Country Mouse. *(From* The Town Mouse & the Country Mouse, *adapted and illustrated by Janet Stevens. Copyright © 1987 by Janet Stevens. Reprinted by permission of Holiday House. All rights reserved.)*

and illustrated. For example, a version of Aesop first published in 1919, *The Aesop for Children*, is in simple narrative form and dialogue. The capture of the mouse in "The Lion and the Mouse" is described in this way:

> A Lion lay asleep in the forest, his great head resting on his paws. A timid little Mouse came upon him unexpectedly, and in her fright and haste to get away, ran across the Lion's nose. Roused from his nap, the Lion laid his huge paw angrily on the tiny creature to kill her.
>
> "Spare me!" begged the poor Mouse. "Please let me go and some day I will surely repay you."
>
> The Lion was much amused to think that a Mouse could ever help him. But he was generous and finally let the Mouse go. (p. 19)

The moral is stated simply in this version: "A kindness is never wasted."

Tom Paxton retells fables in verse in his *Aesop's Fables*. He describes the incident in which the mouse is captured in "The Lion and the Mouse":

> He ran over the lion, who awoke with a roar:
> "Who's treating my back like the jungle floor?"
> He grabbed the poor mouse by his poor little tail.
> "Oh, please, Mister Lion, I swear without fail.
> If you'll please just release me, I promise someday
> The debt will be one that I'll gladly repay."
> The proud lion laughed and let the mouse go.
> (unnumbered)

The moral of this fable is presented in verse form in the last two lines:

> Yes, sometimes the weak and sometimes the strong
> Must help each other to save right from wrong.
> (unnumbered)

The *McElderry Book of Aesop's Fables*, retold by Michael Morpurgo, is another large collection of fables that each end with a short moral; for example, "Kindness is more important than strength" follows "The Lion and the Mouse." The large size of the book and the use of numerous illustrations make it appropriate for sharing with a group. In contrast, Verónica Uribe's *Little Book of Fables* is a small-book format more appropriate for individual reading. Comparisons can also be made with the short morals that end the 20 fables. For example, the moral following "The Lion and the Mouse" states, "Little friends may prove to be great friends." Readers will notice that the morals stated in the Morpurgo and the Uribe texts are paraphrases of the same idea.

Jane Yolen's *A Sip of Aesop* provides an interesting version for comparison with more traditional versions of the fables. Yolen retells the fables in poetic form, including the moral at the end of the fable. For example, "The Dog and the Bone" ends with this moral:

> You may not have time
> For a final correction.
> Don't open your mouth
> Without proper reflection. (unnumbered)

Contemporary versions of fables differ in the illustrator's style as well as the author's style. Michael Hague's *Aesop's Fables* is illustrated with full-page paintings in somber, earthy tones. Fulvio Testa's *Aesop's Fables* also follows each fable with a full-page illustration. Each illustration is framed with a colorful design. Jerry Pinkney's *Aesop's Fables* is illustrated with large watercolor paintings, and Tom Lynch's *Fables From Aesop* is illustrated with fabric collages.

An interesting cross-cultural comparison of texts and illustrations can be made with John Bierhorst's *Doctor Coyote: A Native American Aesop's Fables*. Bierhorst identifies both Spanish-Aztec and ancient Latin connections. He states:

> The Aztec Aesop's was adapted in the 1500s by one or more Indian retellers, using a now-lost Spanish collection of the standard fables. All of these, however, can be traced to Latin and Greek manuscripts of late classical and medieval times. Compared with the originals, the Aztec variants differ mainly in the cast of characters, which includes Coyote and Puma, two of the best-known animal tricksters in Native American folklore. (author's note, unnumbered)

Jon Scieszka and Lane Smith have used the fable format to create their own contemporary interpretations in *Squids Will Be Squids: Fresh Morals, Beastly Fables*. The authors introduce their book by stating: "This book, *Squids Will Be Squids*, is a collection of fables that Aesop might have told if he were alive today and sitting in the back of class, daydreaming and goofing around instead of paying attention and correcting his homework like he was supposed to, because his dog ate it and he didn't have time to run out and buy new paper and do it over again before his bus came to pick him up in the morning" (fore-word). Julius Lester develops another series of humorous literary fables in *Ackamarackus: Julius Lester's Sumptu-ously Silly Fantastically Funny Fables.* These literary fables provide interesting sources for comparisons. In addition, the tales can be used to motivate students to write their own fables.

Myths

Every ancient culture made up stories that answered questions about the creation of the earth, the origins of people, and the reasons for natural phenomena. The Greeks called these explanations *mythos,* which means "tales" or "stories." Today, people sometimes use the word *myth* to describe any story they consider to be untrue. However, in literary terms, a myth is a story con-taining fanciful or supernatural incidents intended to ex-plain nature or tell about the gods and demons of early peoples. In the distant past, as in some traditional cultures today, the stories were taken as fact made sacred by reli-gious belief.

Neil Philip (2004), in his *Mythology of the World,* re-lates the importance of myth to culture: "A culture that is defined by its mythology often shapes its myths to form a type of self-portrait of its people, showing their values, beliefs, and concerns. Myths express the spiritual and in-tellectual life of people, and the content of these myths is central to understanding how the people think" (p. 14).

Myths live on in contemporary literature and provide an understanding of the rich cultural heritage that we have acquired from ancient civilizations all over the world. Greek, Roman, and Norse mythology have been most influential in Western culture. Many terms used in those mythologies are also found in modern language, such as our names for the planets and for the days of the week. Children find these stories exciting, and they be-come interested in this rich literary heritage.

Joseph Campbell (1988) argues that myths are pow-erful literature and should be read and understood by everyone. He believes that four functions related to myths are as important today as they were in earlier times: (1) a mystical function that allows people to experience the awe of the universe, (2) a cosmological one that shows the shape and mystery of the universe, (3) a sociological one that supports and validates a certain social order, and (4) a pedagogical one that teaches people how to live.

James Houston (1990), a reteller of Inuit myths and legends, stresses the importance of preserving the ancient stories of any culture. He states:

Inuit songs and stories, like their carvings, often reveal an enormous freshness and ingenuity. But there is one enormous difference. A carving may be lost in the permafrost near some ancient campsite only to be excavated thousands of years later to tell us much about its maker. An unrecorded story or a song will disappear forever with the last breath of its teller and has no way to return. (p. 106)

Myths provide children with knowledge about ances-tral cultures and allow them to look at other cultures from the inside out. Myths are models for belief; they are seri-ous statements about existence. They provide a frame-work for understanding the things that other people did or thought. Myths are tools for understanding and for ex-panded expression, offering new dimensions for imagina-tion and suggesting ways for children to gain insights from their daydreams. Myths also provide means of introducing children to literary allusions: An author describing some-thing as being "as swift as Diana" or "as mighty as Zeus" is alluding to characteristics of gods.

Greek and Roman Mythology

Probably the best-known myths in Western culture origi-nated in ancient Greece. When the Romans conquered Greece, they adopted many Greek myths, applying them to their own equivalent deities. Helen Sewell states in the introduction to *A Book of Myths, Selections From Bulfinch's Age of Fable* (1942, 1964) that to understand these stories, one must be acquainted with ancient Greek ideas about the structure of the universe. The Greeks believed that the universe had been created out of unorganized matter called *chaos,* swirling and transparent vapor; form and shape resulted in *order* and *cosmos.* The Greeks believed that the first things formed out of chaos were the gods: *Gaia* (meaning "earth"; *Terra* is the Roman name) and *Ouranos* (meaning "sky"; *Uranus* is the Roman name). From the offspring of the female Gaia and the male Oura-nos emerged the remaining Greek gods and goddesses, who lived on Mount Olympus (an actual mountain in Greece) and frequently came into the human world.

According to the Greeks, the earth was flat and cir-cular and their own country was the center. Around the earth flowed the river Ocean. The dawn, the sun, and the moon were supposed to rise out of the eastern Ocean, dri-ven by gods and giving light to gods and mortals. The ma-jority of the stars also rose out of and sank into this river.

The Greeks also believed that the northern part of the earth beyond the mountains was inhabited by a race of people called Hyperboreans. In these mountains were the caverns from which came the piercing north winds that sometimes chilled Greece. To the south lived the Ethiopians, whom the gods favored; on the west lay the Elysian Plain, where mortals favored by the gods were transported to enjoy immortality. Roman myths drew es-sentially the same picture.

Although mythology and folktales contain similar motifs and themes, myths include Bascom's require-

CHART 6.4 A comparison of a myth and a folktale

Cupid and Psyche	"East of the Sun and West of the Moon"
Setting	
Mount Olympus, Greece	Any kingdom
Time	
In a remote past, when gods and goddesses dwelt on the earth	Once upon a time
Attitude	
Sacred—worship of the deity was required or punishment resulted	Secular
Principal Characters	
Venus (the goddess of love) Cupid (the son of Venus) Psyche (a mortal girl who becomes immortal)	Transformed human boy Human girl Troll princess

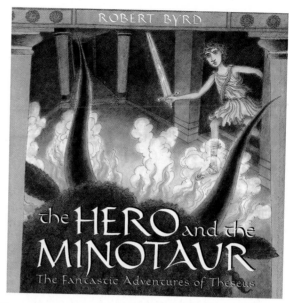

Illustration from The Hero and the Minotaur: The Fantastic Adventures of Theseus, *by Robert Byrd. Copyright © 2005 by Robert Byrd. Used by permission of Dutton Children's Books, a division of Penguin Putnam, Inc.*

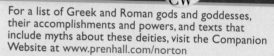

Technology Resources

For a list of Greek and Roman gods and goddesses, their accomplishments and powers, and texts that include myths about these deities, visit the Companion Website at www.prenhall.com/norton

ments for setting, time, attitude, and principal characters. Chart 6.4 compares points in Edna Barth's version of the myth *Cupid and Psyche* and the Norse folktale "East of the Sun and West of the Moon." The plot in the two tales is similar: A young girl breaks a promise, her loved one leaves, she searches for him, and she overcomes obstacles or performs tasks before they are reunited. The principal characters differ in important characteristics, however. Psyche, a beautiful mortal princess, is the object of a goddess's anger and jealousy. She later falls in love with a god, performs tasks stipulated by the goddess, and requires intervention from the most divine ruler, Jupiter.

Barth sees strong religious significance in the Cupid and Psyche myth. The myth, she reminds us, originally represented the progress of the human soul as it travels toward perfection. Symbolized by Psyche, the soul originated in heaven, where all is love, which is symbolized by Cupid. The soul is then condemned for a period of time to wander the earth and undergo hardship and misery. If the soul proves worthy, it is returned to heaven and reunited with love.

Circumstances surrounding the creation of the gods and goddesses, their places within the Olympian family, the consequences of their varied personality traits, and their accomplishments create exciting tales and enjoyable reading for children. Contemporary versions of Greek and Roman myths vary widely in terms of author's style, complexity of text, and illustration. Consider these factors when choosing myths to share with children of various ages and interests. Eight- or nine-year-olds, for example, enjoy Edna Barth's *Cupid and Psyche*. Her rendition of this myth is appropriate for children who enjoy such folktales as "Beauty and the Beast" and "East of the Sun and West of the Moon."

Leonard Everett Fisher's *Theseus and the Minotaur* has bold, full-page illustrations to accompany his version of the story of a brave youth who slays an evil monster. Warwick Hutton's *Theseus and the Minotaur* is illustrated with watercolor paintings that are especially effective in the depiction of the tragic return of the hero.

Gerald McDermott's *Daughter of Earth: A Roman Myth* is a highly illustrated version of the Ceres and Proserpina story. Jeanne Steig's *A Gift From Zeus: Sixteen Favorite Myths* includes myths such as tales of Prometheus and Pandora, Midas, and Echo and Narcissus; the collection is illustrated by William Steig. These three highly illustrated books are appropriate for all ages.

Many older children enjoy longer, more developed versions of the myths. For example, Doris Gates presents stories with fast-paced plots and language that suggests word pictures. Her style reads well, and her books are excellent for sharing orally. For example, her description of the creation of Athena in *The Warrior Goddess:Athena* seems appropriate:

> She sprang from the head of Zeus, father of gods. Born without a mother, she was fully grown and fully armed. Her right hand gripped a spear, while her left steadied a shield on her forearm. The awful aegis, a breast ornament bordered with serpents, hung from her neck, and from her helmeted head to her sandaled feet she was cloaked in radiance, like the flash of weaponry. So the great goddess Athena came to join the family of gods on high Olympus, and, of all Zeus's children, she was his favorite. (p. 11)

Older children can contrast this passage with Gates's description of the creation of the goddess of love and beauty in *Two Queens of Heaven:Aphrodite and Demeter*:

> There appeared a gathering of foam on the water. It resembled the white spindrift that trails behind a great wave as it breaks. But this form did not trail. It formed itself into a raft rising and falling with the sea. Suddenly a woman's figure appeared atop the raft balancing on slender feet. She was young and beautiful beyond anything in human form the sun had ever shone on. (pp. 9–10)

Versions of myths told by Olivia Coolidge, Charles Kingsley, and Padraic Colum are also good choices for older children.

In *Dateline: Troy*, Paul Fleischman retells the Greek myth about the Trojan War and puts the war into a contemporary context by placing appropriate, actual contemporary newspaper articles on pages facing similar content. In his introduction, Fleischman makes readers feel that they are reading about conflicts and people that are still found in the world today: "Listeners and readers had always found real human nature in what had transpired there. Envy-maddened Ajax, lovestruck Paris, crafty Odysseus, and all the others have walked the earth in every age and place. They come from the distant Bronze Age, it's as current as this morning's headlines. The Trojan War is still being fought. Simply open a newspaper . . ." (p. 9).

Norse Mythology

A far different group of gods and heroes existed in the Norse universe of ice, glaciers, and cold mountains. The harsh conditions of the far North helped form the Norse people and their legends. According to Kevin Crossley-Holland (1983), recurring strains in Norse mythology include a strong sense of fate that governs the lives of both gods and humans; a heroic bond between characters that is characterized by physical and moral courage, loyalty, and a willingness to take vengeance; a belief in omens; an ironic wit; a restless spirit of adventure; and a keen sense of wonder in the natural world and a close identification with nature.

Norse mythology influenced subsequent oral and written literature in northern Europe. Shakespeare, for instance, was influenced by an old Norse tale when he wrote *Hamlet*; J. R. R. Tolkien, a professor of Anglo-Saxon literature at Oxford University, relied on his knowledge of the northern sagas when he wrote *The Hobbit* and *The Lord of the Rings*.

The tales of the northern gods and goddesses were collected during the 12th and 13th centuries from the earlier oral tradition; these original tales formed two volumes, the *Elder Edda* and the *Younger Edda*. These texts are now the sources for most of our knowledge about Norse mythology. According to Olivia Coolidge (1951), Norse mythology maintains that the earth began when a frost giant, Ymir, came out of swirling mists. The shifting particles formed a great cow, whose milk nourished Ymir. As time went by, sons and daughters were also created out of the mists. Gods took form when the cow began to lick the great ice blocks that filled the mists. As she licked, a huge god appeared. When he stood up, his descendants were formed from his warm breath.

The frost giants were evil, so the gods vowed to destroy them. A mighty battle resulted between the gods and the frost giants, with the gods finally overpowering the giants. Ymir was destroyed, and the remaining giants fled into the outer regions and created a land of mists and mountains. The mightiest of the gods, Odin, looked at the dead frost giant, Ymir, and suggested that the gods use his body to make a land where they could live. They formed Ymir's body into the round, flat earth, and on its center, they built mountains to contain their home, Asgard. Ymir's skull was used to form the great arch of heaven; his blood was the ocean, a barrier between the earth and giantland. The gods stole sparks from the fiery regions to light the stars, and they built chariots in which they placed sun and moon spirits to ride over the earth.

The Norse world of tales filled with heroism, humor, and wisdom and peopled with gods, goddesses, giants, and dwarfs comes alive in Mary Pope Osborne's *Favorite Norse Myths*. These tales retold from the *Elder Edda* and the *Younger Edda* are introduced with quotes from the *Poetic Edda*, written down in the 10th century. For example, the first myth, "Creation: The Nine Worlds," opens with the following quote:

> Twas the earliest of times
> When Ymir lived:
> There was no sand nor sea
> Nor cooling wave.
> Earth had not been,
> Nor heaven on high,
> There was a yawning void
> And grass no where. (p. 1)

Osborne then begins the tale in a similar manner that places readers into this far distant time: "In the morning of time there was no sand, no sea, and no clouds. There was no heaven, no earth, and no grass. There was only a region of icy mist called Niflheim, a region of fire called Muspell, and a great yawning empty void between them

"The Hammer of Thor" is an excellent choice for storytelling.
(From Legends of the North, *by Olivia Coolidge. Copyright*
© *1951 and renewed 1979 by Olivia E. Coolidge. Reprinted by*
permission of Houghton Mifflin Co.)

called Ginnugagap" (p. 1). The author provides an introduction that places the Norse myths into their historical
time and setting. In addition, sections contain pronunciation guides and identifications of the gods, goddesses, giants, and other creatures; meanings of symbols and runes;
a bibliography; and an index.

Padraic Colum portrays the strong moral code of Odin
in his version of "The Building of the Wall," found in *The
Children of Odin: The Book of Northern Myths.* Even though
a protective wall is built around Asgard, Odin grieves:

> But Odin, the Father of the Gods, as he sat upon his throne
> was sad in his heart, sad that the Gods had got their wall built
> by a trick, that oaths had been broken, and that a blow had
> been struck in injustice in Asgard. (p. 12)

Olivia E. Coolidge's *Legends of the North* is an excellent source of stories about the Norse gods and goddesses
who lived on earth in the mighty citadel of Asgard and the
heroes and heroines who lived under their power. In "The
Apples of Idun," the divine beings often walked on earth
because the mighty Odin believed they should know their
realm intimately, in stone, flower, and leaf.

One humorous selection from this book is "The
Hammer of Thor." In this story, Thor searches loudly for
his missing hammer. Children probably feel close to
Thor as he responds in exasperation when Freyja, the
goddess of beauty, asks him where he put it. He shouts,
"If I knew where I put it, I should not be looking for it
now" (p. 35).

Thor discovers that the giant Thyrm has stolen the
hammer and wants Freyja as ransom. When the goddess
vehemently refuses to become the giant's bride, the suggestion is made that Thor dress up as a bride and go to giantland to retrieve his own hammer.

Thor's courage, loyalty, and willingness to take
vengeance are recurring strains found in this mythology.
The humor and action in this tale make it excellent for
storytelling. Other enjoyable Norse tales suitable for
sharing with children include Ingri and Edgar Parin
D'Aulaire's *Norse Gods and Giants* and Kevin Crossley-
Holland's *The Faber Book of Northern Legends.*

Native American Myths

MULTICULTURAL LITERATURE   There are numerous traditional Native
American tales that emphasize the cre-
ation of the earth and various animal and
plant life. Earth-diver myths are found in
the literature of several North American
Indian tribes. These myths reveal how an animal such as
a turtle dives under the water in a water-covered earth,
brings mud to the surface of the water, and then this mud
forms the earth. For example, Virginia Hamilton includes
two earth-diver myths in *In the Beginning: Creation Stories
From Around the World:* "Turtle Dives to the Bottom of the
Sea: Earth Starter the Creator," a Maidu tale from California, and "The Woman Who Fell From the Sky: Divine
Woman the Creator," a Huron myth from the northeastern United States. Hamilton's collection also includes a
Blackfoot myth in which Na'pi, or Old Man the Creator,
travels around the world creating people and animals, and
an Eskimo myth in which Raven, a trickster god, travels
around the world instructing people how to live.

Creation stories from several tribes are found in
*Keepers of the Earth: Native American Stories and Environ-
mental Activities for Children,* by Michael J. Caduto and
Joseph Bruchac. An Onondaga tale from the northeastern
woodlands, "The Earth on Turtle's Back," tells about how
Great Turtle gives his shell to hold Earth and seeds
brought to Earth by the Great Chief's wife. In a Navajo
tale, "Four Worlds: The Dine Story of Creation," The
Holy People move from the first world to the fourth world
by way of a female reed. This myth shows the disastrous
consequences of not taking care of Earth. The tale concludes with a warning: "So the Fourth World came to be.
However, just as the worlds before it were destroyed when
wrong was done, so too this Fourth World was destined to
be destroyed when the people do not live the right way.
That is what the Dine say to this day" (p. 34).

In *Keepers of the Animals: Native American Stories and
Wildlife Activities for Children,* Caduto and Bruchac discuss
the symbolic meaning of "Salmon Boy," a Haida tale from
the Pacific Northwest. They state: "'Salmon Boy' is an allegory of great importance, revealing a series of interlocking circles which, as the story proceeds, run progressively

From Keepers of the Earth: Native American Stories and Environmental Activities for Children, *by Michael J. Caduto and Joseph Bruchac; illustrations by John Kahionhes Fadden and Carol Wood. Cover illustration copyright © 1988 John Kahionhes Fadden. Published by Fulcrum, Inc., 1988. Reprinted by permission.*

deeper into the life ways of the Haida. . . . There is an important, independent relationship here: The salmon give people food and the people show their appreciation through prayer and reverence" (p. 97).

Caduto and Bruchac identify the first circle as the great circle of life and death and as the reality of the spirit world. Another circle is transformation, depicted when Salmon Boy returns to his people as a healer and a teacher to instruct them in the ways of the Salmon People and to help them when they are sick. This circle shows the sense of interconnectedness between the world and the spirit world, and between animals and people. Finally, Salmon Boy's body is placed in the river, where it circles four times, a sacred number to the Salmon People.

In *Storm Boy*, Paul Owen Lewis bases his original tale on the mythology of the Northwest Coast of North America, focusing on the motifs of separation, initiation, and return. Under "separation" are the motifs that wandering too far from the village invites supernatural encounters and that there is a mysterious entrance in the Spirit World. Under "initiation" are the motifs that animals are encountered in human form and that potlatching or exchanging of gifts and culture are important. Under "return" are the motifs that objects are given to assist the mythological character in this return.

Students of children's literature will discover that like Lewis, many authors use mythology as a foundation for their writings.

MULTICULTURAL LITERATURE

Myths From Other Cultures

All cultures include mythology that allows their peoples to experience and to explain the awe of the universe. As do the Greek and Norse myths, these myths reflect the cultures and the settings from which they originated. For example, Kiri Te Kanawa's *Land of the Long White Cloud: Maori Myths, Tales, and Legends* is a collection of ancient folklore told by the Polynesian sailors who discovered New Zealand—The Land of the Long White Cloud. Here are creation stories, trickster tales, and legends of various Maori tribes. The first tale, "The Birth of Maui," describes the birth of this trickster character and explains why he grew up to be a maker of mischief. The setting is appropriate for a culture that is so influenced by the ocean. Michael Foreman's predominantly blue and green illustrations create a mood of a land surrounded by water.

Diane Wolkstein's *Sun Mother Wakes the World: An Australian Creation Story* is an Aboriginal myth that reveals the creation process. The myth begins: "In the sky, Sun Mother was also asleep. Then a soft voice whispered to her, 'Wake, wake, my child.' When Sun Mother opened her eyes, light appeared. 'My daughter,' the voice spoke again. 'It is time for you to wake the sleeping earth.' Sun Mother smiled, and the light became brighter" (unnumbered). The myth continues as Sun Mother gives the gift of life as she walks all the earth, first waking the vegetation and then the sleeping animal spirits. Finally, she gives birth to a daughter, Moon, and a son, Morning Star. After Moon and Morning Star grow brighter, they give birth to twins, the first woman and the first man. These humans are told to take care of the land by traveling across the earth to know that it is alive. According to Wolkstein, some Australian people still go on walkabouts to renew themselves and keep the earth alive.

Virginia Hamilton's *In the Beginning: Creation Stories From Around the World* presents 25 myths from various cultures. Each myth includes a comment in which Hamilton provides information about the source of the myth and some interpretative information. Barry Moser's illustrations add to the feelings of wonder that are reflected in these myths.

Some of the folklore from the Middle East reflects the common ground between Islam and Christianity. Shulamith Levy Oppenheim's *Iblis*, thought to date back to the ninth century B.C., is both a creation story explaining the beginnings of humankind and our troubles and a cautionary tale showing the dangers of disobeying God's orders. The author tells us that this version of the Adam and Eve story "can be found in the work of Jarir at-Tabari, a famous Islamic scholar who was a religious authority and historian. Born about 839 A.D. in Amul, a city near the southern shore of the Caspian Sea, he traveled throughout the Islamic world as a young man and finally settled in Baghdad, in what is now Iraq. He acquired material for his history of the world from oral storytelling and literary sources, as well as from the Koran" (author's note, unnumbered). You can compare this variant of the Adam and Eve story with the Christian version.

Legends

According to Richard Cavendish, in his introduction to *Legends of the World* (1982):

Legends stand the test of time, better than genuine history does. . . . The territory of legend has history on one of its borders, myth on another and folk-tale on a third. The frontier zones are vague and shifting, and perhaps no two people will ever agree about precisely where the boundary lines fall. . . . Everywhere in the world, legendary stories of what happened in the past have been handed down from generation to generation. They are part of the inherited conglomerate of accepted beliefs, values and attitudes which give a people its identity. These stories consequently provide invaluable evidence about the societies that give birth to them, and insights into human nature in general. (p. 9)

The great legends in traditional literature are closely related to mythology. Many of these legends have been transmitted over the centuries in the form of epics, which are long narrative poems about the deeds of traditional or historical human heroes and heroines of high station. Two of the better-known Greek epics are *The Iliad* and *The Odyssey*. *The Iliad* is an account of the Trojan War. *The Odyssey* reports the journey of Odysseus (Ulysses in Latin) as he defeats the Cyclops, overcomes the song of the sirens, and manages to survive 10 long years of hazardous adventures. Gods, goddesses, and other supernatural beings play important roles in such epics, but the focus is human characters.

"Beowulf," the story of a human warrior, is usually considered the outstanding example of Norse epic poetry. Beowulf's struggle against evil has three main episodes. First, Beowulf fights and kills the monster Grendel. Second, Beowulf dives to the depths of a pool and attacks Grendel's mother, She. Third, Beowulf fights the dragon Firedrake and is mortally wounded.

Versions of this epic are available in both narrative and poetic form. One version, which the author Robert Nye calls a new telling, is written in narrative form for young readers. In this version, Beowulf is strong, but he is also good—loyal, courageous, and willing to take vengeance. His character epitomizes the heroic code found in Norse myths.

Fate, a strong code of honor, and a willingness to avenge wrong are emphasized in Kevin Crossley-Holland's *Beowulf*. He develops the importance of fate as Beowulf ponders the outcome of his forthcoming struggle with the monster Grendel: "Who knows? Fate goes always as it must" (p. 11), and "If a man is brave enough and not doomed to die, fate often spares him to fight another day" (p. 13). The importance of fate is reemphasized after Beowulf's victory, as King Hrothgar declares: "Beowulf, bravest of men, fate's darling! Your friends are fortunate, your enemies not to be envied" (p. 34).

Crossley-Holland develops a strong code of honor when Beowulf refuses to use a sword or a shield because the monster fights without weapons. Crossley-Holland combines honor and vengeance as Beowulf cries that he will avenge the Danes, the people who gave refuge to his father. Honor and vengeance are also part of the monster's code, and Beowulf is pleased when he discovers: "There is honor amongst monsters as there is honor amongst men. Grendel's mother came to the hall to avenge the death of her son" (p. 25).

A newer retelling of the Beowulf epic poem is Seamus Heaney's translation titled *Beowulf*. The text, written in both Old English and modern English, was the 1999 winner of the Whitbread Book of the Year and the Poetry Award.

Many of the heroes and heroines in epic legends reflect a strong sense of goodness as they overcome various worldly evils. The line between legend and myth is often vague, however. The early legends usually enlarged upon the lives of religious figures, such as martyrs and saints. In more recent times, legends developed around royal figures and folk heroes and heroines.

We consider the tales of King Arthur to be legends rather than myths because they are stories primarily about humans rather than supernatural beings and because historical tradition maintains that King Arthur actually existed in fairly recent times. Tales of this legendary British king were so popular in early England that Sir Thomas Malory's *Le Morte d'Arthur* was one of the first books published in England.

Another early version of the tale is Howard Pyle's *The Story of King Arthur and His Knights*. The first section of Pyle's version, "The Book of King Arthur," reveals how Arthur removed the sacred sword Excalibur from a stone and signified that he was the rightful king of England, claimed his birthright, wed Guinevere, and established the Round Table. The second section, "The Book of Three Worthies," tells about Merlin the magician, Sir Pellias, and Sir Gawaine. The original version of this book, with Pyle's illustrations, has been reissued. Other editions of Arthurian legends include Rosemary Sutcliff's *The Sword and the Circle: King Arthur and the Knights of the Round Table, The Light Beyond the Forest, The Road to Camlann: The Death of King Arthur,* and Margaret Hodges's *Merlin and the Making of the King.* In *Parzival: The Quest of the Grail Knight*, Katherine Paterson retells a legendary tale about another knight from Arthur's court.

Selina Hastings's *Sir Gawain and the Loathly Lady* retells one of the Arthurian legends in a picture-book format. Characteristically, the tale includes a challenge, a quest, enchantment, and a promise demanded by the code of chivalry. Juan Wijngaard's illustrations capture both the evil menace of the black knight and the ancient splendor of Arthur's court.

Michael Morpurgo's *Sir Gawain and the Green Night* presents another tale of the legendary character in King Arthur's court. Again, the code of chivalry requires that Sir Gawain accept the challenge of the monstrous, evil challenger after the knight picks up his severed head and demands a return match.

The importance of the Arthurian legends as subjects for more contemporary authors is easily seen by reading Cindy Mediavilla's *Arthurian Fiction: An Annotated Bibliography* (1999). Mediavilla includes more than 200 book-length Arthurian novels that she categorizes under areas such as "Romance of Camelot" and "Merlin, Kingmaker and Mage." To make the bibliography more useful to all readers, she identifies a reading level for each book from middle school to high school.

Another legendary figure in English culture is Robin Hood, the hero of Sherwood Forest. Stories about Robin Hood were told orally for centuries and were mentioned in manuscripts as early as 1360. Legend suggests that he was born Robert Fitzooth, Earl of Huntingdon, in Nottinghamshire, England, in 1160. According to the tales, he was a great archer. He and his band of outlaws poached the king's deer, robbed the rich, and gave to the poor.

Stories of Robin Hood are popular with children. Howard Pyle's *The Merry Adventures of Robin Hood* provides visions of what it would be like to live "in merry England in the time of old" and to interact with Little John, Maid Marian, Friar Tuck, the Sheriff of Nottingham, and King Richard of the Lion's Heart. Margaret Early's *Robin Hood* is a highly illustrated version of the legend. Children enjoy comparing the various editions and describing the strengths and weaknesses of each.

The Outlaws of Sherwood is Robin McKinley's interpretation of the Robin Hood legend. McKinley has created a vivid and readable story that includes both a castle-versus-cottage conflict and the romanticism of the original time. For example, through the words of Alan-a-Dale, she shows the conflict between the outlaws and their wealthier antagonists:

> Indeed, perhaps I have heard of this band for enough of time that I have written a ballad or two about them; a ballad or two received well enough at market day among the yeoman farmers and goodwives, but not so well among those who live in great castles and feel the need to have an eye to their own wealth. (p. 71)

This text is good for reading and for making comparisons among Robin Hood legends. You can also compare Michael Cadnum's *In a Dark Wood,* which is told from the point of view of the sheriff.

The hero in Margaret Hodges's adaptation of the English legend *Saint George and the Dragon* exemplifies the characteristics found in legendary heroes. He is noble, courageous, and willing to avenge a wrong.

Many of the legendary characters battle dragons. Dragons, both evil and good, are also popular in modern fantasy such as Tolkien's *Lord of the Rings,* Paolini's *Eragon,* and Funke's *Dragon Rider.* Consequently, many readers are interested in reading Dugald A. Steer's *Dragonology: The Complete Book of Dragons* and *The Dragonology Handbook: A Practical Course in Dragons.* (One fifth-grade student told me that a number of her classmates carry the books from class to class.) *Dragonology* is a heavily illustrated book that includes a folding map showing locations of various dragons. The text is divided according to subjects such as "Different Species of Dragon: Western Dragons, Eastern Dragons, and Other Dragons." An appendix relates the dragons to legendary characters such as St. George and Beowulf.

A legendary fight for freedom and independence is retold by Margaret Early in *William Tell.* This beautifully illustrated text captures the mood of the historic period as well as the life of the Swiss hero, William Tell.

Page design is enhanced by plain-colored borders on illustrated pages and drawings of plants and scenes bordering text pages. (From Saint George and the Dragon. *Retold by Margaret Hodges and illustrated by Trina Schart Hyman. Illustration copyright © 1984 by Trina Schart Hyman. Used by permission of Holiday House.)*

DRAGONOLOGY

GEORGE OF CAPPADOCIA: IIIrd Century A.D.

George of Cappadocia was a dragonslayer who became confused with a Christian saint. This is partly because they shared the same name and partly because, while George of Cappadocia slew an actual dragon, St. George slew the *symbolic* dragon of paganism. The dragon George of Cappadocia slew was not evil, just hungry. The people of Libya, where the dragon lived, had become rich, and their large flocks grazed on land that was once the habitat of the dragon's natural prey. So it was not surprising that, having eaten all their sheep, the hungry dragon resorted to feeding on townsfolk. Interestingly, Sylene, the town where this took place, seems to have been destroyed, as it cannot be found on the map at all, which leads us to wonder if George was *quite* as successful at ridding the area of dragons as history has since painted him.

BEOWULF: VIth Century A.D.

Beowulf, the famous Danish king, was forced to become a dragonslayer when a local dragon was aroused to fury by the theft of a cup from its hoard. Unable to pacify the dragon, Beowulf decided to face it alone in order to save his subjects. Badly bitten and burned, he would have failed had not his faithful servant Wiglaf stabbed the dragon, enabling Beowulf to finally despatch it, although mortally wounded himself.

FU HSI: MMCMLXII B.C.

Fu Hsi is the first recorded dragonologist. A dragon met him in 2962 B.C. on the banks of China's Yellow River and gave him the vital secret of writing. Fu Hsi used writing to teach people how to become civilised: to use a compass and set-square to take accurate measurements, to make music, to fish, and to domesticate animals. It is not known whether modern dragons regret so generously helping mankind in this way.

Illustration from DRAGONOLOGY: THE COMPLETE BOOK OF DRAGONS. *Illustrations copyright © 2003 by Wayne Anderson, Douglas Carrel, and Helen Ward. Text and design copyright © by the Templar Company plc. Reproduced by permission of the publisher Candlewick Press, Inc.*

The Hawaiian Islands provide the setting for Marcia Brown's *Backbone of the King: The Story of Pakáa and His Son Ku*. The characters display the qualities of other legendary heroes: Bravery, honor, and willingness to avenge a wrong characterize the chief, a trusted adviser to the king, who is wronged and then brought back to honor through the brave actions of his son.

David Wisniewski's *Sundiata: Lion King of Mali*, a legend, is the tale of a ruler who lived in the late 1200s. The tale begins in this fashion: "Listen to me, children of the Bright Country, and hear the great deeds of ages past. The words I speak are those of my father and his father before him, pure and full of truth . . ." (p. 1, unnumbered). Sundiata's courage and leadership are especially valued in this tale.

In endnotes, Wisniewski (1992) provides information about the source of this tale. For example, he states:

> The story of Sundiata has reached modern ears through the unbroken oral tradition provided by griots. Many African ethnic groups rely on the prodigious memories of these people, rather than written accounts, to preserve the history and wisdom of the past. This version of the Sundiata epic is dis-

tilled from the words of Djeli Mamoudou Kouyate, a griot of the Keita clan, in *Sundiata: An Epic of Old Mali*, a compilation written by Djibril Tamsir Niane and translated from the original Malinke by G. D. Pickett (London, 1965). (endnote)

This information is valuable because it allows you to compare Wisniewski's retelling and interpretation with the earlier version.

Jewish legends with Biblical sidelights are important for understanding the Jewish culture. In *Wonders and Miracles: A Passover Companion*, Eric A. Kimmel presents the steps performed in the traditional Passover Seder as well as stories, songs, poetry, prayers, and pictures that celebrate the significance of the holiday for Jews throughout the world. The text begins with an introduction that identifies why Passover is the most important holiday of the Jewish year: "The descendants of Abraham, Isaac, and Jacob emerged from slavery in Egypt to change the course of history. Passover is a holiday of liberation like America's Fourth of July, Mexico's Cinco de Mayo, and France's Bastille Day" (p. 1).

Kimmel's text and illustrations span 3,000 years and are taken from literature throughout the world. The book begins with the poem "Spirit of Seder," by Patrick Lewis, and an illustration from Northern Spain showing a family sitting around the Seder table, mid-14th century. The stories show a diverse people who have lived in many places. The text also includes a collection of art from many time periods. The author provides a bibliography of sources, a list of credits, and an index.

Sandy Eisenberg Sasso's *But God Remembered: Stories of Women From Creation to the Promised Land* includes legends about Lilith, who tradition tells us was Adam's first wife, and other little-known female figures such as Serach, the granddaughter of Jacob, and the five daughters of Zelophehad, who come to Moses after their father dies and ask to inherit their father's land. The characteristics of these women reflect many of the important values found in Jewish folklore. For example, in "The Psalm of Serach," Serach has the characteristics of grace and wisdom. She feels honored because her father taught her the wisdom of the ancestors. Through her beautiful singing voice and the Psalm she writes, the storyteller shows the importance of music and of Psalms to affect knowledge and understanding. Through the Psalm, readers discover the importance of hope, forgiveness, and God's role in Jewish history.

Barbara Diamond Goldin places *Journeys With Elijah: Eight Tales of the Prophet* in different times and in different places "to emphasize the age-old idea that Elijah can appear anywhere, anytime, if people will but welcome him and what he stands for—hope and peace" (p. x). Each of the eight stories includes an introduction that identifies the time, place, and circumstances used in telling the tale.

Three versions of the legend about the Golem provide opportunities for comparisons of both illustrations and text. For example, David Wisniewski's *Golem* is a highly illustrated tale about a rabbi who brings to life a clay giant to help the people during a very dangerous time in 16th-century Prague. The cut-paper illustrations give a three-dimensional appearance to both the architecture and the characters; they also stress the power that is found in the form of the Golem. Within the illustrations are numerous examples of Jewish culture such as Hebrew letters, the rabbi, the holy texts, the yellow circles worn on the left shoulders or sleeves of many of the characters, and the synagogue.

Wisniewski's version can be compared with Barbara Rogasky's *The Golem*, illustrated by Trina Schart Hyman, and Isaac Bashevis Singer's *The Golem*, illustrated by Uri Shulevitz. Both of these books present longer versions of the Golem story and have fewer illustrations. As you read these three texts, compare the power of the writing, consider the information provided in the author's or illustrator's notes, and view the impact of the illustrations.

Additional Traditional Literature With Religious Themes

There are beautifully illustrated texts that present the Christian Christmas story. For example, Kevin Crossley-Holland's *How Many Miles to Bethlehem?* uses spare text and large paintings by Peter Maline. The text in Faith Ringgold's *O Holy Night: Christmas With the Boys Choir of Harlem* includes the words of the Christmas carols sung by the Boys Choir; a CD of the choir singing the carols is packaged in the book. Ringgold's illustrations depict scenes from carols such as "Silent Night," "O Come All Ye Faithful," "O Holy Night," "Hark! The Herald Angels Sing," and "Joy to the World."

Beatriz Vidal's *Federico and the Magi's Gift: A Latin American Christmas Story* is a story of Epiphany, the day the Three Wise Men, or Magi, bring gifts to fill the good children's shoes. The author uses numerous Spanish words that are translated in the glossary. An author's note presents the importance in Latin America of the Feast of the Three Kings, or Epiphany Day, on January 6.

In Jean Little's *Pippin the Christmas Pig*, the farm animals tell Pippin, the young pig, the story of the first Christmas. When they tell Pippin that pigs were not in the first Christmas story, she feels dejected and goes out in a snowstorm, vowing never to return. Along the way, however, Pippin finds a woman and a baby in need of shelter. When she brings the baby and the mother into the warm barn, the animals realize the importance of Pippin and her gift to them.

Legends help children understand the conditions of times that created a need for brave and honorable men and women. These tales of adventure stress the noblest actions of humans. In legends, justice reigns over injustice. Children can feel the magnitude of the oral tradition as they listen to these tales, so reading legends aloud is the best way to introduce them to children.

Folklore for Young Adults

Folklore written for older readers frequently reflects the complexities of the culture from which the stories originated. By reading mythology, for example, young adults discover the historical foundations of a group of people. In this section, we consider some examples of mythology taken from a variety of cultures that require a more sophisticated reading.

Neil Philip's *Mythology of the World* is an example of a text that depicts the complexity and importance of studying the mythology to discover the beliefs and values of the people. Philip develops the following components of a people that are discovered by studying their mythology: (1) Myths reflect the culture by expressing the spiritual and intellectual life of the people; for example, Spider Woman is an important goddess of the Navajo people. (2) Myths are sacred stories often reenacted in religious rituals and depicted through mythical gods; for example, Egyptians had a class of priests who mediated between the human world and the world of the gods. (3) Myths are tied to the social structure of the society, its ideas about kinship, and the development of its arts and crafts; for example, rainmaking is a function of Kachina spirits in Native American tribes of the Southwest. (4) Myths are shaped by the geography of the land; for example, the Warao of South America portray their world as a flat disk surrounded by water because the people live at sea level and see land as a flat strip between water and sky. (5) Myths are influenced by the stars because early people relied on stars to tell them about change, disaster, and renewal; for example, the Inca foresaw their downfall in the stars. Philip's text is divided according to myths from Europe, Asia, America, Australia, and Africa.

Rachel Storm's *The Encyclopedia of Eastern Mythology* presents myths and tales of the heroes, gods, and warriors of ancient Egypt, Arabia, Persia, India, Tibet, China, and Japan. This large reference text is illustrated with photographs of artworks from the various cultures.

Authors of Islamic tales frequently emphasize the difficulty readers have understanding the meanings of the tales. For example, in their *Tales From the Land of the Sufis*, Mojdeh Bayat and Mohammad Ali Jamnia state that although Sufi stories "may seem to be quite simple, their deeper significance may, depending on the student's level of understanding, be subtle and very difficult to grasp" (p. 3). These authors warn that many of the stories are difficult for Westerners to understand because the themes need to be clarified in the light of the stories' culture of origin. For example, misunderstanding may result because Islamic culture and Sufism reflect a masculine bias. In Sufi symbolism, woman stands for one who pursues worldly desires, and man symbolizes the true lover of god. The authors present a history of Sufism and examples of stories that reflect Sufi beliefs.

Much of the folklore from India is more appropriate for young adults, especially if the tales reflect the role of the priestly caste, Brahmans (the most ancient texts of Hindu sacred literature), and Buddha. Books for older readers usually provide background information as well as examples of tales. Sister Nivendita and Ananda K. Coomaraswamy's *Myths and Legends Series: Hindus and Buddhists* includes chapters on the mythology of the Buddha. In Judith Emst's retelling of *The Golden Goose King: A Tale Told by the Buddha,* the storyteller uses another tale told by the Buddha to reveal how a king and queen should rule wisely. As you read the folklore from India, notice the importance of the Hindu and Buddhist religions. The folklore develops such values as devotion to truth, integrity, friendship, and selfless actions.

Most of the Jewish folklore reflects such values as faith, learning, hospitality, knowledge, cooperation, and charity. We have already discussed the cautionary tales, the humorous tales about the people of Chelm, and some of the legends and myths from the Midrash. Jose Patterson's *Angels, Prophets, Rabbis and Kings From the Stories of the Jewish People* includes stories about the patriots, heroes and heroines, kings, and prophets. The anthology concludes with a useful discussion about the symbols in the illustrations that introduce each chapter.

In *Circle Spinning: Jewish Turning and Returning Tales,* Jewish storyteller and author Cherie Karo Schwartz retells stories that represent the types of stories found in Jewish folklore: stories about fire and the world of the spirit, such as "And Then There Was Light"; stories about air, the world of creation, and the intellect, such as "Three Drops of Creation"; stories about water and the world of formation, such as "The Sign, a Rainbow Tale"; and stories about earth, the world of construction, and action, such as "Elijah in the Garden." Schwartz acknowledges that the sources for her tales were the Israel Folktale Archives in Haifa that include over 20,000 folktales from the Jewish world.

Tim Tingle, Choctaw storyteller and author of *Walking the Choctaw Road,* tells folklore that reflects the beliefs and history of members of the Oklahoma Choctaw Nation. The stories are arranged in chronological order "to enable the reader to witness the changes that time and history have rendered upon Choctaw beliefs" (p. 14). Tin-

Cover from Walking the Choctaw Road, *by Tim Tingle, Cinco Puntos Press, 2003. Cover art by Norma Howard © 2001. Untitled.* www.cincopuntos.com.

gle includes symbolism in the folklore such as the owl as the messenger of death, the importance of dreams, and the need for faith. The text is illustrated with historical photographs of the Choctaw people and includes a glossary of Choctaw words and a bibliography of young adult and adult sources.

Roberta H. Markman and Peter T. Markman's *The Flayed God: The Mythology of Mesoamerica* presents several Mayan creation myths, such as "The Birth of the Uinal" (the awakening of the world), "The Birth of All of Heaven and Earth," "The Creation of Animals," "The Human Made of Earth and Mud," and "The Creation of the Sun and Moon." The authors include the sources for each of the translations. The text provides both examples of stories appropriate for storytelling and background information about the stories.

As can be seen from these examples of young adult folklore, the topics in these tales reflect some of the most important aspects and beliefs from the original cultures. Many of the collections also require background knowledge or a willingness to read additional sources if students are to gain an in-depth understanding of the culture.

Through the Eyes of a STORYTELLER

Tim Tingle

Visit the CD-ROM that accompanies this text to generate a complete list of titles written by Tim Tingle.

Selected Titles by Tim Tingle:
Walking the Choctaw Road
Texas Ghost Stories: Fifty Favorites for the Telling
Crossing Bok Chitto
Spooky Texas Tales

I have bonded with my pickup truck in a real Texas kind of way. We've gone together over 200,000 miles. All of my stories have been written in the cab of this truck. As I hear a story, I'll go over it and prepare it and learn it, and I'm doing that in my mind as I drive from one place to the next.

I collect stories like the Grimms would do, but more like Frank Doby, a Texas folklorist, would do. Doby has a quote that we used at the beginning of our collection of ghost stories. If he felt the story could be improved, he'd certainly do that. For example, Crossing Bok Chitto began as a piece of a song, a wedding chant I was learning from an older Choctaw fellow. And I took him out to a sacred mound in central Mississippi and he sang it to me; and on the way back, we saw a run-down shack, and he told me this was where they used to help runaway slaves. Later, I heard of a way Choctaws used to cross the river to be able to hunt in the forest on the other side, which was part of an old plantation. I began to piece these things together. More so than any

of the other stories, Crossing Bok Chitto is a pieced-together stitching of other people's quilt patches.

In the introduction to the book Walking the Choctaw Road, I give credit to the people who told me the stories and try to indicate to what degree each story is patched together and to what degree it's an authentic, straightforward description of something that actually happened to someone. It's created a real interesting dilemma, which I enjoy: People call the publisher and they call me wanting to know whether the book should be fiction or nonfiction. And of course it's a fictional book. In more than half of the stories, the characters are composite characters, but there's no way to document any of the characters in the book; it's a fictional piece. And yet the stories are authentic. It's not as much a collection of legends as a collection of real human experiences.

I was raised in a community in southeast Houston, and this is a time when south Houston was a tiny little isolated farming community. And the hub of our family life was the home of my grandmother, who was full-blood Choctaw Indian with 7 kids and 30 plus cousins. We would spend our time there, with family dinners, and a huge cornfield and gardens, and part of those family gatherings was always the gathering out in the backyard sharing. People didn't think of it as formal stories, but we talk in narrative. We talk in anecdotes when we have time to.

I was the one that would curl up somewhere in the gardenia bushes or the corner of the garage and just listen while other kids

would be off playing. I loved to listen to these old people talk. I really think that's the most important thing a storyteller can have is the nuance of how a voice changes, and for a writer as well, to observe and to see the way no one else sees.

I made one promise, and I think this is important in having people continue to open their doors to me, especially older Choctaws: Every character would have his place of honor. Even the most despicable characters would be given motivation and a moment of understanding. Even just a moment, just a glimpse of understanding. No character would be totally evil and eliminated from any hope of redemption. I'm glad I made that promise. I think it makes for a stronger piece. I noticed a remarkable thing that happened over the years as I worked on giving some piece of sensitivity to every single character. What I found was the emotional work I was doing in giving an aura of hope for every character translated into my personal life, and it's been remarkable to watch myself see people in a way that's so different than before I made that promise. So in a way, I was making that promise to myself as well. It's made me a much more people-friendly person, and it makes my travels just a wonder-filled trip of meeting remarkable, good-hearted people.

Video Profile: The accompanying video contains conversations with Joseph Bruchac, Molly Bang, Leonard Everett Fisher, Keith Baker, and Brian Pinkney on writing and illustrating children's books.

Teaching With Traditional Literature

Traditional tales are among the most memorable that children experience in literature. With their well-defined plots, easily identifiable characters, rapid action, and satisfactory endings, the tales lend themselves to enjoyable experiences. Diane F. Wyzga (2005) reminds storytellers that "each civilization is built on five institutions: social, political, intellectual, religious, and economic and as storytellers we should ask, 'How has storytelling formed the core of civilized life, how do stories shape us as much as we shape stories, and why does the

human appetite for stories persist as the ultimate connection between how we live and view reality?'" (p. 5). This section explores ways to recapture the oral tradition through telling stories, comparing folktales from different countries, investigating folktales from a single country, and motivating writing.

Telling Stories

Learning the ancient art of storytelling is worth the effort in the pleasure it affords both the teller and the audience. This is true whether the storyteller is

Through the Eyes of a CHILD

Donovan

Grade 8

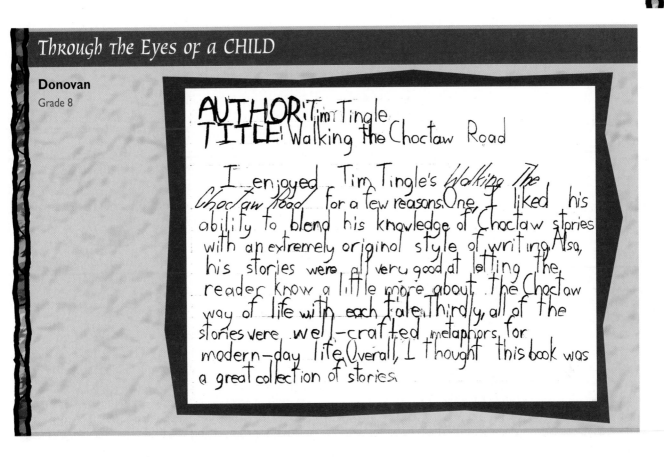

AUTHOR: Tim Tingle
TITLE: Walking the Choctaw Road

I enjoyed Tim Tingle's *Walking The Choctaw Road* for a few reasons. One, I liked his ability to blend his knowledge of Choctaw stories with an extremely original style of writing. Also, his stories were all very good at letting the reader know a little more about the Choctaw way of life with each tale. Thirdly, all of the stories were well-crafted metaphors for modern-day life. Overall, I thought this book was a great collection of stories.

---

an adult or a child. The current emphasis on storytelling is seen not only in the increase of university and public school programs that focus on storytelling, but also in the development of community programs such as "Spellbinders Programs" that connect storytellers, community volunteers, libraries, and children. For example, the values of storytelling as identified by *Spellbinders Volunteer Storytelling* (1999) include the following:

1. Provide children with positive, character-building role models.
2. Provide natural and nourishing communication between generations.
3. Enhance children's language development, listening skills, and aural comprehension.
4. Stimulate children's creative imagination.
5. Acquaint children with the folktales, legends, and true stories of many cultures and many lives, told in traditional oral form.
6. Give older adult volunteers an opportunity to be of traditional significance and purpose to their communities (p. 3).

It was my pleasure to be an observer of and a participant in a Spellbinders Program sponsored by the Pitkin Library in Aspen, Colorado, during the summers of 2001 and 2005. Each of the weekly sessions began with stories told by a professional storyteller. The audience consisted of more than 100 children. Following an interactive storytelling session that involved children with both stories and songs, adult volunteers helped children who had joined a children's storytelling club prepare their own stories for telling. Children first told their stories to small groups and then to larger groups. It was an exciting experience to witness the power of storytelling.

Choosing a Story

The most important factor in choosing a story is selecting one that is really enjoyable. Narrators should enjoy spending time preparing stories and should retell them with conviction and enthusiasm.

Storytelling demands an appreciative audience. Storytellers must be aware of the interests, ages, and experience of the listeners involved. Young children have short attention spans, so story length must be considered when selecting a tale. Children's ages also should influence the subject of the chosen tale. Young children like stories about familiar subjects, such as animals, children, or home life. They respond to the repetitive language in cumulative tales and enjoy joining in when stories such as "Henny Penny" reach their climax. Simple folktales, such as "The Three Bears," "The Three Little Pigs," and "The Three Billy Goats Gruff," are excellent to share with young children. Children from roughly ages 7 through 10 enjoy folktales with longer plots, such as those collected by the Brothers Grimm. "Rapunzel" and "Rumpelstiltskin" are favorites. Other favorites include such Jewish folktales as "It Could Always Be Worse." Older children enjoy adventure tales, myths, and legends. Nadia Grosser Nagarajan's *Pomegranate Seeds: Latin American Jewish Tales* (2005), Anne Pellowski's *Drawing Stories From Around the World* (2005), Daniel A. Kelin's *To Feel as Our Ancestors Did: Collecting and Performing Oral Histories* (2005), Joseph Daniel Sobol's *The House Between Earth and Sky: Harvesting New American Folktales* (2005), Sarah Conover and Freda Crane's *Ayat Jamilah: Beautiful Signs: A Treasury of Islamic Wisdom for Children and Parents* (2004), Patricia Santos Marcantonio's *Red Ridin' in the Hood and Other Cuentos* (2005), Gary Marvin Davison's *Tales From the Taiwanese* (2004), Bonnie C. Marshall's *The Snow Maiden and Other Russian Tales* (2004), and Elvia Perez's *From the Winds of Manguito: Cuban Folktales in English and Spanish* (2004) include recommended stories and suggestions for how to use them.

Folktales have several characteristics that make them appropriate for storytelling: strong beginnings that bring listeners rapidly into the fast-paced action, several characters with whom listeners easily identify, climaxes that are familiar to children, and satisfying endings. These characteristics suggest worthwhile criteria for selecting tales.

Storytellers should also consider the mood that they wish to create, whether it be humorous and lighthearted or serious and scary. For example, if you want to choose a story appropriate for Halloween, then mood is important. Even the site for storytelling may affect the mood and story selection. Assume, for example, that a group of people is sitting on high rocks overlooking Lake Superior: The wind is causing the waves to crash with a mighty roar onto the rocks below. When the people look out over the lake, they can see only a wide stretch of water. No one else is in sight. The view to the north is one of thick forests, ferns, and distant waterfalls. The Norse myth "The Hammer of Thor," from Olivia E. Coolidge's *Legends of the North*, seems ideal for this setting.

Preparing the Story for Telling

Storytelling does not require memorization, but it does require preparation. Certain steps will help you prepare for an enjoyable experience. An experienced storyteller, Patti Hubert (Norton, 2004), recommends the following sequence of steps:

1. Read the story completely through about three times.

2. List mentally the sequence of events. You are giving yourself a mental outline of the important happenings.

3. Reread the story, noting the events you did not remember.

4. Go over the main events again and add the details that you remember. Think about the meaning of the events and ways to express that meaning, rather than memorize the words in the story.

5. When you believe that you know the story, tell it to a mirror. (You will be surprised at how horrible the story sounds the first time.)

6. After you have practiced two or three more times, the wording will improve, and you can change vocal pitch to differentiate characters.

7. Change your posture or hand gestures to represent different characters.

8. Do not be afraid to use pauses to separate scenes.

9. Identify background information, share information about hearing the story for the first time, or share an object related to the story.

Sharing the Story With an Audience

Because you have spent considerable time in preparation, you should present the story effectively. However, you can enhance your presentation by stimulating interest in the story, setting a mood, creating an environment where children can see and hear you, and presenting the story with effective eye contact and voice control. You can use book jackets, giant books, miniature books, travel posters, art objects and everyday objects, puppets, or music to stimulate children's interest in the story. A librarian or teacher who regularly tells stories to large groups of children can use any of these methods so that children will look forward to the story hour.

Colorful book jackets from folktales or myths not only entice children but also help set a mood for storytelling. For example, you might develop a display around the book jacket for Steven Kellogg's *Jack and the Beanstalk*. In addition to the book jacket, you could display a picture of a beanstalk (or even a real beanstalk), a toy chicken, an egg, and a picture of a castle. To show comparative sizes, you might include a picture of a giant and a picture of a boy. Your accompanying questions might include the following: How could a beanstalk make it possible for a boy to reach a castle that is up in the sky? How could a chicken and eggs cause a boy and his mother to obtain great wealth?

Stories about giants also lend themselves to displays of large books. One librarian drew huge figures of giants and beanstalks on large sheets of tagboard and then placed the sheets together to form a gigantic book that stimulated interest in "Jack and the Beanstalk." The giant book worked well in this case: The children speculated about the size or strength of anyone who could read such a large book. Drawings of a huge hammer stimulated interest about Thor when another librarian prepared the Norse myth for telling. Miniature books stimulated children's interest before another story hour when "Tom Thumb" was the story. The storyteller used other tiny objects, many formed out of clay, that would be appropriate for a little person.

Identifying sources for folklore is important. Consequently, information about the sources for the folklore should be included in the introduction.

Travel posters can stimulate interest and provide background information, and are especially appealing when used with folktales from other countries. Travel posters showing ancient English sites might introduce an oral telling of Barbara Cohen's adaptation of Geoffrey Chaucer's *Canterbury Tales*. Likewise, you can use travel posters about Greece and Italy with Greek and Roman mythology. Travel posters showing Norwegian fjords and mountains can accompany Norse myths, and posters showing the Black Forest and old European castles are appropriate for "Snow White and the Seven Dwarfs" and "Sleeping Beauty."

Objects from the story or from the country that is the setting of the story can also increase children's interest. Dolls, plates, figurines, stuffed animals, and numerous other everyday objects and curios can add to the story hour.

After interest is high, concentrate on setting the mood for story time. Many storytellers use story-hour symbols. For example, if a small lamp is the symbol for story hour, children know that when the lamp is lit, it is time to listen. Music can also be a symbol; a certain recording, music box tune, piano introduction, or guitar selection can introduce story hour. These techniques are usually effective, because children learn to associate them with enjoyable listening experiences. Donna E. Norton (2004, p. 228) has the following suggestions for telling the story:

1. Find a place in the room where all of the children can see and hear the presentation.

2. Either stand in front of the children or sit with them.

3. Select an appropriate introduction: Use a prop, tell something about the author, discuss a related event, or ask a question.

4. Maintain eye contact with the children; this engages them more fully in the story.

5. Use an appropriate voice rate and volume for effect.

6. While telling the story, use a short step or shift in footing to indicate a change in scene or character or to heighten the suspense. If seated, lean forward or away from the children.

7. After telling the story, pause to give the audience a chance to soak in everything you said.

Observing Children's Responses to Storytelling

Children may have emotional responses to the story, to the interpretation of the story, or to various literary elements within the story. The responses may be as subtle as facial expressions or as expressive as vocal interactions with the story and the storyteller. Zena Sutherland (1997) recommends that you ask yourself the following questions after telling a story to a group of children:

1. Which children showed response during the story period?

2. What parts of the story evoked the most response?

3. How did the children show their reactions?

4. Did the reactions influence, in any way, your telling of the story?

5. Did any child comment about the story at some time after the story hour? If so, did the comment indicate emotional response? interpretation of the story? attention to literary characteristics such as style?

6. Do their reactions give you ideas for future story choices for this group? (p. 552)

Encouraging Children to Be Storytellers

Storytelling by children is frequently a natural continuation of storytelling by adults because children learn to tell and appreciate oral storytelling by imitating adults. Storytellers Martha Hamilton and Mitch Weiss (1993) believe that when children tell stories, they gain confidence, improve verbal skills, learn how to think inventively, and develop a love of language and stories.

Hamilton and Weiss (1993) provide valuable guidelines for helping children choose, learn, and tell their stories. These storytellers stress that when helping children choose their stories, adults should select a pool of stories from which the children can select so that the children choose stories appropriate to the age and interests of their audience. A sign-up sheet will help children avoid duplicating stories that they are preparing for telling.

The techniques for helping students learn the story are similar to those identified for adults. You should ask children to read their stories a number of times. Use pictorial outlines to help children understand and visualize the sequence of the story rather than memorize the story. It is also helpful to have the children practice their stories by tape-recording them, telling the stories in front of a mirror, telling the stories to only one person, and then telling the stories to a larger audience. Additional guidelines for helping children learn to tell stories are found in Hamilton and Weiss's *Children Tell Stories: A Teaching Guide* (1990).

Using Feltboards to Share Folktales

Storytelling does not require any props. In fact, some of the best storytellers use nothing except their voices and gestures to recapture the plots and characters found in traditional tales. Most storytellers, however, enjoy adding variety to their repertoire. Children also enjoy experimenting with different approaches to storytelling; the flannelboard or feltboard lends itself to storytelling by both adults and children.

A feltboard is a rectangular, lightweight board covered with felt, flannel cloth, or lightweight indoor-outdoor carpeting. This board acts as the backdrop for figures cut from felt, pellon, or another material. Felt or pellon figures will cling directly to a feltboard, and any object, even leather, wood, or foam rubber, will adhere to the felt if backed with a small square or strip of Velcro. Other materials, such as yarn or cotton balls, will also cling to a feltboard and can be used to add interest and texture to a story.

Stories that lend themselves to feltboard interpretations have only a few major characters, plots that depend on oral telling rather than physical action, and settings that do not demand exceptional detail. These characteristics are similar to those already stipulated for the simple folktales that young children enjoy. Pleasing stories to retell on the feltboard include the folktales "The Three Billy Goats Gruff," "The Three Bears," "The Gingerbread Boy," and "Henny Penny." Stories should include actions that can be shown on the board. In addition, the number of figures should not overwhelm the board (see Figure 6.1).

Consider the Norwegian folktale "The Three Billy Goats Gruff." First, use simple cutouts or objects to represent the characters. The three goats range in size from a small goat to a great big goat with curved horns. The ugly old troll has big eyes and a long, long nose. You can show the setting easily: a bridge crossing a stream and green grass on the other side of the bridge. You can illustrate the action effectively: Each goat can go "Trip, trap! Trip, trap!" over the bridge. The troll can challenge each goat with "Who's that tripping over my bridge?" You can also illustrate the climax easily: The big billy goat knocks the troll off the bridge and continues to cross to the other side. The plot develops sequentially from a small billy goat, to a medium-sized billy goat, and finally to a great big billy goat.

Cumulative tales are excellent for feltboard presentations. As you introduce each new character, place it on the feltboard. Have the children join the dialogue as "The Fat Cat," for example, encounters first the gruel, then the pot, the old woman, Skahottentot, Skilinkenlot, five birds, seven dancing girls, the lady with the pink parasol, the parson, and the woodsman.

Through such presentations, children learn about sequential order and improve their language skills. Using feltboard stories with children, you will often find that the children either ask if they can retell the stories or make up

FIGURE 6.1 Stories that lend themselves to feltboard interpretations have only a few major characters, plots that depend on oral telling rather than physical action, and settings that do not demand exceptional detail.

their own feltboard stories to share. If you provide feltboards and materials, children naturally enjoy telling stories in this manner. Whether you tell a story to one child or to a group, storytelling is well worth the effort of preparation and presentation. Watching children as they respond to a magical environment and then make their own efforts as storytellers will prove to you that storytelling should be included in every child's experience.

Storytelling can be used to increase interest in any area of the curriculum. For example, teachers discover ideas for relating storytelling and sources to use by referring to these articles from *Storytelling Magazine, 17,* (May/June, 2005):

Social studies: Jim Cogan's "Crafting Social Studies Story Lifeline," pp. 31–34.

Math: Barbara Lipke's "Crafting Math Stories," pp. 35–38.

Science: Fran Stallings's "Crafting Science Stories," pp. 39–41.

Comparing Folktales From Different Countries

Understanding how various types of traditional stories are related, becoming aware of cultural diffusion, and learning about different countries are benefits of traditional literature. One way to help children gain these benefits is to compare folktales from different countries.

Comparing Different Versions of the Same Tale

Many older children are fascinated to discover that certain tales appear in almost every culture. The names vary, magical objects differ, and settings change, but the basic elements of the story remain the same. Folklorist Alan Dundes (1988) claims that more than 1,000 versions of the Cinderella story have been found throughout the world. Compile questions such as the following with the children's assistance to guide their search and discovery:

1. What caused Cinderella to have a lowly position in the family?
2. What shows that Cinderella has a lowly position in the household?
3. How is Cinderella related to other household members?
4. What happens to keep Cinderella away from the ball?
5. How does Cinderella receive her wishes or transformation?
6. Where does Cinderella meet the prince?
7. What is the test signifying the rightful Cinderella?
8. What happens to the stepsisters?

Sources for comparisons include Mary Ann Nelson's (1972) anthology, Bingham and Scholt's (1974) synopses of 12 variants of the Cinderella story, Sutherland and Livingston's anthology (1984), and folklore collections from around the world. Jerry D. Flack's *From the Land of Enchantment: Creative Teaching With Fairy Tales* (1997) includes "'Cinderella' Resources" such as Tradition Sources (29 summaries), Variations and Other Treatments (12 summaries), Stepmothers and Stepsisters (4 summaries), and Videocassettes (5 summaries). There are also numerous "Cinderella" tales published in single editions, such as Rebecca Hickox's *The Golden Sandal: A Middle Eastern Cinderella Story* (Iraq). Chart 6.5 represents some key variants found in Cinderella tales from different countries.

After children have read, listened to, and discussed many Cinderella tales, they should summarize their comparisons. In addition to these comparisons of "Cinderella" stories, M. Joe Worthy and Janet W. Bloodgood (1992/1993) suggest sources and activities that can accompany the study of three categories of "Cinderella" stories: The heroine is mistreated by stepmother or stepsisters, sibling rivalry, and the daughter flees an unnatural or misunderstanding father.

A search for variant versions of a tale encourages children to develop an understanding of the impact of cultural diffusion on literature. Children also realize that each culture has placed the tale in a context that reflects the society of the storyteller and the audience.

Analyzing Variants

Variants of folktales, especially those that changed as the original audiences moved to new lands, are especially interesting for developing the understanding that folktales frequently change as storytellers adjust to their new environments. In addition, if tales retain the original motifs and themes, use the variants to help students analyze possible sources of the original tales. As a logical extension of a comparative study of Cinderella tales for upper-elementary and middle-school students, use William H. Hooks's *Moss Gown* to analyze variations on themes and motifs, search for references to time and place, and speculate about the country of origin.

To begin, provide some background knowledge gained from other sources of literature and from geography. First, furnish a knowledge of Cinderella-type elements by having the children read many variants of the Cinderella story. This activity can help children understand that most Cinderella-type stories have such characteristics as a girl who is given the hardest tasks, a helper with supernatural powers, and an occasion that the girl wants to attend. Supply a knowledge of the English versions of Cinderella through "Tattercoats" and "Mossycoat" to help the students understand how the English Cinderella stories differ from those in other countries. Also, give the students at least a brief introduction to Shakespeare's *King Lear* to help them identify these elements in the story. A King Lear story written for children is included in E. Nesbit's *Beautiful Stories From Shakespeare* (1907) and in Charles and Mary Lamb's *Tales From Shakespeare* (1986). William H. Hooks's *Moss Gown* is a variant collected from the tidewater section of North Carolina; consequently, there are references to the environment and to the Southern plantations of an earlier time.

After providing these background understandings, ask the students to listen to or to read Hooks's *Moss Gown*. Have them search for (1) Cinderella elements, (2) King Lear elements, (3) references to time and place, and (4) evidence of the European country the early storytellers came from. From this activity, they will discover evidence that is similar to the information in Chart 6.6.

After the students complete this task, ask them to speculate about why *Moss Gown* has a happy ending and not the tragic ending of *King Lear*. They will probably decide that the Cinderella theme requires a happy ending, so the storytellers needed to find a way for the heroine and her father to live happily. Compare the themes in both *King Lear* and *Moss Gown* for an interesting and lively discussion. Additional variants for this type of activity include Gail E. Haley's *Jack and the Bean Tree*, an Appalachian variant of "Jack and the Beanstalk"; John Bierhorst's *Doctor Coyote: A Native American Aesop's Fables*, a Spanish-Aztec variant; and Eva Martin's *Canadian Fairy Tales*, a collection containing Canadian variants from French, German, and English sources.

CHART 6.5   Variations found in Cinderella stories from different countries

Origin	Cause of Lowly Position	Outward Signs of Lowly Position	Cinderella's Relationship to Household	How She Receives Wishes	What Keeps Her From Social Occasion	Where She Meets the Prince	Test of Rightful Cinderella	What Happens to Stepsisters
French Perrault's "Cinderilla"	Mother died. Father remarried.	Sitting in ashes. Vilest household tasks.	Stepdaughter to cruel woman. Unkind stepsisters.	Wishes to fairy godmother.	(Ball) No gown. Family won't let her go.	Castle ball. Beautifully dressed.	Glass slipper.	Forgiven. Live in palace. Marry lords.
German Grimm's "Cinderella"	Mother died. Father remarried.	Wears clogs, old dress. Sleeps in cinders. Heavy work.	Stepdaughter to cruel woman. Cruel stepsisters.	Wishes to bird on tree on mother's grave.	(Ball) Must separate lentils.	Castle ball. Beautifully dressed.	Glass slipper.	Blinded by birds.
English "Tattercoats"	Mother died at her birth. Grandfather blames her.	Ragbag clothes. Scraps for food.	Despised granddaughter. Hated by servants.	Gooseherd plays pipe.	(Ball) Grandfather refuses.	In forest. Dressed in rags.	None.	Grandfather weeps. Hair grows into stones.
Vietnamese "In the Land of Small Dragon"	Mother died. Father's number two wife hates her.	Collects wood. Cares for rice paddies.	Stepdaughter to hateful woman. Hated by half-sisters.	Fairy. Bones of fish.	(Festival) Must separate rice from husks.	Festival. Beautifully dressed.	Jeweled slipper (hai).	Not told.
Chinese "Beauty and Pock Face"	Mother turned into cow.	Straightens hemp. Hard work.	Stepdaughter to cruel woman. Cruel stepsister.	From bones of mother in earthenware pot.	(Theater) Straighten hemp. Separate sesame seeds.	Theater. Scholar picks up shoe from road.	Walks on eggs. Climbs ladder of knives. Jumps into oil.	Roasted in oil.
Micmac— Native American "Little Burnt Face"	Mother died.	Burned face. Ragged garments.	Despised by two jealous sisters.	The Great Chief's sister changes her.	She must make her own dress.	Wigwam by the lake.	Describe the Great Chief.	Sent back to wigwam in disgrace.

CHART 6.6   *An analysis of William H. Hooks's* Moss Gown

Cinderella elements found in Moss Gown:

A helper with supernatural powers.
A gown that changes to rags.
A girl who is given the hardest kitchen work.
An heir who holds a dance.
A heroine who cannot attend the dance because she lacks a dress.
A supernatural being who casts a spell and provides a dress.
An order that must be obeyed.
A handsome heir who dances only with the heroine.
An heir who searches for the heroine.
An heir and a heroine who marry.

King Lear elements found in Moss Gown:

A question asked to prove love.
A father who rejects youngest and most loving daughter's declaration.
A father who wanders after cruel treatment by elder daughters.
A youngest daughter who eventually proves her love for her father.

References to time and place found in Moss Gown:

A great plantation.
A "snow-white house, pillared with eight marble columns on every side" (p. 5).
A reference to fine fields.
A reference to riding and hunting in the murky, mysterious swamp.
A reference to black-green cypress treetops.
A reference to gray Spanish moss.
French words used in the Carolinas to cast a powerful, magical spell.
A party that is called a frolic.

Evidence that the original storytellers came from English backgrounds:

King Lear elements show knowledge of Shakespeare, an English author.
There are similarities to the British Cinderella. For example, in "Tattercoats," servants mistreat a girl, and a man of wealthy position loves the girl even though she is dressed in rags.

MULTICULTURAL LITERATURE

Investigating Themes or Motifs Found in Tales From Many Cultures

Several books provide opportunities for students to read and analyze stories based on a similar theme or motif. For example, *Grandmothers' Stories: Wise Woman Tales From Many Cultures*, retold by Burleigh Mutén, can be used to encourage comparisons among Senegalese, Japanese, Russian, Hawaiian, Mexican, Irish, German, and Swedish tales. Students can search for both commonalities and differences among these tales. If they have been studying tales from specific cultures, they can identify the characteristics that would make them authentic for those cultures.

Two collections of tales retold by Josephine Evetts-Secker are based on specific motifs. *Mother and Son Tales* has 10 tales; the author includes both valuable notes on the stories that can help students conduct an extensive analysis of the symbolism and themes developed in the tales, and a listing of original sources. A similar approach is used in Evetts-Secker's *Father and Son Tales*.

Older students could learn considerable information about justice, resolving disputes, and debating by using Sharon Creeden's *Fair Is Fair: World Folktales of Justice* (1995). In the foreword, a criminal defense attorney states: "In fact, the stories in this collection are themselves the type of archetypal tales that we carry in our heads when attempting to resolve disputes. Thus, 'The Fisherman and the King's Chamberlain' is an expression of the basic principle that being a partner with someone means that you share the bad, as well as the good" (p. 15). Each of the chapters contains introductory comments and sources. The text concludes with "Notes for Legal Commentary." This winner of the Aesop Prize from the Children's Folklore Section of the American Folklore Society could provide interesting sources for debate, dramatization, and discussion.

MULTICULTURAL LITERATURE

Investigating Folktales From a Single Country

Children can learn a great deal about a country and its people by investigating a number of traditional tales from that country. Such an investigation also increases understanding of the multicultural heritage of this country and develops understanding of, and positive attitudes toward, cultures other than one's own.

During the sharing of folktales, some children comment, for example, that Jewish folktales often stress the unselfish desire for a better world or reward sincerity and wisdom. They are also impressed by the fact that the Chinese "Cinderella" married a scholar and not a nobleman. Through the folktales, they learn to respect the values of the people who created them.

A fifth-grade class conducted a successful study of folktales from China. Objects displayed throughout the room stimulated interest. A large, red paper dragon met the children as they entered the room. Other objects included joss sticks (incense), lanterns, Chinese flutes, a tea service, fans, statues of mythical beasts, lacquered boxes and plates, silk, samples of Chinese writing, a blue willow plate, jade, and pictures of artwork, temples, pagodas, people, and animals. Many Chinese folktales were displayed on the library table. A recording of Chinese music played in the background. The chalkboard contained a message, written in Chinese characters, welcoming the children to China.

The students looked at the displays, listened to the music, tried to decipher the message, and discussed what they saw and heard. They located China on a map and on a globe. Then they listed questions about China—questions about the people, country, values, art, music, food, houses, animals, and climate.

The teacher read aloud some of the foreword to Louise and Yuan-hsi Kuo's *Chinese Folk Tales* (1976). She asked the students to close their eyes and imagine the scene, to listen carefully, and then to tell whether the following scene took place in modern times or many centuries ago.

> But suddenly the room echoes with an ear-splitting clash of cymbals and the sonorous boom of a drum and in the street below our window prances a splendid lion. The sound of cymbals and the beat of drums have been heard incessantly since early morning and are merely a prelude to a major part to come: a procession with gay silk banners flying, votive offerings of barbecued pigs . . . golden brown and saffron, cartloads heaped with fruit, red-colored eggs and other delicacies, giant joss sticks, candles and lanterns. A magnificent dragon, gyrating and performing with vigor and intensity to the rapid beat of a drum, will bring the procession to a climax. Throngs crowd the doorways, line the path, as excited onlookers join the ranks to mingle with those on their way to the temple . . . journey's end. This is the day of days . . . the grand finale of five days of celebration in homage to T'ien Ho, the Heavenly Goddess of the Sea . . . she who will bestow blessings on all who worship her, and protect them for the entire year. (p. 7)

After listening to the selection, the children speculated about the time period and gave their reasons for choosing either ancient or modern times. Many children were quite surprised to hear that the festival was held in modern Hong Kong. This discussion led to reading Chinese folktales in order to learn more about the Chinese people and a heritage that still influences people.

Next, the teacher shared several of her favorite Chinese folktales with the children; they included Marilee Heyer's *The Weaving of a Dream: A Chinese Folktale*, Margaret Mahy's *The Seven Chinese Brothers*, Demi's *The Empty Pot*, and several tales from Neil Philip's *The Spring of Butterflies and Other Folktales of China's Minority Peoples*. The selections included "The Tibetan Envoy," which shows the importance of wit and intelligence; "The Story of Washing Horse Pond," which shows the importance of compassion for others; "The King and a Poor Man," which shows the importance of wise ancestors; and "A Crane and Two Brothers," which shows dislike for greed. The teacher also briefly introduced other tales to stimulate the children's interest in reading the tales. The children then chose tales to read independently. As they read, they considered their questions about China. Consequently, when they discovered information about the culture and the people, they jotted the information down so that they could share it with the class.

After collecting their information, the children discussed ways of verifying whether the information was accurate. They compared the information with library reference materials and magazines, such as *National Geographic*. They also invited to the classroom several visitors who either were Chinese or had visited China.

The students used their knowledge about the people, culture, and literature of China in their own art, creative drama, and writing. They drew travel posters as well as book jackets and illustrations for folktales. They also made mobiles of folk-literature objects.

One artistic activity was to create picture storybooks from single folktales. The children chose a favorite tale not already in picture-book format, illustrated it with drawings, and bound the pages together. Because many of the published picture books contained information about the origins of their tales, the children included similar information inside their own front covers. Published book jackets often tell about the illustrator and the research to provide authentic pictures, so the students' books contained this information as well. The children told about themselves and how they prepared for their drawing assignments. They described the media they used for their illustrations. Then they shared their books with one another and other classes and proudly displayed the books in the library.

The class also chose some stories for creative drama. The teacher divided the class into groups according to favorite folktales. Each group then chose a method for sharing the story with the rest of the class: Some groups re-created the stories as plays, others chose puppetry, and one group used pantomime with a narrator who read the lines.

The children invited their parents to attend a Chinese folktale festival. They shared their art projects, picture storybooks, new information, and creative dramas with an appreciative audience.

This unit about one country led to an interest in folktales from other countries. The children next read folktales from Japan and other Asian countries. They discovered the similarities among many of these tales, especially in the symbolic animals found in both Chinese and Japanese tales. The children went on to detect Chinese influence on non-Asian writers when they read the beautiful version of Hans Christian Andersen's *The Nightingale*, illustrated by Nancy Ekholm Burkert.

The discovery of similar mythical animals led to another interesting search through folklore. The teacher read and discussed portions from Dugald A. Steer's *Dragonology: The Complete Book of Dragons*, especially, "It is interesting to note that, while legends of Western dragons portray them as vicious, bloodthirsty monsters, Eastern dragons are for the most part seen as benevolent helpmates to mankind" (unnumbered). Children discovered that both Chinese and Japanese folktales had good and evil dragons; good dragons, a representation of Han nobility, were found in folktales told to ruling classes, but folktales about the common people referred to dragons as evil. With the teacher's guidance, the students searched for and shared examples of Chinese folktales that included good and bad dragons.

Folktales lend themselves well to many activities. Teachers and librarians will find many ways to increase world understanding through literature.

Motivating Writing Through Traditional Tales

Reading and studying traditional tales encourages numerous written activities. The recent examples of adaptations of folktales by Jon Scieszka and William J. Brooke provide exciting motivation for children to write their own versions of folktales. For example, read a traditional version of the folktale "The Three Little Pigs," and discuss the characters and the plot of the story. Ask the children to identify whose point of view the story reflects. Next, read aloud Scieszka's *The True Story of the 3 Little Pigs!* Allow the children to give individual responses to this story. Ask them to identify the point of view in this adaptation and to discuss how they know that the point of view is that of the wolf rather than of the pigs. Encourage the children to compare the characterizations, plots, and point of view in the two versions, then have them write their responses to the two versions.

Use a similar activity to accompany Scieszka's *The Stinky Cheese Man and Other Fairly Stupid Tales.* After students respond to and discuss Scieszka's text and Lane Smith's illustrations, have them choose other folktales and rewrite the stories to reflect another point of view. Place these new writings in the library along with the more traditional tales.

In *A Telling of the Tales: Five Stories*, William J. Brooke tells readers, "The telling of a tale links you with everyone who has told it before. There are no new tales, only new tellers, telling in their own way, and if you listen closely you can hear the voice of everyone who ever told the tale" (introduction). This book tells traditional tales with a new twist: The stories answer such questions as, What if Cinderella did not want to try on the glass slipper? What if Sleeping Beauty did not believe she had been asleep? What if Paul Bunyan, the greatest tree chopper of them all, met Johnny Appleseed, the fastest tree grower? Encourage children to brainstorm other questions to ask characters from folktales, myths, and legends, then have them write their own adaptations of the stories that answer the questions.

Developing Critical Evaluators for Fables

Teachers can motivate older students to conduct critical evaluations of fables by sharing with them evaluations of books published in journals. For example, "Forecast: Children's Books" published in *Publishers Weekly* (August 14, 2000) includes reviews of three editions of Aesop fables: Jerry Pinkney's *Aesop's Fables*, Doris Orgel's *The Lion & the Mouse and Other Aesop Fables*, and Tom Lynch's *Fables From Aesop*. Students can read or listen to the reviews, read each of the books cited, and compare their own analysis with those of professional reviewers. (Make it clear that students do not need to agree with the published evaluations.)

For example, Pinkney's *Aesop's Fables* receives a starred review and comments such as the following: "Pinkney's glorious watercolors, alight with the many creatures who people the tales, from fiddling grasshoppers and diligent ants to wily foxes, clever crows, brave mice and grateful lions. Each of the vigorous retellings concludes with the kind of succinct moral that centuries of readers have come to expect. . . . If there's room on the shelf for only one picture book version of Aesop, this could be it" (p. 354).

The reviewer for Orgel's *The Lion & the Mouse and Other Aesop Fables* is considerably more critical:

> An even dozen of Aesop's fables round out this volume, which ultimately misses the mark. Orgel's retellings, spirited and brisk, engage readers' attention quickly and maintain a lively pace. . . . The problem lies in the fact that the fables do not conclude with a moral. Instead of ending with the expected bang, each of the parables concludes with a mini sidebar that contains a tidbit of information about ancient Greece. . . . Like a symphony that ends on an unresolved cord, the omission will likely leave readers feeling dissatisfied and may result in this otherwise splendid picture book gathering dust on the shelf. (p. 354)

The reviewer for Lynch's *Fables From Aesop* questions the inclusion of lesser-known parables that "may elude younger readers—such as the tale of Zeus refusing a wedding gift from a snake ('Never accept the offerings of a villain,' when nothing in the tale suggests that snake's evil intentions). . . . Still, the sprightly needlework enhances each scene and may well inspire readers to meet the challenge of a few more sophisticated tales" (p. 355).

As students complete this critical analysis activity, they should discuss the different types of features on which reviewers focus. Consequently, they should consider the impact of illustrations, the writing style, and the appropriateness of the text for the audience.

Suggested Activities

For more suggested activities for understanding traditional literature, visit the Companion Website at **CW** www.prenhall.com/norton

- Read the stories in Charles Perrault's *Tales of Mother Goose* and some tales collected by the Brothers Grimm. Note similarities and differences in the characterizations, settings, and actions. Describe the people for whom you believe the stories were originally told.
- Choose a common theme found in folktales, such as that in Cinderella or trickster stories. Find examples of similar

stories in folktales from several countries. What are the similarities and differences? How do the stories reflect cultural characteristics?

- Read a fable in *Caxton's Aesop* and in *The Caldecott Aesop*. Compare these versions of the fables with a modern version. Are there differences in writing style, language, spelling, and illustrations between the earlier and later versions? If so, what do you believe are the reasons for the differences? Share the versions with a child. How does the child respond to each one?

- To gain an understanding of the numerous subjects that are studied within the area of folklore, search editor Thomas A. Green's *Folklore: An Encyclopedia of Beliefs, Customs, Tales, Music, and Art*, Volumes I and II (1997). Share your findings with the class.

Children's Literature

For full descriptions, including plot summaries and award winner notations, of these and other titles for teaching children with traditional literature, please visit the CD-ROM that accompanies this book.

FOLKTALES

African—African American

Aardema, Verna, retold by. *Anansi Does the Impossible: An Ashanti Tale.* Illustrated by Lisa Desimini. Simon & Schuster, 1997 (I:all).

_____. *Bringing the Rain to Kapiti Plain: A Nandi Tale.* Illustrated by Beatriz Vidal. Dial, 1981 (I:5–8).

_____. *The Lonely Lioness and the Ostrich Chicks: A Masai Tale.* Illustrated by Yumi Heo. Knopf, 1996 (I:5–8 R:4).

_____. *Who's in Rabbit's House?* Illustrated by Leo & Diane Dillon. Dial, 1977 (I:7+ R:3).

_____. *Why Mosquitoes Buzz in People's Ears.* Illustrated by Leo & Diane Dillon. Dial, 1975 (I:5–9 R:6).

Ashabranner, Brent, & Russell Davis. *The Lion's Whiskers: And Other Ethiopian Tales.* Illustrated by Helen Siegl. Linnet, 1996 (I:8+).

Bryan, Ashley. *Beat the Story-Drum, Pum-Pum.* Atheneum, 1980 (I:6+ R:5).

_____. *Beautiful Blackbird.* Atheneum, 2003 (I:4–8).

_____. *The Story of Lightning & Thunder.* Atheneum, 1993 (I:6+ R:5).

_____. *Turtle Knows Your Name.* Atheneum, 1989 (I:6+ R:5).

Day, Nancy Raines. *The Lion's Whiskers: An Ethiopian Folktale.* Illustrated by Ann Grifalconi. Scholastic, 1995 (I:5–8 R:5).

Diakite, Baba Wague. *The Magic Gourd.* Scholastic, 2003 (I:6–9).

Grifalconi, Ann. *The Village of Round and Square Houses.* Little, Brown, 1986 (I:4–9 R:6).

Hamilton, Virginia. *Bruh Rabbit and the Tar Baby.* Illustrated by James E. Ransome. Scholastic, 2003 (I:6–9).

_____. *Her Stories: African American Folktales, Fairy Tales, and True Tales.* Illustrated by Leo & Diane Dillon. Scholastic, 1995 (I:all R:6).

_____. *In the Beginning: Creation Stories From Around the World.* Illustrated by Barry Moser. Harcourt Brace, 1988 (I:all R:5).

_____. *The People Could Fly: American Black Folktales.* Illustrated by Leo & Diane Dillon. Knopf, 1988 (I:9+ R:6).

_____. *The People Could Fly: The Picture Book.* Illustrated by Leo & Diane Dillon. Knopf, 2004 (I:all).

_____. *When Birds Could Talk & Bats Could Sing: The Adventures of Bruh Sparrow, Sis Wren, and Their Friends.* Illustrated by Barry Moser. Scholastic, 1997 (I:10+ R:5).

Harris, Joel Chandler. *Jump! The Adventures of Brer Rabbit.* Adapted by Van Dyke Parks. Illustrated by Barry Moser. Harcourt Brace, 1986 (I:all R:4).

_____. *Jump Again! More Adventures of Brer Rabbit.* Adapted by Van Dyke Parks. Illustrated by Barry Moser. Harcourt Brace, 1987 (I:all R:4).

_____. *More Tales of Uncle Remus: Further Adventures of Brer Rabbit.* Retold by Julius Lester. Dial, 1988 (I:all R:4).

_____. *The Tales of Uncle Remus: The Adventures of Brer Rabbit.* Retold by Julius Lester. Illustrated by Jerry Pinkney. Dial, 1989 (I:all).

Kituku, Vincent Muli Wa, retold by. *East African Folktales.* August House, 1997 (I:8+ R:4).

Lester, Julius. *John Henry.* Illustrated by Jerry Pinkney. Dial, 1994 (I:all).

Mandela, Nelson. *Nelson Mandela's Favorite African Folktales.* Norton, 2002 (I:10–YA).

McDermott, Gerald. *Anansi the Spider: A Tale From the Ashanti.* Holt, 1972 (I:7–9).

_____. *Zomo the Rabbit: A Trickster Tale From West Africa.* Harcourt Brace, 1992 (I:4–8 R:4).

McGill, Alice, retold by. *Sure as Sunrise: Stories of Bruh Rabbit and His Walkin' Talkin' Friends.* Illustrated by Don Tate. Houghton Mifflin, 2004 (I:5–10).

Paye, Won-Ldy, & Margaret H. Lippert. *Mrs. Chicken and the Hungry Crocodile.* Illustrated by Julie Paschkis. Henry Holt, 2003 (I:4–8).

Sanfield, Steve. *The Adventures of High John the Conqueror.* Illustrated by John Ward. Watts, 1989 (I:8+ R:4).

San Souci, Robert. *Sukey and the Mermaid.* Illustrated by Brian Pinkney. Four Winds, 1992 (I:5–10 R:5).

_____. *The Talking Eggs.* Illustrated by Jerry Pinkney. Dial, 1989 (I:all).

Shepard, Aaron. *Master Man: A Tall Tale of Nigeria.* Illustrated by David Wisniewski. HarperCollins, 2001 (I:all).

Steptoe, John. *Mufaro's Beautiful Daughters: An African Tale.* Lothrop, Lee & Shepard, 1987 (I:all R:4).

Washington, Donna L. *A Pride of African Tales.* Illustrated by James Ransome. HarperCollins, 2004 (I:6–10).

Asian

Asian Cultural Centre for UNESCO. *Folk Tales From Asia for Children Everywhere.* Book Three. Weatherhill, 1976 (I:8–12 R:6).

_____. *Folk Tales From Asia for Children Everywhere.* Book Five. Weatherhill, 1977 (I:8–12 R:6).

I = Interest by age level.
R = Readability by grade level.

Bang, Molly. *The Paper Crane.* Mulberry, 1987 (I:8+ R:5).

Bodkin, Odds, retold by. *The Crane Wife.* Illustrated by Gennady Spirin. Harcourt Brace, 1998 (I:8+ R:5).

Climo, Shirley. *The Korean Cinderella.* Illustrated by Ruth Heller. HarperCollins, 1993 (I:7–12).

Davison, Gary Marvin. *Tales From the Taiwanese.* Libraries Unlimited, 2004 (I:10–YA).

Demi. *The Empty Pot.* Henry Holt, 1990 (I:5–9 R:4).

Ernst, Judith. *The Golden Goose King: A Tale Told by the Buddha.* Parvardigar, 1995 (I:10+ R:5).

Fang, Linda. *The Ch'i-lin Purse: A Collection of Ancient Chinese Stories.* Illustrated by Jeanne M. Lee. Farrar, Straus & Giroux, 1995 (I:10+ R:5).

Ginsburg, Mirra, ed. *The Chinese Mirror.* Illustrated by Margot Zemach. Harcourt Brace, 1988 (I:5–8 R:4).

Hamanaka, Sheila, retold by. *Screen of Frogs.* Orchard, 1993 (I:5–10 R:5).

Heyer, Marilee. *The Weaving of a Dream: A Chinese Folktale.* Viking, 1986 (I:8+ R:5).

Hong, Lily Toy, retold by. *Two of Everything.* Whitman, 1993 (I:5–8 R:4).

Hyun, Peter, ed. *Korea's Favorite Tales and Lyrics.* Illustrated by Dong-il Park. Tuttle/Seoul International, 1986 (I:5–10 R:6).

Ishii, Momoko. *The Tongue-Cut Sparrow.* Translated by Katherine Paterson. Illustrated by Suekichi Akaba. Dutton, 1987 (I:7–10 R:6).

James, Grace. *Green Willow and Other Japanese Fairy Tales.* Illustrated by Warwick Goble. Avenel, 1987 (I:10+ R:6).

Kimmel, Eric A., retold by. *Three Samurai Cats: A Story From Japan.* Illustrated by Mordicai Gerstein. Holiday House, 2003 (I:all).

Kuo, Louise, & Yuan-hsi Kuo. *Chinese Folktales.* Celestial Arts, 1976 (I:8+ R:6).

Levine, Arthur, retold by. *The Boy Who Drew Cats: A Japanese Folktale.* Illustrated by Frédéric Clément. Dial, 1994 (I:5–9 R:6).

Louie, Ai-Ling. *Yeh Shen: A Cinderella Story From China.* Illustrated by Ed Young. Philomel, 1982 (I:7–9 R:6).

Mahy, Margaret, retold by. *The Seven Chinese Brothers.* Illustrated by Jean & Mou-sien Tseng. Scholastic, 1990 (I:5–8 R:4).

Mehta, Lila, translated by. *The Enchanted Anklet: A Folk Story From India.* Illustrated by Niela Chhaniara. Lilmur, 1985 (I:all R:4).

Mosel, Arlene. *The Funny Little Woman.* Illustrated by Blair Lent. Dutton, 1972 (I:5–8 R:5).

Partridge, Elizabeth, adapted by. *Kogi's Mysterious Journey.* Illustrated by Aki Sogabe. Dutton, 2003 (I:5–9).

Paterson, Katherine. *The Tale of the Mandarin Ducks.* Illustrated by Leo & Diane Dillon. Lodestar, 1990 (I:5–10 R:6).

Philip, Neil, ed. *The Spring of Butterflies and Other Folktales of China's Minority Peoples.* Translated by He Liyi. Illustrated by Pan Aiqing & Li Zhao. Lothrop, Lee & Shepard, 1986 (I:9+ R:6).

Pratt, Davis, and Elsa Kula. *Magic Animals of Japan.* Parnassus, 1967 (I:8–12 R:7).

Rhee, Nami, retold by. *Magic Spring: A Korean Folktale.* Putnam, 1993 (I:7–10 R:5).

Roberts, Moss. *Chinese Fairy Tales and Fantasies.* Pantheon, 1979 (I:10 R:6).

Sanfield, Steve. *Just Reward: Or Who Is That Man in the Moon & What's He Doing Up There Anyway?* Illustrated by Emily Lisker. Orchard, 1996 (I:5–8 R:5).

San Souci, Robert D. *The Samurai's Daughter: A Japanese Legend.* Illustrated by Stephen T. Johnson. Dial, 1992 (I:5–8 R:6).

Sierra, Judy. *Tasty Baby Belly Buttons.* Illustrated by Meilo So. Knopf, 1999 (I:all).

Snyder, Dianne. *The Boy of the Three-Year Nap.* Illustrated by Allen Say. Houghton Mifflin, 1988 (I:all R:6).

So, Meilo, retold by. *Gobble, Gobble, Slip, Slop: A Tale of a Very Greedy Cat.* Knopf, 2004 (I:4–8).

Tseng, Grace, retold by. *White Tiger, Blue Serpent.* Illustrated by Jean & Mou-sien Tseng. Lothrop, Lee & Shepard, 1999 (I:all).

Wang, Rosalind C., retold by. *The Treasure Chest: A Chinese Tale.* Illustrated by Will Hillenbrand. Holiday House, 1995 (I:8–12 R:5).

Yagawa, Sumiko, ed. *The Crane Wife.* Translated by Katherine Paterson. Illustrated by Suekichi Akaba, Morrow, 1981 (I:7–10 R:6).

Yep, Laurence. *The Khan's Daughter: A Mongolian Folktale.* Illustrated by Jean & Mou-sien Tseng. Scholastic, 1997 (I:5–8 R:4).

_____. *The Rainbow People.* Illustrated by David Wiesner. Harper & Row, 1989 (I:9+ R:6).

_____. *Tiger Woman.* Illustrated by Robert Roth. Bridge Water, 1995 (I:5–8 R:5).

Young, Ed. *I, Doko: The Tale of a Basket.* Philomel, 2004 (I:all).

_____, translated by. *Lon Po Po: A Red-Riding Hood Story From China.* Philomel, 1989 (I:all R:5).

British (United Kingdom)

Behan, Brendan. *The King of Ireland's Son.* Illustrated by P. J. Lynch. Orchard, 1997 (I:all).

Brett, Jan. *Goldilocks and the Three Bears.* Dodd, Mead. 1987 (I:3–7 R:6).

Briggs, Katharine. *British Folktales.* Pantheon, 1977. Dorset, 1989 (I:all).

Buchan, David, ed. *Scottish Tradition: A Collection of Scottish Folk Literature.* Routledge & Kegan Paul, 1984 (I:9+ R:5).

Chaucer, Geoffrey, *Canterbury Tales.* Adapted by Barbara Cohen. Illustrated by Trina Schart Hyman. Lothrop, Lee & Shepard, 1988 (I:8+ R:6).

Cooper, Susan, retold by. *The Silver Cow: A Welsh Tale.* Illustrated by Warwick Hutton. Atheneum, 1983 (I:5–8 R:5).

Crossley-Holland, Kevin. *British Folk Tales.* Watts, 1988 (I:8+ R:5).

dePaola, Tomie. *The Friendly Beasts: An Old English Christmas Carol.* Putnam, 1981 (I:3–9).

Galdone, Paul. *The Little Red Hen.* Clarion, 1985 (I:3–7 R:3).

_____. *The Three Bears.* Clarion, 1985 (I:3–7 R:5).

Huck, Charlotte, retold by. *Princess Furball.* Illustrated by Anita Lobel. Greenwillow, 1989 (I:6–10 R:6).

Jacobs, Joseph. *Celtic Fairy Tales.* Illustrated by John D. Batten. David Nutt, 1890; reissued 1968 (I:9+ R:6).

_____. *English Fairy Tales.* Illustrated by John D. Batten. David Nutt, 1890 (I:10+ R:7).

_____. *More English Fairy Tales.* David Nutt, 1894 (I:all R:6).

Jones, Gwyn. *Welsh Legends and Folktales.* Oxford, 1955, Puffin, 1982 (I:9+ R:7).

Kellogg, Steven. *Chicken Little.* Morrow, 1985 (I:5–8 R:5).

_____. *Jack and the Beanstalk.* Morrow, 1991 (I:4–9 R:5).

_____. *The Three Little Pigs.* Morrow, 1997 (I:5–8 R:4).

Kimmel, Eric, retold by. *The Gingerbread Man.* Illustrated by Megan Lloyd. Holiday House, 1993 (I:3–6).

Marshall, James. *Goldilocks and the Three Bears.* Dial, 1988 (I:3–8 R:5).

Myers, Bernice. *Sydney Rella and the Glass Sneaker.* Macmillan, 1985 (I:6–10 R:3).

Philip, Neil, retold by. *Celtic Fairy Tales.* Illustrated by Isabelle Brent. Viking, 1999 (I:7+ R:6).

Rounds, Glen, retold and illustrated by. *Three Little Pigs and the Big Bad Wolf.* Holiday House, 1992 (I:3–8 R:5).

White, Carolyn. *Whuppity Stoorie: A Scottish Folktale.* Illustrated by S. D. Schindler. Putnam, 1997 (I:4–8 R:4).

Wiesner, David, retold by. *The Loathsome Dragon.* Clarion, 2005 (I:all).

Zemach, Harve. *Duffy and the Devil.* Illustrated by Margot Zemach. Farrar, Straus & Giroux, 1973 (I:8–12 R:6).

French

Aylesworth, Jim. *The Gingerbread Man.* Illustrated by Barbara McClintock. Scholastic, 1998 (I:2–6).

Brett, Jan, retold by. *Beauty and the Beast.* Clarion, 1989 (I:8–12 R:6).

de Beaumont, Madame. *Beauty and the Beast.* Translated and illustrated by Diane Goode. Bradbury, 1978 (I:8–14 R:7).

Perrault, Charles. *Cinderella.* Illustrated by Marcia Brown. Scribner, 1954; 2nd ed. 1997 (I:5–8 R:5).

_____. *The Glass Slipper: Charles Perrault's Tales of Time Past.* Translated by John Bierhorst. Illustrated by Mitchell Miller. Four Winds, 1981 (I:9–12 R:6).

_____. *Histories or Tales of Past Times.* Garland, 1977 (I:10+ R:6).

_____. *Puss in Boots.* Retold by Lincoln Kirstein. Illustrated by Alain Vais. Little, Brown, 1992 (I:6–10 R:5).

_____. *Puss in Boots.* Translated by Malcolm Arthur. Illustrated by Fred Marcellino. Farrar, Straus & Giroux, 1990 (I:6–10 R:6).

_____. *The Sleeping Beauty.* Translated and illustrated by David Walker. Crowell, 1976 (I:8–14 R:6).

Wegman, William, retold by. *Cinderella.* Hyperion (I:5–8 R:5).

Willard, Nancy, retold by. *Beauty and the Beast.* Illustrated by Barry Moser. Harcourt Brace, 1992 (I:8+ R:6).

German

Galdone, Paul. *Little Red Riding Hood.* McGraw-Hill, 1974 (I:4–8 R:4).

Grimm, Brothers. *The Brave Little Tailor.* Translated by Anthea Bell. Illustrated by Sergei Goloshapov. North-South, 1997 (I:5–8 R:5).

_____. *The Bremen Town Musicians.* Retold and illustrated by Ilse Plume. Doubleday, 1980 (I:5–8 R:5).

_____. *The Bremen Town Musicians.* Translated by Anthea Bell. Illustrated by Bernadette Watts. North-South, 1997 (I:5–8 R:5).

_____. *The Complete Brothers Grimm Fairy Tales.* Edited by Lily Owens. Avenel, 1981 (I:all R:7).

_____. *The Golden Bird.* Retold by Neil Philip. Illustrated by Isabelle Brent. Little, Brown, 1995 (I:all).

_____. *Hansel and Gretel.* Illustrated by Susan Jeffers. Dial, 1980 (I:5–9 R:6).

_____. *Hansel and Gretel.* Retold by Rika Lesser. Illustrated by Paul O. Zelinsky. Dodd, Mead, 1984 (I:all R:6).

_____. *Little Red Cap.* Translated by Elizabeth Crawford. Illustrated by Lisbeth Zwerger. Morrow, 1983 (I:4–7 R:4).

_____. *Little Red Riding Hood.* Retold and illustrated by Trina Schart Hyman. Holiday House, 1983 (I:6–9 R:7).

_____. *Rapunzel: From the Brothers Grimm.* Retold by Barbara Rogasky. Illustrated by Trina Schart Hyman. Holiday House, 1982 (I:6–9 R:6).

_____. *Rapunzel.* Retold and Illustrated by Paul O. Zelinsky. Dutton, 1997 (I:all).

_____. *Rose Red and Snow White.* Retold by Ruth Sanderson. Little, Brown, 1997 (I:4–8 R:4).

_____. *Rumpelstiltskin.* Retold and illustrated by Paul O. Zelinsky. Dutton, 1986 (I:all R:6).

_____. *The Sleeping Beauty.* Retold and illustrated by Trina Schart Hyman. Little, Brown, Silver Anniversary Edition, 2000 (I:7–12 R:6).

_____. *The Sleeping Beauty.* Illustrated by Warwick Hutton. Atheneum, 1979 (I:7–12 R:6).

_____. *Snow White.* Illustrated by Trina Schart Hyman. Translated by Paul Heins. Little, Brown, Silver Anniversary Edition, 2000 (I:7–12 R:6).

_____. *Snow White and the Seven Dwarfs.* Translated by Randall Jarrell. Illustrated by Nancy Ekholm Burkert. Farrar, Straus & Giroux, 1972 (I:7–12 R:6).

_____. *The Twelve Dancing Princesses.* Illustrated by Errol LeCain. Viking, 1978 (I:7–12 R:7).

_____. *The Twelve Dancing Princesses.* Retold by Marianna Mayer. Illustrated by Kinuko Craft. Morrow, 1989 (I:8+ R:5).

_____. *The Twelve Dancing Princesses.* Retold by Jane Ray. Dutton, 1996 (I:5–8 R:5).

_____. *The Twelve Dancing Princesses.* Retold by Ruth Sanderson. Little, Brown, 1990 (I:7–10 R:5).

_____. *The Turnip.* Retold by Walter de la Mare. Illustrated by Kevin Hawkes. Godine, 1992 (I:5–8 R:4).

_____. *The Water of Life.* Retold by Barbara Rogasky. Illustrated by Trina Schart Hyman. Holiday House, 1986 (I:4–9 R:3).

Grimm, Wihelm. *Dear Mili.* Translated by Ralph Manheim. Illustrated by Maurice Sendak. Farrar, Straus & Giroux, 1988 (I:all R:6).

Long, Laurel, and Jacqueline K. Ogburn, retold by. *The Lady & The Lion: A Brothers Grimm Tale.* Dial, 2003 (I:6–9).

Marshall, James, *Hansel and Gretel.* Dial, 1990 (I:3–8 R:4).

_____. *Red Riding Hood.* Dial, 1987 (I:3–8 R:5).

Orgel, Doris, retold by. *The Bremen Town Musicians and Other Animal Tales From Grimm.* Illustrated by Bert Kitchen. Roaring Brook, 2004 (I:6+).

Wegman, William, retold by. *Little Red Riding Hood.* Hyperion, 1993 (I:5–8 R:5).

Jewish

Geras, Adele. *My Grandmother's Stories: A Collection of Jewish Folk Tales.* Illustrated by Anita Lobel. Knopf, 2003 (I:6–10).

Jaffe, Nina, & Steve Zeitlin. *While Standing on One Foot: Puzzle Stories and Wisdom Tales from the Jewish Tradition.* Illustrated by John Segal. Holt, 1993 (I:8+ R:5).

Patterson, Jose. *Angels, Prophets, Rabbis & Kings From the Stories of the Jewish People.* Illustrated by Claire Bushe. P. Bedrick, 1991 (I:10+ R:6).

Prose, Francine. *The Angel's Mistake: Stories of Chelm.* Illustrated by Mark Podwal. Greenwillow, 1997 (I:all).

Rothenberg, Joan, *Yettele's Feathers.* Hyperion, 1995 (I:5–8 R:6).

Schwartz, Cherie Karo. *Circle Spinning: Jewish Turning and Returning Tales.* Illustrated by Lisa Rauchwerger. Hamsa, 2002 (I:12–YA R:6).

Schwartz, Howard, and Barbara Rush, selected and retold by. *The Diamond Tree: Jewish Tales From Around the World.* Illustrated by Uri Shulevitz. HarperCollins, 1991 (I:8+ R:5).

Singer, Isaac Bashevis. *The Golem.* Illustrated by Uri Shulevitz. Farrar, Straus & Giroux, 1982 (I:8+ R:5).

_____. *Mazel and Shlimazel, or the Milk of the Lioness.* Illustrated by Margot Zemach. Farrar, Straus & Giroux, 1967 (I:8–12 R:4).

_____. *When Shlemiel Went to Warsaw & Other Stories.* Illustrated by Margot Zemach. Farrar, Straus & Giroux, 1968 (I:8–12 R:4).

Zemach, Margot. *It Could Always Be Worse.* Farrar, Straus & Giroux, 1977 (I:5–9 R:2).

Latino

Anaya, Rudolfo. *Maya's Children: The Story of La Llorona.* Illustrated by Maria Baca. Hyperion, 1997 (I:5–9 R:4).

Anzaldua, Gloria. *Prietita and the Ghost Woman.* Children's Book Press, 1996 (I:5–8 R:5).

Bierhorst, John. *Doctor Coyote: A Native American Aesop's Fables.* Illustrated by Wendy Watson. Macmillan, 1987 (I:all).

_____, ed. *Lightning Inside You and Other Native American Riddles.* Illustrated by Louise Brierley. Morrow, 1992 (I:8+).

_____. *The Monkey's Haircut and Other Stories Told by the Maya.* Illustrated by Robert Andrew Parker. Morrow, 1986 (I:8+ R:6).

_____, translated by. *Spirit Child: A Story of the Nativity.* Illustrated by Barbara Cooney. Morrow, 1984 (I:8–12 R:6).

dePaola, Tomie. *The Lady of Guadalupe.* Holiday House, 1980 (I:8+ R:6).

De Spain, Pleasant. *The Dancing Turtle: A Folktale From Brazil.* Illustrated by David Boston. August House, 1998 (I:5–8 R:4).

_____. *The Emerald Lizard: Fifteen Latin American Tales to Tell.* Illustrated by Don Bell. August House, 1999 (I:10+).

Dorson, Mercedes, & Jeanne Wilmot. *Tales From the Rain Forest: Myths and Legends From the Amazonian Indians of Brazil.* Ecco, 1997 (I:8+ R:7).

Ehlert, Lois. *Cuckoo: A Mexican Folktale.* Translated into Spanish by Gloria de Aragon Andujar. Harcourt Brace, 1997 (I:4–8).

_____. *Moon Rope.* Harcourt Brace, 1992 (I: all).

Knutson, Barbara. *Love and Roast Chicken: A Trickster Tale From the Andes Mountains.* Carolrhoda, 2004 (I:6–10).

Marcantonio, Patricia Santos. *Red Ridin' in the Hood: And Other Cuentos.* Illustrated by Renato Alarcão. Farrar, Straus & Giroux, 2005 (I:10+ R:6).

McDermott, Gerald. *Musicians of the Sun.* Simon & Schuster, 1997 (I:all).

Nagarajan, Nadia Grosser. *Pomegranate Seeds: Latin American Jewish Tales.* University of New Mexico Press, 2005 (I:10+ R:7).

Perez, Elvia, retold by. *From the Winds of Manguito: Cuban Folktales in English and Spanish.* Translated by Paula Martin. Illustrated by Victor Francisco Hernández Mora. Libraries Unlimited, 2004 (I:10+ R:7).

Rohmer, Harriet, Octavio Chow, & Morris Vidaure. *The Invisible Hunters.* Illustrated by Joe Sam. Children's Book Press, 1987 (I:all R:5).

Rohmer, Harriet, & Domminster Wilson. *Mother Scorpion Country.* Illustrated by Virginia Steams. Children's Press, 1987 (I:all R:5).

VanLaan, Nancy. *So Say the Little Monkeys.* Illustrated by Yumi Heo. Atheneum, 1998 (I:all).

Volkmer, Jane Anne, retold by. *Song of Chirimia—A Guatemalan Folktale.* Carolrhoda, 1990 (I:6–10 R:5).

Middle Eastern

Ben-Ezer, Ehud. *Hosni the Dreamer: An Arabian Tale.* Illustrated by Uri Shulevitz. Farrar, Straus & Giroux, 1997 (I:4–7 R:4).

Bushnaq, Inea, ed. *Arab Folktales.* Pantheon, 1986 (I:12+ R:7).

Climo, Shirley. *The Egyptian Cinderella.* Illustrated by Ruth Heller. HarperCollins, 1989 (I:7–12).

_____. *The Persian Cinderella.* Illustrated by Ruth Heller. HarperCollins, 1999 (I:7–12).

Demi. *The Hungry Coat: A Tale From Turkey.* McElderry, 2004 (I:6–8).

Dulac, Edmund, illustrated by. *Sinbad the Sailor and Other Stories From the Arabian Nights.* Hodder and Stoughton, 1914; reissued Omega, 1986 (I:12+).

Hickox, Rebecca. *The Golden Sandal: A Middle Eastern Cinderella Story.* Illustrated by Will Hillenbrand. Holiday House, 1998 (I:5–8 R:5).

Kimmel, Eric A., adapted by. *Rimonah of the Flashing Sword: A North African Tale.* Illustrated by Omar Rayyan. Holiday House, 1995 (I:5–9 R:5).

_____. *The Three Princes: A Tale From the Middle East.* Illustrated by Leonard Everett Fisher. Holiday House, 1994 (I:4–8 R:5).

Maugham, W. Somerset. *Appointment.* Adapted by Alan Benjamin. Illustrated by Roger Essley. Simon & Schuster, 1993 (I:all).

Philip, Neil, retold by. *The Arabian Nights.* Illustrated by Sheila Moxley. Orchard, 1994 (I:8+ R:5).

Pullman, Philip, retold by. *Aladdin and the Enchanted Lamp.* Illustrated by Sophy Williams. Scholastic, 2005 (I:8–10).

Sherman, Josepha. *Once Upon a Galaxy.* August House, 1994 (I:8+).

_____, retold by. *Trickster Tales: Forty Folk Stories From Around the World.* Illustrated by David Boston. August House, 1996 (I:7+).

Zeman, Ludmila, retold and illustrated by. *Sindbad: From the Tales of the Thousand and One Nights.* Tundra, 1999 (I:all).

Native American

Baker, Olaf. *Where the Buffaloes Begin.* Illustrated by Stephen Gammell. Warne, 1981 (I:all R:6).

Bania, Michael. *Kumak's Fish: A Tall Tale From the Far North.* Alaska Northwest Books, 2004 (I:4–8).

Bierhorst, John. *The Ring in the Prairie, a Shawnee Legend.* Illustrated by Leo & Diane Dillon. Dial, 1970 (I:all R:6).

Bruchac, Joseph, & James Bruchac. *Raccoon's Last Race.* Illustrated by Jose Aruego & Ariane Dewey. Dial, 2004 (I:4–8).

Caduto, Michael J., & Joseph Bruchac. *Keepers of the Animals: Native American Stories and Wildlife Activities for Children.* Illustrated by John Kahionhes Fadden. Fulcrum, 1991 (I:all).

_____. *Keepers of the Earth: Native American Stories and Environmental Activities for Children.* Illustrated by John Kahionhes Fadden & Carol Wood. Fulcrum, 1988 (I:all).

Cushing, Frank Hamilton. *Zuni Folktales.* University of Arizona Press, 1901, 1986 (I:12+ R:8).

dePaola, Tomie. *The Legend of the Bluebonnet.* Putnam, 1983 (I:all R:6).

Duncan, Lois. *The Magic of Spider Woman.* Illustrated by Shonto Begay. Scholastic (I:all R:7).

Goble, Paul. *Beyond the Ridge.* Bradbury, 1989 (I:all R:5).

_____. *Buffalo Woman.* Bradbury, 1984 (I:all R:6).

_____. *Iktomi and the Berries.* Watts, 1989 (I:4–10 R:4).

_____. *Iktomi and the Boulder: A Plains Indian Story.* Orchard, 1988 (I:4–10 R:4).

McDermott, Gerald. *Raven: A Trickster Tale From the Pacific Northwest.* Harcourt Brace, 1993 (I:all).

Sobol, Joseph Daniel. *The House Between Earth and Sky: Harvesting New American Folktales.* Teacher Ideas Press, 2005 (I:10+ R:7).

Tingle, Tim. *Walking the Choctaw Road.* Cinco Puntos Press, 2003 (I:12+ R:6).

Norwegian

Asbjørnsen, Peter Christen, & Jørgen E. Moe. *East O' the Sun and West O' the Moon.* Translated by George Webbe Dasent. Illustrated by P. J. Lynch. Candlewick, 1992 (I:6–10 R:6).

_____. *The Man Who Kept House.* Illustrated by Otto S. Svend. Macmillan, 1992 (I:5–9 R:5).

_____. *Norwegian Folk Tales.* Illustrated by Erik Werenskiold & Theodor Kittelsen. Viking, 1960 (I:6–10 R:3).

_____. *The Three Billy Goats Gruff.* Illustrated by Marcia Brown. Harcourt Brace, 1957 (I:3–7 R:5).

_____. *Three Billy Goats Gruff.* Retold and illustrated by Glen Rounds. Holiday House, 1993 (I:3–7 R:5).

Booss, Claire, ed. *Scandinavian Folk & Fairy Tales.* Avenel, 1984 (I:10+).

Galdone, Paul. *The Three Billy Goats Gruff.* Seabury, 1973 (I:5–8 R:5).

Hague, Kathleen, & Michael Hague. *East of the Sun and West of the Moon.* Harcourt Brace, 1980 (I:7–9 R:5).

Haviland, Virginia. *Favorite Fairy Tales Told in Norway.* Illustrated by Leonard Weisgard. Little, Brown, 1961 (I:6–10 R:4).

Lunge-Larsen, Lise. *The Hidden Folk: Stories of Fairies, Dwarves, Selkies, and Other Secret Beings.* Illustrated by Beth Krommes. Houghton Mifflin, 2004 (I:4–9 R:4).

_____, retold by. *The Troll With No Heart in His Body and Other Tales of Trolls from Norway.* Illustrated by Betsy Bowen. Houghton Mifflin, 1999 (I:7+ R:4).

Mayer, Mercer. *East of the Sun and West of the Moon.* Four Winds, 1980 (I:8–10 R:4).

Willard, Nancy. *East of the Sun & West of the Moon: A Play.* Illustrated by Barry Moser. Harcourt Brace, 1989 (I:all).

Russian

Afanasyév, Alexander Nikolayevich. *The Fool and the Fish: A Tale from Russia.* Retold by Lenny Hort. Illustrated by Gennady Spirin. Dial, 1990 (I:5–8 R:4).

_____. *Russian Folk Tales.* Translated by Robert Chandler. Illustrated by Ivan I. Bilibin. Random House, 1980 (I:8–12 R:7).

Fonteyn, Margot. *Swan Lake.* Illustrated by Trina Schart Hyman. Harcourt Brace, 1989 (I:all R:6).

Helprin, Mark. *Swan Lake.* Illustrated by Chris Van Allsburg. Houghton Mifflin, 1989 (I:all R:6).

Kimmel, Eric A. *One Eye, Two Eyes, Three Eyes.* Illustrated by Dirk Zimmer. Holiday House, 1996 (I:5–8 R:4).

Lewis, J. Patrick, adapted by. *At the Wish of the Fish: A Russian Folktale.* Illustrated by Katya Krenina. Atheneum, 1999 (I:6–9 R:6).

Marshall, Bonnie C., translated and retold by. *The Snow Maiden and Other Russian Tales.* Libraries Unlimited, 2004 (I:all).

Pushkin, Alexander. *The Golden Cockerel and Other Fairy Tales.* Illustrated by Boris Zvorykin. Doubleday, 1990 (I:8–12 R:6).

_____. *The Tale of Tsar Saltan.* Illustrated by Gennady Spirin. Dial, 1996 (I:7+ R:6).

Ransome, Arthur. *The Fool of the World and the Flying Ship.* Illustrated by Uri Shulevitz. Farrar, Straus & Giroux, 1968 (I:6–10 R:6).

Sanderson, Ruth. *The Golden Mare, the Firebird, and the Magic Ring.* Little, Brown, 2001 (I:all).

Shepard, Aaron, retold by. *The Sea King's Daughter.* Illustrated by Gennady Spirin. Atheneum, 1997 (I:7+ R:5).

Sherman, Josepha. *Vassilisa the Wise: A Tale of Medieval Russia.* Illustrated by Daniel San Souci. Harcourt Brace Jovanovich, 1988 (I:8+ R:6).

Other Folktales

Ahlberg, Janet & Allan. *The Jolly Postman or Other People's Letters.* Little, Brown, 1986 (I:3–8 R:2).

Andersen, Hans Christian. *The Nightingale.* Translated by Eva Le Gallienne. Illustrated by Nancy Ekholm Burkert. Harper & Row, 1965 (I:all R:7).

Baker, Olaf. *Where the Buffaloes Begin.* Illustrated by Stephen Gammell. Warne, 1981 (I:8 R:7).

Bayat, Mojdeh, & Mohammad Ali Jamnia. *Tales From the Land of the Sufis.* Random House, 1994 (I:10–YA R:7).

Blair, Walter. *Tall Tale America: A Legendary History of Our Humorous Heroes.* Illustrated by Glen Rounds. Demco, 1987 (I:8–12 R:5).

Brooke, William J. *A Telling of the Tales: Five Stories.* Harper & Row 1990 (I:8+ R:4).

Chase, Richard, retold by. *The Jack Tales.* Illustrated by Berkeley Williams, Jr. Houghton Mifflin, 1943 (I:all R:5).

Cohn, Amy L., compiled by. *From Sea to Shining Sea: A Treasury of American Folklore and Folk Songs.* Illustrated by Caldecott Award Artists. Scholastic, 1993 (I:all).

Conover, Sarah, & Freda Crane, adapted by. *Ayat Jamilah: Beautiful Signs: A Treasury of Islamic Wisdom for Children and*

Parents. Illustrated by Valerie Wahl. Eastern Washington University Press, 2004 (I:10–YA R:6).

Day, Edward C. *John Tabor's Ride*. Illustrated by Dirk Zimmer. Knopf, 1989 (I:8+ R:5).

Demi. *Buddha Stories*. Holt, 1997 (I:all).

_____. *One Grain of Rice: A Mathematical Folktale*. Scholastic. 1997 (I:5–8 R:4).

dePaola. Tomie. *Days of the Blackbird: A Tale of Northern Italy*. Putnam. 1997 (I:5–9 R:5).

Ernst, Judith, retold by. *The Golden Goose King: A Tale Told by the Buddha*. Parvardigar, 1995 (I:10+ R:6).

Evetts-Secker, Josephine, retold by. *Father and Son Tales*. Illustrated by Helen Cann. Barefoot, 1999 (I:8+ R:5).

_____, retold by. *Mother and Son Tales*. Illustrated by Helen Cann. Barefoot, 1999 (I:8+ R:5).

Haddix, Margaret Patterson. *Just Ella*. Simon & Schuster, 1999 (I:4–7 R:6).

Haley, Gail E. *Jack and the Bean Tree*. Crown, 1986 (I:4–10 R:5).

_____. *Mountain Jack Tales*. Dutton, 1992 (I:8+ R:5).

Harris, Joel Chandler. *Told by Uncle Remus*. McClure, Philips & Co., 1905 (I:all R:4).

_____. *Uncle Remus and His Friends*. Houghton Mifflin, 1892 (I:all R:4).

Highwater, Jamake. *Anpao: An American Indian Odyssey*. Illustrated by Fritz Scholder. Lippincott, 1977 (I:12+ R:6).

Ho, Minfong, & Saphan Ros. *Brother Rabbit: A Cambodian Tale*. Illustrated by Jennifer Hewiston. Lothrop, Lee & Shepard, 1997 (I:5–8 R:4).

Hooks, William H. *Moss Gown*. Illustrated by Donald Carrick. Clarion, 1987 (I:8+ R:5).

Kelin, Daniel A. *To Feel as Our Ancestors Did: Collecting and Performing Oral Histories*. Heinemann, 2005 (I:12–YA).

Kellogg, Stephen, retold by. *Johnny Appleseed*. Morrow, 1988 (I:6–9 R:6).

_____, retold by. *Mike Fink: A Tall Tale*. Morrow, 1992 (I:5–8 R:6).

_____, retold by. *Paul Bunyan*. Morrow, 1984 (I:6–9 R:7).

Ketterman, Helen. *Bubba The Cowboy Prince: A Fractured Texas Tale*. Illustrated by James Warhola. Scholastic, 1997 (I:5–8 R:3).

Levine, Gail. *Ella Enchanted*. HarperCollins, 1997 (I:4–6 R:5).

Manna, Anthony L., & Mitakidou. *Mr. Semolina-Semolinus: A Greek Folktale*. Simon & Schuster, 1997 (I:5–8 R:4).

Martin, Eva, retold by. *Canadian Fairy Tales*. Illustrated by Laszlo Gal. Douglas & McIntyre, 1984 (I:7–10 R:4).

Mayo, Margaret. *Mythical Birds & Beasts From Many Lands*. Illustrated by Jane Ray. Dutton, 1997 (I:all).

McDermott, Gerald. *Arrow to the Sun: A Pueblo Indian Tale*. Viking, 1974 (I:3–9 R:2).

_____. *Raven: A Trickster Tale From the Pacific Northwest*. Harcourt Brace, 1993 (I:all).

Mutén, Burleigh, retold by. *Grandmothers' Stories: Wise Woman Tales From Many Cultures*. Illustrated by Sid Bailey. Barefoot, 1999 (I:all).

Nivendita, Sister, & Ananda K. Coomaraswamy. *Myths and Legends Series: Hindus and Buddhists*. Bracken, 1985.

Osborne, Mary Pope. *Kate and the Beanstalk*. Illustrated by Giselle Potter. Atheneum, 2000.

Pellowski, Anne. *Drawing Stories From Around the World and a Sampling of European Handkerchief Stories*. Libraries Unlimited, 2005 (I:10+ R:6).

Sanderson, Ruth. *Papa Gatto: An Italian Fairy Tale*. Little, Brown, 1995 (I:8+ R:7).

San Souci, Robert D. *Cut From the Same Cloth: American Women of Myth, Legend, and Tall Tale*. Illustrated by Brian Pinkney. Philomel, 1993 (I:8+ R:5).

_____. *A Weave of Words*. Illustrated by Rául Colón. Orchard, 1998 (I:5–9 R:5).

Schroeder, Alan. *Smoky Mountain Rose: An Appalachian Cinderella*. Illustrated by Brad Sneed. Dial, 1997 (I:5–9 R:4).

Scieszka, Jon. *The Stinky Cheese Man and Other Fairly Stupid Tales*. Illustrated by Lane Smith. Viking, 1992 (I:all).

_____. *The True Story of the 3 Little Pigs!* Illustrated by Lane Smith. Viking, 1989 (I:all).

Sierra, Judy. *Multicultural Folktales for the Feltboard and Readers' Theater*. Oryx, 1996 (I:all).

So, Meilo. *Gobble, Gobble, Slip, Slop: A Tale of a Very Greedy Cat*. Knopf, 2004. (I:3–8).

Stanley, Diane. *Rumpelstiltskin's Daughter*. Morrow, 1997 (I:5–9 R:5).

Tchana, Katrin, retold by. *The Serpent Slayer and Other Stories of Strong Women*. Illustrated by Trina Schart Hyman. Little, Brown, 2000 (I:all).

Van Laan, Nancy. *With a Whoop and a Holler: A Bushel of Lore From Way Down South*. Illustrated by Scott Cook. Atheneum, 1998 (I:all).

Walker, Paul Robert. *Little Folk: Stories From Around the World*. Illustrated by James Bernardin. Harcourt Brace, 1997 (I:all).

Yep, Laurence. *The Khan's Daughter: A Mongolian Folktale*. Illustrated by Jean & Mou-sien Tseng. Scholastic, 1997 (I:5–8 R:4).

FABLES

Aesop. *Aesop's Fables*. Illustrated by Fulvio Testa. Barron's, 1989 (I:all R:5).

_____. *Aesop's Fables*. Retold by Tom Paxton. Illustrated by Robert Rayevsky. Morrow, 1988 (I:all).

_____. *Aesop's Fables*. Selected and illustrated by Michael Hague. Holt. Rinehart & Winston, 1985 (I:9–12 R:7).

_____. *Aesop's Fables*. Translated by Sir Roger L'Estrange. Illustrated by Percy J. Billinghurst. Gallery, 1984 (I:9+).

_____. *The Aesop for Children*. Illustrated by Milo Winter. Rand McNally, 1919. (I:all).

Bierhorst, John. *Doctor Coyote: A Native American Aesop's Fables*. Illustrated by Wendy Watson. Macmillan, 1987 (I:all R:5).

Caldecott, Randolph. *The Caldecott Aesop: A Facsimile of the 1883 Edition*. Doubleday, 1978 (I:all R:7).

Craig, Helen. *The Town Mouse and the Country Mouse*. Candlewick, 1992 (I:6–8 R:5).

Lester, Julius. *Ackamarackus: Julius Lester's Sumptuously Silly Fantastically Funny Fables*. Illustrated by Emilie Chollat. Scholastic, 2001 (I:all).

Lynch, Tom, retold by. *Fables From Aesop*. Viking, 2000 (I:4–8).

Morpurgo, Michael. *The McElderry Book of Aesop's Fables*. Illustrated by Emma Chichester Clark. Simon & Schuster, 2004 (I:4–8).

Illustration from *Captain Rapter and the Moon Mystery*. Text copyright © 2005 by Kevin O'Malley, illustrations copyright © 2005 by Patrick O'Brien. Used by permission of Walker Publishing Company, Inc.

Chapter Outline

Time, Space, and Place

- Evaluating Modern Fantasy
- Bridges Between Traditional and Modern Fantasy
- Categories of Modern Fantasy

Teaching With Modern Fantasy

- Helping Children Recognize, Understand, and Enjoy Elements in Fantasy
- Interpreting Modern Fantasy by Identifying Plot Structures
- Involving Children With Science Fiction
- Unit Plan: Using One Book of Modern Fantasy

Time, Space, and Place

When children escape into Beatrix Potter's world, they enter the intriguing sphere of fantasy. With the following rhythmical words from *The Tailor of Gloucester*, one of the most popular authors of modern fantasy takes her readers into a time and setting where the impossible becomes convincingly possible:

> In the time of swords and periwigs and full-skirted coats with flowered lappets—when gentlemen wore ruffles, and gold-laced waistcoats of paduasoy and taffeta—there lived a tailor in Gloucester. (p. 11)

Authors create modern fantasy by altering one or more characteristics of everyday reality. They may create entirely new worlds, as J. R. R. Tolkien does Middle Earth in *The Hobbit*, or they may give their characters extraordinary experiences in the real world, as Donna Jo Napoli does in *Bound*, a story set in the Ming dynasty. A realistic character may go down a rabbit hole and enter another domain, as in Lewis Carroll's *Alice's Adventures in Wonderland*, or nonrealistic characters, such as Mary Norton's little people in *The Borrowers*, may exist in an otherwise realistic setting. In one way or another, however, authors of fantasy permit readers to enter imaginative realms of possibility. More than one fourth of the 63 books listed by the Children's Literature Association in *Touchstones: A List of Distinguished Children's Books* (1985) are modern fantasy. Likewise, one fourth of the books identified as "One Hundred Books That Shaped the Century" (Breen et al., 2000) are fantasy. Within this list are both classics such as Natalie Babbitt's *Tuck Everlasting* and A. A. Milne's *Winnie-the-Pooh* and newer fantasies such as J. K. Rowling's *Harry Potter and the Sorcerer's Stone*. Bonnie Kunzel (2005) states, "There's more quality fantasy being published today than ever before" (p. 46).

Many adults consider modern fantasy to be among the most valuable literature selections for children. For example, Chet Raymo (1992), a scientist and author, maintains that fantasy writing helps children expand their curiosity, become observers of life, learn to be sensitive to rules and variations within the rules, and open their minds to new possibilities. Raymo's favorite fantasy books include C. S. Lewis's "Narnia" series, J. R. R. Tolkien's books set in Middle Earth, Dr. Seuss's various fantasies, and Kenneth Grahame's *The Wind in the Willows*. Raymo recommends these fantasies because in such children's books, "we are at the roots of science—pure, childlike curiosity, eyes open with wonder to the fresh and new, and powers of invention still unfettered by convention and expectation" (p. 567). Another science educator, Lazer Goldberg (1991), concludes, "My study of literature persuaded me that reading fantasy can serve children well. Their suspension of disbelief for the duration of the reading will, among other things, help children deal more effectively with the real world" (p. 38).

This chapter suggests criteria for evaluating modern fantasy. It stresses the ways in which modern authors of fantasy literature follow in the footsteps of the anonymous storytellers who created and transmitted the traditional fantasies of oral literature. It also discusses various types of modern fantasy and recommends numerous outstanding fantasy stories.

Evaluating Modern Fantasy

Like all authors of fiction, authors of high-quality modern fantasy use basic literary elements to create stories that are interesting, engrossing, and believable. In evaluating modern fantasy for children, you should use the criteria recommended in Chapter 3, while considering the special uses of literary elements that the fantasy genre requires. Consider the questions in the Evaluation Criteria box on this page when selecting modern fantasy to share with children. Many books of modern fantasy admirably satisfy these criteria and provide great enjoyment to children and adults alike.

Suspending Disbelief: Plot

The author's ability to make readers suspend disbelief and to accept the possibility that the story could have happened is one of the greatest requirements for modern fantasy. Fantasy writer Patricia Wrightson (1990) states this very well:

> Fantasy is story, and no story has any business to begin by asking you weakly to suspend disbelief. It is the business of story to require and work for your belief. It may be more difficult in fantasy, but that is the writer's affair; no one is forcing him to try. If he invites you to go flying with him, the very least he can do is to build a strong pair of wings. The freedom of fantasy is not license: if it abandons the laws and logic of reality, it must provide other laws and logic to govern itself. It may invent circumstances to suit its purpose, but the purpose must be the story's obligation to explore life and humanity. It has great strengths: the power of the extraordinary, the broad definition of symbol, the evocative voice of poetry; having them, it mustn't also ask for your weak and complaisant credulity. If fantasy is not strong, it is nothing. (p. 75)

A story may seem believable if it begins in a realistic context and then moves into the realm of fantasy. In "The Chronicles of Narnia," for example, C. S. Lewis develops normal human characters who visit a realistic English home and enter into childhood games familiar to most children. When these realistic characters confront the fantastic and believe it, readers believe it too.

When an author constructs a logical framework and develops characters' actions consistently within this framework, there is an internal consistency in the story. This consistency is important. For example, if animals supposedly live and behave like animals, they should do so

consistently unless the author carefully develops when they change, why they change, and how they change.

In *Dragon Rider*, Cornelia Funke writes the story through the vivid storytelling of Firedrake, the dragon who speaks the language of the fabulous animals. Notice in the following example how Firedrake's story retells the plot to a group of believing animals and humans:

> As the moon set outside and the sun began its daily journey across the sky, he told the tale of his quest from the very beginning. His words filled the hall with pictures. He spoke of a clever white rat, enchanted ravens and mountain dwarves, sand-elves and Dubidai. As he went on with the story, the basilisk fell to dust once more, and the blue djinn opened his thousand eyes. The sea serpent swam through the waves, and the great roc bird snatched Ben away. Finally, as the sun outside was sinking in the sky, Nettlebrand climbed the dragons' mountain. His armor melted in blue dragon fire, and a toad hopped out of his mouth. (p. 513)

The author also uses the storyteller to foreshadow stories that may come in the future. The storyteller concludes: "The story ends here he said. The story of Sorrel and Ben the dragon rider, of Firedrake and Nettlebrand, the Golden One, whose servants were his doom. Tomorrow night a new story begins. I don't yet know how it will end, and I will not tell you until I do" (p. 514).

Suspending Disbelief: Characterization

Of course, for readers to suspend disbelief, the character from whose point of view a story is told must be believable. Whether an author humanizes animals and inanimate

The battle between good and evil is found in literature that bridges traditional and modern fantasy. (From Hershel and the Hanukkah Goblins, by Eric A. Kimmel, illustrated by Trina Schart Hyman. Reprinted by permission of Holiday House. Text copyright 1989 by Eric A. Kimmel. Illustrations copyright 1989 by Trina Schart Hyman. All rights reserved.)

basis in fact, whereas most readers of modern fantasy suspend their disbelief only in extraordinary beings and events. Still, to entice their readers into out-of-the-ordinary experiences, authors of modern fantasy play roles similar to those of storytellers of old, who enchanted live audiences with tales that had been orally transmitted over generations. The bridges between traditional fantasy and modern fantasy are evident in many contemporary tales of wonder, but they are especially strong in literary folktales, allegories, and tales about mythical quests and conflicts.

Literary Folktales

In the past hundred years or so, some authors of fantasy have deliberately attempted to replicate the "Once upon a time" of traditional folktales, with their dark forests, castles, princesses and princes, humble people of noble worth, and "happily ever afters." The traditional theme that goodness is rewarded and evil is punished is common in literary folktales, as are motifs involving magic. Betsy Hearne (1992) states that many folklore elements are found in William Steig's *The Amazing Bone,* and archetypal characters from folktales abound in the fantasies of James Marshall.

The foundation for *Bound,* by Donna Jo Napoli, is an ancient Chinese Cinderella tale. Napoli places the tale in the Ming dynasty, 1368–1644. She includes the tradi-

tional Chinese folklore elements: a kind girl whose mother's death results in the changes of her fortunes, the wicked stepmother who cares only for her own daughter, the spirit of the dead mother who looks after her daughter, a fish who is believed to be the spirit of the dead mother, a prince who is searching for a wife, a festival that both girls attend, beautiful clothes provided by the dead mother, and a slipper test for the rightful Cinderella. Within this framework, Napoli develops a full novel by describing a setting that shows the painful tradition of binding feet and a culture that does not encourage the education of women. The Cinderella character, Xing Xing, is her father's favorite daughter and is taught skills such as calligraphy and a love for poetry that are not considered appropriate for females. Even though she is bound into servitude after her father's death, she still honors the spirits of her dead parents and becomes a strong woman. In the end, she is chosen to be the prince's bride even though she does not have bound feet and can read and write.

The author provides the following PostScript in which she describes how and why she changed the tale from the original: "The tale here differs from the traditional Chinese tales I have read in three ways: I have chosen to place it in Ming times rather than in Qin and Han times; in a northern province rather than in a southern province; and in an ordinary community rather than a minority community. These changes allowed me to integrate cultural habits of time, place, and community—notably, the prominence of foot binding and the social revolutions of the first Ming emperor" (p. 186).

Shannon Hale's *The Goose Girl* is a high fantasy built on the foundation of the Grimms' folktales. In folkloric tradition, the author tells readers that some people are born with one of three types of gifts: the gift of people-speaking, in which people listen to them, believe them, and love them; the gift of animal-speaking, in which people can speak with wild things; and the gift of nature-speaking, in which people understand the voices of the fire, wind, and trees. Hale's protagonist has this ability to speak to the swans and eventually to understand nature. The author expands the role of a strong female protagonist who overcomes deception and betrayal and eventually stops a war between neighboring kingdoms. There is both romance and adventure in this tale that is part of a trilogy.

There are several other fantasy stories in which the authors expand on the foundations of a folktale. For example, in *East,* Edith Pattou retells and expands the Scandinavian folktale "East of the Sun, West of the Moon." Gail Carson Levine's *Ella Enchanted* is based on "Cinderella." In this story, which includes wicked stepsisters, fairy godmothers, giants, and ogres, the heroine's quest is to break the curse that has been placed on her. In *The Golden Goose,* Dick King-Smith uses the idea of the traditional golden egg and golden goose. In this book, a

farmer's luck changes after his goose lays a golden egg. However, much of the luck changes for the worse.

Wee Winnie Witch's Skinny: An Original African American Scare Tale, by Virginia Hamilton, is a literary folktale based on witch beliefs in African and African American folklore. Readers can discover folklore elements such as the importance of numbers as Mama Granny tries to rid the house of witches by sprinkling secret potion water around the house for 7 days and chanting seven times: "Remove yourself from here! Remove yourself from here!" (unnumbered). *Basho and the River Stones*, by Tim Myers, includes elements of Japanese folklore. The themes developed in the fantasy are similar to those found in folklore; for example, "Many things are more valuable than gold," and "It is important to keep a promise." The story also incorporates values and beliefs found in Japanese folklore. For example, the poet in the story dedicates his life to appreciating nature through seeing, smelling, tasting, feeling, and hearing. Alan Armstrong's 2006 Newbery Honor winner, *Whittington*, uses a foundation from British folklore.

Hans Christian Andersen. Charles Perrault is usually credited with publishing the first children's book of fairy tales, but Hans Christian Andersen is credited with writing, a century later, the first fairy tale for children. Whereas Perrault wrote down stories from the oral tradition, Andersen created new stories for theater audiences and readers.

Zena Sutherland (1997) points out that although Andersen's first stories for children were

> elaborations of familiar folk and fairy tales, . . . he soon began to allow his imagination full rein in the invention of plot, the shaping of character, and the illumination of human condition. These later creations, solely from Andersen's fertile imagination, are called literary fairy tales, to distinguish them from the fairy tales of unknown origin, those created by common folk. Andersen's work served as inspiration for other writers. (p. 230)

Andersen's "The Wild Swans" is a literary fairy tale quite similar to the Grimms' traditional tale "The Six Swans." Both stories involve enchantment by an evil stepmother and the courage and endurance of a young girl who is willing to suffer in order to free her brothers.

Experts in children's literature believe that some of Andersen's other literary fairy tales are based on his own life. For example, Andersen's unpleasant experiences in school, where the teacher poked fun at the poor boy's lack of knowledge, large size, and looks, may have inspired his story "The Ugly Duckling." Jerry Pinkney's illustrations for a book-length version of this story show the transformation of the ugly duckling into the most beautiful swan in the pond. When the children exclaim that he is the best one of all, "The swan knew that it was worth having undergone all the suffering and loneliness that he had. Otherwise, he would never have known what it was to be really happy" (unnumbered). Compare this version with Robert Ingpen's illustrations for *The Ugly Duckling*.

Illustration from The Tinderbox, *by Hans Christian Andersen, adopted, illustrated, and designed by Barry Moser, copyright © 1990 by Pennyroyal Press, Inc. Used by permission of Little, Brown and Company.*

Andersen's *The Tinderbox*, adapted and illustrated by Barry Moser, includes many of the motifs found in folklore: a poor, tattered soldier who eventually wins riches and the beautiful girl; challenges in the form of three doors, each guarded by a huge dog; a magical object; and a leader who tries to prevent the soldier from marrying his daughter. This book can also be used to analyze the change in setting from the original story. Moser places his adaptation in the Tennessee mountains at the end of the Civil War. His characters include a Confederate soldier and the people who live in a mountain village.

Nancy Ekholm Burkert has beautifully illustrated one of Andersen's stories that reflects the beauty of natural life versus the heartbreak associated with longing for mechanical perfection or metallic glitter. *The Nightingale* tells of a Chinese emperor who turned from the voice of a faithful nightingale to a jeweled, mechanical bird. He learns, however, that only the song of the real, unjeweled bird can bring comfort and truth. Compare Bagram Ibatoulline's illustrations for *The Nightingale* with Burkert's illustrations; both illustrators emphasize the beauty of the Chinese setting.

Amy Lowry Poole also uses a Chinese setting for her retelling of Andersen's *The Pea Blossom*. This is a story in which the fifth and smallest pea in the pod is content with his life, accepts his fate, and shows a caring nature. In contrast, the other peas long for impossible dreams

Illustration from The Pea Blossom, *retold and illustrated by Amy Lowry Poole. Copyright © 2005 by Amy Lowry Poole. Reprinted by permission of Holiday House, Inc.*

such as flying to the sun, flying to the moon, and dining with the emperor. Only the smallest pea's life as a growing pea plant fascinates a sick child, and while watching the pea plant grow, she is nourished back to health. Poole's author's note reveals the Chinese mythological connections that she used in the tale: the raven in the sun and the toad in the moon. She states that the raven's three legs symbolize the three phases of the sun: dawn, midday, and dusk.

There are several collections of Hans Christian Andersen's fairy tales. Some of them, such as *Little Mermaids and Ugly Ducklings: Favorite Fairy Tales by Hans Christian Andersen,* illustrated by Gennady Spirin, *The Stories of Hans Christian Andersen: A New Translation From the Danish,* illustrated by Villhelm Pedersen and Lorenz Frolich, and *Tales of Hans Christian Andersen,* illustrated by Joel Stewart, include a variety of tales appropriate for students in the middle elementary grades. Tiina Nunnally's translation of *Hans Christian Andersen Fairy Tales* is designed for more serious study of the fairy tales. It contains a chronology of the life of Hans Christian Andersen, an introduction to his life and writing, and books for further reading. This edition is of special interest for a study of Andersen's writing because the text includes notes on each of the tales. For example, the following notes accompany "The Tinderbox" (1835):

> "The Tinderbox" opened Andersen's first collection of stories, "Eventyr." It is based on a Danish folktale called "The Spirit of the Candle," which has links with "Aladdin." Andersen also borrows from many other folktales—the princess in the tower from "Rapunzel," the cross on the soldier's door that the dog duplicates along the street from "Ali Baba and the Forty Thieves," the trail of grain from "Hansel and Gretel"—while adapting details of the Aladdin story such as the Arabian minarets, which become Copenhagen's Round Tower.
>
> The Aladdin story had a special emotional significance for Andersen. While he was a poor schoolboy sponsored through grammar school, a turning point in his fortunes came when he was invited to stay with a leading Copenhagen family.... He was given a copy of Shakespeare that Wulff had translated in Danish; ecstatic, he stood at the window of his room and in his diary (December 19, 1825) wrote out lines from Ochlenchlager's play "Aladdin." (p. 423)

Religious and Ethical Allegory

Religious themes provide strong links between traditional and modern fantasy. According to Bruno Bettelheim (1976), "most fairy tales originated in periods when religion was a most important part of life; thus, they deal, directly or by inference, with re-

Illustration from The Wild Swans. *Text copyright © 2005 by Naomi Lewis, illustrations copyright © 2005 by Anne Yvonne Gilbert. Used by permission of Barefoot Books.*

ligious themes" (p. 13). Traditional tales from around the world reflect the religions prominent in their times and places of origins, including Islam, Buddhism, and Judaism, to name but a few.

Some European folktales, such as the German "Our Lady's Child," directly refer to the Roman Catholic beliefs of the Middle Ages. In this tale recorded by the Brothers Grimm, a young girl becomes mute when she disobeys the Virgin Mary and then lies about what she has done. After suffering severe ordeals, she desires only to confess her sin, and the Virgin Mary rewards her confession by renewing her power of speech and granting her happiness. Other European folktales and legends develop less explicit religious themes by using allegory, or prolonged metaphors. Characters representing goodness or wisdom must confront and overcome characters representing evil or foolishness.

Many authors writing in the 1800s created strong stories with ethical and religious themes. John C. Hawley (1989) contends that Charles Kingsley's *The Water-Babies* is a classic example of children's literature employed to disarm and to teach. He states:

> As unusual and even quirky as the water world of Kingsley's novel may be, however, this priest/novelist somehow succeeds in showing readers young and old something very familiar and even comforting in the strange and mysterious, sugaring a pill he considers necessary medicine of his generation. (p. 19)

G. P. Taylor's *Shadowmancer* and *Wormwood* have been identified by some critics as the Christian Harry Potter. The protagonist in Taylor's texts is Abram Richards, an angel. The religious allegory is developed as an 18th-century scientist in London discovers a book that could bring all of creation under the forces of evil. Elizabeth Devereaux (2004) writes the following critique of this religious allegory: "A lurid, even somewhat sadistic flavor taints this enterprise. . . . Most unsetting of all, the sole representative of heaven, Abram/Raphael, traffics in death with a vengeance equal in intensity, if not purpose, to that of the bad group. 'I am nothing but an assassin for righteousness,' he explains. Don't look for faith, hope, or charity. Abram/Raphael doesn't attract, he strikes the deepest fear in other characters" (p. 20). Students of children's literature can read these books and develop their own evaluations and responses.

In our more secular age, as Bettelheim (1976) points out, "these religious themes no longer arouse universal and personally meaningful associations" in the majority of people, as they once did. However, modern authors of fantasy still create religious and ethical allegories. Some authors actually replicate the heroic humans, witches, personified animals, and magical settings of traditional literature. Others use characters and settings consistent with their own times. Readers may respond to these stories on different levels, because they are both allegories and tales of enchantment and high adventure.

George MacDonald.   The strongly moralistic atmosphere of Victorian England and training as a Congregational minister influenced a writer who used allegorical fantasy to portray and condemn the flaws in his society. Cynthia Marshall (1988) states that George MacDonald's concern for distinguishing good from evil leads to "moralizing interventions" (p. 61) in books such as *At the Back of the North Wind*. First published in 1871 and reissued in 1966, this is the story of Diamond, the son of a poor coach driver. Diamond lives two lives: the harsh existence of impoverished working-class Londoners, and a dreamlike existence in which he travels with the North Wind, who takes him to a land of perpetual flowers and gentle breezes, where no one is cold or sick or hungry.

MacDonald uses the North Wind, a beautiful woman with long flowing hair, to express much of his own philosophy. "Good people see good things; bad people, bad things" (p. 37), she tells Diamond, whom MacDonald describes as a good boy, "God's baby." When Diamond questions her reality, she says, "I think . . . that if I were only a dream, you would not have been able to love me so. You love me when you are not with me, don't you?" (p. 363). Diamond clings to the back of the North Wind. With her streaming hair enfolding him, they fly to a land where it is always May. Diamond returns home from that visit, but the end of the story has further allegorical implications:

> I walked up the winding stair, and entered his room. A lovely figure, as white and almost as clear as alabaster, was lying on the bed. I saw at once how it was. They thought he was dead. I knew that he had gone to the back of the North Wind. (p. 378).

C. S. Lewis.   A professor of medieval and Renaissance literature at Cambridge University, C. S. Lewis used his interest in theology and his knowledge about medieval allegory, classical legend, and Norse mythology to create a highly acclaimed and popular fantasy saga. "The Chronicles of Narnia" (winner of the Carnegie Medal for best children's books), beginning with *The Lion, the Witch and the Wardrobe* and ending seven books later with *The Last Battle*, develop marvelous adventure stories interwoven with Christian allegory. Children can enjoy the series for its high drama alone, or they can read it for its allegorical significance.

Although *The Lion, the Witch and the Wardrobe* is the first book in the series, *The Magician's Nephew* explains how the saga began and how the passage between the magical world of Narnia and earth was made possible: The tree grown from the magical Narnia apple has blown over, and its wood is used to build a large wardrobe. This is the same wardrobe through which the daughters of Eve and the sons of Adam enter into the kingdom, meet the wicked White Witch, and help the great lord-lion Aslan defeat the powers of evil.

In *The Lion, the Witch and the Wardrobe*, Alsan gives his life to save Edmund, who has betrayed them all. Aslan, however, rises from the dead and tells the startled, be-reaved children that the deeper magic before the dawn of time has won:

> It means that though the witch knew the Deep Magic, there is a magic deeper still which she did not know. Her knowledge goes back only to the dawn of Time. But if she could have looked a little further back, into the stillness and the darkness before Time dawned, she would have read there a different incantation. She would have known that when a willing vic-tim who has committed no treachery was killed in a traitor's stead, the Table would crack and Death itself would start working backward. (pp. 132–133)

The remaining books in the chronicle tell other fan-tastic tales of adventure in which the characters overcome evil. The final Christian allegory is contained in the last book of the series, *The Last Battle*. Here, the children are reunited with Aslan after their death on earth and dis-cover:

> for them it was only the beginning of the real story. All their life in this world and all their adventures in Narnia had only been the cover and the title page: now at last they were be-ginning Chapter One of the Great Story which no one on earth has read: in which every chapter is better than the one before. (p. 184)

Mythical Quests and Conflicts

Quests for lost or stolen objects of power, descents into darkness to overcome evil, and settings where lightning splinters the world and sets the stage for battles between two opposing forces are found in traditional myths, leg-ends, and modern fantasy. Some authors of modern fantasy borrow magical settings and characters from tradi-tional tales of heroism, and others create new worlds of enchantment. Modern stories may contain some threads of the allegory that characterizes many traditional tales—such as the English legends about King Arthur, his knights of the Round Table, and the quest for the Holy Grail. Most modern fantasies about mythical quests and conflicts, however, emphasize adventure. Their characters acquire new knowledge and learn honorable uses of personal power.

In an interview with Dinitia Smith (2003), Christo-pher Paolini, the author of *Eragon*, identifies how he was inspired to write his high fantasy, a story about a boy with

magical powers who finds a beautiful stone that is actually a dragon's egg and what happens when, after the egg hatches, he and the dragon embark on a quest to avenge the death of his uncle and to defeat an evil king. He states: "The story of the title character, Eragon, who has a mys-terious parentage and wields a magic sword, was inspired by 'Le Morte d'Arthur,' 'Beowulf,' Norse and Icelandic sagas, the 'Ring' cycle and the fantasy books he loves" (p. B1).

The Norse and Icelandic sagas as well as early British history provide foundations for Nancy Farmer's mythical quests and conflicts in *The Sea of Trolls*. Farmer identifies 27 sources used when writing her book that include clas-sic tales such as "Beowulf" and "The Elder Edda" as well as various books about the Norse and the Vikings, the Druids, and Celtic myth and legend. In the appendix, Farmer ties her high fantasy to an actual happening in early Britain: "The abbey of Lindisfarne was founded in A.D. 635, and by 793 it was a center of great learning and art. When the raiders arrived, the monks ran to greet them and to invite them to dinner. The description of what happened next is in *The Sea of Trolls* and is taken from *The Anglo-Saxon Chronicle*. Amazingly one beauti-fully illuminated manuscript survived the fire: the Lindis-farne Bible. This attack was the beginning of two hundered years of Viking raids on the British Isles" (p. 451). Farmer includes historical information as well as myth and legend in her book. The sources and appendix provide enough information for students who would like to explore the use of legends and history in Farmer's book.

Several authors develop fantasies built on various Arthurian legends and characters. For example, Gerald Morris states in his author's note to *The Squire, His Knight, and His Lady:* "I took the battle with the Emperor of Rome from *Le Morte D'Arthur*, by Sir Thomas Malory, and I've borrowed minor characters from *Parzival* by Wolfram von Eschenbach." In *I Am Morgan LeFay: A Tale From Camelot*, Nancy Springer interprets the legend through the viewpoint of the villainous sorceress.

Kevin Crossley-Holland. In his Arthurian trilogy, Kevin Crossley-Holland intertwines the stories of two Arthurs: the legendary King Arthur and his namesake, Arthur de Caldicot, who lives in Britain during the Middle Ages. The author makes the connections between the two char-acters and the conflicts of the two time periods through the use of a seeing stone the current Arthur received from the legendary Merlin. The stone allows the 13-year-old boy to see and learn lessons from images of the legendary King Arthur. These images are related to questions the protagonist asks. For example, in the first book of the tril-ogy, *The Seeing Stone*, winner of the Guardian Children's Fiction Prize, Arthur discovers the meaning and impor-tance of quests for self-discovery when he witnesses this interaction between the legendary knight Sir Pellinores and Merlin: A quest is "a long journey, with many adventures, many setbacks, many dangers. . . . Each of us needs a quest and a person without one is lost to himself. Each of us must have a dream to light our way through this dark world" (p. 164).

Throughout the trilogy, the author uses parallel quests: legendary King Arthur and the Knights of the Round Table and their quest for the Holy Grail, and the protagonist Arthur as he joins the historic Fourth Crusade to free Jerusalem but, more important, to learn the lessons on his own quest for self-discovery.

The themes developed in this trilogy are very similar to those found in legendary high fantasy. For example, "Who we are is not only a matter of blood but also what we make of ourselves." "It is important to be just to both the rich and the poor." "It is important to use our lives to make a difference." Students can compare Crossley-Holland's tale developed on King Arthur with Jane Yolen's *Sword of the Rightful King: A Novel of King Arthur.*

Philip Pullman. *The Golden Compass* is a high fantasy that has numerous fantasy elements that can be identified and analyzed. Characters with supernatural powers include humans with their daemons (spirits, souls in animal form), witches who fly, and talking bears wearing armor. Objects of power include an ancient gold and crystal disk, or alethiometer, that always tells the truth. The symbols on this alethiometer also reveal both themes and possible conflict. For example, the various meanings for the anchor symbol are revealed to be hope, because hope holds you fast like an anchor; steadfastness; snag or prevention; and the sea. The importance of this object of power is revealed through quotes such as the following: "She knew one thing: she was not pleased or proud to be able to read the alethiometer—she was afraid. Whatever power was making that needle swing and stop, it knew things like an intelligent being" (p. 147). Pullman's sequels to *The Golden Compass, The Subtle Knife* and *The Amber Spyglass,* provide other sources for identifying and analyzing fantasy elements.

J. R. R. Tolkien. Destiny, supernatural immortals, evil dragons, and rings of power are found in J. R. R. Tolkien's popular stories. According to Ruth S. Noel (1977), Tolkien's writings "form a continuation of the mythic tradition into modern literature. . . . In no other literary work has such careful balance of mythic tradition and individual imagination been maintained" (pp. 6–7). This balance between myth and imagination is not accidental in Tolkien's writing. Tolkien studied mythology for most of his life; he was a linguistic scholar and professor of Anglo-Saxon literature at Oxford University, where his chief interest was the literary and linguistic tradition of the English West Midlands, especially as revealed in *Beowulf* and *Sir Gawain and the Green Knight.* Tolkien respected the quality in myths that allows evil to be unexpectedly averted and good to succeed. He masterfully develops this battle between good and evil in *The Hobbit* and in *The*

Lord of the Rings, its more complex sequel. According to Tolkien (1965), these stories were at first a philological game in which he invented languages: "The stories were made rather to provide a world for the languages than the reverse. I should have preferred to write in 'Elvish'" (p. 242). These languages with their own alphabets and rules help make Tolkien's characters believable.

Careful attention to detail and vivid descriptions of setting in Middle Earth also add credibility to Tolkien's stories. For example, he introduces the reluctant hobbit, Bilbo Baggins, to the challenge of a quest to regain the dwarfs' treasures by using a dwarfs' chant:

> Far over the misty mountains cold
> To dungeons deep and caverns old
> We must away ere break of day
> To find our long-forgotten gold. (*The Hobbit,* p. 37)

As Bilbo, the wizard Gandalf, and the 13 dwarfs proceed over the mountains toward the lair of the evil dragon Smaug, Tolkien describes a lightning that splinters the peaks and rocks that shiver. When Bilbo descends into the mountain dungeons to confront Smaug, Tolkien's setting befits the climax of a heroic quest: Red light, wisps of vapor, and rumbling noises gradually replace the subterranean darkness and quiet. Ahead, in the bottom-most cellar, lies a huge, red-golden dragon surrounded by precious gold and jewels. As in traditional tales, the quest is successful, the dragon is slain, and the goblins are overthrown. The hero retains his decency, his honor, and his pledge always to help his friends.

The ring found during the hobbit's quest becomes the basis of the plot in the ring trilogy: *The Fellowship of the Ring, The Two Towers,* and *The Return of the King.* In his foreword to *The Fellowship of the Ring,* Tolkien says that he had no intention of writing a story with an inner meaning or message. The story is not meant to be allegorical:

> As the story grew it put down roots (into the past) and threw out unexpected branches; but its main theme was settled from the outset by the inevitable choice of the Ring as the link between it and *The Hobbit.* (*The Fellowship of the Ring* p. 6)

Many junior-high and high school students, college students, and other adults have been brought back into the world of mythology through Tolkien's books.

Lloyd Alexander. The stories that unfold in Lloyd Alexander's mythical land of Prydain reflect Alexander's vivid recollections of Wales, favorite childhood stories, and knowledge of Welsh legends. When Alexander researched the Mabinogion, a collection of traditional Welsh legends, he discovered the characters of Gwydion Son of Don, Arawn Death-Lord of Annuvin, Dallben the enchanter, and Hen Wen the oracular pig (Tunnell & Jacobs, 1989). In Alexander's outstanding Prydain chronicles, these characters become involved in exciting adventures of good versus evil.

Alexander's books take place in a time when fairy folk lived with humans, a time of enchanters and enchantments, a time before the passages between the world of enchantment and the world of humans were closed. In the first Prydain chronicle, *The Book of Three*, Alexander introduces the forces of good and evil and an assistant pig-keeper, Taran, who dreams of discovering his parentage and becoming a hero. (Alexander tells readers that all people are assistant pig-keepers at heart because their capabilities seldom match their aspirations, and they are often unprepared for what is to happen.)

Throughout his Prydain series—*The Black Cauldron, The Castle of Llyr, Taran Wanderer,* and *The High King*—Alexander develops strong, believable characters with whom upper-elementary and older children can identify. The world of fantasy becomes relevant to the world of reality, and the characters gain credibility through Alexander's history of the people and their long struggle against the forces of evil. Alexander encourages readers to believe in the tangible objects of power because the characters place so much faith in the legend of the sword, the prophecies written in *The Book of Three*, and the fearsome black cauldron.

Alexander's literary style also strengthens the credibility of the fantasy, the plot, and the characterization in his other fantasy adventure stories, such as *Westmark, The Iron Ring,* and *The Beggar Queen*. In *The Beggar Queen*, Alexander carefully builds a foundation for the action that follows. He develops strong person-against-person, person-against-self, and person-against-society conflicts. He uses ghosts from the past to introduce the various conflicts and factions; he uses animal symbolism to describe characters; and he concludes each chapter at a point of tension and excitement, foreshadowing the conflict to come.

A detailed map helps make the land of Prydain more credible to readers. (From The High King, by Lloyd Alexander. Map by Evaline Ness. Copyright © 1968 by Lloyd Alexander. Copyright © 1968 by Holt, Rinehart and Winston. Reproduced by permission of Holt, Rinehart and Winston.)

In *The Arkadians*, Alexander develops a high fantasy with foundations in Greek mythology. He encourages readers to suspend disbelief in the mystical setting by introducing the setting through a map showing Arkadia. Alexander's fantasy includes many similarities with Greek mythology such as a wooden animal with a hollow stomach, men with special abilities, winged horses, prophecies that come true, and voyages that include fantastic adventures. In *The Iron Ring*, Alexander develops a high fantasy with foundations in mythology from India.

Ursula K. Le Guin.   Somewhere in the land of fantasy lies Earthsea, an archipelago of imaginary islands where wizards cast their spells and people live in fear of fire-blowing winged dragons. Responsible wizards attempt to retain a balance between the forces of good and evil that seek dominance. Le Guin helps her readers suspend disbelief through detailed descriptions of Earthsea, its inhabitants, and a culture permeated with magic. Her series of Earthsea books develops the theme that responsibility is attached to great power by tracing the life of Sparrowhawk from when he is an apprentice wizard until he is finally the most powerful wizard in the land.

In the first book of the series, *A Wizard of Earthsea*, the young boy has powers strong enough to save his village, but pride and impatience place him in grave danger. A master wizard cautions Sparrowhawk about wanting to learn and use powers of enchantment that he is not yet mature enough to understand:

> Have you never thought how danger must surround power as shadow does light? This sorcery is not a game we play for pleasure or for praise. Think of this: that every act of our Art is said and is done either for good, or for evil. Before you speak or do you must know the price that is to pay! (p. 35)

Sparrowhawk, renamed Ged, does not understand the warning. Conflict with another apprentice leads to a duel of sorcery skills, in which Ged calls up a dead spirit and accidentally unleashes an evil being onto the world. Le Guin's descriptions of the rent in the darkness, the blazing brightness, the hideous black shadow, and Ged's reaction to the beast convince readers that evil really is released, important because the remainder of the book follows Ged as he hunts the shadow-beast across the islands to the farthest waters of Earthsea and develops an understanding that he is responsible for his own actions. The series ends with *Tehanu: The Last Book of Earthsea*.

Alan Garner.   According to John Rowe Townsend (1975), Alan Garner was the most influential writer of fantasy in Great Britain of the 1960s. Garner's books are full of magic: the old magic of sun, moon, and blood that survives from crueler times, as well as the high magic of thoughts and spells that checks the old magic and serves as a potent but uncertain weapon against the old evil. Garner's stories transcend time barriers by allowing children from the present to discover objects that contain ancient spells influential in old legends. The ancient masters of good and evil then emerge either to pursue or to safeguard the children.

Garner creates a believable fantasy in *The Weirdstone of Brisingamen* by first placing two realistic characters into a realistic English country setting. He achieves credibility through the reactions of these children as they discover the powers in a tangible object, a tear-shaped piece of crystal that has been handed down over many generations. The plot then revolves around this "weirdstone," which is sought by both the forces of good and the forces of evil. The children, aided by two dwarfs, set out to return the stone to the good wizard who is its guardian. Along the way, however, they encounter evil characters—a shape-changing witch, giant troll women, and a wolf that chases them through underground tunnels and across the countryside. The final confrontation reveals the power of the weirdstone.

Robin McKinley. Magical objects are the focus of quests in Robin McKinley's *The Blue Sword* and *The Hero and the Crown*. McKinley makes *The Blue Sword* believable by depicting a realistic colony called Daria and realistic characters—colonial officials of Her Majesty's government, career army officers—who are unlikely to be influenced by the extraordinary. Fantasy elements enter the story when Harry is kidnapped by the leader of the Hillfolk and taken to the kingdom of Damar. From Harry's point of view, McKinley reveals a people who have the ability to speak in the old tongue, the language of the gods.

In *The Hero and the Crown*, which McKinley describes as a "prequel" to *The Blue Sword*, the power of a magical object is revealed through the sword that brings power from its original owner, Lady Aerin, who was the savior of her people. There is a strong feeling of destiny as the heroine sets forth to regain the objects of power and restore the power to her kingdom. As in many traditional epics, Aerin's quest results in increasingly difficult tests: She proceeds from slaying small dragons to finally overcoming an evil magician. McKinley strongly emphasizes responsibility, as Aerin discovers that even though the price is high, her destiny and her responsibility to her people require this quest.

Susan Cooper. Students of children's literature may identify the influence of English, Celtic, and Welsh legends and myths in Susan Cooper's series of modern fantasies. Her books about the guardians of light combating the forces of darkness contain references to the legend in which King Arthur does not die but lies resting in a place from which he will arise when the need is greatest. According to Celtic tradition, the words on Arthur's tomb mean "Here lies Arthur, King once and King to be."

Richard Cavendish (1982) reports that the Welsh version of the legend locates Arthur's resting place in a cave in Snowdonia. A similar cave is important in Cooper's *The Grey King*, and Arthur and his knights rise again in *Silver on the Tree* to assist in the final battle against evil. The wizard Merlin, Arthur's legendary confidant, plays a crucial role throughout Cooper's series. Introduced as Merriman Lyon, Merlin has the ability to suspend the laws of nature and to travel into the past as well as the future. Throughout the series, Merriman retains Merlin's profound wisdom from an ancient past that leads the powers of good against the powers of evil.

Legendary objects, places, and occurrences are found throughout the series. For example, the power of a seventh son of a seventh son dominates the characters on heroic quests. Arthur's sword, his ship, and even his dog's name are important in Cooper's books. Quests for the objects of power form a thread of continuity in Cooper's stories. In *Over Sea, Under Stone*, three children visit Cornwall and find an old map that discloses a hidden treasure. This treasure, the grail, could hinder the forces of darkness. With the help of the good Old Ones, the children find the grail, but they lose the manuscript that is the key to its inscriptions.

Cooper encourages readers to suspend disbelief in her fantasies by developing a strong foundation in the reality of the 20th century. When her realistic contemporary characters travel into earlier centuries and mythical worlds, her readers follow them willingly and share their quests for greater knowledge. There is a tie, however, between the past and present. For example, in *The Dark Is Rising*, Will goes back into the past to recover the Sign of Fire. When he has fulfilled his quest, a great crashing roar and rumbling and growling ensue; back in the present, thunder is creating earsplitting sounds. The action is believable, and readers feel that the old ways are actually awakening and that the powers live again.

Cornelia Funke. German writer Cornelia Funke lives up to one of her character's beliefs: "Some books should be tasted, some devoured, but only a few should be chewed and digested thoroughly" (*Inkheart*, p. 8). This quote also reflects the themes in her books: Carefully selected books are powerful, reading aloud is a way to make stories live, and imagination is very important.

Funke's fantasies include *Dragon Rider*, *The Thief Lord*, *Inkheart*, and *Inkspell*. She is known for her vivid descriptive settings, such as this introduction to *Dragon Rider*: "All was still in the valley of the dragons. Mist had drifted in from the sea nearby and was clinging to the mountains. Birds twittered uncertainly in the foggy damp, and clouds hid the sun. . . . It was so dark under the fir trees that you could scarcely see the gaping crevice in the mountainside that swallowed up the mist" (p. 1). This is the forbidding introduction that takes readers along on a

An In-Depth Analysis of Fantasy in the Writings of One Author

What is it about J. K. Rowling's "Harry Potter" books that places them all on the best-seller lists, shows worldwide sales of more than 100 million copies, and encourages the *New York Times* film critic A. O. Scott (2000) to state, "Harry Potter is the biggest mass-culture phenomenon to come out of Britain since the Beatles" (p. 11)? Why does the adult fantasy novelist Stephen King (2000) declare, "Although they bear the trappings of fantasy, and the mingling of the real world and the world of wizards and flying broomsticks is delightful, the Harry Potter books are, at heart, satisfyingly shrewd mystery tales" (p 13)?

The Harry Potter series begins with *Harry Potter and the Sorcerer's Stone,* in which a very unhappy orphan boy is described as living with the Dursleys, his horrible aunt and uncle and their even more despicable son, Dudley. Readers are encouraged to suspend disbelief as they are introduced into this real world of middle-class Britain. Readers along with Harry discover the possibilities that Harry has magical powers. This discovery is reinforced when Harry is accepted into Hogwarts School of Witchcraft and Wizardry and he begins his journey into a parallel world that allows his dismal life to change and his magical powers to develop. Rowling uses a jagged scar to foreshadow the possibilities that Harry is different from those around him.

Rowling suspends disbelief in the fantasy setting by introducing a fantasy environment through detailed descriptions of Diagon Alley, with its wizard's bank and stores selling course books in wizardry, magical wands, cauldrons, and flying broomsticks. There is the journey to the school that begins as the students proceed through Platform Nine and Three-Quarters at King's Cross Station. There are detailed descriptions of Hogwarts School, with its long history of training witches and a sorting hat that uses a student's capabilities and personality to place each student in one of the four divisions of the school, and even Quidditch, which is a school sport played on flying broomsticks.

Rowling also suspends disbelief by presenting universal themes that readers can identify with. There is the importance of friendship and trust as Harry develops close friendships with Ron Weasley and Hermione Granger and the three friends join forces to overcome evil. The author develops through these characters the need to use your own special abilities to solve problems and complete a quest.

Each of the books helps readers to suspend their disbelief and to increase their enjoyment of the series through believable conflicts that exemplify the characteristics of high fantasy: There is a constant battle between good and evil, the characters have a high purpose, the tone is mythically charged, there are objects of power that help the hero, and the conflicts consider high social and moral issues. In *Harry Potter and the Sorcerer's Stone,* Harry and his friends capture the stone that could be used by the evil Lord Voldemort to gain everlasting life. In *Harry Potter and the Chamber of Secrets,* Harry is in danger from a dark power that has the ability to petrify or to kill. In *Harry Potter and the Prisoner of Azkaban,* Harry discovers the secret of his newly found godfather and the relationship among his dead father and Moony, Wormtail, Padfoot, and Prongs. In *Harry Potter and the Goblet of Fire,* Harry discovers the truth about Lord Voldemort and faces him in a deadly combat that could have easily killed Harry. In this fourth book, the author concludes with a chapter titled "The Beginning," which foreshadows the coming dangers and battles caused by Voldemort's return. *Harry Potter and the Half-Blood Prince* reveals many of the purposes for previous activities, but also concludes with a foreshadowing of the dangerous role Harry chooses. In *Exploring Harry Potter* (2000), Elizabeth D. Schafer identifies some of the mythology, legends, and folktale connections that she found in the various Harry Potter books.

---

quest to find the Rim of Heaven, where dragons can live in peace and security.

Words and reading aloud are so powerful in the fantasy world in *Inkheart* and the sequel, *Inkspell,* that Funke's heroine, Meggie, and her father are able to breathe life into the stories and read characters from the book world into the real world. Unfortunately, some of the characters who emerge in *Inkheart* are among the most vile antagonists imaginable. Consequently, the book develops a good-versus-evil conflict.

Funke also uses an intriguing style to introduce each chapter and foreshadow the conflict to come. She uses quotes from children's literature classics that relate to the content of each chapter. For example, a quote from Robert Louis Stevenson's *Treasure Island* introduces a chapter in which Meggie's father is forced to read about gold and treasures from the book. This approach provides an interesting bridge between literary classics and Funke's fantasies.

Categories of Modern Fantasy

Modern fantasies cover a wide range of topics. These topics include articulate animals, toys that come alive, preposterous characters and situations, strange and curious worlds, little people, friendly and frightening spirits, time warps, and science fiction.

Technology Resources

CW

You can link to two excellent Harry Potter websites by visiting the Companion Website at www.prenhall.com/norton

The high fantasy in the Harry Potter books appeals to many readers. (From Harry Potter and the Sorcerer's Stone, by J. K. Rowling.) HARRY POTTER, characters, names, and related indicia are trademarks of and © Warner Bros. (s02)
Harry Potter Publishing Rights © J. K. Rowling

Articulate Animals

Concerned rabbit parents worry about what will happen to their family when new folks move into the house on the hill, a mongoose saves his young owner from a deadly cobra, and a mole and a water rat spend an idyllic season floating down an enchanting river. Animals that talk like people but retain some animal qualities are among the most popular modern fantasy characters. Authors such as Beatrix Potter and Kenneth Grahame have been able to create animal characters that display a balance between animal and human characteristics. This balance is not accidental; many successful authors write from close observations of animal life.

Young children are drawn to the strong feelings of loyalty that the animals in modern fantasies express as they help each other out of dangerous predicaments, stay with friends when they might choose other actions, or protect their human owners while risking their own lives. The memorable animal characters, like all memorable characters in literature, show a wide range of recognizable traits.

Children often see themselves in the actions of their animal friends.

Retaining a consistent point of view is very important in believable modern fantasy. This may be particularly important in articulate animal stories. In Mary James's *Shoebag*, a cockroach changes into a boy. In this humorous story, James's protagonist retains his cockroach point of view.

Robert O'Brien's *Mrs. Frisby and the Rats of NIMH* is an excellent example of an author's use of believable plot, characters, and setting; interesting theme; and consistent point of view in modern fantasy. This consistency continues in Jane Leslie Conly's sequel, *Racso and the Rats of NIMH*, in which the author, who is the daughter of O'Brien, extends the story. In this sequel, the intelligent rat colony must save their Thorn Valley home from the threat of a dam and the accompanying tourism.

Beverly Cleary develops humorous animal stories for young children through imaginative and unusual plots. *The Mouse and the Motorcycle* and Cleary's other books about a mouse named Ralph are good introductions to modern fantasy.

The popular "Golden Hamster Saga" includes *I, Freddy: Book One* and *Freddy in Peril: Book Two*, by Dietlof

The mythological text and illustrations are strongly interrelated in this edition of J. R. R. Tolkien's books, illustrated by Michael Hague. (From The Hobbit by J. R. R. Tolkien, illustrated by Michael Hague. Illustrations copyright © 1984 by Oak, Ash & Thorn, Ltd. Reprinted by permission of Houghton Mifflin Company.)

ISSUE Harry Potter and Censorship

The "Harry Potter" books are among both the most popular books of all time and the most censored or criticized. In 2005, the first six books were all concurrently on various best-seller lists. The books have been highly praised and have won numerous awards; they are also listed on various best books lists such as "Top 10 Fantasy Books for Youth" (*Booklist*, April 15, 2000) and "Best Children's Books, 2000" (*Publishers Weekly*, November 6, 2000). Various letters to the editors also attest to children's positive responses to the books. For example, a letter in *The Horn Book* (March/April 2000) states that fifth through eighth graders in Old Greenwich, Connecticut, voted *Harry Potter and the Sorcerer's Stone* "the best book of 1998, tied for first place with the Newbery winner, *Holes*" (p. 133), and "Children's Voices: A Response to Harry Potter" in *The New Advocate* (Winter, 2001) stresses the importance of being lost in a book and letting your imagination soar. In addition, the author J. K. Rowling has been awarded an honorary doctorate from St. Andrews University in Scotland and is an Officer of the Order of British Empire.

In contrast, the "Harry Potter" series is listed among the top 100 titles identified as banned books for Intellectual Freedom. The Potter books have been attacked because of the witchcraft and wizardry found in them.

Kimbra Wilder Gish (2000) voices the concerns of conservative Christian parents to books such as the "Harry Potter" series and other books that feature magic, witchcraft, and wizardry. For example, Gish cites Deuteronomy 18:9–12 as the reason that some people are concerned about the potential influences on children. "The above-referenced section of Deuteronomy specifically states that witches and wizards are an abomination unto the Lord that will be driven out, [so] one can see why someone who firmly believes this scripture might not want his or her child reading 'Harry Potter.' In these books, witchcraft and wizardry are generally portrayed as having many positive aspects" (p. 267).

In addition to issues related to witchcraft and wizardry, Gish cites problems with divination, Hermione's approval of the Egyptian magicians' work, possession of another person, and trances. Gish's final issue relates to the portrayal of Muggles, the nonmagical people in the books. Gish states, "there remains a tone suggesting more or less overtly that Muggles do not understand magic and that their fear of witches/wizards stems from ignorance or spite rather than sincere and positive faith in a belief system . . . it isn't that we feel other views should be stifled; we are simply concerned about the negative portrayal of non-witches/wizards painted in such sharp contrast to the more positive view of these supernaturally endowed" (pp. 268–299).

Gish concludes her article with ways that she believes conservative, Christian parents should discuss their family's beliefs with their children, talk about what they find of concern in the books, and use interest in the books to spark an in-depth discussion of faith.

As students of children's literature, you should explore different responses to the "Harry Potter" books. Find as many supportive and dissenting views as possible, and share these views with your children's literature class. This would be an interesting topic for debate as you discuss the pros and cons of these books.

Reiche. The author develops articulate animals such as Freddy, a brilliant hamster who can read and write (with the help of a Mac computer); a wise old tom cat; a pair of guinea pigs; and a colony of sewer rats. The plot in *Freddy in Peril* develops as Freddy's special talents are discovered by Professor Fleischkopf, an evil scientist who wants to dissect Freddy's brain to discover why he is literate. Readers will be interested in how Freddy uses his owner's Mac to write his stories and e-mail to send messages. The author also shows how mime can be used to communicate. Two themes are developed as the author shows the importance of working together to solve problems and the debatable practice of conducting certain types of research on animals.

The characterization in Brian Jacques's *Redwall* is effective. For example, Jacques introduces Matthias, an unlikely and frequently clumsy mouse protagonist, with a description that reveals a great deal about the character's physical and emotional characteristics:

> Matthias cut a comical little figure as he wobbled his way along the cloisters, with his large sandals flip-flopping and his tail peeping from beneath the baggy folds of an oversized novice's habit. He paused to gaze upwards at the cloudless blue sky and tripped over the enormous sandals. Hazelnuts scattered out upon the grass from the rush basket he was carrying. Unable to stop, he went tumbling cowl over tail. (p. 13)

After Matthias lands at the feet of Abbot Mortimer, the language reinforces the bumbling nature of the apologetic mouse: "Er, sorry, Father Abbot, I tripped, y'see. Trod on my Abbot, Father Habit. Oh dear, I mean . . ." (p. 13).

Compare the description of Matthias with that of Cluny, the vicious antagonist:

> Cluny was a bilge rat; the biggest, most savage rodent that ever jumped from ship to shore. He was black, with grey and pink scars all over his heavy vermin-ridden back to the enormous whiplike tail which had earned him his title: Cluny the Scourage! (p. 17)

Thus, Jacques sets the tone for a contest between two opposite characters.

Readers who enjoy Jacques's *Redwall* will enjoy additional books in the series. In *Mossflower*, a prequel to *Redwall*, Jacques goes back in time to reveal the story of Martin the Warrior, the original hero of Redwall Abbey and the savior of the land of Mossflower. *Mattimeo*, a sequel to *Redwall*, is about the exploits of Matthias's son, Mattimeo. In *Mariel of Redwall*, a mousemaid leads a battle at sea and saves Redwall animals from a savage pirate rat. As in his other books, Jacques stresses prophecies and provides readers with clues in a poem and a dream. All of Jacques's books have strong characters that reveal the best or the worst of animalkind.

Beatrix Potter. Children of all ages can identify the following sentence as the beginning of an enjoyable story, *The Tale of Peter Rabbit:* "Once upon a time there were four little Rabbits, and their names were—Flopsy,

These articulate animals talk like humans but have the additional power of flight. (From Catwings Return, by Ursula K. Le Guin, illustrated by S. D. Schindler. Copyright © 1989 by Ursula K. Le Guin, illustrations copyright © 1989 by S. D. Schindler. Reprinted by permission of Orchard Books, a division of Franklin Watts, Inc.).

Mopsy, Cotton-tail, and Peter" (p. 3). Beatrix Potter, who wrote so knowledgeably about small animals, spent many holidays in the country observing nature, collecting natural objects, and making detailed drawings. Potter had small pets, including a rabbit, a hedgehog, and mice, that later became very real in her illustrated books for children. As an adult, Potter purchased a farm that offered further stimulation for her stories about articulate animals.

Potter's first book, *The Tale of Peter Rabbit*, began as a letter sent to a sick child. When she later submitted the story to a publisher, it was rejected. She did not let this rejection dissuade her; she had the book printed independently. When young readers accepted Peter Rabbit with great enthusiasm, the publisher asked if he might print the book.

Potter's characters may seem real to children because they show many characteristics that children themselves demonstrate. Peter Rabbit, for example, wants to go to the garden so badly that he disobey's his mother. In a vast store of vegetables, happiness changes rapidly to fright when Peter encounters the enemy, Mr. McGregor. Children can empathize with Peter's fright as he tries unsuccessfully to flee. They also can respond to a satisfying

ending, as Peter narrowly escapes and reaches the security of his mother. Of course, children know that such behavior cannot go unpunished: Peter must take a dose of chamomile tea for a stomachache, while his sisters feast on milk and blackberries.

Potter's carefully detailed illustrations complement the story and suggest the many moods of the main character. For example, Peter stealthily approaches and squeezes under the garden gate. He appears ecstatic as he munches carrots. When Peter discovers that he is too fat to squeeze under the gate, his ears hang dejectedly, a tear trickles down his cheek, one front paw is clenched in fright against his mouth, and his back paws are huddled together. The illustrated moods are so realistic that children feel a close relationship with Peter. *The Tale of Peter Rabbit* is found in a reissue of the 1902 Warne publication, as well as in collections such as *A Treasury of Peter Rabbit and Other Stories* and *Tales of Peter Rabbit and His Friends*.

Michael Bond. Paddington Bear is another animal character whose warmth and appeal are related to the

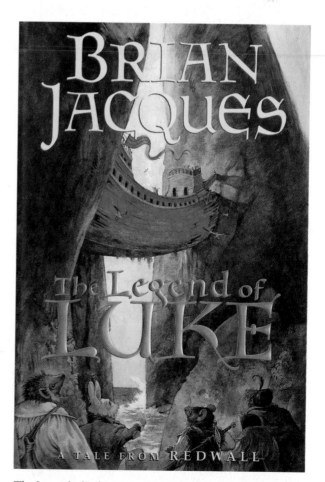

The Legend of Luke is one of the Redwall stories. (Jacket art by Troy Howell, copyright © 2000 by Troy Howell, jacket art, from The Legend of Luke: A Tale From Redwall, by Brian Jacques. Used by permission of Philomel Books, a division of Penguin Putnam, Inc.)

author's ability to encourage children to see themselves in the actions of an animal. Unlike Beatrix Potter's Peter Rabbit, who lives in an animal world, Michael Bond's Paddington lives with an English family after the family discovers the homeless bear in Paddington Station. Acceptance of the bear by the family and neighborhood creates a credible and humorous series of stories beginning with *A Bear Called Paddington*.

Bond's Paddington may seem real to children because Paddington displays many childlike characteristics: He gets himself into trouble, and he tries to hide his errors from people who would be disappointed in or disapprove of his actions. Paddington is hard to communicate with when he is in one of his difficult moods, and like a human child, he often is torn between excitement and perplexity. The excitement of preparing the itinerary for a trip in *Paddington Abroad* is balanced by Paddington's trouble in spelling hard words, his difficulty understanding why the bank does not return the same money that he put into his savings account, and his inability to read his prepared map. Children in the early elementary grades greatly enjoy these humorous episodes.

Rudyard Kipling. Although the majority of articulate animal stories familiar to Americans occur in the woods and farmlands of the United States and Europe, one series uses the jungles of India. Rudyard Kipling spent his early years in Bombay, India, and this time had a great influence on his later writing. He spent much time in the company of Indian *ayahs* (nurses) who told him native tales about the jungle animals. His own young children were the first to hear his most famous stories about the man-cub Mowgli and his brothers, Akela the wolf, Baloo the bear, and Bagheera the panther, published in *The Jungle Book* in 1894.

The story "Mowgli's Brothers" is one of Kipling's most popular. Kipling develops animal characters as diverse as the man-eating tiger Shere Khan, who claims the young Mowgli as his own, and Mother Wolf, who demonstrates her maternal instincts as she protects the man-cub and encourages him to join her own cubs. The law of the jungle is a strong element in the story, as the animals sit in council to decide Mowgli's fate. This story has the flavor of a traditional tale. The suspense rises until old Baloo the bear finally speaks for the man-cub. As in traditional tales about articulate animals, powerful feelings of loyalty grow as Mowgli saves the life of his old friend Akela, the wolf.

The characters, plot, and language of "Rikki-Tikki-Tavi" make it an excellent choice for oral storytelling. The wicked cobras, Nag and Nagaina, live in the garden of a small boy and his parents. They plan a battle against the humans and the heroic mongoose, Rikki-Tikki-Tavi, a hunter with eyeballs of flame and the sworn enemy of all snakes. In keeping with the oral tradition, the action develops rapidly: The boy's loyal mongoose kills Nag, then

Kipling's young children were the first to hear his stories of articulate animals and a boy raised by the jungle animals. Illustration by W. H. Drake. (From The Jungle Book, by Rudyard Kipling. Illustrated by W. H. Drake, copyright © 1894. Macmillan and Co.)

he faces his most deadly peril, a female cobra avenging her mate and protecting her unborn babies. Kipling's language is excellent for oral recitation. As the tension mounts, Rikki-Tikki-Tavi asks:

> What price for a snake's egg? For a young cobra? For a young king-cobra? For the last—the very last of the brood? The ants are eating all the others down by the melon-bed. (p. 117)

A happy-ever-after ending has Rikki-Tikki-Tavi defeating his enemy and remaining on guard so there will not be another threat in the garden.

Humorous incidents and language that is most effective when shared orally are characteristics of Kipling's *Just So Stories*. Young children enjoy the language in such favorite tales as "The Elephant's Child," the story of an adventurous young animal that lives near the banks of the "great, gray-green, greasy Limpopo River."

Kenneth Grahame. Kenneth Grahame first told his stories to his young children; however, scholarly analysis reveals that *The Wind in the Willows* can be read on several levels. For example, Michael Mendelson (1988) analyzed the contrast between the values of the dusty road and the riverbank. Peter Hunt (1988) analyzed the language and class structure. Richard Gillin (1988) searched for evidence of romanticism.

The animals in *The Wind in the Willows* are much more humanlike than are Mowgli's friends in Kipling's jungle (Townsend, 1975). Grahame creates characters that prefer the idyllic life and consider work a bore, that long for wild adventures, that demonstrate human frailties through their actions, and that are loyal to friends. The idyllic life is exemplified in the experiences of Mole and Water-Rat as they explore their river world. Grahame introduces his readers to Mole as the scent of spring is penetrating Mole's dark home with a spirit of longing and discontent. Lured out of his hole, Mole observes the busy animals around him and muses that the best part of a holiday is not resting; instead, it is seeing other animals busy at work. Through detailed description, Grahame communicates this perpetual vacationer's delight and carefree joy to readers:

> He thought his happiness was complete when, as he meandered aimlessly along, suddenly he stood by the edge of a full-fed river. Never in his life had he seen a river before—this sleek, sinuous, full-bodied animal, chasing and chuckling, gripping things with a gurgle and leaving them with a laugh, to fling itself on fresh playmates that shook themselves free, and were caught and held again. All was a-shake and a-shiver—glints and gleams and sparks, rustle and swirl, chatter and bubble. The Mole was bewitched, entranced, fascinated. (p. 6)

Grahame's writing creates strong characters and visual images of the settings. Children often find the text difficult to read, however, so it may be preferable for adults to read this story to children. Many adults find Grahame's writing to be very enjoyable. As illustrator Fritz Eichenberg (1990) states in his Arbuthnot Lecture address, "At my age I can still read with pleasure and profit *The Wind in the Willows*. That should prove a pleasant platform on which we all can meet, peacefully, or better still let's meet at Toad Hall!" (p. 53).

Robert Lawson. This winner of the Newbery Award, the Caldecott Medal, and the Lewis Carroll Shelf Award has created a believable world in which animals retain their individualized characteristics. Unlike the river world of Mole in *The Wind in the Willows*, Robert Lawson's animal kingdom is influenced by humans. Like other distinguished authors of articulate animal stories, Lawson spent time closely observing animals (Weston, 1970). In 1936, Lawson built a house called Rabbit Hill in Connecticut. He says that he had wanted to write a story about the animals that ate everything he planted, the deer that trampled his garden, the skunks that upset his garbage pail, and the foxes that killed his chickens. Instead, when he started to write, he found himself growing fond of Little Georgie, a young rabbit, and the other animals on the hill.

The resulting book, *Rabbit Hill*, presents the impact of humans on the animals from the point of view of the animals. Lawson maintains this point of view to create believable characters. The animals on the hill wait expectantly after they learn that new folks are coming. They wonder if this change will bring about a renewal of older and pleasanter days when the fields were planted, a garden cultivated, and the lawns manicured. However, Mother Rabbit fears that the folks will be lovers of shotguns, traps, and poison gases, or worst of all, will be boys.

Lawson centers his book on the exploits of the exuberant Little Georgie, a rabbit that retains his curiosity and love for a good chase even when his father warns him that misbehavior and parental indulgence can have swift and fatal consequences. The animals believe that all will be well when the new owners put up a sign saying "Please drive carefully on account of small animals." Then, Little Georgie has a dreadful experience with a car on the black road, and the folks from the hill take the limp rabbit into the house. Gloom settles over the animals. Is Georgie alive, and, if so, why does he not appear? What terrible experiences are the folks planning for Little Georgie? The animals learn that the new folks are considerate and caring. The story has a satisfying ending, and the animals pay tribute to their new folks on the hill.

George Selden. Like Robert Lawson, George Selden loves the Connecticut countryside, and he creates animals with strong and believable personalities. His *The Cricket in Times Square*, however, has an urban setting, the subway station at Times Square. Two animal characters, Tucker Mouse and Harry Cat, are city dwellers. The other animal, Chester Cricket, arrives accidentally, having jumped into a picnic basket in Connecticut and been trapped until he arrived in New York.

Selden tells their story from the point of view of the animals and develops additional credibility by retaining some of each animal's natural characteristics: The city-wise Tucker Mouse lives in a cluttered drainpipe because he enjoys scrounging and does not consider neatness important. Chester Cricket is a natural musician and prefers to play when the spirit moves him rather than when people want to hear him. The plot develops around Chester's remarkable ability to play any music he hears and his need for returning kindness to the poor owner of the newsstand in the subway. Selden concludes his story with a longing that might be felt by anyone taken from his native environment. Chester becomes homesick for autumn in Connecticut and leaves the city to return home. When Tucker asks him how he'll know that he has reached home, Chester reassures him, "Oh, I'll . . . I'll smell the trees and I'll feel the air and I'll know" (p. 154).

This is a touching story of friendship, of longing for one's home, and of the love and understanding that can be felt between even a child and a tiny insect. Additional stories about these animals are found in Selden's *Tucker's Countryside, Harry Cat's Pet Puppy*, and *Chester Cricket's Pigeon Ride. Chester Cricket's Pigeon Ride* has a large format and illustrations designed to appeal to young children.

E. B. White.   E. B. White introduces his characters within the reality of an authentically described working farm. His human characters have no unusual powers. They do not treat animals like people, and White does not give his animals human characteristics. The harsh reality is that the farmer must keep only animals that can produce a profit. In this setting, Mr. Arable moves toward the hoghouse with an ax in his hand to kill the runt in a newly born litter of six pigs. His daughter, Fern, pleads with him to let her raise the pig. As Wilbur grows, the profitability of the farm again influences Wilbur's fate. Mr. Arable is not willing to provide for Wilbur's growing appetite. Fern again saves Wilbur, but without a hint of fantasy: She sells him to Uncle Homer Zuckerman, who lives within easy visiting distance.

Wilbur's new home also begins on a firm foundation of reality. White describes the barn in which Wilbur will live and the afternoons when Fern visits Wilbur. On an afternoon when Fern does not arrive, White changes the story from reality to fantasy: Wilbur discovers that he can talk. As he realizes this, his barnyard neighbors begin to talk to him. From this point on, White develops the animal characters into distinct individuals, consistent in speech, actions, and appearance.

Wilbur feels lonely, friendless, and dejected. White answers Wilbur's needs by giving him a barnyard friend. Charlotte A. Cavatica, a beautiful gray spider. Charlotte has quiet manners, and she is intelligent and loyal.

Through the reactions of the farm families, White allows readers to suspend disbelief about the possibility of a spider's spinning a web containing words. When the local residents react in "joyful admiration" and notify their local newspaper (the *Weekly Chronicle*), White's readers tend to believe this could really have happened. Readers can accept even the death of Charlotte, because life and friendship continue through Charlotte's offspring. Wilbur understands this as he welcomes three of Charlotte's daughters to his home:

> Welcome to the barn cellar. You have chosen a hallowed doorway from which to string your webs. I think it is only fair to tell you that I was devoted to your mother. I owe my very life to her. She was brilliant, beautiful, and loyal to the end. I shall always treasure her memory. To you, her daughters, I pledge my friendship, forever and ever. (p. 182)

You may wish to compare E. B. White's *Charlotte's Web* with Dick King-Smith's believable characters and plot in *Pigs Might Fly*. Like Wilbur, Daggie Dogfoot is the runt of the litter. Unlike Wilbur, however, Daggie Dogfoot has a physical disability.

Toys

When children play with dolls or have conversations with their stuffed animals and other toys, they demonstrate belief in the human characteristics they give their playthings. An author who tells a story from the point of view of a toy encourages young readers to draw upon their imaginative experiences with toys and to suspend disbelief.

Rumer Godden.   Telling *The Dolls' House* from the viewpoint of a doll, Godden creates a believable story about a group of small dolls that long to leave a shoebox and live in their own house. Godden tells her readers:

> It is an anxious, sometimes a dangerous thing to be a doll. Dolls cannot choose; they can only be chosen; they cannot "do"; they can only be done by; children who do not understand this often do wrong things, and then the dolls are hurt and abused and lost; and when this happens, dolls cannot speak, nor do anything except be hurt and abused and lost. If you have any dolls, you should remember that. (p. 13)

Godden creates dolls with a range of human characteristics. For example, Mr. and Mrs. Plantagenet are quite ordinary dolls with extraordinary hearts; Tottie is an antique Dutch doll with a warm, friendly character; and Marchpane is an elegant 19th-century china doll with a vile disposition. These characteristics play important roles as the dolls express the desire for a new home. When an elegant dollhouse arrives, Marchpane declares that the house is rightfully hers and that the rest of the dolls are her servants. Godden describes the dolls' increasing unhappiness until a tragedy opens the eyes of the two children and the story ends on a note suggesting that justice is related to one's conduct.

Margery Williams.   *The Velveteen Rabbit* is told from the viewpoint of a stuffed toy that lives in a nursery and learns to know his owner. Conversations between the stuffed rabbit and an old toy horse are especially effective. They allow Williams to share her feelings about the reality of toys. When the rabbit asks the wise, old Skin Horse what it means to be real, the Skin Horse informs him, "Real isn't how you are made. . . . It's a thing that happens to you. When a child loves you for a long, long time, not just to play with, but REALLY loves you, then you become Real" (p. 17). The horse tells the rabbit that becoming real usually happens after a toy's hair has been loved off, its eyes have dropped out, and its joints have loosened. Then, even if the toy is shabby, it does not mind because it has become real to the child who loves it.

The story develops around the growing companionship between a boy and the toy rabbit. Children's reactions to this story suggest how meaningful the toy–child relationship is. Teachers and librarians describe the concern of young children when the rabbit is placed on the rubbish pile because the rabbit spent many hours in bed with the boy when he had scarlet fever. When the nursery fairy appears and turns the toy into a real rabbit, however, children often say that this is the right reward for a toy that has given so much love. These reactions suggest the credibility of a story written from the point of view of a toy. You may wish to compare the versions of this book illustrated by William Nicholson (the original edition), Michael Green, Ilse Plume, Allen Atkinson, and Michael Hague.

Companionship and love between a boy and a toy seem believable in this fantasy. (From The Velveteen Rabbit, *by Margery Williams. Illustrated by Michael Hague. Illustrations copyright © 1983 by Michael Hague. Reprinted by permission of Henry Holt and Company, Inc.)*

A. A. Milne.   According to his creator, A. A. Milne (1966), Winnie-the-Pooh does not like to be called a teddy bear because a teddy bear is just a toy, whereas Pooh is alive. The original Pooh was a present to Milne's son, Christopher Robin, on his first birthday. The boy and Pooh became inseparable, playing together on the nursery floor, hunting wild animals among the chairs that became African jungles, and having lengthy conversations over tea. Christopher Robin's nursery contained other "real" animals, including Piglet, Eeyore, Kanga, and Roo. When Milne wrote his stories about Christopher Robin's adventures with these animals, he was not only thinking about his own son but also remembering himself as a boy.

Winnie-the-Pooh and *The House at Pooh Corner* are filled with stories about Pooh because Pooh likes to hear stories about himself. Milne develops credibility for the actions in his stories by taking Pooh and the others out of the nursery and into the hundred-acre wood, where an inquisitive bear can have many adventures. Several stories suggest Pooh's reality: He climbs trees looking for honey and eats Rabbit's honey when he pays a visit. The text and illustrations leave no doubt that Pooh is a toy, however. No real bear would be so clumsy as to fall from branch to branch or to become stuck in Rabbit's doorway. Children may feel a close relationship with Christopher Robin be-cause every time that Pooh gets into difficulty, the human child must rescue the "silly old bear."

Carlo Collodi.   The adventures of a wooden marionette that is disobedient, prefers the joys of playtime to the rigors of school, and finally learns his lesson and wins an opportunity to become a real boy are similar to the experiences of Carlo Collodi, his creator. The Italian author of *The Adventures of Pinocchio* described himself as "the most irresponsible, the most disobedient and impudent boy in the whole school" (De Wit, 1979, p. 74). Collodi's story reflects a lesson he learned in school:

> I persuaded myself that if one is impudent and disobedient in school he loses the good will of the teachers and the friendship of the scholars. I too became a good boy. I began to respect the others and they in turn respected me. (p. 76)

Pinocchio's insistence on doing only what he wants leads to a series of adventures: He sells his spelling book instead of attending school, he becomes involved with a devious fox and cat, he goes to a land of perpetual playtime, and he is transformed into a donkey. After Pinocchio learns some bitter lessons, he searches for his creator, Geppetto, who works to restore his health. Pinocchio begins to practice his reading and writing, and eventually becomes a real person. Through the words of the blue fairy, Collodi explains why Pinocchio is rewarded:

> Because of your kind heart I forgive you for all your misdeeds. Boys who help other people so willingly and lovingly deserve praise, even if they are not models in other ways. Always listen to good counsel and you will be happy. (p. 193)

The influence of traditional folktales and fables is evident in Collodi's use of animals with human traits to teach lessons. Magical transformations punish and reward Pinocchio on his path to self-improvement (Heins, 1982).

Preposterous Characters and Situations

Children love exaggeration, ridiculous situations, and tongue-twisting language. Stories that appeal to a sense of humor usually include repetition, plays on words, and clever and original figures of speech. The characters in these stories are developed through vivid descriptions of dress, features, or actions.

Floating through the air inside a huge peach propelled by 502 seagulls provides a getaway for an unhappy child in Roald Dahl's *James and the Giant Peach*. Children thoroughly enjoy the freshness and originality of this story. Other enjoyably preposterous journeys occur when a housepainter is granted an unusual wish in *Mr. Popper's Penguins*, by Richard and Florence Atwater; when an eccentric inventor restores an old car in Ian Fleming's *Chitty Chitty Bang Bang;* and when a bed takes flight in Mary Norton's *Bed-Knob and Broomstick*. Pamela L. Travers's preposterous nanny, Mary Poppins, goes on many adventures.

Carl Sandburg.   Readers might expect some unusual characters to be the residents of Rootabaga Country, where the largest city is a village called Liver and Onions. They are usually not disappointed when they hear Carl Sandburg's *Rootabaga Stories*. Told originally to the author's own children, these stories lose part of their humor if they are read rather than heard: The alliteration and nonsensical names are hard for children to read themselves, but they are fun to listen to.

Sandburg begins his ridiculous situation by describing how to get to Rootabaga Country by train: Riders must sell everything they own, put "spot-cash money" into a rag-bag, and then go to the railroad station and ask for a ticket to the place where the railroad tracks run into the sky and never come back. They will know they have arrived when the train begins running on zigzag tracks; when they have traveled through the country of Over and Under, where no one gets out of the way of anyone else; and when they look out the train windows and see pigs wearing bibs.

The residents of Rootabaga Country have tongue-twisting names, such as Ax Me No Questions, Rags Habakuk, Miney Mo, and Henry Hagglyhoagly, and they become involved in tongue-twisting situations. For example, when Blixie Bimber puts a charm around her neck, she falls in love with the first man that she meets with one *x* in his name (Silas Baxby), then with a man with two *x*'s (Fritz Axanbax), and finally with a man with three *x*'s (James Sixbixdix).

Sandburg's characters often talk in alliteration, repeating an initial sound in consecutive words. When the neighbors see a family selling their possessions, for example, they speculate that the family might be going "to Kansas, to Kokomo, to Canada, to Kankakee, to Kamchatka, to the Chattahoochee"(p. 6). The stories are brief enough to share with children during a short story time, but the uncommon names and the language require preparation by a storyteller or an oral reader. *More Rootabagas* is a newer collection of previously unpublished stories. *The Huckabuck Family and How They Raised Popcorn in Nebraska and Quit and Came Back* is one of Sandburg's stories illustrated with humorous drawings by David Small.

Strange and Curious Worlds

While on their way to Carl Sandburg's Rootabaga Country, young readers may find themselves falling down rabbit holes or flying off into even stranger and more curious worlds of modern fantasy.

Lewis Carroll. A remarkable realm unfolds when one falls down a rabbit hole, follows an underground passage, and enters a tiny door into a land of cool fountains, bright flowers, and unusual inhabitants. The guide into this world is also unusual: an articulate white rabbit that wears a waistcoat complete with a pocket watch.

Perhaps even more remarkable is that this world of fantasy was created by a man who was dreadfully shy with adults, had a tendency to stammer, and displayed prim

and precise habits. Charles Lutwidge Dodgson, better known as Lewis Carroll, was a mathematics lecturer at Oxford University during the sedate Victorian period of English history. Warren Weaver (1964) describes the life of this Victorian don:

> Dodgson's adult life symbolized—indeed, really caricatured—the restraints of Victorian society. But he was essentially a wild and free spirit, and he had to burst out of these bonds. The chief outlet was fantasy—the fantasy which children accept with such simplicity, with such intelligence and charm. (p. 16)

Dodgson may have been shy with adults, but he showed a very different personality with children. He kept himself supplied with games to amuse them, made friends with them easily, and enjoyed telling them stories. A story told on a warm July afternoon to three young daughters of the dean of Dodgson's college at Oxford made Lewis Carroll almost immortal. As the children—Alice, Edith, and Lorina Liddell—rested on the riverbank, they asked Dodgson for a story. The result was the remarkable tale that later became *Alice's Adventures in Wonderland*. Even the first line of the story is reminiscent of a warm, leisurely afternoon:

> Alice was beginning to get very tired of sitting by her sister on the bank having nothing to do: Once or twice she had peeped into the book her sister was reading, but it had no pictures or conversations in it, "And what is the use of a book" thought Alice, "without pictures or conversations?" (p. 9)

From that point on, however, the day enters another realm of experience. Alice sees a strange white rabbit muttering to himself and follows him down, down, down into Wonderland, where the unusual is ordinary. Drinking mysterious substances changes one's size; strange animals conduct a race with no beginning and no finish that everyone wins; a hookah-smoking caterpillar gives advice; Dormouse, March Hare, and Mad Hatter have a very odd tea party; Cheshire Cat fades in and out of sight; and the King

A tea party with unusual guests adds to Alice-in-Wonderland's confusion. (From The Nursery "Alice," *by Lewis Carroll. Illustrated by John Tenniel. Published by Macmillan Publishing Co., 1890, 1979.)*

and Queen of Hearts conduct a ridiculous trial. According to Weaver (1964), the strange adventures have a broad appeal to children everywhere because

> something of the essence of childhood is contained in this remarkable book—the innocent fun, the natural acceptance of marvels, combined with a healthy and at times slightly saucy curiosity about them, the element of confusion concerning the strange way in which the adult world behaves, the complete and natural companionship with animals, and an intertwined mixture of the rational and the irrational. For all of these, whatever the accidents of geography, are part and parcel of childhood. (p. 6)

Throughout the book, Alice expresses a natural acceptance of the unusual. When she finds a bottle labeled "Drink Me," she does so without hesitation. When the White Rabbit sends her to look for his missing gloves, she thinks to herself that it is queer to be a messenger for a rabbit, but she goes without question. During her adventures in this strange land she does, however, question her own identity. When the caterpillar opens their conversation by asking, "Who are you?" Alice replies:

> I—I hardly know, Sir, just at present—at least I know who I was when I got up this morning, but I think I must have been changed several times since then. . . . I can't explain myself. I'm afraid, Sir, because I'm not myself, you see. (p. 23)

Lewis Carroll's language is appealing to children, especially if an adult reads the story to them, but children have difficulty reading the story for themselves, and some of the word plays are difficult for them to understand. Carroll's version of the story for young children, *The Nursery "Alice,"* is written as though the author were telling the tale directly to children:

> This is a little bit of the beautiful garden I told you about. You see Alice had managed at last to get quite small, so that she could go through the little door. I suppose she was about as tall as a mouse, if it stood on its hind legs; so of course this was a very tiny rose-tree: and these are very tiny gardeners. (p. 41)

Carroll is noted for his nonsense words as well as for his nonsensical situations. He claimed that even he could not explain the meanings of some words. Myra Cohn Livingston (1973) quotes a letter in which Carroll explains at least some words in his popular poem "Jabberwocky":

> I am afraid I can't explain "vorpal blade" for you—nor yet "tulgey wood:" but I did make an explanation once for "uffish thought"—It seems to suggest a state of mind when the voice is gruffish, the manner roughish, and the temper huffish. Then again, as to "burble"; if you take the three verbs, "<u>b</u>leat," "<u>mur</u>mur" and "wa<u>rble</u>," and select the bits I have underlined, it certainly makes "burble": though I am afraid I can't distinctly remember having made it that way.

You may find it interesting to compare John Tenniel's illustrations in the original version of *Alice's Adventures in Wonderland* with those of two more recent editions: Helen Oxenbury's illustrations for *Alice's Adventures in Wonderland* and Lisbeth Zwerger's illustrations for *Alice in Wonderland.* Both of these editions were published in 1999.

James Barrie. *Peter Pan,* the classic flight of James Barrie's imagination into Never Land, was first presented as a play in 1904. Barrie begins his fantasy in the realm of reality, describing the children of Mr. and Mrs. Darling in their nursery as their parents prepare to leave for a party. When the parents leave the house, the world of fantasy immediately enters it in the form of Peter Pan and Tinker Bell, who are looking for Peter's lost shadow. Thus begins an adventure in which the Darling children fly, with the help of fairy dust, to Never Land, the kingdom that is "second to the right and then straight on till morning" (p. 31).

In Never Land, they meet the lost boys, children who have fallen out of their baby carriages when adults were not looking, and discover that there are no girls in Never Land because girls are too clever to fall out of their baby carriages.

Barrie's description of Mermaids' Lagoon encourages readers to visualize this fantasy land:

> If you shut your eyes and are a lucky one, you may see at times a shapeless pool of lovely pale colours suspended in the darkness; then if you squeeze your eyes tighter, the pool begins to take shape, and the colours become so vivid that with another squeeze they must go on fire. But just before they go on fire you see the lagoon. This is the nearest you ever get to it on the mainland, just one heavenly moment; if there could be two moments you might see the surf and hear the mermaids singing. (p. 111)

The settings and characters seem real, especially to children who do not wish to grow up. Readers who do not want to take on the responsibility of adulthood may empathize with the adult Wendy, who longs to accompany Peter Pan but cannot. The book closes on a touch of nostalgia, as Peter Pan returns to claim each new generation of children who are happy and innocent.

Dave Barry and Ridley Pearson wrote another version of Peter Pan, *Peter and the Starcatchers,* in which the authors add more characters and adventures. Literary critic Michael Gorra (2004) ponders some interesting insights after he shared the book with his daughter: "About halfway through I asked my daughter which version of Peter's origins she preferred, this one or the one she'd gotten from J. M. Barrie. At first she chose this one, excited by the sheer variety of its characters' adventures. But then she asked a question: 'Is that how it really happened, or is it just fake for the book?' That sets a limit; with the best children's tales, the question goes unasked. 'Peter and the Starcatchers' is as satisfying as a popsicle, but don't mistake it for the meal" (p. 23).

Little People

Traditional folktales and fairy tales describe the kingdoms of small trolls, gnomes, and fairies; Hans Christian Andersen wrote about tiny Thumbelina, who sleeps in a walnut shell; and J. R. R. Tolkien created a believable world for the hobbit. In *The Moorchild,* Eloise McGraw creates a world in which the Folk, or fairy people, live in their own world near that of the human occupants of the moor. Saaski, the heroine of the story, cannot survive with the Folk because she does not have their ability to make herself invisible to humans. McGraw creates her fantasy plot when the Folk exchange Saaski for a human child. Contemporary authors of fantasy satisfy children's fascination with people who are a lot like them, only much smaller.

Carol Kendall.   In *The Gammage Cup*, Carol Kendall creates a new world, the Land between the Mountains, in which little people in the valley of the Watercress River live in 12 serene towns with names such as Little Dripping, Great Dripping, and Slipper-on-the-Water. Kendall gives credibility to this setting by tracing its history, carefully describing its building, and creating inhabitants who have lived in the valley for centuries.

The valley has two types of residents. The Periods display smug conformity in their clothing, their insistence on neat houses, and their similar attitudes and values. In contrast, the five Minnipins—whom the Periods refer to as "Oh Them"—insist on being different. Gummy roams the hills rather than working at a suitable job, Curley Green paints pictures and wears a scarlet cloak, Walter the Earl digs for ancient treasure, Muggles refuses to keep her house organized, and Mingy questions the rulers' authority.

Mary Norton.   The little people in Mary Norton's stories do not live in an isolated kingdom of their own. Instead, they are found in "houses which are old and quiet and deep in the country—and where the human beings live to a routine. Routine is their safeguard. They must know which rooms are to be used and when. They do not stay long where there are careless people, or unruly children, or certain household pets" (p. 9). In *The Borrowers*, Norton persuades readers to suspend disbelief by developing a foundation in reality. She describes an old country house in detail, including a clock that has not been moved for more than 80 years. Realistic humans living in the house see and believe in the little people.

Norton describes normal-sized people through the eyes of the Clock family, who are only 6 inches tall. The Clocks' size forces them to lead precarious lives. They borrow their furnishings from the human occupants of the house.

She further encourages readers to suspend disbelief through the effort made to catch the little people. *The Borrowers* reaches an exciting climax when the housekeeper vows to have the borrowers exterminated by all available means: The rat-catcher arrives, complete with dogs, rabbit snares, sacks, spade, gun, and pickax. When a human boy takes an ax and desperately tries to dislodge the grating from the brick wall so that the little people can escape, readers have no doubt that those extraordinary beings are waiting in the shadows for his aid.

The Borrowers Afloat, *The Borrowers Afield*, *The Borrowers Aloft*, and *The Borrowers Avenged* continue the Clocks' adventures in fields and hedgerows. Sights, sounds, smells, and experiences seem original and authentic as readers look at the world from this unusual perspective.

Spirits Friendly and Frightening

Most children love good ghost stories or tales about beings from the spirit realm, whether frightening or friendly. Authors who write about these subjects may develop elements from folklore and the historical past.

Jonathan Stroud's "The Bartimaeus Trilogy" is a series of books set in contemporary London, but a London that is ruled by magicians. The plot and main characters, a 5,000-year-old Djinni and a 12-year-old magician's apprentice, develop both humor and suspense. Stroud begins *The Amulet of Samarkand* with the following setting and mood that are meant to chill: "The temperature of the room dropped fast. Ice formed on the curtains and crusted thickly around the lights in the ceiling. The glowing filaments in each bulb shrank and dimmed, while the candles that sprang from every available surface like a

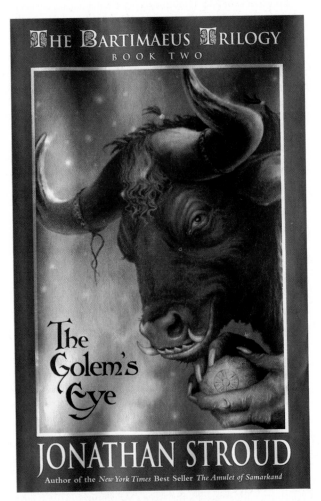

Cover from The Golem's Eye by Jonathan Stroud. Jacket illustration © 2004 by Melvyn Grant. Miramax Books, Hyperion Books for Children. Used by permission.

Through The Eyes of an AUTHOR

Cynthia DeFelice

Visit the CD-ROM that accompanies this text to generate a complete list of titles written by Cynthia DeFelice.

Selected Titles by Cynthia DeFelice:
Nowhere to Call Home
The Apprenticeship of Lucas Whitaker
Ghost of Fossil Glen
Clever Crow
The Ghost of Cutler Creek
The Missing Manatee

As a child, I loved sleepover parties where we would sit around and tell stories to scare each other half to death. And as a school librarian, I loved Halloween time. Spooky but safe—with the kinds of stories that won't give kids nightmares, but kind of give you that great little shiver down your spine.

It was a conscious decision I made to write a ghost story, just because I knew how much I loved them as a child and I know how much kids love them. So I knew I wanted to write a ghost story, but the fact that The Ghost of Fossil Glen was not just a mystery but was about a real ghost came out as I was writing. I see myself as a realistic person, which most

of my books reflect, but I do find something interesting in this supernatural area. When kids ask me, "Do you believe in ghosts?" I think—I don't believe in Casper the ghost or clanking chains or spooky white figures, but I do think there are things in this world that can't be explained. And I have felt that there are people close to me who've died who I do feel I'm still in contact with, in the sense that if you love someone, they are always with you in your heart.

I think being able to write effectively for kids comes from knowing kids and really listening to them, really paying attention to them, and having a lot of respect for them. Then you can write to them in a way that isn't talking down to them. I found that kids are deeply interested in death, whether it's a ghost story or The Apprenticeship of Lucas Whitaker, which deals with sickness and death, or Nowhere to Call Home, which begins with the character's father committing suicide. I've also learned that death is almost the ultimate taboo; parents and teachers and librarians are most afraid of death in books for children, and yet it's something kids are deeply interested in and want to learn about and talk about and know about.

I think kids of that particular age are so fascinating, because they are right on the brink of

so many things. They are sort of teetering between childhood and adulthood, and they are so capable. Of all the characters I've written about, I think Allie is most like me, although she is braver and smarter and cooler than I ever was. Like in The Ghost of Fossil Glen, when the two girls turn on her and decide not to be her friend anymore, that's based on an experience I had. Kids respond to that. They often tell me how much that part of the book meant to them.

I love to try to write about issues that give them credit for all they're capable of. It's so gratifying to have children thank you for writing a book, saying a Mom or Dad was worried about a book because it would be too scary or upsetting, but thanking me for knowing they could handle it. And I think kids can handle a lot of things, if it's done mindfully. I'm not a censor at all, but I do think there are things that are appropriate and inappropriate for 12-, 13-, 14-year-old kids, and I try to write things I know they are deeply, deeply interested in and need to know.

Video Profile: The accompanying video contains interviews with Lynne Cherry, Mary E. Lyons, the late Paula Danziger, and other writers.

---

colony of toadstools had their wicks snuffed out. The darkened room filled with a yellow, choking cloud of brimstone, in which indistinct black shadows writhed and roiled" (p. 3). This setting foreshadows the appearance of the Djinni who, along with the boy, overcomes plots, espionage, and even murder. The two characters outwit the evil magicians and continue their adventures in The Golem's Eye.

In a ghost story, Mary Downing Hahn helps present-day characters deal with their problems. In Wait Till Helen Comes, Hahn's characters overcome their resentment against their stepfather and stepsister when they help the stepsister overcome her fascination with a ghost that is trying to lure the girl to her death. In Ghost Abbey, by Robert Westall, an abbey plays two roles: (1) it protects those who care for it, and (2) it threatens those who harm it. In Whispers From the Dead, by Joan Lowery Nixon, the ghost of a murdered character helps solve a mystery and prevent a second murder.

In The Boggart, Susan Cooper develops a conflict of wills between the Boggart, an ancient spirit, and the children who visit a castle in the western highlands of Scotland. In Cooper's sequel, The Boggart and the Monster, the spirit interacts with the Loch Ness Monster.

Technology Resources

One way to motivate a child to read is to recommend books on a favorite topic. Use the CD-ROM that accompanies this text to generate a list of titles concerning "ghosts" by searching the Title, Description and Topics fields with the term ghost. Add a grade specification to the Grade Level field to streamline your search.

For older readers, Silver Kiss, by Annette Curtis Klause, has a mysterious teenage boy help a girl face her own problems and acquire self-realization. In this book, Zoe, a contemporary girl, and Simon, a 300-year-old vampire, help each other accept what has happened in their lives. Authors of fantasy frequently help characters face issues and overcome problems that could be self-destructive. In Peter Dickinson's The Lion Tamer's Daughter: And Other Stories, teenagers are helped by supernatural friends, and Patricia Windsor's The Blooding is a story of good versus evil.

Lucy Boston. The winner of the Lewis Carroll Shelf Award for The Children of Green Knowe, Lucy Boston uses her own historical manor house at Hemingford Grey near

Through the Eyes of a CHILD

Sarah

Grade 6

Sarah weaver
10-4-05

Author → Cynthia Defelice
Title → The Ghost of Fossil Glen

This book was a great book! It had alot of detail and interesting things that happened in the book that made me keep on reading. I read it every second I could because I couldn't wait to see what happened next. In the book, the character Allie thinks a ghost is following her around and she is trying to figure out why. I recommend this book to anyone who likes mysteries and really good books that you can't put down because it's so good. Once you look at the front page, you know it will be a very good book!

Sarah

Cambridge. England, as the setting for her stories. The house and the way of life that past generations experienced in it provided Boston with ideas for a series of stories written about an old manor house and the friendly presences that return there from generations past.

The first book of a series, *The Children of Green Knowe* introduces the house; its owner, Mrs. Oldknowe; her great-grandson, Tolly; and the children who have previously lived in the house. Boston describes the house through the eyes of Tolly, a lonely, shy boy who comes to live in this old house with furnishings similar to those found in a castle. The past comes alive for Tolly as children who have lived there in previous generations come back to play with each other and bring vitality to the house and gardens.

Other books in this series are *The Treasure of Green Knowe, The River at Green Knowe, A Stranger at Green Knowe,* and *An Enemy at Green Knowe.* In all of the stories, ancestors return because someone wanted to keep their memories alive.

Time Warps

Children who read time-warp stories discover that there are more things in this world than progress and theories about the future. Time-warp stories encourage children to

consider what might have happened in their own towns or geographic location hundreds of years ago, as well as what the future might hold in centuries to come. Symbols and tangible objects unite past, present, and future. Believable characters travel to a distant past or see a future yet to materialize. Unlike many of the modern fantasies that bridge the world between old and new fantasy, time-warp stories focus on human development rather than on the forces of good and evil. The problems are solved by the characters, not by supernatural powers.

Authors frequently use the time-warp technique to allow their characters to make discoveries about themselves, their families, or the past. These discoveries usually allow the characters to gain new understandings. Detailed descriptions of a farm and countryside in the 20th century and during the American Civil War create a believable story in Janet Lunn's time-warp fantasy, *The Root Cellar.* In this book, the problems that an unhappy orphan confronts in both the present and the past encourage her personal development.

Time-warp experiences help children overcome problems related to growing up and to family in Cynthia Voigt's *Building Blocks.* In *Stonewords: A Ghost Story* and the sequel, *Zoe Rising,* Pam Conrad develops a theme of friendship when a contemporary girl interacts with a girl who lived in the same house during a different time. In *Zoe Rising*, 14-year-old Zoe goes back in time to solve a mystery in her estranged mother's past.

Belinda Hurmence uses a historical time and person-against-society conflict to help her protagonist understand a conflict that influenced her family. In *A Girl Called Boy*, Hurmence has a contemporary girl go back in time and experience slavery in 1853. In *Trapped Between the Lash and the Gun*, Arvella Whitmore uses a time-warp experience to help a contemporary African American boy make decisions about his life. When he contemplates running away from home and joining a street gang, he steals his grandfather's watch, which had been owned by an early ancestor. This is the tangible object that unites the present with the past as the boy finds himself transported to the plantation on which his ancestors were slaves.

A contemporary actor is helped to overcome his grief and sorrow when he goes back to the late 1500s in Susan Cooper's *King of Shadows*. In the earlier time, he finds himself in the Globe Theatre acting with Shakespeare. Cooper develops a historically believable earlier setting by describing the theatre, using quotes from Shakespeare, and adding political intrigue associated with the time period. The need for healing from grief is a thread that runs through both time periods and allows the author to develop themes associated with the need to overcome grief and the power of great poetry to transcend time. Jane Yolen uses a similar approach in *The Devil's Arithmetic*. In this book, a contemporary Jewish girl faces the Holocaust.

These books are believable because the authors develop authentic historical backgrounds and characters who are changed by their experiences. The books may seem real because the authors allow their contemporary protagonists to experience the problems of another time.

Science Fiction

Writers of science fiction rely on hypothesized scientific advancements and imagined technology to create their plots. To achieve credibility, they provide detailed descriptions of this technology, portray characters who believe in the technology or its results, and create a world where science interacts with every area of society. Like other modern fantasies, science fiction relies on an internal consistency among plot, characters, and setting to encourage readers' suspension of disbelief. Science fiction written for young children often emphasizes the adventure associated with traveling to distant galaxies or with encountering unusual aliens. Stories for older readers often hypothesize about the future of humanity and stress problem solving in future societies.

Critics do not agree on the identity of the first science fiction novel. Margaret P. Esmonde (1984) identifies Mary Godwin Shelley's *Frankenstein*, published in 1817, as the earliest science fiction story because the protagonist is a scientist, not a wizard, and the central theme is the proper use of knowledge and the moral responsibility of a scientist for his discovery.

Jules Verne published one of the first popular science fiction novels, *Five Weeks in a Balloon*, in 1863. Verne focused that book and later famous books enjoyed by older children and adults, such as *Twenty-Thousand Leagues Under the Sea*, on technology and invention but did not develop a society around them. Later in the 19th century, H. G. Wells began writing science fiction novels, such as *War of the Worlds*, that had a strong influence on the genre. According to Roland J. Green (1977), the writings of Wells differed from those of Jules Verne in that they included the systematic "extrapolation of social trends to create a detailed picture of a future society, revolutionary inventions, interplanetary warfare, and time travel" (p. 46).

After World War I, as technology advanced at an even faster pace, science fiction writing was influenced by the growth of magazines, such as *Amazing Stories*. John W. Campbell, Jr.'s, editorship of *Astounding Science Fiction*, beginning in 1938, was highly influential: Campbell insisted that the authors of stories he published develop strong characters, plausible science and technology, and logical speculation about future societies. He encouraged such talented science fiction writers as Robert A. Heinlein and Isaac Asimov.

In the 1960s, an increasing number of authors began to write science fiction stories. These stories were more suited to older children and young adults than to young children because the plots often relied on a developed sense of time, place, and space. Science fiction became a topic of interest for university and high-school courses. The media were extremely influential during this period. The movie *2001: A Space Odyssey* and the television program "Star Trek" created a devoted science fiction audience and suggested the imaginative potential of science fiction subjects. In the 1970s and 1980s, audiences flocked to such pictures as *Star Wars* and *E.T.* In the 1990s, the possible cloning of dinosaurs became a debated issue in *Jurassic Park*. Young people today read and reread the paperback versions of these movies.

Many writers are creating high-quality science fiction for young people and are considering responses to future catastrophies or scientific possibilities in their plots. The years following the destruction of modern civilization from the Flash provide the setting for Caroline Stevermer's *River Rats*. In this story, a group of teenagers crew an old, salvaged paddle-wheel steamer on the toxic Mississippi River. Their fight for survival is increased after they rescue a man who is being chased because he knows the location of a hoard of weapons. Stevermer presents a setting filled with ruined cities and the consequences of toxic pollution. The protagonists work together and survive in this desolate environment.

Although many of the science fiction books are written for middle- to upper-elementary students and older, Kevin O'Malley's *Captain Raptor and the Moon Mystery* is a heavily illustrated book with dinosaur characters for younger readers. When a mysterious light flashes above the planet Jurassica, Captain Raptor, the hero of a thousand space missions, and his massive spaceship, Megatooth, are called to investigate. The comic-book style builds suspense through such lines as "'Captain. The ship can't take the pressure. The monster is squeezing us like a tube of toothpaste!' Could this be the end of Captain Raptor and his fearless crew?" (unnumbered). This book could easily lead to creative writing and art activities as the captain and his crew are in no hurry to go back to Jurassica because the universe is huge and they are in the mood for adventure.

In *The Giver*, Lois Lowry portrays a future in which poverty, inequality, and unemployment have been eliminated. This society, however, is devoid of conscience, emotion, and even color. Accompanying 12-year-old Jonas as he discovers the truth about his society, readers must ponder and reexamine many of their own beliefs.

In *Messenger*, Lowry reunites characters from *The Giver* and *Gathering Blue*. At the beginning of the book, readers are introduced to the Museum's small, red-painted sled that is a symbol of courage and hope. (To understand the sled's importance, reread the concluding chapter of *The Giver*.) The setting for *Messenger* is Village, a place where people come from places with secrets, places with cruel governments, harsh punishments, desperate poverty, or false comforts. Village is a utopian community where the people value honesty, but must always be aware of forces that threaten the utopia. Lowry develops a strong theme related to honesty, goodness, and freedom when her main character, Matty, uses his healing power and trades himself for all he loves and values in order to overpower the evil that has infected his world. Matty's actions also give him his true name, Healer. This is Lowry's final theme, which suggests that true names must be earned, not merely given to a person.

The transcendent time between the technologically advanced, but polluted, 21st century and the 16th-century world of warriors who plunder the borders of England and Scotland forms the setting for scientists in Susan Price's *The Sterkarm Handshake*. This winner of the Guardian's Children's Fiction Award presents a plot and characters that depict the clashes between two cultures. Readers can consider the responsibilities of and the possibilities for a future culture that might try to solve problems by taking over a culture, a people, and a land.

Kenneth Oppel's *Airborn* combines the descriptions of the high technology needed to fly an airship across the world's oceans and a Victorian-era adventure in which two young people, Matt and Kate, battle pirates who want to capture the airship. The author provides detailed descriptions of the setting in which unusual experiences, the structure of the airship, and the mystical species seem believable.

Notice in the following quote how Oppel develops a setting that foreshadows the plot: "Winds are capricious all through there—that's why it's called the Sisyphus Triangle. There's been airships that went in and never came out. I've heard rumors about garbled distress calls, compass needles spinning madly, instruments all screwy. Luckily there's not much need to use those airways. They don't lead anywhere of particular interest" (p. 91).

This setting becomes important to the story after pirates attack the airship, force it off the usual route, and cause it to land on a mysterious island. The author vividly describes flying mammals that are like birds of prey with faces of a panther, massive wings, and pale fur. "It was a panther's face but altogether more streamlined, designed to cut through wind. Its large eyes danced with intelligence and sunlight. It was exquisite. It was terrifying" (p. 179). Oppel concludes the book with a section, "Six Months Later." Before reading this section, readers could consider what they believe might happen if, like Kate, they discovered an unknown species or if, like Matt, they had always dreamed of going to the Academy and becoming an officer on an airship.

In *Invitation to the Game*, Monica Hughes speculates about what might happen in the year 2154 if there is high unemployment, if workers have been replaced by robots, and if teenagers, after graduating from high school, are given permanent unemployed status rather than jobs. This is the predicament of eight teenagers who are relegated to a Designated Area. As they investigate their area, they discover not only the harsh realities of perpetual unemployment but also the mysterious something referred to as "The Game." When they receive an invitation to participate in the game, they experience lifelike computer simulations that place them in unfamiliar settings and give them challenges in which they must work together. The group discovers that each has unique capabilities.

Hughes provides the ultimate answer to unemployment and overcrowding when the members of the group find themselves on a distant planet and realize that they will not be going back to Earth. In a survival story, the members of the group must use the training that they gained during the simulation sessions and their unique skills to work together and to survive. As in her other science fiction books, Hughes considers the consequences of projected contemporary issues and provides at least a glimmer of hope for the future.

Madeleine L'Engle.   Do we all need each other? Is every atom in the universe dependent on every other? Questions like these confront Madeleine L'Engle's characters as they travel the cosmos, face the problem of being different, fight to overcome evil, understand the need for all things to mature, and discover the power of love.

It is interesting to note L'Engle's thoughts about herself as she wrote *A Wrinkle in Time*:

I was trying to discover a theology by which I could live, because I had learned that I cannot live in a universe where there's no hope of anything, no hope of there being somebody to whom I could say, "Help!" (p. 254)

In *A Wrinkle in Time,* L'Engle creates characters who are different from the people around them but have high intelligence and strong bonds of love and loyalty to one another. Meg Murry and her brother, Charles Wallace, are the children of eminent scientists. Meg worries about the way the people in their town make fun of her brother as backward and strange. Her father consoles her by telling her that Charles Wallace is doing things in his own way and time. In fact, he has very special powers: He can probe the minds of his mother and sister, and he is extremely bright.

L'Engle's development of the characters provides a realistic foundation for the science fiction fantasy that follows. The children discover that their scientist father is fighting the "dark thing"—a thing so evil that it could overshadow a planet, block out the stars, and create fear beyond the possibility of comfort. The children travel in the fifth dimension to a far-distant planet, where their father has been imprisoned by the evil power of "It." L'Engle states that this villain is a naked brain because "the brain tends to be vicious when it's not informed by the heart" (Wintle & Fisher, 1974, p. 254). The heart proves more powerful than the evil It in this story: Meg's ability to love deeply saves her father and Charles.

The battle against evil continues in *A Wind in the Door,* in which Charles appears to be dying. In *A Swiftly Tilting Planet,* readers discover the climactic purpose of Charles's special abilities. L'Engle creates a realistic foundation for the science fiction when 15-year-old Charles and his father construct a model of a tesseract, a square squared and then squared again, which is considered the dimension of time. Because Charles and his father can construct the tesseract, readers feel that the story must be true.

Another credible character adds realism to the story: The president of the United States asks for help. Elements of traditional fantasy enter this science fiction story in the form of an ancient rune designed to call elements of light and hold back evil and a unicorn that aids Charles in a perilous journey. In all of her books, L'Engle emphasizes the mystery and beauty of the cosmos and the necessity of maintaining a natural balance in the order of the universe.

Anne McCaffrey. In Anne McCaffrey's *Dragonsong,* Pern is the third planet of Rukbat, a golden G-type star in the Sagittarian sector. When a wildly erratic, bright red star approaches Pern, spore life, which proliferates at an incredible rate on the red star's surface, spins into space and falls in thin threads toward Pern's hospitable earth. The spore life is not hospitable to life on Pern, however. In order to counteract this menace, the colonists enlist a life form indigenous to the planet. These creatures, called dragons, have two remarkable characteristics: (1) They can travel instantly from place to place by teleportation, and (2) they can emit flaming gas when they chew phosphine-bearing rock. When guided by dragonriders, they can destroy the spore before it reaches the planet.

In this setting, a young girl fights for her dream to become a harpist. Because her father believes that such a desire is disgraceful for a female and forbids her to play her music, Menolly runs away and makes friends with the dragons. After a series of adventures in both *Dragonsong* and *Dragonsinger,* Menolly learns that she need no longer hide her skill or fear her ambitions:

> The last vestige of anxiety lifted from Menolly's mind. As a journeyman in blue, she had rank and status enough to fear no one and nothing. No need to run or hide. She'd a place to fill and a craft that was unique to her. She'd come a long, long way in a sevenday. (*Dragonsinger,* p. 264)

Nancy Farmer. The year is 2194; the location is Harare, Zimbabwe. By analyzing Nancy Farmer's *The Ear, the Eye and the Arm,* a 1995 Newbery Honor book, you will discover several of the themes frequently developed in science fiction: Toxic contamination can change lives, the world of the future may be influenced by technology, and some members of the society search for their traditional heritage. The three main characters have unique characteristics that make them ideal detectives: Arm has a long snaky arm that can outreach all other arms, Ear has extremely sensitive hearing, and Eye has excellent vision. These detectives use their unique abilities to search for the three kidnapped children of the general.

In addition to unusual characters, the text includes both technology and mythology. For example, an automatic doberman guards the mansion, robot gardeners clip the grass, and a programmed pantry prepares the food. The author also uses ancient customs and references to mythology to create a credible history for the country. As in all good science fiction, the author provides detailed descriptions of her futuristic environment.

In *The House of the Scorpion,* a National Book Award winner and a 2003 Newbery Honor book, Farmer again develops a science fiction text based on hypothesized scientific advancements and issues such as human cloning, drugs, and illegal immigration between Mexico and the United States. As in her other books, Farmer creates strong themes such as "It is important to have someone who believes in you," "Power is a drug and people crave power," and "There are moral consequences in life."

John Christopher. The future world that John Christopher envisions in *The White Mountains* is quite different from the world hoped for by people today. In Christopher's future, people have lost free will, and machines called Tripods have taken over. These machines maintain control through a capping ceremony that places a steel plate on the skull, making the wearer docile and obedient. Fourteen-year-old Will Parker, who is angered by the prospect of an inescapable voice inside his head, discovers that a colony of free people lives in the White Mountains, which are far to the south. Will escapes with two other young people, but the Tripods follow them. Will discovers that freedom and hope are the most important luxuries in life.

In *The City of Gold and Lead* and *The Pool of Fire*, the free humans plan battle against the Tripods and then defeat them. Yet quarreling factions defeat Will's attempts to plan for new unity among the victorious humans. Christopher's stories are exciting, but they are also sober reminders of what can happen if humanity allows itself to lose free will.

Modern Fantasy and Science Fiction for Young Adults

Many of the modern fantasies discussed in this chapter under "Mythical Quests and Conflicts" are also enjoyed by young adults (ages 13–18). These stories, with their connections to legends and myths, epic battles between good and evil, and opportunities for young protagonists to make self discoveries, appeal to young adults. Authors such as Philip Pullman, Christopher Paolini, Nancy Farmer, Kevin Crossley-Holland, J. R. R. Tolkien, Lloyd Alexander, Ursula K. Le Guin, Alan Garner, Susan Cooper, J. K. Rowling, and Cornelia Funke are on recommended lists for both children and young adults.

Readers of Alison Croggon's *The Naming* will discover several techniques that the author uses to suspend disbelief. For example, she includes "A Brief History of Edil-Amarandh" in which she states, "The difficulties of dating the extraordinary civilization of Edil-Amarandh, or even of pinpointing its exact geographic location, are well known. Estimates vary wildly, dating its mysterious disappearance from 10,000 to 150,000 years before the beginning of the last Ice Age" (p. 471). She then expands the history by describing various ages associated with the world: "The Age of the Elements," "The Dawn Age," "The Great Silence," and "The Restoration." In addition, she provides a detailed map of Edil-Amarandh, describes the speech of the culture, and expands on the history of the bards, their society, and their culture. To develop the role of believable high fantasy, she also has well-developed characters and a strong plot. *The Naming* is "The First Book of Pellinor," an epic fantasy that has been compared with Tolkien's works.

Books such as O. R. Meling's *The Hunter's Moon* have teenage protagonists. This fantasy, which includes Irish mythology, develops as the two girls share their love for ancient fairy myths and search for the door into other worlds. This search takes them into the land of the Faeries and encounters with the King of the Faeries. Unfortunately, they discover beautiful creatures that lure humans into danger. Now Gwen must try to outwit the fairy creatures and save her Irish cousin, Findabhair. The plot includes a mix of suspense, romance, and humor that is appealing to teenagers.

Reason, the 15-year-old protagonist in Justine Larbalestier's *Magic or Madness*, experiences many of the same feelings and emotions depicted by authors of con-

Cover from THE NAMING. Copyright © 2002 Alison Croggon. Jacket illustration Copyright © 2005 Matt Mahurin. Reproduced by permission of Candlewick Press, Inc., Cambridge, MA, on behalf of Walker Books Ltd., London.

temporary fiction for young adults: She searches for answers related to her own identity and self-worth, she questions physical changes in her body, and she is attracted to members of the opposite sex. Unlike protagonists in realistic fiction, however, she discovers that she has inherited a magical ability. This magical ability leads to both danger and self-discovery. The plot is filled with person-against-person conflict as Reason faces people who want to use her magic for their own gains. Her person-against-self conflict develops as she fights the discovery that she has magic and that magic, if not used with knowledge, can be both dangerous and harmful. The title of the book reveals Reason's inner conflict and her need to develop knowledge: Magic, if not used carefully, leads to early death, or those who have magic but do not use it will go mad. The author develops the strong theme that each of us must learn to use our talents.

According to Alleen Pace Nilsen and Kenneth Donelson (2001), reading and discussing science fiction is of special interest and benefit to young adults. Science fiction encourages young adults to think seriously about societal issues, it may warn them about society's drift to a horrifying future world, and it may suggest disasters caused by ecological carelessness. It also stretches readers' imaginations and offers challenges and hope for the future.

In her author's note, Janet McNaughton expresses the theme found in many science fiction books written for older readers: "The future I've envisioned in *The Secret Under My Skin* is not the way things have to be, but it is the future I'm afraid we'll create if we don't work to change things. I firmly believe the next generation can do a better job of taking care of the earth and its people than we have until now" (p. 263). The futuristic setting in McNaughton's novel is 2368 at a time of dire environmental conditions, a time when the govenrment leads people to believe that technology is dangerous and scientists are imprisoned in concentration camps.

Ethical concerns related to futuristic technologies are the focus for Scott Westerfeld's *Uglies*. What happens in a futuristic society when honesty, justice, and free will are oppressed? This is a world in which children are taught that they are ugly until they are 16, when they have an operation that transforms them into stunningly attractive individuals. Many teenage readers will relate to Tally, the heroine, who is about to turn 16. The conflict and the detrimental characteristics of the society are depicted when Tally's friend, Shay, questions whether to follow society's rules and undergo this change. What happens when the government tries to force changes and oppresses free will?

Many of the science fiction books described in this chapter include issues that can be discussed with young adults. For example, Nancy Farmer's *The House of the Scorpion* presents issues related to human cloning, drugs, and illegal immigration. Although younger readers may read these books for their adventures, older readers can consider and even debate the consequences of the actions described in the books.

Teaching With Modern Fantasy

You can extend the magic that children gain from modern fantasy by providing varied opportunities to interact with the plots, characters, and settings of such stories. In a presentation to the National Council of Teachers of English, Marcia Baghban (2000) provides a strong reason for sharing fantasy with children: "In fantasy, readers are empowered and assured that they can succeed and overcome obstacles. Fantasy-based stories give readers hope—hope to keep on living and hope to keep on reading."

Helping Children Recognize, Understand, and Enjoy Elements in Fantasy

Fantasy is a worthy genre of literature for all children that challenges the intellect, reveals insights, stimulates the imagination, and nurtures the affective domain. However, many children have difficulty comprehending modern fantasy. Unlike realistic fiction, which mirrors a more or less real world, modern fantasy presents an altered picture. One of the first ways to help children understand and appreciate modern fantasy is to have them read several fantasy selections and encourage them to identify and discuss what makes each story modern fantasy. The following questions address the altered literary elements in the stories:

1. How has the author manipulated or altered the literary elements so that the story takes place in a world other than the real world of today?

2. What is the evidence that the setting has been altered? How was the setting altered? How does this setting differ from the real world? (The author does not need to alter all of these elements.)

3. What is the evidence that the characters are different from characters living in the real world? How are the characters altered? How do these characters differ from characters you know in the real world?

4. What is the evidence that time has been altered? How was time altered? How is this experience with time different from experiences with time in the real world?

5. How did the author suspend disbelief and encourage readers to believe in the fanciful experience?

Again, be sure to remind students that they will not find all of these altered elements in every piece of modern fantasy.

Books that vividly describe settings encourage children to visualize the settings, respond to the language, and understand why authors must select words carefully to set the stage for their books. One of the ways to help students recognize the importance of setting in fantasy is to ask them to close their eyes and to listen to a passage. As they listen, have them visualize the setting and then describe what they see.

Numerous books have vivid paragraphs that can be used for visualization and discussion. In *The Wish Giver*, Bill Brittain uses rich and colorful imagery to create a memorable story. Fantasies in picture-book format written for younger children are also excellent selections for this type of activity. For example, have children visualize and describe the settings and the personified characters in Virginia Lee Burton's *The Little House*, Munro Leaf's *The Story of Ferdinand*, and Leo Lionni's *Swimmy*. Pointing out the author's use of similes and metaphors helps students understand the story.

With detailed illustrations and simple plots, picture books can help children understand the more complex elements found in modern fantasy. Picture books can stimulate discussion, illuminate meanings, and form bridges between illusion and understanding. Chart 7.1 identifies elements in modern fantasy and selections that develop and illustrate the elements. The picture books include both modern fantasy and traditional tales. (See the Children's Literature in Chapter 6 for the traditional tales.) Have the children read and discuss the picture books in each category before they read and discuss the fantasy. After children can recognize the literary elements in picture books, they find it easier to identify similar elements in fantasy selections.

Each of the picture books in Chart 7.1 illustrates an important element in fantasy. For example, Hugh Lewin's highly illustrated *Jafta* and *Jafta's Mother* are excellent sources for figurative language. Lewin describes and illustrates Jafta's feelings by comparing them to the feelings and actions of animals in Jafta's African environment. The double-spread illustrations show both the boy and the particular animal demonstrating such actions as skipping (like a spider), stamping (like an elephant), and grumbling (like a warthog). In the modern fantasy *The Wish Giver*, Bill Brittain also uses figurative language to suggest character traits and to enhance the rural setting.

Older students can discover the mythological and legendary foundations of J. R. R Tolkien's modern fantasy by tracing the important motifs in Tolkien's *The Hobbit* back to Norse myths and legends. Have older students identify the elements and motifs in Padraic Colum's *The Children of Odin*, Kevin Crossley-Holland's *The Faber Book of Northern Legends* and *The Norse Myths*, and Michael Harrison's *The Curse of the Ring*.

In addition to identifying the important motifs in *The Children of Odin*, ask older students to identify quotes that show these elements. For example, following are a few of the quotes showing that Norse mythology includes a constant battle between good and evil: "Always there had been war between the Giants and the Gods—between the Giants who would have destroyed the world and the Gods who would have protected the race of men and would have made the world more beautiful" (p. 6), the dwarf Brock's bargain with Loki was an evil bargain and "all its evil consequences you must bear" (p. 42), and "East of Midgard there was a place more evil than any region in Jotunheim. It was Jarnid, the Iron Wood. There dwelt witches who were the most foul of all witches. The son of the most evil witch would be the wolf who would swallow up the Moon and stain the heavens and earth with blood" (p. 168).

Students also can search for references and parallels to Norse mythology in Nancy Farmer's *The Sea of Trolls*. In a review of the book, Lawrence Downes (2005) states that

CHART 7.1   Books for helping children understand modern fantasy

Elements	Picture Books	Modern Fantasy
Allegory	Holder's *Aesop's Fables* Lobel's *Fables*	Lewis's "Chronicles of Narnia"
Irony	Gage's *Cully Cully and the Bear*	Brittain's *The Wish Giver*
Figurative language	Lewin's *Jafta* and *Jafta's Mother*	Brittain's *The Wish Giver* and Dr. Dredd's *Wagon of Wonders*
Folklore elements 　Power in tangible objects	Aylesworth's *The Full Belly Bowl*	Crossley-Holland's *Arthur: 　The Seeing Stone*
A quest	Marshak's *The Month-Brothers* Severo's *The Good-Hearted Youngest 　Brother* Hodges's *Saint George and the Dragon*	Lunn's *The Root Cellar* Funke's *Dragon Rider* McKinley's *The Hero and the Crown*
Magical powers	Grimms's *The Devil With the Three 　Golden Hairs*	McKinley's *The Blue Sword* Pullman's *I Was a Rat!*
Transformations	Andersen's *The Wild Swans* Williams's *The Velveteen Rabbit*	Cooper's *Seaward*
Punishment for misused ability	Van Allsburg's *The Wreck of the Zephyr*	Larbalestier's *Magic or Madness*

"*The Sea of Trolls* blends ancient history and Norse epics with recognizable bits of 'Star Wars' and 'The Lord of the Rings,' which only makes sense, since both of those 20th century sagas owe a conspicuous debt to the mythology of northern Europe" (p. 15). Older students will find Farmer's three pages of sources useful when investigating the Norse connections.

Students can make connections among the themes, plots, or characterizations in two examples of modern fantasy when reading Cornelia Funke's *Inkheart* and *Inkspell*. Each of Funke's chapters is introduced with a quote from another fantasy; students can read the quote and the book from which it is taken and then decide why Funke chose that quote to introduce the chapter. What are the similarities between the two texts? How does the quote from another fantasy foreshadow the plot, characters, or theme developed in Funke's book? For example, the first chapter in *Inkheart*, "A Stranger in the Night," is introduced with a quote from L. M. Boston's *The Children of Green Knowe*. Another chapter, "Going South," is introduced with a quote from Kenneth Grahame's *The Wind in the Willows*. Why is another chapter, "Going Farther South," introduced by a quote from J. R. R. Tolkien's *The Lord of the Rings: The Fellowship of the Ring*? When a group of fifth-grade students did this activity, one student commented: "That author has read a lot of really good books. She has to remember a lot to make those connections." Isn't that the level of comprehension we also want in our students?

Interpreting Modern Fantasy by Identifying Plot Structures

Writings by Joseph Campbell such as *The Power of Myth* (1988) and *The Hero With a Thousand Faces* (1949, 1968) and research by Christopher Vogler in *The Writer's Journey: Mythic Structure for Storytellers and Screenwriters* (1992) suggest that successful authors map the journey or plot of the story by identifying and describing specific stages as the hero or heroine progresses in his or her journey and reaches the ultimate reward. We find these stages of the hero's journey in traditional literature classics such as "The Iliad of Homer," the "Myths of Greece and Rome," and Howard Pyle's *The Story of King Arthur and His Knights*.

Author Katherine Paterson (1995), winner of two Newbery Medals and two National Book Awards, also emphasizes that excellent literature follows the stages in a hero's journey. When writing about the process she uses in writing her own novels, she states, "The hero must leave home, confront fabulous dangers, and return the victor to grant boons to his fellows. Or, a wandering nobody must go out from bondage through the wilderness and by the grace of God become truly someone who can give back something of what she was given. That—incredible as it may seem—is the story of my lives" (p. 154).

These stages in a writer's journey can also be used to help students either analyze structure in literature or to write their own stories. We model this approach using Philip Pullman's *The Golden Compass* (the 1996 Carnegie Medal winner). Students should first read *The Golden Compass* and then become part of the discussion as the plot structures and stages in the hero's journey are identified and discussed.

The first stage in the hero's journey begins by placing the protagonists in the ordinary world before placing them into a new or alien experience. Authors use this technique to create a vivid contrast with the strange new world that the heroes are about to enter.

Pullman begins his story at Oxford University, where the heroine, Lyra, has lived most of her life. The author describes the Hall with pictures of scholars, the library, and the scholars' common room. We see and hear normal people, such as the Master of the college. Pullman's use of dialogue such as "You have been safe here in Jordan, my dear. I think you have been happy" helps readers understand this ordinary world. (You can discuss with students how the author has been successful in creating an ordinary world.)

Vogler's second stage in plot development is the call to adventure, in which the hero is presented with a problem, challenge, or adventure to undertake. Once presented with a call to adventure, the hero can no longer remain indefinitely in the comfort of the ordinary world. Pullman's call to adventure occurs rapidly when the heroine hides in the Oxford Professor's Meeting Room and learns about a problem that could change the nature of the world, especially the easy life she has led at Oxford. The author uses a technique in which Lyra summarizes her discoveries over the previous few weeks and she realizes that she must try to rescue her friends.

The third stage is the refusal of the call, during which experience the protagonist shows fear or expresses reluctance, especially toward facing the unknown. Pullman uses techniques such as avoidance and excuses as his heroine tries to convince herself that she does not want to leave the safety of Oxford University and proceed to the far North and into the unknown.

The fourth stage in plot structure occurs when the protagonist meets the mentor, the wise old man or woman, the Merlin-like character, who assists the hero or heroine. Pullman uses a plot technique in which the Master of Jordan College presents Lyra with an object of power: an alethiometer that tells the truth and gives advice. Pullman also develops a spirit soul in animal form that helps the heroine find her way and gives her advice.

Crossing the first threshold is the fifth stage, in which the hero or heroine commits to the adventure, decides to face the challenge, and fully enters the special world. This plotting occurs when Pullman allows Lyra to discover that Lord Asriel is being held by Armored Beasts and the Oblation Board. Now she knows that she must run away to try to rescue him. The author presents this crossing of the threshold when he states, "Now that Lyra had a task in mind, she felt much better" (p. 110).

Tests, allies, and enemies occur throughout the sixth stage, in which the protagonist encounters new challenges, faces new tests, and makes allies and enemies. These tests allow the author to develop the character of the protagonist and explore the depth of the antagonists that are working against the character. Pullman contrasts the roles of good and bad spirits as the heroine faces various tests along the way.

During the seventh stage, the protagonist approaches the innermost cave, in which he or she comes to the edge of a dangerous place where the object of the quest is hidden. Pullman uses foreshadowing and prophesying in dialogue to reveal the possible dangers: "The witches have spoken of a child such as this, who has a great destiny that can only be fulfilled elsewhere—not in this world, but far beyond. Without this child, we shall all die. . . . But she must fulfill her destiny in ignorance of what she is doing, because only in her ignorance can we be saved" (p. 176).

The supreme ordeal, or eighth stage, occurs when the protagonist faces the greatest fear, the most harrowing moments. This may be a life-or-death moment in which the character or the character's goals are in jeopardy. Pullman uses the encounter between Lyra and Mrs. Coulter, the ultimate evil, to develop the supreme ordeal in which Lyra plans to save the children who are under Mrs. Coulter's power.

The reward occurs during the ninth stage, in which the protagonist takes possession of the treasure or the object of the quest that he or she has come to seek. Pullman uses a device in which Lyra and the children escape as Lyra tries to rescue her father and give him the powerful alethiometer. When she rescues her father, she discovers the meaning of the dust that makes the alethiometer work and also why her enemies are trying to control the dust.

The road back, the tenth stage, deals with the consequences of confronting the dark forces of the supreme ordeal. The character is frequently pursued by the vengeful forces disturbed by seizing the reward. Pullman uses a technique in which the heroine deals with the forces of evil, and the author is now able to reveal the magnitude of this evil. Because this is the first book in a three-volume series, Pullman allows the heroine to confront the dark forces and her own inability to accomplish the total quest through inner thoughts such as "Oh, the bitter anguish! She had thought she was saving Robert, and all the time she'd been diligently working to betray him. Lyra shook and sobbed in a frenzy of emotion. It couldn't be true" (p. 380).

The eleventh stage is the resurrection, in which the hero or heroine is purified, cleansed, or reborn before returning to the ordinary world. It usually occurs when the protagonist is transformed by the experience and returns to the real world with new insights. Pullman allows his heroine to realize that she is not alone in her quest to rid

the world of the terrible evils. Her main realization is that she is not alone. The author uses this resurrection and purification to allow her to continue, with added strength on her journey for the ultimate quest. Lyra's actions reveal this new strength: "She turned away. Behind them lay pain and death and fear; ahead of them lay doubt, and danger, and fathomless mysteries. But they were not alone. So Lyra and her daemon turned away from the world they were born in, and looked toward the sun, and walked into the sky" (p. 399).

The final stage is the return, in which the protagonist journeys back to the ordinary world with some elixir, treasure, or lesson from the special world. Pullman develops the continuation of the plot as Lyra realizes that she has strength and can search for answers. It is interesting that the plot structures found in Pullman's high fantasy parallel those identified by both Campbell and Vogler.

Many high fantasy books can be used for a similar activity. Both Lois Lowry's *The Giver* and Megan Whalen Turner's *The Thief* follow similar plot structures. Although these high fantasy selections have very different contents, they each include stages in plot structures that are similar to those described by Campbell and Vogler. You can ask students to compare the various books and to consider why they believe *The Golden Compass*, *The Giver*, and *The Thief* conclude with strong themes that reveal the importance of being responsible for one's own decisions and the negative situations that are possible when society tries to control people's lives.

Involving Children With Science Fiction

Science fiction stories have inspired children to become scientists and writers. Scientist Carl Sagan (1980), for example, credited the science fiction stories of H. G. Wells with stimulating his boyhood dreams of flying to the moon and Mars and with eventually leading him to become an astronomer. Robert Goddard, the inventor of modern rocketry, read *War of the Worlds*, by Wells. Stories about the space traveler Buck Rogers influenced George Lucas, the creator of the *Star Wars* movies. Science fiction provides enjoyment, but it can also stimulate interaction between science fiction and science or social studies.

Interdisciplinary Studies: Interaction Between Social Studies and Science Fiction

Science fiction relates not only to scientific principles and technology but also to the possible impacts of technological changes, such as mechanization, space travel, and life on other planets, on people and societies. Using science fiction in social studies classrooms allows students to understand and discuss broad themes such as the nature of government, the merits of different types of social organization, and cultural differences. Science fiction can stim-

CHART 7.2 Issues and books to motivate children to consider different viewpoints

Issue: *People who differ from those around them are often misunderstood, feared, and even hated. This treatment is inconsistent with the prevalent belief that fellowship and love are essential if society is to survive. How should people deal with those who are different? What could happen if fellowship and love are not emphasized by society?*

Science Fiction to Share With Children

1 Lowry, Lois. *The Giver.* This world of the future has solved many problems but the inhabitants appear to be devoid of conscience.
2 L'Engle, Madeleine. *A Wrinkle in Time.* People fear and whisper about Charles Wallace because he is different from the other children in the town: He can communicate without speaking.

Issue: *What could happen if people do not strive to retain freedom of choice?*

Science Fiction to Share With Children

1 Christopher, John. *The White Mountains.* People in the 21st century are controlled by machines called Tripods. When human members of the society reach the age of 14, steel plates are inserted into the skulls so that they can be controlled by the state.
2 Christopher, John. *The City of Gold and Lead.* Will tries to discover the secrets of the Tripod culture by spying inside the major Tripod city.
3 Christopher, John. *The Pool of Fire.* People try to set up a new government after defeating the Tripods; dissident groups, however, cannot agree on a unified approach.

ulate debate that is unhindered by children's stereotypes. It also encourages children to acquire a sense of the relationship between cause and effect, and in so doing, children can begin to grasp the sweep of history that is important to any investigation of social studies.

Many science fiction books lend themselves to debates on issues related to society and social studies. Classroom teachers have successfully used the issues and books in Chart 7.2 to motivate children to consider different viewpoints during social studies classes.

Because science fiction stories often describe futuristic cities on earth or on other inhabited planets, they can inspire children to create their own model cities. Have children consider what a city of the future would look like and how it would function if they could build it any way that they wished.

For one such project, sixth graders investigated energy-efficient buildings, transportation systems, sanitation systems, and suburban/urban growth before they began to build. They chose high-rise office and apartment buildings for the efficient use of urban space. For energy efficiency and beauty, their suburban homes were partially or totally below ground and had solar collectors. Shopping centers used below- and above-ground space, and they utilized light shafts to bring in light for plants and people. The children's transportation included clean, electric mass transit; computerized road systems for private cars to ensure safe, steady traffic; and moving sidewalks. Their sanitation system used a three-phase treatment process that produced drinkable water, and their power plant incinerated garbage to provide recycled power. The children planned museums and recreational facilities, including parks, trees, and an arboretum. They considered the issues

of controlling growth, providing an ideal number of people for their city, and satisfying their city's future energy needs.

Unit Plan: Using One Book of Modern Fantasy

Teachers and librarians can develop numerous enjoyable activities around one book of modern fantasy. Madeleine L'Engle's *A Wrinkle in Time,* for example, is a popular science fiction book with a plot, characters, settings, and themes that can stimulate discussion, artwork, and creative dramatization. Many other outstanding books also can serve as bases for such activities. Therefore, you may wish to use the suggestions related to L'Engle's book as guidelines for activities in connection with other books.

Oral Discussion

Some of the suggestions for discussion of L'Engle's text involve questions that require children to consider information presented at different points in the text and then to integrate this information. Leading a discussion, interject appropriate text passages as the children consider their answers. Listen to the children's responses and, if appropriate, ask divergent questions, which encourage more than one "correct" answer. Let the children verbalize different interpretations to the story. Encourage them to consider their own experiences and reactions and thus to interact with the text.

Your discussion of L'Engle's text can focus on plot, characterization, setting, theme, and style, too. The following questions and suggestions are listed in the order of the material in the book (which is indicated by page or chapter). If you wish to focus on plot, characterization, setting, theme, or style at one time, group the following suggestions accordingly.

1. *Characterization.* What did Meg's father mean when he told Meg not to worry about Charles Wallace because "he does things in his own way and in his own time"? Was her father right? What exceptional behavior does Charles Wallace display? Why is Charles Wallace considered strange by the villagers? Why doesn't he want the people in the village to know his real capabilities? (Chapter 2)

2. *Plot.* A tesseract is mentioned in several places in the book. Present ideas about what students think is meant by a tesseract. For example, Mrs. Whatsit informs Mrs. Murry that there is such a thing as a tesseract (p. 21). Mrs. Murry tells the children that she and their father used to have a joke about a thing called a tesseract (p. 23). The term *tessering* is described as traveling in the fifth dimension—going beyond the fourth dimension. The five dimensions are described as first, a line; second, a flat square; third, a cube; fourth, time; and fifth, the square of time, a tesseract in which people can travel through space without going the long way around (p. 76).

3. *Style: Emotional response to language.* Throughout the book, L'Engle makes associations between smells and emotions. Discuss some of these associations: Mrs. Whatsit's statement that she found Charles Wallace's house by the smell; and then her reaction in which she describes how lovely and warm the house is inside (p. 17); or the delicate fragrance that Meg smells when the gentle beast with tentacles relieves her of her pain (p. 175). Express your associations between smells and emotions.

4. *Theme.* Mrs. Who tells Meg that if she wants to help her father, she will need to stake her life on the truth. Mrs. Whatsit agrees, and tells the children that their father is staking his life on the truth. What do Mrs. Who and Mrs. Whatsit mean by their remarks (p. 92)? How does Mrs. Whatsit stake her life in the battle against evil (p. 92)?

5. *Characterization, theme.* Throughout the book, L'Engle develops descriptions and associations around "It." Discuss these associations and meanings:

   p. 72   It is described as a dark thing that blotted out the stars, brought a chill of fear, and is the evil that their father is fighting.

   p. 88   It is described as evil; It is the powers of darkness. It is being fought against throughout the universe. The great people of the earth who have fought against It include Jesus, Leonardo da Vinci, Michelangelo, Madame Curie, Albert Einstein, and Albert Schweitzer. Discuss how these people fought against darkness, and identify other people who fought or are fighting against darkness.

   p. 108   It makes its home in Camazotz, the most oriented city on the planet, the location of the Central Intelligence Center.

   p. 118   The man is frightened about the prospect of being sent to It for reprocessing.

   p. 141   It sometimes calls itself "The Happiest Sadist."

   p. 158   It is a huge brain.

   p. 170   Meg feels iciness because she has gone through the dark thing.

6. *Characterization, plot.* Mrs. Whatsit gives each child a talisman to strengthen the child's greatest ability: For Calvin, it is the ability to communicate with all kinds of people; for Meg, it is her faults; and for Charles Wallace, it is the resilience of his childhood (p. 100). How do the children use these abilities throughout the story in their fight against It and in their endeavors to free Mr. Murry? Which ability is most important? Why?

7. *Characterization, theme, setting.* Why did L'Engle introduce Camazotz by showing the children skipping and bouncing in rhythm, identical houses, and women who opened their doors simultaneously (p. 103)? Why is the woman so frightened about an Aberration? What eventually happened to the Aberration? What is the significance of these actions?

8. *Characterization, theme.* Compare the people living in Camazotz with Meg, Charles Wallace, and Calvin. How do you account for these differences (p. 118)? Could the people living in a city on earth become like the people in Camazotz? Why or why not? Why does the man at Central Intelligence Center tell the children that life will be easier for them if they don't fight It? What would happen if everyone took the man's suggestion (p. 121)? What are the consequences of allowing someone to accept all the pain, responsibility, and burdens of thought and decision? Would this be good or bad? Give a reason for your answer.

9. *Plot.* What is Meg's reason for saying the periodic table of elements when she is standing before It (p. 161)?

10. *Characterization, plot, theme.* What characteristics does Meg have that make her the only one who is able to go back to Camazotz and try to save Charles Wallace from the power of It (p. 195)? What is the only weapon that Meg has that It does not possess (p. 203)? How does Meg use this weapon to free

Charles Wallace? Do any people ever use this weapon? Has anyone here ever used this weapon? Is it a weapon for good or for bad?

ARTWORK

Art activities accompanying *A Wrinkle in Time* can stimulate children's interpretations of setting and characters. Ideally, children can demonstrate their divergent thinking as they interpret the author's descriptions. Following are several suggestions for art interpretations:

1. *Characterization.* Mrs. Whatsit goes through several transformations in the course of the book. Encourage your students to illustrate these transformations. Suggestions include Mrs. Whatsit's appearance as a plump, tramplike character in her blue-and-green paisley scarf, red-and-yellow flowered print, red-and-black bandanna, sparse grayish hair, rough overcoat, shocking-pink stole, and black rubber boots (pp. 16–17). Readers then see her transformed from this comical character into a beautiful winged creature with "wings made of rainbows, of light upon water, of poetry" (p. 64). Readers also discover that Mrs. Whatsit had been a star that gave her life in the battle against It (p. 92).

2. *Setting.* The medium is able to show the children visions through her globe. Ask your students to pretend to be sitting before a magical globe and to draw either the series of visions that the children see or the visions that people would like to see if they could ask the globe to show them anything.

3. *Setting.* Meg, Mr. Murry, and Calvin travel to a planet inhabited by creatures with four arms and five tentacles attached to each hand. The planet also has a different appearance from earth or Uriel. Ask your students to create a shadowbox showing the inhabitants and their planet.

CREATIVE DRAMATIZATION

Creative drama allows children to interact with the characters in a story, interpret aspects of plot, and express their reactions to the author's style. Following are several suggestions for creative dramatizations:

1. *Characterization.* Have your students role-play Mrs. Whatsit's first visit to Charles Wallace's home and Meg's and Mrs. Murry's reactions to her.

2. *Setting, style.* Use chapter 4 to create a Reader's Theater presentation for upper-elementary classes. Have your students accompany their oral readings with music that depicts the mood as Meg describes the light disappearing (p. 56); the sensations of moving with the earth (p. 58); leaving the silver glint of autumn behind and arriving in a golden field filled with light, multicolored flowers, singing birds, and an air of peace and joy (pp. 59–61); the transformation of Mrs. Whatsit into a beautiful winged creature with a voice as warm as a woodwind, with the clarity of a trumpet, and the mystery of an English horn; and ascending into the atmosphere to observe the moon and then seeing the dark, ominous shadow that brought a chill of fear—the dark thing that their father was fighting.

3. *Style.* Have your students pantomime the passages on pages 56 and 57, when Meg experiences the black thing, complete with darkness, the feeling of her body's being gone, legs and arms tingling, traveling through space, and reuniting with Charles and Calvin on Uriel.

4. *Theme.* Have your students debate the argument between Meg and It, talking through Charles Wallace, found on page 160. Have them consider the question, and encourage one group to take It's view—*like* and *equal* are the same thing; people will be happy if they are alike—while another group argues Meg's point—*like* and *equal* are different things; people cannot be happy if they are the same.

5. *Characterization, plot extension.* Have your students pretend that the story continues and role-play the scene in the kitchen after Mr. Murry, Charles Wallace, Meg, and Calvin return home. What would they say to Mrs. Murry and the two boys? What would Mrs. Murry and the boys say to them?

Many science fiction books encourage creative thinking and imagination. If science fiction can inspire children as it did Carl Sagan, then it can open new universes for other children.

Analytical Reading of Nancy Farmer's *The House of the Scorpion*

The following series of lessons applies Adler and Van Doren's (1972) stages in analytical reading to Nancy Farmer's *The House of the Scorpion*, a 2003 Newbery Honor Book and 2002 National Book Award winner. (Teachers and librarians indicate that *The House of the Scorpion* is of considerable interest to middle school students.) This approach can be used with more complex books designed for middle- and upper-elementary grades and middle school. The activity, developed and used with middle school students (Norton, 2005), provides excellent guidelines for teachers when they are leading critical discussions with their students. Use these stages of analytical reading to discuss, analyze, and criticize the book. (The responses shown illustrate the types of discussion you may develop.)

1. *Identify and discuss the kind of literature* The House of the Scorpion *is and its subject matter.* This book is science fiction. Writers of science fiction develop

plots around hypothesized scientific advancements and technology. To develop believable stories, authors must provide detailed descriptions of the technology, develop characters who believe in the technology, and create worlds where science interacts with society. We must decide whether Farmer has developed a credible science fiction world.

2. *Briefly describe the book.* Farmer's book portrays a hypothetical land between Mexico and the United States. The science fiction characteristics include cloning to create human replacement parts, the development of "eejits," who work as slave laborers, and the identification of social conflicts that need to be resolved. Matt, a young boy, is a clone who tries to overcome the conflicts resulting from greed, slave labor, and his own treatment by society because he is a clone.

3. *List the major parts of the book in order.* We can use major incidents in the development of plot and conflict to identify and outline the order of events. Such an outline might include the following parts:

   p. 4   There is a foreshadowing of the types of conflict in the book.

   p. 11   Celia's belief reflects danger.

   p. 60   Matt is so frightened when he interacts with people that he cannot talk.

   p. 122 Matt discovers a clone whose brain has been altered, and he worries he will also be altered.

   p. 127 The author describes Matt's discoveries through his use of the secret passage.

   p. 138 Tam Lin, the man who cares for Matt, treats him as an equal, causing Matt to change his beliefs about himself.

   p. 149 Tam Lin leaves a chest at the oasis for Matt. The contents of the chest foreshadow the possible trouble to come.

   p. 150 A book in the chest gives Matt needed information about the history of the country and the drug traffic.

   p. 246 Matt escapes and begins his quest to find his friend.

   p. 263 Matt is captured and forced into labor.

   p. 368 After many frightening experiences, Matt goes back to El Patron's estate and discovers he is now the new El Patron.

   p. 380 Matt realizes that with help, he can break down the empire of opium and free the slave laborers.

4. *Define the problem.* As seen from the outline of the conflict and the plot, the author has described problems associated with cloning to replace human parts, controlling slave labor through inserts in the brain, illegal immigration, and the drug trade.

5. *Identify and interpret key words.* Some of the words students could identify and interpret include *clones, eejits, illegal immigrants,* and *slave labor.*

6. *Identify and discuss the most important sentences in the text.*

   p. 26   Sentences that identify society's attitudes toward clones.

   p. 145 Sentences describing how people who crossed the borders are turned into eejits.

   p. 147 Sentences that describe the before-and-after operation that allows people to become eejits.

   p. 191 Find the sentences that foreshadow the plot and conflict.

7. *Know the author's arguments by finding them and constructing them out of a sequence of sentences.* One of the best ways to discover Farmer's arguments is to identify and discuss the themes in the book. Many of these themes are developed through the beliefs and values expressed by Tam Lin, a close friend and protector of Matt. For example (these are all paraphrases):

   p. 70   When you are small, you can choose which way to grow. If you're kind and decent, you grow into a kind and decent person, but if you are greedy and evil, you will grow up to be like El Patron.

   p. 139 Matt discovers he needs someone to believe in him. This theme is later displayed through Tam Lin's, Celia's, and Maria's actions and their trust in Matt.

8. *Determine which of the problems the author has solved.* The problems in this book cover major issues in society. Students can decide which of the problems may be solved after Matt takes over as El Patron. Will he be able to solve such problems as those related to slave labor, cloning for use of human parts, the use of illegal immigrants, and even the hoarding of wealth?

9–11. *Criticism.* Before students develop critical judgments of this book, they should conduct their own research into questions like these:

Did Farmer develop a believable description of cloning and the societal issues related to cloning for the use of human part replacements?

Is slave labor a problem along the border? What happens to illegal immigrants and the people who try to influence and control them?

Ask the students to review the author's themes. Why do they or do they not believe the author supported those themes?

Suggested Activities

For more suggested activities for understanding modern fantasy, visit the Companion Website at
CW www.prenhall.com/norton

- Discuss C. S. Lewis's "The Chronicles of Narnia" with another adult who has read the books and with a child who has read them. What are the differences, if any, in the interpretations of the two people? Compare reactions to the book *The Lion, the Witch, and the Wardrobe* with responses to the movie.

- After reading J. R. R. Tolkien's *The Hobbit* or *The Lord of the Rings*, identify common elements and symbols in Tolkien's work and mythology. Consider the use of fate, subterranean descents, denial of death, mortals and immortals, supernatural beings, and power granted to objects.

- Authors who write believably about articulate animals balance reality and fantasy by allowing the animals to talk but still retain some animal characteristics. Choose an animal character such as Beatrix Potter's Peter Rabbit, Little Georgie from Robert Lawson's *Rabbit Hill*, or Mole from Kenneth Grahame's *The Wind in the Willows*. What human characteristics can you identify? What animal characteristics can you identify? Has the author developed a credible character? Why or why not?

- Listen to an audio book of one of the modern fantasies read by an award-winning actor, such as Jim Dale (various "Harry Potter" books), Michael York (*The Lion, the Witch and the Wardrobe*), Gerald Doyle (*Eragon*), and London stage actors (*The Golden Compass*). How do the actors bring the stories to life? Compare your own reading experience with the listening experience.

Children's Literature

For full descriptions, including plot summaries and award winner notations, of these and other titles for teaching children with modern fantasy, please visit the CD-ROM that accompanies this book.

Aiken, Joan. *The Wolves of Willoughby Chase*. Illustrated by Pat Marriott. Doubleday, 1963 (I:7–10 R:5).

Alexander, Lloyd. *The Arkadians*. Dutton, 1995 (I:10+ R:6).

_____. *The Beggar Queen*. Dutton, 1984 (I:10+ R:7).

_____. *The Black Cauldron*. Holt, Rinehart & Winston, 1965 (I:10+ R:7).

_____. *The Book of Three*. Holt, Rinehart & Winston. 1964 (I:10+ R:5).

_____. *The Castle of Llyr*. Holt, Rinehart & Winston, 1966 (I:10+ R:5).

_____. *Gypsy Rizka*. Dutton, 1999 (I:10+ R:5).

_____. *The High King*. Holt, Rinehart & Winston, 1968 (I:10+ R:5).

_____. *The Iron Ring*. Dutton, 1997 (I:10+ R:6).

_____. *The Remarkable Journey of Prince Jen*. Dutton, 1991 (I:10+ R:6).

_____. *Taran Wanderer*. Holt, Rinehart & Winston, 1967 (I:10+ R:5).

_____. *Westmark*. Dutton, 1981 (I:10+ R:7).

Almond, David. *Skellig*. Delacorte, 1999 (I:10+ R:6).

Andersen, Hans Christian. *The Emperor's New Clothes*. Retold by Anne Rockwell. Translated by H. W. Dulcken. Illustrated by Anne Rockwell. Harper & Row, 1982 (I:6–9 R:6).

_____. *The Emperor's New Clothes*. Retold by Riki Levison. Illustrated by Robert Byrd. Dutton. 1991 (I:6–9 R:6).

_____. *The Emperor's New Clothes*. Illustrated by Dorothee Duntz. North-South, 1986 (I:6–9 R:6).

_____. *The Emperor's New Clothes*. Illustrated by S. T. Mendelson. Stewart, Tabori & Chang, 1992 (I:6–9 R:6).

_____. *The Emperor's New Clothes*. Illustrated by Janet Stevens. Holiday House, 1985 (I:6–9 R:6).

_____. *Hans Andersen: His Classic Fairy Tales*. Translated by Erik Haugaard. Illustrated by Michael Foreman. Doubleday, 1974 (I:7–10 R:7).

_____. *Hans Christian Andersen Fairy Tales*. Translated by Tiina Nunnally. Viking, 2004 (I:10–YA R:7).

_____. *The Little Match Girl*. Adapted and illustrated by Jerry Pinkney. Penguin, 1999 (I:6–8).

_____. *The Little Mermaid*. Illustrated by Lisbeth Zwerger. Translated by Anthea Bell. Minedition, 2004 (I:8–10 R:5).

_____. *Little Mermaids and Ugly Ducklings: Favorite Fairy Tales by Hans Christian Andersen*. Illustrated by Gennady Spirin. Chronicle, 2001 (I:8–10 R:6).

_____. *Michael Hague's Favorite Hans Christian Andersen Fairy Tales*. Illustrated by Michael Hague. Holt, Rinehart & Winston, 1981 (I:5–8 R:7).

_____. *The Nightingale*. Translated by Eva Le Gallienne. Illustrated by Nancy Ekholm Burkert. Harper & Row, 1965 (I:all R:7).

_____. *The Nightingale*. Retold by Stephen Mitchell. Illustrated by Bagram Ibatoulline. Candlewick, 2002 (I:7–9).

_____. *The Nightingale*. Retold and illustrated by Jerry Pinkney. Dial, 2002 (I:6–9 R:5).

_____. *The Snow Queen*. Retold by Amy Ehrlich. Illustrated by Susan Jeffers. Dial, 1982 (I:6–9 R:6).

_____. *The Snow Queen*. Adapted by Naomi Lewis. Illustrated by Errol LeCain. Viking, 1979 (I:6–9 R:6).

_____. *The Snow Queen*. Adapted by Naomi Lewis. Illustrated by Angela Barrett. Holt, Rinehart & Winston, 1988 (I:6–9 R:6).

_____. *The Steadfast Tin Soldier*. Illustrated by Thomas DiGrazia. Prentice Hall, 1981 (I:6–8 R:6).

_____. *The Steadfast Tin Soldier*. Retold and illustrated by Rachel Isadora. Putnam, 1996 (I:6–10 R:5).

_____. *The Steadfast Tin Soldier*. Translated by Naomi Lewis. Illustrated by P. J. Lynch. Gulliver, 1992 (I:6–9 R:6).

_____. *The Steadfast Tin Soldier*. Retold by Tor Seidler. Illustrated by Fred Marcellino. HarperCollins, 1992 (I:6–9 R:6).

_____. *The Stories of Hans Christian Andersen: A New Translation From the Danish*. Edited and translated by Diana Crone Frank & Jeffrey Frank. Illustrated by Vilhelm Pedersen & Lorenz Frolich. Houghton Mifflin, 2003 (I:all).

I = Interest by age range.
R = Readability by grade level.

_____. *Tales of Hans Christian Andersen.* Edited and translated by Naomi Lewis. Illustrated by Joel Stewart, 2004 (I:9–12 R:6).

_____. *Thumbelina.* Retold by Amy Ehrlich. Illustrated by Susan Jeffers. Dial, 1979 (I:6–8 R:6).

_____. *Thumbelina.* Retold by Jane Falloon. Illustrated by Emma Chichester Clark. Simon & Schuster, 1997 (I:6–8 R:6).

_____. *Thumbelina.* Retold and illustrated by Brian Pinkney. Greenwillow, 2003 (I:5–8 R:5).

_____. *Thumbelina.* Retold and illustrated by Brad Sneed. Dial, 2004 (I:5–8 R:5).

_____. *Thumbelina.* Translated by Anthea Bell. Illustrated by Lisbeth Zwerger. North-South, 2000 (I:6–8 R:4).

_____. *The Tinderbox.* Adapted and illustrated by Barry Moser. Little, Brown, 1990 (I:4–9 R:5).

_____. *The Ugly Duckling.* Retold and illustrated by Lorinda Bryan Cauley. Harcourt Brace, 1979 (I:6–8 R:2).

_____. *The Ugly Duckling.* Adapted and illustrated by Jerry Pinkney. Morrow, 1999 (I:6–8).

_____. *The Ugly Duckling.* Translated by Anthea Bell. Illustrated by Robert Ingpen. Minedition, 2005 (I:6–8 R:4).

_____. *The Wild Swans.* Retold by Amy Ehrlich. Illustrated by Susan Jeffers. Dial, 1981 (I:7–12 R:7).

_____. *The Wild Swans.* Translated by Naomi Lewis. Illustrated by Anne Yvonne Gilbert. Barefoot, 2005 (I:6–9 R:5).

Armstrong, Alan. *Whittington.* Illustrated by S. D. Schindler. Random House, 2005 (I:7–11 R:3).

Atwater, Richard, & Florence Atwater. *Mr. Popper's Penguins.* Illustrated by Robert Lawson. Little, Brown, 1938 (I:7–11 R:7).

Aylesworth, Jim. *The Full Belly Bowl.* Illustrated by Wendy Anderson Halperin. Atheneum, 1999 (I:5–8).

Babbit, Natalie. *Tuck Everlasting.* Farrar, Straus & Giroux, 1975 (I:8–12 R:6).

Baker, Keith. *The Magic Fan.* Harcourt Brace, 1989 (I:5–8 R:4).

Barker, Clive. *Abarat: Days of Magic, Nights of War.* HarperCollins, 2004 (I:12–YA R:6).

_____. *The Thief of Always.* HarperCollins, 2002 (I:12–YA R:6).

Barrie, James. *Peter Pan.* Illustrated by Nora S. Unwin. Scribner, 1911, 1929, 1950 (I:8–10 R:6).

Barron, T. A. *The Fires of Merlin.* Putnam, 1998 (I:10+ R:6).

_____. *Heartlight.* Philomel, 1990 (I:10+ R:6).

_____. *The Lost Years of Merlin.* Putnam, 1996 (I:10+ R:6).

_____. *The Mirror of Merlin.* Putnam, 1999 (I:10+ R:6).

_____. *The Seven Songs of Merlin.* Putnam, 1997 (I:10+ R:6).

_____. *The Wings of Merlin.* Philomel, 2000 (I:10+ R:6).

Barry, Dave, & Ridley Pearson. *Peter and the Starcatchers.* Illustrated by Greg Call. Hyperion, 2004 (I:8+ R:5).

Bass, L. G. *Sign of the Qin.* Hyperion, 2004 (I:10+ R:6).

Baum, L. Frank. *The Wizard of Oz.* Illustrated by W. W. Denslow. Reilly, 1956 (I:8–11 R:6).

_____. *The Wizard of Oz.* Illustrated by Michael Hague. Holt, Rinehart & Winston, 1982 (I:8–11 R:6).

Bellairs, John. *The Spell of the Sorcerer's Skull.* Dial, 1984 (I:8–12 R:4).

Billingsley, Fanny. *The Folkkeeper.* Atheneum, 1999 (I:10+ R:5).

_____. *Well Wished.* Simon & Schuster, 1997 (I:10+ R:5).

Bond, Michael. *A Bear Called Paddington.* Illustrated by Peggy Fortnum. Houghton Mifflin, 1960 (I:6–9 R:4).

_____. *Paddington Abroad.* Illustrated by Peggy Fortnum. Houghton Mifflin, 1972 (I:6–9 R:4).

_____. *Paddington Helps Out.* Illustrated by Peggy Fortnum. Houghton Mifflin, 1961 (I:6–9 R:4).

_____. *Paddington Marches On.* Illustrated by Peggy Fortnum. Houghton Mifflin, 1965 (I:6–9 R:4).

Boston, Lucy M. *The Children of Green Knowe.* Illustrated by Peter Boston. Harcourt Brace, 1955 (I:8–12 R:6).

_____. *An Enemy at Green Knowe.* Illustrated by Peter Boston. Harcourt Brace, 1964 (I:8–12 R:6).

_____. *The River at Green Knowe.* Illustrated by Peter Boston. Harcourt Brace, 1959 (I:8–12 R:6).

_____. *A Stranger at Green Knowe.* Illustrated by Peter Boston. Harcourt Brace, 1961 (I:8–12 R:6).

_____. *The Treasure of Green Knowe.* Illustrated by Peter Boston. Harcourt Brace, 1958 (I:8–12 R:6).

Brittain, Bill. *Dr. Dredd's Wagon of Wonders.* Illustrated by Andrew Glass. Harper & Row, 1987 (I:9–12 R:6).

_____. *The Wish Giver.* Illustrated by Andrew Glass. Harper & Row, 1983 (I:8–12 R:5).

Burton, Virginia Lee. *The Little House.* Houghton Mifflin, 1942 (I:3–7 R:3).

Cameron, Eleanor. *The Wonderful Flight to the Mushroom Planet.* Illustrated by Robert Henneberger. Little, Brown, 1954 (I:8–10 R:4).

Carman, Patrick. *The Dark Hills Divide: The Land of Elyon.* Scholastic, 2005 (I:8–13 R:5).

Carroll, Lewis. *Alice in Wonderland.* Illustated by Lisbeth Zwerger. North-South, 1999 (I:9+ R:6).

_____. *Alice's Adventures in Wonderland.* Illustrated by Helen Oxenbury. Candlewick, 1999 (I:8+ R:6).

_____. *Alice's Adventures in Wonderland.* Illustrated by S. Michelle Wiggins. Ariel/Knopf, 1983 (I:8+ R:6).

_____. *Alice's Adventures in Wonderland.* Illustrated by Justin Todd. Crown, 1984 (I:8+ R:6).

_____. *Alice's Adventures in Wonderland.* Illustrated by John Tenniel. Macmillan, 1866; Knopf, 1984 (I:8+ R:6).

_____. *Alice's Adventures in Wonderland.* Illustrated by John Tenniel. Macmillan, 1865, 1963 (I:all R:6).

_____. *Alice's Adventures in Wonderland, Through the Looking Glass, and the Hunting of the Snark.* Illustrated by Sir John Tenniel. Chatto, Bodley Head & Jonathan Cape, 1982 (I:all R:6).

_____. *The Nursery "Alice."* Illustrated by John Tenniel. Macmillan, 1890, 1979 (I:6–10 R:5).

_____. *Through the Looking-Glass, and What Alice Found There.* Illustrated by John Tenniel. Macmillan, 1872; Knopf, 1984 (I:8+ R:6).

Christopher, John. *The City of Gold and Lead.* Macmillan, 1967 (I:10+ R:6).

_____. *The Pool of Fire.* Macmillan, 1968 (I:10+ R:6).

_____. *The White Mountains.* Macmillan, 1967 (I:10+ R:6).

Clark, Margaret. *A Treasury of Dragon Stories.* Kingfisher, 1997. (I:8+).

Cleary, Beverly. *The Mouse and the Motorcycle.* Illustrated by Louis Darling. Morrow, 1965 (I:7–11 R:3).

_____. *Ralph S. Mouse*. Illustrated by Paul O. Zelinsky. Morrow, 1982 (I:7–11 R:3).

_____. *Runaway Ralph*. Illustrated by Louis Darling. Morrow, 1970 (I:7–11 R:3).

Colfer, Eoin. *Artemis Fowl: The Oral Deception*. Hyperion, 2005 (I:8–10 R:5).

Collodi, Carlo. *The Adventures of Pinocchio*. Illustrated by Naiad Einsel. Macmillan, 1892, 1963 (I:7–12 R:7).

_____. *The Adventures of Pinocchio*. Retold by Neil Morris. Illustrated by Frank Baber. Rand McNally, 1982 (I:7–12 R:7).

_____. *The Adventures of Pinocchio*. Illustrated by Roberto Innocenti. Knopf, 1988 (I:4–12 R:7).

_____. *The Adventures of Pinocchio: Tale of a Puppet*. Translated by M. L. Rosenthal. Illustrated by Troy Howell. Lothrop, Lee & Shepard, 1983 (I:9+ R:7).

Colum, Padraic. *The Children of Odin: The Book of Northern Myths*. Illustrated by Willy Pogany. Collier, 1984 (I:9+ R:6).

Conly, Jane Leslie. *Racso and the Rats of NIMH*. Harper & Row, 1986 (I:8–12 R:5).

Conrad, Pam. *Stonewords: A Ghost Story*. HarperCollins, 1990 (I:10+ R:6).

_____. *Zoe Rising*. HarperCollins, 1996 (I:10+ R:6).

Cooper, Susan. *The Boggart*. Macmillan, 1993 (I:10+ R:5).

_____. *The Boggart and the Monster*. Simon & Schuster, 1997 (I:10+ R:5).

_____. *The Dark Is Rising*. Illustrated by Alan E. Cober. Atheneum, 1973 (I:10+ R:8).

_____. *Greenwitch*. Atheneum, 1974 (I:10+ R:8).

_____. *The Grey King*. Atheneum, 1975 (I:10+ R:8).

_____. *King of Shadows*. Simon & Schuster, 1999 (I:10+ R:6).

_____. *Over Sea, Under Stone*. Illustrated by Margery Gill. Harcourt Brace, 1965 (I:10+ R:8).

_____. *Seaward*. Atheneum, 1983 (I:10+ R:5).

_____. *Silver on the Tree*. Atheneum, 1977, 1980 (I:10+ R:8).

Croggon, Alison. *The Naming*. Candlewick, 2005 (I:13–YA R:7).

Crossley-Holland, Kevin. *Arthur: The Seeing Stone*. Orion, 2000 (I:8+ R:5).

_____. *At the Crossing Places* (Arthur Trilogy, Book Two). Scholastic, 2002 (I:12–YA R:7).

_____. *The Faber Book of Northern Legends*. Illustrated by Alan Howard. Faber & Faber, 1983 (I:9+ R:6).

_____. *King of the Middle March* (Arthur Trilogy, Book Three). Scholastic, 2004 (I:12–YA R:7).

_____. *The Seeing Stone* (Arthur Trilogy, Book One). Scholastic, 2001 (I:12–YA R:7).

Dahl, Roald. *James and the Giant Peach*. Illustrated by Nancy Ekholm Burkert. Knopf, 1961 (I:7–11 R:7).

DeFelice, Cynthia. *The Ghost of Fossil Glen*. Farrar, Straus & Giroux, 1998 (I:10+ R:5).

Dengler, Marianna. *The Worry Stone*. Illustrated by Sibyl Graber Gerig. Northland, 1996 (I:8+ R:5).

DiCamillo, Kate. *The Tale of Despereaux*. Illustrated by Timothy Basil Ering. Candlewick, 2003 (I:8+ R:4).

Dickinson, Peter. *Eva*. Delacorte, 1989 (I:10+ R:6).

_____. *The Lion Tamer's Daughter: And Other Stories*. Delacorte, 1997 (I:10+ R:5).

Doyle, Arthur Conan. *The Lost World*. Random House, 1959 (I:10+ R:7).

Farmer, Nancy. *The Ear, the Eye and the Arm*. Orchard, 1994 (I:12+ R:6).

_____. *The House of the Scorpion*. Atheneum, 2002 (I:10–YA R:6).

_____. *The Sea of Trolls*. Simon & Schuster, 2004 (I:10–YA R:7).

Fleischman, Paul. *Graven Images*. Illustrated by Andrew Glass. Harper & Row, 1982 (I:10+ R:6).

Fleischman, Sid. *The Midnight Horse*. Illustrated by Peter Sís. Greenwillow, 1990 (I:8–12 R:5).

Fleming, Ian. *Chitty Chitty Bang Bang*. Illustrated by John Burningham. Random House, 1964 (I:7–11 R:6).

Funke, Cornelia. *Dragon Rider*. Translated by Anthea Bell. Scholastic, 2004 (I:8+ R:5).

_____. *Inkheart*. Translated by Anthea Bell. Scholastic, 2003 (I:8+ R:5).

_____. *Inkspell*. Translated by Anthea Bell. Scholastic, 2005 (I:8+ R:5).

_____. *The Thief Lord*. Translated by Oliver Latsch. Scholastic, 2001 (I:8+ R:5).

Gage, Wilson. *Cully Cully and the Bear*. Illustrated by James Stevenson. Greenwillow, 1983 (I:3–8).

Gandolfi, Silvana. *Aldabra, or the Tortoise Who Loved Shakespeare*. Translated by Lynne Sharon Schwartz. Scholastic, 2004 (I:9–12 R:5).

Garner, Alan. *Elidor*. Walck, 1967 (I:10+ R:7).

_____. *The Owl Service*. Walck, 1968 (I:10+ R:5).

_____. *The Weirdstone of Brisingamen*. Walck, 1969 (I:10+ R:5).

Gerstein, Mordicai. *The Mountains of Tibet*. Harper & Row, 1987 (I:6–8 R:4).

Godden, Rumer. *The Dolls' House*. Illustrated by Tasha Tudor. Viking, 1947, 1962 (I:6–10 R:2).

Grahame, Kenneth. *The Reluctant Dragon*. Illustrated by Inga Moore. Candlewick, 2004 (I:5–8 R:5).

_____. *The Wind in the Willows*. Illustrated by E. H. Shepard. Scribner, 1908, 1940 (I:7–12 R:7).

Griffin, Peni R. *Switching Well*. Macmillan, 1993 (I:10+ R:6).

Hahn, Mary Downing. *Wait Till Helen Comes*. Clarion, 1986 (I:8–12 R:5).

Hale, Shannon. *The Goose Girl*. Bloomsbury, 2003 (I:12–YA R:6).

Hamiltion, Virginia. *Dustland*. Greenwillow, 1980 (I:10+ R:7).

_____. *The Gathering*. Greenwillow, 1981 (I:10+ R:7).

_____. *Justice and Her Brothers*. Greenwillow, 1978 (I:10+ R:7).

_____. *The Magical Adventures of Pretty Pearl*. Harper & Row, 1983 (I:10+ R:5).

_____. *Wee Winnie Witch's Skinny: An Original African American Scare Tale*. Illustrated by Barry Moser. Scholastic, 2004 (I:5–10 R:5).

Hogrogian, Nonny, retold and illustrated by. *The Devil With the Three Golden Hairs: A Tale From the Brothers Grimm*. Knopf, 1983 (I:6–9 R:4).

Howe, James. *The Celery Stalks at Midnight*. Illustrated by Leslie Morrill. Atheneum, 1983 (I:8–10 R:5).

Hughes, Carol. *Toots and the Upside-Down House*. Illustrated by Garrett Sheldrewnson & Anthony Stacchi. Random, 1997 (I:8+ R:5).

Hughes, Monica. *Invitation to the Game.* Simon & Schuster, 1991 (I:10+ R:7).

Hunter, Mollie. *The Mermaid Summer.* Harper, 1988 (I:10+ R:6).

Hurmence, Belinda. *A Girl Called Boy.* Houghton Mifflin. 1982 (I:10+ R:6).

Jacques, Brian. *Mariel of Redwall.* Philomel, 1991 (I:10+ R:7).

_____. *Martin the Warrior.* Illustrated by Gary Chalk. Philomel, 1994 (I:10+ R:7).

_____. *Mattimeo.* Putnam, 1990 (I:10+ R:7).

_____. *Mossflower.* Putnam, 1988 (I:10+ R:7).

_____. *Pearls of Leitra.* Philomel, 1997 (I:10+ R:7).

_____. *Redwall.* Philomel, 1986 (I:10+ R:7).

_____. *Seven Strange & Ghostly Tales.* Putnam, 1991 (I:8+ R:6).

_____. *The Legend of Luke. A Tale From Redwall.* Philomel, 2000 (I:10+ R:7).

James, Mary. *Shoebag.* Scholastic, 1990 (I:8+ R:4).

Jennings, Patrick. *Faith and the Electric Dogs.* Scholastic, 1996 (I:8–12 R:5).

Juster, Norton. *The Phantom Tollbooth.* Illustrated by Jules Feiffer. Random House, 1961 (I:9+ R:8).

Kendall, Carol. *The Gammage Cup.* Illustrated by Erik Blegvad. Harcourt Brace, 1959 (I:8–12 R:4).

Key, Alexander. *The Forgotten Door.* Westminster, 1965 (I:8–12 R:6).

Kimmel, Eric A. *Hershel and the Hanukkah Goblins.* Illustrated by Trina Schart Hyman. Holiday House, 1989 (I:all).

King-Smith, Dick. *The Golden Goose.* Illustrated by Ann Kronheimer. Knopf, 2005 (I:6–9 R:4).

_____. *Martin's Mice.* Illustrated by Jez Alborough. Crown, 1989 (I:8–12 R:6).

_____. *Pigs Might Fly.* Illustrated by Mary Rayner. Viking, 1982 (I:9–12 R:6).

Kipling, Rudyard. *The Elephant's Child.* Illustrated by Lorinda Bryan Cauley. Harcourt Brace, 1983 (I:5–7 R:7).

_____. *The Jungle Book.* Doubleday, 1894, 1964 (I:8–12 R:7).

_____. *Just So Stories.* Doubleday, 1902, 1907, 1952 (I:5–7 R:5).

_____. *Just So Stories.* Illustrated by Victor G. Ambrus. Rand McNally, 1982 (I:5–7 R:5).

Klause, Annette Curtis. *Alien Secrets.* Delacorte, 1993 (I:12+ R:6).

_____. *Silver Kiss.* Delacorte, 1990 (I:12+ R:6).

Langrish, Katherine. *Troll Fell.* HarperCollins, 2004 (I:10+ R:6).

Larbalestier, Justine. *Magic or Madness.* Penguin, 2005 (I:12–18 R:7).

Lawrence, Louise. *Dream-Weaver.* Clarion, 1996 (I:12+ R:7).

Lawson, Robert. *Ben and Me.* Little, Brown, 1939 (I:7–11 R:6).

_____. *Rabbit Hill.* Viking, 1944 (I:7–11 R:7).

Leaf, Munro. *The Story of Ferdinand.* Illustrated by Robert Lawson. Viking, 1936 (I:4–10 R:6).

Le Guin, Ursula K. *Catwings.* Illustrated by S. D. Schindler. Watts, 1988 (I:3–8 R:4).

_____. *Catwings Return.* Illustrated by S. D. Schindler. Watts, 1989 (I:3–8 R:4).

_____. *The Farthest Shore.* Illustrated by Gail Garraty. Atheneum, 1972 (I:10+ R:6).

_____. *A Ride on the Red Mare's Back.* Illustrated by Julie Downing. Orchard, 1992 (I:6–10 R:5).

_____. *Tehanu: The Last Book of Earthsea.* Atheneum, 1990 (I:10+ R:6).

_____. *A Wizard of Earthsea.* Illustrated by Ruth Robbins. Parnassus, 1968 (I:10+ R:6).

L'Engle, Madelenie. *A Swiftly Tilting Planet.* Farrar, Straus & Giroux, 1978 (I:10+ R:7).

_____. *A Wind in the Door.* Farrar, Straus & Giroux, 1973 (I:10+ R:7).

_____. *A Wrinkle in Time.* Farrar, Straus & Giroux, 1962 (I:10+ R:5).

Levine, Gail Carson. *Ella Enchanted.* HarperCollins, 1997 (I:8+ R:5).

Lewin, Hugh. *Jafta.* Illustrated by Lisa Kopper. Zimbabwe Publishing House, 1983 (I:3–8).

_____. *Jafta's Mothers.* Illustrated by Lisa Kopper. Carolrhoda, 1983 (I:3–8).

Lewis, C. S. *The Last Battle.* Illustrated by Pauline Baynes. Macmillan, 1956. (I:9+ R:7).

_____. *The Lion, the Witch and the Wardrobe.* Illustrated by Pauline Baynes. Macmillan, 1950 (I:9+ R:7).

_____. *The Magician's Nephew.* Illustrated by Pauline Baynes. Macmillan, 1955 (I:9+ R:7).

_____. *Prince Caspian, the Return to Narnia.* Illustrated by Pauline Baynes. Macmillan, 1951 (I:9+ R:7).

_____. *The Silver Chair.* Illustrated by Pauline Baynes. Macmillan, 1953 (I:9+ R:7).

_____. *The Voyage of the Dawn Treader.* Illustrated by Pauline Baynes. Macmillan, 1952 (I:9+ R:7).

Lewis, Naomi, translated by. *Proud Knight, Fair Lady: The Twelve Lais of Marie de France.* Viking/Kestrel, 1989 (I:10+ R:6).

Lindgren, Astrid. *Pippi Longstocking.* Illustrated by Louis S. Glanzman. Viking, 1950 (I:7–11 R:5).

_____. *Pippi in the South Seas.* Illustrated by Louis S. Glanzman. Viking, 1959 (I:7–11 R:5).

Lionni, Leo. *Swimmy.* Pantheon, 1963 (I:2–6 R:3).

Lowry, Lois. *Gathering Blue.* Houghton Mifflin, 2000 (I:10+ R:5).

_____. *The Giver.* Houghton Mifflin, 1993 (I:10+ R:5).

_____. *Messenger.* Houghton Mifflin, 2004 (I:10+ R:6).

Lunn, Janet. *The Root Cellar.* Scribner, 1983 (I:10+ R:4).

MacDonald, George. *At the Back of the North Wind.* Illustrated by Arthur Hughes. Dutton, 1871, 1966 (I:10+ R:6).

_____. *The Princess and the Goblin.* Illustrated by Nora S. Unwin. Macmillan, 1872, 1951 (I:10+ R:9).

Mahy, Margaret. *The Changeover.* Atheneum, 1984 (I:10 + R:7).

_____. *The Five Sisters.* Illustrated by Patricia MacCarthy. Viking, 1997 (I:7–9 R:5).

Marshak, Samuel, retold by. *The Month-Brothers: A Slavic Tale.* Translated by Thomas P. Whitney. Illustrated by Diane Stanley. Morrow, 1983 (I:6–8 R:4).

McCaffrey, Anne. *Dragonquest.* Ballantine, 1981 (I:10+ R:6).

_____. *The Dragonriders of Pern.* Ballentine, 1988 (I:10 + R:6).

_____. *Dragonsinger.* Atheneum, 1977 (I:10+ R:6).

_____. *Dragonsong.* Atheneum, 1976 (I:10+ R:6).

McGraw, Eloise. *The Moorchild.* Simon & Schuster, 1996 (I:10+ R:5).

McKinley, Robin. *The Blue Sword.* Greenwillow, 1982 (I:10+ R:7).

_____. *The Hero and the Crown.* Greenwillow, 1984 (I:10+ R:7).

_____. *Spindle's End*. Putnam, 2000 (I:10+ R:6).

McNaughton, Janet. *The Secret Under My Skin*. HarperCollins, 2005 (I:12–18 R:6).

Meling, O. R. *The Hunter's Moon*. Abrams, 2004 (I:13–18 R:6).

Mills, Lauren. *Fairy Wings*. Illustrated by Dennis Nolan. Little, Brown, 1995 (I:7–9 R:4).

Milne, A. A. *The House at Pooh Corner*. Illustrated by Ernest H. Shepard. Dutton, 1928, 1956 (I:6–10 R:3).

_____. *Winnie-the-Pooh*. Illustrated by Ernest H. Shepard. Dutton, 1926, 1954 (I:6–10 R:5).

Morris, Gerald. *The Savage Damsel and the Dwarf*. Houghton Mifflin, 2000 (I:10+ R:6).

_____. *The Squire, His Knight, and His Lady*. Houghton Mifflin, 1999 (I:10+ R:6).

_____. *The Squire's Tale*. Houghton Mifflin, 1998 (I:10+ R:6).

Myers, Tim. *Basho and the River Stones*. Illustrated by Oki S. Gab. Cavendish, 2004 (I:5–8 R:4).

Myers, Walter Dean. *The Story of Three Kingdoms*. Illustrated by Ashley Bryan. HarperCollins, 1995 (I:7+ R:5).

Napoli, Donna Jo. *Bound*. Atheneum, 2004 (I:10–YA R:6).

Nix, Garth. *Sabriel*. HarperCollins, 1996 (I:12+ R:7).

Nixon, Joan Lowery. *Whispers From the Dead*. Delacorte, 1989 (I:10+ R:6).

Norton, Mary. *Bed-Knob and Broomstick*. Illustrated by Erik Blegvad. Harcourt Brace, 1943, 1971 (I:7–11 R:6).

_____. *The Borrowers*. Illustrated by Beth and Joe Krush. Harcourt Brace, 1952, 1953 (I:7–11 R:3).

_____. *The Borrowers Afield*. Illustrated by Beth & Joe Krush. Harcourt Brace, 1955 (I:7–11 R:4).

_____. *The Borrowers Afloat*. Harcourt Brace, 1959 (I:7–11 R:4).

_____. *The Borrowers Aloft*. Harcourt Brace, 1961 (I:7–11 R:4).

_____. *The Borrowers Avenged*. Illustrated by Beth & Joe Krush. Harcourt Brace, 1982 (I:7–11 R:4).

O'Brien, Robert C. *Mrs. Frisby and the Rats of NIMH*. Illustrated by Zena Berstein. Atheneum, 1971 (I:8–12 R:4).

O'Malley, Kevin. *Captain Raptor and the Moon Mystery*. Illustrated by Patrick O'Brien. Walker, 2005 (I:5–9 R:4).

Oppel, Kenneth. *Airborn*. HarperCollins, 2004 (I:10+ R:6).

Oppenheim, Shulamith Levy. *The Hundredth Name*. Illustrated by Michael Hays. Boyd Mills, 1995 (I:4–8 R:5).

O'Shea, Pat. *The Hounds of the Morrigan*. Holiday House, 1986 (I:10+ R:6).

Paolini, Christopher. *Eldest*. Knopf, 2005 (I:10–YA R:7).

_____. *Eragon*. Knopf, 2003 (I:10–YA R:7).

Pattou, Edith. *East*. Harcourt, 2003 (I:10+ R:5).

Pearson, Kit. *Awake and Dreaming*. Viking, 1997 (I:8+ R:5).

Philbrick, Rodman. *The Last Book in the Universe*. Scholastic, 2000 (I:9–12 R:6).

Pierce, Mamora. *Circle of Magic*. Brior's, 1999 (I:10+ R:6).

Poole, Amy Lowry. *The Pea Blossom*. Hoilday House, 2005 (I:4–8 R:4).

Potter, Beatrix. *The Tailor of Gloucester, From the Original Manuscript*. Warne, 1969, 1978 (I:5–9 R:8).

_____. *The Tale of Peter Rabbit*. Warne, 1902.

_____. *The Tale of Squirrel Nutkin*. Warne, 1903 (I:3–9 R:6).

_____. *Tales of Peter Rabbit and His Friends*. Chatham, 1964 (I:3–9 R:6).

_____. *A Treasury of Peter Rabbit and Other Stories*. Avenel. 1979 (I:3–7 R:6).

Price, Susan. *The Sterkarm Handshake*. Scholastic, 1998 (I:12+ R:7).

Pullman, Philip. *The Amber Spyglass*. Knopf, 2000 (I:10+ R:7).

_____. *The Golden Compass*. Knopf, 1995 (I:10+ R:7).

_____. *I Was a Rat!* Illustrated by Kevin Hawkes. Knopf, 2000 (I:8+ R:4).

_____. *The Subtle Knife*. Knopf, 1997 (I:10+ R:6).

Reiche, Dietlof. *Freddy in Peril, Book Two*. Translated by John Brownjohn. Illustrated by Joe Cepeda. Scholastic, 2004 (I:7–10 R:4).

_____. *I, Freddy, Book One*. Translated by John Brownjohn. Illustrated by Joe Cepeda. Scholastic, 2003 (I:7–10 R:4).

Rodgers, Mary. *Summer Switch*. Harper & Row, 1982 (I:8–12 R:6).

Rowling. J. K. *Harry Potter and the Chamber of Secrets*. Scholastic, 1999 (I:all).

_____. *Harry Potter and the Goblet of Fire*. Scholastic, 2000 (I:all).

_____. *Harry Potter and the Half-Blood Prince*. Scholastic, 2005 (I:all).

_____. *Harry Potter and the Prisoner of Azkaban*. Scholastic. 1999 (I:all).

_____. *Harry Potter and the Sorcerer's Stone*. Scholastic, 1998 (I:all).

Sandburg, Carl. *The Huckabuck Family and How They Raised Popcorn in Nebraska and Quit and Came Back*. Illustrated by David Small. Farrar, Straus & Giroux, 1999 (I:6–8).

_____. *More Rootabagas*. Illustrated by Paul O. Zelinsky. Knopf, 1993 (I:8–11 R:7).

_____. *Rootabaga Stories*. Illustrated by Maud & Miska Petersham. Harcourt Brace, 1922, 1950 (I:8–11 R:7).

_____. *Rootabaga Stories*. Illustrated by Michael Hague. Harcourt Brace, 1922, 1988 (I:8–11 R:7).

Seabrooke, Brenda. *The Care and Feeding of Dragons*. Illustrated by Mark Robertson. Dutton, 1998 (1:9+).

Sedgwick, Marcus. *The Emperor's New Clothes*. Illustrated by Alison Jay. Chronicle, 2004 (I:6–9 R:5).

Selden, George. *Chester Cricket's Pigeon Ride*. Illustrated by Garth Williams. Farrar, Straus & Giroux, 1981 (I:6–9 R:4).

_____. *The Cricket in Times Square*. Illustrated by Garth Williams. Farrar, Straus & Giroux, 1960 (I:7–11 R:3).

_____. *Harry Cat's Pet Puppy*. Farrar, Straus & Giroux, 1975 (I:7–11 R:3).

_____. *Tucker's Countryside*. Farrar, Straus & Giroux, 1969 (I:7–11 R:3).

Setterington, Ken. *Hans Christian Andersen's The Snow Queen: A Fairy Tale Told in Seven Stories*. Illustrated by Nelly & Emst Hofer. Tundra, 2004 (I:8–10 R:5).

_____. *The Wild Swans: An Adventure in Six Parts*. Illustrated by Nelly & Ernst Hofer. Tundra, 2003 (I:8–10 R:5).

Severo, Emoke de Papp, translated by. *The Good-Hearted Youngest Brother: An Hungarian Folktale*. Illustrated by Diane Goode. Bradbury, 1981 (I:6–8 R:4).

Shinn, Sharon. *The Safe-Keeper's Secret*. Dutton, 2004 (I:10+ R:6).

Shusterman, Neal. *The Dark Side of Nowhere*. Little, Brown, 1997 (I:12+ R:6).

Sleator, William. *Interstellar Pig.* Dutton, 1984 (I:10 R:8).

Smith, Sherwood. *Wren's Quest.* Harcourt Brace, 1993 (I:10+ R:6).

Snyder, Zilpha Keatley. *The Unseen.* Delacorte, 2004 (I:10+ R:5).

Springer, Nancy. *I Am Morgan LeFay: A Tale From Camelot.* Philomel, 2001 (I:12+ R:6).

Steig, William. *The Amazing Bone.* Farrar, Straus & Giroux, 1976 (I:6–9 R:3).

Stevermer, Caroline. *River Rats.* Harcourt Brace, 1992 (I:10+ R:6).

Stroud, Jonathan. *The Amulet of Samarkand.* Hyperion, 2003 (I:10+ R:6).

_____. *The Golem's Eye.* Hyperion, 2004 (I:10+ R:6).

Sutcliff, Rosemary. *The Light Beyond the Forest: The Quest for the Holy Grail.* Penguin, 1980 (I:10+ R:7).

_____. *The Road to Camlann: The Death of King Arthur.* Penguin, 1982 (I:10+ R:7).

_____. *The Sword and the Circle: King Arthur and the Knights of the Round Table.* Penguin, 1981 (I:10+ R:7).

Taylor, G. P. *Shadowmancer.* Charisma House, 2004 (I:10+ R:6).

_____. *Wormwood.* Putnam, 2004 (I:12–YA R:6).

Thurber, James. *Many Moons.* Illustrated by Marc Simont. Harcourt Brace, 1990. Thurber's original copyright, 1943 (I:6–9 R:4).

Tolkien, J. R. R. *Farmer Giles of Ham.* Illustrated by Pauline Baynes. Houghton Mifflin, 1978 (I:7–10 R:6).

_____. *The Fellowship of the Ring.* Houghton Mifflin, 1967 (I:12+ R:8).

_____. *The Hobbit.* Houghton Mifflin, 1938 (I:9–12 R:6).

_____. *The Lord of the Rings.* Houghton Mifflin, 1974 (I:12+ R:8).

_____. *The Return of the King.* Houghton Mifflin, 1967 (I:12+ R:8).

_____. *The Two Towers.* Houghton Mifflin, 1965 (I:12+ R:8).

Travers, Pamela L. *Mary Poppins.* Illustrated by Mary Shepard. Harcourt Brace, 1934, 1962 (I:7–11 R:7).

Tunnell, Michael O. *Wishing Moon.* Dutton, 2004 (I:10+ R:6).

Turner, Megan Whalen. *The Thief.* Greenwillow, 1996 (I:10+ R:6).

Van Allsburg, Chris. *The Wreck of the Zephyr.* Houghton Mifflin, 1983 (I:5–8 R:6).

Voigt, Cynthia. *Building Blocks.* Atheneum, 1984 (I:9 R:7).

Waugh, Sylvia. *Who Goes Home?* Delacorte, 2004 (I:10+ R:6).

Westall, Robert. *Ghost Abbey.* Scholastic, 1989 (I:10+ R:6).

Westerfeld, Scott. *Uglies.* Simon Pulse, 2005 (I:12–YA R:6).

White, E. B. *Charlotte's Web.* Illustrated by Garth Williams. Harper & Row, 1952 (I:7–11 R:3).

_____. *Stuart Little.* Illustrated by Garth Williams. Harper & Row, 1945 (I:7–11 R:6).

Whitmore, Arvella. *Trapped Between the Lash and the Gun.* Dial, 1999 (I:10+ R:6).

Wiesner, David. *Free Fall.* Lothrop, Lee & Shepard, 1988 (I:all).

Williams, Margery. *The Velveteen Rabbit.* Illustrated by Allen Atkinson. Knopf, 1984 (I:6–9 R:5).

_____. *The Velveteen Rabbit.* Illustrated by Michael Hague. Holt, Rinehart & Winston, 1983 (I:6–9 R:5).

_____. *The Velveteen Rabbit.* Illustrated by Ilse Plume. Godine, 1982 (I:6–9 R:5).

_____. *The Velveteen Rabbit: Or, How Toys Become Real.* Illustrated by Michael Green. Running Press, 1982 (I:6–9 R:5).

_____. *The Velveteen Rabbit: Or How Toys Become Real.* Illustrated by William Nicholson. Doubleday, 1958 (I:6–9 R:5).

Windsor, Patricia. *The Blooding.* Scholastic, 1996 (I:12+ R:7).

Wolff, Ferida. *Seven Loaves of Bread.* Illustrated by Katie Keller. Tambourine, 1993 (I:4–8 R:4).

Wright, Betty Ren. *The Ghosts of Mercy Manor.* Scholastic, 1993 (I:10+ R:6).

Yolen, Jane. *The Devil's Arithmetic.* Viking/Kestrel, 1988 (I:8+ R:5).

_____. *Dragon's Blood.* Delacorte, 1982 (I:10+ R:5).

_____. *The Girl Who Loved the Wind.* Illustrated by Ed Young. Crowell, 1972 (I:7–10 R:6).

_____. *Here There Be Witches.* Illustrated by David Wilgus. Harcourt Brace, 1995 (I:8+).

_____. *Hobby.* Harcourt Brace, 1996 (I:10+ R:5).

_____. *Merlin.* Harcourt Brace, 1997 (I:10+ R:5).

_____. *Passager.* Harcourt Brace, 1995 (I:10+ R:5).

_____. *Sword of the Rightful King: A Novel of King Arthur.* Harcourt, 2003 (I:10+ R:6).

The Best-Loved Poems of

JACQUELINE KENNEDY ONASSIS

SELECTED AND INTRODUCED BY

CAROLINE KENNEDY

CHAPTER OUTLINE

Rhythmic Patterns of Language

- The Values of Poetry for Children
- What Poetry Is
- Characteristics of Poems That Children Prefer
- Criteria for Selecting Poetry for Children
- Elements of Poetry
- Forms of Poetry
- Poems and Poets

Teaching With Poetry

- Listening to Poetry
- Moving to Poetry
- Dramatizing Poetry
- Developing Choral Speaking
- Choosing Poetry to Accompany Content
- Writing Poetry

Rhythmic Patterns of Language

According to Eve Merriam, in *Rainbow Writing,* poetry is related to a rainbow because it colors the human mind with the vast spectrum of human experience. As a rainbow inspires an awe of nature, so may a poem inspire an awe for words and the expression of feelings. Poetry often has a musical quality that attracts children and appeals to their emotions. The poet's choice of words can suggest new images and create delightful wordplays.

The Values of Poetry for Children

Children can share feelings, experiences, and visions with poets. Poetry also brings new understandings of the world. It encourages children to play with words and to realize some of the images possible when words are chosen carefully. Through poetry, children can discover the power of words, a power that poets can release. Kathy A. Perfect (1999) states this value:

> Poetry appeals to the near universal fondness children have for rhyme and rhythm. It nurtures a love and appreciation for the sound and power of language. Poetry can help us see differently, understand ourselves and others, and validate our human experience. It is a genre especially suited to the struggling or unmotivated reader. Poetry easily finds a home in all areas of the curriculum, enhances thinking skills, and promotes personal connections to content area subjects. Such attributes deserve a closer look. (p. 728)

When we read why authors are attracted to poetry, we discover many of the values of poetry. For example, poet Kevin Crossley-Holland (2004) states that when reading poems, "I've felt hot, cold, excited, brave, scared; they've made me laugh out loud, and one brought tears to my eyes; they've made me indignant and joyous; they've made me edge forward in my chair. They've shown me how we're all the same and, thank heavens, all completely different" (p. 11).

In *Crosscurrents,* the program for the Aspen Music Festival and *School,* Jane Vial Jaffe (2001) highlights the connections between music and literature, "especially when it comes to poetry; literally thousands of songs bear the shape of verse" (p. 3). She then discusses the impact of literature on various composers such as Leonard Bernstein and Claude Debussy. Debussy was attracted to the poetry of Pierre Loüys, written in 1895. In 1900 and 1901, Debussy staged a reading of the poetry that was accompanied by his newly written compositions. Music can be used today to provide backgrounds for poetry readings.

The connections between poetry and art are shown in Jan Greenberg's *Heart to Heart: New Poems Inspired by Twentieth-Century American Art*. Each of the poems in the collection is paired with the painting that inspired it.

As a young adult, author and critic Harold Bloom (2004) chose poetry because "it raises your consciousness of glory and of grief, of use or wonder" (unnumbered introduction to *The Best Poems of the English Language*). Poet Naomi Shihab Nye, in her introduction to *19 Varieties of Gazelle: Poems of the Middle East*, states, "Poetry slows us down, cherishes small details. . . . We need poetry for nourishment and for noticing, for the way language and imagery reach comfortably into experience, holding and connecting it more successfully than any news channel we could name" (p. xvi). The ultimate value of poetry is cited by David McCullough in his biography of *John Adams* (2001). McCullough describes Adams's love of literature and that he was likely to carry a volume of English poetry with him on journeys because Adams felt that "'you will never be alone with a poet in your pocket'" (p. 19). For teachers of young children, Carolyn Kennedy (2005) provides one of the strongest values of poetry for children in her introduction to *A Family of Poems: My Favorite Poetry for Children*: "Writing a poem forces us to think about what we really want to say, and helps us understand ourselves and shape our lives. If you start when you are young, you will see that words and ideas have the power to change the world" (p. 10).

As we can see, there are numerous values for sharing poetry. First, poetry provides enjoyment, which young children begin to discover by hearing and sharing nonsense poems, Mother Goose rhymes, and tongue twisters. They grow into poetry through story poems, such as those written by A. A. Milne, and they gradually discover the many exciting forms available to poets. Second, poetry provides children with knowledge about concepts in the world around them: size, numbers, colors, and time. Third, because precise and varied words play such important roles in poetic expression, poetry encourages children to appreciate language and to expand their vocabularies: Horses not only run, they clop; kittens jump, but they also pounce; and the moon may be not only bright but also a silver sickle. Fourth, poetry helps children identify with people and situations: With Robert Louis Stevenson, they go up in a swing; with Robert Frost, they share a snowy evening in the woods; and with Mike Makley, they are 'the new kid' on the baseball team who plays just as well as Dutch, PeeWee, or Earl, even though she is a girl. Fifth, poetry expresses moods familiar to children and helps them understand and accept their feelings. Other children empathize with the child in Charlotte Zolotow's "Nobody Loves Me." Sometimes, it seems as if nobody loves the speaker, and sometimes it seems as if everybody loves him—feelings common to all children. Finally, poetry grants children insights into themselves and others,

developing their sensitivity to universal needs and feelings. Through poems written by other children as well as by adults, children discover that others have feelings similar to their poem.

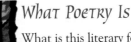

What Poetry Is

What is this literary form that increases enjoyment, develops appreciation for language, and helps children gain insights about themselves? Poetry is not easily defined, nor is it easily measured or classified. There is no single accepted definition of poetry. Some definitions specify the characteristics of poetry, including the poetic elements and the functions of words, but other definitions emphasize its emotional impact. Develop your own definition of poetry as you read the following definitions by poets, critics, and children. Rumer Godden (1988) states, "True poetry, even in its smallest shape, should have form, meter, rhythm bound into a whole with words that so match and express its subject they seem inevitable" (p. 310).

Seventeenth-century Japanese poet Matsuo Basho defines poetry as "a fireplace in summer or a fan in winter" (Hass, p. 236). In "The Bridge," Lebanese poet Kaisser Afif describes poetry as "a river/. . . /Through writing/We cross it,/Through reading/We return" (Nye, *The Space Between Our Footsteps*, p. 83).

Emotional and physical reactions defined poetry for poet Emily Dickinson, who related poetry to a feeling: If she read a book that made "her body so cold no fire could warm" her, she knew it was poetry; if she felt physically as if the top of her head were taken off, she also knew it was poetry. Michael Bedard's *Emily* (1992) is a picture storybook in which a father gives his daughter a similar definition for poetry:

> Listen to Mother play. She practices and practices a piece, and sometimes a magic happens and it seems the music starts to breathe. It sends a shiver through you. You can't explain it, really; it's a mystery. Well, when words do that, we call it poetry. (p. 12, unnumbered)

Poet Valerie Worth (1992) also talks about the power and magic of poetry and the need to select the right words, "the right verbs, the right adjectives, or the precious image would fade away and be gone—and the magic as well" (p. 569). Judson Jerome (1968) contends that poetry is words performed; he stresses that meaning cannot be separated from the sounds of words. Just as visual shape is important to sculptors or painters, tonal shape is important to poets. Jerome compares the work of poets to the composition of musicians; in both forms, tonal quality is essential.

Author Margaret Mahy presents a definition of poetry in her short story "The Cat Who Became a Poet," found in *Nonstop Nonsense*. After the cat cannot stop himself from speaking in poetic form, he thinks, "I became a poet through eating the mouse. Perhaps the mouse became a poet through eating seeds. Perhaps all this poetry stuff is just the world's way of talking about itself" (p. 19). Following the cat's rendition of a poem that tricks a dog, the cat concludes, "If only he knew. I wasn't meaning to praise him. Poetry is very tricky stuff and can be taken two ways" (p. 19).

John Drury (1995) emphasizes that "the writers of children's poems will usually simplify the language and ideas and highlight the rhythms and sound effects. . . . William Blake's *Songs of Innocence and Experience*, while symbolic and profound, are at the same time simple and musical and full of what might be called primary images" (p. 58). Michael Driscoll, in his subtitle for *A Child's Introduction to Poetry*, identifies poetry as "magic words that have moved mountains, won battles and made us laugh and cry" (title page).

Overall, the various definitions of poetry highlight the importance of an original combination of words, distinctive sound, and emotional impact. Visual elements are also significant in poetry. Some poems are like paintings: They must be seen to be appreciated. Poets may use shape and space to increase the impact of their words, grouping lines into stanzas, using open spaces to emphasize words, capitalizing important words, or arranging a whole poem to suggest the subject.

The essential elements of poetry must be savored to be enjoyed. Like painting or sculpture, poetry cannot be experienced rapidly; it must be read slowly, even reread several times to immerse readers or listeners in its sounds and imagery. In other words, children must have time to see, hear, and feel the world of poets.

Characteristics of Poems That Children Prefer

Consider children's individual interests when choosing poetry for them; when children judge honestly what speaks to their imaginations, their judgments must be respected. Even though children's interests and experiences vary widely, research into children's poetry choices contains valuable information. Several researchers have identified poems that children generally enjoy and have analyzed the subjects and elements in them. As you read the results of these studies that were conducted over different time periods, decide whether the results would be the same if conducted today.

Carol Fisher and Margaret Natarella (1982) examined poetry preferences in the first through the third grades, and they found that the children preferred narrative poems and limericks, poems about strange and fantastic events, traditional poems, and poems that rhymed or used alliteration and onomatopoeia to create sound patterns. Karen Sue Kutiper (1985) surveyed preferences of students in the seventh, eighth, and ninth grades; she

concluded that these students prefer rhyme, humorous narrative, and content based on familiar experiences.

Ann Terry (1974) investigated the poetry preferences of children in the fourth, fifth, and sixth grades and analyzed poetic elements in the poems that the children preferred. She concluded the following:

1. Children's enthusiasm for poetry declines as they advance in the elementary grades.
2. Children respond more favorably to contemporary poems than to traditional ones.
3. Children prefer poems dealing with familiar and enjoyable experiences.
4. Children enjoy poems that tell a story or have a strong element of humor.
5. Children prefer poems that feature rhythm and rhyme.
6. Among the least popular poems are those that rely heavily on complex imagery or subtly implied emotion.

In 2003, Sam L. Sebesta and Dianne L. Monson reported studies of poetry preferences that indicate children appreciate poems with rhythm, rhyme, and humor. Studies with middle-grade students suggest that students prefer to read poems rather than listen to them. Sebesta and Monson also concluded that poetry preferences have not changed greatly since the early studies in the 1920s: Students still like poems that are funny, tell a story, include adventure and excitement, have romantic and dramatic qualities, and have rhythm and rhyme.

One reason for the narrow range of poems that children enjoy may be that adults infrequently share poetry with children. The enjoyment of poetry, like the enjoyment of other types of literature, can be increased by an enthusiastic adult who reads poetry to children. Enthusiasm for poetry first must be stimulated among teachers themselves. According to Alexa L. Sandmann (2005), "poetry allows for new ways of visualizing our world. It's the responsibility of educators to broaden students' outlooks. The use of poetry in nontraditional settings makes a powerful statement and adds a bit of magic to lessons. Including poetry provides both form and substance: students learn more about the world, as well as new ways of sharing their growing understandings" (p. 19).

As you begin the study of poetry, you should also heed a warning from William and Betty Greenway (1990): "We may be teaching students the poetry they like as children, but not the poetry they'll like as adults" (p. 138). Poetry, however, is receiving national recognition among adults. Many cities—even boroughs such as Brooklyn—have their own poets laureate. The idea of a national poet laureate follows a 350-year-old tradition in England. The United States has had a poet laureate consultant to the Library of Congress since the 1930s. These poets have included Robert Frost, Louise Glück, Billy Collins, and Robert Pinsky. It is just recently, however, that the idea of poets laureate has emerged throughout the country. Most states and the District of Columbia now have official positions for poets laureate whose purpose is to bring poetry to the public's attention by organizing poetry readings and giving awards to local teachers for their innovative use of poetry in the public school classroom.

In a review of the 53 books chosen by the *School Library Journal* for 2001 (Jones et al., 2001), the editors state: "This was a banner year for poetry. Whether light and funny or serious and thoughtful, the poems and in many cases, their accompanying artwork, made a strong showing in a variety of formats" (p. 44). The following poetry books are included in this list: Kristine O'Connell George's *Toasting Marshmallows: Camping Poems,* Jan Greenberg's *Heart to Heart: New Poems Inspired by Twentieth-Century American Art,* Paul B. Janeczko's *A Poke in the I: A Collection of Concrete Poems,* Henry Wadsworth Longfellow's *The Midnight Ride of Paul Revere,* and Jack Prelutsky's *Awful Ogre's Awful Day.*

CRITERIA FOR SELECTING POETRY FOR CHILDREN

Both Rumer Godden (1988) and Charles Causley (Merrick, 1988) emphasize that a good poem need not be understood all at once. Godden states that a good poem "has a mysterious capacity for growing, unfolding more and more of itself in the mind, and very soon a child whose ear is tuned, mind made alert, is ready to go beyond children's poets and the lively, quickly assimilable poems—far, far beyond" (p. 310).

ELEMENTS OF POETRY

How important to you is a knowledge of the literary elements found in poetry? Avi (1993) states that of the various criteria, "only knowing the elements of good prose and poetry contributes meaningfully to an understanding of what is children's literature" (p. 42).

Poets use everyday language in different ways to encourage readers to see familiar things in a new light, to draw on their senses, and to fantasize. Poets also use certain devices to create medleys of sounds, suggest visual interpretations, and communicate messages. The criteria for selecting poetry for children suggest the importance of such poetic elements as rhythm, rhyme and other sound patterns, repetition, imagery, and shape in the creation of poetry. In their poetry anthology *Knock at a Star: A Child's Introduction to Poetry,* X. J. Kennedy and Dorothy M. Kennedy highlight the elements of poetry through a section titled "What's Inside a Poem?" In this section, they include poems that develop "Images," "Word Music," "Beats that Repeat," "Likenesses," and "Word Play."

EVALUATION CRITERIA

Literary Criticism: Selecting Poetry for Children

1. Poems that are lively, with exciting meters and rhythms, are most likely to appeal to young children.
2. Poems for young children should emphasize the sounds of language and encourage wordplay.
3. Sharply cut visual images and fresh, novel uses of words allow children to expand their imaginations and see or hear the world in a new way.
4. Poems for young children should tell simple stories and introduce stirring scenes of action.
5. The poems selected should not have been written down to children's supposed level.
6. The most effective poems allow children to interpret, to feel, and to put themselves into the poems. They encourage children to extend comparisons, images, and findings.
7. The subjects should delight children, say something to them, enhance their egos, strike happy recollections, tickle their funny bones, or encourage them to explore.
8. Poems should be good enough to stand up under repeated readings.

When you read these poems, you will notice that they develop the elements of poetry.

Rhythm

The word *rhythm* is derived from the Greek *rhythmos,* meaning "to flow." In poetry, this flowing quality refers to the movement of words in the poem. Stress, the number of syllables, and the pattern of syllables direct the feelings expressed in a poem. Many poems have a definite, repetitive cadence, or meter, with certain lines containing a certain number of pronounced beats. For example, limericks have a strict rhythmic structure easily recognizable even when one is hearing them in a foreign language. Free verse, however, usually has a casual, irregular rhythm similar to that of everyday speech.

Poets use rhythm for four specific purposes. First, they use it to increase enjoyment in hearing language. Young children usually enjoy the repetitive cadences of nursery rhymes, chants, and nonsensical verses. Rhythm encourages them to join in orally, experiment with language, and move with it. Second, poets use rhythm to highlight and emphasize specific words. They often use stress to suggest the importance of words. Third, poets use rhythm to

The poems in Knock at a Star: A Child's Introduction to Poetry *are excellent for developing understanding of poetic elements. (Cover from* Knock at a Star: A Child's Introduction to Poetry, *illustrated by Karen Lee Baker. Cover copyright © 1999 by Karen Lee Baker. Published by Little, Brown and Company. Reprinted by permission of Little, Brown and Company.)*

create dramatic effects. Irregular meter or repeatedly stressed words may immediately attract attention. Fourth, poets use rhythm to suggest mood. For example, a rapid rhythm can suggest excitement and involvement, and a slow, leisurely rhythm can suggest laziness and contemplation. David McCord uses rhythm in the following poem to suggest the sounds that a stick might make if a child dragged it along a fence: Rhythm emphasizes specific words, attracts and holds attention, and suggests a certain mood.

The Pickety Fence
The pickety fence
The pickety fence
Give it a lick it's
The pickety fence
Give it a lick it's
A clickety fence
Give it a lick it's
A lickety fence
Give it a lick
Give it a lick
Give it a lick
With a rickety stick

Pickety
Pickety
Pickety
Pick

From Poem "The Pickety Fence" from *Far and Few: Rhymes of the Never Was and Always Is.* p. 7 by David McCord. Copyright © 1974, Little, Brown & Company.

As you share poetry with children, you will notice that the rhythm of a poem works particularly well when it reinforces the content of the poem. Consider, for example, Robert Louis Stevenson's "From a Railway Carriage," whose rhythm suggests the dash and rattle of a train as it crosses the country; you can easily imagine yourself peering out the window as the scenery rushes by.

From a Railway Carriage
Faster than fairies, faster than witches,
Bridges and houses, hedges and ditches;
And charging along like troops in a battle,
All through the meadows the horses and cattle:
All of the sights of the hill and the plain
Fly as thick as driving rain;
And ever again, in the wink of an eye,
Painted stations whistle by.
Here is a child who clambers and scrambles,
All by himself and gathering brambles;
Here is a tramp who stands and gazes;
And here is the green for stringing the daisies!
Here is a cart run away in the road
Lumping along with man and load;
And here is a mill and there is a river:
Each a glimpse and gone forever!

Robert Louis Stevenson
A Child's Garden of Verses, 1885

Rhythm and the sounds of language are important elements in *Talking Like the Rain: A First Book of Poems,* selected by X. J. and Dorothy M. Kennedy. The book is introduced with a quote from Isak Dinesen's *Out of Africa,* in which the workers ask Dinesen to "Speak again, Speak like rain." The poems in the anthology are meant to be read aloud to children and to bring them rhythm and pleasure.

Rhythm and repetition are important poetic elements in Lee Bennett Hopkins's *Good Rhymes, Good Times.* There is the rhythm and sound of the city as "Quiet rumbling/traffic/roars" (p. 8); the rhythm and feel of valentine emotions that go "flippy/fizzy, whoopy, whizzy" (p. 12); and the motion and rhythm of a kite that "flitters/twirls/tumbles/twitters" (p. 14). The repeated line "Sing a song of cities" (p. 5) emphasizes the sound of the city.

Rhyme and Other Sound Patterns

Sound is an important part of the pleasure of poetry. One of the ways in which poets can emphasize sound is with rhyme. Many beloved traditional poems for children—

such as Edward Lear's "The Owl and the Pussy-Cat"—use careful rhyme schemes.

Rhyming words may occur at the ends of lines and within lines. Poets of nonsense verse even create their own words to achieve humorous rhyming effects. Consider, for example, Zilpha Keatley Snyder's use of rhyme in "Poem to Mud." The end rhymes—*ooze–slooze, crud–flood,* and *thickier–sickier*—suggest visual and auditory characteristics of mud. The internal rhymes—*fed–spread, slickier–stickier*—create a tongue-twisting quality.

Poem to Mud

Poem to mud—
Poem to ooze—
Patted in pies, or coating the shoes.
Poem to slooze—
Poem to crud—
Fed by a leak, or spread by a flood.
Wherever, whenever, whyever it goes,
Stirred by your finger, or strained by your toes,
There's nothing sloopier, slipperier, floppier,
There's nothing slickier, stickier, thickier,
There's nothing quickier to make grown-ups sickier,
Trulier coolier,
Than wonderful mud.

Zilpha Keatley Snyder
Today Is Saturday, pp. 18–19

Numerous internal rhymes are found in Robert Southey's classical poem. "The Cataract of Lodore." In the following excerpt from the poem, notice how internal rhymes create the sound and feel of the water as it flows toward a waterfall in the Lake District of England.

Retreating and beating and meeting and sheeting,
Delaying and straying and playing and spraying,
Advancing and prancing and glancing and dancing,
Recoiling, turmoiling and toiling and boiling,
And gleaming and streaming and steaming and beaming,
And rushing and flushing and brushing and gushing,
And flapping and rapping and clapping and slapping,
And curling and whirling and purling and twirling,
And thumping and plumping and bumping and jumping,
And dashing and flashing and splashing and clashing, . . .

Robert Southey, 1774–1843.

Poets also use *alliteration*, the repetition of initial consonants or groups of consonants, to create sound patterns. In "The Tutor," Carolyn Wells repeats the beginning consonant *t* to create a humorous poem about a teacher trying to teach "two young tooters to toot." "The Tutor" is one of the poems in Isabel Wilner's *The Poetry Troupe*, a collection of more than 200 poems that children have selected for reading aloud. Mary Ann Hoberman's four-line poem "Gazelle," also in Wilner's collection, contains 15 words beginning with *g.* If a poem has a great deal of alliteration, a tongue twister results. "Sing Me a Song of Teapots and Trumpets," by N. M. Bodecker, is one of the poems selected for X. J. Kennedy and Dorothy M. Kennedy's *Knock at a Star: A Child's Introduction to Poetry.* Each verse uses a different alliteration. In the first verse are *teapots* and *trumpets, tippets* and *taps,* and *trippers* and *trappers.* The second verse contains *sneakers* and *snoopers, snappers* and *snacks,* and *snorkels* and *snarkles.* By the third verse, the alliteration contains *parsnips* and *pickles, picsnips* and *parkles,* and *pumpkins* and *pears.*

Assonance, the repetition of vowel sounds, is another means of creating interesting and unusual sound patterns. Another poem selected by Kennedy and Kennedy, "Auk Talk," by Mary Ann Hoberman, uses repetitions of vowel sounds in words such as *raucous, auk, squawk,* and *talk.* This poem becomes a tongue twister if read aloud rapidly.

Don't Ever Seize a Weasel by the Tail

You should never squeeze a weasel
for you might displease the weasel,
and don't ever seize the weasel by the tail.
Let his tail blow in the breeze;
if you pull it, he will sneeze,
for the weasel's constitution tends to be little frail.
Yes the weasel wheezes easily;
the weasel freezes easily;
the weasel's tan complexion rather suddenly turns pale.
So don't displease or tease a weasel,
squeeze or freeze or wheeze a weasel
and don't ever seize a weasel by the tail.

Jack Prelutsky
A Gopher in the Garden and Other Animal Poems, p. 19

The sounds of some words suggest the meanings that they are intended to convey. The term *onomatopoeia* refers to words that imitate the actions or sounds with which they are associated. Words such as *plop, jounce,* and *beat* suggest the loud sound of rain hitting the concrete in Aileen Fisher's "Rain."

Eve Merriam effectively uses onomatopoeia in her poem "Owl," found in *Halloween ABC.* Merriam's repeated use of "who" sounds like the subject of her poem. One of her other poems, "Weather," found in Beatrice Schenk de Regniers's *Sing a Song of Popcorn,* begins with "Dot a dot" and continues with words such as "spack a spack speck" to sound like rain. In *Earth Verses and Water Rhymes,* poet J. Patrick Lewis suggests in "Sounds of Winter" that October Ogres lumber in with a "tum-tum-titum."

Repetition

Poets frequently use repetition to enrich or emphasize words, phrases, lines, or even whole verses in poems. David McCord uses repetition of whole lines in "The

Through the Eyes of a POET

Jack Prelutsky

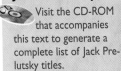

Visit the CD-ROM that accompanies this text to generate a complete list of Jack Prelutsky titles.

Selected Titles by Jack Prelutsky:

The Headless Horseman Rides Tonight

The New Kid on the Block

It's Raining Pigs and Noodles: Poems

Monday's Troll

Nightmares: Poems to Trouble Your Sleep

Poetry Doesn't Have to Be Boring!

Once there was a teacher who had charge of thirty-three open and eager young minds. One Monday morning the teacher opened her curriculum book, which indicated that she should recite a poem to her students. She did, and it came out something like this:

> Blah blah the flower,
> blah blah the tree,
> blah blah the shower,
> blah blah the bee.

When she had finished her recitation she said, "Please open your geography books to page one-hundred-thirty-seven."

On Tuesday morning, the teacher (a wonderful person who happened to be rather fond of poetry) decided, on her own initiative, to read another poem to her class. This poem, which was somewhat longer than the first, came out something like this:

> blah blah blah blah blah blah hill,
> blah blah blah blah blah blah still,

> blah blah blah blah blah blah mill,
> blah blah blah blah daffodil.

Then she said, "Please open your history books to page sixty-two."

She went on like this for the entire week and by Friday, the children (who knew what was coming when she opened her book of verse) began making peculiar faces and shifting restlessly in their seats. The staunchest aesthetes in the group had begun to lose interest in flowers, bees, hills, etc. Many of the children were harboring strange feelings about poetry. They began saying things about poetry to themselves and to each other. Here are some of the things they said:

"Poetry is boring."

"Poetry is dumb."

"Poetry doesn't make any sense."

"Poetry is about things that don't interest me."

"I hate poetry."

Once there was another teacher with a class of thirty-three young students. She was also a wonderful person with a fondness for poetry. One Sunday evening, she opened her curriculum book and saw that a unit of poetry was scheduled for the next day's lesson. "Hmmmmmm," she mused. "Now what poem shall I share with them tomorrow?" After giving it some careful thought, she settled on a poem about a silly monster, which the poet had apparently created out of whole cloth, and which she thought might stimulate her pupils' imaginations. "Hmmmmmm," she mused again. "Now how can I make this poem even more interesting?" She deliberated a bit more and, in the course of memorizing the poem, came up with several ideas. The next morning, this is what happened:

"Children," she said. "Today is a special day. It is the first day of silly monster week, and to honor the occasion I am going to share a silly monster poem with you." She held up a small tin can, and continued. "The monster lives in this can, but I am not going to show it to you yet, because I would like you to imagine what it looks like while I'm reciting the poem."

She then recited the poem, and upon reaching the last word in the last line, suddenly unleashed an expanding snake from the can. The children reacted with squeals of mock terror and real delight. Then they asked her to recite the poem again, which she did. Afterward, she had them draw pictures of the silly monster. No two interpretations were alike.

The drawings were photographed and later presented in an assembly as a slide show, with the children reciting the poem in chorus. She shared a number of other poems during "silly monster week," always showing her honest enthusiasm and finding imaginative methods of presentation. She used masks, musical instruments, dance, sound-effects recordings, and clay sculpture. The children grew so involved that she soon was able to recite poems with no props at all. At the end of the week, these are some of the things her students said about poetry.

"Poetry is exciting."

"Poetry is fun."

"Poetry is interesting."

"Poetry makes you think."

"I love poetry."

Video Profiles: The accompanying video contains conversations with Lynne Cherry, Mary E. Lyons, Keith Baker, and other writers of children's literature.

Pickety Fence," and Lewis Carroll uses repetition to accent his feelings about soup.

Beautiful Soup

> Beautiful Soup, so rich and green,
> Waiting in a hot tureen!
> Who for such dainties would not stoop?
> Soup of the evening, beautiful Soup!
> Soup of the evening, beautiful Soup!
> Beau—ootiful Soo—oop!
> Beau—ootiful Soo—oop!
> Soo—oop of the e—e—evening,
> Beautiful, beautiful Soup!
> Beautiful Soup! Who cares for fish,
> Game, or any other dish?
> Who would not give all else for two

> Pennyworth only of beautiful Soup?
> Beau—ootiful Soo—oop!
> Beau—ootiful Soo—oop!
> Soo—op of the e—e—evening,
> Beautiful, beauti—FUL SOUP!

Lewis Carroll
Alice's Adventures in Wonderland, 1865

"Beautiful Soup" is another favorite for oral reading because children find that they can re-create that marvelous sound of rich, hot soup being taken from the spoon and placed into their mouths.

Lullabies shared with young children are often enhanced by repetition. Christina G. Rossetti's "Lullaby" uses repetition to suggest a musical quality.

Lullaby

Lullaby, oh, lullaby!
Flowers are closed and lambs are sleeping;
Lullaby, oh, lullaby!
Stars are up, the moon is peeping;
Lullaby, oh, lullaby!
While the birds are silence keeping,
(Lullaby, oh, lullaby!)
Sleep, my baby, fall a-sleeping,
Lullaby, oh, lullaby!

Christina Rossetti
Sing-Song, 1872

Imagery

Imagery is a primary element in poetry. It encourages children to see, hear, feel, taste, smell, and touch the worlds created by poets. You have already seen how rhythm, sound patterns, and repetition cause readers to experience what poets describe. Poets also use figurative language (language with nonliteral meanings) to clarify, add vividness, and encourage readers to experience things in new ways. Several types of figurative language are used in poetry.

Through the Eyes of a CHILD

Katie
Grade 4

TITLE: The New kid on the Block
AUTHOR: Jack PreLutsky
Mr. Jack Prelutsky likes to make people laugh by poetry. How James did his illustrations was he drew one picture that represented the poem. He drew black and white pictures. Jack doesn't rhyme that much in his poetry. The tittle is The New Kid on the Block. He does 18 poems in this book. Jack writes funny and fiction poems. James sometimes did funny illustrations. On the front cover it looks like it was painted. But on the inside it looks like it was done in marker. James draws his pictures in detail. Jack doesn't just write about the new kid he also writes about other poems too. I like this book because I like the funny poems. Some poems in this book made me laugh aloud. I dedicate this book to my 10 year old cousin Jennifer Smith because I think this would make her laugh aloud too.
Katie

Metaphors are implied comparisons between things that have something in common but are essentially different. Metaphors highlight certain qualities in things to make readers see them in new ways. In the introduction to *Flashlight and Other Poems,* Judith Thurman (1976) uses metaphor when she asserts that a "poem is a flashlight, too: the flashlight of surprise. Pointed at a skinned knee or at an oil slick, at pretending to sleep or at kisses, at balloons, or snow, or at the soft, scary nuzzle of a mare, a poem lets us feel and know each in a fresh, sudden and strong light" (introduction). Thurman demonstrates her command of metaphor when she compares the Milky Way to thick white breath in cold air, or clay to a clown without bones.

Paul Paolilli and Dan Brewer use metaphors effectively in *Silver Seeds: A Book of Nature Poems.* For example, they compare stars to silver seeds that have been planted in the sky, and the moon is a marvelous melon that offers flavor to the night.

Whereas metaphors are implied comparisons, *similes* are direct comparisons between things that have something in common but are essentially different. The comparisons made by similes are considered direct because the word *like* or *as* is included in the comparison. In "The Path on the Sea," a 13-year-old Russian child uses simile to capture the mystery and allure of moonlight on the ocean. Notice the use of the word *like* in the first line. What are the commonalities between a silver sickle and a new moon?

The Path on the Sea

The moon this night is like a silver sickle
Mowing a field of stars.
It has spread a golden runner
Over the rippling waves.
With its winking shimmer
This magic carpet lures me
To fly to the moon on it.

From the poem "The Path on the Sea" by Inna Miller, from *The Moon Is Like a Silver Sickle* by Miriam Morton. Reprinted by permission.

Insightful comparisons can develop meaning that transcends words. Poetic imagery can open the minds of children to new worlds and can allow them to ascend to different levels of consciousness.

Personification allows poets to give human emotions and characteristics to inanimate objects, abstract ideas, and nonhuman living things. For example, personification is an important element in Byrd Baylor's poetry about Native Americans and Native American legends. In *Moon Song,* Baylor personifies the moon as a mother who gives birth to Coyote Child, wraps him in her magic, caresses him with pale white mist, and shines on him with love.

Hyperbole is exaggeration that creates specific effects. John Ciardi's humorous "Mummy Slept Late and Daddy Fixed Breakfast," for example, says that a waffle is so tough that it cannot be dented by a hacksaw.

Mummy Slept Late and Daddy Fixed Breakfast

Daddy fixed the breakfast.
He made us each a waffle.
It looked like gravel pudding.
It tasted somthing awful.

"Ha, ha," he said, "I'll try again.
This time I'll get it right." But what I got was in
 between
Bituminous and anthracite.

"A little too well done? Oh well,
I'll have to start all over."
That time what landed on my plate
Looked like a manhole cover.

I tried to cut it with a fork:
The fork gave off a spark.
I tried a knife and twisted it
into a question mark.
I tried it with a hack-saw.
I tried it with a torch.
It didn't even make a dent.
It didn't even scorch.

The next time Dad gets breakfast
When Mummy's sleeping late,
I think I'll skip the waffles.
I'd sooner eat the plate!

John Ciardi
You Read to Me, I'll Read to You, p. 18

Shape

Poets may place their words on pages in ways designed to supplement meaning and to create greater visual impact. Word division, line division, punctuation, and capitalization can emphasize content, as when Lewis Carroll writes about "Beau—ootiful Soo—oop!"

The shape of a poem may represent the thing or the physical experience that the poem describes. In e. e. cummings's poem "Hist Wist," included in Michael Driscoll's *A Child's Introduction to Poetry,* the poet uses short words, brief lines, sporadic spaces, and no punctuation so that the words float around the page like the ghosts he describes. In Monica Kulling's poem "Tennis Anyone," found in Paul Janeczko's collection *A Poke in the I,* short words on either side of the page represent a tennis ball as it travels from one side of the net to the other, and the words describe the strain of watching a tennis match, to match the sweep of the swing. In "Seals," by William Jay Smith (anthologized in Stephen Dunning, Edward Lueders, and Hugh Smith's excellent *Reflections on a Gift of Watermelon Pickle . . . and Other Modern Verse*), the poem forms the shape of a supple seal and is reinforced by an accompanying photograph of a seal. Several of the poems in Myra Cohn Livingston's *Space Songs* are shaped like objects in space. For example, "Moon" looks like a crescent, "Meteorites" has a tail, and "Satellites" looks like a mechanical object. In a book for younger children, *Come to My Party and Other Shape Poems,* Heidi Roemer combines her words with Hideko Takahashi's illustrations to capture activities that take place during the four seasons. For example, in a winter poem about sledding, the words move up the illustration of a hill and then down the other side. In Brad Burg's *Outside the Lines,* words join Rebecca Gibbon's illustrations to capture the frenetic energy of the playground. As children read, their eyes follow the path of a Frisbee, skipping stones, and a paper airplane. In "Softball," written in the shape of a baseball diamond, team members are out on the field, and a small verse appears next to each one. Children enjoy discovering that shape may be related to the meaning of a poem and experimenting with shape in their own poetry writing.

Forms of Poetry

Children should be encouraged to write their own poetry. When they write poetry, they enjoy experimenting with different forms. For such experiments, however, they must be immersed in poetry and led through many enjoyable experiences with poems.

Lyric Poetry

Perhaps the earliest and most enduringly popular type of poetry is the lyric. According to Northrop Frye, Sheridan Baker, and George Perkins (1985), a lyric poem is "brief and discontinuous, emphasizing sound and picture imagery rather than narrative or dramatic movement. Lyrical poetry began in ancient Greece in connection with music, as poetry sung, for the most part, to the accompaniment of a lyre" (p. 268). Now, as in the past, lyric poems emphasize musical, pictorial, and emotional qualities. The musical roots of lyric poetry are indicated by the fact that the words of songs are now termed *lyrics.*

John Drury (1995) says that "originally lyric poetry was sung, chanted, or recited to a musical accompaniment. The word lyric refers to the poet's lyre, the harp-like instrument the poet or musician would play. . . . Lyric poetry now tends to be quiet, inward, meditative" (p. 156). Many of the poems discussed in this chapter have lyrical quality.

Children's early experiences with poetry may be through Mother Goose rhymes sung to music and traditional lullabies sung at bedtime. Consider the melody associated with the words in the following traditional lullaby.

Hush, Little Baby
Hush, little baby, don't say a word,
Mama's going to buy you a mocking bird.
And if that mocking bird don't sing,
Mama's going to buy you a diamond ring.
And if that diamond ring turns to brass,
Mama's going to buy you a looking glass.

And if that looking glass gets broke,
Mama's going to buy you a billy goat.
And if that billy goat won't pull,
Mama's going to buy you a cart and bull.
And if that cart and bull turn over,
Mama's going to buy you a dog named Rover.
And if that dog named Rover won't bark,
Mama's going to buy you a horse and cart.
And if that horse and cart fall down,
You'll still be the sweetest little baby in town.

Traditional poem

Children's favorite storybook characters make up verses and sing their poems—as does A. A. Milne's Winnie-the-Pooh, for example. Many poets write poems that have singing qualities. Jack Prelutsky's anthology *The Random House Book of Poetry for Children* contains, for example, Lois Lenski's "Sing a Song of People," which recreates the tempo of people traveling through a city. John Ciardi's "The Myra Song" captures the personality of a little girl who enjoys singing, skipping, chattering, and playing. William Blake's "Introduction to 'Songs of Innocence'" has its piper of "happy songs/Every child may joy to hear."

The songs of two well-known singers and songwriters are the sources for illustrated texts. *Island in the Sun,* by Harry Belafonte and Lord Burgess, pays tribute to Belafonte's island childhood. The lines of the song are divided and illustrated to form a picture book; the text begins and concludes with the music. *This Land Is Your Land,* by Woody Guthrie, is a highly illustrated version of the popular song, with paintings by Kathy Jakobsen. The text includes "A Tribute to Woody Guthrie" and the

The poems and illustrations take readers across America. (From This Land Is Your Land. *Words and music by Woodie Guthrie, paintings by Kathy Jackson. Illustrations © 1998 by Kathy Jakobsen. Published by Little, Brown and Company. Reprinted by permission.)*

From SHE'LL BE COMIN' 'ROUND THE MOUNTAIN by Philemon F. Sturges. Copyright © 2004 by Philemon Sturges (text); copyright © 2004 by Ashley Wolff (illustrations). By permission of Little Brown and Co., Inc.

itor is a librarian in the Six White Horses Book Mobile.

The universality of songs and chants is shown through Nikki Siegen-Smith's *Songs for Survival: Songs and Chants From Tribal Peoples Around the World*. The anthology contains selections from six continents and is divided according to songs about beginnings, songs about the living world, songs that discuss the elements, and songs about survival. An introduction and an appendix present information about the importance of songs and customs of tribal groups.

NARRATIVE POETRY

A poem that tells a story is narrative poetry. The first poets were expert storytellers who told elaborate tales to entertain people and as a way of recording history. The oldest form of the narrative poem is the epic, a long story dealing with heroic events, often with supernatural elements, and divided into several parts, such as Homer's *The Iliad* and *The Odyssey*. In *Voices of the Trojan War*, Kate Hovey uses quotes from classic works about the Trojan War, such as *Metamorphoses*, by Ovid, *The Aeneid*, by Virgil, and *The Iliad*, by Homer, as epigraphs to her own poems that retell the story of the 10-year battle and the ultimate defeat of Troy. She presents multiple perspectives and uses language that is accessible to children in upper-elementary grades. In *Ancient Voices*, Hovey gives poetic voice to the gods and goddesses of Mount Olympus.

Beowulf, composed around the eighth century, is the oldest surviving epic poem in English. *The Hero Beowulf*, adapted by Eric Kimmel, presents the first part of this epic poem and is accessible to children in middle-elementary grades. Kimmel begins his adaptation with Beowulf's youthful experiences slaying trolls and serpents, then moves to the kingdom of Heorot, where the green monster Grendel is wreaking havoc, and ends with Beowulf successfully slaying Grendel and becoming a hero among the Danes. For a complete version of *Beowulf* and for an introduction to the text in its original Old English, older students and teachers can read poet Seamus Heaney's bilingual edition, *Beowulf: A New Verse Translation*.

words and music by Guthrie. The illustrations provide a panorama of the United States. *She'll Be Comin' Round the Mountain*, a favorite American folk song adapted from the African American spiritual "When the Chariot Comes," describes the approach of a horse-drawn stagecoach bringing mail or visitors. In Philemon Sturges's adaptation, along with Ashley Wolff's illustrations, the action of the song is set in a small town in the Southwest where an array of animals prepare a fiesta in anticipation of a visitor's arrival. This version highlights the distinctive rhythm and anticipation of the original song with expanded lyrics: "She'll be comin' 'round the mountain when she comes./She'll be bouncin' 'round the mountain when she comes./She'll be honkin', she'll be hootin', she'll be shoutin', she'll be tootin',/She'll be comin' 'round the mountain when she comes." Throughout the book, a camper can be seen in the background, coming closer as the lyrics progress. Animals are shown preparing for the celebration or are busy reading books. The end, along with the last illustration, reveals that the anticipated vis-

With rapid action and typically chronological order, narrative poems have long been favorites of children. They are excellent for increasing children's interest in, and appreciation of, poetry. Robert Browning's "The Pied Piper of Hamelin," first published in 1882, contains many of the characteristics that make narrative poems appealing to children. The actions of the villainous rats, for example, are easy to visualize.

Rats!
They fought the dogs, and filled the cats,
And bit the babies in the cradles,
And ate the cheeses out of the vats,
And licked the soup from the cook's own ladles,
Split open the kegs of salted sprats,
Made nests inside men's Sunday hats,
And even spoiled the women's chats
By drowning their speaking
With shrieking and squeaking
In fifty different sharps and flats.

The plot develops rapidly, as the townspeople approach the mayor and the town council, demanding action. Into this setting comes the hero.

And in did come the strangest figure!
His queer long coat from heel to head
Was half of yellow and half of red;
And he himself was tall and thin,
With sharp blue eyes, each like a pin,
And light, loose hair, yet swarthy skin,
No tuft on cheek nor beard on chin,
But lips where smiles went out and in—
There was no guessing his kith and kin!
And nobody could enough admire
The tall man and his quaint attire:

With rapidity, the council offers the stranger a thousand gilders to rid the town of its rats, and the piper places the pipe to his lips. At this point, the tempo of the poem resembles the scurrying of rats.

And out of the house the rats came tumbling.
Great rats, small rats, lean rats, brawny rats,
Brown rats, black rats, gray rats, tawny rats,
Grave old plodders, gay young friskers,
Fathers, mothers, uncles, cousins,
Cocking tails and pricking whiskers,
Families by tens and dozens,
Brothers, sisters, husbands, wives—
Followed the piper for their lives.
From street to street he piped advancing,
And step for step they followed dancing,

Robert Browning
The Pied Piper of Hamelin, 1888

Highly illustrated picture books for young children frequently develop a story in rhyme. For example, Kathi Appelt shows the love between a very personified Mama Bird and her child in *Oh My Baby, Little One*. The narrative poem describes Mama's love as her little one goes to school. Similes help depict this love that is always with the young bird, just as the leaves are with the trees, the sand is with the sandbox, or the kite is with the breeze.

Other narrative poems long popular with children include Clement Moore's "A Visit from St. Nicholas" (now better known as "The Night Before Christmas"), which has been produced as books illustrated by Tomie dePaola and by Tasha Tudor; Lewis Carroll's delightful "The Walrus and the Carpenter," in which some young oysters go

for a walk on the beach with one hungry animal and one hungry human; and Henry Wadsworth Longfellow's romantic dramas from early American history, "The Song of Hiawatha" and "Paul Revere's Ride."

Margaret Early's illustrated version of "The Song of Hiawatha" includes historical notes about the poem. She also provides prose descriptions, which summarize the story that occurs between the poetry selections. "Paul Revere's Ride" has been illustrated by Monica Vachula with historically accurate oil paintings of places such as Revere's House, the Old North Church, and the bridge at Lexington and Concord. In another illustrated version of the poem, Christopher Bing uses engravings and watercolors, includes maps that follow the British campaign and Revere's journey on horseback, and re-creates historical documents, including the British general's orders to his troops and Revere's own deposition. His "Miscellany" at the back of the book describes the fictional aspects of the American myth created by Longfellow and gives historical details of Revere and the events surrounding his famous ride. In *Paul Revere's Ride: The Landlord's Tale*, Charles Santore's illustrations and artist's note frame the narrative as Longfellow originally wrote it, as a story being told to a group of friends gathered around a fire in a parlor of the Wayside Inn 100 years after the historic ride took place. Introducing children to three illustrated versions of the poem can show the possibilities artists face when interpreting a classic piece of literature.

Many contemporary poets—including John Ciardi, Jack Prelutsky, and Beatrice Curtis Brown—write narrative poems. Their topics are both nonsensical and realistic. Several contemporary poets have written highly illustrated narrative poems. For example, Nancy Willard's *The Tale I Told Sasha* follows a yellow ball as it rolls over the Bridge of Butterflies and encounters all types of beasts and even the King of Keys. The girl who follows the ball has an imaginative adventure that ends with the girl trying to recapture her strange adventures as she returns home.

Once Upon a Poem: Favorite Poems That Tell Stories, Kevin Crossley-Holland's compilation of 15 narrative poems, contains familiar favorites such as Lewis Carroll's "Jabberwocky," Edward Lear's "The Owl and the Pussycat," and Eugene Field's "Wynken, Blynken, and Nod," as well as lesser-known poems such as C. S. Lewis's "The Late Passenger," A. B. Paterson's "The Man From Snowy River," and W. H. Auden's "O What Is That Sound." Each poem is introduced briefly with a recommendation from a well-known contemporary author such as Avi, Sharon Creech, and J. K. Rowling. The afterword includes biographical sketches of the poets and contemporary authors in the collection.

Ballads

The ballad is a form of narrative folk song or verse popular in Europe during the Middle Ages. *Ballad*, from the Latin *ballare*, meaning "to dance," originally referred to a folk song-and-dance, such as the surviving "London Bridge Is Falling Down." It soon came to refer to a folk song that tells a brief story. Minstrels and bards (*bard* is the Welsh word for "poet") sang the tales of legend or local history, often involving lost love and tragedy, while accompanying themselves on stringed instruments. Marla Frazee's *Hush, Little Baby* is an English folk song that includes a musical accompaniment. Modern poets have used the ballad form for poems to be read rather than sung. However, traditional ballads are part of the oral literary heritage of European culture, passed on by word of mouth.

Beginning in the 16th century and continuing to the present day, some ballads have been printed on large sheets of paper like newspapers and sold as broadside ballads at county fairs. However, most have been sung and passed down by oral tradition, which is why ballads turn up in widely differing versions, such as a Scottish ballad with American-sounding names and locations. Many poets, imitating the folk tradition, have written literary ballads.

Action, usually heroic or tragic, is the focus of literary ballads. Samuel Taylor Coleridge's "The Rime of the Ancient Mariner," a sea ballad published in 1798, was based on the legend that it is fatal to shoot an albatross. The text is dramatic, including memorable lines that are frequently quoted. Notice the drama in the following excerpt from the longer poem.

> The fair breeze blew, the white foam flew,
> The furrow follow'd free;
> We were the first that ever burst
> Into that silent sea.
>
> Down dropt the breeze, the sails dropt down.
> 'Twas sad as sad could be;
> And we did speak only to break
> The silence of the sea!
>
> All in a hot and copper sky,
> The bloody Sun, at noon,
> Right up above the mast did stand,
> No bigger than the Moon.
>
> Day after day, day after day,
> We stuck, nor breath nor motion;
> As idle as a painted ship
> Upon a painted ocean.
>
> Water, water, everywhere,
> And all the boards did shrink;
> Water, water, everywhere
> Nor any drop to drink.

Samuel Taylor Coleridge
From "The Rime of the Ancient Mariner," 1798

Alfred Noyes's "The Highwayman," originally appearing in *Forty Singing Seamen and Other Poems* (1907), is an example of a romantic literary ballad about heartbreak and doomed love. In Murray Kimber's version, illustrations recast the poem into a contemporary setting by re-placing the horse with a motorcycle and King George's soldiers with FBI agents and relocating the action from rural England to the streets of New York City.

Ernest Thayer's "Casey at the Bat" is an example of a ballad inspired by local history. It places the tragic-comic celebration of heroism in the context of a baseball player striking out. This ballad, with the memorable opening lines "The outlook wasn't brilliant for the Mudville nine that day;/The score stood four to two with but one inning more to play," was first published in the *San Francisco Daily Examiner* on June 3, 1888. Readers speculated it was about the losing streak of a California baseball team. A few months later, another version of the ballad appeared in the *New York Sporting Times* with the title "Kelly at the Bat" and references to Boston baseball players.

In one illustrated version of the poem, C. F. Payne includes a "Note About the Poem" that gives historical context to the ballad. In this note, Payne explains how comedian De Wolf Hopper contributed to the ballad's popularity by performing it on stage and on radio more than 10,000 times within a 40-year period. According to Hopper, the ballad has maintained its popularity because "there are one or more Caseys in every league, bush or big, and there is no day in the playing season that this same supreme tragedy . . . does not befall on some field" (unnumbered).

In another illustrated version of the ballad, Christopher Bing, awarded a Caldecott Honor for his illustrations, includes real and *trompe l'oeil* reproductions of period baseball cards, tickets, newspaper clippings, and advertisements.

Limericks

The short, witty poems called *limericks* are popular with children. All limericks have the same basic structure and rhythm: They are five-line poems in which the first, second, and fifth lines rhyme and have three pronounced beats each, and the third and fourth lines rhyme and have two pronounced beats each. The limerick form was popularized by Edward Lear in the 19th century. Following is an example of humorous verse from Lear's *A Book of Nonsense*.

> There was an Old Man with a beard,
> Who said,"It is just as I feared!—
> Two Owls and a Hen,
> Four Larks and a Wren
> Have all built their nests in my beard."

Edward Lear
A Book of Nonsense, 1846

Children enjoy the visual imagery that this poem creates; they can see and laugh at the predicament of having those fowl nesting in a beard. They also enjoy reciting the definite rhythm and rhyme found in the limerick. Fifteen more of Lear's original limericks have been published in the book *Nonsense!*, with humorous illustrations by Valorie Fisher.

In *A Child's Introduction to Poetry*, Michael Driscoll includes several limericks published anonymously such as this favorite among children:

> A flea and a fly in a flue
> Were imprisoned, so what could they do?
> Said the fly, "Let us flee,"
> "Let us fly," said the flea.
> So they flew through a flaw in the flue. (p. 21)

Susan Pearson's modern treatment of the limerick can be found in her book *Grimericks.* These limericks are filled with ghosts, goblins, and monsters, including a limerick about the courtship of Howard the goblin and Gertrude the gremlin.

David McCord (1977), who has written numerous contemporary limericks himself, says that for a limerick to be successful, it must have perfect rhyming and flawless rhythm. McCord's amusing limericks in his *One at a Time: Collected Poems for the Young* illustrate the author's ability to play with words and with the sounds of language. These limericks may also stimulate children to experiment with language by writing their own limericks.

Concrete Poems

Concrete is something that can be seen or touched, something that is physically real. When a poet emphasizes the meaning of a poem by shaping it into the form of a picture, concrete poetry results. Robert Froman's poem "Dead Tree," from *Seeing Things: A Book of Poems*, is lettered in the shape of a dead tree trunk. Mary Ellen Solt was inspired to create both a poem and a picture about the promise of spring in a forsythia bush. This poem is included in Paul Janeczko's collection *A Poke in the I.* Children should turn this poem on its side to read the thoughts of the author. Janeczko's collection also includes John Hollander's poem "Swan and Shadow," in which the words form a swan and the shadow of a swan as it glides on water.

Technically, It's Not My Fault is a collection of humorous and often silly concrete poems by John Grandits, told from the perspective of 11-year-old Robert. The title poem, an account of a science experiment gone awry, appears on the front cover, and its messy result, a smashed tomato, appears on the back; "TyrannosaurBus Rex" features a hungry school bus eating its way along its route; and "The Lay-Up" shows words bouncing up and down a court like a basketball before they go into a basket, move in a circle, and fall to one side while the content of the words expresses disappointment in missing the basket.

The poems in Joan Bransfield Graham's *Flicker Flash* are all written as concrete poetry. Some of these shapes include "Candle," "Firefly," and "Full Moon." Jack Prelutsky's "A Triangular Tale," found in his *A Pizza the Size of the Sun*, is another enjoyable poem that is written in the shape of its content.

Children find concrete poetry exciting to look at. Observing concrete objects and writing picture poems about them also stretch children's imaginations.

Haiku

Haiku is a very old form of Japanese poetry. A traditional haiku has three unrhymed lines; the first line has five syllables, the second line has seven, and the final line has five. According to John Drury (1995), "the essential elements of haiku are brevity, immediacy, spontaneity, imagery, the natural world, a season, and sudden illumination" (p. 125).

Poets of haiku link themselves with nature and the cycle of the seasons. A photograph of a beach scene, in which a stream of water is placing its mark upon the land, accompanies the following example of Ann Atwood's (1971) haiku.

> A blank page of sand—
> at the water's cutting edge
> the pattern shaping.

> From poem *Haiku: The Mood of Earth,*
> by Ann Atwood,
> Scribner's Sons, copyright 1971,
> p. 4, unnumbered

Celeste Davidson Mannis's collection of haiku poems, *One Leaf Rides the Wind: Counting in a Japanese Garden,* follows a young girl as she discovers delights in nature during her walk through a Japanese tranquility garden. Each haiku includes footnotes about Japanese religion and philosophy, such as the tea ceremony and the legend of the koi fish.

Jack Prelutsky uses the haiku form in *If Not For Cat* to describe 17 animals—from elephants to ants. Each animal is presented in the form of a riddle answered in the illustrations.

Japan's most revered poet, Matsuo Basho, is considered the father of the haiku form. According to this 17th-century poet the haiku was an exercise in reflection of the solitary self, and he made his living traveling around Japan teaching this art form. Dawnine Spivak's *Grass Sandals: The Travels of Basho* tells the story of Basho, what he saw and did, and whom he met during his travels. Each page layout includes compressed excerpts from Basho's journals and an original haiku he composed during his walking journey across Japan. Each haiku contains language that appeals to two of the five senses—sight, hearing, smell, touch, and taste—or the additional sense of movement. Illustrations include Japanese characters and Demi's artwork of colored ink on rice paper.

In *Basho and the River Stones*, Tim Myers briefly describes the haiku form and includes an author's note about the poet Basho. In his original trickster tale, Myers presents Basho as a character who considers the act of creating a haiku to be more valuable than gold. Basho's haiku humbles the fox and leads to their lasting friendship.

Climb Mount Fuji,

Snail, but slowly,

slowly!

The illustration reinforces the images of the haiku. (From Cool Melons—Turn to Frogs!: The Life and Poems of Issa. *Story and haiku translations by Matthew Golub. Illustration by Kazuko G. Stone. Illustrations copyright © 1998 by Kazuko G. Stone. Published by Lee & Low Books, Inc. Reprinted by permission of Lee & Low Books, Inc.)*

One of the most interesting introductions both to the 18th-century Japanese poet Issa and to his haiku is Matthew Gollub's *Cool Melons—Turn to Frogs! The Life and Poems of Issa.* The text includes both a brief biography of the poet and haiku translations that highlight Issa's life; Kazuko G. Stone's illustrations add to the impact of the poetry. In addition, Japanese calligraphy adds visual appeal and conveys the feeling of the delicate brush strokes that were part of Issa's skill. As you read these poems, notice how they support Drury's essential elements of haiku. Notice also how the illustrations add to the meaning of both the biography and the haiku. For example, what is the impact of an illustration of a snail on the tree branch overlooking Mount Fuji, the haiku telling readers to climb the mountain slowly like the snail, and the biographical portion on the same page that describes Issa's struggles as he trains under a master poet?

For more information about the history of the haiku and for more examples of this art form, older students and teachers may want to refer to poet Robert Hass's *The Essential Haiku: Versions of Basho, Buson, and Issa.*

Poems and Poets

To share poetry with children, you can select from many classic and contemporary poems. Poets who write for children use subjects interesting to children. Children's poets write humorous poems: nature poems; poems that encourage children to identify with characters, situations, and locations; poems that suggest moods and feelings; animal poems; and poems about witches and ghosts. Although these categories sometimes overlap and some poets write about many different topics, many children's poets focus on certain subjects and types of poetry.

Nonsense and Humor: Poems for Starting Out Right

Nonsense rhymes are logical successors to Mother Goose rhymes for enjoyably introducing children to poetry. The nonsense poems of such great poets as Edward Lear and Lewis Carroll are ideal: They suggest spontaneous fun through emphatic, regular rhythms that are heightened by alliteration. Nonsense verses convey absurd meanings or even no meaning at all. Collections of rhymes, superstitions, and riddles such as those found in Nancy Van Laan's *With a Whoop and a Holler: A Bushel of Lore From Way Down South* suggest that nonsense and humor are universal characteristcs that have appealed to people across time and geographical locations.

Humorous poetry, although closely related to nonsense poetry, deals with amusing happenings that might actually befall a person or an animal. Numerous contemporary poets also write nonsensical or humorous verse to entice children into the fun and life-enriching world of poetry.

Poems in Vadim Levin's *Silly Horse*, translated from Russian by Tanya Wolfson and Tatiana Zunshine, provide humorous viewpoints about animals. For example, we meet a turkey that pushes a trunk, a horse that keeps her shoes inside during inclement weather, a "wicky-wacky-wocky" mouse, Mr. Croakley, and Mr. Quackley. We also meet humans such as Mr. and Mrs. Bockley, who use a telescope to crack nuts on their roof. Evgeny Antonenkov's illustrations add humor to the poems.

Humor is also found in the imagery, situations, and descriptive language in Nancy Willard's *Pish, Posh, Said Hieronymus Bosch*, inspired by the odd creatures found in artist Hieronymus Bosch's paintings. The artist, who painted in the late 1400s and early 1500s, was known for his bizarre creatures. When writing this poetry, Willard speculated about what it would be like to live and work in a household filled with Bosch's creatures. Consequently, the poetry is filled with three-legged thistles, pickle-winged fish, pigeon-toed rats, and a troop of jackdaws.

Several anthologies contain sections of nonsense poetry. Jack Prelutsky's *The Random House Book of Poetry for Children* has a section titled "Nonsense! Nonsense!" *Sing a Song of Popcorn: Every Child's Book of Poems*, by Beatrice Schenk de Regniers et al., includes poems categorized "Mostly Nonsense." A portion of Liz Attenborough's anthology, *Poetry by Heart: A Child's Book of Poems to Remember*, is called "Stuff and Nonsense." *A Family of Poems: My Favorite Poetry for Children*, compiled by Caroline Kennedy, includes poems under the heading "That's So Silly." Lillian Morrison's colletion of lighthearted verse, *It Rained All Day that Night: Autographs, Rhymes & Inscriptions*, is filled with humorous poems, including a section of nonsense verse called "Four Corners of the Round Table." Louise Guinness's attractive anthology, *The Everyman Book of Nonsense Verse*, includes well-known verse by Edward Lear, Lewis Carroll, Ogden Nash, and A. A. Milne as well as nonsense verse by Shakespeare, Elizabeth Bishop, Theodore Roethke, and contemporary poets such as Matthew Sweeney.

Edward Lear. Edward Lear, introduced earlier as the popularizer of the limerick form, had many loyal friends among the leaders and creative artists of Great Britain in the 19th century. He was welcomed into their homes and became an "Adopty Duncle" to their children, for whom he wrote and illustrated the nonsense verses collected in

A Book of Nonsense and *Nonsense Songs and Stories:* limericks, narrative poems, tongue twisters, and alphabet rhymes.

Lear's nonsense poems can be found in many anthologies. They also have been illustrated in single editions by serveral well-known illustrators. *Hilary Knight's The Owl and the Pussy-Cat* is an excellent choice for young children; the highly illustrated text begins with a fantasy situation and presents the poem as a story told by Professor Comfort. A careful search of the illustrations reveals numerous references to Lear's works and interests. Compare Knight's illustrated version with Jan Brett's illustrations for Lear's *The Owl and the Pussycat*; Brett places her characters in a Caribbean setting. Fred Marcellino's illustrated version of *The Pelican Chorus and Other Nonsense*, written by Edward Lear, includes "The New Vestments," "The Owl and the Pussycat," and "The Pelican Chorus." The delightfully humorous illustrations make interesting comparisons with other illustrated versions of Lear's poetry. *The Quangle Wangle's Hat*, highly illustrated by Louise Voce, introduces Mr. Quangle Wangle; Quee, who lives high up in the Crumpety Tree; and the friends he makes as the poem progresses, including the Fimble Fowl and the Pobble who has no toes.

Lewis Carroll. Lewis Carroll was the pen name for Charles Lutwidge Dodgson, a mathematician. Carroll's works are historical milestones of children's literature. His nonsense verses are found in *Alice's Adventures in Wonderland* and *Through the Looking Glass*. One of Carroll's most famous poems is "Jabberwocky," from *Through the Looking Glass*, which introduces the marvelous nonsense words

From THE QUANGLE WANGLE'S HAT, *by Edward Lear. Illustrations copyright © 2005 by Louise Voce. Reproduced by permission of Candlewick Press. Inc., Cambridge, MA.*

brillig, slithy toves, and *borogoves.* This poem has been published as a lovely book illustrated by Jane Breskin Zalben.

Hilaire Belloc. Born in France in 1870 and educated in England, Hilaire Belloc secured his popularity as a children's writer with the publication of *The Bad Child's Book of Beasts* in 1896 and *More Beasts for Worse Children* in 1897. These books, filled with humorous poems of manners about animals such as the whale, the frog, the polar bear, the dodo, and the yak, poked fun at nursery rhymes that were popular at the time.

Belloc followed the success of these books with *A Moral Alphabet* in 1899. These alphabet rhymes include verse such as "E stands for egg. Moral: The moral of this verse is applicable to the Young. Be terse" (*Cautionary Verses,* p. 309) and "X: No reasonable little Child expects/A grown-up Man to make a rhyme on X. Moral: These verses teach a clever child to find/Excuse for doing all that he's inclined" (*Cautionary Verses,* p. 353). Belloc's *Cautionary Tales for Children,* published in 1907, contains poems with instructive lessons and admonishments for children. This collection has titles such as "Henry King, Who Chewed on Bits of String, And Was Early Cut Off In Dreadful Agonies," "Matilda, Who Told Lies, and Was Burned to Death," "Franklin Hyde, Who Caroused in the Dirt and was corrected by His Uncle," "Goldophin Home, Who was cursed with the Sin of Pride, and Became a Boot-Black," and "Algernon, Who Played with a Loaded Gun, and, on missing his Sister, was reprimanded by his Father." These darkly humorous, tongue-in-cheek verses satirized the cautionary tales told to Victorian children.

Children's authors J. K. Rowling and Jack Prelutsky name Belloc as one of their favorite poets for his use of wit. In a 2001 BBC poll, Belloc's cautionary tale "Matilda" was rated the second most favorite children's poem in Great Britain, right after Lear's "The Owl and the Pussy Cat." Belloc's verse is still anthologized and can be found in collections such as Iona and Peter Opie's *The Oxford Book of Children's Verse,* Kevin Crossley-Holland's *Once Upon a Poem: Favorite Poems That Tell Stories,* Michael Driscoll's *A Child's Introduction to Poetry,* and Caroline Kennedy's *A Family of Poems: My Favorite Poetry for Children.* Edward Gorey recently added his own period illustrations to six of Belloc's poems published in *Cautionary Tales for Children.*

Laura E. Richards. Contemporary children may be surprised to discover that a well-known author of nonsense poetry is the daughter of Julia Ward Howe, who wrote a beautiful but somber poem, "The Battle Hymn of the Republic." Like Lear and Carroll, Richards has shared marvelous words and sounds with children. There are *wizzy wizzy woggums, ditty dotty doggums,* and *diddy doddy dorglums.* There are *Rummy-jums, Viddipocks,* and *Orang-Qutang-Tangs.* Richards's collection *Tirra Lirra, Rhymes Old and New* contains many rhymes that emphasize the sound of language and encourage children to play with words. One of her best-loved nonsense poems follows.

Eletelephony

Once there was an elephant,
Who tried to use the telephant—
No!No! I mean an elephone
Who tried to use the telephone—
(Dear me! I am not certain quite
That even now I've got it right.)

Howe'er it was, he got his trunk
Entangled in the telephunk;
The more he tried to get it free,
The louder buzzed the telephee—
(I fear I'd better drop the song
Of elephop and telephong!)

From poem "Eletelephony" from *Tirra Lirra, Rhymes Old and New,* p. 31, by Laura E. Richards. Copyright © 1955, Little, Brown & Company.

Shel Silverstein. One of the most popular children's poets, Shel Silverstein wrote much nonsense and humorous poetry. Librarians report that Silverstein's *Where the Sidewalk Ends* and *A Light in the Attic* are in much demand by young readers. Improbable characters and situations in *A Light in the Attic* include a Quick-Digesting Gink, Sour Ann, and a polar bear in the Frigidaire. Silverstein's *Falling Up* includes poems about additional humorous situations.

Consider Silverstein's use of rhythm, rhyme, sound patterns, and repetition in "Ickle Me, Pickle Me, Tickle Me Too."

Ickle Me, Pickle Me, Tickle Me Too

Ickle Me, Pickle Me, Tickle Me too
Went for a ride in a flying shoe.
"Hooray!"
"What fun!"
"It's time we flew!"
Said Ickle Me, Pickle Me, Tickle Me too.

Ickle was captain, and Pickle was crew
And Tickle served coffee and mulligan stew
As higher
And higher
And higher they flew,
Ickle Me, Pickle Me, Tickle Me too.

Ickle Me, Pickle Me, Tickle Me too.
Over the sun and beyond the blue.
"Hold on!"
"Stay in!"
"I hope we do!"
Cried Ickle Me, Pickle Me, Tickle Me too.

Ickle Me, Pickle Me, Tickle Me too
Never returned to the world they knew,
And nobody
Knows what's
Happened to
Dear Ickle Me, Pickle Me, Tickle Me too.

From poem "Ickle Me, Pickle Me" by Shel Silverstein. Copyright 1974. Reprinted by permission of HarperCollins.

Shel Silverstein's latest collection, *Runny Babbit: A Billy Sook,* which he completed before his death in 1999, introduces children to a world of flip-flopped words and funny poems. As the introductory poem explains, in Runny Babbit's world, "Instead of sayin' 'purple hat,'/They all say 'hurple pat'" (p. 4). We meet Runny Babbit's "funny bamily" and friends, including Toe Jurtle, Ploppy Sig, Skertle Gunk, Rirty Dat, and Dungry Hog who do things such as "bead a rook," visit the "Sharber Bop," and make "puddy mies." Along the way, Runny "shearns to lare the picken chox." The poems require concentration to translate the phrases and may inspire children to create their own verse filled with flip-flopped words.

Jack Prelutsky. The world created by Prelutsky's nonsense and humorous poetry for children could be described as the kingdom of immortal zanies and improbable situations such as those already shown in his poem "Don't Ever Seize a Weasel by the Tail." Within the pages of *The Queen of Eene* are preposterous characters, such as peculiar Mister Gaffe, Poor Old Penelope, Herbert Glerbertt, and the Four Foolish Ladies (Hattie, Harriet, Hope, and Hortense).

Rolling Harvey Down the Hill describes the humorous experiences of a boy and his four friends. In *The Sheriff of Rottenshot,* eccentric characters include Philbert Phlurk, Eddie the spaghetti nut, and a saucy little ocelot. *The Baby Uggs Are Hatching* contains poems about oddly named creatures, such as Sneepies and Slitchs. Prelutsky's *The Dragons Are Singing Tonight* contains poems about all types of dragons, and Peter Sís's illustrations add to the believability. *The Gargoyle on the Roof,* also illustrated by Peter Sís, includes humorous poems about all types of monsters including werewolves, vampires, and, of course, gargoyles. *Awful Ogre's Awful Day,* illustrated by Paul O. Zelinsky, is another collection of humorous poems. Prelutsky's *Monday's Troll* features poems about enchanted characters such as witches and ogres. Other improbable creatures are found in his *A Pizza the Size of the Sun.* Many of the poems in *The Frogs Wore Red Suspenders* use place names such as Tucumcari and Tuscaloosa. In *Scranimals,* illustrated by Peter Sís, Prelutsky introduces children to creatures that are a cross between an animal and a fruit, flower, or vegetable, such as the Porcupineapple, the Avocadodos, the Broccolions, the Mangorilla, and the Pandaffodil.

John Ciardi. A poet who was both a professor of English and a columnist for *Saturday Review World,* Ciardi wrote two books with a simple vocabulary to appeal to children with beginning reading skills: *I Met a Man* and *You Read to Me, I'll Read to You.* In the second book, Ciardi tells readers, "All the poems printed in black, you read to me, and all the poems printed in blue, I'll read to you." This collection contains "Mummy Slept Late and Daddy Fixed Breakfast"; other popular poems in this book tell about such characters as Chang McTang McQuarter Cat and Arvin Marvin Lillisbee Fitch.

Technology Resources

The CD-ROM that accompanies this text can be used to generate a list of appropriate titles to get a class on course to writing their own nature poetry. Begin by searching for "nature" in the Title and Description fields. You might consider using both poetry (P) and information (INF) in the Genre field.

Ciardi's *The Hopeful Trout and Other Limericks* contains numerous poems about funny situations supplemented by tongue-twisting sounds. However, some of Ciardi's poems are better understood by older children. His poems often contain satirical observations about human behavior or problems of society, and the humorous poems in *Doodle Soup* tend to be caustic.

N. M. Bodecker. Poems suggesting that children should wash their hands with number-one dirt, shampoo their hair with molasses, and rinse off in cider are welcomed by young readers. Bodecker uses wordplay in "Bickering" to create humorous verse enjoyed by older children.

> **Bickering**
> The folks in Little Bickering
> they argue quite a lot.
> Is tutoring in bickering
> required for a tot?
> Are figs the best for figuring?
> Is pepper ice cream hot?
> Are wicks the best for wickering
> a wicker chair or cot?
> They find this endless dickering
> and nonsense and nit pickering
> uncommonly invigor'ing
> I find it downright sickering!
> You do agree!

From poem "Bickering" from *Hurry, Hurry Mary Dear!* by N. M. Bodecker, copyright 1976. Reprinted by permission of Atheneum/Macmillan/Simon & Schuster, Inc.

In *Hurry, Hurry Mary Dear!,* the title poem has a harassed woman who is told to pick apples, dill pickles, chop trees, dig turnips, split peas, churn butter, smoke hams, stack wood, take down screens and put up storm windows, close shutters, stoke fires, mend mittens, knit sweaters, and brew tea. This might not be so bad, but the man who is giving the orders sits in a rocking chair all of the time. Finally, Mary has enough: She places the teapot carefully on the demanding gentleman's head.

Nature Poems

Like children, poets have marveled at the opening of the first crocus, seen new visions in a snowflake, or stopped to watch a stream of crystal-clear water tumbling from a mountaintop. They have understood that people should feel reverence and respect for nature. Such reverence and respect require special ways of hearing as well as special ways of looking.

The poetry of Emily Dickinson reflects a reverence for nature. *Poems for Youth* and *Poetry for Young People: Emily Dickinson* include a collection of Dickinson's poetry. Poems such as "The Moon Was But a Chin of Gold" personify nature by describing the moon's forehead, her cheeks, and her lips. In *Emily Dickinson's Letters to the World,* a collection for younger readers, Jeanette Winter tells the story of Dickinson's life from the viewpoint of her sister Lavinia, who discovered almost 1,800 of Dickinson's poems after her death. Winter presents 21 of Dickinson's poems, including poems about snowflakes, her visit to the sea, meadow bees, and how to make a prairie.

Carl Sandburg is another poet who wrote about his reflections on nature. He wrote his best-known poem, "Fog," after a walk along the shores of Lake Michigan:

Fog
The fog comes
on little cat feet.

It sits looking
over harbor and city
on silent haunches
and then moves on.

"Fog," from *Poems of the Midwest,*
by Carl Sandburg, p. 75. 1946,
World Publishing Company.

Penelope Niven's *Carl Sandburg: Adventures of a Poet,* gives biographical details alongside excerpts of Sandburg's works, including several of his poems about nature: "Sunset," "Just Before April Came," "Baby Song of the Four Winds," and "Plowboy," in which Sandburg describes the beauty of the prairie roads and the plowed fields stretching to the horizon.

Charlotte Zolotow's poetry is about childhood experiences and nature. Two editions of Zolotow's *River Winding* make possible interesting comparisons of the effects of illustrations. Children may enjoy evaluating the illustrations by Regina Shekerjian (1970 edition) and by Kazue Mizumura (1978 edition). The poem "Change" demonstrates how Zolotow is able to bring nature and children's experiences together in poetry.

Change
The summer
still hangs
heavy and sweet
with sunlight
as it did last year.

The autumn
still comes
showering gold and crimson
as it did last year.

The winter
still stings
clean and cold and white
as it did last year.

The spring
still comes
like a whisper in the dark night.

It is only I
who have changed.

From poem "Change" from *River Winding,*
by Charlotte Zolotow. Copyright
1978. Reprinted by permission
of Crowell/HarperCollins.

Many poets write about seasons and changes that occur in nature. In *Seasons: A Book of Poems,* Zolotow presents 40 poems about her reflections on the natural world and divides them into the four seasons: "Winter Bits," "Spring Things," "Summer Thoughts," and "The Feel of Fall."

In her collection *Swing Around the Sun,* Barbara Juster Esbensen uses familiar images to evoke the four seasons with poetic flair. For example, in the section "Spring," she describes umbrellas that bloom and concludes with the question "I wonder why tulips/hold their umbrellas upside-down?" In the poem "Snowfall," she asks, "Who shook the night/And made the feathers fly?" Esbensen's effective pairing of poetry with the beautiful artwork of four renowned artists may inspire children to write and illustrate their own seasonal poems.

Douglas Florian combines his lighthearted seasonal verse with his own artwork in *Summersaults,* 28 short poems and paintings that capture a summer filled with bees, seashores, and dandelions. In *Autumnblings: Poems and Paintings,* Florian invents words such as *autumnescent* and *fallicopters* and infuses his poetry and his art with images of ripe apples, falling leaves, pumpkins, and the first frost. In *Leaf by Leaf: Autumn Poems,* Barbara Rogasky pairs the photographs of Marc Tauss with poetry of fall by well-known poets, such as "The Frost," by Tzo Yeh, and "Wind and Silver," by Amy Lowell, and selections from "Come Up From the Fields Father," by Walt Whitman, and "The Window Washer," by Charles Simic.

Poems that illuminate aspects of winter make up Laura Whipple's compilation, *A Snowflake Fell: Poems About Winter.* She includes poems about the natural world, such as "Goose," by Ted Hughes, and "Old Man Winter," by Nancy Wood, as well as poems that reflect the experiences of children, such as "My Mother's Got Me Bundled Up," by Jack Prelutsky, and "Let's Pop the Corn," by Constance Levy.

A creative approach to poetry and the seasons can be found in Betsy Franco's *Mathematickles!* In this book, Franco and illustrator Steven Salerno combine the language of poetry and images of the seasons with simple mathematical concepts. For example, the first poem in the collection brings in the fall with "crisp air shadows tall + cat's thick coat = signs of fall." The last poem reflects the late summer: "lightningbugs × jar = summer lantern." The book includes graphs of a snowball fight and an inchworm climbing a branch. Bird beaks become angles, and a summer storm is evoked with the words "lightning = 2/3 triangle + 2/3 triangle + 2/3 triangle."

Creation and the ancient world are also subjects for poets. Douglas Wood's *Old Turtle* develops an understanding of the earth and our relationship with the beings that inhabit it. Cheng-Khee Chee's watercolors reinforce this fragility.

Nature poems frequently stimulate artists to create the settings described by poets. Ed Young illustrated Robert Frost's poem "Birches"; Susan Jeffers illustrated Frost's poem "Stopping by Woods on a Snowy Evening." Marcia Brown illustrated a series of "Mostly Weather" poems in de Regniers's *Sing a Song of Popcorn: Every Child's Book of Poems*. Wendell Minor's illustrations for Diane Siebert's *Mojave* illuminate the desert landscape, his illustrations in *Heartland* depict the land and people of the Midwest, and his illustrations for *Sierra* show the grandeur of the mountains.

Robert Frost.   The nature poems of Robert Frost are frequently included in anthologies of children's literature or are heavily illustrated in single-poem versions. As you read one of Frost's most famous poems, "Stopping by Woods on a Snowy Evening," visualize nature through the viewpoint of the poet. What emotions do you believe the poet is experiencing?

Stopping by Woods on a Snowy Evening
Whose woods these are I think I know.
His house is in the village though;
He will not see me stopping here
To watch his woods fill up with snow.

My little horse must think it queer
To stop without a farmhouse near
Between the woods and frozen lake
The darkest evening of the year.

He gives his harness bells a shake
To ask if there is some mistake.
The only other sound's the sweep
Of easy wind and downy flake.

The woods are lovely, dark and deep,
But I have promises to keep,
And miles to go before I sleep,
And miles to go before I sleep.

Robert Frost, 1923

Aileen Fisher.   Fisher's poetry communicates the excitement and wonder of discovering nature. Her vision is fresh and full of the magic possible when a person really looks at the natural world. Fisher creates images that are real to children and that children may extend to other observations. In her poems about insects, found in *When It Comes to Bugs,* and her poems about seasons and rabbits, found in *Listen, Rabbit* and *Rabbits, Rabbits,* Fisher encourages readers to closely observe nature.

In Fisher's poems about winter, evergreens after a snowfall wear woolly wraps and snow fills the garden chairs with teddy bears. Her "Frosted-Window World" allows children to visit Winter's house by going inside a frosted windowpane.

Frosted-Window World
The strangest thing,
the strangest thing
came true for me today;
I left myself beneath the quilt
and softly slipped away.

And do you know
the place I went
as shyly as a mouse,
as curious as a cottontail,
as watchful as a grouse?
Inside the frosted windowpane
(it's rather puzzling to explain)
to visit Winter's house!

How bright it was.
How light it was.
How white it was all over,
with twists and turns
through frosted ferns
and crusted weeds and clover,
through frost-grass
reaching up to my knees,
and frost-flowers
thick on all the trees.

The brightest sights,
the whitest sights
kept opening all around,
for everything
was flaked with frost,
the plants, the rocks,
the ground,
and everything was breathless-still
beneath the crusty rime—
there wasn't any clock to tick
or any bell to chime.
Inside the frosted windowpane
(it's rather puzzling to explain)
there wasn't any Time.

How clear it was.
How queer it was.
How near it was to heaven!
Till someone came
and called my name
and said, "It's after seven!"
And heaven vanished like an elf
and I whisked back, inside myself.

From poem "Frosted-Window World" from
*In One Door and Out the Other:
A Book of Poems,* by Aileen Fisher, copyright
1969. Reprinted by permission of Crowell.

Byrd Baylor. The closeness between the land and the creatures who live on it is strikingly presented in Baylor's poetry. She tells readers that they must learn *The Other Way to Listen* if they are to be fortunate enough to hear corn singing, wildflower seeds bursting open, or a rock murmuring to a lizard. The old man in the poem teaches the child that nature will not talk to people who feel superior. A person must respect every aspect of nature, humble as well as grand, and must begin with the small things: one ant, one horned toad, one tree. In several of Baylor's books, Peter Parnall's sensitive illustrations are attuned to both nature and the poet's words.

The poems in *Desert Voices* are written from the viewpoints of various inhabitants of the desert, animal and human. In *The Desert Is Theirs*, a poem about Native Americans, the poetry and accompanying illustrations develop the theme that the land is meant to be shared; it belongs not only to people but also to spiders, scorpions, birds, coyotes, and lizards. This beautifully illustrated poem tells how Earthmaker created the desert, Spider People sewed the sky and earth together, and Elder Brother taught the people to live in the sun and to touch the power of the earth. Readers discover that the Papagos know how to share the earth. Baylor develops the close relationship between people and nature through terms such as *brother* and actions that emphasize respect:

> Papagos try
> not to anger
> their animal brothers.
>
> They don't
> step on
> a snake's track
> in the sand.
>
> They don't disturb
> a fox's bones.
> They don't shove
> a horned toad
> out of the path.
>
> They know
> the land belongs
> to spider and ant
> the same as it does
> to people.
>
> They never say,
> "This is my land
> to do with as I please."
> They say,
> "We share . . .
> we only share."

From poem *The Desert Is Theirs*,
by Byrd Baylor. Reprinted by permission
of Simon & Schuster, Inc.

Paul Fleischman. Sound and motions in nature are strongly depicted in Paul Fleischman's *Joyful Noise: Poems*

for Two Voices and *I Am Phoenix: Poems for Two Voices*. The texts are designed to be read aloud by two readers, one taking the left side, the other taking the right side. The poems are read from top to bottom, with some parts solo and some parts duet. For example, read aloud the poem "Cicadas" in Figure 8.1 with another reader. Notice the effect created by the solo parts and the two voices.

Animals

When reporting a summary of the studies that investigated children's poetry preferences, Dianne Monson and Sam Sebesta (1991) concluded, "The popularity of humorous poems and poems about animals is evident from responses by English as well as U.S. children" (p. 668). Animals, whether teddy bears, cuddly puppies, purring kittens, or preposterous beasts of imagination, hold special places in the hearts of both children and adults. Therefore, it is not surprising that many poets write about animals.

In *Bow Wow Meow Meow: It's Rhyming Cats and Dogs*, Douglas Florian combines his paintings and his poetry to present different breeds of cats and dogs, both wild and domestic. He uses wordplay—"Why ocelots have lots of spots puzzles ocelot" (p. 34)—as well as placement on the page. In one poem, words curl like the hair of a poodle.

In *Mammalabilia*, Florian creates poems about 21 animals in which he depicts often humorous characteristics. He uses considerable rhyming elements, such as when he describes "The Otter" as aquatic, fanatic, acrobatic, and charismatic. *Omnibeasts: Animal Poems and Paintings* presents selections from Florian's seven creature collections. Many of the poems are shaped in the form of the animals they depict, such as the curve of a python or the humps of a camel. Florian continues to play with words in his descriptions: "orange newt./Orange you cute" (p. 75). The poem "The Polliwogs" is an example of how Florian uses rhyme to convey factual information about animals while playing with how words are placed on the page.

The Polliwogs

> We polliwoggle.
> We polliwiggle.
> We shake in lakes,
> Make wakes,
> And wriggle.
> We quiver,
> We shiver,
> We jiggle,
> We jog.
> We're yearning
> To turn ourselves
> Into a frog.

From *Omnibeasts: Animal
Poems and Paintings,*
by Douglas Florian,
p. 24. 2004, Harcourt.

Cicadas	
Afternoon, mid-August Two cicadas singing Five cicadas humming Thunderheads northwestward Twelve cicadas buzzing the mighty choir's assembling Shrill cica- das droning *Three years* spent underground in darkness Now they're breaking ground splitting skins and singing rejoicing fervent praise their hymn sung to the sun Cicadas whin- ing whir- ring pulsing chanting from the treetops sending forth their booming boisterous joyful noise!	Two cicadas singing Air kiln-hot, lead-heavy Five cicadas humming Twelve cicadas buzzing Up and down the street the mighty choir's assembling Ci- cadas droning in the elms *Three years* among the roots in darkness and climbing up the tree trunks and singing Jubilant cicadas pouring out their fervent praise for heat and light their hymn Cicadas whining ci- cadas whirring ci- cadas pulsing chanting from the treetops sending forth their booming joyful noise!

FIGURE 8.1 "Cicadas" (From Paul Fleischman. "Cicadas." *Joyful Noise: Poems for Two Voices*. Text © 1998 by Paul Fleischman. Illustrations © by Eric Beddows. Harper & Row Publishers, Inc. Reprinted by permission of HarperCollins.)

The best-known collection of cat poems by a single author is probably T. S. Eliot's *Old Possum's Book of Practical Cats*. These poems, composed for Eliot's godchildren, are full of vivid language, interesting characterizations, and lyrical quality, as revealed when the poems were set to music in the Broadway show *Cats*. Errol Le Cain has illus-trated two poems from *Old Possum's Book of Practical Cats* in *Mr. Mistoffelees With Mungojerrie and Rumpelteazer*. It is interesting to compare the original illustrations by Edward Gorey with the new ones by Le Cain.

William Blake's "The Tyger," written in the 18th century, begins with the memorable lines "Tyger, Tyger, burning bright/In the forests of the night." In *The Tyger*, more recently illustrated in a single volume, the paintings by Neil Waldman add to the energy, mood, and animals depicted in the poem.

Inspired by Robert Zakanitch's pencil sketchings and oil paintings of dogs, Maya Gottfried's verse in *Good Dog* presents the inner thoughts and distinctive personalities of 16 dogs. In *Fireflies at Midnight*, Marilyn Singer follows the lives of several animals during the span of one summer day. The book begins with a robin at dawn and includes the red fox and the spider that follow the fireflies at midnight; it ends the next dawn with a mole's thoughts on sleep. Diane Ackerman, a poet and naturalist, presents three poems for each of the five senses and each about a different animal in *Animal Sense*. For example, "Hearing" has poems about how bats communicate with pings, how humpback whales send signals through the ocean depths, and how baby birds learn to sing. Peter Sís provides the illustrations. Ackerman combines humor with interesting animal facts, such as that a bat eats 600 bugs an hour.

In *Feathers: Poems About Birds*, Eileen Spinelli uses short rhyming verse to introduce the activities of 28 birds from around the world, including the pelican, the toucan, the cygnet, the fairy tern, and the plover. Illustrations by Lisa McCue present the birds in their natural habitats, and brief notes offering more information about each bird are appended. Kristine O'Connell George chronicles the activities of a hummingbird that builds a nest on her patio in *Hummingbird Nest: A Journal of Poems*. Her subtle rhymes and Barry Moser's watercolor paintings capture the feeling of a nature journal.

In *Song of the Water Boatman & Other Pond Poems*, Joyce Sidman follows the natural drama that unfolds from spring through winter in the world of pond animals. Each of the 11 poems is paired with a paragraph that provides scientific information about a specific creature or aspect of pond life, such as the wood duck, spring peepers, the water bear, the caddis fly, the green darner, and cattails. Beckie Prange's prints are filled with movement and the vibrant greens and subtle browns of pond life.

Several anthologies about animals offer works by various poets. Laura Whipple's *Eric Carle's Animals, Animals* includes poems about a variety of animals. Carle's collage illustrations are vivid. *The Beauty of the Beast: Poems From the Animal Kingdom*, selected by Jack Prelutsky, provides an interesting comparison.

Laura Whipple selected poems about mythical creatures for *Eric Carle's Dragons Dragons & Other Creatures That Never Were*. Carle's large, colorful collages created from painted tissue paper introduce the right mood for poems about dragons, minotaurs, griffins, unicorns, krackens, and manticores. A detailed glossary contains information about these fabulous beasts and their origins. In addition, there are an index of poets and an index of creatures.

Illustration from HUMMINGBIRD NEST: A JOURNAL OF POEMS *by Kristine O'Connell George, illustrations copyright © 2004 by Barry Moser, reproduced by permission of Harcourt, Inc.*

Science

More and more poets are writing about subjects that could easily be used in the science classroom. Poetry can be used to teach subjects such as natural history, astronomy, and earth science. In *Bone Poems*, Jeffrey Moss combines humor with dinosaur facts researched at the American Museum of Natural Science in New York City. He includes poems with titles such as "I'm Going to Ask a Stegosaur to Dinner," he introduces us to a cranky ankylosaurus, and we learn the eating habits of ostracoderms. The end of the book contains a prounciation guide. Tom Leigh's cartoon line drawings soften the features of these ancient creatures. Compare the mood of these illustrations and poems with the influence of Arnold Lobel's watercolor illustrations that accompany Jack Prelutsky's poems in *Tyrannosaurus Was a Beast: Dinosaur Poems* and Murray Tinkelman's black-and-white illustrations in Lee Bennett Hopkins's *Dinosaurs*. You can also compare the mood of these poems with that developed by William Wise in *Dinosaurs Forever*. Wise includes a pronunciation guide to assist the oral reader.

Marilyn Singer explores the elements fire, water, and earth in three collections of poems illustrated by Meilo So. In *Central Heating: Poems About Fire and Warmth*, she writes about fire in poems about subjects such as the Earth's center, forest fires, birthday candles, and less obvious sources of fire such as chili peppers, roasting marshmallows, hot water, fireflies, and inspiration. In *How to Cross a Pond: Poems About Water*, Singer considers different facets of water in 19 poems that range in subject from waves, babbling brooks, wells, and a city river to the less obvious subject of watercolors. In *Footprints on the Roof: Poems About the Earth*, Singer uses poetic language to depict earth elements. For example, she describes volcanoes as sleeping dragons with cool heads and hot bellies.

Lisa Westber Peters uses poetic language and humor in her exploration of geological subjects such as strata, lava, fossils, and tectonic plates in her book *Earthshake: Poems From the Ground Up*. For example, a poem about fault lines is called "Instructions for the Earth's Dishwasher." Other poem titles include "Recipe for Granite," "Earth Charged in Meteor's Fiery Death," and "The Yellowstone Whale."

In *Science Verse*, Jon Scieszka and Lane Smith rewrite classic poems in humorous ways using subjects such as evolution, the food cycle, and the Big Bang. Poems include titles such as "Astronaut Stopping by a Planet on a Snowy Evening," "Scientific Method at the Bat," and "Twas the Night Before Any Thing."

Characters, Situations, and Locations

Poems about experiences that are familiar to children make up a very large category of poetry for children. Familiar experiences may be related to friends or family, may tell about everyday occurrences, or may provide insights into children's environments.

Sharon Creech's poems in *Who's That Baby?* are told from the perspective of a newborn and reflect different aspects of life as he or she meets various relatives and interacts in the world. In Dianna Hutts Aston's *When You Were Born*, a mother recalls the birth of her child and the joy felt by each family member as well as reactions of neighbors and a curious dog. Takayo Noda includes collage and short poems written in a child's voice to express a child's excitement in discovering the world around in *Dear World*. Observations are written as salutations addressing different objects in the world, such as "dear sun," "dear apples," and "dear stars." Elizabeth Garton Scanlon's rhyming verse in *A Sock Is a Pocket for Your Toes: A Pocket Book* encourages children to examine their surroundings as they follow four diverse families throughout the day in settings such as the zoo or a city apartment. Everything is presented in terms of the pocket it contains, such as "A phone is a pocket for a ring." Lee Bennett Hopkins's selection of poems in *Oh, No! Where Are My Pants? And Other Disasters: Poems* has subjects that are familiar to children, such

as a haircut, the first day of school, a friend moving away, and stagefright. The moods in the poems range from the sad, when a classroom pet dies, to the comic: "Hello apple!/Shiny red./CHOMP. CHOMP/Hello worm./Where's your head?" (p. 14).

Eloise Greenfield's *Honey, I Love* emphasizes the things a young girl loves, such as the way her cousin talks, the hose on a hot day, riding in a crowded car, and mama's soft and warm arm. The poems selected by Javaka Steptoe in *In Daddy's Arms I Am Tall: African Americans Celebrating Fathers* explore the bond between fathers and their children. The bond between a father and a son is addressed in Hope Anita Smith's *The Way a Door Closes*. Thirteen-year-old C. J. writes in verse, first to describe his contentment of being part of a close-knit family and then to express his pain, anger, and confusion when his father leaves abruptly and then returns to the family months later. In *Crowning Glory*, Joyce Carol Thomas presents the activities of a family in terms of the virtue and beauty of hair—tending it, adoring it, admiring it—and how this strengthens family bonds, especially among the women in an African American family.

Several stories in verse take children to familar settings surrounded by other students. Laura Nyman Montenegro's *A Bird About to Sing* tells the story of Natalie, who is confident in her writing but is afraid to share her work at a reading hosted by her teacher. On the bus ride home, everything she sees suggests a poem, which inspires her to perform for the students on the bus. In *Speak to Me: And I Will Listen Between the Lines*, Karen English uses six distinct voices to tell the stories of six inner-city third-grade students during one school day in the city. In Helen Frost's *Spinning Through The Universe: A Novel in Poems From Room 214*, students in a fifth-grade class learn details about each other's lives and realize they are a community. Each voice, including the teacher's and night custodian's, speaks in a different poetic form.

R. R. Knudson and May Swenson's *American Sports Poems* is a large anthology of poems about both specific sports and well-known athletes. *At the Crack of the Bat* is a collection of baseball poems compiled by Lillian Morrison. In *Shakespeare Bats Cleanup*, Ron Koertge uses free verse in this novel about 14-year-old Kevin, whose life revolves around baseball. When Kevin is forced to stay home for months because of an illness, he plays with haiku and sonnets and writes about different aspects of his life, including his dreams of baseball stardom. In *Goal*, Robert Burleigh's quick, descriptive poetry and Stephen Johnson's pastel illustrations tell the story of the final moments of a tied soccer game. Charles Smith's *Hoop Kings* is a collection of 12 poems about contemporary basketball players in which Smith mixes terms of the game with poetic language. For example, one player is introduced as a magician whose "3-point illusions/baffle your mind/when toes are behind/the arc/the spark (p. 29). Photographic images include a life-size photo of the sole of Shaquille O'Neal's shoe on a fold-out page. In *Hoop Queens*, Smith gives equal attention to 12 contemporary female basketball stars. At the end of the book, he provides poem notes describing each woman's talent and personality on the court.

Myra Cohn Livingston. Whether about whispers tickling children's ears or celebration of such holidays as Thanksgiving, Christmas, and Martin Luther King Day, Livingston's verses create images and suggest experiences to which children can relate. One child felt his mouth puckering as he read Livingston's poem about learning to whistle.

I Haven't Learned to Whistle

I have't learned to whistle.
I've tried—
But if there's anything like a whistle in me,
It stops
Inside.

Dad whistles.
My brother whistles
And almost everyone I know.

I've tried to put my lips together with wrinkles,
To push my tongue against my teeth
And make a whistle
Come
Out
Slow—

But what happens is nothing but a feeble gasping
Sound
Like a sort of sickly bird.

(Everybody says they never heard
A whistle like *that*
And to tell the truth
Neither did I.)

But Dad says, tonight, when he comes home,
He'll show me again how
To put my lips together with wrinkles,
To push my tongue against my teeth,
To blow my breath out and really make a whistle.

And I'll *try!*

Myra Cohn Livingston
O Sliver of Liver, p. 12

In additional poems, Livingston deals with characters, situations, and locations. Livingston's books of poems include *Celebrations* and *A Circle of Seasons*.

Valerie Worth. In *More Small Poems*, Valerie Worth poetically describes looking at a moth's wing through a magnifying glass, observing a kitten with a stiffly arched back, and seeing fireworks in the night sky. Something as simple as taking off one's shoes becomes a sensual experience for Worth, as in the following poem:

Barefoot

After that tight
Choke of sock
And blunt
Weight of shoe,

The foot can feel
Clover's green
Skin
Growing,

And the fine
Invisible
Teeth
Of gentle grass,

And the cool
Breath
Of the earth
Beneath.

Valerie Worth
Still More Small Poems, p. 13

In Worth's poems, common things in the worlds of children contain magical qualities. In *Still More Small Poems*, she sees common objects with uncommon insights: Grandmother's door with the fancy glass pattern, a kite riding in the air, and rags that are no longer faithful pajamas but crumpled cloths used to wash windows. The poems from all four of Valerie Worth's series of small poems appear in *All the Small Poems*.

David McCord. The poetic genius of McCord won him numerous honors, including the Sarah Josepha Hale Medal, a Guggenheim Fellowship, and, in 1977, the first national award for excellence in children's poetry awarded by the National Council of Teachers of English. Clifton Fadiman (McCord, 1977) said, "David McCord stands among the finest of living writers of children's verse. He is both an acrobat of language and an authentic explorer of the child's inner world" (coverleaf).

One at a Time: Collected Poems for the Young contains more than 200 of McCord's poems: favorite chants, such as "Song of the Train," alphabet verses, riddles, poetic conversations, and numerous poems about animals, children's experiences, nature, and nonsense. The last section of the book, "Write Me Another Verse," shows readers how to write different poetry forms, including the ballad, the tercet, the villanelle, the clerihew, the cinquain, and the haiku. Earlier in the book, McCord gives directions for writing the couplet (two-line verse), the quatrain (four-line verse), the limerick (five-line verse), and the triolet (eight-line verse).

McCord's skill in using shape to supplement meaning is illustrated in the following poem.

Grasshopper

Down
a
deep
well

a
grasshopper
fell.

By kicking about
He thought to get out.
He might have known better,
For that got him wetter.

To kick round and round
Is the way to get drowned,
And drowing is what
I should tell you he got.

But
the
well
had
a
rope
that
dangled
some
hope.
And sure as molasses
On one of his passes
He found the rope handy
And up he went, *and he*

it
up
and
it
up
and

it
up
and
it
up
went
And hopped away proper
As any grasshopper.

From poem "Grasshopper" from
*One at a Time: Collected Poems
for the Young*, pp. 28–30 by David McCord.
Copyright © 1980, Little, Brown & Company.

Moods and Feelings

The many moods and feelings associated with love are reflected in the poems compiled by William Jay Smith in *Here Is My Heart: Love Poems*. These poems range from "My Valentine," by Robert Louis Stevenson, in which love is reflected in bird song at morning and places fit for the loved one, to the humor of Jack Prelutsky, in "I Love You More Than Applesauce," in which love is equated with feelings for lollipops and candy drops.

The many moods related to friendship are also understood by children. The poems selected by Paul B. Janeczko in his anthology *Very Best (Almost) Friend Poems of Friendship* range from the wishful thinking in Janeczko's "If I Could Put a Curse on You," in which the unhappy friend visualizes a locker full of killer bees and busted spokes on a new bike, to the happiness expressed in Barbara Esbensen's "Friends," in which even drawings of the friends' houses lean toward each other as the friend runs up the walk.

The illustrations reinforce the spooky mood of the poems. (From Poems of Halloween Night: Ragged Shadows, *by Lee Bennett Hopkins. Illustrated by Giles Laroche. Copyright © 1993 by Giles Laroche. Reprinted by permission of Little, Brown and Company.)*

In *Danitra Brown Leaves Town*, Nikki Grimes tells the story of best friends Zuri and Danitra who are separated for the summer. Zuri expresses anger when Danitra first tells her she is leaving town and relief when she receives her first letter. The two continue to exchange letters in verse.

A bedtime fantasy forms the setting for the poems in Janet S. Wong's *Night Garden: Poems From the World of Dreams*. Poems such as "Night Garden" are enhanced through the poet's use of visualization, similes, and metaphors. Imagine a setting in which dreams grow wild and are compared with dandelion weeds with feathery heads that are alive with seeds. Or, imagine a world in which the dream person is able to answer a stranger in French that flies out of the mouth as fast as a goose flies south in winter. Or, imagine being able to swim free like a fish following a moonlit path down a stream. These are the fantasy possibilities found in the world of dreams.

Linda Ashman's *Sailing Off to Sleep* offers a bedtime rhyming ritual told in the voices of a parent and a child. Instead of going to sleep, the young girl decides to go sailing to the Arctic. Susan Winter's illustrations in watercolor and pencil show the pajama-clad girl on her imaginative and dreamy expedition. In a humorous treatment of a bedtime ritual, Ashman and illustrator Tricia Tusa tell the story in *How to Make a Night* of a little girl who ends a hectic day by mopping the clouds from the sky, lassoing the sun, and painting the stars. Sally Cook's *Good Night Pillow Fight* captures the excitement children often experience in resisting sleep.

Nikki Grimes explores feelings associated with the grieving process in her novella in verse, *What Is Goodbye?* After their older brother dies, Jesse and Jerilyn help each other cope with the anger, confusion, sadness, and family silence associated with grief. Jesse's rhyming verse faces his older sister's free verse filled with imagery and metaphor. The poems progress through the course of a year, from "Getting the News" to "Ordinary Days" to the final poem, "Photograph—Poem for Two Voices," in which the siblings describe the taking of a new family photograph and Jerilyn exclaims, "one piece missing, but/ we're whole again."

Jacqueline Woodson also explores the grieving process in *Locomotion*, the story of 11-year-old Lonnie, who lost his parents in a house fire when he was 7. Lonnie learns from a teacher how to express his anger and grief through poetry. The poems begin as poetry exercises. As Lonnie's story progresses, the poems become deeper reflections on his life with his foster mother; his experiences as an African American boy; his memories of his family and his childhood; the pain he feels living apart from his younger sister, Lili; and the joy and comfort he finds in being able to express himself with words.

Moods and feelings about loss are expressed in Naomi Shihab Nye's anthology *What Have You Lost?* Many of the poems in this collection for older readers probe deeper feelings such as the lost promises we never return to, as described in Jane Hirshfield's "Autumn Quince," or lamenting the eluded fame that eventually comes after years of desire, as in Nicanor Parra's "Fame." The poems selected by Lydia Omolola Okutoro in the anthology *Quiet Storm: Voices of Young Black Poets* are divided into sections that reflect such areas as "Black Pride," "Keeper of the Oral Tradition," and "Poems That Relfect on Self and Spirit." Moods and feelings also provide the focus in Carol Ann Duffy's *I Wouldn't Thank You for a Valentine: Poems for Young Feminists*. These poems express a variety of feelings, such as humor, anger, and conflict.

Poetry has always offered children consolation and comfort for feelings of sadness and confusion. In response to September 11, 2001, poet Georgia Heard was invited to visit New York City classrooms and read poetry to children who witnessed the event firsthand. Eighteen of these poems have been paired with original illustrations by 18 children's book illustrators and are presented in her compilation *This Place I Know: Poems of Comfort*. This collection contains poems about loss, fear, grief, hope, goodness, love, and consistency in nature, such as Deborah Chandra's poem "Stars" with the line "I like the way they looked down from the sky/And didn't seem to mind the way I cried" (p. 10) and Emily Dickinson's poem " 'Hope' is the thing with feathers—/That perches in the soul—/And sings the tune without the words—/And never stops—at all—" (p. 38).

Some of the poems written by children may reveal very emotional experiences or times of great unhappiness or fear in their lives. For example, the poems in *. . . Never Saw Another Butterfly . . .* , edited by Hana Volavkova, were written in the Terezin Concentration Camp from 1942 through 1944. As you read the following poem, imagine the experiences of and the mood felt by the author, who was also a child.

The Butterfly

The last, the very last,
So richly, brightly, dazzlingly yellow.
Perhaps if the sun's tears would sing
   against a white stone. . . .

Such, such a yellow
Is carried lightly way up high.
It went away I'm sure because it wished to
   kiss the world good-bye.

For seven weeks I've lived in here,
Penned up inside this ghetto.
But I have found what I love here.
The dandelions call to me
And the white chestnut branches in the court.
Only I never saw another butterfly.

That butterfly was the last one.
Butterflies don't live in here, in the ghetto.

Pavel Friedman, 1942

Other colletions of poetry written by children include: *Believe Me I Know,* selected by Valerie Bush; *Soft Hay Will Catch You: Poems by Young People,* compiled by Sandford Lyne; *Salting the Ocean: 100 Poems by Young Poets,* selected by Naomi Shihab Nye; and *Night Is Gone, Day Is Still Coming,* stories and poems by Native American children, selected by Annette Piña Ochoa, Betsy Franco, and Traci L. Gourdine.

Langston Hughes. Although Hughes is not considered primarily a children's poet, his poetry explores feelings, asks difficult questions, and expresses hopes and desires that are meaningful to readers of any age. Some of his poems—such as "Merry-Go-Round," found in *The Dream Keeper*—can be used to help children understand and identify with the feelings and experiences of African Americans in earlier eras of American history. In another poem, Hughes vividly describes what life would be like without dreams.

Dreams

Hold fast to dreams
For if dreams die
Life is a broken-winged bird
That cannot fly.
Hold fast to dreams
For when dreams go
Life is a barren field
Frozen with snow.

Langston Hughes
The Dream Keeper. 1932, 1960

The photograph that accompanies "Dreams" in the anthology *Reflections on a Gift of Watermelon Pickle . . . and Other Modern Verse,* edited by Dunning, Lueders, and Smith, shows a solitary dried weed surrounded by ice crystals. When this poem was shared with a group of fifth graders, one student reminded the class that dreams do not need to die: Like the weed, they can be reborn in the spring.

Cynthia Rylant. Moods and feelings related to growing up form the unifying theme in Rylant's *Waiting to Waltz: A Childhood.* Rylant's poems paint word pitures of a young girl feeling pride in her small town, pondering the relationships within the town, and revealing the experiences that influence her own maturation. In "Teenagers," for example, Rylant explores the longings of a child who is too big for some things and not big enough for others.

Teenagers

Watching the teenagers
in Beaver
using hairspray and
lipstick.
Kissing at ballgames.
Going steady.
And wanting it fast,
Wanting it now.

Because all my pretend
had to be hidden.
All my games
secret.
Wanting to be a wide-open child
but too big,
too big.
No more.
Waiting to shave
and wear nylons
and waltz.
Forgetting when
I was last time
a child.
Never knowing
when it
ended.

Cynthia Rylant
Waiting to Waltz: A Childhood, p. 44.

In *God Went to Beauty School,* Rylant's series of poems blends the familiar and the humorous with the philosophical as she considers what would happen if God lived in a human world with daily tasks and struggles. She ponders a series of "what if" questions with poems such as "God Is a Girl," "God Found Some Fudge," and "God Found God."

Snail

Snail upon the wall,
Have you got at all
Anything to tell
About your shell?

Only this, my child—
When the wind is wild,
Or when the sun is hot,
It's all I've got.

John Drinkwater

Eric Carle's collage illustrations add to the beauty in a poetry collection about animals. (From Eric Carle's Animals, Animals. Illustrations copyright © 1989 by Eric Carle. Philomel Books. Snail, by John Drinkwater, © 1929. Reprinted by permission of Samuel French, Inc.)

Many Voices: Poetry for Young Adults

Naomi Shihab Nye. *A Maze Me: Poems for Girls* is a collection of 70 poems by Naomi Shihab Nye about her observations and memories as a 12-year-old. The moods of the poems in this collection range from the uncertainties of growing up to her feelings of admiration and happiness among family members. Her poem "High Hopes" captures the universal feeling of disappointment that is often part of growing up:

High Hopes

It wasn't that they were so
high, exactly,
they were more
low-down,
close-to-the-ground,
I could rub them
the way you touch a cat
that rubs against your ankles
even if he isn't yours.

So yes I feel lonely without them.
Now that I know the truth,
that I only dreamed someone liked me,
the cat has curled up in a bed of leaves
against the house and I still have to do
everything I had to do before
without a secret hum
inside.

From *A Maze Me: Poems for Girls*,
by Naomi Shihab Nye, p. 52. 2005,
Greenwillow Books.

In addition to writing poems about growing up, Nye is perhaps best known for her poetry about the Arab American experience. In *19 Varieties of Gazelle: Poems of the Middle East*, Nye presents 57 of her original poems about the Middle East and about being Arab American written with elementary school children in mind. Nye includes in her introduction thoughts about the effects of September 11 on her and other Arab Americans. An introductory poem is about that day in particular; the rest are about her family, her visits to the Middle East, and her observations of events there in general. For example, in "My Father and the Fig Tree," Nye writes: "He'd point to cherry trees and say,/'see those? I wish they were figs'/In the evenings he sat by our beds/weaving folktales like vivid little scarves" (p. 6). In her anthology *The Flag of Childhood: Poems From the Middle East*, Nye presents poems by 50 Middle Eastern poets. In the introduction, Nye encourages children to remember "the one flag we all share is the beautiful flag of childhood that flies with hope in every country."

James Berry's *Around the World in Eighty Poems* contains lighthearted and serious verse of poets from 50 countries. *Under the Spell of the Moon: Art for Children From the*

World's Great Illustrators, edited by Patricia Aldana, includes internationally recognized artists as well as those who are known only within their country who have illustrated traditional poems and rhymes.

The life and experiences of Cesar Chavez are told in a collection of poems by Carmen T. Bernier-Grand, *César: ¡Sí, Se Puede! Yes, We Can*. The poems, along with colorful illustrations by David Diaz, pay tribute to Chavez's legacy for helping migrant workers improve their lives by teaching them self-sufficiency. In *The Pot That Juan Built*, Nancy Andrews-Goebel tells the story of Juan Quezada, one of the best-known potters in Mexico, and how he transformed the village of Mata Ortiz from an impoverished village into a prosperous community of artists. One page is told as a cumulative rhyme in the style of "This Is the House That Jack Built" and outlines the process of making a pot; the facing page is in prose and tells the story of the potter's life.

An anthology of poems about important historical figures from Martin Luther King and Gandhi to lesser-known figures such as Roberto Clemente, who rescued earthquake victims of Nicaragua, can be found in J. Patrick Lewis's collection *Heroes and She-Roes: Poems of Amazing and Everyday Heroes*.

In *Ellington Was Not a Street*, Ntozake Shange recalls her childhood home and the innovative people who gathered there, including W. .E. B. DuBois, Paul Robeson, Dizzy Gillespie, and Duke Ellington. Illustrations by Kadir Nelson and the poet's afterword about the "men who changed the world" give more historical detail to the evocative images presented in the poem.

In *Harlem*, Walter Dean Myers uses a songlike poem illustrated by his son, Christopher Myers, to tell the story of a vibrant community where racism was often prevalent. In *Here in Harlem: Poems in Many Voices*, Myers presents 54 poems each titled with the name, age, and occupation of a different fictional narrator that captures the triumphs and tragedies of everyday people who lived in Harlem. In *Blues Journey*, Myers presents the history of the blues told through poetry. In addition to the poems, Myers provides a factual overview of the blues as well as a time line of major events that traces its widespread popularity around the world. A book of poems that celebrates music from multiple perspectives is Jaime Adoff's *The Song Shoots Out of My Mouth*.

Kwame Senu Neville Dawes's poems and Tom Feelings's charcoal portraits present a global journey of people of African descent as seen through young faces in North and South America, Asia, Europe, and the Caribbean in *I Saw Your Face*.

Marilyn Nelson. The poet laureate for the state of Connecticut, Marilyn Nelson effectively places poetry and history side by side in several books for children. *Fortune's Bones: The Manumission Requiem*, a Coretta Scott King Honor Book, is an account of the life of a slave named

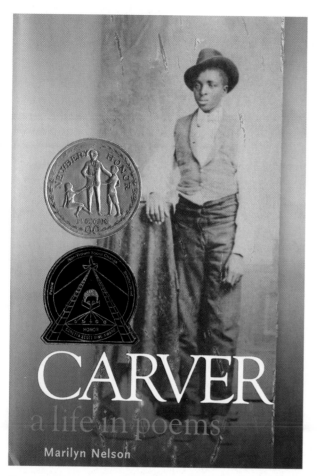

Cover from Carver: A Life in Poems *by Marilyn Nelson (Front Street, 2001). Jacket photograph courtesy of the Tuskegee University Archives. Reprinted with the permission of Boyds Mills Press.*

Fortune who died in 1798. His owner, a doctor, rendered his bones to preserve them for anatomy studies. The skeleton was lost and rediscovered, then hung in a local museum for decades before it was removed from display. In 1996, the museum conducted historical research to discover the provenance of the skeleton and commissioned Nelson to write these six poems in which she uses elements of a traditional requiem as well as a New Orleans jazz funeral. She incorporates multiple viewpoints, such as "Dinah's Lament," told from the perspective of Fortune's wife in which she mourns the husband whose bones she is ordered to dust. Other viewpoints include Fortune's owner, his descendants, museum visitors, and finally, Fortune himself. In "Not My Bones," Fortune states, "You are not your body,/You are not your bones./What's essential about you/is what can't be owned" (p. 27). Each page of verse faces a page containing text and archival graphics that lay out the facts of Fortune's history.

Carver: A Life in Poems, a Newbery Honor Book and a Coretta Scott King Honor Book, also by Nelson, is an account of the life of George Washington Carver, born a slave around 1864 and raised by a childless white couple. Nelson's free-verse poems are told from the different perspectives of those who knew Carver as the first African American student and teacher at Iowa State University, as a friend and colleague of Booker T. Washington, and as a botanist, naturalist, herbalist, inventor, painter, musician, and poet. The poems emphasize Carver's character and dreams and how they survived in the Jim Crow South and the racist attitudes of the North. One of the early poems, "The Drifter," is told from Carver's perspective on a train when he first leaves home in search of an education: "Something says find out/why rain falls, what makes corn proud/and squash so humble, the questions/call like a train whistle . . . /over the receding landscapes the perceiving self/stares back from the darkening window" (p. 16). Black-and-white photographs and historical footnotes authenticate the accompanying poems.

A Wreath for Emmett Till, also by Nelson, tells the story of Emmett Till, a 14-year-old African American boy from Chicago who was kidnapped and murdered while visiting his uncle in Mississippi during the summer of 1955. His lynching for allegedly whistling at a white woman, and the acquittal and confession of those who killed him, helped spark the civil rights movement of the 1950s and 1960s. This poem, a memorial to the lynched teen, is written as a heroic crown of 15 sonnets in which the last line of one is the first line of the next, and then each of the first lines makes up the entirety of the 15th sonnet. Each sonnet takes on a related subject, including a tree that has witnessed lynching and death. There is an introduction by the author, a page about Emmett Till, and literary and poetical footnotes to each sonnet. The book is a 2006 Coretta Scott King Honor Book and received a Printz Honor Award for Young Adult Literature.

The poetry of Marilyn Nelson provides a natural bridge between poetry written for children and poetry written for young adults. The more mature topics in Nelson's poems make them appropriate for the deeper reading of meaning and content required by young adults.

Poetry for Young Adults

What makes poetry so powerful is that the same words can have a different impact depending on the ages and experiences of the readers. What distinguishes books of poetry considered more appropriate for young adults is the use of more mature topics and, at times, more mature language.

The Body Eclectic: An Anthology of Poems, edited by Patrice Vecchione, celebrates all aspects of the body with subjects that include body image, perceptions of the self, sensuality, pride, shame, love, and hate. Poems include Walt Whitman's "I Sing the Body Electric," Mark Doty's

"My Tattoo," Natasha Trethewey's "His Hands," and Andrew Nielsen's "Pimples."

The poems in *Revenge and Forgiveness: An Anthology of Poems* illustrate different ways people deal with grief and anger. Inspired by the events of September 11, Vecchione has selected poems that explore the natural human urge to respond to a wrong either by forgiving or by taking revenge. Poems include Stephen Dunn's "To a Terrorist," Derek Walcott's "Love After Love," about the end of a relationship, and George Herbert's "Love bade me welcome: yet my soul drew back."

In *Truth and Lies: An Anthology of Poems*, Vecchione presents 70 poems that explore truth and lies and the shades of gray. Topics covered include abuse of authority, adults lying to youth, and deceit in love. Vecchione includes William Blake's "A Poison Tree" and Emily Dickinson's poem "Tell All the Truth" as well as poems by Polish, Russian, Irish, Indian, and Spanish poets.

Red Hot Salsa: Bilingual Poems on Being Young and Latino in the United States, an anthology edited by Lori Marie Carlson, presents poems in both Spanish and English by poets such as Gary Soto, Martin Espada, Trinidad Sánchez, Jr., and Luis Rodríguez. Carlson also includes a few poems written by young adults.

Keesha's House is a novel written in verse, by Helen Frost, about seven young adults facing serious situations such as pregnancy, coming out, running away, foster homes, an abusive stepfather, and drunk driving. The first-person narratives written in two poetic forms, the sestina and the sonnet, move in and out of each character's story, but overlap as soon as the characters discover a safe environment at Keesha's house.

In *The Poets' Grimm: 20th Century Poems From Grimm Fairy Tales*, Jeanne Marie Beaumont and Claudia Carlson have collected poems written in English based on tales of the Brothers Grimm. Although many of the poems are humorous and could be read by younger children, the collection as a whole contains poems with subjects more readily accessible to young adults, such as Enid Dame's "The Social Worker Finds Hansel and Gretel Difficult to Place," Wanda Coleman's "Sex and Politics in Fairyland," and Estha Weiner's "Transfiguration Begins at Home." The editors provide a helpful index of poems according to the tale used for inspiration.

Teaching With Poetry

Appreciation for language, knowledge about concepts, empathy with characters and situations, insights about oneself and others, self-expression, and enjoyment are values of poetry for children. According to John Gough (1988), "poetry is an acquired taste, and the taste can only be acquired by using poetry, rolling it around the tongue, spitting out words, chewing ideas, putting oneself into the action, taking risks, allowing oneself to be disturbed" (p. 194). Gough maintains that the disturbing aspect of poetry is especially important because "good poetry is disturbing. That is, it challenges our sense of reality, and breaks down our complacency with strange ideas, new feelings and alternative pictures of the world" (p. 194).

Rumer Godden (1988) stresses that children can be enticed with good poetry. She believes that children should proceed from singing and saying nursery rhymes to exploring lively poems that emphasize movement and rhythm, such as Stevenson's "Windy Nights," to hearing and reading small anthologies of poems to sharing poetry in which poets tell stories, such as Browning's "The Pied Piper of Hamelin," Rossetti's "Goblin Market," Noyes's "The Highwayman," and Scott's "Lochinvar."

University students often say that their aversion to poetry stems from the way it was presented in their elementary, middle school, and high school classrooms. They fondly remember the rhymes and jingles shared in kindergarten and first grade, but the pleasant associations are undercut by later forced memorization of poems and exercises in which everyone had to agree with the teacher's analysis of a poem. One student recalled her feelings of terror every Friday when she had to recite a memorized poem in front of the class and then had points deducted from her presentation for each error she made.

Other university students, however, describe more positive memories of poetry in their elementary classrooms. The students remembered teachers who spontaneously shared a wide variety of poetry with their classes; who encouraged students to write poems and share them with an appreciative audience; and who had their students experiment with choral readings of poetry, sometimes accompanied by rhythm instruments. One student remembered a teacher who always had a poem to reflect the mood of a gentle rain, a smiling jack-o-lantern, or a mischievous child. Another remembered going outside on a warm spring day, looking at the butterflies and wildflowers in a meadow, listening to the world around her, sharing her feelings with the class, and then writing a poem to express the promise of that beautiful day. Yet another remembered a librarian who always included poetry in story-hour presentations.

After university students explore the various ways of sharing poetry with children, many of them sadly conclude that something was left out of their own educations. Hopefully, they can agree with Naomi Shihab Nye. In her introduction to *A Maze Me: Poems for Girls*, Nye states that she writes poetry because "I want to live, every day, inside my timeless brain. . . . If you write three lines down in a notebook every day . . . you will find out what you notice. Uncanny connections will be made visible to you. That's what I started learning when I was twelve, and I never stopped learning it" (pp. 6–7).

Listening to Poetry

Poetry is meant to be read, reread, and shared. The sounds, the rhythms, the vivid words, and the unexpected phrases lend themselves to oral reading. Research shows that poetry is rarely shared with children, and even when poetry is shared, it is often isolated from other experiences. Poet Lee Bennett Hopkins (1987) argues that children may dislike poetry because it is frequently taught as an isolated unit instead of shared at appropriate times throughout the day. Hopkins maintains that poetry deserves to be added to the total curriculum, not limited to the language arts. He provides the following guidelines for reading poetry to children, whether you are a parent, teacher, or librarian:

1. Before reading a poem to an audience, read it aloud several times to get the feel of the words and the rhythm. Mark the words and phrases that you would like to emphasize.

2. Read the poem naturally, following its rhythm. Allow the physical appearance of the poem to dictate the rhythm and mood of the words. Some poems are meant to be read softly and slowly; others must be read at a more rapid pace.

3. Make pauses that are logical and that please you.

4. When reading a poem aloud, speak in a natural voice. Read a poem as though you are interested in the subject.

Reading poetry aloud is also an excellent activity for children. Teacher Lisa Lenz (1992) describes the benefits of immersing her elementary students in reading poetry aloud when she states:

> Listening to poetry and reading it aloud has helped my first and second graders develop a feel for the texture and power of language. The poetry they've read has stepped off the printed page and become part of their lives. The poetry they've written continues to spill out of their own hearts and into those of their listeners. (p. 597)

Lenz describes the process she used with her students to help them prepare for reading their poems aloud. They chose poems they loved and then progressed through a series of rehearsals with peer coaches. These coaches helped them listen to themselves and consider how they wanted each poem to sound. After they could read the poems smoothly, they listened for words or phrases that had interested them and marked up a photocopy of the poem by circling special words and making notes in the margins. When they felt prepared, they videotaped their presentations. In *Let's Do a Poem* (1991), Nancy Larrick emphasizes introducing poetry through such activities as listening, singing, and body movement.

Moving to Poetry

The rhythms, sounds, characters, and images in many poems encourage physical responses from children. An observer of children on a playground is likely to see two children swinging a rope while a third child jumps to the rhythm and the actions described in a chant such as the following:

> Teddy bear, teddy bear, turn around.
> Teddy bear, teddy bear, touch the ground.
> Teddy bear, teddy bear, close your eyes.
> Teddy bear, teddy bear, be surprised.
> Teddy bear, teddy bear, climb up the stairs.
> Teddy bear, teddy bear, say your prayers.
> Teddy bear, teddy bear, turn out the light.
> Teddy bear, teddy bear, say good night.

In a similar way, children may be inspired to move when you slowly read a poem aloud. Valerie Worth's *More Small Poems* provides children with an opportunity to become a "Kitten," arching their backs, dancing sideways, tearing across the floor, crouching against imagined threats, and pouncing with claws ready, or to become "Fireworks," exploding in the air, billowing into bright color, and spilling back down toward earth in waterfalls. They can be spectacular in a much quieter way as a "Soap Bubble" that bends into different shapes, rises shimmering into the air, then pops and disappears. Worth's *Still More Small Poems*, encourages children to experience the free flight of a "Kite" as the wind tears it from a hand and sends it soaring; to become a "Mushroom" pushing up through the soil; or to go "Barefoot," as their feet emerge from choking socks and they feel cool clover and gentle blades of grass between their toes.

Dramatizing Poetry

One of the values of poetry for children is encouragement to identify with characters and situations; narrative poetry is especially good for this purpose. In addition, narrative poetry is a favorite among children. Creative dramatization is one of the ways you can enhance children's enjoyment of the situations found in poetry.

Clement C. Moore's narrative poem "A Visit From St. Nicholas" (now familiarly known as "The Night Before Christmas") suggests several scenes to dramatize. Children can prepare for the Christmas celebration by trimming the tree and decorating the room. They can imagine the sugarplum dreams and act them out. They can reenact the father's response to hearing the clatter of hoofs. They can be reindeer pulling the loaded sleigh or St. Nicholas as he comes down the chimney, fills the stockings, and then bounds up the chimney and drives out of sight.

The poem has many other dramatic possibilities. Children have created the dialogue for an imaginary meeting between the father and St. Nicholas or the children and St. Nicholas. What would they say to each other? How would they act? If the children could ask St. Nicholas questions, what would they ask? If St. Nicholas could ask questions, what would he want to know? Children have imagined themselves as St. Nicholas going into many homes on Christmas Eve: What was the most unusual experience they had? They also have imagined themselves going back to St. Nick's workshop at the North Pole: What kind of a welcome did they receive?

Adults have used the nonsensical situations found in Jack Prelutsky's poems in *The Queen of Eene* to stimulate humorous dramatizations. One group, for example, dramatized the conversation and actions of the four foolish ladies (Hattie, Harriet, Hope, and Hortense) as they roped a rhinoceros and took him to tea. Then, the group imagined and acted out other predicaments that could have been created by the actions of the foolish ladies. "Gretchen in the Kitchen" can stimulate spooky dramatization at Halloween; the quarts of curdled mud, salted spiders, ogre's backbone, and dragon's blood provide a setting appealing to children who are preparing to be spooks, witches, and black cats.

Other poems can be used to stimulate creative dramatizations, including the following:

1. "The Pied Piper of Hamelin," by Robert Browning, located in numerous sources, including Iona and Peter Opie's *The Oxford Book of Children's Verse*. The piper lures rats to their deaths. Then, after the mayor refuses to pay for his services, the piper entices the children of the town to follow him.

2. "The Adventures of Chris," by David McCord, found in *One at a Time: Collected Poems for the Young*. A toad and a boy discuss arithmetic, spelling, and what not to miss on earth.

3. *Sir Cedric*, by Roy Gerrard. Cedric the Good, Black Ned, and Matilda the Pure have knightly adventures.

4. *Sir Francis Drake: His Daring Deeds*, by Roy Gerrard. This explorer has numerous adventures that can stimulate dramatizations.

5. *Night Story*, by Nancy Willard. A small boy has a series of adventures in dreamland.

6. *The Midnight Ride of Paul Revere*, by Henry Wadsworth Longfellow. A classic poem related to history.

7. *A Visit to William Blake's Inn: Poems for Innocent and Experienced Travelers*, by Nancy Willard. Many unusual characters, such as the man in the marmalade hat, visit the inn. The characters and incidents can stimulate many dramatizations.

Developing Choral Speaking

Choral speaking, the interpretation of poetry or other literature by two or more voices speaking as one, is a group activity that allows children to experience, enjoy, and increase their interest in rhymes, jingles, and other types of poetry. During a choral-speaking or choral-reading experience, children discover that speaking voices can be combined as effectively as singing voices. Young children who cannot read can join in during repeated lines or can take part in rhymes and verses that they know from memory; older children can select anything suitable within their reading ability. Choral speaking is useful in a variety of situations: library programs, classrooms, and extracurricular organizations.

Increasing children's enjoyment of poetry and other literature, not developing a perfect performance, is the main purpose for using choral speaking with elementary children. Allow children to enjoy the experience and experiment with various ways of interpreting poetry. Donna Norton (2004) suggests the following guidelines for encouraging children to interact in choral arrangements:

1. For children who cannot read, choose poems or rhymes that are simple enough to memorize.

2. Choose material of interest to children. Young children like nonsense and active words; consequently, humorous poems are enjoyable first experiences that encourage children to have fun with poetry.

3. Select poems or nursery rhymes that use refrains, especially for young children. Refrains are easy for nonreaders to memorize and result in rapid participation from each group member.

4. Let children help select and interpret the poetry. Have them experiment with the rhythm and tempo of a poem, improvise the scenes of the selection, and try different voice combinations and choral arrangements until they decide on the best structure.

5. Let children listen to each other as they try different interpretations within groups.

Adults should also understand the different phases through which children should be guided in their choral interpretations of poetry. First, because young children delight in the rhythm of nursery rhymes, encourage them to explore the rhythm in poetry. They can skip to the rhythm of "Jack and Jill," clap to the rhythm of "Hickory Dickory Dock," and sway to the rhythm of "Little Boy Blue." They can sense fast or slow, happy or sad rhythms through their bodies. They can explore rhythm and tempo as they "hoppity, hoppity, hop" to A. A. Milne's poem "Hoppity" (found in *When We Were Very Young*).

Second, encourage children to experiment with the color and quality of voices available in the choral-speaking choir. Barbara M. McIntyre (1974) says that children do not need to know the meaning of *inflection* (rise and fall within a phrase), *pitch levels* (change between one phrase and another), *emphasis* (pointing out the most important word), and *intensity* (loudness and softness of voices), but adults must understand these terms so that they can recommend materials that excite children and allow them to try different interpretations. Third, encourage children to understand and experiment with different choral arrangements, such as refrain, line, antiphonal, cumulative, and unison arrangements.

Refrain Arrangement

In refrain arrangement, an adult or a child reads or recites the body of a poem, and the other children respond in unison, repeating a refrain or chorus. Poems such as Maurice Sendak's *Pierre: A Cautionary Tale*, Lewis Carroll's "Beautiful Soup," and Jack Prelutsky's "The Yak," in *The Random House Book of Poetry for Children*, have lines that seem to invite group participation.

A nursery rhyme that encourages young children to participate is "A Jolly Old Pig."

Leader:	A jolly old pig once lived in a sty,
	And three little piggies she had,
	And she waddled about saying,
Group:	"Grumph! grumph! grumph!"
Leader:	While the little ones said,
Group:	"Wee! Wee!"
Leader:	And she waddled about saying,
Group:	"Grumph! grumph! grumph!"
Leader:	While the little ones said,
Group:	"Wee! Wee!"

The poetic retelling of "The Fox and the Grapes" in Tom Paxton's version of *Aesop's Fables* contains lines in parentheses, such as "(A very high tree, Yes, a very high tree.)," that encourage group responses.

Line Arrangement

To develop a line arrangement, have one child or a group of children read the first line, another child or group read the next line, a third child or group read the next line, and so forth. Continue this arrangement with a different child or different group reading each line until the poem is finished. Use a familiar nursery rhyme to introduce this arrangement, such as:

Child 1 or Group 1:	One, two, buckle my shoe;
Child 2 or Group 2:	Three, four, shut the door;
Child 3 or Group 3:	Five, six, pick up sticks;
Child 4 or Group 4:	Seven, eight, lay them straight;
Child 5 or Group 5:	Nine, ten, a good fat hen.

Enjoyable poems for line-a-child arrangements include Zilpha Keatley Snyder's "Poem to Mud," Laura E. Richards's "Eletelephony," and from *The Random House Book of Poetry for Children*, Jack Prelutsky's "Pumberly Pott's Unpredictable Niece."

Antiphonal, or Dialogue, Arrangement

This arrangement highlights alternate speaking voices. Boys' voices may be balanced against girls' voices, or high voices may be balanced against low voices. Poems such as "Eskimo Chant," found in *The New Wind Has Wings: Poems From Canada*, compiled by Mary Alice Downie and Barbara Robertson, encourage children to respond in either joyful or fearful voices. Poems with question-and-answer formats or other dialogue between two people are obvious choices for antiphonal arrangements. Poems such as Kaye Starbird's "The Spelling Test," in *The Covered Bridge House and Other Poems*, and the nursery rhyme "Pussy-Cat, Pussy-Cat" are enjoyable in dialogue arrangements. Paul Fleischman's *I Am Phoenix: Poems for Two Voices* includes poems about birds. Fleischman's *Joyful Noise: Poems for Two Voices* allows children to experiment with sounds and movements of insects. The poems are written to be read by more than one person. Children also enjoy chorally reading the lyrics from folk songs. The words of "Yankee Doodle," for example, can be used with one group of children reading each verse and another group responding with the chorus. Many traditional songs are found in Dan Fox's *Go In and Out the Window: An Illustrated Songbook for Young People*. The folk song "A Hole in the Bucket" presents an enjoyable dialogue between Liza and Henry for choral speaking activity.

Try the following Mother Goose rhyme as a dialogue arrangement:

Boys:	The man in the wilderness asked me
	How many strawberries grew in the sea.
Girls:	I answered him as I thought good,
	As many red herrings as grew in the wood.

Cumulative Arrangement

A crescendo arrangement can be used effectively to interpret a poem that builds to a climax. Have the first group read the first line or verse; the first and second groups read the second line or verse; the first, second, and third groups read the third line or verse; and so forth, until the climax. Then, have all of the groups read together.

Edward Lear's "The Owl and the Pussy-Cat" can be read in a cumulative arrangement by six groups; John Ciardi's "Mummy Slept Late and Daddy Fixed Breakfast" is also fun for six groups to develop into a climax, as Daddy's waffles become impossible to eat. Other poems appropriate for cumulative reading include Arnold Lobel's *The*

Rose in My Garden. The nursery rhymes "There Was a Crooked Man" and "This Is the House That Jack Built" are also enjoyable.

Try the following traditional folk song, "Skin and Bones," as a cumulative arrangement:

Group 1:	There was an old woman all skin and bones, Oo—oo—oo!
Groups 1 and 2:	She lived down by the graveyard, Oo—oo—oo!
Group 1, 2, and 3:	One night she thought she'd take a walk, Oo—oo—oo!
Groups 1, 2, 3, and 4:	She went to the closet to get a broom, Oo—oo—oo!
Groups 1, 2, 3, 4, and 5:	She opened the door and BOO!

As a variation, develop a reverse arrangement: Have all groups begin together; then, with each subsequent line or verse, have a group drop out until only one group remains. This arrangement works well with such poems as Barbara Kunz Loots's "Mountain Wind" and James Reeves's "The Wind" because both poems begin with louder expressions and end in silence or quiet. These poems are found in Jack Prelutsky's *The Random House Book of Poetry for Children.*

Unison Arrangement

In unison arrangement, the entire group or class reads or speaks a poem together. This arrangement is often the most difficult to perform, because it tends to create a singsong effect. For this reason, shorter poems, such as Myra Cohn Livingston's "O Sliver of Liver," Bobbi Katz's "Paper Dreams," from Paul Janeczko's collection *A Kick in the Head,* A. A. Milne's "The Engineer," in *There's Always Pooh and Me,* and Judith Thurman's "Campfire," in *Flashlight and Other Poems,* are appropriate.

Choosing Poetry to Accompany Content

An example of a poetry unit developed by a student in a workshop exemplifies how teachers develop understanding of poetry with their students. Jana Wright Prewitt (2001), a fourth-grade teacher, developed "Poetry for the Fourth-Grade Classroom: A Collection of Poems and Activities" as a unit in which she incorporates poems and activities that will allow her also to teach the various content areas of the elementary curriculum, including language arts, science, social studies, and mathematics. Prewitt's introduction to the unit clarifies her purposes:

> I decided to do a poetry collection for fourth grade students and teachers because, in my experience, I have not seen enough teachers integrating poetry into their instruction. I have not used poetry extensively with my students. I have conducted some research and discovered the importance of incorporating poetry on a daily basis in the classroom. The imagery, style, abstract nature, humor, and organization of poetry are all characteristics that attract children. What better way to encourage children to become strong readers and writers than exposing them to poetry that is humorous, descriptive, and thought provoking. I look forward to using this unit in my classroom and adding to this collection in years to come. (introduction)

The following poems are used in the unit. Each poem is followed by discussions that reinforce the following areas:

Language Arts:

Making predictions: Jack Prelutsky's "Chocolate Cake," in Prelutsky's *My Parents Think I'm Sleeping,* Greenwillow, 1985.

Comparing and contrasting things or ideas: Mary Austin's "Rathers," in Helen Ferris's *Favorite Poems Old and New,* Doubleday,1957.

Persuasive writing or speech: Jack Prelutsky's "The Multilingual Mynah Bird," in Prelutsky's *Zoo Doings,* Greenwillow, 1983.

Acrostic poetry and description: Emily Dickinson's "I'm Nobody! Who Are You?," in Dickinson's *The Complete Poems of Emily Dickinson,* Little, Brown, 1924.

Spelling: Robert Pottle's "Bak Too Skool" in "Giggle, Giggle, Snicker, Laugh!" and in the "Gigglepict," <*http://www.robertpottle.com/*>, posted July 2, 2001.

Mathematics:

Studying money: Shel Silverstein's "Smart," in *Where the Sidewalk Ends,* HarperCollins, 1974.

Geometry and shapes: Jack Prelutsky's "A Triangular Tale," in *A Pizza the Size of the Sun,* Greenwillow, 1996.

Science:

Living things: Douglas Florian's "The Daddy Longlegs," in *Insectiopedia,* Harcourt Brace, 1998.

X. J. Kennedy's "Electric Eel," in *Eric Carle's Animals Animals,* edited by Laura Whipple, Philomel, 1989.

Douglas Florian's "The Gorilla" and "The Bear," in *Mammalabilia,* Harcourt, 2000.

Importance of reasearch and experiments: Jack Prelutsky's "Miss Misinformation," in *A Pizza the Size of the Sun,* Greenwillow, 1996.

Jon Scieszka and Lane Smith's "Dino-Sore," in *Science Verse,* Viking, 2004.

Social Studies:

State history: Naomi Shihab Nye's *Is This Forever, or What? Poems and Paintings From Texas,* Greenwillow, 2004.

Prewitt included regional poems on culture, geography, and climate. As you identify social studies poems, expand their use to other regions of the United States and the world. Many excellent poems emphasize U.S. history such as Henry Wadsworth Longfellow's *Paul Revere's Ride* in Ted Rand's illustrated version. Poetry such as Woody Guthrie's *This Land Is Your Land,* illustrated by Kathy Jakobsen, provides many opportunities to incorporate content areas and poetry.

WRITING POETRY

Research conducted by Donald Graves (1988) and George Hillocks (1986) into the development of the writing process of children suggests that adults should work with children during the writing process rather than after the materials are completed. Research emphasizes using phases in the writing process to encourage students to explore, plan, draft, and revise. For example, Jackie Proett and Kent Gill (1986) report a sequence of events and recommend activities from experiences at the Bay Area Writing Project and the University of California. These educators sequence the process according to activities that should be done (1) before the students write (content and idea building through observing, remembering, imagining, experiencing, logging, reading, brainstorming, listing, dramatizing, developing details, and structuring), (2) while the students write (developing rhetorical stance and linguistic choices by deciding voice, audience, purpose, form, word choice, figurative language, structure, and syntax), and (3) after the students write (encouraging revision and highlighting by sharing with editing groups, raising, questions, expanding, clarifying, proofreading, sharing, reading, and publishing).

The various phases are certainly crucial to poetry writing. By reading or listening to poery, children obtain motivational and observational opportunities to develop their awareness and to stimulate their imaginations. Children require opportunities to incubate and clarify ideas, to compose and revise their poetry, and to share their poetry with an appreciative audience. To share poetry writing experinces with children, use the sequence in Chart 8.1 (Norton, 2004).

MOTIVATIONS

The three categories of motivational activities outlined in Chart 8.1 suggest that numerous topics can stimulate the writing of poetry. Many activities already occurring in classrooms, libraries, or extracurricular organizations are natural sources of topics for self-expression through poetry. For example, while teaching a social studies unit, a second-grade teacher showed a film about farm life. The teacher encouraged the children to observe the characteristics and actions of the farm animals and then to write about them in poetic form. A Girl Scout leader encouraged children to describe and write about their feelings following a soccer game. A librarian asked children to write their own color poems after they heard Mary O'Neill's poems about colors in *Hailstones and Halibut Bones*.

University students have used both poetry written by adult authors and poetry written by children as ways of stimulating children to write their own poems. For example, they have used Kenneth Koch's *Wishes, Lies, and Dreams* (1970), reading the poems under a certain topic to children and then using Koch's suggestions to encourage the children to write their own poems. Several of the categories in-

CHART 8.1   An instructional sequence for poetry writing

I. Motivation
   A. Ongoing activities
   B. Everyday experiences
   C. New, adult-introduced experiences
II. Oral exchange of ideas
   A. Questions and answers to extend stimulation activities
   B. Brainstorming of subjects, vocabulary, images, and such
   C. Idea clarifications
III. Transcription
   A. Individual dictation of poems to adults
   B. Individual writing
   C. Teacher interaction to help development
   D. Adult assistance when required
   E. Revision and editing through small-group interaction and teacher interaction during individual writing
IV. Sharing
   A. Reading of the poetry to a group
   B. Audience development
   C. Permanent collections
   D. Poetry extensions, if desired, to poetry dramatizations, choral reading, art interpretations, and so forth
V. Post-transcription
   A. Permanent writing folders
   B. Writing conferences
   C. Modeling of the writing process

clude experiences that are common to children but allow them to think of these experiences in new ways. A third-grade teacher encouraged his students to consider the wishes they might make if they had the opportunity and then asked them to write a poem expressing those wishes. The following is an example of a third grader's wishes.

> I wish I had a puppy,
>   not a dog, a puppy
>   not a cat, a puppy
>   not a kitten, a puppy.
> I wish I was rich
>   not poor, but rich
>   not a little bit of money, a lot
>   so I'm really rich.
> I wish I had a Genie
>   not a pony, a Genie
>   not a pig, a Genie
>   not a pig or a pony
>   a Genie.
> I wish I could
>   have anything
>   know anything
>   be anything
>   see anything
>   and do anything
>   I wish.

> Eight-year-old

Many adults encourage children to write poetry by introducing experiences that allow the children to nurture their awareness and their observational powers. For example, the children may go for a walk in a flowering park or meadow, listen to the noises around them, smell the air in spring, touch trees and flowers, describe their sensations with new feelings, and then write poems about their experiences. The following poem resulted from a sixth grader's visual experiences out-of-doors.

Woodland
Cool crisp air calls me
Late September afternoon
Crimson, gold, green, rust
Falling leaves whisper softly
Come look, what's new in the woods?

Eleven-year-old

Oral Exchanges of Ideas

During an oral exchange of ideas, encourage children to think aloud about a subject. For example, through brainstorming, children may gain many ideas from each other and look at old ideas in new ways.

During an outside observational session, have children look at clouds and share their impressions, describe the ways the light filters through the leaves, or close their eyes and describe the sounds they hear. The librarian who encouraged children to write color poems after listening to Mary O'Neill's poems in *Hailstones and Halibut Bones* asked the children to observe the colors around them. They searched for objects that reminded them of the colors in the poems and talked about their moods as reflected by colors. For example, brainstorming the color white produced the following associations, and more: snowflakes, winter silence, puffy clouds, a wedding veil, the flash of winning, a frost-covered window, quivering vanilla pudding, heaps of popcorn, a plastered wall, apple blossoms, pale lilac blossoms, sails skimming across a lake, a forgotten memory, fog rising from a marsh, a polar bear, and a gift wrapped in tissue paper. After this experience, the children began to look at common objects and feelings with new awareness.

Transcriptions

You can help young children compose by taking dictation. Encourage the children to tell you their thoughts while you write them down. Parents indicate that even very young children like to see their creative jingles, rhymes, and poems in print. Children enjoy playing with language and feeling the tickle of new ways of expression falling off their tongues.

One university student found it meaningful that her mother had kept a notebook of her early experiences writing poetry. Another university student, who had several poems published, felt that his early spontaneous poetry, written down by his mother, had stimulated his desire to become a professional writer. Parents who have been suc-

cessful in this type of dictation have been careful not to force dictation on a child or criticize any thoughts or feelings expressed. The experiences have been warm, trusting relationships, in which children discover that their thoughts can be written down and saved for themselves and for sharing with others.

When children have mastered the mechanics of writing, they usually write their own poems. However, when working with children, continue to interact with them as they progress with their writing. Encourage them to reread their poems aloud, ask questions to help clarify a problem or an idea, or answer questions pertaining to spelling and punctuation.

Sharing

The ideal way to share poetry is to read it to an appreciative audience. Consequently, many adults encourage children to share their creations with others. Attractive bulletin boards of children's poems may also stimulate children to read one another's poems and write more poems.

Children enjoy making permanent collections of their poems. One teacher had each child develop an accordion-pleated poem book (see Figure 8.2). To construct their books, the children folded large sheets of heavy drawing paper in half, connected several sheets with tape, and printed an original poem and an accompanying illustration on each page.

Other classes have made their own books by constructing covers in various appropriate shapes, cutting paper to match the shapes, and binding the covers and pages together. A group of second graders placed Halloween poems inside a jack-o-lantern book, fourth graders wrote city poems inside a book resembling a skyscraper, and third graders placed humorous mythical animal poems inside a book resembling a beast from Dr. Seuss (see Figure 8.3). Although it is not necessary to extend writing of poetry to other activities, children often enjoy using their own poetry for choral reading, art interpretations, or dramatizations.

Various Forms of Poetry

Many children enjoy experimenting with writing different types of poems, such as limericks, cinquains, and diamantes. Limericks, for example, are among the poetry

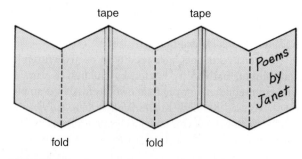

FIGURE 8.2   An accordion-pleated poem book

FIGURE 8.3　Shapes of various poetry books

children enjoy most. David McCord's *One at a Time: Collected Poems for the Young* describes the content and form of limericks and provides examples that you can share with children. Use the nonsense limericks of Edward Lear, N. M. Bodecker, and William Jay Smith to stimulate these five-line poems. Follow this form: Lines 1, 2, and 5 rhyme and have a three-beat rhythm; lines 3 and 4 rhyme and have a two-beat rhythm. Brainstorming words that rhyme helps children complete their rhyming lines. After reading and listening to a number of limericks, a sixth grader wrote about and illustrated the following predicament.

> There once was a girl named Mandy
> Whose hair was dreadfully sandy
> She never did wash it
> Instead she did frost it
> The icing made Mandy smell dandy

> Eleven-year-old

Cinquains are another form of poetry having specific structural requirements. These poems help children realize that descriptive words are important when expressing feelings in poetry and that rhyming words are not necessary. A cinquain uses the following structure.

Line 1:　One word for the title.
Line 2:　Two words that describe the title.
Line 3:　Three words that express action related to the title.

Line 4:　Four words that express a feeling about the title.
Line 5:　One word that either repeats the title or expresses a word closely related to the title.

Brainstorming descriptive words and action words adds to children's enjoyment in writing and sharing their cinquains. The following cinquains were written by middle school children.

Tree
Huge,　woody
Expanding,　reproducing,　entertaining
Leaves　are　colorfully　crisp
Oak

Eleven-year-old

Lasagna
Hot,　delectable
Steaming,　bubbling,　oozing
Always　great　on　Fridays
Paisans

Eleven-year-old

A diamante is a diamond-shaped poem. Poems written in the diamante format progress from one noun to a final noun that contrasts with the first noun. Because this form is more complex than the cinquain, you should describe each line and draw a diagram of the diamante to help children see the relationships among the lines. Diamantes have the following structure.

Line 1:　One noun.
Line 2:　Two adjectives that describe the noun.
Line 3:　Three words that express action related to the noun.
Line 4:　Four nouns or a phrase that expresses a transition in thought between the first noun and the final contrasting noun.
Line 5:　Three words that express action related to the contrasting noun.
Line 6:　Two adjectives that describe the contrasting noun.
Line 7:　One contrasting noun.

Diagramming this type of poem as follows is also helpful:

noun
describing describing
action action action
transition nouns or phrase
action action action
describing describing
noun

Children find it helpful to brainstorm suggestions for contrasting nouns to form the framework for the ideas developed in a diamante. One teacher brainstormed with upper-elementary students and developed the following contrasts.

sun—moon	tears—smiles
day—night	young—old
life—death	happy—sad
friends—enemies	man—woman
summer—winter	war—peace
sky—ground	love—hate
angel—devil	darkness—light
boredom—excitement	dreams—reality

Next, each group wrote a poem. The following poems were created by this experience.

Light
Beautiful, bright
Seeing, glistening, refreshing
Light is sometimes blinding
Groping, cautioning, frightening
Evil, insecure
Dark

Ten-year-old

Friends
Happiness, security
Understanding, caring, laughing
Reaching out your hand
Hating, hurting, fighting
Silence, tension
Enemies

Ten-year-old

POETRY WRITING EXERCISES

Robin Behn and Chase Twichell, the editors of *The Practice of Poetry: Writing Exercises From Poets Who Teach* (1992), provide strong reasons for using poetry writing exercises with anyone who wants to improve his or her writing:

> Poetry, like any art, requires practice. It's easy for us to accept the idea of practice when we think of a painter's figure studies or the sounds coming from the hives of practice rooms in a conservatory. But, since we consider ourselves already fluent in language, we may imagine that talent is the only requirement for writing poetry. . . . The aspiring poet must master the elements of language, the complexities of form and its relation to subject, the feel of the line, the image, the play of sound that make it possible to respond in a voice with subtlety and range when he hears that music in his inner ear, or she sees in the world that image that's the spark of a poem. (p. xi)

Several of the exercises described by various poets in Behn and Twichell's collection are appropriate for students in the elementary and middle grades. For example, to improve an understanding of language and abstract thoughts, have students list their associations with words such as *love* and then ask them to translate the ideas into abstractions and mental pictures, metaphors, or images; these images then become the foundations for poetry. To enhance the visualization of images in a poem, ask them to listen to a poem and then write down all of the evocative words it triggers. To help students structure or organize a poem, ask them to choose an ordinary object, such as a door, and then make a list of the functions for that object. Hopefully, the object has a symbolic meaning, such as a door opens, closes, separates, or blocks the view. Now begin the poem with a title that identifies the object and follow it with a list of functions. Finally, conclude the poem with a summary statement that also suggests the more symbolic meaning.

I have used several of the poetry writing exercises associated with photography described by poet Maggie Anderson (Behn & Twichell, 1992, pp. 231–235). In this case, a photograph provides the details, the images, the setting, and the characters that become the content of the poem. Anderson recommends that students write at least three poems using the same photograph but writing from different viewpoints or perspectives. For example, a poem could be written from the point of view of the photographer or from someone or something that is shown in the photograph. The poem might be written from the perspective of what happened just before, during, or after the photograph was taken. The poem also might be written from the perspective of someone finding the photograph years after it was taken. Photographs of experiences that are close to children or people who are important in their lives are especially meaningful. Students in one classroom created photo albums that included pictures of students and poems that described each of the students. Activities such as a school field trip, sports, music, or drama provide excellent photographic subjects.

Another excellent source of ideas and suggestions for exercises in poetry writing is Stephen Dunning and William Stafford's *Getting the Knack: 20 Poetry Writing Exercises* (1992). Each of the exercises includes an introduction, steps to follow, and examples of poems that were written using the writing exercise.

For more suggested activities for understanding poetry, visit the Companion Website at *www.prenhall.com/norton*

Suggested Activities

For more suggested activities for understanding poetry, visit the Companion Website at www.prenhall. com/norton

■ Compare the poetry selections in the Children's Choices, a list published each year in the October issue of *The Reading Teacher*. What types of poetry are children selecting? Has the poetry changed throughout the years?

■ Look through an anthology of poetry and find some poems that rely on sound patterns to create excitement. Prepare for oral presentation a poem that relies on alliteration (the repetition of initial consonant sounds) or assonance (the repetition of vowel sounds). Share the poem orally with a peer group.

- Compile a list of similes and metaphors found in a poem. What images does the poet suggest? Are similes or metaphors more effective or more easily visualized in word pictures than are realistic words?
- Compare the content and style of a poet who wrote humorous verse in the 19th century (such as Lewis Carroll or Edward Lear) with those of a contemporary author (such as Jack Prelutsky or N. M. Bodecker). What are the similarities and differences between the writers in the two time periods?

Children's Literature

Ackerman, Diane. *Animal Sense*. Illustrated by Peter Sís. Knopf, 2003.

Adedjourna, Davida, ed. *The Palm of My Heart: Poetry by African American Children*. Illustrated by Gregory Christie. Lee, 1996.

Adoff, Arnold. *All the Colors of the Race*. Illustrated by John Steptoe. Lothrop. Lee & Shepard, 1982.

_____. *Love Letters*. Illustrated by Lisa Desimini. Scholastic, 1997.

_____. *My Black Me: A Beginning Book of Black Poetry*. Dutton, 1974.

_____. ed. *The Poetry of Black America: Anthology of the 20th Century*. Harper & Row, 1973.

Adoff, Jaime. *The Song Shoots Out of My Mouth*. Illustrated by Martin French. Dutton, 2002.

Aesop. *Aesop's Fables*. Retold by Tom Paxton. Illustrated by Robert Rayevsky. Morrow, 1988.

Alarcón. Francisco X. *Laughing Tomatoes*. Illustrated by Maya Christina Gonzalez. Children's, 1997.

Aldana, Patricia, selected by. *Under the Spell of the Moon: Art for Children From the World's Great Illustrators*. Groundwood, 2004.

Andrews-Goebel, Nancy. *The Pot That Juan Built*. Illustrated by David Diaz. Lee & Low, 2002.

Angelou, Maya, ed., *Soul Looks Back in Wonder*. Illustrated by Torn Feelings. Dial, 1993.

Appelt, Kathi. *Oh My Baby, Little One*. Illustrated by Jane Dyer. Harcourt, 2000.

Ashman, Linda. *How to Make a Night*. Illustrated by Tricia Tusa. HarperCollins, 2004.

_____. *Sailing Off to Sleep*. Illustrated by Susan Winter. Simon & Schuster, 2001.

Aston, Dianna Hutts. *When You Were Born*. Illustrated by E. B. Lewis. Candlewick, 2004.

Attenborough, Liz, compiled by. *Poetry by Heart: A Child's Book of Poems to Remember*. Illustrated by Helen Stephens et al. Scholastic, 2001.

Atwood, Ann. *Haiku: The Mood of Earth*. Scribner, 1971.

Baylor, Byrd. *The Desert Is Theirs*. Illustrated by Peter Parnall. Scribner, 1975.

_____. *Moon Song*. Illustrated by Ronald Himler. Scribner, 1982.

_____. *The Other Way to Listen*. Illustrated by Peter Parnall. Scribner, 1978.

Baylor, Byrd, and Peter Parnall. *Desert Voices*. Scribner, 1981.

Beaumont, Jeanne Marie, & Claudia Carlson, eds. *The Poets' Grimm: 20th Century Poems From Grimm Fairy Tales*. Story Line, 2003.

Bedard, Michael. *Emily*. Illustated by Barbara Cooney. Doubleday, 1992.

Belafonte, Harry, & Lord Burgess. *Island in the Sun*. Illustrated by Alex Ayliffe. Dial, 1999.

Belloc, Hilaire. *The Bad Child's Book of Beasts*. Illustrated by Basil T. Blackwood. Alden, 1896. Knopf, 1966.

_____. *A Moral Alphabet*. Danton, 1899.

_____. *More Beasts for Worse Children*. Illustrated by Basil T. Blackwood. Arnold, 1897. Knopf, 1966.

_____. *Cautionary Tales for Children*. Illustrated by Edward Gorey. Harcourt, 2002.

_____. *Cautionary Verses*. Illustrated by Basil T: Blackwood & Nicolas Bentley. Knopf, 1973.

Bernier-Grand, Carmen T. *César: ¡Sí, Se Puede! Yes, We Can*. Marshall Cavendish, 2004.

Berry, James. *Around the World in Eighty Poems*. Chronicle, 2002.

Blake William. *The Tyger*. Illustrated by Neil Waldman, Harcourt Brace, 1993.

Bloom, Harold, ed. *The Best Poems of the English Language*. HarperCollins, 2004.

Bodecker, N. M. *Hurry, Hurry Mary Dear!* Atheneum, 1976.

Brenner, Barbara, selected by. *Voices: Poetry and Art From Around the World*. National Geographic, 2000.

Brooks, Gwendolyn. *Bronzeville Boys and Girls*. Illustrated by Ronni Solbert. Harper & Row, 1956.

Browning, Robert. *The Pied Piper of Hamelin*. Illustrated by Kate Greenaway. Warne Classic, 1888.

Bryan, Ashley. *Sing to the Sun*. HarperCollins, 1992.

Burg, Brad. *Outside the Lines*. Illustrated by Rebecca Gibbon. Putnam, 2002.

Burleigh, Robert. *Goal*. Illustrated by Stephen T. Johnson. Silver Whistle, 2001.

_____. *Hoops*. Illustrated by Stephen T. Johnson. Silver Whistle, 1997.

Bush, Valerie Chow, selected by. *Believe Me, I Know*. Small Press, 2002.

Carlson, Lori Marie. *Red Hot Salsa: Bilingual Poems on Being Young and Latino in the United States*. Henry Holt, 2005.

Carroll, Lewis. *Alice's Adventures in Wonderland*. Clarendon, 1865.

_____. *Jabberwocky*. Illustrated by Jane Breskin Zalben. Warne, 1977.

_____. *Poems of Lewis Carroll*. Selected by Myra Cohn Livingston. Crowell, 1973.

_____. *Through the Looking-Glass and What Alice Found There*. Illustrated by Franklin Hughes. Cheshire House, 1931.

Carson, Jo, ed. *Stories I Ain't Told Nobody Yet*. Watts. 1989.

Christian, Peggy. *If You Find A Rock*. Photographs by Barbara Hirsch Lember. Harcourt, 2000.

Ciardi, John. *Doodle Soup*. Illustrated by Merle Nacht. Houghton Mifflin, 1985.

_____. *The Hopeful Trout and Other Limericks*. Illustrated by Susan Meddaugh. Houghton Mifflin, 1989.

_____. *I Met a Man.* Illustrated by Robert Osborn. Houghton Mifflin, 1961.

_____. *You Read to Me, I'll Read to You.* Illustrated by Edward Gorey, Lippincott, 1962.

Cole, William, ed. *Poem Stew.* Illustrated by Karen Ann Weinhaus. Lippincott. 1981.

Cook, Sally. *Good Night Pillow Fight.* Illustrated by Laura Cornell. Joanna Cotler, 2004.

Creech, Sharon. *Heartbeat.* Joanna Cotler, 2004.

_____. *Who's That Baby? New-Baby Songs.* Illustrated by David Diaz. Joanna Cotler, 2005.

Crossley-Holland, Kevin. *Once Upon a Poem: Favorite Poems That Tell Stories.* Illustrated by Peter Bailey et. al. Scholastic, 2004.

Dawes, Kwame Senu Neville. *I Saw Your Face.* Dial, 2005.

Demi, ed. *In the Eyes of the Cat: Japanese Poetry for All Seasons.* Illustrated by Demi. Translated by Tze-si Huang. Holt, 1992.

de Regniers, Beatrice Schenk, Eva Moore, Mary Michaels White, & Jean Carr. *Sing a Song of Popcorn: Every Child's Book of Poems.* Scholastic, 1988.

Dickinson, Emily. *The Complete Poems of Emily Dickinson.* Little, Brown, 1924.

_____. *Poetry for Young People: Emily Dickinson.* Edited by Frances Schoonmaker Bolin. Illustrated by Chi Chung. Sterling, 1994.

_____. *Poems for Youth.* Edited by Alfred Leete Hampson. Illustrated by Thomas B. Allen, Little, Brown, 1996.

Downie, Mary Alice, & Barbara Robertson, eds. *The New Wind Has Wings: Poems From Canada.* Illustrated by Elizabeth Cleaver. Oxford University Press, 1984.

Driscoll, Michael. *A Child's Introduction to Poetry.* Illustrated by Meredith Hamilton. Black Dog & Leventhal, 2003.

Duffy, Carol Ann, ed. *I Wouldn't Thank You for a Valentine: Poems for Young Feminists.* Illustrated by Trisha Rafferty. Holt, 1994.

Dunning, Stephen, Edward Lueders, & Hugh Smith, eds. *Reflections on a Gift of Watermelon Pickle . . . and Other Modern Verse.* Lothrop, Lee & Shepard, 1967.

Dyer, Jane. *Animal Crackers: A Delectable Collection of Pictures, Poems, and Lullabies for the Very Young.* Little, Brown, 1996.

Eliot, T. S. *Mr. Mistoffelees With Mungojerrie and Rumpelteazer.* Illustrated by Errol Le Cain. Harcourt Brace, 1991.

_____. *Old Possum's Book of Practical Cats.* Illustrated by Edward Gorey. Harcourt Brace, 1939, 1967, 1982.

English, Karen. *Speak to Me: And I Will Listen Between the Lines.* Illustrated by Amy June Bates. Farrar, Straus & Giroux, 2004.

Esbensen, Barbara Juster. *Swing Around the Sun: Poems.* Illustrated by Cheng-Khee Chee et al. Lerner, 2003.

_____. *Who Shrank My Grandmother's House? Poems of Discovery.* Illustrated by Eric Beddows. HarperCollins, 1992.

Ferris, Helen, ed. *Favorite Poems Old and New.* Doubleday, 1957.

Field, Eugene. *Wynken, Blynken and Nod.* Illustrated by Susan Jeffers. Dutton, 1982.

Fields, Julia. *The Green Lion of Zion Street.* Illustrated by Jerry Pinkney, Macmillan, 1988.

Fisher, Aileen. *Feathered Ones and Furry.* Illustrated by Eric Carle. Crowell, 1971.

_____. *In One Door and Out the Other: A Book of Poems.* Illustrated by Lillian Hoban. Crowell, 1969.

_____. *Listen, Rabbit.* Illustrated by Simeon Shimin. Crowell, 1964.

_____. *Rabbits, Rabbits.* Illustrated by Gail Nieman. Harper & Row, 1983.

_____. *When It Comes to Bugs.* Illustrated by Chris & Bruce Degen. Harper & Row, 1986.

Fleischman, Paul. *I Am Phoenix: Poems for Two Voices.* Illustrated by Ken Nutt. Harper & Row, 1985.

_____. *Joyful Noise: Poems for Two Voices.* Illustrated by Eric Beddows. Harper & Row, 1988.

Fletcher, Ralph. *Poetry Matters: Writing a Poem From the Inside Out.* HarperCollins, 2002.

Florian, Douglas. *Autumnblings.* Greenwillow, 2003.

_____. *Bow Wow Meow Meow: It's Rhyming Cats and Dogs.* Harcourt, 2003.

_____. *Insectlopedia.* Harcourt Brace, 1998.

_____. *Mammalabilia.* Harcourt, 2000.

_____. *Omnibeasts: Animal Poems and Paintings.* Harcourt, 2004.

_____. *Summersaults.* Greenwillow, 2002.

Fox, Dan. *Go In and Out the Window: An Illustrated Songbook for Young People.* Henry Holt, 1987.

Franco, Betsy. *Mathematickles!* Illustrated by Steven Salerno. McElderry, 2003.

Frazee, Marla. *Hush, Little Baby.* Harcourt, 1999.

Forman, Robert. *Seeing Things: A Book of Poems.* Crowell, 1974.

Frost, Helen. *Keesha's House.* Farrar, Straus & Giroux, 2003.

_____. *Spinning Through The Universe: A Novel in Poems From Room 214.* Farrar, Straus & Giroux, 2004.

Frost, Robert. *Birches.* Illustrated by Ed Young. Holt, Rinehart & Winston, 1988.

_____. *Stopping by Woods on a Snowy Evening.* Illustrated by Susan Jeffers, Dutton, 1978, 2001.

George, Kristine O'Connell. *The Great Frog Race and Other Poems.* Illustrated by Kate Kiesler. Clarion, 1997.

_____. *Hummingbird Nest: A Journal of Poems.* Harcourt, 2004.

_____. *Toasting Marshmallows: Camping Poems.* Illustrated by Kate Kiesler. Clarion, 2001.

Gerrard, Roy. *Sir Cedric.* Farrar, Straus & Giroux, 1984.

_____. *Sir Francis Drake: His Daring Deeds.* Farrar, Straus & Giroux, 1988.

_____. *Wagons West!* Farrar, Straus & Giroux, 1996.

Gollub, Matthew. *Cool Melons—Turn to Frogs! The Life and Poems of Issa.* Illustrated by Kazuko G. Stone. Lee & Low, 1998.

Gordon, Ruth, selected by. *Pierced by a Ray of Sun: Poems About the Times We Feel Alone.* HarperCollins, 1995.

Gottfried, Maya. *Good Dog.* Illustrated by Robert Zakanitch. Knopf, 2005.

Graham, Joan Bransfield. *Flicker Flash.* Illustrated by Nancy Davis. Houghton Mifflin, 1999.

Grandits, John. *Technically, It's Not My Fault: Concrete Poems.* Clarion, 2004.

Greenberg, Jan, ed. *Heart to Heart: New Poems Inspired by Twentieth-Century American Art.* Abrams, 2001.

Greenfield, Eloise, *Honey, I Love.* Illustrated by Jan Spivey Gilchrist. HarperCollins, 1995.

_____. *In the Land of Words: New and Selected Poems.* Illustrated by Jan Spivey Gilchrist. HarperCollins, 2004.

_____. *Nathaniel Talking.* Illustrated by Jan Gilchrist. Black Butterfly Children's Books, 1989.

Grimes Nikki. *Come Sunday.* Illustrated by Michael Bryant. Eerdmans, 1996.

_____. *Danitra Brown Leaves Town.* Amistad Press, 2002.

_____. *My Man Blue.* Illustrated by Jerome Lagarrigue. Dial, 2001.

_____. *A Pocketful of Poems.* Illustrated by Javaka Steptoe. Clarion, 2001.

_____. *What Is Goodbye?* Illustrated by Raúl Colón. Hyperion, 2004.

Guinness, Louise, selected by. *The Everyman Book of Nonsense Verse.* Knopf, 2004.

Guthrie, Woody. *This Land Is Your Land.* Illustrated by Kathy Jakobsen. Little, Brown, 1998.

Hall, Donald, ed. *The Oxford Illustrated Book of American Children's Poems.* Oxford, 1999.

Hass, Robert. *The Essential Haiku: Versions of Basho, Buson, and Issa.* Ecco, 1994.

Heaney, Seamus. *Beowulf: A New Verse Translation.* Farrar, Straus & Giroux, 2000.

Heard, Georgia. *This Place I Know: Poems of Comfort.* Illustrations by Holly Meade et al. Candlewick, 2002.

Hesse, Karen. *Out of the Dust.* Scholastic, 1997.

Hoberman, Mary Ann, adapted by. *There Once Was a Man Named Michael Finnegan.* Illustrated by Nadine Bernard Westcott. Little, Brown, 2001.

Hopkins, Lee Bennett, ed. *Dinosaurs.* Illustrated by Murray Tinkelman. Harcourt Brace, 1987.

_____. *Good Rhymes, Good Times.* Illustrated by Frané Lessac. HarperCollins, 1995.

_____, selected by. *Hoofbeats, Claws & Rippled Fins: Creature Poems.* Illustrated by Stephen Alcorn. HarperCollins, 2002.

_____, selected by. *Oh, No! Where Are My Pants? And Other Disasters: Poems.* Illustrated by Wolf Erlbruch. HarperCollins, 2005.

_____. ed. *Surprises.* Illustrated by Megan Lloyd. Harper & Row, 1984.

_____, selected by. *Wonderful Words: Poems About Reading Writing, Speaking, and Listening.* Illustrated by Karen Barbour. Simon & Schuster, 2004.

Hovey, Kate. *Ancient Voices.* Illustrated by Murray Kimber. McElderry, 2004.

_____. *Voices of the Trojan War.* Illustrated by Leonid Gore. McElderry, 2004.

Hughes, Langston. *The Dream Keeper.* Knopf, 1932, 1960.

_____. *Selected Poems of Langston Hughes.* Knopf, 1942, 1959.

Janeczko, Paul. *A Kick in the Head: An Everyday Guide to Poetic Forms.* Illustrated by Chris Raschka. Candlewick, 2005.

_____. *A Pake in the I: A Collection of Concrete Poems.* Illustrated by Chris Raschka. Candlewick, 2001.

_____. collected by. *Very Best (Almost) Friends: Poems of Friendship.* Illustrated by Christine Davenier. Candlewick, 1999.

Katz, Bobbi. *Truck Talk: Rhymes on Wheels.* Scholastic, 1997.

Kellogg, Steven. *I Was Born About 10,000 Years Ago.* Morrow, 1996.

Kennedy, Caroline, selected by. *The Best-Loved Poems of Jacqueline Kennedy Onassis.* Hyperion, 2001.

Kennedy, Caroline, selected by. *A Family of Poems: My Favorite Poetry for Children.* Illustrated by Jon J. Muth. Hyperion, 2005.

Kennedy X. J., & Dorothy M. Kennedy, eds. *Knock at a Star: A Child's Introduction to Poetry.* Illustrated by Karen Lee Baker. Little, Brown, 1999.

_____, eds. *Talking Like the Rain: A First Book of Poems.* Illustrated by Jane Dyer. Little, Brown, 1992.

Kimmel, Eric A., adapted by. *The Hero Beowulf.* Illustrated by Leonard Everett Fisher. Farrar, Straus & Giroux, 2005.

Kipling, Rudyard, *Gunga Din.* Illustrated by Robert Andrew Parker. Harcourt Brace, 1987.

Knudson, R. R., and May Swenson, eds. *American Sports Poems.* Watts, 1988.

Koch, Kenneth, & Kate Farrell, eds. *Talking to the Sun.* Metropolitan Museum of Art/Holt, Rinehart & Winston, 1985.

Koertge, Ron. *Shakespeare Bats Cleanup.* Candlewick, 2003.

Langstaff, John, foreword by. *On Christmas Day in the Morning.* Illustrated by Melissa Sweet. Candlewick, 1999.

_____, ed. *What a Morning! The Christmas Story in Black Spirituals.* Illustrated by Ashley Bryan. Macmillan, 1987.

Larrick, Nancy, ed. *Songs From Mother Goose.* Illustrated by Robin Spowart. Harper & Row, 1989.

_____, ed. *When the Dark Comes Dancing: A Bedtime Poetry Book.* Illustrated by John Wallner. Philomel, 1982.

Lear, Edward. *A Book of Bosh.* Complied by Brian Alderson. Penguin, 1982.

_____. *A Book of Nonsense.* Thomas McLean, 1846.

_____. *The Complete Nonsense Book.* Dodd, Mead, 1946.

_____. *Hilary Knight's The Owl and the Pussy-Cat.* Illustrated by Hilary Knight. Macmillan, 1983.

_____. *The Nonsense Books of Edward Lear.* New American Library, 1964.

_____. *Nonsense Omnibus.* Warne. 1943.

_____. *Nonsense!* Illustrated by Valorie Fisher. Atheneum, 2004.

_____. *Nonsense Songs.* Illustrated by Bee Willey. Simon & Schuster, 1997.

_____. *The Owl and the Pussycat.* Illustrated by Jan Brett. Putnam, 1991.

_____. *The Pelican Chorus and Other Nonsense.* Illustrated by Fred Marcellino. HarperCollins, 1995.

_____. *The Quangle Wangle's Hat.* Illustrated by Louise Voce. Candlewick, 2005.

Lee, Dennis. *The Ice Cream Store.* Illustrated by David McPhail. HarperCollins, 1991.

Levin, Vadim. *Silly Horse.* Translated by Tanya Wolfson & Tatiana Zunshine. Illustrated by Evgeny Antonenkov. Pumpkin House, 2005.

Levy, Constance. *I'm Going to Pet a Worm Today and Other Poems.* Illustrated by Ronald Himler. Macmillan, 1991.

Lewis, J. Patrick. *Earth Verses and Water Rhymes.* Illustrated by Robert Sabuda. Atheneum, 1991.

_____, selected by. *Heroes and She-Roes: Poems of Amazing and Everyday Heroes.* Dial, 2005.

_____. *Please Bury Me in the Library.* Illustrated by Kyle M. Stone. Gulliver, 2005.

Little, Jean. *Hey World. Here I Am!* Illustrated by Sue Truesdell. Harper & Row, 1989.

Liu, Siyu, and Orel Protopopescu. *A Thousand Peaks: Poems From China.* Illustrated by Siyu Liu. Pacific View, 2002.

Livingston, Myra Cohn. *Celebrations.* Illustrated by Leonard Everett Fisher. Holiday House, 1985.

_____. *A Circle of Seasons.* Illustrated by Leonard Everett Fisher. Holiday House, 1982.

_____. *O Sliver of Liver.* Illustrated by Iris Van Rynbach. Atheneum, 1979.

_____. *Space Songs.* Illustrated by Leonard Everett Fisher. Holiday House, 1988.

Lobel, Arnold. *The Rose in My Garden.* Illustrated by Anita Lobel. Greenwillow, 1984.

_____. *Whiskers and Rhymes.* Greenwillow, 1985.

Longfellow, Henry Wadsworth. *Hiawatha.* Illustrated by Susan Jeffers. Dutton, 1983.

_____. *Hiawatha.* Illustrated by Keith Mosely. Putnam, 1988.

_____. *Hiawatha's Childhood.* Illustrated by Errol LeCain. Farrar, Straus & Giroux, 1984.

_____. *The Midnight Ride of Paul Revere.* Illustrated by Christopher Bing. Handprint, 2001.

_____. *Paul Revere's Ride: The Landlord's Tale.* Illustrated by Charles Santore. HarperCollins, 2003.

_____. *Paul Revere's Ride.* Illustrated by Christopher Bing. Handprint, 2001.

_____. *Paul Revere's Ride.* Illustrated by Monica Vachula. Boyds Mills, 2003.

_____. *Paul Revere's Ride.* Illustrated by Paul Galdone. Crowell, 1963.

_____. *Paul Revere's Ride.* Illustrated by Ted Rand. Dutton, 1990.

_____. *The Song of Hiawatha.* Illustrated by Margaret Early. Handprint, 2003.

Lyne, Sandford, compiled by. *Soft Hay Will Catch You: Poems by Young People.* Illustrated by Julie Monks. Simon & Schuster, 2004.

MacLachlan, Patricia. *What You Know First.* Illustrated by Barry Moser. HarperCollins, 1995.

Mahy, Margaret. *Nonstop Nonsense.* Illustrated by Quentin Blake. Macmillan, 1989.

Mannis, Celeste Davidson. *One Leaf Rides the Wind: Counting in a Japanese Garden.* Illustrated by Susan Kathleen Hartung. Puffin, 2002.

McCord, David. *Far and Few: Rhymes of the Never Was and Always Is.* Illustrated by Henry B. Kane. Little, Brown, 1974.

_____. *One at a Time: Collected Poems for the Young.* Illustrated by Henry B. Kane. Little, Brown. 1977.

McCullough, David. *John Adams.* Simon & Schuster, 2001.

Merriam, Eve. *Halloween ABC.* Illustrated by Lane Smith. Macmillan, 1987.

_____. *Rainbow Writing.* Atheneum, 1976.

_____. *The Singing Green: New and Selected Poems for All Seasons.* Illustrated by Kathleen Collins Howell. Morrow, 1992.

Milne, A. A. *There's Always Pooh and Me.* Illustrated by Ernest H. Shepard. Dutton Children's Books, 2002.

_____. *When We Were Very Young.* Illustrated by Ernest H. Shepard. Dutton, 1961.

_____. *Winnie-the-Pooh.* Illustrated by Ernest H. Shepard. Dutton, 1954.

_____. *The World of Christopher Robin.* Illustrated by E. H. Shepard. Dutton, 1958.

Montenegro, Laura Nyman. *A Bird About to Sing.* Houghton Mifflin, 2003.

Moore, Clement. *The Night Before Christmas.* Illustrated by Tomie dePaola. Holiday House, 1980.

_____. *The Night Before Christmas.* Illustrated by Tasha Tudor. Little, Brown, 1999.

Morrison, Lillian, ed. *At the Crack of the Bat.* Illustrated by Steve Cieslawski. Hyperion, 1972.

_____, compiled by. *It Rained All Day That Night: Autographs, Rhymes & Inscriptions.* Illustrated by Christy Hale. August House, 2003.

Morton, Miriam, ed. *The Moon Is Like a Silver Sickle: A Celebration of Poetry by Russian Children.* Illustrated by Eros Keith. Simon & Schuster, 1972.

Myers, Walter Dean. *Harlem.* Illustrated by Christopher Myers. Scholastic, 1997.

Moss, Jeffrey. *Bone Poems.* Illustrated by Tom Leigh. Workman, 1997.

Myers, Tim. *Basho and the River Stones.* Illustrated by Oki S. Han. Marshall Cavendish, 2004.

Myers, Walter Dean. *Blues Journey.* Illustrated by Christopher Myers. Holiday House, 2003.

_____. *Here in Harlem: Poems in Many Voices.* Holiday House, 2004.

Nelson, Marilyn. *Carver: A Life in Poems.* Front Street, 2001.

_____. *Fortune's Bones: The Manumission Requiem.* Front Street, 2004.

_____. *A Wreath for Emmett Till.* Houghton Mifflin, 2005.

Niven, Penelope. *Carl Sandburg: Adventures of a Poet.* Illustrated by Marc Nadel. Harcourt, 2003.

Noda, Takayo. *Dear World.* Dial, 2003.

Noyes, Alfred. *Forty Seamen and Other Poems.* Blackwood, 1907.

_____. *The Highwayman.* Illustrated by Murray Kimber. Kids Can, 2005.

Nye, Naomi Shihab. *A Maze Me: Poems for Girls.* Greenwillow, 2005.

_____, selected by. *The Flag of Childhood: Poems From the Middle East.* Aladdin, 2002.

_____, selected by. *Is This Forever, or What? Poems & Paintings From Texas.* Greenwillow, 2004.

_____. *19 Varieties of Gazelle: Poems of the Middle East.* Greenwillow, 2002.

_____, selected by. *Salting the Ocean: 100 Poems by Young Poets.* Illustrated by Ashley Bryan. Greenwillow, 2000.

_____, selected by. *The Space Between Our Footsteps: Poems and Paintings From the Middle East.* Simon & Schuster, 1998.

_____, ed. *This Same Sky: A Collection of Poems From Around the World.* Aladdin, 1996.

_____, ed. *What Have You Lost?* Photographs by Michael Nye. Greenwillow, 1999.

Ochoa, Annette Piña, Betsy Franco, & Traci L. Gourdine, selected by. *Night Is Gone, Day Is Still Coming.* Candlewick, 2003.

Okutoro, Lydia Omolola, selected by. *Quiet Storm: Voices of Young Black Poets.* Hyperion, 1999.

O'Neill, Mary. *Hailstones and Halibut Bones.* Illustrated by Leonard Weisgard. Doubleday, 1961.

Opie, Iona, and Peter Opie, eds. *The Oxford Book of Children's Verse.* Oxford University Press, 1984, 2002.

_____. *Tail Feathers From Mother Goose: The Opie Rhyme Book.* Little, Brown, 1988.

Paolilli, Paul, & Dan Brewer. *Silver Seeds: A Book of Nature Poems.* Illustrated by Steve Johnson and Lou Fancher. Viking, 2001.

Pearson, Susan. *Grimericks.* Illustrated by Gris Grimly. Marshall Cavendish, 2005.

Peters, Lisa Westber. *Earthshake: Poems From the Ground Up.* Illustrated by Cathie Felstead. Greenwillow, 2003.

Prelutsky, Jack. *Awful Ogre's Awful Day.* Illustrated by Paul O. Zelinsky. Greenwillow, 2001.

_____. *The Baby Uggs Are Hatching.* Illustrated by James Stevenson. Greenwillow, 1982.

_____, ed. *The Beauty of the Beast: Poems From the Animal Kingdom.* Illustrated by Meilo So. Knopf, 1997.

_____. *The Dragons Are Singing Tonight.* Illustrated by Peter Sís. Greenwillow, 1993.

_____. *The Frogs Wore Red Suspenders.* Illustrated by Petra Mathers. Greenwillow, 2002.

_____. *The Gargoyle on the Roof.* Illustrated by Peter Sís. Greenwillow, 1999.

_____. *A Gopher in the Garden and Other Animal Poems.* Illustrated by Robert Leydenfrost. Macmillan, 1966, 1967.

_____. *The Headless Horseman Rides Tonight.* Illustrated by Arnold Lobel. Greenwillow, 1980.

_____. *If Not For the Cat.* Illustrated by Ted Rand. Greenwillow, 2004.

_____. *Monday's Troll.* Illustrated by Peter Sís. Greenwillow, 1996.

_____. *My Parents Think I'm Sleeping.* Greenwillow, 1985.

_____. *A Pizza the Size of the Sun.* Illustrated by James Stevenson. Greenwillow, 1996.

_____. *The Queen of Eene.* Illustrated by Victoria Chess. Greenwillow, 1978.

_____, ed. *The Random House Book of Poetry for Children.* Illustrated by Arnold Lobel. Random House, 2000.

_____, ed. *Read-Aloud Rhymes for the Very Young.* Illustrated by Marc Brown. Knopf, 1986.

_____. *Rolling Harvey Down the Hill.* Illustrated by Victoria Chess. Greenwillow, 1980.

_____. *Scranimals.* Illustrated by Peter Sís. Greenwillow, 2002.

_____. *The Sheriff of Rottenshot.* Illustrated by Victoria Chess. Greenwillow, 1982.

_____. *Tyrannosaurus Was a Beast: Dinosaur Poems.* Illustrated by Arnold Lobel. Greenwillow, 1988.

_____. *Zoo Doings.* Greenwillow, 1983.

Richards, Laura E. *Tirra Lirra, Rhymes Old and New.* Illustrated by Marguerite Davis. Little, Brown, 1955.

Roemer, Heidi. *Come to My Party and Other Shape Poems.* Illustrated by Hideko Takahashi. Henry Holt, 2004.

Rogasky, Barbara, selected by. *Leaf by Leaf: Autumn Poems.* Illustrated by Marc Tauss. Scholastic, 2001.

Rosen, Michael, ed. *Poems for the Very Young.* Illustrated by Bob Graham. Kingfisher, 1993.

Rossetti, Christina. *Goblin Market.* Illustrated and adapted by Ellen Raskin. Dutton, 1970.

_____. *Sing-Song.* Illustrated by Arthur Hughes. Routledge, 1872.

Rylant, Cynthia. *God Went to Beauty School.* HarperTempest, 2003.

_____. *Waiting to Waltz: A Childhood.* Illustrated by Stephen Gammell. Bradbury, 1984.

Sandburg, Carl. *Poems of the Midwest.* World, 1946.

Sandmann, Alexa L. "What's a Nice Poem Like You Doing in a Place Like This?" Curriculum Connections: A Supplement to *School Library Journal.* Spring 2005, vol. 2, 16–19.

Scanlon, Elizabeth Garton. *A Sock Is a Pocket for Your Toes: A Pocket Book.* Illustrated by Robin Preiss Glasser. HarperCollins, 2004.

Sebesta, Sam L., and Dianne L. Monson. "Reading Preferences." In *Handbook of Research on Teaching the English Language Arts,* 2nd edition. Edited by James Flood, Diane Lapp, James R. Squire, and Julie M. Jensen. Lawrence Erlbaum Associates, 2003, 835–845.

Schwartz, Alvin. *And the Green Grass Grew All Around: Folk Poetry From Everyone.* Illustrated by Sue Truesdell. HarperCollins, 1992.

Scieszka, Jon. *Science Verse.* Illustrated by Lane Smith. Viking, 2004.

Seeger, Ruth Crawford. *American Folksongs for Children—In Home, School, and Nursery School.* Illustrated by Barbara Cooney. Doubleday, 1948.

Sendak, Maurice. *Pierre: A Cautionary Tale.* Harper & Row, 1962.

Seuss, Dr. *The Cat in the Hat.* Random House, 1957.

Shange, Ntozake. *Ellington Was Not a Street.* Illustrated by Kadir Nelson. Simon & Schuster, 2004.

Sidman, Joyce. *Song of the Water Boatman & Other Pond Poems.* Illustrated by Beckie Prange. Houghton Mifflin, 2005.

Siebert, Diane. *Heartland.* Illustrated by Wendell Minor. Crowell, 1989.

_____. *Mojave.* Illustrated by Wendell Minor. Crowell, 1988.

_____. *Sierra.* Illustrated by Wendell Minor. HarperCollins, 1991.

Siegen-Smith, Nikki. *Songs for Survival: Songs and Chants From Tribal Peoples Around the World.* Illustrated by Bernard Lodge. Dutton, 1996.

Silverstein, Shel. *Falling Up.* HarperCollins, 1996.

_____. *A Light in the Attic.* Harper & Row, 1981.

_____. *Runny Babbit: A Billy Sook.* HarperCollins, 2005.

_____. *Where the Sidewalk Ends.* Harper & Row, 1974.

Simon, Seymour, ed. *Star Walk.* Morrow, 1995.

Singer, Marilyn. *Central Heating: Poems About Fire and Warmth.* Illustrated by Meilo So. Knopf, 2005.

_____. *Creature Carnival.* Illustrated by Gris Grimly. Hyperion, 2004.

_____. *Fireflies at Midnight.* Illustrated by Ken Robbins. Atheneum, 2003.

_____. *Footprints on the Roof: Poems About the Earth.* Illustrated by Meilo So. Knopf, 2002.

_____. *How to Cross a Pond: Poems About Water.* Illustrated by Meilo So. Knopf, 2003.

Smith Charles R., Jr. *Hoop Kings.* Candlewick, 2004.

_____. *Hoop Queens.* Candlewick, 2003.

Smith, Hope Anita. *The Way a Door Closes.* Illustrated by Shane W. Evans. Henry Holt, 2003.

Smith, William J., compiled by. *Here Is My Heart: Love Poems.* Illustrated by Jane Dyer. Little, Brown, 1999.

Snyder, Zilpha Keatley. *Today Is Saturday.* Illustrated by John Arms. Atheneum, 1969.

Spinelli, Eileen. *Feathers: Poems About Birds.* Illustrated by Lisa McCue. Henry Holt, 2004.

Spivak, Dawnine. *Grass Sandals: The Travels of Basho.* Illustrated by Demi. Atheneum, 1997.

Southey, Robert. *The Cataract of Lodore.* Illustrated by David Catrow. Holt, 1992.

Starbird, Kaye. *The Covered Bridge House and Other Poems.* Illustrated by Jim Arnosky. Four Winds, 1979.

Steptoe, Javaka edited and illustrated by. *In Daddy's Arms I Am Tall: African Americans Celebrating Fathers.* Lee & Low, 1997.

Stevenson, Robert Louis. *A Child's Garden of Verses.* Longmans, Green, 1885.

Sturges, Philemon. *She'll Be Comin' ' Round the Mountain.* Illustrated by Ashley Wolff. Little, Brown, 2004.

Thayer, Ernest Lawrence. *Casey at the Bat: A Ballad of the Republic Sung in the Year 1888.* Illustrated by Christopher Bing. Handprint, 2000.

_____. *Casey at the Bat: A Ballad of the Republic Sung in the Year 1888.* Illustrated by C. F. Payne. Simon & Schuster, 2003.

Thomas, Joyce Carol. *Crowning Glory.* Illustrated by Brenda Joysmith. Joanna Cotler, 2002.

Thurman, Judith. *Flashlight and Other Poems.* Illustrated by Reina Rubel. Atheneum, 1976.

Tiller, Ruth. *Cats Vanish Slowly.* Illustrated by Laura Seeley. Peachtree. 1995.

Turner, Ann. *Mississppi Mud: Three Prairie Journals.* Illustrated by Robert J. Blake. HarperCollins, 1997.

Van Laan. Nancy. *With a Whoop and a Holler: A Bushel of Lore From Way Down South.* Illustrated by Scott Cook. Atheneum, 1998.

Vecchione, Patrice, ed. *The Body Eclectic: An Anthology of Poems.* Henry Holt, 2002.

_____, ed. *Revenge and Forgiveness: An Anthology of Poems.* Henry Holt, 2004.

_____, ed. *Truth and Lies: An Anthology of Poems.* Henry Holt, 2001.

Viorst, Judith. *If I Were in Charge of the World and Other Worries: Poems for Children and Their Parents.* Illustrated by Lynne Cherry. Atheneum, 1981.

Volavkova, Hana, ed. . . . *Never Saw Another Butterfly . . .* Schocken, 1993.

Westcott, Nadine Bernard. *Peanut Butter and Jelly: A Play Rhyme.* Dutton, 1987.

Whipple, Laura, ed. *Eric Carle's Animals, Animals.* Illustrated by Eric Carle. Philomel, 1989.

_____. *Eric Carle's Dragons Dragons & Other Creatures That Never Were.* Philomel, 1991.

_____. *A Snowflake Fell: Poems About Winter.* Illustrated by Hatsuki Hori. Barefoot, 2003.

Willard, Nancy. *Night Story.* Illustrated by Ilse Plume. Harcourt Brace, 1986.

_____. *Pish, Posh, Said Hieronymus Bosch.* Illustrated by Leo and Diane Dillon. Harcourt Brace, 1991.

_____. *The Tale I Told Sasha.* Illustrated by David Christiana. Little, Brown, 1999.

_____. *A Visit to William Blake's Inn: Poems for Innocent and Experienced Travelers.* Illustrated by Alice and Martin Provensen. Harcourt Brace, 1981.

Wilner, Isabel, ed. *The Poetry Troup: An Anthology to Read Aloud.* Scribner, 1977.

Windham, Sophie, selected by. *The Mermaid: And Other Sea Poems.* Scholastic, 1996.

Winter, Jeanette. *Emily Dickinson's Letters to the World.* Farrar, Straus & Giroux, 2002.

Wise, William. *Dinosaurs Forever.* Illustrated by Lynn Munsinger. Dial, 2000.

Wong, Janet S. *Behind the Wheel: Poems About Driving.* Simon & Schuster, 1999.

_____. *Night Garden: Poems From the World of Dreams.* Illustrated by Julie Paschkis. Simon & Schuster, 2000.

Wood, Douglas. *Old Turtle.* Illustrated by Cheng-Khee Chee. Pfeifer-Hamilton, 1992.

Woodson, Jacqueline. *Locomotion.* Putnam, 2003.

Worth, Valerie. *All the Small Poems.* Illustrated by Natalie Babbitt. Farrar, Straus & Giroux, 1987.

_____. *More Small Poems.* Illustrated by Natalie Babbitt. Farrar, Straus & Giroux, 1976.

_____. *Still More Small Poems.* Illustrated by Natalie Babbitt. Farrar, Straus & Giroux, 1978.

Yolen, Jane. *The Ballad of the Pirate Queens.* Illustrated by David Shannon. Harcourt Brace, 1995.

_____. *The Three Bears Rhyme Book.* Illustrated by Jane Dyer. Harcourt Brace, 1987.

Zemach, Margot. *Some From the Moon, Some From the Sun: Poems and Songs for Everyone.* Farrar, Straus & Giroux, 2001.

Zolotow. Charlotte. *River Winding.* Illustrated by Kazue Mizumura. Crowell, 1978.

_____. *River Winding.* Illustrated by Regina Shekerjian. Abelard-Schuman, 1970.

_____. *Seasons: A Book of Poems.* Illustrated by Erik Blegvad. HarperCollins, 2002.

"HOPE WAS HERE

NEWBERY HONOR BOOK 00

JOAN BAUER

AUTHOR OF RULES OF THE ROAD

CHAPTER OUTLINE

Window on the World

- What Contemporary Realistic Fiction Is
- Values of Realistic Fiction
- Literary Elements— Evaluating Realistic Fiction
- How Realistic Fiction Has Changed
- Literary Criticism: New Realism and the Problem Novel
- Controversial Issues
- Literary Criticism: Guidelines for Selecting Controversial Fiction
- Subjects in Realistic Fiction
- Animal Stories, Mysteries, Sports Stories, and Humor

Teaching With Realistic Fiction

- Using Role Playing
- Using Survival Stories to Motivate Reading and Interaction With Literature
- Developing Questioning Strategies

Window on the World

New terminology enters the discussion of children's books as you leave the realm of Mother Goose, most picture storybooks, traditional literature, and modern fantasy. Such terms as *relevant books, extreme realism, problem novel,* and *everyday occurrences* are found in critiques and discussions of contemporary realistic fiction.

Although some of the books in this genre are among the most popular with older children, they are also among the most controversial. Interest groups, educators, and parents criticize and debate the value of some realistic stories for children. Many adults are concerned about such issues as censorship, sexism, promiscuity, violence, profanity, alienation from society, and racism. This chapter discusses what contemporary realistic fiction is, criteria for evaluating realistic fiction, why it should be shared with children, how realistic fiction has changed, and issues related to realistic fiction.

What Contemporary Realistic Fiction Is

The term *contemporary realistic fiction* implies that everything in a realistic story—including plot, characters, and setting—is consistent with the lives of real people in our contemporary world. The word *realistic* does not mean that the story is true, however; it means only that the story could have happened.

Use of the words *realistic* and *fiction* together is confusing to some children, who have trouble distinguishing contemporary realistic fiction from modern fantasy or from stories that really happened. Certainly, authors of modern fantasy attempt to make their stories realistic in the sense that they create believable plots, characters, and settings; make their stories as internally consistent as possible; and ground their stories in familiar reality before introducing elements of fantasy. Contemporary realistic fiction, however, requires that plots deal with familiar, everyday problems, pleasures, and personal relationships and that characters and settings seem as real as the contemporary world we know. The supernatural has no part in such stories, except occasionally in the beliefs of realistic human characters.

The differences between modern fantasy and contemporary realistic fiction are summarized in Chart 9.1. Two popular animal stories demonstrate the differences. In Beatrix Potter's fantasy *The Tale of Peter Rabbit,* Peter talks, thinks, acts, and dresses like an inquisitive, sometimes greedy, sometimes frightened human child who needs his mother's love and care. Al-

CHART 9.1 Differences between modern fantasy and contemporary realistic fiction

	Modern Fantasy	Contemporary Realistic Fiction
Believable stories	Authors must encourage readers to suspend disbelief	Authors may rely on "relevant subjects," everyday occurrences, or extreme realism
Plot	Conflict may be against supernatural powers Problems may be solved through magical powers	Conflict develops as characters cope with such problems as growing up, survival, family discord, and inner-city tensions Antagonists may be self, other family members, society, or nature
Characters	Personified toys, little people, supernatural beings, real people who have imaginary experiences, animals who behave like people	Characters act like real people Animals always behave like animals
Setting	Past, present, or future Imaginary world May travel through time and space	The contemporary world is as we know it

though the story's garden setting is realistic, Peter's home is furnished with human furniture. In this fantasy, conflict develops because Peter demonstrates believable childlike desires.

In contrast, the three animals in Sheila Burnford's *The Incredible Journey* retain their animal characteristics as they struggle for survival in a realistically depicted Canadian wilderness. A trained hunting dog leads his companions across the wilderness; an English bull terrier, who is a cherished family pet, seeks people to give him food; and a Siamese cat retains her feline independence. Conflict in this realistic story develops as the animals become lost and face problems while trying to return to their home. Burnford does not give the animals human thoughts, values, or other human characteristics. The characters and settings are not only believable but also completely realistic in our everyday world.

Values of Realistic Fiction

One of the greatest values of realistic fiction for children is that many realistic stories allow children to identify with characters their own age who have similar interests and problems. Children like to read about people they can understand; thus, their favorite authors express a clear understanding of children. For example, one girl said about Judy Blume's *Are You There God? It's Me, Margaret*, "I've read this book five times; I could be Margaret."

Realistic fiction can help children discover that their problems and desires are not unique and that they are not alone in experiencing certain feelings and situations. Children who are unhappy about the death of a loved one may identify with Howard Kaplan's *Waiting to Sing* or Audrey

Couloumbis's *Getting Near to Baby*, for example, or children who are having preadolescent anxieties, especially about boy–girl relationships, may find a comrade in Phyllis Naylor's *Alice in Rapture, Sort Of*. The young characters in these books face and overcome their problems while remaining true to themselves.

Realistic fiction also extends children's horizons by broadening their interests, allowing them to experience new adventures, and showing them different ways to view and deal with conflicts in their own lives. Children can vicariously live a survival adventure and mature in the process as they read Scott O'Dell's *Island of the Blue Dolphins*, for example, or experience the death of a father in Vera and Bill Cleaver's *Where the Lilies Bloom*.

According to Joanne Bernstein (1989), reading about children who are facing emotional problems can help children discharge repressed emotions and cope with fear, anger, or grief. For example, books about divorce or abuse may help children cope with a traumatic period in their lives. In Beverly Cleary's *Dear Mr. Henshaw* or Kate DiCamillo's *Because of Winn-Dixie*, readers discover that parents as well as children are hurt by divorce or separation. Children may realize the consequences of wife and child abuse by reading Betsy Byars's *Cracker Jackson*. (A *word of caution*: Realistic fiction should *not* be used to replace professional help in situations that warrant such intervention. Children experiencing severe depression, anger, or grief may require professional help.) Many of the books presented in this chapter can stimulate discussion and help children share their feelings and solve their problems. Of course, realistic fiction also provides children with pleasure and escape. Realistic animal stories, mysteries, sports stories, and humorous stories are enjoyable getaways for young people.

LITERARY ELEMENTS—EVALUATING REALISTIC FICTION

Contemporary realistic fiction should meet the basic literary criteria discussed in Chapter 3. Conflicts that could really occur in our contemporary world should be integral to the plot, characterization, setting, and theme. In realistic contemporary settings, authors should thoroughly develop internal and external conflicts, creating credible stories through believable plots, good characterizations, meaningful themes, and effective styles. (See the Evaluation Criteria box page 365.)

Plot

Conflicts at the center of plots in contemporary realistic fiction may arise from external forces, with characters trying to overcome problems related to families, peers, or the society around them, or they may arise with characters trying to overcome problems related to inner conflicts. However, internal conflicts often result from conflict with external forces. Consequently, person-against-self conflicts are common in contemporary realistic fiction.

As in traditional literature, conflict in contemporary realistic fiction may involve protagonists in quests. Caron Lee Cohen (1985) identifies four major components in person-against-self conflicts: (1) problem, (2) struggle, (3) realization, and (4) achievement of peace or truth. She says:

> The point at which the struggle wanes and the inner strength emerges seems to be the point of self-realization. That point leads immediately to the final sense of peace or truth that is the resolution of the quest. The best books are those which move readers and cause them to identify with the character's struggle. (p. 28)

Of course, if readers are to understand conflicts and empathize with characters' responses, the characters themselves must be convincingly developed. The pressures that characters experience and the motives that characters act upon must be very clear.

As an example of credible conflict, consider the person-against-self conflict that Paula Fox develops in *One-Eyed Cat*. Fox sets the stage for the forthcoming conflict by describing an incident in which Uncle Hilary gives Ned a loaded Daisy air rifle for his 11th birthday. Ned's father, the Reverend Wallace, forbids Ned to use the gun until he is at least 14. Instead of hiding the gun, Ned's father takes it to the attic, where Ned can easily find it. A conflict is developed as Ned considers, "The painful thing was that, though Ned didn't always trust his father, his father trusted him, and that seemed to him unfair, although he couldn't explain why it was so" (p. 40).

Ned cannot resist the temptation of the gun, and he fires it, shooting a wild stray cat. Then the person-against-self conflict deepens. Fox vividly describes Ned's fear and the accompanying guilt when he sees the "gap, the dried blood, the little worm of mucus in the corner next to the cat's nose where the eye had been" (p. 70). Metaphor explains Ned's emotional response as "the gun was like a splinter in his mind" (p. 90). Ned's quest becomes to save the wild cat from sickness and starvation during the approaching winter. It also becomes a quest to overcome his sense of guilt and remorse and to tell the truth about what has happened.

Fox's novel follows Cohen's four major components: The problem results because Ned betrays his parent's trust; the struggle continues when Ned feels increasingly guilty because of his lies as he tries to save the wounded animal; the point of self-realization begins when Ned feels relief by confessing his guilt to a critically ill older neighbor; and peace and truth finally result on a moonlit night when Ned confesses his actions to his mother after they see a one-eyed cat and kittens emerging from the woods. In a satisfying conclusion, Ned and his mother exchange revealing confessions.

This book may be successful because the conflict appeals to more than one age or ability group. Most readers can empathize with the desire to commit a forbidden act and the terror of the consequences. More mature readers can appreciate the portrayal of a boy who overcomes a hurdle in the maturation process.

Characterization

The characterization of Ned in Fox's *One-Eyed Cat* is an integral part of the conflict. For example, Fox describes Ned's actions, clarifies his response to his parents and to the wounded cat, and reveals his thoughts during his traumatic experiences. Readers know Ned intimately: They understand his hopes, his fears, his past, his present, and his relationships with his parents.

Complex characterizations that lead to self-discovery and personal relationships are also important in Cynthia Voigt's books about the Tillerman family. In *Homecoming*, Voigt focuses on the children's experiences after their emotionally ill mother deserts them. In the sequel, *Dicey's Song*, Voigt focuses on the four children and their grandmother: a young girl who is trying to hold her family together, a girl with a learning disability who has a gift for music, a gifted boy who tries to hide his giftedness because he does not want to be different, a younger brother who strikes out in anger, and a grandmother whom the townspeople consider eccentric. In all of Voigt's books, as in Fox's *One-Eyed Cat*, readers discover that the protagonists have many-sided personalities, like their own. Readers come to know these characters intimately, sharing their hopes, fears, pasts, and presents.

Throughout her books, Voigt effectively uses symbolism in her characterizations. The symbolism associated with the blue heron is especially meaningful in *A Solitary Blue*. Consider the implications for Jeff's character in the following examples: When Jeff has low self-esteem, he views the heron as a creature that occupies

Evaluation Criteria

Literary Criticism: Realistic Fiction

1. The content should be presented honestly. Sensationalizing and capitalizing on the novelty of a subject should be avoided.

2. A story should expose personal and social values central to our culture, at the same time revealing how overt expression of those values may have changed.

3. The story should allow readers to draw personal conclusions from the evidence. The author should respect the readers' intelligence.

4. The author should recognize that today's young readers are in the process of growing toward adult sophistication.

5. The language and syntax should reveal the background and the nature of characters and situations.

6. The author should write in a hopeful tone. A story should communicate in an honest way that there is hope in this world.

7. Children's literature should reflect sensitivity to the needs and rights of girls and boys without preference, bias, or negative stereotypes.

8. If violence is included in a story, the author should treat the subject appropriately. Does the author give the necessary facts? Are both sides of the conflict portrayed fully, fairly, and honestly? Is the writing developed with feeling and emotion? Does the author help children gain a perspective about the subject?

9. A story should satisfy children's basic needs and provide them with insights into their own problems and relationships.

10. A story should provide children with enjoyment.

"its own insignificant corner of the landscape in a timeless, long-legged solitude" (p. 45). Later, when Jeff feels angry, broken, and bruised because of his mother's behavior, he again views the heron: "'Just leave me alone,' the heron seemed to be saying. Jeff rowed away, down the quiet creek. The bird did not watch him go" (p. 91). Finally, when Jeff discovers that he is a worthwhile person, he realizes that the solitary heron reminds him of his best friend, Dicey Tillerman. When Dicey laughingly says she was thinking that the bird reminded her of Jeff, he is flattered by the comparison. Jeff knows that he, like the heron, is a "rare bird," with staying power and a gentle spirit.

Norma Fox Mazer also synthesizes symbols and characters in *After the Rain*. She uses the symbolism of rain at the end of the book both to reveal and to review Rachel's changing feelings for her grandfather, Izzy. For example, after Izzy's death, Mazer states:

> Then, behind her closed eyes, she sees a road, a narrow sandy road with tall trees on both sides, and she sees herself walking down this road in the rain . . . dark, blue-green of the trees . . . hard, dark lines of water sleeting down . . . nothing else exists but the wet road, the trees lashed by wind, and herself, a solitary figure walking in the rain. (p. 267)

Later, Rachel uses these words when talking about Izzy to her brother Jeremy:

> "Anyway, I'm glad that I finally _____," she begins, and then she can't say it, can't say she's finally glad she got to know him. The sky is clear and cloudless, the trees are blazing purely with autumn color, but she is all at once in a storm. Hard rain again, this time with thunder and lightning. This time, not grief but anger. Anger at Izzy, hard strikes of anger splitting the blue sky she's created out of their feeling for each other. Anger for all those years he let slip by when they could have been knowing each other, when she could have loved him so much. (p. 278)

After Rachel has spent days searching for Izzy's handprint and initials and finally finds them on the bridge he helped construct, "they are here now she thinks, and they will still be here years from now, when she, herself, is old. And then, though today the whole sky is covered by gray clouds, for a moment she feels the sun on her head, as warm as a loving hand" (p. 288). Mature readers enjoy the development of and the interactions with such characters as Dicey, Jeff, and Rachel. The symbolism makes the reading experience even more vivid and meaningful.

Cynthia Rylant develops both credible characters and the need to overcome personal sorrow after death in *Missing May*. By allowing Summer and Uncle Ob to remember May, Rylant allows readers to understand this remarkable woman. For example, notice how Rylant encourages readers to visualize May by contrasting her with other people:

> May was gardening when she died. That's the word she always used: gardening. Everybody else in Fayette County would say they were going out to work in the garden, and that's the picture you'd get in your mind—people out there laboring and sweating and grunting in the dirt. But Aunt May gardened, and when she said it your mind would see some lovely person in a yellow-flowered hat snipping soft pink roses, little robins landing on her shoulders. (p. 9)

Throughout the book, Rylant develops May's character through such memories. By sharing their memories, both Summer and Uncle Ob can bury their sorrow and finally go on with the life that May would have wanted.

Theme

The underlying ideas that tie the plot, characters, and settings together in contemporary realistic fiction are closely related to the needs of modern children. For example, authors frequently show that children become stronger as they make discoveries about themselves. In *The Outcasts of 19 Schuyler Place*, E. L. Konigsburg's protagonist, Margaret Rose Kane, discovers that even though she is only 12 years old, she can change the course of history. The author uses a plot structure that proceeds from stop to stall to save in order to save an artistic landmark and to develop the theme. Margaret discovers that her main role in saving her uncle's artistic towers from demolition is to stop the destruction of what she considers a national artistic landmark. Adults help with the stalling and saving, but it is Margaret who discovers that she can make things happen. You can compare this theme with that of Carl Hiaasen's *Hoot*, in which a boy and his friends save the habitat of the little burrowing owl. Notice that they also use a procedure of stop, stall, and save to overcome the wishes of adults who are motivated by money. Both authors also include the impact of television and newspapers in winning an environmental decision.

In *Ida B . . . and Her Plans to Maximize Fun, Avoid Disaster, and (Possibly) Save the World*, Katherine Hannigan develops two complementary themes. First, Ida B's father explains to her that "we are the earth's caretakers" (p. 29) because we do not really own land; we only care for it and should leave the land better than we found it. Ida B's response is that the earth takes care of us. To reinforce Ida B's belief about nature, the author develops her character as a child who names the trees, talks to them, and then listens to them in return. Through this interaction with nature, she solves many of her problems.

In Joan Bauer's *Hope Was Here*, the author develops the theme that hope is something that everyone needs. Obtaining and retaining hope, however, are difficult for the heroine as she moves with her aunt to many different locations. It is during their final move, when she discovers the strength and honesty of a man who has cancer, that the heroine makes discoveries about herself and realizes that "hope was here."

The books in this chapter develop many additional themes, such as that children have common hopes and fears, life is filled with important choices that must be carefully considered, and friends should support rather than hurt each other.

Style

An effective literary style greatly enhances plot, characterization, and theme in realistic fiction. Vivid descriptions, believable dialogue, symbolism, figures of speech, and other stylistic techniques subtly provide readers with in-depth understanding of characters and situations. In *Dicey's Song*, for example, Cynthia Voigt develops a synthesis of symbols and character traits. Allusions to familiar music are among Voigt's symbolic means of emphasizing changes in the character.

In *Walk Two Moons*, Sharon Creech develops two parallel stories. As the heroine tells the story of her best friend, Phoebe, and her experiences when her mother left, Sal makes discoveries about her own life and learns to accept her own mother's actions. The author uses considerable symbolism to develop the feelings and characterizations in the story. For example, smoke symbolizes Sal's feelings after her mother leaves: "There goes my mother" and "I watched the trail of smoke disappearing in the air" (p. 74). There is the symbolism of a dream about mother climbing a ladder and never coming down (p. 169). There is also the story of the mother dog as she weans and trains her children to be independent (pp. 257–258), and the symbolism of the singing trees that ends on page 268 at Sal's mother's grave.

To assist the development of her plot in *The Crow-Girl*, Bodil Bredsdorff uses symbolism associated with two crows. After the death of her grandmother, two crows appear to the now-orphaned girl as she buries her grandmother next to her grandfather. The crows appear at several points in the story. They seem to be calling her to leave her isolated home and to search for people. They appear as if to warn her to leave the home of a selfish, heartless woman who is the type of woman her grandmother warned her against. Then they seem to guide her in her journey as she finally discovers the types of warm, caring people her grandmother told her to trust. She also discovers that her grandmother's advice was all correct: She has found the people who will be her new family, and they can live together in her beloved cove by the ocean.

Poetry provides the literary style in Nikki Grimes's *Bronx Masquerade*. Notice in the following quote how the author develops the connection between the Harlem Renaissance and writing poetry: "It's the Harlem Renaissance stuff that got us both going. We spent a month reading poetry from the Harlem Renaissance in our English class. Then Mr. Ward—that's our teacher—asked us to write an essay about it. Make sense to you? Me neither. I mean, what's the point of studying poetry and then writing essays? So I wrote a bunch of poems instead" (p. 4). The book is written through the point of view of various students and includes poetry examples from the characters.

Lauren Myracle's *ttyl*, jargon meaning "talk to you later," displays one of the most contemporary approaches to style. The plot revolves around the instant messages of three high school sophomores, in which the girls share experiences and offer advice. University students can make interesting comparisons between Myracle's text written for high school students and a research study by Gloria E. Jacobs (2004) in which she investigates instant messaging and discusses issues in data collection, transcribing, and data analysis. Jacobs includes actual conversations that are very similar to those of Myracle's characters.

In *Missing May*, Cynthia Rylant uses contrasts to encourage readers to understand the treatment of Summer in two locations, to emphasize how Summer felt about this treatment, and to introduce the special bond that develops between May and Summer. In the following quote, no-

An In-Depth Analysis of a Contemporary Realistic Fiction Novel

How does an author combine a contemporary story about a juvenile detention camp, the irony of a 100-year-old curse that still influences a contemporary plot and the characters, a parallel plot that sounds like a tall tale, and a mysterious search for a buried treasure that is also 100 years old? This is the challenge Louis Sachar took on in *Holes,* the winner of both the 1999 Newbery Medal and a National Book Award. In addition, the book has been listed as a best-seller in the area of children's literature.

Let us first consider the importance of the parallel plots, both of which are built around a treasure that is more than 100 years old. The contemporary story, which is at times extremely humorous and also deadly serious, begins with a boy, Stanley Yelnats, who believes that all of his bad luck is due to the curse that was placed on his great-great-grandfather who had stolen a pig from a one-legged gypsy. Stanley's problem increases when he is sent to Camp Green Lake because he is accused of stealing a pair of shoes valued at more than $5,000 because they belong to a famous athlete. While at this juvenile detention center, he experiences person-against-person conflicts between himself and the warden, the various guards, and a few of his fellow inmates. As the plot progresses, we find Stanley and the other inmates digging large holes in the hot, dry desert. The author identifies the reasons for digging the holes toward the climax of the story when Stanley uncovers evidence pointing toward a treasure that may have been buried in the desert. The story nears a climax when Stanley runs away in order to find a friend who has run from the guards and may be dying of thirst in the desert. After Stanley finds his friend, he helps him reach and climb a mountain in the distance. We later discover that carrying the friend up the mountain is very important as a way to resolve the conflict and the curse. Stanley and his friend eventually go back to camp, dig for the treasure at night, and are finally rewarded with the treasure and a verdict that Stanley was wrongly accused of stealing the shoes.

Without the parallel plots, readers would not understand the humor and irony associated with Stanley's situation and his belief that all of his bad luck is caused by the curse placed on his great-great-grandfather by the one-legged gypsy when he refuses to carry her up the mountain after stealing her pig. This parallel plot resembles a tall tale as the author reveals that the first Stanley Yelnats had made a fortune in the stock market but lost it when he moved from New York to California and the stagecoach was robbed by the outlaw Kissin' Kate Barlow. Periodically, the author interrupts the first story to tell various tales about the family history that add both humor and background. For example, Sachar explains the curse in which Madame Zeroni dooms the descendants because the great-great-grandfather fails to carry the gypsy up the mountain, sing a song to her, and allow her to drink from the stream. Sachar provides stories about the early ancestors, the schoolteacher who later becomes the outlaw Kissin' Kate Barlow, the African American healer who picks and sells onions, and the belief in and the search for Kissin' Kate's treasures—the stolen loot.

The two plots converge when Stanley carries his friend Zero up the mountain, sings him a song they both recognize, and together they dig up a suitcase that belonged to Stanley's great-great-grandfather. The author reveals that Zero is the great-great-grandson of the gypsy who created the curse. We know that the curse is broken when the sky turns dark and rain falls onto the empty lake for the first time in more than 100 years. The contents of the great-great-grandfather's suitcase are stock certificates, deeds of trust, and promissory notes that are worth several million dollars.

Sachar also develops strong characters who support the plot. The main protagonists are Stanley and his friend Zero, and the antagonists are the warden and the guards. A considerable amount of the characterization is developed through actions. For example, Stanley's letters to his mother show his feelings toward her and his desire not to worry her. He is also willing to risk his life to help a friend who is lost in the desert. His friend Zero helps him dig his holes each day so that Stanley will have enough strength left to teach Zero to read. The warden and the guards play the roles of antagonists as they give harsh punishments for disobedience or inability to dig fast enough. The warden's character is revealed as she opens a bottle of fingernail polish containing rattlesnake venom that she claims is harmless when dry but toxic when wet. Later, she reveals that she has been searching for the treasure for years. In an ironic ending, the suitcase that she claims is hers is taken away from her by the attorney general because it is engraved with the name Stanley Yelnats, Stanley's great-great-grandfather.

This is an example of a book that at first glance appears to have a fairly simple plot and characters. Many students, however, indicate that they needed to reread the book when they discovered the importance of the parallel plots.

---

tice the impact of the contrasting situations and the emotional impact of the comparison between the magical girl in Alice in Wonderland and the caged mouse who must beg for every morsel.

I stood there before those shelves, watching these wonders begin to spin as May turned on the fan overhead, and I felt like a magical little girl, a chosen little girl, like Alice who had fallen into Wonderland. This feeling has yet to leave me.

And as if the whirligigs weren't enough. May turned me to the kitchen, where she pulled open all the cabinet doors, plus the refrigerator, and she said, "Summer, whatever you like you can have and whatever you like that isn't here Uncle Ob will go down to Ellet's Grocery and get you. We want you to eat, honey."

Back in Ohio, where I'd been treated like a homework assignment somebody was always having to do, eating was never a joy of any kind. Every house I had ever lived in was so particular about its food, and especially when the food involved me. There's no good way to explain this. But I felt like one of those little mice who has to figure out the right button to push before its food will drop down into the cup. Caged and begging. That's how I felt sometimes. (p. 7)

How Realistic Fiction Has Changed

Synonyms for *realistic* include adjectives such as *lifelike, genuine,* and *authentic.* Of course, what people consider lifelike depends on the social context; what seems realistic to us might seem fantastic to people in different societies or other eras.

In the Victorian era of the late 19th and early 20th centuries, realistic fiction emphasized traditional family roles and ties in warm, close, and stable family units that lived in one place for generations; strict roles for males and females, stressing higher education and careers for males and wifehood and motherhood for females; respect for law and adult authority; strong religious commitment; duty to educate, Christianize, or care for the poor; and problems related to overcoming sinfulness and becoming good.

Realistic fiction continued to emphasize many of these values well into the second half of the 20th century, although the literature began to depict both female and male children gaining more independence. The characters in realistic children's fiction were usually white, middle-class, and members of stable families consisting of a father, a mother, and their children. Nontraditional families and family disturbances were virtually unrepresented in this literature.

Beginning roughly in the 1960s, however, the content of contemporary realistic fiction became more diverse—no doubt reflecting the increasingly diverse and complex social life in the United States and elsewhere. Maria Nikolajeva (1995) states: "Many taboos that existed in children's literature during its early periods are today being withdrawn" (p. 40). Contemporary realistic stories for children depict some unhappy and unstable families, single-parent families, and families in which both parents work outside the home. Career ambitions are not as confined to traditional gender roles as they were in the past. Children often have much responsibility and independence. Fear of or disrespect for law and authority is more common. Education and religion receive less stress. Ethnic and racial minorities are more in evidence, and in general, people's economic, emotional, and social problems receive more emphasis.

John Rowe Townsend (1975) is among the researchers who have pointed out the striking contrasts between children's realistic fiction of the 1950s and the late 1960s. The 1950s was one of the quietest decades in children's literature: In keeping with traditional values, children were pictured as part of a stable community—grandparents were wise, parents were staunch and respected, and childhood was happy and secure. In contrast, children's literature of the late 1960s implied an erosion of adult authority and an apparent widening of the generation gap. It was no longer self-evident that parents knew best and that children could be guided into accepting the established codes and behavior.

Author Betsy Byars (1993), who has been writing for more than 30 years, states that children's publishing has changed a great deal:

> I think there's been a great evolution. When I first started writing, children's books had to be nice. I can remember some editor writing in the margin, "Don't have him lie" or something like that. And now you're very free. You don't feel any pressure, you don't find yourself thinking things like, "I can't say this" or "This will be too tough a subject for kids." (p. 906)

In a study of themes found in contemporary realistic fiction published in the late 1970s, Jane M. Madsen and Elaine B. Wickersham (1980) found that popular themes for young children were overcoming fear and meeting responsibility and that stories about problems related to adoption, divorce, disabilities, and minority social status were more common than in the past. In the 1980s, contemporary realistic fiction for older children often depicted children overcoming family and personal problems. Children confronted quarreling or divorcing parents, deserting or noncaring parents, cruel foster families, conflicts between personal ambitions and parental desires, and death of loved ones. Discovery of self and development of maturity as children face and overcome their fears were other popular themes in stories written for older children. Such stories often stressed the importance of self-esteem and being true to oneself.

Contemporary realistic fiction in the 1990s and 2000s reflects both society's problems and changes that have occurred in books because of past criticisms. An introduction to recommended books titled "Curriculum Connectors: Family Secrets" in *School Library Journal* (1997) highlights many of the characteristics of current realistic fiction: "All of the families in the books listed . . . harbor secrets. Some are dark and grim; others are quirky and quite funny. Abuse, desertion, hidden pasts, feuds, and even a grandmother's elopement play a part. Some of the young protagonists draw on inner strengths they didn't know they had; others turn to siblings and friends for help. What these young people have in common is resilience, resourcefulness, and a feeling of hope for the future" (p. 112).

Literary Criticism: New Realism and the Problem Novel

Alleen Pace Nilsen and Kenneth L. Donelson (2001) characterize books that are identified under the area of new realism as those having serious coming-of-age stories:

> In addition to their candor and the selection of subject matter, they differ from earlier books in four basic ways. The first difference lies in the choice of characters. These protagonists

come mostly from lower-class families, which ties in with the second major difference, setting. Instead of living in idyllic, pleasant suburban homes, the characters in these books come from settings that are harsh, difficult places to live. To get the point across about the characters and where they live, authors used colloquial language, which is the third major difference. Authors began to write the way people really talk (e.g., in dialogue using profanity and ungrammatical constructs). (pp. 113–114)

Nilsen and Donelson identify the fourth difference as a change in attitude, a change in mode in which stories no longer had to have upbeat, happy endings.

Some literary critics question the merit of at least portions of this new realism. Sheila Egoff (1980), for example, applauds realistic novels that have strong literary qualities, including logical flow of narrative, delicate complexity of characterization, insights that convey the conduct of life as characters move from childhood to adolescence and to adulthood, and a quality that touches both the imagination and the emotions. In an outstanding realistic novel, says Egoff, conflict is integral to the plot and characters, and resolution of conflict has wide implications growing out of the personal vision or experience of the writer. In contrast, Egoff maintains, conflict in a problem novel stems from the writer's social standards more than from personal feelings and emotions. The author's intentions may be good, but in an effort to make a point or argue a social position, the author creates a cardboard story instead of one that really comes alive. The conflict is specific rather than universal and narrow rather than far-reaching in its implications. Egoff identifies other typical characteristics of the problem novel:

1. Concern is with externals, with how things look rather than how things are. The author begins with a problem rather than with a plot or characters.

2. The protagonist is burdened with anxieties and grievances that grow out of alienation from the adult world.

3. The protagonist often achieves temporary relief through association with an unconventional adult from outside the family.

4. The narrative is usually in the first person, and its confessional tone is self-centered.

5. The vocabulary is limited, and observation is restricted by the pretense that an ordinary child is the narrator.

6. Sentences and paragraphs are short, the language is flat, without nuance, and the language may be emotionally numb.

7. Inclusion of expletives seems obligatory.

8. Sex is discussed openly.

9. The setting is usually urban.

Jack Forman (1985) adds that in contrast to the fully developed characters in books of literary quality, many topical novels "are peopled with characters who are more mouthpieces of a particular point of view than fully developed protagonists" (p. 470). Beverly Cleary (Connell, 1984) further articulates the difference between stories that focus on problems and stories that focus on people:

I'm more interested in writing about people than problems. *Dear Mr. Henshaw* [the winner of the 1984 Newbery Medal] is about a boy that had a problem, not a problem that had a boy. I don't search for a new problem. (p. IF)

Today's students of children's literature are living in an interesting era of book publishing for children. They may analyze new books of contemporary realistic fiction and contemplate the different directions that authors can choose to pursue.

Controversial Issues

Barbara Feldstein (1993) identifies the major controversies in children's books as political views that differ from those of censors, treatment of minorities, stereotyped roles of women, problems of contemporary society, and profane language. When any of these subjects appear in books, you can expect varied reactions. The degree to which realistic fiction should reflect the reality of the times leads to controversy when writers create characters who face problems relating to sexism, sexuality, violence, and drugs. There is no simple solution: What one group considers controversial, another does not. Realistic fiction has resulted in more controversy and calls for censorship than has any other genre. Therefore, educators must be aware of some concerns in this area of literature, including sexism, sexuality, violence, profanity, and family problems.

Sexism

Sexism has been a major concern for the past few decades. The following position statement by the Association of Women Psychologists (1970), written more than 35 years ago, stresses the dangers of the traditional roles created by society and reflected in literature:

Psychological oppression in the form of sex role socialization clearly conveys to girls from the earliest ages that their nature is to be submissive, servile, and repressed, and their role is to be servant, admirer, sex object and martyr. . . . The psychological consequences of goal depression in young women . . . are all too common. In addition, both men and women have come to realize the effect on men of this type of sex role stereotyping, the crippling pressure to compete, to achieve, to produce, to stifle emotion, sensitivity and gentleness, all taking their toll in psychic and physical traumas.

Marsha M. Sprague and Kara K. Keeling (2000) quote research that concludes: "In the U.S., girls are at risk of academic failure, substance abuse, pregnancy, sexual disease, and suicide to a degree unimaginable to most parents and teachers" (p. 640). These authors recommend that schools use literature as a means for dialogues and real-world learning and especially for creating opportunities that help girls and boys explore and discuss gender issues. Sprague and Keeling recommend using nonstereotypical books in which a central female character searches for her true voice. Three of the recommended contemporary realistic fiction books discussed are Katherine Paterson's *Jacob Have I Loved,* Suzanne Staples's *Shabanu: Daughter of the Wind,* and Cynthia Voigt's *Dicey's Song.*

Colleen A. Ruggieri (2001) also recommends reading and discussing the characteristics of strong female protagonists such as those found in *Shabanu: Daughter of the Wind.* Ruggieri states that "perhaps one of the most important points that *Shabanu* makes for young readers is that no one deserves to be the victim of physical violence" (p. 49).

People concerned with sexism have evaluated the roles of males and females in children's literature and in elementary classrooms; the evaluations are usually harshly critical of the negative forces of sex-role stereotyping. Ramona Frasher (1982), for example, reviewed research on sexism and sex-role stereotyping in children's literature and identified some trends. In Newbery Award–winning books published before the 1970s, male main characters outnumbered female main characters by about 3 to 1. In addition, stereotyping and negative comments about females were common. Frasher's analysis of Newbery Award winners published between 1971 and 1980 showed about equal numbers of male and female characters. In addition, female characters tended to be portrayed with more positive and varied personality characteristics and to exhibit a greater variety of behaviors.

Educators, psychologists, and other concerned adults also criticize the sexism and sex-role stereotyping in realistic picture books. In an earlier study, Alleen Pace Nilsen (1971) analyzed the role of females in 80 Caldecott Medal winners and honor books. She chose picture books because illustrated books are "the ones influencing children at the time they are in the process of developing their own sexual identity. Children decide very early in life what roles are appropriate to male and female" (p. 919). Of the books that were realistic (as compared with fantasy), she found fewer stories having girls as the leading characters. She also compared the number of girl- and boy-centered stories over a 20-year period; the percentage of girl-centered stories had decreased from 46% in 1951–1955 to 26% in 1966–1970. Anita P. Davis and Thomas R. McDaniel (1999) analyzed the percentages of male and female characters in more recent Caldecott Medal winners, and found that 39% of the characters in books published in the 1990s were female.

Many female protagonists in books for older children behave in ways quite different from those of the heroines of traditional literature. They reflect the realization that females also are *heroes,* with intellectual, emotional, and physical potential in their actions. Some of the most memorable girl characters—including Karana in Scott O'Dell's *Island of the Blue Dolphins,* Queenie in Robert Burch's *Queenie Peavy* (who insisted that she would grow up to be a doctor, not a nurse), and Harriet in Louise Fitzhugh's *Harriet the Spy*—are believable and exciting because they do not follow stereotypical behavior patterns.

Nontraditional behaviors, of course, can also result in controversy. Women's roles and women's rights are political issues; advocates express strong opinions on both sides. One of the areas that illustrates women's changed roles is the portrayal of the minor characters in stories: Mothers may be photographers who travel on assignments and join peace marches accompanied by their daughters, as in Norma Klein's *Mom, the Wolf Man and Me;* book illustrators who travel on consulting contracts, as in Lois Lowry's *Anastasia on Her Own;* and authors whose children consider them eccentric, as in Patricia MacLachlan's *The Facts and Fictions of Minna Pratt.* Recent books suggest that the roles of males and females have changed as varied occupations and behavior patterns are found in the books. Teachers, librarians, and parents should be aware, however, that not all people look on these changes favorably.

Sexuality

Today is a time of increasing sophistication and frankness about sexuality. Television programs and movies portray sexual relationships that would not have been shown to earlier generations of adults, let alone children. Premarital and extramarital sex, sexual development, homosexual experiences, and sex education are controversial topics in children's literature. The subjects of books written for older readers may be particularly controversial. For example, M. E. Kerr's *"Hello," I Lied* deals with problems associated with being gay; Julie Anne Peters's *Luna* deals with transgender issues; Suzanne Fisher Staples's *Dangerous Skies* deals with sexual abuse; and Francesca Lia Block's *Girl Goddess #9: Nine Stories* describes a peer world that includes casual sex, drugs, and alcohol. Laurie Halse Anderson's *Speak* deals with a high school freshman's trauma after being raped. The author voices the girl's resolution about her conflict when she thinks: "It happened. There is no avoiding it, no forgetting. No running away, or flying, or burying, or hiding. Andy Evans raped me in August when I was drunk and too young to know what was happening. It wasn't my fault. He hurt me. It wasn't my fault. And I'm not going to let it kill me. I can grow" (p. 197).

Several books written for older children describe nontraditional living situations in which a child's mother lives with a male friend. In Norma Klein's controversial *Mom, the Wolf Man and Me,* Theodore spends weekends with Brett's mother, which leads 11-year-old Brett to ask her mother if she is having sexual relations with him. This results in a frank discussion about sexual intercourse. As might be expected, this book has met with varying reactions.

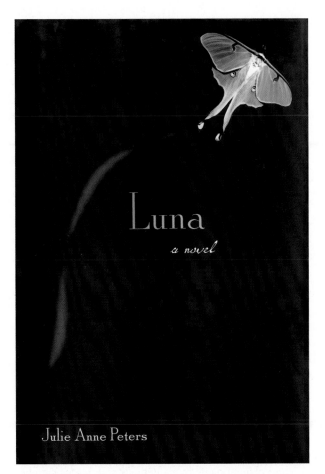

From LUNA, by Julie Anne Peters. Copyright © 2004 by Julie Anne Peters. By permission of Little, Brown and Co., Inc.

In a book for older audiences, *Dear Nobody*, Berlie Doherty deals with feelings and issues associated with the pregnancy of an unmarried high school girl. The author explores the unhappiness and confusion that surround the decision to keep the baby as well as the responses of the mother, the baby's father, and their families.

A study by Joy B. Davis and Laurie MacGillivray (2001) of books that focus on teen pregnancy and parenting found the following eight common messages: Do not have unprotected sex; most mothers keep their babies; having a baby may cause changes in educational plans, but you can still achieve your goals; when pregnant, you are on your own; young men are often portrayed as sexual predators; young women have to live with the consequences, but young men do not; teen pregnancies do not mandate marriage; and teens from troubled homes are more likely to become pregnant.

Books describing children's concerns about their developing sexuality may also be controversial. For example, Judy Blume's popular *Are You There God? It's Me, Margaret* has been reviewed favorably as a book that realistically conveys preadolescent girls' worries over menstruation and body changes. Yet in 1981, this book was one of several taken from library shelves and burned because some adults viewed it as a negative influence on children. In that same year, the national television news showed angry adults criticizing the morality of this book, as well as the morality of many other books, and the resulting flames of protest.

Violence

Television, movies, and books have been accused of portraying too much violence. Children's cartoons are often criticized for their excessive violence. Children's books become the object of controversy when they portray what some people define as inappropriate behavior or excessive violence. Many realistic books containing violence have inner-city settings in which both violence and drugs play a role. For example, drugs figure prominently in Walter Dean Myers's *Scorpions*. Some people believe that children should read about the reality of drugs in the world around them, but others believe that the minds of children should not be contaminated by the mention of drugs.

Shooter, by Walter Dean Myers, depicts the ultimate violence that might occur in a high school. In a book written for older students, Myers uses a writing style that incorporates interviews, reports, and diary entries to trace the possible reasons for a shooting and a suicide, which

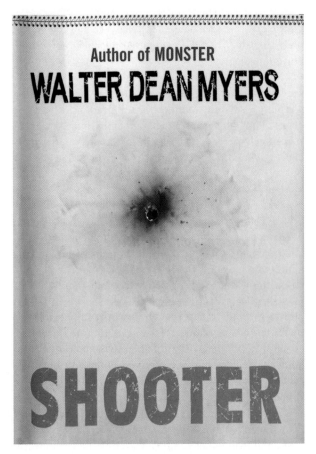

From Shooter, by Walter Dean Myers. Cover art copyright © 2004 by Robert Beck. Used by permission of HarperCollins Publishers.

allows him to develop the many sides of the characters and their emotional problems that led to the tragedy. Sadly, the interviews highlight the bullying the main characters experience. One report summarizes the lack of attention to this person-against-society conflict: "Mr. Gray was the proverbial ticking bomb waiting to go off. His needs were conveniently dismissed at every stage. His reaching out for help was also ignored, and there was no coordinated concept of threat assessment. A conclusion that threat assessment is not the responsibility of the local government today is an invitation to re-create these events" (p. 147). This book would make an interesting discussion tool to highlight the difficulties of some students and the terrible emotional consequences caused by bullies.

Profanity

Profanity and other language objectionable to some people are also controversial. What is considered objectionable has changed over the years, however. Mary Q. Steele (1971) describes her own experiences with writing: In the 1950s, editors deleted "hecks" and "darns" from manuscripts written for children, but now, authors can write relevant dialogue. Ken Donelson's (1985) survey on censorship reports that a committee unsuccessfully challenged the placement of Katherine Paterson's *The Great Gilly Hopkins* in an elementary library because the author used language that the committee members considered objectionable.

In 1990, a teacher in my children's literature class successfully met a challenge to Paterson's *Bridge to Terabithia*. One parent wanted the book removed from the class reading list because of mild profanity, but the teacher successfully defended the book for literary merit, especially the importance of its themes.

Family Problems and Other Controversial Issues

Strong young protagonists in contemporary novels often overcome obstacles related to family problems caused by adult family members. The antagonists are frequently adults who have less than desirable qualities. The lack of strong adult role models in many contemporary books is also controversial. For example, Robert Unsworth (1988) praises the fully developed fathers in several published books, but he also states, "The bad news is the portrayal of that Dad at home. A grander group of adulterers, philanderers, child abusers, wife-beaters, drunks, and all-around ne'er-do-wells hasn't been seen since the fall of Rome" (p. 48).

Award-winning books such as Jack Gantos's *Joey Pigza Loses Control*, Kate DiCamillo's *Because of Winn-Dixie*, and Joan Bauer's *Hope Was Here* include some form of parental abandonment. In *Joey Pigza Loses Control*, Joey spends the summer with an alcoholic father he has never known. In *Because of Winn-Dixie*, the mother has deserted

her daughter and her husband. In *Hope Was Here*, the heroine longs for the father she has never known.

The controversy surrounding the award given to a book in England illustrates issues in contemporary realistic fiction. According to Julie Eccleshare (1997), "the prestigious Carnegie Medal was awarded . . . to Melvin Burgess for *Junk* (Andersen Press). A novel about a group of teenage drug addicts who think that they can handle heroin, *Junk* has attracted enormous media coverage, ranging from adults who find it frightening and even morally wrong that a children's book should deal with these issues, to those who see it as 'a book waiting to be written'" (p. 25). As you read *Junk* and books with similar content, ask yourself, "What is my own response to this content? Is it beneficial? Is it harmful?"

Literary Criticism: Guidelines for Selecting Controversial Fiction

The question of how "realistic" realistic fiction should be is answered differently by various groups. Historically, schools have often been under the pressures of censorship because different groups have tried to impose their values. Although modern censors might laugh at the literary concerns of the Puritans, there is still concern over appropriate subjects for children's literature. Children's books that explore sexuality, violence, moral problems, racism, and religious beliefs are likely to be thought objectionable by individuals and groups who believe that children should not be exposed to such ideas. Arbuthnot Lectures recipient Dorothy Butler (1990) warns that

we must confront those who would cut wild swaths through the body of children's books, rejecting some because they believe them to advance ideas which are in conflict with ones they wish children to espouse, embracing others because they appear to recommend currently approved attitudes—and all with little or no regard to literary merit, or reference to the opinions of those who might advise. We are in danger, in the hands of these well-meaning but misguided evangelists, of banishing at least half the classics of the English language; in vain to protest that the real liberators of the world have always been the informed, the readers; that the burning of books has always been in the cause of human oppression. The dictates of such critics, whether in the cause of antiracism, antisexism, or any other philosophy, denote an arrogance which may be excused as ignorance, but must not be tolerated. Good and true books engender true thought and feeling, and so allow children to think clearly and to feel deeply. (p. 37)

Teachers and librarians need to be knowledgeable about their communities, subjects that may prove controversial, and the merits of controversial books that they would like to share with children. Wholesale avoidance of books containing controversial topics, in addition to encouraging overt censorship, is inappropriate because (1) books about relevant sociological or psychological problems can give young people opportunities to grow in their

Evaluation Criteria

Literary Criticism: Controversial Books

1. Know what might be considered controversial.
2. Determine the author's viewpoint, and weigh the positive influences against perceived negative influences.
3. Be sure the book meets normal literary criteria and is not chosen merely for its high interest and possibly controversial topic.
4. Know and be able to explain your purpose for using a particular book.
5. Review and be able to discuss both sides of the censorship question.

thinking processes and to extend their experiences; (2) problems addressed in books can provide some children with opportunities for identification and allow other children opportunities to empathize with their peers; and (3) problems in books invite decisions, elicit opinions, and afford opportunities to take positions on issues.

Given the controversial issues and the need for books that are relevant to the interests, concerns, and problems of today's children, you should consider some guidelines when choosing realistic fiction for children (see the Evaluation Criteria on this page).

Dianne McAfee Hopkins (1993) provides useful advice for librarians who face challenges to literature. She recommends that you examine your district's materials selection policy carefully, ensure that principals and teachers are aware that the policy is intended for all who challenge the appropriateness of materials, take every challenge seriously, follow the reconsideration section of the policy fully, seek support when an oral or written challenge occurs, communicate at all levels to ensure that challenges are handled effectively and objectively, and recognize that you can be the key person in shaping the outcome of challenges to library materials.

Author Richard Peck (1992) provides an excellent observation for all of those who are developing defenses for books. He states, "Only the nonreader fears books" (p. 816).

In addition to the basic literary criteria, high-quality contemporary realistic fiction should satisfy the following requirements.

Know exactly what might be considered controversial. This means that you have to really read the book; you can't rely on the opinion of someone else or even on a good review. As a member of a school and a community, you must be able to appraise specific content, because what offends in one community might go unnoticed or unchallenged in another.

Ascertain the author's point of view, and weigh the power of the positive influence against exposure to a theme that some people perceive negatively. For example, if an author writes about the drug culture but events in the story clearly point to harmful effects of drug use, then you may miss an opportunity for shaping healthy attitudes if you pass up the book.

Apply literary criteria to the selection of library books so that vulnerability to the arguments of would-be censors is at least partially reduced by the obvious overall quality of the book choices. Occasionally, teachers and librarians select books of inferior quality because they deal with topics having high interest for middle-grade or older children (for example, books involving experimentation with sex). The information in such books may be harmless (or even useful), but the books may fall short of accepted literary criteria. Then, if a book is targeted because it offends community groups, you will have difficulty defending it, and having it in your school collection will suggest that considerations other than literary quality determine choices. In addition, examine books that attempt to counter stereotypes for what can be thought of as overcorrection. Sometimes, in a passion to change images, authors work too hard on issues and neglect plot and characterizations.

Know and be able to explain your purpose for using a particular book. Have answers ready to the following questions:

1. Will the topic be understood by the students with whom I intend to use the book?
2. What merits of this particular book have influenced me to use it rather than another book of comparable literary, sociological, or psychological importance?
3. Is the book an acceptable model for writing style and use of language?
4. Are my objectives in using this book educationally defensible (for example, refinement of attitudes, promotion of reading habits)?

To clarify and maintain your objectivity, review and be prepared to discuss both sides of the censorship question.

Subjects in Realistic Fiction

To help you recommend or choose specific books for children, this section emphasizes personality and social development in children. The various subjects within the genre of contemporary realistic fiction encompass a wide range of themes.

Family Life

The family stories of the late 1930s through the early 1960s depict some of the strongest, warmest family relationships in contemporary realistic fiction for children. Today's children still enjoy the warmth and humor represented by the families in Elizabeth Enright's *Thimble Summer*, Eleanor Estes's *The Moffats*, Sydney Taylor's

Sydney Taylor creates family stories that show warmth, humor, and strong family relationships. (From Ella of All of a Kind Family, by Sydney Taylor. Copyright © 1978 by Sydney Taylor. Illustrations copyright © 1978 by Gail Owens. Reprinted by permission of E. P. Dutton.)

All-of-a-Kind Family, and Madeleine L'Engle's *Meet the Austins.* The actions of the characters suggest that security is gained when family members work together, that each member has responsibility to other members, that consideration for others is desirable, and that family unity and loyalty can overcome hard times and peer conflicts.

Since the early 1960s, many changes have taken place in the characterizations of the American family in realistic fiction: Authors often have focused on the need to overcome family disturbances, as children and adults adjust to new social realities. Death of one or both parents, foster families, single-parent families, children of unmarried females, the disruptions caused by divorce and remarriage, and child abuse are some of the issues related to children and their families that now appear in contemporary realistic fiction for children.

Such literature may help children realize that many family units other than the traditional one are common and legitimate in society today. Children may also see that problems often can be solved if family members work together. Even when depicting the most disturbing of relationships, authors of realistic fiction may show a strong need for family unity and a desire to keep at least some of the members together.

Authors of realistic stories about family disturbances use several literary techniques to create credible plots and characters. Often, they look at painful and potentially destructive situations and feelings that are common in society today. These situations are usually familiar to readers, who may have experienced similar situations, who may have known someone who had such experiences, or who may fear that they will have similar experiences. Authors often tell such stories from the perspective of a child or children involved: First-person or limited omniscient point of view from a child's perspective can successfully depict the emotional and behavioral reactions as the children first discover a problem, experience a wide range of personal difficulties and emotions when they try to change or understand the situation, and finally arrive at acceptance of the situation.

The characterizations may portray the vulnerability of the characters, create sympathy for them, and describe how they handle jolting disruptions and personal discoveries that affect their lives. Symbolism and allusion may emphasize conflicts and characters. Authors often use characters' reactions to change, trouble, and discoveries to trace the development of better relationships with others or personal growth.

However, some authors—such as those making a point about child abuse—use specific situations or discoveries to allow children to escape from all reality. In realistic stories about family life, the antagonist may be a family member or an outside force, such as the death of a parent, divorce, or moving to a new location. To relieve the impact of painful situations, authors may add humor. Humor can make situations bearable, create sympathy for characters, or clarify the nature of confrontations.

Elizabeth Strehle (1999) emphasizes the importance of using literature to help shape children's understandings by providing opportunities to observe characters and experience social issues. She states, "Class discussions provide opportunities for students to understand their own beliefs and reconstruct an existing understanding of a concept such as homelessness. Students form their understandings of the world through knowledge of themselves and personal experiences, as well as from the radio news and the books they read" (p. 219).

Desertion, Divorce, and Remarriage. In *Dear Mr. Henshaw,* Beverly Cleary effectively uses letters and diary entries written by her sixth-grade hero, Leigh Botts, to develop believable characters and plot and to show changes in Leigh as he begins to accept the actuality of his parents' divorce. As a classroom assignment, Leigh sends his favorite author a list of 10 questions. Mr. Henshaw answers Leigh's questions and sends Leigh a list of 10 questions that he wants Leigh to answer about himself.

At first, Leigh refuses to answer the questions, but his mother insists that because Mr. Henshaw answered Leigh's questions, Leigh must answer Mr. Henshaw's questions. The answers to the questions allow Cleary to provide important background information and to reveal Leigh's feelings about himself, his family, and his parents' divorce. Eventually, Leigh begins to write a diary—both because Mr. Henshaw suggests it and because his mother refuses to fix the television.

By midpoint in the book, the diary entries begin to change and Leigh realizes changes in his own character:

> I don't have to pretend to write to Mr. Henshaw anymore. I have learned to say what I think on a piece of paper. And I don't hate my father either. I can't hate him. Maybe things would be easier if I could. (p. 73)

The entries seem believable because Cleary includes both humorous and painful experiences that are important in Leigh's life.

In *Strider*, the sequel to *Dear Mr. Henshaw*, Cleary again uses a series of diary entries to reveal changes in character. By caring for an abandoned dog, 14-year-old Leigh Botts finally learns to accept his parents' divorce and gains self-confidence. Cleary develops parallels to Leigh's divorced parents as Leigh and his best friend argue over the custody of the dog.

A dog is also the means used by Kate DiCamillo in *Because of Winn-Dixie* to help a 10-year-old heroine, Opal,

The companionship of a dog helps a girl make new friends in Because of Winn-Dixie, *by Kate DiCamillo. (Cover illustration by Chris Sheban, © 2001 Candlewick Press, Inc. Reproduced by permission of the publisher Candlewick Press, Inc., Cambridge, MA.)*

make new friends, understand herself, and accept the desertion of her mother. The dog allows her to make discoveries through the wisdom and advice of these new friends. For example, one older friend reminds her that "you got to remember, you can't judge people by the things they done. You got to judge them by what they are doing now" (p. 96). The librarian teaches Opal that most people have their share of sorrow and sadness. When the dog, Winn-Dixie, is lost, the author compares the mother's leaving with Opal's feelings when the dog is lost.

Mother–child relationships and the consequences that occur when mothers are no longer with their children are common plots in current realistic fiction. The plot in Creech's *Walk Two Moons* develops as Sal tries to discover why her mother left. In *Belle Prater's Boy*, Ruth White also deals with the loss of a parent. Notice in the following quote how White uses nature to reveal what the son has learned: "When I first came here, the trees were all in bloom. I never had seen anything so pretty, and thought nothing could ever hurt people who lived in such a beautiful place. Now the summer is gone. The apples are ripe, and I have learned . . . well, I have learned a beautiful place can't shelter you from hurt any more than a shack can" (p. 192). In both of these books, the protagonists make discoveries about tragedy and courage. Through their experiences, they learn to face their problems and realize their personal strength.

Single-Parent Families. Single-parent families have always existed, but recent realistic fiction for children portrays such families more often and sometimes more candidly than did most realistic fiction in the past. In contemporary novels for children, some of the families are doing quite well, but others face serious problems because of the lack of emotional and economic support from a mother or father.

A family's struggle to survive without one parent is popular in contemporary realistic fiction. Authors may suggest that the experience strengthens the children in the family, or that it causes so many difficulties that the children find coping impossible. In Vera and Bill Cleaver's *Where the Lilies Bloom*, a 14-year-old girl experiences conflict between her desire to keep a promise that she made to her dying father and her developing realization that she must break the promise in order to ensure her family's survival.

Although Mary Call's father dies early in the story, the Cleavers characterize him plausibly, as a person who lives by a strong moral and family code. He demands that his daughter take pride in the family name, instill that pride in her brothers and sisters, and hold the family together without accepting charity. Later, this promise becomes a crucial element in the plot and in Mary Call's character development. The Cleavers develop a believable and interesting conflict: Mary Call tries to do as her father demanded, but she gradually realizes that she must accept help if she is to gain the knowledge that she needs and improve her family's welfare.

Jenny Davis's *Good-Bye and Keep Cold* begins with death and continues with adjustments to a single-parent family. Edda, a girl in the Kentucky mining area, first faces her father's accidental death in a strip mine and then grows up as her mother and younger brother must also face the traumatic changes in their lives. Davis uses nature to introduce the conflicting emotions. On the day of the funeral, young Edda retreats to Heaven, the favorite forest sanctuary of Edda and her father. The conflict and grief build as Edda first watches the glasslike water splash and glide over flat rocks and then:

> Suddenly there were birds screaming overhead, loud, horrible screams, like people in pain. I started screaming back at them. . . . Mama was sleeping in her dark room up at the house, and Daddy was dead. There was no one to stop me, and that in itself made it all the more frightening and necessary to do. (p. 22)

Davis's story follows a family's healing process and deals with mature problems. Analyze the symbolic meaning of Davis's title, which is based on Robert Frost's poem, "Good-Bye and Keep Cold." Consider the meaning for Edda in the final paragraph: What does she mean when she thinks the following to herself?

> Mama walked off from the people who raised her and never looked back. I don't want to do that. But I do want to be free of them, want them in perspective, want myself apart. I need to shake them loose, let go. Charlie says everybody has to raise their parents. Is that true? He says the time comes for all of us when we have to kiss them good-bye and trust them to be okay on their own. I've done the best I could with mine. Good-bye, you all, and good luck. Good-bye and keep cold. (p. 210)

Numerous contemporary realistic fiction novels explore themes related to both the need for strong family loyalty during times of severe emotional strain and the person-against-society conflict that results when children fear the possible actions of people in social services. In *Mama, Let's Dance*, by Patricia Hermes, three children fear that they will be separated after their mother deserts them; consequently, they try to keep the desertion a secret. Compare this book and others, such as Janet Taylor Lisle's *Afternoon of the Elves* and Paula Fox's *Monkey Island*, in which children are deserted by a parent.

Authors who place their protagonists in single-parent families frequently develop plots in which the characters

go through unusual circumstances to learn about themselves or their parents. For example, in *Joey Pigza Loses Control*, hyperactive Joey spends the summer with his alcoholic father while his mother worries about how the irresponsible father will care for the boy, who requires medication. By the end of the experience, Joey realizes that his father needs help. He also realizes how much he loves his mother, as revealed in these final sentences: " 'Family hug,' she said, and put her arms around me and Pablo [the dog]. She never could do two things at once, which was good, because when it came to hugging me I wanted her all to myself" (p. 196).

Many of the stories written about single-parent families develop themes in which children become stronger as they make discoveries about themselves and the adults in their lives. The family structures, lifestyles, values, and problems reflect contemporary concerns and issues.

Growing Up

Children face numerous challenges when they venture from the family environment and begin the often difficult process of growing up. Forming and maintaining relationships with peers are important tasks. In addition, children may need to overcome emotional problems, develop or recover self-esteem, and identify their roles in their widening world. As children grow older, they may feel self-conscious about their changing bodies and developing sexuality. They must confront other facts of life as well, including survival and the inevitability of death. Books that explore children's concerns can stimulate discussion with children who are facing these same concerns. Such books also let children know that they are not alone, that other children experience the same problems and overcome them.

Peer Relationships. Children, like adults, need the shared understanding, pleasure, challenge, sense of equality, and security that friendship with peers provides. Peer relationships involve many of the joys and sorrows with which children become familiar in family life, but peer relationships also expand understandings of other people and the world in ways that familiar family ties cannot. Contemporary realistic fiction portrays children who are forming friendships with peers much like themselves in certain ways and with peers who at first seem strange. Books that explore the meaning of real friendship and suggest that best friends should support, rather than hurt, each other may help children overcome the disappointment that results when friends move or may stimulate a discussion about the meaning of friendship.

Friendly relations between best friends as they work together to defeat two bullies provide the plot in Stephanie Greene's *Owen Foote, Frontiersman*. Humorous conflict develops when two second-grade boys decide to wage war on the bullies who are threatening to wreck

Technology Resources

Use the CD-ROM that accompanies this text to generate a list of titles dealing with divorce by searching Titles, Description, and Topics under "divorce." To ensure the highest-quality titles, click on the hot link for each record to check for award winners.

their tree fort. When the boys decide to take on the characteristics of a wolverine and a badger, they discover ways of solving their own problems.

In *Bad Girls*, Cynthia Voigt uses the setting of a fifth-grade classroom and focuses attention on the behaviors of two girls who become best friends. Voigt introduces their attraction to each other early in the book and sets the stage for the mischief to follow: "When Mikey smiled that way, she looked mean, and dangerous—maybe evil. Margalo wanted to be her friend" (p. 11). Quickly, readers discover that Mikey has a closetful of smiles, one appropriate for every occasion. Voigt introduces the title of the book and the plot to follow as the girls are sure that the teacher is saying to herself, "How bad can two fifth-grade girls be?" (p. 23). Through their interactions with each other, their classmates, and their teacher, they learn a great deal about each other, but they really do not change from their original characters. The antics do seem real as one teacher commented, "I'm not sure I want my students to read this. It might give them ideas."

Andrew Clements's *The Landry News* is another book that shows the importance of students' actions. In this book, their actions are very positive. A class of fifth graders develops a newspaper that has the motto "Truth and Mercy." The students learn a great deal about themselves and about democracy when they have to defend the contents of the school paper in front of the school board and the parents. In a happy ending, the students and their teacher make a statement for freedom of speech.

Authors often develop conflict in stories about interpersonal relationships by using person-against-self or person-against-person conflicts. In credible person-against-self conflicts, authors enable readers to identify inner conflicts and to understand why the characters have the conflicts and how they handle them, and what things enable resolution of the conflicts. Resolutions should not be contrived; they should appear as natural outcomes. Contrived endings result when authors try too rapidly or too conveniently to create happy endings for serious and hurtful situations.

In credible person-against-person conflicts, authors develop both believable protagonists and believable opposing forces that serve as antagonists. For example, in Betsy Byars's *Cracker Jackson*, an 11-year-old boy manages to convince adults that his former baby-sitter and her daughter are being abused by their husband and father. Byars uses humor and compassion to lighten the fear in the situation. Readers need to understand why conflicts occur between the forces: Do differences in values, personalities, or character traits cause conflict? An author's development of character should reflect such differences and encourage readers to understand why the characters act and react as they do. The conflicts that authors identify and the ways in which the characters overcome them usually communicate unifying themes about interpersonal relationships. The most successful themes develop natu-

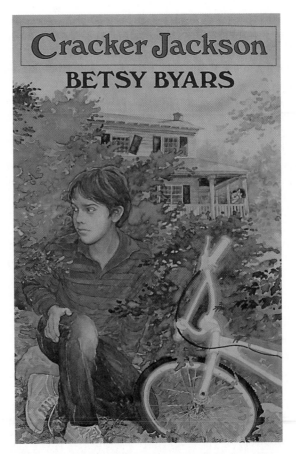

Humor and compassion lighten a story about child abuse. (From *Cracker Jackson*, by Betsy Byars. Jacket illustration by Diane de Groat. Text copyright © Betsy Byars, 1985. Jacket illustration copyright © Viking Penguin, Inc., 1985. Reprinted by permission of Penguin Books.)

rally; the least successful themes are created solely for didactic purposes.

A person-against-self conflict and carefully developed character create a credible story in E. L. Konigsburg's *Jennifer, Hecate, Macbeth, William McKinley, and Me, Elizabeth*. Konigsburg encourages understanding of Elizabeth's inner conflict and need for a friend by emphasizing her shyness. She is a new girl in school, she goes to school alone, and she is afraid that she will cry when she walks into her classroom. Elizabeth's shyness and her need for a friend are reemphasized through her responses when she meets Jennifer, a very imaginative girl. At first, Elizabeth complies with Jennifer's demands and suggestions even when she does not want to do what her new friend asks of her. Later, as she gains confidence in herself, Elizabeth becomes assertive. Her inner conflict is resolved when the friends no longer need the support of the game in which they pretend to be witch and assistant witch. Then, they just can be good friends and act as equals.

The emotional conflicts created when Debbie, a middle school girl, is suddenly dumped by a former best friend provide believable situations for the protagonist in Lynne

Rae Perkins's *All Alone in the Universe*. Debbie reveals a series of believable reactions, including bewilderment, blame, and loneliness, before she discovers that the world has not ended for her and that she can make her own life happen.

Person-against-person and person-against-self conflicts develop in Gennifer Choldenko's *Al Capone Does My Shirts*, a story set on Alcatraz Island in the late 1930s. The family lives on the island because Mr. Flannagan is a guard at the prison. The major conflicts result as Moose Flannagan and his parents face problems resulting from Moose's autistic sister, Natalie. The author vividly describes Natalie's behavior and how it affects the family. The author depicts 12-year-old Moose as a typical boy with special ability playing baseball. Readers understand Moose's conflict when he has to give up his after-school games to watch his sister. There are humorous moments in the book as the youthful, noncriminal inhabitants of the island develop schemes to see or interact with some of the most notorious inmates, including Al Capone. In a satisfying ending, Moose realizes that he loves his sister and that there is actually someone on the island who has enough influence to allow her to be accepted into a special school. An author's note gives more information about Alcatraz and autism; the characters may seem so believable because the author was inspired by her sister who had a severe form of autism.

Physical Changes. To develop credible problems, authors who write about physical maturity often describe embarrassing physical characteristics and explore ways in which the characters, friends, and family members respond to them. The stories may depict both person-against-self and person-against-person conflicts. Person-against-person conflicts include peer victimization of a main character, with the story told from the viewpoint of either the victimized child or a child who is part of the peer group. In the case of a main character who is part of a victimizing peer group, the author may develop the consequences of peer victimization by having the peer group turn against the main character. Some problems have simplistic or humorous resolutions, but other resolutions are complex and express the extreme sensitivity of children who are experiencing changes in their bodies and increased self-consciousness about their appearance as they grow up.

In *The Real Plato Jones*, Nina Bawden combines a 13-year-old boy's concerns over his short stature and his problems reconciling his heritage. Plato Constantine Jones has a Welsh grandfather who fought in World War II and a Greek grandfather who might have been a traitor, conflicts that provide numerous subplots in this coming-of-age story.

In *Are You There God? It's Me, Margaret*, Judy Blume explores a young girl's developing sexuality. Eleven-year-old Margaret has many questions about the physical changes occurring in her body, including breast development and the onset of menstruation. This book discusses a topic that is very serious to girls who are approaching physical maturity.

Emotional Changes. Books that develop plots around emotional maturity—and physical maturity as well—differ in several important ways from the realistic fiction of the past. For example, some authors imply that parents are ineffective in helping a child cope with emotional changes and problems, are unavailable, or are unable to understand the child. Current realistic fiction often suggests that a person outside the family, an understanding grandparent or a knowledgeable friend, is the most important influence in a child's discovery of self—in contrast to the literature of the past, in which strong parents and caring brothers and sisters provide necessary support. Unlike many family stories in the past, current stories also suggest that children who are struggling toward emotional maturity have numerous problems.

Children confront a wide range of emotional issues while growing up. For example, in Lois Lowry's *Anastasia Krupnik*, a 10-year-old girl begins to overcome her desire

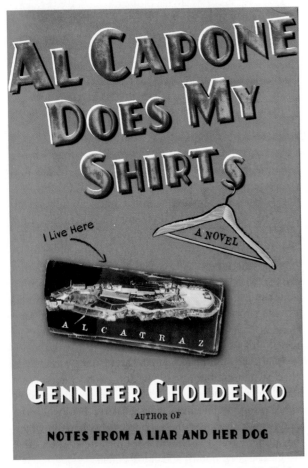

Cover from Al Capone Does My Shirts by Gennifer Choldenko. Copyright © 2004. Used by permission of G. P. Putnam's Sons, a division of Penguin Putnam, Inc.

to be the center of attention and her jealousy when she is able to place her family's new baby on her list of loves instead of her list of hates. Lowry extends the story of the Krupnik family in *Attaboy, Sam!*, focusing on Anastasia's little brother, Sam. The precocious boy's actions result in situations that are both hilarious and disastrous. Sam's story continues in *See You Around, Sam!* when Sam decides that he should run away to Alaska.

The main character in Phyllis Reynolds Naylor's *Alice in Rapture, Sort Of* faces emotional changes caused by boy–girl relationships. Alice and her father live through what the father refers to as the summer of the first boyfriend. Naylor's figurative language effectively introduces the emotional conflict: The summer "stretched out before me like a roller coaster. I didn't want to get off, but I was terrified of what was over the next hill" (p. 2). By the end of the story, Alice concludes that it is more enjoyable to have male friends than boyfriends. In this humorous story, Naylor explores fears and issues associated with relationships, peer pressures, and growing up.

The more serious consequences of growing up are explored in Neal Shusterman's *Speeding Bullet*. The hero, Nick Herrara, is a below-average student who has not received much attention until he saves a young girl from being hit by a subway train. The media and other people in New York City consider him a hero, and he receives all of the attention that he desires. The risks increase, however, when Nick begins to look for other people to rescue. By the end of the book, Nick gains understanding of his needs and reaches self-realization.

Margot, the main character in Susie Morgenstern's *Sixth Grade*, goes through a series of emotions as she anticipates and then actually experiences a new school and sixth grade. The author begins by describing Margot's excitement as she reads the letter that admits her to the school. At this time, she reveals her person-against-self fear that she might be required to repeat fifth grade. The author develops the year in chronological order as Margot searches for what to wear the first day of school, expresses her anxiety that she may look nerdy with her schoolbag, and worries about her new teachers. Her early fears are even reflected in her dreams, as she dreams that she is trapped in a labyrinth with no way out. The author portrays fears of many students as Margot faces the terrifying blank page of paper before writing her first essay. Morgenstern uses a repeated sentence given in advice by Margot's sister and parents every time she complains: "You'll get used to it." As the year progresses, the author lets readers see changes in Margot: "Just as her mother had predicted, Margot was finally starting to feel like an old (very old!) sixth grader. By the time Christmas and New Year's had come and gone, she knew all the ropes, and had gotten used to everything. She was at the top of the class" (p. 77).

Throughout the book, the author uses Margot's fascination with creating alphabetical lists of things. She asks classmates to fill in some of these lists, such as "The Mean Alphapathetic," that frequently get her into trouble. Other lists, such as "The Alphabeautiful" and "The Solidarity ABC for Class 6 F," indicate changes in her attitude.

The protagonist in Pam Muñoz Ryan's *Becoming Naomi León* progresses emotionally from being considered a mouse, because she is unable to speak for herself, to Naomi the Lion, who has considerable self-esteem and feels able to stand up for herself, her great-grandmother, and her younger brother, who has a birth defect. The author uses Naomi's discoveries about her Mexican heritage to help her gain new understandings and to help Gram overcome a custody battle with the mother who deserted her children. Ryan presents cultural and family information as the children and Gram go to Mexico for Christmas, experience Las Posadas, take part in the carvings associated with the Night of the Radishes, and meet the children's father. (The children's parents were divorced.) These carvings, especially those Naomi creates, provide a vehicle in which Naomi discovers her true self as well as the love of her father. The novel concludes with Naomi's new understanding: "I hoped my father was right, that like the figures we carved from wood and soap, I was becoming who I was meant to be, the Naomi Soledad León Outlaw of my wildest dreams" (p. 246).

The title of Mark Peter Hughes's *I Am the Wallpaper* also expresses the emotions of the main character, 13-year-old Floey Parker. Many of these emotions are revealed through diary entries, such as the following entry on her 13th birthday: "Finally, today I'm a teenager! I see the next year of my life waving me onward like Brad Pitt in a loincloth! Great things are about to happen. For example: a. I will say goodbye to tech ed with Mr. Byrd. b. I will say hello to eighth grade. c. Wendel will at long last admit that he likes me. d. Lillian will finally get a real job and move out of the house and I won't have to share a bedroom anymore" (p. 2). It is Floey's popular sister who makes her feel like the title of the book—invisible, like wallpaper. To overcome her feelings about being unnoticed, she tries a number of humorous self-improvement solutions, including violet hair dye. When cousins post Floey's diary entries on the Internet, she becomes noticed, but not in ways that she might choose. This is a humorous book about a girl going through the emotional changes related to becoming a teenager.

Survival

Physical and emotional survival are fundamental challenges. Confrontations with dangers in nature, society, or oneself require and, ideally, develop strength of character in young people and adults. The strong personalities in survival literature are especially popular with older children, who enjoy adventure stories.

Authors of survival literature use several literary techniques to create credible plots and characters. Person-against-nature, person-against-society, and person-against-self conflicts are often the stimuli for complex and exciting plots. Authors may develop forceful natural or social settings as antagonists in stories, clarifiers of conflicts, or means of developing desired moods. Style is also important in survival literature: Careful word selection, imagery, and rhythm patterns can heighten the emotional impact and credibility of adventures outside the realms of experience of most readers. Authors of survival literature usually rely on consistent point of view—often first-person or limited omniscient—to encourage the readers to identify with and believe in the protagonists and their experiences.

Surviving in Nature. In Jean Craighead George's *My Side of the Mountain*, Sam Gribley leaves his home in New York City to live off the land in the Catskill Mountains. George tells part of the story in the form of Sam's diary, which adds a sense of authenticity to the story and creates the feeling that the readers are sharing an autobiographical account of Sam's experiences. Detailed descriptions of Sam's preparing and storing food, tanning and sewing a deerhide suit, and carving and firing the interior of his home in a hemlock tree are told in a matter-of-fact manner, which resembles the writing of someone who is keeping a log of his experiences and observations. The detailed descriptions of wild edible plants and important survival techniques also suggest that Sam prepared carefully for his experiment in the wild. George creates another exciting survival-in-nature story in *Julie of the Wolves*. In this story, a 13-year-old girl lost in the Arctic tundra develops a friendship with wolves.

The consistent first-person point of view used by Scott O'Dell in *Island of the Blue Dolphins* creates a plausible plot, main character, and setting. When Karana, a young Indian girl who survives years alone on a Pacific Island, says, "I will tell you about my island," readers visualize the important features from her viewpoint and believe the description. When she says, "I was afraid," the fear seems real. Later, her discovery of her brother's body justifies her fear. This first-person point of view increases the readers' belief in Karana's personal struggles as she is torn between two forces: Will she adhere to the tribal law that prohibits women from making weapons, or will she construct the weapons that will probably mean the difference between her life or death? Her inner turmoil heightens the suspense, as suggested by the following quote:

> Would the four winds blow in from the four directions of the world and smother me as I made the weapons? Or would the earth tremble, as many said, and bury me beneath its falling rocks? Or, as others said, would the sea rise over the island in a terrible flood? Would the weapons break in my hands at the moment when my life was in danger, which is what my father had said? (p. 54)

Other major decisions are more meaningful, too, because they are told through Karana's point of view. When Karana decides to take a tribal canoe and sail in the direction that her people sailed, readers believe her turmoil

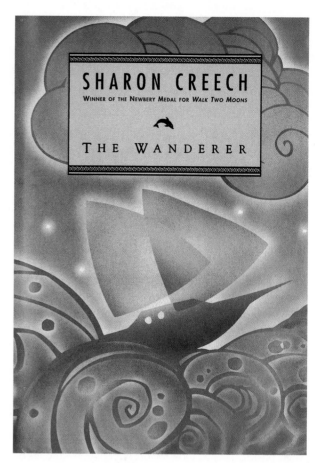

Overcoming problems associated with survival at sea helps a girl make discoveries about herself and her past in Sharon Creech's The Wanderer. *(Cover from* The Wanderer, *by Sharon Creech, illustrated by David Diaz, illustrations copyright © 2001 by David Diaz. Published by HarperCollins, Publisher. Reprinted by permission.)*

as the canoe begins to leak and she must make another difficult decision: Should she go back and face loneliness or go on and risk disaster? Karana decides to return to her island and make it as much of a home as she can.

In the survival story *Hatchet*, Gary Paulsen carefully documents Brian's problem-solving approaches. Each time Brian faces a critical, often life-and-death problem, Paulsen reveals Brian's reasoning processes. Brian thinks about the pros and cons of various actions. For example, he thinks through the various actions that he could take after the pilot has a heart attack and Brian realizes that he is alone (pp. 17–30), the reasons he should have no fear of the bear and return to the raspberry patch (p. 75), the reasons a water animal would come up to the sand (pp. 98–99), a way to create a weapon to effectively catch fish (pp. 111–115), ways to capture birds for meat (pp. 140–141), and a way to make a craft and reach the plane after a tornado reveals the location of the plane (pp. 166–183). Memories of books Brian has read or television programs he has seen frequently help him solve what otherwise would be impossible problems.

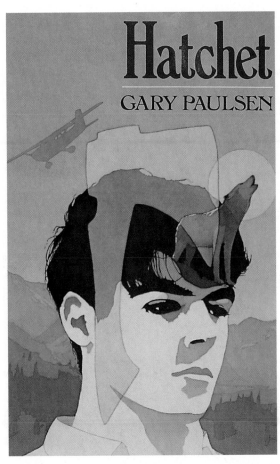

Gary Paulsen develops strong person-against-nature and person-against-self conflicts in Hatchet. *(From* Hatchet, *by Gary Paulsen. Jacket cover by Neil Waldman. Copyright © 1987 by Neil Waldman. Reprinted by permission of Neil Waldman.)*

Paulsen uses contrasts to encourage readers to understand both the gravity and the consequences of many of the problems. For example, Brian compares his experiences in the wilderness with experiences he has had at home. Readers understand that searching for and storing food are more than a simple trip to the grocery store. Unlike Brian's home experiences, his actions in the wilderness are life-and-death matters. The consequences of Brian's survival experiences are extended in Paulsen's sequel, *Brian's Return*. The themes developed in this book indicate that Brian has overcome the person-against-nature conflicts in the earlier book and his understanding of the role of nature in his life: "Never assume anything, expect the unexpected, be ready for everything all the time," and "No matter what he thought would happen, nature would do what it wanted to do. He had to be part of it, part of what it was really like, not what he or some other person thought it should be like" (p. 83).

Surviving Inner-City Reality. Dangerous, polluted, and economically deprived inner cities are the environments in which many American children face the challenges of growing up. A number of authors of realistic fiction portray the problems of overcoming poverty, gang violence, and living without the security of strong, supportive family members. Many of these characters live in homeless situations. It is easy to rely on sensationalism for such stories, and numerous authors do. However, Virginia Hamilton, Walter Dean Myers, and Paula Fox, for example, create inner-city stories with literary merit.

One of the strongest inner-city stories is Virginia Hamilton's *The Planet of Junior Brown*. Her memorable characters enliven a complex story about friendship, loyalty, and learning to live together. The three main characters, all outcasts, live on the fringe of busy New York City. Junior Brown is a talented pianist who should be recognized for his skill, but the fact that he weighs almost 300 pounds causes people to leave him alone. Consequently, he feels ugly and is afraid of being trapped in small spaces. Buddy Clark is an intelligent street boy who has lived on his own since the age of 9. The third outcast is Mr. Pool, a former teacher, who is a school custodian.

Mr. Pool feels that tough black children who know the city streets should be given opportunities to learn, but the rigid school regime causes him to lose heart, give up his teaching job, and move to the school basement. In this basement, however, Mr. Pool has a secret room where he can teach Junior Brown and Buddy Clark. Hamilton uses the symbolism associated with the word *planet* to develop each character's place in the story. Junior Brown's planet is an artistic creation that hangs suspended from metal rods and spherical tracks attached to the ceiling of the hidden room. While the children in the rooms above go through their normal days, the three outcasts build their solar system, create their planets, and learn about science and each other. Hamilton develops a strong theme when Buddy Clark takes the other outcasts to his own planet in the basement of a deserted house and shares with them his own views of life:

> "We are together," Buddy told them, "because we have to learn to live for each other. . . . If you stay here, you each have a voice in what you will do here. But the highest law for us is to live for one another. I can teach you how to do that." (p. 210)

Readers of this story will understand the author's theme: There is danger when people are involved with violent gangs, drugs, and guns.

Stories written for older audiences tend to depict the harsher realities of homelessness. For example, in *Monkey Island*, Paula Fox uses numerous contrasts between Clay's former life with his parents and his life as a homeless boy after his mother's desertion. In the following quotation, Fox depicts Clay's memories:

> Standing there, hidden from the street, trying to breathe shallowly, he had what was almost a vision, or a kind of mist of memory, of being lifted up by his father in the dark warmth of a room, of being carried to the bathroom, where a tiny night-light in a floor socket gave off an amber glow and his father murmuring, "That's good my sweetheart. You can sleep right through now." (p. 26)

On the next page, Fox describes the reality of the streets through Clay's point of view:

> He crossed a street and waited a moment as he heard a very faint murmur—there, and not there—whispers fading into nothing. Now he could see that the black patches were cardboard boxes and heaps of bundles and that there were many long pieces of cardboard lying about on the ground and beneath benches. There were people in the park. On a nearby bench, an old woman lay doubled over, apparently asleep, black plastic bags gathered around her on the bench and on the ground, like big black stones. (p. 27)

As in many stories of homeless people, Fox describes the dangers in the street and develops person-against-society conflicts. Clay thinks about his negative associations with social services, he describes his fear of having an agency take him away so that he cannot find his mother, a character tells Clay that most people think of homeless people as nasty stains on the sidewalk, and he realizes that families can let you down.

You may want to compare the inner-city survival stories set in the United States with one set in Rio de Janeiro: Ineke Holtwijk's *Asphalt Angels*, a 2000 Batchelder Honor book. This book was inspired by a real homeless person living with a street gang in Rio de Janeiro. The author depicts the dangerous world of drugs, suicide, dishonest authorities, sex, and gang violence. The content of the book makes it more appropriate for older, mature audiences.

Surviving in a Dangerous World.   A new type of survival literature is emerging in both American and British children's literature: realistic fiction that mirrors international headlines about new dangers in our modern age. In the person-against-society conflicts of this survival literature, the protagonists are usually innocent children and the antagonists are terrorist groups, oppressive military governments, and mass violence.

Cathryn Clinton uses an interesting technique to introduce the setting and conflict in *A Stone in My Hand*, a novel that explores Jewish–Arab relations during the late 1980s when the Gaza Strip is under Israeli military occupation. She places the main character, Malaak, on the roof of her home where she is feeding seeds to Abdo, a wild bird. The author suggests the importance of the bird and the Moslem heroine's desire for freedom when Malaak states: "I live in Abdo's eyes. I see things my sister and brother will never see. I fly high, high over Gaza City. I soar out of the Gaza Strip. Nothing stops me, not the concrete and razor wire, not the guns, not the soldiers. I stare at them with my hard black Abdo eyes, and they do not shoot me. I am hidden . . . but then I come back to the roof. Someday I may fly away for good, but for now I watch and wait" (p. 1).

The author shows the consequences for Malaak of the occupation and resulting terrorist actions after her father disappears and is killed by a bomb when he travels to Jerusalem to search for work. Clinton shows the conflicts

★ "This story of one young girl and her family is told with compassion and hope. . . . A must-read." —*Kirkus Reviews* (starred review)

A Stone in My Hand

CATHRYN CLINTON

Cover from A STONE IN MY HAND. Copyright © 2002 Cathryn Clinton. Jacket Photographs Copyright © 2005 Matt Mahurin. Reproduced by permission of Candlewick Press, Inc., Cambridge, MA, on behalf of Walker Books, Ltd., London.

within the family as the older brother is drawn to radical groups and brags about being a youth fighter in the uprising that began in December 1987 in the Occupied Territories of the West Bank.

By writing the story through the point of view of Malaak, a Moslem, Clinton shows the fear and conflict faced by innocent families. The author develops a strong antiterrorist theme when Malaak remembers her father's words: "Terrorism is like a wild dog. It only breeds violence" (p. 45).

Rafik Schami's *A Hand Full of Stars* places the hero in the political turmoil of modern Damascus. Showing how dangerous society can be, the story follows a teenager who wants to become a journalist within this suppressed society. His wishes come true when he and his friends begin an underground newspaper. After reading this book, you may speculate about the symbolism in the title. The author states at the end of the book what *A Hand Full of Stars* means: "The Hand is the hand of Uncle Salim, always there to guide the narrator; in the saddest moments, it points the way out of despair. Like the stars that illuminate the dark night sky, the Stars in the hand stand for hope" (endnote).

The political turmoil of Romania provides the setting and conflict in Bel Mooney's *The Voices of Silence*. The major conflict results when a girl betrays her parents to her friend.

In Lois Duncan's *Don't Look Behind You*, a family is threatened by hired assassins. Duncan develops the frightening adjustments that the family must make when it is placed under the federal witness security program. Older readers will understand the conflicts of the teenage girl who tries to salvage parts of her former life.

Death

Part of growing up is realizing and gradually accepting the fact of death. An increasing number of realistic fiction stories develop themes related to the acceptance of death and overcoming emotional problems following the death of a loved one. Louis Rauch Gibson and Laura M. Zaidman (1992) identify the importance of literature that deals with death:

> Since children, like adults, are so deeply affected by the loss of a relative or friend, contemporary realistic fiction and biography help resolve some of the conflicts death presents. Literature about real and fictional people satisfies a desperate need to comfort children who are justifiably bewildered and fearful about death. (p. 233)

As might be expected, different authors treat the subject differently. Treatment also depends on the developmental levels of the intended readers.

Differences in cause of conflict, resolution of conflict, and depth of emotional involvement are apparent in books of realistic fiction about death. Consider how several authors develop these areas in books written for younger readers, preadolescents, and teenagers: Howard Kaplan's *Waiting to Sing*, written for 5- to 8-year-olds; Constance C. Greene's *Beat the Turtle Drum*, written for 10- to 12-year-olds; Richard Peck's *Remembering the Good Times* and Judy Blume's *Tiger Eyes*, written for readers in their early teens; and Robert Cormier's *The Bumblebee Flies Anyway*, written for teenagers and young adults.

In Howard Kaplan's *Waiting to Sing*, the author first depicts a strong family that is nurtured by love for and playing of the piano. This closeness ends with the death of the mother. It is the piano, however, that finally allows father and the son to begin their healing. This begins when "I walked from my bedroom to the piano bench, as if holding on to the music for balance, and sat by my father's side. . . . We let the piano speak for us. It is our way of crying, the way it had once been our way of laughing. . . . I felt as though we could quench our thirst on one bright drop. Sometimes I think the greatest distance to be traveled is that between two beating hearts" (unnumbered).

Stories written for 10- through 12-year-olds have more fully developed characters and deal with more difficult emotions than those written for younger readers. Constance C. Greene's *Beat the Turtle Drum* depicts the basis for a girl's reactions to her sister's accidental death by describing the warm relationship between 10-year-old Joss and her 12-year-old sister, Kate. Kate believes that her parents prefer her younger sister. After Joss falls from a tree and dies, Kate faces both the sorrow of losing a sister and the inner conflict resulting from her belief that her sister was the favorite. Readers glimpse Kate's inner turmoil when she finally admits her feelings to an understanding relative, who responds:

> I bet Joss would've felt the same way. If it'd been you, she might've said the same thing. And both of you would've been wrong. I think when a child dies, it's the saddest thing that could ever happen. And the next saddest is the way the brothers and sisters feel. They feel guilty, because they fought or were jealous or lots of things. And here they are, alive, and the other one is dead. And there's nothing they can do. It'll take time, Kate. (p. 105)

Kate gradually understands that overcoming her grief and conflicting emotions will take more than a moment but that she will receive pleasure from her memories of Joss.

The believable characters in Richard Peck's *Remembering the Good Times* help readers in their teens identify with this story about the suicide of a best friend. Peck first carefully develops the distinct personalities of two boys and a girl in their junior-high years. Kate is involved with people and believes in herself; Buck does not know which group he belongs with; and Trav is angry, unsure of himself, and afraid of the future. Peck develops the main person-against-self conflict by describing Trav's increasing fears as he discusses current events and as he reacts to evidence that he is expected to grow up to be like his successful parents. Trav becomes angry when he feels that he is not being prepared for the realities of life.

Peck develops a strong relationship among the three friends. After Trav kills himself, Kate admonishes herself for not noticing the little things that should have warned them about Trav's approaching suicide. Peck explores various responses to Trav's death, as high school administrators blame the parents, the parents blame the school, a knowledgeable older friend states the community's responsibility, and Kate and Buck discover that they can remember the good times of their friendship.

The causes of the conflict in Blume's story for older readers, *Tiger Eyes*, are the sudden, violent death of a parent and a society that creates such violence. Blume develops a person-against-self conflict as Davey, a teenage girl, tries to adjust emotionally and physically to the death of her father, who was a robbery victim. Blume also develops a person-against-society conflict as the characters respond to and reflect about a society in which there is violent death, vandalism, excessive teenage tension, and powerful weapons. Blume's characterization encourages readers to understand Davey's turmoil. The author shows Davey's emotional ties with her father, her physical reactions when she faces her peers (she faints at school but cannot tell the nurse her problem), her need for a quiet place to reflect, her interactions with a man who is dying from cancer and with an uncle who will not allow her to take chances but designs weapons at Los Alamos, and her interactions with two friends who are also facing inner conflicts. The resolutions of the conflicts take time, but Davey can finally face what happened, tell new friends how her father died, and consider her own future.

Several responses by 14-year-olds to *Tiger Eyes* demonstrate how personal the reactions to realistic fiction can be. One reader said, "This is not a good book to read in class. You need to be by yourself so you can cry if you want to." Another student said, "It's great. You get into the story and forget everything. I was afraid Davey was going to kill herself, but I thought, Judy Blume wouldn't kill her main character." A third reader said that the story was sad but its moral was happy: "Take a chance on your talents; planning someone's life for them doesn't make them happy; it's always better to face the truth rather than run from it; life is a great adventure; you can't go back in time. So pick up the pieces and move ahead; and some changes happen down inside of you and only you know about them." These responses indicate that a 14-year-old grasped many of the complex themes that Blume wove into her novel. It is also interesting to note that the themes identified are positive rather than negative.

The setting in *The Bumblebee Flies Anyway*, Robert Cormier's psychological novel for teenagers and young adults, is a terminal care facility in which Barney, a 16-year-old boy, realizes that his treatment is only experimental and that he actually is dying. Cormier uses symbolism to convey Barney's feelings about being a terminally ill guinea pig: The complex is a facility for experimental medicine; "the Handyman" is a doctor who treats the patients and creates illusions; "the merchandise" is special medicines, chemicals, and drugs that are calculated to produce expected responses; and "the bumblebee" is a sportscar in a junkyard that at first appears to be shining and new but is actually only a cardboard mockup of reality.

Books about death focus on various aspects of death. Books such as Sharon Creech's *Chasing Redbird* deal with a child's struggle to accept her aunt's death. Audrey Couloumbis's *Getting Near to Baby* explores how two sisters, a 13-year-old and a 7-year-old, learn about grief and healing after the tragic death of a sibling. Two recent books deal with responses to death through violence. In Colby Rodowsky's *Remembering Mog*, the author proceeds through a series of family reactions to Mog's murder. The contemporary nightmare of dealing with a missing relative is also developed in Michael Cadnum's *Zero to the Bone*, a book for older readers.

People as Individuals, Not Stereotypes

Stereotypical views of males and females, people with disabilities, and the elderly are becoming less prevalent in children's literature.

Male and Females.   Publishers are sensitive to the need for literature that does not portray either sex in stereotypical roles. For example, since 1981, the Houghton Mifflin Publishing Company has had guidelines for eliminating sex stereotypes in materials that it publishes. Following are several guidelines:

1. Published materials should balance female and male protagonists and female and male contributors to society, and should present females and males in a variety of jobs. Stories should suggest that both females and males can prepare for and succeed in a variety of occupations.

2. Literature should recognize that males and females have the same basic emotions, personality traits, and capabilities. Both sexes should be portrayed in active pastimes and in solitary pursuits.

3. Sensitivity, taste, and nonstereotypic images should be employed in humor used to characterize the sexes.

4. Literature should present a broad range of historical references to women, including women whose contributions are well known and less well known.

5. Where appropriate, literature should include reference to legal, economic, and social issues related to women.

6. Historical books should include coverage of the roles and activities of women in past centuries.

As the roles of females in our society shift away from the stereotypes of the past, female characters in children's literature reflect these changes. Contemporary realistic fiction contains more girls who are distinct individuals: Girls may be brave, they may be tomboys, and they may be unorthodox. Mothers in realistic fiction also are taking on different roles. Often, they work outside the home; they may even have jobs more demanding than those of their husbands. Whatever roles females in recent realistic fiction play, the female characters are quite different from those in earlier children's literature, even literature of the fairly recent past.

Consider, for example, the popular contemporary character Ramona, created by Beverly Cleary. Stories of her exploits span the years from the early 1950s into the 1980s. In *Henry and Beezus*, published in 1952, readers discover that the girls, Beezus and Ramona, are considered worthy playmates *even* by an active boy, such as Henry Huggins. These thoughts at least imply that active pastimes are not usually considered appropriate for girls; girls may not be considered creative playmates.

In later books, however, Ramona comes into her own. In *Ramona the Pest* (1968), she is not the stereotypical quiet girl; instead, she is the "worst rester" in kindergarten. By the time *Ramona and Her Father* was published in the late 1970s, the roles in her family have changed:

Her father loses his job and stays home, and her mother returns to work full-time. Ramona humorously tries to help her father through this change in his life. *Ramona and Her Mother* explores a working mother's life as viewed by her 7-year-old daughter. By 1981, *Ramona Quimby, Age 8* is helping her family while her father returns to college. The Ramona books are popular with children who enjoy reading about the exploits of a spunky, humorous girl.

Louise Fitzhugh's hero in *Harriet the Spy* is an 11-year-old girl whom other characters describe as exceptional, intelligent, and curious. Harriet's actions support these descriptions: she hides in her secret places, observes her neighbors and classmates, and writes down her observations. The extent of this popular character's resourcefulness and self-confidence is revealed when her classmates find her notebook and organize "The Spy Catcher Club." Harriet uses all of her creativity to devise a plan that will persuade her friends to forgive her. She is far from the fainting female of most traditional literature and Victorian fiction, who must be rescued from her failures by the males in the story. She is even able to return to her real loves, spying and writing. More tales about Harriet are found in *The Long Secret*.

E. L. Konigsburg's *From the Mixed-Up Files of Mrs. Basil E. Frankweiler* is another book of realistic fiction in which a female protagonist belies the traditional stereotypes about passive femininity. Claudia Kincaid leads her brother in running away from home and hiding out in the Metropolitan Museum of Art. When the two children are given an hour to search the files and discover the answer to a mystery involving a statue of an angel, Claudia tells her impatient brother that 5 minutes of planning are worth 15 minutes of haphazard looking. Her techniques prove successful, and they discover the answer.

Stereotyped views of males are also changing in our society and in children's literature. In Katherine Paterson's *Bridge to Terabithia*, for example, a boy hates football, aspires to be an artist, and feels pressured by his father's traditionally masculine expectations of him. Although the father is afraid that Jess is becoming a "sissy," Jess finds support for being himself in a strong friendship with the story's other protagonist, a girl named Leslie, who is also a nonconformist in their rural community.

One outstanding book of realistic fiction from the mid-1960s reveals that wider options for males are more prevalent in children's literature today. In Maia Wojciechowska's *Shadow of a Bull*, the son of a famous and supposedly fearless bullfighter learns that a male doesn't have to prove his manliness through acts of physical daring or violence. Manolo's village expects him to follow in his dead father's footsteps. As the men of the village begin training him in the art of bullfighting, Manolo believes that he is a coward because he has no interest in being a bullfighter. He eventually learns that to be truly brave, he must be true to himself and not attempt to satisfy others' expectations.

Individuals Who Are Physically Different or Have a Disability.

Most children and adults dislike standing out because of their appearance or physical capabilities. They also may feel discomfort when they see someone who does not conform to the customary standards of appearance or who is physically disabled. Children's realistic fiction is increasingly sensitive to the importance of overcoming cruel or condescending stereotypes.

In *Blubber*, Judy Blume shows how peer cruelty to someone who is physically different can have negative consequences for all concerned. Classmates torment a girl whom they consider grossly overweight. A strong peer leader manipulates her friends into composing a list entitled "How to Have Fun With Blubber" and forces the girl herself to make demeaning statements, such as "I am Blubber, the smelly whale of class 206" (p. 72). The main character realizes the crushing impact of what she has done when she tries to stop the cruelty and her classmates then turn on her.

Authors who develop realistic plots around credible characters who have physical disabilities often describe details related to a disability, the feelings and experiences of the person who has the disability, and the feelings and experiences of family members and others who interact with the character. Well-written books help other children empathize with and understand children with disabilities. Although adults should evaluate such books by literary standards, they also should evaluate them by their sensitivity.

The resolution of conflict can be a special concern in realistic fiction dealing with physical disabilities. Does the author concoct a happy ending because he or she believes that all children's stories should have happy endings, or does the resolution of conflict evolve naturally and honestly? Through fiction that deals honestly with disabilities, readers can empathize with children who are courageously overcoming their problems and who, with their families, are facing new challenges. Writers of such literature often express the hope that their stories will encourage positive attitudes toward individuals with physical disabilities. As mainstreaming brings more children with disabilities into regular classrooms, this goal becomes even more important.

In *From Anna*, Jean Little develops a credible perspective on visual impairment by describing a girl's frightening experiences as a result of blurred letters and letters that look the same or even appear to jiggle across the page. In *The Gift of the Girl Who Couldn't Hear*, Susan Shreve depicts the interactions between Eliza and her best friend, Lucy, who has been deaf since birth. In this book, Lucy helps Eliza understand her own self-worth. The theme of the book can be used to encourage students to ponder the role of real and self-imposed limitations and to distinguish between the two.

Disabilities include mental capacities that are not up to the social norm. Authors who write plausible books about the relationships between children with mental disabilities and their ordinary siblings often portray the conflicting emotions of characters who experience both protective feelings and feelings of anger toward children with disabilities. In Betsy Byars's *The Summer of the Swans*, Sara is an average teenager who is discontented with her looks, sometimes miserable for no apparent reason, and often frustrated with her mentally retarded brother as she cares for him.

Byars encourages readers to understand and empathize with Charlie's gentle nature. He is fascinated by the swans who glide silently across the lake, but he becomes confused and terrified when he follows the swans and becomes lost. During a frantic search for Charlie, Sara forgets her personal miseries. When the siblings are reunited, Sara discovers that she feels better about herself and life in general than she had before.

Virginia Euwer Wolff's *Probably Still Nick Swansen* develops a many-sided character, Nick, who faces the realities of his learning disability. The author explores the similarities between 16-year-old Nick and other teens as well as individual differences among the students in Nick's special education class. In a strong ending, Nick learns to accept himself. In *Reaching Dustin*, Vicki Grove uses an assignment in which a fifth-grade girl makes discoveries about a classmate's emotional problems when she interviews him.

The Elderly. When students of children's literature evaluate the characterizations of elderly people in children's books, they often discover stereotypes. Some authors of contemporary realistic fiction are exploring the problems related to old age with greater sensitivity than authors expressed in books of the past. When evaluating books dealing with the elderly, you should select those that show elderly people in a wide variety of roles. Close experiences between grandparents and grandchildren are common in books for young children, such as Sharon Bell Mathis's *The Hundred Penny Box* and Benjamin Darling's *Valerie and the Silver Pear*. Books for older children, such as Susan Campbell Bartoletti's *Dancing With Dziadziu*, often stress the worthwhile contributions the elderly make, the warm relationships that can develop between grandparents and grandchildren, and the desire of elderly people to stay out of nursing homes. Some books are very serious; others develop serious themes through humorous stories.

In *Old John*, Peter Hartling explores the need for independence and strong relationships between generations. When a 75-year-old father and grandfather comes to live with his family, Hartling describes a strong elderly man who has not only idiosyncrasies but also needs for love and independence. In *Everywhere*, Bruce Brooks develops the strong bond between grandfather and grandson, which increases after the grandfather suffers a heart attack. The healing power of love is the theme.

The growing relationships and understandings between a girl and her grandfather form the basis for Norma Fox Mazer's *After the Rain*. At first, Rachel resents the time that she is asked to spend with her ailing grandfather, but she mourns the loss of their precious moments together after his death. Well-developed characters help readers understand the needs of the two generations and the changes that can result because people learn to understand each other.

Other outstanding books about the elderly and young people who love and respect them include Gary and Gail Provost's *David and Max* and Patricia MacLachlan's *Journey*. With their diverse, nonstereotyped depictions of elderly people, such books provide discussion material that encourages older children to explore the roles of elderly people in literature and their own feelings about the elderly. Additional books about the elderly are found in Sandra McGuire's bibliography, "Promoting Positive Attitudes Toward Aging" (1993).

Multicultural Topics in Realistic Fiction

Fiction written about African American, Native American, Latino, and Asian characters differs depending on the age of the intended audience. Books written for younger readers emphasize the universal needs of children. Books for children in the middle-elementary grades frequently emphasize searching for the past and understanding one's ancestry. Books for older children and young adults often have the characters face severe personal and social conflicts.

African American Books for Young Children

Fictional stories about African Americans written for young children mainly depict children facing situations and problems common to all young children: overcoming jealousy, adjusting to a new baby, expressing a need for attention, experiencing rivalry with siblings, developing personal relationships, and overcoming family problems. Children from all ethnic backgrounds can realize from these books that African American children have the same needs, desires, and problems that other children have and solve their problems in similar ways.

Books for younger children frequently depict warm relationships between children and their parents or grandparents. Irene Smalls-Hector's *Jonathan and His Mommy* portrays a mother and a son walking in the neighborhood. On this walk, they try various movements, such as zigzag walking, making giant steps, and itsy-bitsy baby steps. Michael Hays's illustrations show the city neighborhood and the people who live there. The actions and the illustrations suggest warm relationships.

Sharon Bell Mathis depicts warm relationships between young children and elderly people in *The Hundred*

Penny Box. In this book, Michael makes friends with his great-great-aunt Dew and learns about the box in which she keeps a penny for every year of life: "It's my old cracked-up, wacky-dacky box with the top broken," says Michael's Aunt Dew. "Them's my years in that box. . . . That's me in that box" (p. 19).

Happy childhood memories also form the background for Donald Crews's *Bigmama's,* a story about warm family relationships that increase as the children visit Bigmama's house in Florida. Crews uses the same Florida setting for *Shortcut.*

In *Working Cotton,* Sherley Anne Williams drew on her own childhood experiences in the cotton fields of Fresno, California. The text and illustrations depict the hardworking life of a migrant family.

Several contemporary realistic picture books for younger children are set in Africa and focus on warm relationships between families and friends. Karen Lynn Williams's *When Africa Was Home* describes relationships between a white boy and his African neighbors. The strength of these relationships is shown when, after the family returns to America, they decide that their home really is in Africa.

Books with African settings may also show the consequences of segregated townships. Rachel Isadora's *At the Crossroads* follows South African children waiting to welcome their fathers, who are working the mines after being separated from their families for 10 months. In *The Day Gogo Went to Vote: South Africa, April 1994,* Elinor Batezat Sisulu creates a strong character in Gogo, Thembi's 100-year-old great-great-grandmother, who has not left her home in many years but who now feels the necessity to leave her home to vote.

African American Books for Children in the Middle-Elementary Grades

Many African American stories for children in the middle-elementary grades are written by authors—black and white—who are sensitive to the black experience. Some themes—such as the discovery of oneself, the need to give and receive love, the problems experienced when children realize that the parents they love are getting a divorce, and the fears associated with nonachievement in school—are universal and suggest that all children have similar needs, fears, and problems. Other themes, such as searching for one's roots in the African past, speak of a special need by black children to know about their ancestry.

Virginia Hamilton's *Zeely* is a warm, sensitive story about an imaginative girl who makes an important discovery about herself and others when she and her brother spend the summer on their Uncle Ross's farm. Elizabeth is not satisfied with the status quo: She calls herself Geeder, renames her younger brother Toeboy, renames her uncle's town Crystal, and calls the asphalt highway Leadback.

When the imaginative Geeder sees her uncle's neighbor, Miss Zeely Tayber, Hamilton describes Zeely's appearance in detail: Zeely is a thin and stately woman over 6 feet tall, with a calm and proud expression, skin the color of rich Ceylon ebony, and the most beautiful face that Geeder has ever seen. When Geeder discovers a photograph of a Watusi queen who looks exactly like Zeely, she decides that Zeely must have royal blood.

Geeder is swept up in this fantasy and shares her beliefs with the village children. Then, Zeely helps Geeder make her greatest discovery: As they talk, Geeder realizes that dreaming is fine, but being yourself is even better. This realization causes Geeder to see everything in a new way. She realizes that Zeely is indeed a queen, but not like the ones in books, with their servants, kingdoms, and wealth. Zeely is queen because she is a self-loving person who always does her work better than anybody else. Geeder realizes that what a person is inside is more important than how a person looks or what a person owns. When Hamilton shares Geeder's final thoughts about her wonderful summer and her discovery that even stars resemble people, readers understand just how much wisdom Elizabeth has gained:

> Some stars were no more than bright arcs in the sky as they burned out. But others lived on and on. There was a blue star in the sky south of Hesperus, the evening star. She thought of naming it Miss Zeely Tayber. There it would be in Uncle Ross' sky forever. (p. 121)

Another book that explores a character's personal discovery and strength of character is *Sister,* by Eloise Greenfield. Sister, whose real name is Doretha, keeps a journal in which she records the hard times—and the good times that "rainbowed" their way through those harder times. Doretha's memory book helps her realize "I'm me." The words of the school song sung in *Sister* are characteristic of the themes found in this and other books by Greenfield:

> We strong black brothers and sisters
> Working in unity,
> We strong black brothers and sisters,
> Building our community,
> We all work together, learn together
> Live in harmony
> We strong black brothers and sisters
> Building for you and for me. (p. 69)

Mildred D. Taylor's *The Gold Cadillac* is a fictionalized story based on Taylor's painful memories, a story about family unity and the consequences of racial prejudice. The prejudice occurs in 1950, when a northern black family buys a gold Cadillac and tries to drive to Mississippi. For the first time, the children experience segregation and racial hostility. As in other books by Taylor, the theme is that family love and unity help them overcome such terrible experiences.

African American Books for Older Children and Young Adults

Outstanding realistic fiction written for older children and young adults is characterized by both strong characters and strong themes. The themes in these stories include searching for freedom and dignity, learning to live together, tackling problems personally rather than waiting for someone else to do so, survival of the body and the spirit, and the more humorous problems involved in living through a first crush.

Virginia Hamilton has written several fine novels that older children find engrossing. She writes about the black experience with a universal appeal that speaks to readers of any heritage. In the suspenseful story *The House of Dies Drear*, Hamilton skillfully presents historical information about slavery and the Underground Railroad through the conversations of a black history professor and his son who are interested in the history of the pre–Civil War mansion they are about to rent. Hamilton provides details for a setting that seems perfect for the mysterious occurrences that begin soon after the family arrives:

> The house of Dies Drear loomed out of mist and murky sky, not only gray and formless, but huge and unnatural. It seemed to crouch on the side of a high hill above the highway. And it had a dark, isolated look about it that set it at odds with all that was living. (p. 26)

Thomas learns that Dies Drear and two escaped slaves were murdered and that rumors say the abolitionist and the slaves haunt the old house and the hidden tunnels below. Mystery fans will enjoy this fast-paced book. In a sequel, *The Mystery of Drear House*, Hamilton answers questions that students may have after reading *The House of Dies Drear*.

In an interview conducted by Hazel Rochman (1992c), Virginia Hamilton discusses her interest in the Underground Railroad and mentions that her grandfather was a fugitive slave who went to Ohio from Virginia. She describes the houses in Ohio that are similar to the one in *The House of Dies Drear*:

> There are houses here with secret rooms and tunnels that were stations on the Underground going north into Oberlin and up to Shawnee territory. There's an octagonal house in Yellow Springs that was specifically designed to hide runaways. It had all these corners that could be cut off into little cubbyholes. (p. 1020)

In *Scorpions*, Walter Dean Myers's characters face person-against-society conflicts created by the contemporary world of drug dealers and gangs. They also face person-against-self conflicts created by inner fears and consequences related to owning a gun. The characters of Mama and her younger son, Jamal, are especially strong. Myers develops Mama's character through numerous con-

Gang violence and guns create conflict in this inner-city setting. (From Scorpions, by Walter Dean Myers, copyright © 1988 by Walter Dean Myers. Cover art: Copyright © 1988 by Bradford Brown. Reprinted by permission of HarperCollins.)

trasts. For example, when Mama thinks about her older son, who is in jail for robbery, she remembers looking at him as a baby and feeling great expectations because "you got a baby and you hope so much for it. . . ." (p. 54). Later, Mama is torn between her need to help this older son and to protect her younger children. Myers develops Mama's inner conflict as she discusses her problems with her minister:

> "And I know they convicted him of taking somebody's life, but that don't mean he ain't my flesh and blood." The minister replies: "Sometimes the herbs we take are bitter, sister, but we got to take them anyway. . . . You got to hold your family here together too. We can't let the bad mess up the good." (p. 153)

In a tragic ending, Jamal discovers the consequences of having the gun and makes an even greater personal discovery. There was "the part of him, a part that was small and afraid, that still wanted that gun" (p. 214). This poignant story reveals the complex problems facing two generations of people who are fighting for personal and family survival in a dangerous world.

In another book that is lighter in tone, *The Mouse Rap*, Walter Dean Myers uses a style that many readers enjoy. Students of children's literature can analyze the impact of the language as the main character, 14-year-old

Mouse, presents many of his views in rap. For example, Myers introduces his character in this way:

> Ka-phoomp! Ka-phoomp! Da Doom Da Dooom!
> Ka-phoomp! Ka-phoomp! Da Doom Da Dooom!
> You can call me Mouse, 'cause that's my tag
> I'm into it all, everything's my bag
> You know I can run, you know I can hoop
> I can do it alone, or in a group
> My ace is Styx, he'll always do
> Add Bev and Sheri, and you got my crew
> My tag is Mouse, and it'll never fail
> And just like a mouse I got me a tale
> Ka-phoomp! Ka-phoomp! Da Doom Da Dooom!
> Ka-phoomp! Ka-phoomp! Da Doom Da Dooom! (p. 3)

Read portions of the book aloud to gain the greatest response to the text.

The characters in all of these stories meet the criteria for outstanding characterization in literature: They are memorable individuals who face the best and the worst that life offers. They are portrayed with dignity and without stereotype.

Native American Books for Young Children

Native American characters frequently explore nature or develop close ties with their traditional roots. In *The Seasons and Someone*, Virginia Kroll uses a question-and-answer format to allow readers to accompany a young Inuit girl as she explores what happens during each of the seasons in the Arctic. For example, she asks in the spring, "What will happen when Wind's roars change to whispers and icicles grow thin?" (unnumbered). The text and illustrations indicate that "lichen will dapple rocks, imitating snowflakes. Ground Squirrel will scurry from her burrow. Ptarmigan's feathers will blend with brown brush again. Fox and Lemming will try to outrun each other. And Someone will laugh aloud to see buds on the berry bushes" (unnumbered). The text develops both descriptions of the environment and the importance of family life.

Like other contemporary realistic fiction for younger children, stories about Native Americans frequently depict themes related to love and family relationships. In Barbara Joosse's *Mama, Do You Love Me?*, set in the Arctic regions, a young girl tests her mother's love. Through satisfactory responses, the girl discovers that her mama loves her "more than the raven loves his treasure, more than the dog loves his tail, more than the whale loves his spout" (pp. 4–5). Each of the questions and responses relates to the culture.

A loving relationship between a Navajo girl and her grandmother provides the foundation in Miska Miles's *Annie and the Old One*. The conflict in the story develops because Annie does not want to accept the natural order of aging and death. In an effort to hold back time, Annie tries to prevent her grandmother from completing the rug that she is weaving because her grandmother has said, "My children, when the new rug is taken from the loom, I will go to Mother Earth" (p. 15). The author emphasizes the way Annie's inner conflict ends, and the theme that we are all part of nature emerges when Annie finally realizes:

> The cactus did not bloom forever. Petals dried and fell to earth. She knew that she was a part of the earth and the things on it. She would always be a part of the earth, just as her grandmother had always been, just as her grandmother would always be, always and forever. And Annie was breathless with the wonder of it. (p. 41)

Annie's actions show that she has accepted nature's inevitable role: She picks up the weaving stick and begins to help her grandmother complete the rug.

Native American Books for Middle- and Upper-Elementary Readers

Symbolism, ancient traditions, and person-against-self conflicts are important elements in Jean Craighead George's *The Talking Earth*, a book for middle-elementary readers in which a Seminole girl who lives on the Big

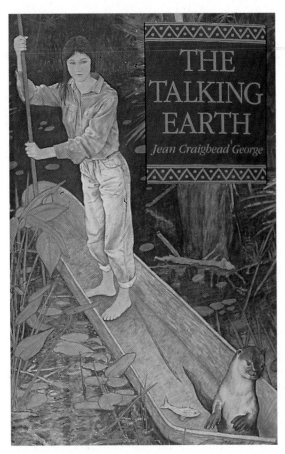

A contemporary Seminole girl searches for her heritage. From The Talking Earth *by Jean Craighead George. Jacket art copyright © 1983 by Bob Marstall. Reprinted by permission of HarperCollins Publishers.*

Cypress Reservation questions the traditions of her people and searches for her heritage as she travels alone through the swamp. Through her journey of self-discovery, she learns the importance of her ancient traditions.

Three stories with Eskimo protagonists show the range of subjects and conflicts that are covered in contemporary literature for this age group. In Jean Craighead George's *Water Sky,* Lincoln, a boy from Massachusetts, journeys to Barrow, Alaska, in search of his uncle. The conflict between cultures is reinforced by the boy's mother, who does not want Lincoln to make his journey. During his quest, Lincoln lives at a whaling camp, where he learns to understand and respect his Eskimo heritage. Throughout this story, George combines vivid settings and information about Eskimo values and beliefs.

In Gary Paulsen's *Dogsong,* Russel, a contemporary Eskimo boy, leaves the mechanized world in which his people hunt seal and caribou by snowmobiles to discover the ways and beliefs that were there in the days of dogsleds. Russel's mentor is an elderly Eskimo who believes that the Eskimo people have lost the songs that made the whales and other animals come to the people in times of need. Russel's search for his own song takes him on a 1,400-mile dogsled trek across the isolated ice and tundra. Through his ordeal with nature, Russel discovers the power of the old Eskimo ways.

In Scott O'Dell's *Black Star, Bright Dawn,* an Eskimo girl drives a dogsled team in the Iditarod Trail sled dog race from Anchorage to Nome. Through her experiences, the girl learns to depend on her dogs and herself. In addition, she discovers the strength in her Eskimo heritage, values, and beliefs.

In *Walk Two Moons,* Sharon Creech's heroine, 13-year-old Sal, is proud of her Native American heritage through her mother. Now she faces conflicts because her mother has left her. The author develops two parallel stories as the heroine tells the story of her best friend, Phoebe, and her experiences when Phoebe's mother left.

Many of the books for this age group focus on motifs of searching for one's heritage and using the information about heritage for self-discovery and to discover self-worth. The books have stronger themes related to the search for heritage than the books written for younger children.

Native American Books for Older Readers and Young Adults

Books written for older readers, especially those read by young adults, have harsher conflicts. Conflicts involving contrasting settings are often used to develop the plots in contemporary realistic fiction; the conflict frequently occurs when a protagonist leaves the reservation and lives in urban environments. For example, the protagonist in Robert Lipsyte's *The Brave* leaves the reservation and the support of his people to try to become a boxer in Manhat-

tan. In the city, he experiences the harsh underworld of violence, drugs, gangs, and prison. It is his heritage, however, and the teachings of his uncle about the Running Braves that make it possible for him to face his problems and control his life. Knowing oneself and relying on traditional teachings and cultural heritage are frequently shown as sources for personal strength.

Symbolism, traditional values, tribal customs, and conflict with contemporary society are common elements in Native American books written for older readers. For example, Jamake Highwater's "Ghost Horse Cycle," which includes *Legend Days, The Ceremony of Innocence,* and *I Wear the Morning Star,* is a series of books that follow three generations of a Northern Plains Indian family as they progress from a proud and powerful people to a people alienated from both their roots and the encroaching white culture. The cycle focuses on the life of Amana, a woman of power, courage, and tragedy, who symbolizes the fate of her people.

The importance of believing in the traditional ways of one's people is a main theme in *Legend Days.* This theme is developed through the "legend days" motif used throughout the book. Omens, powers, visions, and close relationships with animals and nature are important in both the plot and Amana's characterization. That alienation will result if one loses his or her identity is a strong theme in both *The Ceremony of Innocence* and *I Wear the Morning Star.* The theme is developed as Amana finds herself alienated from both her tribal ancestors and her half-French, half-Indian daughter. As she confronts her daughter, she reveals the importance of her tribal heritage and the depth of her alienation. The theme of the destructive force of alienation is reinforced through the unhappiness of two of Amana's children. When the characters try to deny their Native American heritage and struggle to become part of the white culture, they do not know their own identities.

The historical perspective of Highwater's *Legend Days* is based on accounts of life in the Northern Plains as found in the oral history of the Blackfoot Confederacy. The book is grounded in foundations typical of the mythology of the Great Plains. The social context of Highwater's *Ceremony of Innocence* and *I Wear the Morning Star* is similar to the context depicted by Native American authors writing for adult audiences. You will notice that although the books written for older students have harsher plots and conflicts, most of the Native American books portray strong relationships with nature and the importance of understanding one's heritage and traditions.

Latino Literature for Young Children

Values related to the importance of family bonds are central to most Latino literature written for younger readers. These values are reflected in Benjamin Alire Sáenz's *A*

Gift From Papá Diego. The story, written in both English and Spanish, highlights the importance of family relationships through the story of a young boy who wishes to spend his birthday with his grandfather who lives far away. The story has a happy ending and reinforces the importance of family values.

The importance of family bonds and family gatherings are also major values in Diane Gonzales Bertrand's *Uncle Chente's Picnic/El Picnic de Tío Chente.* In this bilingual story about a happy family gathering, the family prepares for a July Fourth celebration to honor a visiting uncle. A rainstorm and the loss of electricity do not ruin the picnic because Uncle Chente tells stories and shows the children how to make shadow animals with a flashlight, and Ernesto plays the guitar for singing and dancing. The time spent together makes a special day that the rain cannot ruin.

A house filled with family is the setting for Lulu Delacre's *Salsa Stories.* The New Year's Day setting is enhanced when Carmen Teresa is given a blank notebook. Family members tell her stories about other holidays and traditions that they believe would make good entries for the empty notebook. Because the stories are all about food, Carmen Teresa decides she will fill her notebook with family recipes. This book could be used to motivate a similar activity with students.

Another book that uses food as a focus is Pat Mora's bilingual text, *The Bakery Lady.* The book includes preparing for the Feast of the Three Kings (January 6) and describes close family relationships. One of the lines by the girl's grandmother highlights the theme of this story about a young girl who helps her grandparents in their bakery: "Bakers share the work, like families" (unnumbered). The text and illustrations are filled with holiday symbols such as piñata invitations, King's Rings, and special lemon cookies as well as frijoles and tamales.

The importance of friendship between an older man and a boy are themes in Avelino Hernandez's bilingual story, *The Boy and the Old Man.* When the boy watches the man going fishing each day without catching any fish, he solves the fishing problem by tossing leftover food into the water to attract the fish before the man arrives. Now the man catches fish, and a friendship results between the man and the boy. The collage illustrations that include seeds and dried flowers add to the visual enjoyment.

Leo Politi has written and illustrated a number of award-winning picture storybooks about Mexican American children living in Southern California. His *Song of the Swallows* tells the story of a young boy whose dear friend is the gardener and bell ringer at the mission of San Juan Capistrano. Politi shares Mexican American history with readers as the gardener tells Juan the story of the mission and of *las golondrinas,* the swallows who always return to the mission in the spring, on Saint Joseph's Day, and remain there until late summer. Politi's illustrations depict the Spanish architecture of the mission and demonstrate a young boy's love for plants and birds.

Song of the Swallows is a good source for readers to search for values and themes. For example, you will discover that Politi develops values such as respect for elders, love of history and nature, responsibility for care of the earth, and a belief in God. These themes show the importance of living in harmony with nature, respect for the past through the lessons of history, and respect for people who have this knowledge of the past.

Marie Hall Ets and Aurora Labastida's *Nine Days to Christmas: A Story of Mexico* tells of a kindergarten child who is excited because she is going to have her own special Christmas party, complete with a piñata. In the midst of numerous other everyday activities, Ceci chooses her piñata at the market, fills it with toys and candy, and joins the La Posada procession. After she sees her beautiful piñata being broken at the party, Ceci is unhappy until she sees a star in the sky that resembles her piñata. When children read this book, they relate to the girl's feelings and learn about the Mexican celebration of Christmas.

Latino Fiction for Middle-Elementary Grades

The fiction written for students in the middle-elementary grades deals with topics such as gaining feelings of self-worth and solving problems that are common for children of that age. Some of the stories that have inner-city settings develop tensions related to racial issues. Maia Wojciechowska's Newbery Award winner set in Spain, *Shadow of a Bull,* develops two themes: It is important to be true to oneself, and facing death is not the only way to demonstrate courage. Another Newbery Award book, Joseph Krumgold's *. . . And Now Miguel,* also has ties to Spain. This book, based on a full-length documentary film feature, is the story of the Chavez family, which has been raising sheep in New Mexico since before their region became part of the United States. Krumgold tells the story from the viewpoint of the middle child, Miguel, who, unlike his older brother, is too young to get everything he wants, and unlike his younger brother, is too old to be happy with everything he has. Miguel has a secret wish to accompany the older family members when they herd the sheep to the summer grazing land in the Sangria de Crest Mountains. With the help of San Ysidro, the patron saint of farmers, Miguel strives to make everyone see he is ready for this responsibility.

The 8-year-old in Nicholasa Mohr's *Felita* has lived in her Puerto Rican neighborhood of New York City for as long as she can remember. Mohr depicts the reasons for Felita's great love of her neighborhood. Conflict results when Felita's father decides that the family must move to a neighborhood with better schools and fewer threats of gang violence. In the new neighborhood, however, Felita experiences racism, and the family must rethink the move. Perhaps the neighborhood and the people in *Felita* seem so real because Mohr herself was born and grew up in a similar neighborhood in New York City.

Latino Fiction Written for Older Readers and Young Adults

Many of the conflicts developed in books for older readers express a harsher and even dangerous world. Some of the stories express conflicts as main characters try to cross borders or survive in the streets of major cities.

Gary Soto has written several contemporary books that appeal to readers. *Taking Sides* is a realistic story about a boy who moves from the barrio to the suburbs. The protagonist, who is a basketball player, must decide how he will respond when his new team plays his old team in a league game. Soto develops themes related to loyalty and friendship. In *Pacific Crossing,* the boys from the barrio participate in an exchange program in Japan.

The harsher, brutal realities of a border-town existence are described in two books for older readers written by Gary Paulsen. In *The Crossing,* the protagonist, Manny, dreams of crossing the border to live in America. In this story of a teenage boy who must use his wits to stay alive, Paulsen develops harsher themes such as you may need to lie as well as use your wits to survive in the streets; life is not always fair, but you should keep up the struggle; and one person can make a difference. *Sisters/Hermanas* also deals with the realities of a border town, including prostitution, prejudice, and explicit language. By telling the story of a young illegal immigrant and an Anglo girl from a wealthier family, Paulsen develops a person-against-society struggle that reflects some of the inequities of life. Even through these conflicts, Paulsen's characters develop positive values such as striving for success, believing in dreams, and working hard.

Sandra Cisneros's *The House on Mango Street* is another book that reflects the complexities of a neighborhood and a family and the conflicting feelings that may be found within a character. Through Esperanza's experiences, readers discover that the same place may be loving and cruel, safe and dangerous, and liked and hated. All of these emotions about a place are expressed as Esperanza struggles with life and the problems associated with growing up. Through the girl's struggles, Cisneros develops strong themes, such as that dreams and goals are always important; family ties are important; and you must be proud of your culture, your family history, and your success.

Asian and Asian American Books for Young Children

Picture books written for young children frequently focus on young Asian American children as they become familiar with various aspects of their culture. For example, in *Chin Chiang and the Dragon's Dance,* Ian Wallace creates a satisfactory conclusion for a person-against-self conflict. Young readers can understand Chin Chiang's conflict. He has practiced for and dreamed of dancing the dragon's dance on the first day of the Year of the Dragon. The time arrives, but he runs away because he fears he will not dance well enough to make his grandfather proud. With the help of a new friend, Chin Chiang discovers his dream can come true. Full-page watercolor paintings capture the beauty of the celebration and depict Asian influences on the city of Vancouver. Kate Waters and Madeline Slovenes-Low's *Lion Dancer: Ernie Wan's Chinese New Year* is a photographic essay that follows a boy as he prepares to take part in the very important lion dance. Readers can make interesting comparisons between these two books.

Numerous experiences in the life of a Vietnamese American are shown through a photographic essay in Diane Hoyt-Goldsmith's *Hoang Anh: A Vietnamese-American Boy.* Lawrence Migdale's photographs show the daily activities of Hoang Anh and his family in San Rafael, California, as they work on their fishing boat, live and play at home, prepare for the New Year, and experience the Tet Festival. Patricia McMahon's *Chi-Hoon: A Korean Girl* is a photograph essay that presents one week in the life of a girl.

Although Takaaki Nomura's picture storybook *Grandpa's Town* is set in Japan rather than in North America, the themes of the story relate to the universality of loving relationships between grandfathers and grandsons, possible loneliness after the death of a loved one, and preferences for staying with old friends. The story, written in

This photographic essay captures many experiences in the life of a Vietnamese American. From Hoang Anh: A Vietnamese-American Boy by Diane Hoyt-Goldsmith. Photographs copyright © 1992 by Lawrence Migdale. Reprinted by permission of Holiday House.

both Japanese and English, includes a great deal of cultural information. A young boy accompanies his grandfather around town, meets his grandfather's friends, and discovers his grandfather is not willing to leave these friends to move with the boy and his mother.

The importance of even small cultural artifacts, such as eating utensils, stimulates a humorous plot in Ina R. Friedman's *How My Parents Learned to Eat*. Friedman suggests the solution to a problem on the first page of this picture storybook: "In our house, some days we eat with chopsticks and some days we eat with knives and forks. For me, it's natural" (p. 1, unnumbered). The remainder of the book tells how an American sailor courts a Japanese girl, and each secretly tries to learn the other's way of eating. The couple reaches a satisfactory compromise because each person still respects the other's culture.

Asian and Asian American Books for Children in Middle-Elementary Grades

The widest range of Asian American experiences in current children's literature is found in the works of Laurence Yep. Yep writes with sensitivity about Chinese Americans who, like him, have lived in San Francisco, California. His characters overcome the stereotypes sometimes found in literature about Asian Americans, and his stories integrate information about Chinese cultural heritage into the everyday lives of his characters. In *Child of the Owl*, Yep develops the story of a heroine, 12-year-old Casey, who discovers she knows more about her father's world of racehorses than about her own Chinese heritage. It is only after she is sent to live with Paw-Paw, her grandmother in San Francisco's Chinatown, that she makes discoveries about, and learns to understand, her Chinese heritage. The author uses a story about the Owl Spirit to help Casey make discoveries about her history; the owl is a symbol that appears throughout the book. In an afterword, Yep states that the owl story "is based upon stories of filial devotion once popular among the Chinese and upon Chinese folklore concerning owls and other animals" (p. 217). In Yep's *Thief of Hearts* and *Later, Gator*, the characters also gain cross-cultural understanding.

Asian and Asian American Books for Upper-Elementary and Young Adult Readers

Two award-winning books appeal to older readers: Cynthia Kadohata's *Kira-Kira* (Newbery Award, 2005) and Gloria Whelan's *Homeless Bird* (National Book Award, 2000). In *Kira-Kira*, Kadohata first develops the strong and loving bonds between two Japanese American sisters, Lynn, the older sister, and Katie, the younger sister. This close relationship makes Katie's anguish believable as she sees her sister progress through the stages of a terminal illness. The author takes Katie through a series of feelings: She feels anger toward her sister for becoming ill, guilt about her own feelings about her sister, and finally accep-

tance of her sister's death. The author uses several techniques to allow readers to understand these emotions. For example, the younger sister writes the eulogy to read at the funeral, composes a school essay about a special memory about her sister, and reads her sister's diary that includes this last entry: "To Kate I leave my diary, my dictionary, and my encyclopedia, which she had *better* use" (p. 242). The book ends with a healing experience for the family as they take a vacation to a location by the Pacific Ocean where Lynn had wanted to visit. The author uses the meaning of the title of the book also to reveal information about the older sister: *Kira-kira* means "glistening" in Japanese. By learning more about Lynn, Katie discovers that her older sister had determination to make life shining. This is the lesson that Katie learns from her sister, a lesson that will influence the rest of her life.

New Immigrants to the United States

A number of authors of contemporary realistic fiction develop their plots on issues related to moving from one culture to a very different culture. Authors may focus on topics such as overcoming cultural differences, facing racial problems, developing friendships, and continuing family relationships. For example, Kashmira Sheth, the author of *Blue Jasmine*, moves the heroine, Seema, and her family from a small town in India where they lived within a tightly knit extended family, to Iowa City, Iowa, where the father has a research position. The author explores Seema's reactions to language differences as she tries to expand her English, to cultural differences such as school behavior, to differences in how holidays are celebrated, and to the very different climate and settings. The author includes racial difficulties as Seema interacts with a classmate who shows considerable prejudice against people she considers to be different.

Sheth uses several techniques to help readers understand Seema's experiences and emotions. For example, Seema writes letters to friends in India in which she describes both joys and frustrations. A considerable amount of Indian history is revealed as Seema delivers her class project: an oral report on Kasturba Gandhi. As she gives this report, the author develops a turning point incident during which Seema feels stronger and calmer as she talks about one of her national heroines. The author summarizes some of Seema's attitudes about the United States when Seema compares her experiences to the game of "Chutes and Ladders": "Many days when I did well in school and talked to my friends, I felt that I'd climbed a ladder, but then there were days when I slid down the chutes" (p. 172). The author uses the symbolism of the blue jasmine found in the title of the book in several places: To show that the main character can bloom in two worlds, Seema compares the sweet-smelling jasmine found in India and a blue hyacinth that blooms in Iowa.

Mitali Perkins's *The Sunita Experiment*, another book with cultural foundations in India, is about a family from

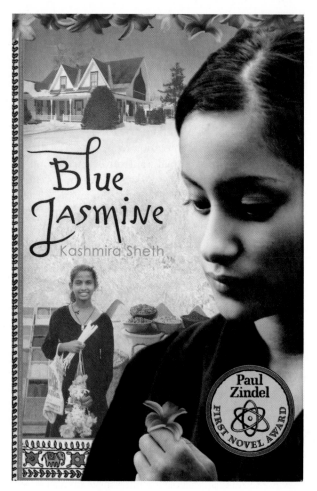

Cover from BLUE JASMINE by Kashmira Sheth. Jacket Illustration © 2004 by Kim McGillivray. Used by permission of Hyperion Books for Children.

India who now lives in California. The book provides strong literary elements of character, conflict, and theme, as well as examples of cultural beliefs. The protagonist, Sunita, is a 13-year-old girl whose life in California changes when her grandparents come for a visit from India. Three generations are represented in the story: the grandparents who have come to visit; the parents, who are from India but who have become Westernized; and their daughter, Sunita, who is totally Westernized and wants to remain that way. The clash of cultures is the main conflict of the story as Sunita struggles to understand her grandparents' culture.

The author depicts changes in Sunita as her character progresses from rejection of her cultural roots to acceptance of and appreciation for her cultural identity. For example, early in the book, she experiences conflict in school because she does not want to identify her "roots" on a *National Geographic* map and then experiences additional feelings of person-against-self conflict when most of the class identifies European ancestry. After her grand-

parents arrive, Sunita is embarrassed by the differences between her home and the homes of her friends. She resents the playing of Indian music in her home because the "twanging sitar music . . . grated on her nerves and made their house sound like a mecca for aging hippies. A grumpy neighbor had already complained three times since Sunita's grandparents had arrived" (p. 19). As you read this book, decide whether the author develops plausible characterization of, and conflict for, a girl living in two cultures.

In *Tangled Threads: A Hmong Girl's Story*, author Pegi Deitz Shea also develops the theme that even though the experiences are challenging, it is possible to live in two cultures without giving up the cultural traditions that are part of a family's foundations. Shea takes her protagonist, Mai, from a crowded refugee camp in Thailand, where she and her grandmother have lived for 10 years, to a Hmong community in Providence, Rhode Island. Mai goes through cultural conflicts such as learning the American language and facing the often negative attitudes of American students. The strong Hmong beliefs are reinforced as her grandmother tries to retain cultural ties, including belief in the shaman's healing powers. The title of the book reflects the Hmong skill of creating beautiful storycloths, but it also suggests that the heroine must untangle the threads in her own life before she can use them to weave a story that allows her to accept and understand her new American way of life.

In *Honeysuckle House*, Andrea Cheng uses alternating chapters to tell the stories of fourth-grade Sarah, a Chinese American, and Ting, a new immigrant from China. This technique allows the author to develop each of their stories in the first person.

Memory, seeds, and traditional beliefs are very important in Sherry Garland's *The Lotus Seed*, a book written for younger children. In this story, a Vietnamese family resettles in the United States. During happier days in Vietnam, the grandmother picks a seed from a lotus plant in the emperor's garden to remember a special occasion. Throughtout her life, she looks at this seed during important moments or when she feels sad. The seed is so important that she brings it to the United States when her family escapes the war. Garland develops a universal theme about how small things and the memories they evoke are important in our lives.

Adjusting to a new culture and gaining understanding of oneself and others are problems many new Americans face. Lensey Namioka's *Yang the Youngest and His Terrible Ear* is a humorous contemporary realistic fiction story that speaks to the needs of many readers. The author portrays a protagonist, 9-year-old Yingtao, who is out of place in his musical family: Although he has a great eye, he has a terrible ear. Students of children's literature can analyze Yingtao's reactions to both learning English and trying to make his family understand he is not, and will never be, a talented musician. The author helps readers visualize the problems by relating them to Yingtao's Chinese background. In a satisfying ending, both the family of his American friend and Yingtao's own family realize the importance of honoring one's gifts. *Yang the Third and Her Impossible Family* is a humorous sequel in which Yingmei Yang, the family's third daughter, tries her best to learn to be an American.

The challenges of many immigrant Latino families are depicted in Susan Middleton Elya's *Home at Last.* When the family moves from Mexico to the United States, they face problems learning English and adjusting to a new culture. As 8-year-old Ana learns English, she practices her new language at home and she and her father encourage her mother to attend English as a Second Language classes. The text shows the importance of the family as they support each other and overcome challenges.

Animal Stories, Mysteries, Sports Stories, and Humor

Animal stories include stories about dogs, horses, and birds. Mysteries use clues and suspense to help readers develop their powers of observation. Sports stories may be about baseball, football, or flying. Humorous stories use ridiculous situations, exaggeration, and the unexpected to create humor.

Animals

The animals in contemporary realistic fiction are quite different from the animals in traditional literature and modern fantasy: Whereas in traditional literature and modern fantasy, animals talk and act like people or have other magical powers, the animals in realistic fiction have a strong sense of reality and sometimes tragedy. Realistic animal stories place specific demands on authors. When evaluating realistic animal stories for children, you should consider the following questions:

1. Does the author portray animals objectively, without giving them human thoughts or motives?

2. Does the behavior of the animal characters agree with information provided by knowledgeable observers of animals and authorities on animal behavior?

3. Does the story encourage children to respond to the needs of animals or the need of people to love animals without being too sentimental or melodramatic?

Authors who write credible animal stories often depict warm relationships between children and pets. The conflict in such stories usually occurs when something happens to disrupt the security of a pet's life. The antagonist may be a physical change in the animal, an environment different from the pet's secure home, or a human character whose treatment of the animal is cruel or even life threatening. Detailed descriptions of physical changes, settings that become antagonists, or cruel human characters may encourage children to understand the vulnerability of animals to such forces.

Credible stories about wild animals usually reflect research about animal behavior and natural habitats. Conflict may arise when animals face natural enemies, when humans take them from natural surroundings and place them in domestic environments, or when humans hunt or trap them.

Some authors use animal-against-society or animal-against-person conflicts to advocate protection of animals. Other authors stress the human development made possible by interaction with animals. Many authors also stress the positive effects of loyalty and devotion between humans and animals.

Consider, for example, the various techniques Theodore Taylor uses in *The Trouble With Tuck.* Taylor first develops a believably close relationship between Helen and her golden Labrador. Helen's love for Tuck and her family's devotion to the dog are strengthened by two incidents in which Tuck saves Helen from harm or possible death. The reactions of the family members when the veterinarian declares that Tuck is going blind and cannot be helped reflect their devotion to the dog and make plausible their acceptance of Helen's resolution of the problem. This story, based on a true incident, emphasizes determination, loyalty, and self-confidence that may develop because of animal and human interaction.

In *Shiloh,* Phyllis Reynolds Naylor uses several techniques to develop the theme that cruelty to animals is wrong. For example, Marty thinks that something really hurts inside when a dog cringes like that. The theme is emphasized when the author compares a jar of lightning bugs to a chained dog: Both are prisoners. The thoughts of others reveal the theme when Marty's father tells Marty to open his eyes and understand that there are many hard-hearted people. In the end, Marty is able to bargain for Shiloh because Judd, Shiloh's cruel owner, illegally killed a deer and Marty saw him. *Shiloh Season* is a sequel to the book and extends the conflict between Marty and Judd.

Horse stories also have qualities that make them marvelous for children. The horses and their owners, or would-be owners, usually have devoted relationships. Often, the little horse that may have been laughed at or scorned becomes the winner of a race and begins a famous line of horses. Sadness in many of these stories results when both horse and owner must overcome severe obstacles and even mistreatment.

Two outstanding authors of horse stories are Marguerite Henry and Walter Farley. Henry's stories reflect research and knowledge about horses and their trainers, and

A strong relationship is developed between an abused dog and a boy. (From Shiloh, by Phyllis Reynolds Naylor. Copyright © 1991 by Phyllis Reynolds Naylor. Published by Atheneum, an imprint of Macmillan Publishing Company. Reprinted by permission of Dilys Evans Fine Illustrations.)

several of them report the history of a breed of horses. One memorable story narrates the ancestry of Man o' War, the greatest racehorse of his time. In *King of the Wind*, readers travel back 200 years to the royal stables of a sultan of Morocco, where Agba, a young horse tender, has a dream of glory for a golden Arabian stallion with a white chest.

The boy and the horse travel from Morocco to France when the Sultan sends six of his best horses to King Louis XV. The king rejects the horses, which have become thin from their voyage. Agba and the once-beautiful Sham are handed over to several degrading and even cruel masters before the English Earl of Godolphin discovers their plight and takes them home with him. In England, Agba's dream comes true. Three of the golden Arabian's offspring win various important races. When the great Arabian horse, renamed the Godolphin Arabian, stands before royalty, Agba's thoughts flash back to a promise that he made in Morocco:

> "My name is Agba. Ba means father. I will be a father to you, Sham, and when I am grown I will ride you before the multitudes. And they will bow before you, and you will be the king of the Wind. I promise it." He had kept his word! (p. 169)

A beautiful black stallion and his descendants are the chief characters in a series of books written by Walter Farley. The first, *The Black Stallion*, introduces a beautiful wild horse that is being loaded onto a large ship. On this same ship is Alec Ramsay, who understands and loves horses. The two are brought together as the ship sinks, and the black horse pulls Alec through the waves to a small deserted island. Friendship develops as the two help each other survive, and Alec discovers the joy of racing on the back of the amazing horse.

Mysteries

Mysteries provide escape and enjoyable reading because of their suspense. They allow children to become involved in the solutions through clues. They also suggest that children themselves—if they are observant, creative, and imaginative—can solve mysteries.

Footsteps on a foggy night, disappearing people, mysterious strangers, and unusual occurrences woven together into exciting, fast-placed plots create mystery stories that appeal to older children. One 11-year-old girl, an avid reader of mysteries, listed the following four characteristics that make a mystery exciting for her: (1) It should have an exciting plot that holds the interest of readers, (2) it should contain suspense, (3) it should have enough clues to allow readers to follow the action, and (4) the clues should be written in such a way that readers can try to discover "who done it." In answer to the question "What has caused your interest in mysteries?" she replied that she had read Donald J. Sobol's *Encyclopedia Brown* in third grade and enjoyed trying to follow the clues. She said that her favorite suspense story was Virginia Hamilton's *The House of Dies Drear*, a tale about the Underground Railroad.

Observation plays an important role in Robert Newman's mysteries, which are set in the London of Sherlock Holmes's time. *The Case of the Baker Street Irregular* includes suspense, sinister characters who must be outwitted, and several mysteries that seem not to be related but actually are.

In *The Original Freddie Ackerman*, Hadley Irwin introduces readers to the two personalities of Trevor Frederick Ackerman, who is going reluctantly to spend the summer with his great-aunts on an island off the coast of Maine. As you read the following quote, notice how Irwin separates the real experience from the imaginary one:

> As they waited for the traffic light to turn green, he wondered what would happen if he opened the car door

Technology Resources Visit the Companion Website at www.prenhall.com/norton to link to a site on which Joan Lowery Nixon guides you through the process of writing a mystery.

and disappeared. Great-Aunt Calla would probably be relieved, and Great-Aunt Louisa, sitting beside him, might not even notice, since she hadn't looked over at him yet and, besides that, seemed to have used up her quota of words for the day.

Freddie Ackerman, World War II ace, his B-24 Liberator bomber shot down in flames and his parachute buried deep in the Black Forest, would never allow himself to be captured alive with all the secret invasion plans he was carrying. Freddie Ackerman would fling open the car door, slide down into the river that bordered the autobahn, and fade like a ghost into the rain and mist of the German countryside. (p. 6)

Trevor's eccentric aunts provide mysterious quests for information to entice his interest. On the island, Trevor searches for physical evidence that will identify whether a book is a first edition. Strong relationships between the aunts and Trevor help him overcome feelings of alienation in his life.

Ellen Raskin's several books challenge readers to join often preposterous characters in working out puzzle clues, which include word puzzles, a series of obscurely written messages, and even observations gained through reading. *The Mysterious Disappearance of Leon (I Mean Noel)* is a humorous word puzzle, a game about names, liberally sprinkled with clues. As the story of Leon and Little Dumpling, the heirs to Mrs. Carillon's Pomato Soup fortune, proceeds, Raskin informs readers that there is a very important clue in a particular section or that they should mark the locations of Leon's 14 messages because they contain important clues. Noel's final words, for example, as he bobs up and down in the water cause Little Dumpling years of searching. What is meant by "Noel glub C blub all . . . I glub new . . ."?

Running With the Reservoir Pups, by Colin Bateman, is an action-packed, fast-paced, humorous caper. The book is full of good and evil characters, a plot filled with mystery, and a boy hero. This mystery involves a group of scrappy gang members who rule the streets of Belfast, a kidnapping plot to steal babies, an evil owner of a cosmetic firm who wants to use the babies to formulate a beauty cream, and a boy hero who thwarts the kidnappers, rescues the babies, and saves his mother from the kidnappers. The author uses a technique that allows readers to review the plot and the increasing tension: Eddie, the protagonist, frequently summarizes to himself how he reaches a certain point in the story. For example, he tries to figure out what makes his life messed up every time he means to do good things: "In a matter of days he had changed from being a nice young fella from the country into a burglar, a liar and a bully. . . . He had made enemies of the Reservoir Pups and the Andytown Albinos, the security guards at the hospital and the police. He had made one new friend in Barney, then stole his bike. And had given it away for the price of a phone call, a call which had landed him in even deeper water" (p. 134).

Suspense, revenge, and mysterious happenings are all part of Robert Cormier's mystery for older readers, *In the Middle of the Night*. The novel begins with a foreshadowing of the suspense to follow: "Ten minutes later, Lulu was dead. And the nightmare began" (p. 9). Cormier uses several techniques to encourage readers to understand the conflict and its influence on the characters. For example, he described the son's reactions to his father as he burns letters, responds to reporters, and sees his face flashing on television. Cormier's *Tenderness*, the portrait of a serial killer, is another taut mystery for older readers.

Sports

Sports stories rate highly with children who are sports enthusiasts. In fact, some quite reluctant readers will finish a book about their favorite sport or sports hero. Many stories deal with the ideal of fair play, the values of sports, the overcoming of conflicts between fathers and sons, and the overcoming of fears connected with sports. Unfortunately, many of the stories are didactic and have familiar plot lines and stock characters.

Sports stories for children are also apparently important to sport franchises. Karen Raugust (1997) reports a merger between major league sports teams and the publishing of sports-related books. According to a director of marketing for the National Hockey League, "the sport depends on the long-term development of fans. Publishing helps to support all of the other fan development programs" (p. 35).

Some authors who write about baseball imply that the sport has therapeutic value. Often, the emphasis in these books is on the role that baseball can play in helping children overcome problems at home, develop new friendships, face physical disabilities, or feel accomplishment. Matt Christopher's *The Fox Steals Home*, for example, tells the story of troubled Bobby Canfield, who is facing his parents' divorce and the prospect of his father's taking a job far from home. His father and his grandfather have coached him and nicknamed him "Fox." His proudest moment comes when he steals home and demonstrates to his father what a good player he has become.

Overcoming a severe accident in which a baseball player loses an eye provides the plot and the conflict in Scott Johnson's *Safe at Second*. This is also a strong story of friendship in which a best friend helps a boy who had been destined for the major leagues.

In *Herbie Jones and the Monster Ball*, Suzy Kline humorously develops a story about a young boy who hates baseball until his uncle coaches a baseball team for 8- and 9-year-olds. The book does not stereotype girls, who play on the team. The boy's older sister also gives him baseball lessons.

Written for older readers, Chris Crutcher's *Athletic Shorts* is a collection of six short stories about various types

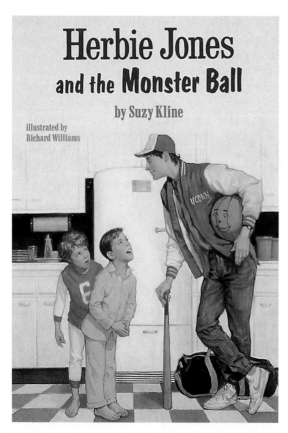

Humor is added to a story about a reluctant ballplayer. (From Herbie Jones and the Monster Ball, by Suzy Kline, illustrations by Richard Williams, copyright © 1988 by Richard Williams. Reprinted by permission of G. P. Putnam's Sons.)

of athletes. The characters in many of these stories are taken from Crutcher's earlier books.

Flying provides the adventure in Betsy Byars's *Coast to Coast.* Developing a strong grandfather-and-grand-daughter relationship, Byars takes readers on an adventurous trip in a Piper Cub when the grandfather and his granddaughter fly from South Carolina to California. This book shows that girls can be just as adventurous as boys.

Matt Christopher's collection of sports stories includes almost every sport. His titles include *Skateboard Renegade,* in which a boy faces a challenge when he tries to fit in with his friends; *Soccer Duel,* in which team rivalry and friendship are in conflict; *Wheel Wizards,* in which a boy learns to play basketball from a wheelchair; and *Tennis Ace,* in which a girl is unhappy when her father ignores her talent and focuses on her brother.

HUMOR

Humorous stories, whether involving figures of fantasy or realistic people living in the contemporary world, are among children's favorites. Authors who write about humorous situations that could happen to real people (these situations and characters may stretch probability) allow

children to understand that life can be highly entertaining and that it is not always serious. Writers may encourage readers to laugh at themselves and at numerous human foibles. Humorous situations and characters also can highlight real problems and make reading about them palatable.

Authors of humorous realistic fiction use many of the sources of humor discussed in Chapter 5—wordplay, surprise and the unexpected, exaggeration, and ridiculous situations. For example, authors may use a play on words or ideas to create humorous situations or clarify characters' feelings. Consider Betsy Byars's *The Cybil War,* an entertaining story about a fifth-grade boy who has a crush on a girl. The war develops as Cybil Ackerman responds in various ways to Simon's advances, which his best friend intentionally misinterprets.

Judy Blume uses a surprising and unexpected situation in *Tales of a Fourth Grade Nothing.* In this story, a humorous conflict between two brothers is brought to a climax when the younger boy swallows the older brother's pet turtle. An unexpected situation provides humor in Lois Lowry's *Anastasia on Her Own* when a naive cook, trying to prepare a gourmet dinner, asks for and receives cooking advice from a stranger who is calling to sell tap dancing lessons.

An unexpected situation in Anne Fine's *Alias Madame Doubtfire* occurs when an ex-husband disguises himself as a cleaning woman and babysitter in his ex-wife's house. The humorous and surprising situations in Joan Bauer's *Squashed* occur when a girl tries to grow the largest pumpkin for the Rock River Pumpkin Weigh-In; she tries everything, including playing motivational tapes to make the pumpkin grow.

Comic twists, flamboyant characters, and humorous situations are part of the pleasure in reading Polly Horvath's *When the Circus Came to Town.* Although most of the incidents are humorous, the actions of the characters reflect and highlight human foibles, and the main characters learn something about themselves when they experience situations that are more humorous to readers than to them.

CONTEMPORARY REALISTIC FICTION FOR YOUNG ADULTS

Books written specifically for young adults frequently have more mature themes and situations that older readers may face. The characters may confront difficult situations and need to make painful decisions. The books, however, usually have a hopeful message as the young protagonists deal with their problems. For example, in *Saving Francesca,* author Melina Marchetta depicts a family facing the severe depression of the normally outspoken and active mother. Her depression is seen primarily through the viewpoint of

Through The Eyes of an AUTHOR

Eve Bunting

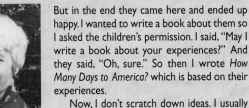

Visit the CD-ROM that accompanies this text to generate a complete list of Eve Bunting titles.

Selected Titles by Eve Bunting:
Butterfly House
Fly Away Home
The Wall
How Many Days to America? A Thanksgiving Story
The Lambkins

When I came from Ireland to the United States, I came in a plane. Actually it was a pretty small plane. When I think about it, I can't imagine coming all the way over the ocean and all the way over the North Pole in a little plane like that. But we came and we had relatives to come to and it was pretty easy for us.

But a friend of mine in Los Angeles who is a teacher had children in her class who spoke something like thirty different languages among them. A lot of them had come to the United States as immigrants, often in small boats, and it was hard for them coming here. I had asked my friend if she could tell me about her students and she said, "No, I'll ask them to write their experiences for you."

So they all wrote their experiences for me, and many of them suffered severe hardships.

But in the end they came here and ended up happy. I wanted to write a book about them so I asked the children's permission. I said, "May I write a book about your experiences?" And they said, "Oh, sure." So then I wrote *How Many Days to America?* which is based on their experiences.

Now, I don't scratch down ideas. I usually have a terrible memory, but when I'm thinking about a book I remember every little detail. I never really make outlines. I think it all out very carefully before I write anything. With a picture book, I would say I know every word before I write it down. So when people ask, "How long did it take you to write a picture book?," I have to really give it some consideration, because sometimes I've been thinking about it off and on for a long, long time. I wrote a book called *The Wall,* which is about the Vietnam Veteran's Memorial in Washington, DC. I really thought about that book for three years before I wrote it. When I actually began to write it, I had every word in my head, so I was able to write it very quickly. It seems silly to say it took three years, but it really did.

I got the idea for *Nasty Stinky Sneakers* because I saw an article in the paper about a competition in some school or town for who had the nastiest, stinkiest sneakers and I thought "Boy, if my two sons were just the right age to go in for that competition, they would win." So I decided to write the *Nasty Stinky Sneakers* book. I had so much fun writ-

ing that book. I have fun writing all of my books, but that was a particularly fun one. Then after I had written it and published it, the publisher decided that they were going to have a nasty, stinky sneaker competition in different classrooms. And so they organized these competitions at different schools. It was really neat because what happened was that first the kids brought their nasty, stinky sneakers into the classroom and then they asked me if I would judge this competition nationwide. I said, "I don't think so." I love my book and I love my work, but I just didn't think I wanted to do that!

So they had the students create poems about their nasty, stinky sneakers or do drawings; some of them even made sculptures. They were really great. My whole house was covered with all of these things while I tried to decide. My husband helped choose the best one, which actually turned out to be a long poem a boy had written. As the prize, his whole class was given new, not nasty, not stinky, but brand new sneakers.

Video Profiles: The accompanying video contains more of this conversation with Eve Bunting, as well as conversations with Lynne Cherry and Mary E. Lyons concerning students' responses to literature.

16-year-old Francesca. The protagonist also faces person-against-person and person-against-society conflicts as she encounters problems when she attends a parochial school that has just turned coed. The author illustrates the devastation in Francesca's life by describing home life with a mother who always plans her daughter's life, motivates her in the morning with music, and requires recitations about activities. When the mother is unable to provide all of this support, Francesca realizes that she does not know who she is without her mother's interactions. By the close of the book, Francesca realizes her mother's struggle and discovers that she, Francesca, has survived the year and is looking forward to her senior year.

Jason Blake, the 16-year-old protagonist in Pete Hautman's National Book Award winner, *Godless,* goes through a cynical response to organized religion, especially to his father's desire to save his soul. As part of his rebellion, he develops his own religion based on the water tower as god. The author provides the reactions of several of his friends as they create sacraments, their own creation

myth, and commandments to accompany their worship. However, when the members start to take the religion seriously, dangerous occurrences result. At this point, Jason realizes that it is a lot easier to invent a religion than to control it. By the end of the book, he learns that faith—in something—is important.

Many of the books written for young adult readers focus on the protagonists' struggle for self-identity and acceptance. For example, in *Orphea Proud,* Sharon Dennis Wyeth develops a story in which 17-year-old Orphea struggles with the realization that she is lesbian. The author uses metaphors to describe Orphea's stages of understanding her emotions. She first feels love for a female friend that resembles a small bubble of surprise. Next, this bubble of joy turns into a small geyser of emotion. She develops feelings of panic as she questions these emotions and realizes that her brother fears and hates lesbians. She finally accepts her feelings, and the dark cloud begins to lift. In addition to developing Orphea's emotional responses, the author explores societal attitudes toward

Through the Eyes of a Child

Riley
Grade 5

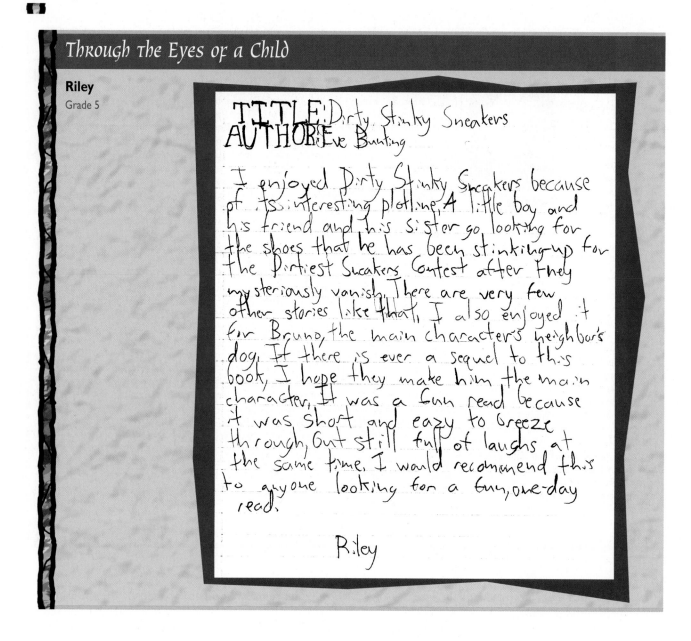

TITLE: Dirty Stinky Sneakers

AUTHOR: Eve Bunting

I enjoyed Dirty Stinky Sneakers because of its interesting plotline. A little boy and his friend and his sister go looking for the shoes that he has been stinking-up for the Dirtiest Sneakers Contest after they mysteriously vanish. There are very few other stories like that. I also enjoyed it for Bruno, the main character's neighbor's dog. If there is ever a sequel to this book, I hope they make him the main character. It was a fun read because it was short and eazy to breeze through, but still full of laughs at the same time. I would recommend this to anyone looking for a fun, one-day read.

Riley

homosexuality that range from hatred and fear to understanding and acceptance.

The conflict in *Luna*, by Julie Anne Peters, results as a teenage boy named Liam struggles with issues of his sex: He feels that he is a girl trapped within his boy's body. In a story that focuses on transgender issues, the author writes through the point of view of the younger sister who witnesses Liam's emotional trauma as he tries to transform himself into Luna by using cosmetics and dressing in girls'

clothing. As in *Orphea Proud,* the author illustrates the negative attitudes of classmates and adults toward people who are different. In a touching conclusion, Liam, now Luna, confesses to his sister: "'You are beautiful. Inside and out. You're kind and generous, compassionate and caring. You're the most caring person in the world. You saved me; you know you did. If you hadn't been there for me, Re, all those years. . . . Don't you know, you're the girl I always wanted to be'" (p. 246).

An In-Depth Analysis of a Contemporary Realistic Fiction Novel for Young Adults

How I Live Now, by Meg Rosoff, is the 2005 winner of the Printz Award for Excellence in Young Adult Literature and the 2004 winner of The Guardian Children's Fiction Prize. The book provides an excellent source for an in-depth analysis because it illustrates how authors frequently use more mature themes and content in young adult literature. This more mature content of this book is expressed by critic Meg McCaffrey (2005) when she states that it "deals with a mix of grief, first love, sex, anorexia, self-discovery, growing up, modern-day warfare, the struggle to survive, and ultimately unconditional love" (p. 47).

The book also shows how authors of contemporary realistic fiction are influenced by the circumstances in which they live. In an interview with McCaffrey, Rosoff describes how she was influenced by the war in Yugoslavia, her feelings about the still-visible destruction in London as a result of World War II, and the United States invasion of Iraq. In *How I Live Now,* the author uses a contemporary setting in which the characters are threatened by terrorists to develop strong characters who have coming-of-age experiences and to express an antiwar theme.

The main characters in the book are 15-year-old Daisy and her cousin Edmond, who are left alone in rural England following a series of terrorist attacks. This contact with modern-day warfare enables Rosoff to develop both the close relationship between Daisy and her cousin and Daisy's character traits that allow her to survive and to eventually help Edmond. Without understanding the loving relationship between Daisy and Edmond, readers would have difficulty believing in Daisy's actions when she happily becomes Edmond's caregiver at the end of the book. This setting and the characters' actions also allow the author to develop the theme: War has terrible consequences.

Rosoff depicts the consequences of war when the cousins' farm is sequestered by soldiers and they are eventually separated. She develops a strong antiwar theme as the teens witness the brutality of the terrorists, and Edmond, after witnessing a massacre by the terrorists, is unable to communicate. The author links the antiwar theme and the coming-of-age content when Daisy and a physically and psychologically disabled Edmond are finally reunited. Notice how the author uses the symbolism of the healing power of a garden to suggest Daisy's maturity and the antiwar theme: After Daisy describes herself as a gardener, she reveals why when she says, "It was the only way to talk to him, not with words, but with hard work and the feel of old tools, and with fat bulbs buried and waiting deep in the rich soil. I watched him and learned from him, digging and planting and making things grow. I needed to be there with him in the sunshine, planting tiny seeds in the crumbling earth and willing them to flower" (p. 194).

The author extends this garden symbolism to Daisy's coming-of-age discoveries and to the antiwar theme when Daisy realizes that this is where she wants to be because she and Edmond are together and because she can give Edmond the two things he needs most: to live in peace and to be loved. Daisy's response to Edmond also reveals the power of unconditional love. The characters in this book for young adults face and eventually overcome difficulties that go beyond the plots in books written for younger readers. There are no simple solutions in this book, or the typical happily-ever-after ending found in most books for younger readers. *How I Live Now* also reflects an author's response to the actual circumstances that could influence the life of young adults in the 21st century.

Teaching With Realistic Fiction

I f realistic fiction is to help children identify with others, extend their horizons, and gain personal insights, then adults who work with children must be aware of a wide range of realistic fiction and activities. It is not necessary, or even advisable, to attach literature-related activities to all realistic fiction that children read, but some activities are appropriate.

This section considers how to use realistic fiction to stimulate role playing that strengthens understanding of the world and offers suggestions for handling real problems. It also takes an in-depth look at a children's literature unit that stresses the theme of island survival. In addition to activities and discussions stressing the influence of settings on the conflicts in stories, a unit may relate literature to the science curriculum through activities that increase understanding of geography and botany. The section concludes with questioning strategies that can accompany realistic fiction or any other genre of literature.

Using Role Playing

Role playing is a creative dramatics activity in which children consider a problem, contemplate possible actions of people in reaction to the problem, and then act out the situation as they believe it might unfold in real life. According to child-development authorities, role playing fosters social development, increases problem-solving capabilities, and enhances creativity. Role playing helps children develop an understanding of the world around them and enhances their understanding of various ways to handle common problems.

Shaffer (1989) provides guidelines that can help you select meaningful role-playing activities. He adapts Robert Selman's stages of social perspective and describes characteristic student responses to others' perspectives. Understanding these typical responses can help you plan activities and observe or interact with students during role playing. For example, 3- to 6-year-olds are unaware of any perspective other than their own; 6- to 8-year-olds recognize that people have perspectives different from theirs; 8- to 10-year-olds know that their points of view can conflict with others'; 10- to 12-year-olds can consider their own and another person's point of view simultaneously; and 12- to 15-year-olds attempt to understand another person's perspective by comparing it with that of the social system in which they operate.

Literature can be the stimulus for activities that satisfy the purposes of role playing. Use realistic picture books about doctors, dentists, and other neighborhood helpers to encourage young children to act out the roles of adults with whom they come in contact. Such role playing can decrease children's fears by allowing them to experience a role before facing a real situation. Use books about families to encourage children to role-play interactions between different members of a family, nuclear or extended.

The plots in realistic fiction provide many opportunities for children to role-play problems. Zena Sutherland (1997) recommends that literature selected for stimulating, thought-provoking problem situations should (1) contain characters who are well developed and have clearly defined problems; (2) have plots that contain logical stopping places so that children can role-play the endings; (3) include problems, such as universal fears and concerns, that allow children to identify with the situations; and (4) present problems that help children develop their personal value systems. In role playing, you can either choose stories in which problems are developed to certain points and then have children role-play the unfinished situations or have children role-play various solutions to problems after they have read or listened to whole stories.

Sutherland recommends the following procedures for role playing: First, encourage students to think about what will happen next in the story, to consider how the story might end, and to identify with the characters. Second, ask the students to describe the characters and then to play those roles. Third, ask the audience to observe and to decide if the solution is a realistic one. Fourth, ask the students who are role playing to decide what they will do to practice dialogue; encourage them to describe the staging they will use. Fifth, have the students role-play the situation, with each student playing the character that he or she represents. The focus should be solving a problem, not acting. Sixth, engage the players and the audience in a discussion of the role playing, the consequences of the actions, and alternative behaviors. Next, have the role players try new interpretations based on the ideas generated from the discussion. Finally, encourage students to assess the outcomes and determine the best ways to deal with the problems.

The books of realistic fiction discussed in this chapter offer many stimuli for role-playing situations. Because the books are categorized according to their content, refer to this chapter when searching for specific situations connected with family life, peer relationships, individuality, and so forth. The following books also contain problem situations that adults have used to stimulate children's role playing in connection with family life (Norton, 1992):

Family Life

1. *Responsibility toward family members (picture books).* Patricia Gauch's *Christina Katerina and the Time She Quit the Family. Problem:* What should happen in a family when a child wants to do only what pleases her and not what would make her part of the family? Mavis Jukes's *Like Jake and Me. Problem:* How should a stepfather and his new son adjust to each other? Phyllis Naylor's *Keeping a Christmas Secret. Problem:* How can a child redeem himself when he reveals an important family secret? How should the rest of the family respond?

2. *Interpersonal relationships.* Sharon Bell Mathis's *The Hundred Penny Box. Problem:* How should a boy respond when he makes friends with his great-great-aunt and tries to explain her feelings about an old box of pennies to his mother? How should the aunt and the mother interact with each other? Patricia C. McKissack's *The Honest-to-Goodness Truth. Problem:* What is the best way to tell the truth without hurting someone's feelings?

3. *Making difficult decisions.* Jeannie Baker's *Where the Forest Meets the Sea. Problem:* How can difficult ecological decisions be made so that the forest and the seashore will be protected? How should the boy let his grandfather know that he understands the problem? Dayal Khalsa's *I Want a Dog. Problem:* How can you convince your family that you are responsible enough to own a pet? Theodore Taylor's *The Trouble With Tuck. Problem:* How should a family respond when the dog goes blind?

4. *Family disturbances.* Carol Lea Benjamin's *The Wicked Stepdog.* Problem: How should a girl, her father, and her new stepmother act when the father remarries? What can they each do to accept each other? Beverly Cleary's *Dear Mr. Henshaw.* Problem: How can a boy overcome his problems related to his parents' divorce? What should the mother, the father, and the boy say to each other? How can the parents help the boy understand what has happened to his family? Janet Taylor Lisle's *Afternoon of the Elves.* Problem: How should a family try to survive when a parent is mentally or physically incompetent? How can a friend help in this situation?

5. *Accepting others and overcoming prejudice.* Judy Blume's *Blubber.* Problem: How can students show sensitivity toward a student who is overweight? Betsy Byars's *The Summer of the Swans.* Problem: How should a sister and society respond to a child who is mentally retarded? Nicholasa Mohr's *Felita* and *Going Home.* Problem: In the first book, how can prejudice toward a Puerto Rican girl in New York be overcome? In the second book, how can the same Puerto Rican American girl overcome prejudice when she visits Puerto Rico?

Such stories allow children to empathize with characters who have problems that many children in elementary school experience. Through role playing, children may discover ways to handle problems and increase their sensitivity to the problems of others.

Using Survival Stories to Motivate Reading and Interaction With Literature

Many realistic fiction adventure stories portray physical survival and increased emotional maturity of the main characters. The plots and strong characterizations in this type of realistic fiction encourage children to live the adventures vicariously. Physical characteristics that cause major conflicts may help children understand the importance of setting.

Two very interesting instructional activities developed by university students and then shared with classrooms of children center on the survival theme. One group developed an in-depth literature unit around physical and emotional survival on islands. Another group chose physical and emotional survival in mountains, on Arctic tundra, and in Canadian wilderness. Each group used the webbing process to organize its unit.

Interdisciplinary Unit: Island Survival

The university students who chose the island survival theme identified the following books for ability to survive physically and grow in maturity through the experiences:

Island of the Blue Dolphins, by Scott O'Dell

Call It Courage, by Armstrong Sperry

The Cay, by Theodore Taylor

The Swiss Family Robinson, by Johann David Wyss

The group read the books and identified the central themes and the main areas that challenged the physical survival: characteristics of the natural environment, including climatic conditions of the islands caused by their geographical locations, and survival needs related to other human needs. This central theme and six subtopics associated with survival were identified in the first phase of the island survival web (see Figure 9.1). During the next phase, the group identified subjects related to each subtopic on the web. The group developed the extended web shown in Figure 9.2.

After finishing the webs, the group planned activities to help children learn the importance of setting, realize that setting may cause major conflicts, and understand

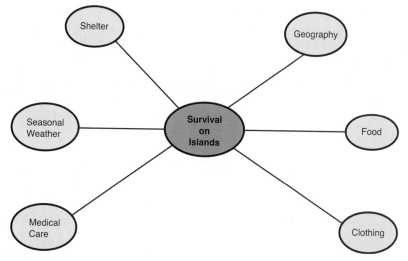

FIGURE 9.1   Island survival web, first phase

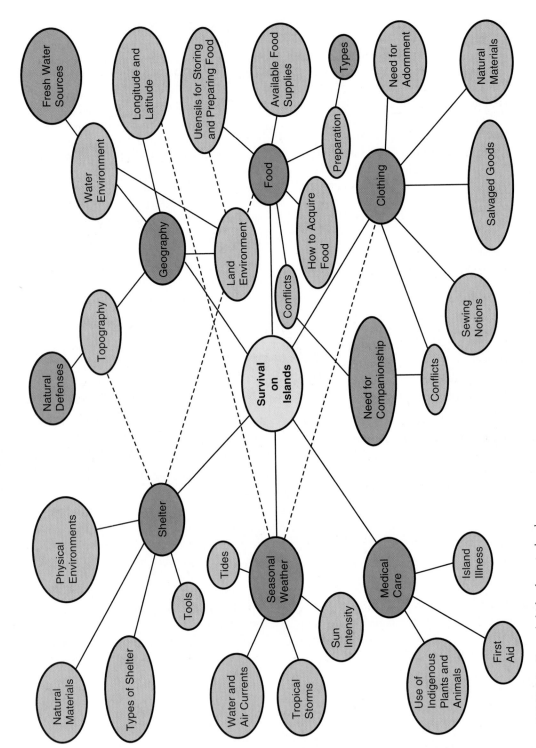

FIGURE 9.2 Extended island survival web

each identified physical survival topic. The university students also identified topics related to an upper-elementary science curriculum. They used interesting literature to increase children's understanding of scientific principles, and they developed activities to stimulate oral language, written language, and artistic interpretations of the plots and characters.

The examples in Chart 9.2 are taken from the physical survival activities developed around Scott O'Dell's *Island of the Blue Dolphins*. Several activities are included for each main subtopic in the web to allow you to visualize the types of physical survival activities that are possible in the classroom. Many of these activities are also appropriate for discussion in the library. The university students developed similar activities around each island survival book. Their discussions and activities stressed the importance of setting in developing the conflict and the effects on the growth of the characters as they overcame

CHART 9.2 Physical survival activities developed around Scott O'Dell's *Island of the Blue Dolphins*

I. Seasonal weather
  A. Karana's life revolves around the seasons; she calculates time and the jobs she must do according to the seasons. Identify the island seasons, the characteristics, and the reasons for Karana's total involvement in the seasons. O'Dell's text provides many clues to seasonal weather: The flowers are plentiful in the spring because of heavy winter rains; in the spring, the birds leave the island and fly to the north; Karana gathers food for the winter; seasonal storms have winds and high waves.
  B. On a large mural, draw the Island of the Blue Dolphins, depicting the different seasons and weather conditions described in the book.
  C. Pretend to be Karana and write a diary with five entries from each season on the island. In the entries, describe seasonal weather and activities during that season.

II. Medical care
  A. *Use of indigenous plants and animals:* In the wilderness, accidents or illnesses are dangerous; there are no doctors or drugstores. Read page 96 to find out what Karana used on Rontu's wound. Find this plant (coral bush) in a reference book and consider why it would help Rontu's wound.
  B. *First aid and use of indigenous plants and animals:* Pretend that you and your family are isolated on an island in the Pacific. Consider the minor illnesses or accidents that could easily occur while on the island. For example, sunburn is common in warm climates. Other problems might include poisonous stings, broken legs, stomach upsets, headaches, and wounds. Research some plants, herbs, and other first aid resources that might be found on the island. Make an illustrated island survival book for medical care. Include drawings of plants, their medical properties, and sketches of first aid measures. Afterward, consider Karana's personal medical needs and how she handled her problems.

III. Clothing
  A. *Natural materials:* Karana and her people lived on an island where the only sources of clothing were natural materials, plant and animal, found on the island or in the sea. What garments did Karana make for herself? What natural materials did she use? Divide into groups and investigate the procedures Karana would need to use and the time it would take to make a skirt from yucca fibers, a belt or a pair of sandals from sealskin, an otter cape, or a skirt of cormorant skins. (Even the needle and thread were made from natural sources.) After describing the natural materials and the procedures, discuss the importance of obtaining clothing in an isolated area and the influence that the need to obtain clothing has on the actions of the characters.
    Consider how your life is different because clothing and materials for clothing are easy to obtain. In your environment, identify natural materials that you could use for clothing and consider what you would need to do to make clothing from them. If possible, try making a garment from natural materials.
  B. *Adornment:* Karana and the women of her island wanted flowers and jewelry that would improve their appearance. Consider why Karana found satisfaction in making a flower wreath for her hair and for Rontu's neck. Investigate the types of flowers that Karana might have used to make her wreath. If possible, make your own flower wreaths using flowers in your area.
    Karana was also fond of jewelry. Consider the implications of Karana's spending five nights to make a circlet of abalone shells as a present for the Aleut girl, Tutok. Examine jewelry made from seashells. If possible, make your own jewelry from seashells. This can also be an opportunity for investigating the types of seashells that might be available on Karana's island.

IV. Food
  A. *Food supplies:* List the foods Karana ate in the story. References are made to the scarlet apples that grow on cactus bushes (tunas) and foods from the sea, such as abalones and scallops. Research the sources that might be available on a Pacific Island. Investigate several cookbooks and make an Island of the Blue Dolphins cookbook using the foods and seasonings Karana might find.

(continues)

CHART 9.2   Continued

B. *Utensils for storing and preparing food:* How did Karana fix her food? Where did she store the food to preserve it and protect it from animals? Karana had to make all of the utensils and storage containers for her food and water. Draw or make a list of five things Karana had to make in order to cook or store her food. Tell or show how she made these utensils or storage containers. Why was it important that Karana create each item? What could have happened if she had not created ways to store food? What impact did preparing and storing food have on her use of time and on the plot of the story?

C. *Acquiring food:* Women in Karana's village were forbidden to make weapons. What is the significance for Karana when, in spite of her fear, she makes weapons to protect herself and to obtain food? Why did she think of destructive winds when she considered the advisability of making weapons? Draw several weapons that Karana created, explain how she made them, and identify the natural resources she used.

D. *Acquiring food and available food supplies:* Rontu and Karana encounter and later hunt a devilfish. From the description on pages 103–104 and 118–124, try to determine another name for a devilfish. Use reference books, and pay close attention to the details. Why did Karana spend her whole winter crafting a special kind of spear to hunt the devilfish?

E. *Conflicts between food or clothing sources and need for companionship:* A conflict arises for Karana when she begins to make friends with some animals on the island. What is the significance of her statement on page 156 that she would never kill another otter, seal, cormorant, or wild dog? Debate this issue as it could relate to your own life. (Another topic for debate is the destruction of animals, such as the sea otter. Karana decided to stop killing the otters even for a cape and would not tell the white men where the otters were located. Investigate the controversy connected with killing or saving the sea otter and then, taking pro and con positions, debate the issue.)

V. Geography

A. *Topography:* Based on Karana's description of the Island of the Blue Dolphins in chapter two and other parts of the book, make a map of the island. The map should include a scale and symbols. To make the scale, you must determine the equivalent length of a league. In her descriptions of where the sun rises and sets, Karana has given the north, south, east, and west directions. Place these symbols on the map. Chart the wind directions on the map. (The island is 2 leagues long and 1 league wide. A league is about 3 miles. The island looks like a dolphin lying on its side. The tail points toward sunrise, which is east, and the nose points toward sunset, which is west.)

B. *Physical environment, longitude and latitude:* The Island of the Blue Dolphins is real. On a large map or atlas that shows the California coastline, find San Nicolas, which is located about 75 miles southwest of Los Angeles. Identify the longitude and latitude of the island. What is the effect of this longitude and latitude on the island? Compare a description of San Nicolas in a reference book with the description of the island in the story. Are there any similarities or differences?

If someone were marooned on an island, what longitude and latitude would have a natural environment most advantageous to survival? Write a short story describing the setting and how one would survive on the island.

C. *Topography, physical environment:* Several geographical terms are used in *Island of the Blue Dolphins.* Following is a list of some of these terms. To develop an understanding of the geography of the island, define each term as used in the story, find pictures illustrating each term, and draw examples of the terms as they looked on Karana's island. Try to see each one through Karana's eyes. What was the significance of each feature for Karana's survival?

mesa	cliffs	ravine
harbor	canyon	spring
cove		

VI. Shelter

A. *Types of shelters:* In her struggles for survival, Karana constructed both a fenced-in house (pp. 74–76) and a cave dwelling (p. 89). Reread the descriptions of each shelter and consider Karana's needs when she constructed them. What was the advantage of each type of shelter? How did each shelter relate to the natural materials found on the island, the physical environment of the island, and the tools that Karana had available for her use? Why did the need for shelter play such an important part in the development of the story and in the use of Karana's time and energy? Build a model of one of her island shelters.

B. *Natural materials:* Look at our own environment. If people were isolated in their physical environments without the houses and other buildings they have now, what types of natural shelter would they construct? Write a short story describing the decision-making processes that people use as they think about the types of shelter they will construct. In this story, consider the need for protection against weather changes, natural predators that might harm people or take their food supplies, the topography of the land that could be used to advantage, the proximity of the shelter to life-sustaining food and water supplies, and the availability of building materials and tools needed for construction. Build a model of this shelter.

problems connected with setting or loneliness. The students also compared the various characters, their settings, and the physical and emotional strategies that led to survival.

In a final activity, the university students set up an elementary-school classroom as an island. They divided the class into groups according to shelter, food, clothing, geography, medical care, and seasonal weather. For Island Day, the elementary-school children chose and developed activities that represented their areas of interest. The children constructed shelters in which they located various interest centers. They shared tool-making and cooking experiences. Art and science displays depicted weather, geography, clothing, food, and shelter. A special demonstration showed possible medical care for island survival. While learning about the impact of setting on characters in survival literature, the children also discovered much about their own environments and how they might conquer their own worlds.

Developing Questioning Strategies

Not all literature selections should be accompanied by questioning. Nevertheless, librarians and teachers responsible for encouraging children to think about and react to literature in a variety of ways benefit from a framework for designing questions to help children examine certain aspects of a story and questions that require higher-level thought processes. Teachers and librarians who wish to develop such questioning strategies will find assistance in taxonomies of reading comprehension, such as those developed by Benjamin Bloom (1956) and Thomas C. Barrett (1972). For example, Barrett identifies four levels of reading comprehension: (1) literal recognition or recall, (2) inference, (3) evaluation, and (4) appreciation.

Develop questions according to levels of reading comprehension in relation to realistic fiction, such as Katherine Paterson's *Jacob Have I Loved*, which is used in the following extended examples. Paterson's book is appropriate for upper-elementary and middle school students. The following questions suggest only the types of questions that might be developed around any book. A librarian or teacher might choose to focus on only a few of these questions. The questions simply illustrate a variety of examples from each subsection of the taxonomy and are not meant to suggest that every question must be discussed.

Literal Recognition

Literal recognition requires children to identify information provided in the literature. You may ask children to recall the information from memory after reading or listening to a story or to locate information while reading a literature selection. Literal-level questions, such as the following, often use the words *who, what, where, when,* and *how.*

1. *Recall of details:* Where does the story *Jacob Have I Loved* take place? When does the story take place? Who are the characters in the story?

2. *Recall of sequence of events:* What sequence of events led Louise to believe that Caroline was the favored child in the family? What sequence of events caused Louise to move from an island to a mountain community?

3. *Recall of comparisons:* Compare the author's physical descriptions of Louise and Caroline. Compare the way Louise thought the family treated her with the way she thought they treated her twin sister, Caroline.

4. *Recall of character traits:* Describe Louise's response to the story about the birth of the twins, Louise and Caroline. How does Grandma respond to Caroline, to Louise, to Captain Wallace, to her son, and to her daughter-in-law?

Inference

When children infer an answer to a question, they go beyond the information the author provides and hypothesize about such things as details, main ideas, and cause-and-effect relationships. Inference is usually considered a higher-level thought process; the answers are not specifically stated within the text. Examples of inferential questions include the following.

1. *Inferring supporting details:* At the end of *Jacob Have I Loved,* Joseph Wojtkiewicz says, "God in heaven's been raising you for this valley from the day you were born." What do you believe he meant by this statement?

2. *Inferring main idea:* What do you believe is the theme of the book? What message do you think the author was trying to express? How does the author develop this theme?

3. *Inferring comparisons:* Think about Captain Wallace, who is such a part of Louise's story. Compare that character with the one who left the island when he was a young man. How do you believe they are alike, and how do you believe they are different?

4. *Inferring cause-and-effect relationships:* If you identified any changes in Captain Wallace, what do you believe might have caused them? Why do you believe Louise dreamed about Caroline's death? Why do you believe Louise felt wild exaltation and then terrible guilt after these dreams?

5. *Inferring character traits:* What do you believe caused Louise to change her mind about wanting Hiram Wallace to be an islander who escaped rather than a Nazi spy? What is Louise saying about herself when she emphasizes the word *escaped*? Why do you believe Louise became so upset whenever she was called "Wheeze"? Why do you think Louise was so upset when Call invited Caroline to join them during their visit to the captain? At the end of the book, after Louise has delivered twins to a mountain family, she becomes very anxious over the healthier twin. Why do you think she gave this advice, "You should hold him. Hold him as much as you can. Or let his mother hold him" (p. 215)? What does this reaction say about Louise's own character and the changes in character that took place in her lifetime?

6. *Inferring outcomes:* There were several places in the book when the action and outcome of the story would have changed if characters had acted differently. Have students read or listen to the book up to a certain point. At various points, ask them to predict the outcomes. For example:

   a. At the end of Chapter Four, a mysterious man leaves the boat and walks alone toward an abandoned house. Who do you think he is? How do you think this man will influence the story?

   b. At the end of Chapter Twelve, Caroline finds and uses Louise's hidden hand lotion. What do you think will happen after Louise angrily breaks the bottle and runs out of the house?

   c. At the end of Chapter Fourteen, the captain has offered to send Caroline to Baltimore to continue her musical education. How do you think Caroline, her parents, and Louise will react to this suggestion?

   d. At the end of Chapter Seventeen, Louise and the captain are discussing what she plans to do with her life. Louise responds that she wants to become a doctor but cannot leave her family. Knowing Louise and her family, how do you think the story will end?

Evaluation

Evaluative questions require children to make judgments about the content of the literature by comparing it with external criteria, such as what authorities on a subject say, or internal criteria, such as experience or knowledge. The following are examples of evaluative questions.

1. *Judgment of adequacy or validity:* Do you agree that Louise in *Jacob Have I Loved* would not have been accepted as a student in a medical college? Why or why not? This story took place in the 1940s; would the author have been able to include the same scene between a woman and a university adviser if the story had taken place today? Why or why not?

2. *Judgment of appropriateness:* What do you think the author meant by the reference to the quote "Jacob have I loved, but Esau have I hated." How does this biblical line relate to the book? Do you think it is a good title for the book? Why or why not?

3. *Judgment of worth, desirability, or acceptability:* Was Louise right in her judgment that her parents always favored Caroline? What caused her to reach her final decision? Do you believe that Louise made the right decision when she left the island? Why or why not?

Appreciation

Appreciation of literature requires a sensitivity to the techniques that authors use in order to have emotional impact on their readers. Questions can encourage children to respond emotionally to the plot, identify with the characters, react to an author's use of language, and react to an author's ability to create a visual image through word choices in the text. The following are examples of questions to stimulate appreciation.

1. *Emotional response to plot or theme:* How did you respond to the plot of *Jacob Have I Loved*? Did the author hold your interest? If so, how? Do you believe the theme of the story was worthwhile? Why or why not? Pretend that you are either recommending this book for someone else to read or recommending that this book not be read; what would you tell that person?

2. *Identification with characters and incidents:* Have you or anyone you know felt like 13-year-old Louise or her twin sister, Caroline? What caused you or that person to feel that way? How would you have reacted if you had been Louise? How would you have reacted if you had been Caroline? Pretend to be a grown-up Louise in Chapter Eighteen talking with your mother about leaving the island. What emotions do you think your mother would feel when you responded, "I'm not going to rot here like Grandma" (p. 200)? How would you feel when she told you, "I chose to leave my own people and build a life for myself somewhere else. I certainly wouldn't deny you that same choice. But . . . oh, Louise, we will miss you, your father and I" (p. 201)?

3. *Imagery:* How did the author encourage you to see the relationship between the island setting and changes in Louise's character over her lifetime?

4. *Appreciative comprehension and identification with characters and incidents:* Have you or anyone you know felt like 13-year-old Louise when she listened to the story about her birth and thought, "I felt cold all over, as though I was the newborn infant a second time, cast aside and forgotten" (p. 15)? How

would you have reacted if you had been Louise and had heard this story repeatedly? What do you think could make you feel cold all over if you were Caroline and heard this story?

MULTICULTURAL LITERATURE

Developing Understanding of Point of View and Motivating Writing With a Native American Story

Byrd Baylor's contemporary story from the Southwest, *Hawk, I'm Your Brother*, is an excellent book to help children recognize differences in point of view and to motivate the writing of a story from another point of view. Such activities help students analyze the characterizations in the book. You can use the following instructional sequence for developing understanding of point of view.

1. Introduce the story and tell the students that they will be listening to a story in which the author describes and develops the hero's aspirations. Ask them to consider how they would feel as Rudy Soto. Also, ask them to consider the feelings and desires of the hawk.

2. After reading *Hawk, I'm Your Brother* aloud, lead a discussion in which the students characterize Rudy and the hawk, and identify the major sequence of events leading up to Rudy's decision to release the hawk.

3. Ask the students to consider the significance of the title of the book. Why did Baylor choose *Hawk, I'm Your Brother*? Is it an accurate description of Rudy Soto's relationship to the hawk? How are Rudy and the hawk alike? How are they different? Why did Rudy release the hawk? How do you think Rudy felt after releasing the hawk? How do you think the hawk felt after being released? What would you do if you were Rudy Soto? How would you react if you were the hawk?

4. Tell the students that an incident may be described in different ways by several people who have the same experience. The details characters describe, the feelings they experience, and their beliefs in the right or wrong of an incident may vary. Consequently, the same story could change drastically, depending on the point of view of the storyteller. Ask the students to tell you whose point of view Baylor develops in *Hawk, I'm Your Brother*. How did they know that the story was told from Rudy Soto's point of view? Then ask the students to consider how the story might be written if the author chose the hawk's point of view.

5. Ask the students to imagine that they are the hawk that Rudy captured. Have them write a story about what happened to them, beginning from the time of the capture from the nest high on Santos Mountain.

Suggested Activities

For more suggested activities for understanding contemporary realistic fiction, visit the Companion Website at **CW** www.prenhall.com/norton

- Sexism in literature, including the harmful sex-role socialization resulting from female- and male-role stereotyping, is a major concern of many educators and psychologists. In a school, public, or university library, choose a random sampling of children's literature selections. If these books were the only sources of information available about male and female roles, what information would be acquired from the books and their illustrations? Is this information accurate?

- Analyze the list of books identified by Marsha M. Sprague and Kara K. Keeling in the April 2000 issue of *Journal of Adolescent & Adult Literacy*. Why do you believe that these 20 books have been identified as books that encourage gender dialogue?

- Interview children's librarians in public or school libraries. Ask them to state the guidelines the library uses when selecting books considered controversial for children. What issues, if any, do the librarians feel are relevant in the community? Can they identify any books that have caused controversy in the libraries? If there are such books, how did they handle the controversy?

- Many realistic fiction stories deal with the problems that children must face and overcome when they experience separation from a friend, a neighborhood, or a parent, or when they face the ultimate separation caused by death. Choose one area, read several books that explore the problem, and recommend books to share with younger children and books more appropriate for older children. Explain your decisions.

Children's Literature

For full descriptions, including plot summaries and award winner notations, of these and other titles for teaching children with contemporary realistic fiction, please visit the CD-ROM that accompanies this book.

Alcott, Louisa M. *Little Women* (first published in 1868). Crowell, 1995 (I:10+ R:7).

Anderson, Laurie Halse. *Speak*. Farrar, Straus & Giroux, 1999 (I:12+ R:5).

Avi. *Nothing But the Truth: A Documentary Novel*. Orchard, 1991 (I:12+).

Baker, Jeannie. *Where the Forest Meets the Sea*. Greenwillow, 1988 (I:4–10).

Bartoletti, Susan Campbell. *Dancing With Dziadziu*. Illustrated by Annika Nelson. Harcourt Brace, 1997 (I:8–12 R:5).

I = Interest by age range.
R = Readability by grade level.

Bateman, Colin. *Running With the Reservoir Pups.* Delacorte, 2005 (I:10+ R:5).

Bauer, Joan. *Backwater.* Putnam, 1999 (I:10+ R:5).

_____. *Hope Was Here.* Putnam, 2000 (I:10+ R:5).

_____. *Rules of the Road.* Putnam, 1998 (I:12+ R:6).

_____. *Squashed.* Delacorte, 1992 (I:10+ R:5).

Bauer, Marion Dane. *On My Honor.* Clarion, 1986 (I:10+ R:4).

Bawden, Nina. *Humbug.* Clarion, 1992 (I:8+ R:5).

_____. *The Real Plato Jones.* Clarion, 1993 (I:12+ R:6).

Baylor, Byrd. *Hawk, I'm Your Brother.* Illustrated by Peter Parnall. Scribner, 1976 (I:all R:6).

Benjamin, Carol Lea. *The Wicked Stepdog.* Crowell, 1982 (I:9–12 R:4).

Berck, Judith. *No Place to Be: Voices of Homeless Children.* Houghton Mifflin, 1991 (I:12+).

Bertrand, Diane Gonzales. *Uncle Chente's Picnic/El Picnic de Tío Chente.* Illustrated by Pauline Rodriguez Howard. Pinata, 2001 (I:7+).

Block, Francesca Lia. *Girl Goddess #9: Nine Stories.* HarperCollins, 1996 (I:14+ R:7).

Blume, Judy. *Are You There God? It's Me, Margaret.* Bradbury, 1970 (I:10+ R:6).

_____. *Blubber.* Bradbury, 1974 (I:10+ R:4).

_____. *Deenie.* Bradbury, 1973 (YA).

_____. *Forever.* Bradbury, 1975 (YA).

_____. *It's Not the End of the World.* Bradbury, 1972 (YA).

_____. *The One in the Middle Is the Green Kangaroo.* Illustrated by Amy Aitken. Bradbury, 1981 (I:6–9 R:2).

_____. *Otherwise Known as Sheila the Great.* Dutton, 1972 (I:9–12 R:6).

_____. *Tales of a Fourth Grade Nothing.* Illustrated by Roy Doty. Dutton, 1972 (I:7–12 R:4).

_____. *Then Again, Maybe I Won't.* Bradbury, 1971 (YA).

_____. *Tiger Eyes.* Bradbury, 1981. (I:12+ R:7).

Bonham, Frank. *Durango Street.* Dutton, 1965 (I:12+ R:5).

Bredsdorff, Bodil. *The Crow-Girl.* Translated by Faith Ingwersen. Farrar, Straus & Giroux, 2004 (I:8+ R:5)

Bridges, Ruby. *Through My Eyes.* Scholastic, 1999.

Brooks, Bruce. *Everywhere.* HarperCollins, 1990 (I:8+ R:4).

_____. *The Moves Make the Man.* Harper & Row, 1984 (I:10+ R:7).

_____. *What Hearts.* HarperCollins, 1992 (I:10+ R:5).

Burch, Robert. *Queenie Peavy.* Illustrated by Jerry Lazare. Viking, 1966 (I:10+ R:6).

Burnford, Sheila. *The Incredible Journey.* Illustrated by Carl Burger. Little, Brown, 1960, 1961 (I:8+ R:8).

Byars, Betsy. *After the Goat Man.* Illustrated by Ronald Himler. Viking, 1974 (I:9–12 R:7).

_____. *The Animal, the Vegetable, and John D. Jones.* Illustrated by Ruth Sanderson. Delacorte, 1982 (I:9–12 R:5).

_____. *Bingo Brown and the Language of Love.* Viking, 1989 (I:10+ R:5).

_____. *The Burning Questions of Bingo Brown.* Viking Kestrel, 1988 (I:10+ R:6).

_____. *Coast to Coast.* Delacorte, 1992 (I:10+ R:5).

_____. *Cracker Jackson.* Viking, 1985 (I:10+ R:6).

_____. *The Cybil War.* Illustrated by Gail Owens. Viking, 1981 (I:9–12 R:6).

_____. *The 18th Emergency.* Illustrated by Robert Grossman. Viking, 1973 (I:8–12 R:3).

_____. *The Night Swimmers.* Illustrated by Troy Howell. Delacorte, 1980 (I:8–12 R:5).

_____. *The Summer of the Swans.* Illustrated by Ted CoConis. Viking, 1970 (I:8–12 R:4).

Cadnum, Michael. *Zero to the Bone.* Viking, 1996 (I:12+ R:7).

Carrick, Carol. *The Accident.* Illustrated by Donald Carrick. Seabury, 1976 (I:5–8 R:4).

_____. *Stay Away From Simon.* Clarion, 1985 (I:7–10 R:3).

Cart, Michael, ed. *Necessary Noise.* HarperCollins, 2003 (I:12+ YA R:7).

Carter, Alden R. *Between a Rock and a Hard Place.* Scholastic, 1995 (I:12+ R:7).

Cheng, Andrea. *Honeysuckle House.* Front Street, 2004 (I:8–10 R:5).

Choldenko, Gennifer. *Al Capone Does My Shirts.* Putnam, 2004 (I:10+ R:6).

Christopher, Matt. *Dirt Bike Racer.* Illustrated by Barry Bomzer. Little, Brown, 1979 (I:10+ R:4).

_____. *Face-Off.* Illustrated by Harvey Kidder. Little, Brown, 1972 (I:8–12 R:4).

_____. *Football Fugitive.* Illustrated by Larry Johnson. Little, Brown, 1976 (I:9–12 R:6).

_____. *The Fox Steals Home.* Illustrated by Larry Johnson. Little, Brown, 1978 (I:8–12 R:6).

_____. *Skateboard Renegade.* Little, Brown, 2000 (I:8–12 R:4).

_____. *Soccer Duel.* Little, Brown, 2000 (I:8–12 R:4).

_____. *Tennis Ace.* Little, Brown, 2000 (I:8–12 R:4).

_____. *Wheel Wizards.* Little, Brown, 2000 (I:8–12 R:4).

Cisneros, Sandra. *The House on Mango Street.* Arte Publico, 1983 (I:12+ R:7).

Cleary, Beverly. *Dear Mr. Henshaw.* Illustrated by Paul O. Zelinsky. Morrow, 1983 (I:9–12 R:5).

_____. *Henry and Beezus.* Illustrated by Louis Darling. Morrow, 1952 (I:7–10 R:6).

_____. *Mitch and Amy.* Illustrated by George Porter. Morrow, 1967 (I:7–10 R:6).

_____. *Muggie Maggie.* Illustrated by Kay Life. Morrow, 1990 (I:7–10 R:5).

_____. *Ramona and Her Father.* Illustrated by Alan Tiegreen. Morrow, 1977 (I:7–10 R:6).

_____. *Ramona and Her Mother.* Illustrated by Alan Tiegreen. Morrow, 1979 (I:7–10 R:6).

_____. *Ramona the Brave.* Illustrated by Alan Tiegreen. Morrow, 1975 (I:7–10 R:6).

_____. *Ramona the Pest.* Illustrated by Louis Darling. Morrow, 1968 (I:7–10 R:4).

_____. *Ramona Quimby, Age 8.* Illustrated by Alan Tiegreen. Morrow, 1981 (I:7–10 R:6).

_____. *Strider.* Illustrated by Paul O. Zelinsky. Morrow, 1991 (I:10+ R:5).

Cleaver, Vera, & Bill Cleaver. *Trial Valley.* Lippincott, 1977 (I:11+ R:5).

_____. *Where the Lilies Bloom.* Illustrated by Jim Spanfeller. Lippincott, 1969 (I:11+ R:5).

Clements, Andrew. *The Janitor's Boy.* Simon & Schuster, 2000 (I:9+ R:5).

_____. *The Landry News.* Illustrated by Brian Selznick. Simon & Schuster, 1999 (I:8+ R:4).

Clinton, Cathryn. *A Stone in My Hand.* Candlewick, 2002 (I:10+–YA R:5).

Cole, Brock. *The Goats.* Farrar, Straus & Giroux, 1987 (I:10+ R:5).

Conly, Jane Leslie. *Crazy Lady!* HarperCollins, 1993 (I:10+ R:5).

Corcoran, Barbara. *The Potato Kit.* Atheneum, 1989 (I:10+ R:6).

Cormier, Robert. *The Bumblebee Flies Anyway.* Pantheon, 1983 (I:14+ R:6).

_____. *In the Middle of the Night.* Delacorte, 1995 (I:12+ R:6).

_____. *Tenderness.* Delacorte, 1997 (I:12+ R:6).

Couloumbis, Audrey. *Getting Near to Baby.* Putnam, 1999 (I:10+ R:4).

Creech, Sharon. *Chasing Redbird.* HarperCollins, 1997 (I:10+ R:6).

_____. *Granny Torrelli Makes Soup.* Illustrated by Chris Raschka. HarperCollins, 2003 (I:9+ R:4).

_____. *Heartbeat.* HarperCollins, 2004 (I:10+).

_____. *Walk Two Moons.* HarperCollins, 1994 (I:12+ R:6).

_____. *The Wanderer.* HarperCollins, 2000 (I:10+ R:6).

Crews, Donald. *Bigmama's.* Greenwillow, 1991 (I:5–7 R:4).

_____. *Shortcut.* Greenwillow, 1992 (I:5–7).

Crutcher, Chris. *Athletic Shorts.* Greenwillow, 1991 (I:10+ R:6).

Cunningham, Julia. *Burnish Me Bright.* Illustrated by Don Freeman. Pantheon, 1970 (I:8–12 R:8).

Curtis, Christopher Paul. *The Watsons Go to Birmingham—1963.* Delacorte, 1995 (I:10+ R:6).

Cutler, Jane. *No Dogs Allowed.* Farrar, Straus & Giroux, 1992 (I:8+ R:4).

_____. *Rats!* Illustrated by Tracey Campbell Pearson. HarperCollins, 1996 (I:8+ R:4).

Danziger, Paula. *Amber Brown Is Not a Crayon.* Illustrated by Tony Ross. Putnam, 1994 (I:6–9 R:4).

_____, and Ann M. Martin. *P. S. Longer Letter Later.* Scholastic, 1998 (I:10+ R:5).

Darling, Benjamin. *Valerie and the Silver Pear.* Illustrated by Dan Lane. Four Winds, 1992 (I:5–8 R:3).

Davis, Jenny. *Good-Bye and Keep Cold.* Orchard, 1987 (I:12+ R:6).

Delacre, Lulu. *Salsa Stories.* Scholastic, 2000 (I:all).

Delton, Judy. *Angel's Mother's Wedding.* Houghton Mifflin, 1987 (I:7–10 R:4).

DiCamillo, Kate. *Because of Winn-Dixie.* Candlewick, 2000 (I:8+ R:4).

Doherty, Berlie. *Dear Nobody.* Orchard, 1992 (I:12+ R:6).

Duncan, Lois. *Don't Look Behind You.* Delacorte, 1989 (I:12+ R:6).

Ellis, Sarah. *Pick-up Sticks.* Macmillan, 1992 (I:10+ R:5).

Elya, Susan Middleton. *Home at Last.* Illustrated by Felipe Davalos. Lee & Low, 2002 (I:8+ R:4).

Enright, Elizabeth. *Thimble Summer.* Holt, Rinehart & Winston, 1938, 1966 (I:7–12 R:5).

Estes, Eleanor. *The Hundred Dresses.* Harcourt Brace, 1974.

_____. *The Moffats.* Illustrated by Louis Slobodkin. Harcourt Brace, 1941 (I:7–10 R:4).

Ets, Marie Hall, & Aurora Labastida. *Nine Days to Christmas: A Story of Mexico.* Viking, 1959 (I:5–8 R:3).

Farley, Walter. *The Black Stallion.* Illustrated by Keith Ward. Random House, 1944 (I:8+ R:3).

_____. *The Black Stallion Returns.* Random House, 1945, 1973 (I:8+).

Fine, Anne. *Alias Madame Doubtfire.* Little, Brown, 1988 (I:9+ R:5).

_____. *Step by Wicked Step.* Little Brown, 1996 (I:10+ R:6).

_____. *The Tulip Touch.* Little, Brown, 1997 (I:10+ R:6).

Fitzhugh, Louise. *Harriet the Spy.* Harper & Row, 1964 (I:8–12 R:3).

_____. *The Long Secret.* Harper & Row, 1965 (I:8–12 R:3).

Fleischman, Paul. *Seedfolks.* Illustrated by Judy Pedersen. HarperCollins, 1997 (I:10+ R:6).

_____. *Whirligig.* Holt, 1998 (I:12+ R:6).

Foreman, Michael. *Seal Surfer.* Harcourt Brace, 1997 (I:5–9 R:4).

Fox, Paula. *Monkey Island.* Orchard, 1991 (I:10+ R:6).

_____. *The Moonlight Man.* Bradbury, 1986 (I:12+ R:5).

_____. *One-Eyed Cat.* Bradbury, 1984 (I:10+ R:5).

_____. *The Village by the Sea.* Watts, 1988 (I:10+ R:6).

_____. *Western Wind.* Orchard, 1993 (I:9+ R:5).

Franklin, Kristine L. *Lone Wolf.* Candlewick, 1997 (I:9+ R:5).

Freeman, Suzanne. *The Cuckoo's Child.* Greenwillow, 1996 (I:10+ R:6).

Friedman, Ina R. *How My Parents Learned to Eat.* Illustrated by Allen Say. Houghton Mifflin, 1984 (I:6–8 R:3).

Gantos, Jack. *Joey Pigza Loses Control.* Farrar, Straus & Giroux, 2000 (I:9+ R:4).

Garland, Sherry. *The Lotus Seed.* Illustrated by Tatsuro Kluchi. Harcourt Brace, 1993 (I:5–8 R:.4).

_____. *The Silent Storm.* Harcourt Brace, 1993 (I:10+ R:6).

Gauch, Patricia. *Christina Katerina and the Time She Quit the Family.* Illustrated by Elise Primavera. Putnam, 1987 (I:4–8).

George, Jean Craighead. *The Cry of the Crow.* Harper & Row, 1980 (I:10+ R:5).

_____. *Julie of the Wolves.* Illustrated by John Schoenherr. Harper & Row, 1972 (I:10+ R:7).

_____. *My Side of the Mountain.* Dutton, 1959 (I:10+ R:6).

_____. *The Talking Earth.* Harper & Row, 1983 (I:10+ R:6).

_____. *Water Sky.* Harper & Row, 1987 (I:10+ R:6).

Gifaldi, David. *Toby Scudder, Ultimate Warrior.* Clarion, 1993 (I:9+ R:5).

Gipson, Fred. *Old Yeller.* Illustrated by Carl Burger. Harper & Row, 1956 (I:10+ R:6).

Greene, Constance. *Beat the Turtle Drum.* Illustrated by Donna Diamond. Viking, 1976 (I:10+ R:7).

Greene, Stephanie. *Owen Foote, Frontiersman.* Illustrated by Martha Weston. Clarion, 1999 (I:6–9 R:4).

Greenfield, Eloise. *Sister.* Illustrated by Moneta Burnett. Crowell, 1974 (I:8–12 R:5).

Grimes, Nikki. *Bronx Masquerade.* Dial, 2002 (I:12+–YA R:6).

Grove, Vicki. *Reaching Dustin.* Putnam, 1998 (I:10+ R:5).

Haas, Jessie. *Keeping Barney.* Greenwillow, 1982 (I:9–12 R:5).

Hall, Lynn. *In Trouble Again, Zelda Hammersmith?* Harcourt Brace, 1987 (I:8–12 R:3).

Hamilton, Virginia. *The House of Dies Drear.* Macmillan, 1968 (I:11+ R:4).

_____. *Plain City.* Scholastic, 1993 (I:10+ R:5).

———. *The Planet of Junior Brown.* Macmillan, 1971 (I:12+ R:6).

———. *Zeely.* Illustrated by Symeon Shimin. Macmillan, 1967 (I:8–12 R:4).

Hanel, Wolfram. *Abby.* Illustrated by Alan Marks. North-South, 1996 (I:7–9 R:4).

Hannigan, Katherine. *Ida B . . . and Her Plans to Maximize Fun, Avoid Disaster, and (Possibly) Save the World.* Greenwillow, 2004 (I:8–12 R:6).

Hartling, Peter. *Old John.* Translated by Elizabeth D. Crawford. Lothrop, Lee & Shepard, 1990 (I:8+ R:5).

Hathorn, Libby. *Thunderwith.* Little, Brown, 1991 (I:10+ R:5).

Hautman, Pete. *Godless.* Simon & Schuster, 2004 (I:14–18 R:7).

Hayes, Daniel. *Flyers.* Simon & Schuster, 1996 (I:12+ R:7).

Henkes, Kevin. *Olive's Ocean.* Greenwillow, 2003 (I:10+ R:6).

———. *Words of Stone.* Greenwillow, 1992 (I:10+ R:5).

Henry, Marguerite. *Black Gold.* Illustrated by Wesley Dennis. Rand McNally, 1957 (I:8–12 R:6).

———. *Justin Morgan Had a Horse.* Illustrated by Wesley Dennis. Rand McNally, 1954 (I:8–12 R:6).

———. *King of the Wind.* Illustrated by Wesley Dennis. Rand McNally, 1948, 1976 (I:8–12 R:6).

———. *Misty of Chincoteague.* Illustrated by Wesley Dennis. Rand McNally, 1947, 1963 (I:8–12 R:6).

———. *San Domingo: The Medicine Hat Stallion.* Illustrated by Robert Lougheed. Rand McNally, 1972 (I:9–14 R:4).

Hermes, Patricia. *Mama, Let's Dance.* Little, Brown, 1991 (I:10+ R:5).

Hernandez, Avelino. *That Boy and that Old Man.* Illustrated by Federico Delicado. Kalandraka, 2002 (I:8+ R:4).

Hiaasen, Carl. *Hoot.* Knopf, 2002 (I:11+–YA R:6).

Highwater, Jamake. *The Ceremony of Innocence.* Harper & Row, 1985 (I:12+ R:6).

———. *I Wear the Morning Star.* Harper & Row, 1986 (I:12+ R:6).

———. *Legend Days.* Harper & Row, 1984 (I:12+ R:6).

Holt, Kimberly Willis. *When Zachary Beaver Came to Town.* Holt, 1999 (I:10+ R:6).

Holtwijk, Ineke. *Asphalt Angels.* Translated by Wanda Boeke. Front Street, 1999 (I:12+ R:6).

Honeycutt, Natalie. *Twilight in Grace Falls.* Orchard, 1997 (I:10+ R:6).

Hopkins, Lee Bennett. *Mama.* Knopf, 1977 (I:7–10 R:6).

Horvath, Polly. *When the Circus Came to Town.* Farrar, Straus & Giroux, 1996 (I:9+ R:6).

Hoyt-Goldsmith, Diane. *Hoang Anh: A Vietnamese-American Boy.* Photographs by Lawrence Migdale. Holiday House, 1992 (I:5–9 R:4).

Hughes, Dean. *Team Picture.* Simon & Schuster, 1996 (I:10+ R:6).

Hughes, Mark Peter. *I Am the Wallpaper.* Delacorte, 2005 (I:11–14 R:5).

Hunt, Irene. *Up a Road Slowly.* Follett, 1966 (I:11+ R:7).

Hurwitz, Johanna. *Russell and Elisa.* Illustrated by Lillian Hoban. Morrow, 1989 (I:3–8 R:3).

Irwin, Hadley. *The Original Freddie Ackerman.* Macmillan, 1992 (I:10+ R:5).

Isadora, Rachel. *At the Crossroads.* Greenwillow, 1991 (I:3–8 R:3).

Johnson, Angela. *Toning the Sweep.* Orchard, 1993 (I:12+ R:4).

Johnson, Scott. *Safe at Second.* Philomel, 1999 (I:10+ R:6).

Joosse, Barbara M. *Mama, Do You Love Me?* Illustrated by Barbara Lavalle. Chronicle, 1991 (I:3–7 R:4).

Jukes, Mavis. *Like Jake and Me.* Illustrated by Lloyd Bloom. Knopf, 1984 (I:6–8).

Kadohata, Cynthia. *Kira-Kira.* Atheneum, 2004 (I:10+ R:6).

Kaplan, Howard. *Waiting to Sing.* Illustrated by Hervé Blondon. DK, 2000 (I:5–8 R:4).

Kerr, M. E. *"Hello," I Lied.* HarperCollins, 1997 (I:14+ R:7).

Khalsa, Dayal. *I Want a Dog.* Clarkson, 1987 (I:4–7).

Kjelgaard, Jim. *Big Red.* Illustrated by Bob Kuhn. Holiday House, 1945, 1956 (I:10+ R:7).

Klein, Norma. *Mom, the Wolf Man and Me.* Pantheon, 1972 (I:12+ R:6).

Kline, Suzy. *Herbie Jones and the Monster Ball.* Illustrated by Richard Williams. Putnam, 1988 (I:8+ R:4).

Konigsburg, E. L. *About the B'nai Bagels.* Atheneum, 1969 (I:8–12 R:7).

———. *From the Mixed-Up Files of Mrs. Basil E. Frankweiler.* Atheneum, 1967 (I:9–12 R:7).

———. *Jennifer, Hecate, Macbeth, William McKinley, and Me, Elizabeth.* Atheneum, 1967, 1976 (I:8–12 R:4).

———. *Journey to an 800 Number.* Atheneum, 1982 (I:10+ R:7).

———. *The Outcasts of 19 Schuyler Place.* Atheneum, 2004 (I:10+ R:6).

———. *T-Backs, T-Shirts, Coat, and Suit.* Atheneum, 1993 (I:10+ R:5).

———. *Throwing Shadows.* Atheneum, 1979 (I:11+ R:7).

———. *The View From Saturday.* Atheneum, 1996 (I:9–12 R:5).

Kroll, Virginia. *The Seasons and Someone.* Illustrated by Tatsuro Kiuchi. Harcourt Brace, 1994 (I:4–8 R:4).

Krumgold, Joseph. *. . . And Now Miguel.* Illustrated by Jean Charlot. Crowell, 1953 (I:10+ R:3).

L'Engle, Madeleine. *Meet the Austins.* Vanguard, 1960 (I:10+ R:6).

Lipsyte, Robert. *The Brave.* HarperCollins, 1991 (I:12+ R:6).

Lisle, Janet Taylor. *Afternoon of the Elves.* Watts, 1989 (I:10+ R:5).

Little, Jean. *Different Dragons.* Illustrated by Laura Fernandez. Viking, 1986 (I:8–10 R:4).

———. *From Anna.* Illustrated by Joan Sandin. Harper & Row, 1972 (I:8–12 R:5).

———. *Willow and Twig.* Viking, 2003 (I:10+ R:6).

London, Jack. *Call of the Wild.* Photographs by Seymour Linden. Harmony, 1903, 1977 (I:10+ R:5).

Lowry, Lois. *All About Sam.* Illustrated by Diane deGroat. Houghton Mifflin, 1988 (I:8–12 R:5).

———. *Anastasia Again!* Illustrated by Diane deGroat. Houghton Mifflin, 1981 (I:8–12 R:6).

———. *Anastasia at Your Service.* Illustrated by Diane deGroat. Houghton Mifflin, 1982 (I:8–12 R:6).

———. *Anastasia Krupnik.* Houghton Mifflin, 1979 (I:8–12 R:6).

———. *Anastasia on Her Own.* Houghton Mifflin, 1985 (I:8–12 R:4).

———. *Anastasia's Chosen Career.* Houghton Mifflin, 1987 (I:10+ R:6).

_____. *Attaboy, Sam!* Illustrated by Diane deGroat. Houghton Mifflin, 1992 (I:8+ R:5).

_____. *The One Hundredth Thing About Caroline.* Houghton Mifflin, 1983 (I:8–12 R:3).

_____. *Rabble Starkey.* Houghton Mifflin, 1987 (I:10+ R:6).

_____. *See You Around, Sam!* Illustrated by Diane deGroat. Houghton Mifflin, 1996 (I:8+ R:5).

_____. *Your Move, J. P.!* Houghton Mifflin, 1990 (I:10+ R:6).

Lynch, Chris, *Shadow Boxer.* HarperCollins, 1993 (I:12+ R:6).

Lyon, George Ella. *Sonny's House of Spies.* Simon & Schuster, 2004 (I:10+ R:6).

MacGregor, Rob. *Hawk Moon.* Simon & Schuster, 1996 (I:12+ R:6).

MacLachlan, Patricia. *The Facts and Fictions of Minna Pratt.* Harper & Row, 1988 (I:7–12 R:4).

_____. *Journey.* Delacorte, 1991 (I:8+ R:4).

_____. *Mama One, Mama Two.* Illustrated by Ruth Lercher Bornstein. Harper & Row, 1982 (I:4–8 R:3).

Manning, Sarra. *Guitar Girl.* Dutton, 2004 (I:14+–YA R:7).

Marchetta, Melina. *Saving Francesca.* Knopf, 2004 (I:14+–YA R:7).

Marino, Jan. *For the Love of Pete.* Little, Brown, 1993 (I:10+ R:5).

Mathis, Sharon Bell. *The Hundred Penny Box.* Puffin, 1986 (I:6–9 R:3).

Mazer, Norma Fox. *After the Rain.* Morrow, 1987 (I:12+ R:5).

McDonald, Joyce. *Comfort Creek.* Delacorte, 1996 (I:10+ R:5).

McKay, Hilary. *The Exiles.* Macmillan, 1992 (I:9+ R:5).

McKissack, C. Patricia. *The Honest-to-Goodness Truth.* Illustrated by Giselle Potter. Atheneum, 2000 (I:5–9 R:4).

McMahon, Patricia. *Chi-Hoon: A Korean Girl.* Photographs by Michael O'Brien. Caroline House, 1993 (I:8+ R:5).

Miles, Miska. *Annie and the Old One.* Illustrated by Peter Parnell. Little, Brown, 1971 (I:6–8 R:3).

Mohr, Nicholasa. *Felita.* Illustrated by Ray Cruz. Dial, 1979 (I:9–12).

_____. *Going Home.* Dial, 1986 (I:10+ R:6).

Mooney, Bel. *The Voices of Silence.* Delacorte, 1997 (I:10+ R:6).

Mora, Pat. *The Bakery Lady.* Illustrated by Pablo Torrecilla. Piñata, 2001 (I:7+ R:4).

Morgenroth, Kate. *Jude.* Simon & Schuster, 2004 (I:14+–YA R:7).

Morgenstern, Susie. *Sixth Grade.* Translated by Gill Rosner. Viking, 2004 (I:10+ R:6).

Mowry, Jess. *Babylon Boyz.* Simon & Schuster, 1997 (I:12+ R:7).

Murray, Martin. *The Slightly True Story of Cedar B. Hartley (Who Planned to Live an Unusual Life).* Scholastic, 2003 (I:10+ R:6).

Myers, Walter Dean. *Map, Moondance, and the Nagasaki Knights.* Delacorte, 1992 (I:9+ R:5).

_____. *The Mouse Rap.* HarperCollins, 1990 (I:10+ R:5).

_____. *Scorpions.* Harper & Row, 1988 (I:10+ R:5).

_____. *Shooter.* HarperCollins, 2004 (I:12+–YA R:6).

Myracle, Lauren. *ttyl.* Abrams, 2004 (I:14+–YA R:7).

Naidoo, Beverly. *Journey to Jo'burg.* Harper, 1986 (I:10+ R:6).

Namioka, Lensey. *Yang the Youngest and Her Impossible Family.* Illustrated by Kees de Kiefte. Little, Brown, 1995 (I:8+ R:4).

_____. *Yang the Youngest and His Terrible Ear.* Illustrated by Kees de Kiefte. Little, Brown, 1995 (I:8+ R:4).

Napoli, Donna Jo. *North.* Greenwillow, 2004 (I:10+ R:6).

Naylor, Phyllis Reynolds. *Alice in Rapture, Sort of.* Atheneum, 1989 (I:10+ R:5).

_____. *All but Alice.* Atheneum, 1992 (I:10+ R:5).

_____. *Josie's Troubles.* Illustrated by Shelley Matheis. Atheneum, 1992 (I:8+ R:4).

_____. *Keeping a Christmas Secret.* Illustrated by Lena Schiffman. Atheneum, 1989 (I:5–8).

_____. *Reluctantly Alice.* Atheneum, 1991 (I:10+ R:5).

_____. *Shiloh.* Atheneum, 1991 (I:10+ R:5).

_____. *Shiloh Season.* Atheneum, 1996 (I:8+ R:5).

Nelson, Theresa. *The Beggars' Ride.* Orchard, 1992 (I:10+ R:5).

Neville, Emily. *It's Like This, Cat.* Illustrated by Emil Weiss. Harper & Row, 1963 (I:8–12 R:6).

Newman, Robert. *The Case of the Baker Street Irregular.* Atheneum, 1978 (I:10+ R:6).

Nomura, Takaaki. *Grandpa's Town.* Translated by Amanda Mayer Stinchecum. Kane-Miller, 1991 (I:3–7 R:4).

O'Connor, Barbara. *Beethoven In Paradise.* Farrar, Straus & Giroux,1997 (I:10+ R:6).

O'Dell, Scott. *Black Star, Bright Dawn.* Houghton Mifflin, 1988 (I:8+ R:6).

_____. *Island of the Blue Dolphins.* Houghton Mifflin, 1960 (I:10+ R:6).

Olsen, Sylvia. *The Girl With a Baby.* Orca, 2004 (I:12+–YA R:6).

Park, Barbara. *Don't Make Me Smile.* Knopf, 1981 (I:9–12 R:5).

_____. *The Kid in the Red Jacket.* Knopf, 1987 (I:7–11 R:3).

_____. *Maxie, Rosie, and Earl—Partners in Crime.* Knopf, 1990 (I:8–12 R:5).

Paterson, Katherine. *Bridge to Terabithia.* Illustrated by Donna Diamond. Crowell, 1977 (I:10–14 R:6).

_____. *Come Sing, Jimmy Jo.* Dutton, 1985 (I:10+ R:4).

_____. *Flip-Flop Girl.* Lodestar, 1994 (I:10+ R:5).

_____. *The Great Gilly Hopkins.* Crowell, 1978 (I:10+ R:6).

_____. *Jacob Have I Loved.* Crowell, 1980 (I:10+ R:7).

_____. *Park's Quest.* Lodestar, 1988 (I:10+ R:5+).

Patron, Susan. *Maybe Yes, Maybe No, Maybe Maybe.* Illustrated by Dorothy Donahue. Orchard, 1993 (I:7–10 R:4).

Paulsen, Gary. *Brian's Return.* Delacorte, 1999 (I:10+ R:6).

_____. *The Car.* Harcourt Brace, 1994 (I:10+ R:6).

_____. *The Crossing.* Doubleday, 1987 (I:12+ R:6).

_____. *Dancing Carl.* Bradbury, 1983 (I:10+ R:4).

_____. *Dogsong.* Bradbury, 1988 (I:10+ R:6).

_____. *Hatchet.* Bradbury, 1987 (I:10+ R:6).

_____. *The Schernoff Discoveries.* Delacorte, 1997 (I:10+ R:6).

_____. *Sisters/Hermanas.* Harcourt Brace, 1993 (I:12+ R:6).

Peck, Richard, *Bel-Air Bambi and the Mall Rats.* Delacorte, 1993 (I:10+ R:5).

_____. *Remembering the Good Times.* Delacorte, 1985 (I:12+ R:4).

Perkins, Lynne Rae. *All Alone in the Universe.* Greenwillow, 1999 (I:10+ R:5).

Perkins, Mitali. *The Sunita Experiment.* Hyperion, 1993 (I:12+ R:6).

Peters, Julie Anne. *Luna.* Little, Brown, 2004 (I:14–18 R:6).

Petersen, P. J. *The Sub.* Illustrated by Meredith Johnson. Dutton, 1993 (I:8–10 R:4).

Philbrick, Rodman. *The Young Man and the Sea.* Scholastic, 2004 (I:10+ R:6).

Politi, Leo. *Song of the Swallows.* Scribner, 1949 (I:5–8 R:4).

Prose, Francine. *After.* HarperCollins, 2003 (I:10+ R:6).

Provost, Gary, & Gail Levine-Provost. *David and Max.* Jewish Publication Society, 1988 (I:10+ R:6).

Rapp, Adam. *The Buffalo Tree.* Front Street, 1997 (I:12+ R:6).

Raskin, Ellen. *Figgs & Phantoms.* Dutton, 1974 (I:10+ R:5).

_____. *The Mysterious Disappearance of Leon (I Mean Noel).* Dutton, 1971 (I:10+ R:5).

_____. *The Westing Game.* Dutton, 1978 (I:10+ R:5).

Riskind, Mary. *Apple Is My Sign.* Houghton Mifflin, 1981 (I:9–12 R:5).

Rocklin, Joanne. *For Your Eyes Only!* Illustrated by Mark Todd. Scholastic, 1997 (I:9–12 R:5).

Rodowsky, Colby. *Remembering Mog.* Farrar, Straus & Giroux, 1996 (I:12+ R:6).

_____. *Sydney, Herself.* Farrar, Straus & Giroux, 1989 (I:12+ R:6).

Rosoff, Meg. *How I Live Now.* Random House, 2004 (I:14+–YA R:7).

Ryan, Pam Muñoz. *Becoming Naomi León.* Scholastic, 2004 (I:10+ R:6).

Rylant, Cynthia. *A Fine White Dust.* Bradbury, 1986 (I:11+ R:6).

_____. *Missing May.* Orchard, 1992 (I:10+ R:6).

Sachar, Louis. *Holes.* Farrar, Straus & Giroux, 1998 (I:10+ R:5).

Sachs, Marilyn. *The Bears' House.* Illustrated by Louis Glanzman, Doubleday, 1971 (I:8–11 R:6).

Sáenz, Benjamin Alire. *A Gift From Papá Diego.* Illustrated by Geronimo Garcia. Cinco Puntos, 1998 (I:7+ R:4).

Savage, Deborah. *Under a Different Sky.* Houghton Mifflin, 1997 (I:12+ R:6).

Schami, Rafik. *A Hand Full of Stars.* Translated by Rika Lesser. Dutton, 1990 (I:12+ R:6).

Schotter, Roni. *Captain Snap and the Children of Vinegar Lane.* Illustrated by Marcia Sewell. Orchard, 1989 (I:5–8).

Shea, Pegi Deitz. *Tangled Thread: A Hmong Girl's Story.* Houghton Mifflin, 2003 (I:10+ R:6).

Sheldon, Dyan. *Confessions of a Teenage Drama Queen.* Candlewick, 1999 (I:12+ R:6).

Sheth, Kashmira. *Blue Jasmine.* Hyperion, 2004 (I:10+ R:6).

Shreve, Susan. *The Gift of the Girl Who Couldn't Hear.* Tambourine, 1991 (I:9+ R:5).

Shusterman, Neal. *Speeding Bullet.* Scholastic, 1992 (I:10+ R:6).

Sisulu, Elinor Batezat. *The Day Gogo Went to Vote: South Africa, April 1994.* Little, Brown, 1996 (I:4–8 R:6).

Slepian, Jan. *The Broccoli Tapes.* Philomel, 1989 (I:10+ R:6).

Slote, Alfred. *Hang Tough, Paul Mather.* Lippincott, 1973 (I:9–12 R:3).

_____. *The Trading Game.* Lippincott, 1990 (I:10+ R:4).

Smalls-Hector, Irene. *Jonathan and His Mommy.* Illustrated by Michael Hays. Little, Brown, 1992 (I:3–8 R:4).

Smith, Janice Lee. *The Show-and-Tell War.* Illustrated by Dick Gackenbach. Harper & Row, 1988 (I:7–9 R:4).

Snyder, Zilpha Keatley. *The Egypt Game.* Illustrated by Alton Raible. Atheneum, 1967 (I:10+ R:6).

Soto, Gary. *Pacific Crossing.* Harcourt Brace, 1992 (I:10+ R:6).

_____. *Taking Sides.* Harcourt, 1991 (I:10+ R:6).

Sperry, Armstrong. *Call It Courage.* Macmillan, 1940 (I:9–13 R:6).

Spinelli, Jerry. *Maniac Magee.* Little, Brown, 1996 (I:8+ R:5).

_____. *Wringer.* HarperCollins, 1997 (I:9+ R:4).

Staples, Suzanne Fisher. *Dangerous Skies.* Farrar, Straus & Giroux, 1996 (I:12+ R:6).

_____. *Shabanu: Daughter of the Wind.* Knopf, 1989 (I:12+ R:6).

Steig, William. *Spinky Sulks.* New York: Farrar, Straus & Giroux, 1988 (I:3–8 R:5).

Stolz, Mary. *Stealing Home.* HarperCollins, 1992 (I:8–12 R:4).

Strachan, Ian. *Flawed Glass.* Little, Brown, 1990 (I:10+ R:6).

Sykes, Shelley. *For Mike.* Delacorte, 1998 (I:12+ R:6).

Taylor, Clark. *The House That Crack Built.* Illustrated by Jan Thompson Dicks. Chronicle, 1992 (I:10+).

Taylor, Mildred D. *The Gold Cadillac.* Illustrated by Michael Hays. Dial, 1987 (I:8–10 R:3).

_____. *Roll of Thunder, Hear My Cry.* Dial, 1976 (I:10+ R:6).

Taylor, Sydney. *All-of-a-Kind Family.* Illustrated by Helen John. Follett, 1951 (I:7–10 R:4).

Taylor, Theodore. *The Cay.* Doubleday, 1969 (I:10+ R:6).

_____. *The Trouble with Tuck.* Doubleday, 1981 (I:6–9 R:5).

Taylor, William. *Agnes the Sheep.* Scholastic, 1991 (I:8+ R:5).

Tolan, Stephanie S. *A Good Courage.* Morrow, 1988 (I:12+ R:6).

_____. *Surviving the Applewhites.* HarperCollins, 2002 (I:10+ R:6).

Voigt, Cynthia. *Bad Girls.* Scholastic, 1996 (I:9+ R:7).

_____. *Dicey's Song.* Atheneum, 1982 (I:10+ R:5).

_____. *Homecoming.* Atheneum, 1981 (I:10+ R:5).

_____. *A Solitary Blue.* Atheneum, 1983 (I:10+ R:6).

_____. *Sons From Afar.* Atheneum, 1987 (I:10+ R:6).

Wallace, Ian. *Chin Chiang and the Dragon's Dance.* Atheneum, 1984 (I:6–9 R:6).

Walter, Virginia. *Making Up Megaboy.* Illustrated by Katrina Roeckelein. DK, 1998 (I:10+ R:6).

Waters, Kate, & Madeline Slovenes-Low. *Lion Dancer: Emie Wan's Chinese New Year.* Scholastic, 1990 (I:5–8 R:4).

Whelan, Gloria. *Homeless Bird.* HarperCollins, 2000 (I:10+ R:5).

White, Ruth. *Belle Prater's Boy.* Farrar, Straus & Giroux, 1996 (I:10+ R:6).

Williams, Carol Lynch. *The True Colors of Caitlynne Jackson.* Delacorte, 1997 (I:10+ R:5).

Williams, Karen Lynn. *When Africa Was Home.* Illustrated by Floyd Cooper. Orchard, 1991 (I:4–8 R:4).

Williams, Sherley Anne. *Working Cotton.* Illustrated by Carole Byard. Harcourt Brace, 1992 (I:all).

Wojciechowska, Maia. *Shadow of a Bull.* Illustrated by Alvin Smith. Atheneum, 1964 (I:10+ R:5).

Wolff, Virginia Euwer. *Probably Still Nick Swansen.* Holt, Rinehart & Winston, 1988 (I:10+ R:6).

Woodson, Jacqueline. *Maizon at Blue Hill.* Delacorte, 1992 (I:10+ R:5).

Wyeth, Sharon Dennis. *Orphea Proud.* Delacorte, 2004 (I:14–17 R:7).

_____. *Something Beautiful.* Bantam, 1998 (I:4–8).

Wynne-Jones, Tim. *The Maestro.* Orchard, 1996 (I:11+ R:6).

Wyss, Johann David. *The Swiss Family Robinson.* Illustrated by Lynd Ward. Grosset & Dunlap, 1949 (I:10+ R:6).

Yep, Laurence. *Child of the Owl.* Harper & Row, 1975 (I:10+ R:7).

_____. *Later, Gator.* Hyperion, 1995 (I:8–12 R:5).

_____. *Skunk Scout.* Hyperion, 2003 (I:9+ R:6).

_____. *Thief of Hearts.* HarperCollins, 1995 (I:10+ R:5).

Jill Esbaum
PICTURES BY **Adam Rex**

Chapter Outline

The People and the Past Come Alive

- Values of Historical Fiction for Children

- Literary Criticism: Using Literary Elements to Evaluate Historical Fiction

- Historical Authenticity

- A Chronology of Historical Fiction

Teaching With Historical Fiction

- Providing Background Through Illustrations

- Interdisciplinary Unit: Looking at Pioneer America

- Creating a Historical Fiction "Books on the Move" Source

The People and the Past Come Alive

The thread of people's lives weaves through the past, through the present, and into the future. Many Americans have a deep desire to trace their roots—here in this hemisphere or back to Europe, Asia, or Africa. What did their ancestors experience? Why did they travel to North America? What were their personal feelings and beliefs? What was life like for the settlers who pioneered the American frontier and for the native North Americans who greeted them? Did people of the past have the same concerns as people of the present? Can their experiences suggest solutions for today's problems?

Through the pages of historical fiction, the past comes alive. It is not just dates, accomplishments, and battles; it is people, famous and unknown. This chapter discusses the values of historical fiction for children, gives criteria for evaluatiang historical fiction, looks at the need for historical authenticity, and provides examples of historical fiction. Books of historical fiction are linked to a short discussion of events in the time period that they reflect in the hope that this chronological framework will give you a better understanding of the sweep of history as portrayed in these books. One way to evaluate the importance of historical fiction is to analyze the genre of books awarded the Batchelder Award, which is presented to the best book translated into English: More than half of the awards presented since 1968 are for historical fiction.

Values of Historical Fiction for Children

Children cannot actually cross the ocean on the *Mayflower* and see a new world for the first time, experience the arrival of the first Europeans on their native shores, or feel the consequences of persecution during World War II. They can imagine these experiences, however, through the pages of historical fiction. With Patricia Clapp's *Constance: A Story of Early Plymouth*, they can imagine that they are standing on the swaying deck of the *Mayflower* and seeing their new home. With Scott O'Dell's *The Feathered Serpent*, they can imagine that they are witnessing Montezuma's tragic encounter with the Spanish conquistador Hernando Cortés. With Paul Fleischman's *Bull Run*, they can understand the various viewpoints associated with the Civil War. With Ida Vos's *Hide and Seek*, they can imagine that they are given sanctuary by Dutch gentiles during World War II.

As children read for enjoyment, they relive the past vicariously. Tales based on authentic historical settings or episodes are alive with adventures that appeal to many children. For example, they can follow the adventures of a young girl living on the Wisconsin frontier in Carol Ryrie Brink's *Caddie Woodlawn*. They can follow the adventures of a girl in Victorian London, interacting with people in the sinister opium trade and conducting a quest for a missing ruby in Philip Pullman's *The Ruby in the Smoke*. They can follow a family preparing for an 1890s Christmas celebration in Virginia Hamilton's *The Bells of Christmas*. They can follow the rescue effort during the evacuation of Dunkirk in May 1940 in Louise Borden's *The Little Ships: The Heroic Rescue at Dunkirk in World War II*.

Children who read historical fiction gain an understanding of their own heritage. The research that precedes the writing of authentic historical stories enables authors to incorporate information about the period naturally. Children gain knowledge about the people, values, beliefs, hardships, and physical surroundings common to various periods. They discover the events that preceded their own time and influenced the present. Through historical fiction, children can begin to visualize the sweep of history. As characters in historical fiction from many time periods face and overcome their problems, children may discover universal truths, identify feelings and behaviors that encourage them to consider alternative ways to handle their own problems, empathize with viewpoints that are different from their own, and realize that history consists of many people who have learned to work together.

Through historical fiction, children can discover that in all times, people have depended on one another and that they have had similar needs. They can learn that when human relationships deteriorate, tragedy usually results. Historical fiction allows children to judge relationships and realize that their present and future are linked to the actions in the past.

One of the strongest values of historical fiction is written by a character who is corresponding with a WW II survivor in Gregory Maguire's *The Good Liar*: "It makes me think that history really happens to ordinary people. That history is even happening to me, right now, even if I don't know it. I like that feeling" (p. 129).

Literary Criticism: Using Literary Elements to Evaluate Historical Fiction

When evaluating historical fiction for children, adults must be certain that a story adheres to the criteria for excellent literature discussed in Chapter 3. Historical fiction must also satisfy special requirements in terms of plot, characterization, setting, and theme. The questions in the Evaluation Criteria box on this page summarize additional criteria you should consider when evaluating historical fiction for children.

Plot

Credible plots in historical fiction emerge from authentically developed time periods. The experiences, conflicts, and resolutions of conflicts must reflect the times—whether the antagonist is another person, society, nature, or internal dilemmas faced by the protagonist. Conflict in historical fiction often develops when characters leave their environments and move into alien ones. Authors may highlight the problems, cultures, or diverse values of time periods by exploring the conflicts developed because of characters' inner turmoil or because of societal pressures.

Author Russell Freedman (1992) presents interesting insights into the search for truth about the interactions between pioneers and Native Americans. He describes his own search for truth about the wagon-train journeys along the Oregon Trail:

> Now, the movies and television have taught us that this journey was fraught with peril, since the hostile Indians were likely to attack at any moment. And yet, as I pursued my research, I found that Indian attacks were few and far between. Attacks were infrequent. I began to wonder, how menacing were the Indians. (p. 2)

In his search for the truth, Freedman describes differences in the impressions gained from diaries written by men and by women: Whereas men emphasized the dangers from Indians and described their battles with Indian war parties, women's diaries frequently showed initial fear of the Indians but usually described the Indians as friendly and

Evaluation Criteria

Literary Criticism: Historical Fiction

1. Do the characters' experiences, conflicts, and resolutions of conflicts reflect what is known about the time period?

2. Do the characters' actions express values and beliefs that are realistic for the time period?

3. Is the language authentic for the period without relying on so many colorful terms or dialects that the story is difficult to understand?

4. Is the setting authentic in every detail?

5. Are details integrated into the story so that they do not overwhelm readers or detract from the story?

6. If the setting is the antagonist, are the relationships between characters and setting clearly developed?

7. Is the theme worthwhile?

8. Does the style enhance the mood and clarify the conflicts, characterizations, settings, and themes?

helpful. Freedman speculates about the accuracy of the depiction of history for this period.

Circle of Fire, by William H. Hooks, explores the moral dilemmas created by prejudice. Hooks's story takes place in North Carolina in the 1930s. In this story, a white boy and his two black friends try to prevent a Ku Klux Klan attack on Irish gypsies. Hooks develops additional believable personal conflict when the 11-year-old boy discovers that his father, whom he loves and respects, is probably involved in the Klan.

Historical fiction stories also develop plausible person-against-society conflicts. The heroines in Karen Cushman's *Catherine, Called Birdy* and *The Midwife's Apprentice* face both person-against-self and person-against-society conflicts caused by society in medieval England and by their needs to overcome inner turmoils. The conflict in *The Captive* develops because of greed and the Spaniards' socially supported prejudice against non-Europeans, which O'Dell portrays compellingly. Likewise, conflict develops in *Circle of Fire* because of social prejudice.

Authors who develop credible person-against-society conflicts must describe the values and beliefs of the time period or the attitudes of a segment of the population so that readers understand the nature of the antagonist. In Kathryn Lasky's *The Night Journey,* deadly anti-Semitism is the antagonist that forces a Jewish family to plan and execute a dangerous flight from czarist Russia. The story seems more credible because a modern-day family in this book believes that these memories would be so painful that the great-grandmother should not be encouraged to remember the experiences.

Well-developed person-against-self and person-against-society conflicts, such as those faced by the 14-year-old hero in Susan Campbell Bartoletti's *No Man's Land: A Young Soldier's Story,* help readers understand the values expressed during a time period and the problems, moral dilemmas, and social issues the people faced. Authors often use these conflicts and their resolutions to develop themes in historical fiction.

Characterization

The actions, beliefs, and values of characters in historical fiction must be realistic for the time period. Authors of historical novels admit that it is sometimes difficult not to give their historical characters contemporary actions and values. Historical fiction author Erik Haugaard (1988) emphasizes the need to accurately depict the beliefs and values of the time period, and he differentiates between technical faults and spiritual errors in historical fiction. He contends that technical faults, such as advancing the petroleum lamp by half a century, are not as troubling as spiritual ones:

> The errors which I have dubbed spiritual I dislike much more, and I would be much harder on them than mere mistake of a date. By spiritual mistakes I mean giving people in one cen-

tury the ideas and opinions of another. A citizen of Rome at the time of Christ might have considered slavery vile. But if he did, he was unique. There is no doubt that the vast majority did not even question the institution. If the author lets the character in his novel have extremely unorthodox views, he must explain why and how he came to hold those opinions. If the characters in a historical novel are merely twentieth century men and women dressed up to perform a masquerade, I see little point in applauding just because their dresses are described accurately. (p. 7)

Choosing the main and supporting characters can cause additional problems. For example, authors of historical fiction rarely use famous people as pivotal characters unless they can document evidence about specific dialogue or sentiments. Authors frequently place historical figures in the role of secondary characters. In Esther Forbes's *Johnny Tremain,* for example, a fictional silversmith's apprentice is the pivotal character, and Paul Revere and Samuel Adams are background characters.

Authors develop characters through dialogue, thoughts, actions, and descriptions. Although all of these elements must appear authentic, the speech of the characters and the language of a period can cause problems for writers of historical fiction. In addition, authors of children's historical fiction must be careful not to use so many colorful terms from a period that the story is difficult for young readers to comprehend. Zena Sutherland (1997) agrees that creating natural conversations is one of the most difficult tasks for writers of historical fiction.

Readers must believe that the characters in historical fiction are human beings like themselves. Belief in individual characters was one of the goals cited by Michael Dorris (1992) in his writing of *Morning Girl,* a story about the Taino people, who lived on the Bahama islands at the time of Columbus's arrival in 1492. Dorris states:

> In the characters of Morning Girl and Star Boy, I allowed myself to speculate freely, to invite onto the page two fully invested children—curious, independent, self-analytical, strong, moving toward independence, whose flaws were the flaws of youth: redeemable with wisdom and maturity. (p. 3)

The resulting novel encourages readers to understand and believe in these characters who lived in a different time.

In *Bud, Not Buddy,* Christopher Paul Curtis uses an interesting technique to increase understanding of his character's motives and behaviors: Throughout the book, he presents rules that Bud expresses when he has problems. For example, Rules and Things Number 328: "When You Make Up Your Mind to Do Something, Hurry Up and Do It, If You Wait You Might Talk Yourself Out of What You Wanted in the First Place" (p. 27).

Technology Resources **CW**

Visit the Companion Website at www.prenhall.com/norton to link to a site dedicated to Christopher Paul Curtis and his works.

In *Shadow Spinner*, Susan Fletcher introduces each chapter with "Lessons for Life and Storytelling." Through this technique, the author develops understanding of the characters and the conflicts in a story with an ancient Persian setting.

SETTING

Because historical fiction must be authentic in every respect, the careful development of setting for a certain time period is essential. Historical fiction author Leon Garfield (1988) states that "historical fiction more than any other kind of fiction must be rooted in a particular place and time" (p. 736). A setting this important to a story is called an *integral setting*.

An integral setting must be described in details so clear that readers understand how the story is related to a time and place. This is of particular concern in historical fiction written for children, because children cannot draw on memory for historical periods. Writers must provide images through vivid descriptions that do not overpower plot and characterization. John Stewig (1989) also emphasizes the need for integral settings when he concludes, "One mark of a skilled writer in any genre is the ability to weave in details so they aren't noticed consciously, yet are available when needed later" (p. 135).

When writing lengthy books for older children, authors have more time to develop settings in which the actions and characters are influenced by both time and place. The setting in historical fiction may guide readers into the plot, create visual images that allow them to accept a character's experiences, and encourage them to feel the excitement of a time period.

For example, the setting for Joëlle Stolz's *The Shadows of Ghadames* is southern Libya, near the Algerian and Tunisian borders, at the close of the 19th century. Within this setting, the author depicts the culture of the city, especially the role of women in a culture that has very different roles for men and women. The author develops details associated with the secret role of women as they live with men in two worlds that are "as necessary and different as the sun and the moon. And the sun and the moon never meet, except at the beginning and end of the night" (p. 10). Readers discover the challenges for Malika, a girl who wants to gain some of the advantages boys experienced, such as learning to read. The author concludes with a foreshadowing of changes to come and the possibilities for women when Malika's father agrees that she should learn to read and he overcomes his wife's concerns that she will never find a husband if she is literate when he says: "Only weak men are afraid of a woman who can read! . . . Don't worry. You'll learn and you'll find a husband because the times are changing—this I know—and change will even come to Ghadames, despite its walls" (p. 117).

Authors of longer historical fiction written for older readers also have more room to include interesting historical details. For example, in *The River Between Us*, Richard Peck provides the following details associated with a Model T Ford touring car in 1916: "You had to crank the car a good ten minutes to get it going, and Dad left that part to me. The knack for starting a Ford was to jack up a rear wheel. . . . But at last the engine caught and turned over. Dad broke a fresh egg into the radiator so that it would hard-boil and seal the leaks" (p. 8). Peck includes descriptions of repairing flat tires, overheating engines, and driving hills that are so steep that they turned the Ford around and drove up the hills in reverse.

Setting plays the role of antagonist in many stories about exploration and pioneering. For example, in Honoré Morrow's *On to Oregon!*, sleet storms, rugged mountains, swift streams, and natural predators act as antagonists. Morrow's descriptions leave little doubt that the children are confronting a beautiful but awesome adversary.

Authors of historical fiction sometimes contrast settings in order to develop conflict; both Ann Petry (*Tituba of Salem Village*) and Elizabeth George Speare (*The Witch of Blackbird Pond*) use this technique. Both authors have taken protagonists from the warm, colorful Caribbean and placed them in the bleak, somber surroundings of a Puritan village. Time and place then influence how other characters react to these protagonists and how these characters respond to their new environments.

Some settings in historical fiction create happy, nostalgic moods. In Cynthia Rylant's picture storybook *When I Was Young in the Mountains*, the illustrations and the text

The illustrations reflect a happy setting in an Appalachian mountain community. (From When I Was Young in the Mountains, by Cynthia Rylant, illustrated by Diane Goode. Illustrations © 1982 by Diane Goode. E. P. Dutton, Inc. Reprinted by permission of E. P. Dutton, Inc.)

Through the Eyes of an AUTHOR

Mary E. Lyons

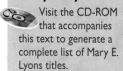

Visit the CD-ROM that accompanies this text to generate a complete list of Mary E. Lyons titles.

Selected Titles by Mary E. Lyons:

Sorrow's Kitchen: The Life and Folklore of Zora Neale Hurston

Raw Head, Bloody Bones: African-American Tales of the Supernatural

Letters From a Slave Girl: The Story of Harriet Jacobs

Catching the Fire: Philip Simmons, Blacksmith

Knockabeg: A Famine Tale

I was a teacher at the middle-school level for seventeen years and school librarian at the elementary, middle- and high-school levels for six years. One day I realized that half of my students were girls and half of my students were African Americans. And I thought, you know, I may just start putting some things in the curriculum that are especially for these two groups of students that I'm teaching. And I became very interested in African

American history and in women's history and did a lot throughout the whole year to celebrate that history.

Many of my books are about women, including my first book, *Sorrow's Kitchen. The Life and Folklore of Zora Neale Hurston.* As I delved into women's history, I found a lot of women writers whose work had been forgotten, and Zora Neale Hurston was one of them. So I collected some of her writings and shared them with my students, and I really liked to tell them the story of her life. She was quite a successful writer and an anthropologist. Sadly, she died alone and poor in a charity home in 1960.

The story of how Zora Neale Hurston educated herself, became a writer, a folklorist, and an anthropologist was so interesting to my students that I told it, and told it, and told it so many times that I finally decided to write it down—that is a short version of how I wrote my first book, *Sorrow's Kitchen.*

My second book, *Raw Head, Bloody Bones: African-American Tales of the Supernatural,* is a book that I edited. I did not write the stories, but I collected stories told by enslaved African Americans all over the world. Some of them are scary, some of them are funny/scary, and some are simply about the supernatural. There

are a lot of wonderful supernatural elements in folklore from all over the world.

Another woman writer in whom I was interested was Harriet Jacobs. Harriet Jacobs was a real person. She was enslaved in North Carolina and for seven years she hid from the slaveholder in the eaves under her grandmother's roof. She finally escaped in 1845, but only when she knew that she could safely have her children join her in the North. She wrote of her experiences in a book called *Incidents of the Life of a Slave Girl.* That's a wonderful book to read when you're ready for it. For my readers, my students, I wanted to retell her story in a childhood voice, in a girlhood voice, so I wrote this historical novel. Writers of historical fiction start with what is true and then we add voice, and dialogue, and thought, and imagination, and for want of a better word, heart. I really felt that Harriet's heart touched mine while I was writing this book.

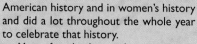

Video Profiles: The accompanying video contains more of this conversation with Mary E. Lyons, as well as conversations with other writers of historical fiction, including Joseph Bruchac, Eve Bunting, and Leonard Everett Fisher.

allow readers to glimpse a girl's happy years of growing up in the Appalachian mountains of Virginia. This peaceful setting includes swimming holes, country stores, and family evenings on the porch. The illustrations help integrate the details of the time period into the story. In contrast, the illustrations in Jo Hoestlandt's *Star of Fear, Star of Hope* reinforce a poignantly sad tale of separation in Nazi-occupied France in 1942.

Smells, sounds, and light create believable settings in Gary Paulsen's *The Winter Room,* a story of farm life in an earlier American setting. Paulsen introduces *The Winter Room* by telling readers that if books could have smells, this book "would have the smell of new-mown hay as it falls off the oiled sickle blade when the horses pull the mower through the field, and the sour smell of manure steaming in a winter barn" (p. 1). If it could have sounds, it "would have the high, keening sound of the six-foot bucksaws as the men pull them back and forth through the trees to cut pine for paper pulp; the grunting-gassy sounds of the work teams snorting and slapping as they hit the harness to jerk the stumps out of the ground" (p. 2). And if the book could have light it would have "the soft gold light—gold with bits of hay dust floating in it—that slips through the crack in the barn wall; the light of the Coleman lantern hissing flat-white in the kitchen; the silver-gray light of a middle winter day, the splattered,

white-night light of a full moon on snow, the new light of dawn at the eastern edge of the pasture behind the cows coming in to be milked on a summer morning" (p. 2). But Paulsen tells readers that because books cannot have smells, sounds, and light, the book needs readers who bring these sensations to the reading. Throughout his book, Paulsen's descriptions help readers visualize and vicariously experience details.

Theme

Themes in historical fiction, as in any literature, should be worthwhile and as relevant in today's society as they were in the historical periods represented. Many books of historical fiction have themes that have been relevant throughout history. The search for freedom is a theme in literature about all time periods. For example, Rosemary Sutcliff's *The Shining Company* is based on the development of a fighting brotherhood to battle the invading Saxons. Sutcliff's books develop stories in which searching for and defending freedom are primary goals. Sutcliff's books are memorable, according to Sutherland (1997), because they are built around great themes. "Her characters live and die for principles they value and that people today still value" (p. 395). Freedom is one of the great themes in historical fiction. Elizabeth Yates's *Amos Fortune, Free Man* tells about an African slave searching for freedom in colo-

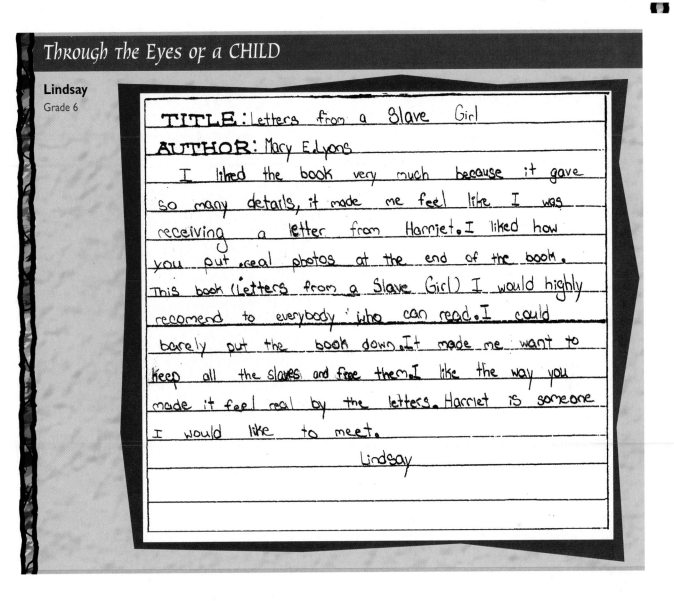

Through the Eyes of a CHILD

Lindsay
Grade 6

TITLE: Letters from a Slave Girl

AUTHOR: Mary E. Lyons

I liked the book very much because it gave so many details, it made me feel like I was receiving a letter from Harriet. I liked how you put real photos at the end of the book. This book (Letters from a Slave Girl) I would highly recomend to everybody who can read. I could barely put the book down. It made me want to keep all the slaves and free them. I like the way you made it feel real by the letters. Harriet is someone I would like to meet.

Lindsay

nial Boston. The importance of justice is developed in many historical fiction books, such as Eve Ibbotson's *Journey to the River Sea*.

Love of the land and the independence it provides are themes in books about the westward expansion of European settlers in North America and about the Native Americans they displaced. Europeans leave relatives and established communities to face unknown dangers and acquire homesteads. Native Americans first attempt to share their beloved natural environment with the new arrivals. Then, they find themselves being pushed out of their homes. Love of land and the consequences caused by loss of land are developed by Scott O'Dell and Elizabeth Hall in *Thunder Rolling in the Mountains*. This book, told through the viewpoint of Chief Joseph's daughter, describes the conflict and pain associated with being forced to leave the Wallowa Valley. Children in both the westward expansion literature and the Native American literature inherit their parents' dreams and fight to retain the land.

Loyalty and honor are also common themes in stories about all time periods. People are loyal to friends and family members, following them on difficult quests and avenging their deaths or dishonor. They are loyal to their principles and defend them. Many books of historical fiction for children stress the cruelty and futility of war, even when honor and adherence to loyalty have helped cause the conflict. Novels about war in various historical periods often develop the themes of overcoming injustice. They also show ways in which people on both sides of a conflict have much in common. For example, Susan Campbell Bartoletti's protagonist in *No Man's Land: A Young Soldier's Story* concludes as he prepares for battle: "It hit Thrasher, all of a sudden, how odd it was. The Yankees and Rebels spoke the same language, knew the same prayers, prayed to the same God" (p. 84). The beliefs of nonviolent people such as the Quakers are the bases of themes in some historical novels. Many themes are relevant today, whether the stories in which they are developed take place in ancient Rome or contemporary America.

Style

An author's style influences the mood in historical fiction. For example, the repetition of the line "When I was young in the mountains" in Cynthia Rylant's text helps create a warm, nostalgic mood, in which harmful occurrences seem improbable. Brett Harvey introduces her mostly happy pioneer adventure *Cassie's Journey: Going West in the 1860s* with a description that suggests anticipation and security: "We're on our way to California! I'm riding up high with Papa, and the wind is rocking the wagon. When I look back I can see a long line of wagons curling behind us like a snake in the dust" (unnumbered).

In contrast, Patricia MacLachlan's introduction to *Sarah, Plain and Tall* suggests that the story will be about a family but that some unhappiness may have entered the family's life:

> "Did Mama sing every day?" asked Caleb. "Every-single-day?" He sat close to the fire, his chin in his hand. It was dusk, and the dogs lay beside him on the warm hearthstones. "Every-single-day," I told him for the second time this week. For the twentieth time this month. The hundredth time this year? And the past few years? (p. 3)

If a historical fiction story has elements of suspense and adventure, the introduction frequently hints at the intrigue to follow. Philip Pullman's *The Ruby in the Smoke* develops mystery and adventure in Victorian England. Pullman introduces his novel about the sinister opium trade and the quest for a missing ruby:

> On a cold, fretful afternoon in early October, 1872, a hansom cab drew up outside the offices of Lockhart and Selby, Shipping Agents, in the financial heart of London, and a young girl got out and paid the driver. She was a person of sixteen or so—alone, and uncommonly pretty. . . . Her name was Sally Lockhart; and within fifteen minutes she was going to kill a man. (p. 3)

Various forms of figurative language may clarify the conflicts, characters, settings, and themes in historical fiction. Figurative language is especially powerful when it provides insights into time, place, and conflict. For example, in *No Hero for the Kaiser*, Rudolf Frank creates vivid images of World War I settings.

Allusions in historical fiction frequently provide insights into plots and characters. These same allusions, however, may require interpretation for less knowledgeable readers. For example, Frank uses allusions to the biblical flood, Napoleon, the skull of an African sultan, and the Maid of Orleans. Some of these allusions are explained in the text, but others are not. Karen Cushman identifies many of her journal entries in *Catherine, Called Birdy* with religious holidays that correspond with the dates. These "Feasts of Saint . . ." imply the importance of religion in medieval England.

Gary D. Schmidt, the author of *Lizzie Bright and the Buckminster Boy*, a novel set in Phippsburg, Maine, in 1912, is another author who uses biblical allusions to help

Historically accurate settings add to this World War I story. (From No Hero for the Kaiser, by Rudolf Frank, translated from the 1931 edition by Patricia Crampton, copyright © 1986. Illustrated by Klaus Steffens. Reprinted by permission of Lothrop, Lee & Shepard.)

develop setting, mood, and characterizations. These allusions seem especially appropriate because the father of the protagonist, Turner Buckminster, is a minister. For example, when Turner is humiliated, he thinks that it is too much to "hope for the Apocalypse" (p. 7); when describing Turner's character, the author writes, "He was as polite as an angel all the way through the roast and potatoes. . . . While carrying out the dishes, he was as helpful as St. Timothy" (p. 40); when Turner experiences the ocean, "it was as if God had just remade the world for him, and he was Adam waking up, an entire globe to explore" (p. 43); and when Turner has a major conflict with his father, the father "started to read from Proverbs; Turner was surprised at how many verses about rebellious children he had been able to collect on such short notice" (p. 49).

Historical Authenticity

In a review of the attitudes expressed by authors of historical fiction, Lawrence R. Sipe (1997) states, "The issue that receives the most attention from authors of historical fiction is how to write authentically" (p. 246). This concern for authenticity emphasizes the use of language, the depiction of the details of everyday life, the faithfulness to the historical record, and the need for readers to perceive that the language, situations, and characters are "true."

The need for authentic historical detail places special demands on authors of historical fiction. Some authors actually lived through the experiences they write about or knew someone who lived through them. Other authors write about historical periods far removed from their personal experiences; to gather their data, they must rely on sources of information far different from the people who vividly remember a historical period. Diane Stanley (1994) emphasizes that authors of historical fiction must set high standards in the hope of coming close to the truth.

Laura Ingalls Wilder, the author of the "Little House" books, lived in the big woods of Wisconsin, traveled by covered wagon through Kansas, lived in a sod house in Minnesota, and shared her life with Pa, Ma, Mary, and Carrie when they finally settled in South Dakota. Wilder's books sound as if they were written immediately after an incident occurred, but Wilder actually wrote the stories describing her life from 1870 through 1889 much later, between 1926 and 1943. Authors who write about their own past experiences need to have both keen powers of observation and excellent memories in order to share the details of their lives with others.

Predominantly happy experiences in the past may be easy to remember. For authors who write about painful experiences in their own lives, however, the doors of memory may be more difficult to open. Johanna Reiss found herself remembering things that she had preferred to forget when she began writing the story of her experiences as a Jewish child hidden by Dutch gentiles during the Holocaust and World War II. According to the publishers of *The Upstairs Room*, Reiss (1972) "did not set out to write a book about her experiences during the Second World War; she simply wanted to record them for her two daughters, who are now about the age she was when she went to stay with the Oastervelds" (p. 197). When Reiss started to write, she began remembering experiences that she had never talked about because they were too painful. To reinforce her memory, she took her children back to Usselo, Holland, where she visited the Dutch family who had protected her and looked again at the upstairs room and the closet in which she had hidden from the Nazis.

Authors such as Carol Ryrie Brink write about relatives' experiences. In *Caddie Woodlawn*, Brink re-creates the story of her grandmother and her grandmother's family. In her author's note to the book, Brink (1973) tells how she lived with her grandmother and loved to listen to her tell stories about her pioneer childhood:

It was many years later that I remembered those stories of Caddie's childhood, and I said to myself, "If I loved them so much perhaps other children would like them too." Caddie was still alive when I was writing, and I sent letters to her, asking about the details that I did not remember clearly. She was pleased when the book was done. "There is only one thing

that I do not understand," she said. "You never knew my mother and father and my brothers—how could you write about them exactly as they were?" "But, Gram," I said, "You told me." (p. 283)

Uri Orlev based his World War II story *The Man From the Other Side* on the memories of a journalist who as a child had lived on the outskirts of the Warsaw Ghetto and had helped his father provide assistance for the Jewish people in the ghetto. Consequently, the setting and the conflict seem very believable.

Of course, modern authors have no firsthand experience of some earlier times and cannot even talk to someone who lived during certain historical periods, so they must use other resources in researching their chosen time periods. To acquire this much knowledge about a time period demands much research. Some authors have chosen to research and write about one period; others have written books covering many different time periods.

Kathryn Lasky reveals the influence of extensive research in her author's note for *Beyond the Divide*. She says that she based the book in part on Theodora Kroeber's biography of the last Yahi Indian, *Ishi: The Last of His Tribe*, and in part on J. Goldsborough Bruff's journal that describes his own experiences during the gold rush. Lasky (1983) describes her own discoveries about the West:

Mrs. Kroeber's story was the first true western tale I had ever read. This was not the West of television, nor was the gold rush the one written about in my school books. The bad guys were worse than I had ever imagined, and the greed for gold was pernicious and deadly to the human spirit. People did not just rob, they killed, and on occasion massacred. The conditions of survival were the most arduous imaginable, but there was one emigrant whose spirit was left miraculously intact. (p. 253)

These discoveries, characterizations, settings, and themes are apparent in her historical novel.

Likewise, Karen Hesse's author's note for *Stowaway* reveals that she based her historical fiction about Captain James Cook's 1768–1771 around-the-world expedition on Cook's and Banks's journals and the "Endeavor" CD-ROM, produced by the National Maritime Museum of Australia and the National Library of Australia.

Lois Lowry based *Number the Stars* on the experiences of the Danish Resistance. She reveals that she was determined to tell the story of the Danish people and the Danish Resistance after seeing a photograph of Kim Malthe-Bruun and reading about his helping Jewish residents of Denmark.

Reading about any of the well-known authors of historical fiction whose books are noted for authentic backgrounds reveals that the authors first spend hundreds of hours researching county courthouse records and old letters, newspapers, and history books; conducting personal interviews; and visiting museums and historical locations. Authors must then write stories that develop believable plots, characters, and settings without sounding like history textbooks. In doing so, they must carefully consider the many conflicting points of view that surround particular events. Writing excellent historical fiction is a very demanding task.

A Chronology of Historical Fiction

In sharing historical fiction with children, you must understand at least some of the history of a time period in order to evaluate stories reflecting that period. Following a 3-year study, Norton found that the understanding, evaluation, and utilization of historical fiction of students in children's literature courses improved if they discussed books of historical fiction in a chronological order, briefly identified the actual historical happenings in each time period, identified major themes

in literature written about a specific period (although, of course, some books have more than one theme), discussed the implications of recurring themes, identified how authors develop believable plots for a time period, and discussed the modern significance of the literature. To assist in the study of historical fiction, this chapter discusses books of historical fiction in an order similar to the one used during this study. Chart 10.1 presents a simple chronology of Western and North American history and the main themes developed in books in each period.

Ancient Times Through the Middle Ages

In pre-Roman times, various Celtic peoples, including the Britons and Gaels, inhabited the British Isles. These people lived in tribes ruled by chiefs and often warred with one another over land and people. In 55 B.C., Julius Cae-

CHART 10.1   Eras and themes in historical fiction

Date	Period	Themes
3000 B.C.	Ancient times through the Middle Ages	Loyalty is one of the noblest human traits. Ignorance, prejudice, and hatred can have destructive consequences for all concerned. Hatred, not people, is the great enemy. Love is stronger than hatred and prevails through times of great trouble. People will always search for freedom and riches. Courage is more important than physical strength. A physical disability does not reduce a person's humanity. People can overcome their handicaps.
A.D. 1492	Changes in the Old World and discovery of the New World	Greed is a strong motivational force and can have destructive consequences. Moral dilemmas must be faced and resolved. People will face severe hardships to acquire the political and religious freedom that they desire. People must work together if they are to survive. Overcoming problems can strengthen character. War creates tragedy. Life is more than physical survival. Land is important: People will endure numerous hardships to acquire land for personal reasons or for the glory of their country.
1692	The Salem witch-hunts	Prejudiced persecution of others is a frightening and destructive social phenomenon. People seek freedom from persecution. Moral obligations require some people to defend the rights of others.
1776	The American Revolution	Freedom is worth fighting for. Strong beliefs require strong commitments.
1780	Early expansion of the United States and Canada	Friendship and faith are important. People long for their own land and the freedom that ownership implies. People will withstand great hardships to retain their dreams. Strong family bonds help physical and spiritual survival. Prejudice and hatred are destructive forces. The greatest strength comes from within. Moral obligations require personal commitment.

sar failed in an attempt to add present-day England and Scotland to the Roman Empire. One hundred years later, Emperor Claudius succeeded in annexing Britain. Roman legions were left behind to subdue the people and to keep peace among the tribes.

The Roman dominance lasted throughout Europe until about A.D. 410, when fierce tribes of Teutonic peoples from northern Europe invaded and sacked Rome, beginning the long medieval period in European history that has sometimes been called the Dark Ages. In their great ships, Vikings from Norway were led by people such as Eric the Red. The Vikings raided the coasts of Europe and demonstrated their remarkable seafaring skills by exploring Greenland and Iceland. In about A.D. 1000, Norse explorers under Leif Ericson's command crossed the Atlantic Ocean and stayed briefly in a place in North America they called "Vinland."

Teutonic Saxons and Angles from the continent invaded and settled Britain. The once-unified Roman empire dissolved into many small domains ruled by competing feudal lords and the warrior nobility that served them in ongoing battles. The lords lived in fortified castles surrounded by cottages and fields in which enslaved peas-

ants produced food and wealth for them. Constant warfare and rampant disease, such as the plague (also known as the Black Death), ravaged the developing towns of England, France, and elsewhere. The strong Christain beliefs of the Middle Ages led to the construction of magnificent cathedrals and to crusades in which Christian warriors attempted to capture Jerusalem for the Roman Catholic Church, which still survived in splendor and power after the fall of Rome.

Authors who write historical fiction about the ancient world and medieval times in Europe often tell their stories from the viewpoint of slaves or other people subjugated by the powerful. Other authors represent the perspectives of the mighty, such as Romans and Vikings, and show the ways in which all people have certain desires and fears in common and confront similar problems. Through these various perspectives, authors of historical fiction for children encourage young readers to imagine and empathize with the personal and social conflicts of people in the distant past. Themes emerge as the characters fight for their beliefs and personal freedoms, follow their dreams, struggle with moral dilemmas, or overcome prejudices or self-doubts that could destroy them.

CHART 10.1   Continued

Date	Period	Themes
1861	The Civil War	War creates tragedy. Moral obligations must be met even if one's life or freedom is in jeopardy. Moral sense does not depend on skin color, but on what is inside a person. People should take pride in themselves and in their accomplishments. Prejudice and hatred are destructive forces. People search for freedom. Personal conscience may not allow some people to kill others. Strong family ties help people persevere.
1860s	The western frontier	People have moral obligations. People have strong dreams of owning land. Families can survive if they work together. People need each other and may work together for their mutual good. Battles can be won through legal means rather than through unlawful actions. Hatred and prejudice are destructive forces. Without spiritual hope, people may lose their will to live.
1900	The early 20th century	People will strive for survival of the physical body and the spirit. Prejudice and discrimination are destructive forces. There is a bond between people who experience injustice. Monetary wealth does not create a rich life.
1939	World War II	People will seek freedom from religious and political persecution. Prejudice and hatred are destructive forces. Moral obligation and personal conscience are strong forces. Freedom is worth fighting for. Family love and loyalty help people endure catastrophic experiences.

In *The Bronze Bow,* Elizabeth George Speare focuses on Israel during Roman rule. She portrays the harshness of the Roman conquerors by telling the story through the eyes of a boy who longs to avenge the death of his parents. (His father was crucified by Roman soldiers, and his mother died from grief and exposure.) Daniel bar Jamin's bitterness intensifies when he joins a guerrilla band and nurtures his hatred of the Romans. His person-against-self conflict comes to a turning point when he almost sacrifices his sister because of his hatred. Speare encourages readers to understand Daniel's real enemy: When Daniel talks to Jesus, both Daniel and readers realize that hatred, not Romans, is the enemy.

Speare's Jewish character shows changes in attitude after he invites a Roman soldier into his home, and the Jewish heroine in Sylvie Weil's *My Guardian Angel* saves the Jewish residents in Troyes, France, from the anti-Semitic hatred of the Crusaders as they march toward the Holy Land in 1096. The author uses two very interesting techniques to develop the attitudes and values of 12-year-old Elvina. First, Elvina talks to and writes letters to Mazal, her guardian angel. It is through these exchanges that Elvina shares her innermost feelings and concerns; they shed light on a heroine who is a many-sided character. The other technique results when Elvina rescues a young Crusader who wants to run away from the Crusades. Elvina answers his questions about Jewish culture when she provides food for him and helps him hide from Peter the Hermit, the leader of this group of Crusaders. The author shows that Christians and Jews can understand and respect each other. A strong love of learning ties the two young people together. The consequence of helping the young Crusader reveals one of the strong themes in the story: Helping others often results in gratitude and protection. The author's afterword also gives historical importance to the actions of the Jewish leaders in Troyes that saved them from the anti-Jewish hatred and destruction that occurred, especially in Germany, as the Crusaders marched toward the Holy Land.

While the Vikings were roaming the seas, knights in armor all across Europe were challenging one another over land and power, and humble people were working in the fields of nobles or serving the mighty in the great halls of castles. In *The Door in the Wall,* Marguerite DeAngeli uses an English castle and its surroundings as the settings for her story about 10-year-old Robin, who is expected to train for knighthood. The plot has an unusual twist when Robin is stricken with a mysterious ailment that paralyzes his legs. The door in the title of the story becomes symbolic. A monk gives unhappy Robin difficult advice: "Thou hast only to follow the wall far enough and there will be a door in it" (p. 16).

This symbol is very important in the story. DeAngeli traces Robin's search for his own door and the preparation necessary to find it. The monk helps Robin by guiding his learning, encouraging him to carve and to read, and expressing the belief that Robin's hands and mind, if not his legs, must be taught because they represent other doors in the wall.

DeAngeli encourages readers to understand the importance of accepting people for what they are, rather than rejecting them because of physical disability, when Robin's father congratulates him: "The courage you have shown, the craftsmanship proven by the harp, and the spirit in your singing all make so bright a light that I cannot see whether or not your legs are misshapen" (p. 120).

Many children enjoy this beautiful story about a child who finds a door in his wall. One girl said that it was her favorite book because she liked the way in which Robin overcame his problem and was happy with his life. The theme is especially appropriate for teaching positive attitudes about people with disabilities.

Three books by Karen Cushman have settings in medieval England in the 13th and 14th centuries. Interesting comparisons can be made among characteristics of the social levels, characterizations of the three heroines, conflicts developed, and themes portrayed in *Catherine, Called Birdy, The Midwife's Apprentice,* and *Matilda Bone.* For example, readers can compare the social structure associated with a medieval English manor and the knight's family in *Catherine, Called Birdy* with the lowest level of poverty described in *The Midwife's Apprentice.* In the latter book, Cushman leaves no doubt about this lowly social level when she introduces both the setting and the heroine, Brat: "When animal droppings and garbage and spoiled straw are piled up in a great heap, the rotting and molding give forth heat. Usually no one gets close enough to notice because of the stench. But the girl noticed and, on that frosty night, burrowed deep into the warm, rotting muck, heedless of the smell. In any event, the dung heap probably smelled little worse than everything else in her life—the food scraps scavenged from kitchen yards, the stables and sties she slept in when she could, and her own unwashed, unnourished, unloved, and unlovely body" (p. 1). Contrasts in social structure are found in *Matilda Bone* as the heroine's life changes from that of a well-educated girl living in a 14th-century manor house to an abandoned orphan who serves as an assistant to a bone setter.

Although the positions of Cushman's three heroines are very different, there are similarities between the characters. Catherine, Brat, and Matilda are strong-willed females who must face conflicts caused by the social structure in order to succeed. There is Catherine's desire for independence and an adventurous life versus society's requirements for females and her father's desire to marry his daughter to a wealthy suitor. There is Brat's need to rise above the ignorance and superstition surrounding her and the antagonism of the village midwife in order to gain the skills and self-respect she needs to succeed. There is Matilda's need to overcome her self-righteous, snobbish attitude before she develops into a compassionate assistant to the bone setter.

There are also similarities in themes in Cushman's books. In each of the books, the heroines discover, through their own actions, that the world is full of possibilities. But to realize these possibilities, they must continue trying. Brat, now Alyce, states this very well when she declares, " 'Jane Sharp! It is I, Alyce, your apprentice. I have come back. And if you do not let me in, I will try again and again. I can do what you tell me and take what you give me, and I know how to try and risk and fail and try again and not give up. I will not go away.' The door opened. Alyce went in. And the cat went with her" (pp. 116–117). This symbol of going through the door could be compared with DeAngeli's *The Door in the Wall.*

Two important themes are developed in Tracy Barrett's *Anna of Byzantium,* which is set in the 11th century during the Byzantine Empire: (1) Searching for and trying to retain power can be destructive, and (2) there were knowledgeable and scholarly women living during the 11th century who should not be forgotten. Barrett develops these two themes by telling a fictional story through the viewpoint of the real Anna Comnena, daughter of the emperor Alexius I. The first theme is developed through the use of tragic Greek myths that Anna's tutor tells her. The theme is reinforced as Anna discovers the intrigue and treachery conducted by her younger brother and her grandmother as they try to replace her as her father's appointed heir. The second theme is developed as the author describes Anna's joy as she writes down her memories, discovers the poetry written by the nun Kassia who wrote about injustice, and her excitement when she receives a gift of Kassia's books and journals. Readers discover that Anna wants to write history because "I admired anyone who could unravel the complicated stories of the past and show them in clear form to a reader" (p. 108).

Fascinating historical fiction books about ancient Asian cultures are available about time periods such as feudal Korea and Japan. For example, Jean Merrill's *The Girl Who Loved Caterpillars* is set in 12th-century Japan. According to the author's note, the story is adapted from an anonymous Japanese story found on a scroll. The author also provides sources for three English translations that were used as the basis for the adaptation. The story presents a strong, clever female character, Izumi, who resists social and family pressures as she develops her own interests. The author contrasts Izumi's interests with those of a noblewoman called "The Lady Who Loved Butterflies," who was considered "The Perfect Lady" because "she dressed exquisitely, wrote poetry in a delicate script, and played with skill on the lute and the sho" (unnumbered). In contrast, Izumi loves caterpillars and other living creatures that most people dislike to touch. In addition, Izumi does not blacken her teeth or trim her busy eyebrows. The story ends with a mystery because, according to Merrill, the original scroll inferred this was part of a longer story that would be found in the second chapter; unfortunately, the second chapter has been lost. Interesting speculations could be made, however, as readers consider what might have happened to this wise woman who was so interested in nature: Would she become a scientist or a philosopher, did she become alienated from her family and society, or did she have some other fate?

The ideas that work gives a person dignity, persistence may result in gaining one's dreams, and courage and loyalty are important human characteristics are all important themes developed in Linda Sue Park's 2002 Newbery Award book, *A Single Shard.* The plot of this story set in 12th-century Korea follows an orphan boy, Tree-ear, as he first longs to become a potter and then has an opportunity to work for one of the most famous potters in Korea. Because he is given the most menial of jobs, he discovers that persistence is necessary if he is ever to gain his dream. The sense of authenticity is developed through the author's use of Korean sayings and proverbs, descriptions of the process used for creating celadon porcelain, and stories told that reveal Korean history. As you read the book, notice the importance of the name change as the orphan Tree-ear becomes Hyung-gu, a name that signifies respect, honor, and attachment to a family.

When writing about how she developed the idea for the book (Johnson & Giorgis, 2002), Park explains that she "happened upon information about how 11th- and 12th-century Korea produced the finest pottery in the world" (p. 396). This information fascinated her so much that she created a story about an orphan boy and how he learned the art of pottery making by watching a master potter create celadon pottery.

Erik Christian Haugaard's *The Boy and the Samurai* is set in feudal Japan during the period of civil wars in the late 1400s and 1500s. As do the authors of many other stories with wartime settings, Haugaard emphasizes the search for peace and the painful realities resulting from war. His settings and characters allow readers to visualize the world of street orphans, warlords, samurai, and priests.

Haugaard uses several techniques to help involve his readers and make the story seem more immediate. For example, in the preface, the author introduces the book in the first person, as if he is telling his autobiography: "As I wrote the tale of my youth, I relived it with each stroke of the brush. When I had finished I felt that a burden had been taken from me. . . . I felt at ease with myself" (p. xxi).

Another technique Haugaard uses is the inclusion of cultural traditions and beliefs throughout the text. For example, as the young boy thinks to himself, he also reveals his belief in the god Oinari-sama: "Oinari-sama is the god

---

Technology Resources CW

Link to more information about the creation of *A Single Shard* from the Chapter 10 Web links on the Companion Website at www.prenhall.com/norton

of rice and has two foxes who serve him. The foxes carry messages and one of them has a roll of paper in his mouth. It is well known that foxes, as well as Tanuki the Badger and the Crane, can change themselves into human beings if they want to. I liked the little fox god and felt that he was nearer to being a child like myself, so I would sometimes pray to him" (p. 8).

As you read Haugaard's book, look for examples of important symbols and beliefs such as the following: the symbol of the monkey (p. 42), the belief in signs of luck (p. 45), belief in ill omens (p. 49), the importance of being able to compose poetry (p. 136), the belief that writing poetry is the noblest of the arts (p. 137), the belief in benefits of honor and the disadvantages of greed (p. 162), and the importance of bravery (p. 168). *The Boy and the Samurai* provides an interesting historical fiction text to use as the basis for searching for beliefs and values that are also depicted in the traditional folklore and in the art of ancient Japan.

Ancient China in the Year of the Dragon, A.D. 1650, provides the setting for Jeff Stone's *Tiger: The Five Ancestors*. The author develops this story based on the martial arts and on Buddhist beliefs and values as five young warrior monks survive the destruction of China's Cangzhen Temple and set out not only to retrieve the stolen scrolls but also to teach their peaceful philosophy of life. Each of these young people is named after an animal—tiger, monkey, snake, crane, and dragon—and they master a style of kung fu that reflects the animal's personality and body type. The themes in the story are developed through teachings of the Grandmaster, Buddhist proverbs, and actions of the characters as they try to live the purpose of the founding monks: to defend truth and deliver justice. For example, taking a life is wrong because violence accomplishes nothing, and for every action there is an equal and opposing reaction that applies to life as well as to the martial arts. This book about the tiger is part of a series of stories about the five ancestors.

The following themes are expressed in historical fiction about ancient and medieval times. Consider how the themes relate to specific happenings in the time periods. Which of them are significant in our modern world?

1. Loyalty is one of the noblest human traits.
2. Ignorance, prejudice, and hatred can have destructive consequences for all concerned.
3. Hatred, not people, is the great enemy.
4. Love is stronger than hatred and prevails through times of great trouble.
5. People will always search for freedom and riches.
6. Courage is more important than physical strength.
7. A physical disability does not reduce a person's humanity.
8. People can overcome their handicaps.

Changes in the Old World and Encounters With the New World

By the 15th century, Europe had entered the Renaissance, a time of cultural rebirth and great social change. Large cities were bustling with trade, and middle-class merchants had attained more social prominence. Protestant Christianity was arising out of medieval Catholicism and challenging the religious and political power of the established church. In Germany, Johann Gutenberg was inventing the printing press, which William Caxton soon used to publish the first printed books in England. Great artists such as Michelangelo and William Shakespeare began to raise the visual arts and literature to new heights of creative glory, inspired by the rediscovery of ancient Greek and Roman culture. Ordinary people were expecting and demanding greater economic, political, and religious freedom. Explorers were sailing off to prove their belief that the world was round and then to acquire great riches in the New World, a land that was inhabited by native peoples in the Western Hemisphere.

The arrival of Christopher Columbus on a Caribbean island in 1492 was soon followed by conquest of ancient Mayan and Aztec cultures in Central America by Spanish explorers. By the late 16th and early 17th centuries, colonies were springing up along the Atlantic coast of North America. People followed their lust for wealth and adventure or their desire for freedom from the religious persecution and political conflicts that were occurring in England and elsewhere.

Several books published in 1992, the 500th anniversary of Columbus's voyage, present the landing of Columbus from the viewpoint of the native peoples. Jane Yolen's picture storybook *Encounter* develops a hypothetical interaction between a Taino Indian boy and Columbus and his men on the island of San Salvador in 1492. The text is developed on the premise that dreams forewarn the boy about the disastrous consequences of interacting with the explorers, who the people believe have flown down from the sky. Yolen includes descriptions of the Taino Indians and their beliefs, details about the loss of culture and human life that resulted because of the Spanish exploration and colonization, and details describing trade between the explorers and the Taino people. Information provided in the author's notes indicates how disastrous this encounter was for the Taino people, who went from a population of 300,000 at the time of Columbus's landing to 500 only 50 years later. The book develops the theme that interaction with people who do not understand or respect your culture can have terrible consequences. As a result of this encounter, the Taino people lost their language, religion, and culture.

In *Morning Girl*, Michael Dorris writes from the perspective of Morning Girl and Star Boy, two Taino children who live on a Bahamian island at the time of Columbus's

The main character in Michael Dorris's Sees Behind Trees encounters "strangers" for the first time. (From Sees Behind Trees, by Michael Dorris, text copyright © 1996. Reprinted by permission of Hyperion Books for Children.)

landing. By developing strong characters and detailing the setting, Dorris encourages readers to understand the nature of the Taino people and their culture. Unlike Yolen, however, Dorris concludes his book at the time of the first sighting of the Spanish sailors. He includes an epilogue that quotes Columbus's journal on October 11, 1492, the day he first encounters the Taino people.

Person-against-self conflicts, settings that depict Mayan and Aztec cultures, and themes that illustrate the consequences of greed are found in Scott O'Dell's historical novels based on the Spanish conquest of Mexico in the early 1500s. O'Dell's *The Captive, The Feathered Serpent,* and *The Amethyst Ring* focus not so much on the events of the time as on the moral dilemmas that a young priest faces in the New World.

A young, idealistic Jesuit seminarian, Julián Escobar, leaves his secure home in Spain and joins an expedition to Central America, inspired by the prospect of saving the souls of native peoples in New Spain. During the long voyage across the Atlantic, he begins to realize that the Spanish grandee leading the expedition actually intends to exploit and enslave the Maya and the Aztecs, rather than convert them to Christianity.

Later, Julián questions whether he has the spirit or the patience to spread the Christian faith within cultures so different from his own. O'Dell explores changes in Julián by stressing the changing conflicts in Julián's life: Should he take on the role of the mythical Kukulcán in order to save his life and make his views palatable to people with their own ancient beliefs? Should he advise attacking a neighboring city before his own Mayan city is attacked? How should he respond to the Mayan rites of sun worship? Why does God permit both good and evil? Julián's defense of his inability to change the Maya and of his own eventual grasping for power demonstrate changes in his character. In *The Feathered Serpent,* for example, Julián thinks back to Augustine's teachings and concludes that evil exists because God wills it. Therefore, idol worship and human sacrifice are beyond his control. Julián does admit, however, that this argument may be only a defense of his own actions.

O'Dell's series of books are rich in cultural information, including values, beliefs, and customs. Students of children's literature will discover in O'Dell's books many beliefs and values that are similar to those found in the traditional literature of the Mayan people. For example, there are beliefs in the legend of Quetzalcoatl's return and in the importance of the ancient gods and the accompanying religious ceremonies; the people value an honorable life and expect to pay the consequences if they do not live such lives. Detailed settings provide extensive cultural information. O'Dell's themes also reflect the time period. For example, there are themes that greed is a powerful force that can ruin lives, and people have moral obligations that must be met.

O'Dell's descriptions of Mayan and Aztec cities and temples and other aspects of the cultures show that an advanced civilization inhabited the Americas long before European exploration and settlement. Readers may also ponder the right of one culture to destroy another whose people worship different gods and possess riches a foreign power desires.

In *The King's Fifth,* O'Dell sets his story in the American Southwest. As in the previous books, his characters reflect the conflicts of the time period. There is Esteban de Sandoval, an adventurous cartographer who accompanies Coronado and the conquistadors on the search for the cities of gold. There is the arrogant and ambitious Captain Mendoza, who goes on the journey in hopes of saving souls. As would be expected from this cast of characters, there are both person-against-society and person-against-self conflicts as the various characters try to achieve their goals. Notice how all four of O'Dell's books about the Spanish conquest develop very similar themes. Students of children's literature can speculate about why these themes are so important for this time period.

In 1620, the *Mayflower* brought the first group of settlers to New England. The Pilgrims made no easy conquest of the wilderness: Their sponsors in England did not provide enough supplies, their first winter was filled with sickness and starvation, and the new settlers were apprehensive about the native peoples who lived beyond their settlement.

Authors who write about the settlement of Plymouth colony often look at the reasons for leaving England and the hardships faced by the Pilgrims. In *Constance: A Story of Early Plymouth,* for example, Patricia Clapp tells about the early settlement of New England from the viewpoint of a 14-year-old girl. Because Constance did not want to leave her cherished London, her first view of the new world from the deck of the *Mayflower* is an unpleasant one. Clapp encourages readers to understand the various viewpoints of the Pilgrims by contrasting Constance's view of a bleak and unfriendly land with the excitement and anticipation expressed by her father, William Bradford, John Alden, and Miles Standish.

While early colonists in North America were struggling to survive, ominous clouds were gathering over England: Conflict between Catholic King Charles I and the staunchly Protestant Parliament led to war in 1642. Authors who set their stories in England during this time frequently develop the theme that war is tragic and explore the influences that shape an awareness of the reality of war.

One of the strongest leaders to emerge during the English Civil War was Oliver Cromwell, an ordinary man but a great military organizer. In Erik Christian Haugaard's *Cromwell's Boy,* a 13-year-old boy discovers the tragic reality of war. The boy, also named Oliver, rides a horse well, does not divulge secrets, and looks inconspicuous. Oliver's ability to serve Cromwell extends beyond messages: He goes into the dangerous stronghold of the king's army as a spy. Haugaard suggests the lessons that Oliver has learned, using a flashback in which Oliver remembers his youthful experiences:

> In my youth there was little time for dreams. Life challenged me early. The leisure to reflect was not my lot; tomorrow was ever knocking on the door of today with new demands. It made me resourceful and sharpened my wit, but the purpose of life must be more than just to survive. You must be able— at least for short moments—to hold your precious soul in your hands and to contemplate that gift with love and understanding. (p. 1)

Elvira Woodruff's *The Ravenmaster's Secret* is set in the Tower of London, 1735. The story focuses on 11-year-old Forrest Harper and his life as the son of the Ravenmaster at the tower. Forrest loves his duties caring for the ravens, but he also wants to prove that he has the courage to guard prisoners in the tower. This second wish is difficult because he abhors the public hangings that are common in the tower. Forrest is tested when he is assigned to guard an 11-year-old girl, Maddy, who is the daughter of a Scottish rebel. Through conversations with the girl, Forrest discovers information about Scottish oppression under the English crown. Forrest faces his greatest person-against-self conflict when Maddy is slated for execution: Should he help her escape and consequently commit treason, or should he obey the law and allow her to be executed? The author increases the authenticity of the time period by including notes on the various uses of the "Tower Through Time," a glossary of English and Scottish words, a bibliography of sources about the tower, and a map of the Tower of London based on a late-16th-century engraving.

Consider the following themes developed in historical fiction about the age of cultural and social change in Europe and about early European settlement of the Western Hemisphere. Why and how are they related to specific happenings in the time periods? What relevance do these themes have in other periods of history, or for us today?

1. Greed is a strong motivational force and can have destructive consequences.
2. Moral dilemmas must be faced and resolved.
3. People will face severe hardships to acquire the political and religious freedom they desire.
4. People must work together if they are to survive.
5. Overcoming problems can strengthen character.
6. War creates tragedy.
7. Life is more than physical survival.
8. Land is important: People will endure numerous hardships to acquire land for personal reasons or for the glory of their country.

The Salem Witch-Hunts

Belief in witchcraft was common in medieval Europe. Thousands of religious and political nonconformists, independent thinkers and artists, mentally ill people, and other unusual people seemed to threaten the established social order. Such people were sometimes accused of witchcraft and were burned at the stake. Belief in witchcraft continued even in the relatively more enlightened 16th and 17th centuries and crossed the Atlantic with the first settlers of North America.

In the New England colonies of the late 1600s, strict Puritan religious beliefs governed every aspect of social life. Any kind of nonconformity was viewed as the work of the devil. The famous witch-hunts of 1692 in Salem, Massachusetts, began when a doctor stated that the hysterical behavior of several teenage girls was due to the "evil eye." Within 6 months, 20 persons had been sentenced to death and 150 had been sent to prison.

Boston minister Cotton Mather was one of those who preached the power of the devil and the need to purge the world of witchcraft. People charged with witchcraft were pardoned in 1693 when Sir William Phipps, royal governor of the Massachusetts Bay Colony, said that the witch-hunt proceedings were too violent and not based on fact. Belief in witchcraft faded in the 1700s as new scientific knowledge began to explain previously frightening phenomena.

The conflict in stories set in this short period of American history is usually person-against-society. Authors often place their characters in a hostile environment, where their usual behaviors create suspicion. For example, is a person a witch because he or she brews tea from herbs to give to the ill? Does spinning thread faster and better prove that a person is a witch? Does speaking to a cat indicate witchcraft? These are the charges that face the protagonist in Ann Petry's *Tituba of Salem Village*.

Contrasts in setting suggest the drama that follows. Petry describes two slaves who are living in comparative freedom by a sparkling sea on the coral-encrusted coastline of Barbados. Tituba and her husband lost their fairly permissive owner in Barbados and in his place acquire a solemn, dark-clothed minister from Boston. The setting changes rapidly from the tropical home to a dark ship that is taking the slaves to New England.

Petry completes the change in setting when she describes the minister's house in Salem. Rotten eggs on the doorstep of the gloomy, neglected building greet Reverend Parris, his family, and the two slaves to their new home. Soon, people in the town are muttering threats, teenage girls are becoming hysterical, and townspeople are testifying that Tituba can transform herself into a wolf or travel without her body. Tituba's crime is not witchcraft; instead, she is not only a strange black person in a predominantly white community but also more capable and intelligent than many of the people around her.

This book develops insights into the consequences of inhumanity, regardless of time or place. Readers are encouraged to see and feel danger in mass accusations and a fear in people to defend what they know is right.

The free white protagonist in Elizabeth George Speare's *The Witch of Blackbird Pond* comes from Barbados, but Kit's life is quite different from Tituba's. Contrasts between the people in Kit's early childhood environment and the people in New England encourage readers to anticipate the conflict. On Barbados, Kit was raised by a loving grandfather, who encouraged her to read history, poetry, and plays.

After the death of her grandfather, Kit travels to New England to live with her aunt. Several experiences on the ship suggest that her former lifestyle will not be appropriate for her new world. For example, when Kit tries to discuss Shakespeare with a fellow passenger, he is shocked because a girl should not read such things: "The proper use of reading is to improve our sinful nature, and to fill our minds with God's holy word" (p. 28). An even harsher response occurs after she jumps into a harbor and swims to rescue a child's doll. (The Puritans believe that only guilty people are able to stay afloat.)

The protagonists in Petry's and Speare's books have courage, high spirits, and honor during trying circumstances. Both remain true to their beliefs, even when faced with hostility and superstition. They cry out against injustices around them. Because of their actions, a few people realize the consequences of blind fear and hatred.

Various attitudes of the times and conflicts caused by the social and religious beliefs of Puritan Boston create person-against-society conflicts in Paul Fleischman's *Saturnalia*. Fleischman's characters strive to survive in a society that is suspicious of knowledge, education, and books; mistrustful of Native Americans; and filled with prejudice. Fleischman develops many of the same themes found in the stories about the Salem witch-hunts.

Consider the following themes developed in historical fiction about the Salem witch-hunts. What consequences of inhumanity and persecution are depicted in other time periods? What historical events coincide with such persecution?

1. Prejudiced persecution of others is a frightening and destructive social phenomenon.
2. People seek freedom from persecution.
3. Moral obligations require some people to defend the rights of others.

The American Revolution

The inhabitants of the 13 American colonies founded by the British came from different countries and had differing sympathies and practices. However, they did have several strong antagonisms in common: They shared a fear of the native peoples of North America; they went through a period when they shared a dread of French conquest; and they came to conflict with their ruler, the British crown. Although they were British subjects, the colonists had no elected representatives in the British Parliament that made decisions affecting their lives. A series of demands made by the British government hastened the uniting of the colonies. In 1765, Britain tried to raise money by passing the Stamp Act, which placed a tax on all paper used in the colonies and declared all unstamped documents to be legally void. Then, the British demanded that British soldiers in the colonies be quartered by the colonists themselves. In 1773, when several British ships bearing tea arrived in Boston Harbor, the Bostonians would not accept the shipment. They refused to pay taxes without the right to vote for those who would represent them. Colonists disguised as Indians boarded the ships and dumped the tea into the harbor. The British Parliament responded by closing Boston Harbor, blocking it from trade. The sympathies of many colonists were in accord with the goal of independence from Great Britain.

Samuel Adams and others like him rallied the colonists in support of this cause. The Declaration of Independence and the long years of the Revolutionary War soon followed—an exciting time in American history. We are all familiar with the famous leaders of this period, but as Elizabeth Yates (1974) points out, many other Americans whose names we do not know played dynamic roles in creating a new nation:

> Those who lived in small towns and villages and on distant farms, who thought and talked about events and made their feelings known: men who left their stock and crops and marched off to fight because they were convinced of the rightness of the stand that had been made, women who took over the work of the farms along with the care of their homes and families. Their names made no news. They did no particular acts of heroism, except as the living of each day was heroic in itself. Hard work they knew well, and hardship they could endure. Giving their lives or living their lives, they were as much the foundation of the new nation as were those whose names have long been known. (p. 6)

Although famous people are found in the background of much historical fiction about the American Revolution that has been written for children, everyday people are the heroes of most such books. In general, two types of stories are written about the revolutionary period: (1) tales about those who defend the home front while others go off to war, and (2) tales about males and females who become actively involved in the war itself.

The best-known children's story about this period is Esther Forbes's *Johnny Tremain*. Forbes creates a superbly authentic setting. Paul Revere and Samuel Adams play important parts in the story, but a silversmith's apprentice named Johnny and other boys like him are the heroes. Through Johnny's observations, actions, and thoughts, Forbes emphasizes the issues of the times, the values of the people, and the feelings about freedom. Johnny discovers the political thinking of the time when he hears a minister preach sermons filled with anger against taxation without representation, delivers messages for the secret anti-British Boston Observers, and rides for the Boston Committee of Correspondence.

Forbes's writing style creates believable action and dialogue, as in this excerpt from a speech calling the rebels to action:

> Friends! Brethren! Countrymen! That worst of Plagues, the detested tea shipped for this Port by the East Indian Company, is now arrived in the Harbour: the hour of destruction, of manly opposition to the machinations of Tyranny, stares you in the Face; Every Friend to his Country, to Himself, and to Posterity, is now called upon to meet. (p. 107)

Johnny is one of the "Indians" who throw the tea into Boston Harbor. He experiences the anger and resulting unity when British troops close the harbor. He is there when British troops and colonial rebels clash at Concord. Unhappily, he is also there when his best friend dies. He makes the discovery that a 16-year-old is considered a boy in times of peace but a man in times of war. As a man, he has the duty to risk his life for what he believes.

Consider the themes and the historical facts from this period. Why do you think the following themes are devel-oped in the literature? How and why are these themes similar to or different from themes in stories about other wartime periods?

1. Freedom is worth fighting for.
2. Strong beliefs require strong commitments.

Early Expansion of the United States and Canada

Many Europeans who came to America during its early existence were escaping from poverty or the lack of freedom in their former lands. For example, the Irish potato famine of 1846–1851 devastated the people and resulted in approximately 2 million people emigrating to North America. Authors who write about this period focus on themes related to survival of the physical and emotional being, the importance of retaining family ties, and the need for friends in times of severe strife.

As more and more settlers came to America, a need for additional land became evident. Many settlers headed away from the Atlantic coastline into the rolling, tree-covered hills to the west, north, and south. These settlers had something in common: With courage, they sought freedom and land. Some settlers developed friendly relationships with the Native Americans, but others experienced hostilities.

Stories about early pioneer expansion are popular with children, who enjoy vivid characters and rapid action. The young characters may be popular with children because they often show extraordinary courage and prove that they can be equal to adults. Many of the stories depict strong family bonds. Vivid descriptions of the new land encourage readers to understand why a family is willing to give up a secure environment to live on a raw and dangerous frontier. Person-against-nature conflicts often appear in these stories, and person-against-self conflicts occur when characters face moral dilemmas, such as racial prejudice.

Themes of friendship, faith, moral obligation, working together, and love for land are found in Elizabeth George Speare's *The Sign of the Beaver*. The Maine wilderness in the 1700s can be either an antagonist or a friend. Matt, the 13-year-old main character, faces a life-and-death struggle when his father leaves him alone to guard their frontier cabin through the winter. Without food or a gun, Matt confronts a harsh natural environment, fear of the local Indians, and the possibility that he will never see his parents again. In spite of conflicts about the ways in which white settlers are changing their land, a Penobscot boy befriends Matt and teaches him how to survive.

The need to believe in oneself and the importance of retaining and respecting one's own beliefs are themes developed in Janet Lunn's person-against-society and person-against-self conflicts set in Hawthorn Bay, On-

Survival and friendship are important in this story set in the 1700s. (From The Sign of the Beaver, *by Elizabeth George Speare. Copyright © 1983 by Elizabeth George Speare. Reprinted by permission of Dell Publishing Company.)*

themes associated with the importance of physical and emotional survival during times of stress and the need for family and friends.

Joan W. Blos's *A Gathering of Days: A New England Girl's Journal, 1830–32* is the fictional journal of a 13-year-old girl on a New Hampshire farm. Blos (1980) says that she tried to develop three types of truthfulness: "the social truthfulness of the situation, the psychological truthfulness of the characters, and the literary truthfulness of the manner of telling" (p. 371). Consequently, the characters are similar to those who stare from New England portraits. Likewise, the tone of the story is similar to that in *Leavitt's Almanac,* written for farmers, with the form and style found in journal writings of that period.

Both Elizabeth George Speare's *Calico Captive* and Lois Lenski's *Indian Captive: The Story of Mary Jemison* are stories about white girls captured by native tribespeople. Both girls face difficult conflicts and harsh circumstances, but their experiences eventually cause them to question their former prejudices. Speare's Miriam learns more about the Indians from Pierre, a *coureur des bois.* After much inner turmoil, Mary Jemison finally decides that the Seneca are her people:

> At that moment she saw Old Shagbark looking at her, his brown eyes overflowing with kindness and understanding. He knew how hard it was for her to decide. . . . She saw the Englishman, too. His lips were smiling, but his eyes of cold gray were hard. Even if she were able to put all her thoughts into words, she knew he would never, never understand. Better to live with those who understood her because they loved her so much, than with one who could never think with her, in sympathy, about anything. . . . Squirrel Woman's scowling face and even Gray Wolf's wicked one no longer held any terrors, because she understood them. (p. 268)

Books written from Native American viewpoints describe the harmful influences of an expanding white population. In *Sweetgrass,* a winner of the Canadian Library Association's Book of the Year Award, Jan Hudson focuses on the struggle for maturity of a young Blackfoot girl as she faces a life-and-death battle in 1837. Smallpox, the "white man's sickness," results in hunger and death. The themes in *Sweetgrass* are that it is important to honor moral obligation toward others and to retain one's dreams.

Hudson employs figurative language involving signs and omens that are meaningful to the characters and that reinforce themes related to retaining one's identity and meeting obligations toward family members. For example, the main character considers the importance of her name: She believes that it is appropriate because sweetgrass is "ordinary to look at but it's fragrant as the spring" (p. 12). Later, her grandmother tells her that sweetgrass has the power of memories. As Sweetgrass considers her future, readers discover that she is joyfully approaching womanhood. She says, "I felt mightier than a brave. . . . I felt I was holding the future like summer berries in my hands" (p. 26). Instead of allowing the signs and omens to control

tario. Lunn's *Shadow in Hawthorn Bay,* winner of the Canadian children's literature award, follows 15-year-old Mary Urquhart as she leaves her Scottish highlands on the shores of Loch Ness to try to find and help her cousin in Canada. As Mary tends sheep in Scotland, she hears her cousin Duncan calling her to come to him. She does not consider this unusual, even though Duncan is more than 3,000 miles away. Her actions and the belief of her Scottish family make her ability to see into the future believable. This same ability, referred to as second sight, causes her conflict when she interacts with a society that not only does not believe in her special powers but also fears and distrusts them.

Lunn develops a related person-against-self conflict as Mary fights her powers and the consequences of her visions. As part of this inner conflict, Mary must overcome her fear of going into the forest, her fear of the black water, and her belief that something evil is trapped in the bay. Mary overcomes her fears and gains the insight she needs to believe in herself and her powers. With this realization, Lunn develops the theme of the book: It is important to keep your beliefs and ways.

The devastation caused by the potato famine in Ireland provides the background for Patricia Reilly Giff's *Nory Ryan's Song.* By writing the story through the viewpoint of 12-year-old Nory, the author is able to develop

JAN HUDSON
Sweetgrass

Canadian Library Association Book of the Year for Children
Canada Council Children's Literature Prize

The language and setting reflect the Blackfoot culture. (From Sweetgrass, by Jan Hudson. Illustration copyright © 1989 by Jan Spivey Gilchrist. Reprinted by permission of Philomel Books, a division of Putnam & Grosset Group.)

her life, Sweetgrass uses them to overcome taboos and to help her family in a time of great trouble. She decides, "I would make Father do what I wanted. I would find the signs, the power to control my own days. I would make my life be what I wanted" (p. 15).

The themes in books of historical fiction about the early expansion of the United States vary widely. Consider the following themes. Why do you think authors who write stories about this period chose them? How do these themes compare to those found in different time periods? How are the themes significant today?

1. Friendship and faith are important.
2. People long for their own land and the freedom that ownership implies.
3. People will withstand great hardships to retain their dreams.
4. Strong family bonds help physical and spiritual survival.
5. Prejudice and hatred are destructive forces.
6. The greatest strength comes from within.
7. Moral obligations require personal commitment.

Slavery, the Civil War, and Overcoming Segregation

In the early centuries of American history, white slave traders brought hundreds of thousands of black Africans to this continent in chains and sold them on auction blocks as field workers, house servants, and skilled craftspeople. Many people in both the North and the South believed that slavery was immoral; therefore, unable to pass laws against it, they assisted slaves in their flight toward Canada and freedom.

Helping runaway slaves was a dangerous undertaking, especially after the passage of the Fugitive Slave Act in 1850 made it a crime. Handbills offering rewards for the return of certain slaves added to the danger by urging slave catchers to hunt for suspected runaways. Because of the dangers and the need for secrecy, an illicit network of people dedicated to assisting fugitive slaves linked the North and the South. Free people led the fugitives from one safe hiding place to another on each part of their journey along the Underground Railroad to Canada.

Conflicts between northern and southern interests that had emerged during the Constitutional Convention increased in the 1850s and led to the outbreak of the Civil War in 1861. The United States was torn apart. In some cases, relatives were on opposite sides of the conflict and faced one another on the battlefields of Bull Run and Gettysburg.

Some authors examine slavery and the experiences of slaves during captivity or as fugitives seeking freedom; others examine the impact of the Civil War on young soldiers or on the people who remained at home. Person-against-society and person-against-self conflicts are common in historical fiction covering this period. Some characters confront prejudice and hatred, and others wrestle with their consciences and discover the tragedy associated with slavery and war. Authors who create credible plots consider not only the historical events but also the conflicting social attitudes of the times. The themes developed in this literature reflect a need for personal freedom, ponder the right of one person to own another, consider the tragedies of war, and question the killing of one human by another.

The attitudes expressed toward blacks create special problems for authors who write about slavery. How accurately should historical fiction reflect the attitudes and circumstances of the times? Should authors use terms of the period that are considered insensitive and offensive today?

A slave ship in which human cargo is chained together in cramped quarters provides the setting for Paula Fox's *The Slave Dancer*. The story is told from the point of view of a 13-year-old white boy from New Orleans who is kidnapped by slave traders to play his fife on their ship.

ISSUE Unbalanced Viewpoints in Historical Fiction

Reporting of history may change depending on the viewpoint of an author. This is also true in the writing of historical fiction. Too many frontier books are written from the perspective of the white settlers rather than from that of the Native Americans. In this context, some critics fear that children will not realize the hardships the Native Americans experienced or the contributions they made. Stories from the perspective of the white settlers emphasize kidnappings of white children, attacks on wagon trains by warring tribes, the burning of white settlements, and rescues of settlers by soldiers. Many frontier heroes created their reputations as Indian fighters.

Some critics believe that historical fiction about the settlement of North America should include more stories told from the native perspective. These stories might include kidnappings of Native American children by white settlers or emphasize the reasons for the kidnappings of white children. They might portray the numerous peaceful tribes, who lived in harmony with settlers, or they might emphasize the diversity of the Native American cultures. Students of children's literature should consider the viewpoints of authors and the consequences of unbalanced narratives of other

time periods, including narratives about early explorers, the Roman invasion of Britain, religious freedom and the settlement of America, the Revolutionary War, the Civil War, and World War II.

Unbalanced viewpoints may be particularly harmful when presenting stories with a World War II Holocaust setting. Leslie Barban[1] emphasizes the importance of viewpoint in this literature when she states:

> George Santayana once said, "Those who cannot remember the past are condemned to repeat it." This famous adage has proved itself to be true in many ways. Children's rooms in public libraries and school media centers across the nation house many important and memorable books not only about the Holocaust but about all types of racial prejudice. However, the Holocaust is often not discussed: many parents believe the subject will depress children, librarians often choose noncontroversial titles for booktalking, and teachers often feel that it's too disturbing or inappropriate to discuss in the classroom. Furthermore, some children are being told that the Holocaust is folklore and that the mass murder of 11 million people never happened. History textbooks mention it, but any true deliberation on the subject seems too much to ask of children. Is it? (p. 25)

In addition to evaluating the balance in historical fiction and in literary discussions, you should encourage students to evaluate and authenticate the historical accuracy in historical fiction. According to the findings of a study in *The Nation's Report Card*,[2] 4th-, 8th-, and 12th-grade students "have a limited grasp of U.S. history." In addition, the study calls for assignments that encourage "thoughtful analytical essays" (p. 4). Evaluating and authenticating the historical accuracy in historical fiction and historical biography encourage such essays.

As you consider the issue of unbalanced viewpoints and accuracy in historical fiction and the findings of *The Nation's Report Card,* what do you think is the role of historical fiction? What viewpoints should the authors of historical fiction express? How could you develop a balanced viewpoint of a historical time period through the use of historical fiction?

---

[1]Barban, Leslie. (1993, March). Remember to never forget. *Book Links, 2,* 25–29.

[2]Knight-Ridder News Service. (1990, April 3). Most students have limited grasp of history, study finds. The Bryan-College Station (TX) *Eagle,* 1–4.

When the ship reaches Africa, Jessie learns about the trade in human "Black Gold" and discovers that in their greed for trade goods, African chiefs sell their own people and people kidnapped from other tribes. For four nights, longboats bring their cargoes to the slave ship: men and women who are half-conscious from the pressure of bodies and bruised by ankle shackles. The detailed descriptions of the conditions on the ship are believable. Jessie describes the holds as pits of misery, is horrified by the low regard for human life, and is shocked when prisoners who die are thrown overboard. He learns the reason for having him aboard when slaves are dragged on deck and forced to dance: A dead or weak slave cannot be sold for profit, and the slave traders believe that dancing keeps their bodies strong.

This book has stirred much controversy. Some have criticized the fact that the slaves in the book are not treated like human beings or even given names. Many college students, however, say that while reading *The Slave Dancer,* they realized for the first time the true inhumanity of slavery. Fox reveals the impact of the experience on Jessie by flashing ahead in time to Jessie's memories:

> At the first note of a tune or a song, I would see once again as though they'd never ceased their dancing in my mind, black

men and women and children lifting their tormented limbs in time to a reedy martial air, the dust rising from their joyless thumping, the sound of the fife finally drowned beneath the clanging of their chains. (p. 176)

You can compare the descriptions in *The Slave Dancer* with Tom Feelings's illustrations in *The Middle Passage: White Ships/Black Cargo.*

A book written for young children explains the purposes of the Underground Railroad: F. N. Monjo's *The Drinking Gourd* tells of a family that is part of the Underground Railroad and the role of that family in helping a fugitive slave family escape. Even though this is an easy-to-read book, it illustrates the importance of one family's contributions. The dialogue between father and sons discloses the purpose of the railroad. Young readers also experience excitement and danger as Tommy accompanies his father and an escaping black family on the next part of their journey.

Kathryn Lasky's *True North* develops themes related to moral obligations and the destructive forces of prejudice as a runaway slave dodges slave catchers while traveling the Underground Railroad on her way to Canada. After a white girl discovers the runaway hiding in her grandfather's house, the two girls join forces on this

Fugitive slaves follow the Underground Railroad to freedom. (From The Drinking Gourd, *by F. N. Monjo. Pictures by Fred Brenner. An* I CAN READ History Book. *Pictures copyright © 1970 by Fred Brenner. Reprinted by permission of Harper & Row Publishers.)*

dangerous journey north. Lasky depicts two strong heroines who are committed to the abolitionist movement. In addition, the author emphasizes the restrictive roles of women during the time period.

The impact of the Civil War on free whites in the United States is the subject of several novels in which idealistic young men come to understand that war is not simply a glamorous time of brass bands and heroic battles led by banner-carrying leaders. Stories about fighting soldiers often show men realizing the true horrors of war. Paul Fleischman's *Bull Run* is a series of short, descriptive pieces that characterize the reactions of 16 people who were involved in the first battle of the Civil War; eight of these people express the Northern point of view, and eight express the Southern point of view. The book is an excellent source for evaluating the importance of point of view when writing about historical time periods and controversial issues. Different points of view are also developed by Carolyn Reeder in *Across the Lines* as Edward and his slave and friend, Simon, struggle with issues of freedom and friendship.

One of the finest books to depict the wartime hardships and conflicts of family members who remain at home is Irene Hunt's *Across Five Aprils.* The beginning conflict is introduced effectively as members of a family in southern Illinois debate the issues related to the Civil War and choose their allegiances: Matt Creighton, the head of the family, argues that a strong union must be maintained; the majority of his sons agree with him, but one son argues that people in the South should be able to live without Northern interference.

Hunt develops a strong personal conflict. Jethro, the youngest son, is emotionally torn between two beloved brothers, one who joins the Union Army and the other who fights for the Confederacy. The consequences of hatred are illustrated when young toughs burn the Creightons' barn and put oil into their well because of the family's divided allegiances. Readers also glimpse a different view of people when neighbors guard the farm, help put in the crops, and rebuild the barn.

This is the touching story of a heroic family overcoming problems at home and awaiting news of fighting sons. In spite of disagreement, the Creightons maintain strong family ties. When the son fighting for the South learns that one of his brothers was killed at Pittsburgh Landing, he sends a message to his mother that he was not in that battle and did not fire the bullet that killed his brother. This story helps children understand the real tragedy of the Civil War: Brothers fought against brothers, and neighbors fought against neighbors.

Southern Illinois is also the setting for *The River Between Us*, by Richard Peck. Peck's story considers both the role of racially mixed people and the consequences of the Civil War. He uses an interesting writers' technique: beginning and closing the novel in the framework of a grown son and his two boys going home in 1916. While the son visits his relatives in southern Illinois, Grandma Tilly tells the story about what happened during the Civil War. She brings back the old times: "She handed over the past like a parcel" (p. 151).

Sixteen characters present their perspectives about the first battle of the Civil War. (From Bull Run, *text copyright © 1993 by Paul Fleischman. Jacket art copyright © 1993 by David Frampton/ jacket copyright © 1993 by HarperCollins Publishers. Used by permission of HarperCollins Publishers.)*

This parcel is filled with wonderful memories of a happy family life, terrible descriptions of Civil War settings, memorable characters, and family secrets. As in *Across Five Aprils*, one of the tragedies of this story is that Noah, the son who fought in the Union Army, unwittingly fought against his father who was in the Confederate Army. Peck's "A Note on the Story" also provides background information on the role of the "free women of color" who play a major role in this story.

No Man's Land: A Young Soldier's Story, by Susan Campbell Bartoletti, is written from the viewpoint of a young Confederate soldier from the Twenty-Sixth Regiment Georgia Volunteer Infantry. The author develops themes related to the tragedy of war by describing the outcomes of the battles, the loss of friends, and the wounding of many young people. Through dialogue, the soldiers express their reasons for joining the army and their belief in the Confederate cause.

Books written with more current settings frequently emphasize the hope to escape segregation and find a better life. For example, *Going North*, a picture book for younger children by Janice Harrington, depicts a young girl as she reluctantly says good-bye to all the things she loves in Alabama. The contrasts in settings are depicted as she reads a sign "Welcome to Nebraska" and declares: "No more cotton fields, no more red sand, no more June bugs on a cotton string. Instead, I see black dirt everywhere, black magic, North magic. Nebraska rolling by on a grassy rug" (unnumbered). The author states that the book is based on her own family's experiences as they moved from Vernon, Alabama, to Lincoln, Nebraska, during the summer of 1964. The text includes a map that shows the bus route from Alabama through Mississippi, Tennessee, Arkansas, Missouri, Kansas, to Nebraska.

Mildred D. Taylor's *The Gold Cadillac* is a fictionalized story based on Taylor's painful memories, a story about family unity and the consequences of racial prejudice. The prejudice occurs in 1950, when a northern African American family buys a gold Cadillac and sets out for Mississippi. For the first time, the children experience segregation and racial hostility. As in other books by Taylor, the theme is that family love and unity help them overcome such terrible experiences.

Outstanding historical fiction written for older children is characterized by both strong characters and strong themes. The themes in these stories include searching for freedom and dignity, learning to live together, tackling problems personally rather than waiting for someone else to do so, and survival of the body and the spirit.

For *Bud, Not Buddy*, Christopher Paul Curtis won both the 2000 Newbery Award and the Coretta Scott King Award. Curtis places his 10-year-old protagonist in the setting of the Great Depression of the 1930s. By developing his main character as a mistreated orphan boy, Curtis describes a very dark side of the Depression as Bud experiences waiting in line for food at missions and living with other people in shantytowns. There is also a very positive side of the story as Bud, clutching the few possessions his mother left him, searches for the man he believes is his father; the search takes Bud into the world of a famous jazz band. Throughout the book, Curtis uses Bud's "Rules and Things for Having a Funner Life" to explore Bud's character and to add humor to the story. It is interesting to learn in the author's afterword that Curtis modeled two of his characters after his own grandfathers: one a redcap for the railroad and the other a bandleader for several musical groups, including "Herman E. Curtis and the Dusky Devastators of the Depression." (An in-depth discussion of Christopher Paul Curtis's use of plot and conflict in *The Watsons Go to Birmingham—1963* is found in Chapter 3 of this text.)

Consider the following themes developed around slavery, the Civil War, and the fight against segregation: Why are so many of the themes related to overcoming great personal and social conflicts? How do these themes relate to the events and values of the times? Are they appropriate for the time period? What other time periods, if any, reflect similar themes, and what do they have in common with the Civil War period? Which of these themes are significant in contemporary life and literature?

1. War creates tragedy.
2. Moral obligations must be met even if one's life or freedom is in jeopardy.
3. Moral sense does not depend on skin color, but on what is inside a person.
4. People should take pride in themselves and in their accomplishments.
5. Prejudice and hatred are destructive forces.
6. People search for freedom.
7. Personal conscience may not allow some people to kill others.
8. Strong family ties help people persevere.

The Western Frontier

The American frontier was extending farther and farther west in the 1800s. White Americans were giving up their settled towns and farms in the East to make their fortunes in unknown territories. Former slaves saw the frontier as a place to make a new start in freedom, and Asian immigrants to the West Coast moved inland to work on the railroads that were beginning to span the Great Plains. The Homestead Act of 1862 promised free land to settlers willing to stake their claims and develop the land. Stories of rich earth in fertile valleys caused families to travel thousands of miles over prairies and mountains to reach Oregon.

Whether the pioneers stopped in the Midwest or went along the Oregon Trail, the journey was perilous; they fought nature, battling blizzards, dust storms, mountain crossings, and swollen rivers. They fought people as they met unfriendly Native Americans, outlaws, and cattle ranchers who did not want them to farm. Some demonstrated noble qualities as they helped each other search for new land and made friends with the Native Americans they encountered; others demonstrated greed and prejudice in their interactions with other pioneers and with Native Americans.

Native peoples themselves were experiencing a time of trauma. Outsiders invaded their ancient territories, staking claims to land that had once been without ownership or boundaries, and killing the buffalo and other wild animals on which the people relied for sustenance. The American government had begun its campaign to relocate Native Americans onto reservatins that were minuscule in size and resources compared with the rich stretches of prairie and mountain that had long been the native peoples' domain.

This period of American history—with its high hopes, dangers, triumphs, and tragic conflicts—still captures the imagination of Americans. Stories about pioneer America are popular with children, as exemplified by the continuing interest in books such as Laura Ingalls Wilder's "Little House" series. Historical fiction for children consists of three general types of stories about this period: (1) adventure stories in which the characters cross the prairies and mountains, (2) stories about family life on pioneer homesteads, and (3) stories about interactions between Native Americans and pioneers or Native Americans and military forces.

Authors who write about crossing the continent explore people's reasons for moving and their strong feelings for the land. Self-discovery may occur in young characters who begin to understand their parents' motivations and values. Detailed descriptions allow readers to understand the awesome continent as both inspiration and antagonist. Stories set on homesteads often depict relationships in which families seek to achieve their dreams. Like earlier stories about Native Americans and colonial settlers, these stories include tales of captive children and of the harsh treatment of Native Americans by white people who alter a traditional way of life.

Moving West. A number of historical fiction books with settings and themes related to moving west are highly illustrated books suitable for younger students or that can be used with older students to enhance understanding of pioneer settings. For example, Deborah Hopkinson's *A Packet of Seeds* introduces the feelings of pioneers moving west in covered wagons. The author develops the conflicting feelings experienced by members of the family when she writes: "All Pa could see was the new land before him. All Momma could feel was the sorrow of leaving everything behind" (unnumbered). The text and illustrations go through the seasons in the new land as Momma sees burned, dry land and Pa sees the land in the spring

when it will be cleared and planted with corn. The author uses seeds brought from home and the creation of a family garden to help Momma overcome her sadness, especially when she finds seeds for poppies, hollyhocks, daisies, and larkspur sent by friends from home. The author's note states that many women who were part of the westward movement created gardens so that they would feel at home in a new place.

In *Apples to Oregon: Being the (Slightly) True Narrative of How a Brave Pioneer Father Brought Apples, Peaches, Plums, Grapes, and Cherries (and Children) Across the Plains*, Deborah Hopkinson uses exaggeration and humor to illustrate the complexities of the trip when a family tries to take fruits that they will transplant from Salem, Iowa, to Milwaukie, Oregon. The author summarizes the family's difficulties when she writes, "But time was running out. Our little trees had almost drowned in the river, got pounded by hailstones, and got withered by drought. How much more could they take? And now we were set for a showdown with the most ornery varmit of all; Jack Frost" (unnumbered). This humorous story about Delicious, the name of the daughter, and her family is based on a true incident.

Another book written for young readers follows pioneer families as they journey westward. Brett Harvey's *Cassie's Journey: Going West in the 1860s* portrays the dangers and hardships as well as the close relationships of pioneers traveling from Illinois to California. The illustrations reinforce the need to work together if the families are to survive.

Honoré Morrow tells the story of earlier pioneers to the far West in *On to Oregon!*, a book for older children. Morrow's novel about pioneers from Missouri in the 1840s is more than an adventure story about crossing the continent; it is also a psychological story about the challenge of surviving in harsh circumstances. After his parents die on the trail, 13-year-old John Sager becomes head of the family and leads his brothers and sisters on to Oregon over 1,000 miles of treacherous mountains, canyons, and rivers. The people in the wagon train do not want responsibility for the Sager children and plan to send them back East.

Morrow shows the strength of the father's dream by describing John's actions. John refuses to forfeit his father's dream; he works out a scheme so that the people think that he and his siblings will be traveling with Kit Carson. The children secretly pack their goods on oxen and head out on the lonely trail. The natural environment becomes the chief antagonist against which the children must struggle before reaching a warm, gentle valley in the Oregon of their dreams.

Morrow looks at the contributions of people who made westward expansion possible. Consider, for example, the possible impact of Morrow's closing statements:

You and I will never hear that magic call of the West, "Catch up! Catch up!" We never shall see the Rockies framed in the opening of our prairie schooner and tingle with the knowledge that if we and our fellow immigrants can reach the valleys in the blue beyond the mountains and there plow enough acreage, that acreage will belong forever to America. (p. 235)

Kathryn Lasky's *Beyond the Divide,* a story of survival set in the ruggedness of the far West just before the Civil War, develops themes related to the destructive nature of greed and prejudice and the constructive power of dreams, hope, and moral obligations. Louise Moeri effectively develops similar themes in *Save Queen of Sheba,* as 12-year-old King David and his young sister, Queen of Sheba (named after biblical characters), survive a Sioux raid and set out alone across the prairie in hope of finding the wagons that separated from their portion of the wagon train. Moeri demonstrates effectively the strength of King David's feeling of responsibility by depicting his varied emotional responses during several emotionally and physically draining experiences.

Two historical fiction texts are based on true events involving railroads. The setting for *Stop the Train,* by Geraldine McCaughrean, is the time of the Oklahoma Land Rush in 1893. Settlers arrive at the future town of Florence in the Red Rock Runner. The conflict develops when the railroad owner is angered because the settlers refuse to sell him their claims; he retaliates by not allowing the train to stop in Florence. A cast of eccentric characters tries, in often humorous ways, to stop the train. The train in Karen Cushman's *Rodzina,* according to the author's note, is based on orphan trains that ran between 1850 and 1929. During this time, nearly 250,000 poor urban children were sent west. Cushman states, "The children had been living on the streets or in overcrowded orphanages. Most of them were orphans; the rest were abandoned, neglected, or sent away by desperate parents. It was thought that hard work in the clean air of the west would offer children a better chance to lead happy and productive lives" (p. 207).

By using a strong and independent protagonist, 12-year-old Rodzina Clara Jadwiga Anastazya Brodski, Cushman is able to show many of the attitudes of the time toward women and orphans. She depicts the rugged frontier by describing the motives of various people who wish to adopt the orphans. Some of them are searching for cheap labor, and others are eager to provide loving families for the children. As the train proceeds through the west, readers catch glimpses of wagon trains where settlers have had to abandon their belongings, wooden crosses that mark the burial sites of some of the settlers, and families living in dugout houses with dirt floors and walls. The author depicts the role of women in the time period by showing interactions between Rodzina and the woman doctor who is accompanying the orphans to California. Miss Doctor reveals the difficulties that she has had being accepted in the medical profession. Likewise, Rodzina's strong-willed nature makes it difficult for her to accept a destination that is not to her liking.

Scott O'Dell's *Carlota* is set in Spanish California in the mid-1800s. O'Dell explores the conflicts that occur between people who expect females to play a traditional role and others who encourage a different type of behavior. Carlota is the strong and independent daughter of Don Saturnino, a native Californian whose ancestors came from Spain; her father supports her brave and adventurous inclinations. Even though Cushman's and O'Dell's female characters come from very different social backgrounds, they still have many characteristics in common: They are both independent characters who show the need for strong beliefs in those who succeed in the western frontier.

Authors who place their characters in the time of the California Gold Rush in the 1850s may develop conflicts related to lawlessness and themes that show that humans may be motivated by greed and even racial hatred. Sid Fleischman's two major characters in *Bandit's Moon* are Annyrose, a newly orphaned girl who finds herself on this lawless frontier, and Joaquin Murieta, a Mexican bandit who some believe is notoriously cruel, and who others believe is a Robin Hood–type character whose major role is to right the wrongs against the Mexican settlers. Through the interactions between Annyrose and Joaquin, readers come to understand the differences between the two individuals and then accompany them on their own road to understanding.

Laurence Yep sets two of his award-winning historical fiction books in the west during the late 1800s and early 1900s. *Dragon's Gate* is set in the Sierra Nevada mountains in 1867 when Chinese immigrants are working on the transcontinental railroad. Yep begins his story in China and provides a historical perspective that allows readers to understand the viewpoint of the Chinese and some of the reasons that Chinese people might have wanted to emigrate to America. As the story progresses, Yep shows the economic need of the characters to learn English and to go to the United States. He also develops the characters' beliefs in the freedom found in the United States when Father explains that the Civil War in America is being fought to free slaves because "everybody there, they free. Everybody, they equal" (p. 3). Yep tells the story through the point of view of a Chinese boy named Otter. Through his experiences on the cold mountain and in the dangerous tunnel, Otter makes discoveries about cooperation and the importance of life and courage.

Yep's *Dragonwings,* set in 1903 San Francisco, is based on a true incident in which a Chinese American built and flew an airplane. The characters are people who retain their values and respect for their heritage while adjusting to a new country. As the story progresses, Moon Shadow, the young protagonist, learns that his stereotype of the white demons is not always accurate. When he and his father move away from the Tang men's protection, Moon Shadow meets and talks to his first demon. Instead of being 10 feet tall, with blue skin and a face covered with warts, the "demon" is a petite woman who is very friendly and considerate. As Moon Shadow and his father get to know this Anglo-Saxon woman and her family, all learn to respect people of different backgrounds as individuals. This book is especially strong in its coverage of Chinese traditions and beliefs; for example, readers learn about the great respect that Chinese Americans feel for the aged and the dead. As Moon Shadow seeks to educate his non-Chinese friend about the nature of dragons, readers discover traditional Chinese tales about a benevolent and wise dragon who is king among reptiles and emperor of animals.

Pioneer Family Life. Many stories about pioneer life depict the power of a family that is working to conquer outside dangers and build a home filled with love and decency. One author in particular has enabled children to vicariously experience family life on the frontier. Laura Ingalls Wilder re-created through her "Little House" books the world of her own frontier family from 1870 through 1889. The "Little House" books have sold in the millions and received literary acclaim. A popular television series introduced the Ingalls family to millions of new friends.

The first book, *Little House in the Big Woods,* takes place in a deep forest in Wisconsin. Unlike the settings in many other pioneer stories, this setting is not antagonistic. Although the woods are filled with bears and other wild animals, the danger never really enters the log cabin in the clearing. Any potential dangers are implied through Pa's stories about his adventures in the big woods, told in a close family environment inside the cabin. Other descriptions of family activities also suggest that the environment, although creating hard work for the pioneer family, is not dangerous. The family clears the land, plants and harvests the crops, gathers sap from the sugar bush, and hitches up the wagon and drives through the woods to Grandpa's house.

Wilder focuses on the interactions of the family members. Pa's actions, for example, imply that he is a warm, loving father. After working all day, he has time to play the fiddle, play mad dog with the children, and tell stories. Likewise, Ma takes care of the physical needs of the children but also helps them create paper dolls. The impact of what it means to live in the relative isolation of the frontier, where a family must be self-sufficient, is also implied through the children's actions and thoughts: They feel secure when the attic is hung with smoked hams and filled with pumpkins, they are excited when they get new mittens and a cloth doll for Christmas, and they are astonished when they visit a town for the first time and see a store filled with marvelous treasures.

In other "Little House" books, Laura and her family leave the big woods of Wisconsin to live in the prairie states: Kansas, Minnesota, and South Dakota. The children go to a one-room school, build a fish trap, have a grasshopper invasion, worry when Pa must walk 300 miles to find a job, and live through a blizzard. Wilder's description of the winter in *Little Town on the Prairie* encourages modern children to share the experience:

> All winter long, they had been crowded in the little kitchen, cold and hungry and working hard in the dark and the cold to twist enough hay to keep the fire going and to grind wheat in the coffee mill for the day's bread. All that long, long winter, the only hope had been that sometime winter must end, sometime blizzards must stop, the sun would shine warm again. (p. 3)

When Laura gets her first job in the little town of De Smet, South Dakota, she earns 25 cents a day and her dinner for sewing shirts. Unselfishly, she saves this money to help send her sister Mary to a college for the blind in Vinton, Iowa. The series ends with stories about Laura's experiences as a schoolteacher, her marriage to Almanzo Wilder, and their early years together on a prairie homestead. One reason that children like these books so much is the feeling of closeness they have with Laura.

Patricia MacLachlan's *Sarah, Plain and Tall* is a more recently published book about pioneer family life. In this book for younger readers, MacLachlan describes the strong need for a loving mother and a happy family life and introduces the children's need for singing in the home by contrasting the singing that took place before the mother's death with the quiet, sad atmosphere that dominates life afterward. The father's needs are revealed through his actions: He places an advertisement for a wife in an eastern newspaper, in response to which "plain and tall" Sarah enters the family's life.

The children's need for a mother and a happy home is reflected in their desire for singing, in their rereading of Sarah's letters until the letters are worn out, their desire to be perfect for Sarah, their frightened reactions when Sarah misses the sea, their trying to bring characteristics of the sea into their prairie farm, and their complete happiness when they realize that Sarah will stay on the prairie. MacLachlan's Sarah is a strong, loving, independent pioneer woman who discovers that her love for her new family is stronger than her feelings of loneliness for the sea. Like Wilder's characters, MacLachlan's characters may seem real because she drew them from her own family history.

Paul Fleischman's *The Borning Room* follows the happenings in a room on an Ohio farm. Family members experience both birth and death in a room set aside for such special occasions. Fleischman focuses on a baby born in 1851 and proceeds through her experiences on the Ohio frontier, through the life cycle of birth, marriage, and death. The time period between Georgina's birth and death allows Fleischman to include happenings that were influenced by changes in history, such as runaway slaves, the Civil War, and the introduction of chloroform. The book concludes as the now older lady, Georgina, awaits her own death in the borning room and thinks about the

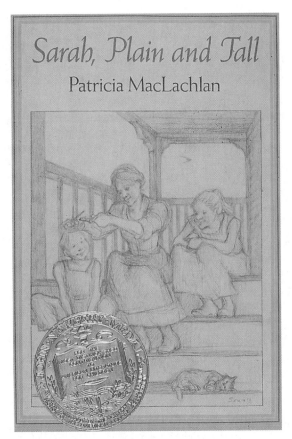

The need for warm family relationships provides the focus for this frontier story. (From Sarah, Plain and Tall, by Patricia MacLachlan. Jacket art copyright © 1985 by Marcia Sewall. Reprinted by permission of HarperCollins.)

changes that have happened in the years between 1851 and 1918. In this conclusion, Fleischman encourages readers to understand the changes that have taken place in this one character's life and on the Ohio frontier:

> I was born in this same month of January. The day might have looked precisely like this one. What a lot, though, has changed between that day and this. Automobiles, telephones, electric lights. And yet, nothing's changed. Here it is 1918 and a woman still can't vote. Over in Europe, we're fighting the Kaiser. A new set of buglers and battles. More dying. It's Shiloh and Vicksburg all over again. But you're too young to know that war. . . . I've got a grandson scuttling through the trenches and a daughter doctoring the wounded. And a son who teaches music at Princeton by day and writes pacifist pamphlets at night. That's Virgil you hear sawing wood. He alone of the four stayed here, as I did. (p. 100)

In *The Winter Room*, Gary Paulsen uses the stories told by family members through the long winter months on a northern farm. Paulsen encourages readers to see, hear, and feel the power of the stories and the memories revealed. He creates a sequence that follows the activities on a farm from spring through winter. The winter nights, however, bring out the stories. The family sits around the stove and watches the fire through the mica windows in the door and wait for the magic that begins, "It was when

I was young . . ." (p. 69). Paulsen shows that stories provide a way to learn about others and to gain feelings of self-worth.

In a book that stresses self-realization, Jennifer L. Holm places her heroine in *Our Only May Amelia* in a Finnish American family on the Washington frontier in 1899. The author based her character on the life of her great-aunt, whose diary she found in an old suitcase. This actual source allows the author to develop settings, conflicts, and characters that are authentic for the time period. Readers will be enticed by adventures such as being trapped on a rope bridge with a growling cougar approaching from one end and a rushing river below.

Pioneers and Native Americans

The West Texas frontier of the 1860s provides the setting for Patricia Beatty's *Wait for Me, Watch for Me, Eula Bee*. The book tells of the capture of two farm children by Comanche and Kiowa Indians, the subsequent escape of the older boy, the changing loyalties of the very young girl who learns to love her Comanche foster parent, and her rescue by her brother. Beatty's descriptions of camp life, food, travel, and behavior create a vivid picture of the period. The author's notes list the sources for her information on Comanche and Kiowa tribes and their treatment of captives.

Although Beatty depicts the Comanches as leading a harsh life built on raiding and warfare, she also depicts the value that they place on children. The little girl and her Comanche foster parent develop a warm, loving relationship. Sadness in this book stems from the tragic results of the lack of understanding of two cultures.

A tragic period in Navaho history, 1863–1865, is the setting for Scott O'Dell's *Sing Down the Moon*. The story of the 300-mile forced march that culminates in holding Navahos prisoner at Fort Sumner, New Mexico, is told through the viewpoint of a Navaho girl, Bright Morning. O'Dell effectively uses both descriptions of physical settings and characterizations to depict tragedy. The Navahos are forced to leave their home, the beautiful Canyon de Chelly, with its fruit trees, green grass, sheep, and cool water, for the harsh, windswept landscape around Fort Sumner.

The greatest tragedy does not result from the loss of home, however, but from the loss of spiritual hope. Still, Bright Morning does not give up her dream of returning to her beautiful canyon, and O'Dell creates a thought-provoking, bittersweet ending, in which Bright Morning and her husband escape from the U.S. Army and return to her hidden valley. It is as she remembers it: The blossoms are on the trees, a sheep and a lamb are grazing on the green land, and the tools that she hid from the soldiers are waiting. However, a menacing shadow looms over their happiness: Readers cannot forget that the Navaho family is hiding from the soldiers they saw on the horizon.

An In-Depth Analysis of One Example of Multicultural Literature—Native American

The Birchbark House, by Louise Erdrich, was a National Book Award finalist. The book is set on an island in Lake Superior in 1847 and describes an Ojibwa girl's life as she experiences four seasons of the year. Consequently, our in-depth analysis must consider both the author's development of Native American values, specifically Ojibwa, and her ability to create credible historical fiction for the time period.

First, Erdrich creates credibility for the story by identifying herself as a member of the Turtle Mountain Band of Ojibwa and explaining that she became interested in writing the book while researching her own family history. In her acknowledgments, Erdrich states: "My mother, Rita Gourneau Erdrich, and my sister, Lise Erdrich, researched our family life and found ancestors on both sides who lived on Madeline Island during the time in which this book is set. One of them was Gatay Manomin, or Old Wild Rice. I'd like to thank him and all of his descendants, my extended family. . . . This book and those that will follow are an attempt to retrace my own family's history" (unpaged acknowledgments).

Two of the evaluative criteria for Native American literature are that the Native American characters belong to a specific identified tribe and are not grouped together under one category referred to as "Indian" and that the customs, values, and beliefs for the specific tribe should be authentic and respected. In this book, the development of Ojibwa values is especially meaningful. For example, Erdrich conveys the value of nature as the girl is taught by her grandmother to listen to and learn from nature. The importance of her lessons is reinforced as she nurses her family during a smallpox epidemic. The author reinforces Ojibwa values and beliefs through traditional stories told by the girl's father and grandmother. One of the grandmother's stories is "Nanabozho and Muskrat Make an Earth." Grandmother uses the stories to teach lessons to her granddaughter. When you read the folklore from various Native American tribes, you will discover that the oral stories were told to pass on various beliefs and to educate the members of the tribe. In addition, the "Earth Diver" story as told by the grandmother is one of the oldest and most common creation stories told among various North American Indian tribes living around the Great Lakes.

Another authentic Native American value and belief is developed as the author explores the importance of messages revealed in dreams and voices heard in nature. Notice in this quote how the grandmother reveals the importance of the fact that her granddaughter, Omakayas, can hear the voices: "Nokomis understood the meaning of what had happened, understood why the voices had spoken, understood what it meant for Omakayas's future and was proud and glad to have a granddaughter who was chosen to be a healer" (p. 206). When you read many of the autobiographies of early Native American leaders, you will discover that showing respect for and relying on messages revealed in dreams and listening to voices found in nature are of considerable value. Consequently, only people of great stature within the tribe are given this special ability.

When analyzing the book for historical accuracy for settings and conflicts, you will notice that the author provides detailed descriptions of the island during each of the four seasons. A map of the general region of the island and Lake Superior and a detailed map of the Ojibwa village are included in the book. The major conflict that the village must overcome is the smallpox epidemic of 1847, when 18 Ojibwa died from the disease. This is the kind of information that can easily be evaluated as you consider the authenticity of both the settings for the island and the major health conflicts of this period. *The Game of Silence* is a sequel to *The Birchbark House.*

Farley Mowat's Canadian Library Association Book of the Year, *Lost in the Barrens,* takes place in the 20th century in a remote Arctic wilderness, hundreds of miles from the nearest town. The two main characters are Awasin, a Woodland Cree, and Jamie, a white Canadian orphan who moves north to live with his uncle. The setting becomes an antagonist for both boys when they accompany the Crees on a hunting expedition and then become separated from the hunters. Mowat vividly describes searching for food and preparing for the rapidly approaching winter. Through long periods of isolation, the boys develop a close relationship and an understanding of each other.

Through all of these stories, children can experience Native American characters who have personal thoughts and emotions and who live within a family as well as within a tribe. In addition, children will begin to understand the impact of white people on the Native American way of life.

Many authors who write about the pioneer period stress the quest for and love of land and the conflicts between different cultures. Consider the following themes developed in historical fiction about pioneer America. How do the themes correspond with historical events? What other periods have similar themes? What are the similarities between times with similar themes?

1. People have moral obligations.
2. People have strong dreams of owning land.
3. Families can survive if they work together.
4. People need each other and may work together for their mutual good.

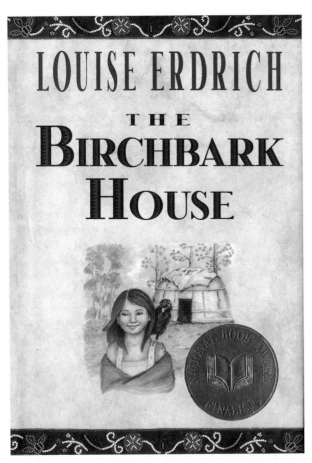

An Ojibwa girl's life is set on an island in Lake Superior in 1847. (From The Birchbark House, *by Louise Erdrich. Text and jacket illustration copyright © 1999 by Louise Erdrich. Reprinted by permission of Hyperion Books for Children.)*

5. Battles can be won through legal means rather than through unlawful actions.

6. Hatred and prejudice are destructive forces.

7. Without spiritual hope, people may lose their will to live.

The Early 20th Century

Recent books of historical fiction with settings in the early 1900s often depict survival of immigrants who flee Europe or social conflicts and the Great Depression, which began in 1929. These stories stress both physical and spiritual survival as people strive to maintain pride and independence. Person-against-society and person-against-self conflicts develop when the characters experience or express racial prejudice and face financial hardships.

Even though Patricia Beatty's *Sarah and Me and the Lady From the Sea* takes place in 1894, shortly before the turn of the century, the father's bankruptcy caused by a flood is as devastating as the financial hardships caused by the Depression. Beatty shows the importance of family unity and a bond between people who are facing hardships. At first, the family reflects prejudices against those who have less social standing than themselves. However, these characters show the family how to survive without servants and how to enjoy their new life. In *The Silent Boy*, Lois Lowry depicts another type of prejudice that was common in the early 1900s: prejudice against people with mental disabilities. Lowry develops strong characters, especially Katy Thatcher, the daughter of the town doctor, who befriends a boy who is shunned because he is considered "retarded." Lowry shows the sad existence related to a boy who is misunderstood and even feared by society, and she adds to the historical time period by introducing each chapter with copies of photographs of real people who lived during that time.

In *Lizzie Bright and the Buckminster Boy*, Gary D. Schmidt's protagonist, Turner Buckminster, the son of a white minister, befriends Lizzie Bright Griffin, the granddaughter of an African American minister. The main character faces two types of conflicts, those imposed on him by the very conservative members of his father's church and the racial attitudes of the people who do not want him to befriend Lizzie and who want to demolish the homes of the former slaves who live on nearby Malaga Island. According to the author's note, the incidents on Malaga Island and the subsequent destruction of the former slaves' homes happened in the early 1900s. The author develops both the strong anti–African American attitudes of the community and the powerful insights Turner gains as he interacts with this wise girl. Schmidt states the theme when Turner realizes that "the world turns and the world spins, the tide runs in and the tide runs out, and there is nothing in the world more beautiful and more wonderful in all its evolving forms than two souls who look at each other straight on. And there is nothing more woeful and soul-saddening than when they are parted. Turner knew that everything in the world rejoices in the touch, and everything in the world laments in the losing. And he had lost Malaga" (p. 216).

In Karen Hesse's *Letters From Rifka*, a Jewish family flees Russia in 1919. The plot unfolds as Rifka writes letters to her cousin, Tovah. The details show that degrading experiences and terror do not overcome the family's will to escape and survive. Rifka endures additional conflict when she is prohibited from sailing to America because she has ringworm. Later, she is kept in detention at Ellis Island. Finally, after months of separation, she is reunited with her family. The story may be so believable because it is based on the experiences of the author's great-aunt.

Anna Myers's *Fire in the Hills*, set in rural Oklahoma during World War I, develops themes related to prejudice and discrimination. For example, during the interactions between a conscientious objector and a German immigrant family, the author develops the themes that prejudice and discrimination are destructive forces and that there is a bond between people who experience injustice. Through the actions of Hallie, the 16-year-old heroine, the author also develops themes related to the importance of dreams and working for a goal as Hallie discovers that her goal to become a teacher is possible, that women deserve to find a place for themselves in the world, and that women can work together to make their desires known.

Mildred D. Taylor's *Roll of Thunder, Hear My Cry* explores both the subtle and the explicit racial prejudice of many white Americans in the early 20th century. Consider, for example, the subtle discrimination Taylor describes. Cassie and her brother, who live in rural Mississippi, excitedly await their new schoolbooks, only to receive badly worn, dirty castoffs from the white elementary school. When Cassie's brother looks at the inside cover of his book, he sees that on its 12th date of issue—to him—it is described as being in very poor condition, and the race of the student is listed as "nigra."

Other expressions of racism portrayed in this book are far less subtle, however, and they include the family's experiences with night riders and cross burnings. Understandably, the family feels fear as well as humiliation and indignation. In a sequel to this book, *Let the Circle Be Unbroken*, Taylor helps readers see how the estrangement of white and black people from each other results from ingrained social prejudices. The family in *Roll of Thunder, Hear My Cry* owns its own land, the mother has graduated from a teacher's college, and the children consistently attend school. The family experiences injustice, but a loving environment helps protect and strengthen the members.

The experiences in William H. Armstrong's *Sounder* are harsher and filled with tragedy. An early 20th-century family of African American sharecroppers lives in one of numerous ramshackle cabins scattered across the vast fields of the white landlord. When the poverty-stricken father steals a ham to feed his hungry family, he is handcuffed, chained, and taken to jail. The futility of protest is suggested as Sounder, the family's faithful coon dog, tries to save the father and is wounded by the white sheriff's shotgun.

Comparisons between the two incidents are developed as both the father and Sounder are gone: the father to jail and then to a succession of chain gangs, and Sounder to the woods to heal his wounds. A strong bond between man and dog is implied when Sounder returns, a crippled remnant of his former self. He does not bark until the father returns home, himself crippled by a dynamite blast in the prison quarry. The two old friends are physically and emotionally tired and have only a short life together. The final vision of the two friends is one of remembered strength, as the son, grown to manhood, recalls his father and the faithful dog as they were before the tragic happenings:

> The pine trees would look down forever on a lantern burning out of oil but not going out. A harvest moon would cast shadows forever of a man walking upright, his dog, bouncing after him. And the quiet of the night would fill and echo again with the deep voice of Sounder, the great coon dog. (p. 116)

Critics of *Sounder* believe that because the dog is the only character in the book with a name, the book implies that the characters need not be respected as human beings. Critics also object to the black family's being characterized as submissive and spiritless. Others argue that the family should be nameless because the tragedy depicted in the story was one shared by many poor black sharecroppers during that period. In the latter view, tragedy is seen as a strong bond between all people who experience injustice. Readers can consider both viewpoints and form their own evaluations of *Sounder*.

The themes developed in historical fiction set in the early 20th century highlight both negative and positive attitudes and values. Consider the following themes found in the literature: How do they relate to the historical events? Are these themes found during any other time period in historical fiction?

1. People will strive for survival of the body and the spirit.
2. Prejudice and discrimination are destructive forces.
3. There is a bond between people who experience injustice.
4. Monetary wealth does not create a rich life.

World War II

In 1933, Adolf Hitler took power in Germany, and Germany resigned from the League of Nations. In 1935, Hitler reintroduced conscription of German soldiers and recommended rearmament, contrary to the Treaty of Versailles. Along with a rapid increase in military power came an obsessive hatred of the Jewish people. In March 1938, Hitler's war machine began moving across Europe. Austria was occupied, and imprisonment of Jews began. World War II became a reality when the Germans invaded Poland on September 1, 1939.

The 1940s saw the invasions of Norway, Belgium, and Holland; the defeat of the French army; and the heroic evacuation of British soldiers from Dunkirk. From the start of the invasions through the defeat of Hitler's forces in 1945, these years have inspired many tales of both sorrow and heroism.

Authors who write children's historical fiction set in World War II often focus on the experiences of Jewish people in hiding and concentration camps, the experiences of Japanese Americans in internment centers in the United States, or the perseverance of people in occupied lands. Because some of these stories are written by people who lived similar experiences, the stories tend to be emotional. The authors often create vivid conflicts.

Authors explore the consequences of war and prejudice by having characters ponder why their lives are in turmoil, by describing the characters' fears and their reactions to their situations and to one another, and by re-

An In-Depth Analysis of One Book of Historical Fiction

Two Suns in the Sky received the Scott O'Dell Award for Historical Fiction. The author, Miriam Bat-Ami, uses an interesting author's style and technique to chronicle both the problems of Jewish refugees in America during World War II and the responses to the refugees by Americans living near the refugee shelters: Parallel voices express two points of view. One point of view belongs to Chris, a teenage girl who lives near the camp in Oswego, New York; the other belongs to Adam, a Jewish youth whose family first escaped from Yugoslavia and then from hiding in Italy.

This parallel-voice approach allows Bat-Ami to explore the many sides of the refugee experience. For example, early in the book when writing from Chris's point of view, the author explores the local and national society's attitudes toward the refugees by having Chris read editorials and comments from the newspapers. Here the attitudes range from "Make one camp, and you invite trouble because the entire United States will soon be a camp filled with refugees" to "This country was built by refugees, they will add to America." When Chris reads the positive editorials and news articles, she hopes they will stop her father and her relatives from making nasty remarks.

Two of the most important evaluations for historical fiction relate to the authenticity of the setting and the conflicts: Do the conflicts and their resolutions reflect what is known about the time period? In addition to expressing various attitudes about refugees found in the time period, Bat-Ami includes considerable background material that can easily be authenticated and that provides insights into the historical conflicts. For example, when writing from Adam's point of view, she presents historical information.

Russia and America were in Germany. President Roosevelt returned from Yalta, where the Allies talked of peace. Belgrade had been liberated since October; Tito and the Soviets joined together. It was the spring of 1945, and the world was a busy place. In the camp we argued over whether Yugoslavia would become a Communist country while we made a circle around the post office and waited like hungry wolves. Every so often a few of us trotted off to Building #188, where a list that had made its way from Switzerland was posted. On it were the names of people who had made it to the free world. Mama, Mira, and I were on the list. We searched for Papa's and Villi's and Grandmama's names. Perhaps they had gone to Israel or were in England. (p. 169)

Bat-Ami reinforces many of the themes and conflicts developed in the book by introducing each chapter with quotes from former refugees or other historical personages. For example, notice in the following quote how the author reveals the meaning of the title of the book and one of the themes she develops in the novel: "'One night I looked into the sky and it appeared like two suns. I remembered an old legend: he who sees two suns in the sky will never be the same.' Walter Greenberg, former resident of Emergency Refugee Shelter" (p. 32).

Probably the most important quote used to reinforce the themes and conflicts related to the time period is this one by Franklin Delano Roosevelt, found at the end of the author's note: "We have learned that we cannot live alone, at peace; that our own well-being is dependent upon the well-being of other nations far away. We have learned that we must live as men [and women], and not as ostriches nor as dogs in the manger. We have learned to be citizens of the world, members of the human community" (p. 218).

vealing what happens to the characters or their families as a result of war. As might be expected, the themes of these stories include the consequences of hatred and prejudice, the search for religious and personal freedom, the role of conscience, and obligation toward others.

Louise Borden's *The Greatest Skating Race: A World War II Story From the Netherlands* introduces younger readers to both the dangers of World War II and the resourcefulness and bravery of children living in the shadows of the Nazi regime. In this strong story of bravery, a 10-year-old skater leads two young neighbors to safety in Belgium after their father is arrested for sending messages to the Allies. The frozen canals provide the escape route in this suspenseful book. The subdued colors in the watercolors used by the illustrator, Niki Daly, add to the tension of the 16-kilometer journey in which the children escape while in possible view of German soldiers.

Borden's *The Little Ships: The Heroic Rescue at Dunkirk in World War II* presents this rescue through the eyes of a young girl who joins her father in the rescue. Michael Foreman's illustrations of the fishing boats and the rescue add drama to this story. In a book for older readers, *Wish Me Luck*, James Heneghan presents another type of rescue, as children are on a ship that is torpedoed on the journey from England to Canada.

John and Katherine Paterson based *Blueberries for the Queen* on a true incident in 1942 when Queen Wilhelmina of the Netherlands lived in exile after the Nazi invasion of her country. During that time, she lived in Lee, Massachusetts, with her daughter and granddaughters. In a historical note, the authors tell how a young boy brought blueberries to the queen. The text reveals that the young boy, William, felt left out of the war because he was too young to fight or to be useful for the war effort; consequently, he dreamed at night about being a brave knight, fighting dragons, and winning battles. When he hears about the Queen, he remembers what his mother always does for people when bad things happen: She takes them

Parallel voices are used to express the points of view of an American girl and a Jewish boy from Yugoslovia. (Cover from Two Suns in the Sky, *by Miriam Bat-Ami. Cover illustration by Hilary Mosberg, copyright © 1999. Published by Front Street/Cricket Books. Reprinted by permission.)*

something to eat. William decides that freshly picked blueberries are about the best food imaginable. Even though people tell him that he will never be able to give his berries to the Queen, he insists. He not only is invited into the house, but also hands the berries to the Queen. The boy tells the Queen, "I picked these blueberries in our field this morning because I . . . I . . . didn't want you to be sad" (unnumbered).

Peter Hartling's *Crutches* develop a theme associated with the terrible consequences of war and the struggle for freedom. The protagonist in *Crutches* is separated from his mother as a consequence of World War II. Hartling develops strong bonds between the homeless boy and a survivor of the war who now walks on crutches. In a story that shows the importance of friendship and the triumph of family loyalty, the boy and the survivor eventually find the mother and reunite the family. Stressing the consequences of war on European families, Hartling shows the inhumanity associated with war and the spirits that survive even in war-torn countries.

Mary Downing Hahn develops person-against-society and person-against-self conflicts in *Stepping on the Cracks*. Person-against-society conflicts emerge as children living in College Park, Maryland, discover a deserter from the army. Through various conversations and reactions, Hahn shows the attitudes of society toward a man who is an army deserter and a conscientious objector. Person-against-self conflicts are explored as the children make decisions about helping the man. Hahn shows that moral obligations and personal conscience are strong forces, war is terrible, and friendship is powerful. Janet Taylor Lisle sets *The Art of Keeping Cool* in a New England village during the war. As in *Stepping on the Cracks*, the major characters face personal struggles. Is the German painter who lives in a shack near the beach an innocent artist who must be protected, or is he a dangerous spy who must be hunted down and prosecuted? The major conflict in Robert Cormier's *Other Bells for Us to Ring*, a story set in America, is person-against-self for the protagonist, who faces questions about faith. The authors of these books present numerous details about the war years in the United States to authenticate the settings.

The Holocaust. The Nazis' terrible crimes against Jewish people are familiar to adults and children alike. Stories about the Holocaust help children sense the bewilderment and terror of a time when innocent people were the subject of irrational hatred and persecution.

In a picture storybook for younger children, *Star of Fear, Star of Hope*, Jo Hoestlandt writes a poignant account of two friends who are separated in Nazi-occupied France in 1942. The story begins, "My name is Helen, and I'm nearly an old woman now. When I'm gone, who will remember Lydia? That is why I want to tell you our story" (unnumbered). The author places the Holocaust on a very personal level by telling the story of the two friends. The personal conflict begins on the eve of Helen's 9th birthday when her Jewish friend, Lydia, is invited to stay overnight. It is on this night when the Nazis begin their roundup of the Jews. Helen does not understand why her friend leaves hurriedly, and she responds with words she has always regretted: "You're not my friend anymore!" (unnumbered). Unfortunately, this is the last time that Helen sees her friend. The book ends on a hopeful note, however, as Helen remembers the rhyme they used to say:

> "Stars at morning, better take warning.
> Stars at night, hope is in sight.
> I'll always have hope . . ." (unnumbered)

Patricia Polacco also chose the picture storybook format to develop a story of Jews hiding in German-occupied France in *The Butterfly*. The author uses butterflies to develop themes within the story. When the Jewish and French girls see a butterfly, it becomes for them a symbol of freedom. At the end of the book, Polacco again uses the butterflies as a symbol of freedom. After the Jewish family

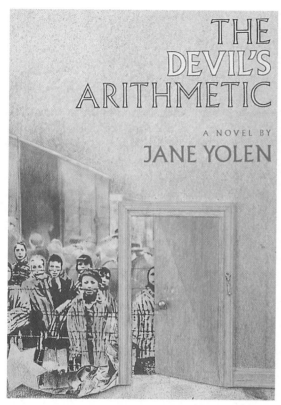

A time-warp experience develops a girl's understanding of the Holocaust. (From The Devil's Arithmetic, *by Jane Yolen, copyright © 1988. Reprinted by permission of Viking Penguin.)*

Technology Resources

Use the CD-ROM that accompanies this text to generate a list of Holocaust books by searching Title, Description, and Topic fields under "Holocaust." Limit the search by including a specific grade in the Grade Level field.

attempts an escape, the French girl searches for a sign that the family is safe. At this point, numerous butterflies land in the garden and one even lands on the girl's finger. She now believes that the butterflies are a sign of the family having reached safety.

Karen Hesse's *The Cats in Krasinski Square* is another picture storybook about a Holocaust experience. According to the author, she read a story about cats outfoxing the Gestapo at the train station in Warsaw during World War II. She includes information in the historical note about Jewish Resistance members who fought the Nazis in April 1943 in the Warsaw Ghetto. In a satisfying story, the Resistance members gather cats into baskets and head to the station behind the Gestapo and their snarling dogs. Before the dogs can reach their human prey, the Resistance members open the baskets and let the cats loose. Now the dogs chase the cats who easily escape, and the

humans smuggle food through the cracks in the wall and into the Ghetto.

Doreen Rappaport's *The Secret Seder* is another picture storybook based on a true experience. The author develops a theme illustrating that people will take considerable risks to practice their religion, even in times of war when their lives are in danger. The family, who is hiding in a small town in France, risks exposure by attending a Seder in a hidden mountain cabin because "we promised Grandpapa that we would celebrate all the holidays, no matter what" (unnumbered). Rappaport includes additional information about the Jewish experience, the Passover, and other books about the Passover and the experiences of children during the Holocaust.

Johanna Reiss tells about her childhood in *The Upstairs Room*. Reiss allows readers to glimpse varying consequences of prejudice and hatred. A young girl, Johanna, hears news of the war and asks why Hitler hates her people. The girl is barred from restaurants and the public school, and she learns that many Jewish people are being taken to forced-labor camps. Reiss depicts the obligations of one person to another when a Dutch family offers, in spite of great danger, to hide Johanna and her sister on their farm. The farmer builds a secret space in an upstairs closet to provide a hiding place for the two girls. At first, Johanna does not understand why she and her sister must hide, but gradually, she realizes their serious predicament, as word of the Holocaust spreads.

In several scenes, Reiss's style and first-person point of view reveal the breathless fear of the children. For example, as the children hide in the cramped closet:

> Footsteps. Loud ones. Boots. Coming up the stairs. Wooden shoes. Coming behind. Sini put her arms around me and pushed my head against her shoulder. Loud voices. Ugly ones. Furniture being moved. And Opoe's protesting voice. The closet door was thrown open. Hands fumbled on the shelves. Sini was trembling. She tightened her arms around me. I no longer breathed through my nose. Breathing through my mouth made less noise. (p. 149)

The girls and the family protecting them are brave during this unsuccessful search by Nazi troops. The story ends happily: Canadian troops liberate the town, and at last, Johanna and her sister can leave their room. This is a powerful story of the experiences of common people during the German occupation. (Some adults have criticized this book because of realistic dialogue, in which members of the farm family use swear words.)

Trust in and loyalty toward a parent are the motivational forces in Uri Orlev's story of survival set in the Jewish ghetto of Warsaw, Poland. *The Island on Bird Street* chronicles the experiences of Alex, who turns a bombed-out building into a refuge while he waits for his father's return. Surrounded by houses emptied of food, Alex feels that his refuge is similar to the desert island in his favorite book, *Robinson Crusoe*. Orlev develops the symbolism of a

Illustration from The Secret Seder *by Doreen Rappaport. Illustration copyright ©
2005 by Emily Arnold McCully. Used by permission of Hyperion Books for Children.*

to! Get someone to teach you how to act
like a Christian, how to cross yourself and
how to pray. Find a farmer you can stay with
until the war ends. Always go to the poor
people. They're more willing to help. . . .
The most important thing is to forget your
name. Wipe it from your memory. . . . But
even if you forget everything—even if you
forget me and Mama—never forget that
you're a Jew" (p. 64).

Srulik follows his father's advice.
While running and hiding from the Nazis,
he encounters all types of people. Some risk
their own lives to hide him and even give
him lessons on becoming a Christian; others either fear Srulik because they believe
he is a Jew or threaten to turn him over to
the Gestapo. The story is an account of a
young boy's struggle to stay alive and to live
up to his father's wishes. This struggle continues even after he loses an arm in a farming accident. This incident illustrates the
hatred for the Jews when a doctor who
could have saved Srulik's arm but refuses to
operate when he discovers the boy is a Jew.
Orlev presents considerable historical data
such as the impact of the partisans, the terrible life forced on those who are hiding for
their lives, the consequences of the Russian
victory, and the search carried on by Jewish
organizations to find lost children after the
war is over. Through Srulik's struggles to stay alive and the
actions of various people, Orlev reinforces themes such as
that freedom is worth fighting for and prejudice and hatred are destructive forces.

Orlev's *Lydia, Queen of Palestine* is a lighter story in
which 10-year-old Lydia escapes from Romania to Palestine, where she becomes a resident of a kibbutz. Readers
enjoy this often humorous story of a free-spirited child
who considers herself "a terror." Lydia has many of the
characteristics needed to be a survivor.

Several books describe the role of the resistance or
friendly gentile families in the Jewish struggle for survival.
Ida Vos's *Hide and Seek* presents the cruel world of the
Holocaust as it changes the lives of Jewish people living
in the Netherlands under German occupation. Vos encourages readers to respond to the book in her foreword
remarks:

> Can you imagine how it feels when you find out that people
> you love are dead, all of a sudden? Imagine what it would be
> like not ever to be allowed to go outside, year after year. Imag-
> ine being able to do your shopping only between three and
> five o'clock. Imagine. . . . I know how difficult it is to imagine
> such things; that is the reason I wrote *Hide and Seek*. To let
> you feel how terrible it is to be discriminated against, and to
> let you know how terrible it was to be a Jewish child in Hol-
> land during those years. (p. ix)

lonely island, on which Alex, like Robinson Crusoe, must
learn how to survive, and the terrifying historical background of the Holocaust, in which Alex witnesses the capture of his Jewish family and friends, experiences fear and
loneliness, and nurses a resistance fighter's wounds. The
book concludes on a note of hope: Alex's father returns,
finds Alex where he promised to wait, and takes him to
the forest to be with the partisans who are resisting the
Nazis.

Orlev also sets *The Man From the Other Side* in the
Warsaw Ghetto during World War II. In this story, a Polish boy and his father risk detection and punishment for
taking supplies to the Jewish people who are enclosed on
the other side of the walls. This gripping story ends with
the Warsaw Ghetto uprising. Orlev presents much history
of the Jewish people in Poland through dialogue. He also
describes the feelings of anti-Semitism that many of the
people held.

According to Orlev's epilogue, *Run, Boy, Run* is based
on a the real experiences of 8-year-old Srulik, who is
forced to leave his family, live in the woods, and try to survive. Imagine being 8 years old and having the following
conversation with your father, who is also in hiding and
running: "Srulik, there's no time. I want you to remember
what I'm going to tell you. You have to stay alive. You have

Symbolic and historical settings are integral to a story set in the Warsaw ghetto. (From The Island on Bird Street, *by Uri Orlev. Jacket illustration copyright © 1984 by Jean Titherington. Reprinted by permission of Houghton Mifflin Company.)*

The author also wants readers to understand both the courage of the Jewish people and the determination of the Dutch gentiles who risked their lives for their neighbors. Compare this book with Lois Lowry's *Number the Stars*, a book about the Danish endeavor to move Jewish residents to Sweden and safety.

Two authors place their Holocaust books in occupied France. Gregory Maguire's *The Good Liar* uses an interesting technique by introducing the book as a class project in which children write or talk to someone who experienced World War II. The remainder of the book is the answer sent to the children by an artist who at the time was a young boy living in France. The family's experiences during the German occupation are told through the viewpoint of the boy, who did not know that his mother was hiding Jewish refugees in the crawl space—thus the title *The Good Liar*. (This book could be used to motivate a class project.)

You can compare *The Good Liar* with Norma Fox Mazer's *Good Night, Maman*. Mazer develops her story through the viewpoint of 12-year-old Karin and her older brother as they experience hiding in an attic, escaping to Italy, and finally arriving in a refugee camp in Oswego, New York. There is both a sad and a hopeful conclusion

to the book. Sadness results when Karin discovers that both of her parents are dead. The hopeful message results when Karin decides to continue writing to her mother and to write about her experiences so that she will never forget what happened. She calls her book her "dream book" and hopes that someday she will share it with her own daughter.

After reading such stories, children often are concerned about the implications of not acting when other people are unjustly accused of crimes.

Internment of Japanese Americans and the Pacific Conflict

The Jewish people weren't the only ones to live through persecution and fear during World War II. Many children are surprised to read stories about the American treatment of Japanese Americans during the war. Two books by Yoshiko Uchida tell about a Japanese American family's experiences after the bombing of Pearl Harbor. (Although the stories are fictional, they are based on what happened to Uchida and her family.)

In *Journey to Topaz*, the police take away Yuki's father, a businessman in Berkeley, California, and send Yuki, her mother, and her older brother to a permanent internment center in Utah, called Topaz. Uchida creates vivid pictures of the internment camp. She describes, for example, latrines without doors, lines of people waiting to use them, and the wind blowing across the desert into the barracks. The fear of the interned people and their wardens climaxes when the grandfather of Yuki's best friend goes searching for arrowheads and is shot by a guard who believes that he is trying to escape. Family members experience conflicting feelings when Yuki's brother, wishing to prove his loyalty to America, joins an army unit composed of Japanese Americans.

Yuki's story continues in *Journey Home*, in which the family returns to Berkeley, only to discover distrust, difficulty finding work, and anti-Japanese violence. The family feels hope and strength more than bitterness, however. Yuki discovers that coming home is having everyone she cares about around her.

Historical fiction set in World War II includes stories about the Pacific conflict. These books develop similar themes as those of other nonfictional war texts. For example, *Shin's Tricycle*, by Tatsuharu Kodama, develops the theme that wars are brutal and that we should try to keep the dream of peace alive for all children. In this true story, a young boy and his best friend are killed by an atomic bomb while riding the prized tricycle. The tricycle is now located at the Peace Museum in Hiroshima.

Adeline Yen Mah's *Chinese Cinderella and the Secret Dragon Society* is set in Shanghai during the 1940s and the Japanese invasion of China. As in the folktale, the young girl, CC, escapes from an unhappy homelife. In this story,

allow readers to understand how characters face and overcome these issues. All of the books suggest that there is hope for the future.

The themes in children's historical fiction with settings during World War II resemble those found during other times of great peril. Consider the following themes. How do they relate to historical events? What are characteristics of other historical periods that have similar themes?

1. People will seek freedom from religious and political persecution.
2. Prejudice and hatred are destructive forces.
3. Moral obligation and personal conscience are strong forces.
4. Freedom is worth fighting for.
5. Family love and loyalty help people endure catastrophic experiences.

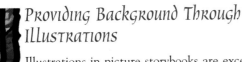

Teaching With Historical Fiction

Children can learn to love and respect history when they vicariously share the experiences of a character with whom they identify. Surrounding themselves with the flavor and spirit of a historical period, they also can visualize how people are affected by the times in which they live. Historical fiction helps children acquire the idea that history is people rather than merely a series of events. You can bring history to life by guiding children toward individual reading selections, reading historical fiction aloud to students, encouraging dramatic presentations of short scenes from favorite books, and using literature in pleasant ways to develop attitudes and general concepts about history. Historical fiction allows children to learn about the continuity of events, to understand human relationships, and to immerse themselves in the settings characteristic of specific times.

Providing Background Through Illustrations

Illustrations in picture storybooks are excellent for helping children visualize the settings for various time periods in historical fiction. If the illustrations have carefully researched details, children can both visualize the characteristics associated with the time period and authenticate the textual descriptions. The following picture storybooks reflect historical settings (many of these books are discussed in Chapters 4 and 5 in this text):

Middle Ages:	Uri Shulevitz's *The Travels of Benjamin of Tudela*
	David Macaulay's *Castle*
	Richard Platt's *Castle Diary: The Journal of Tobias Burgess, Page*
Early Native American cultures:	Stephen Trimble's *The Village of Blue Stone*
	Jane Yolen's *Encounter*

Pioneer America:	Jim Aylesworth's *The Folks in the Valley: A Pennsylvania Dutch ABC*
	Byrd Baylor's *The Best Town in the World*
	Donald Hall's *Ox-Cart Man*
	Brett Harvey's *Cassie's Journey: Going West in the 1860s*
	Brett Harvey's *My Prairie Year: Based on the Diary of Elenore Plaisted*
	Reeve Lindbergh's *Johnny Appleseed*
	Patricia MacLachlan's *Three Names*
Early 1900s:	Gloria Houston's *My Great-Aunt Arizona*
	Megan McDonald's *The Great Pumpkin Switch*
	Janice Shefelman's *A Peddler's Dream*
Mid-1990s:	Judith Hendershot's *In Coal Country*
	William Kurelek's *A Prairie Boy's Summer*
	Cynthia Rylant's *Appalachia: The Voices of Sleeping Birds*
	Jane Yolen's *Letting Swift River Go*
World War II:	Michael Foreman's *War Boy*
	Roberto Innocenti's *Rose Blanche*
	Patricia Polacco's *The Butterfly*
Migrant families:	Sherley Anne Williams's *Working Cotton*

These picture storybooks will add background information as children read about or research various time periods.

Interdisciplinary Unit: Looking at Pioneer America

Most children are fascinated with the time in American history when courageous adults and children were struggling across the country on foot, on horseback, or in covered wagons. They like to hear about children who rode on canal barges, floated on rafts down the

Ohio, or traveled on steamboats down the Mississippi. They also enjoy vicariously experiencing the frontier years after the covered wagons were unloaded and families began their new lives in sod houses or log cabins.

Teachers of social studies find this period exciting. They use the fiction of the pioneer period to help children develop closer ties with the past, understand the physical environment of the time, and discover the links between the pioneer past and the present. Ways of developing these understandings range from sharing an individual story with children to developing total units that encourage children to identify with the period through music, art, stories, games, foods, values, home remedies, and research of historical characters.

Values From the Past

Children can learn about the past and relate it to the present when they identify the values held and problems overcome by people living in pioneer America. Children can compare these values and problems and the solutions of problems, as depicted in historical fiction, with those of today. The pioneer period is filled with stories that stress love of the land and the need for positive relationships among family members, neighbors, pioneers, and Native Americans, including the struggle for survival and the need for bravery. The following experiences encourage children to clarify their own values as well as those of others.

Love of the Land.   Pioneers were drawn to the West because of the opportunity to own rich farmland. Some people left their homes in the East when their land no longer produced good crops. Others traveled to the West because they wanted more room or fewer neighbors. Still others acquired the free land provided under the Homestead Act (see Figure 10.1). After children have read one of the books that place this emphasis on the land (such as Honoré Morrow's *On to Oregon!*, Barbara Brenner's *Wagon Wheels*, and Harold Keith's *The Obstinate Land*), ask them to identify the pioneers' reasons for moving and

conflicts that family members felt when they were deciding whether to move.

At this point, use role playing to help clarify the attitudes of pioneer family members. Ask the students to imagine that the year is 1866; the Civil War ended the year before. They are living on a small New England farm. They are sitting at the evening meal with their immediate family and their visiting aunt and uncle. Their aunt begins talking excitedly about an article in the paper telling how many people are going west to claim free land provided under the Homestead Act of 1862. The aunt and uncle are ready to sell their farm, pack a few belongings, and travel to the West in a covered wagon. The aunt wants her brother's family to join them. Have the students role-play the reactions of the different family members and decide whether they should go. Based on characteristics found in historical fiction stories, they might express these concerns:

- *Mother:* She knows that her husband wants to own a better farm, but her family lives in the East and she doesn't want to leave. In addition, she has lost one child, who is buried on the old farm. She is also concerned about living on the frontier away from a church, a school, and the protection of close neighbors.
- *Father:* He is unhappy with his rocky farm and its poor production. He has dreamed of a farm with rich soil to produce better crops and support his family.
- *Twelve-year-old daughter:* She is filled with the excitement of a new adventure. She wants to see new lands and Indians. In addition, she is not displeased with the prospect of leaving school for a while.
- *Seven-year-old son:* The farmhouse is the only home he has ever known; his best friend and his relatives live in the surrounding countryside. He'd love to see some Indians and he wants to please his father, but he doesn't know what to expect in a land that far from home.

Have the students consider each person's arguments and decide if they would have moved to a new land. Have the students continue by talking about what they would take with them if they decided to homestead.

Finally, draw the discussion into the present time. Do people still have a strong loyalty to the land? Do they want to own their own land? Encourage the students to provide reasons for their arguments. Place the desire for unspoiled land as well as adventure into a modern framework by having students pretend that their families are moving to a wilderness area in Alaska. Why would they or would they not want to move? What problems do they think they would encounter before moving? How would they solve them? What problems would they encounter in the Alaskan wilderness? How would they solve them? Finally, do they believe that these problems and their solutions are similar to those experienced by pioneers?

Human Relations.   Many stories about pioneer days present different ways of dealing with Native Americans

FIGURE 10.1   A poster for the Homestead Act

and diverse attitudes toward them. The only solution that many books give is a battle between the Native Americans and whites. In contrast, Alice Dalgliesh's *The Courage of Sarah Noble* presents a family who settles on land for which the native people have been given a fair price, with the provision that they retain their right to fish in the river. Sarah's parents believe that all people must be treated fairly. Encourage children to discuss the reasons for various actions, the beliefs of the pioneers, and the consequences.

After children have read the "Massacre" and "Ambassador to the Enemy" chapters in Carol Ryrie Brink's *Caddie Woodlawn*, ask them to discuss the settlers' decision to attack the Indians because they thought the Indians were going to attack them. Why did the settlers reach their decision? Was it accurate? Why or why not?

Then, ask the students to place themselves in Caddie's role: If they were Caddie, would they have warned the Indians? Why or why not? What might have been the results if Caddie had not made her evening ride?

Finally, bring the discussion to contemporary times. Ask the students if there are times when people today might decide to act out of fright rather than out of knowledge. What events would they consider important enough to risk their own safety?

Books about pioneers also include many stories about the need to help others; neighbors and family members help each other and provide moral support during times of crisis. The "Little House" series, by Laura Ingalls Wilder, contains many incidents of family support and working with neighbors. *Sarah, Plain and Tall*, by Patricia MacLachlan, emphasizes the need for a mother and a wife in pioneer times. Encourage children to discuss the values of positive relationships during both pioneer and contemporary times.

The Pioneer Environment

Pioneer stories are rich in descriptions of the homes, crafts, store goods, food, transportation, books, and pleasures of the pioneers.

Amusements of the Pioneer Family.   Allowing children to take part in the same experiences that entertained pioneer children is a good way to help them feel closer to their counterparts in the past. For example, Laura Ingalls Wilder's *Little House in the Big Woods* describes happy moments that can be re-created with children:

1. For a special birthday treat, Pa played and sang "Pop Goes the Weasel" for Laura. Some of her happiest memories were related to Pa's fiddle. Other songs mentioned in the book are "Rock of Ages" (the fiddler could not play weekday songs on Sunday) and "Yankee Doodle."

2. The family traveled through the woods to a square dance at Grandpa's house. At the dance, the fiddler played and the square-dance caller called the squares for "Buffalo Gals," "The Irish Washerwoman," and "The Arkansas Traveler."

3. After the day's work was finished, Ma sometimes cut paper dolls for the girls out of stiff white paper and made dresses, hats, ribbons, and laces out of colored paper.

4. In the winter evenings, Laura and Mary begged Pa to tell them stories. He told them about "Grandpa and the Panther," "Pa and the Bear in the Way," "Pa and the Voice in the Woods," and "Grandpa's Sled and the Pig." Enough details are included in these stories so that they can be retold to children.

A School Day With the Pioneer Family.   A day in school for pioneer children (if a school was available) was quite different from a contemporary day in school. Historical fiction and other sources provide enough information about schools attended, books read, and parables memorized to interest children and re-create a school day that emphasizes spelling, reading, and arithmetic.

Modern children may be surprised that Ma in Laura Ingalls Wilder's *On the Banks of Plum Creek* considered three books on the subjects of spelling, reading, and arithmetic among her "best things" and gave them solemnly to the girls with the advice that they care for them and study faithfully.

A number of early textbooks and other stories have been reissued in their original form and can be shared with children. For example, children can read the rhyming alphabet; practice their letters; and learn to read words of one, two, three, four, and five syllables from *The New England Primer* (Ford, 1962).

Pioneer children also read and copied maxims to practice their handwriting or as punishment for bad behavior. Joan W. Blos's *A Gathering of Days: A New England Girl's Journal, 1830–32* tells of this experience in the 1830s and lists some maxims that were written, such as:

> Speak the truth and lie not.
> To thine own self be true.
> Give to them that want.

Additional methods of instruction are described in other stories. Carol Ryrie Brink's *Caddie Woodlawn* describes an 1860 method for memorizing the multiplication tables: The children sang them to the tune of "Yankee Doodle." Re-creating a typical school day during which children read from the primer, recite and copy parables, have a spelling bee, and sing their multiplication tables would help them visualize the pioneer child's life and develop an understanding that education was considered important in earlier times.

A Day in the General Store.   The country store was very different from the contemporary department store or large shopping mall. It fascinated children, however, just as malls create excitement in today's children. Laura Ingalls Wilder's first experience in a general store is described in *Little House in the Big Woods.* This store included bright materials, kegs of nails and shot, barrels of candy, cooking utensils, plowshares, knives, shoes, and dishes. In fact, it had just about everything.

A source of information about the kinds of materials that might be available to a pioneer family in the late 1800s is a reissue of an early Sears, Roebuck and Company catalogue (1997). Through these pages, children can acquire an understanding of the merchandise available and the fashions of the day. They can use the information found in such sources either to create a child-sized general store in one corner of the room or miniature stores in boxes.

Because pioneer families had no refrigerators or freezers, they had to find other ways to preserve their foods. If they lived in the North, they used nature's icebox in the winter. In Joan W. Blos's *A Gathering of Days: A New England Girl's Journal, 1830–32,* children read about chopping off a wedge of frozen soup and heating it in the kettle. Other stories describe the feeling of well-being when the pantry, shed, attic, and cellar were filled with food. In contrast, people experienced great concern when only seed corn remained between the family and starvation.

Children can learn about different ways that the pioneers preserved fruits and vegetables by reading Eliot Wigginton's *The Foxfire Book* (1972). Children enjoy drying their own apples and then having them for a special snack. Other books in this series provide details for many additional pioneer activities.

The people in pioneer fiction come alive for children who cannot actually live on a prairie homestead. Children can sing the same songs pioneer children sang, dance to the music of a pioneer fiddle, listen to the pioneer storyteller, imagine they attend a pioneer school, imagine they go to the general store, and do the chores of the homestead.

Trails in Westward Expansion

Deep ruts across a sea of prairie grass, markers along river crossings, and scars created by oxen hooves sliding down the rock sides of canyons were the pioneer equivalent of modern interstate highways. Like highways, these trails were important for moving people and commerce across the country; without them, the West could not have been opened for expansion. It is hard to imagine 1,000 men, women, and children with 200 covered wagons following such rough trails across prairies, deserts, and mountains to reach California or Oregon.

Have children discuss the purpose for the trails (such as cattle drives, wagon trails, fast movement of mail), their locations, the physical hardships found along the trails, forts built along them, and distances they covered. Have them draw a large map of the United States, place on it the major westward trails, and then trace, using different colored pencils, the routes taken by pioneers in various books of historical fiction. The following books provide enough descriptions of locations to be of value in this activity:

1. Alice Dalgliesh, *The Courage of Sarah Noble.* Westfield, Massachusetts, to New Milford, Connecticut, by foot and horse backpack, 1707.
2. Brett Harvey, *Cassie's Journey: Going West in the 1860s.* Map shows the trail from Independence, Missouri, to Sacramento, California.
3. Honoré Morrow, *On to Oregon!* Missouri to Oregon by covered wagon, horse, and foot, 1844.
4. Laura Ingalls Wilder, "Little House" books. Pepin, Wisconsin, to Kansas, to Minnesota, and to Dakota Territory near De Smet by covered wagon, 1870s.
5. Deborah Hopkinson, *Apples to Oregon.* Salem, Iowa, to Milwaukie, Oregon.

Research Skills

Many historical fiction books describe the sources the authors used to develop the settings and authenticity of periods. Encouraging children to choose a specific time period and location and then to discover as much as possible about the people and their times will help them develop respect for research skills and gain new insights.

In one class, children researched their own small city during the late 1800s. The group investigated documents at the historical society; searched old newspapers; found old family albums, journals, and letters; searched documents at the courthouse; interviewed people whose relatives had lived in the town during that time; read references to discover information about fashions, transportation, and food; and located buildings that would have existed during that time. After they had gathered this information, they pretended that they were living 100 years earlier and wrote stories about themselves. The stories contained only authentic background information.

Additional Activities

Have children pretend that they are newspaper reporters sent from an eastern paper to discover what living on the frontier is really like. Encourage them to write news stories to send back to the newspaper. In addition, have them pretend that they can take tintype pictures to accompany their stories; have them draw pictures of the scenes that they would like to photograph.

Many pioneers moved to the West because they received encouraging letters from friends and relatives. Have children write letters to friends or relatives telling the Easterners why they should or should not sell all their property and move to _____.

A number of books of historical fiction, such as Joan W. Blos's *A Gathering of Days: A New England Girl's Journal, 1830–32,* are written in journal format. Have children select a character from a historical fiction story and write several journal entries for a specific period in the story.

Many scenes from historical fiction about the pioneer period can be dramatized. For example, the experiences of Alice Dalgliesh's Sarah Noble in playing and living with the Indian family when her father leaves her to return for his wife are interesting to dramatize.

You might try activities recommended by Frances F. Jacobson (2000) to bring a pioneer project into the 21st century. Jacobson describes how a group of elementary children combined an oral history project and research using primary sources to make history come alive. The teacher and the librarian first provided background on family farming through class lectures and assigned reading. The students took a tour of the Farm Security Administration/Office of War Information collection of the Library of Congress American Memory website (*http:// lcweb2.loc.gov/ammem/fsahtml*). They searched the collection, chose a photograph, answered questions about it, and interpreted what they saw. Next, they wrote stories about the people in the photographs and projected their stories into two succeeding imaginary generations. The students speculated about how the characters might have survived the Depression and about the role of farming in the lives of their descendants. Finally, they conducted oral history interviews with people involved with farming. Jacobson stated, "The project succeeded on a number of levels. First, the students had fun. They enjoyed searching the collection and debating the fate of their characters. Second, the fiction format was liberating, giving students a chance to use different literary techniques. . . . Finally, and the most important, the students got the point of the research. Even if their stories weren't always historically detailed and precise, they developed an understanding of the family farming tradition in this country, of its vibrant legacy and cyclical nature" (p. 35).

A Culminating Activity

Children enjoy sharing their knowledge about pioneer days with their parents or other children. Have a class plan a pioneer day in which the children display pioneer objects, food, arts, and crafts; demonstrate songs or dances learned; and share information gained, creative writing completed, and art projects made during their study of pioneer life and historical fiction.

Creating a Historical Fiction "Books on the Move" Source

Students in one class used Susan M. Knorr and Margaret Knorr's *Books on the Move: A Read-About-It Go-There Guide to America's Best Family Destinations* (1993) to create their own "Books on the Move" source. First, they looked at and discussed the authors' Chapter 8, "Stepping Into the Past." In this chapter, the authors include children's books on such topics as history museums, dolls and toys, teddy bears, mummies, early American settlements, 19th-century New England, frontier living, the journey of Lewis and Clark, settling the West, gold rush days, cowhands and mountaineers, Native Americans, pueblo and cliff dwellers, striving for freedom, historical homes and sites, and various battles. In addition, the book includes destinations where people can see and discover more information about these time periods in history.

Next, the students conducted research on their own city and state. What historical sources did they have? What museums or other sites were found in their state? After selecting several of these sites, the students identified books they could use to make connections with those sites and to learn more about the historical time period. They wrote to or visited various sites and wrote descriptions of the destinations that were similar to those developed by Knorr and Knorr. As a class, they read all of the material they could find associated with a site near their school and then visited the site and wrote their impressions of the visit.

Finally, they published their own state source for historical sites and placed it in the school library. The activity and the book also provided motivation for family and group excursions.

Recognizing Similarities

One value of sharing the multicultural literature discussed in this historical fiction chapter is increasing children's understanding that those who belong to different groups have feelings, emotions, and needs similar to their own. Many multicultural books, especially those written for young children, have themes suggesting that children everywhere have more similarities than differences. These books can stimulate discussions in which children relate similar experiences they have had, tell how they handled similar problems, suggest how they would feel if they had a similar experience, or relate ways they might respond to similar circumstances. For example, the following books suggest experiences that could be universal.

Book	Experience
Janice Harrington's *Going North* (African American)	Making adjustments when moving to a new location
Jan Hudson's *Sweetgrass* (Native American)	Meeting obligartions toward family members
Jean Merrill's *The Girl Who Loved Caterpillars* (Japanese)	Resisting societal pressures in order to develop one's own interests
Scott O'Dell's *Carlota* (Latino)	Being independent people with strong beliefs
Sylvie Wells's *My Guardian Angel* (Jewish)	Helping others often results in gratitude and protection

Suggested Activities

For more suggested activities for understanding historical fiction, visit the Companion Website at **CW** www.prenhall.com/norton.

- Locate a story in which the setting takes on the role of antagonist (for example, Honoré Morrow's *On to Oregon!*). How has the author developed the setting as the antagonist? How do the characters overcome the obstacles of nature? What happens to the characters as they face and overcome the antagonist?

- Writers of historical fiction often place famous people in the backgrounds of their stories but make the pivotal character fictional. Read a story such as Erik Christian Haugaard's *Cromwell's Boy* and compare the roles of the little-known 11-year-old Oliver Cutter with the well-known Oliver Cromwell. Why did the author choose a little-known person as the main character?

- Read the acceptance speech of an award-winning author of historical fiction, for example, Joan Blos (1980), winner of the Newbery Medal, and David Almond (2005), winner of the Boston Globe–Horn Book Award. What were the author's reasons for choosing to write about that period in history? Does the author discuss the sources used?

- Using Chart 10.1, "Eras and Themes in Historical Fiction," make a list of historical literature that develops each theme during a selected time period.

Children's Literature

For full descriptions, including plot summaries and award winner notations, of these and other titles for teaching children with historical fiction, visit the CD-ROM that accompanies this book.

Adler, David A. *The Babe & I.* Illustrated by Terry Widener. Harcourt Brace, 1999 (I:7+ R:4).

Alder, Elizabeth. *The King's Shadow.* Farrar, Straus & Giroux, 1995 (I:11+ R:7).

Almond, David. *The Fire-Eaters.* Delacorte, 2003 (I:12+–YA R:7).

Ames, Mildred. *Grandpa Jake and the Grand Christmas.* Scribner, 1990 (I:8+ R:5).

Armstrong, William H. *Sounder.* Illustrated by James Barkley. Harper & Row, 1969 (I:10+ R:6).

Auch, Mary Jane. *Frozen Summer.* Holt, 1998 (I:10+ R:5).

Avi. *The Fighting Ground.* Lippincott, 1984 (I:10+ R:6).

_____. *The True Confessions of Charlotte Doyle.* Orchard, 1990 (I:10+ R:6).

Barrett, Tracy. *Anna of Byzantium.* Delacorte, 1999 (I:10+ R:5).

Bartoletti, Susan Campbell. *No Man's Land: A Young Soldier's Story.* Blue Sky, 1999 (I:10+ R:5).

Bat-Ami, Miriam. *Two Suns in the Sky.* Front Street, 1999 (I:12+ R:6).

I = Interest by age range.
R = Readability by grade level.

Beatty, Patricia. *Sarah and Me and the Lady From the Sea.* Morrow, 1989 (I:10+ R:6).

_____. *Wait for Me, Watch for Me, Eula Bee.* Morrow, 1978 (I:12+ R:7).

Blackwood, Gary. *Shakespeare's Scribe.* Dutton, 2000 (I:10+ R:5).

Blos, Joan W. *A Gathering of Days: A New England Girl's Journal, 1830–32.* Scribner, 1979 (I:8–14 R:6).

Borden, Louise. *The Greatest Skating Race: A World War II Story From the Netherlands.* Illustrated by Niki Daly. Simon & Schuster, 2004 (I:7–10 R:5).

_____. *The Little Ships: The Heroic Rescue at Dunkirk in World War II.* Illustrated by Michael Foreman. Simon & Schuster, 1997 (I:8+ R:4).

Bradley, Kimberly Brubaker. *Ruthie's Gift.* Delacorte, 1998 (I:7–12 R:5).

Branford, Henrietta. *Fire, Bed, and Bone.* Candlewick, 1998 (I:10+ R:5).

Brenner, Barbara. *Wagon Wheels.* Illustrated by Don Bolognese. Harper & Row, 1978 (I:6–9 R:I).

Brink, Carol Ryrie. *Caddie Woodlawn.* Illustrated by Trina Schart Hyman. Macmillan, 1935, 1963, 1973 (I:8–12 R:6).

Bruchac, Joseph. *Code Talker.* Dial, 2005 (I:12–YA R:7).

Bunting, Eve. *So Far From the Sea.* Clarion, 1998 (I:5–8).

Cadnum, Michael. *Blood Gold.* Dial, 2004 (I:10+ R:6).

Calvert, Patricia. *Bigger.* Scribner, 1994 (I:8+ R:5).

Carrick, Carol. *Stay Away From Simon!* Illustrated by Donald Carrick. Clarion, 1985 (I:7–10 R:3).

Chotjewitz, David. *Daniel Half Human and the Good Nazi.* Translated by Doris Orgel. Atheneum, 2004 (I:14–YA R:7).

Clapp, Patricia. *Constance: A Story of Early Plymouth.* Lothrop, Lee & Shepard, 1968 (I:12+ R:7).

Conrad, Pam. *My Daniel.* Harper & Row, 1989 (I:10+ R:5).

Cooper, Michael. *Dust to Eat: Drought and Depression in the 1930s.* Clarion, 2004 (I:9+ R:6).

Cormier, Robert. *Other Bells for Us to Ring.* Illustrated by Deborah Kogan Ray. Delacorte, 1990 (I:8+ R:5).

Curtis, Christopher Paul. *Bud, Not Buddy.* Delacorte, 1999 (I:10+ R:5).

Cushman, Karen. *The Ballad of Lucy Whipple.* Clarion, 1996 (I:10+ R:8).

_____. *Catherine, Called Birdy.* Clarion, 1994 (I:12+ R:9).

_____. *Matilda Bone.* Clarion, 2000 (I:9+ R:8).

_____. *The Midwife's Apprentice.* Clarion, 1995 (I:12+ R:8).

_____. *Rodzina.* Clarion, 2003 (I:10+ R:5).

Dalgliesh, Alice. *The Courage of Sarah Noble.* Illustrated by Leonard Weisgard. Scribner, 1954 (I:6–9 R:3).

DeAngeli, Marguerite. *The Door in the Wall.* Doubleday, 1949 (I:8–12 R:6).

Disher, Garry. *The Bamboo Flute.* Ticknor & Fields, 1993 (I:10+ R:5).

Donnelly, Jennifer. *A Northern Light.* Harcourt, 2003 (I:12+–YA R:7).

Dorris, Michael. *Morning Girl.* Hyperion, 1992 (I:8+ R:4).

_____. *Sees Behind Trees.* Hyperion, 1966 (I:9+ R:5).

Erdrich, Louise. *The Birchbark House.* Hyperion, 1999 (I:8+ R:6).

_____. *The Game of Silence.* HarperCollins, 2005 (I:8+ R:6).

Feelings, Tom. *The Middle Passage: White Ships/Black Cargo.* Dial, 1995 (I:12–YA).

Fleischman, Paul. *The Borning Room.* HarperCollins, 1991 (I:10+ R:5).

_____. *Bull Run.* HarperCollins, 1993 (I:10+ R:5).

_____. *Path of the Pale Horse.* Harper & Row, 1983 (I:10+ R:6).

_____. *Saturnalia.* HarperCollins, 1990 (I:12+ R:6).

Fleischman, Sid. *Bandit's Moon.* Illustrated by Jos. A. Smith. Greenwillow, 1998 (I:8+ R:5).

Fletcher, Susan. *Shadow Spinner.* Atheneum, 1998 (I:10+ R:6).

Forbes, Esther. *Johnny Tremain.* Illustrated by Lynd Ward. Houghton Mifflin, 1943 (I:10–14 R:6).

Foreman, Michael. *War Boy: A Country Childhood.* Arcade, 1990 (I:all).

Fox, Paula. *The Slave Dancer.* Illustrated by Eros Keith. Bradbury, 1973 (I:12+ R:7).

Frank, Rudolf. *No Hero for the Kaiser.* Translated by Patricia Crampton. Illustrated by Klaus Steffens. Lothrop, Lee & Shepard, 1986 (I:10+ R:7).

Giff, Patricia Reilly. *Lily's Crossing.* Delacorte, 1997 (I:10+ R:6).

_____. *Nory Ryan's Song.* Delacorte, 2000 (I:10+ R:5).

Graham, Harriet. *A Boy and His Bear.* Simon & Schuster, 1996 (I:9+ R:6).

Gray, Elizabeth Janet. *Adam of the Road.* Illustrated by Robert Lawson. Viking, 1942, 1970 (I:8–12 R:6).

Guarnieri, Paolo. *A Boy Named Giotto.* Translated by Jonathan Galassi. Illustrated by Bimba Landman. Farrar, Straus & Giroux, 1999 (I:5–8 R:4).

Haas, Jessie. *Westminster West.* Greenwillow, 1997 (I:11+ R:6).

Hahn, Mary Downing. *Following My Own Footsteps.* Clarion, 1996 (I:10+ R:6).

_____. *Stepping on the Cracks.* Clarion, 1991 (I:10+ R:6).

Hamilton, Virginia. *The Bells of Christmas.* Illustrated by Lambert Davis. Harcourt Brace, 1989 (I:8+ R:5).

Harrington, Janice N. *Going North.* Illustrated by Jerome Lagarrigue. Farrar, Straus & Giroux, 2004 (I:6–9).

Hartling, Peter. *Crutches.* Translated by Elizabeth D. Crawford. Lothrop, Lee & Shepard, 1988 (I:10+ R:6).

Harvey, Brett. *Cassie's Journey: Going West in the 1860s.* Illustrated by Deborah Kogan Ray. Holiday House, 1988 (I:7–9 R:3).

_____. *My Prairie Year: Based on the Diary of Elenore Plaisted.* Illustrated by Deborah Kogan Ray. Holiday House, 1986 (I:6–8 R:4).

Haugaard, Erik Christian. *The Boy and the Samurai.* Houghton Mifflin, 1991 (I:11+ R:6).

_____. *Cromwell's Boy.* Houghton Mifflin, 1978 (I:11+ R:5).

Hautzig, Esther. *The Endless Steppe: A Girl in Exile.* Harper Junior Books, 1968 (I:12+ R:7).

Heneghan, James. *Wish Me Luck.* Farrar, Straus & Giroux, 1997 (I:12+ R:7).

Hesse, Karen. *The Cats in Krasinski Square.* Illustrated by Wendy Watson. Scholastic, 2004 (I:all).

_____. *Letters From Rifka.* Holt, 1992 (I:10+ R:6).

_____. *Out of the Dust.* Scholastic, 1997 (I:10+ R:6).

_____. *Stowaway.* Simon & Schuster, 2000 (I:10+ R:6).

Hoestlandt, Jo. *Star of Fear, Star of Hope.* Translated by Mark Polizzotti. Illustrated by Johanna Kang. Walker, 1995 (I:7–10 R:3).

Holm, Jennifer L. *Our Only May Amelia.* HarperCollins, 1999 (I:10+ R:5)

Holub, Josef. *An Innocent Soldier.* Translated by Michael Hofman. Scholastic, 2005 (I:II+ R:5)

Hooks, William H. *Circle of Fire.* Atheneum, 1983 (I:10+ R:6).

Hopkinson, Deborah. *Apples to Oregon: Being the (Slightly) True Narrative of How a Brave Pioneer Father Brought Apples, Peaches, Plums, Grapes, and Cherries (and Children) Across the Plains.* Illustrated by Nancy Carpenter. Atheneum, 2004 (I:5–9 R:5).

_____. *A Packet of Seeds.* Illustrated by Bethanne Andersen. Greenwillow, 2004 (I:5–9 R:5).

Hudson, Jan. *Sweetgrass.* Tree Frog, 1984, Philomel, 1989 (I:10+ R:4).

Hunt, Irene. *Across Five Aprils.* Follett, 1964 (I:10+ R:7).

Ibbotson, Eva. *Journey to the River Sea.* Illustrated by Kevin Hawkes. Dutton, 2002 (I:9+ R:5).

_____. *The Star of Kazan.* Illustrated by Kevin Hawkes. Dutton, 2004 (I:10+ R:6).

Johnston, Julie. *Hero of Lesser Causes.* Little, Brown, 1993 (I:10+ R:5).

Karr, Kathleen. *The Great Turkey Walk.* Farrar, Straus & Giroux, 1998 (I:7+ R:5).

Keith, Harold. *The Obstinate Land.* Crowell, 1977 (I:12–YA R:7).

_____. *Rifles for Watie.* Crowell, 1957 (I:12+ R:7).

Kinsey-Warnock, Natalie. *The Canada Geese Quilt.* Illustrated by Leslie W. Bowman. Dutton, 1989 (I:8+ R:5).

Kirkpatrick, Katherine. *Keeping the Good Light.* Delacorte, 1995 (I:12+ R:6).

Kodama, Tatsuharu. *Shin's Tricycle.* Illustrated by Noriyuki Ando. Walker, 1995 (I:all).

Kurelek, William. *A Prairie Boy's Summer.* Houghton Mifflin, 1970 (I:6–8 R:4).

Lasky, Kathryn. *Beyond the Divide.* Macmillan, 1983 (I:9+ R:6).

_____. *The Night Journey.* Illustrated by Trina Schart Hyman. Warne, 1981 (I:10+ R:6).

_____. *True North.* Scholastic, 1996 (I:12+ R:7).

Lenski, Lois. *Indian Captive: The Story of Mary Jemison.* Stokes, 1941 (I:10+ R:7).

Levitin, Sonia. *Annie's Promise.* Atheneum, 1993 (I:12+ R:6).

_____. *Journey to America.* Illustrated by Charles Robinson, Atheneum, 1970 (I:12+ R:6).

_____. *Silver Days.* Atheneum, 1989 (I:12+ R:6).

Lindbergh, Reeve. *Johnny Appleseed: A Poem.* Illustrated by Kathy Jakobsen. Joy Street, 1990 (I:all).

Lisle, Janet Taylor. *The Art of Keeping Cool.* Simon & Schuster, 2000 (I:9+ R:5).

Longfellow, Henry Wadsworth. *Paul Revere's Ride.* Illustrated by Adrian J. Iorio and Frederick J. Alford. Houghton Mifflin (I:8+).

Lowry, Lois. *Number the Stars.* Houghton Mifflin, 1989 (I:10+ R:6).

_____. *The Silent Boy.* Houghton Mifflin, 2003 (I:10+ R:5).

Lunn, Janet. *Shadow in Hawthorn Bay.* Scribner, 1986 (I:10+ R:5).

Lyon, George Ella. *Borrowed Children.* Watts, 1988 (I:10+ R:5).

Macaulay, David. *Castle.* Houghton Mifflin, 1977 (I: all).

MacLachlan, Patricia. *Sarah, Plain and Tall.* Harper & Row, 1985 (I:7–10 R:3).

_____. *Three Names*. Illustrated by Alexander Pertzoff. HarperCollins, 1991 (I:6–8 R:4).

Maguire, Gregory. *The Good Liar*. Clarion, 1999 (I:9+ R:5).

Mah, Adeline Yen. *Chinese Cinderella and the Secret Dragon Society*. HarperCollins, 2005 (I:10+ R:5).

Mazer, Norma Fox. *Good Night, Maman*. Harcourt Brace, 1999 (I:12+ R:6).

McCaughrean, Geraldine. *Stop the Train*. HarperCollins, 2003 (I:10+ R:6).

McDonald, Megan. *The Great Pumpkin Switch*. Illustrated by Ted Lewin. Orchard, 1992 (I:6–8 R:4).

McGuigan, Mary Ann. *Where You Belong*. Simon & Schuster, 1997 (I:10+ R:6).

Merrill, Jean, adapted by. *The Girl Who Loved Caterpillars*. Illustrated by Floyd Cooper. Putnam, 1992 (I:5–8 R:5).

Moeri, Louise. *Save Queen of Sheba*. Dutton, 1981 (I:10+ R:5).

Monjo, F. N. *The Drinking Gourd*. Illustrated by Fred Brenner. Harper & Row, 1970 (I:7–9 R:2).

Morpurgo, Michael. *Private Peaceful*. Scholastic, 2004 (I:12+–YA R:6).

Morrow, Honoré. *On to Oregon!* Illustrated by Edward Shenton, Morrow, 1926, 1948, 1954 (I:10+ R:6).

Mowat, Farley. *Lost in the Barrens*. Illustrated by Charles Geer. Little, Brown, 1956 (I:9+ R:6).

Myers, Anna. *Fire in the Hills*. Walker, 1996 (I:10+ R:8).

Namioka, Lensey. *The Coming of the Bear*. HarperCollins, 1992 (I:9+ R:6).

O'Dell, Scott. *The Amethyst Ring*. Houghton Mifflin, 1983 (I:10+ R:6).

_____. *The Captive*. Houghton Mifflin, 1979 (I:10+ R:6).

_____. *Carlota*. Houghton Mifflin, 1977 (I:9+ R:4).

_____. *The Feathered Serpent*. Houghton Mifflin, 1981 (I:10+ R:6).

_____. *The King's Fifth*. Illustrated by Samuel Bryant. Houghton Mifflin, 1966 (I:10+ R:6).

_____. *Sing Down the Moon*. Houghton Mifflin, 1970 (I:10+ R:6).

_____ & Elizabeth Hall. *Thunder Rolling in the Mountains*. Houghton Mifflin, 1992 (I:10+ R:6).

Orlev, Uri. *The Island on Bird Street*. Translated by Hillel Halkin. Houghton Mifflin, 1984 (I:10+ R:6).

_____. *The Lady With the Hat*. Houghton Mifflin, 1995 (I:12+ R:5).

_____. *The Man From the Other Side*. Houghton Mifflin, 1991 (I:10+ R:6).

_____. *Run, Boy, Run*. Translated by Hillel Halkin. Houghton Mifflin, 2003 (I:9–12 R:5).

Oughton, Jerrie. *The War in Georgia*. Houghton Mifflin, 1997 (I:12+ R:6).

Park, Linda Sue. *A Single Shard*. Clarion, 2001 (I:11+–YA R:6).

Paterson, John, & Katherine Paterson. *Blueberries for the Queen*. Illustrated by Susan Jeffers. HarperCollins, 2004 (I:6–9 R:5).

Paterson, Katherine. *Preacher's Boy*. Clarion, 1999 (I:10+ R:6).

Patneaude, David. *Thin Wood Walls*. Houghton Mifflin, 2004 (I:10+–YA R:6).

Paulsen, Gary. *The Winter Room*. Orchard, 1989 (I:8+ R:5).

Pearson, Kit. *The Sky Is Falling*. Viking, 1989 (I:10+ R:6).

Peck, Richard. *The River Between Us*. Dial, 2003 (I:12–YA R:6).

_____. *The Teacher's Funeral: A Comedy in Three Parts*. Dial, 2004 (I:10+ R:6).

Petry, Ann. *Tituba of Salem Village*. Crowell, 1964 (I:11+ R:6).

Platt, Richard. *Castle Diary: The Journal of Tobias Burgess, Page*. Illustrated by Chris Riddell. Candlewick, 1999 (I:all).

Polacco, Patricia. *The Butterfly*. Philomel, 2000 (I:6–9 R:5).

Pullman, Philip. *The Ruby in the Smoke*. Knopf, 1985 (I:10+ R:6).

Rappaport, Doreen. *The Secret Seder*. Illustrated by Emily Arnold McCully. Hyperion, 2005 (I:5–9 R:4).

Reeder, Carolyn. *Across the Lines*. Simon & Schuster, 1997 (I:9+ R:6).

_____. *Shades of Gray*. Macmillan. 1989 (I:10+ R:6).

Reiss, Johanna. *The Upstairs Room*. Crowell, 1972 (I:11+ R:4).

Rinaldi, Ann. *The Fifth of March: A Story of the Boston Massacre*. Harcourt Brace, 1993 (I:10+ R:6).

Rylant, Cynthia. *Appalachia: The Voices of Sleeping Birds*. Illustrated by Barry Moser. Harcourt Brace, 1991 (I:all).

_____. *When I Was Young in the Mountains*. Dutton, 1982 (I:4–9 R:3).

Salisbury, Graham. *Under the Blood Red Sun*. Delacorte, 1995 (I:8+ R:6).

Sandin, Joan. *The Long Way to a New Land*. Harper & Row, 1981 (I:7–9 R:3).

Schmidt, Gary D. *Lizzie Bright and the Buckminster Boy*. Clarion, 2004 (I:10+ R:6).

Shefelman, Janice. *A Peddler's Dream*. Illustrated by Tom Shefelman. Houghton Mifflin, 1992 (I:6–8 R:8).

Shulevitz, Uri. *The Travels of Benjamin of Tudela: Through Three Continents in the Twelfth Century*. Farrar, Straus & Giroux, 2005 (I:8+ R:5).

Siegal, Aranka. *Grace in the Wilderness: After the Liberation, 1945–1948*. Farrar, Straus & Giroux, 1985 (I:10+ R:7).

_____. *Upon the Head of the Goat: A Childhood in Hungary 1939–1944*. Farrar, Straus & Giroux, 1981 (I:10+ R:7).

Siegelson, Kim. *Trembling Earth*. Dial, 2004 (I:10+ R:5).

Skolsky, Mindy Warshaw. *Love From Your Friend, Hannah*. DK, 1998 (I:8+ R:5).

Snyder, Zilpha Keatley. *Gib Rides Home*. Delacorte, 1998 (I:9+ R:5).

Speare, Elizabeth George. *The Bronze Bow*. Houghton Mifflin, 1961 (I:10+ R:6).

_____. *Calico Captive*. Illustrated by W. T. Mars. Houghton Mifflin, 1957 (I:10+ R:6).

_____. *The Sign of the Beaver*. Houghton Mifflin, 1983 (I:8–12 R:5).

_____. *The Witch of Blackbird Pond*. Houghton Mifflin, 1958 (I:9–14 R:4).

Stevens, Carla. *Anna, Grandpa, and the Big Storm*. Illustrated by Margot Tomes. Houghton Mifflin, 1982 (I:6–9 R:3).

Stolz, Joëlle. *The Shadows of Ghadames*. Delacorte, 2004 (I:10+ R:6).

Stone, Jeff. *Tiger*. Random House, 2005 (I:10+ R:6).

Sutcliff, Rosemary. *The Eagle of the Ninth*. Illustrated by C. Walter Hodges. Walck, 1954 (I:11+ R:8).

_____. *The Lantern Bearers*. Illustrated by Charles Keeping. Walck, 1959 (I:11+ R:7).

_____. *The Shining Company*. Farrar, Straus & Giroux, 1990 (I:11+ R:8).

_____. *The Silver Branch*. Illustrated by Charles Keeping. Walck, 1958 (I:10+ R:8).

Taylor, Mildred D. *The Gold Cadillac*. Illustrated by Michael Hays. Dial, 1987 (I:8–10 R:3).

_____. *Let the Circle Be Unbroken*. Dial, 1981 (I:10 R:6).

_____. *Roll of Thunder, Hear My Cry*. Illustrated by Jerry Pinkney. Dial, 1976 (I:10+ R:6).

Trimble, Stephen. *The Village of Blue Stone*. Illustrated by Jennifer Owings Dewey & Deborah Reade. Macmillan, 1990 (I:6–9 R:4).

Uchida, Yoshiko. *Journey Home*. Illustrated by Charles Robinson. Atheneum, 1978 (I:10+ R:5).

_____. *Journey to Topaz*. Illustrated by Donald Carrick. Scribner, 1971 (I:10+ R:5).

Van Leeuwen, Jean. *Cabin on Trouble Creek*. Dial, 2004 (I:10+ R:6).

Vos, Ida. *Hide and Seek*. Translated by Terese Edelstein & Inez Smidt. Houghton Mifflin, 1991 (I:8+ R:5).

Weil, Sylvie. *My Guardian Angel*. Translated by Gillian Rosner. Scholastic, 2004 (I:9–12 R:5).

Westall, Robert. *Time of Fire*. Scholastic, 1997 (I:10+ R:5).

Wigginton, Eliot. *The Foxfire Book*. Doubleday, 1972 (I:12–YA R:6).

Wilder, Laura Ingalls. *By the Shores of Silver Lake*. Illustrated by Garth Williams. Harper & Row, 1939, 1953 (I:8–12 R:6).

_____. *The First Four Years*. Illustrated by Garth Williams. Harper & Row, 1971 (I:8–12 R:6).

_____. *Little House in the Big Woods*. Illustrated by Garth Williams. Harper & Row, 1932, 1953 (I:8–12 R:6).

_____. *Little House on the Prairie*. Illustrated by Garth Williams. Harper & Row, 1935, 1953 (I:8–12 R:8).

_____. *Little Town on the Prairie*. Illustrated by Garth Williams. Harper & Row, 1941, 1953 (I:8–12 R:8).

_____. *The Long Winter*. Illustrated by Garth Williams. Harper & Row, 1940, 1953 (I:8–12 R:6).

_____. *On the Banks of Plum Creek*. Illustrated by Garth Williams. Harper & Row, 1937, 1953 (I:8–12 R:6).

_____. *These Happy Golden Years*. Illustrated by Garth Williams. Harper & Row, 1943, 1953 (I:8–12 R:6).

Williams, Laura. *Behind the Bedroom Wall*. Milkweed, 1996 (I:9+ R:5).

Woodruff, Elvira. *The Ravenmaster's Secret*. Scholastic, 2003 (I:9–12 R:5).

Yates, Elizabeth. *Amos Fortune, Free Man*. Illustrated by Nora S. Unwin. Dutton, 1950 (I:10+ R:6).

Yep, Laurence. *Dragon's Gate*. HarperCollins, 1993 (I:10+ R:6).

_____. *Dragonwings*. Harper & Row, 1975 (I:10+ R:6).

_____. *Hiroshima*. Scholastic, 1995 (I:9+ R:4).

Yolen, Jane. *The Devil's Arithmetic*. Viking/Kestrel, 1988 (I:8+ R:5).

_____. *Encounter*. Illustrated by David Shannon. Harcourt Brace, 1992 (I:6–10 R:5).

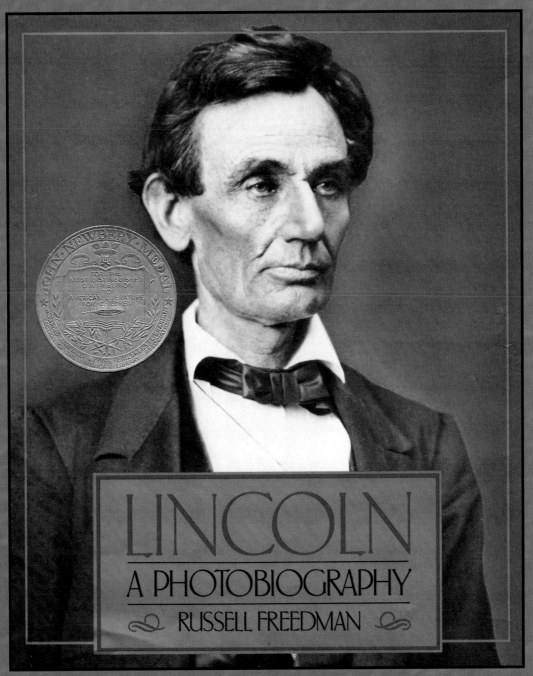

Russell Freedman develops a carefully documented biography in his book. (From Lincoln: A Photobiography, by Russell Freedman, copyright © 1987. Reprinted by permission of Clarion Books, a Houghton Mifflin Company.)

CHAPTER OUTLINE

People Who Change Lives

- **Changing Ideas About Biographies for Children**

- **Literary Criticism: Evaluating Biographies**

- **Biographical Subjects**

Teaching With Biographies

- **Unit Plan: Using Biographies in Creative Dramatizations**

- **Reader Response: Developing Hypothetical Interviews With Authors**

- **Common Themes in Lives of Scientists and Inventors**

- **Developing Comprehension Through Time Lines of Biographical Characters**

- **Analyzing Values and Beliefs**

- **Motivating Additional Reading and Discussion**

- **Developing Appreciation for the Lives and the Music of Biographical Characters**

People Who Change Lives

Many children who read well-written biographies feel as if the biographical subjects become personal friends. Often, these children carry with them into adulthood a love of nonfiction that portrays the lives of interesting people with whom they can identify and from whom they can learn. Biography offers children the high adventure and engrossing drama that fiction also supplies, but it also offers the special satisfaction of knowing that the people and events described are "really real."

Writers of biographies have a vast pool of real people from which to choose. There are brave men and women who conquer seas, encounter new continents, and explore space. There are equally brave and intelligent women and men who fight discrimination, change lives through their ministering or inventions, and overcome disabilities in their efforts to achieve. The ways in which writers of children's literature choose to portray these figures, however, change with historical time periods.

Changing Ideas About Biographies for Children

A brief review of biographies for children shows that the authors have been influenced by social attitudes toward children and attitudes about appropriate content. Children's biographies written in the 17th through the 19th centuries in Europe and North America were affected by the didactic themes of the Puritan era, the Victorian emphasis on duty to God and parents, the values associated with the American frontier, and the belief that children should be educated in a highly structured environment. In addition, early biographers believed that children's biographies should be tools for religious, political, or social education. Emulation of biographical heroes was considered desirable (Norton, 1984). Consequently, many pre-20th-century biographies reflected the belief that literature should save children's souls. Jon Stott (1979) concludes that this time produced numerous "biographies of good little children who died early and went to Heaven and of bad little children who died early and went to Hell" (p. 177). For example, in 1671, leading Puritan writer James Janeway published a series of stories about children who died at an early age after leading saintly lives.

In the mid-1800s, the religious zeal of many early Americans was replaced by concern for the nation and the acquisition of the "American dream." Salvation was no longer the primary goal. The supreme achievements were acquisition of power, fame, and wealth. Consequently, biography changed from a religious tool to a political tool.

Alan Wolfe (2001) describes changes between the 19th and 20th centuries when he states:

> In the 19th century, principles of economic liberty were instrumental in creating a society in which the right to own property, to hire workers, and to manufacture and dispose of goods was accepted as the most productive way for a society to create and distribute its wealth. This was followed, in the 20th century, by the spread of political freedom. By the century's end, the idea that people had a right to vote and to run for office—and that such a right could not be denied them on the basis of ownership of property, race or gender—had become so widely accepted that no society could be considered good unless its political system was organized along democratic lines. (p. 48)

These changing attitudes are also apparent in biographies written during different time periods.

The early 20th century also brought new insights into child development. The growing science of psychology emphasized the vulnerability of youth and a need for protective legislation. Religious training placed less emphasis on sinfulness and more emphasis on moral development and responsibility toward others. In keeping with these ideas, biographers also protected children from the indiscretions of biographical subjects. Because idealized heroes were still believed to be desirable and necessary, biographers avoided areas concerning sensitive political beliefs and private lives. Taboos imposed by society included writing about infamous people, unsavory or undistinguishing actions, and controversial subjects.

Furthermore, in the early 1900s, as in earlier periods of American history, the contributions of female and nonwhite Americans were either not highly regarded or considered too controversial. Traditional social patterns kept most women and members of minority groups out of the positions of power and the fame that produced what American society considered the most appropriate subjects of biography. Consequently, few biographies dealt with women, African Americans, Native Americans, and members of other ethnic and racial minorities.

Biographies of most political leaders published through the 1960s continued to present role models for political and social instruction. Omissions and distortions allowed biographers to stress important contributions and to highlight dates of accomplishment. Biographers still did not explore motives. Literary critic Margery Fisher (1976) maintains that biographies for children were controlled by an establishment that exercised a powerful invisible influence. William Epstein (1987) argues, "State-supported American education is more or less a product of middle-class values and aspirations, and biography has almost always been an ally of the dominant structures of authority" (p. 179).

In an effort to increase the ability of children to empathize with political heroes, biographers writing for young readers often focused on the boyhood years of their characters. Still, these biographers tended to glorify the individuals. For example, the titles of several biographies published by Bobbs-Merrill before 1980 indicated the accomplishments that the subjects would achieve: *Thomas Paine: Common Sense Boy* and *John D. Rockefeller: Boy Financier.*

During the late 1960s and the 1970s, traditional social, family, and personal values were changing, and the new openness was reflected in fiction for children. In addition, the previous instructional uses of, and role models in, children's biography were challenged. Some literary critics, educators, and authors of children's biographies maintained that idealizing subjects distorted not only history but also development. According to this argument, if prominent men and women were shown only in a favorable light, children would assume that because they themselves make errors, they could never be great. In an effort to overcome past shortcomings in biographies for children, Marilyn Jurich (1972) advocated a greater variety in the choice of subjects—including great people who were not famous, ordinary people, and antiheroes—as well as a fuller and more honest treatment of all subjects. Biographer Russell Freedman (1988) summarizes the changes when he concludes:

> The hero worship of the past has given way to a more realistic approach, which recognizes the warts and weaknesses that humanize the great. And fictionalization has become a naughty word. Many current biographies for children adhere as closely to documented evidence as any scholarly work. And the best of them manage to do so without becoming tedious or abstract or any less exciting than the most imaginative fictionalization. (p. 447)

As with realistic fiction, educators, authors, publishers, and parents today have different opinions about what the content of children's biographies should be. Jean Fritz (1976), a well-known author of historical biographies for young children, says:

> Biographies have for the most part lagged behind other types of children's literature, bogged down, for one thing, by didacticism. Famous men and women must be shown in their best colors so children can emulate them. The idea of emulation has been a powerful factor in determining the nature of biography for children: you see the word over and over again in textbooks and courses of study. And I think it has done great harm in distorting history and breeding cynicism; the great men are all gone, the implication is. Because history is old, educators are often guilty of simply repeating it instead of taking a fresh look at it. Because it is complicated, they tend to simplify by watering down material for children, whereas children need more meat rather than less, but selected for their own interests. This, of course, involves original research, a great deal of it, which twenty years ago, I think was rather rare in children's biographies. (p. 125)

This rarity in children's biographies and Jean Fritz's role in changing biographies were recognized by Breen, Fader, Odean, and Sutherland (2000) when they identified Fritz's *And Then What Happened, Paul Revere?* as one of the

"One Hundred Books That Shaped the Century." The authors of the article define Fritz's role when they conclude: "Starting with this book, Fritz enlivened the field of biography with short illustrated books that use well-chosen details and humor to attract young people to the genre" (p. 54).

Biographies now depict many sides of a person's character—as well as people who are female and nonwhite, like many young readers themselves. Readers may discover, through the work of such authors as Jean Fritz, that the heroes of biography were real people who, like other humans, often demonstrated negative qualities. In fact, a biographical subject who is a believable human being may be easier for children to emulate than one who is not.

The current increase in the number and quality of biographies is also highlighted by the editorial staff of the Cooperative Children's Book Center in their *CCBC Choices for 2004* and *CCBC Choices for 2005*. In their 2004 volume, they state: "In the past few years, we have been amazed by the number and variety of excellent biographies, autobiographies, and memoirs for children and teens" (2004, p. 13). In their 2005 volume, they note the works of biographies such as Russell Freedman's *The Voice That Challenged a Nation*, about Marian Anderson, and Albert Marrin's *Old Hickory*, about President Andrew Jackson. They conclude that such biographies "give children and teenagers opportunities to connect with the past in meaningful ways that will deepen their understanding of who we are as a nation today" (2005, p. 16).

Literary Criticism: Evaluating Biographies

Like other literature, biographies should be evaluated according to the criteria for good literature. They should carefully avoid negative stereotypes based on gender, race, ethnicity, and physical ability. With regard to literary elements, characterization is of primary concern, and authors of biography must place special emphasis on accuracy of detail and use sound research methods. (See the Evaluation Criteria box on this page.)

Like other authors, biographers have a responsibility to portray their subjects three-dimensionally. Unlike authors of fiction, however, biographers are restricted from inventing characters and indicating unsupported thoughts and actions.

It is interesting how Tonya Bolden addresses supported and unsupported actions in her biography *Maritcha: A Nineteenth-Century American Girl*. Bolden based her biography on Maritcha Rémond Lyons's unpublished memoir, *Memories of Yesterday: All of Which I Saw and Part of Which I Was*, dated 1928. This is a biography of a free African American girl whose family inspired her to succeed despite the difficult times. Bolden discusses how she used the memoir as her source, but that she needed to conduct extensive research to fill gaps caused by faint typescript and spotted pages. Notice in this description of

---

Evaluation Criteria

Literary Criticism: Biography

1. Does the biography meet the criteria for good literature?
2. Is the subject of the biography worth reading about?
3. Is the biography factually accurate in relation to characters, plots, and settings?
4. Does the biographer distinguish between fact and judgment and between fact and fiction?
5. Does the biographer use primary sources when conducting research for the text? Are these sources identified in the bibliographies or other notes to the readers?
6. Does the biographer include photographs and other documents that increase the credibility of the text?
7. If the biographer uses illustrations other than photographs, are the illustrations accurate according to the life and time of the person?
8. Does the writing style appeal to readers?

Maritcha's actions the terminology Bolden uses when she fills in the gaps: "One can only wonder about her day-to-day activities—and spats with sisters Therese and Pauline. There is no indication that the Lyons family had servants, so it is likely that Maritcha was helping with housekeeping by the time she was six or seven. Her chores may have included sweeping floors, featherdusting furniture, washing clothes on a washboard in a tin tub, and ironing with a five-pound or even heavier flatiron heated on a wood-or-coal-fueled cast-iron cookstove" (p. 7). In contrast, when Bolden describes supported actions of the character, she says Maritcha "recalled day trips across the Hudson," "Maritcha took pride in," "Maritcha treasured her grandmother's memory," and "Maritcha knew never to breathe a word about her parents' Underground Railroad work" (p. 23).

Characterization

Author Virginia Hamilton (1992) believes that characterization in biography must go beyond the known facts of a life. After the research,

> then one proceeds in the same way as with a question. How did this person really move in time and space? Who was he inside, where no one is the wiser about him but himself? Is there any light in there, any way to see? The researcher-novelist must find an opening within the real person of the biography so that the life is in the spotlight in full view, and exists again. (p. 678)

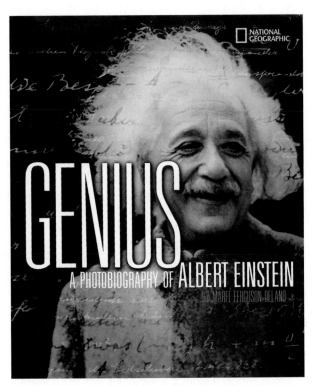

Cover of Genius: A Photobiography of Albert Einstein, *by Marfé Ferguson Delano. Copyright © 2005 Marfé Ferguson Delano. Jacket copyright © 2005 National Geographic Society. All rights reserved. Used by permission.*

Factual Accuracy

Comparisons between biographies for children and for adults and between biographies and reference books often reveal differences in facts. Ann W. Moore (1985) reports:

> Errors in contemporary children's biographies fall into one of the following three categories: (1) inaccuracies in numbers, dates, and names, items easily checked in reference books or authorized and/or reputable adult titles; (2) incomplete, unclear, or misleading statements caused by attempts at simplification; and (3) patently false, incorrect information. (p. 34)

Moore emphasizes the need for writers and publishers to improve the accuracy of biographies for children and for reviewers to check the facts against reputable sources. Biographies have a special responsibility to be accurate and authentic in characters and settings. Extensive research should use recent scholarly works and historical materials that indicate what the subjects and others of the time actually said and wrote.

Alessandra Stanley (2001) emphasizes changes in the perception of a historical character, arguing that as cultural mores change, so does the writing of biographies. Consequently, historical viewpoints can influence biographical writing.

In a critical review of two biographies written about Roald Dahl and Dr. Seuss, Mark I. West (1996) concludes that "most biographies do not simply record the events in the lives of their subjects; they also interpret these events" (p. 244). When selecting and evaluating biographies, this is a point to be considered: How accurate or biased is the interpretation of events in a person's life?

Any search for accuracy should include a wide range of sources. For example, Russell Freedman (1988), author of the 1988 Newbery Medal winner *Lincoln: A Photobiography,* stresses the importance of visiting original sites and studying original materials:

> There's something magic about being able to lay your eyes on the real thing—something you can't get from your reading alone. As I sat at my desk in New York City and described Lincoln's arrival in New Salem at the age of twenty-two, I could picture the scene in my mind's eye, because I had walked down those same dusty lanes, where cattle still graze behind split-rail fences and geese flap about underfoot. When I wrote about Lincoln's morning walk from his house to his law office in downtown Springfield, I knew the route because I had walked it myself. (p. 449)

Frank J. Dempsey (1988) verifies Freedman's research in Springfield, Illinois, when he describes Freedman's fervor for on-site research. Other authors often mention research in historical societies, newspaper records, diaries, and letters. Often, they visit actual locations. Even simple biographies for young children must be accurate in the illustrations, as well as in the text, because young children acquire much of their knowledge about a time or a setting from the illustrations rather than from detailed descriptions.

It is helpful if a biographer provides a bibliography. For example, Freedman includes "A Lincoln Sampler" (a listing of quotes from Lincoln's speeches), "In Lincoln's Footsteps" (a listing of historical sites), and "Books About Lincoln" (a listing of additional sources).

In his 2005 Newbery Honor book, *The Voice That Challenged a Nation: Marian Anderson and the Struggle for Equal Rights,* Freedman again stresses accuracy and the quality of his references. He says, "Allan Keiler's *Marian Anderson: A Singer's Journey* [New York: Scribner, 2000], the only definitive biography, is the first truly complete, accurate, and documented account. Written with the cooperation of Anderson's family and with full access to her private papers, Keiler's book proved indispensable to my own research" (p. 104).

Biographers must also distinguish fact from judgment. A good biographer is concerned with the effect a biographical subject has on other people or the environment, and with scientific knowledge. For example, in *Genius: A Photobiography of Albert Einstein,* Marfé Ferguson Delano presents first the judgments of Einstein's contemporaries and then the current scientific attitudes toward his work: "Einstein spent the last 30 years or so of his life in the unsuccessful pursuit of a unified field theory—one simple theory that could explain the laws of physics. Some of his contemporaries considered this work a waste of time. But now it seems that Einstein was actually a couple of generations ahead of his time. Today, one of the hottest topics in physics is the search for a 'theory of everything'" (p. 60).

In addition to separating fact and judgment, biographers must contend with separating fact and legend. In her biography, *Calamity Jane: Her Life and Her Legend*, Doris Faber introduces her character by asking "Who Was She?" Then she states:

> But was she a real person or just a made-up character in adventure stories? The answer to this question is a little complicated. Yes, there was a real woman nicknamed Calamity Jane, who loved to talk about having lived through many exciting adventures—but much of what she said could not really have happened the way she told it. There also was a writer who somehow got the idea of calling the imaginary heroine of some of his most popular tales Calamity Jane. Then, around a hundred years ago, the actual person and the fictional heroine began merging in the public mind, creating the same kind of legendary figure as Johnny Appleseed, for instance. (p. 1)

Throughout her biography, Faber separates fact from legend.

Worthiness of Subject

The subject of a biography should be worth reading about, just as she or he should be worthy of the meticulous research and time that the author spends in writing. Has the subject made a significant impact on the world—for good or for ill—that children should be aware of? Will children have a better understanding of the complexities of human nature after they have read the biography? Will they discover that history is made up of real people when they read the book? Will they appreciate the contributions of their ancestors or their heritage through the life of the person in the biography?

Tobie Brandriss (1999) stresses the importance of choosing biographies about scientists who could be models for students as they shape their own goals and values. In addition, Brandriss chooses biographies that help students "gaze into the lives of scientists whose discoveries we study" (p. 108). Biographies of scientists and inventors that focus on the lives that students study might include the following: Marfé Ferguson Delano's *Genius: A Photobiography of Albert Einstein* and Don Brown's *Odd Boy Out: Young Albert Einstein*; Peter Sís's *The Tree of Life: A Book Depicting the Life of Charles Darwin*; Amy Ehrlich's *Rachel: The Story of Rachel Carson*; Peter Busby's *First to Fly: How Wilbur & Orville Wright Invented the Airplane*, Richard Maurer's *The Wright Sister: Katharine Wright and Her Famous Brothers*, and Russell Freedman's *The Wright Brothers: How They Invented the Airplane*; and Peter Sís's *Starry Messenger: Galileo Galilei*.

The subjects of biography and autobiography need not be famous, infamous, or outstanding in a worldly sense for their lives to communicate important lessons about people and society. The subjects should be portrayed in believable ways, however. Whether a notable personage or an unsung hero of everyday life, the person upon whom a biographer focuses should have a many-faceted character, just like the people children know. Jean Fritz, for example, has written a series of historical biographies

suggesting that leaders of the American Revolution were very human. She portrays Patrick Henry as a practical joker who did not appreciate school in his youth, and Samuel Adams as a man who was not afraid to speak out against the British but who refused to ride a horse.

Balance Between Fact and Story Line

Writers of biographies for children must balance the requirement for accuracy with the requirement for a narrative that appeals to children. For example, authors may emphasize humorous facts as they develop plots and characters that present information in story formats. A poor balance between fact and story line may cause problems for young readers. Children have difficulty evaluating differences between fiction and nonfiction. Jean Fritz's (1982) foreword to her own fictionalized autobiography *Homesick: My Own Story*, clarifies differences between fiction and biography:

> Since my childhood feels like a story, I decided to tell it that way, letting the events fall as they would into the shape of a story, lacing them together with fictional bits, adding a piece here and there when memory didn't give me all I needed. I would use conversation freely, for I cannot think of my childhood without hearing voices. So although this book takes place within two years from October 1925 to September 1927, the events are drawn from the entire period of my childhood, but they are all, except in minor details, basically true. The people are real people; the places are dear to me. But most important, the form I have used has given me the freedom to recreate the emotions that I remember so vividly. Strictly speaking, I have to call this book fiction, but it does not feel like fiction to me. It is my story, told as truly as I can tell it. (foreword)

Writers of biographies for older children usually provide extensive factual detail. For example, in his biography *Einstein: Visionary Scientist*, John B. Severance presents the theory of relativity in a way that readers can understand. This is extremely important when writing scientific biographies.

Biographies in Picture-Book Format

There are numerous biographies written as picture books in which much of the information about the subject, the setting, and the times is reflected in the illustrations. The illustrations in many biographies written for younger children are especially important, according to Katheleen Odean (1996), because they supplement the spare texts by providing details about the historical era. John Malam's *Beatrix Potter*, for example, includes photographs of the author and her family, illustrations from her most famous work, *Peter Rabbit*, and paintings showing Hill Top Farm in the Lake District.

The dangers associated with being the country's first female steamboat captain are captured in Holly Meade's illustrations for Judith Heide Gilliland's *Steamboat! The Story of Captain Blanche Leathers*. By illustrating the often-hidden dangers of the river, the biography depicts the strong courage associated with Captain Leathers. Sheila Moxley's illustrations for Laurence Anholt's *Stone Girl,*

Bone Girl: The Story of Mary Anning show the Dorset Coast in England during the early 1800s. The illustrations reinforce the character of a young girl who is fascinated by the hunt for fossils and show her excitement when at the age of 12, she discovers the skeleton of an ichthyosaur and later expands her interest in paleontology.

When the illustrations provide this type of detail for a person's life, it is very important to evaluate them critically. Joanna Rudge Long (1997) provides several guidelines for evaluating illustrated biographies. For example, the style and visual references should be appropriate for the intended audience. The pictorial motifs should suit the text. The author and the illustrator should provide sources. The attitudes and points of view conveyed by the illustrations should be in harmony with the subject's true spirit. Long believes that illustrated biographies can enhance understandings of a person's life. She states, "An artist's eloquently expressed vision can transform a subject; at best, it can enhance understanding by heightening perceptions, or by presenting a familiar realm in an unexpected light" (p. 48). Long believes that Diane Stanley's *Leonardo da Vinci* and Peter Sís's *Starry Messenger* meet these guidelines for illustrated biographies.

Drawings, diagrams, and maps help readers follow and understand complex theories in Peter Sís's *The Tree of Life: A Book Depicting the Life of Charles Darwin: Naturalist, Geologist & Thinker.* The author/illustrator depicts Darwin's life, beginning in childhood; provides information about his private life; and presents his various hypotheses. Excerpts from his journals add to the information in the biography. Amy Ehrlich's *Rachel: The Story of Rachel Carson* is another biography of a scientist in picture-book format. The illustrations emphasize the importance of nature in Carson's life and the influence of a supporting parent who nurtured her interests. Thomas Locker's full-page paintings in Joseph Bruchac's *Rachel Carson: Preserving a Sense of Wonder* present the beauty of nature as envisioned by Carson.

Locker uses a similar approach to illustrate *John Muir: America's Naturalist.* Beautiful oil paintings of wilderness settings depict Muir quotes, such as "Go to Nature's School—the one true university" (p. 12), and "People are beginning to find out that

Illustration from Rachel Carson: Preserving A Sense of Wonder, *by Joseph Bruchac. Text and paintings copyright © 2004 Joseph Bruchac and Thomas Locker. Used by permission of Fulcrum Publishing.*

Illustration from John Muir: America's Naturalist, *by Thomas Locker. Text and paintings copyright © 2003 Thomas Locker. Used by permission of Fulcrum Publishing.*

going to the mountains is going home, that wilderness is a necessity" (p. 16).

Biographies of naturalists appear to be popular subjects for biographies in picture-book format. For example, *The Flower Hunter: William Bartram, America's First Naturalist*, by Deborah Kogan Ray, includes a map of the naturalist's travels between 1773 and 1776, and numerous drawings of labeled plants. In these biographies, the illustrations reinforce the naturalists' love for nature and the environment.

Don Brown's *Odd Boy Out: Young Albert Einstein* provides an introduction to the work and early life of the 20th-century physicist whose theory of relativity revolutionized scientific thinking. This heavily illustrated text shows a many-sided individual who was sometimes cruel to his sister, but who brought a single-minded focus to his work. The author shows how Einstein's parents encouraged his independence. The title of the text refers to his difficulties in school because he did not like sports and because his classmates insulted him because he was Jewish. He also liked math and playing Mozart on the violin, but he ignored topics that he disliked. The author expresses Einstein's philosophy through his words: "I believe that love [of a subject] is a better teacher than a sense of duty—at least for me" (unnumbered).

The Dinosaurs of Waterhouse Hawkins, by Barbara Kerley and illustrated by Brian Selznick, presents a look at the works of another creative person who, 150 years ago, designed models of dinosaurs. The book, which won a Caldecott Honor Award, shows Hawkins's process of creating his dinosaurs, starting with a drawing, developing a small model in clay and then a life-size model in clay, creating the mold, building the iron skeleton to support tons of dinosaur, and finally the finished dinosaur. Even though vandals destroyed his New York City models, his love for dinosaurs continued in his work for Princeton University and the Smithsonian Institute. The author shows the importance of living for a dream: "Just as he hoped, his models were the start of something wonderful: the world's first encounter with these ancient animals" (unnumbered). The illustrations on the final three pages go from the time of Victorian England with people looking at brown models, to the next page with dinosaurs in more lifelike color as viewed by a contemporary family, and finally to a setting in New York's Central Park that shows a boy drawing a bird while pieces of Waterhouse Hawkins's dinosaurs are buried below him in Central Park. An extensive author's note and illustrator's note add considerable information. The final illustration contrasts "Then," information about the structures of dinosaurs as what

was known or believed in the time of Waterhouse Hawkins, and "Now," what is currently known about dinosaurs.

The Man Who Walked Between the Towers, by Mordicai Gerstein, also won a Caldecott Medal. The author tells the story of the French aerialist who, in 1974, walked on a tightrope between the World Trade Center towers. Although the story and the illustrations center on Philippe Petit's preparations for and actual walk between the towers, the final illustration and text show what happens following the 9/11 attacks on the towers. The text states, "But in memory, as if imprinted on the sky, the towers are still there. And part of that memory is the joyful morning, August 7, 1974, when Philippe Petit walked between them in the air" (unnumbered). The illustrations show the towers with the tightroper in a soft silhouette behind the New York skyline.

In *Walt Whitman: Words for America*, author Barbara Kerley and illustrator Brian Selznick combine poetry, biographical information, and illustrations that depict the historical setting for one of America's greatest poets. For example, the text and the illustrations show how Whitman traveled from New York to New Orleans and filled his notebooks with reactions to people and issues, especially those connected with slavery. The author then reveals how Whitman spent the next 7 years writing poetry celebrating America. She includes text from "Leaves of Grass." Kerley addresses both praise and criticism for the poems when she states, "Walt's new style of poetry struck

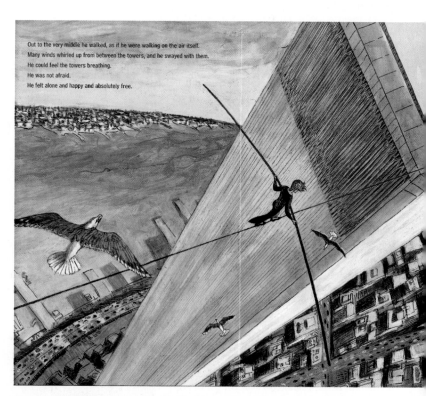

Illustration from The Man Who Walked Between the Towers *by Mordicai Gerstein. Copyright © 2003 by Mordicai Gerstein. Reprinted by permission of Roaring Brook Press.*

some readers with its freshness and vigor. Others, however, thought the poems clumsy and crude" (unnumbered). One of the most moving portions of the book is Whitman's reactions to the Civil War, especially to the death of soldiers and to the assassination of Abraham Lincoln. Now the biographer shows Whitman's grief by telling readers that he spent the next several months composing poems that illustrated this grief. To show the extent of this grief, the author includes a portion of "O Captain! My Captain!" The author's note and illustrator's note add useful information. A "Note on the Poems" contains longer excerpts from "Leaves of Grass" and sources.

Joseph Bruchac's *Jim Thorpe's Bright Path* is a picture-book biography of the Native American athlete. Bruchac's text and S. D. Nelson's illustrations focus on Thorpe's boyhood education, which prepared him for athletic achievement, international fame, and Olympic gold medals. The text includes "Important Dates in Jim Thorpe's Life and Legacy" from birth in 1887 to 1999, when he was recognized in Congress as America's Athlete of the Century. The author includes information that shows Thorpe's determination, such as that he ran almost 300 miles home when he heard that his father was injured.

The style and format in M. D. Usher's *Wise Guy: The Life and Philosophy of Socrates* provide an illustrated biography appropriate for both younger readers and young adults. Meghan Cox Gurdon (2006) evaluates the style in this way: "In a neat device, two typographically separate texts run through the book. These enable parents to read aloud a simple version to younger children (or let them read it themselves) while giving young-adult readers a more sophisticated explanation of the ideas and provocations that eventually put Socrates in jail and led him, at the age of 70, to down a cup of hemlock" (p. 8).

This two-tiered format places the simple text on the left side of each illustrated page and a more adult version of the same incidents and details of Socrates's life printed as long scrolls on the right side. Both sides of the biography, however, depict a personage who searches for the meaning of wisdom, courage, and justice by asking tough, probing questions. The author includes several additional resources that make the biography appropriate for older readers. Two pages of short biographical sketches identify various scholars who were influenced by Socrates, including Thomas Jefferson, Mahatma Gandhi, and Martin Luther King Jr. The author also includes a list of ancient sources used when writing the text and a list of current sources that are appropriate for further reading by young adult readers.

Biographical Subjects

The subjects of biographies and autobiographies for children range from early European explorers and rulers to American space travelers and ordinary people of today. Political leaders rise to eminence in times of need, and social activists speak out against oppression. Great achievers make contributions in science, art, literature, and sports. Common people display uncommon courage in their daily struggle for survival.

Explorers of Earth and Space

People who question existing boundaries and explore the unknown fascinate children and adults alike, and they are the subjects of numerous biographies. The consequences of the quest of Columbus are familiar to every schoolchild and are portrayed in many biographies. These biographies differ in literary style, focus, amount of detail, and development of character; consequently, they are good for evaluation and comparison.

One of the earliest biographical subjects for explorers of earth and space is found in Kathryn Lasky's *The Librarian Who Measured the Earth*. Lasky depicts the wonder associated with the Greek geographer Eratosthenes, who determined the circumference of the earth using techniques such as trying to calculate how long it took camels to get from one city to another, dropping plumb lines, and measuring the angles of shadows. Surprisingly, his measurements accomplished more than 2,000 years ago are within 200 miles of those measured with the latest technology. Kevin Hawkes's illustrations portray the ancient setting, the importance of the Alexandria Museum, and Eratosthenes's quest to answer questions about the earth.

Biographies of Christopher Columbus are found in both highly illustrated versions for young children and carefully documented texts for older readers. Ingri and Edgar Parin D'Aulaire's *Columbus*, written for slightly older children, includes details that describe a Columbus quite different from the one in many highly illustrated versions. Additional information enables children to visualize an explorer who did not recognize the magnitude of his discovery and who considered himself a failure because he had not reached the Far East. The D'Aulaires say: "Old and tired, Columbus returned to Spain from his fourth and last voyage. While he was searching in vain, the Portuguese had found the seaway to the East by sailing south around Africa. Now Columbus stood in the shadow" (p. 54).

Jean Fritz's *Where Do You Think You're Going, Christopher Columbus?* is written in a light style that appeals to many children. Through detailed background information, Fritz creates a lively history inhabited by realistic people. For example, Columbus's sponsor, Queen Isabella of Spain, "was so religious that if she even found Christians who were not sincere Christians, she had them burned at the stake. (Choir boys sang during the burning so Isabella wouldn't have to hear the screams.)" (p. 17). Fritz ends her book with additional historical notes and an index of people and locations discussed in the book.

In the 15th and 16th centuries, astronomers such as Nicolaus Copernicus and Galileo Galilei shared and proved the belief of Christopher Columbus that the world is round. Through their explorations of the stars—by means of mathematical equations, naked-eye observations, and the earliest telescopes—such early explorers of space further shook the foundations of European worldviews. The astronomers discovered that the earth is not only round but also one of numerous planets rotating around the sun and that the sun itself is only one of many astral bodies moving through the universe. In a time when the church insisted that the earth was the stationary center of the one solar system created by God, these discoveries were radical.

In *Starry Messenger: Galileo Galilei,* Peter Sís presents a highly illustrated version of the scientist's life. Students who read this biography discover Galileo's search for truth in a world in which the church considered his findings to be dangerous. Sís adds authenticity to the biography by including Galileo's own writings in the text. The highly detailed illustrations provide the major strength of the biography. As you read the text and view the illustrations, search for the techniques that Sís uses to depict the time period and to add important information about Galileo and the time.

Two biographies about Albert Einstein demonstrate to readers the importance of the scientist who gave the world $E = mc^2$ and the theory of relativity; the two biographies also illustrate differences between biographies written for younger readers and for older readers. Don Brown's *Odd Boy Out: Young Albert Einstein,* written for readers in the lower-elementary grades, focuses on Einstein as a young boy who is curious about subjects such as the secrets of geometry and is great at problem solving. The author also depicts Einstein as an angry boy with few friends and a capacity to irritate his teachers: consequently, the title of the book. In a book for older readers, Marfé Ferguson Delano's *Genius: A Photobiography of Albert Einstein,* the author spends more time explaining Einstein's theories. The photographs follow Einstein from early childhood to old age. The longer format of Delano's text allows space for Einstein's thoughts and feelings, such as his thoughts about his work: "I occupy myself exclusively with the problem of gravitation. . . . Compared with this problem, the original theory of relativity is child's play" (p. 36). Quotes such as the following reflect Einstein's feelings: "In the past it never occurred to me that every casual remark of mine would be snatched up and recorded. Otherwise I would have crept further into my shell" (p. 45). After reading these biographies, readers may understand Richard Panek's (2005) comment that Einstein's "dizzying discoveries in 1905 would forever change our understanding of the universe" (p. 109).

The inventions of the Wright Brothers encouraged explorers to open the next great frontier. In *The Wright Brothers: How They Invented the Airplane,* Russell Freedman places readers into the historical context of the time, provides information about the history of flight, places the inventions of the Wright Brothers into the context of this historical development, supports his text with numerous photographs, and documents his sources.

An interesting accompanying text to Freedman's biography is Richard Maurer's *The Wright Sister: Katharine Wright and Her Famous Brothers.* The biographer's sources include letters in which the sister of the Wright Brothers describes her brothers' work as they develop their invention of the airplane. The biography provides an interesting perspective on the social constraints placed on women during this time. Black-and-white photographs illustrate the biography. In *First to Fly: How Wilbur & Orville Wright Invented the Airplane,* Peter Busby stresses the importance of growing up in a household that encourages discovery and learning. The text shows the importance of using diagrams and photographs to help readers improve their comprehension of complex ideas.

Talkin' About Bessie: The Story of Aviator Elizabeth Coleman, by Nikki Grimes, displays an interesting style: The biographer tells the story of Coleman by developing imagined monologues by friends and acquaintances. *Tomboy of the Air: Daredevil Pilot Blanche Stuart Scott,* by Julie Cummins, is a biography of another trailblazer who was the first woman to fly in the United States and the first woman test pilot. Later in her career she became a writer and a talk show host on radio.

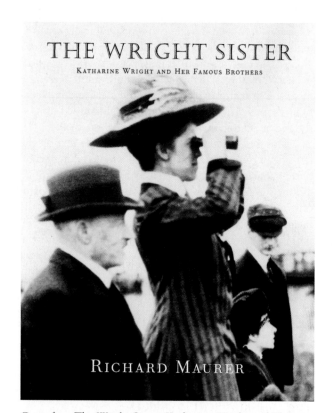

Cover from The Wright Sister: Katharine Wright and Her Famous Brothers *by Richard Maurer. Copyright © 2003 by Richard Maurer. Photograph from Wright State University Archives. Used by permission of Roaring Brook Press.*

Political Leaders and Social Activists

Men and women who have achieved noteworthy political power or who have attempted to bring about social change are common subjects of biography. Often, these public figures are controversial—adored by some, deplored by others. As a result, biographers sometimes create unbalanced portraits of their subjects. Because biographers usually choose to write about people they admire, hagiography (the biography of saints), rather than objective biography, may result. Even authors who create well-rounded portrayals of political leaders and social activists inevitably express their own perspectives. For example, after reading three books about a certain political leader, one student of children's literature commented that she could have been reading about three different people. Because each author had a specific purpose in writing a biography, characterization of the person, choice of events to discuss, style, and tone created a different bias. If possible, read several biographies about the same person and draw your own conclusions.

Several biographies depict the lives of people who lived in early time periods. Biographies of Cleopatra, born in 69 B.C., are among the most common biographies of people living in the Middle East during this early time. *Cleopatra*, by Diane Stanley and Peter Vennema, is a highly illustrated biography about the Queen of Egypt. The authors provide an interesting note on ancient sources that might influence how readers approach these biographies: "Everything we know about Cleopatra was written by her enemies. It is not surprising, then, that she was portrayed as a conniving, immoral woman" (unnumbered note). The authors present a queen who was strong willed, ambitious, and brilliant with a fine education and who also longed to return her country to the glory of its earlier years. The characterization suggests that her strength was her intelligence, courage, and charm. The text includes her relationships first with Caesar and then with Mark Antony. The illustrations, which depict the grandeur of Egypt, look like mosaics. The biography includes a historical atlas of Egypt and Roman Provinces during the accession of Cleopatra, a bibliography, and a pronunciation guide.

Many of the biographies of early religious leaders portray personages whose beliefs are still felt today. In *Muhammad*, Demi focuses on the prophet born in Mecca in A.D. 570. The author presents the life and basic teachings of the man who, at the age of 40, received his first revelation from Allah. His recorded words are in the Koran and became the foundations of the Islamic faith. Demi illustrates her biography in the style of Persian miniatures. Islamic tradition forbids pictorial representations of Muhammad, so Demi represents his image as a golden silhouette. She also provides a bibliography and art references.

Diane Stanley's *Saladin: Noble Prince of Islam* also focuses on the life of an Islamic leader who, in 1138, was welcomed into the world with words of faith: "La ilaba illa Allah; Muhammad rasul Allah—There is no god but Allah, and Muhammad is his Prophet" (unnumbered). Stanley presents a vivid description of the factions fighting during the Crusades. She also summarizes the beliefs of Saladin when he gives the following advice to his son: "Win the hearts of your people and watch over their prosperity; for it is to secure their happiness that you are appointed by God and by me. . . . I have become as great as I am because I have won men's hearts by gentleness and kindness" (unnumbered). By reading this biography, students will discover an Islamic viewpoint associated with the Crusades.

Russell Freedman's *Confucius: The Golden Rule* is the biography of a religious leader who lived more than 2,500 years ago and whose teachings have influenced millions of followers. Freedman tells his readers that all of the dialogue developed in the biography is from the *Analects* of Confucius. This dialogue provides important beliefs from Confucius's life. Notice in the following example how Freedman uses these sayings to make his character seem believable and to reflect Confucius's values: "Somehow he was able to study, perhaps with a teacher, though he seems to have been largely self-taught. And throughout his life, he never lost his love of books and learning. 'Study as if you'll never know enough,' he later told his students, 'as if you're afraid of losing what you've already gained'" (p. 10). Freedman includes an author's note that explains the importance of the biographical research that, for him, included visitations to the Chinese city of Qufu in Shandong Province, where Confucius was born. Freedman includes suggested readings of the *Analects* that are translated and annotated into English. The endpapers are printed with sayings from the *Analects*, such as "Don't worry when people fail to recognize your merits. Worry when you fail to recognize theirs" (frontispiece).

Another early personage who demonstrated a love of learning and of books is found in Don Brown's *Across a Dark and Wild Sea*. Brown develops a biography about Crimthann, who lived in sixth-century Ireland. Unfortunately, his love of books eventually causes a dispute over the ownership of a book, and he seeks refuge on Iona, off the coast of Scotland. On Iona, he establishes a monastery and is reported to have transcribed more than 300 books. (Remember, at the time, books were transcribed by hand.) Illustrations in the text show how books were produced before the invention of the printing press.

The biographer of the following book uses many techniques to make the book an excellent example of biography. Polly Schoyer Brooks develops the characters and settings to capture the people and the times in *Queen Eleanor: Independent Spirit of the Medieval World*. She portrays Eleanor of Aquitaine as she develops from a frivolous, immature girl who acts to satisfy her whims to a mature queen who has a shrewd talent for politics. Brooks uses a variety of techniques to develop colorful characters.

In Ten Queens: Portraits of Women of Power, *short biographies of portraits such as this one of Eleanor of Aquitaine provide a glimpse of some of the most powerful women in history. (From* Ten Queens: Portraits of Women of Power, *by Milton Meltzer, illustrated by Bethanne Andersen. Copyright © 1998 by Bethanne Andersen, illustrations. Used by permission of Dutton Children's Books, an imprint of Penguin Putnam Books for Young Readers, a division of Penguin Putnam, Inc.*

Consider, for example, the picture that Brooks paints of Eleanor and her husband, Henry II, through the following comparisons:

> Eleanor gradually restored some measure of peace and order to her duchy, using persuasion where Henry had used force. (p. 100)

> While Eleanor had become serene, Henry had become more irascible. (p. 126)

> From a queen of the troubadours, who had inspired romance and poetry, she became a queen with as much authority as a king. . . . Henry had been admired and feared; Eleanor was admired and loved. (p. 132)

Brooks includes verses composed about Eleanor to describe the attitudes expressed toward the queen and to reinforce the mood of medieval chivalry. The following lyrics were written by troubadour Bernard de Ventadour and were included as an integral part of the text:

> Lady, I'm yours and yours shall be
> Vowed to your service constantly
> This is the oath of fealty
> I pledged to you this long time past,
> As my first joy was all in you,
> So shall my last be found there too,
> So long as life in me shall last. (p. 107)

Founding Fathers and Mothers of America. *George Washington, Spymaster: How the Americans Outspied the British and Won the Revolutionary War,* by Thomas B. Allen, focuses on an interesting portion of Washington's life as Revolutionary War general and first president of the United States by describing his use of spies to gather intelligence that helped the colonies win the war. The text begins with a Spy Chart that portrays both the British and American spies, for example, Samuel Adams and the Sons of Liberty, Benjamin Franklin and the Committee of Safety, and John Jay and the Committee for Detecting and Defeating Conspiracies. The design of the book is meant to take readers back to the days when George Washington used printed leaflets to spread the word about the revolution; the print is a digital version of the Carlson typeface used in 1774. The text includes a War Time Line and an example of code in which readers learn how to decipher the numbers in Tallmadge's code. This book should add interesting information for older students and young adult readers.

Jean Fritz's stories about Patrick Henry, Samuel Adams, John Hancock, Benjamin Franklin, James Madison, and Sam Houston seem to come alive through Fritz's inclusion of little-known information. In these books, children discover that heroes, like themselves, have fears, display good and bad characteristics, and are liked by some and disliked by others. For example, Fritz adds humor to *Where Was Patrick Henry on the 29th of May?* by developing the theory that unusual things always seemed to happen to Henry on the date of his birth. She characterizes Henry as not only a great patriot but also a practical joker and a person filled with "passion for fiddling, dancing, and pleasantry."

Similar insights enliven Fritz's biographies of other beloved figures from the Revolutionary War period. Fritz doesn't limit her writing to supporters of American independence from Great Britain, however. In *Traitor: The Case of Benedict Arnold,* Fritz describes a man who wanted to be a success and a hero. She attracts interest in Arnold and prepares readers for the apparently dramatic changes in a man who chose to support the British by suggesting early in the book the complete reversal of Arnold's popularity. In 1777, following Arnold's successes in the assault on Quebec and in the Saratoga Campaign, George Washington called him "the bravest of the brave." But by 1780, after his plot with John André to betray the American post at West Point, he was regarded as "the veriest villain of centuries past." The incidents that Fritz chooses to include portray many sides of Arnold's character and en-

Technology Resources

The accompanying CD-ROM is ideal for generating a list of titles to support a unit on explorers, a discussion of inventors, a career week focus, or a study of a specific historical figure.

courage readers to understand why Arnold joined forces with the British.

In *Benjamin Franklin: The New American*, Milton Meltzer carefully introduces readers to the historical background of Franklin. In the following quotation, Meltzer encourages readers to understand the time and place:

> It is almost three hundred years since Benjamin Franklin was born in Boston. (The date was January 17, 1706.) It is hard to put yourself back in that time and grasp what it was like. About 12,000 people lived in Boston, and in all the English colonies of North America there were only 250,000. (That's about the same as the population of Rochester, New York, today.) Most of the people were clustered around Boston, the Connecticut and Hudson river valleys. . . . They had little connection with one another. Roads were really paths, and bad weather made them almost impassable. (p. 15)

Meltzer depicts a many-sided person by revealing both strengths and weaknesses in Franklin, adding credibility to the characterization through numerous quotations drawn from Franklin's writings and speeches.

Candace Fleming's *Ben Franklin's Almanac: Being a True Account of the Good Gentleman's Life* uses Franklin's almanac not only to provide information for the biography, but also to formulate the design of the book: Each two-page spread resembles an almanac entry and depicts some aspect of Franklin's life. The author includes reproductions of photographs, paintings, and engravings that help readers understand the historical events surrounding Franklin's life. A bibliography, notes on sources, and an index make the book very useful for readers.

Another viewpoint of the Revolutionary War is found in Jim Murphy's *A Young Patriot: The American Revolution as Experienced by One Boy*, the biography of a 15-year-old who enlisted in the army in 1776. *George Washington and the Founding of a Nation*, by Albert Marrin, includes quotes from Washington's writings, historical drawings, and maps. Marrin carefully develops a biographical character who is both someone to be admired and a personality with flaws. The biography also depicts the harshness of war.

Cheryl Harness's *Thomas Jefferson* is a highly illustrated biography for younger readers. The author's lively style interests many readers; for example, she uses similes to describe Jefferson's attitudes toward the French Revolution: "America was like a mouse batted around by French and English cats. John Adams wanted the mouse to be neutral—and uneaten! But talk grew so hot that his Federalist Party in Congress passed laws against criticizing the government. Foreign critics could be thrown in jail or out of the country. Dark days for civil rights, Thomas thought. He saw the election of 1800 as being 'as real a revolution in the principles of our government as that of 1776.'" (p. 31). As in many other biographies written for younger readers, the illustrations provide details about the time period that are not included in the text.

Harness presents information about Jefferson that would not have been found in biographies written during an earlier time: In "A Note From the Author," Harness tells about Jefferson's slave, Sally Hemings. Notice in the following quote how the author shares this information and also includes questions about the relationship:

> One part of his story is the story of Sally Hemings. She was the daughter of her mother's white master and half-sister of Jefferson's wife, Martha. When his father-in-law died, Thomas inherited 135 slaves, including Sally. Evidence now suggests that in the long years after Martha died, Sally Hemings and Thomas Jefferson, her owner, produced six children. Were Thomas and Sally in love, or was this a case of master exploiting his slave? The wondering will never end. (p. 7)

Fiery words and bold actions are not the only forms of patriotism and leadership. Elizabeth Yates's *Amos Fortune, Free Man* depicts a man who advanced freedom. Fortune was an African who was brought to slavery in Boston, learned a trade, and eventually acquired freedom. He represents thousands of unsung heroes of the American Revolution—black and white, male and female. The words on his tombstone, erected in 1801, suggest the fundamental American values that Fortune exemplified: "Born free in Africa, a slave in America, he purchased liberty, professed Christianity, lived reputably, and died hopefully" (p. 181).

Leaders of a Growing America. As the United States became more confident in itself as a nation, it began to expand its interests overseas. Rhoda Blumberg's *Commodore Perry in the Land of the Shogun* depicts the attempts of the American naval officer Matthew Perry to open Japanese harbors to American trade in 1853. This book, an excellent choice for multicultural studies, strongly emphasizes the dramatic interactions between Perry and the Japanese. Reproductions of the original drawings that recorded the expedition, Japanese scrolls and handbills, and photographs provide documentation and enhance children's understanding of the setting and Japanese culture.

Albert Marrin combines history and analysis of the time period in his biography *Old Hickory: Andrew Jackson and the American People*. The author emphasizes Jackson's background as a soldier, judge, and legislator as well as his experiences as the seventh president of the United States (1829–1837). As a soldier, Jackson defeated the British at the Battle of New Orleans in 1815; as a politician, he advocated increased participation in government from farmers and owners of small businesses. The time period is made more interesting through Marrin's inclusion of political cartoons and documents that reflect the time. The sources and additional readings make the book an excellent reference for students conducting research on topics such as the Industrial Revolution.

The best-known biographer of Abraham Lincoln is probably Carl Sandburg, whose *Abraham Lincoln: The Prairie Years* was the basis for his biography for children, *Abe Lincoln Grows Up*. In this biography, children vicariously share the youth of a great American leader. They discover an impoverished young man of the backwoods who is starved for books, hungry for knowledge, eager to

In-Depth Analysis of a Biography

In 2000, Russell Freedman's biography *Lincoln: A Photobiography* was chosen unanimously as one of the "One Hundred Books That Shaped the Century" (Breen et al., 2000). In this 1988 Newbery Medal winner, Russell Freedman uses numerous techniques that students of children's literature should consider. First, he introduces each of the seven chapters with quotations from Lincoln's own writing. For example, Freedman introduces chapter two, "A Backwoods Boy," with this quotation:

It is a great piece of folly to attempt to make anything out of my early life. It can all be condensed into a simple sentence, and that sentence you will find in Gray's Elegy—"the short and simple annals of the poor." That's my life, and that's all you or anyone else can make out of it. (p. 7)

Second, Freedman clearly separates legend from fact. For example, in chapter three, "Law and Politics," Freedman states:

He also fell in love—apparently for the first time in his life. Legend tells us that Lincoln once had a tragic love affair with Ann Rutledge . . . who died at the age of twenty-two. While this story has become part of American folklore, there isn't a shred of evidence that Lincoln ever had a romantic attachment with Ann. Historians believe that they were just good friends. (p. 28)

Third, Freedman supports his text with photographs of various documents of Lincoln's own writing. For example, the text includes a page of Lincoln's autobiographical sketch written in 1859 (p. 6), a page from Lincoln's homemade copybook (p. 13), and a copy of the handwritten Gettysburg Address (p. 103).

Fourth, Freedman includes historical photographs that support the settings and people. There are photographs of battlefields and of Lincoln and his family.

Fifth, the text contains photographs of authentic posters, newspaper ads, and documents. For example, readers find a photograph of the marriage license of Abraham Lincoln and Mary Todd (p. 33), a wanted poster for a runaway slave (p. 44), a victory poster from 1860 (p. 62), and a newspaper cartoon from a Baltimore paper (p. 71).

Sixth, Freedman supports the text with references to sources for quotations and major speeches, lists of historical sites, sources for additional books about Lincoln, and lists of acknowledgments and picture credits. You can compare Freedman's biography with Albert Marrin's *Commander in Chief: Abraham Lincoln in the Civil War.*

have fun, and ambitious to test himself and his principles in a wider world. Sandburg says:

It seemed that Abe made the books tell him more than they told other people. . . . Abe picked out questions . . . such as

"Who has the most right to complain, the Indian or the Negro?" and Abe would talk about it, up one way and down the other, while they were in the cornfield pulling fodder for the winter. (p. 135)

In *Abraham Lincoln*, a highly illustrated biography for younger readers, Amy L. Cohn and Suzy Schmidt use a writing style that encourages readers to interact with the text. For example, they ask readers, "See that tall, tall man in that tall black hat? Know who he is?" (unnumbered). They continue by introducing information about the 16th president. They focus on developing a many-sided character who reflects humor and warmth, but also frustration and pain as he takes the country into the Civil War.

The man who changed the course of United States history by assassinating Lincoln is the subject of James Cross Giblin's *Good Brother, Bad Brother: The Story of Edwin Booth & John Wilkes Booth.* This dual portrait of two brothers written for older readers provides an interesting study in point of view and influences that change a life.

Biographies of Charles Eastman and Theodore Roosevelt depict people who had great impact on the growth of America. Charles Eastman, the most famous Native American of his time, was a Sioux of the Great Plains, born in 1858. Eastman overcame poverty and racial prejudice to become a physician and a crusader for Native American rights. Peter Anderson's *Charles Eastman: Physician, Reformer, and Native American Leader* looks at the influences that combined to make Eastman a spokesperson for his people, including the forced migration of the Sioux from Minnesota, Eastman's medical education, and his efforts to provide medical treatment and better living conditions for the Sioux. Eastman worked to restore broken treaties and to encourage Indians and whites to respect Native American culture. Anderson describes Eastman's motives for publishing his first book:

It was Charles's intention to present an accurate picture of the Indian people and their way of life. Too often white people looked upon the Indian people as ignorant and backward. In his writing and lecturing, Charles was quick to correct them, pointing out the many strengths and contributions of America's native people. In addition to their deep respect for nature, Charles wrote about the beauty of their arts and crafts. Indian people, he said, also had developed their own herbal medicines and farming techniques. They knew, as well as anyone, how to live off the land. (p. 90)

James Rumford's *Sequoyah: The Man Who Gave His People Writing* presents another milestone for political leaders and social activists. Rumford's biography is the story of the man who created a writing system for the Cherokee people. The text, written in both English and Cherokee, should appeal to all grades. The biographer begins with a reference to the strong, tall sequoyah tree and proceeds to the man called Sequoyah, born in the 1760s in eastern Tennessee. He is described as a man who did not want his people to disappear into the white man's world; he did not want Cherokee voices to fade away. He believed that writing would make his people strong. The author shows Sequoyah's hardships when neighbors feared his signs were evil and burned his cabin. This did not deter him, however, and he invented letters that matched the sounds of the language. In 1824, the Cherokee Nation gave him a silver medal.

Bully for You, Teddy Roosevelt! by Jean Fritz, is a biography of the 26th president, who worked especially hard for conservation issues. Fritz's biography includes notes, a bibliography, and an index. Betsy Harvey Kraft begins her biography, *Theodore Roosevelt: Champion of the American Spirit*, with an introduction to Roosevelt's life as a boy, when he was frequently ill. The biographer stresses how his youthful experiences influenced his later life as a fighter for environmental protection and social justice. It is interesting for readers to see how his beliefs were influenced by his family's belief in social reform. The author portrays a many-sided figure who began as a sickly child and emerged as a vigorous, healthy adult.

Numerous biographies of escaped slaves develop the importance of freedom and the inhumanity of slavery. Virginia Hamilton's *Anthony Burns: The Defeat and Triumph of a Fugitive Slave* is a narrative history of events surrounding the life of Burns as well as a biography. In the research material, however, there existed no day-to-day calendar of the activities and movements of Burns as an ordinary slave child and youth. The life of Burns became well documented only after his 20th year, when he was hired out to Richmond, Virginia, and carefully began to plan his escape. Because of the lack of documentation, Hamilton draws from supporting materials to re-create Burns's early life.

Hamilton uses an interesting technique to allow readers to understand the early life of Burns. After Burns is captured as a fugitive slave, he goes within himself and remembers his happier childhood days. In the following quotation, Hamilton transfers her character from his unhappy days of imprisonment to his memories: "Anthony was not aware Suttle had gone anywhere, for he had left first and gone deep inside himself, to his childhood. These days seemed endless, perfect. There mornings and waking up were the times he could hardly wait for, he loved them so" (p. 7).

Tonya Bolden uses an unpublished memoir and family materials to develop the story of an African American girl in *Maritcha: A Nineteenth-Century American Girl*. The biographer describes the life of a free African American child living in New York City before and after the Civil War. She focuses on the influences of both Maritcha's family and her education to help her through these difficult times, including the Draft Riots of 1863 and the destruction of her family's home and business. An afterword discusses her adulthood, during which she spent 50 years

as an educator. The depiction of the 19th-century New York City setting is enhanced with photographs and family documents.

Twentieth-Century Leaders in America and Abroad. Biographies written for young children and for older children differ in tone, focus, choice of content, amount of detail, and development of character. Because of the range in intended audiences, biographies about political leaders and social activists in the 20th century provide opportunities to compare the authors' techniques and the content they include.

First, consider two biographies written for young children: Barbara Cooney's *Eleanor* and Kathleen Krull's *Harvesting Hope: The Story of Cesar Chavez*. The books share several features. The readability levels are for the fourth grade, indicating that the books are meant for independent reading. The books contain numerous illustrations, and they emphasize very positive characteristics and situations.

Cooney's *Eleanor* focuses on Roosevelt as a young girl. Both Cooney's text and illustrations develop characterization that shows her as a lonely and insecure child, especially after her father's death. The biography has a happy ending as the child realizes that she has special talents. Cooney's illustrations depict the time period and recreate the era of mansions and a wealthy social life. Krull's *Harvesting Hope: The Story of Cesar Chavez* shows the future labor activist as a young boy living on his family's ranch in Arizona. The author then stresses how his life changes when drought destroys the ranch and forces the family to move to California. Now Chavez experiences discrimination toward migrant workers and is forced to speak English in school. These experiences result in positive activities for social justice because they cause him to organize the National Farm Workers Association and fight discrimination through strikes and nonviolent demonstrations. Krull stresses the positive activities and experiences that allow Chavez to negotiate the first contract for farm workers.

Next, consider several biographies that have been written for older children. Longer formats allow authors to include more details and to develop more information about the historical periods.

Appropriately for an older audience, Russell Freedman's *Franklin Delano Roosevelt* includes many photographs, lists books about Roosevelt, and provides acknowledgments for picture credits. Many of these photographs are from the Franklin D. Roosevelt Library, the Library of Congress, the Bettmann Archive, and the National Archives. The biography includes an in-depth look at Roosevelt's activities during World War II. Consequently, it is a valuable source for authenticating historical fiction about World War II. In *Eleanor Roosevelt: A Life of Discovery*, Freedman realistically portrays

Eleanor Roosevelt by drawing heavily on her memoirs. Unlike biographies written for younger readers, Freedman's *Eleanor Roosevelt* includes her reactions when she discovers her husband's love affair. As in Freedman's other biographies, numerous photographs add to the depiction of this political leader's life.

Photobiographies are important for introducing both a biographical subject and a time period; younger readers learn a great deal from the photographs, and older readers can use them to support the information in more advanced biographies. The photographs in Deborah Heiligman's *High Hopes: A Photobiography of John F. Kennedy*, for example, provide readers with a visual representation of both Kennedy's youth and his presidency. In addition to the text and the photographs, the author highlights quotations that illustrate Kennedy's beliefs and values, such as "Political action is the highest responsibility of a citizen" (p. 23); "The stories of past courage . . . can teach, they can offer hope, they can provide inspiration. But they cannot supply courage itself. For this each man must look into his own soul" (p. 28); and "We stand today on the edge of a new frontier—The frontier of the 1960s—A frontier of unknown opportunities and perils—A frontier of unfulfilled hopes and threats" (p. 40).

Demi is another biographer who uses quotes from a biographical subject to bring the person to life. In *Mother Teresa*, Demi provides numerous prayers and sayings to develop character and values. For example, the following words are printed on Mother Teresa's business card: "The fruit of Silence is Prayer, The fruit of Prayer is Faith, The fruit of Faith is Love, The fruit of Love is Service, The fruit of Service is Peace" (unnumbered). The biography chronicles the life of the woman who founded the Missionaries of Charity in 1950 and then oversaw thousands of nuns as they ministered to the poor. Demi's illustrations, surrounded by rich gold borders, develop both a formal feeling to the biography and a sacred quality to Mother Teresa's life. A map showing the locations of the Missionary of Charity Foundations and the route of Mother Teresa's journey from Skopie to Calcutta adds to the international quality of her life. The author provides a listing of awards and honors, including the Nobel Prize and the Albert Schweitzer Award for humanitarian work in the United States.

John B. Severance's *Gandhi, Great Soul* begins with a chapter that develops the impact of Gandhi's beliefs on other world leaders such as Martin Luther King, Jr. and Nelson Mandela. Severance's biography includes interesting details about Gandhi's personal life as well as historical events and struggles with the British and various religious groups.

Elizabeth Ferber's *Yasir Arafat: A Life of War and Peace* is the biography of the Palestinian leader. The biographer combines the story of his life with information about the Arab and Israeli conflict. Ferber presents both points of view about the man: a popular leader among displaced Palestinians and a reviled figure in the occupied territories after the Hebron massacre in 1994. Labeled black-and-white photographs accompany the text. There is also a chronology of important dates, source notes for each chapter, a bibliography, and an index.

How does a biographer write about biographical subjects who have had a dire impact on history? James Cross Giblin begins his biography *The Life and Death of Adolf Hitler* with questions, such as, "What sort of man could plan and carry out such horrendous schemes?" He then presents the details associated with Hilter's formative years that affected his beliefs and led to his ability to influence crowds of Germans. Giblin portrays Hitler as a personality who is both very disturbed and hungry for power. Photographs from the time period illustrate Hitler's rise to power. In *Good Brother, Bad Brother: The Story of Edwin Booth & John Wilkes Booth*, Giblin contrasts two brothers: one who built a reputation as a classical actor and the other who assassinated Abraham Lincoln. Giblin's biography incorporates careful research including firsthand accounts and photographs from the Harvard Theatre Collection. Giblin discusses John Wilkes Booth's love for the Confederacy, the events leading to the assassination, and the effect of the assassination on his family and the country.

The importance of memories and friendship is developed in Vedat Dalokay's *Sister Shako and Kolo the Goat: Memories of My Childhood in Turkey*. This book, the winner of the 1995 Mildred Batchelder Honor Award, is a personal remembrance of the former mayor of Ankara, Turkey, in which he lovingly recalls his childhood in rural Turkey and his special friendship with a widow and her remarkable goat, Kolo. The author describes many of the values and beliefs identified in Turkish folklore. For example, the importance of hospitality is shown when the new goat comes into the family unexpectedly and is considered a "Guest of God," because "if a traveler needs shelter or food, he knocks at the door of any house along the way. The host offers him whatever he needs, because the traveler is considered a guest sent by God. This is a very old Turkish tradition that is still practiced today" (p. 14).

Dalokay presents many of these Turkish values as he remembers Sister Shako's thoughts and advice about subjects such as holy places and death. For example, Sister Shako states her beliefs about death: "Now I am here in this hut, but after death, I shall be in the caterpillar on the black earth, I shall be in the rain seeping into the earth. Blowing winds and rapid rivers will carry me around this world. May death come nicely, smoothly, without pain, without suffering" (p. 58). To clarify understanding, the author includes footnotes that describe various customs and beliefs developed in the story. The cultural atmosphere is reinforced by the use of regional words, idioms, sayings, and traditions of eastern Turkey.

Achievers and American heroes are always popular subjects for children's biographies. In *The American Hero:*

The True Story of Charles A. Lindbergh, Barry Denenberg uses several techniques that stimulate interest in the controversial aviator's life and add a feeling of authenticity. For example, he introduces each of the chapters with quotes from Charles or Anne Lindbergh's own writings. The introduction to the second chapter includes insights into the motivation to learn to fly an airplane: "When I was a child on our Minnesota farm, I spent hours lying on my back . . . hidden from passersby, watching white cumulus clouds drift overhead, staring into the sky. It was a different world up there. You had to be flat on your back, screened in by the grass stalks, to live in it. Those clouds, how far away were they? Nearer than the neighbor's house, untouchable as the moon—unless you had an airplane. How wonderful it would be, I'd thought, if I had an airplane—wings with which I could fly up to the clouds and explore their caves and canyons—wings like the hawk circling above me. Then, I would ride on the wind and be part of the sky . . . —Charles Lindbergh" (p. 19). In addition, photographs showing Lindbergh's experiences, charts, and maps illustrate the biography. The text includes source notes, a bibliography, and an index.

In *America's Champion Swimmer: Gertrude Ederle,* David A. Adler presents a biography of the first woman to swim the English channel. He uses newspaper comments that describe her as courageous, determined, modest, and poised to help define the character of the woman who also won three medals in the 1924 Olympics and set 29 U.S. and world records.

When children do library research, they discover some of the techniques that biographers use. Such investigations may also lead children to outstanding, recently published biographies of other social leaders.

Civil Rights Leaders

Biographies about civil rights leaders encourage readers to examine historical, political, and social perspectives of the movement. For example, James Haskins's *Thurgood Marshall: A Life for Justice* presents the fight against racism and segregation waged by the first African American Supreme Court justice. The text includes bibliographies of books, articles, and other sources, and indexes that encourage older readers to conduct specific research.

There are several biographies of Martin Luther King Jr. that can be used for comparative studies and analysis. Lillie Patterson's *Martin Luther King, Jr. and the Freedom Movement* begins with an account of the 1955–1956 Montgomery, Alabama, bus boycott and King's involvement in it. Patterson then explores King's background and discovers some of the influences that caused him to become a leader in the boycott and the civil rights movement. James Haskins's *The Life and Death of Martin Luther King, Jr.* presents a stirring account of King's triumphs and tragedies. Haskins's *I Have a Dream: The Life and Words of Martin Luther King, Jr.* focuses on King's involvement with the civil rights movement. You may wish to compare these biographies of Martin Luther King Jr. with the revised edition of *My Life With Martin Luther King, Jr.,* by Coretta Scott King.

Interesting comparisons can be made between two highly illustrated biographies of Martin Luther King Jr.: one by Faith Ringgold and the other by Rosemary L. Bray. Ringgold's *My Dream of Martin Luther King* develops the biography of the civil rights leader through a dream sequence. The text and illustrations present various stages in King's vision for a better world, tracing events in King's life such as joining demonstrations, being arrested, listening to his father's sermons, being influenced by the teachings of Mahatma Gandhi, becoming an adult minister, and dying from an assassin's bullet. The text and the dream sequence end as people in a crowd scene trade bags filled with prejudice, hate, ignorance, violence, and fear for Martin Luther King's dream for the promised land. The text includes a chronology of important dates in King's life.

Bray's biography, *Martin Luther King,* is illustrated with folk-art paintings by Malcah Zeldis. This biography includes more details about King's life than the one by Ringgold. It also contains a chronology of dates, but neither book provides source notes. Students of children's literature can compare the impact of the illustrations and the depiction of King's life in these two highly illustrated biographies written to appeal to younger readers.

Another biography of Martin Luther King Jr. written for younger readers is Christine King Farris's *My Brother Martin: A Sister Remembers Growing Up With the Rev. Dr. Martin Luther King Jr.* This biography by King's older sister presents incidents in his childhood that influenced his lifelong commitment to fighting injustice. For example, after two childhood friends tell him that they can no longer play with him, he asks his mother why and she answers, "Because they just don't understand that everyone is the same but someday it will be better." King responds, "Mother Dear, one day I'm going to turn this world upside down" (unnumbered). This incident helps readers understand how a young boy's life can be changed through racism.

There are several biographies of Malcolm X that lend themselves to comparative studies and analysis. For example, Arnold Adoff's *Malcolm X* stresses how and why Malcolm X urged African Americans to be proud of their heritage and of themselves. In a book written for older readers, *Malcolm X: By Any Means Necessary*, Walter Dean Myers sets Malcolm X's life against the history of segregation and the civil rights movement.

Eloise Greenfield's *Rosa Parks* focuses on the life of the seamstress in Montgomery who refused to give up her seat on the bus. Nikki Giovanni's *Rosa* is a highly illustrated version of this experience. Ruby Bridges's *Through My Eyes* focuses on the experiences of a 6-year-old girl during the integration of her school in New Orleans in 1960.

The Power of One: Daisy Bates and the Little Rock Nine, by Judith Bloom Fradin and Dennis Brindell Fradin, focuses on the Little Rock Central High School crisis of 1957–1958 and the influence of a woman who worked for desegregation as the publisher of the *Arkansas State Press*, an influential African American newspaper, and as the president of the Arkansas branch of the National Association for the Advancement of Colored People. A listing of a few of the chapter titles shows the focus of the book: "Hate Can Destroy You, Daisy," "Birth of the Arkansas State Press," and "They're In!" Photographs from the time period, such as one that shows the National Guard barring African American students and another showing the United States Army escorting Little Rock students into the school, depict the racial feelings of the period. The authors provide nine pages of source notes, a bibliography, picture credits, and an index.

Artists and Authors

One of the most interesting newer biographies develops both the biography of a world-famous photographer and a chronological view of history as shown through her photographs. In *Margaret Bourke-White: Her Pictures Were Her Life*, Susan Goldman Rubin uses a photobiography approach to blend the personal and professional life of this renowned photographer who was able to make a reputation in a profession that at the time was dominated by men. The biographer introduces her subject in a way that suggests to readers that they will be reading about a courageous and dedicated photographer by beginning as Bourke-White is ordered to abandon ship while she is on a troop carrier in World War II headed for North Africa and she takes pictures of the sinking ship while she is in a lifeboat. The major portion of the biography chronicles her development as one of the world's best-known photojournalists. Her importance is reinforced through the reproductions of such photographs as the one of Churchill and Stalin that was on the cover of *Life* magazine.

Through the Eyes of a Biographer

David A. Adler

Visit the CD-ROM that accompanies the text to generate a complete list of titles written by David A. Adler.

Selected Biographies by David A. Adler:
George Washington: An Illustrated Biography
Joe Louis: America's Fighter
Lou Gehrig: The Luckiest Man
The Picture Book of Sojourner Truth
America's Champion Swimmer: Gertrude Ederle
B. Franklin, Printer

I have to be interested in writing the book, and the publisher has to be interested in publishing the book. But it usually starts with me. What I generally do is find a subject I'd be interested in, and then do a little research to see if I'm still interested. I end up reading so much about this person, and if I'm not that interested, it's homework. And I find if I'm interested, I do a better job writing and I enjoy the process a lot more. It's the same thing if you tell a child to read a book. If the child's interested, it's a joy. If they're not interested, first of all it's hard to read, and then, the child doesn't retain anything.

George Washington is interesting. There's almost unlimited information. The things Washington did really told you about his personality. He was a really exacting man. Once when he was away, Martha had an upstairs room replastered, and when he returned, he measured the room to see how much the plasterer should have been paid, and he discovered that Martha had overpaid by a few schillings. The plasterer had died, and his widow had remarried, so Washington collected the extra schillings from the new husband. And it wasn't because he was cheap—he wasn't cheap—he was just that exacting. All this tells you a lot about him as a person. I could have just listed his accomplishments, but I felt this was a better way to tell you about him.

With biographies, I always want somebody who was important to history. Actually, the first biography I wanted to write was Gertrude Ederle, because she was so important to history. She's so important because she excelled on the same level as men—not separate but equal. It was amazing that she'd been somehow skipped over. But I couldn't get that published at first, so after a number of other biographies, a publisher asked me, "Who would be a good biography?" And I said, "How about Gertrude Ederle?"

Writing somebody's biography can become a problem when the negatives outweigh the positives. There are some people I don't even want to write about because I don't like them. Christopher Columbus was a product of his time. It's unfortunate he didn't step above it, like Ben Franklin did, or George Washington did in later life. But take Thomas Jefferson, for example. You can't avoid that he was a slave holder who said all men are created equal. It's hard to understand what that means. I sat down with that and looked at Ben Franklin and said I'd just rather do Franklin.

Anything I write is accurate, but that doesn't mean I write everything. I'm not completely forthright; I can't write everything because I'm limited in the number of words I can use. And a reader might wonder, "Why did you skip this or that?" But that's my decision. That's how you learn what an author finds important. And it's OK to wonder why something was skipped, as long as you don't ask why I got it wrong.

Video Profile: Find conversations with children's book authors Brian Pinkney, Joseph Bruchac, Roland Smith, and Leonard Everett Fisher on the video that accompanies this text.

Through the Eyes of a Child

Julia
Grade 5

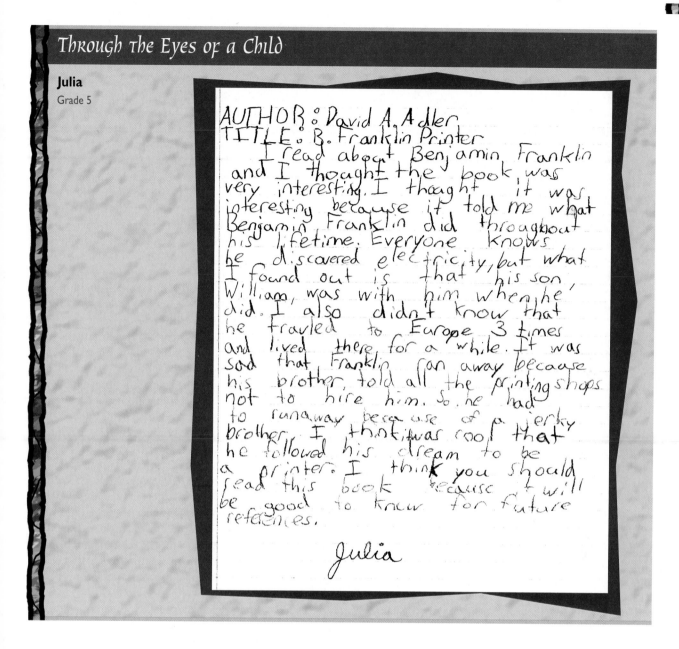

AUTHOR: David A. Adler
TITLE: B. Franklin Printer
    I read about Benjamin Franklin and I thought the book was very interesting. I thought it was interesting because it told me what Benjamin Franklin did throughout his lifetime. Everyone knows he discovered electricity, but what I found out is that his son, William, was with him when he did. I also didn't know that he travled to Europe 3 times and lived there for a while. It was said that Franklin ran away because his brother told all the printing shops not to hire him. So he had to runaway because of a jerky brother. I think it was cool that he followed his dream to be a printer. I think you should read this book because it will be good to know for future references.

Julia

The series of books "Portraits of Women Artists for Children" includes both brief biographical sketches of the artists and color reproductions of their works. Titles in this series include Robyn Montana Turner's *Frida Kahlo, Mary Cassatt, Georgia O'Keeffe,* and *Rosa Bonheur.* These books also provide much information about art.

In *Leonardo da Vinci,* Diane Stanley introduces readers to the art of the Renaissance artist. Through this biography, Stanley presents da Vinci's accomplishments both as a painter and as a scientist. She incorporates miniature reproductions of da Vinci's paintings into her illustrations. Stanley uses a similar approach in *Michelangelo.* In this biography, she also presents a historical perspective that allows readers to better understand how artists who worked during the Italian Renaissance were controlled by the desires of religious leaders and the wishes of wealthy patrons.

In *Leonardo: Beautiful Dreamer,* Robert Byrd develops a picture-book biography that includes a time line of da Vinci's life and accomplishments. The author presents an individual who was interested in solving the intricate problems that he found exhilarating. Byrd introduces the text in this way: "Five hundred years ago, a man lived and worked who thrived on the hard parts. A painter and engineer, he wasn't content simply to accept other people's explanations. He wanted to figure things out for himself—everything! How birds fly. How we see. What makes the blood move in the body. What gives an arch its strength or the sky its depth. How to make a painting alive with emotion, reality, mystery" (unnumbered). The text and illustrations present each of these challenges in the artist's life.

Several additional texts provide both biographical information about artists and introductions to their art.

Gary Schwartz's *Rembrandt* and Richard Meryman's *Andrew Wyeth* include information that helps readers understand and interpret their works. Both texts are heavily illustrated with color reproductions of each artist's paintings. Schwartz and Meryman are both considered leading authorities in art interpretations. Jan Greenberg and Sandra Jordan use numerous reproductions of the visionist artist's work in *Chuck Close, Up Close*. The authors list museums that show Close's art as well as a bibliography.

Some biographies combine art and science. In *The Boy Who Drew Birds: A Story of John James Audubon*, biographer Jacqueline Davies presents a vivid interpretation of the life of the man who in the 1800s pioneered a technique for banding birds' legs to track their movements. Audubon's theories were published in his *Ornithological Biography*. Scientists later used his banding technique to prove that small birds migrate. The author describes Audubon's enthusiasm for bird research and his love for painting life-size accurate images of birds. Melissa Sweet's illustrations were inspired by Audubon's art, which she studied while at the Audubon Wildlife Sanctuary, Mill Grove, Pennsylvania. Sweet states, "It was the cadence of his handwriting and the quality of the handmade papers he used that became the starting point of my paintings and collages" (Illustrator's Source Note, unnumbered).

Anne Elizabeth Rector's biography *Anne Elizabeth's Diary: A Young Artist's True Story* combines diary entries, art, and tips for keeping a diary. The biography presents the life of a 12-year-old girl living in New York City in 1912. Sidebars describe the author/illustrator's life and family and significant events of the time period. For example, the diary entry for January 6 reads: "In front of the entire art class, Miss Pratt asked me to make a poster. It is for a lecture by Ernest Thompson Seton, who is coming to our school. She chose me out of all the good artists in class. Daddy gave me the paper to make it" (p. 6). The accompanying illustration shows the teacher at her desk and a row of students. The sidebar gives information about Ernest Thompson Seton, the cofounder of the Boy Scouts of America. The text includes "What Happened Next?," which focuses on Anne Elizabeth, "A Note From Anne Elizabeth's Granddaughter," "Some Tips for Keeping a Diary," and an "Author's Note."

Jan Greenberg and Sandra Jordan collaborated again in the biography *Action Jackson*, a picture-book biography of artist Jackson Pollack. The biographers stress the influence of Pollack's early life and his experiences watching gulls near his home. Robert Andrew Parker's illustrations support Pollack's energy and his visions.

In *Romare Bearden: Collage of Memories*, Jan Greenberg illustrates her biography with the artwork of this 20th-century artist. The text and accompanying art show the influence on his work of the civil rights movement and his life in Harlem. Greenberg and Jordan's *Andy Warhol: Prince of Pop* follows the artist's life from "Pittsburgh Days,

1928–1940" to "Last Years, 1982–1987." The chapters begin with quotes such as: "Artists are never intellectuals, that's why they're artists"—Andy Warhol (p. 16). The biography is illustrated with labeled copies of Warhol's art. The text includes important dates in his life, selected films and books by Andy Warhol, a glossary of art terms, notes, and sources.

Winfred Rembert's *Don't Hold Me Back: My Life and Art* is an autobiography of an African American artist who grew up in the segregated South where he experienced discrimination, beatings, and prison. It was in prison that he learned to tool leather and began to paint scenes from his childhood and early experiences on the leather.

Jonah Winter's *Frida* is a picture-book biography of the Mexican artist Frida Kahlo. The author depicts the importance of art as Kahlo uses her art to overcome the pain she experienced from a bus accident. An author's note provides additional information about Kahlo, including her marriage to Diego Rivera.

Biographies of Latino figures provide interesting sources for analysis and comparisons; this is especially true if biographies available about the same person are written for different age levels. For example, students of children's literature can compare the coverage, characterizations, and conflicts developed in three biographies about the artist Diego Rivera: Jeanette Winter's *Diego*, written for younger children; James Cockcroft's *Diego Rivera*, written for adolescent audiences; and Cynthia Newman Helms's *Diego Rivera: A Retrospective* (1986), an adult biography. By studying all three biographies, readers can find characterizations, values, and beliefs similar to those found in other genres of Latino literature: for example, the importance of fiestas, the role of women in sustaining religion, belief in healers, belief in the supernatural, belief that people should be good and should work hard, and pride in one's heritage.

Each book, however, has a slightly different point of view about Rivera. Winter's biography for younger readers portrays Rivera as a hero of the people whose mural paintings were influenced by the cultural events around him and the economic depression in Mexico. There is a strong theme in the book that one must be proud of one's heritage. Cockcroft's biography, written for young adult audiences, includes more information about Rivera's personality, his character flaws, and his political affiliations. As in the biography written for younger readers, there is a strong theme about being proud of one's heritage. The adult biography explains the inspirations of Rivera's artistic works. This biography presents a chronology of his art and life and discusses Rivera's influences on other artists. The text includes reproductions of Rivera's murals and gives explanations about his artwork. All of the biographies emphasize that Rivera was considered an artistic genius.

Other current biographies and autobiographies provide insights into the authors and illustrators of children's books. Read about the lives of the authors of *Little Women* and *Charlotte's Web* and then compare the lives of the authors with those of their fictional heroines and heroes.

In *Louisa May: The World and Works of Louisa May Alcott*, Norma Johnston chronicles the life of Louisa May Alcott. Readers will be interested in Johnston's motivation for writing this biography and her point of view. For example, Johnston states:

> Like generations of readers, I grew up envying the March family everything but their poverty—their closeness, the way they never stayed angry, the way they always, always loved each other. As a young teen, I wept bitterly because I couldn't make my family as picture-perfect as the Marches, and resolved to be, like Louisa, a writer of books for girls. (author's note)

Beverly Gherman's *E. B. White: Some Writer!* presents the life of the popular author of *Charlotte's Web, Stuart Little*, and *The Trumpet of the Swan* and contributor to such journals as *The New Yorker*. Throughout her biography, Gherman relates White's character to scenes from and characters developed in his children's stories. For example, she introduces the book in such a way that readers can visualize a many-sided person:

> Whenever E. B. White was asked to accept an award for one of his books, he found an excuse for not attending the ceremony. In 1970, when *Charlotte's Web* won the Claremont Center's Award, he sent them a speech describing how Wilbur fainted with excitement after he won his special prize at the fair. It took a bite from Templeton the rat to revive him. White said he would faint just as Wilbur had if he were forced to stand up before the audience and read his own speech. But he thanked them for liking *Charlotte* and said he felt "very lucky to have gained the ear of children." (p. 1)

In *Beatrix*, by Jeanette Winter, children can read about another of their favorite authors, Beatrix Potter, the author of the various Peter Rabbit books. Winter depicts the relationship between the young girl and the characters in her books such as Peter Rabbit and the hedgehog, Mrs. Tiggy-Winkle. Winter focuses on Potter as a young woman who leads a lonely life in London, but who is inspired by the animal friends she discovers during her summers in rural England. The biographer shows how Potter, as an adult, used the stories to create her beloved series.

Milton Meltzer's *Carl Sandburg: A Biography* chronicles the life of the poet and biographer who became known for his ability to speak for the common man. Meltzer describes early work that shows Sandburg as a journalist for the *International Socialist Review* as well as his extensive poetry focusing on working conditions in Chicago. He presents a clear vision of the author by discussing Sandburg's poems and his reasons for writing them. A considerable portion of the biography focuses on Sandburg's role as a biographer of Lincoln and the success and recognition that came as a consequence of the Lincoln biographies.

Carl Sandburg: Adventures of a Poet, by Penelope Niven, is a combination of poetry and biography. The format matches a poem with appropriate biographical information about the writer's life. The narratives cover information about his life such as his involvement in the Spanish American War, his life as a journalist, and his work as a storyteller. The text includes notes on Marc Nadel's illustrations that encourage readers to search for details in the art.

In Don Brown's heavily illustrated biography, *American Boy: The Adventures of Mark Twain*, the biographer presents various incidents and characters in Twain's life that later become parts of his stories. Readers will discover how boyhood friends became characters in *Tom Sawyer* and *Huckleberry Finn*. Brown shows how various characters such as Uncle Dan, a slave owned by Clemens's uncle, influenced a love of storytelling and may have motivated the creation of Jim, the runaway slave.

Jane Yolen's *The Perfect Wizard: Hans Christian Andersen* is one of the more interesting and motivating biographies. Yolen combines the life of the author of popular literary fairy tales with the fairy tales that are associated with Andersen's life experiences. For example, each two-page spread provides a brief introduction to some part of Andersen's life, an illustration by Dennis Nolan that corresponds to the biographical information, a reference to one of Andersen's fairy tales that reflects the experience, and an illustration from the fairy tale. For example, Yolen describes Andersen's joyful experience following a production of one of his plays at the Royal Theater. Then she presents a quote from "The Nightingale" that reflects Andersen's feelings: "I shall never forget that the very first time I sang for you, you wept, and to a poet's heart, such tears are jewels" (unnumbered). Yolen includes a listing of Andersen's fairy tales and their publication dates. Adults find this text very motivating because children can read the fairy tales that were inspired by Andersen's life and discuss how they reflected Andersen's experiences. (An activity involving Andersen's biography and his fairy tales appears later in this chapter.)

Erica Silverman's *Sholom's Treasure: How Sholom Aleichem Became a Writer* focuses on the childhood of the Jewish writer whose Yiddish stories became the basis for the musical "Fiddler on the Roof." The biographer emphasizes the experiences in the writer's early life that appeal to young readers, such as his ability to make classmates laugh, his early humorous writings, and his use of humor to battle bullies. Silverman reveals how Sholom felt when his father first recognizes the quality of his writing. The biography ends with a foreshadowing of the future: "Sholom smiled to himself. So! He was going to be a somebody. He knew exactly what that meant. He was going to be a writer. That was the treasure Sholom would give Father" (unnumbered).

Russell Freedman's *The Voice That Challenged a Nation: Marian Anderson and the Struggle for Equal Rights* is a biography appropriate for the study of the civil rights movement and of great musicians. The book has won numerous awards: the Newbery Honor for 2005, the *Horn Book* Fanfare Award, the *School Library Journal* Best Books, the Robert F. Sibert International Award for 2005, the ALA/YALSA Best Books for Young Adults 2005, and ALA Notable Children's Books for 2005. Consequently, it is an excellent source for studying the techniques of an award-winning biographer.

Freedman begins his biography with one of the greatest controversies in Anderson's life, her 1939 Easter concert at the Lincoln Memorial and the controversy when she was not allowed to sing at Constitution Hall. Freedman goes back to her earlier life and presents a chronological account that goes from her childhood in Philadelphia through her American and European concert tours in the 1920s and 1930s.

Each chapter begins with a quote from Marian Anderson that reveals both her stature as an artist and her struggle for equal rights; for example, "I knew that I had to test myself as a serious artist in my own country" (p. 33), and "The essential point about wanting to appear in [Constitution Hall] was that I wanted to do so because I felt I had that right as an artist" (p. 71). To authenticate his text, Freedman draws from photographs from the time period, photographs of Marian Anderson and her family during different times in her life, and copies of programs of her performances. Many of the photographs show the racism Anderson faced, such as colored waiting rooms in train depots and colored taxicab stands. The enormity of Anderson's struggle for equal rights is shown when the DAR (Daughters of the American Revolution) bans her from singing. A copy of a newspaper article shows Eleanor Roosevelt resigning from the DAR in protest for Anderson's treatment. Freedman provides a list of selected recordings by Anderson and, as in all of his biographies, extensive chapter notes and a bibliography.

When Marian Sang, a biography of Anderson in picture-book format by Pam Muñoz Ryan, presents the difficulties the singer faced because of discrimination. Brian Selznick's illustrations depict the mood of the period and reflect Anderson's stunning voice, especially as she sings at the Lincoln Memorial after she is invited to the occasion by Eleanor Roosevelt. Additional information about Anderson is found in the author's note. This biography of Marian Anderson may provide older readers who have difficulties reading Freedman's biography for more mature readers with an easier, pictorial representation of her life.

Andrea Davis Pinkney's *Ella Fitzgerald: The Tale of a Vocal Virtuosa* is another picture-book biography of an African American singer. Brian Pinkney's illustrations add an appropriate feeling of movement to the mood of the text. Notice how each of the titles for the four parts of the biography also reflects a feeling of movement: "Hoofin' in Harlem," "Jammin' at Yale," "Stompin' at the Savoy," and "Carnegie Hall Scat." The biography includes both an author's note and an illustrator's note.

Quincy Troupe's *Little Stevie Wonder* introduces readers to the blind African American musician. The author stresses Stevie Wonder's fascination with sound and instruments when he was very young. Lisa Cohen's acrylic paintings add to the vibrant mood of the text.

Elizabeth Partridge, the biographer of *This Land Was Made for You and Me: The Life and Songs of Woody Guthrie,* emphasizes not only Guthrie's music but also how the music reflects the struggles for social justice. The biographer used information from interviews with Guthrie's son, folksinger Pete Seeger, and other people who knew Guthrie. Another American composer is the subject of Mordicai Gerstein's picture-book biography, *What Charlie Heard.* Gerstein's biography of composer Charles Ives focuses on the sounds he heard from childhood through adulthood; for example, he heard sounds such as his father's fiddle and fire truck bells. In a moving remembrance to the death of Ives's father, the page shows no sounds because "Charlie heard a great silence" (unnumbered). This page without sounds suggests Ives's strong relationship with his father and the sorrow he felt at his death.

Autobiographies give children insights into the illustrators and authors of children's books. *Bill Peet: An Autobiography* provides information about the artist's experiences as a Disney cartoonist who worked on such films as *Dumbo* and *Fantasia.* This text is heavily illustrated with Peet's drawings. Beverly Cleary's *A Girl From Yamhill: A Memoir* is a chronicle of the early life of the popular realistic fiction author. Numerous photographs should intrigue readers of the "Ramona" series and *Dear Mr. Henshaw.*

Readers will discover the author's experiences when he was a young boy by reading Tomie dePaola's *26 Fairmount Avenue.* The autobiography begins with a hurricane in 1938 and includes such exciting memories as watching his house being built, spending time with his grandmothers, and attending kindergarten. The author reveals emotions that seem very real to many young children as he discovers that he will not learn to read until next year and he is infuriated when Walt Disney changes "Snow White and the Seven Dwarfs" from the "true" story in his folktale book.

In *War Boy: A Country Childhood,* British author and illustrator Michael Foreman describes his life growing up in England during the 1940s. This is not the normal life of a young boy; it is complicated by bombs, gas masks, and guns. It is also filled, however, with excitement, working together, and new friends. Foreman's detailed illustrations provide background for stories set in World War II. In *After the War Was Over,* Foreman continues illustrating and describing his experiences into his teenage years. His text and watercolor illustrations present a warm personal account of his post–World War II years in England.

By reading *Open Your Eyes: Extraordinary Experiences in Faraway Places,* a collection of autobiographies edited by Jill Davis, readers discover how authors such as Jean

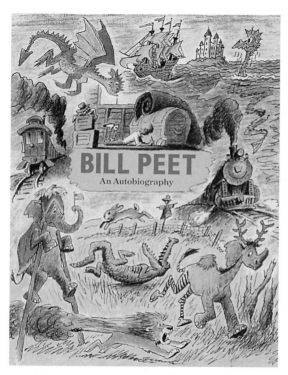

The humorous illustrations show the work of the author. (From Bill Peet: An Autobiography, *by Bill Peet, copyright © 1989 by Bill Peet. Reprinted by permission of Houghton Mifflin Company.)*

Fritz, Lois Lowry, and Katherine Paterson used their personal experiences to develop their understanding of the world. The individual autobiographies then reveal how these understandings influenced their writing. Many of these are moving experiences, such as this one written by Lois Lowry: "The time period contained in this story was probably no more than twenty minutes, and it happened over fifty years ago. But it seems like yesterday, because I was changed by it. Such small encounters—a brief meeting, a look exchanged, a tiny moment of surprise or pleasure—are the times I return to most often in my memory" (p. 27).

People Who Have Persevered

Biographies are not always written about famous people or people of great material success; some excellent biographies and autobiographies portray the courage and perseverance of ordinary people. For example, Lisa Ketchum's *Into a New Country: Eight Remarkable Women of the West* focuses on women such as Mary McGladery Tape, who came to America as a Chinese immigrant and sought equal rights for Chinese, and Katherine Ryan, a nurse who joined the Gold Rush in the Klondike.

Ginger Wadsworth's *Words West: Voices of Young Pioneers* uses letters, diaries, and memoirs to tell the stories of pioneers who traveled west between 1830 and 1870. Wadsworth begins the book with an author's note that attracts the reader's interest: "Cook beans and coffee over an open fire of sagebrush or buffalo chips. Wear the same dress for six months. Sleep in a new place every night. Leave my friends forever. No way!" (p. xi). She then informs readers about why she researched and wrote the book that begins with information about opening the west and then presents the experiences of young people as they encounter everything from extreme cold and hunger to the excitement of reaching "the promised land." The author provides a listing of sources that describe the personages in the book. The text includes a chronology that extends from 1801 to 1912, a map of the major trails, a list of books for further reading, and a selected bibliography divided between adult books and juvenile books.

Biographies of immigrants to the United States frequently depict the harsh circumstances that forced them to leave their home countries. Rosemary Wells's *Streets of Gold* is based on Mary Austin's memoir written in the early 20th century. The biography begins with her early life in Russia during which she experienced anti-Semitism, continues with her travels to America after her father earns enough money for his family's passage, and concludes with her life in Boston where she is finally able to attend school.

Another extraordinary woman is the subject of Rosemary Wells's *Mary on Horseback: Three Mountain Stories.* This biography chronicles many of the experiences of Mary Breckinridge, the first nurse to go to the Appalachian Mountains and provide medical services to families living in isolated locations. The influence of her work is shown through her formation of the Frontier Nursing Service, which began in 1925 with three nurses and grew to a service that visited about 35,000 mountain homes each year. Joan Dash's *The World at Her Fingertips: The Story of Helen Keller* emphasizes how Keller influenced opinions about and treatment of the blind.

Biographies of Native Americans, especially those written about historical personages, often portray people who have persevered. Several biographies look at famous Native Americans who interacted with white settlers of this continent. For example, *Sacajawea, Wilderness Guide,* by Kate Jassem, is the biography of the Shoshone woman who guided the Lewis and Clark expedition across the Rocky Mountains to the Pacific Ocean. This book is appropriate for young readers.

Albert Marrin's *Sitting Bull and His World* places Sitting Bull into the context of the world he inhabited and the customs, culture, and spiritual beliefs that shaped his character. The author adds to the biography by including maps, drawings, and photographs.

Eleven-year-old Georgia Salois is the Cree Indian survivor in Pamela Porter's *Sky.* The story set in Montana in 1964 depicts the harsh realities and hope for the future after a terrible flood. Even though Salois's family loses their home and all their possessions in the terrible destruction caused by a flood, Georgia finds and cares for a small foal who also survives the catastrophe. In addition to being a biography of Georgia's life, *Sky* details the racism that is felt toward Native Americans. For example, white families are given free food and shelter after the flood, but the Native peoples are crushed together in a single classroom and forced to pay for their food. Georgia, however, is not defeated: As she rides the colt for the first time, she realizes that even though she does not always get what she needs, her family has each other.

Conflicts between worlds provide numerous opportunities for character and plot development in Jean Fritz's *The Double Life of Pocahontas*. Fritz effectively develops a character who is torn between loyalty to her father's tribe and to her new friends in the Jamestown colony. As in her other biographies, Fritz documents her historical interpretations. Notes, a bibliography, an index, and a map add to the authenticity.

Russell Freedman's *Indian Chiefs* includes short biographies about Red Cloud, Satanta, Quanah Parker, Washakie, Joseph, and Sitting Bull. The text is supported with photographs, a bibliography, and an index. Dorothy Morrison's *Chief Sarah: Sarah Winnemucca's Fight for Indian Rights* is one of the strongest biographies of this period. Morrison depicts conflicts through contrasts when she describes Sarah's confusion:

> The whites killed—but they had made her well. They took the Indians' meadows—but gave them horses and presents. They burned stores of food—but they gave food, too. Would she ever understand these strange people who were overrunning the land? (p. 31)

Morrison shows Sarah's battle for retention of Paiute culture when she describes Sarah's dream:

> All this time Sarah had been lecturing and saving every penny, for she had another dream—of a school for Indian children, taught by Indians themselves, a school that would train its students as teachers for their own people. Up to then, Indian schools, both private and under the Bureau, had been taught and managed by white people who tried to "civilize" the students by wiping out native language and culture. Sarah, however, was sure her people's culture was worth preserving. (p. 149)

As Long as the Rivers Flow, by Larry Loyie, is the autobiography of a Cree Indian boy in Alberta, Canada, who is sent to a residential school for Native American children. The consequences of a change of life for Loyie and other First Nations children is shown dramatically as the book begins with the description of an idyllic summer in 1944 when Loyie accompanies his family to their summer camp. This life changes as the children are forcibly taken away in trucks to attend a distant boarding school. An epilogue states that residential schools began in 1880 and continued into the 1980s.

Biographies of historical people frequently stress the difficulties they encountered from racism. For example, Rhoda Blumberg's *York's Adventures With Lewis and Clark: An African-American's Part in the Great Expedition* begins in 1784 with the early years of York's life when he is a slave on a plantation in Virginia and where he is eventually assigned to be William Clark's personal body servant. The majority of the biography follows York as part of the Lewis and Clark expedition (1804–1806). Blumberg's illustrations show the western movement as the expedition visits Native Americans in a Mandan village, in a Hidalsa village, and during buffalo hunts; these photographs provide a strong feeling for the setting of the book. Blumberg presents an ending in which she separates truth from fiction: "It would be wonderful to end this true story with a happy ending. According to some fanciful accounts, York escaped to freedom and spent the rest of his life living contentedly in the Rocky Mountains among the Crow Indians, where he was honored as one of their chiefs. Other fictitious versions relate that Clark gave York his freedom in 1806, as a reward for his valuable contributions to the two-and-a-half-year, eight-thousand-mile Lewis and Clark expedition. How fine it would feel to be sure that York lived happily ever after. But that was not to be" (p. 79–80).

In *Knockin' on Wood*, Lynne Barasch presents the story of a world-famous tap dancer, Peg Leg Bates, who eventually performed for the king and queen of England. The biography is impressive because he lost his left leg in an accident in 1919 when he was 12 and then became a dancer using a wooden leg. The author ends the biography with Bates's words that show the importance of perseverance: "Don't look at me in sympathy. I'm glad that I'm this way. I feel good, knockin' on wood" (unnumbered).

Biographies of sports stars frequently show perseverance. For example, Sharon Robinson, the daughter of one of baseball's greatest players, chronicles the life of her fa-

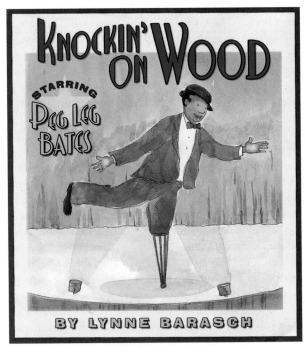

Cover from Knockin' on Wood: Starring Peg Leg Bates, *by Lynne Barasch. Copyright © 2004 by Lynne Barasch. Permission arranged with Lee & Low Books, Inc., New York, NY 10016.*

ther in *Promises to Keep: How Jackie Robinson Changed America.* Her biography makes the character come alive by using family photographs, newspaper headlines, and letters. In addition to insights into Robinson's life, the biography provides details about the struggle for civil rights. Jonah Winter's *Roberto Clemente: Pride of the Pittsburgh Pirates* is a picture-book biography that emphasizes not only Clemente's baseball accomplishments with his record of 3,000 hits, but also his struggles in overcoming negative attitudes because he was Latino. The biography concludes with Clemente's tragic death in a plane crash while he was taking aid to victims of an earthquake in Central America. Readers will learn that Clemente was a very generous person as well as a hero for Latino youth.

Females also have struggled for recognition in sports. *Girl Wonder: A Baseball Story in Nine Innings,* by Deborah Hopkinson, is based on the life of Alta Weiss, who in the early 20th century played baseball for a semiprofessional team in Ohio. The biography presents the story of a girl who broke down barriers not only in baseball, but also in medical school where she was the only girl in her class.

Peter Golenbock's biography *Hank Aaron: Brave in Every Way* portrays the life of a major league baseball star who was born during the Depression and during a time when the major leagues excluded black players. However, his father taught him to play baseball, and his mother taught him determination. Through the biography, the author shows that determination can overcome obstacles.

Persevering may require the survival of body and soul through such terrible experiences as the Holocaust. When children of the Holocaust write their autobiographical experiences as adults, they frequently emphasize both the tragedies of their experiences and the hopes for the future that kept them alive during their hiding or internment.

An effective author's style may be one of the most important literary elements used to increase understanding of the Jewish experience during World War II. In *No Pretty Pictures: A Child of War,* Anita Lobel, the future Caldecott Honor winner, describes her own life experiences during the years in Krakow, in hiding in the countryside, while living in the ghetto, and during internment in various concentration camps. Lobel does not end her autobiography, however, with liberation. Instead, she tells about her life of recuperation in Sweden following her imprisonment by the Nazis. Lobel uses an especially effective writing style to allow readers to understand the full meaning of the changes in her life.

In the second part of her autobiography, which is set in Sweden, Lobel uses contrasting descriptions of settings, personal responses to food, and emotional reactions to help readers understand the differences. For example, notice in the following quote how Lobel helps readers visualize the changes in her life by contrasting settings:

> At first I had spent a lot of time in bed, getting up only to go to the toilet and to wash in the bathroom down the corridor. I don't know how soon I came to take for granted the luxury of the flushing toilet, the sink to wash in, the fresh towels. I had no lice in my stubby hair anymore, no lice in the seams of my pajamas. The sheets on my bed were so white, so clean. . . . These were miraculous pleasures after the filthy bunks barely filled with hay and burlap. For years my body, my skin had not felt the wrappings of such comfort. (p. 13)

Lobel contrasts the memories brought on by such simple things as smells, sounds, bus rides, gates, weather, and announcements. Through these contrasts, readers also gain an understanding of the fear and suspicion that became a part of Lobel's life and how difficult it was for her to overcome her suspicious reactions. Lobel creates a many-sided character by contrasting and describing her own reactions and conflicting person-against-self conflicts. By the conclusion of the autobiography, the author has developed a strong character who understands her own need for self-realization, especially through her artwork.

David A. Adler develops a strong personage in his *A Hero and the Holocaust: The Story of Janusz Korczak and His Children.* As the director of the Jewish orphans' home in Warsaw, Poland, Korczak refused to leave the children even after a wall was built around the Warsaw Ghetto or after the children were placed on trains that took them to Treblinka and death. Oil paintings depict Korczak's love for the children and the serious mood of the time period.

Andrea Warren chronicles the experiences of an orphaned Amerasian boy in *Escape From Saigon: How a Vietnam War Orphan Became an American Boy.* The biography follows the boy from his birth and early childhood in Saigon through his departure from Vietnam in the 1975 Operation Babylift and his subsequent life as the adopted son of an American family in Ohio, and his return visit to Vietnam. The author includes an afterword that provides information on Operation Babylift and international adoption. There are multimedia recommendations for young readers, for middle readers, and for mature readers as well as recommended websites.

Biographies of children who have persevered are popular subjects in the "Children of Conflict" series. For example, in *Children of Israel, Children of Palestine: Our Own True Stories,* Laurel Holliday includes memoirs from more than 30 Jewish and Arab subjects who tell about the struggle between Israeli Jews and Palestinians.

Authors who write biographies about people who have overcome physical disabilities frequently focus on the biographical subject's ability to achieve success against considerable odds. In *Out of Darkness: The Story of Louis Braille,* Russell Freedman focuses on Braille's struggle to communicate after he loses his own sight and his additional difficulties in having his system accepted. In *Wilma Unlimited: How Wilma Rudolph Became the World's Fastest Woman,* Kathleen Krull stresses how Rudolph overcame her childhood polio to become at age 20 the first woman to win three gold medals in a single Olympics.

Eloise Greenfield and Lessie Jones Little's *Childtimes: A Three-Generation Memoir* traces a family's experiences.

In three parts, an African American grandmother, mother, and daughter tell about growing up in time periods ranging from the late 1800s through the 1940s. Both Greenfield and Little are well-known authors of children's books. This book concludes poignantly:

> It's been good, stopping for a while to catch up to the past. It has filled me with both great sadness and great joy. Sadness to look back at suffering, joy to feel the unbreakable threads of strength. Now, it's time for us to look forward again, to see where it is that we're going. Maybe years from now, our descendants will want to stop and tell the story of their time and their place in this procession of children. A childtime is a mighty thing. (p. 175)

The words provide a fitting conclusion to this discussion of biographies written for children. What better purposes are there for sharing biographies with children than allowing them to feel good, to catch up to the past, and to experience the sadness and great joy of other people's lives?

Biographies Written for Young Adults

Biographies and autobiographies written for young adults frequently develop powerful portrayals of the subjects, especially if they have faced difficult experiences. These books may have more mature coverage of the subjects as the biographical characters face and overcome various personal or societal difficulties.

First-person accounts of an incident are among the most powerful portrayals of the Holocaust experience. For example, *The Diary of a Young Girl: The Definitive Edition* certainly is among the most widely read autobiographies of the Holocaust. The diary, written by Anne Frank while she was in hiding in the attic of a house in Amsterdam, provides an intimate view of family life during the Holocaust.

The following entry from the diary is an excellent example of the power of Anne Frank's story:

Friday, October 9, 1942

Dear Kitty,

Today I have nothing but dismal and depressing news to report. Our many Jewish friends and acquaintances are being taken away in droves. The Gestapo is treating them very roughly and transporting them in cattle cars to Westerbork, the big camp in Drenthe to which they're sending all the Jews. Miep told us about someone who'd managed to escape from there. It must be terrible in Westerbork. The people get almost nothing to eat, much less to drink, as the water is available only one hour a day, and there's only one toilet and sink for several thousand people. Men and women sleep in the same room, and women and children often have their heads shaved. Escape is almost impossible; many people look Jewish, and they're branded by their shorn heads. (p. 54)

Through her diary, Anne Frank reflects not only growing fear but also love for life. This ability is highlighted in Patricia Hampl's review of the book published in the *New York Times Book Review* (1995). Hempl states, "The 'Diary,' now 50 years old, remains astonishing and excruciating. It is a work almost sick with terror and tension, even as it performs its miracle of lucidity. . . . All that remains is this diary, evidence of her ferocious appetite for life. It gnaws at us still" (p. 21).

Barry Denenberg's *Shadow Life: A Portrait of Anne Frank and Her Family* is classified as biography, except the author uses nonfiction sources to create a fictional diary written from Margot Frank's perspective. Readers can make interesting comparisons and use the author's extensive bibliography to discover additional information about the Frank family and the Holocaust.

You can compare Anne Frank's autobiography with Livia Bitton-Jackson's *I Have Lived a Thousand Years: Growing Up in the Holocaust.* This autobiography focuses on the life of a 13-year-old Hungarian girl and her family's experiences as they live in ghettos, forced labor camps, and in both Auschwitz and Dachau. Readers understand the severe consequences of their experiences when Livia is finally liberated and someone assumes she is 60 years old.

Ilse Koehn's *Mischling, Second Degree: My Childhood in Nazi Germany* provides insights into history and the values of both the Jewish and the German people. The title of the book is based on one of the three basic designations of Jewish people under the Nazis. The first is Jew—anyone with three racially full Jewish grandparents, or a person belonging to the Jewish religious community. The second is Mischling, first degree—anyone with two Jewish grandparents. The third is Mischling, second degree—anyone with one Jewish grandparent and not of the Jewish faith or married to a Jew. Additional history is revealed as Koehn discusses German philosophies. For example, she talks about "Blood and Soil," which means old German soil soaked with German blood: The Nazi government believed that they had the right to capture any country in which German blood had been spilled in battle. There is a description of the big bonfire in front of the Berlin University after Hitler ordered the burning of books that were "un-German." The response of her Jewish father to this incident reveals his love of books when he buries his forbidden literature in the garden. By contrasting the German and Jewish sides of her family, the author reveals many Jewish values that were not as respected by her German relatives, such as the value of books and studying.

In her introduction to *Persepolis: The Story of a Childhood,* Marjane Satrapi reveals her purpose for writing the book, which explains the harsher content in many young adult biographies: She states that since the Islamic Revolution in 1979, she must reveal her story because "this old and great civilization has been discussed mostly in connection with fundamentalism, fanaticism, and terrorism.

As an Iranian who has lived more than half of my life in Iran, I know that this image is far from the truth. This is why writing *Persepolis* was so important to me. I believe that an entire nation should not be judged by the wrongdoings of a few extremists. I also don't want those Iranians who lost their lives in prisons defending freedom, who died in the war against Iraq, who suffered under various repressive regimes, or who were forced to leave their families and flee their homeland to be forgotten. One can forgive but one should never forget" (Introduction).

Persepolis is a graphic memoir told in black-and-white cartoon images. The memoir begins before 1979, when Strapi attends a coeducational, nonreligious school. The text and setting change rapidly in 1980 when these schools are closed and boys and girls attend separate classes. The cartoon illustrations show dramatic contrasts between life before and after the Islamic Revolution and between being at home with her liberal parents and living under the Islamic constraints in school and broader society where she questions the wearing of the veil. The text depicts a well-rounded character who displays contrasting emotions, both fear and laughter. Some of the illustrations are very graphic, showing arrests, torture, and the horrors of war. The book ends as Satrapi is sent to live in Europe after she contradicts a teacher and her parents fear for her safety.

The experiences of young people following apartheid in South Africa are included in interviews by Tim McKee in *No More Strangers Now: Young Voices From a New South Africa*. The choice of interviews from numerous people presents a well-rounded view of the overall situation in South Africa for all the citizens. The interview with Pfano Takalani, the son of the chief, is especially interesting because Takalani stresses the values of his traditional life, which include respect for elders, learning traditional dances, and expectations for children. Takalani summarizes the importance of traditions when he states: "If these traditions are lost, we will lose a lot of human dignity" (p. 76).

Ange Zhang's *Red Land, Yellow River: A Story From the Cultural Revolution* is an autobiography of a young man who was a teenager during the time of Mao's Cultural Revolution in China. The author describes his experiences when, as the son of a famous writer and intellectual, he is labeled a black kid and is unable to join the Red Guard. He describes seeing his father publicly humiliated, finding his father's study ransacked and his antiques destroyed, being forced to join millions of urban youth as they are sent into the country to work with the peasants, and reading only the works of Chairman Mao. The turning point in his life occurs when he returns to his home and finds and reads his father's hidden books. He states: "Over the following months, I stayed home and read almost everything that was in those bookcases. Most of the books were banned material, especially books by Western

authors like Victor Hugo, Charles Dickens and Jack London. Day after day, I buried myself in these books. For the first time I realized that there were many different kinds of people in the world—some good, some evil, some strong, some weak. Yet each one of us had to face our own destiny, pursue our own future" (p. 28).

In *Runaway Girl: The Artist Louise Bourgeois*, Jan Greenberg and Sandra Jordan develop the biography of a controversial painter and sculptor. The biography stresses how Bourgeois broke down barriers in the male-dominated art world and how she ran away from a past controlled by her father. The authors emphasize the contrasts in her life that influenced her art: love versus anger, loyalty versus betrayal. Photographs of her artwork illustrate how her art reflects these contrasting emotions. As opposed to a book written for younger readers, this biography provides harsher insights into why she felt alienated. The text includes a time line of important dates, from her birth in Paris in 1911 through 2003, when she received a commission for a large-scale project for the Tate Museum of Modern Art in London. In addition, the text includes "How to Look at a Sculpture," "Where to View Artworks by Louise Bourgeois," a glossary of art terms, and a bibliography of articles and books.

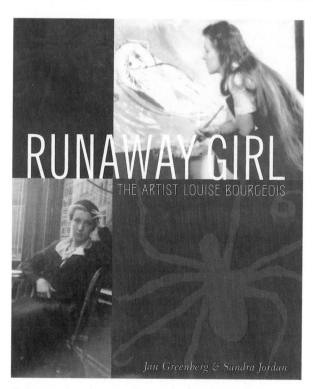

Cover from Runaway Girl: The Artist Louise Bourgeois by Jan Greenberg and Sandra Jordan. Text Copyright © 2003 by Jan Greenberg and Sandra Jordan. Images of Louise Bourgeois are © Louise Bourgeois. Published by Henry N. Adams, Inc. Used by permission.

As noted, these biographies for young adults develop more in-depth characterizations and conflicts than are found in biographies for younger readers. Biographies for younger readers frequently focus on the early years of a biographical character; in contrast, the biographies for young adults often focus on the teenage and adult years. They also may develop harsher person-against-society conflicts. Many develop themes and values that are important to the cultures and to the biographical characters.

Teaching With Biographies

 hildren often find biographies and other informational books more exciting than textbooks. The lively dialogues, the confrontations between people and ideas, and the joys and sorrows in many biographies are natural sources for creative dramatizations and discussions. Thus, you can use biographies to help children understand people of the past and present. Librarians and teachers indicate that biographies and other nonfiction texts are among the most used genres of literature when students are searching for sources for school reports. This use is reinforced in a report of literacy education in New York public schools (Herszenhorn & Saulny, 2005); these journalists quote teachers who state that increased literacy scores in fifth grade are related, in part, to a reading curriculum that specifies "a literacy genre to focus on each month, like autobiography or mystery, and weekly skills like making inferences" (p. 30). Biographies are excellent sources for this type of study.

Unit Plan: Using Biographies in Creative Dramatizations

The biographies of significant people of the past and present are filled with lively dialogue, confrontations, and the joys connected with discovery. Consequently, biographies provide many opportunities for children to dramatize the momentous experiences in people's lives. Children can create "You Are There" dramas based on scenes of historical significance. They also can create imaginary conversations between two people from the past or present or from different time periods who had some common traits but were never able to communicate because of time or distance. The following ideas are only samples of the creative dramatizations that can result from using biographies in the classroom.

Jean Fritz's stories of Revolutionary War heroes, with their humorous and human portrayals, are excellent sources for dramatizations. For example, you can read *Where Was Patrick Henry on the 29th of May?* and ask children how Patrick Henry acted and how they would act if they were Patrick Henry. Then read the story a second time, letting the children dramatize it.

There is another way to approach this dramatization: After the children listen to or read the book, have them identify and discuss scenes they would like to depict and then act out each one. Children have identified the following scenes in Patrick Henry's life as being of special interest:

1. Going fishing with a pole over his shoulder.
2. Going hunting for deer or opossum, with a rifle in his hands, accompanied by a dog at his heels.
3. Walking barefoot through the woods, and then lying down while listening to the rippling of a creek or the singing of birds and imitating their songs.
4. Listening to rain on the roof, his father's fox horn, and the music of flutes and fiddles.
5. Teaching himself to play the flute while he is recovering from a broken collarbone.
6. Listening to his Uncle Langloo Winston making speeches.
7. Waiting for the school day to end.
8. Playing practical jokes on his friends, including upsetting a canoe.
9. Trying without success to be a storekeeper.
10. Attempting to be a tobacco farmer.
11. Attending court and discovering that he likes to watch and listen to lawyers.
12. Beginning his law practice and not finding many clients.
13. Defending his first big case in court and winning.
14. Arguing against taxation without representation as a member of Virginia's House of Burgesses.
15. Delivering his "give me liberty or give me death" speech at St. John's Church.
16. Governing Virginia.
17. Hearing the news that the Continental army has defeated the English troops at Saratoga, New York.

18. Speaking against the enactment of the Constitution of the United States and for individual and states rights after the war is over.

19. Retiring on his estate in western Virginia.

These scenes can also be developed into a sequence game that involves careful observation by all players, who must interpret what someone else is doing and, according to directions written on their cue cards, stand and perform the next action at the correct time. (Players must be able to read to do this activity.) Prepare cue cards for scenes from Patrick Henry's life. The first cue card would look approximately like this:

Cue: Begin the game.

Pretend that you are a young, barefoot Patrick Henry happily going fishing with a pole over your shoulder.

When you are finished, sit down in your seat.

The second card would read:

Cue: Someone pretends to be a young Patrick Henry going fishing with a pole over his shoulder.

You are a young Patrick Henry happily going hunting for deer or opossum, with a rifle in your hands and accompanied by a dog running at your heels.

When you are finished, sit down in your seat.

Place the rest of the scenes, written in a similar manner, on cards. It is helpful if the cue and the directions for the dramatization are written in different colors. Mix the cards and distribute them randomly. There should be at least one cue card for each player, but you may add more scenes if a whole class is taking part in the activity. If there are fewer players, you can reduce the number of scenes or give each player more than one cue card. Ask the children to pay close attention and wait for each player to complete the dramatization.

It is helpful to have a master cue sheet with all of the cues in correct order so that you can help if someone misinterprets a scene, if the children seem uncertain, or if the group loses its direction. To involve as many children as possible, you may divide large groups into three small groups. Have each small group dramatize a set of identical cue cards independently. Let a child act as leader of each group and follow the master sheet.

Incidents in the lives of other Fritz heroes—described in *Why Don't You Get a Horse, Sam Adams?*, *The Great Little Madison*, *What's the Big Idea, Ben Franklin?*, and *Bully for You, Teddy Roosevelt!*—also make enjoyable dramas.

Following a drama using Fritz's *What's the Big Idea, Ben Franklin?* students could dramatize incidents from Candace Fleming's *Ben Franklin's Almanac: Being a True Account of the Good Gentleman's Life*. For example, "Traveling by His Wits" reports an incident in which Franklin got a seat by a crowded fireplace by asking the tavern keeper's son to "get my horse a quart of oysters" (p. 42). Following this request, the men around the fire hurried out to see a horse who ate oysters. Consequently, Franklin got his seat by the fire and also the oysters when the horse would not eat them. The almanac is filled with humorous, witty, and historical incidents that help students understand Franklin's personality and his role in American history. Additional examples include:

p. 5:   Franklin's experiences with a screechy tin whistle and what he learns from the incident.

p. 7:   Franklin's experience and lessons learned from building a wharf out of stones.

pp. 22–23: Franklin's experience that resulted in this belief: "If you would not be forgotten, as soon as you are dead and rotten, either write things worth the reading, or do things worth the writing" (Poor Richard's Almanac, 1738, p. 22).

p. 35:   Franklin's "Project Perfection."

p. 39:   Franklin's promotion of schools to give boys a formal education.

p. 41:   Franklin's first experiment.

pp. 60–62: Franklin's involvement with the Stamp Act.

pp. 58–77: Incidents in the "Revolutionary Memorabilia."

p. 94:   Responses to and reasons for Franklin's quote from his letter to George Whitefield, 1756: "Life, like a dramatic piece, should not only be conducted with regularity, but should finish handsomely. Being now in the last act, I begin to cast about for something fit to end with . . . I am very desirous of concluding on a bright point" (p. 94).

Reader Response: Developing Hypothetical Interviews With Authors

One reader response activity that is recommended for biographies, autobiographies, and other nonfictional literature is to have students develop hypothetical question-and-answer interviews between students and authors (Reissman, 1996). Reissman describes how she encourages sixth and seventh graders to read published interviews; to critically read, write, and interact with the issues and questions in the interview; and to develop their own imagined question-and-answer interviews with authors. She also asks her students to research the autobiographies and biographies of their favorite authors and to place quotations from the authors into the hypothetical interviews.

There are numerous sources for interviews that allow students to read, discuss, and respond to the format for published interviews. Students could begin with interviews with favorite authors of fictional or informational books that they are currently reading. For example, the following interviews use a question-and-answer format: Roxanne Feldman's interview with J. K. Rowling, the author of the "Harry Potter" books (1999); Kathleen T. Isaacs's interview with Gloria Whelan, the National Book Award–winning author of *Homeless Bird* (2001); Leonard Marcus's interviews with Bruce Brooks, Nicholasa Mohr, and Laurence Yep (2000); Marc Aronson's interview with the Grolier Award winner Michael Cart (2000); and Susan Faust's interview with Newbery Award winner Cynthia Kadohata (2005). All of these interviews are published in *School Library Journal* and are readily available in most libraries.

Ask the students to read the interviews critically and to respond to the questions and answers found in them. For example, they could respond to Gloria Whelan's answers about how she accomplished the research for *Homeless Bird* and her need to write daily. Quotes from Michael Cart (Aronson, 2000) such as "Nonfiction can educate the mind, fiction can educate the heart" (p. 56) foster numerous responses. After students have read and discussed these interviews, they should develop a list of effective questions that they would ask if they had the opportunity to conduct an interview.

Books such as *Popular Nonfiction Authors for Children: A Biographical and Thematic Guide* (Wyatt, Coggins, & Imber, 1998) provide numerous examples of authors of nonfictional literature as well as a two-page biographical sketch, a message from the biographical subject, and a selected bibliography of each author's works. These biographical sketches, messages to students, and lists of books could easily form the structure for the question-and-answer interviews. Another source for selecting potential interview characters is Sharron L. McElmeel's *100 Most Popular Children's Authors' Biographical Sketches and Bibliographies* (1999). A "Genre Index" identifies the authors with their type of writing. There is a listing for both biographies and nonfiction.

If desired, students can develop and conduct their interviews in pairs or in small groups. An interesting activity results if students prepare an interview that is similar to those found when political leaders or scientists come to college campuses. For example, the speaker usually makes a formal presentation that is followed by questions written on cards by the audience and asked by the moderator of the session. This type of activity involves many of the class members in researching to determine what the speaker might say, acting the part of the speaker, and interviewing the personage.

Imaginary Conversations Between People of Two Time Periods

Children enjoy contemplating what historical personalities might say to each other if they had the opportunity to meet. Because this is impossible except through imagination, children can be motivated to read biographies in order to enter into such conversations. For example, an exciting conversation could result if Theodore Roosevelt (Jean Fritz's *Bully for You, Teddy Roosevelt!*) met with a panel of loggers from the Northwest and with the administration in Washington, DC, as the group tries to develop policies about logging and the endangering of the owl (use newspaper, journal, or television reports).

Other historical biographical characters might have stimulating conversations if they could meet with world figures of the 2000s. What views would emerge if Patrick Henry could share his opinions on states' rights and the rights of individuals with the current president of the United States? What would be Amelia Earhart's or the Wright Brothers' response to space travel and exploration? What questions would they ask of a contemporary astronaut? What role would they want if they could be involved in the space program? When children read in order to role-play a character's actions, express a character's feelings, or state dialogue that a character might express, they interact with the character on a human level and often read until they feel empathy with that character and the historical time period.

Common Themes in Lives of Scientists and Inventors

One of the activities Tobie Brandriss (1999) used in a study of biographies is to search for common themes in the lives of the scientists. The following themes emerged: The scientists exhibited a total preoccupation with the problem; they were undaunted by lack of money because each found a way to obtain funds; they had confidence in their experimental abilities; they had conviction that there was a solution; they had an independence of mind; they believed in intuition; they understood the importance of observation; and women scientists emphasized the importance of their fathers in encouraging their studies. This activity would be equally interesting when investigating the lives of other biographical subjects such as artists or authors.

Biographies of scientists and inventors that students can use in their search include:

Don Brown's *Odd Boy Out: Young Albert Einstein*

Peter Busby's *First to Fly: How Wilbur & Orville Wright Invented the Airplane*

Marfé Ferguson Delano's *Genius: A Photobiography of Albert Einstein*

Joseph Bruchac and Thomas Locker's *Rachel Carson: Preserving a Sense of Wonder*

Richard Maurer's *The Wright Sister: Katharine Wright and Her Famous Brothers*

Peter Sís's *Starry Messenger: Galileo Galilei*

Peter Sís's *The Tree of Life: A Book Depicting the Life of Charles Darwin: Naturalist, Geologist & Thinker*

Developing Comprehension Through Time Lines of Biographical Characters

Time lines help students understand the sequence of events in a person's life as well as the conflicts that influenced the personage and the time period. For example, if studying World War II, you may use biographies such as Russell Freedman's *Franklin Delano Roosevelt* and *Eleanor Roosevelt: A Life of Discovery*. Here we use *Franklin Delano Roosevelt* as an example.

Introduce the time period for Franklin Delano Roosevelt, 1882–1945, and the historical significance of his life as president during the Depression and World War II. Ask the students questions such as "Why is it necessary that the setting, conflict, and plot is accurate? What might happen if these elements are not accurate?"

Ask the students to look briefly at the text and the photographs. Do they notice dates, happenings, and locations that can be verified? Do they think the book would be easy to verify? Make sure students understand that the historical background for this book covers two of the most dynamic occurrences in American life: the Depression and World War II. They should understand that information about these time periods and Roosevelt's actions during those periods is found in numerous nonfiction sources.

As students read this book, have them, individually or in groups, develop time lines of the most important occurrences in Roosevelt's life. Some teachers ask groups to draw time lines from the whole book, and other teachers ask students to draw time lines for specific chapters. The time line in Figure 11.1 was drawn by a group of seventh-grade students.

After the students draw the time lines, have them share these important historical happenings with the class. Ask them to state why they chose certain times and occurrences. Next, ask them to verify the accuracy of these dates and occurrences through library research. They can use sources such as history books, other biographies about Roosevelt, and newspaper and magazine stories from the time period. They might find it valuable to interview people who lived during this time period. A map could be available so that students can locate the important geographical settings in the book.

After students have completed this analysis of historical settings, conflict, and plot, ask them to evaluate Russell Freedman's ability to create an accurate biography that includes authentic information.

Analyzing Values and Beliefs

Biographies of African Americans can be used to help students identify and compare values, beliefs, and themes; identify the sources of conflict; and research the historical happenings and evaluate their accuracy. Chart 11.1 shows these literary elements found in two biographies of African Americans who lived during the time of slavery: Elizabeth Yates's *Amos Fortune, Free Man* and Jeri Ferris's *Go Free or Die: A Story About Harriet Tubman*. Students can discuss reasons for the similarities in the themes and values found in the two biographies and the types of conflicts the authors developed.

1882	Growing up	1896+	1900+	1913+	1933+	1941+	1945
Born: Hyde Park, New York	Spent time with adults, traveled to Europe eight times Hobbies: photography and stamps Sports: tennis and boating Summers at Campobello	Groton Boarding School: Learned about social responsibility Manager of baseball team	Harvard University: Major in history and government, minor in English and public speaking Editor of Harvard Crimson Columbia Law School Married Eleanor Roosevelt	Assistant Secretary of Navy Victim of polio Governor of New York during stock market crash and Depression	President of the United States: Fireside Chats New Deal CCC WPA Social Security	WWII: Signs declaration of war with Japan after Pearl Harbor War with Germany Meeting of the Big Three: Stalin, Churchill, and Roosevelt	Died: Warm Springs, Georgia

FIGURE 11.1   Time line of Franklin D. Roosevelt's life

CHART 11.1   Analyzing historical biography and autobiography

Literature	Evidence of Philosophy, Values, Beliefs, and Language	Sources of Conflict	Historical Happenings and Evaluations
Yates's *Amos Fortune, Free Man*	African story told by Amos is in the style of African storytellers, using repetition, chants, and audience participation. *Theme:* Freedom is important. *Values:* Work, family, retribution, generosity, love of nature.	Person against society, as Amos fights mistreatment, injustice, and separation. Person against self, as Amos considers consequences of his actions.	New Hampshire, 1725–1801. Blacks are taken from Africa and sold as slaves. The horrors of the slave block are avoided in the text, so acceptance of the situations may be too easy.
Ferris's *Go Free or Die: A Story of Harriet Tubman*	*Themes:* Freedom is worth risking one's life. We must help others obtain their freedom. *Values:* Obligations to family and people, wit, trickery when needed for balance, responsibility, and gratitude.	Person against society, as Harriet fights to free blacks and to combat injustice.	America, mid-1800s to the end of the Civil War. This story is based on facts related to slavery, the Underground Railroad, the 1850 Fugitive Slave Act, and the 1863 Emancipation Proclamation. Tubman freed more than 300 slaves in 10 years.

Motivating Additional Reading and Discussion

Biographies, especially those written about authors, can be used to encourage students to read and discuss the books written by the biographical subject. For example, Jane Yolen's *The Perfect Wizard: Hans Christian Andersen* provides information about Andersen's life and then lists a title of one of his fairy tales and a quote that reflects a similar theme and experience from Andersen's life. Students can search for similarities between Andersen's life experiences and the topics chosen for his stories. They can discuss how the fairy tales might correspond with Yolen's biography and compare the various editions of the tales. For example, students can read the following fairy tales discussed by Yolen, either in collections or in single volumes. (The stories are listed in the Children's Literature for Chapter 7, "Modern Fantasy.")

Collections by Hans Christian Andersen:

Little Mermaids and Ugly Ducklings: Favorite Fairy Tales of Hans Christian Andersen, illustrated by Gennady Spirin

The Stories of Hans Christian Andersen: A New Translation From the Danish, illustrated by Vilhelm Pedersen and Lorenz Frolich

Tales of Hans Christian Andersen, illustrated by Joel Stewart

Single Volumes by Hans Christian Andersen:

The Nightingale, illustrated by Jerry Pinkney

The Princess and the Pea, illustrated by Janet Stevens

Thumbelina, illustrated by Bryan Pinkney

Thumbelina, illustrated by Brad Sneed

Thumbelina, illustrated by Lisbeth Zweger

The Ugly Duckling, illustrated by Robert Ingpen

The Ugly Duckling, illustrated by Jerry Pinkney

The Emperor's New Clothes: A Tale Set in China, illustrated by Demi

Older students can gain considerable information about the tales by reading *Hans Christian Andersen: Fairy Tales*, translated by Tina Nunnally. This text contains 30 tales with notes about the tales. They also can consult Harold Bloom's (2004) *Bloom's Modern Critical Views: Hans Christian Andersen*, in which 12 writers examine Andersen's life and writing.

Another biography that is popular for this activity is Kathleen Krull's *The Boy on Fairfield Street: How Ted Geisel Grew Up to Become Dr. Seuss*. The author includes a list of the "Great Works Written and Illustrated by Dr. Seuss" and a Further Reading list, the Dr. Seuss books from which illustrations were used. Students can search through the various Dr. Seuss books to locate the drawings included in the biography. A list of these drawings is found at the end of Krull's book.

Developing Appreciation for the Lives and the Music of Biographical Characters

My university students frequently develop units that combine biography and music. For example, Ramona T. Pittman (2005) developed a unit around the works of African American musicians for grades six through eight. She focused on two biographies about Marian Anderson: Russell Freedman's *The Voice That Challenged a Nation: Marian Anderson and the Struggle for Equal Rights* and Pam Muñoz Ryan's *When Marian Sang* (a picture-book biography). She had students choose and read one of the texts, draw a graphic organizer to portray the characterization of Marian Anderson, and compare the characterizations developed in the two texts. The students created a collage showing the life of Marian Anderson in which they developed a common theme for her life. Working in groups, they used the texts to create a Reader's Theater presentation of her life. They wrote journal entries in which they responded to the social injustice reflected in the biographies.

The teacher used the "Selected Discography" in the Freedman text to locate recent Marian Anderson CDs. The class listened to and discussed the following CDs:

"Marian Anderson: Schubert and Schumann Lieder, 1945–1951" (RCA #63575, 2000)

"Softly Awakes My Heart: Arias, Songs, & Spirituals, 1928–1946" (ASV Living Era #5262, 1999)

"Marian Anderson: Rare and Unpublished Recordings, 1936–1952" (Video Arts Intl #1168, 1999)

"Marian Anderson Spirituals: He's Got the Whole World in His Hands, 1961–1964" (RCA #61960, 1994)

Students responded to both the texts and the CDs. They listened to Anderson's music while they wrote reader responses, created collages, and wrote poetry about Marian Anderson. A similar activity could accompany Elizabeth Partridge's *John Lennon: All I Want Is the Truth*, the 2006 Printz Honor Award for Young Adult Literature, for a British biography.

Motivating Discussions With Young Adult Readers

Teachers of young adult students can motivate both reading and discussions by using evaluation concerns cited by Ann W. Moore (2005). Her article includes the subtitle "A reviewer seeks books that inspire and instruct teen readers" (p. 38). Teachers can use Moore's evaluation and her discussions of biographies that do or do not meet her criteria. Students can read these books, compare the content, and discuss the qualifications of highly recommended biographies and the reasons why biographies may not be highly recommended.

1. Authors of biographies should not assume that readers have the necessary historical knowledge to understand the content. They should incorporate background information as part of the text so that readers understand the settings, the characterizations, and the issues and themes.

Meet the Criteria
Albert Marrin's *Old Hickory: Andrew Jackson and the American People* (Places historical information within the text without losing sight of the story.)

Do Not Meet the Criteria
Silvia Anne Sheafer's *Aimee Semple McPherson* (2004). (There is no background information on religion. Readers need information on basic Christian beliefs.)

2. Illustrations should never contradict the text. The illustrations should clarify such areas as personal appearance and dress, and should provide accurate information.

Meet the Criteria
Choose various illustrated biographies discussed earlier in this chapter.

Do Not Meet the Criteria
Elizabeth Silverthorne's *Joan of Arc* (2005). (Five illustrations show Joan with long hair after the text states that her hair was cut short.)

3. Terms in a biography should be clarified, especially if they have historical meanings that contemporary readers would not understand.

Meet the Criteria
James Cross Giblin's *Good Brother, Bad Brother: The Story of Edwin Booth & John Wilkes Booth* (The author clarifies the meanings of historical terms such as "simple," meaning "slow-witted.")

Do Not Meet the Criteria
Nick Fauchald's *William Lloyd Garrison: Abolitionist and Journalist* (2005). (The author does not clarify the meanings of archaic terms.)

4. The biography should have a balanced view of the personage as well as distinguish between supposition and fact.

Meet the Criteria
James Cross Giblin's *Good Brother, Bad Brother* (The author includes anecdotes and states that they may or may not be true.)

Do Not Meet the Criteria
Brenda Haugen's *Frederick Douglass: Slave, Writer, Abolitionist* (2005) (The author devotes 60 pages to Douglass's life, but only 24 pages to his years as an influential writer and abolitionist.)

5. The writing should be clear and inspiring. It should convey a vivid sense of the individual without merely listing events.

Meet the Criteria	Do Not Meet the Criteria
Russell Freedman's *The Voice That Challenged a Nation: Marian Anderson and the Struggle for Equal Rights* (The author writes a vivid biography and includes an evaluation of Anderson's life and influence.)	David Hilliam's *Thomas Becket: English Saint and Martyr* (2005). (The author overuses the passive voice, has an awkward writing style, and lists events without creating a sense of the individual.)

6. Biographies for young adults should include complete footnotes or source notes. Sloppy footnoting implies inadequate research and is a poor example for students.

Meet the Criteria	Do Not Meet the Criteria
Freedman's *The Voice That Challenged a Nation*. (Biography includes "Chapter Notes," "Selected Bibliography," "Selected Discography," "Acknowledgments and Picture Credits," and "Index.")	Nancy Whitelaw's *Queen Victoria and the British Empire* (2004). (Incorrect page numbers; quotes have incorrect dates, places, and events.)

The biographies listed under "Meet the Criteria" are all discussed in this chapter. Teachers and students can search for, highlight, and discuss the qualities that make these books outstanding. Those listed under "Do Not Meet the Criteria" are included in the References at the back of this text. As students read, compare, and discuss biographies, they may discover why Moore states that teachers and librarians should expand their horizons by "holding biographies to higher standards, and enthusiastically promoting good books about intriguing, noteworthy people" (p. 39). As they complete this activity, students should add their own examples to each of the categories and provide support for why they placed the biographies in those categories.

Suggested Activities

For more suggested activities for understanding biographies, visit the Companion Website at **CW** www.prenhall.com/norton

■ Select a well-known author who has written several biographies for older readers, such as Milton Meltzer, and another biographer who has written several biographies for younger children, such as Jean Fritz. What techniques does each author use to write a biography that appeals to a specific age group?

■ Listen to a recording of an adult biography, such as Walter Isaacson's *Benjamin Franklin: An American Life*, read by Boyd Gaines (2003); David McCullough's *Truman*, read by David McCullough (2003); or Geoffrey C. Ward, Dayton Duncan, and Ken Burns's *Mark Twain*, read by Bill Meisle (2001). What techniques do the authors and the readers use to make the biographical characters seem believable?

■ Search the listings of the books identified as "Teachers' Choices" in November issues of *The Reading Teacher*. Identify the books that are biographies and the reasons for selecting the books as "Teachers' Choices." What percentage of the books are biographies?

■ Read an autobiography of an author of children's literature. What information do you find that relates to his or her writing of the literature? For example, in *Surprised by Joy: The Shape of My Early Life*, C. S. Lewis (1955) identifies fantasies such as those by Beatrix Potter and E. Nesbit that influenced him. He also created and mapped "Animal-Land," which he stated was how he trained himself to be a novelist. How would these early experiences have influenced the author of "The Chronicles of Narnia"?

■ Select a biography in picture-book format, such as Don Brown's *Odd Boy Out: Young Albert Einstein* or Amy Ehrlich's *Rachel: The Story of Rachel Carson*. Study several of the illustrations, and list the biographical information that is shown through them.

■ Read an adult biography or autobiography and a children's biography about the same figure. Compare the two texts using the literary elements discussed in this text.

■ Respond to the reviews on the back cover of Marjane Satrapi's *Persepolis: The Story of a Childhood*, a biography that has appealed to both young adult and adult audiences. Why do you believe the *Philadelphia Inquirer* called it "cause for celebration . . . Superb" and the *Los Angeles Times* reviewed it as "one of the freshest and most original memoirs of our day. Satrapi's is a voice calling out to the rest of us, reminding us to embrace this child's fervent desire that human dignity reign supreme"? Why do you agree or disagree with the reviews?

Children's Literature

For full descriptions, including plot summaries and award winner notations, of these and other titles for teaching children with biographies, visit the CD-ROM that accompanies this book.

Adler, David A. *America's Champion Swimmer: Gertrude Ederle.* Illustrated by Terry Widener. Harcourt, 2000 (I:7–9 R:4).

———. *A Hero and the Holocaust: The Story of Janusz Korczak and His Children.* Illustrated by Bill Farnsworth. Holiday House, 2002 (I:8–12 R:5).

Adoff, Arnold. *Malcolm X.* Crowell, 1970 (I:7–12 R:5).

Aliki. *The King's Day: Louis XIV of France.* Crowell, 1989 (I:8+ R:6).

I = Interest by age range.
R = Readability by grade level.

Allen, Thomas B. *George Washington, Spymaster: How the Americans Outspied the British and Won the Revolutionary War.* Illustrated by Cheryl Harness. National Geographic, 2004 (I:8+ R:5).

Anderson, Peter. *Charles Eastman: Physician, Reformer, and Native American Leader.* Children's Press, 1992 (I:9+ R:5).

Anderson, William. *Pioneer Girl.* Illustrated by Dan Andreasen. HarperCollins, 1998 (I:7+ R:4).

Anholt, Laurence. *Stone Girl, Bone Girl: The Story of Mary Anning.* Illustrated by Sheila Moxley. Orchard, 1999 (I:all).

Ashby, Ruth, & Deborah Gore Ohrn, eds. *HerStory: Women Who Changed the World.* Viking, 1995 (I:9+ R:6).

Barasch, Lynne. *Knockin' on Wood.* Lee & Low, 2004 (I:5–8 R:4).

Binns, Tristan Boyer. *Winston Churchill.* Watts, 2005 (I:10+ R:5).

Bitton-Jackson, Livia. *I Have Lived a Thousand Years: Growing Up in the Holocaust.* Simon & Schuster, 1997 (I:12+ R:6).

Blumberg, Rhoda. *Commodore Perry in the Land of the Shogun.* Lothrop. Lee & Shepard, 1985 (I:10+ R:6).

_____. *York's Adventures With Lewis and Clark: An African-American's Part in the Great Expedition.* HarperCollins, 2004 (I:10+ R:5).

Bolden, Tonya. *Maritcha: A Nineteenth-Century American Girl.* Abrams, 2005 (I:9+ R:5).

Borden, Louise, & Mary Kay Kroeger. *Fly High! The Story of Bessie Coleman.* Illustrated by Teresa Flavin. Simon & Schuster, 2001 (I:8+).

Bradley, Kimberly Brubaker. *The President's Daughter.* Delacorte, 2004 (I:8–10 R:5).

Bray, Rosemary L. *Martin Luther King.* Illustrated by Malcah Zeldis. Greenwillow, 1995 (I:7–10 R:4).

Brenner, Barbara. *The Boy Who Loved to Draw: Benjamin West.* Illustrated by Olivier Dunrea. Houghton Mifflin, 1999 (I:all).

Brewster, Hugh. *Anastasia's Album.* Hyperion, 1996 (I:10+ R:6).

Bridges, Ruby. *Through My Eyes.* Scholastic, 1999 (I:all R:5).

Brighton, Catherine. *The Fossil Girl: Mary Anning's Dinosaur Discovery.* Millbrook, 1999 (I:7+).

Brooks, Polly Schoyer. *Queen Eleanor: Independent Spirit of the Medieval World.* Lippincott, 1983 (I:10+ R:8).

Brown, Don. *Across a Dark and Wild Sea.* Illustrated by Deborah Nadel. Roaring Brook, 2002 (I:7–10 R:5).

_____. *American Boy: The Adventures of Mark Twain.* Houghton Mifflin, 2003 (I:8+ R:5).

_____. *Odd Boy Out: Young Albert Einstein.* Houghton Mifflin, 2004 (I:6–8 R:4).

_____. *Uncommon Traveler: Mary Kingsley in Africa.* Houghton Mifflin, 2000 (I:4–8).

Bruchac, Joseph. *Jim Thorpe's Bright Path.* Illustrated by S. D. Nelson. Lee & Low, 2004 (I:6+ R:4).

_____. *Rachel Carson: Preserving a Sense of Wonder.* Illustrated by Thomas Locker. Fulcrum, 2004 (I:all R:4).

Busby, Peter. *First to Fly: How Wilbur & Orville Wright Invented the Airplane.* Illustrated by David Craig. Crown, 2003 (I:7–11 R:4).

Byrd, Robert. *Leonardo: Beautiful Dreamer.* Dutton, 2003 (I:9+ R:5).

Carpenter, Angelica Shirley, & Jean Shirley. *Frances Hodgson Burnett: Beyond the Secret Garden.* Lerner, 1990 (I:8+ R:5).

Christopher, Matt. *In the Huddle With . . . Steve Young.* Little, Brown, 1996 (I:9+ R:5).

Cleary, Beverly. *A Girl From Yamhill: A Memoir.* Morrow, 1988 (I:8+ R:5).

Cockcroft, James. *Diego Rivera.* Chelsea House, 1991 (I:10+ R:6).

Cohn, Amy L., & Suzy Schmidt. *Abraham Lincoln.* Illustrated by David A. Johnson. Scholastic, 2002 (I:5–9 R:4).

Cooney, Barbara. *Eleanor.* Viking, 1996 (I:5–9 R:4).

Cummins, Julie. *Tomboy of the Air: Daredevil Pilot Blanche Stuart Scott.* HarperCollins, 2001 (I:8–12 R:5).

Dalokay, Vedat. *Sister Shako and Kolo the Goat: Memories of My Childhood in Turkey.* Translated by Guner Ener. Lothrop, Lee & Shepard, 1994 (I:10+ R:5).

Dash, Joan. *The World at Her Fingertips: The Story of Helen Keller.* Scholastic, 2001 (I:10+ R:5).

D'Aulaire, Ingri, & Edgar Parin D'Aulaire. *Abraham Lincoln.* Doubleday, 1939, 1957 (I:8–11 R:5).

Davies, Jacqueline. *The Boy Who Drew Birds: A Story of John James Audubon.* Illustrated by Melissa Sweet. Houghton Mifflin, 2004 (I:5–9 R:5).

Davis, Jill, ed. *Open Your Eyes: Extraordinary Experiences in Faraway Places.* Viking, 2003 (I:8+ R:5).

Delano, Marfé Ferguson. *Genius: A Photobiography of Albert Einstein.* National Geographic, 2005 (I:10+ R:6).

Demi. *Mother Teresa.* McElderry, 2005 (I:all R:5).

_____. *Muhammad.* Simon & Schuster, 2003 (I:8+ R:5).

_____. *Columbus.* Doubleday, 1955 (I:7–10 R:5).

Denenberg, Barry. *An American Hero: The True Story of Charles A. Lindbergh.* Scholastic, 1996 (I:12+ R:8).

_____. *Shadow Life: A Portait of Anne Frank and Her Family.* Scholastic, 2005 (I:11–YA R:6).

dePaola, Tomie. *26 Fairmount Avenue.* Putnam, 1999 (I:6+ R:4).

Duggleby, John. *Artist in Overalls: The Life of Grant Wood.* Chronicle, 1995 (I:8+ R:8).

_____. *Story Painter: The Life of Jacob Lawrence.* Chronicle, 1998 (I:6–12 R:6).

Ehrlich, Amy. *Rachel: The Story of Rachel Carson.* Illustrated by Wendell Minor. Harcourt, 2003 (I:5–9 R:4).

Faber, Doris. *Calamity Jane: Her Life and Her Legend.* Houghton Mifflin, 1992 (I:8+ R:4).

Farris, Christine King. *My Brother Martin: A Sister Remembers Growing Up With the Rev. Dr. Martin Luther King Jr.* Illustrated by Chris Soentpiet. Simon & Schuster, 2003 (I:4–8 R:4).

Ferber, Elizabeth. *Yasir Arafat: A Life of War and Peace.* Millbrook, 1995 (I:12+ R:12).

Ferris, Jeri. *Go Free or Die: A Story About Harriet Tubman.* Carolrhoda, 1988 (I:7+ R:4).

Fisher, Leonard Everett. *Alexander Graham Bell.* Atheneum, 1999 (I:7–10 R:5).

Fleischman, Sid. *The Abracadabra Kid: A Writer's Life.* Greenwillow, 1996 (I:10+ R:6).

Fleming, Candace. *Ben Franklin's Almanac: Being a True Account of the Good Gentleman's Life.* Atheneum, 2003 (I:9+ R:5).

Foreman, Michael. *After the War Was Over.* Arcade, 1996 (I:all R:5).

_____. *War Boy: A Country Childhood.* Arcade, 1990 (I:all R:5).

Fradin, Dennis Brindell. *Hiawatha: Messenger of Peace.* Macmillan, 1992 (I:10+ R:5).

Fradin, Judith Bloom, & Dennis Brindell Fradin. *The Power of One: Daisy Bates and the Little Rock Nine.* Clarion, 2004 (I:10+ R:5).

Frank, Anne. *Anne Frank: The Diary of a Young Girl: The Definitive Edition.* Edited by Otto H. Frank & Mirjam Pressler. Translated by Susan Massotty. Doubleday, 1995 (I:12–YA R:6).

Freedman, Russell. *Confucius: The Golden Rule.* Illustrated by Frédéric Clément. Scholastic, 2002 (I:9+ R:5).

_____. *Eleanor Roosevelt: A Life of Discovery.* Clarion, 1993 (I:8+ R:5).

_____. *Franklin Delano Roosevelt.* Clarion, 1990 (I:8+ R:5).

_____. *Indian Chiefs.* Holiday House, 1987 (I:10+ R:6).

_____. *The Life and Death of Crazy Horse.* Photographs by Amos Bad Heart Bull. Holiday House, 1996 (I:10+ R:5).

_____. *Lincoln: A Photobiography.* Clarion, 1987 (I:8+ R:6).

_____. *Out of Darkness: The Story of Louis Braille.* Illustrated by Kate Kiesler. Clarion, 1997 (I:8+ R:5).

_____. *The Voice That Challenged a Nation: Marian Anderson and the Struggle for Equal Rights.* Clarion, 2004 (I:10+ R:6).

_____. *The Wright Brothers: How They Invented the Airplane.* Holiday House, 1991 (I:all R:5).

Fritz, Jean. *And Then What Happened, Paul Revere?* Illustrated by Margot Tomes. Putnam, 1996 (I:8+ R:5).

_____. *Bully for You, Teddy Roosevelt!* Illustrated by Mike Wimmer. Putnam, 1991 (I:8+ R:5).

_____. *The Double Life of Pocahontas.* Illustrated by Ed Young. Putnam, 1983 (I:8–10 R:7).

_____. *The Great Little Madison.* Putnam, 1989 (I:9+ R:6).

_____. *Make Way for Sam Houston.* Illustrated by Elise Primavera. Putnam, 1986 (I:9 R:6).

_____. *Stonewall.* Illustrated by Stephen Gammell. Putnam, 1979 (I:10+ R:6).

_____. *Traitor: The Case of Benedict Arnold.* Putnam, 1981 (I:8+ R:5).

_____. *What's the Big Idea, Ben Franklin?* Illustrated by Margot Tomes. Coward, McCann, 1978 (I:7–10 R:5).

_____. *Where Do You Think You're Going, Christopher Columbus?* Illustrated by Margot Tomes. Putnam, 1980 (I:7–12 R:5).

_____. *Where Was Patrick Henry on the 29th of May?* Illustrated by Margot Tomes. Coward, McCann, 1975 (I:7–10 R:5).

_____. *Why Don't You Get a Horse, Sam Adams?* Illustrated by Trina Schart Hyman. Coward, McCann, 1974 (I:7–10 R:5).

Gerstein, Mordicai. *The Man Who Walked Between the Towers.* Roaring Brook, 2003 (I:all R:4).

_____. *What Charlie Heard.* Farrar, Straus & Giroux, 2002 (I:all R:4).

Gherman, Beverly. *E. B. White: Some Writer!* Atheneum, 1992 (I:10+ R:5).

Giblin, James Cross. *Good Brother, Bad Brother: The Story of Edwin Booth & John Wilkes Booth.* Clarion, 2005 (I:10–YA R:7).

_____. *The Life and Death of Adolf Hitler.* Clarion, 2002 (I:14–YA R:7).

Gilliland, Judith Heide. *Steamboat! The Story of Captain Blanche Leathers.* Illustrated by Holly Meade. DK, 2000 (I:7+ R:4).

Giovanni, Nikki. *Rosa.* Illustrated by Brian Collier. Henry Holt, 2005 (I:all R:4).

Gold, Alison Leslie. *Memories of Anne Frank: Reflections of a Childhood Friend.* Scholastic, 1997 (I:8+ R:6).

Golenbock, Peter. *Hank Aaron: Brave in Every Way.* Illustrated by Paul Lee. Harcourt, 2001 (I:6–9 R:4).

Goodman, Joan Elizabeth. *A Long and Uncertain Journey: The 27,000-Mile Voyage of Vasco da Gama.* Illustrated by Tom McNeely. Mikaya, 2001 (I:10+ R:5).

Goodsell, Jane. *Eleanor Roosevelt.* Illustrated by Wendell Minor. Crowell, 1970 (I:7–10 R:2).

Greenberg, Jan. *Romare Bearden: Collage of Memories.* Abrams, 2003 (I:8–14 R:6).

_____, & Sandra Jordan. *Action Jackson.* Illustrated by Robert Andrew Parker. Roaring Brook, 2002 (I:8+ R:6).

_____. *Andy Warhol: Prince of Pop.* Delacorte, 2004 (I:12+ R:6).

_____. *Chuck Close, Up Close.* DK, 1998 (I:10+ R:5).

_____. *Runaway Girl: The Artist Louise Bourgeois.* Abrams, 2003 (I:12–YA).

Greenfield, Eloise. *Rosa Parks.* Illustrated by Eric Marglow. Crowell, 1973 (I:7–10 R:4).

_____, & Lessie Jones Little. *Childtimes: A Three-Generation Memoir.* Crowell, 1979 (I:10+ R:5).

Grimes, Nikki. *Talkin' About Bessie: The Story of Aviator Elizabeth Coleman.* Illustrated by E. B. Lewis. Orchard, 2002 (I:8+ R:4).

Gross, Ruth Belov. *True Stories About Abraham Lincoln.* Illustrated by Jill Kastner. Lothrop, Lee & Shepard, 1990 (I:7–10 R:4).

Hamilton, Virginia. *Anthony Burns: The Defeat and Triumph of a Fugitive Slave.* Knopf, 1988 (I:10+ R:6).

Harness, Cheryl. *Abe Lincoln Goes to Washington: 1837–1865.* National Geographic, 1997 (I:5–9 R:4).

_____. *Thomas Jefferson.* National Geographic, 2004 (I:8+ R:4).

Haskins, James. *I Have a Dream: The Life and Words of Martin Luther King, Jr.* Millbrook, 1993 (I:10+ R:6).

_____. *The Life and Death of Martin Luther King, Jr.* Beech Tree, 1992 (I:10+ R:7).

_____. *Spike Lee: By Any Means Necessary.* Walker, 1997 (I:12+ R:6).

_____. *Thurgood Marshall: A Life for Justice.* Holt, 1992 (I:10+ R:6).

Heiligman, Deborah. *High Hopes: A Photobiography of John F. Kennedy.* National Geographic, 2003 (I:8+ R:5).

Helms, Cynthia Newman. *Diego Rivera: A Retrospective.* Founders Society, Detroit Institute of Arts, 1986.

Holliday, Laurel. *Children of Israel, Children of Palestine: Our Own True Stories.* Pocket Books, 1998 (I:12+).

Hopkinson, Deborah. *Girl Wonder: A Baseball Story in Nine Innings.* Illustrated by Terry Widener. Atheneum, 2003 (I:5–9 R:4).

Hurwitz, Johanna. *Anne Frank: Life in Hiding.* Illustrated by Vera Rosenberry. Jewish Publication Society, 1988 (I:8–12 R:5).

Jakes, John. *Susanna of the Alamo.* Illustrated by Paul Bacon. Harcourt Brace, 1986 (I:7–12 R:6).

Jassem, Kate. *Sacajawea, Wilderness Guide.* Illustrated by Jan Palmer. Troll Associates, 1979 (I:6–9 R:2).

Johnson, Rebecca L. *Braving the Frozen Frontier: Women Working in Antarctica.* Lerner, 1997 (I:9+ R:6).

Johnston, Norma. *Louisa May: The World and Works of Louisa May Alcott.* Four Winds, 1991 (I:10+ R:6).

Josephson, Judith Pinkerton. *Mother Jones: Fierce Fighter for Workers' Rights.* Lerner, 1997 (I:10+ R:6).

Kent, Zachary. *Andrew Carnegie: Steel King and Friend to Libraries.* Enslow, 1999 (I:10+ R:6).

Kerley, Barbara. *The Dinosaurs of Waterhouse Hawkins.* Illustrated by Brian Selznick. Scholastic, 2002 (I:all R:5).

_____. *Walt Whitman: Words for America.* Illustrated by Brian Selznick. Scholastic, 2004 (I:all R:5).

Ketchum, Lisa. *Into a New Country: Eight Remarkable Women of the West.* Little, Brown, 2000 (I:10+ R:6).

Kherdian, David. *The Road From Home: The Story of an Armenian Girl.* Greenwillow, 1979 (I:12+ R:6).

King, Coretta Scott. *My Life With Martin Luther King, Jr.* Holt, 1993 (I:10+ R:5).

Koehn, Ilse. *Mischling, Second Degree: My Childhood in Nazi Germany.* Puffin, 1990 (I:10–YA R:6).

Kraft, Betsy Harvey. *Theodore Roosevelt: Champion of the American Spirit.* Clarion, 2003 (I:10+–YA R:6).

Krull, Kathleen. *The Boy on Fairfield Street: How Ted Geisel Grew Up to Become Dr. Seuss.* Random House, 2004 (I:all R:5).

_____. *Harvesting Hope: The Story of Cesar Chavez.* Illustrated by Yuyi Morales. Harcourt, 2003 (I:5–9 R:4).

_____. *Lives of the Musicians: Good Times, Bad Times (And What the Neighbors Thought).* Harcourt Brace, 1993 (I:9+ R:5).

_____. *Wilma Unlimited: How Wilma Rudolph Became the World's Fastest Woman.* Illustrated by David Diaz. Harcourt Brace, 1996 (I:8+ R:5).

Kunhardt, Edith. *Honest Abe.* Illustrated by Malcah Zeldis. Greenwillow, 1993 (I:5–8 R:4).

Lalicki, Tom. *Spellbinder: The Life of Harry Houdini.* Holiday House, 2000 (I:9+ R:5).

Lasky, Kathryn. *The Librarian Who Measured the Earth.* Illustrated by Kevin Hawkes. Little, Brown, 1994 (I:8+ R:6).

_____. *Vision of Beauty: The Story of Sarah Breedlove Walker.* Illustrated by Nneka Bennett. Candlewick, 2000 (I:8–10 R:6).

Lawlor, Laurie. *Shadow Catcher: The Life and Work of Edward S. Curtis.* Walker, 1994 (I:10+ R:7).

Leiner, Katherine. *First Children: Growing Up in the White House.* Illustrated by Katie Keller. Tambourine, 1996 (I:10+ R:9).

Lester, Helen. *Author: A True Story.* Houghton Mifflin, 1997 (I:all).

Levine, Ellen. *Anna Pavlova: Genius of the Dance.* Scholastic, 1995 (I:12+ R:9).

Lipman, Jean, and Margaret Aspinwall. *Alexander Calder and His Magical Mobiles.* Hudson Hills, 1981 (I:9+ R:6).

Lobel, Anita. *No Pretty Pictures: A Child of War.* Greenwillow, 1989 (I:10+ R:6).

Locker, Thomas. *John Muir: America's Naturalist.* Fulcrum, 2003 (I:all R:4).

Loyie, Larry. *As Long as the Rivers Flow.* Illustrated by Heather D. Holmlund. Douglas & McIntyre, 2003 (I:8–12 R:5).

Macy, Sue. *Winning Ways: A Photohistory of American Women in Sports.* Holt, 1996 (I:12+ R:7).

Malam, John. *Beatrix Potter.* Carolrhoda, 1998 (I:all R:4).

Marrin, Albert. *Commander In Chief: Abraham Lincoln and the Civil War.* Dutton, 1997 (I:10+ R:7).

_____. *George Washington and the Founding of a Nation.* Dutton, 2001 (I:10+ R:7).

_____. *Old Hickory: Andrew Jackson and the American People.* Dutton, 2004 (I:12–YA R:6).

_____. *Plains Warrior: Chief Quanah Parker and the Comanches.* Simon & Schuster, 1996 (I:10+ R:6).

_____. *Sitting Bull and His World.* Dutton, 2000 (I:10+ R:7).

_____. *Stalin: Russia's Man of Steel.* Viking, 1988 (I:10+ R:7).

Maurer, Richard. *The Wright Sister: Katharine Wright and Her Famous Brothers.* Roaring Brook, 2003 (I:10+ R:6).

McCully, Emily Arnold. *Squirrel and John Muir.* Farrar, Straus & Giroux, 2004 (I:6–9 R:4).

McKee, Tim. *No More Strangers Now: Young Voices From a New South Africa.* Photographs by Anne Blackshaw. DK, 1998 (I:10–YA R:6).

Meltzer, Milton. *Andrew Jackson and His America.* Watts, 1993 (I:10+ R:6).

_____. *Benjamin Franklin: The New American.* Franklin Watts, 1988 (I:10+ R:6).

_____. *Carl Sandburg: A Biography.* Millbrook, 1999 (I:10+ R:5).

_____. *Ten Queens: Portraits of Women to Power.* Illustrated by Bethanne Andersen. Dutton, 1998 (I:9+ R:5).

Meryman, Richard. *Andrew Wyeth.* Abrams, 1991 (I:10+ R:6).

Miller, Douglas. *Frederick Douglass and the Fight for Freedom.* Facts on File, 1988 (I:10+ R:6).

Morrison, Dorothy Nafus. *Chief Sarah: Sarah Winnemucca's Fight for Indian Rights.* Atheneum, 1980 (I:10+–YA R:6).

Murphy, Jim. *A Young Patriot: The American Revolution as Experienced by One Boy.* Clarion, 1996 (I:10+ R:6).

Myers, Elizabeth. *John D. Rockefeller: Boy Financier.* Bobbs-Merrill, 1973 (I:8+ R:5).

_____. *Thomas Paine: Common Sense Boy.* Bobbs-Merrill, 1976 (I:8+ R:5).

Myers, Walter Dean. *Malcolm X: By Any Means Necessary.* Scholastic, 1993 (I:10+ R:6).

Niven, Penelope. *Carl Sandburg: Adventures of a Poet.* Illustrated by Marc Nadel. Harcourt, 2003 (I:8–10 R:5).

Novac, Ana. *The Beautiful Days of My Youth: My Six Months in Auschwitz and Plaszow.* Translated by George L. Newman. Holt, 1997 (I:12+ R:6).

Partridge, Elizabeth. *John Lennon: All I Want Is the Truth.* Viking, 2005 (I:12–YA R:7).

_____. *This Land Was Made for You and Me: The Life and Songs of Woody Guthrie.* Viking, 2002 (I:all).

Pasachoff, Naomi. *Alexander Graham Bell: Making Connections.* Oxford University Press, 1996 (I:10+ R:6).

Patterson, Lillie. *Martin Luther King, Jr. and the Freedom Movement.* Facts on File, 1989 (I:10+ R:6).

Paulsen, Gary. *Woodsong.* Bradbury, 1990 (I:10+ R:6).

Peet, Bill. *Bill Peet: An Autobiography.* Houghton Mifflin, 1989 (I:all R:5).

Pinkney, Andrea Davis. *Ella Fitzgerald: The Tale of a Vocal Virtuosa.* Illustrated by Brian Pinkney. Hyperion, 2002 (I:all R:4).

Porter, A. P. *Jump at de Sun: The Story of Zora Neale Hurston.* Carolrhoda, 1992 (I:8+ R:5).

Porter, Pamela. *Sky.* Illustrated by Mary Jane Gerber. Douglas & McIntyre, 2004 (I:8–11 R:5).

Provensen, Alice, and Martin Provensen. *The Glorious Flight Across the Channel With Louis Bleriot, July 25, 1909.* Viking, 1983 (I:all R:4).

Ray, Deborah Kogan. *The Flower Hunter: William Bartram, America's First Naturalist.* Farrar, Straus & Giroux, 2004 (I:all R:5).

Rector, Anne Elizabeth. *Anne Elizabeth's Diary: A Young Artist's True Story.* Little, Brown, 2004 (I:9+ R:5).

Reiss, Johanna. *The Upstairs Room.* Crowell, 1972 (I:11 R:4).

Rembert, Winfred. *Don't Hold Me Back: My Life and Art.* Cricket, 2003 (I:10–YA R:6).

Ringgold, Faith. *My Dream of Martin Luther King.* Crown, 1995 (I:6–9 R:5).

Robinson, Sharon. *Promises to Keep: How Jackie Robinson Changed America.* Scholastic, 2004 (I:8+ R:4).

Roop, Peter, & Connie Roop, eds. *I, Columbus—My Journal 1492.* Illustrated by Peter Hanson. Walker, 1900 (I:all R:5).

Roosevelt, Elliott. *Eleanor Roosevelt, With Love.* Dutton, 1984 (I:10+ R:7).

Rubin, Susan Goldman. *Margaret Bourke-White: Her Pictures Were Her Life.* Photographs by Margaret Bourke-White. Abrams, 1999 (I:10+ R:5).

Rumford, James. *Sequoyah: The Man Who Gave His People Writing.* Houghton Mifflin, 2004 (I:all R:4).

Ryan, Pam Muñoz. *When Marian Sang.* Illustrated by Brian Selznick. Scholastic, 2002 (I:all R:5).

Sandburg, Carl. *Abe Lincoln Grows Up.* Illustrated by James Daugherty. Harcourt Brace, 1926, 1928, 1954 (I:10+ R:6).

———. *Abraham Lincoln: The Prairie Years.* Harcourt Brace, 1926 (I:12+ R:7).

Satrapi, Marjane. *Persepolis: The Story of a Childhood.* Pantheon, 2003 (I:14–YA).

Schwartz, Gary. *Rembrandt.* Abrams, 1992 (I:10+ R:6).

Severance, John B. *Einstein: Visionary Scientist.* Clarion, 1999 (I:10+ R:6).

———. *Gandhi, Great Soul.* Clarion, 1997 (I:10+ R:6).

Shange, Ntozake. *Ellington Was Not a Street.* Illustrated by Kadir Nelson. Simon & Schuster, 2004 (I:all R:4).

Sills, Leslie. *Visions: Stories About Women Artists.* Whitman, 1993 (I:8+ R:5).

Silverman, Erica. *Sholom's Treasure: How Sholom Aleichem Became a Writer.* Illustrated by Mordicai Gerstein. Farrar, Straus & Giroux, 2005 (I:all R:4).

Sís, Peter. *Follow the Dream.* Knopf, 1991 (I:5–9 R:4).

———. *Starry Messenger: Galileo Galilei.* Farrar, Straus & Giroux, 1996 (I:all).

———. *The Tree of Life: A Book Depicting the Life of Charles Darwin: Naturalist, Geologist & Thinker.* Farrar, Straus & Giroux, 2003 (I:9+ R:5).

Sofer, Barbara. *Shalom, Haver: Goodbye, Friend.* Kar-Ben, 1996 (I:7–9 R:5).

Stanley, Diane. *Leonardo da Vinci.* Morrow, 1996 (I:all R:5).

———. *Michelangelo.* HarperCollins, 2000 (I:all R:5).

———. *Peter the Great.* Four Winds, 1986 (I:8+ R:7).

———. *Saladin: Noble Prince of Islam.* HarperCollins, 2002 (I:9+ R:5).

———. *Good Queen Bess: The Story of Elizabeth I of England.* Four Winds, 1990 (I:7–10 R:5).

———. *Shaka: King of the Zulus.* Illustrated by Diane Stanley. Morrow, 1988 (I:8+ R:5).

———, & Peter Vennema. *Cleopatra.* Illustrated by Diane Stanley. Morrow, 1994 (I:all R:5).

Stanley, Fay. *The Last Princess: The Story of Princess Ka'iulani of Hawaii.* Illustrated by Diane Stanley. Four Winds, 1991 (I:7–10 R:6).

St. George, Judith. *To See With the Heart: The Life of Sitting Bull.* Putnam, 1996 (I:10+ R:6).

Swain, Gwenyth. *Little Crow (Taoyateduta): Leader of the Dakota.* Borealis, 2004 (I:10+ R:6).

Szabo, Corinne. *Sky Pioneer: A Photobiography of Amelia Earhart.* National Geographic, 1997 (I:8–12 R:5).

Troupe, Quincy. *Little Stevie Wonder.* Illustrated by Lisa Cohen. Houghton Mifflin, 2005 (I:5–9 R:4).

Turner, Ann. *Abe Lincoln Remembers.* Illustrated by Wendell Minor. HarperCollins, 2001 (I:6+ R:5).

Turner, Robyn Montana. *Portraits of Women Artists for Children: Frida Kahlo.* Little, Brown, 1993 (I:8+ R:5).

———. *Portraits of Women Artists for Children: Georgia O'Keeffe.* Little, Brown, 1991 (I:8+ R:5).

———. *Portraits of Women Artists for Children: Mary Cassatt.* Little, Brown, 1992 (I:8+ R:5).

———. *Portraits of Women Artists for Children: Rosa Bonheur.* Little, Brown, 1991 (I:8+ R:5).

Usher, M. D. *Wise Guy: The Life and Philosophy of Socrates.* Illustrated by William Bramhall. Farrar, Straus & Giroux, 2005 (I:all).

Van der Rol, Ruud, & Verhoeven Rian. *Anne Frank: Beyond the Diary.* Viking, 1993 (I:8+ R:4).

Wadsworth, Ginger. *Words West: Voices of Young Pioneers.* Clarion, 2003 (I:10+ R:5).

Warren, Andrea. *Escape From Saigon: How a Vietnam War Orphan Became an American Boy.* Farrar, Straus & Giroux, 2004 (I:10+ R:6).

Wells, Rosemary. *Mary on Horseback: Three Mountain Stories.* Dial, 1998 (I:6+ R:5).

———. *Streets of Gold.* Illustrated by Dan Andreasen. Dial Books, 1999 (I:6+ R:5).

Whitney, Sharon. *Eleanor Roosevelt.* Watts, 1982 (I:10+ R:5).

Winter, Jeanette. *Beatrix.* Farrar, Straus & Giroux, 2003 (I:6–9 R:5).

———. *Diego.* Scholastic, 1991 (I:8+ R:5).

———. *My Name Is Georgia.* Harcourt Brace, 1998 (I:5–9 R:4).

Winter, Jonah. *Frida.* Illustrated by Ana Juan. Scholastic, 2002 (I:all R:5).

———. *Roberto Clemente: Pride of the Pittsburgh Pirates.* Illustrated by Raúl Colón. Simon & Schuster, 2005 (I:7–10 R:4).

Yates, Elizabeth. *Amos Fortune, Free Man.* Illustrated by Nora S. Unwin. Dutton, 1950 (I:10+ R:6).

Yolen, Jane. *The Perfect Wizard: Hans Christian Andersen.* Illustrated by Dennis Nolan. Dutton, 2005 (I:all R:5).

Zhang, Ange. *Red Land, Yellow River: A Story From the Cultural Revolution.* Groundwood & Douglas McIntyre, 2004 (I:10–YA R:6).

INFORMATIONAL BOOKS

Illustration by the National Park Service from Volcanoes, *by Seymour Simon, 1988. William Morrow and Company, Inc.*

Chapter Outline

From History to How Things Work

- Values of Informational Books
- Evaluating Informational Books
- History and Culture
- Nature
- Discoveries and How Things Work
- Hobbies, Crafts, and How-To Books

Teaching With Informational Books

- Incorporating Literature Into the Science Curriculum

From History to How Things Work

Books about subjects such as history, space, animals, plants, geography, and how things work are among the most-used books in school and public libraries. These are the books that students use when writing reports and expanding their knowledge about subjects studied in the content areas. They are valued by children, teachers, parents, and librarians. This nonfiction, however, requires careful evaluation of the contents.

Values of Informational Books

"I am curious." "It is easier to find the answer from reading than it is to ask my teacher." "I want to learn to take better pictures." "I want to learn about a career I might enjoy." "I like reading the books." These are reasons children gave when I asked them why they read informational books. The range of answers also reflects the many values of informational books for children. Nonfiction books provide information about hobbies, experiments, the way things work, the characteristics of plants and animals, and many other phenomena.

Gaining knowledge is a good reason for reading informational books. Many recently published books contain information on timely subjects that children hear about on television or radio or read about in newspapers. For example, children excited by NASA's space explorations can consult Seymour Simon's *Jupiter* and *Saturn* for color photographs and information obtained during NASA's *Pioneer* and *Voyager* space explorations. Nic Bishop's *Digging for Bird-Dinosaurs: An Expedition to Madagascar* and Don Lessem's *Dinosaur Worlds* encourage children to expand their knowledge about dinosaurs and fossils and to learn about the work and discoveries of paleontologists. Joy Cowley's text and Nic Bishop's photographs help young children imagine the precarious life of the *Red-Eyed Tree Frog* in the rain forests of Costa Rica.

Informational books also provide opportunities for children to experience the excitement of new discoveries. For example, they can read Phillip Hoose's *The Race to Save the Lord God Bird* and discover the excitement developed by the discovery of a bird believed to be extinct. This book also has an important message about the need to preserve our natural heritage.

Another value of informational books is introduction to the scientific method. Through firsthand experience and reading about the work of scientists, children discover how scientists observe, compare, formulate and test hypotheses, and draw conclusions or withhold them until

Color photographs taken during actual space explorations clarify the content of an informational book. (From Jupiter, by Seymour Simon. Published by William Morrow & Company, Inc., 1985. Photograph courtesy of NASA.)

they uncover more evidence. Children also become familiar with the instruments used by scientists. As children learn about the scientific method, they gain appreciation for the attitudes of the people who use it. They discover the importance of careful observation over long periods of time, the need for gathering data from many sources, and the requirement that scientists, whatever the field, make no conclusions before all the data have been collected. Books such as *Guinea Pig Scientists: Bold Self-Experiments in Science and Medicine,* by Leslie Dendy and Mel Boring, include detailed methodologies of scientists who risked their own lives to find answers to medical problems such as the spread of yellow fever and the development of the first heart catheter. This book emphasizes the dedication of these scientists and how their discoveries changed the lives of people living today. Books such as Susan E. Goodman's *Stones, Bones, and Petroglyphs: Digging Into Southwest Archaeology* not only introduce the scientific method, but also motivate students to take part in field trips. Goodman's text and Michael J. Doolittle's photographs accompany a group of eighth graders as they go on a field trip to the Mesa Verde region in Colorado.

Informational books also encourage self-reliance: One enjoyable discovery can motivate children to make further investigations. Parents and educators need to provide books such as David Macaulay's *The Way Things Work* to pique children's interest and then help them explore their environment. A high school student who likes to read informational books emphasizes the satisfaction in following his curiosity into broader and deeper exploration:

I enjoy reading to answer my own curiosity. Fictional books don't have the information that I want. I am more interested

in real things. When I was in first grade, astronomy was the first science that interested me; the more I read, the more I learned I didn't know. As I became older I read a lot of books about the stars, space exploration, and theories about the black hole. I discovered that reality is stranger and more exciting than any fiction could be. I could not take fiction and transfer it into the real world; factual books help me learn about the real world.

Informational books can encourage children to develop critical reading and thinking skills. While reading books written on one subject by different authors, children can compare the books to evaluate the objectivity of the authors and determine their qualifications to write about the subject. They can check the copyright dates to see if the information is current.

Of course, informational books encourage children to stretch their minds. Chet Raymo (1992), a professor of physics and a science author, stresses:

Creative science depends crucially upon habits of mind that are most readily acquired by children: curiosity; voracious observation; sensitivity to rules and variations within the rules; and fantasy. Children's books that instill these habits of mind sustain science. (p. 561)

When children read Lola M. Schaefer's *Arrowhawk,* they may discover the perilous balance between animals, the environment, and humans and begin to think of ways in which their generation can conserve animals, plants, and other natural resources. Informational books also inform children about values, beliefs, lifestyles, and behaviors different from their own.

Many well-written informational books expand children's vocabularies by introducing new words, including technical terms. Meanings of technical terms are often enriched through photographs or detailed illustrations. For example, in *The Life and Times of the Apple,* Charles Micucci develops the concept of grafting by presenting a series of illustrations that show how a cleft graft joins a scion to a rootstock. Detailed, labeled illustrations show each step in the grafting process.

Books that include well-defined vocabulary help students improve their reading skills and discover the importance of reading for meaning. They learn that authors frequently provide context clues that help them understand the content. For example, in *Outside and Inside Killer Bees,* Sandra Markle defines scientific terms within the text. Notice in the following example how she defines *larva* and *pupa:*

These are honeybee eggs and larvae (shown in photograph). Like all bees, killer bees go through three stages as they develop: egg; larva, the stage that needs to be fed; and pupa, the stage that changes into an adult. (You will see the pupa on page 28.) The terms egg, larva, and pupa are also printed in red. Words printed in red are further defined and the locations in which they are discussed are listed in the "Glossary/Index."

Remember that one of the greatest values in informational books is *enjoyment,* which is often the primary reason children read informational literature. In addition, books such as Sue Macy's *Winning Ways: A Photohistory of American Women in Sports* or Steve Jenkins's *The Top of the World: Climbing Mount Everest* may inspire the next generation of climbers and adventurers.

Evaluating Informational Books

Several science associations concerned with the education of elementary school children provide valuable guidelines for selecting informational books for children. These guidelines are specifically tailored to science books but are equally valid for all types of informational books. The guidelines in the Evaluation Criteria box on this page are taken from recommendations made by the National Science Teachers Association (1997) and the American Association for the Advancement of Science (Johnston, 1991).

In addition to these criteria, Raymo (1992) emphasizes that good science books should develop "an attitude toward the world—curious, skeptical, undogmatic, forward-looking" (p. 562). Raymo recommends books that convey an "extraordinary adventure story of how the information was obtained, why we understand it to be true, or how it might embellish the landscape of the mind" (p. 561).

Accuracy

Does the author have the scientific qualifications to write a book on the particular subject? Phillip Hoose, the author of *The Race to Save the Lord God Bird*, is a graduate of Yale School of Forestry and Environmental Sciences and is on the staff of the Nature Conservancy. The stature of the scientists who have praised his book also reflects respect for his work. For example, Paul R. Ehrlich, president of the Center for Conservation Biology at Stanford University, refers to the book as "groundbreaking." Other critical evaluations come from the past president of the American Society of Naturalists and the author of *The Sibley Guide to Birds*. The review journal of the Cooperative Children's Book Center of the University of Wisconsin (*CCBC Choices*, 2005) states that

> Hoose blends environmental, social, and political history in a compelling narrative that traces the multiple factors that contributed to the demise of this grand species, and he shows

how scientists and conservationists were in a race against time as events hurled toward a tragic and seemingly inevitable conclusion. At the same time, he chronicles the many positive efforts that sprung from the growing awareness of the Ivory-bill's extinction, among them national conservation efforts like the Audubon Society. (p. 15)

Sylvia A. Earle, the author of *Hello, Fish!: Visiting the Coral Reef*, is a marine biologist and was the National Geographic Society's explorer-in-residence for 1998 and 1999. Mark A. Norell and Lowell Dingus, authors of *A Nest of Dinosaurs: The Story of Oviraptor*, are both scientists with the American Museum of Natural History and have led expeditions in the Gobi Desert in search of dinosaur fossils. Many books, however, provide little or no helpful information by which to evaluate the qualifications of the author.

Are facts and theory clearly distinguished? Children should know if something is a fact or if it is a theory that has not been substantiated. For example, in Jim Murphy's *An American Plague: The True and Terrifying Story of the Yellow Fever Epidemic of 1793*, the author includes the chapter "A Modern-Day Time Bomb," in which he presents current information about yellow fever with terms such as "we know" and "research shows us." He also emphasizes that despite years of research, "there is still no cure for yellow fever." Notice in the following paragraph how Murphy separates what is known from theories that may lead to cures for yellow fever:

> We know, too, that the antimosquito breeding campaigns in Cuba and Panama were very effective in halting the infections and that massive insecticide campaigns can control the populations of Aedes aegypti. Prompt warning and fast (if unpleasant) action have kept yellow fever and related diseases in check over recent decades as well, and the same will be true in the future. Meanwhile, dedicated scientists develop theories and test them, hoping to discover a safe and effective cure. (p. 139)

One of the chapters in *Bones Rock! Everything You Need to Know to Be a Paleontologist*, by Peter Larson and Kristin Donnan, is "Developing and Testing a Theory: The Scientific Guessing Game." The chapter begins with the question "Are dinosaurs the direct ancestors of birds?" This question is followed by "The Observations" and then discussions of various hypothetical answers, such as "Hypothesis #1: Birds descended from dinosaurs," "Hypothesis #2: Birds did not descend from dinosaurs, but instead from some other, unknown animal," and "Hypothesis #3—The Sequel: Birds did too descend from dinosaurs." This discussion is followed by "More Evidence," "The Theory," and "Possible Conclusions."

Are significant facts provided? Authors should present enough significant facts to make the text accurate. Specialized books that give complete histories of certain animals are valuable because they help children understand the evolution of a species, as well as its characteristics and its needs, if any, for protection. To acquire a balanced viewpoint on some topics, readers may require a book with a different focus for comparison. For example, Sneed B.

Evaluation Criteria

Literary Criticism: Informational Books

1. All facts should be accurate.
2. Stereotypes should be eliminated.
3. Illustrations should clarify the text.
4. Analytical thinking should be encouraged.
5. The organization should aid understanding.
6. The style should stimulate interest.

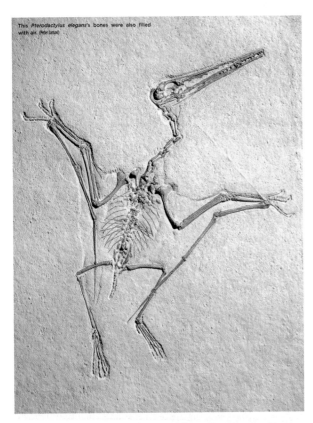

Illustration from Bones Rock!: Everything You Need to Know to Be a Paleontologist *by Peter Larson and Kristin Donnan. Copyright © 2004 by Peter Larson and Kristin Donnan. Published by Invisible Cities Press. Used by permission.*

Collard's *Animal Dads* could be used to show that not only the mother protects, feeds, and teaches the young. Texts giving historical information should also provide enough facts for readers to understand the concepts. For example, in *Smoke and Ashes: The Story of the Holocaust*, Barbara Rogasky traces the roots of anti-Semitism before presenting the World War II experiences.

Are differing views on controversial subjects presented? Subjects such as ecology and nuclear energy are controversial. A biased author should identify that his or her personal point of view is not necessarily a universally held position.

History texts should present both sides of controversial issues. For example, Natalie Bober uses an interesting technique in *Countdown to Independence: A Revolution of Ideas in England and Her American Colonies: 1760–1776:* She provides alternating viewpoints and actions. Reproductions of documents and portraits add to the depiction of differing views.

Authors who write about sports frequently address both heroic subjects and controversies that may mar reputations. For example, several chapters in *Swifter, Higher, Stronger: A Photographic History of the Summer Olympics*, by Sue Macy, highlight the accomplishments of the athletes. However, in the chapter "Controversies Cast a Shadow," Macy says,

Although the Olympic Games often bring out the best in the world's athletes, they also have given rise to a whole host of controversies. Issues from conflicts over amateur status to gender testing, from drug use to political boycotts and confrontations have cast a shadow over the Games as a joyous celebration of athletic achievement. The opportunities for scandal and wrongdoing have increased as the Games have grown to massive proportions. It is inevitable that these negative influences, too, would shape the history of the Summer Olympics. (p. 47)

The author includes such controversies as resulted when a 1976 German swimming team was found to have taken steroids or when a water polo match was called in 1954 because of excessive violence. Macy also discusses the influence of political tensions such as the discrimination against Jews and other minorities during the Winter and Summer Games in Germany in 1936.

Is the information presented without relying on anthropomorphism? Although it is perfectly acceptable for authors of fantasy to write about animals that think, talk, act, and dress like people, authors of informational books should not ascribe human thoughts, motives, or emotions to animals or to plants and other nonhuman things (a practice called *anthropomorphism*). Writers of animal information books should describe the animals in terms that can be substantiated through careful observation. For example, in *The Snake Scientist*, Sy Montgomery describes information discovered about snakes at the Narcisse Wildlife Area in Manitoba, Canada. Notice in the following quote how the author relies on observations to answer questions about snakes:

Bob felt sure the males were searching for some clue to tell them which snake was the female. Bob checked off the information the snake could glean from its senses. Could the male snakes see which one was female? No—from the top and sides, males and females look similar (though the females are usually bigger). Could they tell by their sense of touch? That was unlikely, too. Males and females feel alike when you touch them: smoother than satin, softer than silk. How about hearing? Snakes can't talk to one another, and if they could, they couldn't hear what the others were saying—they don't have ears. Most researchers believe that snakes don't have the sense of taste as we know it, either. So that left only the sense of smell—a sense that is highly developed in snakes. (pp. 26–27)

Is the information as up to date as possible? Because knowledge in some areas is changing rapidly, copyright dates are very important for certain types of informational books. For example, the copyright date is very important in books about space, such as Gloria Skurzynski's *Are We Alone? Scientists Search for Life in Space.*

Attitudes and values also change. Comparing older factual books with more recent ones is one way to illustrate how attitudes and biases change. No educator or publisher today would condone the untrue and highly offensive descriptions of Native Americans presented in *Carpenter's Geographical Reader, North America* published by Frank G. Carpenter in 1898. For example, the following is Carpenter's depiction of the historical background of Native Americans:

> The savage Indians were in former times dangerous and cruel foes. They took delight in killing women and children. They hid behind rocks and bushes to fight. . . . They used tomahawks to brain their victims, and delighted in torturing their captives and in burning them at the stake. (p. 293)

Information about Australian native people is just as biased in Charles Redway Dryer's *Geography, Physical, Economic, and Regional,* published in 1911, and V. M. Hillyer's 1929 text, *A Child's Geography of the World,* says that the most curious animals in Africa are the people. Students of children's literature may not realize how outdated, misinformed, and biased informational books can be until they discover books such as these that influenced the thinking of schoolchildren early in the 20th century.

STEREOTYPES

Does the book respect basic principles against racism and sexism? As the preceding examples make clear, informational books, like all books, should be without demeaning racist or sexist stereotypes.

Some contemporary books reflect stereotypes through inclusion or exclusion of certain types of people in certain professions. For example, are both men and women and various racial and ethnic groups shown in illustrations of science or science professions? The illustrations in Joanna Cole's *The Magic School Bus: On the Ocean Floor* show that both boys and girls are interested in scientific subjects, and those in Donna M. Jackson's *The Bone Detectives: How Forensic Anthropologists Solve Crimes and Uncover Mysteries of the Dead* show that both boys and girls are interested in the subject. In addition, the text includes photographs of both male and female scientists. Informational books such as Nancy Loewen and Ann Bancroft's *Four to the Pole!: The American Women's Expedition to Antarctica, 1992–93* show that women can succeed in very dangerous endeavours and environments.

ILLUSTRATIONS

Are the illustrations accurate? Illustrations should be as accurate as the text and should add to its clarity. Photographs and drawings should be accompanied by explanatory legends keyed directly to the text to allow children to expand their understanding of the principles or terminology presented. Literary critic Barbara Elleman (1992) emphasizes the importance of illustrations when evaluating trends in nonfiction. She states, "When done well, today's visuals are directly connected to the text, are made up of either meticulous, accurately produced drawings or clear, full-color photographs, and have captions that extend the information" (p. 30). David Macaulay's detailed illustrations in *The Way Things Work* are labeled to clarify concepts. *The Incredible Journey of Lewis and Clark,* by Rhoda Blumberg, includes maps showing both the journey west and the return journey

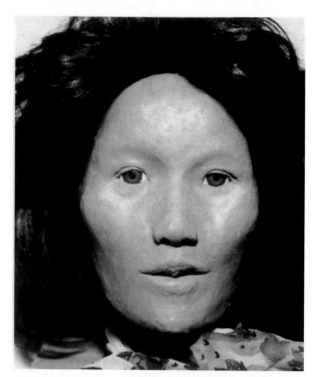

Children discover the importance of careful observation and research in Donna M. Jackson's The Bone Detectives: How Forensic Anthropologists Solve Crimes and Uncover Mysteries of the Dead. *(From* The Bone Detectives: How Forensic Anthropologists Solve Crimes and Uncover Mysteries of the Dead, *by Donna M. Jackson, photographs by Charlie Fellenbaum, copyright © 1996. Photo courtesy of the Missouri State Highway Patrol.)*

east. Important locations are numbered and keyed to dates and pages of discussion within the text. *Money, Money, Money: The Meaning of the Art and Symbols on United States Paper Currency,* by Nancy Winslow Parker, includes detailed, labeled illustrations showing the symbols on the front and back of United States currency from $1 to $100,000. In *A Drop of Blood,* Paul Showers uses diagrams and close-up photographs of subjects as seen under a microscope to present science concepts related to the role of blood in the human body. The monsters shown in some of the illustrations add a lighter tone that appeals to younger readers.

Analytical Thinking

Do children have an opportunity to become involved in solving problems logically? Many informational books, particularly scientific ones, should encourage children to observe, gather data, experiment, compare, and formulate hypotheses. Informational books should encourage children to withhold judgment until enough data have been gathered or enough facts have been explored. Books that demonstrate scientific facts and principles should encourage children to do more experiments on their own and should stress the value of additional background reading.

For example, in *How to Be an Ocean Scientist in Your Own Home*, by Seymour Simon, a series of experiments proceeds from "Let's Find Out" to "Here's What You Will Need" to "Here's What to Do." In addition, Simon includes a bibliography of books about the topics.

Good science writing should also encourage children to become involved with their world. Science writer Patricia Lauber (1992) states that the best science books, like any other literature, "have a point of view. They involve readers by making them care—care about the people, the animals, a town, an idea, and most of all, care how it all comes out. In short, they inspire feeling" (p. 13). This point of view is important when Lauber describes her own aims in writing science books: "Overall, my aims are to help children understand how the earth (or its parts) works and to try to imbue them with some of my own sense of wonderment, in the hope that they will grow up to be good stewards, who will take care of the earth, not just use (or abuse) it" (p. 14). As children read some of Lauber's books, such as *Volcano: The Eruption and Healing of Mount St. Helens*, *Flood: Wrestling With the Mississippi*, and *Hurricanes: Earth's Mightiest Storms*, decide if Lauber is able to involve her readers by making them care about the earth.

Excellent science-related books should encourage students to understand that scientists conduct research studies that support or reject their theories. Donna M. Jackson's *In Your Face: The Facts About Your Features* includes sufficient references to research studies to show readers the importance of such studies. The studies cited also show that scientific research can reach contradictory conclusions. Readers can also become part of the observational and research process, as shown by Joe Rhatigan and Rain Newcomb in *Out-of-This-World Astronomy: 50 Amazing Activities & Projects*. The authors provide suggestions for developing a "Stargazer's Notebook," "What you need," "What you do," and Why take notes." They then describe a series of projects that readers can accomplish. The text also separates facts and theories. For example, one section lists "Solar System Stats and Facts." This section is followed by "How the Solar System Formed: A Theory" (p. 71).

Organization

Is the organization logical? Ideas in informational books should be broken down into easily understood components. Authors often use an organization that progresses from the simple to the more complex, from the familiar to the unfamiliar, or from early to later development. In Stephen R. Swinburne's *Once a Wolf: How Wildlife Biologists Fought to Bring Back the Gray Wolf*, the organization progresses from early attitudes to more contemporary ones. The author begins with a history of hatred toward wolves and their depiction as an enemy and a symbol of savagery that goes back as early as 5000 B.C. Swinburne brings the conflict to America by describing how ranchers

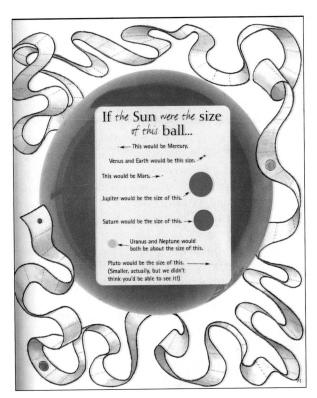

Illustration from Out-of-This World Astronomy: 50 Amazing Activities & Projects, *by Joe Rhatigan and Rain Newcomb. Copyright © 2003 by Lark Books. Reprinted with permission of Sterling Publishing Co., Inc., New York, NY.*

massacred the animals. He progresses to changing attitudes expressed by early conservationists and finally to the conservation movement that is bringing the gray wolf back to areas such as Yellowstone National Park.

Are organizational aids included? Reference aids such as a table of contents, an index, a glossary, a bibliography, and a list of suggested readings can encourage children to use organized reference skills. Although very young children do not need all of these aids, older children find them helpful. For example, in *Commodore Perry in the Land of the Shogun*, Rhoda Blumberg includes a table of contents, notes, information about the illustrations, a bibliography, an index, and five appendixes of additional information about the time period. Blumberg uses a similar approach in *What's the Deal? Jefferson, Napoleon, and the Louisiana Purchase*.

The organization, including the illustrations, should clarify the text. In *Empire State Building: When New York Reached for the Skies*, Elizabeth Mann uses black-and-white photographs to depict the sequence in the construction process of the 86-story building. Labeled, full-page color illustrations explain concepts, and a gatefold provides a sense of the height of the building.

Patricia Lauber uses diagrams, maps, and information boxes that clarify concepts such as carbon-14 dating in *Who Came First? New Clues to Prehistoric Americans*. A time line increases interest and comprehension for this complex subject. In *Vote*, Eileen Christelow also uses a time line of voting rights, starting with 1776, that extends to the Help America Act in 2002.

Style

Is the writing style lively and not too difficult for children of a certain age to understand? Kathryn Lasky's *Sugaring Time* is an excellent example of both stimulating literary style and careful documentation. For example, Lasky describes corn snow, large and granular snow crystals, as follows: "When Jonathan skis it sounds as if he is skimming across the thick frosting of a wedding cake" (p. 7). The maple sap "runs like streams of Christmas tinsel" (p. 19). The environment in the sugarhouse is "like sitting in a maple cloud surrounded by the muffled roar of the fire and the bubbling tumble of boiling sap" (p. 34). The photographs reinforce the language, following the family during all aspects of collecting and processing maple syrup.

Comparisons can help clarify complex ideas or startling facts. For example, in *Shadows of the Night: The Hidden World of the Little Brown Bat*, Barbara Bash compares the weight of a young bat with that of a pencil and pro-

vides diagrams that compare the structures of human hands and the wings of a bat.

Challenging questions and understandable analogies bring readers into the world of paleontology in Peter Larson and Kristin Donnan's *Bones Rock! Everything You Need to Know to Be a Paleontologist*. The time-consuming work of a paleontologist is emphasized when the authors report that it takes 25,000 hours to clean a T Rex skeleton. The text includes a teacher's guide, color photographs, diagrams, and drawings.

Children's publisher and author of nonfiction James Cross Giblin (1992) emphasizes the importance of style when writing nonfiction and also presents some of the similarities and differences between writing nonfiction and fiction:

> A nonfiction author is telling a story the same as any other author. The only difference is that it's a true story. So there's nothing wrong with using fictional techniques of scene setting and atmosphere building to make factual materials more interesting and involving for the reader. . . . A cautionary note: fictional techniques should never be confused by authors, editors, or book selectors with a distortion of the facts. Anthropomorphizing animals in natural history should be

An In-Depth Analysis of an Informational Book

Life: Our Century in Pictures for Young People, edited by Richard B. Stolley, has been identified by *Publishers Weekly* as one of the best books published in 2000. Let us consider why the book might be so designated and how it meets the evaluation criteria for informational books.

First, the book is a large, glossy text using labeled photographs that have appeared in *Life* magazine. This format is one that is very appealing to readers of all ages.

Second, the format aids understanding and helps readers clarify the major occurrences in each of nine important time periods of the last century. The text uses a chronological order beginning in 1900 and progressing to 1999. Within each time period, the text follows a similar format: An introduction by a children's author, numerous labeled photographs, a turning point incident, and a requiem. For example, the section "1900–1913: Across the Threshold" begins with an essay by Katherine Paterson titled "The Dawn of the American Century"; includes 13 pages of descriptive text with labeled photographs, such as Teddy Roosevelt and his family, the receiving of the first Morse code message by Marconi, and the first flight of Orville Wright; features the turning point incident of the sinking of the *Titanic*; and concludes with a requiem section that includes labeled photographs and descriptions of Harriet Tubman, Geronimo, Florence Nightingale, Susan B. Anthony, and Mark Twain.

Third, the text continues in chronological order with the same inner format through the following historical periods: "1914–1919: The War to End All Wars," "1920–1929: All That

Glitters," "1930–1939: Empty Pockets," "1940–1945: World on Fire," "1946–1963: Spreading the Wealth," "1976–1992: A Global Burst of Freedom," and "1993–1999: Our Future.Com."

Fourth, the writing styles of the various children's authors provide a lively introduction to the period and also challenge and stimulate readers' interests. For example, notice how Gary Paulsen stimulates interest and even debate in his essay "Liberty for All" that introduces the 1976–1992 time period: "It can of course be argued that there have been many outbursts of liberty in our history. Certainly America's declaration in 1776 that it would be independent from England. . . . And yet . . . there was something about the period between 1976 and 1992 that sets it apart, or perhaps more accurately, several things that make it a unique time in history. When viewed from a whole world perspective, this was the most volatile period since World War II" (p. 186). Paulsen then presents his reasons for his belief. These various essays lend themselves to discussions and additional research.

Fifth, the author of an informational book should have the expertise to write about the subject. Richard B. Stolley, the editor of the book, is also senior editorial adviser of Time Inc. Previously, he was a staff member for *Life* magazine for 19 years. His expertise is visible in the editing of the book.

Finally, the text should be a useful companion to historical fiction units, biographical studies, and historical investigations. This text is extremely useful for authenticating literature that is written from one of the historical perspectives developed in the book.

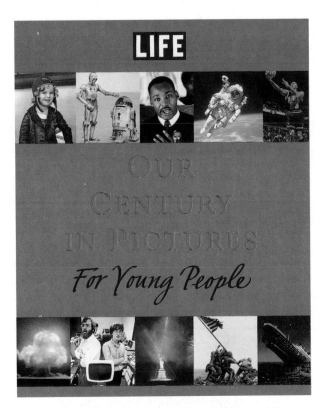

Photographs from Life *magazine provide a vivid history. (Cover from* Our Century in Pictures for Young People, *edited by Richard B. Stolley. Copyright © 2000 by Little, Brown and Company. Reprinted by permission of the publisher.)*

avoided at all costs, and invented dialogue should never be put into the mouths of the figures in biographies; anachronisms and inaccuracies of any type do not belong in nonfiction books. (p. 20)

Authors of credible informational books meet many of these guidelines. Consider in the following sections how authors develop credible books that can stimulate and inform readers.

History and Culture

Informational books about history and culture include books about ancient civilizations as well as more recent ones. The illustrations and photographs in many of the books help children visualize the past.

The Ancient World

Books on archaeology help readers understand the magnitude of history and develop an awareness of how archaeologists help uncover the past. In Kate Duke's *Archaeologists Dig for Clues*, a highly illustrated book for younger readers, an archaeologist explains the science of archaeology to three children who accompany her on a dig. Lively dialogue, realistic questions, and descriptions of the Archaic Era of 6,000 years ago are discussed through such findings as stone knives. Sidebars add information about the content. In *Stone Age Farmers Beside the*

Sea: Scotland's Prehistoric Village of Skara Brae, Caroline Arnold focuses on the work of archaeologists to uncover and preserve a prehistoric village inhabited from 3100 to 2500 B.C. Colored photographs, maps, and diagrams add to an understanding of the time period.

The discovery of an ancient world even older than described in these previous books is explored in Patricia Lauber's *Painters of the Caves.* Lauber begins with the discovery of Chauvet in southeastern France, a cave that holds paintings of Stone Age animals that lived about 32,000 years ago. Lauber accompanies her descriptions of the Ice Age and Stone Age artists with labeled photographs showing the paintings discovered in the caves. The author includes a map of Europe that shows the locations of the caves, a discussion about how scientists date ancient artifacts, a bibliography of related reading, and an index.

John S. Major's *The Silk Route: 7,000 Miles of History* follows the silk route from Chang'an, China, to Byzantium during the Tang Dynasty (A.D. 618–906). A map introduces the text. The remainder of the text and the illustrations focus on the major cities, geography, and obstacles along the route. Stephen Fieser's large, colored illustrations show people, culture, and settings. The book

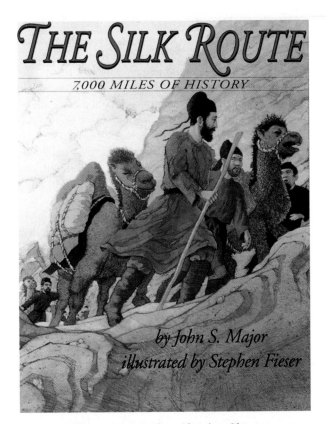

Illustrations focus on the route from Chang'an, China, to Byzantium. (From The Silk Route: 7,000 Miles of History. *Text copyright © 1995 by John S. Major. Illustrations copyright © 1995 by Stephen Fieser. Used by permission of HarperCollins Publishers.)*

ISSUE Is There a Shortage of History Books for Children? Should Authors of History Books for Children Include Controversial Subjects?

Two writers of history informational books, Dorothy and Thomas Hoobler,[1] explore some of the issues associated with history books for children. They begin their article with the following concern:

> Studies show that children in the United States have little knowledge of history. . . . Certainly one of the most important reasons is that the subject is just not taught in the lower grades. This lack of knowledge has its effect on the reading students choose outside the classroom. Children who have no background in this area are unlikely to read it for recreation. . . . A look at the children's section of a bookstore will show little more than a few biographies, and many of these are about current sports figures and celebrities. (p. 37)

The Hooblers then suggest several additional reasons why few history books are written for children. For example, they argue that publishers are not interested in publishing children's books about periods before World War II. In addition, discussion of issues associated with conflicts in history may make the books controversial.

The Hooblers summarize their own experiences with the mixed reviews of *Vietnam: Why We Fought: An Illustrated History*. They state: "Unfortunately, we found that after almost 20 years, the controversy over the conflict is still very much alive. Our approach offended some people, although many publications praised our book" (p. 38).

After reading this article, discuss some of the following issues:

1. How pervasive is the lack of historical understanding in children in the elementary and middle grades? If there is a lack of understanding, how does it influence the history books read by children?
2. What should the publisher's role be in publishing and promoting books about history before World War II?
3. Should authors write controversial history books for children? Why or why not?

[1]Hoobler, Dorothy, & Hoobler, Thomas. (1992, January). Writing history for children. *School Library Journal, 38,* 37–38.

concludes with a section called "A Closer Look" in which the author provides additional background information on topics such as caravan life, invasion routes of inner Asia, and the religions of Central Asia.

Authors who write about the ancient world may develop credible books by citing the latest information gained from their own research or from that of others and by describing details so that readers can visualize an ancient world. Because readers cannot verify facts about the ancient world through their own experiences, authors may include drawings that clarify information or use photographs of museum objects or archaeological sites.

Ancient civilizations in Central America are the subjects of several books. Patricia Calvert's *The Ancient Inca* includes photographs of ancient ruins and artifacts. Illustrated time lines help readers understand the early origins and cultures of the Inca people. The text presents information about their daily life, agriculture, childhood, lifestyles, religion, building techniques, and the effect of the Spanish conquest. Jean Fritz et al. present the history of the various parts of the world at the time of Columbus in *The World in 1492*. The section titled "The Americas in 1492" is written by Jamake Highwater; this chapter discusses the Aztecs, the Incas, and other native peoples. Maps show the Aztec and Inca empires, and illustrations show art from the time period.

Elizebeth Mann's *Machu Picchu* provides an excellent introduction to the Inca empire. The author begins with the 1911 discovery of the city, which the Inca considered sacred. The author then goes back in time to when the Incas and Machu Picchu represented a viable, living culture. Mann's style is one that both captures interest and formulates the book. She asks, "How can we ever really understand a culture so widely different from our own, where

Information about the Aztecs and Incas focuses on the accomplishments of the native peoples. (From The World in 1492. Copyright © 1992 by Henry Holt and Company, Inc. Illustrations copyright © 1992 by Stefano Vitale. Reprinted by permission of Henry Holt and Company, Inc.)

people celebrated rocks as sacred, thought strips of finely woven cloth were more precious than gold, administered a vast empire without knowledge of money or writing, and sacrificed children on mountain peaks?" The author then provides answers to her questions.

Informational books also explore the lives of early Native American populations. Carolyn Arnold's *The Ancient Cliff Dwellers of Mesa Verde* describes the lives of the Anasazi, or ancient ones, through color photographs and text describing the cliff dwellings found in Mesa Verde National Park. Topics Arnold discusses include the discovery of Mesa Verde, uncovering the past, the history and the daily life of the Anasazi, and speculations about why the Anasazi left Mesa Verde.

Raymond Bial's *The Chumash* begins with the early history of the Native American people who lived in southern and central California. The text includes chapters on "Origins," "Villages," "Lifeways," and "Beliefs." The book ends with chapters that focus on the changing world of the Chumash. The author includes a time line starting with 9,000–6,000 B.C. and extends to 2002 with the construction of new buildings for a tribal hall and a health clinic on the Santa Ynez Reservation. There is a bibliography of both adult and children's books and websites that can be consulted to learn more about the Chumash Indians.

Archaeological investigations in Europe provide the sources for information in Susan Woodford's *The Parthenon*. Woodford's book, part of the Cambridge History Library, presents a detailed account of the building of the Greek Parthenon. This book follows a chronological order beginning in 490 B.C. and extending through current problems caused by air pollution. Use the labeled drawings, captioned photographs, and detailed descriptions of ancient Greek life and religious practices to expand a study of Greek culture and Greek mythology.

Eric Shanower combines the legend of Troy and recent archaeological evidence to create *Sacrifice: Age of Bronze: The Story of the Trojan War*. The writing style may appeal to many older students because it is illustrated in comic-book form. The contents include maps of the Bronze Age, a glossary of names, genealogical charts, and a bibliography.

Several books provide glimpses into the Roman Empire, which lasted from about 27 B.C. to about A.D. 476. According to Dyan Blacklock's *The Roman Army: The Legendary Soldiers Who Created an Empire*, "at the height of its power it extended from Syria in the east and northern Africa in the south, to Britain and Germany in the north. Such a broad and diverse empire was difficult to control. This complex and dangerous work was the job of one of the most fearsome forces the world has ever seen—the Roman army" (p. 3). The text contains a map showing the Roman empire and illustrations of various facets of army life, including housing, weapons, and camp plans. Moira Butterfield's *Going to War in Roman Times* provides additional background information about the Roman army.

Kathryn Hinds is the author of a series of books that focus on various aspects of Roman life. Books in the *Life in the Roman Empire* series include *The Patricians*, in which the author tells about the emperors, the imperial court, the imperial women, and children of the empire. *The City* presents various aspects of urban life, including important public places such as the Forum, a large rectangular plaza where citizens gathered for political meetings and ceremonies. *The Countryside* covers the country communities, country homes, and working the land. Each of the books has a glossary, a list of further readings, on-line information, a bibliography, sources for quotations, and an index.

Shelley Tanaka's *Secrets of the Mummies* covers subjects related to creation of the mummies and building of elaborate tombs. In a section titled "Treasures of the Afterlife," Tanaka focuses on the work of Howard Carter and his discovery of Tutankhamen's tomb in the Valley of the Kings. Photographs and illustrations add understanding to both the historical times and the process of creating mummies.

James Cross Giblin's *Secrets of the Sphinx* begins with a map of Egypt that includes a time line clarifying the time periods of the artifacts and monuments that he discusses; the time line extends from the Predynastic period (5000–2920 B.C.) to the Late Period (712 B.C.–A.D. 332). He discusses the most famous monuments and artifacts, including the pyramids, the Rosetta Stone, and the Great Sphinx. Notice how the author's style develops a sense of mystery in this introduction:

> Before dawn, the giant creature is almost invisible. It sits in shadow in its rocky, horseshoe-shaped hollow. Then, as the sun slowly rises in the east, the creature's body is gradually revealed. First, the huge paws of a lion appear, followed by the animal's powerful haunches and shoulders. As the sun rises higher, the creature's face catches the light. But it is not the face of a lion. No, it is the face of a man . . . This creature—part man, part beast—is the Great Sphinx. (p. 4)

Giblin includes source notes, a bibliography, and an index.

Informational books may trace the history of important developments that have changed the world. In *Just What the Doctor Ordered: The History of American Medicine*, Brandon Marie Miller begins with descriptions of early Native American ceremonies and herbal remedies and continues through more modern times, such as the impact on medical developments that resulted from the Revolutionary War and Civil War.

The Story of Clocks and Calendars: Making a Millennium, by Betsy Maestro, traces the history of calendars and clocks from early cave dwellers through modern atomic clocks. Giulio Maestro's illustrations are especially effective for depicting important milestones in the development of ways to mark the passing of time.

History also includes religious traditions. Betsy Maestro develops an introduction to various beliefs in *The Story of Religion*. She begins with a discussion of early polytheistic beliefs and continues into a discussion of other religions such as Taoism, Hinduism, Christianity, and Islam. Giulio Maestro's illustrations relate to the culture of the religion. In *The Passover Journey: A Seder Companion*,

Barbara Goldin explains the traditions associated with Passover. Gail Gibbons's *Santa Who?* provides both a religious and a secular history of Santa Claus. This history proceeds from the Wise Men bringing gifts to the Christ child to Saint Nicholas and the Dutch Sinter Cleas, and finally to many of the customs associated with contemporary practices.

Patricia Lauber's *Who Came First? New Clues to Prehistoric Americans* presents recent archaeological finds that challenge prevailing theories about the arrival of prehistoric people to the Americas. Lauber describes the work of physical anthropologists, archaeologists, geneticists, and linguists. She also discusses how new finds may change prevailing theories. Readers can compare Lauber's text with Christopher Sloan's *The Human Story: Our Evolution From Prehistoric Ancestors to Today.* A foreword by paleontologists Meave and Louise Leakey states: "Sloan teaches us about the history we all share. We are the only surviving hominin, and we all have a common African origin and a common future. Every individual must play his or her part in securing this future not only for our own species, but also for all those species with whom we have the privilege to share this fragile Earth" (p. 5). The highly illustrated text includes a glossary; a pronunciation guide; a bibliography listing books, articles in *National Geographic*, and websites; and an index.

The Modern World

The data in informational books about the modern world can be made credible by citing research, quoting authorities, quoting original sources, and providing detailed descriptions of the setting, circumstances, or situations. Photographs also often add authenticity.

In *The Golden City: Jerusalem's 3,000 Years,* a book for older readers, Neil Waldman focuses on the history of this sacred city and includes information about the early conflicts. To add to the feeling of historical change, Waldman's water-color illustrations are labeled with both time and place. The author also includes Biblical text. Even though he covers the historical conflicts, he concludes his book on a positive note: "Just as in centuries past, thousands of people from faraway places come to visit Jerusalem each year. They are drawn by the splendor of the place, the magnificent domed mosques and the narrow alleyways, the delicate carvings and the massive ramparts, the ancient shrines and modern museums. But hidden beneath all these visible things is the mysterious feeling that, as you pass through the city gates, you are actually drifting back past the days of fabled knights and prophets, to the time when a young boy slew a giant with a slingshot" (unnumbered). In *Talking Walls,* a book for readers in the middle-elementary grades, Margy Burns Knight presents a history of some of the most famous walls in the world, including the Great Wall of China, the Vietnam Veterans Memorial, and the Berlin Wall.

The photographs in Ruth Ashby's *Elizabethan England* provide an interesting introduction to 16th-century England. The author includes a cultural history that encourages readers to understand and to value the Golden Age of the Renaissance through poetry, Shakespearean theater, art, architecture, and music.

Jim Murphy's *The Great Fire* presents details associated with the Chicago fire of 1871. In addition to being selected a 1996 Newbery Honor award winner, the book received starred reviews in *Booklist, Horn Book,* and *School Library Journal.* Consequently, it provides an excellent source for applying the evaluation criteria for information literature. For example, under accuracy of facts, students of children's literature will discover that Murphy provides a bibliography and sources for accounts that are presented in the book, and he uses carefully selected documents and personal accounts to provide the details associated with the fire. The author frequently distinguishes between fact and theory, or in this case, facts and rumors. For example, when Murphy reports the common belief that the fire department had given up because they could do nothing, Murphy states, "That wasn't exactly accurate. Much of the fire department was still at work, even though they knew the fire was completely out of control. Engines and men had scattered as the fire advanced and were now operating on their own, essentially trying to save individual buildings here and there. Chief Marshall Williams, for instance, had jumped aboard a passing engine and was now at one of the remaining bridge crossings, hosing it down" (p. 67). The author also separates facts from rumors in the concluding chapter, "Myth and Reality," in which he discusses questions such as "Did Mrs. O'Leary's cow cause the fire?" and "Was the drunken fire department to blame for the spread of the fire?"

The book is illustrated with reproductions of drawings that originated at the time of the event. Each drawing is labeled and includes its source and date of origin. For example, the drawing on page 44 shows fire ravaging the Crosby Opera House and identifies the source as *Harper's Weekly,* October 28, 1871.

In *Blizzard!* Murphy uses a similar approach to document the 1888 storm that paralyzed the northeastern United States.

In *An American Plague: The True and Terrifying Story of the Yellow Fever Epidemic of 1793,* Jim Murphy chronicles Philadelphia's yellow fever epidemic that killed 4,000 to 5,000 people and caused the evacuation of about 20,000 citizens. Murphy again proves his ability to research and write authentic nonfiction: He immediately brings readers into the time period by including copies of newspaper articles published during the epidemic and engravings depicting the time. He provides 13 pages of sources that he consulted, including books, newspapers, magazines, personal journals, and letters. These sources are divided according to topics such as "Firsthand Accounts: Nonmedical" and "Firsthand Accounts: Medical."

Murphy's writing style also encourages readers to place themselves in the setting and understand the conflict. Notice in the following quote how the author uses sounds and nature to develop the mood of fear and disaster: "On Sunday, August 25, a savage storm hit the city, bringing winds and torrents of rain. Water cascaded off roofs, splashed loudly onto the sidewalks, and ran in burbling rivers through the streets. The howling wind and pounding rain made a frightful noise, and yet through it all a single, chilling sound could still be heard—the awful tolling of the church bells" (p. 19). Later, Murphy again uses the image of the tolling bells to reflect the panic. Notice the influence of the bells in this quote: "Philadelphia was a city in panic and flight. It did not even help when Mayor Clarkson acted on another recommendation from the College of Physicians. The tolling bells that had so thoroughly terrified everyone were ordered to remain still. The great silence that followed did little to comfort those left behind. It was too much like the eternal silence of the grave" (p. 33).

The history of the early postal service is depicted in Steven Kroll's *Pony Express!*. Kroll attracts readers' attention by beginning the book with a help wanted ad:

Wanted.
YOUNG SKINNY WIRY FELLOWS
not over eighteen. Must be expert riders willing
to risk death daily. Orphans preferred. WAGES $25
perweek. Apply, Central Overland Express,
Alta Bldg., Montgomery St. (unnumbered)

He then places the need for the pony express in its historical context by discussing the Gold Rush in California and the need to get mail from New York to California in less than the 6 months required for a ship to travel around Cape Horn. Kroll highlights the development of the overland routes, including stagecoach travel and the impact of additional gold discoveries in Colorado and Nevada. The major part of the text then describes the pony express beginning with the first ride on April 3–April 13, 1860. Dan Andreasen's illustrations place the text into its historical context. The book concludes with an author's note that discusses the mail service through modern time. The text contains a map of the Pony Express Route, a Mini Photo Museum that traces the mail service from clipper ships to bar code sorters in a modern post office, a bibliography, and an index.

The influences of the Gold Rush in the late 1890s on developing transportation and on human lives are found in Charlotte Foltz Jones's *Yukon Gold: The Story of the Klondike Gold Rush*. The text includes maps, photographs, posters, a glossary, and a bibliography. Authors of various books about gold rushes may not agree about the human potential gained from the experience. Do you agree or disagree with Jones's conclusion about the Gold Rush?

The men and women who rushed to the Klondike for gold were changed forever. They had achieved a goal they might never have attempted had they not been victims of gold fever. Almost everyone who survived was a better person for the experience. As the hardships faded in their memories, they realized they had endured conditions and accomplished a feat they would never have believed possible. Each man and woman had a new sense of his or her own incredible potential. (p. 88)

You can compare Jones's text with Claire Rudolf Murphy and Jane G. Haigh's *Children of the Gold Rush*.

The competition of the transcontinental railroad is one of the most historic developments in the United States. Monica Halpern's *Railroad Fever: Building the Transcontinental Railroad, 1830–1870* places the development of the railroad within the historical, environmental, and social contexts of the United States. Maps, photographs, a glossary, and index make the book very useful for writing reports. It can be compared with Rhoda Blumberg's *Full Steam Ahead*.

Russell Freedman has written books that reflect a Native American perspective on the railroad and on the influence of European Americans. In *Buffalo Hunt*, for example, Freedman shows the importance of the buffaloes to the Indians living on the Great Plains. His text includes descriptions of the hunts, attitudes of the Indians toward the buffaloes, and the consequences to the Indians when the white culture all but eliminated the buffaloes. The text is illustrated with reproductions of paintings by such artists as George Catlin and Karl Bodmer, who actually saw the buffalo hunts. The titled and dated illustrations add interest to the text. Freedman uses a similar approach in *An Indian Winter*, accompanying his description of traditional Mandan life in the 1800s with paintings and drawings created by Karl Bodmer in 1832.

Michael Cooper's *Indian School: Teaching the White Man's Way* presents a sad time in the lives of many Native American youth. The author traces the importance of boarding schools in changing the lifestyles of young people who were separated from their families and land and sometimes moved thousands of miles away. He begins the text by describing the experiences of 84 Lakota Sioux as they journey from the Great Plains to a boarding school in Carlisle, Pennsylvania, providing anecdotes that reveal the conflicts the youth suffer as they are exposed to and are expected to adapt to the ways of the white people. The author also presents the debates about the schooling that the government held during this time.

In *Good Women of a Well-Blessed Land: Women's Lives in Colonial America*, Brandon Marie Miller also presents anecdotes and numerous details that depict the lives of Native American, African American, and European American women who lived in the 13 English colonies. The author explains his reasons for writing the book: "Part of my curiosity about women in colonial America is personal. One twig of my family tree set roots in seventeenth-century Virginia. Virginia court records show that one of my ancestors, newly widowed Cecily Jordan, accepted a

Illustration, "Mih-Tutta-Hang-Kusch, Mandan Village" by Karl Bodmer. (From An Indian Winter, by Russell Freedman, illustration of "Mih-Tutta-Hang-Kusch, Mandan Village," by Karl Bodmer. Copyright © 1992. Reprinted by permission of Joslyn Art Museum, Omaha, Nebraska; gift of Enron Art Foundation.)

marriage proposal. She later refused to marry the man, choosing a different suitor instead. Cecily's change of heart was recorded when she was sued in the colony's first breach of promise case" (p. 7).

Nancy Winslow Parker's *Money, Money, Money: The Meaning of the Art and Symbols on United States Paper Currency* is both an informative text about the meaning of each of the figures or symbols on various paper currencies and a history that provides information about the people or symbols pictured on the bills. Parker introduces the subject with an enlarged $50 bill, identifying each of the symbols on the portrait. In the remainder of the book, she provides information about the Secretary of the Treasury, the people whose portraits are on the bills, the seal of the United States, the White House, Independence Hall, engraving and printing, counterfeiters, the Federal Reserve System, and architectural capitals. To add clarity to the text, each of the illustrations are labeled.

The presidency and the White House are interesting subjects for authors of informational books. Alice Provensen's *The Buck Stops Here: The Presidents of the United States* is a pictorial representation of the presidents and the major happenings during each time period. This heavily illustrated book contains excellent information for readers at all levels. The book also provides interesting

background information for children reading stories set in various time periods.

Jane O'Connor's *If the Walls Could Talk: Family Life at the White House* focuses on each president through brief text and almost cartoonlike illustrations. Notice the type of lively information that is included in the following 1901–1909 presentation of Theodore Roosevelt:

Vice President Teddy Roosevelt (26) became president after William McKinley died. He was only 42 years old, and right away he loved being president. What energy he had! After a new tennis court was installed, the president is said to have played 91 games in one day. The six rambunctious Roosevelt kids liked to sled down the stairs on cookie trays, walk on stilts through the hallways, roller-skate in the East Room, and shinny up the flagpole. (unnumbered)

Humorous illustrations show many of these activities.

An interesting book to accompany texts about male presidents is Catherine Thimmesh's *Madam President: The Extraordinary, True (and Evolving) Story of Women in Politics*. In response to a girl who is chided because she wants to grow up to be president, the author presents a history of women who were or are influential in politics. The book concludes with female leaders from other countries, such as Margaret Thatcher of Great Britain; requirements for the presidency from the United States

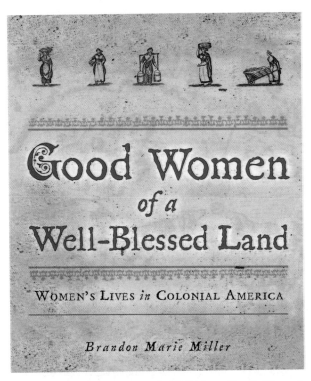

Illustration from Good Women of a Well-Blessed Land: Women's Lives in Colonial America, *by Brandon Marie Miller. Copyright © 2003 by Brandon Marie Miller. Lerner Publications Company, a division of Lerner Publishing Group. Used by permission.*

Constitution; and a time line of women in politics. A focus on female suffragists allows readers to understand the problems women faced in politics. For example, the author provides the following quote about one of the most influential suffragists:

Susan B. Anthony and other suffragists heard countless excuses for why women shouldn't vote: women weren't educated enough; they were too controlled by their emotions; they were too pure for the rough-and-tumble world of politics; they were too weak to make their way through the crowds to the voting box; and undoubtedly they would conceal extra ballots in their bulky sleeves, secretly slipping multiple votes into the ballot box. (p. 28)

Many informational books about the modern world help children understand the varied peoples on the earth, including their struggles and achievements and their impact on history. Students can make interesting comparisons between books related to the writing of the Constitution and the people of that time. Jean Fritz's *Shh! We're Writing the Constitution* is for younger children. Fritz writes about the constitutional leaders in the lighter, often humorous style found in her biographies.

Milton Meltzer's *The American Revolutionaries: A History in Their Own Words, 1750–1800* is an excellent source for the original writings of the people who fought in the Revolutionary War or designed the Constitution. The text includes actual letters, diaries, journals, and speeches.

Peter Sís's *The Train of States* is another book that presents a history of the United States. The illustrations provide information about each state, including capital, motto, state tree, bird, source of name, and date of statehood. The drawings are modeled after antique circus train cars found at the Circus World Museum in Baraboo, Wisconsin. The details should provide hours of observation for students.

Rosalyn Schanzer's *George vs. George: The American Revolution as Seen From Both Sides* develops the controversy by describing the differing views of George Washington and King George III of England. The text presents

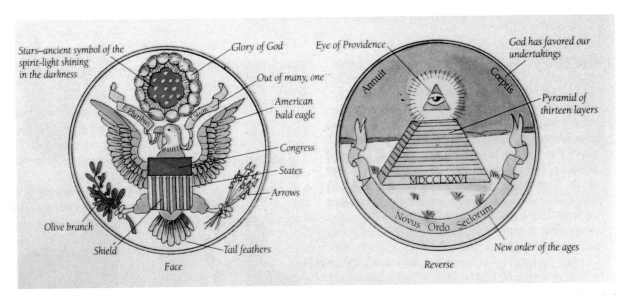

Detailed, labeled illustrations enhance understanding of currency. (From Money, Money, Money: The Meaning of the Art and Symbols on United States Paper Currency, *copyright © 1995 by Nancy Winslow Parker. HarperCollins Children's Books, a division of HarperCollins Publishers. Used by permission of HarperCollins Publishers.*)

both points of view by alternating between the two figures. The author compares the American and British governments, views on taxation, the Boston Tea Party, and the major battles. By reading this book, students discover the importance of research and inquiry projects that cover both sides of an issue.

In Richard Ammon's *Valley Forge*, the author uses a time line to show important war dates for the Revolutionary War. Readers develop an understanding of the harsh living conditions the soldiers experienced. Sidebars within the text present personalities and events associated with Valley Forge.

The American flag is another topic found in information books. Susan Campbell Bartoletti's *The Flag Maker: A Story of the Star-Spangled Banner* begins with the setting and the need for a flag: "It was 1812, and the United States was at war with Britain. A country at war needed plenty of flags" (p. 3). The book continues as three military officers visit the flag shop and order a flag for Fort McHenry. This is the story about the flag that inspired Francis Scott Key to write the words for "The Star-Spangled Banner." Additional interesting information about the flag is included in the author's note and in "Flag Facts."

Several current books explore the history of the United States at war. In *A Nation Torn: The Story of How the Civil War Began*, Delia Ray explores the causes of the Civil War. This book includes a map of the United States that designates free states and slave states, a glossary, a bibliography, and an index. Catherine Clinton's *Scholastic Encyclopedia of the Civil War* proceeds in chronological order from incidents that caused tensions before the war through 1865 and the consequences of the war.

Early photographs of military camps, battlefields, and soldiers provide the setting for Jennifer Armstrong's photographic essay, *Photo by Brady: A Picture of the Civil War.* The photographs portray Lincoln's life from his election to his death. Armstrong's book chronicles the Civil War as well as provides an introduction to early photography. *Secrets of a Civil War Submarine: Solving the Mysteries of the H. L. Hunley*, by Sally M. Walker, tells the story of how Horace L. Hunley created a submarine that could circumvent the Union blockade of the Southern ports. The first portion of the book discusses the design and construction of the submarine, and the second portion presents the puzzle about what happened in 1864 when the submarine and her crew disappeared. Both text and pictures document the archaeological process related to the search. The author includes maps, illustrations, and primary sources. The book won the 2006 Sibert Information Award.

Robert D. Ballard led the expedition that discovered the lost *Titanic* in 1985, which he describes in *Exploring the Titanic.* Photographs from the 1912 *Titanic* are used extensively to show what the ship and its interior looked like before the "unsinkable" ship sank. The text and color photographs document the finding of the ship and its subsequent exploration. A glossary of terms and a time line add to the text.

In *Always Remember Me: How One Family Survived World War II*, Marisabina Russo uses a storytelling technique to allow a grandmother to tell her granddaughter about her life that begins with a happy "first life" in Germany before the war and proceeds to her "second life" after the war. By telling the story of her life, she talks about her husband's death after World War I, the rise of the Nazi party and the persecution of the Jews in concentration camps, and a happy conclusion when the grandmother is reunited with her three daughters in America. The importance of the title of the book is revealed when the grandmother gives her granddaughter the necklace that her own grandmother gave her when the family left Poland to go to Germany. That grandmother said: "When you wear this . . . always remember me" (unnumbered).

Barbara Rogasky's *Smoke and Ashes: The Story of the Holocaust* begins with the history of anti-Semitism and proceeds to

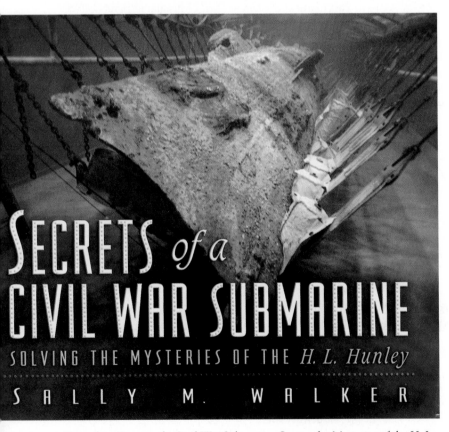

Cover from Secrets of a Civil War Submarine: Saving the Mysteries of the H. L. Hunley, by Sally M. Walker. Copyright © by Sally M. Walker. Published by Carolrhoda Books, Inc., a division of Lerner Publishing Group. Used by permission.

the 1933–1945 experience. This text shows life in the camps and explores such questions as these: Why and how did the Holocaust happen? Didn't anyone try to stop it? Photographs add to the feeling of tragedy. Milton Meltzer's *Rescue: The Story of How Gentiles Saved Jews in the Holocaust* reveals another side of the Holocaust and shows that many people risked their lives to help the Jewish people. Michael Leapman uses the experiences of eight children to depict the reality and cruelty of the Holocaust in *Witnesses to War: Eight True-Life Stories of Nazi Persecution*. In the introduction, Leapman provides information about the children as well as his purposes for writing the book. The text concludes with a listing of sources from which Leapman gained his information.

Ellen Levine's *Darkness Over Denmark: The Danish Resistance and the Rescue of the Jews* is a comprehensive text that progresses from the invasion of Denmark in April 1940 through the liberation of Denmark in May 1945. The text includes source notes, a "Who's Who," a chronology, a bibliography, and an index.

Another interesting perspective on the history of Nazi Germany is developed in Susan D. Bachrach's *The Nazi Olympics: Berlin 1936*. The text, based on an exhibit at the United States Holocaust Memorial, includes numerous photographs taken during the time period. Readers will discover how a government can use a sporting event as a propaganda tool. This book could lead to interesting research and debates about political considerations that are identified in current Olympic games.

Through a photojournalism format, Stephen Ambrose surveys important incidents in *The Good Fight: How World War II Was Won*. Photographs and textual information cover topics from the D-Day invasion through the bombing of Hiroshima and Nagasaki. Ambrose uses quotes to reinforce experiences shown in the photographs.

Writing World War II events in Europe in chronological order helps readers understand the sequences in Ronald J. Drez's *Remember D-Day: The Plan, The Invasion, Survivor Stories*. The author discusses problems, tactics, and strategies as well as the invasion. Photographs, a bibliography, and an index add to the usefulness of the book.

Susan Campbell Bartoletti develops another point of view associated with World War II in *Hitler Youth: Growing Up in Hitler's Shadow*. She tells a history that shows how Hitler developed the *Hitlerjugend* (Hitler Youth) because he believed that the future of Germany was closely related to its young people. The author focuses on 12 young people and how they were indoctrinated into believing the goals of the Third Reich. The characters' responses reflect a wide variety of attitudes, from patriotic zeal to confusion about Hitler's goals to disillusionment.

History is made up of people who immigrate to a new country, as shown in Dorothy and Thomas Hoobler's *The Jewish American Family Album*. According to the authors, about 2.5 million Jewish immigrants arrived in the United States between 1880 and 1924. This nonfictional book describe families as they leave Europe, arrive in America, begin new lives, and become part of American life. Photographs and firsthand descriptions add to the authenticity of the book. It is interesting to compare these experiences with those described in historical fiction. Many of the Jewish immigrants express desires for education and freedom, which mirror the conflicts, settings, and themes found in many historical fiction books written about this same time period. There are many excerpts from this book that can be used for comparisons and for authentication of historical fiction.

Detailed illustrations provide a strong sense of history in Andrew Langley's *Shakespeare's Theatre*. June Everett's paintings both provide historical views of Shakespeare's time and depict the modern reconstruction of the Globe Theatre. The illustrations for the book were selected from more than 150 pictures drawn by Everett, who was the "Artist of Record" for the project.

Two books on history use both photographs of the times and writings by children's authors to present a history of the previous century. *Life: Our Century in Pictures for Young People*, edited by Richard B. Stolley, contains labeled photographs that have appeared in *Life* magazine. (See In-Depth Analysis on page 506.) *The Century That Was: Reflections on the Last One Hundred Years*, edited by James Cross Giblin, is a collection of essays written by authors of juvenile literature in which they reflect on various aspects of life in the 20th century. For example, Russell Freedman discusses "Looking Back at Looking Forward: Predicting the Twentieth Century" in an essay that begins with predictions made by Jules Verne more than 100 years ago. Eve Bunting writes about immigration, Albert Marrin explores World War I, and Milton Meltzer discusses politics from William McKinley through William Clinton. The text contains 11 essays, an introduction, a section of additional readings, and an index.

In *With Courage and Cloth: Winning the Fight for a Woman's Right to Vote*, author Ann Bausum presents in chronological order the history of women's rights. This history extends from 1913 to 1920. The momentum of the time period is highlighted by photographs showing women struggling for equality. Each chapter includes quotes from historical personages. For example, Chapter 1 begins, "Yesterday the government, which is supposed to exist for the good of all, left women while passing in peaceful procession . . . at the mercy of a howling mob"—Harriot Stanton Blatch, March 4, 1913. This is a quote from a telegram sent to President Woodrow Wilson as he started his inaugural parade. The text includes profiles of personages such as Susan B. Anthony and Sojourner Truth; a chronology from 1788–1929; a resource guide that lists books, videos, places to visit, and websites; sources and acknowledgments; a bibliography; and an index. These references provide excellent information for reports.

What will a person do to safeguard a national treasure in time of war? *The Librarian of Basra: A True Story From*

Book cover from THE LIBRARIAN OF BASRA: A TRUE STORY FROM IRAQ, Copyright © 2005 by Jeannette Winter, reprinted by permission of Harcourt, Inc.

Iraq, by Jeanette Winter, reveals how Alia Muhammad Baker, chief librarian of Basra's Central Library, rescued 70% of the library's collection prior to the burning of the library. This picture storybook depicts the importance of a woman's actions when she dreams of peace "and dreams of a new library. But until then, the books are safe—safe with the librarian of Basra" (unnumbered).

History of Civil Rights for African Americans

The struggle for civil rights for African Americans is described in several recent books. Older students will discover considerable information in Diane McWhorter's *A Dream of Freedom: The Civil Rights Movement From 1954 to 1968*. In 2002, the author won the Pulitzer Prize for her adult book on the civil rights movement. She explores the sacrifices and triumphs of African Americans in their pursuit of social and political equality, profiling the accomplishments of major people such as Rosa Parks, John Lewis, Fred Shuttlesworth, and Martin Luther King Jr. The book is very well written, using a chronological organization that highlights the major incidents of the movement.

As in many books about the struggle for African American rights, McWhorter introduces her book with a warning: "What you are about to read goes against our national self-portrait of fairness. Be warned, you will hear whites using the word 'nigger' in these pages; to sanitize the language of segregation is to mute its destructive force. As disturbing as some of the material in this book is, it will enable you to appreciate the hardships faced by those without power and to admire their strength to overcome so much" (p. 11). Photographs, a bibliography, further readings, an index, and websites make this a readable and useful source.

Toni Morrison's *Remember: The Journey to School Integration* tells in pictures and words the history and impact of school integration and the 1954 Supreme Court decision, *Brown v. Board of Education*. The text includes a time line of "Key Events in Civil Rights and School Integration History." The time line extends from 1896, when the U.S. Supreme Court legalized separate but equal facilities in *Plessy v. Ferguson*, through November 1999, when the Little Rock Nine were awarded the Congressional Gold Medal. Diane Telgen's *Brown v. Board of Education* includes a section on "Important People, Places, and Terms" and covers information beginning with an 1849 school segregation case and concludes with the 2003 University of Michigan rulings on student diversity. The text is illustrated with archival photographs.

Herb Boyd writes *We Shall Overcome: A Living History of the Civil Rights Struggle Told in Words, Pictures and Voices of the Participants* in a journalistic style. This book, also appropriate for older readers, includes two CDs, recordings of speeches and protest songs. Doreen Rappaport's *Free At Last!: Stories and Songs of Emancipation* covers a longer period, from emancipation in 1863 to the Supreme Court decision declaring school segregation illegal. The text begins with a poem by Lucille Clifton, "Listen Children." The author presents short stories about Booker T. Washington, Harriot Postle, John Solomon Lewis, Ida B. Wells, Jackie Robinson, and Thurgood Marshall. Poetry and songs depict working while shackled. The author includes a list of important dates and an author's note.

Walter Dean Myers's *Now Is Your Time! The African-American Struggle for Freedom* consists of shorter episodes that explore the African American experience from slavery through the civil rights movement and into contemporary times. This book includes sources, a bibliography, and an index. The text of Patricia and Fredrick McKissack's *The Civil Rights Movement in America From 1865 to the Present* is supported by numerous photographs and descriptions of people who influenced the civil rights movement.

Numerous books reflect the contributions of African Americans to the fine arts. James Weldon Johnson's "Lift Every Voice and Sing" is often referred to as the African American national anthem. His book of the same name combines the song with linocut prints that were created in the 1940s by Elizabeth Catlett. Laban Carrick Hill's *Harlem Stomp! A Cultural History of the Harlem Renaissance* includes poetry, prose, photographs, paintings, and historical documents associated with the Harlem Renaissance. According to the foreword by Nikki Giovanni, "In the early part of the twentieth century, Harlem was a hotbed of intellectual, artistic, literary, and political blossoming for Black people. . . . They came to St. Louis, Chicago, and ultimately to Harlem seeking peace, prosperity, and freedom. Stepping out on faith, they both preserved and created a culture" (p. 2). The chapters are written in chronological order, beginning with 1900–1910 and the great migration of 1911–1920. The chapters focus on areas such as arts, music, and theater. Numerous photographs and reproductions of art make this an exciting volume. It is a National Book Award finalist.

Nature

Effective informational books about nature encourage children to understand their own bodies, observe nature, explore the life cycles of animals, consider the impact of endangered species, experiment with plants, understand the balance of the smallest ecosystem, and explore the earth's geology. To create effective and credible books, authors must blend fact into narrative. The authors must gain these facts from observation and research. Close-up photography is especially effective in clarifying information and stimulating interest. For example, photographs may illustrate what happens inside an egg or a nest or follow the life cycle of an animal or a plant. Labeled diagrams may clarify text descriptions. Maps may show natural habitats of animals, migration patterns of birds, or locations of earthquakes. If authors present new vocabulary or concepts, they should define the terms, illustrate them with diagrams or photographs, and proceed from known to unknown information. Clearly developed activities that encourage children to observe and experiment can make a book even more useful. A bibliography, an index, and a list of additional readings are helpful, too.

Effective books about nature written for younger readers should use child-friendly examples and comparisons. For example, April Pulley Sayre's heavily illustrated book *Stars Beneath Your Bed: The Surprising Story of Dust* is written in a pleasing style that can be shared orally with young children. The accompanying illustrations depict the content. For example, the text reads: "Dust is made everywhere, every day. A flower drops pollen. A dog shakes dirt from its fur. A butterfly flutters, and scales fall off its wings" (unnumbered); the illustration shows pollen dropping from a flower, a dog shaking dirt, and scales falling from a butterfly's wings. Then the author tells readers, "That's dust. Dust is little bits of things." She continues by showing and telling about all types and sources of dust: bike wheels that scatter dust, animals that raise dust as they race across the savanna, ash from an erupting volcano, and dust that comes from outer space. Illustrations such as one from an Egyptian tomb inform readers that the dust that made King Tut sneeze is still on the Earth and might even be on their floor. The book concludes with additional information about how dust influences sunsets.

The Human Body

Informational books about the human body are especially interesting to readers who are curious about their own bodies and how they function. Books for children about the human body range from overviews to detailed discussions of one aspect of the body, such as the brain or the eyes. Some books also discuss body-related issues, such as the right to live or to die, genetic engineering, and human origins.

Books on the human body illustrate the importance of labeled diagrams when studying anatomy. Robie H. Harris's *It's So Amazing!: A Book About Eggs, Sperm, Birth, Babies and Families* contains numerous labeled drawings. For example, Michael Emberley's drawings include detailed illustrations of an unborn child from a ball of cells through a full-term fetus drawn in actual size. Seymour Simon also includes numerous labeled diagrams in his *Guts: Our Digestive System*. The book begins with a drawing of the human body with the various parts of the digestive system labeled and each drawn in a different color. The author traces how chewed food enters the stomach through the esophagus, passes through the stomach and into the small intestine and finally into the large intestine and out of the body. Simon explains how food is broken down into the substances used by the body and shows that the body is related to the food that is eaten.

Paul Showers's *A Drop of Blood* is part of the "Let's-Read-And-Find-Out Science" series. The text presents a simple introduction to the composition and functions of blood. The author writes in a child-friendly language and includes numerous labeled drawings depicting the heart, lungs, vessels, and white blood cells. The text gives advice on "How to make sure your heart stays healthy"—do not smoke, eat healthy foods, exercise, and get regular medical checkups.

Authors who write about subjects that have conflicting viewpoints frequently present both sides of the argument. For example, in *The Human Story: Our Evolution From Prehistoric Ancestors to Today*, Christopher Sloan presents two theories of evolution: the replacement model and the multiregional model. He includes evidence that shows how fossils, artwork, and tools provide knowledge about early humans.

Younger readers learn about racial differences when interacting with Julius Lester's *Talk About Race*. Lester uses an interactive style when he tells readers to press their fingers against their faces and tells them: "Beneath everyone's skin are the same hard bones" (unnumbered); consequently, without skin, we would all look the same.

Texts on the AIDS virus are available for both younger and older readers. For example, Deborah Stanley's *Sexual Health Information for Teens* provides information on HIV and AIDS. It includes Internet resources and lists organizations that can be contacted.

The world of forensics is explored in Donna M. Jackson's *The Bone Detectives: How Forensic Anthropologists Solve Crimes and Uncover Mysteries of the Dead.* The text discusses several cases in which forensic anthropology was used to solve crimes. The text includes labeled photographs. Several of the photographs clarify size by a measurement device; for example, one photograph is labeled, "Back at the police station, detectives organize and photograph evidence collected at the scene. A yardstick or ruler is usually included in such photographs to indicate scale" (p. 13). The text explains how sex, race, and age can be determined; how markings on bones can establish cause of death; and how a clay reconstructed face can help solve crimes.

Animals

Authors who write effectively about prehistoric animals or about modern-day reptiles and amphibians, birds, land invertebrates (earthworms), insects, and mammals must present their facts clearly, and they must not give their animals human qualities and emotions. Because books about animals are popular with many different age groups, authors must consider the readers' backgrounds when they develop new concepts.

Dinosaurs. With scientists as detectives and fossils as clues, 21st-century children can experience the thrill of investigating the earth's prehuman past. Children who learn about dinosaurs in books, study about them in museums, search for fossilized footprints or bones, and make dinosaur models often become enthusiastic amateur paleontologists. Books depicting excavation sites, such as Caroline Arnold's *Dinosaur Mountain: Graveyard of the Past* and Margery Facklam's *Tracking Dinosaurs in the Gobi,* present the work of paleontologists and show the careful work that has provided answers about dinosaurs. Books on dinosaurs range from highly illustrated texts for younger children, such as Gail Gibbons's *Dinosaurs,* to texts for older children that provide extensive scientific details. Nic Bishop's *Digging for Bird-Dinosaurs: An Expedition to Madagascar* follows the work of paleontologist Cathy Foster as she works in her laboratory and out on the dig. The author uses several techniques to create interest in the subject. For example, he introduces Foster's interest in the relationship between dinosaurs and birds by stating: "It's natural to wonder how they evolved. What did their ancestors look like? What events led to the evolution of flight?" (p. 4). Some of the greatest excitement occurs when the scientists begin to examine the bones brought back from Madagascar. The author details the sci-

entific process used, the excitement when a sickle claw is found, and the evidence revealed through computer analysis. By reading this book, young scientists will discover the dedication and perseverance required to be a professional scientist.

Vivian French writes *T. Rex* as a conversation between a grandfather and his grandson as they go through a T. Rex exhibition in a museum. The grandson asks many questions, and the grandfather tries to answer them. Many of the questions do not have known answers, and the grandfather answers questions such as "Did he hunt with his friends? Did he hunt with his mate?" (p. 20) with "He probably hunted and ate alone, but then again—we don't really know. It was millions and millions of years ago . . . " (p. 20). The book ends with a challenge to readers: "Maybe one day we'll really know . . . Maybe we'll know what's really true. The person to tell us might just be you!" (pp. 26–27).

The authors of books about dinosaurs may develop their content through a question-and-answer approach. In *New Questions and Answers About Dinosaurs,* Seymour Simon asks and answers 22 questions, which range from "What are dinosaurs?" to "Why did the dinosaurs become extinct?" and "What are some new discoveries about dinosaurs?" A helpful index includes a pronunciation guide.

J. Lynett Gillette focuses on one type of dinosaur in *Dinosaur Ghosts: The Mystery of Coelophysis.* The author attracts readers' attention by showing the remains of 300 dinosaurs that died very rapidly. Gillette explores various theories about their extinction. In *The News About*

Illustrations and text present old and new information about dinosaurs. (From The News About Dinosaurs, by Patricia Lauber, copyright © 1989 by Patricia Lauber. Reprinted by permission of Bradbury Press.)

Dinosaurs, Patricia Lauber presents past beliefs as well as newer information that often refutes earlier beliefs.

Two books on dinosaurs cover expeditions in Mongolia. Brian Floca's *Dinosaurs at the Ends of the Earth: The Story of the Central Asian Expeditions* presents the story of the 1920s expeditions led by Dr. Roy Chapman Andrews that found the first fossilized eggs. This finding proved "that dinosaurs were not born, but hatched" (unnumbered). Floca effectively conveys both the excitement of and the requirements for being a paleontologist. In *A Nest of Dinosaurs; The Story of Oviraptor*, authors Mark A. Norell and Lowell Dingus begin by describing the 1920 expeditions in Mongolia and proceed to more recent expeditions, such as one in 1993.

Insects, Spiders, Snakes, and Turtles. Sy Montgomery's *The Tarantula Scientist* is a Sibert Information Honor Book for 2005 and an American Library Association Notable Children's Book. The author begins with a map showing French Guiana, where spider scientist Sam Marshall explores for tarantulas. Her introduction intrigues readers and even suggests a hint of danger: "Sam Marshall is lying on his belly in the rainforest, his freckled face just inches from a fist-sized hole in the dirt. He turns on his headlamp. He gently pokes a twig into the tunnel and wiggles it. 'Come out!' he says into the hole. 'I want to meet you!'" (p. 7). Nic Bishop's accompanying photographs show the scientist poking a twig in the hole and then a large tarantula emerging. The text also suggests that scientists working in the rainforest must be very knowledgeable before they poke sticks into burrows because the burrow might contain something very dangerous. The text has labeled photographs, spider statistics, definitions of terms, a bibliography, and websites.

One of the strengths of Sandra Markle's writing style in *Outside and Inside Killer Bees* is her ability to provide definitions of scientific vocabulary. For example: "Africanized honeybees also do something else European honeybees don't do. They *migrate*. This means that the whole colony leaves the nest and moves to a new location. Killer bees migrate when workers have trouble finding a supply of nectar or when their nest is disturbed" (p. 27). In addition, the vocabulary words presented in the text are further defined in the glossary. Markle also provides labeling for illustrations such as an enlarged photograph that identifies the head, thorax, abdomen, and legs of the bee.

Books for younger children frequently present nature in familiar environments. Margery Facklam's *Creepy, Crawly Caterpillars* presents details about 13 types of caterpillars, including a close-up of each of the caterpillars that provides information about its habitat. A band on the lower part of each double-page spread pictures the life cycle from eggs to caterpillar to cocoon to moth. The text includes a glossary of terms. Sandra Markle's *Creepy,*

Crawly Baby Bugs provides color close-up photographs of various insects. Molly McLaughlin's *Dragonflies* follows the life cycle of these insects. Photographs of dragonflies resting on hands indicate sizes. Other photographs are magnified to reveal physical characteristics.

I Love Bugs!, by Philemon Sturges, follows a boy and his camera as he excitedly explores his environment. The text in this book for young children is simple, as the boy explains that he likes "bugs that creep, bugs that crawl" (unnumbered). Shari Halpern's large, colorful illustrations correspond with the text as the boy sees bugs that hop, fly, paddle, weave, burrow, chew, and swoop and buzz. The simple text and illustrations encourage vocabulary development and observation. The content is extended on the inside front and back covers as each bug is pictured as if in a photograph ready to place in a scrapbook of bugs, identified by name, and labeled with three or four lines.

Books about butterflies provide both basic facts about and beautiful illustrations of butterflies. Laurence Pringle's *An Extraordinary Life: The Story of a Monarch Butterfly* follows the often perilous route of the butterfly as it migrates from New England to Mexico. The illustrations and captions provide details about various aspects of the life cycle of the monarch. The text includes maps and diagrams that clarify information. There is also a list of further reading and an index.

Steve Jenkins uses size comparisons to increase readers' understanding in *Actual Size*. For example, beautiful collage illustrations show textures of the atlas moth with a wingspan of 12 inches. In contrast, a dwarf goby is illustrated as ¼ inch. The cover of the book has a 12-inch measuring tape that allows readers to interact with the story. The text includes additional information about the animals, their sizes, and their habitats.

Authors of informational books may entice children by presenting challenges or comparisons. Kathryn Lasky's *Interrupted Journey: Saving Endangered Sea Turtles* begins when a boy finds a nearly dead sea turtle and continues with the attempts by veterinarians to save the life of the endangered turtle. Christopher Knight's photographs and Lasky's text document various activities in different parts of the world designed to help save sea turtles.

Frank Staub's *Sea Turtles* stimulates reader involvement by asking readers to be word detectives as they search for words in the text and try to identify meaning. A glossary is included to help readers verify the meanings. Labeled color photographs also clarify the meanings. Another way the author clarifies meaning is by comparing characteristics of the turtles with known objects. For example, "Leatherbacks are the biggest reptiles alive today. They can grow as big as a bathtub" (p. 13).

Photographs and text in Sy Montgomery's *The Snake Scientist* describe the habitat of the red-sided garter snakes in Manitoba, Canada, as well as the work of scientists who study them. Nic Bishop's photographs show

Through the Eyes of an AUTHOR

Laurence Pringle

Visit the CD-ROM that accompanies this text to generate a complete list of titles written by Laurence Pringle.

Selected Titles by Laurence Pringle:

An Extraordinary Life: The Story of a Monarch Butterfly

Snakes! Strange and Wonderful

Bats! Strange and Wonderful

Sharks! Strange and Wonderful

Dog of Discovery: A Newfoundland's Adventures With Lewis and Clark

Come to the Ocean's Edge

Neither of my parents had finished high school, but they aimed high. They were determined that all of their children would graduate from high school. There were no expectations about college at all.

When I decided to go to college and considered what to major in, I thought I could either study biology at Cornell or journalism at Syracuse. At that point, at the age 17 or 18, there was definitely the thought that I might pursue a writing career of some kind, but I chose Cornell because it was cheaper. Later on, I did take some journalism courses at Syracuse, and I started getting magazine articles published, so my writing craft began that way.

There was one key writing course I took. This was after I had a BS and MS in wildlife biology, and I had been taking some journalism courses at Syracuse. There was a professor there from *Better Homes and Gardens* named, oddly enough, George Bush. He had a two-week course. We met every day about writing magazine articles, and those courses traditionally dwell on how to write a query letter and how to study a magazine in terms of market analysis so you don't foolishly send the wrong kind of article to the magazine. By about the third day, he told us he thought most of us needed more help writing a clear English sentence than analyzing magazine markets. And I was one of those people. He really helped me enormously. No doubt I had been taught some of this stuff before, but it finally sank in.

Later in the fall of that year, I had an interview for a rookie editing job with *Nature and Science*, and I had to write a trial article, and I got the job. If I hadn't had that class and that professor, I don't think I would have gotten the job, and it was a crucial job because it was with a children's magazine. If I hadn't gotten that, I might have never written for children.

It was at that magazine that I had an important experience. We represented the American Museum of Natural History in New York, so as I would finish an article, I'd send it on to some museum staffer to check it for accuracy. Often I would discover that it was inaccurate. There was something left out or something depicted inaccurately, and I learned that there is an awful lot of information that goes into this kind of writing, so I always need an expert reader.

Ideally—like in *Snakes!*—the expert doesn't just see my words but also the art. I'm very involved in the illustrations. When I submit a manuscript, I also tell the artist, spread by spread, what should be on that page. Sometimes the artist has quite a bit of freedom, and sometimes they don't. In *Snakes!*, there's a certain page where I've written several sentences about the snake skeleton and backbone, so obviously I needed a painting of a snake skeleton. But later I write about constrictors. The artist could have picked a python or a boa, but she picked an anaconda squeezing a caiman, so the artist had some freedom there. It varies, but I understand how important the illustrations are, so I am very involved.

Belatedly, I also realize how important story is, whether in fiction or nonfiction. I think it was my 77th book, *An Extraordinary Life: The Story of a Monarch Butterfly*, which won the Orbis Pictus Award. The idea was to follow one individual critter and tell the story of its journey in life. And I hadn't really thought about it as story before, but then I looked back at my very first book about dinosaurs and it described the flow of ideas and the flow of investigation and how scientists figure out something, and I realized there was a story there. I unconsciously was using story in my writing a lot.

I think writing is terribly hard work, but I would hate to stop doing it.

Video Profile: The accompanying video contains conversations with Mary E. Lyons, Eve Bunting, Jack Gantos, Roland Smith, Earl B. Lewis, and other writers for children.

---

the annual gathering of thousands of the snakes in the Narcisse National Management Area. Photographs show that people of all ages and both sexes are involved in the experiments.

Laurence Pringle begins *Snakes! Strange and Wonderful* with a series of questions designed to create reader curiosity and interest: "Can you eat without using hands? Snakes can. Can you climb a tree without using arms or legs? Snakes can. Can you smell odors by wiggling your tongue in the air? Snakes can" (p. 3). Pringle's text and Meryl Henderson's illustrations explore the answers to these questions about snakes and show many kinds of snakes from around the world. Labeled illustrations indicate length, motions, senses, and eating habits. One child commented that the snakes appeared so lifelike that he dropped the book after first opening it.

Vivian French encourages reader involvement in *Growing Frogs* by providing directions for collecting frog eggs, placing them in a fish tank, watching the eggs hatch into tadpoles, and observing various stages as the tadpoles grow into frogs. Alison Barlett's illustrations show each of these stages of growth. The book concludes with the need to return the frogs to the pond from which the eggs were collected.

Mammals. *National Geographic Prehistoric Mammals*, by Alan Turner, is a good introduction to the world of mammals. The text begins with a general introduction that answers questions such as What is a mammal?: "Mammals are warm-blooded, air-breathing animals with backbones and fur or hair, and they feed their young milk. But not all of these defining features show up on fossils" (p. 10). This section includes maps that show the "Age of Mammals," full-page illustrations of early mammals, reconstructions from fossils, social behavior, classifications, and mammal groupings. The text includes discussions and examples

Through the Eyes of a CHILD

Caleb
Grade 6

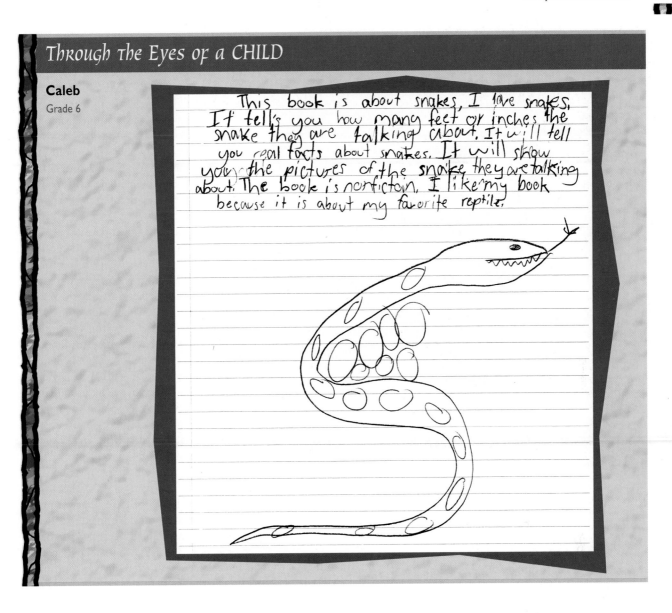

This book is about snakes, I love snakes, It tell's you how many feet or inches the snake they are talking about. It will tell you real facts about snakes. It will show you the pictures of the snake they are talking about. The book is nonfictoin, I like my book because it is about my favorite reptile.

that range from mammal-like reptiles to brontotheres. Each two-page presentation contains discussion, a map showing locations, fact files, and a time frame. The text concludes with a listing of museums, a glossary of terms, and an index.

Several books on animals are especially appropriate for young readers because the subjects are familiar. In *My Puppy Is Born*, Joanna Cole presents the birth of miniature dachshund puppies. Jerome Wexler's photographs show the pregnant dog going into her box; the emergence of the first puppy, born inside a sac; and the mother tearing the sac and licking the puppy. The book follows the growth of the puppies during their first 8 weeks, as they are unable to see or hear, as they nurse, and then as they open their eyes and take their first steps.

William Muñoz's photographs for Dorothy Hinshaw Patent's *The Right Dog for the Job: Ira's Path From Service Dog to Guide Dog* follows the training of a Guide Dog for the Blind in California. The text concludes as the trained dog is paired with a blind person.

By reading Sy Montgomery's *Search for the Golden Moon Bear: Science and Adventure in the Asian Tropics*, readers follow the activities of a scientific expedition to Southeast Asia to find and verify the existence of an unusual bear. The text describes the scientific process used to verify a species, such as DNA analysis. The author includes recently discovered information about mammals; her tone suggests the excitement felt among scientists as they search for new discoveries. Notice in the following quote how the author presents details that describe the bear:

> The sight of her took our breath away. She was as unusual as she was beautiful. Framed by the cream-colored fur of her face, her brown eyes were ringed in black, almost like a panda's. But she was no panda. Her ears were big and round, and stood up like those on Mickey Mouse. She had a furry

From Snakes! Strange and Wonderful, *text copyright © 2004 by Laurence Pringle, illustrations copyright © 2004 by Meryl Henderson. Published by Boyds Mills Press, Inc. Reprinted by permission.*

wolf: "The wolf had come almost full circle. From the centuries-long war against them to the early research by scientists such as Olson, Murie, and Leopold and finally to the twenty-five-year battle to bring them back, the wolves destiny was once again to be shaped by humans. And yet this is a unique experiment. Would wolves adjust to a new environment? Would they turn north and walk back to their home in Canada? Would ranchers shoot them? No one knew" (p. 28).

The beauty and adventure associated with searching for an endangered species are developed in Phyllis Root's *If You Want to See a Caribou.* Jim Meyer's woodblock print illustrations depict the wonders of nature found on the Canadian State Islands of Lake Superior; they show trails churned black by caribou hooves while surrounded with spruce trees and logs gnawed by beavers. Root tells readers that if they are quiet and wait, they may see a caribou. She ends the book with a list of places you might go to see a caribou and information about why the woodland caribou are endangered in the United States and threatened in Canada. Her text includes information about how in the early 1900s, the herd crossed over the ice of Lake Superior in a rare winter when the lake froze. Readers understand the importance of protecting endangered species when she states: "These caribou have lived there ever since because no predators crossed over the ice with the caribou, and because the government protects the islands, these caribou have thrived, eating the lichens, moss, fungi, twigs, grass, leaves, and plants growing on the islands" (Concluding Facts About Caribou).

The Firefly Animal Rescue Series has two recent titles emphasizing threats to animals' survival and ways that animals can be rescued. Dan Bortololli's *Panda Rescue: Changing the Future for Endangered Wildlife* and *Tiger Rescue: Changing the Future of Endangered Wildlife* emphasize both the obstacles to survival, such as using tiger parts for traditional medicine, and ways that readers can join in the efforts to save endangered animals. Full-color photographs and websites encourage readers to support rescue attempts.

Through text and acrylic illustrations, Jonathan London's *Baby Whale's Journey* presents the world of sperm whales as the pods travel the seas. To increase interest for younger readers, the author focuses on the experiences of a young whale. The author uses comparisons to help understanding. Notice in the following quote how the author compares the characteristics of a giant squid

mane, like an adult male lion's. On her chest was a V, like on a college sweater. But what was most exciting was her amazing color. The fur of her back, sides, and belly—most of the bear, in fact—was different shades of gold. She was like no other bear we'd seen before, not even in a photo or on television. (p. 7)

In this quote, Montgomery uses similes that compare the bear to animals and objects known to the readers. Also note that the tone of the writing suggests the excitement of a new discovery and a scientific search.

In *Lions: Animal Predators,* Sandra Markle introduces her heavily illustrated text with a definition for *predator.* She encourages reader interaction with the text feature "Looking Back." For example, she states, "Check out the lion's long claws on page 13. Just like human fingernails, the claws keep growing. Why would that be important for the hunter?" (p. 38). The author includes numerous photographs, a glossary, further information sources, and an index.

The life of an endangered species is described in Stephen R. Swinburne's *Once a Wolf: How Wildlife Biologists Fought to Bring Back the Gray Wolf.* Notice how the author summarizes the various conflicts associated with the

The Chimpanzee Family Book
Jane Goodall

The photographs follow a day in the life of Jane Goodall, the British naturalist. (From The Chimpanzee Family Book, *by Jane Goodall, copyright © 1989 by the Jane Goodall Institute for Wildlife Research, Education and Conservation. Photos copyright © 1989 by Michael Neugebauer. Reprinted by permission of Picture Book Studio.)*

with known objects and also infers the dangerous battles between squids and sperm whales: "A giant squid has tentacles 60 feet long (18 meters) and can weigh 1 to 2 tons. It has eyes the size of basketballs and a huge parrot-like beak. The beak and suction cups of a giant squid leave scars on the sperm whales who battle them" (Afterword, unnumbered).

Other excellent books about wild animals and protection of species include Dorothy Hinshaw Patent's *Back to the Wild* and Nicholas and Theodore Nirgiotis's *No More Dodos: How Zoos Help Endangered Wildlife*.

Another animal that is often hunted is described in Ted and Betsy Lewin's *Gorilla Walk*. The authors introduce the relationship between mountain gorillas and humans as being tragic for animals. The text then describes an expedition to the native habitat in southern Uganda. Maps, a gorilla fact sheet, and an index add to the text.

Birds. The topics of informational books about birds range from common barnyard fowl to exotic tropical birds. In these books, the authors use various techniques to create interest for young children and to present new concepts to older children. The introduction to *The Emperor's Egg*, by Martin Jenkins, begins with a male Emperor penguin taking care of the egg laid by his mate. Notice in the following quote how the style of writing interests the reader by providing questions and statements: "Can you imagine it? Standing around in the freezing cold with an egg on your feet for two whole months" (unnumbered).

In *My Seasons With Penguins: An Antarctic Journal*, Sophie Webb uses journal entries and illustrations to cover her 2-month expedition to study Adélie penguins. The author includes a glossary of technical vocabulary and the questions studied by the scientists. This approach helps readers understand the scientific method that is essential for animal study.

In a book for younger readers, Barbara Juster Esbensen focuses on specific birds and their habitats. In *Tiger With Wings: The Great Horned Owl*, Esbensen and Mary Barrett Brown present insights into the life and habitat of horned owls. A combination of illustration and text allows vivid comparisons. For example, Esbensen describes the horned owl in this way:

> The great horned owl is such a fierce hunter that it is often compared to a tiger. Like the tiger, the great horned owl hunts in the dark, and it kills instantly. Its stripes let it blend with the forest patterns of dim light and shadow. Its two-inch feather tufts look like a tiger's ears, and it has a face like an angry cat. It is a tiger with wings—a tiger that can fly almost unseen through the darkness. (p. 2, unnumbered)

Brown's two-page illustration shows an owl flying through the woods as a transparent tiger follows behind.

Think Like an Eagle: At Work With a Wildlife Photographer, a book for older readers, depicts both animal behavior and the requirements to be a wildlife photographer. In this book, Kathryn Lasky uses many effective writing techniques to appeal to older readers. For example, she introduces the book with a language style that encourages readers to visualize the setting and the life of the wildlife photographer:

> He follows a silver thread of moonlight through the forest. The tangled shadows of bare-branched trees spread across the snowy ground. . . . Now Jack crosses a stream that feeds into the reservoir. The water slides like a black satin ribbon under snow bridges and curls around billowing white banks. . . . Jack is wrapped in the silence of the forest when suddenly from somewhere behind him, deep in the heart of the woods, comes the flat hooo hoooo of the great horned owl. Hooo hoooo. The call thrums through the forest. (p. 5)

Such vivid language is found throughout the text. Lasky also makes comparisons that readers understand, such as the following comparison of time spent watching animals with time spent watching television:

> But the most important part of the blind is the rectangular window slot. This slot is Jack's window on the world. He has spent as much time peering through it as many people spend in front of a television. He can't switch the channel. He can't change the scene. He must wait for the real-life action to happen in front of this small rectangle. It does. (p. 8)

Later, Lasky contrasts hunting and photography. Finally, she encourages critical thinking by suggesting to readers that an animal photographer must become a student of animal behavior and think like the animal, whether the animal is an eagle, a great egret, a beaver, or a deer. This concept provides interesting discussions when readers consider, What would a photographer of _____ need to know about the animal's behavior?

Phillip Hoose's *The Race to Save the Lord God Bird* (also called the ivory-bill woodpecker) is listed on three "Best Books" lists for both children and young adults. The author explores evolving attitudes toward understanding species and protecting habitats. His introduction provides an excellent definition of *extinction*: "To become extinct is the greatest tragedy in nature. Extinction means that all the members of an entire species are dead; that an entire genetic family is gone, forever" (p. 3).

Hoose states that the extinction described in this book is different from earlier extinctions because humans are responsible; humans delete the habitats and alter the earth's resources. He presents the history of the destruction of the ivory-bill woodpecker as well as the efforts to save the bird. Maps showing the reduction of the habitat from pre-1800 to the 1980s bolster his points effectively. The text includes "Important Dates for the Protection of Birds," a glossary of terms, a list of sources, picture credits, and an index.

In *Arrowhawk*, Lola M. Schaefer develops a text based on a true story of efforts to save an endangered bird of prey. The author and her fourth-grade students followed Michigan and Indiana news stories about a red-tailed hawk that was injured by a poacher's arrow. This text tells the efforts to save an endangered bird and discusses the importance of saving endangered species.

Plants

Informational books about plants should present clear details in logical order, include diagrams and photographs that illustrate terminology, and encourage children to become involved in learning. Detailed, labeled photographs and illustrations enhance books on plants.

Aileen Fisher's *The Story Goes On* uses collage illustrations and rhyming text to demonstrate not only the cycle of life but also a theme that life is interdependent. The cycle begins as a seed sprouts, and continues as a bug munching on a leaf is eaten by a frog. A snake swallows the frog, but the snake is grabbed by a hawk and flown away in the hawk's claws. A farmer shoots the hawk that later provides food for a coyote. Crows peck at the remains, and beetles finish the remains by burying them in the soil. Thus the soil is enriched, and the cycle begins again. The book ends in a visual representation of the cycle in which the illustrator, Mique Morinchi, shows each animal in order of appearance.

The natural world of plants and the environment are depicted by Thomas Locker. Locker's *Sky Tree: Seeing Science Through Art* follows the sequence of the seasons through paintings of the same tree. The book concludes with the section "Connecting Art and Science in Sky Tree," in which the author asks questions such as, "This is the same tree in the same place. What makes this painting different?" (unnumbered). The author then discusses the painting.

Desert Giant: The World of the Saguaro Cactus, by Barbara Bash, is part of the "Tree Tales" series of Sierra Club Books. This book, written for young readers, emphasizes that the cactus provides food and shelter for desert inhabitants. Large illustrations show the interior as well as the exterior of the cactus. Labeled drawings clarify flower fertilization and detail seed interiors.

Charles Micucci's *The Life and Times of the Apple* combines information about the tree and its history. Detailed, labeled drawings show a cross-section of an apple and illustrate such concepts as cross-fertilization of apples, grafting, parts of an apple flower, pollination, growth, and harvesting. The text then discusses uses for apples, leading apple-growing states and countries, and apple varieties. The author provides a time line to show the history of the apple from 2,500,000 B.C. through the 1600s. An illustrated map of the United States shows the impact of the apple on America, from the first grafting of domestic apples in Virginia in 1647, to the legend of Johnny Appleseed, to the Franciscan priests who planted orchards in New Mexico and other Spanish territories, and to pioneers who brought apples west in covered wagons. *The Life and Times of the Apple* provides lessons in geography and history as well as plant science. Micucci uses a similar approach in *The Life and Times of the Peanut*. Catherine Paladino's *One Good Apple: Growing Our Food for the Sake of the Earth* explores one of the issues related to growing food: Do pesticides and fertilizers have a destructive influence on the earth? The author focuses on the benefits of organic farming.

Geology and Geography

Geology and geography books encourage readers to develop insights into changes in the earth, to understand the consequences of natural and human-produced disasters, and to understand the importance of developing cultural awareness. Changes in a region resulting from interactions with humans are the major focus for Steve Noon's illustrations in Anne Millard's *A Street Through Time: A 12,000-Year Walk Through History*. The text and illustrations highlight changing times as a riverside settlement first draws Stone Age hunters seeking water and proceeds through modern times. The author suggests that readers "trace the changing the role of the river from age to age as the story of the street unfolds" (p. 3).

Because children often see the results of earthquakes and other disasters on television, geology may be a subject that interests them. Seymour Simon's *Earthquakes* has vivid photographs that show the consequences of earthquakes in various parts of North America. Books about earthquakes provide interesting background information for children who also read Laurence Yep's novel *Dragonwings*, which describes the great San Francisco earthquake of 1906.

PATRICIA LAUBER

VOLCANO

The Eruption and Healing of Mount St. Helens

BRADBURY PRESS · NEW YORK

Color photographs show important sequences in the Mount St. Helens eruption. (From Volcano: The Eruption and Healing of Mount St. Helens, *by Patricia Lauber, copyright © 1986. Reprinted by permission of Bradbury Press.)*

Since the eruption of Mount St. Helens, several books emphasizing volcanic activity have appeared. Patricia Lauber's *Volcano: The Eruption and Healing of Mount St. Helens* is an excellent photographic essay of the eruption and of the changes since it took place. Photographs showing minute changes in time are effective, as are photographs of specific settings taken before and after the eruption.

Storms and other natural disasters are popular subjects for informational books. In *Hurricanes: Earth's Mightiest Storms*, Patricia Lauber discusses the weather conditions that create the storms and the technological developments that allow meteorologists to track them. Color photographs, maps, and lists of further readings help clarify the subject. In *Flood: Wrestling With the Mississippi*, Lauber presents the history of the river, highlights the 1927 and 1993 floods, and discusses ways that people have tried to control the river. Color photographs provide dramatic examples of various types of storms, including hurricanes and tornadoes, in Stephen Kramer's *Eye of the Storm: Chasing Storms With Warren Faidley.*

The consequences of the Dust Bowl are depicted in Michael L. Cooper's *Dust to Eat: Drought and Depression in the 1930s.* Notice in the following introduction how the author describes the consequences for humans who lived

during this time period: "Thousands of them are crossing the borders in ancient rattling automobiles, destitute and hungry and homeless, ready to accept any pay so they may eat and feed their children" (p. 1). This quote is from a story written by John Steinbeck in a 1936 article for the *San Francisco News.* The text is illustrated with photographs that show the destruction caused by the dust and drought. The author includes a list of books, videos, Internet sources, and places to visit, and an index. This nonfiction book would be good to accompany *Out of the Dust,* a historical fiction novel by Karen Hesse.

Weather reporters frequently discuss the influences of El Niño or La Niña on the weather patterns, especially excessive rain or drought. Patricia Seibert's *Discovering El Niño: How Fable and Fact Together Help Explain the Weather* traces the weather phenomenon from its influence on early fishermen in Peruvian villages to recent times. The text includes maps that illustrate weather patterns.

In *Poles Apart: Why Penguins and Polar Bears Will Never Be Neighbors,* Elaine Scott shares historical information about the North and South Poles and their scientific importance. The text answers questions such as "What makes a compass point north?," "Why did a tropical island, once home to alligators and dinosaurs, become one of the coldest spots on earth?," and "Why do penguins survive on that island today?" The author discusses the theory of the continental drift by showing maps that explain the concept and fossil evidence of Triassic land reptiles and fossils of ferns found in southern continents, and she uses contrasting photographs to show the changing ice cap. For example, in 1979, the polar ice cap covered much of the Arctic Sea; in contrast, 2003 photographs show that much of the ice cap has melted. The text also discusses early humans who explored the polar regions.

Interactions among people and geography are developed in Rebecca L. Johnson's *Braving the Frozen Frontier: Women Working in Antarctica,* Will Steger and Jon Bowermaster's *Over the Top of the World: Explorer Will Steger's Trek Across the Arctic,* and Lawrie Raskin and Debora Pearson's *My Sahara Adventure: 52 Days by Camel.*

The undersea world of the marine biologist is presented in Diane Swanson's *Safari Beneath the Sea: The Wonder World of the North Pacific Coast.* The large color photographs by the Royal British Columbia Museum present a beautiful world of creatures such as jellyfish, mud crabs, sea stars, and sea anemone. This book won the Orbis Pictus Award for Outstanding Nonfiction for Children. Consequently, students of children's literature might analyze the book to decide what features make it an award-winning text.

Books on ecology and conservation frequently introduce the importance of and the beauty associated with the subject and then present a plea to readers to help solve the problem. In *Everglades*, Jean Craighead George introduces the subject through a Native American storyteller who is taking five children through the Everglades and telling them a story about the environment. George allows readers to ponder the changes in the Everglades as the children question the storyteller: "Where are the clouds of egrets?" and "Where are the quantities of alligators?" The storyteller now tells the children why the numbers have diminished. George ends the ecology tale on a hopeful note in which the children grow up, run the earth, and return the Everglades to its former glory. The children have learned their lesson as George concludes, " 'That's a much better story,' said the children. 'Now pole us home quickly so we can grow up'" (unnumbered).

Other books about the earth and the need for environmental changes highlight actual projects that have resulted in change. One example is Molly Cone's *Come Back, Salmon*. The text and photographs by Sidnee Wheelwright follow the actions of a group of students in Everett, Washington, who cleaned up a stream, stocked it with salmon, and watched carefully to see if their efforts to improve the fish habitat succeeded. When reading this book, many children are moved by the students' efforts and are ready to try a similar project in their own neighborhoods. Most children understand the underlying message of the book: We can and must make a difference if we want the planet to improve.

Discoveries and How Things Work

Some informational books answer children's questions about discoveries of the past and present or provide explanations of how machines work. Authors may clarify their texts through step-by-step directions, carefully labeled diagrams, photographs that illustrate concepts, and content that proceeds from the simple to the complex or from the known to the unknown.

Discoveries

Books about discoveries may describe the basic principles of past discoveries or the latest space or computer technology. Some books combine information about discoveries with experiments designed to help children understand and duplicate earlier experiments. One such book is Seymour Simon's *How to Be an Ocean Scientist in Your Own Home*. Simon first asks a question, such as How can you make fresh water from seawater? Next, he presents information in a "Let's Find Out" section. Then, he tells students "Here's What You Will Need" and provides detailed directions in "Here's What to Do."

Joy Hakim's *The Story of Science: Aristotle Leads the Way* uses myths, history, physics, and mathematics to present the history of modern science. The book is supported with photographs, illustrations, quotes, and sidebars. In *Are We Alone? Scientists Search for Life in Space*, Gloria Skurzynski describes scientists' efforts to find and communicate with possible life on other planets. The author states, "All the scientists I spoke with were eager to share information about this exciting new field, and about their hopes for the future. They believe that the next ten, or twenty, or hundred years will open up the universe for human discovery and exploration and perhaps for our first encounter with E.T." (unnumbered). The text includes sidebars profiling the work of various scientists. The author also discusses topics such as UFOs and aliens. Students who are conducting research will find websites, sources, and a bibliography.

Patrick Moore's series of beginning astronomy books designed for children in the lower-elementary grades presents basic information about comets, planets, stars, and the moon. The text and illustrations are presented to clarify understandings for young readers or listeners. For example, in *Comets and Shooting Stars*, the author introduces the subject "What makes a shooting star?" and the friction in meteors this way: "If you pump up a bicycle tire, you will find that the pump gets hot, because the air inside is being squashed; this sets up friction, and this causes heat. A meteor moving into the upper air sets up so much heat by friction against the air that it catches fire, and burns away" (p. 11). In *The Planets*, photographs of a child pointing a flashlight at a ball held by another child show how the planets are illuminated by the sun. Illustrations in *The Stars* compare the size of the sun with Vega and Spica and show diagrams of the Great Bear, or Big Dipper. In *The Sun and Moon*, the illustrations show the various phases of an eclipse.

Out-of-This-World Astronomy: 50 Amazing Activities & Projects, by Joe Rhatigan and Rain Newcomb, presents a series of illustrated activities that include the following information: "What You Need," "What You Do," and "What Just Happened." Some of the beginning activities, such as "Calculate Your Moon Weight," are easily completed because the authors give readers a list of easily obtained materials such as a measuring tape and a scale. The authors then provide details about weighing yourself and multiplying the weight by .162. Finally, they explain why gravity on the moon results in such a difference in weight. The book is divided into sections such as "The Moon," "The Sun," "The Solar System," and "The Stars and Beyond."

Informational books about space and space travel should reflect current knowledge. Copyright dates, therefore, may be a very important consideration when selecting these books. Seymour Simon has written several readable books that, through words and photographs, take young readers into the far reaches of space and explain comets and planets. Simon's *The Long View Into Space, Saturn, Jupiter,* and *Galaxies* provide information in a simple and illuminating way. For example, in *The Long View Into Space*, Simon explains why space distances between earth and the planets are not measured in miles by saying that to measure in miles would be like "trying to measure the distance between New York and London in inches" (p. 4).

A humorous and very visual introduction to the solar system is provided in Joanna Cole's *The Magic School Bus: Lost in the Solar System*. The facts about the solar system are introduced when Ms. Frizzle and her class enter the magic school bus, find themselves in outer space, and explore the planets in the solar system. Information about the solar system also is provided in reports written by the students in the class. Many of these reports use a question-and-answer format, such as What is the solar system?, What makes night and day?, Why are spaceships launched with rockets?, What is gravity?, and Why is it so hot on Venus? This book includes a planet chart and a mobile of the solar system. As with the other books in "The Magic School Bus" series, you can use this book to suggest various projects.

How Things Work

Numerous informational books appeal to children's curiosity about how common home appliances and bigger machines actually work. These books usually contain detailed diagrams or photographs that accompany two or three pages of descriptive text about each item. Although the readability and interest levels are usually considered upper-elementary and above, many younger children ask questions about how percolators, dishwashers, or Thermos bottles work. Therefore, parents may find these books helpful when answering the questions of young children. (One mother said that her 6-year-old son's favorite book was one containing diagrams of machines at work.)

David Macaulay's *The Way Things Work* includes more than 300 pages of detailed diagrams of almost every conceivable instrument. The text is arranged in four sections: "The Mechanics of Movement," "Harnessing the Elements," "Working With Waves," and "Electricity & Automation." The book includes a glossary of technical terms and an index. The humorous analogies used throughout the text appeal to many readers. Macaulay's *Building Big* is a highly illustrated book with drawings of bridges, domes, and skyscrapers. Ronnie Krauss's *Take a Look, It's in a Book: How Television Is Made at Reading Rainbow* follows the process of producing the children's television show.

Molly Bang's *My Light* explores the mysteries behind the light switch. Bang also describes how the sun's light is transformed into energy. Natalie M. Rosinsky's *Light: Shadows, Mirrors, and Rainbows* is a highly illustrated book in which the author answers questions such as "What makes shadows?," "How do mirrors work?," and "What makes a rainbow?" The text gives directions for experiments such as making shadow creatures with hands, making a rainbow, and playing shadow tag. Rosinsky's *Water: Up, Down, and All Around* uses large, colorful illustrations and rhythmic language to describe the water cycle. The author provides directions for simple experiments such as "Make your own dew" and "Make your own frost."

What You Never Knew About Tubs, Toilets, and Showers, by Patricia Lauber, traces the history of these devices beginning with the Stone Age and progressing through various cultures. The book presents a fascinating way to look at history.

Chronological order is an important concept in many books that explain how things work. Byron Barton's *Airport*, an excellent picture book for young children, answers many questions about airports and airline travel, following passengers from arrival at the airport to boarding the plane. *Inside the Hindenburg: A Giant Cutaway Book*, written by Mireille Majoor and illustrated by Ken Marschall, includes both the history of and detailed drawings showing the interior of the famous zeppelin. The illustrations and the text follow a chronological order beginning with the maiden voyage on April 4, 1936, and concluding on May 6, 1937, with the tragic fire that killed 35 passengers and crew.

Interactive texts are important for discovering how things work. In *Top Secret: A Handbook of Codes, Ciphers, and Secret Writings*, Paul B. Janeczko introduces students to the world of codemaking and secret codes. Notice how he motivates readers to become involved with the text: "If you are nuts about codes and ciphers and secret writing, this guide has it all: codes, ciphers, invisible inks, concealment techniques, spy stories, and even a little bit of history (but only the exciting parts). Find a friend and start building your codemaker's field kit. The fun has just begun!" (p. 3). The illustrations show examples of various codes. In an interactive text, the author presents several challenges to encipher and to decipher. The answers are included in the book.

Hobbies, Crafts, and How-To Books

One of the main reasons that older elementary-school children give for reading is to learn more about their hobbies and interests. Children told one educator who asked how to increase the enjoyment of reading that teachers should ask them about their hobbies and help them find books about them. Informational books cover almost every hobby and craft. The more useful books contain clearly written directions, provide guidelines for choosing equipment or other materials, or give interesting background information.

Books on hobbies, crafts, and how-to projects are important for expanding children's interests. Developing art appreciation is a goal found in a number of information books. For example, a series of books written by Colleen Carroll focuses on different subjects in art including animals, people, elements, and weather. In each of the books, Carroll discusses the art in a way that stimulates the imagination and the senses. The books in this series include *How Artists See Animals: Mammal Fish Bird Reptile; How*

This topic is debated in two journal articles in *School Library Journal*. In May 1991, Marsha Broadway and Malia Howland[1] published results of their research in "Science Books for Young People: Who Writes Them?" These researchers analyzed the qualifications of authors of children's science books reviewed over a 5-year period in the journal *Science Books and Films,* published by the American Association for the Advancement of Science. Broadway and Howland found that 43% of the authors had degrees in English, journalism, or the humanities, and 37% of the authors had degrees in science-related fields. Only 12% of the respondents had science-related primary occupations. In addition, 19% of the authors indicated that they selected topics on the basis of their own experience and expertise. After analyzing the results of the returned questionnaires, Broadway and Howland conclude:

The findings suggest an insufficient concern about the qualifications and authority of those who write science and technology books for children and adolescents. Perhaps too many publishers and authors may believe that writing ability and interest qualify authors to write science books for children, regardless of credentials in a particular subject. (p. 37)

These researchers then provide several guidelines that they believe should be used for the authors of science books:

1. Ideally, the authors of science books for children and adolescents would be experts in their fields.
2. Another useful step in increasing the quality of informational books is to help make those who work with young people— and the young people themselves—more aware of the authors writing informational books and their credentials.
3. Publishers should recruit authors who are knowledgeable about specific topics and who have appropriate credentials and experience. (p. 38)

In the October 1992 issue of *School Library Journal,*[2] nonfiction author Gloria Skurzynski, who is an experienced writer but not a scientist, challenges Broadway and Howland's conclusions. Skurzynski argues that experienced writers are better at creating science books than are scientists, because experienced writers, even though they are not experienced in that specific scientific field

know how to bring the subject to life. Whether they write fiction or nonfiction, they're storytellers. They've learned all the ways to hook young readers. In contrast, books written by experts tend to be bogged down in the very weight of their expertise. (p. 46)

Further, Skurzynski believes:

Since experienced writers are generally not sci-tech savants, they'll be curious about the same as-

pects of a subject as the audience. They'll want to know what readers want to know. Experts are so familiar with their own spheres of knowledge that they rarely have a clue as to what fascinates, or bewilders, general readers. (p. 46)

Skurzynski also defends a technique used by many writers of nonfictional works, blending fact and story within the book. She states:

I'm willing to sugarcoat hardcore information with every sweetener in the storyteller's bag of tricks, provided the coating doesn't obscure the facts. My job is twofold: to attract young readers to the book, and to make sure the information in it is absolutely correct. (p. 46)

After reading these two articles, debate the following issues:

1. Should there be any requirements about who writes children's informational books that have scientific content?
2. What should be the qualifications of writers of nonfictional books for children?
3. What role does fiction have in nonfictional books written for children?

[1]Broadway, Marsha D., & Howland, Malia. (1991, May). Science books for young people: Who writes them? *School Library Journal, 37,* 35–38.
[2]Skurzynski, Gloria. (1992, October). Blended books. *School Library Journal, 38,* 46–47.

Artists See People: Boy Girl Man Woman; How Artists See the Elements: Earth Air Fire Water; and *How Artists See the Weather: Sun Rain Wind Snow.*

Joy Richardson's *Looking at Pictures: An Introduction to Art for Young People* uses art from the National Gallery in London to show children how they can observe and appreciate paintings. Lucy Micklethwait's *A Child's Book of Play in Art* encourages children not only to look at art but to create their own works of art. Peggy Thomson and Barbara Moore's *The Nine-Ton Cat: Behind the Scenes at an Art Museum* takes readers behind the scenes at the National Gallery in Washington, D.C. This book may increase interest in visiting a museum or even in exploring careers associated with art and museums.

Some how-to books provide directions and information to expand special interests. For example, Colleen Aagesen and Marcia Blumberg's *Shakespeare for Kids: His Life and Times* presents both an introduction to Shakespeare and Elizabethan England and detailed directions for constructing objects associated with the period such as

pomander balls, a juggler's beanbag, and games. This book provides interesting background and activities that might accompany a study of historical fiction set during Shakespeare's time period.

Lisa Bany-Winters's *Show Time!: Music, Dance, and Drama Activities for Kids* includes ideas that could be adapted for various ages. The book is divided into eight chapters, beginning with "The History of Musical Theater" and concluding with "Show Time." The text includes "Suggested Musicals for Young Actors" and "Summaries of Plays Mentioned in the Book."

CREATIVE ARTS

Clear, detailed drawings that illustrate the points made in the text are important in informational books. Detailed directions and illustrations are particularly important in books that show how to make various objects. Joan Irvine's *How to Make Super Pop-Ups* includes explicit, step-by-step directions and drawings to help readers measure, fold, cut, draw, or connect various parts to each project. *The Elements of Pop-Up,* by David A. Carter and James Diaz, provides detailed written and visual directions for making three-dimensional pop-up books. Examples of each type of paper engineering encourage readers to create their own artwork.

In Laura C. Martin's *Nature's Art Box,* the author suggests that nature provides sources for art supplies. She classifies the 65 projects described in the book according to the materials required such as leaves, shells, and cones. Each chapter includes information about ethnic and historical uses for the materials. Line drawings and numbered steps clarify the directions for the projects.

Step-by-step instructions for 11 art projects designed to be completed by young children are found in Denis Roche's *Loo-Loo, Boo, and Art You Can Do.* In addition to directions for such art projects as making potato prints, the author provides helpful hints that make cleaning up easier.

How-to-books should have clear directions for projects that readers can accomplish. Diane Rhoades's *Garden Crafts for Kids: 50 Great Reasons to Get Your Hands Dirty* has detailed step-by-step directions for various outdoor projects. For example, chapter 4, "Starting Your Garden," includes a list of needed materials, instructions that are numbered in the appropriate sequence, photographs that show children completing the various tasks, lists of plants that are grown from seeds and those that are set from transplants, and tips to make the activity successful. The section concludes with an experiment in which readers can try planting according to a moon planting calendar.

Marion Dane Bauer, a Newbery Medal author, provides guidance for young writers in her *What's Your Story? A Young Person's Guide to Writing Fiction.* The content covers such important subjects as developing a story plan, choosing your best idea, developing strong characters, focusing your story, developing the plot, choosing a point of view, and polishing the story. Bauer relates many of the subjects to her own writing. This book also provides guidelines for readers to use when they are evaluating literature.

In *Past Perfect, Present Tense: New and Collected Stories,* author Richard Peck uses his own short stories to provide helpful hints about writing. His theme is closely related to reading because he maintains that it is impossible to become a writer without being a reader. Both teachers and students will find Loreen Leedy's *Look at My Book: How Kids Can Write & Illustrate Terrific Books* motivating and useful. The book describes the creation of a book, from brainstorming ideas to a finished product. Illustrations, websites, and a list of further readings add to the interest.

Rachel Isadora, a professional dancer, focuses on her daughter's training in *Lili at Ballet.* The illustrations and the text show various aspects of ballet classes. Captioned drawings clarify the text and provide practical information for readers who may themselves become future ballet professionals.

Deborah Dunleavy's *The Jumbo Book of Drama* provides an introduction to the theater. The text is divided into four parts: physical movement, including mime and dance drama; voice, including reader's theater, puppetry, and radio plays; characters and plots of comedy, melodrama, and tragedy; and costumes, set designs, sound, lighting, and props. The text includes activities for students to develop. Dana Amendola's *A Day at the New Amsterdam Theatre* presents a day in the life of a Broadway musical: Disney's "The Lion King."

Children who read frontier stories and survival stories may be interested in discovering more about the foods the characters ate. Barbara M. Walker's *The Little House Cookbook: Frontier Foods From Laura Ingalls Wilder's Classic Stories* presents frontier foods that Wilder wrote about in her "Little House" stories. Walker searched for authentic recipes by reading the writings of Wilder and her daughter Rose, pioneer diaries, and local recipe collections. Her hope in sharing this collection is that children will rediscover basic connections between the foods on the table and the grains in the field and the cows in the pasture, as well as between people in the past and today. Walker uses liberal excerpts from the "Little House" books and the original Garth Williams illustrations in discussing the foods and their preparation.

A PARENTS' CHOICE APPROVED AWARD WINNER

From t-shirts to twig baskets, **65 cool projects** for crafty kids

to **make with natural materials** you can find anywhere

Written by Laura C. Martin with drawings by David Cain

STOREY KIDS

Cover from Nature's Art Box, *by Laura C. Martin. Text copyright © 2003 by Laura C. Martin. Illustrations copyright © 2003 by David Cain. Storey Publishing. Used by permission.*

One of the criteria for effective cookbooks is the author's ability to develop clear directions that can be followed easily. For example, Angela Wilkes's *The Children's Step-by-Step Cookbook* has colored photographs that show ingredients and utensils. There are step-by-step instructions for the recipes, such as those for stuffed potatoes. A picture glossary of cooking terms helps develop understandings. Megan Carle's *Teens Cook: How to Cook What You Want to Eat* includes sidebars that highlight amusing cooking mistakes and how to adapt recipes to meet the needs of a vegetarian diet. Kari Cornell's *Holiday Cooking Around the World* includes holiday traditions from various countries as well as recipes and international menus. The text presents recipes such as Danish Rice Pudding and Thai Egg Rolls, and provides shopping lists and lists of ethnic ingredients.

Many books encourage children to consider new hobbies or to learn more about existing ones.

Informational Books for Young Adults

Books on American and world history, along with biographies that relate to the time periods, are among the most popular informational books for both young adults and adults. Reading and evaluating the books, however, requires specific requirements. Susan Wise Bauer (2003) identifies the following approach for readers of history:

> As you read history, you'll ask yourself the classic detective (and journalist) questions: Who? What? When? Where? Why? At the first level of inquiry, ask these questions about the story the writer tells: Who is this history about? What happened to them? When does it take place, and where? Why are the characters of this history able to rise above their challenges? Or why do they fail? On the second level of inquiry, you'll scrutinize the historian's argument: What proof does she offer? How does she defend her assertions? What historical evidence does she use? Finally, on your third level of inquiry, ask: What does this historian tell us about human existence? How does the history explain who men and women are, and what place they are to take in the world? (p. 187)

As noted from these questions, young adults may read some of the same history books discussed earlier in this text, but at a much deeper level of understanding and criticism. It is also interesting to note that the very first Newbery Award was presented in 1922 to a history book, *The Story of Mankind*, by Hendrik Willem Van Loon. Bertha Mahony Miller's (1955) evaluation of the book states:

> It is significant that the first Newbery Award should have been this particular book. It is an awakening book, an arousing book, a book to catch the imagination of a young and alert mind. For the first time it presents young people with a history of the world, a global history that breaks down conventional walls, that deals with ideas and movements, not dry-as-dust information and precise dates. Reading the book again in 1955 it is startlingly interesting to find how often the

author sent a searchlight into the future; how clearly he foretold problems that would face the world of the future, even of our troubled world of today, as he analyzed the trends and events of the past. (p. 10).

Students of children's literature will find this book fascinating as they read and compare the insights into history with those published in more recent times.

There are numerous informational books about the history of and issues related to the United States at war or fighting for independence. Books about the American Revolution range from Doris and Harold Faber's *We the People: The Story of the United States Constitution Since 1787* to David McCullough's adult text *1776* (2005). McCullough's books-on-tape version, which is read by the author, can be used by students who do not have the appropriate reading ability to read his text. Students may be interested to know that McCullough won the Pulitzer Prize for his adult biographies *John Adams* and *Truman.*

In *Reconstruction*, Claudine L. Ferrell discusses the complex issues surrounding the Civil War. The author includes the personalities who debated the issues and the economic and social problems that divided the North and the South. In another book covering the same time period, *Cause: Reconstruction America 1863–1877,* Tonya Bolden discusses topics such as Lincoln's Proclamation of Amnesty, the Civil Rights Act of 1866, and issues related to freed slaves and national expansion. Tom Lalicki's *Grierson's Raid: A Daring Cavalry Strike Through the Heart of the Confederacy* presents an account of a secret Union mission into Confederate territory. Sources include diaries, letters, and photographs that present day-to-day progress of the cavalry. Jennifer Armstrong's *Photo By Brady: A Picture of the Civil War* is illustrated with photographs taken by Mathew B. Brady during the Civil War. Sally M. Walker's *Secrets of a Civil War Submarine: Solving the Mysteries of the* H. L. Hunley follows the design, building, sinking, and recovery of a submarine that made history in 1864 as the first submarine to sink an enemy ship. These four books allow students to develop in-depth understandings of the time period, the conflicts, and the issues.

Some history books appropriate for young adults focus on one issue. For example, Diane McWhorter's *A Dream of Freedom: The Civil Rights Movement From 1954 to 1968* can be read by different age groups. Young adult readers may develop deeper levels of understanding and criticism because the author includes both sides of such issues as *Brown v. Board of Education*, the Little Rock Nine, and the violence that accompanied the freedom riders and the Black Panthers. A related book is Patricia McKissack and Arlene Zarembka's *To Establish Justice: Citizenship and the Constitution*, in which the authors present a history of selected Supreme Court decisions and develop the argument that Supreme Court rulings have the power to support or deny civil rights.

Young adults will receive an overview of the major happenings in the 20th century by reading Richard B. Stolley's *Life: Our Century in Pictures for Young People* and James Cross Giblin's *The Century That Was: Reflections on the Last One Hundred Years.*

Informational books on current events and contemporary issues for young adults encourage readers to consider the issues that may be discussed in the 21st century. To acquire these insights, they can read and discuss books such as W. Patrick Lang's *Intelligence: The Human Factor,* which focuses on issues of national security since 9/11; James Haley's *Foreign Oil Dependence,* which includes articles about topics such as drilling for oil in Alaska; and Auriana Ojeda's *Civil Liberties,* which discusses current responses to freedom of expression, privacy, and separation of church and state. The content of these books makes the questions Bauer (2003) recommends even more important if students are to read with understanding and become critical readers of their books.

Teaching With Informational Books

nformational books provide excellent sources for teaching in the content areas if the books follow the definition for truth in informational books. Kathleen Isaacs (2005) reaffirms the importance of truth in informational books when she cites the definition presented by The Robert F. Sibert Informational Book Award: "Informational books are defined as those written and illustrated to present, organize, and interpret documentable factual material for children" (p. 28). If these books are well written by authors who have considerable knowledge in their areas, they provide valuable sources for the classroom. Literature discussed in this chapter—especially that discussed under nature, including the human body, animals, plants, and geology and geography—are subjects that are also found in the science curriculum.

Incorporating Literature Into The Science Curriculum

James Rutherford (1991), the chief education officer of the American Association for the Advancement of Science, argues that trade books rather than textbooks should be a primary source of science materials in the early grades. He states:

> I would say that the elementary school classroom, in the earliest grades, should not have science textbooks. They are too ordered, too assertive by their nature, too given to explanations. . . . Furthermore, textbooks are rarely very relevant to the real neighborhoods where the children go to school. . . . Nevertheless, despite this ban on textbooks in the early grades, books should be an essential part of science learning. What that means is that once we rule out the conventional textbook, we have to think very carefully and more creatively about the role that books really should play. (p. 27)

When recommending the types of books that should be used in the early grades, Rutherford states, "The kind I am recommending are those which are adventurous, in which the story is built around finding things out, and which emphasize the excitement of discovery" (p. 29). He concludes: "Elementary classroom books should promote the legitimacy of imaginative thinking, just as much as they promote activity. It is just this combination of action, thought, and imagination that makes science so powerful" (p. 30).

Lazer Goldberg (1991) reinforces Rutherford's beliefs about the quality of trade books in the science curriculum. He believes that good science books should foster questions and critical thinking because "critical thinking is at the heart of science" (p. 34).

Science author Laurence Pringle (1991) also argues the benefits of trade books over textbooks in the science curriculum. He states:

> It is the process of science, and how scientists think, that needs more attention in children's books. Textbooks do a lot of telling and defining; they're often curiosity-killers. They usually fail to convey a sense of excitement in scientific research. (p. 52)

Pringle also believes that good trade books should foster critical thinking and reasoning. He warns, however, that science trade books must be chosen with the same scrutiny used in choosing textbooks. Poorly written trade books can also kill curiosity and restrict critical thinking and reasoning.

Several values of informational books relate to the science curriculum. Interesting books—such as those by Seymour Simon, Millicent Selsam, and Laurence Pringle—allow children to experience the excitement of discovery. Through books such as Simon's *How to Be an Ocean Scientist in Your Own Home,* children can observe, experiment, compare, formulate and test hypotheses, draw conclusions, and evaluate their evidence. Children can become directly involved in the scientific method. Even fairly young children can become interested in the scientific method by reading Kathryn Lasky's humorous *Science Fair Bunnies,* in which two first graders (bunny characters) first face the problem of a failed project and then solve the problem by developing a new project. Through the project, readers discover the importance of keeping careful records as well as relying on originality and independent work. Through the experiments and information found in many informational books, children can learn about the world of nature. Because many informational books that deal with science subjects have greater depth of coverage than do science textbooks, such informational books are valuable for extending knowledge and understanding.

Communication abilities, such as graphing, illustrating, recording, and reporting, are especially important to science. Authors of science informational books frequently use these communication abilities when writing. Consequently, children are introduced to reading and interpreting graphs and can present their own ideas and findings in graphic form. Children need many opportunities to interpret data and to make predictions from them. Such experiences help children become actively involved in reading and discovery.

However, the nature of science materials—with their heavy concentration of facts and details, new scientific principles, and new technical vocabulary—may cause reading problems for children who are accustomed to the narrative writing style. Use excellent informational materials on science-related topics to encourage children to develop their abilities to read science-related materials and to understand science-related concepts. This text considers abilities that relate to both literature and the content areas: using the parts of the book, locating sources of information, using science vocabulary, reading for meaning, evaluating science materials, and applying data from reading to practical problems. The specific books mentioned are only examples of the numerous books that you can use in the classroom. You may wish to add other informational books.

Using the Parts of a Book

Science informational books reinforce the ability to use parts of a book because many books contain a table of contents, a glossary, a bibliography of further readings, and an index. Children can use the table of contents in conjunction with an index to locate specific content. For example:

1. Find the chapter describing "The Battle to Bring the Gray Wolf Home" in Stephen R. Swinburne's *Once a Wolf: How Wildlife Biologists Fought to Bring Back the Gray Wolf* (Chapter 3, pp. 21 and 28).

2. Find the page that describes the migration of caterpillars in Sy Montgomery's *The Snake Scientist* (p. 33).

3. Find the chapter on "All Was Not Right" in Jim Murphy's *An American Plague* (chapter 2, p. 11).

4. Find the number of entries that are classified as fossils in Nic Bishop's *Digging for Bird-Dinosaurs: An Expedition to Madagascar* (11 entries plus "See also dinosaurs").

5. Find the chapter describing damage caused by mudflows in Patricia Lauber's *Volcano: The Eruption and Healing of Mount St. Helens* (Chapter 2, pp. 15–17).

Laurence Pringle's books usually have a glossary of technical terms, an index, and a list of further readings that provide additional information about a subject. Use these books to reinforce the importance of each part of the book, the kind of information that is available, and locational aids. Books that include lists of further reading and biographical sources, such as Rhoda Blumberg's *Commodore Perry in the Land of the Shogun* and Jim Murphy's *The Great Fire*, provide opportunities for students to locate additional subjects.

Locating Sources of Information

Helping children learn how to make their own discoveries about a subject fosters important scientific goals. You can use the lists of references at the back of many informational books to show children how to use a library filing system for more information. For example, Joe Rhatigan and Rain Newcomb's *Out-of-This-World Astronomy* includes 37 on-line resources. Jim Murphy's *The Great Fire* lists 17 additional books about the Chicago fire. Murphy's *An American Plague* includes 13 pages of sources. Charlotte and David Yue's *Christopher Columbus: How He Did It* includes 22 additional books that provide further information.

Using Science Vocabulary

The glossary in many informational books is also a source of information about the meaning of technical terminology found in the book. Authors such as Caroline Arnold, in *Saving the Peregrine Falcon*, and Sally Walker, in *Glaciers: Ice on the Move* and *Rhinos*, use boldface type to identify terms that are defined in the glossary. Authors of informational books for children often present the meaning of new words through their context in the text. You should specifically point out this technique to children to help them understand the meanings of words. In *Almost the Real Thing: Simulation in Your High-Tech World*, Gloria Skurzynski presents meaning in both the text and a glossary. For example, in the text, she states: "Simulations are imitations of things that exist in the real world. Almost anything can be simulated—in images, in solid models you can touch, in sound, in motion, or in elements that you can feel, like the wind" (p. 7). In the glossary, she provides additional information for *simulation*: "an imitation that represents a real object, like an airplane's cockpit; or represents a force, like the wind; or an abstract idea, such as nuclear winter" (p. 63).

Authors also clarify the meanings of technical terminology through photographs, diagrams, and charts. Even books written for young children often use labeled drawings to clarify meanings of technical terminology. Millicent Selsam and Joyce Hunt's books for young children, including *A First Look at Caterpillars* and *A First Look at Seals, Sea Lions, and Walruses*, discuss specific characteristics that are easy to observe in illustrations. Selsam and Hunt use technical terms frequently and ask children to use their knowledge to answer questions. In *Creepy, Crawly Caterpillars*, Margery Facklam's terms are reinforced by Paul Facklam's illustrations that include labeled details in the lower portion of the page. For example, on a page showing the monarch caterpillar, the lower illustrations depict the changes from egg to butterfly.

Reading for Meaning

A major reason that many students give for reading informational science books is to acquire facts; therefore, comprehending the meaning is important. Unlike writings that stress make-believe, informational science books are based on accuracy. Children often need encouragement to note main ideas and supporting details and to see organization. Books on reading methods usually include several chapters about these comprehension abilities, but the approaches considered here allow content-area teachers and parents to reinforce and encourage the abilities through informational books.

Noting Main Ideas. Because many informational books written for children have a main idea as a topic sentence at the beginning of a paragraph, many teachers have children read a paragraph and then visualize the author's organization of the material according to the main idea and important details. (This technique may also help children evaluate whether the author uses a logical organization and help them use similar structures in their own nonfiction writing.) A typical paragraph may follow this organization (Norton, 2004):

Main Idea
Supporting Detail
Supporting Detail
Supporting Detail
Supporting Detail

Seymour Simon's writing tends to follow this structure. Use this diagram with material from *New Questions and Answers About Dinosaurs* to help children identify the main idea and supporting details and to evaluate whether the organization is logical. On page 4 of Simon's book are two paragraphs that answer the question "What are dinosaurs?" Arrange the paragraph in the following way:

Main idea: Answer the question What are dinosaurs?
Supporting details:
A group of reptiles that appeared about 225 million years ago.
Dinosaurs lived during the Mesozoic era, sometimes called the Age of Reptiles.

Dinosaurs died about 65 million years ago, long before there were humans.
There were hundreds of different kinds and sizes of dinosaurs.
Some dinosaurs were meat-eaters and some were plant-eaters.
Dinosaurs were spread across the world.
Dinosaurs lived for 160 million years.

Have children discuss whether Simon developed his main idea and answered the question with sufficient supporting details. The remainder of Simon's book uses a similar approach. Each two-page spread answers a question with one or two short paragraphs. The text includes such questions as Were all ancient reptiles dinosaurs?, How else are new dinosaurs discovered?, How are dinosaurs named?, and Were dinosaurs cold-blooded or warm-blooded? If children do not receive sufficient answers to any of their questions, encourage them to expand their knowledge through further reading and investigations.

Noting Supporting Details. When noting main ideas, children should learn to identify supporting details in diagrams and questions. In informational science books, size, color, number, location, and texture are also supporting details. Have the children listen to or read a description from an informational science book and then draw a picture that shows the important details. The following descriptions are examples of sources that you can use:

1. The description of the process associated with grafting found on pages 8–9 in Charles Micucci's *The Life and Times of the Apple*.

2. The description of lightning found in Stephen Kramer's *Lightning* (various sections of this book).

Seeing an Author's Organization. A logical organization of information is often critical in the science content areas. Use books that emphasize the life cycles of plants and animals, the correct steps to use in an experiment, or a chain of events to help children increase their ability to note scientific organization and to evaluate an author's ability to organize logically. Also use books that organize content according to subject. For example, discuss why David Macaulay chose the following organizational plan for the relationships among the objects pictured in *The Way Things Work*: (1) the mechanics of movement, (2) harnessing the elements, (3) working with waves, and (4) electricity and automation.

To organize content according to geographic area, mark on a large world map in different colors the six areas identified in Joyce Pope's *Kenneth Lilly's Animals: A Portfolio of Paintings*—(1) hot forests, (2) cool forests, (3) seas and rivers, (4) grasslands, (5) deserts, and (6) mountains. Have students list the characteristics of the areas, the animals in each area, and the characteristics of the animals. Have the students search through geography texts to identify additional characteristics of these areas. Ask them to consider why Pope's organization seems logical. Have them compare the effectiveness of Pope's organization with that in other texts in the library that use maps to identify locations of animals. Another book that encourages students to analyze organization through a map is John S. Major's *The Silk Route: 7,000 Miles of History;* the text follows the ancient route from Chang'an to Byzantium.

Evaluating Science Materials

Evaluation requires critical thinking. Critical reading and thinking go beyond factual comprehension; they require identifying the problem, weighing the validity of facts, making judgments, interpreting implied ideas, distinguishing fact from opinion, drawing conclusions, determining the adequacy of a source of information, and suspending judgment until all of the facts have been accumulated. For example, have students develop questions to ask when evaluating science materials. For this activity, have them consider the evaluation criteria used by the book review journal *Appraisal: Science Books for Young People* and develop questions around the following guidelines recommended by Diane Holzheimer (1991) for that journal. First, accuracy is extremely important. Consequently, materials should be correct and up to date. Second, the organization should be logical for the book. Third, the writing should be clear and logical. Fourth, writers should use language with precision and grace and should encourage readers to participate in the subject. Fifth, the illustrations should aid understanding and be appealing. Sixth, if the book has activities and experiments, the instructions should be clear. Seventh, the book should exemplify scientific attitudes, stimulate imagination, and encourage readers to examine firsthand the wonders of the world.

In addition to questions that allow the students to evaluate the text, develop questions that allow them to consider authors' qualifications. For example, help students answer the following list of questions about the authors:

1. *Why did the author write this book?* Was it to present information? to promote a point of view? to advertise? to propagandize? to entertain?

2. *How qualified is the author to write on this topic for this purpose?* What is the author's background? What is the author's reputation? Does the author have any vested interest in this topic? What is the author's professional position?

To help children critically evaluate authors of informational books (this list and activity are excellent for all informational books, not just those related to science), provide access to many books by different authors and biographical information about the authors. One teacher of upper-elementary students divided a class into five research groups according to a category of interest that each group chose to investigate: botany, birds, earth and geology, land mammals, and insects. (You can use the list of authors and books in the Children's Literature at the end of this chapter to help you and your students identify books and topics.)

Next, the students found as many books as possible on these categories in the library, including each author's most recent publications on the subject. They read the information about the author on the dust jacket or elsewhere in the book and searched for biographical data and magazine or journal articles written by the author. Then the students evaluated the author's background and read and reread the books, searching for each author's point of view and purpose for writing the book.

After the students had carefully read the books, they evaluated the content of the materials according to the criteria developed earlier.

The children also read background information in science textbooks, encyclopedias, and magazines or journals. They checked the copyright dates of the materials; scrutinized the photographs, graphs, charts, and diagrams; and evaluated whether the author differentiated fact from opinion. If the students found more than one viewpoint on the subject, they tried to determine whether the author presented them all.

Finally, the groups presented their information on the authors and their books to the rest of the class. The students learned how to critically evaluate informational books and authors. They also learned much about the content area and the procedures that writers of informational books should use when they research their subjects.

A number of authors of informational science books develop themes related to endangered species and ecology. Books with these themes can provide stimulating sources for topics of debate and independent research. Have students use the criteria for evaluating authors and content that were given earlier in this section. In addition, have them test the validity of an argument presented in written materials. For example, have them strip the argument of any excess words or sentences; identify all of the premises upon which an author's conclusion rests; determine whether the author is referring to all of a group, some of a group, or none of a group; and determine whether the conclusion logically follows from the premises.

Next, have students independently evaluate whether the author's conclusion is logical and supported by facts. Also, have them enter into debates, choosing different sides of an issue, researching outside sources, and developing contrasting viewpoints. For example, use Stephen R. Swinburne's *Once a Wolf: How Wildlife Biologists Fought to*

Bring Back the Gray Wolf to help students debate about the plight of the wolf and the role of humans in this plight.

Have the students choose sides in these issues, complete additional research, and present their positions in debate format. They may include the following points that show humans as friends of wolves:

1. Wildlife biologists are attempting to bring the gray wolf back to its natural habitat in Yellowstone National Park.

2. The 1960s and 1970s saw sweeping environmental changes influenced by Rachel Carson's publication *Silent Spring.*

3. The Endangered Species Act guaranteed protection of wolves by imposing a $10,000 fine and a jail sentence on anyone killing a wolf.

4. Overpopulation of elk, moose, and deer resulted without the wolf as predator to control their numbers. Animals killed by wolves were often diseased or crippled.

5. A 1991 environmental impact statement favored releasing Canadian wolves in Yellowstone.

6. The Native Americans, especially the Lakota, Blackfoot, and Shoshone, believed that the wolf was their spiritual brother and respected its endurance and its hunting ability.

The following points show humans as foes to wolves:

1. Wolves have been hated and feared by Europeans throughout history.

2. Europeans who settled America in the 17th century brought their hatred of wolves with them. They feared wolves would kill cattle, horses, and sheep.

3. The wolf was killed because it was seen as an obstacle to civilization and progress.

4. Ranchers set cattle loose on the western ranges and attacked wolves when the wolves killed livestock.

5. Ranchers believed that wolf recovery was forced on them by easterners and city residents.

Some animals are not endangered because people hunt or poison them; instead, pollution or land development has endangered their survival. Books on this subject can spark debates whether the interests of people are in opposition to the interests of animals and whether the protective measures designed for animals also protect humans. You also can use Nicholas and Theodore Nirgiotis's *No More Dodos: How Zoos Help Endangered Wildlife* for this purpose.

Other books about animals that have been endangered include Phillip Hoose's *The Race to Save the Lord God Bird,* Lola M. Schaefer's *Arrowhawk,* and Brenda Z. Guiberson's *Into the Sea.*

Suggested Activities

For more suggested activities for understanding nonfiction, visit the Companion Website at www.prenhall.com/norton

- Select a content area, such as science or social studies, that is taught in an elementary or middle school grade. From the curriculum, identify men and women who are discussed in that content area. Develop an annotated bibliography of literature on a subject, such as biology, to stimulate interest in the subject and provide additional information about the contributors.

- Develop a bibliography of websites that can be used to add to or to evaluate the accuracy of one of the topics in the informational books discussed in the chapter. Students can use the evaluation criteria of reviewers of websites for *School Library Journal* (Ishizuka, 2005). Highly recommended websites are chosen "for accuracy, authority, developmental appropriateness, clear design, and navigation" (p. 69).

- Select the work of an outstanding author of informational books for children, such as Millicent E. Selsam, Seymour Simon, or Laurence Pringle. Evaluate the books according to the criteria listed in this chapter. Share with the class the characteristics of the books that make them highly recommended.

- Following suggestions recommended by Bamford and Kristo (2000), locate examples of books that use on-site research, books that identify the author's research process, books that present the author's credentials, books that allow readers to detect author bias, and books in which authors speculate using limited information. With a peer group, evaluate the effectiveness of each category of book.

- Search journals that include recommended informational books for specific content areas such as *Book Links, The Reading Teacher,* and *Curriculum Connections* (a supplement to *School Library Journal*). What are the characteristics of books recommended for specific content areas?

Children's Literature

For full descriptions, including plot summaries and award winner notations, of these and other titles for teaching children with nonfiction, visit the CD-ROM that accompanies this book.

Aagesen, Colleen, and Marcia Blumberg. *Shakespeare for Kids: His Life and Times.* Chicago Review Press, 1999 (I:9+).

Alonso, Karen. *Schenck v. United States: Restrictions on Free Speech.* Enslow, 1999 (I:10+ R:6).

Altman, Linda Jacobs. *Slavery and Abolition in American History.* Enslow, 1999 (I:10+ R:6).

Ambrose, Stephen E. *The Good Fight: How World War II Was Won.* Simon & Schuster, 2001 (I:9+ R:5).

Amendola, Dana. *A Day at the New Amsterdam Theatre.* Photographs by Gino Domenico. Disney, 2004 (I:9–YA R:6).

I = Interest by age range.
R = Readability by grade level.

Amendola, Dana. *A Day at the New Amsterdam Theatre.* Photographs by Gino Domenico. Disney, 2004 (I:10+–YA R:6).

Ammon, Richard. *Conestoga Wagons.* Illustrated by Bill Farnsworth. Holiday House, 2000 (I:7+ R:4).

_____. *Valley Forge.* Illustrated by Bill Farnsworth. Holiday House, 2004 (I:8–12 R:6).

Appelbaum, Diana. *Giants in the Land.* Illustrated by Michael McCurdy. Houghton Mifflin, 1993 (I:6–9 R:4).

Armstrong, Jennifer. *Photo by Brady: A Picture of the Civil War.* Simon & Schuster, 2005 (I:10–YA R:7).

Arnold, Caroline. *The Ancient Cliff Dwellers of Mesa Verde.* Photographs by Richard Hewett. Clarion, 1992 (I:8+ R:6).

_____. *Stone Age Farmers Beside the Sea: Scotland's Prehistoric Village of Skara Brae.* Photographs by Arthur P. Arnold. Clarion, 1997 (I:8–12 R:6).

Arnosky, Jim. *Freshwater Fish and Fishing.* Four Winds, 1982 (I:8–12 R:5).

Arthur, Alex. *Shell.* Knopf, 1989 (I:9+ R:6).

Ashabranner, Brent. *To Seek a Better World: The Haitian Minority in America.* Photographs by Paul Conklin. Cobblehill, 1997 (I:10+ R:6).

Ashby, Ruth. *Elizabethan England.* Cavendish, 1999 (I:10+ R:6).

Bachrach, Susan D. *The Nazi Olympics: Berlin 1936.* Little, Brown, 2000 (I:10+ R:6).

Ballard, Robert D. *Exploring the Titanic.* Scholastic, 1988 (I:8+ R:5).

Bang, Molly. *My Light.* Scholastic, 2004 (I:5–10 R:4).

Bany-Winters, Lisa. *Show Time!: Music, Dance, and Drama Activities for Kids.* Chicago Review Press, 2000 (I:7+ R:5).

Barnes, Peter W., and Cheryl Shaw Barnes. *Woodrow for President: A Tail of Voting, Campaigns and Elections.* VSP, 1999 (I:7+ R:4).

Bartoletti, Susan Campbell. *The Flag Maker: A Story of the Star-Spangled Banner.* Illustrated by Claire A. Nivola. Houghton Mifflin, 2004 (I:8+ R:4).

_____. *Growing Up in Coal Country.* Houghton Mifflin, 1996 (I:10+ R:5).

_____. *Hitler Youth: Growing Up in Hitler's Shadow.* Scholastic, 2005 (I:10–YA R:6).

Barton, Byron. *Airport.* Crowell, 1982 (I:3–8).

Bash, Barbara. *Desert Giant: The World of the Saguaro Cactus.* Sierra Club/Little Brown, 1989 (I:5–9 R:4).

_____. *Shadows of Night: The Hidden World of the Little Brown Bat.* Sierra Club, 1993 (I:5–9 R:4).

_____. *Urban Roosts: Where Birds Nest in the City.* Little, Brown, 1990 (I:4–9 R:5).

Bauer, Marion Dane. *What's Your Story? A Young Person's Guide to Writing Fiction.* Clarion, 1992 (I:10+ R:5).

Bausum, Ann. *With Courage and Cloth: Winning the Fight for a Woman's Right to Vote.* National Geographic, 2004 (I:12–YA R:8).

Beattie, Owen, and John Geiger. *Buried in Ice: The Mystery of a Lost Arctic Expedition.* Scholastic, 1992 (I:9+ R:4).

Bial, Raymond. *The Chumash.* Benchmark, 2004 (I:8+ R:5).

Birdseye, Debbie Holsclaw, & Tom Birdseye. *What I Believe: Kids Talk About Faith.* Photographs by Robert Crum. Holiday House, 1996 (I:8+ R:4).

Bishop, Nic. *Digging for Bird-Dinosaurs: An Expedition to Madagascar.* Houghton Mifflin, 2000 (I:8+ R:5).

_____. *The Secrets of Animal Flight.* Illustrated by Amy Bartlett Wright. Houghton Mifflin, 1997 (I:8+ R:4).

Bitton-Jackson, Livia. *I Have Lived a Thousand Years: Growing Up in the Holocaust.* Simon & Schuster, 1997 (I:12+ R:6).

Blacklock, Dyan. *The Roman Army: The Legendary Soldiers Who Created an Empire.* Illustrated by David Kennett. Walker, 2004 (I:9+ R:6)

Blumberg, Rhoda. *Commodore Perry in the Land of the Shogun.* Lothrop, Lee & Shepard, 1985 (I:9+ R:6).

_____. *Full Steam Ahead: The Race to Build a Transcontinental Railroad.* National Geographic, 1996 (I:9+ R:6).

_____. *The Incredible Journey of Lewis and Clark.* Lothrop, Lee & Shepard, 1987 (I:9+ R:6).

_____. *What's the Deal? Jefferson, Napoleon, and the Louisiana Purchase.* National Geographic, 1999 (I:9+ R:6).

Bober, Natalie. *Countdown to Independence: A Revolution of Ideas in England and Her American Colonies: 1760–1776.* Simon & Schuster, 2001 (I:12+ R:7).

Boitano, Brian, & Suzanne Harper. *Boitano's Edge: Inside the Real World of Figure Skating.* Simon & Schuster, 1997 (I:8+ R:4).

Bolden, Tonya. *Cause: Reconstruction America 1863–1877.* Knopf, 2005 (I:14–YA R:7).

_____. *Wake Up Our Souls: A Celebration of Black American Artists.* Abrams, 2004 (I:10+ R:6).

Bortolotti, Dan. *Panda Rescue: Changing the Future for Endangered Wildlife.* Firefly, 2003 (I:8+ R:4).

_____. *Tiger Rescue: Changing the Future for Endangered Wildlife.* Firefly, 2003 (I:8+ R:4).

Boyd, Herb. *We Shall Overcome: A Living History of the Civil Rights Struggle Told in Words, Pictures and Voices of the Participants.* SourceBooks Media Fusion, 2004 (I:15+–YA).

Brandenburg, Jim. *An American Safari: Adventures on the North American Prairie.* Walker, 1995 (I:8+ R:5).

_____. *Sand and Fog: Adventures in Southern Africa.* Walker, 1994 (I:10+ R:5).

Brenner, Barbara. *If You Were There in 1492.* Macmillan, 1991 (I:8+ R:5).

Brown, Laurie Krasny, and Marc Brown. *Dinosaurs to the Rescue! A Guide to Protecting Our Planet.* Little, Brown, 1992 (I:5–8 R:4).

Brown, Mary Barrett. *Wings Along the Waterway.* Orchard, 1992 (I:10+ R:6).

Bunting, Eve. *I Am the Mummy Heb-Nefert.* Illustrated by David Christiana. Harcourt Brace, 1997 (I:all R:4).

Burandt, Harriet, & Shelly Dale. *Tales From the Homeplace: Adventures of a Texas Farm Girl.* Holt, 1997 (I:9+ R:5).

Butterfield, Moira. *Going to War in Roman Times.* Watts, 2001 (I:9+ R:6).

Calvert, Patricia. *The Ancient Inca.* Franklin Watts, 2004 (I:9+ R:5).

Carle, Megan, & Jill Carle, with Judi Carle. *Teens Cook: How to Cook What You Want to Eat.* Photographs by Jessica Boone. Ten Speed, 2004 (I:12–YA R:6).

Carrick, Carol. *Whaling Days.* Illustrated by David Frampton. Clarion, 1993 (I:8+ R:4).

Carroll, Colleen. *How Artists See Animals: Mammal Fish Bird Reptile*. Abbeville, 1996 (I:all).

_____. *How Artists See the Elements: Earth Air Fire Water*. Abbeville, 1996 (I:all).

_____. *How Artists See People: Boy Girl Man Woman*. Abbeville, 1996 (I:all).

_____. *How Artists See the Weather: Sun Wind Snow Rain*. Abbeville, 1996 (I:all).

Carter, David A., and James Diaz. *The Elements of Pop-Up*. Simon & Schuster, 1999 (I:10+).

Cerullo, Mary M. *The Octopus: Phantom of the Sea*. Photographs by Jeffery L. Rotman. Cobblehill, 1997 (I:9+ R:5).

Christelow, Eileen. *Vote*. Clarion, 2003 (I:all).

Christian, Peggy. *If You Find a Rock*. Photographs by Barbara Hirsch Lember. Harcourt, 2000 (I:6–9 R:4).

Clinton, Catherine. *Scholastic Encyclopedia of the Civil War*. Scholastic, 1999 (I:10+ R:6).

Cole, Joanna. *How You Were Born*. Photographs by Margaret Miller. Morrow, 1993 (I:4–8 R:4).

_____. *The Magic School Bus: Inside the Earth*. Illustrated by Bruce Degen. Scholastic, 1987 (I:6–8 R:4).

_____. *The Magic School Bus: Lost in the Solar System*. Illustrated by Bruce Degen. Scholastic, 1990 (I:6–8 R:4).

_____. *The Magic School Bus: On the Ocean Floor*. Illustrated by Bruce Degen. Scholastic, 1992 (I:6–8 R:4).

_____. *My Puppy Is Born*. Photographs by Jerome Wexler. Morrow, 1991 (I:7–9 R:2).

Collard, Sneed B. *Animal Dads*. Illustrated by Steve Jenkins. Houghton Mifflin, 1997 (I:5–8 R:4).

Colman, Penny. *Carpses, Coffins, and Crypts; A History of Burial*. Holt, 1997 (I:10+ R:6).

Cone, Molly. *Come Back Salmon*. Photographs by Sidnee Wheelwright. Sierra Club, 1992 (I:8+ R:5).

_____. *Squishy, Misty, Damp & Muddy: The In-Between World of Wetlands*. Sierra Club, 1996 (I:all R:7).

Cooper, Michael L. *Dust to Eat: Drought and Depression in the 1930s*. Clarion, 2004 (I:8+ R:5).

_____. *Indian School: Teaching the White Man's Way*. Clarion, 1999 (I:9+ R:5).

Cornell, Kari A. *Holiday Cooking Around the World*. Lerner, 2002 (I:9+ R:6).

Cowley, Joy. *Red-Eyed Tree Frog*. Photographs by Nic Bishop. Scholastic, 1999 (I:5+ R:4).

Curlee, Lynn. *Liberty*. Atheneum, 2000 (I:9+ R:5).

_____. *Rushmore*. Scholastic, 1999 (I:9+ R:5).

Dendy, Leslie, & Mel Boring. *Guinea Pig Scientists: Bold Self-Experiments in Science and Medicine*. Illustrated by C. B. Mordan. Henry Holt, 2005 (I:10–YA R:7).

dePaola, Tomie. *The Popcorn Book*. Holiday House, 1978 (I:3–8 R:5).

Drez, Ronald J. *Remember D-Day: The Plan, the Invasion, Survivor Stories*. National Georgraphic, 2004 (I:10+ R:6).

Duke, Kate. *Archaeologists Dig for Clues*. HarperCollins, 1997 (I:6–9 R:5).

Dunleavy, Deborah. *The Jumbo Book of Drama*. Illustrated by Jane Kurisu. Kids Can, 2004 (I:8+ R:5).

Earle, Sylvia A. *Hello, Fish!: Visiting the Coral Reef*. Photographs by Wolcott Henry. National Geographic, 1999 (I:all R:4).

Englander, Roger. *Opera, What's All the Screaming About?* Walker, 1983 (I:10+ R:7).

Erbensen, Barbara Juster. *Tiger With Wings: The Great Horned Owl*. Illustrated by Mary Barrett Brown. Orchard, 1991 (I:5–9 R:4).

Faber, Doris, & Harold Faber. *We the People: The Story of the United States Constitution Since 1787*. Scribners, 1987 (I:10–YA R:6).

Faber, Harold. *The Discoverers of America*. Scribner, 1992 (I:10+ R:7).

Facklam, Margery. *Creepy, Crawly Caterpillars*. Little, Brown, 1996 (I:4–9 R:7).

_____. *Tracking Dinosaurs in the Gobi*. 21st Century, 1997 (I:10+ R:6).

Falk, John H., et al. *Bubble Monster: And Other Science Fun*. Illustrated by Charles C. Somerville. Chicago Review, 1996 (I:4–8).

Ferrell, Claudine I. *Reconstruction*. Greenwood, 2003 (I:12–YA R:7).

Finkelstein, Norman. *The Other Fourteen Ninety-Two: Jewish Settlement in the New World*. Scribner, 1989 (I:10+ R:6).

Fischer-Nagel, Heiderose, & Andraes Fischer-Nagel. *Life of the Honey Bee*. Carolrhoda, 1986 (I:6–10 R:6).

Fisher, Aileen. *The Story Goes On*. Illustrated by Mique Moriuchi. Roaring Brook, 2005 (I:all).

Fleisher, Paul. *Life Cycles of a Dozen Diverse Creatures*. Millbrook, 1996 (I:9+ R:6).

Floca, Brian. *Dinosaurs at the Ends of the Earth: The Story of the Central Asiatic Expeditions*. Dorling Kindersley, 2000 (I:8+ R:6).

Fraser, Mary Ann. *Vicksburg: The Battle That Won the Civil War*. Henry Holt, 1999 (I:10+ R:5).

Freedman, Russell. *Buffalo Hunt*. Holiday House, 1988 (I:8+ R:6).

_____. *An Indian Winter*. Illustrated by Karl Bodmer. Holiday House, 1992 (I:8+ R:6).

French, Vivian. *Growing Frogs*. Illustrated by Alison Bartlett. Candlewick, 2000 (I:5+ R:4).

_____. *T. Rex*. Illustrated by Alison Bartlett. Candlewick, 2004 (I:2–5 R:4).

Fritz, Jean. *Shh! We're Writing the Constitution*. Illustrated by Tomie dePaola. Putnam, 1987 (I:7–10 R:5).

_____, Katherine Paterson, Patricia McKissack, Fredrick McKissack, Margaret Mahy, & Jamake Highwater. *The World in 1492*. Illustrated by Stefano Vitale. Holt, 1992 (I:8+ R:6).

Gatti, Anne, retold by. *The Magic Flute*. Illustrated by Peter Malone. Chronicle, 1997 (I:8+).

George, Jean Craighead. *Everglades*. Illustrated by Wendell Minor. HarperCollins, 1995 (I:7+ R:5).

George, Lindsay Barrett. *Around the World: Who's Been Here?* Greenwillow, 1999 (I:8+ R:5).

George, William T. *Box Turtle at Long Pond*. Illustrated by Lindsay Barrett George. Greenwillow, 1989 (I:3–8 R:3).

Gibbons, Gail. *Beacons of Light: Lighthouses*. Morrow, 1990 (I:7–9 R:4).

_____. *Dinosaurs*. Holiday House, 1987 (I:4–8 R:3).

_____. *Santa Who?* Morrow, 1999 (I:all R:4).

Giblin, James Cross, ed. *The Century That Was: Reflections on the Last One Hundred Years.* Atheneum, 2000 (I:10+ R:4).

_____. *Secrets of the Sphinx.* Illustrated by Bagram Ibatoulline. Scholastic, 2004 (I:10+ R:6).

Gillette, J. Lynett. *Dinosaur Ghosts: The Mystery of Coelophysis.* Illustrated by Douglas Henderson. Dial, 1997 (I:9+ R:6).

Goldin, Barbara. *The Passover Journey: A Seder Companion.* Illustrated by Neil Waldman. Viking, 1994 (I:all R:4).

Goodall, Jane. *The Chimpanzee Family Book.* Photographs by Michael Neugebauer. Picture Book Studio, 1989 (I:8+ R:5).

_____. *The Chimpanzees I Love: Saving Their World and Ours.* Scholastic, 2001 (I:10+ R:5).

Goodman, Susan E. *Stones, Bones, and Petroglyphs: Digging Into Southwest Archaeology.* Photographs by Michael J. Doolittle. Atheneum, 1998 (I:10+ R:6).

Gourley, Catherine. *Hunting Neptune's Giants: True Stories of American Whaling.* Millbrook, 1995 (I:10+ R:8).

Grace, Eric S. *Seals.* Photographs by Fred Bruemmer. Sierra Club/Little, Brown, 1991 (I:8+ R:6).

Graff, Nancy Price. *The Strength of the Hills: A Portrait of a Family Farm.* Photographs by Richard Howard. Little, Brown, 1989 (I:all R:5).

Granfield, Linda. *Circus: An Album.* DK, 1998 (I:8+ R:6).

_____. *In Flanders Fields: The Story of the Poem by John McCrae.* Doubleday, 1996 (I:9+ R:6).

Greene, Carol. *Police Officers Protect People.* Child's World, 1996 (I:4–7 R:4).

Greenwald, Michelle. *The Magical Melting Pot: The All-American Cookbook That Celebrates America's Diversity.* Cherry, 2003 (I:12+–YA R:6).

Guiberson, Brenda Z. *Into the Sea.* Illustrated by Alix Berenzy. Holt, 1996 (I:5–8 R:4).

_____. *Spoonbill Swamp.* Illustrated by Megan Lloyd. Holt, 1992 (I:4–7 R:4).

Hakim, Joy. *The Story of Science: Aristotle Leads the Way.* Smithsonian, 2004 (I:12+–YA R:8).

Haley, James, ed. *Foreign Oil Dependence.* Greenhaven, 2004 (I:12–YA R:7).

Halpern, Monica. *Railroad Fever: Building the Transcontinental Railroad 1830–1870.* National Geographic, 2004 (I:8+ R:5).

Harris, Robie H. *It's So Amazing!: A Book About Eggs, Sperm, Birth, Babies, and Families.* Illustrated by Michael Emberley. Candlewick, 1999 (I:7+ R:4).

Hearne, Betsy. *Seven Brave Women.* Illustrated by Bethanne Andersen. Greenwillow, 1997 (I:5–8 R:5).

Heiligman, Deborah. *From Caterpillar to Butterfly.* Illustrated by Bari Weissman. HarperCollins, 1996 (I:5–8 R:4).

High, Linda Oatman. *Barn Savers.* Illustrated by Ted Lewin. Boyds Mills, 1999 (I:8+ R:5).

Hill, Laban Carrick. *Harlem Stomp! A Cultural History of the Harlem Renaissance.* Little, Brown, 2003 (I:10+ R:6).

Hinds, Kathryn. *Life in the Roman Empire: The City.* Benchmark, 2005 (I:8+ R:4).

_____. *Life in the Roman Empire: The Countryside.* Benchmark, 2005 (I:8+ R:4).

_____. *Life in the Roman Empire: The Patricians.* Benchmark, 2005 (I:8+ R:4).

Hirst, Robin, and Sally Hirst. *My Place in Space.* Illustrated by Roland Harvey & Joe Levine. Orchard, 1990 (I:5–8 R:5).

Hoban, Tana. *A Children's Zoo.* Greenwillow, 1985 (I:2–6).

Hoobler, Dorothy, & Thomas Hoobler. *The Jewish American Family Album.* Oxford, 1995 (I:all R:10).

Hoose, Phillip. *The Race to Save the Lord God Bird.* Farrar, Straus & Giroux, 2004 (I:10+–YA R:6).

_____. *We Were There, Too!: Young People in U.S. History.* Farrar, Straus & Giroux, 2001 (I:10+ R:6).

Hopkinson, Deborah. *Shutting Out the Sky: Life in the Tenements of New York: 1880–1924.* Scholastic, 2004 (I:8–12 R:6).

Irvine, Joan. *How to Make Super Pop-Ups.* Illustrated by Linda Hendry. Morrow, 1992 (I:8+ R:4).

Isadora, Rachel. *Lili at Ballet.* Putnam, 1993 (I:4–8 R:5).

Jackson, Donna M. *The Bone Detectives: How Forensic Anthropologists Solve Crimes and Uncover Mysteries of the Dead.* Photographs by Charlie Fellenbaum. Little, Brown, 1996 (I:10+ R:9).

_____. *In Your Face: The Facts About Your Features.* Viking, 2004 (I:8–12 R:5).

Janeczko, Paul B. *Top Secret: A Handbook of Codes, Ciphers, and Secret Writing.* Illustrated by Jenna LaReau. Candlewick, 2004 (I:9+ R:5).

Jarrow, Gail, & Paul Sherman. *The Naked Mole-Rat Mystery: Scientific Sleuths at Work.* Lerner, 1996 (I:9+ R:6).

Jenkins, Martin. *The Emperor's Egg.* Illustrated by Jane Chapman. Candlewick, 1999 (I:3–8).

Jenkins, Steve. *Actual Size.* Houghton Mifflin, 2004 (I:4–8 R:4).

_____. *The Top of the World: Climbing Mount Everest.* Houghton Mifflin, 1999 (I:7+).

Johnson, James Weldon. *Lift Every Voice and Sing.* Illustrated by Elizabeth Catlett. Walker, 1993 (I:all).

Johnson, Neil. *All in a Day's Work: Twelve Americans Talk About Their Jobs.* Little, Brown, 1989 (I:10+ R:6).

Johnson, Rebecca L. *Braving the Frozen Frontier: Women Working in Antarctica.* Lerner, 1997 (I:9+ R:6).

Jones, Charlotte Foltz. *Yukon Gold: The Story of the Klondike Gold Rush.* Holiday, 1999 (I:8+ R:5).

Kay, Verla. *Iron Horses.* Illustrated by Michael McCurdy. Putnam, 1999 (I:5+).

King, Casey, & Linda Barrett Osborne. *Kids Talk About the Civil Rights Movement With the People Who Made It Happen.* Knopf, 1997 (I:9+).

King-Smith, Dick. *I Love Guinea Pigs.* Illustrated by Anita Jeram. Candlewick, 1995 (I:4–8 R:4).

Knight, Margy Burns. *Talking Walls.* Illustrated by Anne Sibley O'Brien. Tilbury House, 1992 (I:8+ R:5).

Koch, Michelle. *World Water Watch.* Greenwillow, 1993 (I:4–8 R:4).

Koscielniak, Bruce. *The Story of the Incredible Orchestra.* Houghton Mifflin, 2000 (I:8+ R:5).

Kramer, Stephen. *Eye of the Storm: Chasing Storms With Warren Faidley.* Putnam, 1997 (I:9+ R:5).

_____. *Lightning.* Photographs by Warren Faidley. Carolrhoda, 1992 (I:8+ R:6).

Krauss, Ronnie. *Take a Look, It's in a Book: How Television Is Made at Reading Rainbow.* Walker, 1997 (I:all R:5).

Krensky, Steven B. *Breaking Into Print: Before and After Invention of the Printing Press.* Little, Brown, 1996 (I:8+ R:5).

Kroll, Steven. *Pony Express!* Illustrated by Dan Andreasen. Scholastic, 1996 (I:10+ R:9).

Kuskin, Karla. *Jerusalem, Shining Still.* Illustrated by David Frampton. Harper & Row, 1987 (I:8+ R:5).

Lalicki, Tom. *Grierson's Raid: A Daring Cavalry Strike Through the Heart of the Confederacy.* Farrar, Straus & Giroux, 2004 (I:12–YA R:8).

Lang, W. Patrick. *Intelligence: The Human Factor.* Chelsea House, 2004 (I:14–YA R:8).

Langley, Andrew. *Shakespeare's Theatre.* Illustrated by June Everett. Oxford, 1999 (I:10+ R:6).

Larson, Peter, & Kriston Donnan. *Bones Rock! Everything You Need to Know to Be a Paleontologist.* Invisible Cities, 2004 (I:10+ R:5).

Lasky, Kathryn. *Interrupted Journey: Saving Endangered Sea Turtles.* Photographs by Christopher Knight. Candlewick, 2001 (I:8+ R:5).

_____. *Monarchs.* Photographs by Christopher Knight. Harcourt Brace: 1993 (I:all R:5).

_____. *The Most Beautiful Roof in the World: Exploring the Rainforest Canopy.* Photographs by Christopher G. Knight. Harcourt Brace, 1997 (I:9+ R:6).

_____. *Science Fair Bunnies.* Illustrated by Marylin Hafner. Candlewick, 2000 (I:6+ R:4).

_____. *Sugaring Time.* Photographs by Christopher Knight. Macmillan, 1983 (I:all R:6).

_____. *Think Like an Eagle: At Work With a Wildlife Photographer.* Photographs by Christopher G. Knight & Jack Swedberg. Little, Brown, 1992 (I:8+ R:6).

Lauber, Patricia. *Flood: Wrestling With the Mississippi.* National Geographic, 1996 (I:8+ R:6).

_____. *How Dinosaurs Came to Be.* Illustrated by Douglas Henderson. Simon & Schuster, 1996 (I:6–10 R:4).

_____. *Hurricanes: Earth's Mightiest Storms.* Scholastic, 1996 (I:9+ R:6).

_____. *Living with Dinosaurs.* Illustrated by Douglas Henderson. Bradbury, 1991 (I:8+ R:6).

_____. *The News About Dinosaurs.* Bradbury, 1989 (I:8+ R:6).

_____. *Painters of the Caves.* National Geographic, 1998 (I:all R:6).

_____. *Snakes Are Hunters.* Illustrated by Holly Keller. Crowell, 1988 (I:4–8 R:3).

_____. *Volcano: The Eruption and Healing of Mount St. Helens.* Bradbury, 1986 (I:all R:6).

_____. *What You Never Knew About Tubs, Toilets, and Showers.* Illustrated by John Manders. Simon & Schuster, 2001 (I:all R:6).

_____. *Who Came First? New Clues to Prehistoric Americans.* National Geographic, 2003 (I:10+ R:6).

Lawlor, Laurie. *Where Will This Shoe Take You?: A Walk Through the History of Footwear.* Walker, 1996 (I:10+ R:5).

Leapman, Michael. *Witnesses to War: Eight True-Life Stories of Nazi Persecution.* Viking, 1998 (I:10+ R:5).

Leedy, Loreen. *Look at My Book: How Kids Can Write & Illustrate Terrific Books.* Holiday House, 2004 (I:7–10 R:5).

Lessem, Don. *Bigger Than T. Rex.* Illustrated by Robert F. Walters. Crown, 1997 (I:9+ R:5).

_____. *Dinosaur Worlds.* Boyds Mills, 1996 (I:10+ R:6).

Lesser, Carolyn. *Storm on the Desert.* Illustrated by Ted Rand. Harcourt Brace, 1997 (I:all R:4).

Lester, Julius. *Let's Talk About Race.* Illustrated by Karen Barbour. HarperCollins, 2005 (I:6–10 R:5).

Levine, Ellen. *Darkness Over Denmark: The Danish Resistance and the Rescue of the Jews.* Holiday House, 2000 (I:10+ R:6).

_____. *The Tree That Would Not Die.* Illustrated by Ted Rand. Scholastic, 1995 (I:6–9 R:4).

Lewin Ted, and Betsy Lewin. *Gorilla Walk.* Lothrop, Lee & Shepard, 1999 (I:10+ R:6).

Lindberg, Reeve. *Our Nest.* Illustrated by Jill McElmurry. Candlewick, 2004 (I:3–5).

Locker, Thomas. *Sky Tree: Seeing Science Through Art.* HarperCollins, 1995 (I:6–8 R:5).

Loewen, Nancy, and Ann Bancroft. *Four to the Pole!: The American Women's Expedition to Antarctica, 1992–93.* Linnet, 2001 (I:10+ R:6).

London, Jonathan. *Baby Whale's Journey.* Illustrated by Jon VanZyle. Chronicle, 1999 (I:6–9 R:4).

Macaulay, David. *Building Big.* Houghton Mifflin, 2000 (I:all R:5).

_____. *Building the Book Cathedral.* Houghton Mifflin, 1999 (I:all R:5).

_____. *Cathedral: The Story of Its Construction.* Houghton Mifflin, 1973 (I:all R:5).

_____. *Mill.* Houghton Mifflin, 1983 (I:9+ R:5).

_____. *Ship.* Houghton Mifflin, 1993 (I:10+ R:5).

_____. *The Way Things Work.* Houghton Mifflin, 1988 (I:all R:6).

Macy, Sue. *Swifter, Higher, Stronger: A Photographic History of the Summer Olympics.* National Geographic, 2004 (I:10+ R:6).

_____. *A Whole New Ball Game: The Story of the All-American Girls Professional Baseball League.* Holt, 1993 (I:10+ R:5).

_____. *Winning Ways: A Photohistory of American Women in Sports.* Henry Holt, 1996 (I:10+ R:7).

Maestro, Betsy. *The Story of Clocks and Calendars: Marking a Millennium.* Illustrated by Giulio Maestro. Lothrop, Lee & Shepard, 1999 (I:9+ R:5).

_____. *The Story of Money.* Illustrated by Giulio Maestro. Clarion, 1993 (I:8+ R:4).

_____. *The Story of Religion.* Illustrated by Giulio Maestro. Clarion, 1996 (I:8+ R:6).

Majoor, Mireille. *Inside the Hindenburg: A Giant Cutaway Book.* Illustrated by Ken Marschall. Little, Brown, 2000 (I:all).

Major, John S. *The Silk Route: 7,000 Miles of History.* Illustrated by Stephen Fieser. HarperCollins, 1995 (I:8+ R:6).

Mann, Elizabeth. *The Brooklyn Bridge.* Illustrated by Alan Witschonke. Mikaya, 1996 (I:9+ R:5).

_____. *Empire State Building: When New York Reached for the Skies.* Illustrated by Alan Witschonke. Mikaya, 2003 (I:8+ R:4).

_____. *The Great Pyramid.* Illustrated by Laura Lo Turco. Mikaya, 1996 (I:9+ R:5).

_____. *Machu Picchu.* Mikaya, 2000 (I:9+ R:5).

Markle. Sandra. *Creepy, Crawly Baby Bugs.* Walker, 1996 (I:7–9 R:4).

_____. *Lions: Animal Predators.* Carolrhoda, 2005 (I:8+ R:5).

_____. *Outside and Inside Killer Bees.* Walker, 2004 (I:8+ R:5).

_____. *Outside and Inside Spiders.* Atheneum, 1994 (I:7–9 R:4).

Martin, Laura C. *Nature's Art Box.* Illustrated by David Cain. Storey, 2003 (I:9+ R:5).

Maruki, Toshi. *Hiroshima No Pika.* Lothrop, Lee & Shepard, 1982 (I:8–12 R:4).

Maynard, Caitlin, & Thane Maynard. *Rain Forests & Reefs: A Kid's-Eye View of the Tropics.* Photographs by Stan Rullman. Watts, 1996 (I:9+ R:5).

McClung, Robert. *Lost Wild America: The Story of Our Extinct and Vanishing Wildlife.* Illustrated by Bob Hines, Linnet. 1993 (I:12+ R:7).

McDonald, Megan. *Is This a House for Hermit Crab?* Illustrated by S. D. Schindler. Orchard, 1990 (I:3–6 R:3).

McKissack, Patricia, & Fredrick McKissack. *The Civil Rights Movement in America: From 1865 to the Present,* 2nd ed. Children's Press, 1991 (I:10+ R:6).

McKissack, Patricia, & Arlene Zarembka. *To Establish Justice: Citizenship and the Constitution.* Knopf, 2004 (I:12–YA R:7).

McLaughlin, Molly. *Dragonflies.* Walker, 1989 (I:7–12 R:5).

McMillan, Bruce. *Going on a Whale Watch,* Scholastic, 1992 (I:3–8 R:3).

McPhail, David. *Farm Morning.* Harcourt Brace, 1985 (I:2–5).

McWhorter, Diane. *A Dream of Freedom: The Civil Rights Movement From 1954 to 1968.* Scholastic, 2004 (I:10+–YA R:6).

Meltzer, Milton, ed. *The American Revolutionaries: A History in Their Own Words, 1750–1800.* Crowell, 1987 (I:10+).

_____. *Rescue: The Story of How Gentiles Saved Jews in the Holocaust.* Harper & Row, 1988 (I:10+ R:7).

Merriman, Nick. *Early Humans.* Knopf, 1989 (I:all R:5).

Micklethwait, Lucy. *A Child's Book of Play in Art.* Dorling Kindersley, 1996 (I:4–9 R:5).

Micucci, Charles. *The Life and Times of the Apple.* Orchard, 1992 (I:all R:4).

_____. *The Life and Times of the Peanut.* Houghton Mifflin, 1997 (I:5–9 R:4).

Millard, Anne. *A Street Through Time: A 12,000-Year Walk Through History.* Illustrated by Steve Noon. DK, 1998 (I:all).

Miller, Brandon Marie. *Good Women of a Well-Blessed Land: Women's Lives in Colonial America.* Lerner, 2003 (I:10–YA R:6).

_____. *Just What the Doctor Ordered: The History of American Medicine.* Lerner, 1997 (I:10+ R:6).

Miller, Debbie S. *Disappearing Lake: Nature's Magic in Denali National Park.* Illustrated by Jon Van Zyle. Walker, 1997 (I:all R:5).

_____. *Flight of the Golden Plover: The Amazing Migration Between Hawaii and Alaska.* Illustrated by Daniel Van Zyle. Alaska Northwest, 1996 (I:8+ R:5).

Miller, Debra A., ed. *North Korea.* Gaale, 2004 (I:12–YA R:7).

Miller, Margaret. *Who Uses This?* Greenwillow, 1990 (I:2–5).

Montgomery, Sy. *Search for the Golden Moon Bear: Science and Adventure in the Asian Tropics.* Houghton Mifflin, 2004 (I:10+ R:6).

_____. *The Snake Scientist.* Photographs by Nic Bishop. Houghton Mifflin, 1999 (I:8+ R:5).

_____. *The Tarantula Scientist.* Photographs by Nic Bishop. Houghton Mifflin, 2004 (I:8+ R:6).

Moore, Patrick. *Comets and Shooting Stars.* Illustrated by Paul Doherty. Copper Beech, 1995 (I:6–9 R:6).

_____. *The Planets.* Illustrated by Paul Doherty. Copper Beech, 1995 (I:6–9 R:6).

_____. *The Stars.* Illustrated by Paul Doherty. Copper Beech, 1995 (I:6–9 R:6).

_____. *The Sun and Moon.* Illustrated by Paul Doherty. Copper Beech, 1995 (I:6–9 R:5).

Morrison, Toni. *Remember: The Journey to School Integration.* Houghton Mifflin, 2004 (I:all R:5).

Moses, Amy. *Doctors Help People.* Child's World, 1996 (I:5–7 R:4).

Murphy, Claire Rudolf, & Jane G. Haigh, *Children of the Gold Rush.* Rinehart, 1999 (I:10+ R:5).

Murphy, Jim. *An American Plague: The True and Terrifying Story of the Yellow Fever Epidemic of 1793.* Clarion, 2003 (I:10–YA R:6).

_____. *Blizzard!* Scholastic, 2000 (I:10+ R:7).

_____. *The Great Fire.* Scholastic, 1995 (I:10+ R:7).

_____. *The Long Road to Gettysburg.* Clarion, 1992 (I:10+ R:5).

Myers, Walter Dean. *Now Is Your Time! The African-American Struggle for Freedom.* HarperCollins, 1991 (I:10+ R:6).

Nathan, Amy. *Count on Us: American Women in the Military.* National Geographic, 2004 (I:10+ R:6).

Nirgiotis, Nicholas, & Theodore Nirgiotis. *No More Dodos: How Zoos Help Endangered Wildlife.* Lerner, 1996 (I:10+ R:6).

Norell, Mark A., and Lowell Dingus. *A Nest of Dinosaurs: The Story of Oviraptor.* Doubleday, 1999 (I:7+ R:5).

O'Connor, Jane. *If the Walls Could Talk: Family Life at the White House.* Illustrated by Gary Hovland. Simon & Schuster, 2004 (I:all).

Ojeda, Auriana, ed. *Civil Liberties.* Greenhaven, 2004 (I:12–YA R:7).

Paladino, Catherine. *One Good Apple: Growing Our Food for the Sake of the Earth.* Houghton Mifflin, 1999 (I:8+ R:4).

Pandell, Karen, *Animal Action ABC.* Photographs by Art Wolfe & Nancy Sheehan. Dutton, 1996 (I:all).

Parker, Nancy Winslow. *Money, Money, Money: The Meaning of the Art and Symbols on United States Paper Currency.* HarperCollins, 1995 (I:9+ R:6).

Parker, Steve. *Mammal.* Knopf, 1989 (I:8–12 R:7).

Pascoe, Elaine. *The Right to Vote.* Millbrook, 1997 (I:8+ R:4).

Patent, Dorothy Hinshaw. *Back to the Wild.* Illustrated by William Muñoz. Harcourt Brace, 1997 (I:9+ R:6).

_____. *Biodiversity.* Photographs by William Muñoz. Clarion, 1996 (I:9+ R:6).

_____. *Prairies.* Photographs by William Muñoz. Holiday, 1996 (I:8+ R:6).

_____. *The Right Dog for the Job: Ira's Path From Service Dog to Guide Dog.* Photographs by William Muñoz. Walker, 2004 (I:6–10 R:5).

_____. *The Whooping Crane: A Comeback Story.* Photographs by William Muñoz. Clarion, 1988 (I:8+ R:6).

Peck, Richard. *Past Perfect, Present Tense: New and Collected Stories.* Dial, 2004 (I:10+ R:6).

Perry, Robert. *Focus on Nicotine and Caffeine.* Illustrated by David Neuhaus. 21st Century, 1990 (I:10+ R:5).

Platt. Richard. *Castle Diary: The Journal of Tobias Burgess, Page.* Illustrated by Chris Riddell. Candlewick, 1999 (I:all).

Pope, Joyce. *Kenneth Lilly's Animals: A Portfolio of Paintings.* Illustrated by Kenneth Lilly. Lothrop, Lee & Shepard, 1988 (I:all R:7).

Priceman, Majorie. *How to Make an Apple Pie and See the World.* Knopf, 1994 (I:5–8 R:4).

Pringle, Laurence. *An Extraordinary Life: The Story of a Monarch Butterfly.* Illustrated by Bob Marstall. Orchard, 1997 (I:8+ R:6).

_____. *Snakes! Strange and Wonderful.* Illustrated by Merl Henderson. Boyds Mills, 2004 (I:7–10 R:6).

Provensen, Alice. *The Buck Stops Here: The Presidents of the United States.* HarperCollins, 1990 (I:all).

Rappaport, Doreen. *Free at Last! Stories and Songs of Emancipation.* Illustrated by Shane W. Evans. Candlewick, 2004 (I:all).

Raskin, Lawrie, & Debora Pearson. *My Sahara Adventure: 52 Days by Camel.* Annick, 1998 (I:9+ R:5).

Ray, Delia. *A Nation Torn: The Story of How the Civil War Began.* Lodestar, 1990 (I:10+ R:6).

Relf, Pat. *A Dinosaur Named Sue: The Story of the Colossal Fossil: The World's Most Complete T. Rex.* Scholastic, 2000 (I:10+ R:6).

Rhatigan, Joe, and Rain Newcomb. *Out-of-This-World Astronomy: 50 Amazing Activities & Projects.* Sterling, 2003 (I:10+ R:5).

Rhoades, Diane. *Garden Crafts for Kids: 50 Great Reasons to Get Your Hands Dirty.* Sterling, 1995 (I:9+ R:8).

Richardson, Joy. *Looking at Pictures: An Introduction to Art for Young People.* Illustrated by Charlotte Voake. Abrams, 1997 (I:10+ R:5).

Roche, Denis. *Loo-Loo, Boo, and Art You Can Do.* Houghton Mifflin, 1996 (I:4–9).

Rogasky, Barbara. *Smoke and Ashes: The Story of the Holocaust.* Holiday House, 1988 (I:10+ R:6).

Roop, Peter, & Connie Roop. *Seasons of the Cranes.* Walker, 1989 (I:8+ R:5).

Root, Phyllis. *If You Want to See a Caribou.* Illustrated by Jim Meyer. Houghton Mifflin, 2004 (I:6–9 R:4).

Rosinsky, Natalie M. *Light: Shadows, Mirrors, and Rainbows.* Illustrated by Sheree Boyd. Picture Window, 2003 (I:7–9 R:4).

_____. *Water: Up, Down, and All Around.* Illustrated by Matthew John. Picture Window, 2003 (I:7–9 R:4).

Rossel, Seymour. *The Holocaust.* Watts, 1981 (I:9+ R:6).

Russo, Marisabina. *Always Remember Me: How One Family Survived World War II.* Atheneum, 2005 (I:6–9 R:4).

Ryder, Joan. *Dancers in the Garden.* Illustrated by Judith Lopez. Sierra Club, 1992 (I:all).

Sattler, Helen Roney. *The Earliest Americans.* Illustrated by Jean Day Zallinger. Clarion, 1993 (I:10+ R:6).

Sayre, April Pulley. *Put on Some Antlers and Walk Like a Moose: How Scientists Find, Follow, and Study Wild Animals.* 21st Century, 1997 (I:10+ R:5).

_____. *Stars Beneath Your Bed: The Surprising Story of Dust.* Illustrated by Ann Jonas. Greenwillow, 2005 (I:5–8 R:5).

Sayre, Henry. *Cave Paintings to Picasso: The Inside Scoop on 50 Art Masterpieces.* Chronicle, 2004 (I:all).

Schaefer, Lola M. *Arrowhawk.* Illustrated by Gabi Swiatkowska. Henry Holt, 2004 (I:5–10 R:4).

Schanzer, Rosalyn. *George vs. George: The American Revolution as Seen From Both Sides.* National Geographic, 2004 (I:8–12 R:5).

Schmandt-Besserat, Denise. *The History of Counting.* Illustrated by Michael Hays. Morrow, 1999 (I:all).

Schyffert, Bea Uusma. *The Man Who Went to the Far Side of the Moon: The Story of Apollo 11 Astronaut Michael Collins.* Chronicle, 2003 (I:all R:6).

Scott, Elaine. *Poles Apart: Why Penguins and Polar Bears Will Never Be Neighbors.* Viking, 2004 (I:8+ R:5).

Seibert, Patricia. *Discovering El Niño: How Fable and Fact Together Help Explain the Weather.* Illustrated by Jan Davey Ellis. Millbrook, 1999 (I:8+ R:5).

Selsam, Millicent E. *How to Be a Nature Detective.* Illustrated by Ezra Jack Keats. Harper & Row, 1958, 1963 (I:5–8 R:4).

_____, & Joyce Hunt. *A First Look at Caterpillars.* Illustrated by Harriett Springer. Walker, 1987 (I:5–8 R:3).

_____. *A First Look at Seals, Sea Lions, and Walruses.* Illustrated by Harriett Springer. Walker, 1988 (I:5–8 R:3).

Shahan, Sherry. *Dashing Through the Snow: The Story of the Jr. Iditarod.* Millbrook, 1997 (I:8+ R:5).

Shanower, Eric. *Sacrifice: Age of Bronze: The Story of the Trojan War.* Image Comics, 2004 (I:13–YA R:7).

Shemie, Bonnie. *Houses of Snow, Skin, and Bones.* Tundra, 1989 (I:7–12 R:5).

Showers, Paul. *A Drop of Blood.* Illustrated by Edward Miller. HarperCollins, 2004 (I:5–8 R:4).

Sierra Club. *Sierra Club Book of Great Mammals.* Sierra Club, 1992 (I:8+ R:5).

_____. *The Sierra Club Book of Small Mammals.* Sierra Club. 1993 (I:8+ R:5).

Sill, Cathryn. *About Birds: A Guide for Children.* Illustrated by John Sill. Peachtree, 1991 (I:3–8).

Simon, Seymour: *Earthquakes.* Morrow, 1991 (I:8+ R:6).

_____. *Galaxies.* Morrow, 1988 (I:5–8 R:5).

_____. *Guts: Our Digestive System.* HarperCollins, 2005 (I:8+ R:4).

_____. *How to Be an Ocean Scientist in Your Own Home.* Illustrated by David A. Carter. Lippincott, 1988 (I:8+ R:5).

_____. *Jupiter.* Morrow, 1985 (I:5–8 R:5).

_____. *Lightning.* Morrow, 1997 (I:8+ R:6).

_____. *The Long View Into Space.* Knopf, 1987 (I:8+ R:5).

_____. *New Questions and Answers About Dinosaurs.* Illustrated by Jennifer Dewey. Morrow, 1990 (I:7+ R:5).

_____. *Poisonous Snakes.* Illustrated by William R. Downey. Four Winds, 1981 (I:7–10 R:5).

_____. *Saturn.* Morrow, 1985 (I:5–8 R:5).

_____. *Storms.* Morrow, 1989 (I:8–12 R:5).

_____. *Volcanoes.* Morrow, 1988 (I:8–12 R:5).

Sís, Peter. *The Train of States.* Greenwillow, 2004 (I:all).

Skurzynski, Gloria. *Almost the Real Thing: Simulation in Your High-Tech World.* Bradbury, 1991 (I:10+ R:5).

_____. *Are We Alone? Scientists Search for Life in Space.* National Geographic, 2004 (I:10+ R:5).

Sloan, Christopher. *The Human Story: Our Evolution From Prehistoric Ancestors to Today.* Photographs by Kenneth Garrett. Illustrated by Alfons Kennis & Adrie Kennis. National Geographic, 2004 (I:10+ R:6).

Sobol, Richard. *An Elephant in the Backyard.* Dutton, 2004 (I:7–9 R:4).

Stanley, Deborah A., ed. *Sexual Health Information for Teens.* Omnigraphics, 2003 (I:14+ R:8).

Staub, Frank. *Sea Turtles.* Lerner, 1995 (I:7+ R:5).

Stefoff, Rebecca. *Finding the Lost Cities.* Oxford, 1997 (I:8+ R:5).

Steger, Will, and Jon Bowermaster. *Over the Top of the World: Explorer Will Steger's Trek Across the Arctic.* Scholastic, 1997 (I:9+ R:6).

Stevens, Leonard A. *The Case of Roe v. Wade.* Putnam, 1996 (I:12+ R:7).

Stokes, Philip. *Philosophy: 100 Essential Thinkers.* Enchanted Lion, 2003 (I:10+ R:6).

Stolley, Richard B., ed. *Life: Our Century in Pictures for Young People.* Little, Brown, 2000 (I:10+ R:5).

Sturges, Philemon. *I Love Bugs!* Illustrated by Shari Halpern. HarperCollins, 2005 (I:2–5).

Swain, Ruth Freeman. *Bedtime!* Illustrated by Cat Bowman Smith. Holiday House, 1999 (I:6–9 R:4).

Swanson, Diane. *Buffalo Sunrise: The Story of a North American Giant.* Little, Brown, 1996 (I:10+ R:8).

_____. *Safari Beneath the Sea: The Wonder World of the North Pacific Coast.* Photographs by the Royal British Columbia Museum. Sierra Club, 1994 (I:all R:6).

Swinburne, Stephen R. *Once a Wolf: How Wildlife Biologists Fought to Bring Back the Gray Wolf.* Photographs by Jim Brandenburg. Houghton Mifflin, 1999 (I:10+ R:6).

Tanaka, Shelley. *Secrets of the Mummies.* Illustrated by Greg Ruhl. Hyperion, 1999 (I:10+ R:6).

_____, & Hugh Brewster, eds. *Anastasia's Album.* Hyperion, 1996 (I:10+ R:6).

Telgen, Diane. *Brown v. Board of Education.* Defining Moments Series. Omnigraphics, 2005 (I:12+ R:6).

Thimmesh, Catherine. *Madam President: The Extraordinary, True (and Evolving) Story of Women in Politics.* Illustrated by Douglas B. Jones. Houghton Mifflin, 2004 (I:8+ R:5).

Thomson, Peggy, & Barbara Moore. *The Nine-Ton Cat: Behind the Scenes at an Art Museum.* Houghton Mifflin, 1997 (I:9+ R:6).

Turner, Alan. *National Geographic Prehistoric Mammals.* Illustrated by Muricio Anton. National Geographic, 2004 (I:9+ R:7).

Van Loon, Hendrik Willem. *The Story of Mankind.* Liveright, 1921, 1984 (I:9+ R:5).

Vogt, Gregory L. *Disasters in Space Exploration.* Millbrook, 2001 (I:9+ R:5).

Waldman, Neil. *The Golden City: Jerusalem's 3,000 Years.* Atheneum, 1995 (I:8–12 R:10).

Walker, Barbara M. *The Little House Cookbook: Frontier Foods From Laura Ingalls Wilder's Classic Stories.* Illustrated by Garth Williams. Harper & Row, 1979 (I:8–12 R:7).

Walker, Sally. *Glaciers: Ice on the Move.* Carolrhoda, 1990 (I:9+ R:5).

_____. *Rhinos.* Photographs by Gerry Ellis. Carolrhoda, 1996 (I:8+ R:5).

_____. *Secrets of a Civil War Submarine: Solving the Mysteries of the H. L. Hunley.* Carolrhoda, 2005 (I:8+ R:7).

Wallace, Karen. *Imagine You Are a Crocodile.* Holt, 1997 (I:3–6).

Warren, James A. *Cold War: The American Crusade Against World Communism, 1945–1991.* Lothrop, Lee & Shepard, 1996 (I:12+ R:7).

Weatherford, Carole Boston. *Freedom on the Menu: The Greensboro Sit-Ins.* Illustrated by Jerome Lagarrigue. Dial, 2005 (I:10+ R:5).

Webb, Sophie. *My Seasons With Penguins: An Antarctic Journal.* Houghton Mifflin, 2000 (I:9+ R:5).

Weitzman, David. *Old Ironsides: Americans Build a Fighting Ship.* Houghton Mifflin, 1997 (I:9+ R:6).

Wilcox, Charlotte. *Mummies & Their Mysteries.* Carolrhoda, 1993 (I:8–12 R:5).

_____. *Trash!* Photographs by Jerry Bushey. Carolrhoda, 1988 (I:8–12 R:5).

Wilkes, Angela. *The Children's Step-by-Step Cookbook.* Dorling Kindersley, 1994 (I:all).

Winter, Jeanette. *The Librarian of Basra: A True Story From Iraq.* Harcourt, 2005 (I:6–9 R:4).

Woodford, Susan. *The Parthenon.* Cambridge/Lerner, 1983 (I:10+ R:7).

Yue, Charlotte. *Shoes: Their History in Words and Pictures.* Illustrated by David Yue. Houghton Mifflin, 1997 (I:8+ R:6).

References

Adams, Dennis, & Mary Hamm. *Media and Literacy,* 2nd ed. Springfield, IL: Charles C. Thomas, 2000.

Adams, Karen I. "The 'Born Again' Phenomenon and Children's Books." *Children's Literature Association Quarterly* 14 (Spring 1989): 5–9.

Adler, Mortimer J., & Charles Van Doren. *How to Read a Book.* New York: Simon & Schuster, 1972.

Aiken, Joan. "Interpreting the Past." *Children's Literature in Education* 16 (Summer 1985): 67–83.

Alderson, Brian. "Children Who Live in Boxes." *The New York Times Book Review* (November 14, 1993a): 17.

_____. "Compass, Knife and Spyglass." *The New York Times Book Review* (November 19, 2000): 22.

_____. *Ezra Jack Keats: Artist and Picture-Book Maker.* Gretna, Louisiana: Pelican, 1994.

_____. "Harry Potter, Dido Twite, and Mr. Beowulf." *The Horn Book Magazine* LXXVI (May/June 2000): 349–352.

_____. "Maurice Before Max: The Yonder Side of the See-Saw." *The Horn Book* (May/June 1993b): 291–295.

_____. *Sing a Song of Sixpence.* New York: Cambridge University Press, 1986.

_____, ed. and trans. *Three Centuries of Children's Books in Europe.* Cleveland: World, 1959.

Allen, Marjorie N. *What Are Little Girls Made Of? A Guide to Female Role Models in Children's Books.* New York: Facts On File, 1999.

Almond, David. "Fiction and Poetry Award Winner." *The Horn Book* LXXXI (January/February 2005): 31–36.

Amaki, Amalia, ed. *A Century of African American Art.* New Brunswick, NJ: Rutgers University Press, 2004.

"An Adventure With Books." *Reading Today* (June/July 2001): 15.

Aoki, M. Elaine. "Are You Chinese? Are You Japanese? Or Are You Just a Mixed-Up Kid?—Using Asian American Children's Literature." *The Reading Teacher* 34 (January 1981): 382–385.

Applebee, Arthur S. "Children and Stories: Learning the Rules of the Game." *Language Arts* 56 (September 1979).

Apseloff, Marilyn Fain. "Abandonment: The New Realism of the Eighties." *Children's Literature in Education* 23 (December 1992): 101–106.

_____. "New Trends in Children's Books From Europe and Japan." *School Library Journal* 32 (November 1985): 30–32.

Arbuthnot, May Hill, & Dorothy M. Broderick. *Time for Biography.* Glenview, IL: Scott, Foresman, 1969.

Arnold, Renea. "Charming the Next Generation." *School Library Journal* 51 (July 2005): 30–32.

Aronson, Marc. "The World According to Cart." *School Library Journal* 46 (September 2000): 54–57.

Art Museum, Princeton University. *The Olmec World: Ritual and Rulership.* New York: Abrams, 1996.

Ashe, Rosalind, & Lisa Tuttle. *Children's Literary Houses: Famous Dwellings in Children's Fiction.* New York: Facts on File, 1984.

Ashton, John. *Chap-Books of the Eighteenth Century.* London: Chatto & Windus, 1882.

Association of Women Psychologists. "Statement of Resolutions and Motions." Miami: American Psychological Association Convention, September 1970.

Atwood, Ann. *Haiku: The Mood of Earth.* New York: Scribner, 1971.

Au, Kathryn H. *Literacy Instruction in Multicultural Settings.* Orlando: Harcourt Brace, 1993.

Avery, Gillian. "Beginnings of Children's Reading to c. 1700." In *Children's Literature: An Illustrated History,* edited by Peter Hunt. Oxford: Oxford University Press, 1995, 1–25.

Avi. "The Child in Children's Literature." *The Horn Book* 69 (January/February 1993): 40–50.

Babbitt, Natalie. "Read This, It's Good For You." *The New York Times Book Review.* (May 18, 1997): 23–24.

Bader, Barbara. "'They Shall Not Wither': John Biehorst's Quiet Crusade for Native American Literature." *The Horn Book* 73 (May/June 1997): 268–281.

Baghban, Marcia. "Too Serious Too Soon: Where Is the Childishness in Children's Fiction?" New York: National Council of Teachers of English, March 16–18, 2000.

Bagley, Ayers. *An Invitation to Wisdom and Schooling.* Society of Professors of Education Monograph Series, 1985.

Baird, Merrily. *Symbols of Japan: Thematic Motifs in Art and Design.* New York: Rizzoli, 2001.

Baker, Gwendolyn C. "The Role of the School in Transmitting the Culture of All Learners in a Free and Democratic Society." *Educational Leadership* 36 (November 1978): 134–138.

Ballinger, Franchot. "A Matter of Emphasis: Teaching the 'Literature' in Native American Literature Courses." *American Indian Culture and Research Journal* 8 (1984): 1–12.

Bamford, Rosemary, & Janice V. Kristo. *Checking Out Nonfiction K–8: Good Choices for Best Learning.* Norwood, MA: Christopher-Gordon, 2000.

Banfield, Beryle. "Racism in Children's Books: An Afro-American Perspective." In *The Black American in Books for Children: Readings in Racism,* edited by Donnarae MacCann & Gloria Woodard. Metuchen, NJ: Scarecrow, 1985.

Barclay, Donald A. "Interpreted Well Enough: Two Illustrators' Visions of Adventures of Huckleberry Finn." *The Horn Book* 68 (May/June 1992): 311–319.

Barnes, B. "Using Children's Literature in the Early Anthropology Curriculum." *Social Education* (January 1991): 17–18.

Barr, Rebecca, & Marilyn W. Sadow. "Influence of Basal Programs on Fourth-Grade Reading Instruction." *Reading Research Quarterly* 24 (Winter 1989): 44–71.

Barrett, Thomas C. "Taxonomy of Reading Comprehension." In *Reading 360 Monograph.* Lexington, MA: Ginn, 1972.

Barsam, Richard. *A Peaceable Kingdom: The Shaker Abecedarius.* New York: Viking, 1978.

Bartel, Nettie. "Assessing and Remediating Problems in Language Development." In *Teaching Children With Learning and Behavior Problems,* edited by Donald Hammill & Nettie Bartel. Boston: Allyn & Bacon, 1990.

Bascom, William. "The Forms of Folklore: Prose Narratives." *Journal of American Folklore* 78 (January/March 1965): 3–20.

Bauer, Susan Wise. *The Well-Educated Mind.* New York: Norton, 2003.

Bauermeister, Erica, & Holly Smith. *Let's Hear It for the Girls.* New York: Penguin, 1997.

Baylor, Byrd. *And It Is Still That Way.* New York: Scribner, 1976.

Bean, Thomas W., & Nicole Rigoni. "Exploring the Intergenerational Dialogue Journal Discussion of a Multicultural Young Adult Novel." *Reading Research Quarterly* 36 (July/August/September 2001): 232–248.

Beckham, Stephen Dow. In *Echoes of the Elders: The Stories and Paintings of Chief Lelooska,* by Christine Normandin. New York: DK, 1997, 4–5.

Bedard, Michael. *Emily.* New York: Delacorte, 1992.

Beer, Robert. *The Handbook of Tibetan Buddhist Symbols.* Boston: Shambhala, 2003.

Behn, Harry. *Chrysalis, Concerning Children and Poetry.* New York: Harcourt Brace, 1968.

Behn, Robin, & Chase Twichell, eds. *The Practice of Poetry: Writing Exercises From Poets Who Teach.* New York: HarperCollins, 1992.

Bernstein, Joanne E. "Bibliotherapy: How Books Can Help Young Children Cope." In *Children's Literature: Resource for the Classroom,* edited by Masha Kabakow Rudman. Norwood, MA: Christopher-Gordon, 1989.

———. *Books to Help Children Cope With Separation and Loss,* 2nd ed. New York: Bowker, 1983.

Bettelheim, Bruno. *The Uses of Enchantment: The Meaning and Importance of Fairy Tales.* New York: Knopf, 1976.

Bierhorst, John. "Children's Books." *New York Times Book Review* (May 23, 1993).

———. *The Mythology of North America,* New York: Morrow, 1985.

———. ed. *The Red Swan: Myths and Tales of the American Indians.* New York: Farrar, Straus & Giroux, 1976.

Bingham, Jane, & Grayce Scholt. *Fifteen Centuries of Children's Literature: An Annotated Chronology of British and American Works in Historical Context.* Westport, CT: Greenwood, 1980.

———. "The Great Glass Slipper Search: Using Folk Tales With Older Children." *Elementary English* 51 (October 1974): 990–998.

Bitzer, Lucy. "The Art of Picture Books: Beautiful Treasures of Bookmaking." *Top-of-the-News* 38 (Spring 1992): 226–232.

Blair, Sheila S., & Jonathan M. Bloom. *The Art and Architecture of Islam, 1250–1800.* New Haven: Yale University Press, 1994.

Blatt, Gloria Toby. "Violence in Children's Literature: A Content Analysis of a Select Sampling of Children's Literature and a Study of Children's Responses to Literary Episodes Depicting Violence." East Lansing: Michigan State University, 1972. University Microfilm No. 72-29, 931.

Blenz-Clucas, Beth. "History's Forgotten Heroes: Women on the Frontier." *School Library Journal* 39 (March 1993): 118–123.

Bloom, Benjamin. *Taxonomy of Educational Objectives.* New York: Longman, 1956.

Bloom, Harold, selected by. *The Best Poems of the English Language.* New York: HarperCollins, 2004.

———, ed. *Bloom's Modern Critical Views: Hans Christian Andersen.* Philadelphia: Chelsea House, 2004.

Blos, Joan W. "Newbery Medal Acceptance." *The Horn Book* 56 (August 1980): 369–377.

Blough, Glenn O. "The Author and the Science Book." *Library Trends* 22 (April 1974): 419–424.

Bond, Nancy. "Conflict in Children's Fiction." *The Horn Book* 60 (June 1984): 297–306.

Book Review Subcommittee of the National Council for the Social Studies—Children's Book Council Joint Committee. "Notable 1991 Children's Trade Books in the Field of Social Studies." *Social Education* 56 (April/May 1992): 253–264.

Booss, Claire. *Scandinavian Folk & Fairy Tales.* New York: Avenel Books, 1984.

Booth, David. "Imaginary Gardens With Real Toads: Reading and Drama in Education." *Theory Into Practice* 24 (1985): 193–198.

Booth, William. "Diversity and Division: America's New Wave of Immigration Is Changing Its 'Melting Pot' Image." *The Washington Post National Weekly Edition* 15 (March 2, 1998): 6–8.

Borgman, Harry. *Art and Illustration Techniques.* New York: Watson-Guptill, 1979.

Bossert, Jill. *Children's Book Illustration: Step by Step Techniques.* New York: Watson-Guptill, 1998.

Boulanger, Susan. "Language, Imagination, Vision: Art Books for Children." *The Horn Book* 72 (May/June 1996): 295–304.

Braga, Laurie, & Joseph Braga. *Learning and Growing: A Guide to Child Development.* Englewood Cliffs, NJ: Prentice Hall, 1975.

Braine, Martin. "The Ontogeny of English Phrase Structure: The First Phase." In *Readings in Language Development,* edited by Lois Bloom. New York: Wiley, 1978.

Brandriss, Tobie. "Heroes for Our Students." *The American Biology Teacher* 61 (February 1999): 108–114.

Breen, Karen, Ellen Fader, Kathleen Odean, & Zena Sutherland. "One Hundred Books That Shaped the Century." *School Library Journal* 46 (January 2000): 50–58.

Bridge, Ethel Brooks. "Using Children's Choices of and Reactions to Poetry as Determinants in Enriching Literary Experience in the Middle Grades." Philadelphia: Temple University, 1966. University Microfilm No. 67-6246.

Briggs, Katharine. *Dictionary of British Folk-Tales.* 4 volumes. London: Routledge & Kegan Paul, 1970–1971.

Briggs, Nancy E., & Joseph A. Wagner. *Children's Literature Through Storytelling and Drama.* Dubuque, IA: Brown, 1979.

Brink, Carol Ryrie. *Caddie Woodlawn.* Illustrated by Trina Schart Hyman. New York: Macmillan, 1935, 1973.

Broderick, Dorothy May. *The Image of the Black in Popular and Recommended American Juvenile Fiction, 1827–1967.* New York: Columbia University, 1971. University Microfilm No. 71-4090.

Broudy, H. S. "Arts Education as Artistic Perception." In G. W. Hardiman & T. Zernich (Eds.), *Foundations for Curriculum Development and Evaluation in Art Education.* Champaign, IL: Stipes, 1981, 9–17.

———. "How Basic Is Aesthetic Education? or Is It the Fourth R?" *Language Arts* 54 (September 1977): 631–637.

Brown, Jennifer M. "Flying Starts: Ian Falconer." *Publishers Weekly* 247 (December 18, 2000): 26.

Brown, June. "Critical Questions." *The Reading Teacher* 52 (February 1999): 520–521.

Brown, Roger. *A First Language/The Early Stages.* Cambridge, MA: Harvard University Press, 1973.

Browne, C. A. *The Story of Our National Ballads.* Edited by Willard Heaps. New York: Crowell, 1960.

Bruchac, Joseph. *Tell Me a Tale.* San Diego: Harcourt Brace, 1997.

Bryan, Ashley. *The Dancing Granny and Other African Stories.* New York: Caedmon. 1985.

Buckley, Marilyn Hanf. "Focus on Research: We Listen a Book a Day: We Speak a Book a Week: Learning From Walter Loban." *Language Arts* 69 (December 1992): 622–626.

Bulzone, Marisa. "Children's Book Illustration: Is This the New Golden Age?" *Communication Arts* 34 (January/February 1993): 94–106.

Burke, Eileen M. *Early Childhood Literature: For Love of Child and Book.* Boston: Allyn & Bacon, 1986.

Burton, Hester. "The Writing of Historical Novels." In *Children and Literature: Views and Reviews,* edited by Virginia Haviland. Glenview, IL: Scott, Foresman, 1973, 299–304.

Bushnaq, Inea, ed. *Arab Folk Tales.* New York: Pantheon, 1986.

Butler, Dorothy. "From Books to Buttons: Reflections From the Thirties to the Eighties." *The Arbuthnot Lectures: 1980–1989.* Chicago: American Library Association, 1990.

Byars, Betsy. Interview conducted by Ilene Cooper. "The Booklist Interview." *Booklist* 89 (January 15, 1993): 906–907.

Byler, Mary Gloyne. "American Indian Authors for Young Readers." In *Cultural Conformity in Books for Children,* edited by Donnarae MacCann & Gloria Woodard. Metuchen, NJ: Scarecrow, 1977.

Cadogan, Mary, & Patricia Craig. *You're a Brick, Angela! A New Look at Girls' Fiction From 1839 to 1975.* London: Gollancz, 1976.

Caduto, Michael J., & Joseph Bruchac. *Keepers of the Animals: Native American Stories and Wildlife Activities for Children.* Golden, CO: Fulcrum, 1991.

———. *Keepers of the Earth: Native American Stories and Environmental Activities for Children.* Golden, CO: Fulcrum, 1989.

Cafakum, Leslie. "Alphabet Books Grow Up!" *Book Links* 2 (May 1993): 41–45.

Cai, Mingshui. "A Balanced View of Acculturation: Comments on Laurence Yep's Three Novels." *Children's Literature in Education* 23 (June 1992): 107–118.

———. "Folks, Friends and Foes: Relationships Between Humans and Animals in Some Eastern and Western Folktales." *Children's Literature in Education* 24 (1993): 73–83.

Campbell, Joseph. *The Hero With a Thousand Faces.* Princeton, NJ: Princeton University Press, 1949, 1968.

———. *The Power of Myth.* New York: Doubleday, 1988.

———. *Transformations of Myth Through Time.* New York: Harper & Row, 1990.

Carlson, Julia Ann. *A Comparison of the Treatment of the Negro in Children's Literature in the Periods 1929–1938 and 1959–1968.* Storrs: University of Connecticut, 1969. University Microfilm No. 70-1245.

Carlson, Ruth Kearney. "World Understanding Through the Folktale." In *Folklore and Folk Tales Around the World,* edited by

Ruth Kearney Carlson. Newark, DE: International Reading Association, 1972.

Carmichael, Carolyn Wilson. "A Study of Selected Social Values as Reflected in Contemporary Realistic Fiction for Children," East Lansing: Michigan State University, 1971, University Microfilm No. 71-31.

Caroff, Susan, & Elizabeth Moje. "A Conversation With David Wiesner: 1992 Caldecott Medal Winner." *The Reading Teacher* 46 (December 1992/January 1993): 284–289.

Carpenter, Frank G. *Carpenter's Geographical Reader, North America.* New York: American Book, 1898.

Carter, Betty. "Hold the Applause! Do Accelerated Reader & Electronic Bookshelf Send the Right Message?" *School Library Journal* 42 (October 1996): 22–25.

Carter, James. *Talking Books.* New York: Routledge, 1999.

Carvajal, Doreen. "In Kids' Pop Culture, Fear Rules." *The New York Times* (Sunday, June 1, 1997): E. 5.

Cavendish, Richard, ed. *Legends of the World.* New York: Schocken Books, 1982.

Cecil, Nancy Lee, & Patricia L. Roberts. *Families in Children's Literature: A Resource Guide, Grades 4–8.* Englewood, CO: Teacher Ideas Press, 1998.

Chall, Jeanne S., & Emily W. Marston. "The Reluctant Reader: Suggestions From Research and Practice." *Catholic Library World* 47 (February 1976): 274–275.

Chance, Rosemary. "A Portrait of Popularity: An Analysis of Characteristics of Novels From Young Adults' Choices for 1997." *The Alan Review* 27 (Fall 1999): 65–67.

Chang, Margaret A. "The Travels of Benjamin of Tudela: Through Three Continents in the Twelfth Century." *School Library Journal* 51 (April 2005): 142.

Chapman, Raymond. *The Victorian Debate: English Literature and Society 1832–1901.* New York: Basic Books, 1968.

Charpenel, Mauricio. "Literature About Mexican American Children." College Station: Texas A&M University, Children's Literature Conference, 1980.

Cheatham, Bertha M. "News of '85: SLJ's Annual Roundup." *School Library Journal* 32 (December 1985): 19–27.

"Children's Choices for 1992." *The Reading Teacher* 46 (October 1992): 127–141.

"Children's Choices for 1993: A Project of the International Reading Association and the Children's Book Council." *The Reading Teacher* 47 (October 1993): 127–141.

Children's Literature Association. *Touchstones: A List of Distinguished Children' Books.* Lafayette, IN: Purdue University; Children's Literature Association, 1985.

"Children's Voices: A Response to Harry Potter." *The New Advocate* 14 (Winter 2001): 86–87.

Cianciolo, Patricia J. "A Look at the Illustrations in Children's Favorite Picture Books." In *Children's Choices: Teaching With Books Children Like,* edited by Nancy Roser & Margaret Frith. Newark, DE: International Reading Assocation, 1983.

———. *Picture Books for Children,* 3rd ed. Chicago: American Library Association, 1990.

———. *Picture Books for Children,* 4th ed. Chicago: American Library Association, 1997.

———. "Reading Literature, and Writing From Writers' Perspectives." *English Journal* 74 (December 1985): 65–69.

Cirker, Blanche. *The Book of Kells: Selected Plates in Full Color.* New York: Dover, 1982.

Clark, Anne. "Books in the Classroom: Poetry." *The Horn Book* 68 (September/October 1992): 624–627.

Clark, Beverly Lyon, & Margaret R. Higonnet, eds. *Girls, Boys, Books, Toys: Gender in Children's Literature and Culture.* Baltimore, MD: Johns Hopkins University Press, 1999.

Clark, Leonard. "Poetry for the Youngest." In *Horn Book Reflections,* edited by Elinor Whitney Field. Boston: Horn Book, 1969.

Clay, Marie M. "Child Development." In *Handbook of Research on Teaching the English Language Arts,* 2nd ed. edited by James Flood, Julie M. Jensen, Diane Lapp, & James R. Squire. Upper Saddle River, NJ: Merrill/Prentice Hall, 2003, 46–52.

Coe, Michael. *The Maya,* 4th ed. New York: Thames & Hudson, 1992.

———, Dean Snow, & Elizabeth Benson. *Atlas of Ancient America.* New York: Facts on File, 1986.

Cohen, Caron Lee. "The Quest in Children's Literature." *School Library Journal* 31 (August 1985): 28–29.

Commire, Anne. *Something About the Author: Facts and Pictures About Contemporary Authors and Illustrators of Books for Young People.* Detroit: Gale, 1971.

Committee on Geographic Education. *Guidelines for Geographic Education: Elementary and Secondary Schools.* Washington, DC: National Council for Geographic Education and the Association of American Geographers, 1983.

Connell, Christopher. "Middle-Class House-wife Writes High-Class Children's Tales." The Bryan-College Station (TX) Eagle (March 28, 1984): 1F.

Cook, Elizabeth. The Ordinary and the Fabulous: An Introduction to Myths. Legends, and Fairy Tales, 2d ed. New York: Cambridge University Press, 1976.

Coolidge, Olivia E. Legends of the North. Boston: Houghton Mifflin, 1951.

_____. "My Struggle With Facts." Wilson Library Bulletin 49 (October 1974): 146–151.

Cooper, Ilene. "The African American Experience in Picture Books." Booklist 88 (February 1,1992): 1036–1037.

Cooper-Solomon, Debra. "A Look at Eric Carle." School Arts 98 (May/June 1999): 18–19.

Council on Interracial Books for Children. "Chicano Culture in Children's Literature: Stereotypes, Distortions and Omissions." In Cultural Conformity in Books for Children, edited by Donnarae MacCann & Gloria Woodard. Metuchen, NJ: Scarecrow, 1977a.

_____. "Criteria for Analyzing Books on Asian Americans." In Cultural Conformity in Books for Children, edited by Donnarae MacCann & Gloria Woodard. Metuchen, NJ: Scarecrow, 1977b.

Courlander, Harold. A Treasury of African Folklore. New York: Crown, 1975.

Cowen, John E. "Conversations With Poet Jose Garcia Villa on Teaching Poetry to Children." In Teaching Reading Through the Arts, edited by John E. Cowen. Newark, DE: International Reading Association, 1983, 78–87.

Crane, Walter. The Decorative Illustration of Books Old and New. London: Bracken, 1984.

Creeden, Sharon. Fair Is Fair: World Folktales of Justice. Little Rock, AR: August House, 1995.

Crosscurrents, Aspen, CO: Aspen Music Festival and School, 2001.

Crossley-Holland, Kevin. The Faber Book of Northern Legends. Boston: Faber & Faber, 1983.

_____. Once Upon a Poem: Favorite Poems That Tell Stories. Illustrated by Peter Bailey et al. New York: Scholastic, 2004.

Crowley, Daniel. Foreword to "On Another Day . . ." Tales Told Among the Nkundo of Zaire, collected by Mabel Ross & Barbara Walker. Hamden, CT: Archon, 1979.

Cullinan, Beatrice, Marilyn C. Scalo, & Virginia Schroeder. Three Voices: An Invitation to Poetry Across the Curriculum. York, ME: Stenhouse, 1995.

Cullingford, Cedric. Children's Literature and its Effects: The Formative Years. London: Cassell, 1998.

Cullum, Carolyn N. The Storytime Sourcebook: A Compendium of Ideas and Resources for Storytellers, 2nd ed. New York: Neal-Schuman, 1999.

Cummins, Julie. "Taste Trends: A Cookie Lover's Assortment of Picture Book Art." School Library Journal 42 (September 1996): 118–123.

"Curriculum Connectors: Family Secrets." School Library Journal 43 (March 1997): 112–113.

Cushing, Frank Hamilton. Zuni Folktales, Tucson: University of Arizona Press, 1986.

D'Alleva, Anne. Look Again!: Art History and Critical Theory. Upper Saddle River, NJ: Prentice Hall, 2005.

Danoff, Michael. Quoted in The Art of Nancy Ekholm Burkert, edited by David Larkin, New York: Harper & Row, 1977.

Darton, F. J. Harvey. Children's Books in England: Five Centuries of Social Life. New York: Cambridge University Press, 1932, 1966.

Davis, Anita P., & Thomas R. McDaniel. "You've Come a Long Way, Baby—Or Have You: Research Evaluating Gender Portrayal in Recent Caldecott-Winning Books." The Reading Teacher 52 (February 1999): 532–536.

Davis, Joann. "Trade News: Sendak on Sendak." As told to Jean F. Mercier. Publishers Weekly (April 10, 1981): 45–46.

Davis, J. Madison. Creating Plot. Cincinnati: Writers Digest Books, 2000.

Davis, Joy B., & Laurie MacGillivray. "Books About Teen Parents: Messages and Omissions." English Journal 90 (January 2001): 90–96.

Day-Lewis, Cecil. Poetry for You. New York: Oxford University Press, 1947.

deCaro, Frank, ed. The Folktale Cat. Little Rock, AR: August House, 1992.

DelFattore, Joan. What Johnny Shouldn't Read: Textbook Censorship in America. New Haven: Yale University Press, 1992.

Dempsey, Frank J. "Russell Freedman." The Horn Book (July/August 1988): 452–456.

Devereaux, Elizabeth. "Chronicle Fantasy Series: Of Trolls and Men." The New York Times Book Review (November 14, 2004): 20.

De Wit, Dorothy. Children's Faces Looking Up: Program Building for the Storyteller. Chicago: American Library Association, 1979.

Diakiw, J. "Children's Literature and Global Education: Understanding the Develop-ing World." The Reading Teacher 43 (1990): 296–300.

Dole, J., G. Duffy, L. Roehler, & P. D. Pearson. "Moving From the Old to the New: Research on Reading Comprehension Instruction." Review of Educational Research 61 (1991): 239–264.

Donelson, Ken. "Almost 13 Years of Book Protests—Now What?" School Library Journal 31 (March 1985): 93–98.

Dorris, Michael. "Native American Literature in an Ethnohistorical Context." College English 41 (October 1979): 147–162.

_____. "On Morning Girl." Press Release by Hyperion, 1992.

Dressel, Janice Hartwick. "Abstraction in Illustration: Is It Appropriate for Children?" Children's Literature in Education 15 (Summer 1984): 103–112.

Drury, John. The Poetry Dictionary. Cincinnati: Story Press, 1995.

Dryer, Charles Redway. Geography, Physical, Economic, and Regional. New York: American Books, 1911.

Duffy, Gerald G. "Crucial Elements in the Teaching of Poetry Writing." In The Language Arts in the Middle School, edited by Martha L. King, Robert Emans, & Patricia J. Cianciolo. Urbana, IL: National Council of Teachers of English, 1973.

Dundes, Alan. "Interpreting Little Red Riding Hood Psychoanalytically." In The Brothers Grimm and Folktale, edited by James M. McGlathey. Urbana: University of Illinois Press, 1988, 16–51.

Dunning, Stephen, & William Stafford. Getting the Knack: 20 Poetry Writing Exercises. Urbana, IL: National Council of Teachers of English, 1992.

Early, Margaret. "What Ever Happened To . . .?" The Reading Teacher 46 (December 1992/January 1993): 302–308.

Eccleshare, Julie. "Children's Books: Letter From London." Publishers Weekly 244 (August 18, 1997): 25.

Egoff, Sheila. "The Problem Novel." In Only Connect: Readings on Children's Literature, edited by Sheila Egoff, G. T. Stubbs, & L. F. Ashley. Toronto: Oxford University Press, 1980.

_____. Worlds Within: Children's Fantasy From the Middle Ages to Today. Chicago: American Library Association, 1988.

Eichenberg, Fritz. "Bell, Book and Candle." In The Arbuthnot Lectures: 1980–1989. Chicago: American Library Association, 1990, 51–66.

Eisenman, Stephen F., & Thomas E. Crow. Nineteenth Century Art: A Critical History. New York: Thames & Hudson, 2002.

Elleman, Barbara. "The Nonfiction Scene: What's Happening." In *Using Nonfiction Trade Books in the Elementary Classroom*, edited by Evelyn Freedman & Diane Person. Urbana, IL: National Council of Teachers of English, 1992, 26–33.

Ellis, Rex M. *Beneath the Blazing Sun*. Little Rock, AR: August House, 1997.

Engelfried, Steven. "The ABCs of ABCs: A Look at 26 of the Most Innovative Alphabet Books Around." *School Library Journal* 47 (January 2001): 32–33.

English Journal Forum. "When Minority Becomes Majority." *English Journal* 79 (January 1990): 15.

Epstein, William H. "Introducing Biography." *Children's Literature Association Quarterly* 12 (Winter, 1987): 177–179.

Erisman, Fred Raymond. "There Was a Child Went Forth: A Study of St. Nicholas Magazine and Selected Children's Authors, 1890–1915." Minneapolis: University of Minnesota, 1966, University Microfilm No. 66–12.

Ernest, Edward. *The Kate Greenaway Treasury*. Cleveland: World, 1967.

Esmonde, Margaret P. "Children's Science Fiction." In *The First Steps: Best of the Early ChLA Quarterly*. Compiled by Patricia Dooley. Lafayette, IN: Purdue University; Children's Literature Association, 1984.

Evans, Dilys. "An Extraordinary Vision: Picture Books of the Nineties." *The Horn Book* 68 (November/December 1992): 759–763.

Evans, Janet, ed. *What's in the Pictures?* London: Paul Chapman, 1998.

Fauchald, Nick. *William Lloyd Garrison: Abolitionist and Journalist*. Minneapolis: Compass Point, 2005.

Faulkner, William J. *The Days When the Animals Talked*. Illustrated by Troy Howell. Chicago: Follett, 1977.

Faust, Susan. "The Comeback Kid." *School Library Journal* 51 (May 2005): 38–40.

Favat, F. André. *Child and Tale: The Origins of Interest*. Urbana, IL: National Council of Teachers of English, 1977.

"Federal Technology Funding for Schools Jumps 450 Percent." *School Library Journal* 42 (November 1996): 14.

Feitelson, D., B. Kita, & Z. Goldstein. "Effects of Listening to Series Stories on First Graders' Comprehension and Use of Language." *Research in the Teaching of English* 20 (1986): 339–355.

Feldman, Edmund Burke. *Varieties of Visual Experience*. New York: Abrams, 1992.

Feldman, Roxanne. "The Truth About Harry." *School Library Journal* 45 (September 1999): 136–139.

Feldstein, Barbara. "Selection as a Means of Diffusing Censorship." In *Children's Literature: Resource for the Classroom*, edited by Masha Kabakow Rudman. Norwood, MA: Christopher-Gordon, 1993, 147–167.

Fillmore, Lily Wong. "Educating Citizens for a Multicultural 21st Century." *Multicultural Education* 1 (Summer 1993): 10–12, 37.

Fisher, Carol, & Margaret Natarella. "Young Children's Preferences in Poetry: A National Survey of First, Second, and Third Graders." *Research in the Teaching of English* 16 (December 1982): 339–354.

Fisher, Leonard Everett. "The Artist at Work: Creating Nonfiction." *The Horn Book* (May/June 1988): 315–323.

Fisher, Margery. "Life Course or Screaming Farce?" *Children's Literature in Education* 7 (Autumn 1976): 108–115.

Flack, Jerry D. *From the Land of Enchantment: Creative Teaching With Fairy Tales*. Englewood, CO: Libraries Unlimited, 1997.

Fleming, Margaret, & Jo McGinnis, eds. *Portraits: Biography and Autobiography in the Secondary School*. Urbana, IL: National Council of Teachers of English, 1985.

Flender, Mary G. "Charting Book Discussions: A Method of Presenting Literature in the Elementary Grades." *Children's Literature in Education* 16 (Summer 1985): 84–92.

Fohr, Samuel Denis. *Cinderella's Gold Slipper: Spiritual Symbolism in the Grimms' Tales*. Wheaton, IL: Quest Books, 1991.

Ford, Paul Leicester. *The New-England Primer*. New York: Columbia University, Teachers College, 1962.

"Forecasts: Children's Books." *Publishers Weekly* 247 (August 14, 2000): 354–356.

Forman, Jack. "Young Adult Books: Politics—The Last Taboo." *The Horn Book* 61 (July/August 1985): 469–471.

Fowke, Edith, & Joe Glazer. *Songs of Work and Protest*. New York: Dover, 1973.

Fox, Dan. *Go In and Out the Window: An Illustrated Songbook for Young People*. New York: The Metropolitan Museum of Art and H. Holt, 1987.

Frankel, Ellen, ed. *The Jewish Spirit: Celebration in Stories and Art*. New York: Stewart, Tabori & Chang, 1997.

Fraser, James H., ed. *Society and Children's Literature*. Boston: Godine, 1978.

Frasher, Ramona. "A Feminist Look at Literature for Children: Ten Years Later." In *Sex Stereotypes and Reading: Research and Strategies*, edited by E. Marcia Sheridan. Newark, NJ: International Reading Association, 1982.

Freedman, Russell. "Fact or Fiction?" In *Using Nonfiction Trade Books in the Elementary Classroom*, edited by Evelyn Freeman & Diane Person. Urbana, IL: National Council of Teachers of English, 1992, 2–10.

_____. "Newbery Medal Acceptance." *The Horn Book* (July/August 1988): 444–451.

Friedan, Betty. "My Quest for the Fountain of Age." *Time* 142 (September 6, 1993): 61–64.

Fritz, Jean. *Homesick: My Own Story*. New York: Putnam. 1982.

_____. "Making It Real." *Children's Literature in Education* 22 (Autumn 1976): 125–127.

Frobenius, Leo, & Douglas Fox. *African Genesis*. Berkeley, CA: Turtle Island for the Netzahualcoyal Historical Society, 1983.

Fry, Edward. "Fry's Readability Graph: Clarifications, Validity, and Extension." *Journal of Reading* 21 (December 1977): 249.

Frye, Northrop, Sheridan Baker, & George Perkins. *The Harper Handbook to Literature*. New York: Harper & Row, 1985.

Furnivall, Frederick J., ed. *Caxton's Book of Curtesye*. London: Oxford University Press, 1868.

Gage, N. L., & David C. Berliner. *Educational Psychology*. Chicago: Rand McNally, 1979.

_____. *Educational Psychology*, 5th ed. Boston: Houghton Mifflin, 1992.

Galda, Lee. "Accent on Art." *The Reading Teacher* 44 (February 1991): 406–414.

_____. "Readers, Texts and Contexts: A Response-Based View of Literature in the Classroom." *The New Advocate* 1 (Spring, 1988): 92–102.

Garfield, Leon. "Historical Fiction for Our Global Times." *The Horn Book* (November/December 1988): 736–742.

Garrett, Jeffrey. "Far-Away Wisdom: Three Nominees for the 1992 Andersen Prize." *The Reading Teacher* 46 (December 1992/January 1993): 310–314.

Gay, Carol. "Children's Literature and the Bicentennial." *Language Arts* 53 (January 1976): 11–16.

Geller, Linda Gibson. *Wordplay and Language Learning for Children*. Urbana, IL: National Council of Teachers of English, 1985.

Gensler, Kinereth, & Nina Nyhart. *The Poetry Connection: An Anthology of Contemporary Poems With Ideas to Stimulate Children's Writing*. New York: Teachers & Writers, 1978.

GEO News Handbook (November 11–17, 1990): 7.

George, Jean Craighead. "Science Is Stories." In *Vital Connections: Children, Science, and Books*, edited by Wendy Saul & Sybille A. Jagusch. Washington, DC: Library of Congress, 1991, 67–70.

Gerke, Pamela. *Multicultural Plays for Children, Volume II, Grades 4–6.* Lyme, NH: Smith & Kraus, 1996.

Giblin, James Cross. "The Rise and Fall and Rise of Juvenile Nonfiction, 1961–1988." In *Using Nonfiction Trade Books in the Elementary Classroom,* edited by Evelyn Freedman & Diane Person. Urbana IL: National Council of Teachers of English, 1992, 17–25.

Gibson, Louis Rauch, & Laura M. Zaidman. "Death in Children's Literature: Taboo or Not Taboo?" *Children's Literature Association Quarterly* 16 (Winter 1992): 232–234.

Gillespie, Margaret C. *Literature for Children: History and Trends.* Dubuque, IA: Brown, 1970.

Gillin, Richard. "Romantic Echoes in the Willow." *Children's Literature* 16 (1988): 169–174.

Gillmor, Frances. *The King Danced in the Marketplace.* Salt Lake City: University of Utah Press, 1977.

Gish, Kimbra Wilder. "Hunting Down Harry Potter: An Exploration of Religious Concerns About Children's Literature." *The Horn Book* LXXVI (May/June 2000): 262–271.

Glazer, Joan. *Literature for Young Children.* Upper Saddle River, NJ: Merrill/Prentice Hall, 1991.

Glazer, Tom. *A New Treasury of Folk Songs.* New York: Bantam, 1961.

Gleason, Katherine. *Native American Literature.* New York: Chelsea, 1996.

Glenn, Wendy J. "Brock Cole: The Good, the Bad, and the Humorously Ironic." *The Alan Review* 26 (Winter 1999): 26–29.

Gloria, Alberta. "Battling Against Attrition." *The Newsletter of the University of Wisconsin (Madison)* (Spring 2001): 14, 16.

Goble, Paul. *Notes by Goble About the Illustrations for* The Girl Who Loved Wild Horses. New York: Bradbury Press, 1978.

Godden, Rumer. "Shining Popocatapetl: Poetry for Children." *The Horn Book* (May/June 1988): 305–314.

"Going Places." *Reading Today* 18 (February/March 2001): 3.

Goldberg, Lazer. "Gaps and Emphases." In *Vital Connections: Children, Science, and Books,* edited by Wendy Saul & Sybille A. Jagusch. Washington, DC: Library of Congress, 1991, 31–41.

Golman, Daniel. *Emotional Intelligence.* New York: Bantam, 1995.

Good, Carter. *Dictionary of Education.* New York: McGraw-Hill, 1973.

Gordon, Christine J. "Modeling Inference Awareness Across the Curriculum." *Journal of Reading* 28 (February 1985): 444–447.

Gorman, James. "Woodpecker Flies By and the Critics Soon Follow." *The New York Times* (July 24, 2005): A1.

Gorra, Michael. "Next Stop, Neverland." *The New York Times Book Review* (November 14, 2004): 23.

Gosa, Cheryl. "Moral Development in Current Fiction for Children and Young Adults." *Language Arts* 54 (May 1977): 529–536.

Gough, John. "Experiencing a Sequence of Poem: Ted Hughes's *Season Songs.*" *Children's Literature Association Quarterly* 13 (Winter 1988): 191–194.

————. "Poems in a Context: Breaking the Anthology Trap." *Children's Literature in Education* 15 (Winter 1984): 204–210.

Granstrom, Jane, & Anita Silvey. "A Call for Help: Exploring the Black Experience in Children's Books." In *Cultural Conformity in Books for Children,* edited by Donnarae MacCann & Gloria Woodard. Metuchen, NJ: Scarecrow, 1977.

Graves, Donald. *Writing: Teachers and Children at Work.* Exeter, NH: Heinemann, 1988.

Greaney, Vincent. "Factors Related to Amount and Type of Leisure Time Reading." *Reading Research Quarterly* 15 (1980): 337–357.

Green, Roland J. "Modern Science Fiction and Fantasy: A Frame of Reference." *Illinois School Journal* 57 (Fall 1977): 45–53.

Green, Thomas A., ed. *Folklore: An Encyclopedia of Beliefs, Customs, Tales, Music and Art,* Vol. II. Santa Barbara, CA: ABC-CLIO, 1997.

Greenfield, Eloise. "Writing for Children—A Joy and a Responsibility." In *The Black American in Books for Children: Readings in Racism,* edited by Donnarae MacCann & Gloria Woodard. Metuchen, NJ: Scarecrow, 1985.

Greenway, William, & Betty Greenway. "Meeting the Muse: Teaching Contemporary Poetry by Teaching Poetry Writing." *Children's Literature Association Quarterly* 15 (1990): 138–142.

Griego y Maestas, Jose, & Rudolfo A. Anaya. *Cuentos: Tales From the Hispanic Southwest.* Santa Fe: Museum of New Mexico, 1980.

Griffiths, Antony, ed. *Landmarks in Print Collecting.* London: British Museum, 1996.

Groce, Robin, & Patricia Wiese. *A Mosaic of Stories: Celebrating Cultures Through Classroom Storytelling.* College Station: Texas A & M University, 2000.

Groff, Patrick. "Where Are We Going With Poetry for Children?" In *Horn Book Reflections,* edited by Elinor Whitney Field. Boston: Horn Book, 1969.

Gross, John. "Pop-Up Books: The Magical Art of Making Movable Pictures Over the Years." *The New York Times* (Sunday, January 17, 1988): 33H.

Guggenheim Museum. *Marc Chagall and the Jewish Theater.* New York: Guggenheim Museum, 1992.

Gurdon, Meghan Cox. "Children's Books." *The Wall Street Journal* (January 1, 2006): 8.

Gurjar, Nandita. "Position of Women in Indian Culture and Literature." Paper Presented at Multicultural Conference. Texas A & M University, 1995.

Haight, Anne Lyon. *Banned Books: 387 B.C to 1978 A.D.* New York: R. R. Bowker, 1978.

Haining, Peter. *Movable Books: An Illustrated History.* London: New English Library Limited, 1979.

Haley, Gail E. "From the Ananse Stories to the Jack Tales: My Work With Folktales." *Children's Literature Association Quarterly* 11 (Fall 1986): 118–121.

Hall, Ann E. "Contemporary Realism in American Children's Books." *Choice* (November 1977): 1171–1178.

Hall, Christine, & Martin Coles. *Children's Reading Choices.* New York: Routledge, 1999.

Hall, Edwin S., Jr. *The Eskimo Storyteller: Folktales From Noatak, Alaska.* Knoxville: The University of Tennessee Press, 1976.

Hamilton, Martha, & Mitch Weiss. "Children as Storytellers: Teaching the Basic Tools." *School Library Journal* 39 (April 1993): 30–33.

————. *Children Tell Stories: A Teaching Guide.* Katonah, NY: Richard C. Owen, 1990.

————. *How & Why Stories: World Tales Kids Can Read & Tell.* Little Rock, AR: August House, 1999.

Hamilton, Virginia. *The People Could Fly: American Black Folktales.* New York: Knopf, 1985.

————. "Planting Seeds." *The Horn Book* 68 (November/December 1992): 674–680.

Hammill, Donald, & Nettie R. Bartel. *Teaching Students With Learning and Behavior Problems: Managing Mild-to-Moderate Difficulties in Resource and Inclusive Settings.* Austin, TX: Pro-Ed, 1995.

Hampl, Patricia. "A Review of *The Diary of a Young Girl: Anne Frank, the Definitive Edition.*" *The New York Times Book Review* (March 5, 1995): 21.

Handler, Daniel. "Aladdin and the Enchanted Lamp." *The New York Times Book Review* (June 5, 2005): 39.

Hanson, W. D., & M. O. Eisenbise. *Human Behavior and American Indians.* Rockville, MD: National Institute of Mental Health, 1983. ERIC Document Reproduction Service, ED 231–589.

Harms, Jeanne McLain, & Lucille J. Lettow. "Book Design Elements: Integrating the Whole." *Childhood Education* 75 (Fall 1998): 17–24.

Harris, Violet. "Multiethnic Children's Literature." In *Exploring Literature in the Classroom: Content and Methods,* edited by K. D. Wood & A. Moss. Norwood, MA: Christopher-Gordon, 1992, 169–201.

Harrison, Barbara. "Howl Like the Wolves." *Children's Literature* 15 (1987): 67–90.

Harvey, Karen D., Lisa D. Harjo, & Jane K. Jackson, *Teaching About Native Americans.* Washington, DC: National Council for the Social Studies, 1990.

Haugaard, Erik. "When Does the Past Become History?" In *The Child and the Family: Selected Papers From International Conference of the Children's Literature Association,* edited by Susan R. Gannon & Ruth Anne Thompson. New York: Pace University, 1988, 5–11.

Haugen, Brenda. *Frederick Douglass: Slave, Writer, Abolitionist.* Minneapolis: Compass Point, 2005.

Haven, Kendall. *Super Simple Storytelling: A Can-Do Guide for Every Classroom, Every Day.* Englewood, CO: Libraries Unlimited, 2000.

Haviland, Virginia. *Children and Literature: View and Reviews.* Glenview, IL: Scott, Foresman, 1973.

———. *North American Legends.* New York: Collins, 1979.

Hawley, John C. "The Water-Babies as Catechetical Paradigm." *Children's Literature Association Quarterly* 14 (Spring 1989): 19–21.

Hayden, Carla D., ed. *Venture Into Cultures: A Resource Book of Multicultural Materials and Programs.* Chicago: American Library Association, 1992.

Hayden, Gretchen Purtell. "A Descriptive Study of the Treatment of Personal Development in Selected Children's Fiction Books Awarded the Newbery Medal." Detroit: Wayne State University, 1969, University Microfilm No. 70-19, 060.

Hearn, Michael Patrick. Preface to *Histories or Tales of Past Times,* by Charles Perrault. New York: Garland, 1977.

Hearne, Betsy. *Beauty and the Beast: Visions and Revisions of an Old Tale.* Chicago: University of Chicago Press, 1989.

———. "Booking the Brothers Grimm: Art, Adaptations, and Economics." In *The Brothers Grimm and Folktale,* edited by James M. McGlathery. Urbana, IL: University of Illinois Press, 1988, 220–233.

———. "Circling Tuck: An Interview With Natalie Babbitt." *The Horn Book* LXXVI (March/April 2000): 153–161.

———. "Cite the Source: Reducing Cultural Chaos in Picture Books, Part One." *School Library Journal* 39 (July 1993a): 22–27.

———. "Contemporary Issues—Child Abuse." *Booklist* 81 (May 1, 1985): 1261–1262.

———. "Patterns of Sound, Sight, and Story: From Literature to Literacy." *The Lion and the Unicorn* 16 (June 1992): 17–42.

———. "Picture Books: More Than a Story." *Booklist* 30 (December 1, 1983): 577–578.

———. "Respect the Source: Reducing Cultural Chaos in Picture Books, Part Two." *School Library Journal* 39 (August 1993b): 33–37.

Heins, Paul. "Coming to Terms With Criticism." In *Crosscurrents of Criticism: Horn Book Essays 1968–1977.* Boston: Horn Book, 1978a, 82–87.

———. "Out on a Limb With the Critics: Some Random Thoughts on the Present State of the Criticism of Children's Literature." In *Crosscurrents of Criticism: Horn Book Essays 1968–1977.* Boston: Horn Book, 1978b, 72–81.

———. "A Second Look: The Adventures of Pinocchio." *The Horn Book* (April 1982): 200–204.

Helms, Cynthia Newman, ed. *Diego Rivera: A Retrospective.* Founders Society, Detroit Institute of Arts, 1986.

Hendrick, Joanne. *The Whole Child,* 4th ed. Upper Saddle River, NJ: Merrill/Prentice Hall, 1992.

———. *The Whole Child: Developmental Education for the Early Years,* 6th ed. Englewood Cliffs, NJ: Merrill, 1996.

Henke, James T. "Dicey, Odysseus, and Hansel and Gretel: The Lost Children of Voigt's *Homecoming.*" *Children's Literature in Education* 16 (Spring 1985): 45–52.

Hepler, Susan Ingrid. "Profile, Tomie de Paola: A Gift to Children." *Language Arts* 56 (March 1979): 269–301.

Herb, Steve. "Building Blocks for Literacy: What Current Research Shows." *School Library Journal* 43 (July 1997): 23.

Herbst, Laura. "That's One Good Indian: Unacceptable Images in Children's Novels." In *Cultural Conformity in Books for Children,* edited by Donnarae MacCann & Gloria Woodard. Metuchen, NJ: Scarecrow, 1977.

Herman, Gertrude B. " 'Footprints on the Sands of Time': Biography for Children." *Children's Literature in Education* 9 (Summer 1977): 85–94.

Herring, William A. "Creating Rhythm With Color and Line." *American Artist* 61 (March 1997): 40–43.

Herszenhorn, David M., & Susan Saulny. "As Far as Teachers and Students Are Concerned, Scores Rose on Hard Work, Period." *The New York Times* (June 12, 2005): 30–31.

Hewett, Gloria J., & Jean C. Rush. "Finding Buried Treasures: Aesthetic Scanning With Children." *Art Education* 40 (January 1987): 41–43.

Hilliam, David. *Thomas Becket: English Saint and Martyr.* New York: Rosen, 2005.

Hillocks, George. *Research on Written Composition: New Directions for Teaching.* Urbana, IL: National Conference on Research in English, 1986.

Hillyer, V. M. *A Child's Geography of the World.* Illustrated by Mary Sherwood Wright Jones. New York: Century, 1929.

Hilts, Paul. "The Road Ahead: Publishing Visionaries Look at the Change That Digital Technology Might Bring." *Publishers Weekly* 244 (July 1997): 125–128.

Hipple, Ted, & Amy B. Maupin. "What's Good About the Best?" *English Journal* 90 (January 2001): 40–42.

Hockwald, Lambeth. "Little Book, Big Controversy." *Publishers Weekly,* 243 (July 29, 1996): 32–33.

Hoffman, James, & P. David Pearson. "Reading Teacher Education in the Next Millennium: What Your Grandmother's Teacher Didn't Know That Your Granddaughter's Teacher Should." *Reading Research Quarterly* 35 (January/February/March 2000): 28–44.

Hoffman, Lynn. "Picture Books at the Museum." *Joys* 14 (Fall 2000): 16–17.

Holt, David, & Bill Mooney, eds. *Ready-to-Tell Tales.* Little Rock, AR: August House, 1994.

Holzheimer, Diane. "Appraisal: A Book Review Journal." In *Vital Connections: Children, Science, and Books,* edited by Wendy Saul & Sybille A. Jagusch. Washington, DC: Library of Congress, 1991, 91–96.

Homze, Alma Cross. "Interpersonal Relationships in Children's Literature From 1920 to 1960." University Park: Pennsylvania State University, 1963. University Microfilm No. 64-5366.

Hopkins, Dianne McAfee. "Put It in Writing: What You Should Know About Challenges to School Library Materials."

School Library Journal 39 (January 1993): 26–30.

Hopkins, Lee Bennett. *Pass the Poetry, Please!* New York: Harper & Row, 1987.

"The Horn Book Guide to Children's and Young Adult Books." *The Horn Book* 4 (Spring 1993): 18–51.

Horning, Kathleen T. "The Tale of DiCamillo." *School Library Journal* 50 (April 2004): 44–47.

_____, Merri V. Lindgren, Hollis Rudiger, & Megan Schliesman. *CCBC Choices 2005.* Madison: University of Wisconsin, Co-operative Children's Book Center, School of Education, 2005.

_____. *CCBC Choices 2004.* Madison: University of Wisconsin, Cooperative Children's Book Center, School of Education, 2004.

Houghton Mifflin Company. *Eliminating Stereotypes, School Division Guidelines.* Boston: Houghton Mifflin, 1981.

Houston, James. "A Primitive View of the World." In *The Arbuthnot Lectures, 1980–1989.* Chicago: American Library Association, 1990, 99–111.

Hsu, Richard C., & William E. Mitchell. "Books Have Endured for a Reason . . ." *The New York Times* 3 (May 25, 1997): 12.

Huck, Charlotte S., Susan Hepler, & Janet Hickman. *Children's Literature in the Elementary School.* Madison, WI: Brown & Benchmark, 1997.

Hunt, Peter. "Censorship and Children's Literature in Britain Now, or, The Return of Abigail." *Children's Literature in Education* 28 (1997): 95–103.

_____, ed. *Children's Literature: An Illustrated History.* New York: Oxford University Press, 1995.

_____. "Dialogue and Dialectic: Language and Class in *The Wind in the Willows.*" *Children's Literature* 16 (1988): 159–168.

Hürlimann, Bettina. "Fortunate Moments in Children's Books." In *The Arbuthnot Lectures, 1970–1979,* compiled by Zena Sutherland. Chicago: American Library Association, 1980, 61–80.

Huus, Helen. "Teaching Literature at the Elementary School Level." *The Reading Teacher* 26 (May 1973): 795–801.

Isaacs, Kathleen T. "Flying High." *School Library Journal* 47 (March 2001): 52–55.

_____. "Truth in Information Books." *School Library Journal* 51 (July 2005): 28–29.

Ishizuka, Kathy, ed. "Web Site Review." *School Library Journal* 51 (December 2005): 69–70.

Jacobs, Gloria E. "Complicating Contexts: Issues of Methodology in Researching the Language and Literacies of Instant Messaging." *Reading Research Quarterly* 39 (October/November/December 2004): 394–406.

Jacobs, Melville. *The Content and Style of an Oral Literature: Clackamas Chinook Myths and Tales.* Chicago: University of Chicago Press, 1959.

Jacobson, Frances F. "Remembrance of Things Past: Making History Come Alive With Primary Sources." *School Library Journal* 46 (December 2000): 35.

Jaffe, Jane Vial. "Introduction." *Crosscurrents.* Aspen, CO: Aspen Music Festival and School, 2001, 3.

Jaffe, Nina. "Reflections on the Work of Harold Courlander." *School Library Journal* 42 (September 1996): 132–133.

James, Grace. *Green Willow and Other Japanese Fairy Tales.* New York: Avenel, 1987.

Janson, H. W., & Anthony F. Janson. *History of Art,* 5th ed. New York: Abrams, 1997.

_____. *History of Art for Young People,* 4th ed. New York: Abrams, 1992.

_____. *History of Art for Young People,* 6th ed. New York: Abrams, 1999.

_____. *A Short History of Art.* Upper Saddle River, NJ: Prentice Hall, 2006.

Jerome, Judson. *Poetry: Premeditated Art.* Boston: Houghton Mifflin, 1968.

Johannessen, Larry R. *Teaching the Literature of the Vietnam War.* Urbana, IL: National Council of Teachers of English, 1992.

Johnson, Nancy J., & Cyndia Giorgis. "Interview With the 2002 Newbery Medal Winner, Linda Sue Park." *The Reading Teacher* 56 (December 2002/January 2003): 394–398.

Johnston, Kathleen S. "Choosing Books." In *Vital Connections: Children, Science, and Books,* edited by Wendy Saul & Sybille A. Jagusch. Washington, DC: Library of Congress, 1991, 97–103.

Jones, Leigh Ann. "Better Libraries Through Censorship." *School Library Journal* 42 (October 1996): 54.

Jones, Trevelyn E. "Annual Policy Statement." *School Library Journal* 51 (January 2005): 84.

Jones, Trev, Luann Toth, Marlene Charnizon, Daryl Grabarek, & Joy Fleishhacker, selected by. "The Year's Best Books." *School Library Journal* (December 2001): 44–49.

Jorgensen, Karin. "Making the Reading, Writing, Social Studies Connection." *Social Studies and the Young Learner* 2 (March/April 1990): 20–22.

Judson, Hallowell. "What Is in a Picture?" *Children's Literature in Education* 20 (March 1989): 59–68.

Jurich, Marilyn. "What's Left Out of Biography for Children?" *Children's Literature: The Great Excluded* 1 (1972): 143–151.

Kaminski, Winfred. "War and Peace in Recent German Children's Literature." *Children's Literature* 15 (1987): 55–66.

Karl, Jean E. *How to Write and Sell Children's Books.* Cincinnati: Writers Digest Books, 1994.

_____. "What Sells—What's Good?" *The Horn Book* 63 (July/August 1987): 505–508.

Kean, John M., & Carl Personke. *The Language Arts: Teaching and Learning in the Elementary School.* New York: St. Martin, 1976.

Kehret, Peg. "Encouraging Empathy." *School Library Journal* 47 (August 2001): 44–45.

Keith, Harold. *The Obstinate Land.* New York: Crowell, 1977.

Keller, Sharon. *The Jews: A Treasury of Art and Literature.* New York: Macmillan, 1992.

Kelly, Robert Gordon. "Mother Was a Lady: Self and Society in Selected American Children's Periodicals, 1865–1890," Iowa City: University of Iowa, 1970, University Microfilm No. 71–5770.

_____. "Social Factors Shaping Some Nineteenth-Century Children's Periodical Fiction." In *Society and Children's Literature,* edited by James H. Fraser. Boston: Godine, 1978.

Kennedy, Caroline, selected by. *A Family of Poems: My Favorite Poetry for Children.* Illustrated by Jon J. Muth. New York: Hyperion, 2005.

Kennemer, Phyllis K. "Reviews of Fiction Books: How They Differ." *Top of the News* 40 (Summer 1984): 419–421.

Kherdian, David. *Feathers and Tails: Animal Fables From Around the World.* New York: Philomel, 1992.

Killheffer, Robert K. J. "Fantasy Charts New Realms." *Publishers Weekly* 244 (June 16, 1997): 34–40.

Kimmel, Mary, & Elizabeth Segel. *For Reading Out Loud.* New York: Dell, 1983.

King, Stephen. "Wild About Harry." *The New York Times Book Review* (July 23, 2000): 13–14.

Kingsbury, Mary. "Perspectives on Criticism." *The Horn Book* 60 (February 1984): 17–23.

Kingsley, Mary. *West African Studies,* 3rd ed. New York: Barnes & Noble, 1964.

Kiska, Paula. "Slavic Wonder Tales: An Overview." *Children's Literature Association Quarterly* 11 (Fall 1986): 123–128.

Knorr, Susan M., & Margaret Knorr. *Books on the Move: A Read-About-It Go-There*

Guide to America's Best Family Destinations. Minneapolis: Free Spirit, 1993.

Kobus, Doni Kwolek. "Multicultural/Global Education: An Educational Agenda for the Rights of the Child." *Social Education* 56 (April/May 1992): 224–227.

Koch, Kenneth. *Wishes, Lies, and Dreams.* New York: Vintage Books/Chelsea House, 1970.

Koelling, Holly. *Classic Connections: Turning Teens on to Great Literature.* Westport, CT: Libraries Unlimited, 2004.

Kohlberg, Lawrence. *Essays on Moral Development: The Philosophy of Moral Development.* New York: Harper & Row, 1981.

Kukla, Kaile. "David Booth: Drama as a Way of Knowing." *Language Arts* 64 (January 1987): 73–78.

Kun-yu, Bu. "Between Two Cultures." *Social Education* 52 (September 1988): 378–383.

Kunzel, Bonnie. "Hooray for Harry." *School Library Journal* 51 (February 2005): 46–49.

Kuo, Louise, & Yuan-hsi Kuo. *Chinese Folk Tales.* Millbrae, CA: Celestial Arts, 1976.

Kutiper, Karen Sue. "A Survey of the Adolescent Poetry Preferences of Seventh, Eighth, and Ninth Graders." University of Houston: Ed.D. Dissertation, 1985. DAI 47:451–452A.

Lacy, Lyn Ellen. *Art and Design in Children's Picture Books: An Analysis of Caldecott Award-Winning Illustrations.* Chicago: American Library Association, 1986.

Laliberté, Norman, and Alex Mogelon. *The Reinhold Book of Art Ideas.* New York: Van Nostrand Reinhold, 1976.

Lamb, Charles, & Mary Lamb. *Tales From Shakespeare.* New York: Children's Classics, 1986.

Lamme, Linda Leonard. "Reading Aloud to Young Children." *Language Arts* 53 (November/December 1976): 886–888.

_____, & Frances Kane. "Children, Books, and Collage." *Language Arts* 53 (November/December 1976): 902–905.

Lanes, Selma. *The Art of Maurice Sendak.* New York: Abradale Press, 1980.

Larrick, Nancy. *Let's Do a Poem.* New York: Delacorte, 1991.

Lasky, Kathryn. *Beyond the Divide.* New York: Macmillan, 1983.

Latimer, Bettye I. *Starting Out Right: Choosing Books About Black People for Young Children.* Madison: Wisconsin Department of Public Instruction, 1972, Bulletin No. 2314.

_____. "Telegraphing Messages to Children About Minorities." *The Reading Teacher* 30 (November 1976): 151–156.

Lauber, Patricia. "The Evolution of a Science Writer." In *Using Nonfiction Trade Books in the Elementary Classroom,* edited by Evelyn Freedman & Diane Person. Urbana, IL: National Council of Teachers of English, 1992, 11–16.

_____. "The Heart of the Matter." In *Vital Connections: Children, Science, and Books,* edited by Wendy Saul & Sybille A. Jagusch. Washington, DC: Library of Congress, 1991, 45–50.

Laws, Frederick. "Randolph Caldecott." In *Only Connect: Readings on Children's Literature,* edited by Sheila Egoff, G. T. Stubbs, & L. F. Ashley. 2nd ed. Toronto: Oxford University Press, 1980.

Lee, Sherman E. *A History of Far Eastern Art,* 5th ed. Upper Saddle River, NJ: Prentice Hall, 1994.

Leeson, Robert. *Children's Books and Class Society.* London: Writers & Readers, 1977.

Leggo, Carl. *Teaching to Wonder: Responding to Poetry in the Secondary Classroom.* Vancouver: Pacific Educational Press, 1997.

Lehr, Susan, ed. *Battling Dragons: Issues and Controversy in Children's Literature.* Portsmouth, NH: Heinemann, 1995.

Lenaghan, R. T., ed. *Caxton's Aesop.* Cambridge, MA: Harvard University Press, 1967.

Lenz, Lisa. "Crossroads of Literacy and Orality: Reading Poetry Aloud. *Language Arts* 69 (December 1992): 597–603.

Le Pere, Jean. "For Every Occasion: Poetry in the Reading Program." Albuquerque, NM: Eighth Southwest Regional Conference, International Reading Association, 1980.

Lepman-Logan, Claudia. "Books in the Classroom: Moral Choices in Literature." *The Horn Book* (January/February 1989): 108–111.

Leroi-Gourhan, Andre. *Treasures of Prehistoric Art.* New York: Abrams.

Levenson, Jay. *Circa 1492: Art in the Age of Exploration.* Washington, DC: National Gallery of Art, 1991.

Lewis, C. S. *Surprised by Joy: The Shape of My Early Life.* London: G. Bles, 1955.

Lewis, Naomi. "Introduction." In Peter Christen Asbjørnsen & Jørgen Moe's *East O' the Sun and West O' the Moon.* Cambridge, MA: Candlewick, 1991.

Lewis, Rena, & Donald Doorlag. *Teaching Special Students in the Mainstream,* 2nd ed. Upper Saddle River, NJ: Merrill/Prentice Hall, 1987.

Lindauer, Shelley L. Knudsen. "Wordless Books: An Approach to Visual Literacy."

Children's Literature in Education 19 (1988): 136–142.

Linder, Enid, & Leslie Linder. *The Art of Beatrix Potter.* London: Warne, 1980.

Lipkis, Rita. "Books in the Classroom: Young Hands on Old Books." *The Horn Book* 69 (January/February 1993): 115–118.

Lipman, Doug. *Improving Your Storytelling: Beyond the Basics for All Who Tell Stories in Work or Play.* Little Rock, AR: August House, 1999.

_____. *The Storytelling Coach.* Little Rock, AR: August House, 1995.

Lipson, Eden Ross. "Summer and the Reading Can Be Easy." *The New York Times Book Review* (May 20, 2001): 26–27.

Livingston, Myra Cohn. "Not the Rose . . ." In *Horn Book Reflections,* edited by Elinor Whitney Field. Boston: Horn Book, 1969.

_____. *Poems of Lewis Carroll.* New York: Crowell, 1973.

_____. *Poetry-Making: Ways to Begin Writing Poetry.* New York: HarperCollins, 1991.

Loban, Walter. *Language Development: Kindergarten Through Grade Twelve.* Urbana, IL: National Council of Teachers of English, 1976.

Lobsenz, Norman. "News From the Home Front." *Family Weekly* (August 2, 1981): 9.

Locke, John. "Some Thoughts Concerning Education." In *English Philosophers,* edited by Charles W. Eliot. New York: Villier, 1910.

Lodge, Sally, compiled by. "Children's Books for Fall." *Publishers Weekly* 243 (July 22, 1996): 158–205.

_____. "Rolling Out the Green Carpet: Environmental Books for Kids." *Publishers Weekly* 239 (March 2, 1992): 22–25.

_____. "Spanish-Language Publishing for Kids in the U.S. Picks Up Speed." *Publishers Weekly* Special Supplement (August 25, 1997): 548–549.

Lofaro, Michael A. *The Tall Tales of Davy Crockett: The Second Nashville Series of Crockett Almanacs, 1839–1841.* Knoxville: University of Tennessee Press, 1987.

Long, Joanna Rudge. "Eloquent Visions: Perspectives In Picture Book Biography." *School Library Journal* 43 (April 1997): 48–49.

Lonsdale, Bernard J., & Helen K. Macintosh. *Children Experience Literature.* New York: Random House, 1973.

Lottman, Herbert R. "In the Studio With Satomi Ichikawa." *Publishers Weekly* 240 (June 7, 1993): 19.

Lowell, Amy. *Poetry and Poets.* New York: Biblo, 1971.

Lukens, Rebecca J. *A Critical Handbook of Children's Literature,* 6th ed. Reading, MA: Addison-Wesley, 1999.

Lunstrum, John P., & Bob L. Taylor. *Teaching Reading in the Social Studies.* Newark, DE: International Reading Association, 1978.

Lustig, Arnost. "What We Will Never Understand About the Holocaust." Unexpected Encounters With the Holocaust Conference: Texas A&M University, College Station, TX, April 2, 1997.

Lystad, Mary. *From Dr. Mather to Dr. Seuss: Two Hundred Years of American Books for Children.* Boston: G. K. Hall, 1980.

MacCann, Donnarae, & Olga Richard. *The Child's First Books: A Critical Study of Pictures and Texts.* New York: Wilson, 1973.

MacDonald, Margaret Read. *The Story-Teller's Start-Up Book.* Little Rock, AR: August House, 1993.

MacDonald, Robert. "Signs From the Imperial Quarter: Illustrations in Chums, 1892–1914." *Children's Literature* 16 (1988): 31–55.

MacLeod, Anne Scott. *American Childhood.* Athens: University of Georgia Press, 1994.

————. "Children's Literature in America from the Puritan Beginnings to 1870." In *Children's Literature: An illustrated History,* edited by Peter Hunt. Oxford: Oxford University Press, 1995, 102–129.

Madsen, Jane M., & Elaine B. Wickersham. "A Look at Young Children's Realistic Fiction." *The Reading Teacher* 34 (December 1980): 273–279.

Maguire, Jack. "Sounds and Sensibilities: Storytelling as an Educational Process." *Children's Literature Association Quarterly* 13 (Spring, 1988): 6–9.

Maher, Susan Naramore. "Encountering Others: The Meeting of Cultures in Scott O'Dell's *Island of the Blue Dolphins* and *Sing Down the Moon.*" *Children's Literature in Education* 23 (1992): 215–227.

————. "Recasting Crusoe: Frederick Marryat, R. M. Ballantyne and the Nineteenth-Century Robinsonade." *Children's Literature Association Quarterly* 13 (Winter 1988): 169–175.

Mandela, Nelson. *Nelson Mandela's Favorite African Folktales.* Cape Town, South Africa: Tafelberg, 2002.

Manguel, Alberto. *A History of Reading.* New York: Viking, 1996.

————, & Gianni Guadalupi. *The Dictionary of Imaginary Places.* Illustrated by Graham Greenfield, Eric Beddows, & James Cook. New York: Harcourt Brace, 2000.

Marantz, Sylvia S. *Picture Books for Looking and Learning: Awakening Visual Perceptions Through the Art of Children's Books.* Phoenix: Oryx Press, 1992.

Marcus, Leonard S. "Awakened by the Moon." *Publishers Weekly* 238 (July 26, 1991): 16–20.

————. "Song of Myself." *School Library Journal* 46 (September 2000): 50–53.

Margolis, Rick. "Will You Still Read Me When I'm 64?" *School Library Journal* 50 (November 2004): 58–61.

Marshall, Cynthia. "Allegory, Orthodoxy, Ambivalence: MacDonald's *The Day Boy and the Night Girl.*" *Children's Literature* 16 (1988): 57–75.

Martin, Sue Anne Gillespi. "The Caldecott Medal Award Books, 1938–1968: Their Literary and Oral Characteristics as They Relate to Storytelling." Detroit, MI: Wayne State University, 1969. University Microfilm No. 72-16, 219.

Martinez, Miriam, & Nancy Roser. "Children's Responses to Literature." In *Handbook of Research on Teaching the English Language Arts,* 2nd ed., edited by James Flood, Diane Lapp, & James R. Squire, Julie M. Jensen. Mahwah, NJ: Erlbaum, 2003, 799–813.

Maryles, Daisy. "Behind the Bestsellers." *Publishers Weekly* 243 (July 22, 1996): 141.

Mason, Penelope. *History of Japanese Art,* 2nd ed. Upper Saddle River, NJ: Prentice Hall, 2005.

Maughan, Shannon. "Dealing the Straight Dope." *Publishers Weekly* 239 (April 13, 1992): 23.

Maxim, George. *The Very Young: Guiding Children From Infancy Through the Early Years.* Upper Saddle River, NJ: Merrill/Prentice Hall, 1993.

————. *The Very Young: Guiding Children From Infancy Through the Early Years* (5th ed.). Upper Saddle River, NJ: Merrill/Prentice Hall, 1997.

McCaffrey, Meg. "Answering the Call." *School Library Journal* 51 (March 2005): 46–48.

McCall, Cecelia. "A Historical Quest for Literacy." *Interracial Books for Children Bulletin* 19 (1989): 3–5.

McClenathan, Day Ann K. "Realism in Books for Young People. Some Thoughts on Management of Controversy." In *Developing Active Readers: Ideas for Parents, Teachers, and Librarians,* edited by Dianne L. Monson & Day Ann K. McClenathan. Newark, DE: International Reading Association, 1979.

McCord, David. *One at a Time: Collected Poems for the Young.* Boston: Little, Brown, 1977.

McCord, Sue. *The Storybook Journey: Pathways to Literacy Through Story and Play.* Upper Saddle River, NJ: Merrill/Prentice Hall, 1995.

McCulloch, Lou J. *An Introduction to Children's Literature: Children's Books of the 19th Century.* Des Moines, IA: Wallace-Honestead, 1979.

McCullough, David. *1776.* New York: Simon & Schuster, 2005.

McDermott, Beverly Brodsky. *The Golem.* Philadelphia: Lippincott, 1976.

McElderry, Margaret. "The Best Times, the Worst Times, Children's Book Publishing 1917–1974." *The Horn Book* (October 1974): 85–94.

McElmeel, Sharron L. *100 Most Popular Children's Authors: Biographical Sketches and Bibliographies.* Englewood, CO: Libraries Unlimited, 1999.

McElveen, Susan, & Connie Dierking, *Literature Modes to Teach Expository Writing.* Gainesville, FL: Maupin House, 2001.

————. *Teaching Writing Skills With Children's Literature.* Gainesville, FL: Maupin House, 1999.

McGarvey, Jack. ". . . But Computers Are Clearly the Future." *The New York Times* (May 25, 1997): 12.

McGavran, James Holt, ed. *Literature and the Child: Romantic Continuations, Postmodern Contestations.* Iowa City: University of Iowa Press, 1999.

McGrath, Robin. "Words Melt Away Like Hills in Fog: Putting Inuit Legends Into Print." *Children's Literature Association Quarterly* 13 (Spring 1988): 9–12.

McGuire, Sandra. "Promoting Positive Attitudes Toward Aging." *Childhood Education* 69 (Summer 1993): 204–210.

McIntyre, Barbara M. *Creative Drama in the Elementary School.* Itasca, IL: Peacock, 1974.

McKay, Gwendda. "Poetry and the Young Child." *English in Australia* (June 1986): 52–58.

Mediavilla, Cindy. *Arthurian Fiction: An Annotated Bibliography.* Lanham, MD: Scarecrow Press. 1999.

Meigs, Cornelia, Elizabeth Nesbitt, Anne Thaxter Eaton, & Ruth Hill. *A Critical History of Children's Literature: A Survey of Children's Books in English.* New York: Macmillan, 1969.

Mendelson, Michael. "The Wind in the Willows and the Plotting of Contrast." *Children's Literature* 16 (1988): 125–144.

Mendoza, Alicia. "Reading to Children: Their Preferences." *The Reading Teacher* 38 (February 1985): 522–527.

Merriam, Eve. *Rainbow Writing.* New York: Atheneum, 1976.

Merrick, Brian. "With a Straight Eye: An Interview with Charles Causley." *Children's Literature in Education* 19 (Winter 1988): 123–135.

Metcalf, Eva-Maria, and Michael J. Meyer. "Society, Child Abuse, and Children's Literature." *Children's Literature Association Quarterly* 17 (Fall 1992): 2–3.

Miers, Charles, ed. *Harlem Renaissance: Art of Black America*. New York: Abrams, 1987.

Miller, Bertha Mahony, ed. *Newbery Medal Books: 1922–1955*. Boston: Horn Book, 1955.

Miller, Peggy J. "Peter Rabbit and Mr. McGregor Reconciled, Charlotte Lives: Preschoolers Recreate the Classics." *The Horn Book* 73 (May/June 1997): 282–283.

Miller, Winifred. "Dragons—Fact or Fantasy?" *Elementary English* 52 (April, 1975): 582–585.

Milne, A. A. *The Christopher Robin Story Book*. New York: Dutton. 1966.

Mittelstadt, Michelle. "Texas High on Watchdog Group's Censorship List." Associated Press. The Bryan-College Station (TX) *Eagle* (September 2, 1993): A9.

Monson, Dianne, & Sam Sebesta. "Reading Preferences." In *Handbook of Research on Teaching the English Language Arts*, edited by James Flood, Julie M. Jensen, Diane Lapp, & James R. Squire. New York: Macmillan, 1991, 664–673.

Moore, Ann W. "Setting the Bar for Biography: A Reviewer Seeks Books That Inspire and Instruct Teen Readers." *School Library Journal* 51 (November 2005): 38–39.

_____. "A Question of Accuracy: Errors in Children's Biographies." *School Library Journal* 31 (February 1985): 34–35.

Moore, Eva. *The Fairy Tale Life of Hans Christian Andersen*. Illustrated by Trina Schart Hyman. New York: Scholastic, 1969.

Moore, Lilian. "A Second Look: Small Poems." *The Horn Book* (July/August 1988): 470–473.

_____. "A Second Look: The Poetry of Lillian Morrison." *The Horn Book* 69 (May/June 1993): 303–306.

Moore, Robin. *Creating a Family Storytelling Tradition: Awakening the Hidden Storyteller*. Little Rock, AR: August House, 1999.

Morache, Jette. "Use of Quotes in Teaching Literature." *English Journal* 76 (October 1987): 61–63.

Morgan, Betty M. *An Investigation of Children's Books Containing Characters From Selected Minority Groups Based on Specified Criteria*. Carbondale: Southern Illinois University, 1973. University Microfilm No. 74-6232.

Moritz, Charles. *Current Biography Yearbook*. New York: Wilson, 1968.

Morrison, Lillian. *The Sidewalk Racer and Other Poems of Sport and Motion*. New York: Lothrop, Lee & Shepard, 1977.

Morrow, Lesley Mandel. "Promoting Voluntary Reading." In *Handbook of Research on Teaching the English Language Arts*, edited by James Flood, Julie M. Jensen, Diane Lapp, & James R. Squire. New York: Macmillan, 1991, 681–690.

Morse, Samuel French. "Speaking of the Imagination." In *Horn Book Reflections*, edited by Elinor Whitney Field. Boston: Horn Book, 1969.

Muir, Percy. *English Children's Books, 1600 to 1900*. New York: Praeger, 1954.

Musleah, Rahel. "Rediscovering the Jewish Folktale." *Publishers Weekly* 239 (September 21, 1992): 42–43.

Mussen, Paul Henry, John Janeway Conger, & Jerome Kagan. *Child Development and Personality*. New York: Harper & Row, 1989.

National Council for the Social Studies. "The Columbian Quincentenary: An Educational Opportunity." *Social Education* 56 (April/May 1992): 248–249.

National Geographic. *Through the Lens: National Geographic Greatest Photographs*. Washington, DC: National Geographic, 2003.

National Science Teachers Association. "Criteria for Selection—Outstanding Science Trade Books for Children." *Science and Children* 34 (March 1997): 23.

Natov, Roni. "Internal and External Journeys: The Child Hero in *The Zabajaba Jungle* and *Linnea in Monet's Garden*." *Children's Literature In Education* 20 (June 1989): 91–101.

Nelson, Mary Ann. *A Comparative Anthology of Children's Literature*. New York: Holt, Rinehart & Winston, 1972.

Nesbit, E., retold by. *Beautiful Stories From Shakespeare*. New York: Weathervane. Facsimile of 1907 edition.

Neufeld, John. "Preaching to the Unconverted." *School Library Journal* 42 (July 1996): 36.

New York Times Book Review. "Best Illustrated Books." *The New York Times* (November 14, 2004): 38–39.

Newcomb, Franc J. *Navajo Folk Tales*. Santa Fe: Museum of Navajo Ceremonial Art, 1967, xvi.

Nikolajeva, Maria, ed. *Aspects and Issues in the History of Children's Literature*. Westport, CT: Greenwood, 1995.

Nikola-Lisa, W. "Scribbles, Scrawls, and Scratches: Graphic Play as Subtext in the Picture Books of Ezra Jack Keats." *Children's Literature in Education* 22 (December 1991): 247–255.

Nilsen, Alleen Pace. "Women in Children's Literature." *College English* 32 (May 1971): 918–926.

_____, & Kenneth L. Donelson. *Literature for Today's Young Adults*, 4th ed. New York: HarperCollins, 1993.

_____. *Literature for Today's Young Adults*, 6th ed. New York: Longman, 2001.

Nitschke, August. "The Importance of Fairy Tales in German Families Before the Grimms." In *The Brothers Grimm and Folktale*, edited by James M. McGlathery. Urbana: University of Illinois Press, 1988, 164–177.

Noble, Judith Ann. "The Home, the Church, and the School as Portrayed in American Realistic Fiction for Children 1965–1969." East Lansing: Michigan State University, 1971. University Microfilm No. 31-271.

Noble, William. *Bookbanning in America: Who Bans Books?—and Why*. Middlebury, VT: Eriksson, 1990.

Nodelman, Perry. "How Children Respond to Art." *School Library Journal* 31 (December 1984a): 40–41.

_____. "Some Presumptuous Generalizations About Fantasy." In *The First Steps: Best of the Early ChLA Quarterly*. Compiled by Patricia Dooley. Purdue University; Children's Literature Association, 1984b, 15–16.

_____. "Which Children? Some Audiences for Children's Books." *The Horn Book* 63 (January/February 1987): 35–40.

_____. *Words About Pictures*. Athens: University of Georgia Press, 1988.

_____. *Words About Pictures*, 2nd ed. Athens: University of Georgia Press, 1990.

Noel, Ruth S. *The Mythology of Middle Earth*. Boston: Houghton Mifflin, 1977.

Norton, Donna E. "Centuries of Biographies for Childhood." *Vitae Scholasticae* 3 (Spring 1984): 113–129.

_____. *The Effective Teaching of Language Arts*, 6th ed. Upper Saddle River, NJ: Merrill/Prentice Hall, 2004.

_____. "The Expansion and Evaluation of a Multiethnic Reading/Language Arts Program Designed for 5th, 6th, 7th, and 8th Grade Children." Meadows Foundation Grant, No. 55614. A Three Year Longitudinal Study. Texas A&M University, 1984–1987.

_____. "Folklore and the Language Arts." In *Language Arts Instruction and the*

Beginning Teacher, edited by Dale Johnson & Carl Personke. Englewood Cliffs, NJ: Prentice Hall, 1987a.

_____. "Genres in Children's Literature: Identifying, Analyzing, and Appreciating." In *Children's Literature: Resource for the Classroom,* edited by Masha Kabakow Rudman. Norwood, MA: Christopher-Gordon, 1993, 75–94.

_____. *The Impact of Literature-Based Reading.* Upper Saddle River, NJ: Merrill/Prentice Hall, 1992.

_____. "The Intrusion of an Alien Culture: The Impact and Reactions as Seen Through Biographies and Autobiographies of Native Americans." *Vitae Scholasticae* 6 (Spring 1987b): 59–75.

_____. "Moral Stages of Children's Biographical Literature: 1800s–1900s." *Vitae Scholasticae* (Fall 1986).

_____. *Multicultural Literature: Through the Eyes of Many Children.* Upper Saddle River, NJ: Merrill/Prentice Hall, 2005.

_____. "Teaching Multicultural Literature in the Reading Program." *The Reading Teacher* 44 (September 1990): 28–40.

_____. "A Three-Year Study Developing and Evaluating Children's Literature Courses." Paper presented at the College Reading Association, National Conference, Baltimore, MD, October, 1980.

_____. "A Web of Interest." *Language Arts* 54 (November 1977): 928–932.

_____, & James F. McNamara. *An Evaluation of the Multicultural Reading/Language Arts Program for Elementary and Junior High School Students.* College Station: Texas A&M University, 1988.

_____, & Saundra E. Norton. *Language Arts Activities for Children,* 5th ed. Upper Saddle River, NJ: Merrill/Prentice Hall, 2003.

Noss, Philip A. "Description in Gbaya Literary Art." In *African Folklore,* edited by Richard Dorse. Bloomington: Indiana University Press, 1972.

"Notable Children's Trade Books in the Field of Social Studies." *Social Education* (April/May 1992): 253–264.

Odean, Kathleen. "Adventures and Accomplishments: Picture-Book Biographies of Women." *School Library Journal* 42 (December 1996): 664–665.

_____. "The Story Master." *School Library Journal* 46 (October 2000): 50–54.

O'Donnell, Liam. "Are Canadian Boys Redefining Literacy?" *Reading Today* 22 (February/March 2005): 19.

Olson, Renee. "When It Comes To Technology . . . The Postman Always Thinks Twice." *School Library Journal* 42 (May 1996): 19–22.

Opler, Morris Edward. *Myths and Tales of the Jicarilla Apache Indians.* Memoirs 31. New York: American Folklore Society, 1938.

Parsons, Elsie Clews. *Folktales of Andros Island, Bahamas.* New York: American Folklore Society, 1918.

Paterson, Katherine. *A Sense of Wonder: On Reading and Writing Books for Children.* New York: Penguin, 1995.

Paul, Lissa. "A Second Look: The Return of the Iron Man." *The Horn Book* LXXVI (March/April 2000): 218–225.

Paulin, Mary Ann. *Creative Uses of Children's Literature.* Hamden, CT: Library Professional Pubs., 1985.

Peck, Richard. "The Great Library-Shelf Witch Hunt." *Booklist* 88 (January 1, 1992): 816–817.

Pellowski, Anne. *The Family Story-Telling Handbook.* New York: Macmillan, 1987.

_____. *Hidden Stories in Plants.* New York: Macmillan, 1990.

_____. *The World of Storytelling.* New York: Bowker, 1977.

Penney, David W. *Art of the American Indian Frontier.* Seattle: University of Washington Press, 1992.

Perfect, Kathy A. "Rhyme and Reason: Poetry for the Heart and Head." *The Reading Teacher* 52 (April 1999): 728–737.

Perrine, Laurence. *Literature: Structure, Sound, and Sense,* 4th ed. San Diego: Harcourt Brace, 1983.

Phelan, Carolyn. "Talking With Mem Fox." *Book Links* 2 (May 1993): 29–32.

Phelps, Ruth M. "A Comparison of Newbery Award Winners in the First and Last Decade of the Award (1922–31 and 1976–85). Miami University, 1985, DAI 47: 453A.

Phillips, Tom, ed. *Africa: The Art of a Continent.* New York: Prestel, 1999.

Piaget, Jean, & B. Inhelder. *The Psychology of the Child.* New York: Basic Books, 1969.

Piper, David. "Language Growth in the Multiethnic Classroom." *Language Arts* 63 (January 1986): 23–36.

Pittman, Ramona. "African American Musicians." College Station, TX: Texas A&M University, 2005.

Polking, Kirk, ed. *Writing A to Z.* Cincinnati: Writer's Digest Books, 1990.

Poole, Roger. "The Books Teachers Use." *Children's Literature in Education* 17 (Fall 1986): 159–180.

Powell, Richard. *Black Art: A Cultural History.* London and New York: Thames & Hudson, 2002.

Preble, Duane. *Art Forms.* New York: Harper & Row, 1978.

Prewitt, Jana Wright. "Poetry for the Fourth-Grade Classroom." Paper, Texas A&M University, 2001.

Pringle, Laurence. "The Thinking Gap." In *Vital Connections: Children, Science, and Books,* edited by Wendy Saul & Sybille A. Jagusch. Washington, DC: Library of Congress, 1991, 51–56.

_____. *Wild Foods: A Beginner's Guide to Identifying, Harvesting and Preparing Safe and Tasty Plants From the Outdoors.* Illustrated by Paul Breeden. New York: Four Winds, 1978.

Probst, Robert. "Response to Literature." In *Handbook of Research on Teaching the English Language Arts,* edited by James Flood, Julie M. Jensen, Diane Lapp, & James R. Squire. New York: Macmillan, 1991, 633–655.

_____. "Teaching the Reading of Literature." In *Content Area Reading and Learning: Instructional Strategies,* edited by Diane Lapp, James Flood, & N. Farnan. Englewood Cliffs, NJ: Prentice Hall, 1989, 179–186.

Proett, Jackie, & Kent Gill. *The Writing Process in Action: A Handbook for Teachers.* Urbana, IL: National Council of Teachers of English, 1986.

Propp, Vladimir. *Morphology of the Folktale.* Translated by Laurence Scott. Austin: University of Texas, 1968.

"Publishers Weekly: Children's Bestsellers." *Publishers Weekly* 244 (July 21, 1997): 177.

Publishers Weekly. "The 2004 Cuffies." *Publishers Weekly,* January 10, 2005.

Purves, Alan C. "The School Subject Literature." In *Handbook of Research on Teaching the English Language Arts,* edited by James Flood, Julie M. Jensen, Diane Lapp, & James R. Squire. New York: Macmillan, 1991, 674–680.

_____, & Dianne L. Monson. *Experiencing Children's Literature.* Glenview IL: Scott, Foresman, 1984.

Quammen, David. "The Look of the Wild: How Styles of Illustration Have Changed the Way We Look at Animals." *The New York Times Book Review* (November 7, 1993): 12.

Quayle, Eric. *The Collector's Book of Children's Books.* New York: Clarkson N. Potter, 1971.

Querry, Ron. "Discovery of America: Stories Told by Indian Voices." In *American Diversity, American Identity: The Lives and Works of 145 Writers Who Define the American Experience,* edited by John K. Roth. New York: Holt, 1995.

Rauch, Alan. "A World of Faith on a Foundation of Science: Science and Religion in

British Children's Literature: 1761–1878." *Children's Literature Association Quarterly* 14 (Spring 1989): 13–19.

Raugust, Karen. "Sports Leagues Target Young Fans With Books." *Publishers Weekly* 244 (August 18, 1997): 34–35.

Raymo, Chet. "Dr. Seuss and Dr. Einstein: Children's Books and Scientific Imagination." *The Horn Book* 68 (September/October 1992): 560–567.

Reading Today. "Lord of the Rings Tops List of Favorite Books in UK." *Reading Today* 21 (February/March 2004): 15.

Reed, Susan Nugent. "Career Idea: Meet the Poet at His Craft." In *Using Literature and Poetry Affectively,* edited by Jon E. Shapiro. Newark, DE: International Reading Association, 1979.

Rees, David. "The Virtues of Improbability: Joan Aiken." *Children's Literature in Education* 19 (Spring 1988): 42–54.

Rees-Williams, Gwladys, and Brian Rees-Williams, eds. *What I Cannot Tell My Mother Is Not Fit for Me to Know.* New York: Oxford University Press, 1981.

Reichard, Gladys A. *An Analysis of Coeur d'Alene Indian Myths.* Philadelphia: American Folklore Society, 1974.

Reid, Donna K. *Thinking and Writing About Art History,* 3rd ed. Upper Saddle River, NJ: Prentice Hall, 2004.

Reiss, Johanna. *The Upstairs Room.* New York: Crowell, 1972.

Reissman, Rose. "Writer/Author Q & A—Technology Takes the Published Interview to the Next Generation of Reader Response." *English Journal* 85 (February 1996): 78–79.

Reynolds, Kimberley, & Nicholas Tucker, eds. *Children's Book Publishing in Britain Since 1945.* Brookfield, VT: Ashgate, 1998.

Rice, Daniel. "Vision and Culture: The Role of Museums in Visual Literacy." *The Journal of Museum Education* 13 (1988): 13–17.

Riley, Gail Blasser. *Censorship.* New York: Facts On File, 1998.

Roback, Diane, & Cindi Di Marzo. "Children's Book Survey: Consumer Awareness." *Publishers Weekly* 244 (June 16, 1997): 28–31.

Roback, Diane, & Shannon Maughan, eds. "Fall 1996 Children's Books: The Road Ahead." *Publishers Weekly* 243 (July 22, 1996): 151–153.

Robertson, Elizabeth, & Jo McGinnis. "Biography as Art: A Formal Approach." In *Portraits: Biography and Autobiography in the Secondary School,* edited by Margaret Fleming & Jo McGinnis. Urbana, IL: National Council of Teachers of English, 1985.

Rochman, Hazel. "The African American Journey: From Slavery to Freedom." *Booklist* 89 (February 15, 1993): 1052–1053.

_____. *Against Borders: Promoting Books for a Multicultural World.* Chicago: American Library Association, 1992a.

_____. "The Booklist Interview: Maurice Sendak." *Booklist* 88 (June 15, 1992b): 1848–1849.

_____. "The Booklist Interview: Virginia Hamilton." *Booklist* 88 (February 1, 1992c): 1020–1021.

_____. "Booktalking: Going Global." *The Horn Book* (January–February 1989): 30–35.

_____. "How Not to Write About the Holocaust." *Booklist* 89 (October 15, 1992): 416.

_____. "Loose Canon." *Booklist* 92 (September 1, 1996): 114–115.

_____. "Young Adult Books: Childhood Terror." *The Horn Book* 61 (September/October 1985): 598–602.

Roehler, Laura, & Gerald G. Duffy. "Direct Explanation of Comprehension Processes." In *Comprehension Instruction,* edited by Gerald G. Duffy, Laura R. Roehler, & Jana Mason. New York: Longman, 1984, 265–280.

Roller, Cathy. "Classroom Interaction Patterns: Reflections of a Stratified Society." *Language Arts* 66 (September 1989): 492–500.

Root, Shelton L. "The New Realism—Some Personal Reflections." *Language Arts* 54 (January 1977): 19–24.

Rosenberg, Liz. "Has Poetry for Kids Become a Child's Garden of Rubbish?" *The New York Times Book Review* (November 10, 1991): 55.

Rosenblatt, Louise. "Language, Literature, and Values." In *Language, Schooling, and Society,* edited by S. N. Tchudi. Upper Montclair, NJ: Boynton/Cook, 1985, 64–80.

_____. "Literary Theory." In *Handbook of Research on Teaching the English Language Arts,* edited by James Flood, Julie M. Jensen, Diane Lapp, & James R. Squire. Upper Saddle River, NJ: Merrill/Prentice Hall, 1991, 57–62.

_____. *The Reader, the Text, and the Literary Work.* Carbondale: Southern Illinois Press, 1978.

Ross, A. C., & D. Brave Eagle. *Value Orientation—A Strategy for Removing Barriers.* Denver, CO: Coalition of Indian Controlled School Boards, 1975. ERIC Document Reproduction, ED 125–811.

Ross, Elinor P. "Comparison of Folk Tale Variants." *Language Arts* 56 (April 1979): 422–426.

Ross, Jan. "Small Is Tall—Children and Self-Esteem." *Book Links* 2 (January 1993): 53–59.

Ross, Mabel, & Barbara Walker. "*On Another Day . . .*" *Tales Told Among the Nkundo of Zaire.* Hamden, CT: Archon, 1979.

Ross, Ramon R. *Storyteller,* 2nd ed. Upper Saddle River, NJ: Merrill/Prentice Hall, 1980.

Routman, Regle. *Literacy at the Crossroads: Crucial Talk About Reading, Writing, and Other Teaching Dilemmas.* Portsmouth, NH: Heinemann, 1996.

Rovenger, Judith. "Fostering Emotional Intelligence: A Librarian Looks at the Role of Literature in a Child's Development." *School Library Journal* 46 (December 2000): 40–41.

Ruddell, Robert. "A Whole Language and Literature Perspective: Creating a Meaning-Making Instructional Environment." *Language Arts* 69 (December 1992): 612–619.

Rudman, Masha Kabakow. *Children's Literature: An Issues Approach,* 2nd ed. New York: Longman, 1984.

_____. "Children's Literature in the Reading Program." In *Children's Literature: Resource for the Classroom,* edited by Masha Kabakow Rudman. Norwood, MA: Christopher-Gordon, 1993a, 171–199.

_____. "People Behind the Books: Illustrators." In *Children's Literature: Resource for the Classroom,* edited by Masha Kabakow Rudman. Norwood, MA: Christopher-Gordon, 1993b, 19–41.

_____, & Anna Markus Pearce. *For Love of Reading: A Parent's Guide to Encouraging Young Readers From Infancy Through Age 5.* Mount Vernon, NY: Consumers Union, 1988.

Ruggieri, Colleen A. "What About Our Girls? Considering Gender Roles With *Shabanu.*" *English Journal* 90 (January 2001): 48–53.

Russell, David L. *Scott O'Dell.* New York: Twayne, 1999.

Rutherford, James. "Vital Connections: Children, Books, and Science." In *Vital Connections: Children, Books, and Science,* edited by Wendy Saul & Sybille A. Jagusch, Washington DC: Library of Congress, 1991, 21–30.

Sacks, David. "Breathing New Life Into Ancient Greece and Rome." *School Library Journal,* 42 (November 1996): 38–39.

Sagan, Carl. *Cosmos.* Public Broadcasting System, October 26, 1980.

Sage, Mary. "A Study of the Handicapped in Children's Literature." In *Children's Literature, Selected Essays and Bibliographies,* edited by Anne S. MacLeod. College

Park: University of Maryland College of Library and Informational Services, 1977.

Sale, Roger. *Fairy Tales and After: From Snow White to E. B. White.* Cambridge, MA: Harvard University Press, 1978.

Sam Houston Area Reading Conference, Sam Houston State University, February 1981.

Sandburg, Carl. *The American Songbag.* New York: Harcourt Brace, 1927.

San Diego Museum of Art. *Dr. Seuss From Then to Now.* New York: Random House, 1986.

Sandmann, Alexa L. "What's a Nice Poem Like You Doing in a Place Like This?" *School Library Journal* 51 (April 2005): 16–19.

Sarafino, Edward P., & James W. Armstrong. *Child and Adolescent Development.* Glenview, IL: Scott, Foresman, 1986.

Saturday Review 48 (September 11, 1965), 63–65, 84–85.

Saul, Wendy. "Introduction." In *Vital Connections: Children, Science, and Books,* edited by Wendy Saul & Sybille A. Jagusch. Washington, DC: Library of Congress, 1991, 3–18.

Saylor, David. "Look Again." *School Library Journal* 46 (January 2000): 37–38.

Schafer, Elizabeth D. *Beacham's Sourcebook for Teaching Young Adult Fiction: Exploring Harry Potter.* Osprey, FL: Beacham, 2000a

_____. *Exploring Harry Potter.* Osprey, FL: Beacham, 2000b.

Schamel, Wynell Burroughs, & Jean West. "The Fight for Equal Rights: A Recruiting Poster for Black Soldiers in the Civil War." *Social Education* 56 (February 1992): 118–120.

Schoenherr, John. "Caldecott Medal Acceptance." *The Horn Book* 64 (July/August 1988): 457–459.

School Library Journal 46 (September 2000). Cover.

Schwarcz, Joseph. Ways of the *Illustrator: Visual Communication in Children's Literature.* Chicago: American Library Association, 1982.

Schwartz, Alvin. *And the Green Grass Grew All Around.* New York: HarperCollins, 1992.

Scott, A. O. "The End of Innocence." *The New York Times Magazine* (July 2, 2000): 11–12.

Sealey, D. Bruce. "Measuring the Multicultural Quotient of a School." *TESL Canada Journal/Revue TESL du Canada* 1 (March 1984): 21–28.

Sears, Roebuck and Co., Consumers Guide: 1900. Reprint. Northfield, IL: DBI Books, 1970.

Sebesta, Sam. "Choosing Poetry." In *Children's Choices,* edited by Nancy Roser & Margaret Frith. Newark, DE: International Reading Association, 1983.

_____. "What Do Young People Think About the Literature They Read?" *Reading Newsletter,* no. 8. Rockleigh, NJ: Allyn & Bacon, 1979.

_____, & Dianne L. Monson. "Reading Preferences." In *Handbook of Research on Teaching the English Language Arts,* 2nd ed., edited by James Flood, Diane Lapp, James R. Squire, & Julie M. Jensen. Mahwah, NJ: Erlbaum, 2003.

Seeger, Ruth Crawford. *American Folksongs for Children—In Home, School, and Nursery School.* New York: Doubleday, 1948.

Seki, Keigo, ed. *Folktales of Japan.* Translated by Robert J. Adams. Chicago: University of Chicago, 1963, xv.

Sendak, Maurice. *Posters by Maurice Sendak.* New York: Harmony Books, 1986.

Sender, Ruth Minsky. *The Holocaust Lady.* New York: Macmillan, 1992.

Sewell, Helen. *A Book of Myths, Selections From Bulfinch's Age of Fable.* New York: Macmillan, 1942, 1962.

Shaffer, David R. *Developmental Psychology: Childhood and Adolescence,* 2nd ed. Pacific Grove, CA: Brooks/Cole, 1989.

Shannon, George. "Once and Forever a Platypus: Child Reader to Writing Adult." *Children's Literature Association Quarterly* 13 (Fall 1988): 122–124.

_____. "Sharing Honey From the Hive." *Children's Literature Association Quarterly* 11 (Fall, 1986): 115–118.

Shapiro, Jon E., ed. *Using Literature and Poetry Affectively.* Newark, DE: International Reading Association, 1979.

Shavit, Zohar. "The Historical Model of the Development of Children's Literature." In *Aspects and Issues in the History of Children's Literature,* edited by Maria Nikolajeva. Westport, CT: Greenwood, 1995, 27–38.

Shaw, Jean Duncan. "An Historical Survey of Themes Recurrent in Selected Children's Books Published in America Since 1850," Philadelphia: Temple University, 1966, University Microfilm No. 67-11, 437.

Sheafer, Silvia Anne. *Aimee Semple McPherson.* Broomall, PA: Chelsea House, 2004.

Short, Geoffrey. "Learning Through Literature: Historical Fiction, Autobiography and the Holocaust." *Children's Literature in Education* 28 (1997): 179–189.

Shulevitz, Uri. *Writing With Pictures: How to Write and Illustrate Children's Books.* New York: Watson-Guptill, 1985.

Sibley, Brian. *The Land of Narnia.* New York: Harper & Row, 1989.

Sidney, Sir Philip. *An Apologie for Poetrie.* London: 1595.

Sierra, Judy. *Multicultural Folktales for the Feltboard and Readers' Theater.* Phoenix: Oryx, 1996.

Siks, Geraldine. *Drama With Children.* New York: Harper & Row, 1983.

Silvey, Anita. "Evaluation and Criticism: The Quest for Quality in Children's Books." In *Children's Literature: Resources for the Classroom,* edited by Masha Kabakow Rudman. Norwood, MA: Christopher-Gordon, 1993.

_____. "The Goats." *The Horn Book* (January/February 1988): 23.

_____. *100 Best Books for Children.* Boston: Houghton Mifflin, 2004.

Simmons, John S. *Censorship: A Threat to Reading, Learning, Thinking.* Newark, DE: International Reading Association, 1994.

Sipe, Lawrence R. "In Their Own Words: Author's Views on Issues in Historical Fiction." *The New Advocate* 10 (Summer 1997): 243–258.

Sís, Peter. "The Artist at Work." *The Horn Book* 68 (November/December 1992): 681–687.

Smith, Amanda. "The Lively Art of Leo Lionni." *Publishers Weekly* 238 (April 5, 1991): 118–119.

Smith, Dinitia. "Finding a Middle Earth in Montana." *The New York Times* (October 7, 2003): B1.

Smith, Lane. "The Artist at Work." *The Horn Book* 69 (January/February 1993): 64–70.

Smith, Sally A. "Talking About 'Real Stuff': Explorations of Agency and Romance in an All-Girls' Book Club." *Language Arts* 78 (September 2000): 30–37.

Smuskiewicz, Ted. *Oil Painting: Step by Step.* Cincinnati: North Light Books, 1992.

Spang, A. "Counseling the Indian." *Journal of American Indian Education* 5 (1965): 10–15.

Spellbinders Volunteer Storytelling. Aspen, CO: Pitkin County Library, 1999.

Spiegel, Dixie Lee. "Reader Response Approaches and the Growth of Readers." *Language Arts* 76 (September 1998): 41–48.

Sprague, Marsha M., & Kara K. Keeling. "A Library for Ophelia." *Journal of Adolescent & Adult Literacy* 43 (April 2000): 640–647.

Stacks, John F. "Aftershocks of the 'Me' Decade." *Time* (August 3, 1981): 18.

Stander, Bella. "Spring Titles for Kids Highlight Heroes and Their Times." *Publishers*

Weekly 239 (December 14, 1992): 28–29.

Stanley, Alessandra. "Cleopatra, Career Woman." *The New York Times* (January 20, 2001): A21, A23.

Stanley, Diane. "Is That Book Politically Correct? Truth and Trends in Historical Literature for Young People. A Writer Speaks . . ." *Journal of Youth Services in Libraries* 7 (Winter 1994): 172–175.

Stark, Myra. *Florence Nightingale.* New York: Feminist Press, 1979.

St. Clair, Jean. "Recreating Black Life in Children's Literature." *Interracial Books for Children Bulletin* 19 (1989): 7–11.

Steele, Mary Q. "Realism, Truth, and Honesty." *The Horn Book* 46 (February 1971): 17–27.

Sterck, Kenneth. "Landscape and Figures in the Poetry of De la Mare." *Children's Literature in Education* 19 (Spring 1988): 17–31.

Stewig, John Warren. "The Emperor's New Clothes." *Book Links* 2 (May 1993): 35–38.

_____. "A Literary and Linguistic Analysis of Scott O'Dell's *The Captive.*" *Children's Literature Association Quarterly* 14 (Fall 1989): 135–138.

_____. *Reading Pictures: Exploring Illustrations with Children.* New Berlin, WI: Jenson, 1988.

Stokstad, Marilyn. *Art History: Volume One.* New York: Abrams, 1995a.

_____. *Art History: Volume Two.* New York: Abrams, 1995b.

Storey, Denise C. "Fifth Graders Meet Elderly Book Characters." *Language Arts* 56 (April 1979): 408–412.

Stott, Jon C. "Biographies of Sports Heroes and the American Dream." *Children's Literature in Education* 10 (Winter 1979): 174–185.

_____. "Native Tales and Traditions in Books for Children." *The American Indian Quarterly* 16 (Summer 1992): 373–380.

Strehle, Elizabeth. "Social Issues: Connecting Children With Their World." *Children's Literature in Education* 30 (1999): 213–220.

Strickland, Dorothy S. "Prompting Language and Concept Development." In *Literature and Young Children,* edited by Bernice Cullinan. Urbana, IL: National Conference of Teachers of English, 1977.

Sutherland, Zena. *Children and Books,* 9th ed. New York: Longman, 1997.

_____, & Betsy Hearne. "In Search of the Perfect Picture Book Definition." In *Jump Over the Moon: Selected Professional Readings,* edited by Pamela Barron &

Jennifer Burley. New York: Holt, Rinehart & Winston, 1984.

_____, & Myra Cohn Livingston. *The Scott, Foresman Anthology of Children's Literature.* Glenview. IL: Scott, Foresman, 1984.

Sutton, Roger. "Where's That Renaissance?" *The Horn Book* 72 (November/December 1996): 664–665.

Swanton, Susan. "Minds Alive: What and Why Gifted Students Read for Pleasure." *School Library Journal* 30 (March 1984): 99–102.

Symons, Ann K. "Sizing Up Sites: How to Judge What You Find on the Web." *School Library Journal* 43 (April 1997): 22–25.

Taggart, James. " 'Hansel and Gretel' in Spain and Mexico." *Journal of American Folklore* 99 (1986): 435–460.

Tanner, Fran. *Creative Communication: Projects in Acting, Speaking, Oral Reading.* Pocatello, ID: Clark, 1979.

Tarbox, Gwen Athene, ed. *The Clubwomen's Daughters: Collective Impulses in Progressive-Era Girl's Fiction, 1890–1940.* New York: Garland, 2000.

Temple, Frances. *Taste of Salt: A Story of Modern Haiti.* New York: Orchard, 1992.

Terry, Ann. *Children's Poetry Preferences: A National Survey of the Upper Elementary Grades.* Urbana, IL: National Council of Teachers of English, 1974.

Thomas, Joyce. "The Tales of the Brothers Grimm: In the Black Forest." In *Touchstones: Reflections on the Best in Children's Literature,* edited by Perry Nodelman. West Lafayette, IN: Children's Literature Association, 1987, 104–117.

Thompson, Stith. *The Folktale.* Berkeley: University of California Press, 1977.

Thurman, Judith. *Flashlight and Other Poems.* New York: Atheneum, 1976.

Tolkien, J. R. R. *Fellowship of the Ring.* Boston: Houghton Mifflin, 1965.

Totten, Herman L., Carolyn Garner, & Risa W. Brown. *Culturally Diverse Library Collections for Youth.* New York: Neal-Schuman, 1996.

Townsend, John Rowe. *Written for Children: An Outline of English-Language Children's Literature.* New York: Lippincott, 1975.

Trafzer, Clifford E. "The Word Is Sacred to the Child: American Indians and Children's Literature." *The American Indian Quarterly* 16 (Summer 1992): 381–396.

Travers, P. L. *About the Sleeping Beauty.* Illustrated by Charles Keeping. New York: McGraw-Hill, 1975.

Trease, Geoffrey. "The Historical Story: Is It Relevant Today?" *The Horn Book* (February 1977): 21–28.

Trelease, Jim. *The New Read-Aloud Handbook.* New York: Viking, 1989.

Tremearne, A. J. *Hausa Superstitions and Customs: An Introduction to the Folklore and the Folk.* London: Frank Cass, 1970.

Tuer, Andrew W. *Stories From Forgotten Children's Books.* London: Leadenhall Press, 1898; Bracken Books, 1986.

Tunnell, Michael O. "Alexander's Chronicles of Prydain: Twenty Years Later." *School Library Journal* 34 (April 1988): 27–31.

_____. "Books in the Classroom." *The Horn Book* 63 (July/August 1987): 509–511.

_____, & James S. Jacobs. "Using 'Real' Books: Research Findings on Literature Based Reading Instruction." *The Reading Teacher* 42 (March 1989): 470–477.

Tway, Eileen. "Dimensions of Multicultural Literature for Children." In *Children's Literature: Resource for the Classroom,* edited by Masha Kabakow Rudman. Needham Heights, MA: Christopher-Gordon, 1989, 109–138.

Unsworth, Robert. "Welcome Home . . . I Think." *School Library Journal* 35 (May 1988): 48–49.

Uribe, Verónica. *Little Book of Fables.* Toronto: Douglas & McIntyre, 2004.

Vallone, Lynne. "The Crisis of Education: Eighteenth-Century Adolescent Fiction for Girls." *Children's Literature Association Quarterly* 14 (Summer 1988): 63–67.

Vasilakis, Nancy. "Young Adult Books: An Eighties Perspective." *The Horn Book* 61 (November/December 1985): 768–769.

Vogler, Christopher. *Writer's Journey: Mythic Structure for Storytellers & Screenwriters.* Studio City, CA: Michael Wiese Productions, 1992.

Vrooman, Diana. "Characterization Techniques in *Sarah, Plain and Tall.*" College Station: Texas A&M University, 1989.

Walker, Barbara. *The Dancing Palm Tree and Other Nigerian Folktales.* Illustrated by Helen Siegl. Lubbock: Texas Tech University Press, 1990.

Walmsley, S. A., & T. P. Walp. *Teaching Literature in Elementary School: A Report on the Elementary School Antecedents of Secondary School Literature Instruction.* Report Series 1.3. Albany, NY: Center for the Teaching and Learning of Literature. University at Albany, State University of New York (ERIC No. ED 315 754), 1989.

Ward, Nel, & Patrick Jones. "Homelessness in America." *Booklist* 89 (October 1, 1992): 340–341.

Weaver, Warren. *Alice in Many Tongues.* Madison, WI: University of Wisconsin, 1964.

Weinberg, Steve. "Biography: Telling the Untold Story." *The Writer* (February 1993): 23–25.

Werner, Craig, & Frank P. Riga. "The Persistence of Religion in Children's Literature." *Children's Literature Association Quarterly* 14 (Spring, 1989): 2–3.

West, Mark I. "Essay Review: The Contrasting Biographies of Roald Dahl and Dr. Seuss." *Children's Literature in Education* 27 (1996): 243–247.

———. *Trust Your Children: Voices Against Censorship in Children's Literature.* New York: Neal-Schuman, 1988.

Western, Linda. "A Comparative Study of Literature Through Folk Tale Variants." *Language Arts* 57 (April 1980): 395–402.

Weston, Annette H. "Robert Lawson: Author and Illustrator." *Elementary English* 47 (January 1970): 74–84.

Whalen-Levitt, Peggy. "Making Picture Books Real: Reflections on a Child's-Eye View." In *The First Steps: Best of the Early ChLA Quarterly,* compiled by Patricia Dooley. Lafayette, IN: Purdue University, Children's Literature Association, 1984.

Whitehead, Jane. "'This Is Not What I Wrote!': The Americanization of British Children's Books—Part I." *The Horn Book* (November/December 1996): 687–693.

———. "'This Is Not What I Wrote!': The Americanization of British Children's Books—Part II." *The Horn Book* (January/February 1997): 27–34.

Whitelaw, Nancy. *Queen Victoria and the British Empire.* Greensboro, NC: Morgan Reynolds, 2004.

Whitson, Kathy J. *Native American Literatures: An Encyclopedia of Works, Characters, Authors, and Themes.* Santa Barbara, CA: ABC-CLIO, 1999.

Wigginton, Eliot. *The Foxfire Book.* New York: Doubleday, 1972.

Wilkin, Binnie Tate. *Survival Themes in Fiction for Children and Young People.* Metuchen, NJ: Scarecrow, 1978.

Wilkins, David G., Bernard Schulz, & Katheryn Linduff. *Art Past Art Present,* 5th ed. Upper Saddle River, NJ: Prentice Hall, 2005.

Williams, Mary E., ed. *The Family: Opposing Viewpoints.* San Diego: Greenhaven Press, 1998.

Wineke, William R. "Caldecott for Henkes." *Wisconsin State Journal* (January 18, 2005): C1.

Winkler, Karen J. "Academe and Children's Literature: Will They Live Happily Ever After?" *Chronicle of Higher Education* (June 15, 1981).

Wintle, Justin, & Emma Fisher. *The Pied Pipers: Interviews With the Influential Creators of Children's Literature.* New York: Paddington, 1974.

Wisniewski, David. *Sundiata: Lion King of Mali.* New York: Clarion, 1992.

Wolfe, Alan. "The Final Freedom." *The New York Times Magazine* (March 18, 2001): 48–51.

Wolkomir, Joyce, & Richard Wolkomir. "When Bandogs Howl & Spirits Walk." *Smithsonian* 31 (January 2001): 38–44.

Wolkstein, Diane. "Twenty-Five Years of Storytelling: The Spirit of the Art." *The Horn Book* 68 (November/December 1992): 702–708.

Worth, Valerie. "Capturing Objects in Words." *The Horn Book* 68 (September/October 1992): 568–569.

Worthy, M. Jo, & Janet W. Bloodgood. "Enhancing Reading Instruction Through Cinderella Tales." *The Reading Teacher* 46

(December 1992/January 1993): 290–301.

Wright, Jone P., & Elizabeth G. Allen. "Sixth-Graders Ride With Paul Revere." *Language Arts* 53 (January 1976): 46–50.

Wrightson, Patricia. "Stones Into Pools." In *The Arbuthnot Lectures: 1980–1989.* Chicago: American Library Association, 1990, 67–77.

Wyatt, Flora R., Margaret Coggins, & Jane Hunter Imber. *Popular Nonfiction Authors for Children.* Englewood, CO: Libraries Unlimited, 1998.

Wyndham, Robert. *Tales the People Tell in China.* New York: Messner, 1971.

Yates, Elizabeth. *We, the People.* Illustrated by Nora Unwin. Hanover, NH: Regional Center for Educational Training, 1974.

Yep, Laurence. *The Rainbow People.* New York: Harper & Row, 1989.

Yolen, Jane. "Magic Mirrors: Society Reflected in the Glass of Fantasy." *Children's Literature Association Quarterly* 11 (Summer 1986): 88–90.

———. "Past Time: The Writing of the Picture Book Encounter." *The New Advocate* (September 1992): 234–239.

———. "Taking Time: On How Things Have Changed in the Last Thirty-Five Years of Children's Publishing." *The New Advocate* 10 (Fall 1997): 285–291.

Young, Beverly. "The Young Female Protagonist in Juvenile Fiction: Three Decades of Evolution." Washington State University, 1985, DAI 46: 3276A.

Zamora, Martha. *Frida Kahlo: The Brush of Anguish.* San Francisco: Chronicle, 1990.

Author, Illustrator, and Title Index

A: Apple Pie (Greenaway), 124, 156, 199
A, B, See! (Hoban), 199
Aagesen, Colleen, 528, 535
Aardema, Verna, 6, 31, 80, 111, 137, 154, 182, 201, 233, 234, 262
Aardvarks, Disembark! (Jonas), 169, 199
Aarne-Thompson, 229
Abarat: Days of Magic, Nights of War (Barker), 310
Abby (Hanel), 412
Abe Lincoln Goes to Washington: 1837–1867 (Harness), 496
Abe Lincoln Grows Up (Sandburg), 63, 473–474, 498
Abe Lincoln Remembers (Turner), 498
Abells, Chana Byers, 148, 154
Abel's Island, 102
Abolafia, Yossi, 204
About Birds: A Guide for Children (Sill), 541
About the B'nai Bagels (Konigsburg), 412
Abracadabra Kid, The: A Writer's Life (Fleischman), 495
Abraham Lincoln: The Prairie Years (Sandburg), 473, 498
Abraham Lincoln (Cohn & Schmidt), 474, 495
Abraham Lincoln (D'Aulaire & D'Aulaire), 495
Absurd ABC, The (Crane), 54
Accident, The (Carrick), 410
Ackamarackus: Julius Lester's Sumptuously Silly Fantastically Funny Fables (Lester), 242, 267
Ackerman, Diane, 338, 355
Ackerman, Karen, 25, 106–107, 111, 123–124, 154, 179, 201
Across a Dark and Wild Sea (Brown), 471, 495
Across Five Aprils (Hunt), 64, 436, 458
Across the Lines (Reeder), 436, 459
Action Jackson (Greenberg & Jordan), 480, 496
Actual Size (Jenkins), 519, 538
Adadjourna, Davida, 355
Adam of the Road (Gray), 458
Adams, Karen I., 67
Adler, David A., 32, 457, 477, 478, 479, 485, 494
Adler, Mortimer J., 307
Adoff, Arnold, 201, 355, 477–478, 494
Adoff, Jaime, 344, 355
"Adventures of Chris, The" (McCord), 348
Adventures of High John the Conqueror, The (Sanfield), 262
Adventures of Huckleberry Finn, The (Twain), 60, 66, 71
Adventures of Odysseus, The (Philip), 268
Adventures of Pinocchio, The: Tale of a Puppet (Collodi), 63, 291, 311
Adventures of Pinocchio, The (Morris), 311
Adventures of Sherlock Holmes, The (Doyle), 63
Adventures of Spider, The: West African Folktales (Arkhurst), 154

Adventures of Tom Sawyer, The (Twain), 63, 71
Aenid (Virgil), 326
Aesop for Children, The (Winter), 241, 267
Aesop's Fables, 17, 239, 240, 257, 267
Aesop's Fables (Hague), 241, 267
Aesop's Fables (Holder), 302
Aesop's Fables (L'Estrange), 240, 267
Aesop's Fables (Newbery), 51
Aesop's Fables (Paxton), 241, 267, 349, 355
Aesop's Fables (Pinkney), 17, 241, 261, 268
Aesop's Fables (Sneed), 268
Aesop's Fables (Testa), 241, 267
Afanasyév, Alexander Nikolayevich, 227, 266
Afif, Kaisser, 317
Africa: The Art of Continent (Phillips), 147
After (Prose), 414
Afternoon of the Elves (Lisle), 33, 64, 91, 113, 376, 403, 412
After the Goat Man (Byars), 410
After the Rain (Mazer), 365, 386, 413
After the War Was Over (Foreman), 482, 495
Age of Shakespeare, The (Kermode), 7
Agnes the Sheep (Taylor), 414
Ahlberg, Allan, 32, 196, 201, 266
Ahlberg, Janet, 196, 201, 266
Ahlender, David, 70
Aiken, Joan, 274, 309
Aimee Semple McPherson (Sheafer), 493
Aiqing, Pan, 263
Airborn (Oppel), 15, 275, 298, 313
Airport (Barton), 527, 536
A Is For…? A Photographer's Alphabet of Animals (Horenstein), 169, 199
A Is for Asia (Chin-Lee), 170, 198
Akaba, Suekichi, 128, 230, 263
Aladdin and the Enchanted Lamp (Pullman), 232, 265
"Aladdin and the Magic Lamp," 219, 231
Alarcão, Francisco X., 355
Alarcão, Renato, 265
Alborough, Jez, 312
Al Capone Does My Shirts (Choldenko), 20, 22, 102, 378, 410
Alcorn, Stephen, 357
Alcott, Louisa May, 45, 61, 63, 67–68, 108, 111, 409, 481
Alcott, May, 67
Aldabra, or The Tortoise Who Loved Shakespeare (Gandolfi), 274, 311
Aldana, Patricia, 144, 154, 344, 355
Alder, Elizabeth, 457
Alderson, Brian W., 54, 58, 59, 138–139, 144, 357
Aldrich, Thomas Bailey, 60, 63, 67, 68
Aleshire, Peter, 33
Alexander, Lloyd, 13, 20, 40, 64, 111, 281–282, 300, 309

Alexander and the Terrible, Horrible, No Good, Very Bad Day (Viorst), 64, 128, 160, 179, 180, 205
Alexander and the Wind-up Mouse (Lionni), 157, 204
Alexander Calder and His Magical Mobiles (Lipman & Aspinwall), 497
Alexander Graham Bell: Making Connections (Pasachoff), 497
Alexander Graham Bell (Fisher), 495
Alex and the Cat (Griffith), 200
Alfie Gives a Hand (Hughes), 203
Alford, Frederick J., 458
"Algernon, Who Played with a Loaded Gun, and, on missing his Sister, was reprimanded by his Father" (Belloc), 332
Alias Madame Doubtfire (Fine), 398, 411
Alice in Rapture, Sort Of (Naylor), 363, 379, 413
Alice's Adventures in Wonderland: A Pop-Up Adaptation (Sabuda), 24
Alice's Adventures in Wonderland (Carroll), 45, 55, 58, 59, 63, 108, 144, 155, 272, 292–293, 310, 322, 331, 355
Alice the Fairy (Shannon), 5, 178, 205
Alien Secrets (Klause), 312
Aliki, 33, 494
Alison's Zinnia (Lobel), 199
All About Sam (Lowry), 412
All Alone in the Universe (Perkins), 377–378, 413
All But Alice (Naylor), 413
Allen, Kit, 168, 198
Allen, Laura Jean, 200
Allen, Marjorie N., 3
Allen, Thomas B., 88, 356, 472, 495
All in a Day's Work: Twelve Americans Talk About Their Jobs (Johnson), 538
Allington, Richard, 2
Allison (Say), 159
All-of-a-Kind Family (Taylor), 68, 69, 373–374, 414
All the Colors of the Race (Adoff), 355
All the Small Poems (Worth), 340, 360
Almond, David, 22, 33, 88, 102, 111, 275, 309, 451, 457
Almost the Real Thing: Simulation in Your High-Tech World (Skurzynski), 532, 541
Alonso, Karen, 535
Alphabatics (MacDonald), 11, 169, 199
Alphabears: An ABC Book (Hague), 199
Alphabet City (Johnson), 11–12, 123, 157, 169, 199
Alphabet from Z to A, The (With Much Confusion on the Way) (Viorst), 199
Alphabet of Animals, An (Wormell), 144, 160
Altman, Linda Jacobs, 535
Always Remember Me: How One Family Survived World War II (Russo), 148, 159, 514, 541
Amaki, Amalia K., 147
A Maze Me: Poems for Girls (Nye), 344, 347, 358

Amazing Bone, The (Steig), 159, 205, 276, 314
Amazing Stories, 297
Amber Brown Is Not a Crayon (Danziger), 411
Amber Spyglass, The (Pullman), 87, 92, 114, 281, 313
Ambrose, Stephen E., 515, 535
Ambrus, Victor G., 268, 269, 312
Amendola, Dana, 529, 535, 537
American Association for the Advancement of Science, 502
American Boy: The Adventures of Mark Twain (Brown), 480, 495
American Folksongs for Children—In Home, School, and Nursery School (Seeger), 359
American Hero, The: The True Story of Charles Lindbergh (Denenberg), 476–477, 495
American Plague, A: The True and Terrifying Story of the Yellow Fever Epidemic of 1793 (Murphy), 64, 89, 114, 502, 510–511, 532, 540
American Revolutionaries, The: A History in Their Own Words, 1750-1800 (Meltzer), 513, 540
American Safari, An: Adventures on the North American Prairie (Brandenburg), 536
American Sports Poems (Knudson & Swenson), 339, 357
American Winter, A (Freedman), 151
America's Champion Swimmer: Gertrude Ederle (Adler), 32, 477, 478, 494
America the Beautiful: A Pop-Up Book (Sabuda), 24
Ames, Mildred, 457
Amethyst Ring, The (O'Dell), 429, 459
Amman, Jost, 53
Ammon, Richard, 14, 18–19, 514, 536
Amos Fortune, Free Man (Yates), 32, 420–421, 460, 473, 491, 492, 498
Amulet of Samarkand, The (Stroud), 294–295, 314
Anansi Does the Impossible!: An Ashanti Tale (Aardema), 233, 262
"Anansi's Fishing Expedition" (Washington), 234
Anansi the Spider: A Tale from the Ashanti (McDermott), 262
Anastasia Again! (Lowry), 412
Anastasia at Your Service (Lowry), 412
Anastasia Krupnik (Lowry), 378–379, 412
Anastasia on Her Own (Lowry), 370, 398, 412
Anastasia's Album (Brewster), 495, 542
Anastasia's Chosen Career (Lowry), 412
Anaya, Rudolfo A., 236, 265
Ancient Cliff Dwellers of Mesa Verde, The (Arnold), 509, 536
Ancient Inca, The (Calvert), 508, 536
Ancient Voices (Hovey), 326, 357
Ancona, George, 172, 199
Andersen, Bethanne, 269, 458, 472, 497, 538
Andersen, Hans Christian, 45, 52, 63, 124, 154, 260, 266, 277–278, 293, 302, 309, 492
Anderson, Alexander, 53
Anderson, Laurie Halse, 370, 409
Anderson, Lena, 154
Anderson, Maggie, 354
Anderson, Peter, 474, 495
Anderson, Wayne, 249
Anderson, Wendy, 154
Anderson, William, 495
And if the Moon Could Talk (Banks), 107, 111, 154
... And Now Miguel (Krumgold), 391, 412
Ando, Noriyuki, 157, 203, 458

Andreasen, Dan, 495, 498, 511, 538
Andrew, Ian, 150
Andrew Carnegie: Steel King and Friend to Libraries (Kent), 497
Andrew Jackson and His America (Meltzer), 497
Andrews-Goebel, Nancy, 14, 146, 154, 344, 355
Andrew Wyeth (Meryman), 158, 480, 497
And the Green Grass Grew All Around: Folk Poetry from Everyone (Schwartz), 359
"And Then There Was Light" (Schwartz), 251
And Then What Happened, Paul Revere? (Fritz), 463–464, 496
And to Think That I Saw It on Mulberry Street (Seuss), 6, 55, 63, 177, 205
Andujar, Gloria de Aragon, 265
Andy Warhol: Prince of Pop (Greenberg & Jordan), 480, 496
Angel and the Soldier Boy, The (Collington), 9
Angelou, Maya, 66, 355
Angels, Prophets, Rabbis and Kings from the Stories of the Jewish People (Patterson), 251, 265
Angel's Mistake, The: Stories of Chelm (Prose), 229, 265
Angel's Mother's Wedding (Delton), 411
Anholt, Laurence, 29, 466–467, 495
Animal Action ABC (Pandell), 540
Animal Alphabet (Kitchen), 169, 199
Animal Crackers: A Delectable Collection of Pictures, Poems, and Lullabies for the Very Young (Dyer), 8–9, 356
Animal Dads (Collard), 502–503, 537
Animal Sense (Ackerman), 338, 355
Animal, the Vegetable, and John D. Jones, The (Byars), 32, 410
Animal Tales (Nister), 158
Annabelle Swift, Kindergartner (Schwartz), 31, 205
Anna, Grandpa, and the Big Storm (Stevens), 459
Anna of Byzantium (Barrett), 40, 111, 427, 457
Anna Pavlova: Genius of the Dance (Levine), 497
Anne Elizabeth's Diary: A Young Artist's True Story (Rector), 480, 498
Anne Frank—Beyond the Diary: A Photographic Remembrance (van der Rol & Verhoeven), 498
Anne Frank: Diary of a Young Girl, The: The Definitive Edition (Frank), 77, 112, 486, 496
Anne Frank: Life in Hiding (Hurwitz), 496
Annie and the Old One (Miles), 389, 413
Annie's Promise (Levitin), 458
Anno, Mitsumasa, 14, 16, 176, 199, 200
Anno's Counting Book (Anno), 14, 199
Anno's Journey (Anno), 176, 200
Anno's Math Games II (Anno), 14
Anno's U.S.A. (Anno), 16
Annotated Mona Lisa, The: A Crash Course in Art History from Prehistoric to Post-Modern (Strickland), 159
Anpao: An American Indian Odyssey (Highwater), 32, 64, 110, 113, 267
Anthony Burns: The Defeat and Triumph of a Fugitive Slave (Hamilton), 113, 475, 496
Antics! (Hepworth), 170, 199
Antler, Bear, Canoe: A Northwoods Alphabet Year (Bowen), 154, 170, 198
Anton, Muricio, 542
Antonenkov, Evgeny, 330, 357
Anzaldua, Gloria, 236, 265

Appalachia: The Voices of Sleeping Birds (Rylant), 88, 114, 452, 459
Appelbaum, Diana, 536
Appelemando's Dreams (Polacco), 91, 114, 204
Appelt, Kathi, 6, 201, 327, 355
Apple, Margot, 202
Apple Is My Sign (Riskind), 414
Apples to Oregon: Being the (Slightly) True Narrative of How a Brave Pioneer Father Brought Apples, Peaches, Plums, Grapes, and Cherries (and Children) Across the Plains (Hopkinson), 438, 455, 458
Appointment (Maugham), 265
Appraisal: Science Books for Young People, 534
Apprenticeship of Lucas Whitaker, The (Defelice), 295
Apt. 3 (Keats), 137–138, 157
Arab Folktales (Bushnaq), 232, 265
Arabian Nights, The: Tales from a Thousand and One Nights (Burton), 150, 154, 232
Arabian Nights, The (Philip), 232, 265
Archaeologists Dig for Clues (Duke), 507, 537
Archambault, John, 170, 199, 204
Archuleta, Leroy Ramon, 199
Are We Alone? Scientists Search for Life in Space (Skurzynski), 503, 526, 541
Are You There God? It's Me, Margaret (Blume), 64, 77, 112, 363, 371, 378, 410
Argent, Kerry, 202, 203
Arkadians, The (Alexander), 20, 111, 282, 309
Arkhurst, Joyce Cooper, 154
Arms, John, 360
Armstrong, Jennifer, 128, 154, 514, 530, 536
Armstrong, Thomas, 22
Armstrong, William H., 64, 444, 457
Arnold, Arthur P., 536
Arnold, Caroline, 32, 507, 509, 518, 532, 536
Arnold, Renea, 195
Arnold, Tim, 204
Arnosky, Jim, 360, 536
Aronson, Marc, 490
Around the World: Who's Been Here? (George), 537
Around the World in Eighty Days (Verne), 60, 63
Around the World in Eighty Poems (Berry), 344, 355
Arrowhawk (Schaefer), 501, 524, 535, 541
Arrow to the Sun: A Pueblo Indian Tale (McDermott), 122–123, 158, 267
Arrowville (Boedoe), 122, 152, 154, 181–182, 201
Art Against the Odds: From Slave Quilts to Prison Paintings (Rubin), 147, 159
Art and Architecture of Islam 1250–1800, The (Blair & Bloom), 150
Art and Design in Children's Picture Books (Lacy), 143
Artemis Fowl: The Oral Deception (Colfer), 311
Arthur: The Seeing Stone (Crossley-Holland), 131, 155, 302, 311
Arthur, Alex, 536
Arthur, Malcolm, 264
Arthur and the Sword (Sabuda), 24
Arthur Goes to Camp (Brown), 201
Arthurian Fiction: An Annotated Bibliography (Mediavilla), 248
Arthur's Baby (Brown), 201
Arthur's Family Vacation (Brown), 185–186, 201

Arthur's Great Big Valentine (Hoban), 110, 113
Artist in Overalls: The Life of Grant Wood
    (Duggleby), 155, 495
Art of Japan (Finley), 130–131, 156
Art of Keeping Cool, The (Lisle), 446, 458
Art of Maurice Sendak, The (Lanes), 139
Art of Reading, The: Forty Illustrators Celebrate RIF's
    40th Anniversary, 127–128, 158
Art of the Far North: Inuit Sculpture, Drawing, and
    Printmaking (Finley), 140, 151, 156
Art Past Art Present (Wilkins), 148, 150
Art Up Close: From Ancient to Modern
    (d'Harcourt), 141, 155
Aruego, Ariane, 203
Aruego, José, 64, 159, 203, 266
Asbjørnsen, Peter Christian, 12, 225, 226–227, 266
Asch, Frank, 31, 201
Ashabranner, Brent, 234, 262, 536
Ashanti to Zulu: African Traditions (Musgrove), 64,
    129, 158, 170, 199
Ashby, Ruth, 495, 510, 536
Ashe, Rosalind, 108
Ashley Bryan's ABC of African American Poetry
    (Bryan), 198
Ashman, Linda, 342, 355
Ashton, John, 47
Asian Cultural Centre for UNESCO, 231, 262
Asimov, Isaac, 297
As Long as the Rivers Flow (Loyie), 484, 497
Aspects and Issues in the History of Children's
    Literature (Nikolajeva), 44
Asphalt Angels (Holtwijk), 382, 412
Aspinwall, Margaret, 497
Association of Women Psychologists, 369
Aston, Dianna Hutts, 339, 355
Astounding Science Fiction, 297
Astro Bunnies (Loomis), 204
"Astronaut Stopping by a Planet on a Snowy
    Evening" (Scieszka), 339
Athletic Shorts (Crutcher), 397–398, 411
Atkin, S. Beth, 149
Atkinson, Allen, 16, 290, 314
Attaboy, Sam! (Lowry), 14, 379, 413
Attenborough, Liz, 331, 355
At the Back of the North Wind (MacDonald), 63,
    275, 279, 312
At the Crack of the Bat (Morrison), 339, 358
At the Crossing Places (Crossley-Holland), 311
At the Crossroads (Isadora), 387, 412
At the Wish of the Fish: A Russian Folktale
    (Lewis), 227, 266
Atwater, Florence, 291, 310
Atwater, Richard, 291, 310
Atwater-Rhodes, Amelia, 310
Atwood, Ann, 329, 355
Auch, Mary Jane, 201, 457
Auden, W. H., 327
"Auk Talk" (Hoberman), 321
Austin, Mary, 350, 483
Author: A True Story (Lester), 29, 497
Autumnblings: Poems and Paintings (Florian),
    334, 356
"Autumn Quince" (Hirshfield), 342
Avery, Gillian, 46
Avi, 15, 40, 64, 97–98, 111, 319, 327, 409, 457
Awake and Dreaming (Pearson), 313
Awful Ogre's Awful Day (Prelutsky), 319, 333, 359

Ayat Jamilah: Beautiful Signs: A Treasury of Islamic
    Wisdom for Children and Parents (Conover &
    Crane), 254, 266–267
Aylesworth, Jim, 154, 170, 198, 264, 302, 310, 452
Ayliffe, Alex, 355

Babar's Anniversary Album: 6 Favorite Stories
    (de Brunhoff & de Brunhoff), 202
Babbit, Natalie, 77, 101, 107, 111, 201, 272,
    310, 360
Babe & I, The (Adler), 457
Baber, Frank, 311
Baboon King, The (Quintana), 83, 114
Babushka Baba Yaga (Polacco), 204
Baby Babka, The Gorgeous Genius (Zalban), 31, 206
Baby Buggy (Ziefert), 168, 198
Baby Duck and the Bad Eyeglasses (Hest), 203
Baby Goes Beep, The (O'Connell), 5
Baby Radar (Nye), 12
Baby Sister for Frances, A (Hoban), 184, 203
"Baby Song of the Four Winds" (Sandburg), 334
Baby's Opera, The (Crane), 124, 155
Baby's Own Aesop, The (Crane), 54
Baby Uggs Are Hatching, The (Prelutsky), 333, 359
Baby Whale's Journey (London), 157,
    522–523, 539
Baca, Maria, 265
Bachrach, Susan D., 148, 154, 515, 536
Backbone of the King: The Story of Pakáa and His
    Son Ku (Brown), 249, 268
Back to the Wild (Patent), 523, 540
Backwater (Bauer), 410
Bacon, Paul, 496
Bad Boy, a Memoir (Myers), 22
Bad Child's Book of Beasts, The (Belloc), 332, 355
Bad Girls (Voigt), 115, 377, 414
Bad Heart, Amos, 496
Baer, Edith, 18
Baghban, Marcia, 301
Bagley, Ayers, 53
Baicker, Karen, 5
Bailey, Peter, 356
Bailey, Sid, 267
Baird, Anne, 40
Baker, Jeannie, 6, 154, 176, 193, 195, 196, 200,
    201, 402, 409
Baker, Karen Lee, 320, 357
Baker, Keith, 11, 201, 310
Baker, Olaf, 154, 237, 265, 266
Baker, Sheridan, 76, 325
Bakery Lady, The (Mora), 391, 413
Baldwin, Ruth M., 198
Ballad of Lucy Whipple, The (Cushman), 457
Ballad of the Pirate Queens, The (Yolen), 360
Ballard, Robert D., 514, 536
Ballot Box Battle, The (McCully), 113, 158
Bamboo Flute, The (Disher), 457
Bamford, Rosemary, 535
Bancroft, Ann, 504, 539
Bancroft, Bronwyn, 268
Bandit's Moon (Fleischman), 439, 458
Bang, Molly, 12, 21, 171, 199, 201, 230, 263,
    527, 536
Bania, Michael, 266
Banks, Kate, 30, 107, 111, 154
Banned Books: 387 B.C. to 1978 A.D. (Haight), 65

Bannerman, Helen, 175, 201
Bany-Winters, Lisa, 528, 536
Barasch, Lynn, 21, 484, 495
Barban, Leslie, 435
Barbour, Karen, 268, 357, 539
Barclay, Donald A., 60
Bard of Avon: The Story of William Shakespeare
    (Stanley & Vennema), 40
"Barefoot" (Worth), 340, 347
Bargain for Frances, A (Hoban), 203
Barker, Clive, 310
Barkley, James, 457
Barlett, Alison, 520
Barnes, Cheryl Shaw, 536
Barnes, Peter W., 536
Barn Savers (High), 538
Barrett, Angela, 309
Barrett, Peter, 203
Barrett, Thomas C., 407
Barrett, Tracy, 40, 111, 427, 457
Barrie, J. M., 63, 293, 310
Barron, T. A., 310
Barry, Dave, 293, 310
Barth, Edna, 243, 268
Bartlett, Alison, 537
Bartoletti, Susan Campbell, 386, 409, 418, 421,
    437, 457, 514, 515, 536
Barton, Byron, 5, 111, 200, 527, 536
Barton, Jill, 185, 203
Bascom, William, 209, 211, 242–243
Bash, Barbara, 506, 524, 536
Basho, Matsuo, 317, 329
Basho and the River Stones (Myers), 6, 178, 194,
    204, 277, 329, 358
Basket Moon (Ray), 135, 158
Bass, L. G., 310
Bat-Ami, Miriam, 32, 33, 112, 445, 446, 457
Bateman, Colin, 397, 410
Bates, Amy June, 356
Bats! Strange and Wonderful! (Pringle), 520
Batten, John D., 263
Bauer, Joan, 112, 361, 366, 372, 398, 410
Bauer, Marion Dane, 17, 104, 112, 410, 529,
    531, 536
Bauer, Susan Wise, 74–75, 530
Baum, L. Frank, 310
Bausum, Ann, 515, 536
Bawden, Nina, 64, 378, 410
Bayat, Mojdeh, 250–251, 266
Bayberry Bluff (Lent), 157
Baylor, Byrd, 181, 201, 324, 336, 355, 409, 410, 452
Baylor, Frances Courtenay, 60
Baynes, Pauline, 312, 314
Beacons of Light: Lighthouses (Gibbons), 537
Bean, Thomas W., 36
"Bear, The" (Florian), 350
"Bear and the Children, The," 229
Bear Called Paddington, A (Bond), 64, 288, 310
Bearden, Romare, 147, 154
Bearobics: A Hip-Hop Counting Story (Parker), 13
Bears (Kraus), 5, 31, 93
Bears' House, The (Sachs), 414
Bearskin (Pyle), 158
Bear Snores On (Wilson), 5
Beast of Monsieur Racine, The (Ungerer), 205
Beaton, Clare, 197
Beatrix (Winter), 480, 498

Beatrix Potter (Malam), 466, 497
Beat the Story-Drum, Pum-Pum (Bryan), 233, 262
Beat the Turtle Drum (Greene), 383, 411
Beattie, Owen, 536
Beatty, Patricia, 441, 443, 457
Beaumont, Jeanne Marie, 346, 355
Beaumont, Karen, 182, 201
Beautiful Blackbird (Bryan), 262
Beautiful Days of My Youth, The: My Six Months in Auschwitz and Plaszow (Novac), 497
"Beautiful Girl of the Moon Tower, The" (Hamilton), 238
"Beautiful Soup" (Carroll), 322, 324, 349
Beautiful Stories from Shakespeare (Nesbit), 17, 257
Beautiful Warrior: The Legend of the Nun's Kung Fu (McCully), 269
"Beauty and Pock Face," 258
"Beauty and the Beast," 211, 213, 217, 219, 220, 223, 226, 239, 243
Beauty and the Beast (Brett), 264
Beauty and the Beast (de Beaumont), 217, 222, 264
Beauty and the Beast (Willard), 264
Beauty of the Beast, The: Poems from the Animal Kingdom (Prelutsky), 338, 359
Because of Winn-Dixie (DiCamillo), 32, 363, 372, 375, 411
Beck, Robert, 371
Beckett, Sister Wendy, 154
Beckham, Stephen Dow, 237
Becoming Naomi León (Ryan), 22, 379, 414
Bedard, Michael, 135, 154, 201, 317, 355
Beddows, Eric, 337, 356
Bed-Knob and Broomstick (Norton), 291, 313
Bedtime! (Swain), 542
Beethoven in Paradise (O'Connor), 413
Beethoven Lives Upstairs (Nichol), 14
Bee Tree, The (Polacco), 204
Begay, Shonto, 17, 151, 154, 266
Beggar Queen, The (Alexander), 282, 309
Beggars' Ride, The (Nelson), 413
Behan, Brendan, 221, 263
Behind the Bedroom Wall (Williams), 460
Behind the Wheel: Poems About Driving (Wong), 360
Behn, Robin, 354
Behren, June, 149, 154
Belafonte, Harry, 325, 355
Bel-Air Bambi and the Mall Rats (Peck), 413
Believe Me, I Know (Bush), 343, 355
Bell, Anthea, 264, 309, 310, 311
Bell, Don, 265
Bellairs, John, 310
"Belle au Bois Dormant, La, or The Sleeping Beauty in the Wood" (Perrault). *See* "Sleeping Beauty"
Belle Prater's Boy (White), 70, 71, 83, 115, 375, 414
Belloc, Hilaire, 332, 355
Bells of Christmas, The (Hamilton), 417, 458
Bemelmans, Ludwig, 30, 77, 112, 144, 154
Ben and Me (Lawson), 157, 312
Benchley, Nathaniel, 200
Beneath the Blazing Sun (Ellis), 239
Ben-Ezer, Ehud, 112, 265
Ben Franklin's Almanac: Being a True Account of the Good Gentleman's Life (Fleming), 473, 489, 495

Benjamin, Alan, 265
Benjamin, Carol Lea, 112, 403, 410
Benjamin Franklin: An American Life (Isaacson), 494
Benjamin Franklin: The New American (Meltzer), 473, 497
Bennett, Nneka, 497
Benny: An Adventure Story (Graham), 24, 198, 202
Beowulf: A New Verse Translation (Heaney), 247, 269, 326, 357
"Beowulf," 15, 45, 247, 280, 281, 326
Beowulf (Crossley-Holland), 155, 268
Beowulf, A New Telling (Nye), 269
Berck, Judith, 410
Berenzy, Alix, 112, 538
Berlioz the Bear (Brett), 154
Bernardin, James, 267
Bernier-Grand, Carmen, 22, 344, 355
Bernstein, Joanne, 363
Bernstein, Zena, 93, 114
Berry, James, 344, 355
Berstein, Zena, 313
Bertrand, Diane Gonzales, 391, 410
Best, Cari, 201
Best Cat in the World, The (Newman), 25
Best Friends for Frances (Hoban), 30, 34, 203
Best Friends Think Alike (Reiser), 30, 182, 204
Bestiary: An Illuminated Alphabet of Medieval Beasts (Hunt), 199
Best-Loved Poems of Jacqueline Kennedy Onassis (Kennedy), 7, 315, 357
Best Place, The (Meddaugh), 204
Best Poems of the English Language, The (Bloom), 317, 355
Best Town in the World, The (Baylor), 181, 201, 452
Best Valentine in the World, The (Sharmat), 205
Bettelheim, Bruno, 213, 278–279
Between a Rock and a Hard Place (Carter), 410
Beverly Billingsly Can't Catch (Stadler), 21
Bewick, John, 55
Bewick, Thomas, 54, 55, 144
Beyond the Divide (Lasky), 423, 439, 458
Beyond the Ridge (Goble), 156, 238, 266
B. Franklin, Printer (Adler), 478, 479
Bial, Raymond, 509, 536
Bianco, Margery Williams. *See* Williams, Margery
Bible, 66
"Bickering" (Bodecker), 333
Bierhorst, John, 235, 237, 241, 257, 264, 265, 266, 267
Big & Little (Jenkins), 13, 200
Big & Little (Parr), 168, 198
Big Anthony and the Magic Ring (dePaola), 155
Big Box, The (Morrison), 34
Big Boy, 187
Bigger (Calvert), 457
Bigger Than T. Rex (Lessem), 539
Biggest Bear, The (Ward), 63, 133, 160, 205
Big Mama (Crunk), 202
Bigmama's (Crews), 387, 411
Big Red (Kjelgaard), 412
Bileck, Marvin, 126, 159
Bilibin, Ivan I., 227, 266
Billinghurst, Percy J., 267
Billingsley, Fanny, 310

Bill Peet: An Autobiography (Peet), 32, 40, 158, 482, 483, 497
Bing, Christopher, 327, 328, 358, 360
Bingham, Jane M., 47, 48, 50, 53, 257
Bingo Brown and the Language of Love (Byars), 410
Binns, Tristan Boyer, 495
Biodiversity (Patent), 540
Birchbark House, The (Erdrich), 442, 443, 457
"Birches" (Frost), 335, 356
Bird About to Sing, A (Montenegro), 339, 358
Birdseye, Debbie Holsclaw, 536
Birdseye, Tom, 536
Birmingham, Christian, 124, 158
Birthday Basket for Tía, A (Mora), 40
"Birth of All of Heaven and Earth, The" (Markman & Markman), 251
"Birth of the Uinal, The" (Markman & Markman), 251
Bishop, Elizabeth, 331
Bishop, Nic, 498, 518, 519, 532, 536, 537, 540
Bittle (MacLachlan & MacLachlan), 183, 204
Bitton-Jackson, Livia, 28, 486, 495, 536
Bitzer, Lucy, 128–129
Björk, Christina, 146, 154
Black Americans, The: A History in Their Own Words, 1599–1983 (Meltzer), 114
Black & White (Parr), 168, 198
Black Art: A Cultural History (Powell), 146, 147
Black Beauty (Sewell), 63, 127
Black Cauldron, The (Alexander), 282, 309
Black Gold (Henry), 412
Black Is Brown Is Tan (Adoff), 201
Blacklock, Dyan, 509, 536
Blackshaw, Anne, 497
Black Stallion, The (Farley), 396, 411
Black Stallion Returns, The (Farley), 411
Black Star, Bright Dawn (O'Dell), 390, 413
Blackwood, Basil T., 355
Blackwood, Gary, 457
Blair, Sheila, 150
Blair, Walter, 239, 266
Blake, Quentin, 358
Blake, Robert J., 360
Blake, William, 45, 52, 55, 63, 138, 143, 318, 325, 337–338, 346, 355
Blegvad, Erik, 312, 313, 360
Bliss, Harry, 202
Blizzard! (Murphy), 510, 540
Blizzard, Gladys S., 149, 154
Blizzard's Robe, The (Sabuda), 159
Block, Francesca Lisa, 370, 410
Blondon, Hervé, 412
Blood Gold (Cadnum), 457
Bloodgood, Janet W., 257
Blooding, The (Windsor), 295, 314
Bloom, Benjamin, 407
Bloom, Harold, 317, 355, 492
Bloom, Jonathan, 150
Bloom, Lloyd, 203, 412
Bloom, Suzanne, 30, 201
Bloom's Modern Critical Views: Hans Christian Andersen (Bloom), 492
Blos, Joan W., 89, 90, 93, 112, 433, 454, 455, 457
Blubber (Blume), 81, 112, 385, 403, 410
"Blue Beard" (Perrault), 71, 221
Blueberries for Sal (McCloskey), 138, 144, 158, 187, 204

Blueberries for the Queen (Paterson & Paterson), 445–446, 459

Blue Fairy Book, The (Lang), 63

Blue Jasmine (Sheth), 33, 393, 394, 414

Blue Sea (Kalan), 200

Blues Journey (Myers), 344, 358

Blue Sword, The (McKinley), 283, 302, 312

Blue Willow (Gates), 63

Blumberg, Marcia, 528, 535

Blumberg, Rhoda, 15, 19, 64, 148, 154, 473, 484, 495, 504, 505, 511, 532, 536

Blume, Judy, 14, 31, 64, 77, 81, 112, 363, 371, 378, 383–384, 385, 398, 403, 410

Blushing: Expressions of Love in Poems & Letters (Janeczko), 7

Bluthenthal, Diana Caine, 197

Bobbin Girl, The (McCully), 158

Bobbsey Twins, The; or Merry Days Indoors and Out (Garis), 63

"Bobby Shafto," 164

Bober, Natalie, 112, 503, 536

Bodecker, N. M., 321, 333, 353, 355

Bodkin, Odds, 263

Bodmer, Karl, 156, 511, 512, 537

Bodnár, Judit Z., 124–125, 154

Body Eclectic, The: An Anthology of Poems (Vecchione), 345–346, 360

Boedoe, Geefwee, 122, 152, 154, 181–182, 201

Boeke, Wanda, 412

Bogacki, Tomek, 201

Boggart, The (Cooper), 39, 295, 311

Boggart and the Monster, The (Cooper), 295, 311

Boitano, Brian, 536

Boitano's Edge: Inside the Real World of Figure Skating (Boitano & Harper), 536

Bolden, Tonya, 147, 154, 464, 465, 475, 495, 530, 536

Bolin, Frances Schoonmaker, 356

Bolognese, Don, 200, 268, 457

Bomzer, Barry, 410

Bond, Michael, 64, 287–288, 310

Bone Detectives, The: How Forensic Anthropologists Solve Crimes and Uncover Mysteries of the Dead (Jackson), 504, 518, 538

Bone Poems (Moss), 338, 358

Bones Rock! Everything You Need to Know to Be a Paleontologist (Larson & Donnan), 502, 503, 506, 539

Bonham, Frank, 410

Bonsall, Crosby, 200

Bookbanning in America: Who Bans Books? (Noble), 65

Book Links, 535

Booklist, 76, 163, 168, 286

Book of Bosh, A (Lear), 357

Book of Myths, A (Bulfinch), 268

Book of Myths, A: Selections from Bulfinch's Age of Fable (Sewell), 242

Book of Nonsense, A (Lear), 45, 58, 63, 328, 331, 357

Book of the Subtyl Historyes and Fables of Esope (Caxton), 47, 55, 63, 71, 240, 262

Book of Three, The (Alexander), 64, 282, 309

Books on the Move: A Read-About-It Go-There Guide to America's Best Family Destinations (Knorr & Knorr), 456

Boone, Jessica, 536

Booss, Claire, 266

Borden, Louise, 35, 417, 445, 457, 495

Borgman, Harry, 127

Boring, Mel, 501, 537

Borning Room, The (Fleischman), 80, 112, 440–441, 458

Bornstein, Ruth Lercher, 413

Borrowed Children (Lyon), 458

Borrowers, The (Norton), 63, 272, 275, 294, 313

Borrowers Afield, The (Norton), 294, 313

Borrowers Afloat, The (Norton), 274, 294, 313

Borrowers Aloft, The (Norton), 294, 313

Borrowers Avenged, The (Norton), 294, 313

Bortololli, Dan, 522, 536

Bosch, Hieronymus, 144, 330–331

Bossert, Jill, 146

Boston, David, 265

Boston, Lucy M., 63, 295–296, 303, 310

Boston, Peter, 310

Bottner, Barbara, 181, 201

Boulanger, Susan, 140

Bound (Napoli), 33, 272, 276, 313

Bourke-White, Margaret, 159, 498

Boutet de Monvel, Maurice, 144

Bowen, Betsy, 131, 154, 157, 170, 198, 266

Bowermaster, John, 525, 542

Bowman, Leslie W., 458

Bow Wow Meow Meow: It's Rhyming Cats and Dogs (Florian), 336, 356

Box Turtle at Long Pond (George), 537

Boy, a Dog, a Frog, and a Friend, A (Mayer), 200

Boy, a Dog, and a Frog, A (Mayer), 200

Boy, the Bear, the Baron, the Bard, The (Rogers), 7, 9–10, 40, 153, 158, 190, 191, 200

Boy and His Bear, A (Graham), 458

"Boy and the Northwind, The" (Lunge-Larsen), 226

Boy and the Old Man, The (Hernandez), 391

Boy and the Samurai, The (Haugaard), 427–428, 458

Boyd, Herb, 516, 536

Boyd, Sheree, 541

"Boy in Girl's Dress, The" (Bushnaq), 232

Boy Named Giotto, A (Guarnieri), 156, 458

Boy of the Three-Year Nap, The (Snyder), 104, 114, 230, 263

Boy on Fairfield Street, The: How Ted Geisel Grew Up to Become Dr. Seuss (Krull), 21, 492, 497

"Boy Who Became a Lion, a Falcon, and an Ant, The" (Lunge-Larsen), 226

Boy Who Drew Birds, The: A Story of John James Audubon (Davies), 131, 155, 230, 480, 495

Boy Who Drew Cats, The: A Japanese Folktale (Levine), 7, 263

Boy Who Loved to Draw, The: Benjamin West (Brenner), 495

Boy Who Would Not Go to Bed, The (Cooper), 202

Bradley, Kimberly Brubaker, 457, 495

Bramhall, William, 498

Brandenburg, Jim, 536, 542

Brandriss, Tobie, 466, 490

Branford, Henrietta, 457

Brave, The (Lipsyte), 390, 412

Brave and Bold (Alger), 58

"Brave Little Tailor, The," 239, 264

Braving the Frozen Frontier: Women Working in Antarctica (Johnson), 33, 496, 525, 538

Bravo, Constanza, 268

Bray, Rosemary L., 147, 154, 477, 495

Bread and Jam for Frances (Hoban), 184, 203

Breaking Into Print: Before and After the Invention of the Printing Press (Krensky), 157, 538

Bredsdorff, Bodil, 22, 366, 410

Breen, Karen, 77, 272, 463

"Bremen Town Musicians, The," 211, 223

Bremen Town Musicians, The (Grimm & Grimm), 264

Bremen Town Musicians, The (Plume), 264

Bremen Town Musicians and Other Animal Tales from Grimm, The (Orgel), 31, 223, 264

Brenner, Barbara, 200, 355, 453, 457, 495, 536

Brenner, Fred, 436, 459

Brent, Isabelle, 156, 264

"Brer Rabbit Finds His Match" (Parks), 239

Brett, Jan, 5, 110, 154, 201, 221, 263, 264, 331, 357

Bretts-Secker, Josephine, 224, 259, 267

Breughel, Pieter, 144

Brewer, Dan, 7, 324, 359

Brewster, Hugh, 495, 542

Brian's Return (Paulsen), 413

Bridges, Ruby, 410, 478, 495

Bridges Are to Cross (Sturges), 132

Bridge to Terabithia (Paterson), 64, 77, 90–91, 102, 114, 372, 385, 413

Brierley, Louise, 265

Briggs, Katharine, 263

Brighton, Catherine, 26–27, 29, 495

Bringing the Rain to Kapiti Plain: A Nandi Tale (Aardema), 6, 80, 111, 233, 262

Brink, Carol Ryrie, 417, 423, 454, 457

British Folk Tales (Briggs), 263

British Folk Tales (Crossley-Holland), 221, 263

Brittain, Bill, 302, 310

Broadway, Marsha, 528

Broccoli Tapes, The (Slepian), 414

Bronx Masquerade (Grimes), 7, 95, 113, 366, 411

Bronze Bow, The (Speare), 17, 426, 459

Bronze Cauldron, The: Myths and Legends of the World (McGaughrean), 268

Bronzeville Boys and Girls (Brooks), 355

Brooke, L. Leslie, 63, 124, 154

Brooke, William J., 17, 261, 266

Brooker, Kyrsten, 205

Brooklyn Bridge, The (Mann), 539

Brooks, Bruce, 33, 85, 112, 410, 490

Brooks, Gwendolyn, 355

Brooks, Polly Schoyer, 471–472, 495

Brother Eagle, Sister Sky (Jeffers), 157

Brother Rabbit: A Cambodian Tale (Ho & Ros), 267

Brothers Grimm, 45, 52, 53, 55, 63, 113, 124, 130, 156, 209, 214, 218, 219, 222, 223, 225, 226, 254, 261, 276, 277, 279, 302

Brothers of Pity, and Other Tales (Ewing), 56

Brother to the Wind (Walter), 7, 136–137, 160

Broudy, H. S., 141

Brown, Beatrice Curtis, 327

Brown, Bradford, 388

Brown, Don, 102, 466, 468, 470, 471, 481, 490, 494, 495

Brown, Jennifer, 154

Brown, Jennifer M., 144

Brown, June, 194–195, 197

Brown, Kathryn, 205
Brown, Laurie Krasny, 25, 154, 536
Brown, Marc, 21, 25, 110, 154, 185–186, 198, 201, 359, 536
Brown, Marcia, 63, 106, 120, 121, 132, 153, 154, 155, 158, 201, 221–222, 249, 264, 266, 268, 335
Brown, Margaret Wise, 77, 112, 144, 154, 168, 180, 198, 201
Brown, Mary Barrett, 523, 536, 537
Brown, Richard, 198
Brown, Tricia, 151, 154
Browne, Anthony, 16, 110, 112, 145–146, 154
Browning, Elizabeth Barrett, 57
Browning, Robert, 43, 55, 326–327, 346, 348, 355
Brownjohn, John, 313
Brown v. Board of Education (Telgen), 516, 542
Bruchac, James, 266
Bruchac, Joseph, 245–246, 266, 451, 457, 467, 469, 490, 495
Bruemmer, Fred, 538
Bruff, J. Goldsborough, 423
Bruh Rabbit and the Tar Baby (Hamilton), 262
Brundibar (Kushner & Sendak), 148, 157, 191, 203
Bryan, Ashley, 17, 145, 154, 198, 233, 234, 262, 313, 355, 357, 358
Bryant, Michael, 357
Bryant, Samuel, 459
BUB: Or the Very Best Thing (Babbit), 201
Bubba the Cowboy Prince: A Fractured Texas Tale (Ketterman), 267
Bubble Monster: And Other Science Fun (Falk et al.), 537
Buchan, David, 263
Buchholz, Quint, 196, 201
Buckley, Marilyn Hanf, 9
Bucks, Betsy L., 156, 197
Buck Stops Here, The: The Presidents of the United States (Provensen), 512, 541
Bud, Not Buddy (Curtis), 32, 418, 437, 457
Buddha Stories (Demi), 267
Buehner, Mark, 204
Buffalo Hunt (Freedman), 151, 156, 511, 537
Buffalo Sunrise: The Story of a North American Giant (Swanson), 542
Buffalo Tree, The (Rapp), 414
Buffalo Woman (Goble), 156, 238, 266
Building Big (Macaulay), 527, 539
Building Blocks (Voigt), 296, 314
"Building of the Wall, The" (Colum), 245
Building the Book Cathedral (Macaulay), 539
Bulfinch, Thomas, 268
Bulla, Clyde Robert, 200
Bulletin of the Center for Children's Books, 76
Bull Run (Fleischman), 98, 112, 416, 436, 458
Bully for You, Teddy Roosevelt! (Fritz), 19, 113, 475, 489, 490, 496
Bulzone, Marisa, 129–130
Bumblebee Flies Anyway, The (Cormier), 383, 384, 411
"Bun, The," 209
Bunny Cakes (Wells), 205
Bunting, Eve, 19, 30, 102, 112, 122, 123, 132, 149, 153, 154, 196, 201, 399, 400, 457, 515, 536
Bunyan, John, 45, 48–49, 63
Burandt, Harriet, 536
Burch, Robert, 370, 410

Burg, Brad, 325, 355
Burger, Carl, 113, 410, 411
Burgess, Lord, 325, 355
Burgess, Melvin, 372
Buried in Ice: The Mystery of a Lost Arctic Expedition (Beattie & Geiger), 536
Burkert, Nancy Ekholm, 154, 156, 223, 260, 264, 266, 277, 309, 311
Burleigh, Robert, 7, 339, 355
Burnett, Frances Hodgson, 14, 63, 90, 108, 112
Burnett, Moneta, 411
Burnford, Sheila, 363, 410
Burningham, John, 30, 311
Burning Questions of Bingo Brown, The (Byars), 410
Burnish Me Bright (Cunningham), 411
Burns, Ken, 494
Burton, Sir Richard Francis, 150, 154, 232
Burton, Virginia Lee, 6, 30, 63, 109–110, 112, 125, 126, 154, 186–187, 201, 302, 310
Busby, Peter, 466, 470, 490, 495
Bush, Valerie Chow, 343, 355
Bushe, Claire, 265
Bushey, Jerry, 542
Bushnaq, Inea, 232, 233, 265
Busy Busy Moose (Van Laan), 201
Busy Dog (Julian), 198
But God Remembered: Stories of Women from Creation to the Promised Land (Sasso), 249, 269
Butler, Dorothy, 372
Butterfield, Moira, 509, 536
Butterfly, The (Polacco), 31, 35, 36, 182, 204, 446–447, 452, 459
Butterfly House (Bunting), 19, 399
Buttons (Cole), 179, 202
Buzzy Bones and the Lost Quilt (Martin), 204
Byard, Carole, 17, 180, 206, 414
Byars, Betsy, 13, 32, 33, 64, 200, 363, 368, 377, 386, 398, 403, 410
Byrd, Robert, 146, 154, 309, 479, 495
By the Shores of Silver Lake (Wilder), 460

Cabin Faced West, The (Fritz), 63, 113
Cabin on Trouble Creek (Van Leeuwen), 460
Caddie Woodlawn (Brink), 417, 423, 454, 457
Cadnum, Michael, 112, 248, 268, 384, 410, 457
Caduto, Michael J., 245–246, 266
Cai, Mingshui, 211
Cain, David, 539
Calabash Cat and His Amazing Journey (Rumford), 13
"Calabash Flower" (Diakite), 234
Calamity Jane: Her Life and Her Legend (Faber), 466, 495
Calavera Abecedario: A Day of the Dead Alphabet Book (Winter), 170, 199
Caldecott, Randolph, 45, 54, 55, 56, 71, 143–144, 154, 240, 262, 267
Caldecott Aesop, The (Caldecott), 240, 262, 267
Caldecott Celebration, A: Six Artists and Their Paths to the Caldecott Medal (Marcus), 158
Caleb & Kate (Steig), 194, 196, 205
Calico Captive (Speare), 433, 459
Call, Greg, 310
Call It Courage (Sperry), 28, 63, 82–83, 85, 93, 94, 96, 114, 194, 403, 414
Call Me Ahnighito (Conrad), 202
Call of the Wild (London), 412

Calmenson, Stephanie, 177–178, 197, 200, 201
Calvert, Patricia, 457, 508, 536
Cameron, Eleanor, 310
Campbell, John W., Jr., 297
Campbell, Joseph, 242, 303, 304
Campbell, Rod, 12, 198
"Campfire" (Thurman), 350
Canada Geese Quilt, The (Kinsey-Warnock), 458
Canadian ABC, A (Cook), 198
Canadian Fairy Tales (Martin), 126, 158, 239, 257, 267
"Candle" (Graham), 329
Cann, Helen, 267
Cannon, Janell, 201
Canterbury Tales, The (Chaucer), 79, 112, 155, 255, 263
Can't You Sleep, Little Bear? (Waddell), 23, 186, 205
Captain Raptor and the Moon Mystery (O'Malley), 271, 297–298, 313
Captain Snap and the Children of Vinegar Lane (Schotter), 32, 180, 205, 414
Captive, The (O'Dell), 418, 429, 459
Car, The (Paulsen), 413
Care and Feeding of Dragons, The (Seabrooke), 313
Caribou Alphabet, A (Owens), 169, 199
Carle, Eric, 12, 13, 17, 24, 30, 110, 131, 146, 155, 160, 168, 171, 173, 198, 199, 200, 338, 343, 356, 360
Carle, Jill, 536
Carle, Judi, 536
Carle, Megan, 530, 536
Carlota (O'Dell), 439, 456, 459
Carl Sandburg: A Biography (Meltzer), 481, 497
Carl Sandburg: Adventures of a Poet (Niven), 334, 358, 481, 497
Carlson, Claudia, 346, 355
Carlson, Lori Marie, 346, 355
Carlstrom, Nancy White, 201
Carman, Patrick, 310
Carmi, Gloria, 203
Caroff, Susan, 139, 144
Carousel (Crews), 200
Carpenter, Angelica Shirley, 34, 495
Carpenter, Frank G., 503–504
Carpenter, Nancy, 458
Carpenter's Geographical Reader (Carpenter), 503–504
"Carpenter's Son, The," 231
Carr, Jean, 356
Carrell, Douglas, 249
Carrick, Carol, 112, 410, 457, 536
Carrick, Donald, 122, 154, 201, 267, 410, 457, 460
Carroll, Colleen, 155, 527–528, 536–537
Carroll, Lewis, 45, 55, 58–59, 63, 108, 144, 155, 272, 291–292, 310, 324, 327, 330, 331–332, 349, 355
Carson, Jo, 355
Cart, Michael, 410, 490
Carter, Alden R., 410
Carter, David A., 155, 529, 537, 541
Carver: A Life in Poems (Nelson), 7, 11, 95, 114, 345, 358
Case of Roe v. Wade, The (Stevens), 542
Case of the Baker Street Irregular, The (Newman), 396, 413

Case of the Hungry Stranger, The (Bonsall), 200
"Casey at the Bat" (Thayer), 328, 360
Cassie's Journey: Going West in the 1860s (Harvey), 422, 438, 452, 455, 458
Castle (Macaulay), 452, 459
Castle Diary: The Journal of Tobias Burgess, Page (Platt), 452, 459, 540
Castle of Llyr, The (Alexander), 282, 309
Catalanotto, Peter, 155, 203, 204
Cat and Mouse (Bogacki), 201
Cataract of Lodore, The (Southey), 321, 360
Catching the Fire: Philip Simmons, Blacksmith (Lyons), 420
Catch the Ball (Carle), 155
Cathedral: The Story of Its Construction (Macaulay), 539
Catherine, Called Birdy (Cushman), 110, 111, 112, 418, 422, 426, 457
Cat in the Hat, The (Seuss), 13, 77, 110, 114, 177, 201, 359
Cat in the Hat Comes Back, The (Seuss), 201
Catlett, Elizabeth, 517, 538
Catlin, George, 511
Catrow, David, 182, 201, 360
Cats, 337
Cats, Cats, Cats! (Newman), 6, 8, 204
Cats in Krasinski Square, The (Hesse), 447, 458
Cats Vanish Slowly (Tiller), 360
"Cat Who Became a Poet, The" (Mahy), 317–318
"Cat Who Went to Mecca, The" (Bushnaq), 233
Catwings (LeGuin), 312
Catwings Return (LeGuin), 287, 312
Cauley, Lorinda Bryan, 310, 312
Cause: Reconstruction America 1863–1877 (Bolden), 530, 536
Causley, Charles, 319
Cautionary Tales for Children (Belloc), 332, 355
Cautionary Verses (Belloc), 332, 355
Cavendish, Richard, 247, 283
Cave Paintings to Picasso: The Inside Scoop on 50 Art Masterpieces (Sayre), 19, 127, 145, 159, 541
Caxton, William, 46, 55, 63, 71, 240, 262
Caxton's Aesop. See Book of the Subtyl Historyes and Fables of Esope
Caxton's Book of Curtesye (Caxton), 47, 63
Cay, The (Taylor), 64, 93, 115, 403, 414
Cazet, Denys, 201
Ceceoli, Nicoletta, 224
Cecil, Nancy Lee, 69
Cecil, Randy, 199
Celebrate America: In Poetry and Art (Panzer), 144, 158
Celebrations (Livingston), 340, 358
Celery Stalks at Midnight, The (Howe), 311
Cello of Mr. O, The (Couch), 129, 155, 202
Celtic Fairy Tales (Jacobs), 263
Celtic Fairy Tales (Philip), 221, 264
Cendrars, Blaise, 106, 112, 132, 155, 201
Cendrillon: A Caribbean Cinderella (San Souci), 114
Censorship (Riley), 65
Central Heating: Poems, About Fire and Warmth (Singer), 339, 359
Century of African American Art, A (Amaki), 147
Century That Was, The: Reflections on the Last One Hundred Years (Giblin), 32, 33, 515, 531, 537

Cepeda, Joe, 313
Ceremony of Innocence, The (Highwater), 390, 412
Cerullo, Mary M., 537
César: ¡Sí, Se Puede! Yes, We Can (Bernier-Grand), 344, 355
Cezanne Pinto: A Memoir (Stolz), 92, 114
Chaikin, Miriam, 268
Chair for My Mother, A (Williams), 30, 188, 206
Chalk, Gary, 312
Chance, Rosemary, 84
Chandler, Robert, 266
Chandra, Deborah, 342
Chang, Margaret A., 76
"Change" (Zolotow), 334
Changeover, The (Mahy), 312
Changes, Changes (Hutchins), 12, 13, 174, 175, 200
Chanticleer and the Fox (Cooney), 135, 155
Chanukkah Guest, The (Kimmel), 197, 203
Chanukkah Tree, The (Kimmel), 184, 203
Chap-Books of the Eighteenth Century (Ashton), 47
Chapman, Jane, 205, 538
Chapman, Raymond, 58, 157
Charles Eastman: Physician, Reformer, and Native American Leader (Anderson), 474, 495
"Charlie Balch's Metamorphosis," 57
Charlie Needs a Cloak (dePaola), 155
Charlip, Remy, 172, 199
Charlot, Jean, 412
Charlotte's Web (White), 14, 39, 77, 86, 110, 115, 194, 290, 314, 481
Chase, Richard, 266
Chasing Redbird (Creech), 384, 411
Chaucer, Geoffrey, 79, 112, 155, 255, 263
Cheatham, Bertha M.
Chee, Cheng-Khee, 160, 335, 356, 360
Chen, Chih-Yuan, 31, 186, 201
Cheng, Andrea, 394, 410
Cherry, Lynne, 360
Chess, Victoria, 206, 359
Chester (Hoff), 200
Chester Cricket's Pigeon Ride (Selden), 289, 313
Chhaniara, Niela, 263
Chicka Chicka Boom Boom (Martin & Archambault), 170, 199
Chicken Little (Kellogg), 264
Chicken Sisters, The (Numeroff), 204
Chief Sarah: Sarah Winnemucca's Fight for Indian Rights (Morrison), 484, 497
Chi-Hoon: A Korean Girl (McMahon), 148, 158, 392, 413
Child, Lauren, 185, 202
Child of the Owl (Yep), 393, 414
Children of Green Knowe, The (Boston), 63, 295, 296, 303, 310
Children of Israel, Children of Palestine: Our Own True Stories (Holliday), 485, 496
Children of Lir, The (MacGill-Callahan), 158
Children of Odin, The: The Book of Northern Myths (Colum), 245, 268, 302, 311
Children of the Gold Rush (Murphy & Haigh), 511, 540
Children of the Midnight Sun: Young Native Voices of Alaska (Brown), 151, 154
Children's Book Illustration: Step by Step Techniques (Bossert), 146
Children's Book Publishing in Britain Since 1945 (Reynolds & Tucker), 44

Children's Literary Houses: Famous Dwellings in Children's Fiction (Ashe & Tuttle), 108
Children's Literature and Its Effects (Cullingford), 44
Children's Step-by-Step Cookbook, The (Wilkes), 530, 542
Children's Zoo, A (Hoban), 538
Children Tell Stories: A Teaching Guide (Hamilton & Weiss), 255
Children We Remember, The (Abells), 148, 154
Children Who Smelled a Rat, The (Ahlberg), 32
Child's Book of Art, A: Great Pictures, First Words (Micklethwait), 32, 140–141, 158
Child's Book of Play in Art, A: Great Pictures, Great Fun (Micklethwait), 14, 15, 528, 540
Child's Book of Prayer in Art, A (Beckett), 154
Child's Christmas in Wales, A (Thomas), 7, 96, 115, 152, 159, 190, 205
Child's Garden of Verses, A (Stevenson), 5, 63, 320, 360
Child's Geography of the World, A (Hillyer), 504
Child's Introduction to Poetry, A (Driscoll), 10, 318, 324, 329, 332, 356
Childtimes: A Three-Generation Memoir (Greenfield & Little), 485–486, 496
Chi-Lin Purse, The: A Collection of Ancient Chinese Stories (Fang), 263
Chimpanzee Family Book, The (Goodall), 523, 538
Chimpanzees I Love, The: Saving Their World and Ours (Goodall), 538
Chin Chiang and the Dragon's Dance (Wallace), 148, 160, 392, 414
Chinese Cinderella and the Secret Dragon Society (Mah), 449–450, 459
Chinese Fairy Tales and Fantasies (Roberts), 218, 263
Chinese Folk Tales (Kuo & Kuo), 260, 263
Chinese Mirror, The (Ginsburg), 263
Chinese Mother Goose Rhymes (Wyndham), 166, 198
Chin-Lee, Cynthia, 170, 198
Chipman, Liz, 88, 112
Chitty Chitty Bang Bang (Fleming), 291, 311
"Chocolate Cake" (Prelutsky), 350
Chocolate War, The (Cormier), 66, 77, 112
Choldenko, Gennifer, 20, 22, 102, 378, 410
Chollat, Emilie, 267
Choose the Right College & Get Accepted (Hutchins), 22
Chotjewitz, David, 82, 112, 451, 457
Chow, Octavio, 265
Christelow, Eileen, 12, 14, 199, 506, 537
Christensen, Bonnie, 157
Christian, Peggy, 355, 537
Christiana, David, 360, 536
Christie, Gregory, 355
Christie, R. Gregory, 203
Christina Katerina and the Time She Quit the Family (Gauch), 202, 402, 411
Christmas Carol, A (Dickens), 63, 155
Christopher: The Holy Giant (dePaola), 136, 155
Christopher, John, 64, 299–300, 305, 310
Christopher, Matt, 397, 398, 410, 495
Christopher Columbus: How He Did It (Yue & Yue), 532
Chrysanthemum (Henkes), 25
Chuck Close, Up Close (Greenberg & Jordan), 480, 496

Chumash, The (Bial), 509, 536
Chums, 57
Chung, Chi, 356
Church, Caroline Jayne, 160, 205
Cianciolo, Patricia, 163, 192
Ciardi, John, 324, 325, 327, 333, 349, 355–356
"Cicadas" (Fleischman), 336, 337
Cieslawski, Steve, 98, 358
"Cinderella," 80, 209, 211, 219, 232, 239, 257–259, 276
Cinderella (Brown), 120, 121, 153, 158, 221–222
Cinderella (Crane), 54
Cinderella (Ehrlich), 158
"Cinderella" (Grimm & Grimm), 52, 223, 258
Cinderella (Perrault), 71, 221, 222, 258, 264
Cinderella (Wegman), 264
"Cinderella: or The Little Glass Slipper" (Perrault), 217
"Cinnamon Tree in the Moon, The," 217
Circa 1492: Art in the Age of Exploration (Levenson), 149, 151
Circle of Fire (Hooks), 418, 458
Circle of Magic (Pierce), 313
Circle of Seasons, A (Livingston), 134, 157, 340, 358
Circles, Triangles, and Squares (Hoban), 12, 200
Circle Spinning: Jewish Turning and Returning Tales (Schwartz), 251, 265
Circus: An Album (Granfield), 538
Cisneros, Sandra, 392, 410
"Cite the Source: Reducing Cultural Chaos in Picture Books, Part One" (Hearne), 214
City of Gold and Lead, The (Christopher), 300, 305, 310
Civil Liberties (Ojeda), 531, 540
Civil Rights Movement in America from 1865 to the Present, The (McKissack & McKissack), 32, 516, 540
Clapp, Patricia, 64, 416, 430, 457
Clark, Emma Chichester, 267, 268, 310
Clark, Margaret, 310
Classic Connections: Turning Teens on to Great Literature (Koelling), 44
Clatter Bash! A Day of the Dead Celebration (Keep), 132, 149, 152, 157
Clay, Marie, 9
Cleary, Beverly, 14, 33, 63, 80, 112, 285, 310–311, 363, 369, 374–375, 384–385, 403, 410, 482, 495
Cleaver, Bill, 64, 70, 71, 363, 375–376, 410
Cleaver, Elizabeth, 356
Cleaver, Vera, 64, 70, 71, 363, 375–376, 410
Clee, Paul, 15
Clemens, Samuel. See Twain, Mark
Clément, Frédéric, 263, 496
Clements, Andrew, 377, 410–411
Clemesha, David, 206
Cleopatra (Stanley & Vennema), 471, 498
Clever Crow (Defelice), 295
"Clever Wife, The," 217
Clever Woman of the Family, The (Yonge), 45, 57
Click, Clack, Moo: Cows That Type (Cronin), 6, 107, 112, 128, 155, 183, 194, 202
Clickety Clack (Spence & Spence), 8
Clifton, Lucille, 516
Climo, Shirley, 263, 265
Clinton, Catherine, 382, 411, 514, 537
Clouds of Glory (Chaikin), 268

Clown of God, The (dePaola), 64, 135–136, 155, 202
Clubwomen's Daughters, The: Collective Impulses in Progressive-Era Girl's Fiction, 1890–1940 (Tarbox), 44
Cluck O'Clock (Gray), 18
Coast to Coast (Byars), 398, 410
Cober, Allan E., 269, 311
Cocca-Leffler, Maryann, 201
Cock-A-Doodle-DOO (Lavis), 199
Cockcroft, James, 149, 155, 480, 495
CoConis, Constantinos, 268
CoConis, Ted, 410
Code Talker (Bruchac), 451, 457
Coerr, Eleanor, 32
Cogan, Jim, 256
Coggins, Margaret, 490
Cohen, Barbara, 112, 155, 255, 263
Cohen, Caron Lee, 104, 199, 364
Cohen, Lisa, 482, 498
Cohen, Miriam, 24
Cohn, Amy L., 236, 266, 474, 495
Cold War: The American Crusade Against World Communism (Warren), 542
Cole, Brock, 33, 80–81, 112, 179, 202, 411
Cole, Joanna, 40, 177–178, 197, 200, 201, 504, 521, 527, 537
Cole, William, 356
Coleman, Wanda, 346
Coleridge, Samuel Taylor, 328
Coles, Martin, 101
Colfer, Eoin, 311
Collard, Sneed B., 502–503, 537
Collector of Moments, The (Buchholz), 196, 201
Collicott, Sharleen, 204
Collier, Brian, 202
Collier, Christopher, 66
Collier, James, 66
Collington, Peter, 9
Collins, Billy, 319
Collodi, Carlo, 63, 291, 311
Colman, Penny, 537
Colón, Raúl, 202, 267, 357, 498
Color of His Own, A (Lionni), 157
Colum, Padraic, 244, 245, 268, 302, 311
Columbus (D'Aulaire & D'Aulaire), 469
Columbus (Demi), 495
Come a Tide (Lyon), 204
Come Back, Salmon (Cone), 39, 526, 537
Come Lasses and Lads (Caldecott), 54, 154
Come Look with Me: World of Play (Blizzard), 149, 154
Comenius, Johann Amos, 53, 54, 55
Come Sing, Jimmy Jo (Paterson), 413
Come Sunday (Grimes), 357
Come to My Party and Other Shape Poems (Roemer), 324–325, 359
Come to the Ocean's Edge (Pringle), 520
Comets and Shooting Stars (Moore), 526, 540
"Come Up From the Fields Farther" (Whitman), 334
Comfort Creek (McDonald), 413
Coming of the Bear, The (Namioka), 459
Coming On Home Soon (Woodson), 152, 160, 189, 190, 206
Commander in Chief: Abraham Lincoln in the Civil War (Marrin), 474, 497

Commodore Perry in the Land of the Shogun (Blumberg), 19, 64, 148, 154, 473, 495, 505, 532, 536
Complete Brothers Grimm Fairy Tales (Grimm & Grimm), 223, 264 See also Brothers Grimm
Complete Nonsense Book, The (Lear), 357
Complete Poems of Emily Dickinson, The (Dickinson), 350, 356
Condra, Estelle, 202
Cone, Molly, 39, 526, 537
Conestoga Wagons (Ammon), 536
Confessions of a Teenage Drama Queen (Sheldon), 414
Confucius: The Golden Rule (Freedman), 471, 496
Conger, John Janeway, 11
Conklin, Paul, 536
Conly, Jane Leslie, 285, 311, 411
Conover, Sarah, 254, 266–267
Conrad, Pam, 202, 296–297, 311, 457
Constance: A Story of Early Plymouth (Clapp), 416, 430, 457
Contes de ma Mère l'Oye (Perrault). See Tales of Mother Goose
Cook, Lyn, 198
Cook, Sally, 202, 342, 356
Cook, Scott, 204, 239, 267, 360
Coolidge, Olivia, 63, 244, 245, 254, 268
Cool Melons—Turn to Frogs! The Life and Poems of Issa (Gollub), 330, 356
Coomaraswamy, Ananda K., 251, 267
Cooney, Barbara, 121, 135, 153, 154, 155, 156, 158, 160, 197, 201, 202, 206, 235, 265, 355, 359, 475, 495
Cooper, Floyd, 414, 459
Cooper, Helen, 5, 112, 126, 155, 202
Cooper, James Fenimore, 63
Cooper, Michael L., 14, 17, 457, 511, 525, 537
Cooper, Susan, 10, 33, 39, 102, 221, 263, 283, 295, 297, 300, 302, 311
Cooperative Children's Book Center, 464, 502
Cooper-Solomon, Debra, 146, 195
Coorper, Floyd, 202
Copley, John Singleton, 130
Corcoran, Barbara, 411
Cormier, Robert, 66, 77, 112, 383, 384, 397, 411, 446, 457
Cornell, Kari, 530, 537
Cornell, Laura, 202, 356
Corpses, Coffins, and Crypts: A History of Burial (Colman), 537
Corral, Roy, 154
Couch, Greg, 129, 155, 202
Could Be Worse! (Stevenson), 183, 196, 205
Couloumbis, Audrey, 104, 112, 363, 384, 411
Count! (Fleming), 12, 199
Count and See (Hoban), 172, 199
Countdown to Independence: A Revolution of Ideas in England and Her American Colonies: 1760–1776 (Bober), 112, 503, 536
Counting Crocodiles (Sierra), 13, 199
Count on Us: American Women in the Military (Nathan), 540
Country Crossing (Aylesworth), 154
Count with Maisy (Cousins), 168, 198
Count Your Way Through Italy (Haskins), 14, 173, 199
Courage of Sarah Noble, The (Dalgliesh), 454, 455, 456, 457

Courlander, Harold, 213
Cousins, Lucy, 168, 198
Covered Bridge House and Other Poems, The (Starbird), 349, 360
Cowan, Catherine, 204
Cowley, Joy, 498, 537
Cow Who Wouldn't Come Down, The (Johnson), 203
Cracker Jackson (Byars), 363, 377, 410
Craft, Kinoko Y., 225, 264
"Crafting Math Stories" (Lipke), 256
"Crafting Science Stories" (Stallings), 256
"Crafting Social Studies Story Lifeline" (Cogan), 256
Craig, David, 495
Craig, Helen, 267
Crampton, Patricia, 112, 154, 422, 458
Crandell, Rachel, 149, 155
Crane, Freda, 254, 266–267
Crane, Walter, 45, 54, 55, 71, 124, 155
"Crane and Two Brothers, A" (Philip), 260
"Crane Wife, The," 210, 211, 219, 220
Crane Wife, The (Bodkin), 263
Crane Wife, The (Yagawa), 128, 160, 230, 263
Crawford, Elizabeth, 264, 412, 458
Crazy Lady! (Conly), 411
Creation, The (Johnson), 157
"Creation of Animals, The" (Markman & Markman), 251
"Creation of the Sun and Moon, The" (Markman & Markman), 251
Creature Carnival (Singer), 359
Creech, Sharon, 20, 22, 86, 88–89, 92, 112, 327, 339, 356, 366, 375, 380, 384, 390, 411
Creeden, Sharon, 259
Creepy, Crawly Baby Bugs (Markle), 519, 539
Creepy, Crawly Caterpillars (Facklam), 519, 533, 537
Crews, Donald, 12, 173–174, 199, 200, 202, 387, 411
Crews, Nina, 165, 197
Cricket in Times Square, The (Selden), 289, 313
Crockett-Blassingame, Linda, 202
Croggon, Alison, 300, 311
Cromwell's Boy (Haugaard), 430, 458
Cronin, Doreen, 6, 107, 112, 128, 152, 155, 180, 183, 194, 202
"Crooked Road Walker" (Diakite), 234
Crossing, The (Paulsen), 392, 413
Crossing Bok Chitto (Tingle), 252
Crossley-Holland, Kevin, 107, 112, 131, 155, 221, 244, 245, 247, 250, 263, 268, 269, 280–281, 300, 302, 311, 316, 327, 332, 356
Crow, Thomas, 153
Crow Boy (Yashima), 123, 153, 160
Crow-Girl, The: The Children of Crow Cove (Bredsdorff), 22, 366, 410
Crowley, Joy, 168, 198
Crowning Glory (Thomas), 339, 360
Cruikshank, George, 55
Crum, Robert, 536
Crunk, Tony, 202
Crutcher, Chris, 397–398, 411
Crutches (Hartling), 446, 458
Cruz, Ray, 128, 160, 205, 413
"Cry of the Children, The" (Browning), 57
Cry of the Crow, The (George), 411
Cuckoo: A Mexican Folktale (Ehlert), 155, 235, 265
Cuckoo's Child, The (Freeman), 411

Cullingford, Cedric, 37, 39, 44
Cully, Cully and the Bear (Gage), 302, 311
Cummings, Pat, 33, 40, 146, 155
Cummins, Julie, 470, 495
"Cunning Cat, The," 219
Cunningham, Julia, 411
Cunningham, Patria, 2
Cupid and Psyche (Barth), 243, 268
Curious George (Rey), 186, 204
Curlee, Lynn, 537
Curriculum Connections, 535
Curse of the Ring, The (Harrison), 268, 302
Curtis, Carolyn, 4, 6, 129, 130, 155, 182, 202
Curtis, Christopher Paul, 32, 81, 112, 418, 437, 457
Curtis, Jamie Lee, 21, 28, 202
Cushing, Frank Hamilton, 237, 266
Cushman, Doug, 115, 200
Cushman, Karen, 96, 110, 111, 112, 418, 422, 426–427, 439, 457
Cut from the Same Cloth: American Women of Myth, Legend, and Tall Tale (San Souci), 239, 267
Cutler, Jane, 129, 155, 181, 202, 411
Cybil War, The (Byars), 33, 398, 410
Cyrus the Unsinkable Sea Serpent (Peet), 204

Dabcovich, Lydia, 112
Daddy Darwin's Dovecot (Ewing), 56
"Daddy Longlegs, The" (Florian), 350
Dadey, Debbie, 202
Dahl, Roald, 291, 311
Daisy Chain, The (Yonge), 45, 57, 63, 67
Daisy Says "Goo!" (Simmons), 5, 168, 198
Daisy's Day Out (Simmons), 168, 198
Daisy's Hide and Seek (Simmons), 168, 198
Dale, Jim, 309
Dale, Shelly, 536
Dalgliesh, Alice, 454, 455, 456, 457
D'Alleva, Anne, 151, 153
Dalokay, Vedat, 476, 495
Daly, Niki, 31, 203, 445, 457
Dame, Enid, 346
Dance Away (Shannon), 159
Dancers in the Garden (Ryder), 541
Dancing Carl (Paulsen), 413
Dancing Turtle, The: A Folktale from Brazil (De Spain), 235, 265
Dancing with Dziadziu (Bartoletti), 386, 409
Dangerous Skies (Staples), 370, 414
Daniel Boone (Daugherty), 63
Daniel Half Human and the Good Nazi (Chotjewitz), 82, 112, 451, 457
Daniel's Duck (Bulla), 200
Danitra Brown Leaves Town (Grimes), 342, 357
Dante Alighieri, 66
Danziger, Paula, 411
Darcy and Gran Don't Like Babies (Cutler), 181, 202
Dark Hills Divide, The: The Land of Elyon (Carman), 310
Dark Is Rising, The (Cooper), 283, 311
Darkness and the Butterfly (Grifalconi), 109, 113
Darkness over Denmark: The Danish Resistance and the Rescue of the Jews (Levine), 515, 539
Dark Side of Nowhere, The (Shusterman), 313
Darling, Benjamin, 386, 411
Darling, Louis, 112, 310, 311, 410
Darton, F. J. Harvey, 52
Dasent, Sir George Webbe, 225–226, 266
Dash, Joan, 483, 495

Dashing Through the Snow: The Story of the Jr. Iditarod (Shahan), 541
Dateline: Troy (Fleischman), 112, 244, 268
Daugherty, James, 63, 498
Daughter of Earth: A Roman Myth (McDermott), 243, 268
D'Aulaire, Edgar Parin, 245, 268, 469, 495
D'Aulaire, Ingri, 245, 268, 469, 495
D'Aulaires' Book of Greek Myths (D'Aulaire & D'Aulaire), 268
Davalos, Felipe, 411
Davenier, Christine, 203, 357
David and Max (Provost & Levine-Provost), 386, 414
Davie, Helen K., 126
Davies, Jacqueline, 131, 155, 480, 495
Davis, Anita P., 370
Davis, Jenny, 376, 411
Davis, Jill, 482–483, 495
Davis, Joann, 138
Davis, Joy B., 371
Davis, Lambert, 458
Davis, Marguerite, 359
Davis, Nancy, 356
Davis, Russell, 234
Davison, Marvin Gary, 254, 263
Dawes, Kwame Senu Neville, 344, 356
Day, Alexandra, 107, 110, 112
Day, Edward C., 239, 267
Day, Nancy Raine, 155, 233, 262
Day at the New Amsterdam Theatre, A (Amendola), 529, 535, 537
Day Gogo Went to Vote, The: South Africa, April 1994 (Sisulu), 188, 205, 387, 414
Day of Ahmed's Secret, The (Heide & Gilliland), 28–29
Days of the Blackbird: A Tale of Northern Italy (dePaola), 267
Day the Babies Crawled Away, The (Rathmann), 102
Day the Goose Got Loose, The (Lindbergh), 197, 204
Deacon, Alexis, 203
"Dead Princess and the Seven Heroes, The" (Pushkin), 227
"Dead Tree" (Froman), 329
DeAngeli, Marguerite, 426, 427, 457
Dear Mili (Grimm), 156, 264
Dear Mr. Blueberry (James), 203
Dear Mr. Henshaw (Cleary), 363, 374–375, 403, 410
Dear Nobody (Doherty), 371, 411
Dear World (Noda), 339, 358
Dear Zoo (Campbell), 12, 198
Death of the Iron Horse (Goble), 156
de Beaumont, Madame, 217, 222, 264
de Brunhoff, Jean, 63, 144, 155, 186, 202
de Brunhoff, Laurent, 202
Debussy, Claude, 316
Deenie (Blume), 410
Defelice, Cynthia, 6, 202, 295, 296, 311
Defoe, Daniel, 45, 49–50, 51, 60, 63, 66
Degan, Bruce, 537
Degas and the Dance: The Painter and the Petits Rats, Perfecting Their Art (Rubin), 146, 159
Degen, Bruce, 201, 356
Degen, Chris, 356
deGroat, Diane, 375, 412, 413

Dejong, Meindert, 110
DeKay, James T.
de Kiefte, Kees, 413
Delacre, Lulu, 391, 411
de la Mare, Walter, 264
Delano, Marfé Ferguson, 465, 466, 470, 490, 495
Delicado, Federico, 412
Delton, Judy, 411
de Marcken, Gail, 17
Demarest, Chris L., 6, 169, 198
Demi, 32, 233, 260, 263, 265, 267, 356, 360, 471, 476, 492, 495
Dempsey, Frank J., 465
Dendy, Leslie, 501, 537
Denenberg, Barry, 476–477, 486, 495
Dengler, Marianna, 311
Dennis, Wesley, 412
Dennison, Amy, 22
Denslow, W. W., 310
Denton, Terry, 202
dePaola, Tomie, 64, 110, 112, 125, 135–136, 137, 155, 158, 165, 166, 188, 197, 200, 202, 235, 237, 263, 265, 266, 267, 327, 358, 482, 495, 537
de Regniers, Beatrice Schenk, 321, 331, 335, 356
Desert Giant: The World of Saguaro Cactus (Bash), 524, 536
Desert Is Theirs, The (Baylor), 336, 355
Desert Song (Johnston), 157
Desert Voices (Baylor), 336, 355
Desimini, Lisa, 262, 355
De Spain, Pleasant, 235, 265
Devereaux, Elizabeth, 279
Devil's Arithmetic, The (Yolen), 108, 115, 297, 314, 447, 460
Devil with the Three Golden Hairs, The (Grimm & Grimm), 302
Devil with the Three Golden Hairs, The (Hogrogian), 311
Dewey, Ariane, 64, 159, 266
Dewey, Jennifer Owings, 151, 155, 460, 541
Dewey, John, 67
De Wit, Dorothy, 291
d'Harcourt, Claire, 141, 155
Diakite, Baba Wague, 234, 262
Diamond, Donna, 91, 114, 411, 413
"Diamond and the Toads" (Perrault), 221
Diamond Tree, The: Jewish Tales from Around the World (Schwartz & Rush), 228, 229, 265
Diaz, David, 123, 132, 153, 154, 196, 199, 201, 355, 356, 380, 497
Diaz, James, 155, 529, 537
DiCamillo, Kate, 7, 32, 64, 94, 96, 112, 274, 311, 363, 372, 375, 411
Dicey's Song (Voigt), 110, 115, 364, 366, 370, 414
Dickens, Charles, 57, 63, 155
Dickinson, Emily, 317, 334, 342, 346, 350, 356
Dickinson, Peter, 295, 311
Dicks, Jan Thompson, 414
"Dick Whittington," 211
Dictionary of Imaginary Places, The (Manguel & Guadalupi), 108
"Diddle Diddle Dumpling," 164
Diego (Winter), 160, 480, 498
Diego Rivera (Cockcroft), 149, 155, 480, 495
Diego Rivera: A Retrospective (Helms), 480, 496
Diego Velásquez (Venezia), 15, 146, 159
Different Dragons (Little), 412

Digging for Bird-Dinosaurs: An Expedition to Madagascar (Bishop), 498, 518, 532, 536
DiGrazia, Thomas, 309
Dillon, Diane, 111, 113, 126, 129, 136–137, 146, 152, 153, 154, 156, 158, 160, 170, 199, 201, 204, 262, 263, 266, 360
Dillon, Leo, 111, 113, 126, 129, 136–137, 146, 152, 153, 154, 156, 158, 160, 170, 199, 201, 204, 262, 263, 266, 360
Dinesen, Isak, 320
Dingus, Lowell, 502, 519, 540
Dinosaur! (Sís), 176, 200
Dinosaur Bob and His Adventures with the Family Lazardo (Joyce), 203
Dinosaur Ghosts: The Mysteries of Coelophysis (Gillette), 518–519, 538
Dinosaur Mountain: Graveyard of the Past (Arnold), 518
Dinosaur Named Sue, A: The Story of the Colossal Fossil: The World's Most Complete T. Rex (Relf), 541
Dinosaurs (Gibbons), 518, 537
Dinosaurs (Hopkins), 338, 357
Dinosaurs Are Back and It's All Your Fault Edward, The! (Hartmann & Daly), 31, 203
Dinosaurs at the Ends of the Earth: The Story of the Central Asian Expeditions (Floca), 519, 537
Dinosaurs Forever (Wise), 338, 360
Dinosaurs of Waterhouse Hawkins, The (Kerley), 153, 157, 468, 497
Dinosaurs to the Rescue! A Guide to Protecting Our Planet (Brown & Brown), 536
Dinosaur Worlds (Lessem), 498, 539
"Dino-Sore" (Scieszka), 350
Dirt Bike Racer (Christopher), 410
Dirty Stinky Sneakers (Bunting), 400
Disappearing Alphabet, The (Wilbur), 169, 199
Disappearing Lake: Nature's Magic in Denali National Park (Miller), 540
Disasters in Space Exploration (Vogt), 542
Discoverers of America, The (Faber), 537
Discovering El Niño: How Fable and Fact Together Help Explain the Weather (Seibert), 525, 541
Disher, Garry, 457
Diterlizzi, Tony, 157
Diverting History of John Gilpin, The (Caldecott), 54, 55
"Dizzy" (Fleming), 8
Doctor Coyote: A Native American Aesop's Fables (Bierhorst), 241, 257, 265, 267
Doctor De Soto (Steig), 102
Doctors Help People (Moses), 540
Dodge, Mary Elizabeth Mapes, 62, 63
Dodgson, Charles L.. See Carroll, Lewis
"Dog and the Bone, The" (Yolen), 241
Dog of Discovery: A Newfoundland's Adventures with Lewis and Clark (Pringle), 520
Dogsong (Paulsen), 32, 390, 413
Doherty, Berlie, 371, 411
Doherty, Paul, 540
Dole, J. G., 105
Dolls' House, The (Godden), 290, 311
Domenico, Gino, 535, 537
Donahue, Dorothy, 413
Donelson, Kenneth L., 77, 99, 100, 195, 300–301, 368–369, 372
"Dong with the Luminous Nose, The" (Lear), 58
"Donkey, the Table, and the Stick, The," 212

Donnan, Kristin, 502, 503, 506, 539
Donnelly, Jennifer, 22, 451–452, 457
Don Quixote and the Windmills (Kimmel), 22
"Don't Ever Seize a Weasel by the Tail" (Prelutsky), 321, 333
Don't Forget to Come Back! (Harris), 21, 180, 202
Don't Hold Me Back: My Life and Art (Rembert), 147, 158, 480, 498
Don't Look Behind You (Duncan), 383, 411
Don't Make Me Smile (Park), 413
Don't You Know There's a War On? (Stevenson), 205
Doodler Doodling (Gelman), 156
Doodle Soup (Ciardi), 333, 355
Doolittle, Michael J., 538
Door in the Wall, The (DeAngeli), 426, 427, 457
Doorlag, Donald, 77
Dora's Eggs (Sykes), 205
Dorris, Michael, 112, 418, 428–429, 457
Dorson, Mercedes, 236, 265
Doty, Mark, 345–346
Double Life of Pocahontas, The (Fritz), 484, 496
Downes, Lawrence, 302–303
Downey, William R., 541
Downie, Mary Alice, 349, 356
Downing, Julie, 205, 312
Doyle, Arthur Conan, 63, 311
Doyle, Gerald, 309
Do You Want to Be My Friend? (Carle), 24, 200
Do You Want to Play? A Book About Being Friends (Kolar), 157
Dragonflies (McLaughlin), 519, 540
Dragonology: The Complete Book of Dragons (Steer), 248, 249, 260–261, 269
Dragonology Handbook, The: A Practical Course in Dragons (Steer), 248, 269
Dragonquest (McCaffrey), 312
Dragon Rider (Funke), 248, 273, 283–284, 302, 311
Dragonriders of Pern, The (McCaffrey), 312
Dragons Are Singing Tonight, The (Prelutsky), 333, 359
Dragon's Blood (Yolen), 314
Dragon's Gate (Yep), 439, 460
Dragonsinger (McCaffrey), 299, 312
Dragonsong (McCaffrey), 299, 312
Dragonwings (Yep), 64, 439–440, 460, 524
Drake, W. H., 288
Drawing Stories from Around the World (Pellowski), 254, 267
Dr. Dredd's Wagon of Wonders (Brittain), 302, 310
Dream Keeper, The (Hughes), 343, 357
Dream of Freedom, A: The Civil Rights Movement from 1954 to 1968 (McWhorter), 11, 92, 113, 516, 530, 540
Dreamplace (Lyon), 204
"Dreams" (Hughes), 343
Dreams (Keats), 203
Dream-Weaver (Lawrence), 312
Drescher, Henrik, 144
Dressel, Janice Hartwick, 134
Dressing (Oxenbury), 4, 5, 198
Drez, Ronald J., 515, 537
"Drifter, The" (Nelson), 345
Drinking Gourd, The (Monjo), 32, 35, 435, 459
Drinkwater, John, 343
Driscoll, Michael, 10, 318, 324, 329, 332, 356
Drop of Blood, A (Showers), 19, 504, 517, 541
Drummer Hoff (Emberley), 155, 198, 202

Drums of Noto Hanto, The (James), 126, 157
Drury, John, 318, 325, 329, 330
Dryer, Charles Redway, 504
Duck for President (Cronin), 152, 155, 180, 202
Duffy, Carol Ann, 342, 356
Duffy, Gerald, 105
Duffy and the Devil (Zemach), 221, 264
Duggleby, John, 155, 495
Duke, Kate, 507, 537
Dulac, Edmund, 128, 150, 155, 158, 265
Dulcken, H. W., 309
Dunbar, Paul Laurence, 17, 155
Duncan, Dayton, 494
Duncan, Lois, 17, 238, 266, 383, 411
Dundes, Alan, 257
Dunleavy, Deborah, 7, 529, 537
Dunn, Stephen, 346
Dunning, Stephen, 40, 324, 343, 354, 356
Dunrea, Olivier, 29, 155, 495
Duntz, Dorothee, 309
Durango Street (Bonham), 410
Dürer, Albrecht, 130
Dustland (Hamilton), 311
Dust to Eat: Drought and Depression in the 1930s (Cooper), 14, 17, 457, 525, 537
Duvoisin, Roger, 186, 202
Dyer, Jane, 8–9, 21, 185, 202, 355, 356, 357, 360

Each Orange Had Eight Slices: A Counting Book (Giganti), 199
Each Peach Pear Plum: An I-Spy Story (Ahlberg & Ahlberg), 201
Eagle of the Ninth, The (Sutcliff), 63, 459
Earle, Sylvia A., 502, 537
Earliest Americans, The (Sattler), 541
Early, Margaret, 100, 248, 268–269, 327, 358
Early American Christmas, An (dePaola), 136, 155, 202
Early Humans (Merriman), 540
Early Morning in the Barn (Tafuri), 5
"Earth Charged in Meteor's Fiery Death" (Peters), 339
Ear, the Eye, and the Arm, The (Farmer), 102, 299, 311
"Earth on Turtle's Back, The" (Caduto & Bruchac), 245
Earthquakes (Simon), 524, 541
Earthshake: Poems From the Ground Up (Peters), 339, 359
Earth Verses and Water Rhymes (Lewis), 321, 357
East (Pattou), 276, 313
East African Folktales (Kituku), 234, 262
Easter Egg Farm, The (Auch), 201
"East of the Sun and West of the Moon," 211, 217, 219, 223, 243, 276
East of the Sun and West of the Moon (Hague & Hague), 266
East of the Sun and West of the Moon (Mayer), 226, 266
East of the Sun & West of the Moon: A Play (Willard), 226, 266
East O' the Sun and West O' the Moon (Dasent), 226, 266
Eating Fractions (McMillan), 14, 199
Eating the Alphabet: Fruits and Vegetables from A to Z (Ehlert), 170, 198
E.B. White: Some Writer! (Gherman), 481, 496
Eccleshare, Julie, 372

Echoes of the Elders: The Stories and Paintings of Chief Lelooska (Normandin), 237
Edelstein, Terese, 460
Ed Emberley's Picture Pie 2: A Drawing Book and Stencil (Emberley), 19, 155
Edens, Cooper, 197
Edmonds, Walter D., 112
Edward and the Pirates (McPhail), 10, 204
Edward Lear Alphabet, An (Lear), 199
Edwards, Michelle, 32
Edwards, Pamela Duncan, 6, 165, 192, 197
Eggleston, Edward, 60
Egielski, Richard, 124, 127–128, 153, 160, 179, 202, 206
Egoff, Sheila, 369
Egypt Game, The (Snyder), 414
Egyptian Cinderella, The (Climo), 265
Egyptology: Search for the Tomb of Osiris (Sands), 145, 150, 159
Ehlert, Lois, 40, 117, 145, 155, 170, 198, 202, 235, 265
Ehrlich, Amy, 158, 309, 310, 466, 467, 494, 495
Ehrlich, Paul R., 502
Eichenberg, Fritz, 289
Eight Cousins (Alcott), 61
18th Emergency, The (Byars), 410
Einsel, Naiad, 311
Einstein: Visionary Scientist (Severance), 466, 498
Einzig, Susan, 114
Eisenman, Stephen F., 153
Eises, Rachel, 234
Eitan, Ora, 202, 204
Elder Edda, 244, 280
Eleanor (Cooney), 155, 475, 495
Eleanor Roosevelt (Goodsell), 496
Eleanor Roosevelt (Whitney), 498
Eleanor Roosevelt: A Life of Discovery (Freedman), 19, 33, 80, 112, 475–476, 491, 496
Eleanor Roosevelt, with Love (Roosevelt), 498
"Electric Eel" (Kennedy), 350
Elements of Pop-Up, The (Carter & Diaz), 155, 537
Elena's Serenade (Geeslin), 21, 129, 156, 202
Elephant in the Backyard, An (Sobol), 541
"Elephant's Child, The" (Kipling), 288, 312
"Eletelephony" (Richards), 332, 349
Elidor (Garner), 311
Eliot, T. S., 337, 356
Elisabeth (Nivola), 204
Elizabethan England (Ashby), 510, 536
Ella Enchanted (Levine), 113, 267, 276, 312
Ella Fitzgerald: The Tale of a Vocal Virtuoso (Pinkney), 482, 497
Ella's Big Chance (Hughes), 31
Elleman, Barbara, 504
Ellington Was Not a Street (Shange), 152, 153, 159, 180, 205, 344, 359, 498
Elliott, Elizabeth Shippen Green, 113
Ellis, Jan Davey, 541
Ellis, Rex M., 239
Ellis, Sarah, 411
"Elves and the Shoemaker, The" (Grimm & Grimm), 52
Elya, Susan Middleton, 395, 411
Emberley, Barbara, 155, 198, 202
Emberley, Ed, 14, 19, 20, 155, 198, 202
Emberley, Michael, 194, 203, 517, 538

Emerald Lizard, The: Fifteen Latin American Tales to Tell (De Spain), 265
Emile (Rousseau), 45, 51, 66
Emily (Bedard), 135, 154, 201, 317, 355
Emily Dickinson's Letters to the World (Winter), 334, 360
Emily's Art (Catalanotto), 155
Emily's First 100 Days of School (Wells), 14, 172, 174, 200
Emma's Strange Pet (Little), 200
Emperor's Egg, The (Jenkins), 523, 538
Emperor's New Clothes: A Tale Set in China (Demi), 492
Emperor's New Clothes (Duntz), 309
Emperor's New Clothes (Levison), 309
Emperor's New Clothes (Rockwell), 309
Emperor's New Clothes, The (Sedgwick), 313
Empire State Building: When New York Reached for the Skies (Mann), 19, 505, 539
Empty Pot, The (Demi), 260, 263
Enchanted Anklet, The (Mehta), 263
Encounter (Yolen), 428, 452, 460
Encyclopedia Brown (Sobol), 396
Encyclopedia of Eastern Mythology, The (Storm), 250, 268
Encyclopedia Prehistoria Dinosaurs: The Definitive Pop-Up (Sabuda), 24
Endless Steppe, The: A Girl in Exile (Hautzig), 458
Enemy at Green Knowe, An (Boston), 296, 310
Ener, Guner, 495
Engel, Diana, 110, 112, 202
Engelfried, Steven, 169
"Engineer, The" (Milne), 350
Englander, Roger, 537
English, Karen, 131, 155, 181, 202, 339, 356
English Fairy Tales (Jacobs), 220, 263
Enright, Elizabeth, 68, 69, 373, 411
Epstein, William, 463
Eragon (Paolini), 248, 269, 274–275, 280, 309, 313
Erdrich, Louise, 442, 443, 457
Eric Carle's Animals Animals (Whipple), 131, 155, 338, 343, 350, 360
Eric Carle's Dragons Dragons and Other Creatures That Never Were (Whipple), 131, 160, 338, 360
Ericsson, Jennifer A., 202
Erikson, Erik, 23
Eriksson, Eva, 168, 198
Eriksson, Inga-Karin, 154
Ering, Timothy Basil, 112, 311
Erisman, Fred Raymond, 56
Erlbruch, Wolf, 357
Ernest, Edward, 54, 55
Ernst, Judith, 231, 250, 263, 267
Ernst, Lisa Campbell, 30, 184, 202
Esbaum, Jill, 9, 182, 202, 415
Esbensen, Barbara Juster, 126, 155, 334, 341, 356, 523, 537
Escape from Saigon: How a Vietnam War Orphan Became an American Boy (Warren), 485, 498
Escape from Slavery: The Boyhood of Frederick Douglass in His Own Words (McCurdy), 15
Eschenbach, Wolfram von, 280
"Eskimo Chant," 349
Esmonde, Margaret P., 297
Espada, Martin, 346
Essential Haiku, The: Versions of Basho, Buson, and Issa (Hass), 330, 357

Essley, Roger, 265
Estes, Eleanor, 68, 69, 373, 411
E.T., 297
Ets, Marie Hall, 149, 155, 391, 411
Euvremer, Teryl, 205
Eva (Dickinson), 311
Evans, Dilys, 121
Evans, Edmund, 54, 55
Evans, Leslie, 121
Evans, Shane W., 360, 541
Everett, Gwen, 156
Everett, June, 539
Everglades (George), 526, 537
Everyman Book of Nonsense Verse, The
  (Guinness), 331, 357
Everywhere (Brooks), 410
Evslin, Bernard, 268
Ewart, Claire, 202
Ewing, Juliana Horatia, 56
Exiles, The (McKay), 413
Exodus (Wildsmith), 160
Exploring Harry Potter (Schafer), 284
Exploring the Titanic (Ballard), 514, 536
Extraordinary Life, A: The Story of a Monarch
  Butterfly (Pringle), 519, 520, 541
Eye of the Storm: Chasing Storms with Warren
  Faidley (Kramer), 525, 538

Faber, Doris, 466, 495, 530, 537
Faber, Harold, 530, 537
Faber Book of Northern Legends, The (Crossley-
  Holland), 245, 268, 302, 311
"Fable of the Fig Tree, The," 217
Fables (Lobel), 126, 157, 302
Fables from Aesop (Lynch), 17, 241, 261, 267
Fables Sénégalaises, Recueillies de l'Oulof, 233
Face At the Window, The (Hanson), 32, 202
Face-Off (Christopher), 410
Facklam, Margery, 518, 519, 533, 537
Facklam, Paul, 533
Facts and Fictions of Minna Pratt, The
  (MacLachlan), 113, 370, 413
Fadden, John Kahionhes, 246, 266
Fader, Ellen, 77, 463
Faidley, Warren, 538
Fain, Moira, 156
"Fair, Brown and Trembling" (Philip), 221
Fair is Fair: World Folktales of Justice
  (Creeden), 259
Fairy Library (Cruikshank), 55
Fairy Tales Told for Children (Andersen), 52
Fairy Wings (Mills), 313
Faith and the Electric Dogs (Jennings), 312
Falconer, Ian, 144, 154, 156, 185, 202
"Falcon Under the Hat, The," 209
Falk, John H., 537
Falling Up (Silverstein), 359
Falloon, Jane, 310
Falwell, Cathryn, 200
"Fame" (Parra), 342
Fame and Fortune (Alger), 58
Family (Oxenbury), 30, 198
Family of Poems, A: My Favorite Poetry for Children
  (Kennedy), 317, 331, 332, 357
Family Pictures/Cuadros de familia (Garza),
  149, 156
Fancher, Lou, 359
Fang, Linda, 263

Far and Few: Rhymes of the Never Was and the
  Always Is (McCord), 63, 320, 358
Faraway Home (Kurtz), 203
Farley, Walter, 395, 396, 411
Farmer, Nancy, 33, 83, 102, 112, 275, 280, 299,
  300, 301, 302–303, 307–308, 311
Farmer Duck (Waddell), 160, 186, 205
Farmer Giles of Ham (Tolkien), 314
Farm Morning (McPhail), 540
Farmyard Alphabet, The (Crane), 54
Farnsworth, Bill, 494, 536
Farrell, Kate, 357
Farris, Christine King, 477, 495
Farthest Shore, The (LeGuin), 312
"Fat Cat, The," 209
Father and Son Tales (Evetts-Secker), 259, 267
Father Who Had 10 Children, The (Guettier), 199
Fatus, Sophie, 198
Fauchald, Nick, 493
Faust, Susan, 490
Favat, F. André, 213, 216
Favorite Fairy Tales Told in Norway (Haviland), 266
Favorite Norse Myths (Osborne), 244–245, 268
Favorite Poems Old and New (Ferris), 350, 356
Feathered Ones and Furry (Fisher), 356
Feathered Serpent, The (O'Dell), 416, 429, 459
Feathers: Poems About Birds (Spinelli), 338, 360
Federico and the Magi's Gift: A Latin American
  Christmas Story (Vidal), 250, 269
Feelings, Muriel, 14, 64, 170, 172–173, 198, 199
Feelings, Tom, 147, 156, 172–173, 177, 190–191,
  199, 200, 344, 355, 435, 457
Feiffer, Jules, 312
Feldman, Edmund Burke, 119
Feldman, Roxanne, 490
Feldstein, Barbara, 369
Felita (Mohr), 391–392, 403, 413
Fellenbaum, Charlie, 504, 538
Fellowship of the Ring, The (Tolkien), 281, 303, 314
Felstead, Cathie, 359
Felts, Shirley, 269
Fenner, Carol, 20, 85, 112
Ferber, Elizabeth, 476, 495
Ferrell, Claudine L., 530, 537
Ferris, Helen, 350, 356, 492
Ferris, Jeri, 491, 495
Feyerabend, Sigmund, 53
Field, Edward, 151, 156
Field, Eugene, 156, 327, 356
Field, Rachel, 63
Fields, Julia, 356
Fieser, Stephen, 507–508, 539
Fiesta! (Behren), 149, 154
Fiesta! (Guy), 173, 199
Fifth of March, The: A Story of the Boston
  Massacre (Rinaldi), 459
Figgs & Phantoms (Raskin), 414
Fighting Ground, The (Avi), 457
Finding the Lost Cities (Stefoff), 542
Fine, Anne, 398, 411
Fine White Dust, A (Rylant), 104, 114, 414
Finkelstein, Norman, 537
Finley, Carol, 130–131, 140, 151, 156
Fire, Bed, and Bone (Branford), 457
"Firebird, The," 217
"Fire Bringer, The," 215
Fire-Eaters, The (Almond), 22, 33, 88, 111, 451, 457
Firefighters A to Z (Demarest), 6, 169, 198

Fireflies at Midnight (Singer), 338, 360
"Firefly" (Graham), 329
Fire in the Hills (Myers), 443–444, 459
Fire on the Mountain, 187
Fires of Merlin, The (Barron), 310
"Fireworks" (Worth), 347
First Children: Growing Up in the White House
  (Leiner), 497
First Comes Spring (Rockwell), 13, 200
First Four Years, The (Wilder), 460
First Look at Caterpillars, A (Selsam & Hunt),
  533, 541
First Look at Seals, Sea Lions, and Walruses, A
  (Selsam & Hunt), 533, 541
First Song Ever Sung, The (Melmed), 204
First Thanksgiving, The (George), 130, 156
First to Fly: How Wilbur & Orville Wright Invented
  the Airplane (Busby), 466, 470, 490, 495
Firth, Barbara, 33, 205
Fischer-Nagel, Andraes, 537
Fischer-Nagel, Heiderose, 537
Fisher, Aileen, 321, 335, 356, 524, 537
Fisher, Carol, 318
Fisher, Emma, 299
Fisher, Leonard Everett, 134, 157, 243, 265, 268,
  357, 358, 495
Fisher, Margery, 463
Fisher, Valerie, 328, 357
"Fisherman and His Wife, The," 219
Fish in His Pocket, A (Cazet), 201
Fitzhugh, Louise, 64, 77, 112, 370, 411
500 Hats of Bartholomew Cubbins, The (Seuss),
  124, 144, 159, 190, 194, 205
Five Little Monkeys Jumping on the Bed
  (Christelow), 12, 199
Five Little Peppers and How They Grew, The
  (Sidney), 45, 61, 63, 67–68
Five Little Peppers Grown Up, The (Sidney), 61
Five Little Peppers Midway, The (Sidney), 61
Five Sisters, The (Mahy), 312
Five Trucks (Floca), 174, 200
Five Weeks in a Balloon (Verne), 60, 297
Fix-It (McPhail), 204
Flack, Jerry D., 257
Flack, Marjorie, 55
Flag Maker, The: A Story of the Star-Spangled
  Banner (Bartoletti), 513, 536
Flag of Childhood, The: Poems From the Middle
  East (Nye), 344, 358
Flashlight and Other Poems (Thurman), 324, 350,
  360
Flavin, Teresa, 495
Flawed Glass, The (Strachan), 18, 114, 414
Flayed God, The: The Mythology of Mesoamerica
  (Markman & Markman), 251, 268
Fleischman, Paul, 5, 10, 13, 15–16, 19, 64, 80, 98,
  102, 112, 175, 200, 202, 244, 268, 311, 336, 337,
  349, 356, 411, 416, 431, 436, 440–441, 458
Fleischman, Sid, 31, 92, 94, 112, 126, 156,
  179–180, 202, 311, 439, 458, 495
Fleisher, Paul, 537
Fleming, Candace, 202, 473, 489, 495
Fleming, Denise, 5, 12, 122, 156, 199, 202
Fleming, Ian, 291, 311
Fleming, Maria, 8
Fleser, Stephen, 158
Fletcher, Ralph, 202, 356
Fletcher, Susan, 419, 458

Flicker Flash (Graham), 329, 356
Flip-Flop Girl (Paterson), 413
Floca, Brian, 174, 200, 519, 537
Flood: Wrestling with the Mississippi (Lauber), 505, 525, 539
Florian, Douglas, 334, 336, 350
Flournoy, Valerie, 156
Flower Garden (Bunting), 201
Flower Hunter, The: William Bartram, America's First Naturalist (Ray), 468, 498
Fly Away Home (Bunting), 399
Flyers (Hayes), 412
Fly High! The Story of Bessie Coleman (Borden & Kroeger), 495
Flying Dragon Room, The (Wood), 10, 183, 206
"Flying Ship, The," 209
Foa, Maryclare, 268
Focus on Nicotine and Caffeine (Perry), 540
"Fog" (Sandburg), 334
Fohr, Samuel Dennis, 223
Folkkeeper, The (Billingsley), 310
Folklore: An Encyclopedia of Beliefs, Customs, Tales, Music, and Art (Green), 262
Folks in the Valley, The: A Pennsylvania Dutch ABC (Aylesworth), 170, 198, 452
Folk Tales from Asia for Children Everywhere (Asian Cultural Centre for UNESCO), 231, 262
Following My Own Footsteps (Hahn), 458
Follow the Dream (Sis), 498
Fonteyn, Margot, 266
Food for Thought: The Complete Book of Concepts for Growing Minds (Freymann), 173, 200
Fool and the Fish, The: A Tale from Russia (Afanasyév), 227, 266
"Fool of the World and the Flying Ship, The," 211, 215, 218, 219
Fool of the World and the Flying Ship, The (Ransome), 158, 184, 204, 227–228, 266
Football Fugitive (Christopher), 410
Footprints on the Roof: Poems, About the Earth (Singer), 339, 360
Forberg, Ati, 268
Forbes, Esther, 15, 63, 108, 112, 194, 418, 432, 458
Ford, H. J., 113
Ford, Paul Leicester, 454
Foreign Oil Dependence (Haley), 531, 538
Foreman, Michael, 112, 114, 121, 156, 165–166, 197, 246, 268, 269, 309, 411, 452, 457, 458, 482, 495
Forever (Blume), 410
Forgotten Door, The (Key), 312
Forman, Jack, 369
Forman, Robert, 356
For Mike (Sykes), 414
For the Love of Pete (Marino), 413
Fortnum, Peggy, 310
Fortune's Bones: The Manumission Requiem (Nelson), 11, 344–345, 358
Fortune-Tellers, The (Alexander), 13, 40
Forty Singing Seamen and Other Poems (Noyes), 328, 358
Forward, Toby, 31
For Your Eyes Only! (Rocklin), 414
Fossil Girl, The: Mary Anning's Dinosaur Discovery (Brighton), 26–27, 29, 495
Four Hungry Kittens (McCully), 200
Four on the Shore (Marshall), 201
"Four Puppets, The," 231

Four to the Pole! The American Women's Expedition to Antarctica, 1992–93 (Loewen & Bancroft), 504, 539
"Four Worlds: The Dine Story of Creation" (Caduto & Bruchac), 245
Fox, Dan, 349, 356
Fox, Mem, 21, 168, 182, 198, 202
Fox, Paula, 17, 64, 70, 71, 92, 104, 110, 112, 364, 376, 381–382, 411, 434–435, 458
"Fox and the Geese, The" (Grimm & Grimm), 223
"Fox and the Grapes, The" (Aesop), 349
"Fox and the Mole, The," 235
Foxfire Book, The (Wigginton), 455, 460
Fox Jumps Over the Parson's Gate, The (Caldecott), 54, 155
Fox Steals Home, The (Christopher), 397, 410
Fox Went Out on a Chilly Night, The (Spier), 159
Fradin, Dennis Brindell, 478, 495, 496
Fradin, Judith Bloom, 478, 496
Frampton, David, 112, 156, 157, 268, 436, 536, 539
Frances Hodgson Burnett: Beyond the Secret Garden (Carpenter & Shirley), 34, 495
Francisco, Victor, 265
Francisco Goya (Waldron), 144, 160
Franco, Betsy, 334–335, 343, 356, 359
Frank, Anne, 77, 112, 486, 496
Frank, Diana Crone, 309
Frank, Jeffrey, 309
Frank, John, 202
Frank, Rudolf, 66, 92, 112, 422, 458
Frank and Ernest on the Road (Day), 110, 112
Frank and Ernest Play Ball (Day), 107, 112
Frankel, Ellen, 148
Frankenstein (Shelley), 297
Frankfeldt, Gwen, 112, 268
Franklin, Kristine L., 411
Franklin Delano Roosevelt (Freedman), 475, 491, 496
"Franklin Hyde, Who Caroused in the Dirt and was corrected by His Uncle" (Belloc), 332
Franklin's Big Search-and-Solve Flap Book (Jeffrey), 168, 198
Frank's Campaign (Alger), 58
Fraser, James H., 60
Fraser, Mary Ann, 537
Frasher, Ramona, 370
Frazee, Marla, 328, 356
Freddy in Peril: Book Two (Reiche), 285–286, 313
Frederick Douglass: Slave, Writer, Abolitionist (Haugen), 493
Frederick Douglass and the Fight for Freedom (Miller), 497
Free at Last!: Stories and Songs of Emancipation (Rappaport), 516, 541
Freedman, Russell, 14, 15, 18, 19, 32, 33, 64, 77, 80, 92, 112, 151, 156, 417–418, 461, 463, 464, 465, 466, 470, 471, 474, 475, 481–482, 484, 485, 491, 493, 494, 496, 511, 512, 515, 537
Freedom Riders (Haskins), 33
Freedom's Children: Young Civil Activists Tell Their Own Stories (Levine), 35, 113
Free Fall (Wiesner), 5, 10, 13, 40, 139, 160, 175, 176, 193, 200, 314
Freeman, Don, 411
Freeman, Suzanne, 411
Freeom on the Menu: The Greensboro Sit-Ins (Weatherford), 542

Freight Train (Crews), 12, 173–174, 200
French, Martin, 355
French, Vivian, 19–20, 518, 520, 537
Freshwater Fish and Fishing (Arnosky), 536
Freymann, Saxton, 173, 200
Frida (Winter), 480, 498
Frida Kahlo: The Artist in the Blue House (Holzhey), 15, 146, 156
Frida Kahlo: The Brush of Anguish (Zamora), 149
Frida Kahlo (Luis-Martin), 149
Frida Kahlo (Turner), 149, 159, 479, 498
Frida Kahlo Masterpieces (von Waberer), 149
Friedman, Ina R., 32, 393, 411
Friedman, Pavel, 342
Friend, The (Stewart), 102
Friendly Beasts, The: An Old English Christmas Carol (dePaola), 263
"Friends" (Esbensen), 341
Fritz, Jean, 19, 63, 64, 80, 113, 149, 151, 156, 463–464, 466, 469, 472–473, 475, 482–483, 484, 488–489, 490, 494, 496, 508, 513, 537
Frog and Toad All Year (Lobel), 13, 31, 200
Frog and Toad Are Friends (Lobel), 64, 77, 113, 177, 200
Frog and Toad Together (Lobel), 200
Froggie Went a-Courting (Priceman), 158
Frog Goes to Dinner (Mayer), 174, 193, 200
Frog He Would A-Wooing Go, A (Caldecott), 155
"Frog King, The" (Grimm & Grimm), 218
"Frog Prince, The," 220
Frog Prince, The (Berenzy), 112
"Frog Prince, The" (Grimm & Grimm), 52
Frogs Wore Red Suspenders, The (Prelutsky), 333, 359
Frolich, Lorenz, 278, 309, 492
Froman, Robert, 329
From Anna (Little), 385, 412
"From a Railway Carriage" (Stevenson), 320
From Caterpillar to Butterfly (Heiligman), 538
From Dr. Mather to Dr. Seuss: Two Hundred Years of American Books for Children (Lystad), 44
From Farm Boy to Senator: Being the History of the Boyhood and Manhood of Daniel Webster (Alger), 58
From Head to Toe (Carle), 131, 155
From Sea to Shining Sea: A Treasury of American Folklore and Folk Songs (Cohn), 236, 266
From the Land of Enchantment: Creative Teaching with Fairy Tales (Flack), 257
From the Lighthouse (Chipman), 88, 112
From the Mixed-Up Files of Mrs. Basil E. Frankweiler (Konigsburg), 77, 113, 385, 412
From the Winds of Manguito: Cuban Folktales in English and Spanish (Perez), 254, 265
Frost, Helen, 339, 346, 356
Frost, Robert, 317, 319, 335, 356, 376
"Frost, The" (Yeh), 334
"Frosted-Window World" (Fisher), 335
Frozen Summer (Auch), 457
Fry, Edward, 177
Frye, Northrop, 76, 325
Full Belly Bowl, The (Aylesworth), 154, 302, 310
Fuller, Elizabeth, 198
"Full Moon" (Graham), 329
Full Steam Ahead: The Race to Build a Transcontinental Railroad (Blumberg), 511, 536
Fun (Mark), 25

Funke, Cornelia, 248, 273, 283–284, 300, 302, 303, 311
Funny Little Woman, The (Mosel), 263
Further Tales of Uncle Remus (Lester), 157

Gab, Oki S., 313
Gaber, Susan, 128, 154, 204
Gackenbach, Dick, 414
Gág, Wanda, 6, 12, 21, 63, 124, 126, 127, 156, 202
Gage, Wilson, 302, 311
Gal, Laszlo, 126, 158, 267
Galassi, Jonathan, 458
Galaxies (Simon), 526, 541
Galbraith, Kathryn O., 202
Galda, Lee, 36–37
Galdone, Paul, 12, 13, 30, 214–215, 221, 263, 264, 266, 358
Gallenkamp, Charles, 15
Gallienne, Eva Lee, 266
Galoshes (Allen), 168, 198
Galston, William A., 70
Game of Silence, The (Erdrich), 442, 457
Gammage Cup, The (Kendall), 294, 312
Gammell, Stephen, 17, 107, 111, 123–124, 126–127, 154, 158, 179, 201, 202, 204, 237, 265, 266, 359, 496
Gandhi, Great Soul (Severance), 32, 476, 498
Gandolfi, Silvana, 272, 311
Gantos, Jack, 14, 70, 71, 202, 372, 376, 411
Garcia, Geronimo, 414
Garden Crafts for Kids: 50 Great Reasons to Get Your Hands Dirty, 529, 541
Gardener, The (Stewart), 124, 159, 205
Garden of Abdul Gasazi, The (Van Allsburg), 139, 159
Garfield, Leon, 17, 418
Gargoyle on the Roof, The (Prelutsky), 333, 359
Garis, Howard, 63
Garland, Sherry, 394, 411
Garner, Alan, 282–283, 300, 311
Garraty, Gail, 312
Garrett, Kenneth, 541
Garza, Camen Lomas, 149, 156
Gates, Doris, 63, 243–244, 268
Gathering, The (Hamilton), 311
Gathering Blue (Lowry), 298, 312
Gathering of Days, A: A New England Girl's Journal, 1830-32 (Blos), 89, 93, 112, 433, 454, 455, 457
Gatti, Anne, 537
Gauch, Patricia Lee, 156, 202, 402, 411
Gaugin, Paul, 130
"Gazelle" (Hoberman), 321
Geer, Charles, 114, 459
Geeslin, Campbell, 21, 129, 156, 202
Geiger, John, 536
Geisel, Theodor. *See* Seuss, Dr.
Geisert, Arthur, 40, 169, 171, 199
Gelman, Rita Golden, 156
Genius: A Photobiography of Albert Einstein (Delano), 465, 466, 470, 490, 495
Geography, Physical, Economic, and Regional (Dryer), 504
George, Jean Craighead, 63, 77, 82, 87, 88, 113, 130, 156, 380, 389–390, 411, 526, 537
George, Kristine O'Connell, 6, 319, 338, 356
George, Lindsay Barrett, 537
George, William T., 537

George and Martha One Fine Day (Marshall), 204
George vs. George: The American Revolution as Seen from Both Sides (Schanzer), 15, 73, 98, 114, 513–514, 541
George Washington: An Illustrated Biography (Adler), 478
George Washington, Spymaster: How the Americans Outspied the British and Won the Revolutionary War (Allen), 472, 495
George Washington and the Founding of a Nation (Marrin), 473, 497
Georgia O'Keefe (Turner), 159, 479, 498
Geras, Adele, 228, 264
Gerber, Carole, 5, 212
Gerber, Mary Jane, 498
Gerig, Sibyl Graber, 311
German Popular Stories (Grimm & Grimm), 52, 53 *See also* Brothers Grimm
Gerrard, Roy, 348, 356
Gerstein, Mordicai, 153, 156, 263, 311, 468, 482, 496, 498
Getting Near to Baby (Couloumbis), 104, 112, 363, 384, 411
Getting the Knack: 20 Poetry Writing Exercises (Dunning & Stafford), 354
"Getting the News" (Grimes), 342
Gherman, Beverly, 481, 496
Ghost Abbey (Westall), 295, 314
Ghost of Cutler Creek, The (Defelice), 295
Ghost of Fossil Glen, The (Defelice), 295, 296, 311
Ghost's Hour, Spook's Hour (Bunting), 30, 122, 154, 201
Ghosts of Mercy Manor, The (Wright), 314
Giants in the Land (Appelbaum), 536
Gibbons, Gail, 200, 510, 518, 537
Gibbons, Rebecca, 325, 355
Giblin, James Cross, 32, 33, 474, 476, 493, 496, 506–507, 509, 515, 531, 537–538
Gib Rides Home (Snyder), 459
Gibson, Louis Rauch, 383
Gifaldi, David, 411
Giff, Patricia Reilly, 433, 458
Gift for Abuelita, A: Celebrating the Day of the Dead (Luenn), 149, 157
Gift from Papá Diego, A (Sáenz), 391, 414
Gift from Zeus, A: Sixteen Favorite Myths (Steig), 243, 268
Gift of the Girl Who Couldn't Hear, The (Shreve), 385, 414
Gift of the Sacred Dog, The (Goble), 156
Giganti, Paul, Jr., 199
"Giggle, Giggle, Snigger, Laugh!" (Pottle), 350
"Gigglepict" (Pottle), 350
Gilbert, Anne Yvonne, 278, 310
Gilbert, Sharon S., 156, 197
Gilchrist, Jan Spivey, 17, 356, 357, 434
Gill, Kent, 351
Gillespie, Margaret C., 51
Gillette, J. Lynett, 518–519, 538
Gilliland, Judith Heide, 28–29, 132, 156, 466, 496
Gillin, Richard, 289
"Gingerbread Boy, The," 209, 255
Gingerbread Boy, The (Galdone), 12
Gingerbread Man, The (Aylesworth), 264
Gingerbread Man, The (Kimmel), 264
Ginger Jumps (Ernst), 30
Ginsburg, Mirra, 263
Giorgio's Village (dePaola), 136, 155

Giorgis, Cyndia, 427
Giovanni, Nikki, 202, 517
Gipson, Fred, 113, 411
Girl Called Boy, A (Hurmence), 35, 113, 297, 312
Girl from Yamhill, A: A Memoir (Cleary), 33, 482, 495
Girl Goddess #9: Nine Stories (Block), 370, 410
Girl Named Disaster, A (Farmer), 83, 112
Girl Who Dreamed Only Geese and Other Tales of the Far North, The (Howard), 137, 158
Girl Who Loved Caterpillars, The (Merrill), 427, 456, 459
Girl Who Loved the Wind, The (Yolen), 314
Girl Who Loved Wild Horses, The (Goble), 32, 34, 93–94, 113, 119–120, 121, 142, 153, 156
Girl With a Baby, The (Olsen), 413
Girl Wonder: A Baseball Story in Nine Innings (Hopkinson), 485, 496
Gish, Kimbra Wilder, 286
Giver, The (Lowry), 64, 66, 101, 102, 110, 113, 298, 304, 305, 312
Giving Thanks: A Native American Morning Message (Swamp), 151, 159
Giving Tree, The (Silverstein), 110
Glaciers: Ice on the Move (Walker), 532, 542
Glanzman, Louis S., 312, 414
Glass, Andrew, 310, 311, 496
Glasser, Robin Preiss, 359
Glass Slipper, The: Charles Perrault's Tales of Time Past (Perrault), 264
Glazer, Joan, 23
Glorious Flight Across the Channel with Louis Bleriot, July 25, 1909 (Provensen & Provensen), 138, 158, 498
Glorious Mother Goose, The (Edens), 197
Glück, Louise, 319
Gnats of Knotty Pine, The (Peet), 204
Goal (Burleigh), 339, 355
Goats, The (Cole), 80–81, 112, 411
Gobble, Slip, Slop: A Tale of A Very Greedy Cat (So), 205, 211, 263, 267
Goble, Paul, 32, 34, 93–94, 113, 119–120, 121, 142, 153, 156, 237–238, 266
Goble, Warwick, 263
Goblin Market (Rossetti), 63, 346, 359
Goddard, Robert, 303
Godden, Rumer, 290, 311, 317, 319, 346
"God Found God" (Rylant), 343
"God Found Some Fudge" (Rylant), 343
"God Is a Girl" (Rylant), 343
Godless (Hautman), 83–84, 113, 399, 412
God Went to Beauty School (Rylant), 343, 359
Go Free or Die: A Story of Harriet Tubman (Ferris), 491, 492, 495
Goggles! (Keats), 137, 157, 203
Go In and Out the Window: An Illustrated Songbook for Young People (Fox), 349, 356
Going Home (Bunting), 149, 154
Going Home (Mohr), 403, 413
Going North (Harrington), 81, 113, 437, 456, 458
Going on a Whale Watch (McMillan), 540
Going to War in Roman Times (Butterfield), 509, 536
Gold, Alison Leslie, 496
Goldberg, Lazer, 272–273, 531
Gold Cadillac, The (Taylor), 387, 414, 437, 460
Golden Bird, The (Philip), 156, 264

Golden City, The: Jerusalem's 3,000 Years (Waldman), 148, 160, 510, 542

Golden Cockerel and Other Fairy Tales, The (Pushkin), 227, 266

Golden Compass, The (Pullman), 7, 87, 90, 114, 281, 303–304, 309, 313

Golden Fleece and the Heroes Who Lived Before Achilles, The (Colum), 268

Golden God, The: Apollo (Gates), 268

"Golden Goose, The," 209

"Golden Goose, The" (Grimm & Grimm), 218, 223, 226

Golden Goose, The (King-Smith), 276–277, 312

Golden Goose King, The: A Tale Told By the Buddha (Ernst), 231, 250, 263, 267

Golden Mare, the Firebird, and the Magic Ring, The (Sanderson), 227, 266

Golden Sandal, The: A Middle Eastern Cinderella Story (Hickox), 232, 257, 265

"Golden Sheng, The," 215, 219

"Goldilocks and the Three Bears," 221

Goldilocks and the Three Bears (Brett), 5, 221, 263

Goldilocks and the Three Bears (Marshall), 221, 264

Goldin, Barbara Diamond, 156, 249–250, 269, 509–510, 538

"Goldophine Home, Who was cursed with the Sin of Pride, and Became a Boot-Black" (Belloc), 332

Golem (McDermott), 123, 134, 158

Golem (Wisniewski), 84, 133, 153, 160, 250, 269

Golem, The (Rogasky), 158, 250, 269

Golem, The (Singer), 159, 250, 265, 269

Golembe, Carla, 157

Golem's Eye, The (Stroud), 294, 295, 314

Golenbock, Peter, 485, 496

Gollub, Matthew, 330, 356

Golman, Daniel, 3

Goloshapov, Sergei, 264

Gonzalez, Maya Christina, 355

Goodall, Jane, 523, 538

Good Brother, Bad Brother: The Story of Edwin Booth & John Wilkes Booth (Giblin), 474, 476, 493, 496

Good-Bye and Keep Cold (Davis), 376, 411

Good Courage, A (Tolan), 414

Good Dog (Gottfried), 338, 356

Goode, Diane, 114, 222, 264, 313, 419

Good Fight, The: How World War II Was Won (Ambrose), 515, 535

Good-Hearted Youngest Brother, The: An Hungarian Folktale (Severo), 302, 313

Good Liar, The (Maguire), 417, 449, 459

Goodman, Joan Elizabeth, 496

Goodman, Susan E., 501, 538

Good Night, Harry (Lewis), 5, 181, 203

Good Night Maman (Mazer), 449, 459

Goodnight Moon (Brown), 77, 112, 144, 154

Goodnight Moon Room, The: A Pop-Up Book (Brown), 168, 198

Good Night Pillow Fight (Cook), 202, 342, 356

Good Queen Bess: The Story of Elizabeth I of England (Stanley & Vennema), 34, 40, 498

Good Rhymes, Good Times (Hopkins), 320, 357

Goodsell, Jane, 496

Good Times on Grandfather Mountain (Martin), 204

Good Women of a Well-Blessed Land: Women's Lives in Colonial America (Miller), 511–512, 513, 540

Good Zap, Little Grog (Wilson), 8, 183, 206

Goose (Bang), 201

"Goose" (Hughes), 334

"Goosebumps" series (Stine), 110

Goose Girl, The (Hale), 276, 311

Goose That Almost Got Cooked, The (Simont), 159

Gopher in the Garden and Other Animal Poems, A (Prelutsky), 321, 359

Gordon, Christine, 105

Gordon, Ruth, 356

Gore, Leonid, 357

Gorey, Edward, 332, 337, 356

Gorilla (Browne), 110, 112

"Gorilla, The" (Florian), 350

Gorilla Walk (Lewin & Lewin), 523, 539

Gorra, Michael, 293

Gotcha! (Jorgensen), 203

Goto, Scott, 202

Gottfried, Maya, 338, 356

Gough, John, 346

Gourdine, Traci L., 343, 359

Gourley, Catherine, 538

Goya, Francisco, 144

Grace, Eric S., 538

Grace in the Wilderness: After the Liberation, 1945–1948 (Siegel), 459

Graff, Nancy Price, 538

Graham, Bob, 24, 185, 198, 202, 359

Graham, Harriet, 458

Graham, Joan Bransfield, 329, 356

Grahame, Kenneth, 14, 55, 63, 113, 272, 285, 288–289, 303, 309, 311

Grandaddy and Janetta (Griffith), 202

Grandaddy's Place (Griffith), 31, 196, 202

Grandfather's Journey (Say), 31, 148, 159

Grandits, John, 329, 356

Grandmothers' Stories: Wise Woman Tales from Many Cultures (Mutén), 259, 267

Grandpa Jake and the Grand Christmas (Ames), 457

Grandpa's Town (Nomura), 31, 392–393, 413

Granfield, Linda, 538

Granny Torelli Makes Soup (Creech), 22, 411

Grant, Melvyn, 294

Graphic Alphabet, The (Pelletier), 123, 158, 169–170, 199

"Grasshopper, The" (McCord), 340–341

Grasshopper on the Road (Lobel), 177, 201

Grass Sandals: The Travels of Basho (Spivak), 329, 360

Graven Images (Fleischman), 311

Graves, Donald, 351

Gray, Elizabeth Janet, 458

Gray, Kes, 18

Gray, Libba Moore, 8, 202

Great Art Adventure, The (Knox), 157

Greatest Skating Race, The: A World War II Story from the Netherlands (Borden), 445, 457

Greatest Skating Race, The (Borden), 35

Great Fire, The (Murphy), 510, 532, 540

Great Frog Race and Other Poems, The (George), 356

Great Gilly Hopkins, The (Paterson), 372, 413

Great Little Madison, The (Fritz), 80, 113, 489, 496

Great Pumpkin Switch, The (McDonald), 204, 452, 459

Great Pyramid, The (Mann), 539

Great Turkey Walk, The (Karr), 458

Greek Myths (Coolidge), 268

Greek Myths (McCaughrean), 268

Green, Michael, 290, 314

Green, Roland J., 297

Green, Thomas A., 262

Greenaway, Kate, 43, 45, 54–55, 56, 71, 124, 156, 165, 197, 199, 355

Greenberg, Jan, 33, 144, 146, 156, 317, 319, 356, 480, 487, 496

Greene, Carol, 538

Greene, Constance C., 383, 411

Greene, Ellin, 268

Greene, Stephanie, 376–377, 411

Green Eggs and Ham (Seuss), 110

Greenfield, Eloise, 4, 339, 356–357, 387, 411, 478, 485–486, 496

Green Lion of Zion Street, The (Fields), 356

Greenspun, Adele, 21

Greenway, Betty, 318

Greenway, Michelle, 538

Greenway, William, 318

Green Willow and Other Japanese Folktales (James), 229–230, 263

Greenwitch (Cooper), 311

Gregory Griggs and Other Nursery Rhyme People (Lobel), 165, 197

"Gretchen in the Kitchen" (Prelutsky), 348

Grey King, The (Cooper), 283, 311

Grierson's Raid: A Daring Cavalry Strike Through the Heart of the Confederacy (Lalicki), 530, 539

Grifalconi, Ann, 109, 113, 155, 233, 262

Griffin, Peni R., 311

Griffith, Helen V., 31, 196, 200, 202

Grimericks (Pearson), 329, 359

Grimes, Nikki, 7, 15, 34, 95, 113, 156, 342, 357, 366, 411, 470, 496

Grimly, Gris, 359

Grimm, Wilhelm, 52, 156, 264 See also Brothers Grimm

Grimm Brothers. See Brothers Grimm

Gross, Ruth Belov, 496

Grossman, Bill, 14, 199

Grossman, Robert, 410

Grouchy Ladybug, The (Carle), 200

Grove, Vicki, 386, 411

Growing Frogs (French), 19–20, 520, 537

Growing Up in Coal Country (Bartoletti), 536

Guadalupi, Gianni, 108

Guarnieri, Paolo, 156, 458

Guess How Much I Love You (McBratney), 33

Guettier, Bénédicte, 199

Guiberson, Brenda Z., 535, 538

Guinea Pig Scientists: Bold Self-Experiments in Science and Medicine (Dendy & Boring), 501, 537

Guinness, Louise, 331, 357

Guitar Girl (Manning), 413

Guji Guji (Chen), 31, 186, 201

"Guleesh" (Jacobs), 221

Gulliver's Travels (Swift), 45, 50, 51, 63, 66

Gunga Din (Kipling), 357

Gunson, Christopher, 12

Gurdon, Meghan Cox, 469

Gutenberg, Johannes, 46

Guthrie, Woody, 4, 325–326, 350, 357

Guts: Our Digestive System (Simon), 517, 541

Guy, Ginger Foglesong, 173, 199
Gypsy Rizka (Alexander), 309

Haas, Irene, 5, 202
Haas, Jessie, 411, 458
Haas, Merle S., 155
Haddix, Margaret Peterson, 267
Hague, Kathleen, 199, 266
Hague, Michael, 16, 199, 241, 266, 267, 290, 291, 309, 310, 313, 314
Hahn, Mary Downing, 33, 295, 311, 446, 458
Haigh, Jane G., 511, 540
Haight, Anne Lyon, 65
Haiku: The Mood of Earth (Atwood), 329, 355
Hailstones and Halibut Bones (O'Neill), 351, 352, 359
Hakim, Joy, 526, 538
Hale, Christy, 203, 358
Hale, Sarah Josepha, 166, 197
Hale, Shannon, 274, 311
Haley, Gail E., 131, 156, 182, 202, 213, 239, 257, 267
Haley, James, 531, 538
Halkin, Hillel, 459
Hall, Bruce Edward, 98, 113, 202
Hall, Christine, 101
Hall, Donald, 18, 121, 126, 135, 153, 156, 357, 452
Hall, Elizabeth, 421, 459
Hall, Lynn, 411
Hallensleben, Georg, 111, 154
Halloween ABC (Merriam), 66, 114, 170, 199, 321, 358
Halperin, Wendy Anderson, 91, 113, 156, 310
Halpern, Monica, 511, 538
Halpern, Shari, 519, 542
Halsey, Megan, 201
Hamanaka, Sheila, 231, 263
Hamilton, Martha, 255
Hamilton, Meredith, 356
Hamilton, Virginia, 35, 64, 110, 113, 126, 137, 152, 153, 156, 238, 245, 246, 262, 268, 277, 311, 381, 387, 388, 396, 411–412, 417, 458, 464–465, 475, 496
Hamlet (Shakespeare), 244
"Hammer of Thor, The" (Coolidge), 245, 254
Hampl, Patricia, 486
Hampson, Alfred Leete, 356
Han, Oki S., 204, 358
Hand Full of Stars, A (Schami), 382, 414
Handler, David, 232
Hands of the Maya: Villagers at Work and Play (Crandell), 149, 155
Handtalk Birthday: A Number & Story Book in Sign Language (Charlip, Miller & Ancona), 172, 199
Handville, Robert, 268
Hanel, Wolfram, 412
Hang Tough, Paul Mather (Slote), 414
Hank Aaron: Brave in Every Way (Golenbock), 485, 496
Hannah, Jonny, 147, 156
Hannigan, Katherine, 86, 102, 113, 366, 412
Hans Andersen: His Classic Fairy Tales (Foreman), 309
Hans Brinker, or the Silver Skates (Dodge), 62, 63
Hans Christian Andersen Fairy Tales (Andersen), 278, 309, 492

Hans Christian Andersen's The Snow Queen: A Fairy Tale Told in Seven Stories (Setterington), 313
"Hansel and Gretel," 80, 215, 216, 218
"Hansel and Gretel" (Grimm & Grimm), 52, 223, 264
Hansel and Gretel (Jeffers), 156, 264
Hansel and Gretel (Lesser), 130, 131, 156, 223, 264
Hansel and Gretel (Marshall), 223, 264
Hansen, Joyce, 113
Hanson, Peter, 498
Hanson, Regina, 32, 202
Hanukkah Lights: Holiday Poetry (Hopkins), 8
Happy Birthday, Sam (Hutchins), 203
Happy Cockerel (Julian), 168, 198
Harbor (Crews), 200
"Hare and the Frog, The," 210
"Hare and the Hedgehog, The" (Grimm & Grimm), 223
"Hare and the Tortoise, The," 211
Harlem (Myers), 196, 204, 344, 358
Harlem Renaissance: Art of Black America (Miers), 147
Harlem Stomp! A Cultural History of the Harlem Renaissance (Hill), 15, 147, 156, 517, 538
Harms, Jeanne McLain, 125
Harness, Cheryl, 473, 495, 496
Harper, Suzanne, 536
Harriet the Spy (Fitzhugh), 77, 112, 370, 385, 411
Harrington, Janice N., 81, 113, 437, 456, 458
Harris, Joel Chandler, 63, 238, 239, 262, 267
Harris, Robie H., 21, 180, 202, 517, 538
Harris, Violet, 77
Harrison, Michael, 268, 302
Harry Cat's Pet Puppy (Selden), 289, 313
Harry in Trouble (Porte), 204
Harry Potter and the Chamber of Secrets (Rowling), 284, 313
Harry Potter and the Goblet of Fire (Rowling), 90, 114, 284, 313
Harry Potter and the Half-Blood Prince (Rowling), 64, 284, 285, 313
Harry Potter and the Prisoner of Azkaban (Rowling), 284, 313
Harry Potter and the Sorcerer's Stone (Rowling), 272, 284, 285, 286, 313
Hartling, Peter, 386, 412, 446, 458
Hartmann, Wendy, 31, 203
Hartung, Susan Kathleen, 358
Harvesting Hope: The Story of Cesar Chavez (Krull), 475, 497
Harvey, Brett, 422, 438, 452, 455, 458
Harvey, Roland, 538
Haskins, James, 14, 33, 173, 199, 477, 496
Hass, Robert, 317, 330, 357
Hassall, Joan, 198
Hastings, Selina, 113, 247–248, 269
Hatchet (Paulsen), 7, 17, 28, 83, 110, 114, 380–381, 413
Hathorn, Libby, 412
Hatmaker's Sign, The: A Story by Benjamin Franklin (Fleming), 202
Hattie and the Fox (Fox), 202
Haugaard, Erik Christian, 309, 418, 427–428, 430, 458
Haugen, Brenda, 493
Haunted House (Pienkowski), 114
Hautman, Pete, 83–84, 113, 399, 412

Hautzig, Esther, 458
Have You Seen Trees? (Oppenheim), 158
Haviland, Virginia, 266
Hawk, I'm Your Brother (Baylor), 409, 410
Hawkes, Kevin, 15–16, 175, 199, 200, 202, 264, 458, 469, 497
Hawk Moon (MacGregor), 413
Hawksong (Atwater-Rhodes), 310
Hawley, John C., 279
Hayden, Gretchen Purtell, 93
Hayes, Daniel, 412
Hays, Michael, 313, 386, 414, 460, 541
Headless Horseman Rides Tonight, The (Prelutsky), 322, 359
Heaney, Seamus, 247, 269, 326, 357
Heard, Georgia, 342, 357
Hearne, Betsy, 62, 163–164, 192, 209, 212, 214, 217, 276, 538
Heartbeat (Creech), 22, 112, 356, 411
Heartland (Siebert), 335, 359
Heartlight (Barron), 310
Heart to Heart: New Poems Inspired by Twentieth-Century American Art (Greenberg), 144, 156, 317, 319, 356
Heath, Shirley Brice, 3
Hector Protector (Sendak), 144
Heide, Florence Parry, 28–29
Heidi (Spyri), 45, 62, 63
Heiligman, Deborah, 476, 496, 538
Heinlein, Robert A., 297
Heins, Paul, 264, 291
Helga's Dowry: A Troll Love Story (dePaola), 155
Heller, Nicholas, 169, 199
Heller, Ruth, 263, 265
Hello, Fish! Visiting the Coral Reef (Earle), 502, 537
Hello, Goodbye Window, The (Juster), 203
"Hello," I Lied (Kerr), 370, 412
Helms, Cynthia Newman, 480, 496
Helprin, Mark, 266
Hendershot, Judith, 88, 452
Henderson, Douglas, 538, 539
Henderson, Merl, 540
Hendrick, Joanne, 20
Hendry, Linda, 538
Heneghan, James, 445, 458
Henkes, Kevin, 4, 6, 22, 25, 30, 31, 102, 107, 113, 120, 152, 156, 168, 181, 185, 198, 203, 412
Henneberger, Robert, 310
"Henny Penny," 209, 253, 255
Henry, Marguerite, 395–396, 412
Henry, O., 63
Henry, Wolcott, 537
Henry and Beezus (Cleary), 384, 410
Henry and Mudge and the Bedtime Thumps (Rylant), 177, 201
Henry and Mudge and the Great Grandpas (Rylant), 201
Henry and Mudge and the Happy Cat (Rylant), 177
Henry and Mudge and the Long Weekend (Rylant), 13, 177, 201
Henry and the Kite Dragon (Hall), 98, 113, 202
Henry Hikes to Fitchburg (Johnson), 16, 185, 203
Henry Huggins (Cleary), 63
"Henry King, Who Chewed on Bits of String, And Was Early Cut Off in Dreadful Agonies" (Belloc), 332
Henry's First-Moon Birthday (Look), 24
Henterley, Jamichael, 269

Heo, Yumi, 198, 262, 265
Hepler, Susan Ingrid, 135, 136, 228
Hepworth, Cathi, 170, 199
Herb, Steven, 4
Herbert, George, 346
Herbie Jones and the Monster Ball (Kline), 397, 398, 412
Hercules (Evslin), 268
Here Comes Mother Goose (Opie), 5, 198
Here in Harlem: Poems in Many Voices (Myers), 344, 358
Here Is My Heart: Love Poems (Smith), 341, 360
Here There Be Witches (Yolen), 314
Hermes, Patricia, 376, 412
Hernandez, Avelino, 391, 412
Hero and the Crown, The (McKinley), 7, 113, 283, 302, 312
Hero and the Holocaust, A: The Story of Janusz Korczak and His Children (Adler), 485, 494
Hero Beowulf, The (Kimmel), 326, 357
Heroes, The (Kingsley), 268
Heroes and She-Roes: Poems of Amazing and Everyday Heroes (Lewis), 344, 357
Hero of Lesser Causes (Johnston), 458
Hero with a Thousand Faces, The (Campbell), 303
Herring, William A., 119
Herriot, James, 202
Hershel and the Hanukkah Goblins (Kimmel), 276, 312
Her Stories: African American Folktales, Fairy Tales, and True Tales (Hamilton), 137, 156, 262
HerStory: Women Who Changed the World (Ashby & Ohrn), 495
Herszenhorn, David M., 488
Hesse, Karen, 17, 101, 102, 104, 113, 357, 423, 443, 447, 458, 525
Hest, Amy, 24, 183, 185, 203
Hewett, Gloria J., 141, 143
Hewiston, Jennifer, 267
Hewitt, Kathryn, 201
Hey, Al (Yorinks), 104, 115, 124, 153, 160, 178, 179, 206
"Hey Diddle Diddle," 164, 192
Hey Diddle Diddle and Baby Bunting (Caldecott), 155
Hey Diddle Diddle Picture Book, The (Caldecott), 55
Heyer, Marilee, 229, 260, 263
Hey World, Here I Am! (Little), 358
Hiaasen, Carl, 360, 412
"Hiawatha" (Longfellow). See "Song of Hiawatha, The"
Hiawatha: Messenger of Peace (Fradin), 495
Hiawatha's Childhood (Longfellow), 126, 157, 358
Hichens, Robert, 234
Hickman, Janet, 64, 228
"Hickory, Dickory, Dock," 164, 349
Hickox, Rebecca, 232, 257, 265
Hicks, Barbara Jean, 203
Hidden Alphabet, The (Seeger), 199
Hidden Folk, The: Stories of Fairies, Dwarves and Other Secret Beings (Lunge-Larsen), 226, 266
Hide and Seek (Vos), 89, 115, 416, 448–449, 460
Hide and Snake (Baker), 11
Higgins, Jasan, 70
High, Linda Oatman, 538
High Hopes: A Photobiography of John F. Kennedy (Heiligman), 476, 496

"High Hopes" (Nye), 344
High King, The (Alexander), 282, 309
Highwater, Jamake, 32, 64, 110, 113, 267, 390, 412, 508, 537
Highwayman, The (Noyes), 114, 158, 328, 346, 358
Hilary Knight's The Owl and the Pussycat (Lear), 331, 357
Hilary Knight's The Twelve Days of Christmas (Knight), 199
Hill, Eric, 5, 168, 198
Hill, Laban Carrick, 15, 147, 156, 517, 538
Hillenbrand, Will, 199, 263, 265
Hilliam, David, 494
Hillocks, George, 351
Hillyer, V. M., 504
Hinds, Kathryn, 509, 538
Hines, Bob, 540
Hipple, Ted, 101
"Hippopotamus Called Isantim, The," 221
Hiroshima (Yep), 450, 460
Hiroshima No Pika (The Flash of Hiroshima) (Maruki), 113, 134, 148, 158, 204, 540
Hirshfield, Jane, 342
Hirst, Robin, 538
Hirst, Sally, 538
"His Hands" (Trethewey), 346
Histories or Tales of Past Time (Perrault), 264
History of Art for Young People (Janson & Janson), 150, 157
History of Counting, The (Schmandt-Besserat), 173, 199, 541
History of Far Eastern Art, A (Lee), 148
History of Japanese Art (Mason), 147, 148
History of Little Goody Two-Shoes (Newbery), 45, 51
History of Reading, A (Manguel), 3, 65
"Hist Wist" (Driscoll), 324
Hitler (Marrin), 107–108, 113
Hitler Youth: Growing Up in Hitler's Shadow (Bartoletti), 515, 536
Hitty, Her First Hundred Years (Field), 63
Ho, Minfong, 5, 156, 180, 182, 203, 267
Hoang Anh: A Vietnamese-American Boy (Hoyt-Goldsmith), 148, 157, 392, 412
Hoban, Lillian, 110, 113, 203, 356, 412
Hoban, Russell, 30, 34, 184, 203
Hoban, Tana, 12, 14, 17, 18, 19, 156, 168, 172, 173, 198, 199, 200, 538
Hobbit, The (Tolkien), 40, 63, 108, 115, 244, 272, 274, 281, 302, 309, 314
Hobby (Yolen), 314
Hoberman, Mary Ann, 6, 31, 194, 203, 321, 357
Hodges, C. Walter, 459
Hodges, Margaret, 126, 156, 247, 248, 269, 302
Hoestlandt, Jo, 189, 203, 420, 446, 458
Hofer, Ernst, 313
Hofer, Nelly, 313
Hoff, Syd, 200
Hoffman, Lynn, 143
Hogrogian, Nonny, 311
Holder, Heidi, 302
"Hole in the Bucket, A," 349
Hole Is to Dig, A (Krauss), 157
Holes (Fatus), 198
Holes (Sachar), 32, 64, 101, 110, 114, 194, 366, 414
Holiday, Laurel, 485

Holiday Cooking Around the World (Cornell), 530, 537
Hollander, John, 329
Holliday, Laurel, 496
Holling, Holling Clancy, 133, 156
Holm, Jennifer L., 441, 458
Holmlund, Heather D., 497
Holocaust, The (Rossel), 541
Holt, Kimberly, 412
Holtwijk, Ineke, 382, 412
Holub, Josef, 458
Holzheimer, Diane, 534
Holzhey, Magdelena, 15, 146, 156
Home at Last (Elya), 395, 411
Homecoming (Voigt), 364, 414
Homeless Bird (Whelan), 7, 95, 96, 115, 194, 393, 414
Homer, 66, 247, 326
Homesick: My Own Story (Fritz), 466
Homze, Alma Cross, 69
Honest Abe (Kunhardt), 497
Honest-to-Goodness Truth, The (McKissack), 204, 402, 413
Honey, I Love (Greenfield), 339, 356
Honeybee and the Robber, The: A Moving/Picture Book (Carle), 155
Honeycutt, Natalie, 412
Honeysuckle House (Cheng), 394, 410
Hong, Lily Toy, 229, 263
Hoobler, Dorothy, 148, 157, 508, 515, 538
Hoobler, Thomas, 148, 157, 508, 515, 538
Hoofbeats, Claws & Rippled Fins: Creature Poems (Hopkins), 357
hooks, bell, 6, 14, 34, 182, 203
Hooks, William H., 239, 257, 259, 267, 418, 458
Hoop Kings (Smith), 22, 339–340, 360
Hoop Queens (Smith), 340, 360
Hoops (Burleigh), 355
Hooray, A Pinata! (Kleven), 157
Hoose, Phillip, 102, 498, 502, 524, 535, 538
Hoosier School Boy, The (Eggleston), 60
Hoot (Hiaasen), 360, 412
Hooway for Wodney Wat (Lester), 24, 203
"Hope" (Dickinson), 342
Hopeful Trout and Other Limericks, The (Ciardi), 333, 355
Hope Was Here (Bauer), 112, 361, 366, 372, 410
Hopkins, Dianne McAfee, 373
Hopkins, Lee Bennett, 8, 200, 320, 338, 339, 340, 347, 357, 412
Hopkinson, Deborah, 438, 455, 458, 485, 496, 538
Hopper, De Wolf, 328
"Hoppity" (Milne), 349
Horace and Morris But Mostly Delores (Howe), 30, 92, 113
Horenstein, Henry, 169, 199
Hori, Hatsuki, 360
Horn Book, The, 76, 163, 197, 286
Horning, Kathleen T., 94, 274
Horse, Harry, 30, 185, 203
Hort, Lenny, 227, 266
Horton Hatches the Egg (Seuss), 190, 205
Horvath, Polly, 102, 398, 412
Hosni the Dreamer: An Arabian Tale (Ben-Ezer), 112, 265
Hot City (Joosse), 6, 181, 203
Hot Day on Abbott Avenue (English), 131, 155, 181, 202

Hot Jazz Special (Hannah), 147, 156
Hounds of the Morrigan, The (O'Shea), 313
House at Pooh Corner, The (Milne), 13, 291, 313
House Between Earth and Sky, The: Harvesting New American Folktales (Sobol), 254, 266
Household Tales (Grimm & Grimm), *See also* Brothers Grimm
House of Dies Drear, The (Hamilton), 388, 396, 411
House of the Scorpion, The (Farmer), 299, 301, 307–308, 311
House on Mango Street (Cisneros), 392, 410
Houses of Snow, Skin, and Bones (Shemie), 541
House That Crack Built, The (Taylor), 414
"House That Jack Built, The," 80
House That Jack Built, The (Crane), 54, 55
Houston, Gloria, 180, 203, 452
Houston, James, 242
Hovey, Kate, 326, 357
Hovland, Gary, 540
How Angel Peterson Got His Name: And Other Outrageous Tales About Extreme Sports (Paulsen), 22
Howard, Alan, 268
Howard, Arthur, 201
Howard, Norma, 251
Howard, Pauline Rodriguez, 410
Howard, Richard, 538
How Artists See Animals: Mammal Fish Bird Reptile (Carroll), 155, 527, 536
How Artists See People: Boy Girl Man Woman (Carroll), 155, 527–528, 536
How Artists See the Elements: Earth Air Fire Water (Carroll), 155, 528, 536
How Artists See the Weather: Sun Rain Wind Snow (Carroll), 155, 528, 537
How Dinosaurs Came to Be (Lauber), 539
Howe, James, 30, 92, 113, 311
Howell, Kathleen Collins, 358
Howell, Troy, 268, 287, 311, 410
How I Captured a Dinosaur (Schwartz), 18
How I Live Now (Rosoff), 22, 70, 71, 401, 414
Howitt, Mary, 157
Howland, Malia, 528
How Many Days to America? A Thanksgiving Story (Bunting), 399
How Many Fish? (Cohen), 199
How Many Miles to Bethlehem? (Crossley-Holland), 155, 250, 269
How Many Snails? A Counting Book (Giganti), 199
How My Parents Learned to Eat (Friedman), 32, 393, 411
"How Spider Got a Thin Waist," 215
How to Be a Nature Detective (Selsam), 541
How to Be an Ocean Scientist in Your Own Home (Simon), 505, 526, 531, 541
How to Cross a Pond: Poems About Water (Singer), 339, 360
How to Make an Apple Pie and See the World (Priceman), 14, 541
How to Make a Night (Ashman), 342, 355
How to Make Super Pop-Ups (Irvine), 528–529, 538
How You Were Born (Cole), 537
Hoyt-Goldsmith, Diane, 148, 157, 392, 412
Hu, Ying-Hwa, 205
Huang, Tze-si, 356

Hubert, Patti, 254
Huck, Charlotte, 228, 263
Huckabuck Family and How They Raised Popcorn in Nebraska and Quit and Came Back, The (Sandburg), 291, 313
Huckaby, Anna Sixkiller, 159
Hudson, Cheryl Willis, 147, 157
Hudson, Jan, 94, 110, 113, 433–434, 456, 458
Hudson, Wade, 147, 157
Hughes, Arthur, 312, 359
Hughes, Carol, 311
Hughes, Dean, 412
Hughes, Franklin, 355
Hughes, Langston, 157, 343, 357
Hughes, Mark Peter, 379, 412
Hughes, Monica, 298, 312
Hughes, Shirley, 31, 203
Hughes, Ted, 334
Hull, Richard, 199
"Human Made of Earth and Mud, The" (Markman & Markman), 251
Human Story, The: Our Evolution from Prehistoric Ancestors to Today (Sloan), 510, 517, 541
Humbug (Bawden), 410
Hummingbird Nest: A Journal of Poems (George), 338, 356
Humphries, Tudor, 268
"Humpty Dumpty," 103
Hunches in Bunches (Seuss), 205
Hundred Dresses, The (Estes), 411
Hundred Penny Box, The (Mathis), 188, 204, 386–387, 402, 413
Hundredth Name, The (Oppenheim), 313
Hungry Coat, The: A Tale from Turkey (Demi), 32, 233, 265
Hungry Hen (Waring), 160, 205
Hungry Pig (Julian), 198
Hunt, Irene, 64, 412, 436, 458
Hunt, Jonathan, 199
Hunt, Joyce, 533, 541
Hunt, Peter, 65, 288–289
Hunter, Anne, 203
Hunter, Mollie, 312
Hunter and the Animals, The: A Wordless Picture Book (dePaola), 200
Hunter's Moon, The (Meling), 300, 313
Hunting Neptune's Giants: True Stories of American Whaling (Gourley), 538
Hunting of the Snark, The (Carroll), 310
Hurd, Clement, 112, 144, 154, 198, 201
Hurd, Edith Thacher, 6, 203
Hürlimann, Bettina, 52, 53–54
Hurmence, Belinda, 35, 113, 297, 312
Hurricanes: Earth's Mightiest Storms (Lauber), 505, 525, 539
Hurry, Hurry Mary Dear (Bodecker), 333, 355
Hurwitz, Johanna, 412, 496
"Husband Who Counted the Spoonfuls, The" (Bryan), 233
"Husband Who Has to Mind the House, The," 209, 211
Hush!: A Thai Lullaby (Ho), 5, 156, 180, 182, 203
"Hush, Little Baby," 325
Hush, Little Baby (Frazee), 328, 356
Hutchins, Megan, 22
Hutchins, Pat, 6, 12, 13, 30, 174, 175, 200, 203
Hutton, Warwick, 243, 263, 264, 268

Huxley, Dee, 206
Hyman, Trina Schart, 112, 125–126, 155, 156, 158, 223, 224, 248, 263, 264, 266, 267, 268, 269, 276, 312, 457, 458, 496
Hyun, Peter, 263

I, Columbus—My Journal 1492 (Roop & Roop), 498
I, Doko: The Tale of a Basket (Young), 13, 17, 148, 160, 231, 263
I, Freddy: Book One (Reiche), 285–286, 313
I Ain't Gonna Paint No More! (Beaumont), 182, 201
I Am Morgan LeFay: A Tale from Camelot (Springer), 280, 314
I Am Phoenix: Poems for Two Voices (Fleischman), 336, 349, 356
I Am the Mummy Heb-Nefert (Bunting), 536
I Am the Wallpaper (Hughes), 379, 412
I Am Too Absolutely Small for School (Child), 185, 202
Ibatoulline, Bagram, 277, 309, 538
Ibbotson, Eve, 113, 421, 458
Iblis (Oppenheim), 246–247, 268
Iceberg and Its Shadow, The (Greenberg), 33
Ice Cream Store, The (Lee), 357
Ichikawa, Satomi, 144, 156
"Ickle Me, Pickle Me, Tickle Me Too" (Silverstein), 332
Ida B … and Her Plans to Maximize Fun, Avoid Disaster, and (Possibly) Save the World (Hannigan), 86, 102, 113, 366, 412
I Dance in My Red Pajamas (Hurd), 6, 203
"If I Could Put a Curse on You" (Janeczko), 341
If I Only Had a Horn: Young Louis Armstrong (Orgill), 497
If I Ran the Zoo (Seuss), 183, 205
If I Were in Charge of the World and Other Worries: Poems for Children and Their Parents (Viorst), 360
If Not For the Cat (Prelutsky), 329, 359
If the Walls Could Talk: Family Life at the White House (O'Connor), 512, 540
If You Find a Rock (Christian), 355, 537
If You Want to See a Caribou (Root), 522, 541
If You Were There in 1492 (Brenner), 536
I Have a Dream: The Life and Words of Martin Luther King, Jr. (Haskins), 477, 496
I Have a Friend (Narahashi), 5
I Have Lived A Thousand Years: Growing Up in the Holocaust (Bitton-Jackson), 28, 486, 495, 536
"I Haven't Learned to Whistle" (Livingston), 340
I Hear (Oxenbury), 198
I Know Why the Caged Bird Sings (Angelou), 66
Iktomi and the Berries (Goble), 156, 238, 266
Iktomi and the Boulder: A Plains Indian Story (Goble), 156, 237–238, 266
Iliad, The (Homer), 247, 303, 326
I Like It When … (Murphy), 204
I Love Bugs! (Sturges), 519, 542
I Love Guinea Pigs (King-Smith), 538
"I Love You More Than Applesauce" (Prelutsky), 341
Imagine You Are a Crocodile (Wallace), 542
Imber, Jane Hunter, 490
I'm Deborah Sampson: A Soldier in the War of the Revolution (Clapp), 64
I Met a Man (Ciardi), 333, 356

"I'm Going to Ask a Stegosaur to Dinner" (Moss), 338

I'm Going to Pet a Worm Today and Other Poems (Levy), 357

I'm Going to Sing: Black American Spirituals (Bryan), 145, 154

"I'm Nobody! Who Are You?" (Dickinson), 350

Imogene's Antlers (Small), 184, 205

Important Book, The (Brown), 201

Impressionism (Welton), 146, 160

In a Dark, Dark Room (Schwartz), 201

In a Dark Wood (Cadnum), 112, 248, 268

In Coal Country (Hendershot), 88, 452

Incredible Journey, The (Burnford), 363, 410

Incredible Journey of Lewis & Clark, The (Blumberg), 15, 19, 504, 536

In Daddy's Arms I Am Tall: African Americans Celebrating Fathers (Steptoe), 159, 339, 360

Index of Forbidden Books, 66

Indian Captive, The Story of Mary Jemison (Lenski), 63, 433, 458

Indian Chiefs (Freedman), 484, 496

Indian School: Teaching the White Man's Way (Cooper), 511, 537

Indian Winter, An (Freedman), 32, 156, 511, 512, 537

... I Never Saw Another Butterfly ... (Volavkova), 148, 149, 160, 342, 360

In Flanders Fields: The Story of the Poem by John McCrae (Granfield), 538

Ingersoll, 2

Ingpen, Robert, 277, 310, 492

Ingwersen, Faith, 410

Inhelder, B., 11, 35

Inkheart (Funke), 283, 284, 303, 311

Inkpen, Mick, 14, 169, 199

Inkspell (Funke), 283, 284, 303, 311

Innocenti, Roberto, 155, 157, 188, 203, 311, 452

In November (Rylant), 159

In One Door and Out the Other: A Book of Poems (Fisher), 335, 356

In Praise of Our Fathers and Our Mothers: A Black Family Treasury by Outstanding Authors and Artists (Hudson & Hudson), 147, 157

Insectopedia (Florian), 350, 356

Inside the Hindenburg: A Giant Cutaway Book (Majoor), 527, 539

Inspector Hopper's Mystery Year (Cushman), 200

"Instructions for the Earth's Dishwasher" (Peters), 339

Intelligence: The Human Factor (Lang), 531, 539

Interrupted Journey: Saving Endangered Sea Turtles (Lasky), 519, 539

Interstellar Pig (Sleator), 314

In the Beginning: Creation Stories from Around the World (Hamilton), 245, 246, 262, 268

In the Eyes of the Cat: Japanese Poetry for All Seasons (Demi), 356

In the Huddle With ... Steve Young (Christopher), 495

"In the Land of Small Dragon," 258

In the Land of Words: New and Selected Poems (Greenfield), 4, 356

In the Middle of the Night (Cormier), 397, 411

In the Night Kitchen (Sendak), 159, 175, 205

In the Rain with Baby Duck (Hest), 24, 183, 203

In the Small, Small Pond (Fleming), 5, 122, 156

In the Tall, Tall Grass (Fleming), 5, 8

Into a New Country: Eight Remarkable Women of the West (Ketchum), 483, 497

Into the Mummy's Tomb: The Real-Life Discovery of Tutankhamun's Treasures (Reeves), 150, 158

Into the Sea (Guiberson), 535, 538

In Trouble Again, Zelda Hammersmith? (Hall), 411

Invisible Hunters, The (Rohmer, Chow & Vidaure), 235, 236, 265

Invitation to the Game (Hughes), 298, 312

In Your Face: The Facts About Your Features (Jackson), 15, 505, 538

Iorio, Adrian J., 458

Iron Horses (Kay), 538

Iron Ring, The (Alexander), 282, 309

Irvine, Joan, 528–529, 538

Irving, Washington, 129–130, 157

Irwin, Hadley, 396–397, 412

Isaacs, Anne, 157, 183–184, 203

Isaacs, Kathleen T., 490, 531

Isaacson, Walter, 494

Isadora, Rachel, 203, 309, 387, 412, 529, 538

I Saw Esau: The Schoolchild's Pocket Book (Opie & Opie), 165, 198

I Saw Your Face (Dawes), 344, 356

I See (Oxenbury), 12, 198

Ishi: The Last of His Tribe (Kroeber), 423

Ishii, Momoko, 263

Ishizuka, Kathy, 535

"I Sing the Body Electric" (Whitman), 345

Island Boy (Cooney), 135, 155

Islander, The (Rylant), 114

Island in the Sun (Belafonte & Burgess), 325, 355

Island of the Blue Dolphins (O'Dell), 28, 77, 86, 114, 363, 370, 380, 403–407, 413

Island of the Mighty: Stories of Old Britain (Middleton), 268

Island on Bird Street, The (Orlev), 81–82, 92, 108, 114, 447–448, 449, 459

I Spy: An Alphabet of Art (Micklethwait), 199

I Spy Shapes in Art (Micklethwait), 16, 173, 200

Issa, 330

Is This a House for Hermit Crab? (McDonald), 540

Is This Forever, Or What? Poems and Paintings from Texas (Nye), 350, 358

"It Could Always Be Worse," 254

It Could Always Be Worse: A Yiddish Folktale (Zemach), 13, 206, 228, 265

I Thought My Soul Would Rise and Fly: The Diary of Patsy, a Freed Girl (Hansen), 113

I Took the Moon for a Walk (Curtis), 4, 6, 129, 130, 155, 182, 202

It Rained All Day That Night: Autographs, Rhymes & Inscriptions (Morrison), 331, 358

It's Like This, Cat (Neville), 413

It's Not the End of the World (Blume), 410

It's Raining Pigs and Noodles: Poems (Prelutsky), 322

It's So Amazing! A Book About Eggs, Sperm, Birth, Babies, and Families (Harris), 517, 538

Ivanhoe: A Romance (Scott), 60, 63

"Ivory Cups, The" (Lunge-Larsen), 226

Iwa, Melissa, 205

I Want a Dog (Khalsa), 203, 402, 412

I Want to Be an Astronaut (Barton), 111

I Was a Rat! (Pullman), 302, 313

I Was Born About 10,000 Years Ago (Kellogg), 203, 357

I Wear the Morning Star (Highwater), 390, 412

I Wonder If I'll See a Whale (Weller), 129, 160

I Wouldn't Thank You for a Valentine: Poems for Young Feminists (Duffy), 342, 356

"Jabberwocky" (Carroll), 293, 327, 331–332, 355

Jackanapes (Ewing), 56

"Jack and Jill," 103, 165, 192, 349

"Jack and the Beanstalk," 218, 220, 239, 257

Jack and the Beanstalk (Kellogg), 61, 220, 254, 264

Jack and the Bean Tree (Haley), 239, 257, 267

"Jack and the Varmints," 219, 239

"Jack Be Nimble," 192

Jackson, Donna M., 15, 504, 505, 518, 538

Jackson, Shelley, 106, 113, 202

Jack Tales, The (Chase), 266

"Jack the Giant Killer," 45, 47, 209, 215, 216, 217, 219, 220

Jacob Have I Loved (Paterson), 80, 82, 114, 370, 407–409, 413

Jacobs, Francine, 20

Jacobs, Gloria E., 360

Jacobs, James S., 281

Jacobs, Joseph, 220, 221, 263

Jacobson, Frances F., 456

Jacobson, Jennifer, 22

Jacques, Brian, 286, 287, 312

Jaffe, Jane Vial, 316

Jaffe, Nina, 213, 265, 269

Jaffe, Steven H.

Jafta (Lewin), 6, 302, 312

Jafta's Mothers (Lewin), 302, 312

Jakes, John, 496

Jakobsen, Kathy, 16, 157, 325, 350, 357, 458

Jambo Means Hello: Swahili Alphabet Book (Feelings), 170, 198

James, Grace, 229, 263

James, J. Alison, 126, 157

James, Mary, 285, 312

James, Simon, 203

James and the Giant Peach (Dahl), 291, 311

Jamnia, Mohammad Ali, 250–251, 266

Janeczko, Paul B., 7, 319, 324, 329, 341, 350, 357, 527, 538

Janeway, James, 48, 462

Janisch, Heinz, 193, 203

Janitor's Boy, The (Clements), 410

Jan of the Windmill (Ewing), 56

Janson, Anthony F., 119, 121, 134, 143, 146–147, 150, 157

Janson, H. W., 119, 121, 134, 143, 146–147, 150, 157

Jarrell, Randall, 264

Jarrow, Gail, 538

Jassem, Kate, 483, 496

Jay, Alison, 129, 130, 182, 202, 313

Jeffers, Susan, 156, 157, 158, 206, 264, 309, 310, 335, 356, 358, 459

Jeffrey, Sean, 168, 198

Jenkins, Leonard, 497

Jenkins, Martin, 523, 538

Jenkins, Steve, 13, 157, 200, 501–502, 519, 537, 538

Jennifer, Hecate, MacBeth, William McKinley and Me, Elizabeth (Konigsburg), 64, 377, 412

Jennings, Patrick, 312

Jeram, Anita, 538

Jerome, Judson, 317

Jerusalem, Shining Still (Kuskin), 148, 157, 539
Jesse Bear, What Will You Wear? (Carlstrom), 201
Jessica (Henkes), 30, 203
Jewish American Family Album, The (Hoobler & Hoobler), 148, 157, 515, 538
Jewish Spirit, The: A Celebration in Stories and Art (Frankel), 148
Jews, The: A Treasury of Art and Literature (Keller), 148
Jim Thorpe's Bright Path (Bruchac), 469, 495
Jitter-Bug Jam: A Monster Tale (Hicks & Deacon), 203
Joan of Arc (Silverthorne), 493
Joe Louis: America's Fighter (Adler), 478
Joey Pigza Loses Control (Gantos), 14, 70, 71, 372, 376, 411
John, Helen, 414
John, Matthew, 541
John Adams (McCullough), 317, 358, 530
John D. Rockefeller: Boy Financier (Myers), 497
John Henry (Lester), 262
John Muir: America's Naturalist (Locker), 467–468, 497
Johnny Appleseed: A Poem (Lindbergh), 157, 452, 458
Johnny Appleseed (Kellogg), 267
"Johnny Cake," 209
Johnny Crow's Garden (Brooke), 63, 124, 154
Johnny Tremain (Forbes), 15, 63, 108, 112, 194, 418, 432, 458
John Philip Duck (Polacco), 183, 204
Johnson, Adrian, 204
Johnson, Angela, 107, 113, 203, 412
Johnson, David A., 495
Johnson, D. B., 16, 185, 203
Johnson, James Weldon, 157, 516–517, 538
Johnson, Jean, 199
Johnson, Larry, 410
Johnson, Meredith, 413
Johnson, Nancy J., 427
Johnson, Neil, 538
Johnson, Paul Brett, 203
Johnson, Rebecca L., 33, 496, 525, 538
Johnson, Scott, 397, 412
Johnson, Stephen, 339
Johnson, Stephen T., 11–12, 123, 157, 169, 199, 263, 355
Johnson, Steve, 359
Johnson, William H., 156
Johnston, Julie, 458
Johnston, Kathleen S., 502
Johnston, Norma, 34, 481, 497
Johnston, Tony, 157
John Tabor's Ride (Day), 239, 267
"Jolly Old Pig, A," 349
Jolly Postman or Other People's Letters, The (Ahlberg & Ahlberg), 196, 201, 266
Jonas, Ann, 169, 199, 541
Jonathan and His Mommy (Smalls-Hector), 31, 386, 414
Jones, Charlotte Foltz, 511, 538
Jones, Douglas B., 542
Jones, Gwyn, 264
Jones, Trev, 319
Jones, Trevelyn E., 76
Joosse, Barbara, 6, 181, 203, 389, 412
Jordan, Sandra, 146, 156, 480, 487, 496

Jorgensen, Gail, 203
Joseph Had a Little Overcoat (Taback), 18, 132, 159, 178, 205
Josephina Hates Her Name (Engel), 110, 112, 202
Josephson, Judith Pinkerton, 497
Josie's Troubles (Naylor), 413
Journey (MacLachlan), 386, 413
Journey Home (Uchida), 449, 460
Journey Home, The (Lester), 10
Journeys with Elijah: Eight Tales of the Prophet (Goldin), 156, 249–250, 269
Journey to America (Levitin), 458
Journey to an 800 Number (Konigsburg), 113, 412
Journey to Jo'burg (Naidoo), 413
Journey to the River Sea (Ibbotson), 113, 421, 458
Journey to Topaz (Uchida), 449, 460
Joyce, William, 203
Joyful Noise: Poems for Two Voices (Fleischman), 64, 336, 337, 349, 356
Joysmith, Brenda, 360
Juan, Ana, 6, 129, 156, 202, 498
Juan and Juanita (Baylor), 60
Jubela (Kessler), 203
Jude (Morgenroth), 413
Judson, Hallowell, 141
Jukes, Mavis, 179, 203, 402, 412
Julian, Russell, 168, 198
Julie of the Wolves (George), 77, 82, 87, 88, 113, 380, 411
Julius (Johnson), 107, 113, 203
Julius's Candy Corn (Henkes), 168, 198
July (Stevenson), 205
Jumanji (Van Allsburg), 139, 159, 190, 197, 205
Jumbo Book of Drama, The (Dunleavy), 7, 529, 537
Jump Again! More Adventures of Brer Rabbit (Parks), 238, 262
Jump at de Sun: The Story of Zora Neale Hurston (Porter), 497
Jump Back Honey: The Poems of Paul Laurence Dunbar (Dunbar), 17, 155
Jump! The Adventures of Brer Rabbit (Parks), 238–239, 262
June 29, 1999 (Wiesner), 139, 160, 196, 206
Jungle Book, The (Kipling), 63, 288, 312
Junk (Burgess), 372
Jupiter (Simon), 159, 498, 501, 526, 541
Jurassic Park, 297
Jurich, Marilyn, 463
Just a Minute: A Trickster Tale and Counting Book (Morales), 199
"Just Before April Came" (Sandburg), 334
Just Ella (Haddix), 267
Juster, Norton, 203, 312
Justice and Her Brothers (Hamilton), 311
Justin Morgan Had a Horse (Henry), 412
Just My Dad & Me (Komaiko), 33
Just Reward: Or Who Is That Man in the Moon & What's He Doing Up There Anyway? (Sanfield), 263
Just So Stories (Kipling), 288, 312
Just What the Doctor Ordered: The History of American Medicine (Miller), 509, 540

Kadohata, Cynthia, 393, 412, 490
Kagan, Jerome, 11
Kalan, Robert, 200
Kalman, Maira, 14
Kamishibai Man (Say), 32

Kane, Henry B., 358
Kang, Johanna, 203, 458
Kaplan, Howard, 363, 383, 412
Karas, G. Brian, 159, 202
Karl, Jean, 75
Karr, Kathleen, 458
Kastner, Jill, 159, 496
Kasza, Keiko, 21
Kate and the Beanstalk (Osborne), 239, 267
Kate Greenaway (Greenaway), 156
Kate Greenaway's Birthday Book (Greenaway), 55
Kate Greenaway's Mother Goose (Greenaway), 165
Kate Greenaway Treasury, The (Ernest), 54
Katy and the Big Snow (Burton), 186–187, 201
Katz, Bobbi, 6, 350, 357
Kay, Verla, 538
Keats, Ezra Jack, 5, 24, 28, 30, 31, 64, 77, 113, 131–132, 137–138, 157, 187, 188, 195, 196, 203
Keeling, Kara K., 369–370, 409
Keep, Richard, 132, 149, 152, 157
Keepers of the Animals: Native American Stories and Wildlife Activities for Children (Caduto & Bruchac), 245–246, 266
Keepers of the Earth: Native American Stories and Environmental Activities for Children (Caduto & Bruchac), 245, 246, 266
Keeping, Charles, 114, 155, 158, 268, 460
Keeping a Christmas Secret (Naylor), 204, 402, 413
Keeping Barney (Haas), 411
Keeping Quilt, The (Polacco), 148
Keeping the Good Light (Kirkpatrick), 458
Keesha's House (Frost), 346, 356
Keiler, Allan, 464
Keith, Eros, 112, 358, 458
Keith, Harold, 453, 458
Kelin, Daniel A., 254, 267
Keller, Holly, 539
Keller, Katie, 314, 497
Keller, Sharon, 148
Kelley, Gary, 129–130, 157
Kelley, True, 206
Kellogg, Steven, 61, 127, 146, 194, 203, 204, 220, 239, 254, 264, 267, 357
Kelly, Robert Gordon, 44, 57
Kendall, Carol, 294, 312
Kennedy, Caroline, 7, 315, 317, 331, 332, 357
Kennedy, Dorothy M., 319, 320, 321, 357
Kennedy, X. J., 319, 320, 321, 350, 357
Kennemer, Phyllis K., 76
Kenneth Lilly's Animals: A Portfolio of Paintings (Pope), 125, 158, 533–534, 540
Kennett, David, 536
Kennis, Adrie, 541
Kennis, Alfons, 541
Kensuke's Kingdom (Morpurgo), 114
Kent, Zachary, 497
Kept in the Dark (Bawden), 64
Kerley, Barbara, 32, 152, 153, 157, 468–469, 497
Kermode, Frank, 7
Kerr, Judith, 458
Kerr, M. E., 69, 370, 412
Kessler, Christina, 203
Kessler, Leonard, 200
Ketchum, Lisa, 483, 497
Ketterman, Helen, 267

Key, Alexander, 312
Khalsa, Dayal Kaur, 203, 402, 412
Khan's Daughter, The: A Mongolian Folktale (Yep),
    231, 263, 267
Kherdian, David, 497
Kick, Pass, and Run (Kessler), 200
Kick in the Head, A (Janeczko), 350, 357
Kidder, Harvey, 410
Kid in the Red Jacket, The (Park), 413
Kidnapped (Stevenson), 59
Kids Talk About the Civil Rights Movement
    With the People Who Made It Happen
    (King & Osborne), 538
Kiesler, Kate, 202, 356, 496
Kim, Joung Un, 204
Kimball, Laurel H., 156, 197
Kimber, Murray, 328, 357, 358
Kimmel, Eric A., 22, 148, 157, 184, 197, 203,
    230–231, 232, 249, 263, 264, 265, 266, 269,
    276, 312, 326, 357
Kinder- und Hausmärchen (Grimm & Grimm), 63,
    225. See also Brothers Grimm
Kindle, Patrice, 102
King, Casey, 538
King, Coretta Scott, 477, 497
King, Stephen, 284
"King and a Poor Man, The" (Philip), 260
King Arthur and the Knights of the Round Table
    (Williams), 269
"King Arthur Tales," 210
King Bidgood's in the Bathtub (Wood), 39, 160
King Lear (Shakespeare), 257, 259
King of Ireland's Son, The (Behan), 221, 263
King of Shadows, The (Cooper), 297, 311
"King of the Birds" (Grimm & Grimm), 223
King of the Golden River (Ruskin), 63
King of the Middle March (Crossley-Holland), 311
King of the Wind (Henry), 396, 412
King's Day, The: Louis XIV of France (Aliki), 494
King's Fifth, The (O'Dell), 429, 459
Kingsley, Charles, 63, 244, 268, 279
King-Smith, Dick, 276–277, 290, 312, 538
King's Shadow, The (Alder), 457
Kinsey-Warnock, Natalie, 458
Kipling, Rudyard, 63, 288, 312, 357
Kipper's A to Z: An Alphabet Adventure (Inkpen),
    14, 169, 199
Kira-Kira (Kadohata), 393, 412
Kirk, Connie Ann, 180–181, 203
Kirkpatrick, Katherine, 458
Kirkus Reviews, 76
Kirstein, Lincoln, 222, 264
Kiss Hello, Kiss Goodbye (Brown), 21, 198
Kitchen, Bert, 169, 199, 264, 268
"Kite" (Worth), 347
Kittelsen, Theodor, 266
"Kitten" (Worth), 347
Kitten's First Full Moon (Henkes), 4, 6, 120, 152,
    156, 203
Kituku, Vincent Muli Wa, 234, 262
Kiuchi, Tatsuro, 411, 412
Kjelgaard, Jim, 412
Klause, Annette Curtis, 295, 312
Klee, Paul, 144
Klein, Norma, 70–71, 370, 412
Kleven, Elisa, 157, 203
Kline, Suzy, 397, 398, 412
Knight, Christopher G., 519, 539

Knight, Hilary, 199, 331
Knight, Margy Burns, 510, 538
Knockabag: A Famine Tale (Lyons), 420
Knock at a Star: A Child's Introduction to Poetry
    (Kennedy & Kennedy), 319, 320, 321, 357
Knockin' on Wood (Barasch), 21, 484, 495
Knorr, Margaret, 456
Knorr, Susan M., 456
Knox, Bob, 157
Knudson, R. R., 339, 357
Knuffle Bunny: A Cautionary Tale (Willems), 152,
    153, 160, 187, 188, 206
Knutson, Barbara, 235, 265
Kobus, Doni Kwolek, 77
Koch, Kenneth, 351, 357
Koch, Michelle, 538
Kodama, Tatsuharu, 148, 157, 189, 203,
    449, 458
Koehn, Ilse, 486, 497
Koelling, Holly, 44
Koertge, Ron, 339, 357
Kogi's Mysterious Journey (Partridge), 231, 263
Kohlberg, Lawrence, 35–36
Kolar, Bob, 157
Komaiko, Leah, 33
Konigsburg, E. L., 14, 22, 39, 64, 77, 86, 93, 102,
    113, 366, 377, 385, 412
Kopper, Lisa, 312
Korean Cinderella, The (Climo), 263
Korea's Favorite Tales and Lyrics (Hyun), 263
Koscielniak, Bruce, 14, 538
Kraft, Betsy Harvey, 475, 497
Kramer, Stephen, 525, 533, 538
Kraus, Robert, 31, 64, 184–185, 194, 203
Kraus, Ruth, 5, 31, 93
Krauss, Ronnie, 527, 538
Krauss, Ruth, 157
Krenina, Katya, 266
Krensky, Steven B., 157, 538
Kreutzberger, Paul, 53
Kristo, Janice V., 535
Kroeber, Theodora, 423
Kroeger, Mary Kay, 495
Kroll, Steven, 511, 538
Kroll, Virginia, 40, 389, 412
Krommes, Beth, 266
Kronheimer, Ann, 312
Kruglik, Gerald, 181, 201
Krull, Kathleen, 21, 29, 475, 485, 492, 497
Krumgold, Joseph, 391, 412
Krush, Beth, 313
Krush, Joe, 313
Kuhn, Bob, 412
Kula, Elsa, 263
Kulling, Monica, 324
Kumak's Fish: A Tall Tale from the Far North
    (Bania), 266
Kunhardt, Edith, 497
Kunst und Lehrbüchlein, 53
Kunzel, Bonnie, 272
Kuo, Louise, 229, 260, 263
Kuo, Yuan-hsi, 229, 260, 263
Kurelek, William, 452, 458
Kurisu, Jane, 537
Kurtz, Jane, 203
Kushner, Tony, 148, 157, 191, 203
Kuskin, Karla, 148, 157, 539
Kutiper, Karen Sue, 318

Labastida, Aurora, 149, 155, 391, 411
Lacy, Lyn Ellen, 121, 126, 138, 143
"Lad Who Went to the North Wind, The,"
    211, 212, 215, 219, 220
Lady & the Lion, The: A Brothers Grimm Tale
    (Long & Ogburn), 217, 223, 264
Lady of Guadalupe, The (dePaola), 235, 265
Lady of the Lake, The (Scott), 60
Lady with the Hat, The (Orlev), 459
Lagarrigue, Jerone, 113, 156, 357, 458, 542
Lagerlof, Selma, 268
Lalicki, Tom, 497, 530, 539
Lamb, Charles, 17, 113, 257
Lamb, Mary, 17, 113, 257
Lamb, Susan Condie, 180, 203
Lambkins, The (Bunting), 399
Landman, Bimba, 156, 458
Land of the Long White Cloud: Maori Myths, Tales,
    and Legends (Te Kanawa), 246, 268
Landry News, The (Clements), 377, 411
Landstrom, Olof, 201
"Land Where Time Stood Still, The," 217
Lane, Dan, 411
Lanes, Selma, 139
Lang, Andrew, 63, 88, 113
Lang, W. Patrick, 531, 539
Langley, Andrew, 515, 539
Langrish, Katherine, 312
Langstaff, John, 357
Lanning, Rosemary, 203
Lantern Bearers, The (Sutcliff), 460
Larbalestier, Justine, 300, 302, 312
LaReau, Jenna, 538
Laroche, Giles, 132, 157, 341
Larrick, Nancy, 347, 357
Larson, Peter, 502, 503, 506, 539
Lasky, Kathryn, 18, 20, 24, 32, 40, 418, 423,
    435–436, 439, 458, 469, 497, 506, 519, 523,
    531–532, 539
Last Battle, The (Lewis), 279, 280, 312
Last Book in the Universe, The (Philbrick), 313
"Last Camel of Emir Hamid, The"
    (Bushnaq), 232
Last of the Mohicans, The (Cooper), 63
Last Princess, The: The Story of Princess Ka'iulani of
    Hawaii (Stanley), 498
Last Tales of Uncle Remus, The (Lester), 13
"Late Passenger, The" (Lewis), 327
Later, Gator (Yep), 393, 414
Latsch, Oliver, 311
Lauber, Patricia, 15, 18, 19, 96, 505–506, 507, 510,
    518–519, 525, 527, 532, 539
Laughable Lyrics (Lear), 58
Laughing Tomatoes (Alarcão), 355
Laura Charlotte (Galbraith), 202
Lavis, Steve, 199
Lawlor, Laurie, 151, 157, 497, 539
Lawrence, John, 205
Lawrence, Louise, 312
Laws, Frederick, 55
Lawson, Robert, 63, 157, 203, 289, 309, 310,
    312, 458
"Lay-Up, The" (Grandits), 329
Lazare, Jerry, 410
Leaf, Munro, 31, 40, 157, 186, 203, 302, 312
Leaf by Leaf: Autumn Poems (Rogasky), 334, 359
Leaf Jumpers (Gerber), 5, 121
Leaf Man (Ehlert), 117, 145, 155

Leapman, Michael, 107, 113, 515, 539
Lear, Edward, 45, 58–59, 63, 129, 157, 199, 321, 327, 328, 330, 331, 332, 349, 353, 357
Least of All (Purdy), 204
LeCain, Errol, 126, 157, 264, 309, 337, 356, 358
Lee, Dennis, 357
Lee, Jeanne M., 263
Lee, Paul, 496
Lee, Sherman E., 148
Leedy, Loreen, 21, 157, 529, 539
Leeson, Robert, 46
LeGalliene, Eva, 154, 309
Legend Days (Highwater), 390, 412
Legend of Luke, The (Jacques), 287, 312
Legend of Sleepy Hollow, The (Irving), 129–130, 157
Legend of the Bluebonnet, The (dePaola), 136, 155, 237, 266
Legend of the Christmas Rose, The (Lagerlof), 268
Legend of the Indian Paintbrush, The (dePaola), 136, 155
Legends of the North (Coolidge), 63, 245, 254, 268
Legends of the World (Cavendish), 247
LeGuin, Ursula K., 282, 287, 300, 312
Lehman, Barbara, 7, 18, 152, 157, 175, 196–197, 200
Leigh, Tom, 338, 358
Leiner, Katherine, 497
Lember, Barbara Hirsch, 355, 537
Lemons Are Not Red (Seeger), 12, 173, 200
Lenaghan, R. T., 240
L'Engle, Madeleine, 7, 64, 69, 77, 113, 194, 203, 298–299, 305–307, 312, 374, 412
Lenski, Lois, 63, 157, 325, 433, 458
Lent, Blair, 157, 158, 263
Lentil (McCloskey), 16, 158, 194, 204
Lenz, Lisa, 347
Leonardo: Beautiful Dreamer (Byrd), 146, 154, 479, 495
Leonardo da Vinci (McLanathan), 146, 158
Leonardo da Vinci (Stanley), 147, 159, 467, 479, 498
Leo the Late Bloomer (Kraus), 31, 64, 184–185, 194, 203
Lepman, Jella, 144
Leroy's Zoo (Lowe & Lowe), 199
Lessac, Frané, 357
Lessem, Don, 498, 539
Lesser, Carolyn, 539
Lesser, Rika, 131, 156, 223, 414
Lester, Alison, 10
Lester, Helen, 24, 29, 203, 497
Lester, Julius, 13, 157, 203, 238, 239, 242, 262, 267, 269, 517–518, 539
L'Estrange, Roger, 240, 267
Let's Do a Poem (Larrick), 347
Let's Eat! (Zamorano), 179, 206
Let's Fly from A to Z (Magee & Newman), 199
Let's Go Home, Little Bear (Waddell), 5, 205
Let's Paint a Rainbow (Carle), 155
"Let's Pop the Corn" (Levy), 334
Let's Talk About It: Divorce (Rogers), 25, 28
Let's Talk About Race (Lester), 517–518, 539
Letters from a Slave Girl: The Story of Harriet Jacobs (Lyons), 420, 421
Letters from Rifka (Hesse), 443, 458
Letter to Amy, A (Keats), 203
Let the Celebrations Begin! (Wild), 160, 188–189, 206

Let the Circle Be Unbroken (Taylor), 35, 444, 460
Letting Swift River Go (Yolen), 135, 160, 206, 452
Lettow, Lucille J., 125
Leuck, Laura, 13, 171, 199
Levenson, Jay, 149, 151
Levin, Betty, 18
Levin, Vadim, 330, 357
Levine, Arthur A., 7, 230, 263
Levine, Ellen, 35, 113, 497, 515, 539
Levine, Gail Carson, 113, 267, 276, 312
Levine, Joe, 538
Levine-Provost, Gail, 414
Levinson, Nancy Smiler, 200
Levison, Riki, 309
Levitin, Sonia, 458
Levy, Constance, 334, 357
Lewin, Betsy, 112, 128, 152, 155, 180, 202, 523, 539
Lewin, Hugh, 6, 302, 312
Lewin, Ted, 129, 160, 204, 459, 523, 538, 539
Lewis, C. S., 14, 64, 77, 108, 113, 194, 272, 273, 279–280, 302, 309, 312, 327, 494
Lewis, E. B., 152, 160, 187, 189, 190, 203, 206, 355, 496
Lewis, J. Patrick, 227, 266, 321, 344, 357–358
Lewis, Kim, 5, 181, 203
Lewis, Naomi, 53, 225–226, 278, 309, 310, 312
Lewis, Patrick, 249
Lewis, Paul Owen, 157, 161, 203, 246, 268
Lewis, Rena, 77
Leydenfrost, Robert, 359
Liberty (Curlee), 537
Librarian of Basra, The: A True Story from Iraq (Winter), 515–516, 542
Librarian Who Measured the Earth, The (Lasky), 469, 497
"Li Chi Slays the Serpent," 218
Life: Our Century in Pictures for Young People (Stolley), 15, 506, 507, 515, 531, 542
Life, Kay, 410
Life and Death of Adolf Hitler, The (Giblin), 476, 496
Life and Death of Crazy Horse, The (Freedman), 496
Life and Death of Martin Luther King, Jr., The (Haskins), 477, 496
Life and Times of the Apple, The (Micucci), 501, 524, 533, 540
Life and Times of the Peanut, The (Micucci), 524, 540
Life Cycles of a Dozen Diverse Creatures (Fleisher), 537
Life in the Roman Empire: The City (Hinds), 509, 538
Life in the Roman Empire: The Countryside (Hinds), 509, 538
Life in the Roman Empire: The Patricians (Hinds), 509, 538
Life of the Honey Bee, The (Fischer-Nagel & Fischer-Nagel), 537
Lift Every Voice and Sing (Johnson), 516–517, 538
Light: Shadows, Mirrors, and Rainbows (Rosinsky), 527, 541
Light Beyond the Forest, The: The Quest for the Holy Grail (Sutcliff), 247, 269, 314
Light in the Attic, A (Silverstein), 6, 332, 359
Lightning (Kramer), 533, 538
Lightning (Simon), 541

Lightning Inside You and Other Native American Riddles (Belting), 265
Like Jake and Me (Jukes), 179, 203, 402, 412
Li'l Dan the Drummer Boy (Bearden), 147, 154
Lili at Ballet (Isadora), 529, 538
Lilly, Kenneth, 125, 158, 533–534, 540
Lilly's Purple Plastic Purse (Henkes), 31, 102, 202
Li'l Sis and Uncle Willie: A Story Based on the Life and Paintings of William H. Johnson (Everett), 156
Lily's Crossing (Giff), 458
Linch, Tanya, 159
Lincoln: A Photobiography (Freedman), 15, 64, 77, 80, 112, 461, 465, 474, 496
Lindbergh, Reeve, 157, 197, 204, 452, 458, 539
Linden, Seymour, 412
Lindgren, Astrid, 312
Lindgren, Barbro, 30, 168, 198
Linduff, Katheryn, 133
Linnea in Monet's Garden (Björk), 146, 154
"Lion and the Mouse, The" (Morpurgo), 241
"Lion and the Mouse, The" (Paxton), 241
"Lion and the Mouse, The" (Uribe), 241
Lion & the Mouse and Other Aesop Fables, The (Orgel), 17, 261, 268
"Lion and the Mouse, The" (Aesop), 241
Lion Dance: Ernie Wan's Chinese New Year (Waters & Slovenz-Law), 148, 160, 392, 414
Lionel, 168, 198
Lion Named Shirley Williamson, A (Waber), 160, 205
Lionni, Leo, 63, 134, 157, 193–194, 195, 204, 302, 312
Lions: Animal Predators (Markle), 522, 539
Lion's Whiskers, The: And Other Ethiopian Tales (Ashabranner & Davis), 234, 262
Lion's Whiskers, The: An Ethiopian Folktale (Day), 155, 233, 262
Lion Tamer's Daughter, The: And Other Stories (Dickinson), 295, 311
Lion, the Witch, and the Wardrobe, The (Lewis), 14, 77, 108, 113, 194, 279, 280, 309, 312
Lipke, Barbara, 256
Lipman, Jean, 497
Lippert, Margaret H., 262
Lipson, Eden Ross, 99
Lipsyte, Robert, 390, 412
Lisker, Emily, 263, 269
Lisle, Janet Taylor, 33, 64, 91, 113, 376, 403, 412, 446, 458
Listen, Rabbit (Fisher), 335, 356
"Listen Children" (Clifton), 516
Literature and the Child: Romantic Continuations, Postmodern Contestations (McGavran), 44
Little, Jean, 22, 200, 250, 269, 358, 385, 412
Little, Lessie Jones, 485–486, 496
Little Bear (Minarik), 63
Little Black Sambo (Bannerman), 175
Little Blue and Little Yellow (Lionni), 63
Little Book of Fables (Uribe), 241, 268
"Little Boy Blue," 192, 349
Little Brown Bear Won't Go to School! (Dyer), 21, 185, 202
"Little Burnt Face," 258
Littlechild, George, 151, 157
Little Cliff and the Porch People (Taulbert), 187
Little Crow (Taoyateduta): Leader of the Dakota (Swain), 498

Little Folk: Stories from Around the World (Walker), 214, 267

Little Green (Baker), 201

Little House, The (Burton), 6, 63, 109–110, 112, 125, 126, 154, 187, 201, 302, 310

Little House Cookbook, The: Frontier Foods from Laura Ingalls Wilder's Classic Stories (Walker), 529, 542

Little House in the Big Woods (Wilder), 14, 40, 63, 77, 84, 115, 440, 454–455, 460

Little House on the Prairie (Wilder), 460

Little Lord Fauntleroy (Burnett), 63

Little Match Girl, The (Pinkney), 309

Little Men (Alcott), 61

"Little Mermaid, The" (Andersen), 52, 309

Little Mermaids and Ugly Ducklings: Favorite Fairy Tales by Hans Christian Andersen (Andersen), 278, 309, 492

"Little Miss Muffet," 164, 192

Little Pretty Pocket Book, A (Newbery), 45, 50–51, 63

Little Rabbit Goes to School (Horse), 30, 185, 203

Little Red Cap (Grimm & Grimm), 264

"Little Red Hen, The," 209, 211, 213

Little Red Hen, The (Galdone), 30, 214–215, 263

"Little Red Riding Hood," 80, 218, 219

Little Red Riding Hood (Evetts-Secker), 224

Little Red Riding Hood (Galdone), 264

"Little Red Riding Hood" (Grimm & Grimm), 52, 223, 224, 264

Little Red Riding Hood (Hyman), 156, 223, 224, 264

Little Red Riding Hood (Marshall), 223, 224

"Little Red Riding Hood" (Perrault), 71, 221

Little Red Riding Hood (Wegman), 223, 264

Little Ships, The: The Heroic Rescue at Dunkirk in World War II (Borden), 417, 445, 457

Little Stevie Wonder (Troupe), 482, 498

Littlesugar, Amy, 204

"Little Thumb" (Perrault), 71, 221

Little Town on the Prairie (Wilder), 440, 460

Little Women (Alcott), 45, 61, 63, 67–68, 108, 111, 409, 481

Liu, Siyu, 358

Lives of the Musicians: Good Times, Bad Times (And What the Neighbors Thought) (Krull), 497

Livingston, Myra Cohn, 134, 157, 257, 293, 324, 340, 350, 355, 358

Living with Dinosaurs (Lauber), 539

Liyi, He, 263

Lizzie Bright and the Buckminster Boy (Schmidt), 87, 114, 422, 443, 459

"Llorona, La," 236

Lloyd, Megan, 200, 264, 357, 538

Loathsome Dragon, The (Jacobs), 220, 264

Loban, Walter, 9

Lobel, Anita, 19, 170, 171, 199, 263, 264, 358, 485, 497

Lobel, Arnold, 5, 13, 31, 64, 77, 113, 126, 157, 165, 170, 177, 197, 199, 200, 201, 302, 338, 349–350, 358, 359

"Lochinvar" (Scott), 346

Locke, John, 45, 49, 51

Locker, Thomas, 18, 130, 134, 156, 157, 467–468, 490, 495, 497, 524, 539

Locomotion (Woodson), 342, 360

Lodge, Bernard, 359

Loewen, Nancy, 504, 539

London, Jack, 412

London, Jonathan, 157, 522–523, 539

"London Bridge Is Falling Down," 328

Lonely Lioness and the Ostrich Chicks: A Masai Tale (Aardema), 262

Lone Wolf (Franklin), 411

Long, Joanna Rudge, 467

Long, Laurel, 217, 223, 264

Long and Uncertain Journey, A: The 27,000- Mile Voyage of Vasco da Gama (Goodman), 496

Longfellow, Henry Wadsworth, 110, 126, 157, 319, 327, 348, 350, 358, 458

Longjohns (Allen), 168, 198

Long Road to Gettysburg, The (Murphy), 540

Long Secret, The (Fitzhugh), 385, 411

Long View into Space, The (Simon), 526–527, 541

Long Way from Chicago, A (Peck), 96, 114

Long Way to a New Land, The (Sandin), 459

Long Winter, The (Wilder), 460

Lon Po Po: A Red Riding Hood Story from China (Young), 7, 160, 224, 225, 229, 263

Lonsdale, Bernard J., 48, 59

Look: Body Language in Art (Wolfe), 141, 160

Look, Lenore, 24, 33–34

Look at My Book: How Kids Can Write and Illustrate Terrific Books (Leedy), 21, 157, 529, 539

Looking at Pictures: An Introduction to Art for Young People (Richardson), 528, 541

Look! Look! Look! (Hoban), 12, 18, 168, 198, 200

Look Whooo's Counting (MacDonald), 158, 199

Loo-Loo, Boo, And Art You Can Do (Roche), 19, 529, 541

Loomis, Christine, 204

Loots, Barbara Kunz, 350

Lopez, Judith, 541

Lord of the Rings, The (Tolkien), 244, 248, 269, 274, 281, 303, 309, 314

Lord of the Sky: Zeus (Gates), 268

Lost Calf (Julian), 198

Lost in the Barrens (Mowat), 114, 442, 459

Lost Wild America: The Story of Our Extinct and Vanishing Wildlife (McClung), 540

Lost World, The (Doyle), 311

Lost Years of Merlin, The (Barron), 310

Lots of Feelings (Rotner), 21, 25, 173, 200

Lottman, Herbert R., 144

Lotus Seed, The (Garland), 394, 411

Loud Emily (O'Neill), 21

Lou Gehrig: The Luckiest Man (Adler), 478

Lougheed, Robert, 412

Louie (Keats), 137, 157

Louie, Ai-Lang, 263

Louisa May: The World and Works of Louisa May Alcott (Johnston), 34, 481, 497

Louÿs, Pierre, 316

"Love After Love" (Walcott), 346

Love and Roast Chicken: A Trickster Tale from the Andes Mountains (Knutson), 235, 265

Love as Strong as Ginger (Look), 33–34

"Love bade me welcome; yet my soul drew back" (Herbert), 346

Love From Your Friend, Hannah (Skolsky), 459

Love Is … (Halperin), 91, 113, 156

Love Letters (Adoff), 355

Love You Forever (Munsch), 110

Low, Alice, 160

Low, Joseph, 200

Low, William, 113, 202

Lowe, Sylvia, 199

Lowe, Warren, 199

Lowell, Amy, 334

Lowry, Lois, 14, 22, 32, 64, 66, 90, 101, 102, 108, 110, 113, 298, 304, 305, 312, 370, 378–379, 398, 412–413, 423, 443, 458, 483

Loyie, Larry, 484, 497

Lucas, George, 303

Lueders, Edward, 40, 324, 343, 356

Luenn, Nancy, 149, 157

Luis-Martin, 149

Lukens, Rebecca J., 80, 275

"Lullaby" (Rossetti), 322–323

Lum, Kate, 184, 204

Luna (Peters), 370, 371, 400, 413

Lunch (Fleming), 202

Lunch Bunnies (Lasky), 24

Lunge-Larsen, Lise, 131, 157, 212, 226, 266

Lunn, Janet, 33, 274, 296, 302, 312, 432–433, 458

Luther, Martin, 66

Lydia, Queen of Palestine (Orlev), 448

Lynch, Chris, 413

Lynch, Patrick J., 17, 226, 263, 266, 309

Lynch, Tom, 17, 241, 261, 267

Lyne, Sanford, 343, 358, 359

Lyon, George Ella, 89, 113, 204, 413, 458

Lyons, Maritcha Rémond, 464

Lyons, Mary E., 420, 421

Lystad, Mary, 44

Macaulay, David, 32, 150, 157, 204, 452, 459, 501, 504, 527, 533, 539

MacCarthy, Patricia, 312

MacDonald, Fiona, 158

MacDonald, George, 63, 69, 275, 279, 312

MacDonald, Robert, 57

MacDonald, Suse, 11, 158, 169, 199

MacGill-Callahan, Sheila, 158

MacGillivray, Laurie, 371

MacGregor, Rob, 413

Machines at Work (Barton), 5, 200

Machu Picchu (Mann), 508, 539

Macintosh, Helen K., 48, 59

MacLachlan, Emily, 183, 204

MacLachlan, Patricia, 33, 77, 105–106, 113, 158, 183, 204, 358, 370, 386, 413, 422, 440, 441, 452, 454, 459

MacLeod, Anne Scott, 48

Macy, Sue, 29, 33, 497, 501, 503, 539

Madam President: The Extraordinary, True (and Evolving) Story of Women in Politics (Thimmesh), 512–513, 542

Madeline (Bemelmans), 30, 77, 112, 144, 154

Madeline in London (Bemelmans), 154

Mad Man's Drum (Ward), 144

Madsen, Jane M., 368

Maestro, Betsy, 509, 539

Maestro, Guilio, 539

Maestro, The (Wynne-Jones), 414

Magee, Doug, 199

Maggie and the Pirate (Keats), 196, 203

Magical Adventures of Pretty Pearl, The (Hamilton), 311

Magical Melting Pot, The: The All-American Cookbook That Celebrates America's Diversity (Greenway), 538

Magic Animals of Japan (Pratt & Kula), 263

Magic Fan, The (Baker), 310

Magic Flute, The (Gatti), 537

Magic Gourd, The (Diakite), 234, 262
Magician's Nephew, The (Lewis), 280
Magic of Spider Woman, The (Duncan), 17, 238, 266
Magic or Madness (Larbalestier), 300, 302, 312
Magic School Bus, The: Inside the Earth (Cole), 537
Magic School Bus, The: Lost in the Solar System (Cole), 527, 537
Magic School Bus, The: On the Ocean Floor (Cole), 40, 504, 537
Magic Spring: A Korean Folktale (Rhee), 231, 263
Magic Words: Poems (Field), 151, 156
Maguire, Gregory, 417, 449, 459
Mah, Adeline Yen, 449–450, 459
Mahurin, Matt, 300, 382
Mahy, Margaret, 260, 263, 312, 317–318, 358, 537
Maisy Goes to School (Cousins), 168, 198
Maisy Goes to the Playground (Cousins), 168, 198
Maisy's Colors (Cousins), 168, 198
Maizlish, Lisa, 175, 200
Maizon at Blue Hill (Woodson), 414
Majoor, Mireille, 527, 539
Major, John S., 148, 158, 507–508, 534, 539
Make Way for Ducklings (McCloskey), 6, 31, 63, 121, 124, 138, 158, 194, 204
Make Way for Sam Houston (Fritz), 64, 113, 496
Making Up Megaboy (Walter), 414
Makley, Mike, 317
Malam, John, 466, 497
Malcolm X (Adoff), 477–478, 494
Malcolm X: By Any Means Necessary (Myers), 478, 497
Maline, Peter, 250
Mallat, Kathy, 158
Malone, Peter, 155, 268, 269, 537
Malory, Sir Thomas, 47, 247, 280
Mama (Hopkins), 412
Mama, Do You Love Me? (Joosse), 389, 412
Mama, Let's Dance (Hermes), 376, 412
Mama One, Mama Two (MacLachlan), 113, 413
Mama's Coming Home (Banks), 30
Mammal (Parker), 540
Mammalabilia (Florian), 336, 350, 356
Mandela, Nelson, 233, 234, 262
Manders, John, 539
Manet (Wright), 160
"Man From Snowy River, The" (Paterson), 327
Man from the Other Side, The (Orlev), 15, 108, 114, 423, 448, 459
Manguel, Alberto, 3, 65, 108
Manheim, Ralph, 156, 264
Maniac Magee (Spinelli), 414
Mann, Elizabeth, 19, 505, 508, 539
Manna, Anthony L., 267
Manning, Sarra, 413
Mannis, Celeste Davidson, 329, 358
Man Who Kept House, The (Asbjørnsen & Moe), 266
Man Who Walked Between the Towers, The (Gerstein), 153, 156, 468, 496
Man Who Went to the Far Side of the Moon, The: The Story of Apollo 11 Astronaut Michael Collins (Schyffert), 541
Many Moons (Thurber), 314
Many Thousand Gone: African Americans from Slavery to Freedom (Hamilton), 35, 113
Manzano, Sonia, 188, 204

Map, Moondance, and the Nagasaki Knights (Myers), 413
"Marandenboni," 219
Marantz, Sylvia S., 140
Marcantonio, Patricia Santos, 254, 265
Marc Chagall and the Jewish Theater (Guggenheim Museum), 148
Marcellino, Fred, 127, 201, 264, 309, 331, 357
Marchetta, Melina, 102, 398–399, 413
Marcus, Leonard S., 102, 144, 158, 490
Margaret Bourke-White: Her Pictures Were Her Life (Rubin), 122, 159, 478, 498
Marglow, Eric, 496
Margolis, Rick, 102
"Maria Morevna," 216
Marian Anderson: A Singer's Journey (Keiler), 465
Marie in Fourth Position: The Story of Degas' "The Little Dancer" (Littlesugar), 204
Mariel of Redwall (Jacques), 286, 312
Marino, Jan, 413
Maritcha: A Nineteenth-Century American Girl (Bolden), 464, 465, 475, 495
Mark, Jan, 25
Markes, Julie, 5
Markle, Sandra, 501, 519, 522, 539
Markman, Peter T., 251, 268
Markman, Roberta H., 251, 268
Marks, Alan, 112, 412
Mark Twain (Ward, Duncan, & Burns), 494
Marrin, Albert, 107–108, 113, 464, 473, 474, 483, 493, 497, 515
Marriott, Pat, 309
Marschall, Ken, 527, 539
Marshak, Samuel, 302, 312
Marshall, Bonnie C., 254, 266
Marshall, Cynthia, 279
Marshall, Edward, 201
Marshall, James, 129, 157, 201, 204, 221, 223, 224, 264, 276
Marshmallow (Newberry), 158
Marstall, Bob, 541
Martha Speaks (Meddaugh), 107, 113, 204
Martin, Ann M., 411
Martin, Bill, Jr., 170, 199, 204
Martin, Cyd, 199
Martin, Eva, 126, 158, 239, 257, 267
Martin, Jacqueline Briggs, 204
Martin, Laura C., 14, 529, 539
Martin, Paula, 265
Martin, Rafe, 6, 17, 18, 31, 126–127, 158, 204
Martin, Sue Anne, 182–183
Martinez, Miriam, 37
Martin Luther King (Bray), 147, 154, 477, 495
Martin Luther King, Jr. and the Freedom Movement (Patterson), 477, 497
Martin's Mice (King-Smith), 312
Martin the Warrior (Jacques), 312
Maruki, Toshi, 113, 134, 148, 158, 204, 540
Mary Cassatt (Turner), 479, 498
Mary Had a Little Lamb (Hale), 166, 197
Mary on Horseback: Three Mountain Stories (Wells), 483, 498
Mary Poppins (Travers), 291, 314
Masai and I (Kroll), 40
"Ma Sheep Thunder and Son Ram Lightning" (Bryan), 234
Mason, Penelope, 146, 148

Massotty, Susan, 496
Master Man: A Tall Tale of Nigeria (Shepard), 133, 159, 234, 262
Matchlock Gun, The (Edmonds), 112
Mathematickles! (Franco), 334–335, 356
Mathers, Petra, 359
Mathis, Sharon Bell, 188, 204, 386–387, 402, 413
"Matilda, Who Told Lies, and Was Burned to Death" (Belloc), 332
Matilda Bone (Cushman), 426, 457
Matthew's Dragon (Cooper), 10
Mattimeo (Jacques), 312
Maugham, W. Somerset, 265
Maughan, Shannon, 70
Maupin, Amy B., 101
Maurer, Richard, 466, 470, 490, 497
Max Found Two Sticks (Pinkney), 102
Maxie, Rosie, and Earl—Partners in Crime (Park), 413
Maxim, George, 11, 20, 29
Max's Bath (Wells), 168, 198
Max's Bedtime (Wells), 168, 198
Max's Breakfast (Wells), 168, 198
Max's Chocolate Chicken (Wells), 115
Maya's Children: The Story of La Llorona (Anaya), 236, 265
Maybe Yes, Maybe No, Maybe Maybe (Patron), 413
Mayer, Marianna, 200, 225, 264
Mayer, Mercer, 174, 177, 193, 200, 204, 226, 266
Maynard, Caitlin, 540
Maynard, Thane, 540
Mayo, Margaret, 219, 267
"Mazel and Schlimazel," 215
Mazel and Schlimazel, or the Milk of the Lioness (Singer), 217, 228, 265
Mazer, Norma Fox, 365, 386, 413, 449, 459
McAllister, JoEllen, 203
McBratney, Sam, 33
McCaffrey, Anne, 299, 312
McCaffrey, Meg, 401
McCaughrean, Geraldine, 268, 439, 459
McClintock, Barbara, 264
McCloskey, Robert, 6, 16, 31, 63, 121, 124, 138, 144, 158, 187, 194, 204
McClung, Robert, 540
McCord, David, 63, 320, 321–322, 329, 340–341, 348, 353, 358
McCue, Lisa, 338, 360
McCulloch, Lou J., 47
McCullough, David, 317, 358, 494, 530
McCully, Emily Arnold, 5, 6, 9, 113, 124, 146, 158, 174, 175, 188, 193, 200, 201, 203, 204, 269, 448, 459, 497
McCurdy, Michael, 15, 536, 538
McDaniel, Thomas R., 370
McDermott, Beverly Brodsky, 134, 158
McDermott, Gerald, 122–123, 158, 235, 237, 243, 262, 265, 266, 267, 268
McDonald, Joyce, 413
McDonald, Megan, 204, 452, 459, 540
McDuff Moves In (Wells), 206
McElderry, Margaret, 67
McElderry Book of Aesop's Fables, The (Morpurgo), 241, 267
McElmeel, Sharron L., 490
McElmurry, Jill, 539
McGavran, James Holt, 44

McGill, Alice, 262
McGillivray, Kim, 394, 450
McGraw, Eloise, 293–294, 312
McGuigan, Mary Ann, 459
McGuire, Sandra, 386
McIntyre, Barbara M., 349
McKay, Hilary, 413
McKee, Tim, 487, 497
McKinley, Robin, 7, 113, 248, 269, 283, 302, 312–313
McKissack, Frederick, 32, 516, 537, 540
McKissack, Patricia C., 32, 113, 204, 402, 413, 516, 530, 537, 540
McLanathan, Richard, 146, 158
McLaughlin, Molly, 519, 540
McMahon, Patricia, 148, 158, 392, 413
McMillan, Bruce, 14, 158, 197, 199, 540
McMullan, Kate, 21
McNaughton, Janet, 301, 313
McNeely, Tom, 496
McPhail, David, 10, 204, 357, 540
McWhorter, Diane, 11, 92, 113, 516, 530, 540
Meade, Holly, 132, 156, 180, 202, 357, 466, 496
Meddaugh, Susan, 107, 113, 204, 206, 355
Mediavilla, Cindy, 248
Meet the Austins (L'Engle), 69, 374, 412
Mehta, Lila, 263
Meigs, Cornelia, 47, 49, 58
Mei-Mei Loves the Morning (Tsubakiyama), 188, 205
Meisle, Bill, 494
Melchior's Dream and Other Stories (Ewing), 56
Meling, O. R., 300, 313
Melmed, Laura Krauss, 204
Meltzer, Milton, 107, 114, 472, 473, 481, 494, 497, 513, 515, 540
Melville, Herman, 127
Memories of Anne Frank: Reflections of a Childhood Friend (Gold), 496
Memories of Yesterday: All of Which I Saw and Part of Which I Was (Lyons), 464
Mendelson, Michael, 288
Mendelson, S. T., 309
Merlin (Yolen), 314
Merlin and the Making of the King (Hodges), 247, 269
Mermaid, The: And Other Sea Poems (Windham), 360
Mermaid Summer, The (Hunter), 312
Merriam, Eve, 66, 114, 170, 199, 321
Merrick, Brian, 319
Merrill, Jean, 427, 456, 459
Merriman, Nick, 540
Merry Adventures of Robin Hood, The (Pyle), 45, 55, 59–60, 63, 248, 269
"Merry-Go-Round" (Hughes), 343
Meryman, Richard, 158, 480, 497
Messenger (Lowry), 298, 312
Metamorphoses (Ovid), 326
Meteor! (Polacco), 107, 114, 183, 204
"Meteorites" (Livingston), 324
Meyer, Carolyn, 15
Meyer, Jim, 522, 541
Miami Giant, The (Yorinks), 160, 197, 206
Michael Foreman's Mother Goose (Foreman), 121, 156, 165–166, 197

Michael Hague's Favorite Hans Christian Andersen Fairy Tales (Hague), 309
Michael Rosen's ABC (Rosen), 199
Michelangelo (Stanley), 479, 498
Micklethwait, Lucy, 14, 15, 16, 32, 140–141, 158, 173, 199, 200, 528, 540
Micucci, Charles, 501, 524, 533, 540
Middle Passage, The: White Ships/Black Cargo (Feelings), 147, 156, 177, 190–191, 200, 435, 457
Middleton, Haydn, 268
Midnight Horse, The (Fleischman), 94, 112, 311
"Midnight Ride of Paul Revere, The" (Longfellow), 319, 327, 348, 350, 358, 458
Midwife's Apprentice, The (Cushman), 110, 112, 418, 426–427, 457
Miers, Charles, 147
Migdale, Lawrence, 157, 392, 412
Mighty Asparagus, The (Radunsky), 153, 158
Mike Fink: A Tall Tale (Kellogg), 239, 267
Mike Mulligan and His Steam Shovel (Burton), 30, 154, 187, 201
Mikolaycak, Charles, 268
Miles, Bernard, 268
Miles, Miska, 389, 413
Milgrim, David, 201
Milkmaid, The (Caldecott), 54
Mill (Macaulay), 539
Millard, Anne, 18, 90, 114, 524, 540
Miller, Bertha Mahony, 530
Miller, Brandon Marie, 509, 511–512, 513, 540
Miller, Debbie S., 124, 158, 540
Miller, Debra A., 540
Miller, Douglas, 497
Miller, Edward, 541
Miller, Inna, 324
Miller, Margaret, 537, 540
Miller, Mary Beth, 172, 199
Miller, Mitchell, 264
Millions of Cats (Gág), 6, 12, 21, 63, 124, 126, 127, 156, 202
Mills, Lauren, 313
Milne, A. A., 13, 40, 55, 63, 77, 114, 194, 204, 272, 291, 313, 317, 325, 331, 349, 350, 358
Minarik, Else Holmelund, 63, 177
Minor, Wendell, 205, 335, 359, 361, 495, 496, 498, 537
Minty: A Story of Young Harriet Tubman (Schroeder), 159
Mirette on the High Wire (McCully), 124, 158, 188, 204
Mirror of Merlin, The (Barron), 310
Mischling, Second Degree: My Childhood in Nazi Germany (Koehn), 486, 497
Miss Bindergarten Gets Ready for Kindergarten (Slate), 24
Missing Manatee, The (Defelice), 295, 366–368
Missing May (Rylant), 40, 80, 114, 365, 414
Mississippi Mud: Three Prairie Journals (Turner), 360
Miss Mary Mac: And Other Children's Street Rhymes (Cole & Calmenson), 197
"Miss Misinformation" (Prelutsky), 350
Miss Rumphius (Cooney), 202
Mister Seahorse (Carle), 132, 155
Misty of Chincoteague (Henry), 412
Mitakidou, 267
Mitch and Amy (Cleary), 410

Mitchell, Steven, 309
Mitten, The (Brett), 110
Mixed-Up Chameleon, The (Carle), 17, 30, 146, 155, 200
Mizumura, Kazue, 334, 360
Moby-Dick (Melville), 127–128
Moe, Jörgen E., 225, 226–227, 266
Moeri, Louise, 439, 459
Moffats, The (Estes), 68, 69, 373, 411
Mohr, Nicholasa, 391–392, 403, 413, 490
Moja Means One: Swahili Counting Book (Feelings), 14, 64, 172–173, 199
Mojave (Siebert), 335, 359
Moje, Elizabeth, 139, 144
"Mole Catcher, The" (Bierhorst), 235
Mole's Hill (Ehlert), 202
Molk, Laurel, 129, 160
Mom, the Wolf Man, and Me (Klein), 70–71, 370, 412
Monarchs (Lasky), 539
Monday's Troll (Prelutsky), 322, 333, 359
Mondrian, Piet, 134
Monet (Welton), 146, 160
Monet, Claude, 133
Money, Money, Money: The Meaning of the Art and Symbols on United States Paper Currency (Parker), 504, 512, 513, 540
Monjo, F. N., 32, 35, 435, 459
Monkey Island (Fox), 112, 376, 381–382, 411
Monkey's Haircut and Other Stories Told by the Maya, The (Bierhorst), 235, 265
Monks, Julie, 358
Monson, A. M., 182, 204
Monson, Dianne L., 38, 39, 100, 182, 318, 336, 359
Montenegro, Laura Nyman, 339, 358
Montgomery, Sy, 503, 519–520, 521–522, 532, 540
Month-Brothers, The: A Slavic Tale (Marshak), 302, 312
"Moon" (Livingston), 324
Moonbear's Pet (Asch), 31, 201
Mooney, Bel, 383, 413
Moon Is Like a Silver Sickle, The: A Celebration of Poetry by Russian Children (Morton), 324, 358
Moon Jumpers, The (Udry), 138, 159
Moonlight Man, The (Fox), 70, 71, 411
Moon Rope (Ehlert), 235, 265
Moon Song (Baylor), 324, 355
"Moon Was But a Chin of Gold, The" (Dickinson), 334
Moorchild, The (McGraw), 293–294, 312
Moore, Ann W., 64, 465, 493, 494
Moore, Barbara, 528, 542
Moore, Clement C., 63, 125, 158, 327, 348, 358
Moore, Eva, 356
Moore, Inga, 311
Moore, Patrick, 526, 540
Mora, Pat, 40, 181, 391, 413
Morache, Jette, 110
Moral Alphabet, A (Belloc), 332, 355
Morales, Yuyi, 199
Mordan, C. B., 537
More Beasts for Worse Children (Belloc), 332, 355
More English Fairy Tales (Jacobs), 221, 263
Moreno, Rene King, 199
More Nonsense (Lear), 58
More Rootabagas (Sandburg), 7, 291, 313

More Scary Stories to Tell in the Dark (Schwartz), 66
More Small Poems (Worth), 340, 347, 360
More Tales of Oliver Pig (Van Leeuwen), 31, 201
More Tales of Uncle Remus: Further Adventures of Brer Rabbit, His Friends, Enemies, and Others (Lester), 262
Morgenroth, Kate, 413
Morgenstern, Susie, 379, 413
Moritz, Charles, 138
Moriuchi, Mique, 537
Morning Girl (Dorris), 112, 418, 428–429, 457
Morpurgo, Michael, 83, 114, 124, 158, 241, 248, 267, 269, 450–451, 459
Morrill, Leslie, 311
Morris, Gerald, 280, 313
Morris, Neil, 311
Morris Goes to School (Wiseman), 201
Morrison, Dorothy Nafus, 484, 497
Morrison, Lillian, 331, 339, 358
Morrison, Toni, 34, 147, 158, 516, 540
Morrow, Glenn, 112, 268
Morrow, Honoré, 419, 438–439, 453, 455, 457, 459
Morrow, Lesley Mandel, 99
Morte d'Arthur, Le (Malory), 47, 63, 71, 247, 280
Morton, Miriam, 324, 358
Mosberg, Hilary, 446
Mosel, Arlene, 158, 263
Mosely, Keith, 358
Moser, Barry, 13, 17, 88, 114, 158, 238, 246, 262, 264, 266, 268, 277, 310, 311, 338, 358, 459
Moses, Amy, 540
Moses, Will, 157
Moses the Kitten (Herriot), 203
Mosher, Richard, 102
Mosque (Macaulay), 150, 157
Moss, Jeffrey, 338, 358
Moss, Lloyd, 6, 8, 120, 158, 194, 204
Mossflower (Jacques), 286, 312
Moss Gown (Hooks), 239, 257, 259, 267
"Mossycoat," 257
"Mossycoat" (Crossley-Holland), 221
Most Beautiful Roof in the World, The: Exploring the Rain Forest Canopy (Lasky), 539
Mother and Son Tales (Evetts-Secker), 259, 267
Mother Goose (Newbery), 51
Mother Goose: Or, the Old Nursery Rhymes (Greenaway), 197
Mother Goose Remembers (Beaton), 197
Mother Jones: Fierce Fighter for Workers' Rights (Josephson), 497
Mother Scorpion Country (Rohmer & Wilson), 235–236, 265
Mother's Day Mice, The (Bunting), 201
Mother Teresa (Demi), 476, 495
"Mother Was a Lady: Self and Society in Selected American Children's Periodicals" (Kelly), 44
Mountain Jack Tales (Haley), 239, 267
Mountain Men: True Grit and Tall Tales (Glass), 496
Mountains of Tibet, The (Gerstein), 311
"Mountain Wind" (Loots), 350
Mouse and the Motorcycle, The (Cleary), 112, 285, 310
Mouse Count (Walsh), 200
Mouse Mess (Riley), 194

Mouse Rap, The (Myers), 388–389, 413
Moves Make the Man, The (Brooks), 33, 85, 112, 410
Mowat, Farley, 114, 442, 459
"Mowgli's Brothers" (Kipling), 288
Mowry, Jess, 413
Moxley, Sheila, 265, 466–467, 495
Mr. and Mrs. Muddle (Hoberman), 31
"Mr. and Mrs. Vinegar," 211
Mr. Griggs' Work (Rylant), 205
Mr. Gumpy's Outing (Burningham), 30
Mr. Mistoffelees with Mungojerrie and Rumpelteazer (Eliot), 337, 356
Mr. Nick's Knitting (Wild), 32, 206
Mr. Popper's Penguins (Atwater & Atwater), 291, 310
Mr. Putter and Tabby Pour the Tea (Rylant), 13, 177, 201
Mr. Putter and Tabby Walk the Dog (Rylant), 177, 201
Mr. Rabbit and the Lovely Present (Zolotow), 160
Mrs. Chicken and the Hungry Crocodile (Paye & Lippert), 262
Mr. Semolina-Semolinus: A Greek Folktale (Manna & Mitakidou), 267
Mrs. Frisby and the Rats of NIMH (O'Brien), 93, 114, 285, 313
Mrs. Goose's Baby (Voake), 12, 205
Mrs. Overtheway's Remembrances (Ewing), 56
Mrs. Wishy-Washy's Scrubbing Machine (Crowley), 168, 198
Mrs. Wishy-Washy's Splishy-Sploshy (Crowley), 168, 198
Ms. MacDonald Has a Class (Ormerod), 166, 198
Mufaros's Beautiful Daughters: An African Tale (Steptoe), 7, 109, 114, 234, 262
Muggie Maggie (Cleary), 410
Muhammad (Demi), 471, 495
Muir, Percy, 49
Mullins, Patricia, 202
Multicultural Folktales for the Feltboard and Readers' Theater (Sierra), 267
Multicultural Literature: Through the Eyes of Many Children (Norton), 214
"Multilingual Mynah Bird, The" (Prelutsky), 350
Mulvihill, Margaret, 146, 158
Mummies & Their Mysteries (Wilcox), 542
"Mummy Slept Late and Daddy Fixed Breakfast" (Ciardi), 324, 333, 349
Munch, Edvard, 134
Muncha! Muncha! Muncha! (Fleming), 202
Muñoz, William, 540
Munsch, Robert N., 110
Munsinger, Lynn, 201, 203, 204, 360
Murphy, Claire Rudolf, 511, 540
Murphy, Jim, 64, 89, 114, 473, 497, 502, 510–511, 532, 540
Murphy, Mary, 204
Murray, Martin, 413
Musgrove, Margaret, 64, 129, 158, 170, 199
"Mushroom" (Worth), 347
Musicians of the Sun (McDermott), 235, 265
Musleah, Rahel, 228
Mussen, Paul Henry, 11
Mutén, Burleigh, 259, 267
Muth, Jon J., 204, 357
My Backpack (Bunting), 201

My Best Friend (Rodman), 31, 182, 187, 205
My Black Me: A Beginning Book of Black Poetry (Adoff), 355
My Brother, Ant (Byars), 13, 200
My Brother Martin: A Sister Remembers Growing Up with the Rev. Dr. Martin Luther King, Jr. (Farris), 477, 495
My Brother Sam Is Dead (Collier & Collier), 66
My Daniel (Conrad), 457
My Dog Toby (Zimmerman & Clemesha), 206
My Dream of Martin Luther King (Ringgold), 147, 158, 477, 498
Myers, Anna, 443–444, 459
Myers, Bernice, 264
Myers, Christopher, 158, 196, 204, 358
Myers, Elizabeth, 497
Myers, Tim, 6, 178, 194, 204, 277, 313, 329, 358
Myers, Walter Dean, 22, 114, 196, 204, 313, 344, 358, 371–372, 381, 388–389, 413, 478, 497, 516, 540
"My Father and the Fig Tree" (Nye), 344
My First Mother Goose (Opie & Opie), 198
My Friend Rabbit (Rohman), 5, 120, 159
My Grandmother's Stories: A Collection of Jewish Folk Tales (Geras), 228, 264
My Great-Aunt Arizona (Houston), 180, 203, 452
My Guardian Angel (Weil), 20, 426, 456, 460
My Kindergarten (Wells), 21, 185, 206
My Life with Martin Luther King, Jr. (King), 477, 497
My Life with the Wave (Paz), 204
My Light (Bang), 527, 536
My Little Sister Ate One Hare (Grossman), 14, 199
My Little Toolbox (Reed), 198
My Mama Had a Dancing Heart (Gray), 202
My Man Blue (Grimes), 34, 156, 357
"My Mother's Got Me Bundled Up" (Prelutsky), 334
My Name is Georgia (Winter), 40
My Name Is Yoon (Recorvits), 21
My New York (Jakobsen), 16
My Parents Think I'm Sleeping (Prelutsky), 350, 359
My Place in Space (Hirst & Hirst), 538
My Prairie Year: Based on the Diary of Elenor Plaisted (Harvey), 452, 458
My Puppy Is Born (Cole), 521, 537
Myracle, Lauren, 22, 366, 413
"Myra Song, The" (Ciardi), 325
My Sahara Adventure: 52 Days by Camel (Raskin & Pearson), 525, 541
My Seasons with Penguins: An Antarctic Journal (Webb), 523, 542
My Shadow (Stevenson), 159
My Side of the Mountain (George), 63, 87, 380, 411
Mysteries of Harris Burdick, The (Van Allsburg), 13, 139, 159, 193, 200
Mysterious Disappearance of Leon (I Mean Noel) (Raskin), 397, 414
Mysterious Island, The (Verne), 60
Mysterious Visitor, The: Stories of the Prophet Elijah (Jaffe), 268
Mystery of Drear House, The (Hamilton), 388
Mystery of the Ancient Maya, The (Meyer & Gallenkamp), 15
Mystery of the Missing Red Mitten, The (Kellogg), 61
Mystic Horse (Goble), 156
"My Tattoo" (Doty), 345–346

Mythical Birds and Beasts from Many Lands (Mayo), 219, 267

Mythology of the World (Philip), 242, 250, 268

Myths and Legends Series: Hindus and Buddhists (Nivendita & Coomaraswamy), 251, 267

Myths of Greece & Rome (Bulfinch), 268

"My Valentine" (Stevenson), 341

My Very First Book of Colors (Carle), 12, 17, 173, 200

My Very First Book of Numbers (Carle), 12, 171, 199

My Very First Book of Shapes (Carle), 12, 17, 200

My Very First Mother Goose (Opie), 6

Nacht, Merle, 355

Nadel, Deborah, 495

Nadel, Marc, 358, 497

Nagarajan, Nadia Grosser, 254, 265

Naidoo, Beverly, 413

Naked Mole-Rat Mystery, The: Scientific Sleuths at Work (Jarrow & Sherman), 538

Naming, The (Croggon), 300, 311

Namioka, Lensey, 394–395, 413, 459

Nana Upstairs and Nana Downstairs (dePaola), 202

Napoli, Donna Jo, 22, 33, 272, 276, 313, 413

Narahashi, Keiko, 5, 200

Nash, Ogden, 331

Natarella, Margaret, 318

Nathan, Amy, 540

Nathaniel Talking (Greenfield), 357

National Council for the Social Studies, 76

National Geographic Prehistoric Mammals (Turner), 520–521, 542

National Science Teachers Association, 502

Nation's Report Card, 435

Nation Torn, A: The Story of How the Civil War Began (Ray), 514, 541

Nature's Art Box (Martin), 14, 529, 539

Navajo: Visions and Voices Across the Mesa (Begay), 17, 151, 154

Naylor, Phyllis Reynolds, 110, 114, 204, 363, 379, 395, 396, 402, 413

Nazi Olympics, The: Berlin 1936 (Bachrach), 515, 536

Neat Line, The: Scribbling Through Mother Goose (Edwards), 6, 165, 192, 197

Necessary Noise (Cart), 410

Neighborhood Mother Goose, The (Crews), 165, 197

Neighborhood Odes (Soto), 32

"Nellie in the Light House," 57

Nelson, Annika, 409

Nelson, Kadir, 152, 153, 159, 180, 205, 344, 359, 498

Nelson, Marilyn, 7, 11, 95, 114, 344–345, 358

Nelson, Mary Ann, 257

Nelson, S. D., 495

Nelson, Theresa, 413

Nelson Mandela's Favorite African Folktales (Mandela), 234, 262

Nemean Lion, The (Evslin), 268

Nesbit, E., 17, 257

Ness, Evaline, 31, 104, 114, 204, 282

Nest of Dinosaurs, A: The Story of Oviraptor (Norell & Dingus), 502, 519, 540

Nettie Jo's Friends (Potter), 204

Neufeld, John, 101

Neugebauer, Michael, 538

Neuhaus, David, 540

Neumeyer, Peter F., 201

Neville, Emily, 413

Newberry, Clare Turlay, 158

Newbery, John, 45, 50–51, 63, 165, 198

Newcomb, Rain, 505, 526, 532, 541

New England Primer, The, 49

New Kid on the Block, The (Prelutsky), 32, 322, 323

New Lottery Book of Birds and Beasts, The (Bewick), 54, 55

Newman, George L., 497

Newman, Lesléa, 6, 8, 21, 25, 204

Newman, Robert, 199, 396, 413

New Questions and Answers About Dinosaurs (Simon), 518, 533, 541

News About Dinosaurs, The (Lauber), 18, 518–519, 539

Newsom, Carol, 199

"New Vestments, The" (Lear), 331

New Wind Has Wings, The: Poems from Canada (Downie & Robertson), 349, 356

Nichol, Barbara, 14

Nicholson, William, 115, 290, 314

Nielsen, Andrew, 346

Nieman, Gail, 356

Night at the Fair (Crews), 202

Night Before Christmas, The (Moore), 125, 158, 327, 348, 358

Night Eater, The (Juan), 6

Night Garden: Poems from the World of Dreams (Wong), 342, 360

"Night Garden" (Wong), 342

Nightingale, The (Andersen), 154, 260, 266, 277, 309, 481, 492

Nightingale, The (Mitchell), 309

Nightingale, The (Pinkney), 309, 492

Night Is Gone, Day Is Still Coming (Ochoa, Franco, & Gourdine), 343, 359

Nightjohn (Paulsen), 81, 114

Night Journey, The (Lasky), 32, 418, 458

Night Knight (Ziefert), 168, 198

Night Noises (Fox), 21, 202

Night Shift Daddy (Spinelli), 30, 181, 205

Night Story (Willard), 6, 348, 360

Night Swimmers, The (Byars), 410

Nikolajeva, Maria, 44, 368

Nilsen, Alleen Pace, 2, 77, 99, 100, 195, 300–301, 368–369, 370

Nine Days to Christmas: A Story of Mexico (Ets & Labastida), 149, 155, 391, 411

19 Varieties of Gazelle: Poems of the Middle East (Nye), 317, 344, 358

Nine-Ton Cat, The: Behind the Scenes at an Art Museum (Thomson & Moore), 528, 542

Nirgiotis, Nicholas, 523, 535, 540

Nirgiotis, Theodore, 523, 535, 540

Nister, Ernest, 158

Nitschke, August, 46, 222

Niven, Penelope, 334, 358, 481, 497

Nivendita, Sister, 251, 267

Nivola, Claire A., 204, 536

Nix, Garth, 313

Nixon, Joan Lowery, 295, 313

Noah's Ark (Janisch), 193, 203

Noah's Ark (Spier), 159, 176, 193, 200

Noble, William, 65

"Nobody Loves Me" (Zolotow), 317

Noda, Takayo, 339, 358

Nodelman, Perry, 140, 162

No Dogs Allowed (Cutler), 411

No Dogs Allowed! (Manzano), 188, 204

Noel, Ruth S., 274, 281

No Hero for the Kaiser (Frank), 66, 92, 112, 422, 458

Noisy Way to Bed, The (Whybrow), 5, 8, 21

Nolan, Dennis, 313, 498

Noll, Sally, 6

No Man's Land: A Young Soldier's Story (Bartoletti), 418, 421, 437, 457

No Milk! (Ericsson), 202

No More Dodos: How Zoos Help Endangered Wildlife (Nirgiotis & Nirgiotis), 523, 535, 540

No More Strangers Now: Young Voices from a New South Africa (McKee), 487, 497

Nomura, Takaaki, 31, 392–393, 413

Nonsense! (Lear), 328, 357

Nonsense Books of Edward Lear, The (Lear), 357

Nonsense Omnibus (Lear), 357

Nonsense Songs (Lear), 357

Nonsense Songs, Botany and Alphabets (Lear), 58

Nonsense Songs and Stories (Lear), 331

Nonstop Nonsense (Mahy), 317–318, 358

Noon, Steve, 90, 114, 524, 540

No Place to Be: Voices of Homeless Children (Berck), 410

No Pretty Pictures: A Child of War (Lobel), 485, 497

Norell, Mark A., 502, 519, 540

Norman, Howard, 137, 158

Norse Gods and Giants (D'Aulaire), 245, 268

Norse Myths, The (Crossley-Holland), 302

North (Napoli), 22, 413

Northern Light, A (Donnelly), 22, 451–452, 457

North Korea (Miller), 540

North, Sterling, 114

Norton, Donna E., 75, 78, 101, 105, 110, 111, 196, 214, 254, 255, 307, 348, 351, 402, 462, 533

Norton, Mary, 63, 272, 274, 275, 291, 294, 313

Norton, Saundra E., 554

Norwegian Folk Tales (Asbjørnsen & Moe), 266

Nory Ryan's Song (Giff), 433, 458

No Such Things (Peet), 183, 204

Nothing But the Truth: A Documentary Novel (Avi), 15, 40, 64, 97–98, 111, 409

Nothing Ever Happens on 90th Street (Schotter), 7, 205

"Not My Bones" (Nelson), 345

Novac, Ana, 497

Nowhere to Call Home (Defelice), 295

Now Is Your Time! The African-American Struggle for Freedom (Myers), 114, 516, 540

Noyes, Alfred, 114, 158, 328, 346, 358

Number the Stars (Lowry), 32, 90, 108, 113, 423, 458

Numeroff, Laura, 204

Nunnally, Tina, 309, 492

Nursery "Alice," The (Carroll), 292, 293, 310

Nursery Companion, A (Opie & Opie), 50, 165, 198

Nurse Truelove's New Year's Gift (Newbery), 51

Nutt, Ken, 356

Nye, Michael, 358

Nye, Naomi Shihab, 12, 150, 158, 317, 342, 343, 344, 347, 350, 358
Nye, Robert, 247, 269

Obligado, Lilian, 205
O'Brian, Patrick, 313
O'Brien, Anne Sibley, 538
O'Brien, Michael, 158, 413
O'Brien, Patrick, 271
O'Brien, Robert C., 93, 114, 285, 313
Obstinate Land, The (Keith), 453, 458
Ochoa, Annette Piña, 343, 359
O'Connell, Rebecca, 5
O'Connor, Barbara, 413
O'Connor, Jane, 512, 540
October Smiled Back (Peters), 12, 18
Octopus, The: Phantom of the Sea (Cerullo), 537
Odd Boy Out: Young Albert Einstein (Brown), 466, 468, 470, 490, 494, 495
Odean, Katheleen, 77, 463, 466
O'Dell, Scott, 3, 28, 64, 77, 86, 110, 114, 363, 370, 380, 390, 403–407, 413, 416, 418, 421, 429, 439, 441, 456, 459
Odin's Family: Myths of the Vikings (Philip), 268
O'Donnell, Liam, 100
Odyssey, The (Homer), 66, 247, 326
Of Colors and Things (Hoban), 12, 173, 200
Officer Buckle and Gloria (Rathmann), 182, 183, 194, 204
Off to School, Baby Duck! (Hest), 185, 203
Off We Go! (Yolen), 4, 8, 129, 160
Of Mice and Men (Steinbeck), 66
Ogburn, Jacqueline K., 217, 223, 264
Ogres! Ogres! Ogres! A Feasting Frenzy from A to Z (Heller), 169, 199
Oh, David! (Shannon), 198
Oh, Lewis! (Rice), 41
Oh, No! Where Are My Pants? And Other Disasters (Hopkins), 339, 357
Oh, the Places You'll Go! (Seuss), 64
Oh My Baby, Little One (Appelt), 327, 355
O Holy Night: Christmas with the Boys Choir of Harlem (Ringgold), 250, 269
Ohrn, Deborah Gore, 495
Ojeda, Auriana, 22, 531, 540
Okutoro, Lydia Omolola, 342, 359
Old-Fashioned Girl, An (Alcott), 61
Old Hickory: Andrew Jackson and the American People (Marrin), 464, 473, 493, 497
Old Home Day (Hall), 18
Old Ironsides: Americans Build a Fighting Ship (Weitzman), 542
Old John (Hartling), 386, 412
"Old King Cole," 192
"Old MacDonald Had a Farm," 166
"Old Man Winter" (Wood), 334
"Old Mother Hubbard," 192
Old Possum's Book of Practical Cats (Eliot), 337, 356
Old Turtle (Wood), 160, 335, 360
Old Woman and the Wave, The (Jackson), 106, 113
Old Woman Who Named Things, The (Rylant), 205
Old Yeller (Gipson), 113, 411
Oliver and Amanda's Halloween (Van Leeuwen), 201
Oliver Button Is a Sissy (dePaola), 188, 202
Oliver Pig at School (Van Leeuwen), 13, 201
Oliver the Mighty Pig (Van Leeuwen), 21

Oliver Twist (Dickens), 57
Olive's Ocean (Henkes), 22, 412
Olivia (Falconer), 144, 154, 156, 185, 202
Olivia Saves the Circus (Falconer), 202
Oller, Erika, 204
Olmec World, The: Ritual and Rulership (Art Museum, Princeton University), 149
Olsen, Sylvia, 413
O'Malley, Kevin, 271, 297–298, 313
Omnibeasts: Animal Poems and Paintings (Florian), 336, 356
Once a Mouse (Brown), 154
Once a Wolf: How Wildlife Biologists Fought to Bring Back the Gray Wolf (Swinburne), 505, 522, 532, 534–535, 542
Once Upon a Galaxy (Sherman), 265
Once Upon a Poem: Favorite Poems That Tell Stories (Crossley-Holland), 327, 332, 356
On Christmas Day in the Morning (Langstaff), 357
On Christmas Eve (Brown), 201
100 Best Books for Children (Silvey), 153
One at a Time: Collected Poems for the Young (McCord), 329, 340–341, 348, 353, 358
One Eye, Two Eyes (Kimmel), 266
One-Eyed Cat (Fox), 17, 64, 104, 112, 364, 411
One Frog Too Many (Mayer & Mayer), 200
One Good Apple: Growing Our Food for the Sake of the Earth (Paladino), 524, 540
One Grain of Rice: A Mathematical Folktale (Demi), 267
"One Hundred Books That Shaped the Century" (Breen, Fader, Odean, & Sutherland), 77, 272, 463–464
100 Most Popular Children's Authors' Biographical Sketches and Bibliographies (McElmeel), 490
One Hundred Nineteenth-Century Rhyming Alphabets in English (Baldwin), 198
One Hundredth Thing About Caroline, The (Lowry), 413
O'Neill, Alexis, 21
O'Neill, Mary, 351, 352, 359
One in the Middle Is the Green Kangaroo, The (Blume), 31, 410
One Is a Snail, Ten Is a Crab: A Counting by Feet Book (Sayre & Sayre), 199
One Leaf Rides the Wind: Counting in a Japanese Garden (Mannis), 329, 358
One Lighthouse, One Moon (Lobel), 19, 171, 199
One Lucky Girl (Lyon), 89, 113
"One Misty Moisty Morning," 164
One Morning in Maine (McCloskey), 144, 158, 204
1, 2, 3 (Hoban), 12
One Witch (Leuck), 13, 171, 199
On Market Street (Lobel), 13, 170, 199
On My Honor (Bauer), 17, 104, 112, 410
On the Banks of Plum Creek (Wilder), 454, 460
On to Oregon! (Morrow), 419, 438–439, 453, 455, 457, 459
Oops! (Shannon), 168, 198
Open Your Eyes: Extraordinary Experiences in Faraway Places (Davis), 482–483, 495
Opera, What's All the Screaming About? (Englander), 537
Opie, Iona, 5, 6, 165, 198, 332, 348, 359
Opie, Peter, 165, 198, 332, 348, 359
Oppel, Kenneth, 15, 275, 298, 313
Oppenheim, Joanne, 158
Oppenheim, Shulamith Levy, 246–247, 268, 313

Orbis Pictus (Comenius), 53, 54, 55
"Ordinary Days" (Grimes), 342
Orgel, Doris, 17, 31, 112, 223, 261, 264, 268, 457
Orgill, Roxane, 497
Original Freddie Ackerman, The (Irwin), 396–397, 412
Original Mother Goose's Melody, The (Newbery), 165, 198
Orlev, Uri, 15, 81–82, 92, 114, 423, 447–448, 449, 459
Ormai, Stella, 204
Ormerod, Jan, 166, 198
Orphea Proud (Wyeth), 399–400, 414
Orr, Tamara, 22
Osborn, Robert, 356
Osborne, Linda Barrett, 538
Osborne, Mary Pope, 239, 244–245, 267, 268
Oscar Otter (Benchley), 200
O'Shea, Pat, 313
"O Sliver of Liver" (Livingston), 350
O Sliver of Liver (Livingston), 340, 358
Other Bells for Us to Ring (Cormier), 446, 457
Other Dog, The (L'Engle), 203
Other Fourteen Ninety-Two, The: Jewish Settlement in the New World (Finkelstein), 537
Other Side, The (Woodson), 187, 189, 206
Other Way to Listen, The (Baylor), 336, 355
Otherwise Known as Sheila the Great (Blume), 410
"Otter, The" (Florian), 336
Oughton, Jerrie, 459
Our Century in Pictures for Young People (Stolley), 33
Our Dad Died (Dennison), 22
Our Granny (Wild), 107, 115
Ouriou, Susan, 268
"Our Lady's Child" (Grimm & Grimm), 279
Our Nest (Lindbergh), 539
Our Only May Amelia (Holm), 441, 458
Outcasts of 19 Schuyler Place, The (Konigsburg), 22, 39, 86, 113, 366, 412
Outlaws of Sherwood, The (McKinley), 248, 269
Out of Africa (Dinesen), 320
Out of Darkness: The Story of Louis Braille (Freedman), 485, 496
Out of the Dust (Hesse), 17, 101, 102, 104, 113, 357, 458, 525
Out-of-This-World Astronomy: 50 Amazing Activities & Projects (Rhatigan & Newcomb), 505, 526, 532, 541
Outside and Inside Killer Bees (Markle), 501, 519, 539
Outside and Inside Spiders (Markle), 539
Outside Dog (Pomerantz), 177, 201
Outside Over There (Sendak), 138, 143, 159
Outside the Lines (Burg), 325, 355
Over, Under and Through and Other Spatial Concepts (Hoban), 173, 200
Over on the Farm: A Counting Picture Book Rhyme (Gunson), 12
Over Sea, Under Stone (Cooper), 283, 311
Over the Top of the World: Explorer Will Steger's Trek Across the Arctic (Bowermaster), 525, 542
Ovid, 66, 326
Owen (Henkes), 107, 113, 181, 185, 202
Owen Foote, Frontiersman (Greene), 376–377, 411
Owens, Gail, 410
Owens, Lily, 264
Owens, Mary Beth, 169, 199

"O What Is That Sound" (Auden), 327
"Owl" (Merriam), 321
"Owl and the Pussy-Cat, The" (Lear), 129, 157, 321, 327, 331, 332, 349, 357
Owl at Home (Lobel), 201
Owl in Love (Kindle), 102
Owl Moon (Yolen), 10, 21, 25, 40, 124, 160
Owl Service, The (Garner), 311
Ox-Cart Man, The (Hall), 121, 126, 135, 153, 156, 452
Oxenbury, Helen, 4, 5, 12, 30, 115, 122, 159, 160, 186, 198, 205, 293, 310
Oxford Book of Children's Verse, The (Opie & Opie), 332, 348, 359
Oxford Illustrated Book of American Children's Poems, The (Hall), 357
Oxford Nursery Rhyme Book, The (Opie & Opie), 165, 198
Oxford Spanish Dictionary, 7

Pacific Crossing (Soto), 392, 414
Packer, Tina, 17
Packet of Seeds, A (Hopkinson), 438, 458
Paddington Abroad (Bond), 288, 310
Paddington Helps Out (Bond), 310
Paddington Marches On (Bond), 310
Paddle-to-the-Sea (Holling), 133, 156
Painters of the Caves (Lauber), 507, 539
Painter Who Loved Chickens, The (Dunrea), 29
Pak, Soyung, 204
Paladino, Catherine, 524, 540
Palin, Nicki, 268
Palmer, Jan, 496
Palm of My Heart, The: Poetry by African American Children (Adadjourna), 355
"Pancake, The," 209
Pancakes for Breakfast (dePaola), 200
Panda Rescue: Changing the Future for Endangered Wildlife (Bortololli), 522, 536
Pandell, Karen, 540
Panek, Richard, 470
Panzer, Nora, 144, 158
Paolilli, Paul, 7, 10, 324, 359
Paolini, Christopher, 248, 269, 274–275, 280, 300, 313
Papa Gatto, An Italian Fairy Tale (Sanderson), 207, 217, 267
Paper Crane, The (Bang), 230, 263
"Paper Dreams" (Katz), 350
Park, Barbara, 413
Park, Dong-il, 263
Park, Linda Sue, 11, 94–95, 114, 146, 158, 427, 459
Parker, Nancy Winslow, 504, 512, 513, 540
Parker, Robert Andrew, 202, 265, 357, 480, 496
Parker, Steve, 540
Parker, Vic, 13
Parks, Van Dyke, 238–239, 262
Park's Quest (Paterson), 413
Parnall, Peter, 336, 355, 410, 413
Parr, Todd, 168, 198
Parra, Nicanor, 342
Parthenon, The (Woodford), 509, 542
Partridge, Elizabeth, 231, 263, 482, 497
Parzival (Eschenbach), 280
Parzival: The Quest of the Grail Knight (Paterson), 247, 269
Pasachoff, Naomi, 497
Paschkis, Julie, 262, 360

Pascoe, Elaine, 540
Passager (Yolen), 314
Passover Journey, The: A Seder Companion (Goldin), 509–510, 538
Past Perfect, Present Tense: New and Collected Stories (Peck), 529, 540
"Pat-a-Cake, Pat-a-Cake, Baker's Man," 103
Patchwork Quilt, The (Flournoy), 156
Patent, Dorothy Hinshaw, 521, 523, 540
Paterson, A. B., 327
Paterson, John, 445–446, 459
Paterson, Katherine, 64, 66, 77, 80, 82, 90–91, 102, 114, 160, 230, 247, 263, 269, 303, 370, 372, 385, 407–409, 413, 445, 459, 483, 506, 537
Path of the Pale Horse (Fleischman), 458
"Path on the Sea, The" (Miller), 324
Patneaude, David, 20, 22, 450, 459
Patron, Susan, 413
Patterson, Jose, 251, 265
Patterson, Lillie, 477, 497
Pattou, Edith, 276, 313
Paul Bunyan (Kellogg), 61, 267
Paul Revere's Ride: The Landlord's Tale (Santore), 327, 358
"Paul Revere's Ride" (Longfellow). See "Midnight Ride of Paul Revere, The"
Paulsen, Gary, 7, 17, 22, 28, 32, 81, 83, 110, 114, 380–381, 390, 392, 420, 441, 459, 497
Paxton, Tom, 241, 267, 349, 355
Paye, Won-Ldy, 262
Payne, C. F., 328, 360
Paz, Octavio, 204
Pea Blossom, The (Poole), 277–278, 313
Peale, Charles Wilson, 130
Peanut Butter and Jelly: A Play Rhyme (Westcott), 360
Pearce, Anna Markus, 20
Pearce, Phillippa, 114
Pearl and Wagner: Three Secrets (McMullan), 21
Pearls of Leitra (Jacques), 312
Pearson, Debora, 525, 541
Pearson, Kit, 313, 459
Pearson, P. D., 105
Pearson, Ridley, 293, 310
Pearson, Susan, 329, 359
Pearson, Tracy Campbell, 411
"Peasant's Pea Patch," 211
Peck, Richard, 64, 96, 98, 114, 373, 383, 413, 419, 436–437, 459, 529, 540
Peddler's Dream, A (Shefelman), 452, 459
Pedersen, Villhelm, 278, 309, 492
Peekaboo Babies: A Counting Book (Lionel), 168, 198
Peeping Beauty (Auch), 201
Peet, Bill, 32, 40, 158, 183, 204, 482, 483, 497
"Pelican Chorus, The" (Lear), 331
Pelican Chorus and Other Nonsense, The (Lear), 331, 357
Pelletier, David, 123, 158, 169–170, 199
Pellowski, Anne, 254, 267
Péne du Bois, William, 206
Penguin Pup for Pinkerton, A (Kellogg), 194, 203
People Could Fly, The: American Black Folktales (Hamilton), 137, 156, 238, 262
People Could Fly, The: The Picture Book (Hamilton), 126, 137, 152, 153, 156, 238, 262
Perez, Elvia, 254, 265

Perfect Wizard, The: Hans Christian Andersen (Yolen), 480, 492, 498
Perkins, George, 76, 325
Perkins, Lynne Rae, 377–378, 413
Perkins, Mitali, 393–394, 413
Perrault, Charles, 45, 49, 52, 63, 71, 153, 158, 209, 217, 221–222, 261, 264, 277
Perrault d'Armancour, Pierre, 49, 63
Perrine, Laurence, 91
Perry, Robert, 540
Persephone (Hutton), 268
Persepolis: The Story of a Childhood (Satrapi), 486–487, 494, 498
Persian Cinderella, The (Climo), 265
Pertzoff, Alexander, 459
Peter and the Starcatchers (Barry & Pearson), 293, 310
Peter Pan; or The Boy Who Would Not Grow Up (Barrie), 63, 293, 310
"Peter Piper," 164
Peter Rabbit. See Tale of Peter Rabbit, The
Peters, Julie Anne, 370, 371, 400, 413
Peters, Lisa Westberg, 12, 14, 18, 339, 359
Peter's Chair (Keats), 24, 131–132, 137, 157, 203
Petersen, P. J., 413
Petersham, Maud, 313
Petersham, Miska, 313
Peterson, Katherine, 230
Peter the Great (Stanley), 498
"Petrosinella," 219
Petry, Ann, 419, 431, 459
Petunia (Duvoisin), 186, 202
Phantom Tollbooth, The (Juster), 312
Phelan, Carolyn, 182
Philbrick, Rodman, 313, 413
Philip, Neil, 156, 221, 232, 242, 250, 260, 263, 264, 265, 268
Phillips, Tom, 147
Philosophy: 100 Essential Thinkers (Stokes), 542
Photo by Brady: A Picture of the Civil War (Armstrong), 514, 530, 536
"Photograph—Poem for Two Voices" (Grimes), 342
Photography and the Making of the American West (Clee), 15
Piaget, Jean, 11, 35
Picasso, Pablo, 134
"Pickety Fence, The" (McCord), 320, 321–322
Pick-up Sticks (Ellis), 411
Picnic (McCully), 6, 174, 175, 193, 200
Picture Book of Sojourner Truth, The (Adler), 478
Picture That Mom Drew, The (Mallat & McMillan), 158
Pied Piper of Hamelin (Browning), 43, 55, 326–327, 346, 348, 355
Pienkowski, Jan, 114
Pierce, Mamora, 313
Pierced By a Ray of Sun: Poems About the Times We Feel Alone (Gordon), 356
Pierre: A Cautionary Tale (Sendak), 349, 359
Pierre's Dream (Armstrong), 128, 154
Piggies (Wood), 206
Pigs from A to Z (Geisert), 169, 199
Pigs from 1 to 10 (Geisert), 40, 171, 202
Pigs in the Mud in the Middle of the Rud (Plourde), 204
Pigs Might Fly (King-Smith), 290, 312
Pilgrim's Progress, The (Bunyan), 45, 48, 63

Pilkey, Dav, 113, 203
"Pimples" (Nielsen), 346
Pinkney, Andrea Davis, 482, 497
Pinkney, Brian, 17, 102, 113, 114, 262, 267, 310, 497
Pinkney, Jerry, 9, 17, 124, 146, 154, 156, 157, 159, 203, 241, 261, 262, 268, 269, 277, 309, 310, 356, 460, 492
Pinocchio. See Adventures of Pinocchio, The
Pinsky, Robert, 319
Pioneer Girl (Anderson), 495
Pipkin of Pepper for the Pumpkin Soup, The (Cooper), 126, 155
Pippi in the South Seas (Lindgren), 312
Pippi Longstocking (Lindgren), 312
Pippin the Christmas Pig (Little), 250, 269
Pish, Posh, Said Hieronymus Bosch (Willard), 10, 40, 160, 330–331, 360
Pittman, Ramona T., 493
Pizza the Size of the Sun, A (Prelutsky), 329, 333, 350, 359
Plain City (Hamilton), 411
Plains Warrior: Chief Quanah Parker and the Comanches (Marrin), 497
Planet of Junior Brown, The (Hamilton), 381, 412
Planets, The (Moore), 526, 540
Platt, Richard, 452, 459, 540
Playing (Oxenbury), 198
Please Bury Me in the Library (Lewis), 358
Plecas, Jennifer, 200, 201
Plourde, Lynn, 204
"Plowboy" (Sandburg), 334
Plume, Ilse, 16, 264, 290, 314, 360
Pocketful of Poems, A (Grimes), 156, 357
Pocket Poems (Katz), 6
Podwal, Mark, 265
Poems for the Very Young (Rosen), 359
Poems for Youth (Dickinson), 334, 356
Poems of Halloween Night: Ragged Shadows (Hopkins), 340
Poems of Lewis Carroll (Livingston), 355
Poems of the Midwest (Sandburg), 334, 359
Poem Stew (Cole), 356
"Poem to Mud" (Snyder), 321, 349
Poetic Edda, 244
Poetry by Heart: A Child's Book of Poems to Remember (Attenborough), 331, 355
Poetry for Young People: Emily Dickinson (Dickinson), 334, 356
Poetry Matters: Writing a Poem from the Inside Out (Fletcher), 356
Poetry of Black America, The: Anthology of the 20th Century (Adoff), 355
Poetry Troupe, The: An Anthology to Read Aloud (Wilner), 321, 360
Poets' Grimm, The: 20th Century Poems From Grimm Fairy Tales (Beaumont & Carlson), 346, 355
Pogany, Willy, 268, 311
Poisonous Snakes (Simon), 541
"Poison Tree, A" (Blake), 346
Poke in the I, A: A Collection of Concrete Poems (Janeczko), 319, 324, 329, 357
Polacco, Patricia, 31, 35, 36, 91, 107, 114, 148, 179, 182, 183, 204, 446–447, 452, 459
Polar Bear Journey, A (Miller), 158
Polar Bear Night (Thompson), 4, 5, 123, 153, 159, 181, 205

Polar Express, The (Van Allsburg), 13, 110, 139, 140, 159, 205
Poles Apart: Why Penguins and Polar Bears Will Never Be Neighbors (Scott), 525, 541
Police Officers Protect People (Greene), 538
Politi, Leo, 391, 413
Polizzotti, Mark, 458
Polking, Kirk, 65
"Polliwogs, The" (Florian), 336
Pollock, Jackson, 134
Pollyanna (Porter), 63
Pomegranate Seeds: Latin American Jewish Tales (Nagarajan), 254, 265
Pomerantz, Charlotte, 177, 201
Pomeroy, Diana, 199
Pony Express! (Kroll), 511, 538
Poole, Amy Lowry, 277–278, 313
Pool of Fire, The (Christopher), 300, 305, 310
"Poor Turkey Girl, The" (Cushing), 237
Popcorn Book, The (dePaola), 537
Pope, Joyce, 125, 158, 533–534, 540
Poppleton (Rylant), 177, 201
Popular Nonfiction Authors for Children: A Biographical and Thematic Guide (Wyatt, Coggins, & Imber), 490
Porte, Barbara Ann, 204
Porter, A. P., 497
Porter, Eleanor H., 63
Porter, George, 410
Porter, Pamela, 483–484, 498
Possum's Harvest Moon (Hunter), 203
Postal Workers A to Z (Johnson), 199
Posters by Maurice Sendak (Sendak), 139
Potato Kit, The (Corcoran), 411
Potter, Beatrix, 5, 55, 63, 77, 80, 96, 114, 158, 194, 272, 275, 285, 286–287, 309, 313, 362–363
Potter, Giselle, 201, 202, 204, 413
Pot That Juan Built, The (Andrews-Goebel), 14, 146, 154, 344, 355
Pottle, Robert, 350
Powell, Richard J., 146, 147
Power of Myth, The (Campbell), 303
Power of One, The: Daisy Bates and the Little Rock Nine (Fradin & Fradin), 478, 496
Practice of Poetry, The: Writing Exercises from Poets Who Teach (Behn & Twichell), 354
Prairie Boy's Summer, A (Kurelek), 452, 458
Prairies (Patent), 540
Prange, Beckie, 338, 359
Pratt, Davis, 263
Pratt, Kristin Joy, 201
Preacher's Boy (Paterson), 459
Prelutsky, Jack, 32, 319, 321, 322, 323, 325, 327, 329, 331, 332, 333, 334, 338, 341, 348, 349, 350
Presenting Tanya the Ugly Duckling (Gauch), 156
President's Daughter, The (Bradley), 495
Pretty Book of Pictures for Little Masters and Misses; or Tommy Trip's History of Beasts and Birds (Bewick), 54
Prewitt, Jana Wright, 350
Price, Susan, 298, 313
Priceman, Marjorie, 14, 120, 158, 204, 541
Pride of African Tales, A (Washington), 6, 234, 262
Prietita and the Ghost Woman (Anzaldua), 236, 265
Primavera, Elise, 113, 202, 411, 496
Prince Caspian, the Return to Narnia (Lewis), 312

"Princess and the Glass Hill, The," 209
Princess and the Goblin, The (MacDonald), 312
Princess and the Pea, The (Stevens), 492
Princess Furball (Huck), 263
Pringle, Laurence, 64, 519, 520, 522, 531, 535, 541
Printup, Erwin, Jr., 151, 159
Private Peaceful (Morpurgo), 83, 114, 450–451, 459
Probably Still Nick Swansen (Wolf), 386, 414
Probst, Robert, 37
Proett, Jackie, 351
Project Mulberry (Park), 11, 94–95, 114
Promises to Keep: How Jackie Robinson Changed America (Robinson), 484–485, 498
"Promoting Positive Attitudes Toward Aging" (McGuire), 386
Propp, Vladimir, 216
Prose, Francine, 229, 265, 414
Protagoras, 66
Protopopescu, Orel, 358
Proud Knight, Fair Lady: The Twelve Lais of Marie de France (Lewis), 312
Provensen, Alice, 136, 138, 158, 160, 360, 498, 512, 541
Provensen, Martin, 136, 138, 158, 160, 360, 498
Provost, Gail, 386
Provost, Gary, 386, 414
"Psalm of Serach, The" (Sasso), 249
P.S. Longer Letter Later (Danziger & Martin), 411
Publisher's Weekly, 163, 286
Puddle Pail, The (Kleven), 203
Pullen, Zachary, 202
Pullman, Philip, 7, 87, 90, 92, 114, 232, 265, 281, 300, 302, 303–304, 417, 422, 459
"Pumberly Pott's Unpredictable Niece" (Prelutsky), 349
Pumpkin Soup (Cooper), 5, 112, 126, 155
Pup Just for Me, A: A Boy Just for Me (Seeber), 6, 16, 114, 198
Purdy, Carol, 204
Purves, Alan C., 38, 39, 75
Pushkin, Alexander, 227, 266
"Puss in Boots," 216, 219
Puss in Boots (Kirstein), 222, 264
"Puss in Boots" (Perrault), 216, 219, 221, 264
"Pussy-Cat, Pussy-Cat," 349
Put on Some Antlers and Walk Like a Moose: How Scientists Find, Follow, and Study Wild Animals (Sayre), 541
Pyle, Howard, 45, 55, 59–60, 63, 158, 247, 248, 269, 303

Quammen, David, 130
"Quangle Wangle's Hat, The" (Lear), 58, 331, 357
Quayle, Eric, 53
Queen Eleanor: Independent Spirit of the Medieval World (Brooks), 471–472, 495
Queenie Peavy (Burch), 370, 410
Queen of Eene, The (Prelutsky), 333, 348, 359
Queen Victoria and the British Empire (Whitelaw), 494
Quiet Storm: Voices of Young Black Poets (Okutoro), 342, 359
Quiller-Couch, Sir Arthur, 158
Quintana, Anton, 83, 114

"Rabbit and Coyote" (Bierhorst), 235
Rabbit Hill (Lawson), 63, 157, 289, 309, 312

Rabbits, Rabbits (Fisher), 335, 356
Rabbit's Wedding, The (Williams), 175, 206
Rabble Starkey (Lowry), 413
Raccoon's Last Race (Bruchac & Bruchac), 266
Race to Save the Lord God Bird, The (Hoose), 102, 498, 502, 524, 535, 538
Rachel: The Story of Rachel Carson (Ehrlich), 466, 467, 494, 495
Rachel Carson: Preserving a Sense of Wonder (Bruchac), 467, 490, 495
Rackham, Arthur, 55, 128
Racso and the Rats of NIMH (Conly), 285, 311
Radunsky, Vladimir, 153, 158
Rafferty, Trisha, 356
"Ragged Dick" series (Alger), 57–58
Raible, Alton, 414
Railroad Fever: Building the Transcontinental Railroad, 1830–1870 (Halpern), 511, 538
"Rain" (Fisher), 321
Rainbow People, The (Yep), 229, 263
Rainbow Writing (Merriam), 358
Rain Forests & Reefs: A Kid's-Eye View of the Tropics (Maynard & Maynard), 540
Rain Makes Applesauce (Scheer), 126, 159
Rain Player (Wisniewski), 84, 132–133, 160
Ralph S. Mouse (Cleary), 311
Ralph's Secret Weapon (Kellogg), 61
Ramona and Her Father (Cleary), 14, 80, 112, 384–385, 410
Ramona and Her Mother (Cleary), 385, 410
Ramona Quimby, Age 8 (Cleary), 112, 385, 410
Ramona the Brave (Cleary), 410
Ramona the Pest (Cleary), 384, 410
Rand, Ted, 154, 159, 204, 350, 358, 359, 539
Random House Book of Mother Goose, The (Lobel), 5, 197
Random House Book of Poetry for Children, The (Prelutsky), 325, 331, 349, 350, 359
Ransome, Arthur, 158, 184, 204, 227–228, 266
Ransome, James E., 262
Ransom of Red Chief, The (Henry), 63
Rapp, Adam, 414
Rappaport, Doreen, 447, 448, 459, 516, 541
Rapunzel: From the Brothers Grimm (Rogasky), 264
"Rapunzel," 219
"Rapunzel" (Grimm & Grimm), 124, 254, 264
Rapunzel (Zelinsky), 130, 156, 264
Rascal (North), 114
Raschka, Chris, 34, 96, 115, 152, 159, 179, 190, 202, 203, 204, 205, 357, 411
Raskin, Ellen, 114, 359, 397, 414
Raskin, Lawrie, 525, 541
"Rathers" (Austin), 350
Rathmann, Peggy, 25, 102, 114, 182, 183, 194, 204
Rats! (Cutler), 411
Rauch, Alan, 56
Rauchwerger, Lisa, 265
Raugust, Karen, 397
Raven: A Trickster Tale from the Pacific Northwest (McDermott), 237, 266, 267
Ravenmaster's Secret, The (Woodruff), 430, 460
Raw Head, Bloody Bones: African-American Tales of the Supernatural (Lyons), 420
Rawls, Wilson, 110
Ray, Deborah Kogan, 457, 458, 468, 498
Ray, Delia, 514, 541

Ray, Jane, 264, 267
Ray, Mary Lyn, 135, 158
Rayevsky, Robert, 355
Raymo, Chet, 11, 272, 501, 502
Rayner, Mary, 312
Rayyan, Omar, 265
Reaching Dustin (Grove), 386, 411
Read-Aloud Rhymes for the Very Young (Prelutsky), 359
Reade, Deborah, 460
"Reading Preferences" (Sebesta & Monson), 359
Reading Teacher, The, 101, 354, 535
Ready ... Set ... Read! (Cole & Calmenson), 177–178, 200
Real Plato Jones, The (Bawden), 378, 410
Reaping the Whirlwind: The Apache Wars (Aleshire), 33
Rebecca of Sunnybrook Farm (Wiggins), 60, 63, 67–68
"Recipe for Granite" (Peters), 339
Reconstruction (Ferrell), 530, 537
Recorvits, Helen, 21
Rector, Anne Elizabeth, 480, 498
Red Book, The (Lehman), 7, 18, 152, 157, 175, 196–197, 200
Red-Eyed Tree Frog (Cowley), 498, 537
Red Fairy Book, The (Lang), 88, 113
Red Hot Salsa: Bilingual Poems on Being Young and Latino in the United States (Carlson), 346, 355
Red Land, Yellow River: A Story from the Cultural Revolution (Zhang), 487, 498
Red Leaf, Yellow Leaf (Ehlert), 40, 155
Red Racer, The (Wood), 206
Red Riding Hood (Marshall), 223, 264
Red Ridin' in the Hood and Other Cuentos (Marcantonio), 254, 265
"Red Shoes, The" (Andersen), 52
Redwall (Jacques), 286, 312
Reed, Nathan, 198
Reeder, Carolyn, 436, 459
Rees, David, 274
Rees-Williams, Brian, 58
Rees-Williams, Gwladys, 58
Reeves, James, 350
Reeves, Nicholas, 150, 158
Reflections on a Gift of Watermelon Pickle ... and Other Modern Verse (Dunning, Lueders & Smith), 40, 324, 343, 356
Regan, Laura, 206
Regards to the Man in the Moon (Keats), 157, 187, 203
Reiche, Dietlof, 285–286, 313
Reid, Donna K., 150–152
Reiser, Lynn, 12, 30, 182, 199, 204
Reiss, Johanna, 423, 447, 459, 498
Reiss, John J., 17
Reissman, Rose, 489
Relf, Pat, 541
Reluctant Dragon, The (Grahame), 311
Reluctantly Alice (Naylor), 413
Remarkable Journey of Prince Jen, The (Alexander), 309
Rembert, Winfred, 147, 158, 480, 498
Rembrandt (Schwartz), 20, 159, 480, 498
Remember: The Journey to School Integration (Morrison), 147, 158, 516, 540

Remember D-Day: The Plan, the Invasion, Survivor Stories (Drez), 515, 537
Remembering Mog (Rodowsky), 384, 414
Remembering the Good Times (Peck), 383, 413
Rescue: The Story of How Gentiles Saved Jews in the Holocaust (Meltzer), 107, 114, 515, 540
"Respect the Source: Reducing Cultural Chaos in Picture Books, Part Two" (Hearne), 214
Return of the King, The (Tolkien), 281, 314
Revenge and Forgiveness: An Anthology of Poems (Vecchione), 22, 346, 360
Rex, Adam, 202, 415
Rey, Hans, 186, 204
Reynart the Foxe (Caxton), 47, 71
Reynolds, Kimberley, 44
Rhatigan, Joe, 505, 526, 532, 541
Rhee, Nami, 231, 263
Rhinos (Walker), 532, 542
Rhoades, Diane, 529, 541
Rice, Eve, 41
Richards, Laura E., 63, 332, 349, 359
Richardson, Joy, 528, 541
Riddell, Chris, 459, 540
"Riddle of the Drum, The," 219
Ride a Cock Horse to Banbury Cross & A Farmer Went Trotting Upon His Grey Mare (Caldecott), 155
Ride on the Red Mare's Back, A (LeGuin), 312
Rifles for Watie (Keith), 458
Riga, Frank, 69
Right Dog for the Job, The: Ira's Path from Service Dog to Guide Dog (Patent), 521, 540
Right to Vote, The (Pascoe), 540
Rigoni, Nicole, 36
"Rikki-Tikki-Tavi" (Kipling), 288
Riley, Gail Blasser, 65
Riley, Linnea, 194, 204
Rime of the Ancient Mariner, The (Coleridge), 328
Rimonah of the Flashing Sword: A North African Tale (Kimmel), 265
Rinaldi, Ann, 459
Ring, The (Maizlish), 175, 200
Ringgold, Faith, 17, 147, 158, 250, 269, 477, 498
"Ring in the Prairie, The," 219, 220
Ring in the Prairie, The: A Shawnee Legend (Bierhorst), 266
Riordan, James, 269
Risen from the Ranks (Alger), 58
Riskind, Mary, 414
River at Green Knowe, The (Boston), 296, 310
River Between Us, The (Peck), 419, 436–437, 459
River Rats (Stevermer), 297, 314
Riverside Magazine for Young People, 57
River Winding (Zolotow), 334, 360
Road From Home, Thee: The Story of an American Girl (Kherdian), 497
Road to Camlann, The: The Death of King Arthur (Sutcliff), 247, 269, 314
Roback, Diane, 70
Robber and Me, The (Holub), 458
Robbins, Ken, 360
Robbins, Ruth, 312
Roberto Clemente: Pride of the Pittsburgh Pirates (Winter), 485, 498
Roberts, Moss, 218, 263
Roberts, Patricia L., 69
Robertson, Barbara, 349, 356

Robertson, Mark, 313
Robin Hood: His Life and Legend (Miles), 268
Robin Hood (Early), 248, 268
Robin of Sherwood (Morpurgo), 269
Robins, Arthur, 205
Robinson, Charles, 460
Robinson, Sharon, 484–485, 498
Robinson Crusoe (Defoe), 45, 49–50, 51, 60, 63, 66
Rob Roy (Scott), 60
Roche, Denis, 19, 529, 541
Rochman, Hazel, 118–119, 388
"Rock-a-Bye Baby," 103
Rockin' Reptiles (Calmenson & Cole), 201
Rocklin, Joanne, 414
Rockwell, Anne, 13, 200, 309
Rodgers, Mary, 313
Rodman, Mary Ann, 31, 182, 205
Rodowsky, Colby F., 114, 384, 414
Rodríguez, Luis, 346
Rodzina (Cushman), 96, 112, 439, 457
Roeckelein, Katrina, 414
Roehler, L., 105
Roemer, Heidi, 324–325, 359
Roethke, Theodore, 331
Rogasky, Barbara, 107, 114, 148, 158, 250, 264, 269,
    334, 359, 503, 514–515, 541
Roger, Jacques-François, 233
Rogers, Fred, 25, 28
Rogers, Gregory, 7, 10, 40, 153, 158, 190, 191, 200
Rohman, Eric, 5, 120, 127, 158
Rohmer, Harriet, 235–236, 265
Rojankousky, Feodor, 113
Rolling Harvey Down the Hill (Prelutsky), 333, 359
Rolling Store, The (Johnson), 203
Rollo and Tweedy and the Ghost at Dougal Castle
    (Allen), 200
Roll of Thunder, Hear My Cry (Taylor), 64, 92, 114,
    414, 444, 460
*Roman Army, The: The Legendary Soldiers Who
    Created an Empire* (Blacklock), 509, 536
Romare Bearden: Collage of Memories
    (Greenberg), 480, 496
Roop, Connie, 498, 541
Roop, Peter, 498, 541
Roosevelt, Elliott, 498
Root, Phyllis, 522, 541
Rootabaga Stories (Sandburg), 291–292, 313
Root Cellar, The (Lunn), 274, 296, 302, 312
Ros, Saphan, 267
Rosa (Giovanni), 202
Rosa Bonheur (Turner), 479, 498
Rosa Parks (Greenfield), 478, 496
Rose Blanche (Innocenti), 157, 188, 203, 452
Rose for Pinkerton, A (Kellogg), 203
Rose in My Garden, The (Lobel), 349–350, 358
Rosen, Michael, 5, 122, 159, 194, 195, 199, 205, 359
Rosenberry, Vera, 496
Rosenblatt, Louise, 38, 39, 74
Rosenthal, M. L., 311
Roser, Nancy, 37
Rose Red and Snow White (Sanderson), 264
Rosinsky, Natalie M., 527, 541
Rosner, Gill, 413, 460
Rosoff, Meg, 22, 70, 71, 401, 414
Rossel, Seymour, 541
Rossetti, Christina Georgina, 63, 322–323,
    346, 359
Roth, Robert, 263

Rothenberg, Joan, 228, 265
Rotman, Jeffery L., 537
Rotner, Shelley, 21, 25, 173, 200
Rotten Ralph's Rotten Romance (Gantos), 202
Roualt, Georges, 144
Rounds, Glen, 220, 264, 266
Rousseau, Jean Jacques, 45, 51, 52, 66
Rowling, J. K., 64, 86, 90, 114, 194, 272, 284, 285,
    286, 300, 313, 327, 332, 490
Roxburgh, Stephen, 70
"Rub a Dub Dub," 164
Rubel, Reina, 360
Rubin, Susan Goldman, 122, 146, 147, 159,
    478, 498
Ruby in the Smoke, The (Pullman), 417, 422, 459
Ruby the Copycat (Rathmann), 25, 114
Ruddell, Robert, 38, 39
Rudman, Masha Kabakow, 20, 136, 145
Ruggieri, Colleen A., 370
Ruhl, Greg, 542
Rules of the Road (Bauer), 410
Rullman, Stan, 540
Rumford, James, 10, 13, 129, 159, 474–475, 498
"Rumpelstiltskin," 214, 221
"Rumpelstiltskin" (Grimm & Grimm), 52, 113,
    214, 254, 264
Rumpelstiltskin (Zelinsky), 130, 156, 264
Rumpelstiltskin's Daughter (Stanley), 267
Run, Boy, Run (Orlev), 448, 459
Runaway Bunny, The (Brown), 180, 201
Runaway Girl: The Artist Louise Bourgeois
    (Greenberg & Jordan), 146, 156, 487, 496
Runaway Ralph (Cleary), 311
Running with the Reservoir Pups (Bateman),
    397, 410
Runny Babbit: A Billy Sook (Silverstein), 333, 359
Rusch, Amy, 201
Rush, Barbara, 228, 229, 265
Rush, Jean C., 141, 143
Rushmore (Curlee), 537
Ruskin, John, 55, 63
Russell, David L., 3
Russell and Elisa (Hurwitz), 412
Russian Folk Tales (Afanasyév), 227, 266
Russo, Marisabina, 148, 159, 514, 541
Rutherford, James, 531
Ruthie's Gift (Bradley), 457
Ryan, Pam Muñoz, 22, 379, 414, 482, 493, 498
Ryan, Susannah, 202
Ryder, Joan, 541
Rylant, Cynthia, 13, 30, 40, 64, 69, 80, 88, 104,
    107, 114, 159, 177, 201, 205, 343, 359, 365,
    366–368, 414, 419–420, 422, 452, 459

Sabriel (Nix), 313
Sabuda, Robert, 24, 159, 357
Sacajawea, Wilderness Guide (Jassem), 483, 496
Sachar, Louis, 32, 64, 101, 110, 114, 194, 366, 414
Sachs, Marilyn, 414
Sacks, David, 213
*Sacrifice: Age of Bronze: The Story of the Trojan
    War* (Shanower), 509, 541
Sadako and the Thousand Paper Cranes (Coerr), 32
Sáenz, Benjamin Alire, 390–391, 414
*Safari Beneath the Sea: The Wonder World of the
    North Pacific Coast* (Swanson), 525, 542
Safe at Second (Johnson), 397, 412
Safe-Keeper's Secret, The (Shinn), 313

Sagan, Carl, 303, 307
Sailing Off to Sleep (Ashman), 342, 355
Sailing With the Wind (Locker), 134, 157
Saint George and the Dragon (Hodges), 126, 156,
    248, 269, 302
Saladin: Noble Prince of Islam (Stanley), 471, 498
Salerno, Steven, 334, 356
Salisbury, Graham, 114, 450, 459
"Salmon Boy" (Caduto & Bruchac), 245–246
Salsa Stories (Delacre), 391, 411
Salting the Ocean: 100 Poems by Young Poets
    (Nye), 343, 358
Sam, Bangs and Moonshine (Ness), 31, 104,
    114, 204
Sam, Joe, 265
*Sam and the Tigers: A New Telling of Little Black
    Sambo* (Lester), 157, 203
Sammy the Seal (Hoff), 200
Sam's Ball (Lindgren), 30, 168, 198
Sam's Bath (Lindgren), 168, 198
Samurai's Daughter, The: A Japanese Legend (San
    Souci), 263
Sánchez, Trinidad, Jr., 346
Sand and Fog: Adventures in Southern Africa
    (Brandenburg), 536
Sandburg, Carl, 7, 63, 291–292, 313, 334, 359,
    473–474, 498
Sanderson, Ruth, 207, 217, 227, 264, 266, 267, 410
Sandford, John, 154
Sandin, Joan, 200, 459
Sandmann, Alexa L., 318, 359
San Domingo: The Medicine Hat Stallion
    (Henry), 412
Sandoz, Edouard, 268
Sands, Emily, 145, 150, 159
Sanfield, Steve, 262, 263
Sanford, John, 124–125
San Souci, Daniel, 266
San Souci, Robert D., 9, 13, 114, 239, 262, 263,
    267, 269
Santa Calls (Joyce), 203
Santa Who? (Gibbons), 510, 537
Santore, Charles, 146, 327, 358
Saport, Linda, 202
Sarah and Me and the Lady from the Sea (Beatty),
    443, 457
Sarah, Plain and Tall (MacLachlan), 77, 105–106,
    113, 440, 441, 454, 459
Sasso, Sandy Eisenberg, 249, 269
"Satellites" (Livingston), 324
Satrapi, Marjane, 486–487, 494, 498
Sattler, Helen Roney, 541
Saturn (Simon), 498, 526, 541
Saturnalia (Fleischman), 431, 458
Saulny, Susan, 488
Savadier, Elivia, 268
Savage, Deborah, 414
Savage, Stephen, 123, 153, 159, 205
Savage Damsel and the Dwarf, The (Morris), 313
Save Queen of Sheba (Moeri), 439, 459
Saving Francesca (Marchetta), 102, 398–399, 413
Saving Sweetness (Stanley), 159
Saving the Peregrine Falcon (Arnold), 32, 532
Say, Allen, 31, 32, 34–35, 114, 148, 159, 263, 411
Saylor, David, 118
Sayre, April Pulley, 199, 517, 541
Sayre, Henry, 19, 127, 145, 159, 541
Sayre, Jeff, 199

Say the Magic Word (Brown), 198

Scandinavian Folk & Fairy Tales (Booss), 266

Scanlon, Elizabeth Garton, 339, 359

Scarebird, The (Fleischman), 31, 126, 156, 179–180, 202

Scary Stories 3: More Tales to Chill Your Bones (Schwartz), 66

Scary Stories to Tell in the Dark (Schwartz), 66

Schaefer, Carole Lexa, 18, 30

Schaefer, Lola M., 501, 524, 535, 541

Schafer, Elizabeth D., 284

Schami, Rafik, 382, 414

Schanzer, Rosalyn, 15, 73, 98, 114, 513–514, 541

Scheer, Julian, 126, 159

Schenck v. United States: Restrictions on Free Speech (Alonso), 535

Schernoff Discoveries, The (Paulsen), 413

Schindler, S. D., 199, 264, 287, 312, 540

Schmandt-Besserat, Denise, 173, 199, 541

Schmidt, Gary D., 87, 114, 422, 443, 459

Schmidt, Suzy, 474, 495

Schoenherr, John, 113, 124, 160, 204, 206, 411

Scholastic Encyclopedia of the Civil War (Clinton), 514, 537

Scholder, Fritz, 113, 267

Scholt, Grayce, 47, 48, 50, 53, 257

School (McCully), 5, 9, 174, 193, 200

School Library Journal, The, 76, 163, 319, 368, 528, 535

Schotter, Roni, 7, 32, 180, 205, 414

Schroeder, Alan, 159, 267

Schulevitz, Uri, 76

Schultz, Bernard, 133

Schwarcz, Joseph, 137–138

Schwartz, Alvin, 66, 201, 359

Schwartz, Amy, 16, 21, 31, 205

Schwartz, Cherie Karo, 251, 265

Schwartz, Gary, 20, 159, 480, 498

Schwartz, Henry, 18

Schwartz, Howard, 228, 229, 265

Schwartz, Lyyne Sharon, 311

Schweninger, Ann, 201

Schyffert, Bea Uusma, 541

"Science Books for Young People: Who Writes Them?" (Broadway & Howland), 528

Science Fair Bunnies (Lasky), 20, 531–532, 539

Science Verse (Scieszka), 102, 339, 350, 359

"Scientific Method at the Bat" (Scieszka), 339

Scieszka, Jon, 10, 17, 102, 114, 130, 159, 241–242, 261, 267, 268, 339, 350, 359

Scorpion House (Farmer), 33

Scorpions (Myers), 371, 388, 413

Scott, A. O., 284

Scott, Elaine, 525, 541

Scott, Sir Walter, 52, 60, 63, 346

Scottish Tradition: A Collection of Scottish Folk Literature (Buchan), 263

Scranimials (Prelutsky), 333, 359

Screen of Frogs (Hamanaka), 231, 263

Sea, The: Exploring Life on an Ocean Planet (Burleigh), 7

Seabird (Holling), 133, 156

Seabrooke, Brenda, 313

Seadogs: An Epic Ocean Operetta (Wheeler), 124, 160

Sea King's Daughter, The: A Russian Legend (Shepard), 159, 227, 266

Seals (Grace), 538

"Seals" (Smith), 324

Seal Surfer (Foreman), 411

Sea of Trolls, The (Farmer), 102, 275, 280, 302–303, 311

Search for the Golden Moon Bear: Science and Adventure in the Asian Tropics (Montgomery), 521–522, 540

Seasons: A Book of Poems (Zolotow), 334, 360

Seasons and Someone, The (Kroll), 389, 412

Seasons of the Cranes (Roop & Roop), 541

Sea Turtles (Staub), 519, 542

Seaward (Cooper), 302, 311

Sebesta, Sam Leaton, 100, 182, 318, 336, 359

Secret Garden, The (Burnett), 14, 63, 90, 108, 112

Secret Knowledge of Grownups, The (Wisniewski), 84

Secret Seder, The (Rappaport), 447, 448, 459

Secrets of a Civil War Submarine: Solving the Mysteries of the H.L. Hunley (Walker), 514, 530, 542

Secrets of Animal Flight, The (Bishop), 536

Secrets of the Mummies (Tanaka), 509, 542

Secrets of the Sphinx (Giblin), 509, 538

Secret Under My Skin, The (McNaughton), 301, 313

Sector 7 (Wiesner), 13, 175, 196, 200

Sedgwick, Marcus, 313

Seeber, Dorothea P., 6, 16, 114, 198

Seedfolks (Fleischman), 411

Seeger, Laura Vaccaro, 12, 173, 199, 200

Seeger, Ruth Crawford, 359

Seeing Stone, The (Crossley-Holland), 280–281, 311

Seeing Things: A Book of Poems (Froman), 329, 356

Seeley, Laura, 360

Seen Art? (Scieszka & Smith), 159

See Pip Paint (Milgrim), 201

Sees Behind Trees (Dorris), 429, 457

See the Ocean (Condra), 202

See You Around, Sam! (Lowry), 22, 379, 413

Segal, John, 265

Seibert, Patricia, 525, 541

Seidler, Tor, 309

Selden, George, 289, 313

Selected Poems of Langston Hughes (Hughes), 357

Select Fables of Aesop and Others, The (Bewick & Bewick), 55

Selman, Robert, 402

Selsam, Millicent E., 531, 533, 535, 541

Selznick, Brian, 152, 153, 157, 411, 468–469, 482, 497, 498

Sendak, Maurice, 10, 31, 77, 86, 110, 114, 118–119, 129, 138–139, 143–144, 148, 153, 156, 157, 159, 160, 166, 167, 175, 178, 179, 191, 197, 198, 203, 205, 206, 264, 349, 359

Sequoyah: The Cherokee Man Who Gave His People Writing (Rumford), 10, 129, 159, 474–475, 498

Seredy, Kate, 114, 269

Serfozo, Mary, 18, 200

"Serpent of the Sea, The," 211

Serpent Slayer and Other Stories of Strong Women, The (Tchana), 267

Serpent's Tongue, The: Prose, Poetry, and Art of the New Mexico Pueblos (Wood), 151, 160

Setterington, Ken, 313

Seurat, George, 146

Seuss, Dr., 6, 13, 55, 63, 64, 77, 110, 114, 124, 144, 159, 177, 183, 190, 194, 201, 205, 272, 359, 492

Seven Blind Mice (Young), 31, 160

Seven Brave Women (Hearne), 538

Seven Chinese Brothers, The (Mahy), 260, 263

Seven Little Monsters (Sendak), 205

Seven Loaves of Bread (Wolff), 314

Seven Songs of Merlin, The (Barron), 310

Seven Strange & Ghostly Tales (Jacques), 312

1776 (McCullough), 530

Severance, John B., 32, 466, 476, 498

Severo, Emoke de Papp, 302, 313

Sewall, Marcia, 180, 205, 441

Sewell, Anna, 63, 127

Sewell, Helen, 242, 268

Sewell, Marcia, 414

"Sex and Politics in Fairyland" (Coleman), 346

Sexual Health Information for Teens (Stanley), 518, 542

Shabanu: Daughter of the Wind (Staples), 89–90, 114, 370, 414

Shades of Gray (Reeder), 459

Shadow (Cendrars), 106, 112, 132, 155, 201

Shadow Boxer (Lynch), 413

Shadow Catcher (Levin), 18

Shadow Catcher: The Life and Work of Edward S. Curtis (Lawlor), 151, 157, 497

Shadow in Hawthorn Bay (Lunn), 433, 458

Shadow Life: A Portrait of Anne Frank and Her Family (Denenberg), 486, 495

Shadowmancer (Taylor), 279, 314

Shadow of a Bull (Wojciechowska), 17, 385, 391, 414

Shadows and Reflections (Hoban), 156

Shadows of Ghadames, The (Stolz), 22, 89, 114, 419, 459

Shadows of the Night: The Hidden World of the Little Brown Bat (Bash), 506, 536

Shadow Spinner (Fletcher), 419, 458

Shaffer, David, 11, 29

Shahan, Sherry, 541

Shaka: King of the Zulus (Stanley & Vennema), 40, 498

Shaker Hearts (Turner), 205

Shakespeare, William, 17, 244, 257, 259, 331

Shakespeare Bats Cleanup (Koertge), 339, 357

Shakespeare for Kids: His Life and Times (Aagesen & Blumberg), 528, 535

Shakespeare's Scribe (Blackwood), 457

Shakespeare's Theatre (Langley), 515, 539

Shakespeare Stories (Garfield), 17

Shalom, Haver: Goodbye Friend (Sofer), 498

Shange, Ntozake, 152, 153, 159, 180, 205, 344, 359, 498

Shannon, David, 5, 168, 178, 198, 205, 360, 460

Shannon, George, 159

Shanower, Eric, 509, 541

Shape Game, The (Browne), 16

Shapes (Reiss), 17

Shapes, Shapes, Shapes (Hoban), 12, 17, 173, 200

Shape Space (Falwell), 200

Shapiro, Ellen S., 229–230

Sharks! Strange and Wonderful! (Pringle), 520

Sharmat, Marjorie Weinman, 205

Shavit, Zohar, 48

Shea, Pegi Dietz, 22, 33, 394, 414

Sheafer, Silvia Anne, 493

Sheban, Chris, 375

Shefelman, Janice, 452, 459
Shefelman, Tom, 459
Shekerjian, Regina, 334, 360
Sheldon, Dyan, 414
Sheldrewnson, Garrett, 311
Shell (Arthur), 536
She'll Be Comin' 'Round the Mountain (Sturges), 6, 8, 326, 360
Shelley, Mary Godwin, 297
Shemie, Bonnie, 541
Shenton, Edward, 459
Shepard, Aaron, 133, 159, 227, 234, 262, 266
Shepard, Ernest H., 55, 113, 204, 311, 313, 358
Shepard, Mary, 314
Sheriff of Rottenshot, The (Prelutsky), 333, 359
Sherman, Josepha, 228, 265, 266
Sherman, Paul, 538
Sheth, Kashmira, 33, 393, 394, 414
Shhhhh! Everybody's Sleeping (Markes), 5
Shh! We're Writing the Constitution (Fritz), 513, 537
Shiffman, Lena, 204
Shih Huang-ti, 66
Shiloh (Naylor), 110, 114, 395, 396, 413
Shiloh Season (Naylor), 413
Shimin, Simeon, 356, 412
Shining Company, The (Sutcliff), 420, 460
Shinn, Sharon, 313
Shin's Tricycle (Kodama), 148, 157, 189, 203, 449, 458
Ship (Macaulay), 539
Shirley, Jean, 34, 495
Shiva's Fire (Staples), 92, 114
Shoebag (James), 285, 312
Shoes: Their History in Words and Pictures (Yue & Yue), 542
Sholom's Treasure: How Sholom Aleichem Became a Writer (Silverman), 480, 498
Shooter (Myers), 22, 371–372, 413
Shooting Star: Annie Oakley, the Legend (Dadey), 202
Shortcut (Crews), 202, 411
Show-and-Tell War, The (Smith), 414
Showers, Paul, 19, 504, 517, 541
Show Time!: Music, Dance, and Drama Activities for Kids (Bany-Winters), 528, 536
Shreve, Susan, 385, 414
"Shrewd Todie & Lyzer the Miser" (Singer), 228
Shrinking Violet (Best), 201
Shulevitz, Uri, 112, 114, 123, 158, 159, 204, 228, 250, 265, 266, 269, 452, 459
Shusterman, Neal, 313, 379, 414
Shutting Out the Sky: Life in the Tenements of New York 1880–1924 (Hopkinson), 538
"Sickle Blade, The" (Diakite), 234
Sidewalk Circus (Fleischman), 5, 13, 15–16, 175, 200
Sidman, Joyce, 338, 359
Sidney, Margaret, 45, 61, 63, 67–68
Sidney, Sir Philip, 46
Siebert, Diane, 335, 359
Siegel, Aranka, 459
Siegel, Mark, 160
Siegelson, Kim, 459
Siegen-Smith, Nikki, 326, 359
Siegl, Helen, 262
Sierra (Siebert), 335, 359
Sierra, Judy, 7, 13, 230, 263, 267
Sierra, Lucy, 199
Sierra Club Book of Great Mammals, 541

Sierra Club Book of Small Mammals, 541
"Sign, The, a Rainbow Tale" (Schwartz), 251
Sign of the Beaver, The (Speare), 15, 108, 114, 432, 433, 459
Sign of the Qin (Bass), 310
Sign on Rosie's Door, The (Sendak), 205
Silent Boy, The (Lowry), 443, 458
Silent Storm, The (Garland), 411
Silk Route, The: 7,000 Miles of History (Major), 148, 158, 507–508, 534, 539
Sill, Cathryn, 541
Sill, John, 541
Sills, Leslie, 498
Silly Horse (Levin), 330, 357
Silver Branch, The (Sutcliff), 460
Silver Chair, The (Lewis), 312
Silver Cow, The: A Welsh Tale (Cooper), 221, 263
Silver Days (Levitin), 458
Silver Kiss (Klause), 295, 312
Silverman, Erica, 480, 498
Silver on the Tree (Cooper), 283, 311
Silver Seeds: A Book of Nature Poems (Paolilli & Brewer), 7, 10, 324, 359
Silverstein, Shel, 6, 110, 332–333, 350, 359
Silverthorne, Elizabeth, 493
Silver Treasure, The: Myths and Legends of the World (McCaughrean), 268
Silvey, Anita, 3, 75, 153
Simic, Charles, 334
Simmons, Jane, 5, 168, 198
Simon, Seymour, 159, 359, 499, 501, 505, 517, 518, 524, 526–527, 531, 533, 535, 541
Simont, Marc, 159, 200, 205, 314
"Simple Simon," 164, 165, 192
Sinbad: From the Tales of the Thousand and One Nights (Zeman), 126, 160, 232, 265
Sinbad the Sailor and Other Stories from the Arabian Nights (Dulac), 150, 155, 265
Sing a Song of People (Lenski), 157, 325
Sing a Song of Popcorn: Every Child's Book of Poems (de Regniers et al.), 321, 331, 335, 356
"Sing a Song of Sixpence," 164
Sing a Song of Sixpence (Alderson), 54
Sing Down the Moon (O'Dell), 441, 459
Singer, Isaac Bashevis, 159, 217, 228, 250, 265, 269
Singer, Marilyn, 102, 338, 339, 359–360
Singing Green, The: New and Selected Poems for All Seasons (Merriam), 358
Single Shard, A (Park), 146, 158, 427, 459
"Sing Me a Song of Teapots and Trumpets" (Bodecker), 321
Sing-Song (Rossetti), 322–323, 359
Sing to the Sun (Bryan), 355
Sink or Swim (Alger), 58
Sipe, Lawrence R., 422
Sip of Aesop, A (Yolen), 241, 268
Sir Cedric (Gerrard), 348, 356
Sir Francis Drake: His Daring Deeds (Gerrard), 348, 356
Sir Gawain and the Green Knight, 281
Sir Gawain and the Green Knight (Hastings), 269
Sir Gawain and the Green Knight (Morpurgo), 248, 269
Sir Gawain and the Loathly Lady (Hastings), 113, 247–248, 269
Sís, Peter, 12, 102, 126, 144, 153, 156, 159, 176, 198, 200, 202, 205, 311, 333, 338, 355, 359, 466, 467, 470, 490, 498, 513, 541

Sister (Greenfield), 387, 411
Sister Shako and Kolo the Goat: Memories of My Childhood in Turkey (Dalokay), 476, 495
Sisters/Hermanas (Paulsen), 413
Sisulu, Elinor Batezal, 188, 205, 387, 414
Sitting Bull and His World (Marrin), 483, 497
"Six Swans, The" (Grimm & Grimm), 211, 223, 277
16th Century Mosque, A (MacDonald), 150, 158
Sixth Grade (Morgenstern), 379, 413
Skateboard Renegade (Christopher), 398, 410
Skellig (Almond), 102, 275, 309
Skin Again (hooks), 6, 14, 34, 182, 203
"Skin and Bones," 350
Skira-Venturi, Rosabianca, 146, 159
Skolsky, Mindy Warshaw, 459
Skunk Scout (Yep), 22, 414
Skurzynski, Gloria, 503, 526, 528, 532, 541
Sky (Porter), 483–484, 498
Sky Dancers (Kirk), 180–181, 203
Sky Is Falling, The (Pearson), 459
Sky Pioneer: A Photobiography of Amelia Earhart (Szabo), 498
Sky Tree: Seeing Science through Art (Locker), 18, 524, 539
Slate, Joseph, 24
Slave Dancer, The (Fox), 92, 112, 434–435, 458
Slavery and Abolition in American History (Altman), 535
Sleator, William, 314
"Sleeping Beauty," 80, 215, 219, 255
"Sleeping Beauty" (Perrault), 71, 209, 221, 222
Sleeping Beauty, The (Hutton), 264
Sleeping Beauty, The (Hyman), 223, 264
Sleeping Beauty, The (Walker), 264
Sleeping Beauty and Other Fairy Tales, The (Quiller-Couch), 158
Sleepy Bear (Dabcovich), 112
Slepian, Jan, 414
Slightly True Story of Cedar B. Hartley (Who Planned to Live an Unusual Life), The (Murray), 413
Sloan, Christopher, 510, 517, 541
Slobodkin, Louis, 411
Slote, Alfred, 414
Slovenz-Law, Madeline, 148, 160, 392, 414
Small, David, 1, 124, 159, 184, 205, 291, 313
Smalls-Hector, Irene, 31, 386, 414
Small Wolf (Benchley), 200
"Smart" (Silverstein), 350
Smidt, Inez, 460
Smith, Alvin, 414
Smith, Amanda, 193–194
Smith, Cat Bowman, 542
Smith, Charles, 22, 339–340, 360
Smith, Dinitia, 280
Smith, Doris, 64
Smith, Hope Anita, 339, 360
Smith, Hugh, 40, 324, 343, 356
Smith, Janice Lee, 414
Smith, Jos. A., 169, 199, 268, 458
Smith, Lane, 114, 121, 130, 144, 146, 159, 199, 241–242, 261, 267, 268, 339, 350, 358, 359
Smith, Rosie, 170–171, 199
Smith, Sherwood, 314
Smith, William Jay, 324, 341, 353, 360
Smoke and Ashes: The Story of the Holocaust (Rogasky), 107, 114, 148, 158, 503, 514–515, 541

Smoky Mountain Rose: An Appalachian Cinderella (Schroeder), 267

Smoky Night (Bunting), 123, 132, 153, 154, 196, 201

"Snail" (Drinkwater), 343

Snakes Are Hunters (Lauber), 539

Snake Scientist, The (Montgomery), 503, 519–520, 532, 540

Snakes! Strange and Wonderful! (Pringle), 520, 522, 541

Sneed, Brad, 267, 268, 310

"Snowfall," (Esbensen), 334

Snowflake Fell, A: Poems About Winter (Whipple), 334, 360

"Snow Maiden, The," 219, 227

Snow Maiden and Other Russian Tales, The (Marshall), 254, 266

Snow Pumpkin (Schaefer), 30

Snow Queen, The (Ehrlich), 309

Snow Queen, The (Lewis), 309

Snowshoe Thompson (Levinson), 200

Snow White (Heins), 223

Snow White (Hyman), 264

"Snow White and the Seven Dwarfs," 209, 210, 217, 255

"Snow White and the Seven Dwarfs" (Grimm & Grimm), 52, 223, 227, 264

Snow White and the Seven Dwarfs (Jarrell), 156, 223, 264

Snowy Day (Fain), 156

Snowy Day, The (Keats), 5, 31, 77, 113, 137, 157

Snyder, Dianne, 104, 114, 230, 263

Snyder, Zilpha Keatley, 314, 321, 349, 360, 414, 459

So, Meilo, 205, 263, 267, 339, 359, 360

"Soap Bubble" (Worth), 347

Sobol, Daniel Joseph, 254, 266

Sobol, Donald J., 396

Sobol, Richard, 541

Soccer Duel (Christopher), 398, 410

"Social Worker Finds Hansel and Gretel Difficult to Place, The" (Dame), 346

Sock Is a Pocket for Your Toes, A: A Pocket Book (Scanlon), 339, 359

Soentpiet, Chris, 495

So Far From the Sea (Bunting), 457

Sofer, Barbara, 498

"Softball" (Burg), 325

Soft Hay Will Catch You: Poems by Young People (Lyne), 343, 358, 359

Sogabe, Aki, 263

Solbert, Ranni, 355

Solitary Blue, A (Voigt), 364–365, 414

Solt, Mary Ellen, 329

Soman, David, 113

So Many Circles, So Many Squares (Hoban), 12, 173, 200

Some From the Moon, Some From the Sun: Poems and Songs for Everyone (Zemach), 360

Somerville, Charles C., 537

Something Beautiful (Wyeth), 414

Something Special for Me (Williams), 180, 206

Some Thoughts Concerning Education (Locke), 45, 49

Song and Dance Man (Ackerman), 25, 106–107, 111, 123–124, 154, 179, 201

Song of Chirimia-A Guatemalan Folktale (Volkmer), 235, 265

"Song of Hiawatha, The" (Longfellow), 110, 327, 358

"Song of Roland, The," 208

Song of the Swallows (Politi), 391, 413

"Song of the Train" (McCord), 340

Song of the Water Boatman & Other Pond Poems (Sidman), 338, 359

Songs for Survival: Songs and Chants from Tribal Peoples Around the World (Siegen-Smith), 326, 359

Songs From Mother Goose (Larrick), 357

Song Shoots Out of My Mouth, The (Adoff), 344, 355

Songs of Experience (Blake), 52, 318

Songs of Innocence (Blake), 45, 52, 55, 63, 318, 325

Sonny's House of Spies (Lyon), 413

Sons from Afar (Voigt), 414

Sorrow's Kitchen: The Life and Folklore of Zora Neale Hurston (Lyons), 420

So Say the Little Monkeys (Van Laan), 235, 265

Soto, Gary, 32, 346, 392, 414

Soul Looks Back in Wonder (Angelou), 355

Sounder (Armstrong), 64, 444, 457

"Sounds of Winter" (Lewis), 321

Southey, Robert, 321, 360

So You Want to Be President? (St. George), 1

Space Between Our Footsteps, The: Poems and Paintings from the Middle East (Nye), 150, 158, 358

Space Camp: The Great Adventure for NASA Hopefuls (Baird), 40

Space Songs (Livingston), 324, 358

Spanfeller, Jim, 410

Speak (Anderson), 370, 409

Speak to Me: And I Will Listen Between the Lines (English), 339, 356

Speare, Elizabeth George, 15, 17, 63, 92, 108, 114, 419, 426, 431, 432, 433, 459

Speed, Lancelot, 113

Speeding Bullet (Shusterman), 379, 414

Spellbinder: The Life of Harry Houdini (Lalicki), 497

Spellbinders Volunteer Storytelling, 253

"Spelling Test, The" (Starbird), 349

Spell of the Sorcerer's Skull, The (Bellairs), 310

Spence, Amy, 8

Spence, Rob, 8

Sperry, Armstrong, 28, 63, 82–83, 85, 93, 94, 96, 114, 194, 403, 414

Spider and the Fly, The (Howitt), 157

Spier, Peter, 159, 176, 193, 200, 205

Spike Lee: By Any Means Necessary (Haskins), 496

Spindle's End (McKinley), 313

Spinelli, Eileen, 30, 181, 205, 338, 360

Spinelli, Jerry, 83, 114, 414

Spinky Sulks (Steig), 196, 205, 414

Spinning Through the Universe: A Novel in Poems From Room 214 (Frost), 339, 356

Spirin, Gennady, 158, 159, 227, 263, 266, 278, 309, 492

Spirit Child: A Story of the Nativity (Bierhorst), 235, 265

"Spirit of Seder" (Lewis), 249

Spiritual Milk for Boston Babes in Either England, Drawn from the Breasts of Both Testaments for Their Souls' Nourishment, 45, 48–49

Spivak, Dawnine, 329, 360

Splendid Friend, Indeed, A (Bloom), 30, 201

Spooky Texas Tales (Tingle), 252

Spoonbill Swamp (Guiberson), 538

Spot Goes to School (Hill), 5, 198

Spots (Fatus), 198

Spot's Birthday Party (Hill), 198

Spowart, Robin, 205, 357

Sprague, Marsha M., 369–370, 409

Springer, Harriett, 541

Springer, Nancy, 280, 314

Spring of Butterflies and Other Folktales of China's Minority Peoples, The (Philip), 260, 263

Spyri, Johanna, 45, 62, 63

Squares (Fatus), 198

Squashed (Bauer), 398, 410

Squids Will Be Squids: Fresh Morals, Beastly Fables (Scieszka & Smith), 241–242, 268

Squiggle, The (Schaefer), 18

Squire, His Knight, and His Lady, The (Morris), 280, 313

Squire's Tale, The (Morris), 313

Squirrel and John Muir (McCully), 497

Squishy, Misty, Damp & Muddy: The In-Between World of Wetlands (Cone), 537

Stacchi, Anthony, 311

Stacks, John F., 69

Stadler, Alexander, 21

Stadler, John, 168, 198

Stafford, William, 354

Stagestruck (dePaola), 137

Stalin: Russia's Man of Steel (Marrin), 497

Stallings, Fran, 256

Stanley, Alessandra, 465

Stanley, Deborah A., 518, 542

Stanley, Diane, 34, 146, 159, 267, 312, 423, 467, 471, 479, 498

Stanley, Fay, 498

Staples, Suzanne Fisher, 89–90, 92, 114, 370, 414

Starbird, Kaye, 349, 360

Star Boy (Goble), 156

Stark, Myra, 57

Star Maiden, The (Esbensen), 126, 155

Star of Fear, Star of Hope (Hoestlandt), 189, 203, 420, 446, 458

Star of Kazan, The (Hawkes), 458

Starring Mirette & Bellini (McCully), 188, 204

Starry Messenger: Galileo Galilei (Sis), 153, 159, 205, 466, 470, 490, 498

"Stars" (Chandra), 342

Stars, The (Moore), 526, 540

Stars Beneath Your Bed: The Surprising Story of Dust (Sayre), 517, 541

Star-Spangled Banner, The (Spier), 159, 205

"Star Trek," 297

Star Walk (Simon), 359

Star Wars, 297, 304

Staub, Frank, 519, 542

Stay Away from Simon! (Carrick), 410, 457

Steadfast Tin Soldier, The (Andersen), 309

Steadfast Tin Soldier, The (Isadora), 309

Steadfast Tin Soldier, The (Lewis), 309

Steadfast Tin Soldier, The (Seidler), 309

Stealing Home (Stolz), 414

Steamboat! The Story of Captain Blanche Leathers (Gilliland), 132, 156, 466, 496

Stearns, Virginia, 265

Ste-e-e-eam Boat A-Comin'! (Esbaum), 9, 182, 202, 415

Steele, Mary Q., 372

Steer, Dugald A., 248, 249, 260–261, 269
Steffens, Klaus, 112, 422, 458
Stefoff, Rebecca, 542
Steger, Will, 525, 542
Steig, Jeanne, 243, 268
Steig, William, 64, 102, 159, 175, 186, 194, 196, 205, 243, 268, 276, 314, 414
Steinbeck, John, 66, 525
Step by Wicked Step (Fine), 411
Stephens, Helen, 355
Stepping on the Cracks (Hahn), 33, 446, 458
Steptoe, Javaka, 131, 155, 156, 159, 202, 339, 360
Steptoe, John, 7, 34, 64, 109, 114, 124, 144, 159, 234, 262, 355, 357
Sterkarm Handshake, The (Price), 298, 313
Stevens, Carla, 459
Stevens, James, 311
Stevens, Janet, 18, 126, 159, 184, 205, 240, 268, 309
Stevens, Leonard A., 542
Stevenson, James, 183, 196, 202, 205, 359
Stevenson, Robert Louis, 40, 45, 59, 63, 159, 284, 317, 320, 341, 346, 360
Stevenson, Sucie, 201
Stevermer, Caroline, 297, 314
Stevie (Steptoe), 34, 64, 144, 159
Stewart, Joel, 278, 310, 492
Stewart, Sarah, 102, 124, 159, 205
Stewig, John Warren, 419
St. George, Judith, 1, 498
Still More Small Poems (Worth), 340, 347, 360
Stinchecum, Amanda Myer, 413
Stine, R. L., 110
Stinky Cheese Man and Other Fairly Stupid Tales, The (Scieszka), 17, 114, 130, 159, 261, 267
Stinky Stern Forever (Edwards), 32
St. Nicholas: Scribner's Illustrated Magazine for Girls and Boys, 56, 63
Stokes, Philip, 542
Stolley, Richard B., 15, 33, 506, 507, 515, 531, 542
Stolz, Joëlle, 22, 89, 114, 419, 459
Stolz, Mary, 92, 114, 414
Stone, Jeff, 428, 459
Stone, Kazuko G., 330, 356
Stone, Kyle M., 358
Stone Age Farmers Beside the Sea: Scotland's Prehistoric Village of Skara Brae (Arnold), 507, 536
Stone Girl, Bone Girl: The Story of Mary Anning (Anholt), 29, 466–467, 495
Stone in My Hand, A (Clinton), 382, 411
Stones, Bones, and Petroglyphs: Digging Into Southwest Archaeology (Goodman), 501, 538
Stone Soup (Brown), 63
Stonewall (Fritz), 496
Stonewords: A Ghost Story (Conrad), 296–297, 311
"Stopping by Woods on a Snowy Evening" (Frost), 335, 356
Stop the Train (McCaughrean), 438, 459
Stories from Forgotten Children's Books (Tuer), 58
Stories I Ain't Told Nobody Yet (Carson), 355
Stories of Hans Christian Andersen, The: A New Translation from the Danish (Andersen), 278, 309
Stories on Stone: Rock Art: Images from the Ancient Ones (Dewey), 151, 155
Storm (Crossley-Holland), 107, 112
Storm, Rachel, 250, 268

Storm Boy (Lewis), 157, 161, 203, 246, 268
Storm on the Desert (Lesser), 539
Storms (Simon), 541
"Story" (Greenfield), 4
"Story, a Story, A," 217
Story, a Story, A (Haley), 131, 156, 182, 202
Story Goes On, The (Fisher), 524, 537
Story of a Bad Boy, The (Aldrich), 60, 63, 67, 68
Story of Babar, The (de Brunhoff), 63, 144, 155, 202
Story of Clocks and Calendars, The: Making a Millennium (Maestro), 509, 539
Story of Ferdinand, The (Leaf), 31, 40, 157, 186, 203, 302, 312
Story of Jumping Mouse, The (Steptoe), 124, 159
Story of King Arthur and His Knights, The (Pyle), 247, 269, 303
Story of Lightning & Thunder, The (Bryan), 234, 262
Story of Little Babaji, The (Bannerman), 201
Story of Mankind, The (Van Loon), 63, 530, 542
Story of Money, The (Maestro), 539
Story of Ping, The (Flack), 55
Story of Religion, The (Maestro), 509, 539
Story of Science, The: Aristotle Leads the Way (Hakim), 526, 538
Story of the Champions of the Round Table, The (Pyle), 269
Story of the Incredible Orchestra, The (Koscielniak), 14, 538
Story of Three Kingdoms, The (Myers), 313
"Story of Washing Horse Pond, The" (Philip), 260
Story Painter: The Life of Jacob Lawrence (Duggleby), 495
Stott, Jon C., 462
Stowaway (Hesse), 113, 423, 458
Stowe, Harriet Beecher, 66
Strachan, Ian, 18, 114, 414
Stranger at Green Knowe, A (Boston), 296, 310
Stray Dog, The: From a True Story by Reiko Sassa (Simont), 205
Streets of Gold (Wells), 483, 498
Street Through Time, A: A 12,000-Year Walk Through History (Millard), 18, 90, 114, 524, 540
Strega Nona (dePaola), 136
Strehle, Elizabeth, 374
Strength of the Hills, The: A Portrait of a Family Farm (Graff), 538
Strickland, Carol, 159
Strider (Cleary), 375, 410
Stringbean's Trip to the Shining Sea (Williams), 115, 196, 206
Stripes (Fatus), 198
Strong and Steady (Alger), 58
Stroud, Jonathan, 294–295, 314
Stuart Little (White), 194, 314
Sturges, Philemon, 6, 8, 132, 199, 326, 360, 519, 542
Sub, The (Petersen), 413
Subtle Knife, The (Pullman), 87, 114, 281, 313
Sugaring Time (Lasky), 18, 506, 539
Sukey and the Mermaid (San Souci), 262
Sumi's First Day of School Ever (Pak), 204
Summer of the Swans, The (Byars), 64, 386, 403, 410
Summersaults (Florian), 334, 356
Summer Song, A (Haas), 202
Summer Switch (Rodgers), 313
Summertime Song, A (Haas), 5
Sun and Moon, The (Moore), 526, 540

Sundiata: Lion King of Mali (Wisniewski), 84, 249, 269
Sunita Experiment, The (Perkins), 393–394, 413
Sun Mother Wakes the World: An Australian Creation Story (Wolkstein), 246, 268
"Sunset" (Sandburg), 334
Sun, the Wind and the Rain, The (Peters), 14
Sure as Sunrise: Stories of Bruh Rabbit and His Walkin' Talkin' Friends (McGill), 262
Surprised by Joy: The Shape of My Early Life (Lewis), 494
Surprises (Hopkins), 200, 357
Surviving the Applewhites (Tolan), 22, 414
Susanna of the Alamo (Jakes), 496
Sutcliff, Rosemary, 63, 247, 269, 314, 420, 459–460
Sutherland, Zena, 77, 163, 255, 257, 277, 402, 418, 420, 463
Svend, Otto S., 266
Swain, Gwenyth, 498
Swain, Ruth Freeman, 542
Swamp, Chief Jake, 151, 159
Swamp Angel (Isaacs), 157, 183–184, 203
"Swan and Shadow" (Hollander), 329
Swan Lake (Fonteyn), 266
Swan Lake (Helprin), 266
Swanson, Diane, 525, 542
Swanton, Susan, 99
Sweater (Allen), 168, 198
Swedberg, Jack, 539
Sweeney, Matthew, 331
Sweet, Melissa, 131, 155, 357, 480, 495
Sweet and Sour Animal Book, The (Hughes), 157
Sweetest Fig, The (Van Allsburg), 139, 159, 205
Sweetgrass (Hudson), 94, 110, 113, 433–434, 456, 458
Swenson, May, 339, 357
Swiatkowska, Gabi, 541
Swift, Jonathan, 45, 50, 51, 63, 66
Swifter, Higher, Stronger: A Photographic History of the Summer Olympics (Macy), 503, 539
Swiftly Tilting Planet, A (L'Engle), 7, 299, 312
Swimmy (Lionni), 134, 157, 302, 312
Swimsuit (Allen), 168, 198
Swinburne, Stephen R., 505, 522, 532, 534–535, 542
Swing Around the Sun (Esbensen), 334, 356
Swiss Family Robinson (Wyss), 50, 63, 403, 414
Switching Well (Griffin), 311
Sword and the Circle, The: King Arthur and the Knights of the Round Table (Sutcliff), 247, 269, 314
Sword in the Stone, The (White), 108, 115
Sword of the Rightful King: A Novel of King Arthur (Yolen), 281, 314
Sydney Herself (Rodowsky), 114, 414
Sydney Rella and the Glass Sneaker (Myers), 264
Sykes, Julie, 159, 205
Sykes, Shelley, 414
Sylvester and the Magic Pebble (Steig), 64, 175, 186, 205
Syme, Ronald, 64
Szabo, Corinne, 498

Taback, Simms, 6, 18, 107, 114, 124, 132, 159, 178, 205
"Table, the Donkey, and the Stick, The," 212
Tafuri, Nancy, 5, 199

Tai Chi Morning: Snapshots of China (Grimes), 15

Tail Feathers from Mother Goose: The Opie Rhyme Book (Opie & Opie), 165, 198, 359

Tailor of Gloucester, The (Potter), 269, 313

Tainos, The: The People Who Welcomed Columbus (Jacobs), 20

Takahashi, Hideko, 325, 359

Take a Look, It's in a Book: How Television Is Made at Reading Rainbow (Krauss), 527, 538

Take Me Out to the Ball Game (Stadler), 168, 198

Taking Sides (Soto), 32, 392, 414

Tale I Told Sasha, The (Willard), 327, 360

Tale of a Tail (Bodnár), 124–125, 154

Tale of Despereaux, The (DiCamillo), 7, 64, 94, 96, 112, 274, 311

Tale of Peter Rabbit, The (Potter), 5, 63, 77, 80, 114, 158, 194, 275, 286–287, 313, 362–363

Tale of Squirrel Nutkin, The (Potter), 313

Tale of the Mandarin Ducks, The (Paterson), 230, 263

Tale of Tsar Saltan, The (Pushkin), 266

Tales from Shakespeare (Lamb & Lamb), 17, 113, 257

Tales from Shakespeare (Packer), 17

Tales from the Homeplace: Adventures of a Texas Farm Girl (Burandt & Dale), 536

Tales from the Land of the Sufis (Bayat & Jamnia), 250–251, 266

Tales from the Rain Forest (Dorson & Wilmot), 236, 265

Tales from the Taiwanese (Davison), 254, 263

Tales from the Waterhole (Graham), 185, 202

Tales of a Fourth Grade Nothing (Blume), 14, 398, 410

Tales of Hans Christian Andersen (Andersen), 278, 310, 492

Tales of King Arthur (Riordan), 269

Tales of Mother Goose (Perrault), 45, 49, 63, 209, 221, 261 *See also* Perrault, Charles

Tales of Oliver Pig (Van Leeuwen), 201

Tales of Peter Rabbit and His Friends (Potter), 287, 313

Tales of the Crusaders (Scott), 60

Tales of Uncle Remus, The: The Adventures of Brer Rabbit (Lester), 157, 239, 262

Talkin' About Bessie: The Story of Aviator Elizabeth Coleman (Grimes), 470, 496

Talking Earth, The (George), 389–390, 411

Talking Eggs, The: A Folktale from the American South (San Souci), 9, 13, 262

Talking Like the Rain: A First Book of Poems (Kennedy & Kennedy), 320, 357

Talking to the Sun (Farrell), 357

Talking Walls (Knight), 510, 538

Talking with Artists (Cummings), 33, 40, 146, 155

Tall Tale America: A Legendary History of Our Humorous Heroes (Blair), 239, 266

Tanaka, Shelley, 509, 542

Tang, Tracy, 70

Tangled Threads: A Hmong Girl's Story (Shea), 22, 33, 394, 414

Tanya's Reunion (Flournoy), 156

"Taper Tom" (Asbjørnsen & Moe), 226–227

Tarantula Scientist, The (Montgomery), 519, 540

Taran Wanderer (Alexander), 282, 309

Tarbox, Gwen Athene, 44

Taste of Blackberries, A (Smith), 64

Tasty Baby Belly Buttons (Sierra), 7, 230, 263

Tate, Don, 262

"Tattercoats," 221, 257, 258, 259

Taulbert, Clifton L.

Tauss, Marc, 334, 359

Taylor, Clark, 414

Taylor, G. P., 279, 314

Taylor, Mildred D., 35, 64, 92, 114, 387, 414, 437, 444, 460

Taylor, Scott, 154

Taylor, Sydney, 68, 69, 373, 374–375, 414

Taylor, Theodore, 64, 93, 115, 395, 402, 403, 414

Taylor, William, 414

T-Backs, T-Shirts, Coat, and Suit (Konigsburg), 412

Tchana, Katrin, 267

Teacher's Funeral, The: A Comedy in Three Parts (Peck), 459

Teague, Mark, 10, 183, 201, 206

Team Picture (Hughes), 412

Technically, It's Not My Fault (Grandits), 329, 356

"Teenagers" (Rylant), 343

Teens at Risk: Opposing Viewpoints (Ojeda), 22

Teens Cook: How to Cook What You Want to Eat (Carle & Carle), 530, 536

Teeth, Tails, & Tentacles: An Animal Counting Book (Wormell), 131, 144, 152, 160, 171, 172, 200

Tehanu: The Last Book of Earthsea (LeGuin), 282, 312

Te Kanawa, Kiri, 246, 268

Telgen, Diane, 516, 542

"Tell All the Truth" (Dickinson), 346

Telling of the Tales, A: Five Stories (Brooke), 261, 266

Tell Me Again About the Night I Was Born (Curtis), 21, 28, 202

Tell Me a Story, Mama (Johnson), 113

Tell Them We Remember: The Story of the Holocaust (Bachrach), 148, 154

Ten, Nine, Eight (Bang), 12, 171, 199

10 Little Rubber Ducks (Carle), 13, 131, 155, 171, 173, 199

Tenderness (Cormier), 397, 411

Ten Flashing Fireflies (Sturges), 199

Tenniel, John, 55, 59, 144, 155, 292, 293, 310

Tennis Ace (Christopher), 398, 410

"Tennis Anyone" (Kulling), 324

Ten Puppies (Reiser), 12, 199

Ten Queens: Portraits of Women in Power (Meltzer), 472, 497

Tenth Good Thing About Barney, The (Viorst), 102

Terry, Ann, 318

Testa, Fulvio, 241, 267

Texas Ghost Stories: Fifty Favorites for the Telling (Tingle), 252

That Boy and That Old Man (Hernandez), 412

Thayer, Ernest Lawrence, 328, 360

Then Again, Maybe I Won't (Blume), 410

Theodore Roosevelt: Champion of the American Spirit (Kraft), 475, 497

There Once Was a Man Named Michael Finnegan (Hoberman), 357

There's Always Pooh and Me (Milne), 350, 358

There's a Nightmare in My Closet (Mayer), 204

"There Was A Crooked Man," 350

There Was An Old Lady Who Swallowed A Fly (Taback), 6, 107, 114, 124, 159

These Happy Golden Years (Wilder), 460

Theseus and the Minotaur (Fisher), 243, 268

Theseus and the Minotaur (Hutton), 243, 268

Thief, The (Turner), 115, 304, 314

Thief Lord, The (Funke), 283, 311

Thief of Always, The (Barker), 310

Thief of Hearts (Yep), 393, 414

Thimble Summer (Enright), 68, 69, 411

Thimmesh, Catherine, 512–513, 542

Things I Learned in Second Grade (Schwartz), 21

Think Like an Eagle: At Work with a Wildlife Photographer (Lasky), 18, 40, 523, 539

Thin Wood Walls (Patneaude), 20, 22, 450, 459

This and That (Sykes), 159

"This Is the House That Jack Built," 350

This is the Way We Go to School: A Book About Children Around the World (Baer), 18

This Land Is My Land (Littlechild), 151, 157

This Land Is Your Land (Guthrie), 325–326, 350, 357

This Land Was Made for You and Me: The Life and Songs of Woody Guthrie (Partridge), 482, 497

This Place I Know: Poems of Comfort (Heard), 342, 357

This Same Sky: A Collection of Poems From Around the World (Nye), 358

Thomas, Dylan, 7, 96, 115, 152, 159, 190, 205

Thomas, Joyce Carol, 339, 360

Thomas and the Library Lady (Mora), 181

Thomas Becket: English Saint and Martyr (Hilliam), 494

Thomas Jefferson: The Revolutionary Aristocrat (Meltzer), 114

Thomas Jefferson (Harness), 473, 496

Thomas Paine: Common Sense (Myers), 497

Thompson, Lauren, 4, 5, 123, 153, 159, 181, 205

Thompson, Stith, 208

Thomson, Peggy, 528, 542

Thornhill, Jan, 199

Those Summers (Aliki), 33

Thousand Peaks, A: Poems From China (Liu & Protopopescu), 358

"Three Bears, The," 17, 209, 213, 220, 253, 255

Three Bears, The (Crane), 54

Three Bears, The (Galdone), 221, 263

Three Bears Rhyme Book, The (Yolen), 5, 360

"Three Billy Goats Gruff, The," 103, 211, 219, 253, 255

Three Billy Goats Gruff, The (Asbjørnsen & Moe), 12, 266

Three Billy Goats Gruff, The (Brown), 266

Three Billy Goats Gruff, The (Galdone), 13, 266

"Three Billy Goats Gruff, The" (Lunge-Larsen), 226

Three Billy Goats Gruff, The (Rounds), 266

"Three Drops of Creation" (Schwartz), 251

Three Jovial Huntsmen (Jeffers), 157

"Three Little Pigs, The," 80, 213, 219, 220, 221, 253, 261

Three Little Pigs, The (Kellogg), 220, 264

Three Little Pigs, The (Moser), 13, 158

Three Little Pigs and the Big Bad Wolf, The (Rounds), 220, 264

Three Little Wolves and the Big Bad Pig, The (Trivizas), 17, 115, 194, 205

Three Names (MacLachlan), 452, 459

Three Princes, The: A Tale from the Middle East (Kimmel), 232, 265

Three Samurai Cats: A Story From Japan (Kimmel), 230–231, 263

Through My Eyes (Bridges), 410, 478, 495

Through the Eyes of Many Children: An Introduction to Multicultural Literature (Norton), 214

Through the Lens: National Geographic Greatest Photographs (National Geographic), 148, 150

Through the Looking Glass, and What Alice Found There (Carroll), 58, 310, 331–332, 355

Throwing Shadows (Konigsburg), 412

Thumbelina (Andersen), 310, 492

Thumbelina (Ehrlich), 310

Thumbelina (Falloon), 310

Thumbelina (Pinkney), 310, 492

Thumbelina (Sneed), 310, 492

Thumbelina (Zweger), 492

Thunder Cake (Polacco), 179, 204

Thunder Rolling in the Mountains (O'Dell & Hall), 421, 459

Thunderwith (Hathorn), 412

Thurber, James, 314

Thurgood Marshall: A Life for Justice (Haskins), 477, 496

Thurman, Judith, 324, 350, 360

"Tibetan Envoy, The" (Philip), 260

Tiegreen, Alan, 112, 197, 410

Tiger: The Five Ancestors (Stone), 428, 459

Tiger Eyes (Blume), 383–384, 410

Tiger Rescue: Changing the Future for Endangered Wildlife (Bortololli), 522, 536

Tiger with Wings: The Great Horned Owl (Esbensen), 523, 537

Tiger Woman (Yep), 229, 263

Tikki Tikki Tembo (Mosel), 158

Tiller, Ruth, 360

Time for Bed (Fox), 168, 198

Time of Fire (Westall), 460

Time of Wonder (McCloskey), 138, 158, 204

Time Train (Fleischman), 10, 202

Timothy Goes to School (Wells), 24, 31, 206

"Tinderbox, The" (Andersen), 277, 278, 310

Tinderbox, The (Moser), 277, 310

Tingle, Tim, 251, 252, 253, 266

Tinkelman, Murray, 338, 357

Tiny's Big Adventure (Waddell), 21, 181, 205

Tirra Lirra: Rhymes Old and New (Richards), 63, 332, 359

Titherington, Jean, 449

Tituba of Salem Village (Petry), 419, 431, 459

Toasting Marshmallows: Camping Poems (George), 6, 319, 356

"To a Terrorist" (Dunn), 346

Toby Scudder, Ultimate Warrior (Gifaldi), 411

Toby Where Are You? (Steig), 205

Today Is Saturday (Snyder), 321, 360

Todd, Justin, 310

Todd, Mark, 414

To Establish Justice: Citizenship and the Constitution (McKissack & Zarembka), 530, 540

To Feel as Our Ancestors Did: Collecting and Performing Oral Histories (Kelin), 254, 267

Token for Children, A, Being an Exact Account of the Conversion, Holy and Exemplary Lives, and Joyful Deaths of Several Young Children (Janeway), 48

Tolan, Stephanie S., 22, 414

Told by Uncle Remus (Harris), 267

Tolkien, J. R. R., 40, 63, 108, 115, 244, 248, 269, 272, 274, 281, 293, 300, 302, 303, 309, 314

Tomboy of the Air: Daredevil Pilot Blanche Stuart Scott (Cummins), 470, 495

Tomes, Margot, 459, 496

Tomie dePaola's Mother Goose (dePaola), 136, 155, 165, 166, 197

Tom's Midnight Garden (Pearce), 114

"Tom Thumb," 254–255

Tom Thumb's Folio (Newbery), 51

"Tom Tit Tot," 214

Tongue-Cut Sparrow, The (Ishii), 263

Toorchen, Anthea, 268

Toots and the Upside-Down House (Hughes), 311

Top of the World, The: Climbing Mount Everest (Jenkins), 157, 501–502, 538

Tops & Bottoms (Stevens), 18, 126, 159, 184, 205

Top Secret: A Handbook of Codes, Ciphers, and Secret Writings (Janeczko), 527, 538

To Rabbittown (Wayland), 205

Torrecilla, Pablo, 413

Tortillitas para Mama and Other Spanish Nursery Rhymes (Griego et al.), 5, 8, 135, 156, 166, 197

"Tortoise and the Hare, The" (Aesop), 239

Tortoise and the Hare, The (Stevens), 240, 268

To Seek a Better World: The Haitian Minority in America (Ashabranner), 536

To See With the Heart: The Life of Sitting Bull (St. George), 498

Touchstones: A List of Distinguished Children's Books (Children's Literature Association), 272

Toughest Cowboy, The: Or How the West Was Won (Frank), 202

Town Mouse and the Country Mouse, The (Craig), 267

Town Mouse & the Country Mouse, The (Stevens), 268

Townsend, John Rowe, 49, 68, 69, 282, 289, 368

Tracking Dinosaurs in the Gobi (Facklam), 518, 537

Trading Game, The (Slote), 414

Trafzer, Clifford E., 237

Train of States, The (Sís), 513, 541

Trains (Gibbons), 200

Traitor: The Case of Benedict Arnold (Fritz), 113, 472–473, 496

"Transfiguration Begins at Home" (Weiner), 346

Trapped Between the Lash and the Gun (Whitmore), 297, 314

Trash! (Wilcox), 542

Travels of Benjamin of Tudela, The: Through Three Continents in the Twelfth Century (Schulevitz), 76, 114, 452, 459

Travers, Pamela L., 291, 314

Treasure Chest, The: A Chinese Tale (Wang), 229, 263

Treasure Island (Stevenson), 40, 45, 59, 63, 284

Treasure of Green Knowe, The (Boston), 296, 310

Treasury of Dragon Stories, A (Clark), 310

Treasury of Peter Rabbit and Other Stories, A (Potter), 287, 313

Treasury of Saints and Martyrs, The (Mulvihill), 146, 158

Tree of Cranes (Say), 34–35

Tree of Life, The: A Book Depicting the Life of Charles Darwin (Sís), 466, 467, 490, 498

Tree That Would Not Die, The (Levine), 539

Trembling Earth (Siegelson), 459

Trethewey, Natasha, 346

T. Rex (French), 518, 537

Trial Valley (Cleaver & Cleaver), 410

"Triangular Tale, A" (Prelutsky), 329, 350

Trickster Tales: Forty Folk Stories From Around the World (Sherman), 265

Trimble, Stephen, 452, 460

Trip, The (Keats), 132, 137, 157, 187, 196, 203

Trivas, Irene, 89, 113

Trivizas, Eugene, 17, 115, 194, 205

Trojan Horse, The (Hutton), 268

Troll Fell (Langrish), 312

Troll with No Heart in His Body and Other Tales of Trolls from Norway, The (Lunge-Larsen), 131, 157, 212, 226, 266

Trouble with Tuck, The (Taylor), 395, 402, 414

Troupe, Quincy, 482, 498

Trow-Wife's Treasure, The (Dunrea), 155

Trucks Trucks Trucks (Sís), 12, 198

Truck Talk: Rhymes on Wheels (Katz), 357

True Colors of Caitlynne Jackson, The (Williams), 414

True Confessions of Charlotte Doyle, The (Avi), 111, 457

True North (Lasky), 435–436, 458

Truesdell, Sue, 358, 359

True Stories About Abraham Lincoln (Gross), 496

True Story of the 3 Little Pigs, The! (Scieszka), 130, 159, 261, 267

Truly Winnie (Jacobson), 22

Truman (McCullough), 494, 530

Trumpet of the Swan, The (White), 115, 194

Truth and Lies: An Anthology of Poems (Vecchione), 346, 360

Tseng, Grace, 159, 229, 263

Tseng, Jean, 158, 159, 263, 267

Tseng, Mou-sien, 158, 159, 263, 267

Tsubakiyama, Margaret Holloway, 188, 205

Tsukushi, 157

ttyl (Myracle), 22, 366, 413

Tucker, Nicholas, 44

Tucker's Countryside (Selden), 289, 313

Tuck Everlasting (Babbit), 77, 107, 111, 272, 310

Tudor, Tasha, 112, 311, 327, 358

Tuer, Andrew, 58

Tuesday (Wiesner), 5, 10, 13, 129, 139, 160, 175–176, 200

Tulip Touch, The (Fine), 411

Tumble Me Tumbily (Baicker), 5

Tunnell, Michael O., 281, 314

"Tup and the Ants" (Bierhorst), 235

Turner, Alan, 520–521, 542

Turner, Ann, 205, 360, 498

Turner, Megan Whalen, 115, 304, 314

Turner, Robyn Montana, 149, 159, 479, 498

Turnip, The (de la Mare), 264

"Turtle Dives to the Bottom of the Sea: Earth Starter the Creator" (Hamilton), 245

Turtle Knows Your Name (Bryan), 262

Tusa, Tricia, 342, 355

"Tutor, The" (Wells), 321

Tuttle, Lisa, 108

Twain, Mark, 60, 63, 66, 71

"Twas the Night Before Any Thing" (Scieszka), 339

"Twelve Dancing Princesses, The," 219

Twelve Dancing Princesses, The (Grimm & Grimm), 264

Twelve Dancing Princesses, The (LeCain), 264

Twelve Dancing Princesses, The (Mayer), 225, 264
Twelve Dancing Princesses, The (Ray), 264
Twelve Dancing Princesses, The (Sanderson), 264
26 Fairmount Avenue (dePaola), 110, 112, 482, 495
26 Letters and 99 Cents (Hoban), 14, 19, 172, 199
Twenty Thousand Leagues Under the Sea (Verne), 45, 60, 297
Twichell, Chase, 354
Twilight Comes Twice (Fletcher), 202
Twilight in Grace Falls (Honeycutt), 412
"Two Children in the Wood, The," 47
Two of Everything (Hong), 229, 263
Two Queens of Heaven: Aphrodite and Demeter (Gates), 244, 268
Two Suns in the Sky (Bat-Ami), 32, 33, 112, 445, 446, 457
2001: A Space Odyssey, 297
Two Towers, The (Tolkien), 281, 314
Tyger, The (Blake), 337–338, 355
"TyrannosaurBus Rex" (Grandits), 329
Tyrannosaurus Was a Beast: Dinosaur Poems (Prelutsky), 338, 359
"Tyrant who Became a Just Ruler, The," 210

Uchida, Yoshiko, 449, 460
Udry, Janice May, 138, 159
Uglies (Westerfield), 301, 314
"Ugly Duckling, The" (Andersen), 52, 124, 154, 277, 310, 492
Ugly Duckling, The (Cauley), 310
Ugly Duckling, The (Ingpen), 492
Ugly Duckling, The (Pinkney), 310, 492
Umbrella (Yashima), 160
Uncle Chente's Picnic/El Picnic de Tío Chente (Bertrand), 391, 410
Uncle Elephant (Lobel), 201
Uncle Remus; His Songs and Sayings: The Folklore of the Old Plantation (Harris), 63, 238
Uncle Remus and His Friends (Harris), 267
Uncle Tom's Cabin (Stowe), 66
Uncommon Traveler: Mary Kingsley in Africa (Brown), 102, 495
Under a Different Sky (Savage), 414
Under the Blood-Red Sun (Salisbury), 114, 450, 459
Under the Spell of the Moon: Art for Children From This World's Great Illustrators (Aldana), 144, 154, 344, 355
Under the Window (Greenaway), 55
Ungerer, Tomi, 205
Unseen, The (Snyder), 314
Unsworth, Robert, 372
Untold Tales (Brooke), 17
Unwin, Nora S., 310, 312, 460, 498
Unwitting Wisdom: An Anthology of Aesop's Fables (Ward), 102, 240, 268
Up and Down on the Merry-Go-Round (Martin & Archambault), 204
Up a Road Slowly (Hunt), 412
Upon the Head of the Goat: A Childhood in Hungary 1939-1944 (Siegel), 459
Upstairs Room, The (Reiss), 423, 447, 459, 498
"Urashima Taro," 211
Urban Roosts: Where Birds Nest in the City (Bash), 536
Uribe, Verónica, 240, 241, 268

Uses of Enchantment, The: The Meaning and Importance of Fairy Tales (Bettelheim), 213
Usher, M. D., 469, 498

Vachula, Paul, 327, 358
Vais, Alain, 222, 264
Valerie and the Silver Pear (Darling), 386, 411
"Valiant Little Tailor, The," 219
Valley Forge (Ammon), 14, 18–19, 514, 536
Valley of the Shadow, The (Hickman), 64
Van Allsburg, Chris, 13, 18, 110, 139, 140, 146, 159, 170, 181, 190, 193, 197, 199, 200, 205, 266, 302, 314
van der Rol, Ruud, 498
Van Doren, Charles, 307
van Gogh, Vincent, 134
Van Laan, Nancy, 201, 235, 239, 265, 267, 330, 360
Van Leeuwen, Jean, 13, 21, 31, 201, 460
Van Loon, Hendrik Willem, 63, 530, 542
Van Rynbach, Iris, 358
Van Wright, Cornelius, 205
Van Zyle, Jon, 124, 157, 158, 539, 540
Vassilisa the Wise: A Tale of Medieval Russia (Sherman), 228, 266
"Vassilissa the Fair," 227
Vecchione, Patrice, 22, 345–346, 360
Velveteen Rabbit, The (Williams), 16, 63, 110, 115, 290, 291, 302, 314
Vendela in Venice (Björk), 146, 154
Venezia, Mike, 15, 146, 159
Vennema, Peter, 34, 40, 471, 498
Verdi (Cannon), 201
Verhoeven, Rian, 498
Verne, Jules, 45, 60, 63, 297
Very Best (Almost) Friend: Poems of Friendship (Janeczko), 341, 357
Very Clumsy Click Beetle, The (Carle), 131, 155, 168, 198
Very Hungry Caterpillar, The (Carle), 110, 131, 155, 199
Very Quiet Cricket, The (Carle), 198
Vicksburg: The Battle That Won the Civil War (Fraser), 537
Vidal, Beatriz, 250, 262, 269
Vidaure, Morris, 265
Vietnam: Why We Fought: An Illustrated History (Hoobler & Hoobler), 508
View From Saturday, The (Konigsburg), 14, 64, 93, 113, 412
Viguers, Ruth Hill, 54
Village by the Sea, The (Fox), 411
Village of Blue Stone, The (Trimble), 452, 460
Village of Round and Square Houses, The (Grifalconi), 233, 262
Violence in Our Schools (Orr), 22
Viorst, Judith, 64, 102, 128, 160, 179, 180, 199, 205, 360
Virgie Goes to School with Us Boys, 187
Virgil, 66, 326
"Virgin of Guadalupe, The," 235
Vision of Beauty: The Story of Sarah Breedlove Walker (Lasky), 497
Visions: Stories About Women Artists (Sills), 498
Visit from St. Nicholas, A (Moore). *See Night Before Christmas, The*
Visiting the Art Museum (Brown & Brown), 154

Visit to William Blake's Inn, A: Poems for Innocent and Experienced Travelers (Willard), 64, 138, 160, 348, 360
Vitale, Stefano, 156, 160, 198, 537
Vivas, Julie, 160, 188, 206
Voake, Charlotte, 12, 205, 541
Voce, Louise, 331, 357
Vogler, Christopher, 303–304
Vogt, Gregory L., 542
Voices: Poetry and Art From Around the World (Brenner), 355
Voices from the Fields: Children of Migrant Farmworkers Tell Their Stories (Atkins), 149
Voices of Silence, The (Mooney), 383, 413
Voices of the Trojan War (Hovey), 326, 357
Voice That Challenged a Nation, The: Marian Anderson and the Struggle for Equal Rights (Freedman), 92, 112, 464, 465, 481–482, 493, 494, 496
Voigt, Cynthia, 110, 115, 296, 314, 364–365, 366, 370, 377, 414
Vojtech, Anna, 199
Volavkova, Hana, 148, 149, 160, 342, 360
Volcano: The Eruption and Healing of Mount St. Helens (Lauber), 19, 505, 525, 532, 539
Volcanoes (Simon), 499, 541
Volkmer, Jane Anne, 235, 265
von Waberer, Keto, 149
Vos, Ida, 89, 115, 416, 448–449, 460
Vote (Christelow), 506, 537
Voyage of the Dawn Treader, The (Lewis), 312
Voyage of the Frog, The (Paulsen), 17
Vrooman, Diana, 105

Waber, Bernard, 160, 205
Waddell, Martin, 5, 21, 23–24, 29, 33, 160, 181, 186, 205
Wadsworth, Ginger, 483, 498
Wagons West! (Gerrard), 356
Wagon Wheels (Brenner), 200, 453, 457
Wahl, Valerie, 267
Wait for Me, Watch for Me, Eula Bee (Beatty), 441, 457
Waiting to Sing (Kaplan), 363, 383, 412
Waiting to Waltz: A Childhood (Rylant), 343, 359
Wait Till Helen Comes (Hahn), 295, 311
Wake Up Bear … It's Christmas! (Gammell), 202
Wake Up Our Souls: A Celebration of Black American Artists (Bolden), 147, 154, 536
Walcott, Derek, 346
Waldman, Neil, 148, 160, 337, 355, 380, 510, 538, 542
Waldo, Amy, 113
Waldron, Ann, 144, 160
Walker, Barbara M., 529, 542
Walker, David, 264
Walker, Paul Robert, 214, 267
Walker, Sally M., 514, 530, 532, 542
Walking the Choctaw Road (Tingle), 251, 252, 253, 266
Walk in the Rainforest, A (Pratt), 199
Walk Two Moons (Creech), 20, 92, 112, 366, 375, 390, 411
Wall, The (Bunting), 399
Wallace, Ian, 148, 160, 392, 414
Wallace, Karen, 542
Wallace's Lists (Bottner & Kruglik), 181, 201

Wallner, John, 357
"Walrus and the Carpenter, The" (Carroll), 327
Walsh, Ellen Stoll, 200
Walter, Mildred Pitts, 7, 136–137, 160
Walter, Virginia, 414
Walters, Robert F., 539
Walter's Tail (Ernst), 202
Walt Whitman: Words for America (Kerley), 32, 152, 157, 468–469, 497
Wanderer, The (Creech), 86, 88–89, 112, 380, 411
Wang, Rosalind C., 229, 263
Wanted: Best Friend (Monson), 182, 204
War Boy: A Country Childhood (Foreman), 112, 452, 458, 482, 495
Ward, Geoffrey C., 494
Ward, Helen, 102, 240, 249, 268
Ward, John, 262
Ward, Lynd, 63, 112, 133, 144, 160, 205, 414, 458
Warhola, James, 267
Waring, Richard, 160, 205
War in Georgia, The (Oughton), 459
War of the Worlds (Wells), 297, 303
Warren, Andrea, 485, 498
Warren, James A., 542
Warrior and the Wise Man, The (Wisniewski), 84, 86
Warrior Goddess, The: Athena (Gates), 244, 268
"Warrior Goddess Athena, The," 210
Washington, Donna L., 6, 234, 262
Watch Out for the Chicken Feet in Your Soup (dePaola), 136, 155
Watch Where You Go (Noll), 6
Water: The Next Great Resource Battle (Pringle), 64
Water: Up, Down, and All Around (Rosinsky), 527, 541
Water-Babies, The (Kingsley), 63, 279
Water of Life, The (Rogasky), 264
Waters, Kate, 148, 160, 392, 414
Water Sky (George), 87, 390, 411
Watson, Wendy, 265, 267
Watsons Go to Birmingham—1963, The (Curtis), 81, 112, 411, 437
Watts, Bernadette, 264
Waugh, Sylvia, 314
Waverly: Or, 'Tis Sixty Years Since (Scott), 60
Way a Door Closes, The (Smith), 339, 360
Wayland, April Halprin, 205
Way Things Work, The (Macaulay), 501, 504, 527, 533, 539
We Are All in the Dumps with Jack and Guy (Sendak), 139, 143–144, 159, 166, 167, 197, 198
"Weather" (Merriam), 321
Weatherford, Carole Boston, 542
Weave of Words, A (San Souci), 267
Weaver, Warren, 291, 293
Weaving of a Dream, The: A Chinese Folktale (Heyer), 229, 260, 263
Webb, Sophie, 523, 542
Wednesday Surprise, The (Bunting), 112, 201
Weekend with Leonardo da Vinci, A (Skira-Venturi), 146, 159
Wee Winnie Witch's Skinny: An Original African American Scare Tale (Hamilton), 277, 311
Wegman, William, 205, 223, 264
We Hide, You Seek (Aruego & Dewey), 64
Weideman, George, 234
Weil, Sylvie, 20, 33, 426, 456, 460

Weiner, Estha, 346
Weinhaus, Karen Ann, 356
Weirdstone of Brisingamen, The (Garner), 283, 311
Weisgard, Leonard, 201, 266, 359, 457
Weiss, Emil, 413
Weiss, Mitch, 255
Weissman, Barry, 538
Weitzman, David, 542
Welcome to the Sea of Sand (Yolen), 206
Weller, Frances Ward, 129, 160
Wells, Carolyn, 321
Wells, H. G., 297, 303
Wells, Rosemary, 14, 21, 24, 30, 31, 115, 168, 172, 174, 185, 198, 200, 205, 483, 498
Well Wished (Billingsley), 310
Welsh Legends and Folktales (Jones), 264
Welton, Jude, 146, 160
Wemberly's Ice-Cream Star (Henkes), 168, 198
We're Going On a Bear Hunt (Rosen), 5, 122, 159, 194, 195, 205
Werenskiold, Erik, 266
Werner, Craig, 69
We Shall Overcome: A Living History of the Civil Rights Struggle Told in Words, Pictures and Voices of the Participants (Boyd), 516, 536
Weslandia (Fleischman), 19, 202
West, Mark I., 465
Westall, Robert, 295, 314, 460
Westcott, Nadine Bernard, 357, 360
Westerfield, Scott, 301, 314
Western Wind (Fox), 411
Westing Game, The (Raskin), 114, 414
Westmark (Alexander), 282, 309
Westminster West (Haas), 458
Weston, Annette H., 289
Weston, Martha, 411
We the People: The Story of the United States Constitution Since 1787 (Faber & Faber), 530, 537
We Were There, Too! Young People in U.S. History (Hoose), 538
Wexler, Jerome, 521, 537
Whaling Days (Carrick), 536
What a Morning! The Christmas Story in Black Spirituals (Langstaff), 357
What Charlie Heard (Gerstein), 482, 496
What! Cried Granny: An Almost Bedtime Story (Lum), 184, 204
What Dads Can't Do (Wood), 92, 115
What Did You Do Today? (Forward), 31
What Game Shall We Play? (Hutchins), 6, 200
What Have You Lost? (Nye), 342, 358
What Hearts (Brooks), 112, 410
What I Believe: Kids Talk About Faith (Birdseye & Birdseye), 536
What I Cannot Tell My Mother Is Not Fit for Me to Know (Rees-Williams & Rees-Williams), 56
What Is Goodbye? (Grimes), 342, 357
What James Likes Best (Schwartz), 16
Whatley, Bruce, 170–171, 199
Whatley's Quest (Whatley & Smith), 170–171, 199
What Pete Ate from A-Z: (Really!) (Kalman), 14
"What's a Nice Poem Like You Doing in a Place Like This?" (Sandmann), 359
What's the Big Idea, Ben Franklin? (Fritz), 489, 496
What's the Deal? Jefferson, Napoleon, and the Louisiana Purchase (Blumberg), 505, 536

What's What?: A Guessing Game (Serfozo), 18, 200
What's Your Story? A Young Person's Guide to Writing Fiction (Bauer), 529, 536
What Use Is a Moose? (Waddell), 205
What You Know First (MacLachlan), 158, 358
What You Never Knew About Tubs, Toilets, and Showers (Lauber), 18, 527, 539
Wheeler, Lisa, 124, 160
Wheel Wizards (Christopher), 398, 410
Whelan, Gloria, 7, 95, 96, 115, 194, 393, 414, 490
When Africa Was Home (Williams), 387, 414
When Agnes Caws (Fleming), 202
When Birds Could Talk & Bats Could Sing: The Adventures of Brush Sparrow, Sis Wren, and Their Friends (Hamilton), 238, 262
When Bluebell Sang (Ernst), 184, 202
When Dinosaurs Die: A Guide to Understanding Death (Brown & Brown), 25
When Hitler Stole Pink Rabbit (Kerr), 458
When It Comes to Bugs (Fisher), 335, 356
When I Was Young in the Mountains (Rylant), 30, 64, 107, 114, 205, 419–420, 459
When Marian Sang (Ryan), 482, 493, 498
When Shlemiel Went to Warsaw & Other Stories (Singer), 228
When the Beginning Began: Stories About God, the Creatures, and Us (Lester), 269
"When the Birds and the Beasts Went to War" (Grimm & Grimm), 223
When the Circus Came to Town (Horvath), 398, 412
When the Dark Comes Dancing: A Bedtime Poetry Book (Larrick), 357
When the Wind Stops (Zolotow), 160
When Uncle Took the Fiddle (Gray), 8
When We Were Very Young (Milne), 55, 63, 349, 358
When You Were Born (Aston), 339, 355
When Zachary Beaver Came to Town (Holt), 412
Where, Where Is Swamp Bear? (Appelt), 6, 201
Where Do You Think You're Going, Christopher Columbus? (Fritz), 469, 496
Where's Spot? (Hill), 168, 198
Where's the Baby? (Hutchins), 30, 203
Where the Buffaloes Begin (Baker), 154, 237, 265, 266
Where the Forest Meets the Sea (Baker), 154, 196, 201, 402, 409
Where the Lilies Bloom (Cleaver & Cleaver), 64, 70, 71, 363, 375–376, 410
Where the Red Fern Grows (Rawls), 110
Where the River Begins (Locker), 134, 157
Where the Sidewalk Ends (Silverstein), 332, 350, 359
Where the Wild Things Are (Sendak), 10, 31, 77, 86, 110, 114, 138, 153, 159, 178, 179, 205
Where Was Patrick Henry on the 29th of May? (Fritz), 472, 488–489, 496
Where Will This Shoe Take You? A Walk Through the History of Footwear (Lawlor), 539
Where You Belong (McGuigan), 459
While Standing on One Foot: Puzzle Stories and Wisdom Tales from the Jewish Tradition (Jaffe & Zeitlin), 265
Whipping Boy, The (Fleischman), 92, 112
Whipple, Laura, 160, 334, 338, 350, 360
Whirligig (Fleischman), 411

Whiskers and Rhymes (Lobel), 358
Whispers from the Dead (Nixon), 295, 313
Whistle for Willie (Keats), 28
White, Carolyn, 264
White, E. B., 14, 39, 63, 77, 86, 110, 115, 194, 290
White, Mary Michaels, 356
White, Ruth, 70, 71, 83, 102, 115, 414
White, T. H., 108, 115
"White Archer, The," 210
Whitelaw, Nancy, 494
White Mountains, The (Christopher), 64, 299, 305, 310
White Stag, The (Seredy), 114, 269
White Tiger, Blue Serpent (Tseng), 159, 229, 263
Whitman, Walt, 334, 345
Whitmore, Arvella, 297, 314
Whitney, Sharon, 498
Whitney, Thomas P., 312
Who Came First? New Clues to Prehistoric Americans (Lauber), 15, 505–506, 510, 539
Who Goes Home? (Waugh), 314
Whole New Ball Game, A: The Story of the All-American Girls Professional Baseball League (Macy), 539
Whole Night Through, The: A Lullaby (Frampton), 156
Whooping Crane, The: A Comeback Story (Patent), 540
Who's Counting? (Tafuri), 199
Who Shrank My Grandmother's House: Poems of Discovery (Esbensen), 356
Who's in Rabbit's House? (Aardema), 31, 262
Who's That Baby? New-Baby Songs (Creech), 339, 356
Who Uses This? (Miller), 540
Who Was That Masked Man, Anyway? (Avi), 40
Whuppity Stoorie: A Scottish Folktale (White), 264
Whybrow, Ian, 5, 8, 21
Why Don't You Get a Horse, Sam Adams? (Fritz), 489, 496
Why Mosquitoes Buzz in People's Ears: A West African Tale (Aardema), 80, 111, 137, 154, 182, 201, 234, 262
"Why Mosquitoes Buzz in People's Ears," 209
Why Not? (Wormell), 24
Why the Chicken Crossed the Road (Macaulay), 204
"Why the Sea Is Salt," 219
Wicked Stepdog, The (Benjamin), 112, 403, 410
Wickersham, Elaine B., 368
Widener, Terry, 457, 494, 496
Widow's Broom, The (Van Allsburg), 139, 159, 190, 205
Wiese, Kurt, 55
Wiesner, David, 5, 10, 13, 40, 121, 129, 139, 144, 146, 160, 175–176, 193, 196, 200, 206, 220, 263, 264, 314
Wiggins, Kate Douglas, 60, 63, 67–68
Wiggins, S. Michelle, 310
Wigginton, Eliot, 455, 460
Wijngaard, Juan, 113, 248, 269
Wilbur, Richard, 169, 199
Wilcox, Charlotte, 542
Wild, Margaret, 32, 107, 115, 160, 188–189, 206
Wilder, Laura Ingalls, 14, 40, 63, 77, 84, 110, 115, 118, 423, 438, 440, 454–455, 460

Wildflower ABC: An Alphabet of Potato Prints (Pomeroy), 199
Wildlife ABC, The: A Nature Alphabet Book (Thornhill), 199
Wildsmith, Brian, 160
Wild Swans, The: An Adventure in Six Parts (Setterington), 313
Wild Swans, The (Andersen), 277, 278, 302
Wild Swans, The (Ehrlich), 310
Wilkes, Angela, 530, 542
Wilkin, Binnie Tate, 69
Wilkins, David G., 133, 148, 150
Willard, Nancy, 6, 10, 40, 64, 138, 160, 226, 264, 266, 327, 330–331, 348, 360
Willems, Mo, 152, 153, 160, 187, 188, 206
Willey, Bee, 199, 268
William Lloyd Garrison: Abolitionist and Journalist (Fauchald), 493
Williams, Berkeley, Jr., 266
Williams, Carol Lynch, 414
Williams, Garth, 115, 175, 206, 313, 314, 460, 529, 542
Williams, Jennifer, 115
Williams, Karen Lynn, 387, 414
Williams, Laura, 460
Williams, Marcia, 269
Williams, Margery, 16, 63, 110, 115, 290, 291, 302, 314
Williams, Mary E., 70
Williams, Richard, 398, 412
Williams, Sherley Anne, 180, 206, 387, 414, 452
Williams, Sophy, 265
Williams, Vera B., 30, 115, 180, 188, 196, 206
William's Doll (Zolotow), 188, 206
William Tell (Early), 248, 269
William Wegman's Farm (Wegman), 205
Will I Have a Friend? (Cohen), 24
Willow and Twig (Little), 22, 412
Will's Mammoth (Martin), 6, 17, 18, 31, 126–127, 158, 204
Willy's Pictures (Browne), 16, 145–146, 154
Willy's Silly Grandma (Defelice), 6, 202
Wilma Unlimited: How Wilma Rudolph Became the World's Fastest Woman (Krull), 29, 485, 497
Wilmot, Jeanne, 236, 265
Wilner, Isabel, 321, 360
Wilson, Dorminster, 265
Wilson, Karma, 5
Wilson, Sarah, 8, 183, 206
Wilson, Sharon, 205
Wimmer, Mike, 113, 496
"Wind, The" (Reeves), 350
"Wind and Silver" (Lowell), 334
Wind Blew, The (Hutchins), 203
Windham, Sophie, 360
Wind in the Door, A (L'Engle), 299, 312
"Wind in the Pine Tree, The" (James), 230
Wind in the Willows, The (Grahame), 14, 55, 63, 113, 272, 288–289, 309, 311
Window (Baker), 6, 154, 176, 193, 196, 200
"Window Washer, The" (Simic), 334
Windsor, Patricia, 295, 314
"Windy Nights" (Stevenson), 346
Wineke, William R., 120
Wing on a Flea, The: A Book About Shapes (Emberley), 14, 19, 20

Wings (Myers), 158
Wings Along the Waterway (Brown), 536
Wings of Merlin, The (Barron), 310
Winnie-the-Pooh (Milne), 40, 63, 77, 114, 194, 204, 272, 291, 313, 325, 358
Winning Ways: A Photohistory of American Women in Sports (Macy), 29, 33, 497, 501, 539
Winston Churchill (Binns), 495
Winter, Jeanette, 40, 160, 170, 199, 334, 360, 481, 498, 515–516, 542
Winter, Jonah, 160, 480, 484, 498
Winter, Milo, 267
Winter, Susan, 342, 355
Winter Room, The (Paulsen), 7, 420, 441, 459
Winter's Tale (Sabuda), 24
Winthrop, Elizabeth, 30
Wintle, Justin, 299
Wise, William, 338, 360
Wise Guy: The Life and Philosophy of Socrates (Usher), 469, 498
Wiseman, Bernard, 177, 201
Wishes, Lies, and Dreams (Koch), 351
Wish Giver, The (Brittain), 302, 310
Wishing Moon (Tunnell), 314
Wish Me Luck (Heneghan), 445, 458
Wisniewski, David, 73, 84, 86, 121, 123, 132–133, 153, 159, 160, 195, 234, 249, 250, 262, 269
Witch of Blackbird Pond, The (Speare), 63, 92, 114, 419, 431, 459
With a Whoop and a Holler: A Bushel of Lore from Way Down South (Van Laan), 239, 267, 330, 360
With Courage and Cloth: Winning the Fight for a Woman's Right to Vote (Bausum), 515, 536
Witnesses to War: Eight True-Life Stories of Nazi Persecution (Leapman), 107, 113, 515, 539
Witschonke, Alan, 539
Wizard of Earthsea, A (LeGuin), 282, 312
Wizard of Oz (Baum), 310
Wojciechowska, Maia, 17, 385, 391, 414
"Wolf and the Dog, The" (Ellis), 239
Wolf and the Seven Little Kids, The (Grimm & Grimm), 219, 223
Wolfe, Alan, 463
Wolfe, Gillian, 141, 160
Wolff, Ashley, 326, 360
Wolff, Ferida, 314
Wolff, Virginia Euwer, 102, 386, 414
Wolfson, Tanya, 330, 357
Wolkstein, Diane, 212, 246, 268
Wolves of Willoughby Chase, The (Aiken), 274, 309
"Woman of the Well, The," 219
"Woman Who Fell from the Sky, The: Divine Woman the Creator" (Hamilton), 245
Wombat Divine (Fox), 202
Wombat Goes Walkabout (Morpurgo), 124, 158
Wonderful Flight to the Mushroom Planet, The (Cameron), 310
Wonderful Wizard of Oz, The: A Commemmorative Pop-Up (Sabuda), 24
Wonderful Words: Poems About Reading, Writing, Speaking, and Listening (Hopkins), 357
Wonders and Miracles: A Passover Companion (Kimmel), 148, 157, 249, 269
Wong, Janet S., 342, 360
Wood, Audrey, 10, 39, 160, 183, 206
Wood, Carol, 246, 266

Wood, Don, 160, 206
Wood, Douglas, 92, 115, 160, 335, 360
Wood, Nancy, 151, 160, 334
Woodford, Susan, 509, 542
Woodrow for President: A Tail of Voting, Campaigns and Elections (Barnes & Barnes), 536
Woodruff, Elvira, 430, 460
Woodson, Jacqueline, 152, 160, 189, 190, 206, 342, 360, 414
Woodsong (Paulsen), 497
Woody's 20 Grow Big Songs (Guthrie), 4
Woolly Mammoth Journey, A (Miller), 124, 158
Words of Stone (Henkes), 412
Words West: Voices of Young Pioneers (Wadsworth), 483, 498
Working (Oxenbury), 198
Working Cotton (Williams), 180, 206, 387, 414, 452
World at Her Fingertips, The: The Story of Helen Keller (Dash), 483, 495
World in 1492, The (Fritz et al.), 149, 151, 156, 508, 537
World of Christopher Robin, The (Milne), 358
World Water Watch (Koch), 538
Wormell, Christopher, 131, 144, 152, 160, 171, 172, 200
Wormell, Mary, 21, 24
Wormwood (Taylor), 279
Worry Stone, The (Dengler), 311
Worth, Valerie, 317, 340, 347, 360
Worthy, M. Joe, 257
Wreath for Emmett Till, A (Nelson), 345, 358
Wreck of the Zephyr, The (Van Allsburg), 139, 159, 181, 205, 302, 314
Wren's Quest (Smith), 314
Wretched Stone, The (Van Allsburg), 139, 159, 205
Wright, Amy Bartlett, 536
Wright, Beth, 173, 199
Wright, Betty Wren, 314
Wright, Patricia, 160
Wright Brothers, The: How They Invented the Airplane (Freedman), 14, 18, 80, 112, 466, 470, 496
Wright Sister, The: Katharine Wright and Her Famous Brothers (Maurer), 466, 470, 490, 497
Wrightson, Patricia, 273
Wringer (Spinelli), 83, 114, 414
Wrinkle in Time, A (L'Engle), 77, 113, 194, 298–299, 305–307, 312
"Write Me Another Verse" (McCord), 340
Writer's Journey, The: Mythic Structure for Storytellers and Screenwriters (Vogler), 303
Wyatt, Flora R., 490
Wyeth, Sharon Dennis, 399–400, 414
Wyndham, Robert, 166, 198, 229

Wynken, Blynken and Nod (Field), 156, 327, 356
Wynne-Jones, Tim, 414
Wyss, Johann David, 50, 63, 403, 414
Wyzga, Diane F., 252

Yaccarino, Dan, 204
Yagawa, Sumiko, 128, 160, 230, 263
"Yak, The" (Prelutsky), 349
Yang the Third and Her Impossible Family (Namioka), 395, 413
Yang the Youngest and His Terrible Ear (Namioka), 394–395, 413
"Yankee Doodle," 349
Yankee Doodle (Kellogg), 61
Yashima, Taro, 123, 153, 160
Yasir Arafat: A Life of War and Peace (Ferber), 476, 495
Yates, Elizabeth, 32, 420–421, 432, 460, 473, 491, 492, 498
Year Down Yonder, A (Peck), 64, 96, 98, 114
Yeh, Tso, 334
Yeh Shen: A Cinderella Story from China (Louie), 263
Yellowstone ABC, A (Martin), 199
"Yellowstone Whale, The" (Peters), 339
Yep, Laurence, 22, 64, 229, 231, 263, 267, 393, 414, 439–440, 450, 460, 490, 524
Yes, We Can (Bernier-Grand), 22
Yettele's Feathers (Rothenberg), 228, 265
Yolanda's Genius (Fenner), 20, 85, 112
Yolen, Jane, 4, 5, 8, 10, 21, 25, 40, 108, 115, 123–124, 129, 135, 160, 206, 241, 268, 275, 281, 297, 314, 360, 428, 447, 452, 460, 481, 492, 498
Yonge, Charlotte, 45, 57, 63, 67
Yorinks, Arthur, 104, 115, 124, 153, 160, 178, 179, 197, 206
York, Michael, 309
York's Adventures with Lewis and Clark: An African-American's Part in the Great Expedition (Blumberg), 484, 495
You and Me, Little Bear (Waddell), 29, 33, 205
"Youghy-Bonghy-Bo, The" (Lear), 58
Young, Beverly, 69
Young, Ed, 7, 13, 18, 31, 114, 148, 157, 160, 198, 204, 224, 225, 229, 231, 263, 268, 314, 335, 356, 496
Younger Edda, 244
Young Guinevere (San Souci), 269
Young Lancelot (San Souci), 269
Young Man and the Sea, The (Philbrick), 413
Young Mozart (Isadora), 203
Young Painter: The Life and Paintings of Wang Yani—China's Extraordinary Young Artist (Zheng & Low), 160

Young Patriot, A: The American Revolution as Experienced by One Boy (Murphy), 473, 497
You Read to Me, I'll Read to You: Very Short Stories to Read Together (Hoberman), 6, 194, 203, 324, 333, 356
You're Smarter Than You Think (Armstrong), 22
Your Mother Was a Neanderthal (Scieszka), 10
Your Move, J.P.! (Lowry), 413
Yo! Yes? (Raschka), 179, 204
Yue, Charlotte, 532, 542
Yue, David, 532, 542
Yukon Gold: The Story of the Klondike Gold Rush (Jones), 511, 538

Zaidman, Laura M., 383
Zakanitch, Robert, 338, 356
Zalben, Jane Breskin, 31, 206, 355
Zallinger, Jean Day, 541
Zamora, Martha, 149
Zamorano, Ana, 179, 206
Zarembka, Arlene, 530, 540
Zazoo (Mosher), 102
Zeely (Hamilton), 64, 387, 412
Zeitlin, Steve, 265
Zeldis, Malcah, 154, 477, 495, 497
Zelinsky, Paul O., 113, 124, 130, 131, 156, 157, 183–184, 203, 223, 264, 311, 313, 333, 359, 410
Zemach, Harve, 221, 264
Zemach, Margot, 13, 206, 228, 263, 264, 265, 360
Zeman, Ludmila, 126, 160, 232, 265
Zen Shorts (Muth), 204
Zero to the Bone (Cadnum), 384, 410
Zhang, Ange, 487, 498
Zhao, Li, 263
Zheng, Zhensun, 160
Ziefert, Harriet, 168, 198
Zimmer, Dirk, 201, 266, 267
Zimmerman, Andrea, 206
Zimmerman, H. Werner, 269
Zin! Zin! Zin! A Violin (Moss), 6, 8, 120, 158, 194, 204
Zlateh the Goat (Shulevitz), 159
Zoe Rising (Conrad), 296–297, 311
Zolotow, Charlotte, 160, 188, 206, 317, 334, 360
Zomo the Rabbit: A Trickster Tale from West Africa (McDermott), 262
Zoo Doings (Prelutsky), 350, 359
"Zuñi Creation Myth," 210
Zuni Folk Tales (Cushing), 237, 266
Zunshine, Tatiana, 330, 357
Zvorykin, Boris, 266
Z Was Zapped, The (Van Allsburg), 18, 170, 199
Zweger, Lisbeth, 492
Zwerger, Lisbeth, 193, 203, 264, 293, 309, 310

Subject Index

Aaron, Hank, 485
Aboriginal myths, 246
Abstract art, 134
Abstract expressionism, 134
Accessibility, 99
Accuracy
   in biographies, 465–466
   in informational books, 502–504
Acrylics, 129
Activities, suggested
   biographies, 494
   child development, 41
   contemporary realistic fiction, 409
   evaluation criteria, 110
   historical fiction, 457
   history of children's literature, 71
   illustrations, 153–154
   informational books, 535
   modern fantasy, 309
   picture books, 197
   poetry, 354–355
   traditional literature, 261–262
Adoption, 28
Adventure stories, early, 49–50, 51, 59–60
Aesop's fables. See Fables
Aesthetic responses, 38–39. See also Art
  appreciation
   aesthetic scanning, 141–143
   and motivation, 39, 40
   and picture books, 195–196
Aesthetic scanning, 141–143
Afghan folktales, 231
Africa, books about. See also African folktales;
  African legends
   biographies, 487
   contemporary realistic fiction, 387
   historical fiction, 89, 419
   informational books, 129, 170, 172–173
   picture storybooks, 188, 302
   survival stories, 83
African American literature. See also Slavery,
  books about
   art appreciation, 147
   biographies, 465, 473, 475, 477–478, 480,
     481–482, 484–486, 491–492
   contemporary realistic fiction, 381,
     386–389
   folktales, 136–137, 219, 238–239
   historical fiction, 418, 443, 444
   illustrations, 152
   informational books, 516–517, 530
   literary folktales, 277
   picture storybooks, 181, 189, 190
   poetry, 339, 343, 344–345
African folktales, 233–234
   cross-cultural comparisons, 209, 215, 221
   illustrations, 131, 137, 234
   literary elements in, 217

   and oral tradition, 45
   style in, 182
African legends, 212, 249
AIDS, 518
Alcott, Louisa May, 481
Aleichem, Sholom, 481
Allegory, 278–280, 302
Alliteration, 164, 171, 292, 321
Allusions, 422
Alphabet books, 168–171, 332
   animal themes, 169
   and cognitive development, 15
   early, 54
   illustrations, 123
American Revolution, books about
   biographies, 472–473, 488–489
   historical fiction, 418, 431–432
   informational books, 503, 513–514, 530
Ancient world
   biographies, 469, 471
   historical fiction, 424–426
   informational books, 507–510
Andersen, Hans Christian, 481, 492
Anderson, Marian, 465, 481–482, 493
Animals, books about. See also Fables; Trickster
  characters
   alphabet books, 169
   contemporary realistic fiction, 363, 395–396
   counting books, 171, 172
   easy-to-read books, 177
   folktales, 211, 218–219, 223, 230, 233,
     237–238
   illustrations, 131, 133
   informational books, 505, 506, 518–524
   modern fantasy, 274, 285–290, 309, 362, 363
   myths, 245–246
   and personality development, 23–24
   picture storybooks, 180, 181, 183, 184–186
   plot in, 80
   poetry, 329, 330–331, 333, 336–338
   and social development, 29, 33
   theme in, 93
   wordless picture books, 174
Anning, Mary, 26–27, 466–467
Antagonists. See Conflict
Anthropomorphism, 503
Antiphonal arrangement for choral speaking, 349
Applying/responding, 19–20
Arab folktales. See Middle Eastern literature
Arafat, Yasir, 476
Archaeology, 507, 510
Arnold, Benedict, 472
Art activities. See also Art appreciation; How-to
  books
   folktales, 260
   how-to books, 528–529
   modern fantasy, 108, 298
   picture books, 195–196

Art appreciation, 140–146. See also Art
  activities; Illustrations
   aesthetic scanning, 141–143
   and artistic media, 127, 130–131
   and cognitive development, 16, 19
   concept books, 173
   great artists, 145–146
   how-to books, 527–528
   multicultural, 146–150, 151
   and poetry, 317
   for young adults, 150–153
Arthurian legends, 47, 131, 247–248,
  280–281
Artistic media, 127–133
Asian American literature. See also Asian
  folktales
   art appreciation, 148
   biographies, 485
   contemporary realistic fiction, 392–393
   historical fiction, 439–440
   myths, 250
   picture storybooks, 178, 188
Asian cultures/history. See also Asian folktales
   biographies, 487
   historical fiction, 427–428
Asian folktales, 229–231
   cross-cultural comparisons, 211, 212,
     215, 258
   illustrations, 128
   literary elements in, 217
   motifs in, 211, 218–219
   nursery rhymes, 166
   and oral tradition, 45–46
   unit study, 259–261
   for young adults, 251
Assonance, 321
Astronomy, 517, 526–527
Audubon, John James, 480
Authenticity
   historical fiction, 422–424, 442, 445
   multicultural literature, 78
   traditional literature, 213, 214, 237
Author interviews, 489–490
Autobiographies, 3, 466, 476, 480, 482, 494. See
  also Biographies
Aztec folktales, 234–235

Ballads, 47, 327–328
Bartram, William, 468
Basque folktales, 220
Bates, Daisy, 478
Bates, Peg Leg, 484
Battledores, 47
Bearden, Romare, 480
Beast tales, 211. See also Folktales
Bedouin folktales, 232. See also Middle Eastern
  literature
Bibliotherapy, 20, 39

Biographies, 462–498
    artists/authors, 478–483
    autobiographies, 3, 466, 476, 480, 482, 494
    book list, 494–498
    and child development, 20, 26–27, 29, 34, 463
    evaluation criteria, 64, 78, 464–466, 493–494
    explorers, 469–470
    history of, 462–464
    illustrations, 122, 129, 131, 135, 466–467
    literary elements in, 80, 464–465, 466
    and motivation, 40
    perseverance, 483–486
    picture books, 466–469, 494
    plot in, 80, 466
    political leaders, 471–478
    professional perspectives, 478
    setting in, 90
    suggested activities, 494
    teaching methods, 488–494
    values of, 3
    for young adults, 486–488, 493–494
Birds, books about, 523–524
Board books, 4, 168
Book awards, 77, 102, 152–153
Book charts
    cognitive development, 12–15
    language development, 5–7
    personality development, 21–22
    social development, 30–33
Book lists
    biographies, 494–498
    contemporary realistic fiction, 409–414
    historical fiction, 457–460
    history of children's literature, 45, 55, 66
    illustrations, 154–160
    informational books, 535–542
    modern fantasy, 309–314
    picture books, 197–206
    poetry, 355–360
    traditional literature, 262–269
"Books on the Move" unit, 456
Booth, John Wilkes and Edwin, 474, 476
Borders, 125–126
Bourgeois, Louise, 487–488
Bourke-White, Margaret, 478
Boys/men. See Nonsexist literature; Sexism
Braille, Louis, 485
Breckinridge, Mary, 483
Bride stories, 211
British folktales, 220–221
    cross-cultural comparisons, 212, 215, 258
    history of, 208, 209
    literary elements in, 215, 217, 218
    motifs in, 218, 220
    North American variants, 239
British legends, 47, 131, 247–248, 280–281
Burmese folktales, 231
Burns, Anthony, 475

Calamity Jane, 466
Canadian folktales, 126, 239
Caricatures, 184
Carson, Rachel, 467
Cartooning, 196
Carver, George Washington, 345
Castle tales, 46, 208. See also Folktales

Censorship. See also Controversial issues
    contemporary realistic fiction, 372, 373
    history of, 65–66
    modern fantasy, 286
Change-of-heart stories, 57
Chapbooks, 47–48, 54
Chapter titles, 18
Characterization
    analysis example, 85
    in biographies, 464–465, 466, 494
    and cognitive development, 17, 20
    in contemporary realistic fiction, 85, 364–365, 367, 374, 389
    in easy-to-read books, 177
    evaluation criteria, 65
    in folktales, 216–217
    in historical fiction, 105–106, 418–419
    and illustrations, 138, 153
    in modern fantasy, 273–274, 286, 287, 288, 299, 306, 307
    overview, 84–86
    in picture storybooks, 179–180
    and style, 94, 95, 109–110
    suggested activities, 110
    teaching methods, 104–106
    and theme, 91, 92
Chart stories, 193
Chavez, Cesar, 344, 475
Chicago fire, 510
Child abuse, books about, 377
Child development, 4–36
    and biographies, 20, 26–27, 29, 34, 463
    cognitive, 11–20, 41, 65, 172, 192–193, 213–214, 501, 504–505
    language, 4–11, 163–164, 171, 174, 176, 193, 501, 532–533
    moral, 35–36, 213
    personality, 20–29
    Rousseau on, 51
    social, 29–36, 213
    suggested activities, 41
Children's preferences
    and evaluation criteria, 100–102
    folktales, 213–214, 217
    and literary elements, 84, 101–102
    picture books, 163
    poetry, 318–319, 354
    and style, 93
    suggested activities, 110
Children's responses to literature, 36–40. See also Children's preferences
    aesthetic/efferent, 38–39, 40, 141–143, 195–196
    biographies, 479
    and cognitive development, 19–20
    contemporary realistic fiction, 384, 400
    historical fiction, 421
    and illustrations, 28, 62, 137, 150–153
    informational books, 521
    modern fantasy, 296, 309
    multicultural literature, 86
    nursery rhymes, 164, 167, 192
    picture storybooks, 189
    poetry, 323
    storytelling, 255
    traditional literature, 253
Chinese Americans, 394–395

Chinese folktales, 229
    cross-cultural comparisons, 212, 215, 225, 258
    literary elements in, 217
    motifs in, 208, 209, 218
    nursery rhymes, 166
    unit study, 259–261
Chinese myths, 278
Choral speaking, 336, 337, 348–350
Christmas, 250, 348
Cinquains, 353
Civil rights movement, 477–478, 516–517, 530. See also Prejudice, books about
Civil War, books about
    biographies, 469
    historical fiction, 98, 421, 434, 436–437
    informational books, 514, 530
    modern fantasy, 274, 296
Classic literature. See History of children's literature
Classifying, 17–18
Clemente, Roberto, 485
Cleopatra, 471
Close, Chuck, 480
Cognitive development, 11–20
    applying/responding, 19–20
    book chart, 12–15
    classifying, 17–18
    comparing, 16–17
    and counting books, 172
    criticizing, 20
    and evaluation criteria, 65
    and folktales, 213–214
    hypothesizing, 18
    and informational books, 501, 504–505
    observing, 11, 15–16
    organizing, 18–19
    suggested activities, 41
    summarizing, 19
    and wordless picture books, 15–16, 192–193
Coleman, Elizabeth, 470
Collage
    activities, 195–196
    in illustrations, 131–133, 137, 176
Color
    concept books, 173
    in illustrations, 54, 120, 121–122, 130, 131, 139, 154
Columbus, Christopher, 428–429, 469
Community. See Friendship
Comparing activities
    biographies, 491–492, 494
    fables, 17, 240–241, 262
    folktales, 224–225, 256–259
    historical fiction, 456
    illustrations, 16–17, 127–128, 143–144, 224–225
    myths, 244
    nursery rhymes, 197
    plot, 104
    wordless picture books, 193
Composition. See Design
Concept books, 171, 173–174
    and cognitive development, 16, 17, 18, 19
    values of, 3
Concrete poetry, 329

Conflict. *See also* Plot
   and cognitive development, 17, 20
   in contemporary realistic fiction, 80–81, 364,
       369, 375–376, 377–378, 379–380, 388,
       390, 399, 400
   in folktales, 214, 216
   in historical fiction, 88, 417, 418, 429, 431,
       432, 433, 434, 446
   and illustrations, 179
   in modern fantasy, 282, 297
   overview, 80–84
   and personality development, 24–25
   and setting, 88, 107–108
   suggested activities, 110
   teaching methods, 104
   and theme, 92
Confucius, 471
Contemporary realistic fiction, 362–414
   African American, 381, 386–389
   animals in, 363, 395–396
   Asian American, 392–393
   book list, 409–414
   changes in, 368
   characterization in, 85, 364–365, 367,
       374, 389
   controversial issues in, 369–373, 409
   death in, 365, 375–376, 383–384
   defined, 362–363
   evaluation criteria, 365, 373, 408
   family life in, 68–71, 368, 372, 373–376, 378,
       386–387, 389, 391, 402–403
   growing-up themes in, 376–379
   humor in, 374, 398
   immigration in, 393–395
   Latino, 390–392, 395
   mysteries, 388, 396–397
   Native American, 389–390, 409
   new realism, 368–369
   and personality development, 23
   plot in, 80–81, 83–84, 364, 366, 367
   point of view in, 98, 374, 380, 409
   professional perspectives, 399
   questioning strategies, 407–409
   setting in, 90–91
   sports stories, 85, 397–398
   and stereotypes, 384–386
   style in, 366–368, 380, 388–389
   suggested activities, 409
   survival stories, 379–383
   teaching methods, 401–409
   theme in, 92, 365–366
   values of, 3, 363
   for young adults, 388, 390, 392, 398–401
Controversial issues. *See also* Censorship;
   Racially stereotyped literature; Sexism
   children's publishing, 70
   contemporary realistic fiction, 369–373, 409
   evaluation criteria, 101
   historical fiction, 435
   informational books, 503, 508
   modern fantasy, 286
   nursery rhymes, 166, 167
   picture books, 175, 188–189, 197
   traditional literature, 213
Cookbooks, 530
Cottage tales, 46, 208–209, 229. *See also*
   Folktales

Counting books, 131, 171–173
Crafts. *See* Art activities; How-to books
Creation stories, 242, 244, 245
Creative dramatization
   biographies, 488–489
   folktales, 260
   and language development, 4, 8, 10
   nursery rhymes, 192
   and personification, 110
   picture books, 192, 195
   and plot, 103
   poetry, 347–348
Creative writing. *See* Writing activities
Crimthann, 471
Criticizing, 20
Cultural authenticity. *See* Authenticity
Cultural diversity. *See* Multicultural literature;
   Racially stereotyped literature
Cumulative arrangement for choral speaking,
   349–350
Cumulative tales, 80, 209, 211, 253, 256
Curtis, Edward S.

Dance, 529
Darwin, Charles, 467
Death, books about, 25, 101, 104, 342
   contemporary realistic fiction, 365, 375–376,
       383–384
Decision making. *See* Moral development
Design, 125–127
Dialects, 79
Dialogic reading, 195
Dialogue arrangement for choral speaking, 349
Diamante, 353–354
Dictation, 352
Didactic literature, 56, 57, 67–68, 101, 279–280
Dinosaurs, books about, 502, 518–519
Disabilities, people with, 18, 29, 485
Discussion activities
   aesthetic scanning, 141–143
   biographies, 493–494
   contemporary realistic fiction, 374
   folktales, 260
   informational books, 534–535
   picture books, 176, 195–196
   poetry, 352
Displays, 254–255
Divorce, books about, 25, 28, 70, 71, 374, 375.
   See also Family life
Dolls, in modern fantasy, 290
Dominance, 125
Dragons, 248
Drama. *See* Creative dramatization

Earth-diver myths, 245
East Indian Americans, 393–394
Eastman, Charles, 474
Easy-to-read books, 177–178, 194, 333
Ecology, 525–526
Ederle, Gertrude, 477
Efferent responses, 38–39, 40
Egypt, ancient, 471, 509
Einstein, Albert, 465, 468, 470
Eleanor of Aquitaine, 471–472
Elizabeth I, 34, 40, 498
Emotional development. *See* Personality
   development

Emotional intelligence, 3
Emphasis, 349
English Civil War, 430
English traditional literature. *See* British folktales;
   British legends
Epics, 247, 326
Eratosthenes, 469
Escape literature, 40
Evaluation criteria, 74–79. *See also* Literary
   elements
   accessibility, 99
   biographies, 64, 78, 464–466, 493–494
   and children's interests, 100
   and children's preferences, 100–102
   contemporary realistic fiction, 365, 373, 408
   controversial issues, 101
   historical fiction, 65, 79, 417
   illustrations, 79, 118–119
   informational books, 64, 65, 76, 502–507,
       534–535
   modern fantasy, 273–275
   multicultural literature, 77–79
   picture books, 163
   poetry, 319
   and program objectives, 74–75
   readability, 99–100
   and stereotypes, 65, 78, 100
   suggested activities, 110
   traditional literature, 212, 261
   wordless picture books, 176
   young adult literature, 64–65
Exaggeration, 183–184
Explorers
   biographies, 469–470
   historical fiction, 428
   informational books, 514
Expressionism, 134

Fables, 240–242
   and African American folktales, 238, 239
   and cognitive development, 17
   defined, 210, 211, 240
   history of, 47, 49
   suggested activities, 262
Fairy tales. *See* Folktales; Literary folktales
Family life
   in contemporary realistic fiction, 68–71, 368,
       372, 373–376, 378, 386–387, 389, 391,
       402–403
   in historical fiction, 440–441
   and history of children's literature, 57, 60–61,
       67–71
   in modern fantasy, 296–297
   and personality development, 25, 28
   in picture storybooks, 181, 185–186
   in poetry, 339
   and social development, 29, 33–34
Fantasy. *See* Literary folktales; Modern fantasy
Feltboard stories, 17–18, 255–256
Figurative language, 93–94, 95
   and language development, 10
   in modern fantasy, 291, 302
   in poetry, 321, 323–324, 354–355
First-person point of view, 98, 374
Fitzgerald, Ella, 482
Flannelboard stories. *See* Feltboard stories
Flap books, 168

Flashbacks, 80
Folk songs. See Music
Folktale illustrations
    African, 131, 137, 234
    African American, 136–137
    Asian, 128
    British, 221
    French, 120, 221–222
    German, 130, 224–225
    Hungarian, 124–125
    Jewish, 133
    Latino, 132–133, 235
    Native American, 119–120, 121, 122–123,
        126, 142
    Norwegian, 131
Folktales, 214–239. See also Folktale illustrations;
    specific countries and cultural groups
    authenticity, 213, 214, 237
    characterization in, 216–217
    and child development, 16–18, 213–214
    cross-cultural comparisons, 209, 211, 212,
        215, 221, 239, 256–259, 261–262
    defined, 209, 210, 211
    dePaola on, 136
    history of, 45–46, 47, 48, 49, 52–53, 54, 71,
        208–209, 221, 222, 225
    literary, 52–53, 276–278
    little people in, 221
    and modern fantasy, 302
    vs. myths, 242–243
    and oral tradition, 3, 45–46
    plot in, 80, 103, 179, 214, 216
    and poetry, 346
    professional perspectives, 252
    setting in, 88, 108, 217
    single-country study, 259–261
    style in, 182, 217–218, 221, 230
    suggested activities, 261–262
    theme in, 109, 209, 217, 259
    values of, 3, 212–214
    and writing activities, 197, 261
Forensics, 518
Formality/informality, 126
Fortune, Amos, 473, 491–492
Frank, Anne, 486
Franklin, Benjamin, 473, 489
French folktales, 221–222
    cross-cultural comparisons, 215, 226, 258
    history of, 49, 208, 209, 221
    illustrations, 120, 221–222
    literary elements in, 216, 217
    motifs in, 216, 219
Friendship
    in contemporary realistic fiction, 376–378
    in picture storybooks, 179–180, 181–182
    in poetry, 341–342
    and social development, 34
Fry Readability Formula, 177

Galilei, Galileo, 469–470
Gandhi, Mohandas, 476
Gender. See Sexism; Sex roles
Geography, 525–526
Geology, 524–525
German folktales, 222–225
    cross-cultural comparisons, 209, 211, 212,
        215, 258
    history of, 52, 209, 222

illustrations, 130, 224–225
literary elements in, 216, 217, 218
motifs in, 216, 218, 219
religion in, 279
and storytelling, 223, 225, 254
Ghosts. See Spirit world
Gifted students, 99
Girls/women. See Nonsexist literature; Sexism
Gold Rush, 439, 511
Grandparents. See Older people
Greek mythology, 46, 212, 242–244
Growing-up themes, 376–379
Guthrie, Woody, 482

Haiku, 329–330
Hawaiian legends, 249
Hawkins, Waterhouse, 468
Hemings, Sally, 473
Henry, Patrick, 472, 488–489
Hiroshima, books about, 134, 189, 449, 450
Hispanic American literature. See Latino
    literature
Historical fiction, 416–460. See also Native
    Americans, historical fiction about; Western
    frontier, books about
    American Revolution, 418, 431–432
    ancient and medieval times, 424–428
    authenticity, 422–424, 442, 445
    book list, 457–460
    "Books on the Move" unit, 456
    characterization in, 105–106, 418–419
    chronology overview, 424–425
    Civil War, 98, 421, 434, 436–437
    and cognitive development, 20
    controversial issues, 435
    early, 60
    early twentieth century, 443–444, 451–452
    evaluation criteria, 65, 79, 417
    figurative language in, 94
    illustrations, 138, 153, 452
    and motivation, 40
    North American expansion, 432–434
    plot in, 81, 88, 417–418
    point of view in, 97, 98, 445, 447
    professional perspectives, 420
    Renaissance and New World encounters,
        428–430
    Salem witch-hunts, 430–431
    setting in, 88, 89–90, 108, 274, 419–420, 432,
        454–455, 457
    slavery, 434–436
    style in, 96, 422
    suggested activities, 457
    teaching methods, 452–456
    theme in, 420–421, 428, 430, 434, 437,
        442–443, 444, 452
    values of, 3, 416–417
    webbing literary elements, 110, 111
    wordless picture books, 190
    World War II, 444–450
    for young adults, 450–452
History of children's literature, 44–71
    adventure stories, 49–50, 51, 59–60
    alphabet books, 54
    biographies, 462–464
    Blake's poetry, 52
    book lists, 45, 55, 66
    censorship, 65–66

early printed books, 46–48, 71
family life, 57, 60–61, 67–71
fantasy, 58–59
folktales, 45–46, 47, 48, 49, 52–53, 54, 71,
    208–209, 221, 222, 225
illustrations, 53–55, 57, 71
Locke's influence, 49
milestone lists, 45, 55, 66
Newbery's books, 50–51
notable authors, 63–64
oral tradition, 45–46
Puritan influence, 48–49, 209
Rousseau's influence, 51
science fiction, 60, 297
suggested activities, 71
Victorian influence, 56–58, 60–61, 67–68
Hitler, Adolf, 476
Hmong Americans, 394
Hobbies. See How-to books
Holocaust, books about
    biographies, 107–108, 485, 486
    and child development, 35, 36
    historical fiction, 81–82, 89, 90, 108, 423,
        446–449, 451
    informational books, 107, 503, 514–515
    modern fantasy, 297
    and personality development, 28
    picture storybooks, 182, 188–189, 191,
        446–447
    setting in, 107–108
    and social development, 36
Homelessness, books about, 381–382
Hornbooks, 46, 47
Horse stories. See Animals, books about
How-to books, 19, 527–530
Human body, 517–518
Humor
    and cognitive development, 19
    in contemporary realistic fiction, 374, 398
    in fables, 241–242
    in folktales, 184, 211, 228
    and language development, 8
    in modern fantasy, 58–59, 288, 291–292
    and mood, 107
    in myths, 245
    in nursery rhymes, 164, 165
    in picture storybooks, 182–184, 190
    in poetry, 129, 183, 318, 321, 329, 330–333,
        336, 348, 355
    in wordless picture books, 174
Humorous tales. See also Folktales; Humor
Hungarian folktales, 124–125, 220
Hyperbole, 164, 324
Hypothesizing, 18

Identification, 29
Illustrations, 118–160. See also Art appreciation;
    Folktale illustrations; Picture books; Picture
    storybooks
    artistic media, 127–133
    artistic style, 133–134
    biographies, 122, 129, 131, 135, 466–467
    book list, 154–160
    and cognitive development, 15, 16–17, 18, 19
    color in, 54, 120, 121–122, 130, 131, 139, 154
    design in, 125–127
    evaluation criteria, 79, 118–119
    fables, 241

historical fiction, 138, 153, 452
history of, 53–55, 57, 71
informational books, 3, 28, 125, 129, 131, 133, 504, 515
inspirations for, 143–144
legends, 133, 134, 248, 249
line in, 119–121, 128, 131, 138, 139, 153, 165
modern fantasy, 277, 287
and mood, 88, 106–107, 122, 123–124, 153
multicultural literature, 79, 132, 135
myths, 243
nursery rhymes, 135, 139, 164, 165–166
outstanding illustrators, 134–140, 154
and plot, 79–80, 122, 138, 153, 179
poetry, 126, 129, 134, 144, 327, 329, 330, 335
professional perspectives, 24, 61, 136, 187
and reading aloud, 194, 195–196
and setting, 88, 89, 108, 138
shape in, 122–124
suggested activities, 153–154
teaching methods, 140–146
texture in, 124–125, 131
Imagery. See Figurative language
Imaginary conversations, 490
Imagination, development of, 3, 10, 178
Immigration, 393–395, 483, 515
Impressionism, 133–134
Incas, books about, 508
India, folktales from, 211, 231, 251
Inferencing, 105–106, 407–408
Inflection, 349
Informational books, 500–542
    alphabet format, 170
    ancient world, 507–510
    animals, 505, 506, 518–524
    book list, 535–542
    and child development, 18–19, 20, 25, 28, 501, 504–505, 532–533
    controversial issues, 503, 508
    counting book format, 171, 172–173
    discoveries, 526–527
    earth science, 524–527
    evaluation criteria, 64, 65, 76, 502–507, 534–535
    how-to books, 19, 527–530
    human body, 517–518
    illustrations, 3, 28, 125, 129, 131, 133, 504, 515
    machines, 527
    modern world, 510–517
    and motivation, 40
    plants, 524
    point of view in, 98
    professional perspectives, 520
    and setting, 89, 90
    suggested activities, 535
    teaching methods, 531–535
    values of, 3, 500–502
    for young adults, 530–531
Inner-city survival. See Survival stories
Instant messaging, 366
Intensity, 349
Interdisciplinary units. See Unit studies
Iran, 486–487
Iraq War, 515–516
Irish folktales, 221
Irony, 183, 302
Islam, 150, 246–247, 250–251, 471, 486–487

Italian folktales, 217
Ives, Charles, 482

Jackson, Andrew, 473
Jack tales, 239
Japanese American internment, books about, 449–450
Japanese literature
    biographies, 473
    folktales, 128, 211, 218–219, 220, 229–231, 260, 277
    haiku, 329–330
    historical fiction, 427
Jealousy, 24
Jefferson, Thomas, 473
Jewish culture/history. See also Holocaust, books about; Jewish folktales; Jewish legends
    art appreciation, 148, 149
    historical fiction, 418, 426, 443, 445
Jewish folktales, 228–229. See also Jewish legends
    characterization in, 217
    cross-cultural comparisons, 212, 215
    humor in, 184, 228
    and storytelling, 254
    theme in, 217
    writing activities, 197
    for young adults, 251
Jewish legends, 133, 134, 249–250
Joan of Arc legends, 212
Journals. See Literature journals

Kahlo, Frida, 480
Kennedy, John F., 476
King, Martin Luther, Jr., 477
Korczak, Januscz, 485
Korean folktales, 231

Language. See Language development; Style
Language development
    adolescents, 7, 11
    book chart, 5–7
    and counting books, 171
    elementary-age children, 6–7
    and informational books, 501, 532–533
    and nursery rhymes, 163–164
    and picture books, 193
    preschool children, 4, 5–6, 8–9
    and wordless picture books, 9–10, 174, 176
Language experience approach, 193
Lap reading. See Reading aloud
Latino literature
    art appreciation, 149
    biographies, 480
    contemporary realistic fiction, 390–392, 395
    counting books, 173
    easy-to-read books, 177
    folktales, 45, 132–133, 234–236
    informational books, 132
    nursery rhymes, 135, 166
    picture storybooks, 188
    poetry, 344, 346
Leathers, Blanche, 466
Legends, 247–250
    and biographies, 466
    British legends, 47, 131, 247–248, 280–281
    defined, 210, 212, 247
    illustrations, 133, 134, 248, 249

and modern fantasy, 280–281
and oral tradition, 46
Robin Hood legends, 59–60, 212, 248
Leonardo da Vinci, 146, 479
Lesson plans. See Activities, suggested
Lewis, C. S., 494
Limericks, 319, 328–329, 352–353
Limited omniscient point of view, 98, 374
Lincoln, Abraham, 465, 473–474
Lindbergh, Charles, 477
Line, 119–121, 128, 131, 138, 139, 153, 165
Line arrangement for choral speaking, 349
Literal recognition, 407
Literary criticism, 65, 75–76, 78–79. See also Evaluation criteria
Literary elements, 79–99. See also Characterization; Plot; Point of view; Setting; Style; Theme
    in biographies, 80, 464–465, 466
    characterization overview, 84–86
    and children's preferences, 84, 101–102
    in contemporary realistic fiction, 364–368
    in folktales, 214–218
    in modern fantasy, 273–275, 301–303
    plot overview, 79–84
    point of view overview, 96–99
    setting overview, 87–91
    style overview, 93–96
    teaching methods, 103–111
    theme overview, 91–93
    webbing, 110, 111
Literary folktales, 52–53, 276–278
Literature journals, 76, 153, 163, 197, 261
Literature program objectives, 74–75
Lithuanian folktales, 220
Little people, 221, 274, 275, 293–294
Local-color stories, 60
Logicomathematical ability, 11
Lullabies, 322–323, 325
Lyric poetry, 325–326

Magic and wonder tales, 211, 232. See also Folktales
Malcolm X, 477–478
Maori myths, 246
Maps, 108, 274–275
Marshall, Thurgood, 477
Marxist criticism approach, 153
Mathematics, 11, 171
Maya, books about, 235, 251, 429
Medieval Europe
    ballads, 327–328
    books about, 59–60, 422, 426–427
    storytelling, 46, 208–209
Messages. See Didactic literature
Metaphors, 10, 94, 107, 324, 355
Middle Ages. See Medieval Europe
Middle Eastern literature
    art appreciation, 150
    folktales, 212, 232–233, 250–251
    myths, 246–247
    poetry, 344
Modeling techniques, 104, 105–106
Modern fantasy, 272–314. See also Setting in modern fantasy
    allegory in, 278–280, 302
    animals in, 274, 285–290, 309, 362, 363
    book list, 309–314

characterization in, 273–274, 286, 287, 288, 299, 306, 307
vs. contemporary realistic fiction, 362–363
controversial issues, 286
early precursors, 58–59
evaluation criteria, 273–275
humor in, 58–59, 288, 291–292
illustrations, 277, 287
and language development, 10
literary elements in, 273–275, 301–303
and literary folktales, 52–53, 276–278
little people in, 274, 275, 293–294
and motivation, 40
and myths, 280–284, 299, 302–303, 309
picture books, 190, 302
plot in, 273, 303–304, 306
point of view in, 99, 275, 285, 289
professional perspectives, 295
science fiction, 3, 90, 297–300, 304–308
spirit world in, 294–296
strange worlds in, 292–293
style in, 274, 292, 293, 302, 306, 307
suggested activities, 309
teaching methods, 301–308
theme in, 275, 306, 307
time warps in, 296–297
toys in, 290–291
and traditional literature, 275–276
unit study, 304–308
values of, 272–273
wordless picture books, 175–176
for young adults, 300–301
Money, 512
Mongolian folktales, 231
Mood
and color, 122, 139
in modern fantasy, 294–295
in poetry, 106, 320, 341–345
and setting, 88, 106–107
and shape, 123–124
and storytelling, 254
suggested activities, 153
Moral development, 35–36, 213
Moralizing. See Didactic literature
Mother Goose rhymes. See Nursery rhymes
Mother Teresa, 476
Motifs, in folktales, 209, 211, 216, 218–220, 259
Motivation, 39–40, 65, 193, 254–255, 351–352.
    See also Children's responses to literature;
    Values of children's literature
Movable books. See also Toy books
Movement activities, 347. See also Creative
    dramatization
Muhammad, 471
Muir, John, 467–468
Multicultural literature. See also specific cultural
    groups
alphabet books, 170
art appreciation, 146–150, 151
evaluation criteria, 77–79
illustrations, 79, 132, 135
music, 326
nursery rhymes, 135, 166
professional perspectives, 84
and social development, 34–35
values of, 3, 77–78
Music, 316, 325–326, 327–328, 493

Mysteries, 388, 396–397
Myths, 242–247
authenticity, 213
Chinese, 278
defined, 210, 211–212
vs. folktales, 242–243
Greek/Roman, 46, 212, 242–244
history of, 45–46
and legends, 247
and modern fantasy, 280–284, 299,
    302–303, 309
Native American, 245–246
Norse, 244–245, 254, 280, 302–303
for young adults, 250

Narrative poetry, 326–327, 347–348
Native American folktales, 237–238
cross-cultural comparisons, 215, 258
illustrations, 119–120, 121, 122–123,
    126, 142
motifs in, 211, 219, 220
and oral tradition, 45
setting in, 217
for young adults, 251
Native American literature. See also Native
    American folktales; Native Americans,
    historical fiction about
art appreciation, 151
biographies, 129, 474–475, 483–484
contemporary realistic fiction, 389–390, 409
informational books, 509, 511
myths, 245–246
picture storybooks, 180–181
stereotypes in, 503–504
Native Americans, historical fiction about
authenticity, 423, 442
characterization in, 418
controversial issues, 435
European encounters, 428–430
North American expansion, 433–434
theme in, 421
and Western frontier, 438, 441–443,
    453–454
for young adults, 451
Nature poetry, 333–336
Nature survival. See Survival stories
Nepalese folktales, 231
New realism, 368–369
Nonfiction. See Biographies; Informational
    books
Nonrepresentational art, 134
Nonsense poetry, 183, 321, 330–333
Nonsexist literature. See also Sexism; Sex roles
and child development, 34
contemporary realistic fiction, 370,
    384–385, 409
folktales, 228
historical fiction, 439
informational books, 504
picture books, 188
Norse mythology, 244–245, 254, 280, 302–303
North American expansion, books about,
    432–434
North American folktales, 236–239. See also
    African American literature; Native American
    folktales
tall tales, 183–184

Norwegian folktales, 225–227
cross-cultural comparisons, 209, 211,
    212, 215
illustrations, 131
motifs in, 220
storytelling, 256
Numbers. See Counting books
Nursery rhymes, 163–166, 167
choral speaking, 349, 350
controversial issues, 166, 167
history of, 165
illustrations, 135, 139, 164, 165–166
and language development, 163–164
multicultural, 135, 166
plot in, 80, 103
and poetry, 325
rhythm in, 164, 182
suggested activities, 197
teaching methods, 192

Objective point of view, 98
Observing, 11, 15–16, 29, 169–170, 171,
    192–193
"Off the Cuff" awards, 102
Oils, 130
Older people
in contemporary realistic fiction,
    386–387, 389
in picture storybooks, 180, 188
Older students. See Young adult literature
Omniscient point of view, 98
Onomatopoeia, 8, 182, 238, 321
Oral language. See Discussion activities; Language
    development; Storytelling
Oral reading. See Reading aloud
Oral summaries, 19
Oral tradition, 3, 45–46, 328. See also Folktales
Ordeal stories, 57
Organizing, 18–19

Paleontology. See Dinosaurs, books about
Pantomime. See Creative dramatization
Parks, Rosa, 478
Pastels, 129–130
Peer relationships. See Friendship
Pen-and-ink drawings, 128
Perry, Matthew, 473
Person-against-nature conflict, 82–83, 88, 107,
    432. See also Survival stories
Person-against-person conflict, 80, 84, 377, 378
Person-against-self conflict, 83–84, 88, 104
in contemporary realistic fiction, 364, 377,
    378, 388
in historical fiction, 418, 429, 433, 434, 446
Person-against-society conflict, 80–82,
    107–108
in contemporary realistic fiction, 80–81, 388
in historical fiction, 88, 418, 429, 431,
    434, 446
in modern fantasy, 297
Personality development, 20–29
and biographies, 26–27, 29
book chart, 21–22
Personification
in folktales, 238–239
in picture storybooks, 109–110, 186–187
and plot, 83

in poetry, 324
and setting, 107
Pets. See Animals, books about
Photographs
in alphabet books, 169
in biographies, 474
in concept books, 173
in informational books, 28, 506, 507, 514, 515
and mood, 122
in nursery rhymes, 165
and poetry, 354
Physical knowledge, 11
Picture books, 162–206. See also Alphabet
books; Illustrations; Nursery rhymes; Picture
storybooks; Reading aloud; Wordless picture
books
alphabet books, 168–171
biographies, 466–469, 494
book list, 197–206
and child development, 4, 11, 15–16
children's preferences, 163
concept books, 173–174
controversial issues, 175, 188–189, 197
counting books, 131, 171–173
defined, 162–163
easy-to-read books, 177–178, 194
evaluation criteria, 163
modern fantasy, 190, 302
and motivation, 40
narrative poetry, 327
nursery rhymes, 163–166
setting in, 89, 180–181
suggested activities, 197
teaching methods, 191–197
toy books, 166, 168
wordless picture books, 174–177
Picture storybooks, 178–191. See also
Illustrations; Picture books
animals in, 180, 181, 183, 184–186
characterization in, 179–180
and child development, 25
vs. easy-to-read books, 177
and historical fiction, 419–420, 446–447, 452
humor in, 182–184, 190
and motivation, 40
personification in, 109–110, 186–187
plot in, 79–80, 104, 178–179
reading aloud, 194
realism in, 187–190
setting in, 180–181
style in, 182
theme in, 91–92, 181–182
and writing activities, 196
for young adults, 190–191
Pioneers. See Western frontier, books about
Pitch levels, 349
Plants, 524
Plot, 79–84. See also Conflict
analysis example, 81
in biographies, 80, 466
and cognitive development, 18
in contemporary realistic fiction, 80–81,
83–84, 364, 366, 367
diagramming, 103–104
in folktales, 80, 103, 179, 214, 216
in historical fiction, 81, 88, 417–418
and illustrations, 79–80, 122, 138, 153, 179

in modern fantasy, 273, 303–304, 306
in narrative poetry, 326–327
in picture storybooks, 79–80, 104, 178–179
and style, 94
teaching methods, 103–104
in wordless picture books, 174, 175–176
Pocahontas, 484
Poetry, 316–360
alphabet books, 170
animals in, 329, 330–331, 333, 336–338
ballads, 47, 327–328
book list, 355–360
characterization in, 95
children's preferences, 318–319, 354
choral speaking, 336, 337, 348–350
and cognitive development, 17
concrete, 329
and contemporary realistic fiction, 366
creative dramatization, 347–348
defined, 317–318
evaluation criteria, 319
familiar experiences in, 339–341
figurative language in, 321, 323–324,
354–355
haiku, 329–330
humor in, 129, 183, 318, 321, 329, 330–333,
336, 348, 355
illustrations, 126, 129, 134, 144, 327, 329,
330, 335
and language development, 8–9, 10
limericks, 319, 328–329, 352–353
lyric, 325–326
moods and feelings in, 106, 320, 341–345
and motivation, 40
movement to, 347
narrative, 326–327, 347–348
nature, 333–336
professional perspectives, 322
reading aloud, 318, 322, 347, 352
repetition in, 319, 320, 321–323
rhyme in, 318, 320–321, 327, 329
rhythm in, 318, 319–320, 329
and science, 338–339
setting in, 106, 342
shape in, 324–325
suggested activities, 354–355
teaching methods, 346–354
unit studies, 350
values of, 316–317
writing, 340, 351–354
for young adults, 344–346
Point of view
analysis example, 97
in contemporary realistic fiction, 98, 374,
380, 409
in folktales, 261
in historical fiction, 97, 98, 445, 447
in modern fantasy, 99, 275, 285, 289
overview, 96–99
and writing activities, 197
Political leaders
biographies, 471–478
informational books, 512–513
Pollack, Jackson, 480
Pony Express, 511
Pop-up books, 168
Potter, Beatrix, 466, 481

Pourquoi tales, 211, 235. See also Folktales
Prejudice, books about. See also Holocaust,
books about; Slavery, books about
biographies, 483, 484–485
and child development, 35
contemporary realistic fiction, 387,
391–392, 403
historical fiction, 418, 434, 437, 443–444
Japanese American internment, 449–450
picture storybooks, 182
plot in, 81
poetry, 344–345
theme in, 92
Prestige, 39–40
Pride, 28–29, 78
Problem novels, 368–369. See also
Contemporary realistic fiction
Problem-solving
in contemporary realistic fiction, 368,
376–377
and motivation, 39
in multicultural literature, 78
in nursery rhymes, 165
and personality development, 28
in picture storybooks, 188
and point of view, 98
suggested activities, 41
and theme, 93
in Victorian literature, 68
and wordless picture books, 174
Profanity, 372
Professional perspectives
David A. Adler, 478
Eve Bunting, 399
Cynthia DeFelice, 295
Tomie dePaola, 136
Steven Kellogg, 61
E. B. Lewis, 187
Mary E. Lyons, 420
Jack Prelutsky, 322
Laurence Pringle, 520
Robert Sabuda, 24
Tim Tingle, 252
David Wisniewski, 84
Publishing trends, 70, 209, 397
Puritan influence, 48–49, 209, 430

Questioning strategies
aesthetic scanning, 141–143
art appreciation, 150–153
contemporary realistic fiction, 407–409
and reading aloud, 195
Quezada, Juan, 344
Quotations, gathering, 110

Racially stereotyped literature, 175, 463
Racism, books about. See Civil rights movement;
Prejudice, books about; Slavery, books about
Rags-to-riches stories, 57–58
Readability, 99–100, 177
Reading aloud, 193–196
contemporary realistic fiction, 389
and illustrations, 194, 195–196
and language development, 4, 7
modern fantasy, 292, 293, 309
nursery rhymes, 165
poetry, 318, 322, 347, 352

and readability, 177
and repetition, 182, 194, 195
and style, 93, 109, 194
Realistic art, 133–134
Realistic fiction. See also Contemporary realistic
fiction
early, 60–62
picture storybooks, 187–190
Realistic tales, 211. See also Folktales
Refrain arrangement for choral speaking, 349
Religion
and Asian folktales, 251
in contemporary realistic fiction, 83–84, 399
and historical fiction, 429, 430–431, 447, 448
and history of children's literature, 46, 47, 48,
67, 69
informational books, 509–510
and Latino literature, 235
and legends, 249–250
and Middle Eastern literature, 246–247
and modern fantasy, 278–280
and myths, 243
Rembrandt van Rijn, 480
Repetition
and design, 125
in folktales, 221, 253
and language development, 4, 7
in modern fantasy, 291
in nursery rhymes, 164
in picture storybooks, 182, 184–185
in poetry, 319, 320, 321–323
and reading aloud, 182, 194, 195
Representational art, 133–134
Research activities, 145, 455
Responses. See Children's responses to literature
Reviews. See Literature journals
Reward/punishment, 29
Rhyme
in alphabet books, 169
in counting books, 171
and language development, 4, 8, 9
in nursery rhymes, 164, 165
in picture storybooks, 182, 183
in poetry, 318, 320–321, 327, 329
and style, 93
Rhythm
and language development, 8
in nursery rhymes, 164, 182
in picture storybooks, 182
in poetry, 318, 319–320, 329
Riddles, 235
Rivera, Diego, 480
Robin Hood legends, 59–60, 212, 248
Robinson, Jackie, 484–485
Role playing, 39, 402–403, 453. See also Creative
dramatization
Romanian folktales, 217
Roman mythology, 46, 242–244
Romantic movement, 209
Roosevelt, Eleanor, 475–476
Roosevelt, Franklin, 475, 491
Roosevelt, Theodore, 475
Rudolph, Wilma, 485
Russian folktales, 227–228
cross-cultural comparisons, 209, 215
humor in, 184
literary elements in, 216, 217
motifs in, 216, 218

Saladin, 471
Salem witch-hunts, books about, 430–431
Salois, Georgia, 483–484
Sandburg, Carl, 481
Science books, 517–527. See also Informational
books
animals, 505, 506, 518–524
astronomy, 517
and cognitive development, 19–20, 504–505
earth science, 524–527
evaluation criteria, 502–503, 504–505,
534–535
human body, 517–518
literature in curriculum, 531–535
machines, 527
plants, 524
poetry, 338–339
values of, 500–501
Victorian didacticism, 56
Science fiction, 297–300
early, 60, 297
setting in, 90
unit study, 304–308
values of, 3
Scientific imagination, 11, 272
Scientific method, 500–501
Scott, Blanche Stuart, 470
Self-concept, 25, 28–29, 123
September 11, 2001 terrorist attacks. See
Terrorism, books about
Sequoyah, 474–475
Setting. See also Setting in modern fantasy
analysis example, 87
in biographies, 90
and characterization, 106
evaluation criteria, 65, 79
in folktales, 88, 108, 217
in historical fiction, 88, 89–90, 108, 274,
419–420, 432, 454–455, 457
and illustrations, 88, 89, 108, 138
overview, 87–91
in picture storybooks, 180–181
in poetry, 106, 342
and style, 94
in survival stories, 403, 405
teaching methods, 106–108
Setting in modern fantasy, 274–275
in-depth analysis, 87
literary folktales, 277
and maps, 108
and mood, 107
and myths, 281
science fiction, 297, 298
and spirit world, 294–295
and symbolism, 90
teaching methods, 301–302
and unit studies, 306, 307
Seuss, Dr., 492
Sexism
biographies, 463
contemporary realistic fiction, 369–370, 409
Sex roles, 34, 57, 65, 67–68, 79, 175. See also
Nonsexist literature; Sexism
Sexuality
contemporary realistic fiction, 370–371, 378,
399–400
informational books, 518
Shako, Sister, 476

Shape
concept books, 16, 17, 173
in illustrations, 122–124
in poetry, 324–325
Sibling rivalry, 34, 80
Sign language, 172
Similes, 10, 93, 94, 324, 355
Single-parent families, books about, 375–376
Sitting Bull, 483
Slavery, books about. See also African American
literature
biographies, 473, 475
contemporary realistic fiction, 388
historical fiction, 434–436
modern fantasy, 297
picture storybooks, 190–191
plot in, 81
poetry, 344–345
Social development, 29–36
book chart, 30–33
moral development, 35–36, 213
socialization, 29, 34–35
Social issues
and art criticism, 153
in contemporary realistic fiction, 369
in modern fantasy, 298, 299–300, 301, 305
in nursery rhymes, 166, 167
and picture books, 175
in poetry, 333
Socialization, 29, 34–35. See also Social
development
Social studies, 304–305. See also Historical fiction
Socrates, 469
Songs. See Music; Nursery rhymes; Poetry
Sound effects, 168
South Africa, 487
Spanish language books
contemporary realistic fiction, 391
counting books, 173
easy-to-read books, 177
folktales, 235
nursery rhymes, 135, 166
poetry, 346
Spirit world
in folktales, 218, 238
in modern fantasy, 294–296
Sports, books about, 85, 339–340, 397–398,
484–485, 503
Standards. See Evaluation criteria
Stereotypes. See also Nonsexist literature;
Racially stereotyped literature; Sexism
and contemporary realistic fiction, 384–386
and evaluation criteria, 65, 78, 100
and informational books, 503–504
and picture storybooks, 182
Storytelling, 252–256. See also Folktales
by children, 176, 255
cumulative tales, 209, 211, 253, 256
feltboard stories, 17–18, 255–256
German folktales, 223, 225, 254
medieval Europe, 46, 208–209
modern fantasy, 188
and poetry, 326
professional perspectives, 252
Story time. See Reading aloud
Style
analysis example, 95
artistic, 133–134

in contemporary realistic fiction, 366–368, 380, 388–389
in folktales, 182, 217–218, 221, 230
in historical fiction, 96, 422
in informational books, 506–507, 511
in modern fantasy, 274, 292, 293, 302, 306, 307
overview, 93–96
in picture storybooks, 182
and reading aloud, 93, 109, 194
teaching methods, 109–110
Suicide, books about, 71, 383
Summarizing, 19, 105
Superiority, 184
Supernatural. See Spirit world
Surprise, in picture storybooks, 183
Survival stories, 379–383
and cognitive development, 17
and how-to books, 529
literary elements in, 81–83, 85, 87, 88–89, 94, 403, 405
and personality development, 28
unit studies, 403–407
Symbolism
and artistic style, 134
and characterization, 364–365, 366
in contemporary realistic fiction, 364–365, 366
in folktales, 217, 223, 234, 238, 239
in modern fantasy, 90, 282
and plot, 83
and setting, 90–91, 108, 217
Symmetry, 125, 138, 139

Tabula rasa, 49
Tall tales, 183–184, 239
Teaching methods. See also Activities, suggested
biographies, 488–494
contemporary realistic fiction, 401–409
historical fiction, 452–456
illustrations, 140–146
informational books, 531–535
literary elements, 103–111
modern fantasy, 301–308
picture books, 191–197
poetry, 346–354
traditional literature, 252–261
Telegraphic speech, 4
Terrorism, books about, 71, 342, 344, 346, 382, 401, 468
Test, 44, 45, 55, 56
Texture, 124–125, 131
Theater, 529
Thematic studies. See Unit studies
Theme
analysis example, 92
in biographies, 490
and cognitive development, 20
in contemporary realistic fiction, 92, 365–366
evaluation criteria, 65
in folktales, 109, 209, 217, 259
in historical fiction, 420–421, 428, 430, 434, 437, 442–443, 444, 452
in modern fantasy, 275, 306, 307
overview, 91–93

in picture storybooks, 91–92, 181–182
teaching methods, 108–109
Thorpe, Jim, 34, 469
"Through the Eyes" boxes. See Children's responses to literature; Professional perspectives
Till, Emmett, 345
Time lines, 491
Time-warp stories, 108, 296–297
Titanic, 514
Toy books, 166, 168
Toys, in modern fantasy, 290–291
Traditional literature, 208–269, 247–250. See also Folktales; Legends; Myths; Storytelling
book list, 262–269
and cognitive development, 16–17
comparison chart, 210
controversial issues, 213
evaluation criteria, 212, 261
fables, 240–242
legends, 247–250
and modern fantasy, 275–276
myths, 242–247
oral tradition, 3, 45–46
suggested activities, 261–262
teaching methods, 252–261
types of, 209–212
values of, 3, 212–214, 242
for young adults, 250–251
Trickster characters, 178, 212, 218–219, 235, 237–238
Tubman, Harriet, 491–492
Twain, Mark, 481

Unison arrangement for choral speaking, 350
Unit studies
Asian American literature, 259–261
biographies, 488–489
modern fantasy, 304–308
poetry, 350
survival stories, 403–407
Western frontier, 452–456

Values of children's literature, 2, 3–4
contemporary realistic fiction, 3, 363
historical fiction, 3, 416–417
informational books, 3, 500–502
modern fantasy, 272–273
multicultural literature, 3, 77–78
poetry, 316–317
traditional literature, 3, 212–214, 242
Victorian influence, 56–58, 60–61, 67–68, 279
Vietnamese folktales, 258
Vietnam War, 485
Violence, in contemporary realistic fiction, 371–372, 383–384
Visual elements
aesthetic scanning, 141–143
color, 54, 120, 121–122, 130, 131, 139, 154
design, 125–127
line, 119–121, 128, 131, 138, 139, 153, 165
shape, 122–124
texture, 124–125, 131

Washes, 128
Washington, George, 472, 473

Watercolors, 128–129, 138
Webbing, 110, 111, 403, 404
Weiss, Alta, 485
Welsh folktales, 221
Western frontier, books about, 437–443
authenticity, 423
biographies, 483
how-to books, 529
setting in, 419
style in, 422
theme in, 421
unit study, 452–456
"What if" stories, 10
White, E. B., 481
Whitman, Walt, 468–469
"Why" tales. See Pourquoi tales
Woodcuts, 130–131
Wordless picture books, 174–177
and child development, 9–10, 15–16, 174, 176, 192–193
design in, 126–127
evaluation criteria, 176
historical fiction, 190
outstanding illustrators, 139, 144
teaching methods, 192–193, 196–197
World War I, books about, 92, 422, 443–444, 450–451
World War II, books about, 444–450. See also Holocaust, books about
informational books, 515
picture storybooks, 189, 190
for young adults, 451
Wright Brothers, 470
Writing activities
and alphabet books, 170
and cognitive development, 19
and contemporary realistic fiction, 409
and folktales, 197, 261
and historical fiction, 455
and language development, 10
and modern fantasy, 298
and nursery rhymes, 192
and picture books, 193, 196–197
poetry, 340, 351–354
Wyeth, Andrew, 480

Yiddish folktales. See Jewish folktales
York, 484
Young adult literature
art appreciation, 150–153
biographies, 486–488, 493–494
characterization in, 84
and cognitive development, 15
contemporary realistic fiction, 388, 390, 392, 398–401
evaluation criteria, 64–65
historical fiction, 450–452
informational books, 530–531
and language development, 7, 11
modern fantasy, 300–301
and personality development, 22
picture storybooks, 190–191
plot in, 83–84
poetry, 344–346
reading preferences, 100
and social development, 33
traditional literature, 250–251

Credits

About the Author

Donna Norton

Following the completion of her doctorate at the University of Wisconsin, Madison, Donna E. Norton joined the College of Education faculty at Texas A&M University where she now holds the rank of professor. She teaches courses in children's literature, language arts, and reading. Dr. Norton is the recipient of the Texas A&M Faculty Distinguished Achievement Award in Teaching. This award is given "in recognition and appreciation of ability, personality, and methods which have resulted in distinguished achievements in the teaching and the inspiration of students." She is also the recipient of the Virginia Hamilton Essay Award, presented by the Virginia Hamilton Conference Advisory Board at Kent State University. This annual award recognizes an article that "makes a significant contribution to the professional literature concerning multicultural literature experiences for youth." She is listed in *Who's Who of American Women, Who's Who in America,* and *Who's Who in the World.* Several of her articles and chapters from books have been translated into Chinese and are used in Chinese universities.

Dr. Norton is the author of four books in addition to this volume: *The Effective Teaching of Language Arts,* 6th edition, *Language Arts Activities for Children,* 5th edition, *Multicultural Children's Literature: Through the Eyes of Many Children,* and *The Impact of Literature-Based Reading.* Her publications include 20 textbooks and over 100 journal articles. At the international level, she has been on the International Reading Association's Lee Bennett Hopkins Promising Poet Committee, President of the International Society of Educational Biography, on numerous editorial boards for professional journals, and presenter at international conferences including the Conference on Children's Literature at Providence University in Taiwan. The focus of her current research is on the authentication of biographical literature, historical fiction, and multicultural literature. She is also researching the literature and writing connection. Funded research has supported institutes in children's literature and the literacy connection as well as graduate courses that enable students to study children's literature and reading instruction in England and Scotland. She is currently the Grant Writing Chair for the Bush Museum Storytellers Guild. Her work with the Texas A&M University Evans Library and the Bush Library has resulted in several Storytelling Festivals that highlight the work of distinguished storytellers and provide training for university students in the art of storytelling.

Prior to her college teaching experience, Dr. Norton was an elementary teacher in River Falls, Wisconsin and in Madison, Wisconsin. She was a Language Arts/Reading Consultant for federally funded kindergarten through adult basic education programs. In this capacity she developed, provided in-service instruction, and evaluated kindergarten programs, summer reading and library programs, remedial reading programs, learning disability programs for middle school children, elementary and secondary literature programs for the gifted, and diagnostic and intervention programs for reading-disabled adults. Dr. Norton's continuing concern for literature results in frequent consultations with educators from various disciplines, librarians, and school administrators and teachers.

Saundra Norton

Saundra Norton completed her master's degree at Texas A&M University where she majored in American literature with an emphasis in children's literature and textual bibliography. Under the sponsorship of a Jordan Fellowship she studied German language, culture, and folklore at the Goethe Institute in Germany. Her current academic concentration is in 19th century American literature and biographical studies. She is a frequent participant at national and international conferences. Her paper presented at the 15th International Ezra Pound Conference in Italy was presented the Bates Award for the best essay written by a graduate student while in the doctoral program at the University of South Carolina. Saundra has won numerous competitions for her writing including being selected for the Prague Summer Seminars, the Paris Writer's Workshop, Bread Loaf Writer's Conference at Middlebury College, in Middlebury, Vermont, and Sewanee Writer's Conference at the University of the South. Her poetry has been published in several scholarly journals and she has given poetry readings in Prague, Key West, Paris, and at Wesleyan College. She is listed in *Who's Who Among Students in American Universities and Colleges.* Saundra is the co-author of *Language Arts Activities for Children,* 5th edition.